Transport for London

UNDERGROUND

*You pay no more than 5p per minute if calling
from a BT landline. There may be a connection charge.
Charges from mobiles or other landline providers may vary.

Improvement works may affect your journey, please check before you travel

Version A TfL 12.2011

D1187246

LONDON

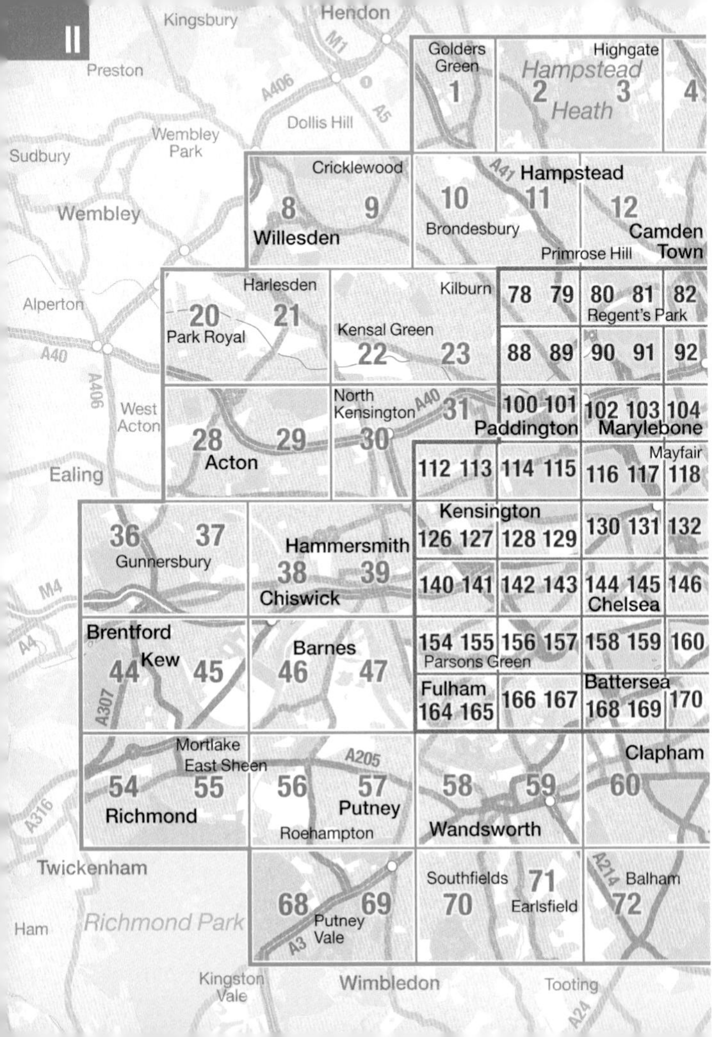

Kingsbury

Hendon

Preston

Golders
Green
1

Highgate

Hampstead
2

3

4

Heath

A406

M1

A5

Dollis Hill

Sudbury

Wembley
Park

Cricklewood

A41 Hampstead

10

11

12

Camden
Town

Wembley

8

9

Brondesbury

Willesden

Primrose Hill

Alperton

Harlesden

20

21

Kilburn

78 79

80 81 82

Regent's Park

Park Royal

Kensal Green

22

23

88 89

90 91 92

A40

West
Acton

North
Kensington

A40

31

100 101

Paddington

102 103 104

Marylebone

28

29

30

112 113

114 115

116 117

Mayfair

118

Acton

Ealing

Kensington

126 127

128 129

130 131 132

36

37

Gunnersbury

Hammersmith

38

39

Chiswick

140 141

142 143

144 145 146

Chelsea

M4

A4

Brentford

Kew

Barnes

154 155

Parsons Green

156 157

158 159 160

44

45

46

47

Fulham

164 165

166 167

Battersea

168 169

170

A307

Mortlake
East Sheen

A205

Clapham

54

55

56

57

58

59

60

Richmond

Putney

Roehampton

Wandsworth

A316

Twickenham

A214

Balham

Ham

Richmond Park

68

69

Putney
Vale

Southfields

70

71

Earlsfield

72

A3

Kingston
Vale

Wimbledon

Tooting

A24

III

Key to map pages

Atlas pages at
3½ inches to 1 mile
are shown in blue

Central London
atlas pages at
7 inches to 1 mile
are shown in red
(See page 77)

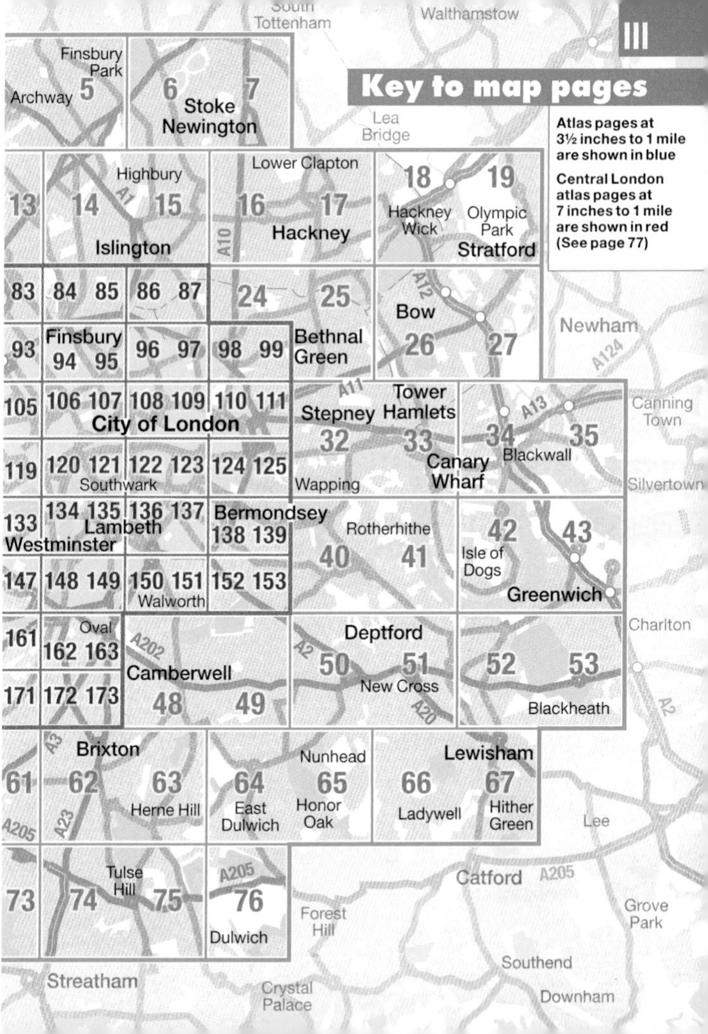

South Tottenham

Walthamstow

Finsbury Park

Archway **5**

6

7

Stoke Newington

Lea Bridge

Highbury

Lower Clapton

18

19

Hackney Wick

Olympic Park

13

14 **15**

16

17

Islington

Hackney

A10

A1

Stratford

83 **84** **85** **86** **87**

24

25

Bow

Newham

A124

93 Finsbury **94** **95** **96** **97** **98** **99**

Bethnal Green

26

27

105 **106 107 108 109 110 111**

City of London

Tower Stepney Hamlets

32 **33**

34 **35**

Canning Town

A13

119 **120 121 122 123 124 125**

Southwark

Wapping

Canary Wharf

Blackwall

Silvertown

133 **134 135 136 137**

138 139

Lambeth

Bermondsey

Rotherhithe

42 **43**

Westminster

Isle of Dogs

147 **148 149 150 151 152 153**

Walworth

40 **41**

Greenwich

161 Oval

A202

Deptford

52 **53**

Charlton

162 163

50 **51**

Camberwell

New Cross

Blackheath

A2

171 172 173

48 **49**

A2

A20

Brixton

Nunhead

Lewisham

61 **62** **63**

64 **65**

66 **67**

Lee

Herne Hill

East Dulwich

Honor Oak

Ladywell

Hither Green

A23

A205

A3

73 **74** **75** **76**

Tulse Hill

Catford

A205

Grove Park

A205

A3

Dulwich

Forest Hill

Southend

Streatham

Crystal Palace

Downham

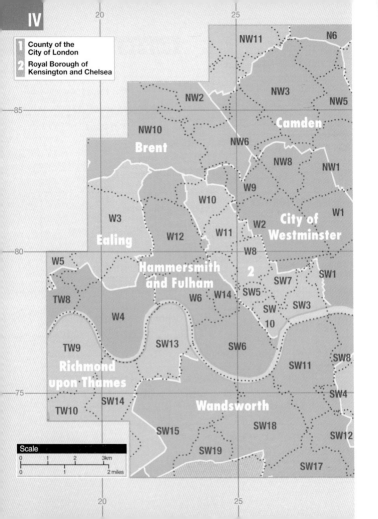

1 County of the City of London

2 Royal Borough of Kensington and Chelsea

N6

NW11

NW2

NW3

NW5

Camden

NW10

Brent

NW6

NW8

NW1

W9

W1

W10

W3

W2

City of Westminster

Ealing

W12

W11

W8

W5

Hammersmith and Fulham

SW7

SW1

TW8

W6

W14

SW5

SW3

W4

SW

10

SW13

SW6

SW11

SW8

TW9

Richmond upon Thames

SW4

TW10

SW14

Wandsworth

SW18

SW12

SW15

SW19

SW17

Scale

0   1   2   3km

0   1   2 miles

20

25

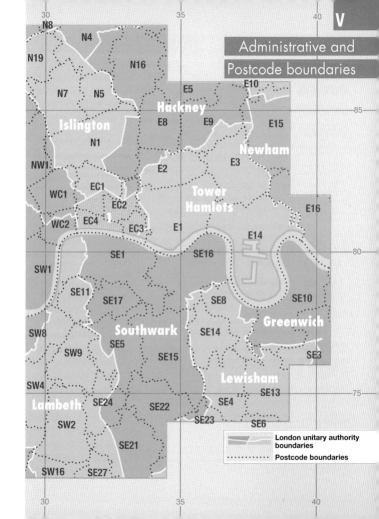

Key to map symbols

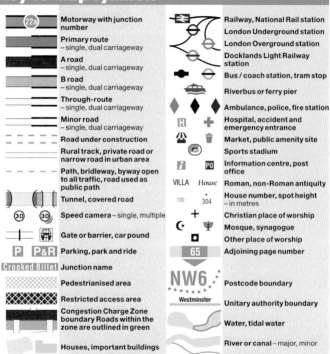

Motorway with junction number	
Primary route – single, dual carriageway	
A road – single, dual carriageway	
B road – single, dual carriageway	
Through-route – single, dual carriageway	
Minor road – single, dual carriageway	
Road under construction	
Rural track, private road or narrow road in urban area	
Path, bridleway, byway open to all traffic, road used as public path	
Tunnel, covered road	
Speed camera – single, multiple	
Gate or barrier, car pound	
Parking, park and ride	
Junction name	
Pedestrianised area	
Restricted access area	
Congestion Charge Zone boundary Roads within the zone are outlined in green	
Houses, important buildings	
Woods, parkland/common	

Railway, National Rail station

London Underground station

London Overground station

Docklands Light Railway station

Bus / coach station, tram stop

Riverbus or ferry pier

Ambulance, police, fire station

Hospital, accident and emergency entrance

Market, public amenity site

Sports stadium

Information centre, post office

VILLA House   Roman, non-Roman antiquity

100   304   House number, spot height – in metres

Christian place of worship

Mosque, synagogue

Other place of worship

65   Adjoining page number

NW6   Postcode boundary

Westminster   Unitary authority boundary

Water, tidal water

River or canal – major, minor

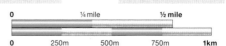

The map scale on the pages numbered in blue is 3½ inches to 1 mile
5.52 cm to 1 km • 1:18 103

0   ¼ mile   ½ mile

0   250m   500m   750m   1km

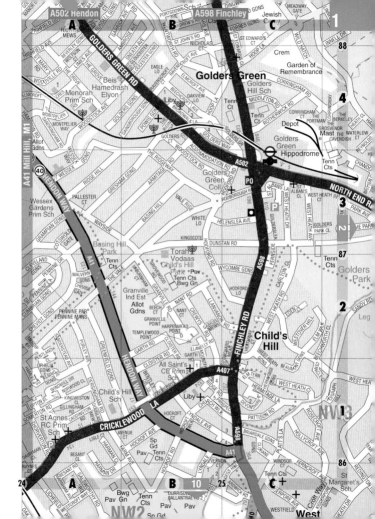

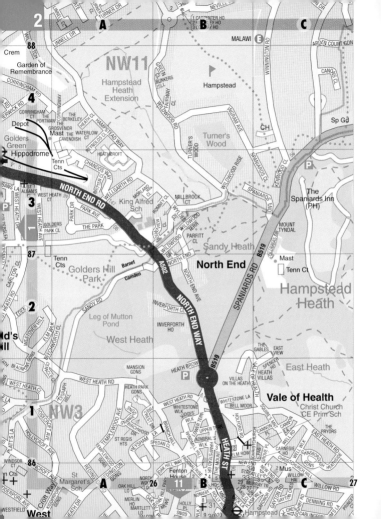

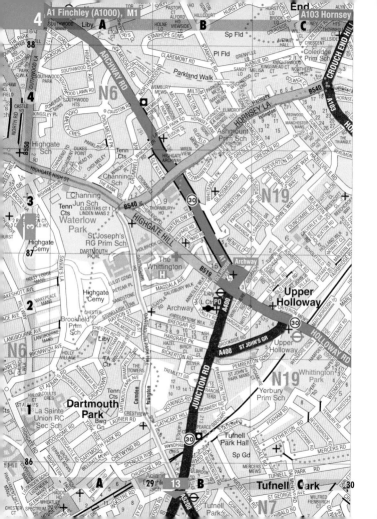

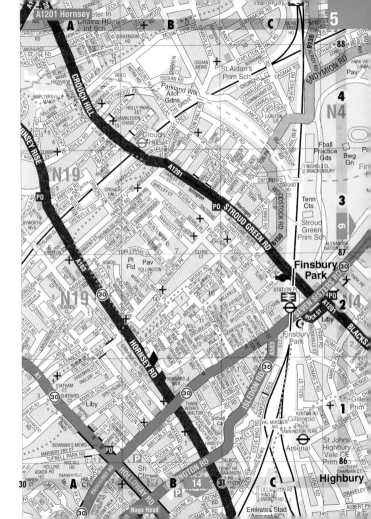

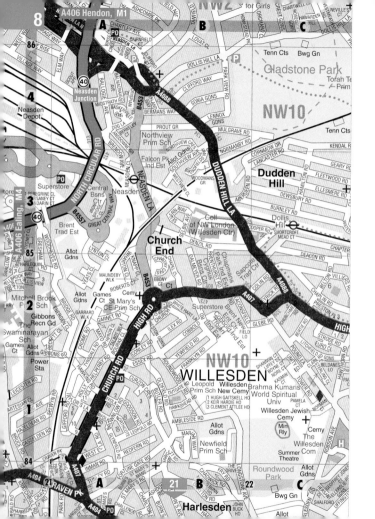

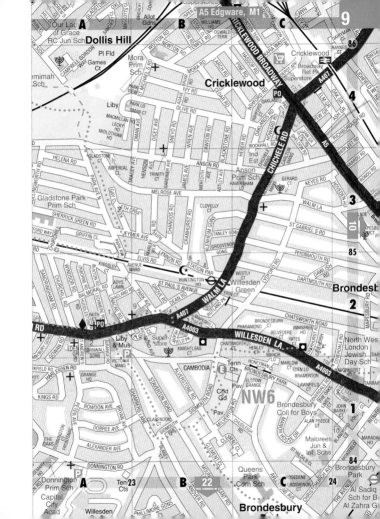

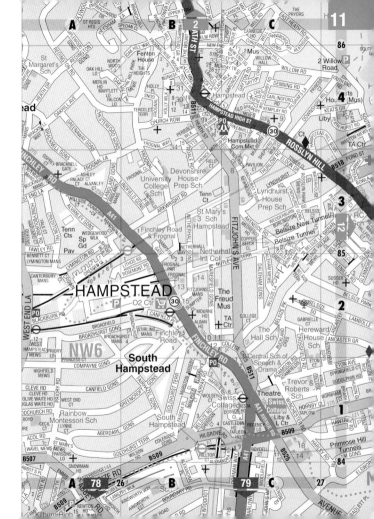

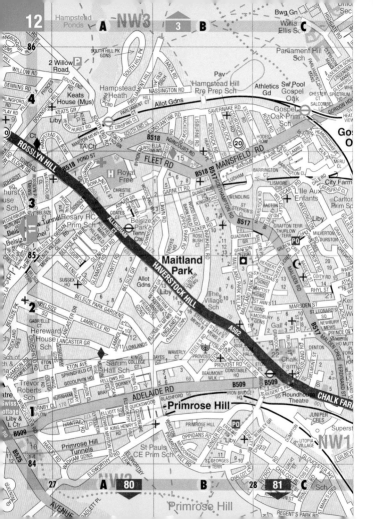

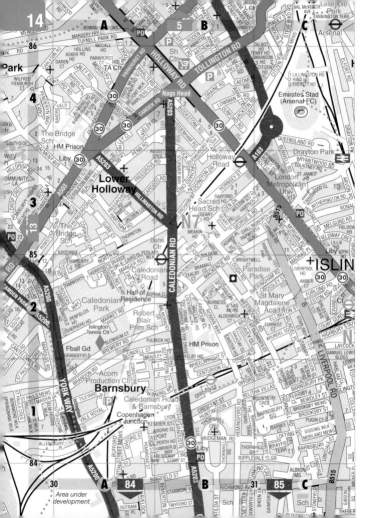

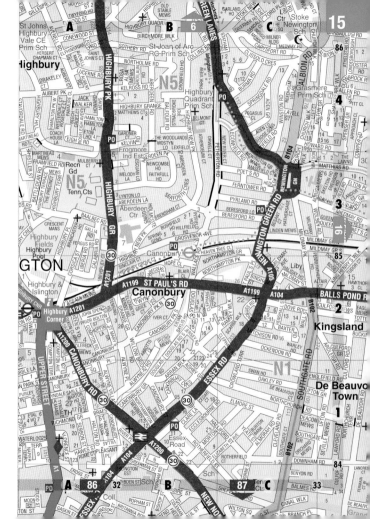

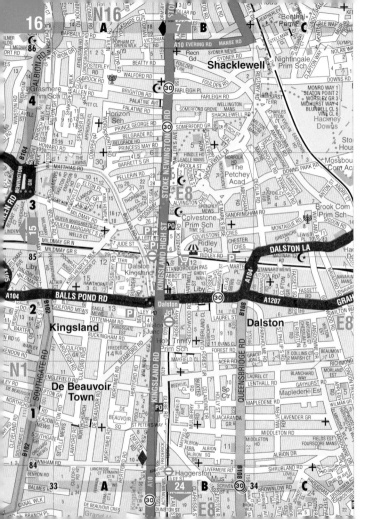

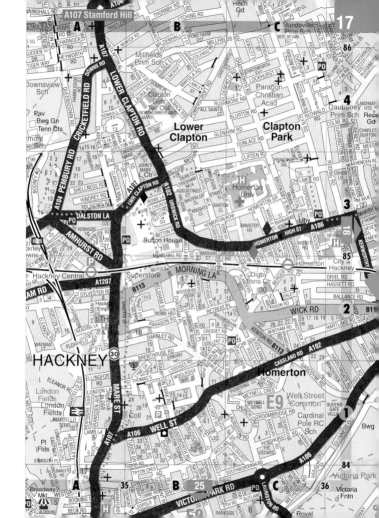

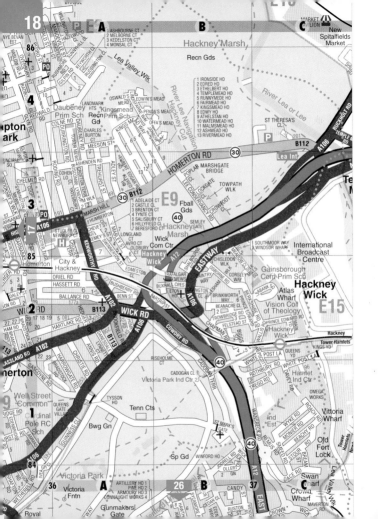

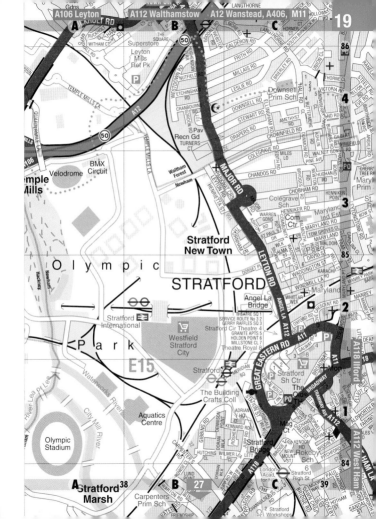

A106 Leyton
A112 Walthamstow
A12 Wanstead, A406, M11

A
B
C

86
ALNWICK RD
LANGTHORNE
THE SQUARE
Superstore
Leyton
Mills
Ret Pk
CALDERON RD
FRITH RD
MILLAIS RD
LESLIE RD
Downsell
Prim Sch
4
TEMPLE MILLS LA
A12
CRANBOURNE RD
Pav
Recn Gd
TURNERS
CT
DOWNSELL RD
STEWART RD
DRAPERS RD
CROWNFIELD RD
AMETHYST
COLEGRAVE RD
WALNUT GDNS
MILES
PINE AVE

CHANDOS RD

MAJOR RD

Velodrome
BMX
Circuit

Waltham
Forest
Newham

CHOBHAM RD

Colegrave
Sch
HENNIKER RD

3
85

Temple
Mills

Stratford
New Town

O l y m p i c

STRATFORD

Com
Ctr

LEYTON RD

Maryland

Angel La
Bridge

THEATRE SQ 1
SERVICE ROUTE No 3 2
GERRY RAFFLES SQ 3
Stratford Cir Theatre 4
GRANITE APTS 5
HOLDEN POINT 6
MILLSTONE CL 7
Theatre Royal 8

2

Stratford
International

Westfield
Stratford
City

P a r k

E15

Stratford

GREAT EASTERN RD

A11

Stratford
Sh Ctr
The
PO

A112
A11

1

18

Mon

The Building
Crafts Coll

Aquatics
Centre

Stratford
Bridge

Mag
Ct

Stratford
Rokeby
Sch

84

Olympic
Stadium

A Stratford 38
Marsh

B 27

Carpenters
Prim Sch

Stratford
High St

C 39

2 Stratford
Workshops

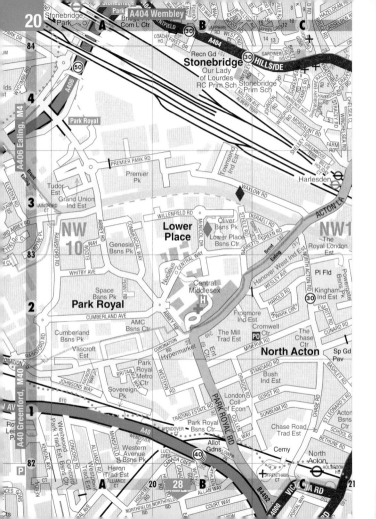

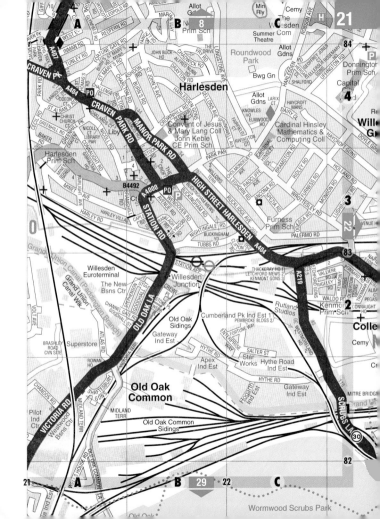

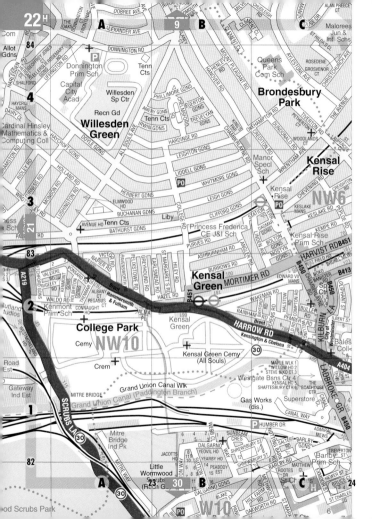

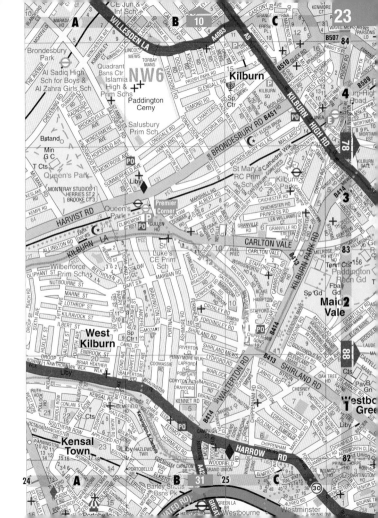

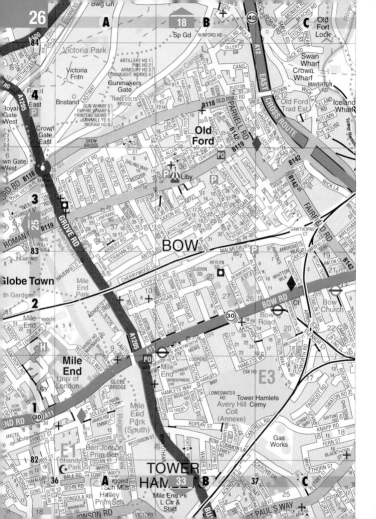

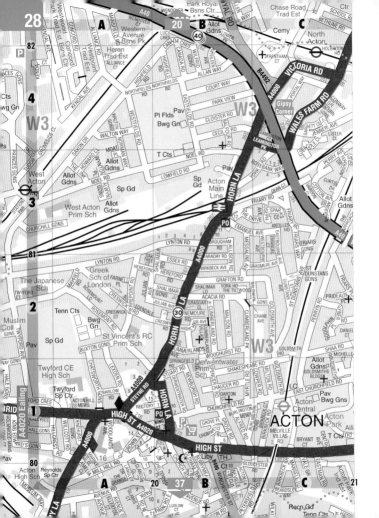

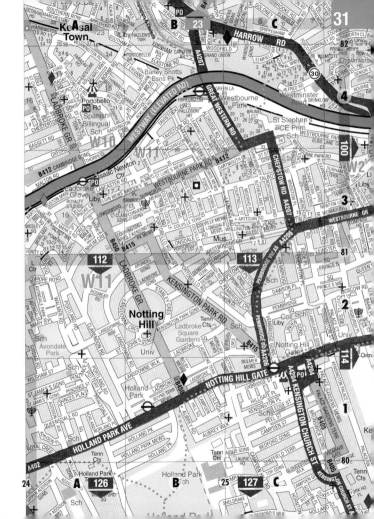

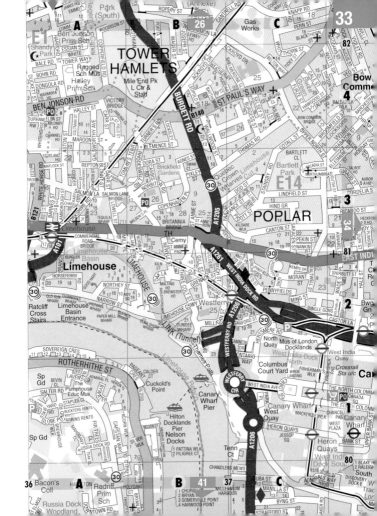

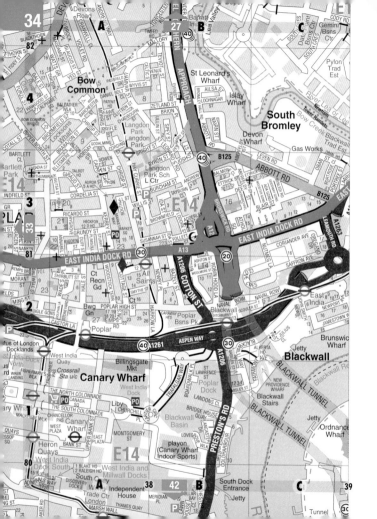

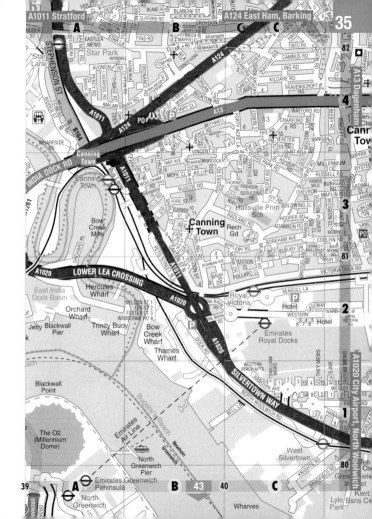

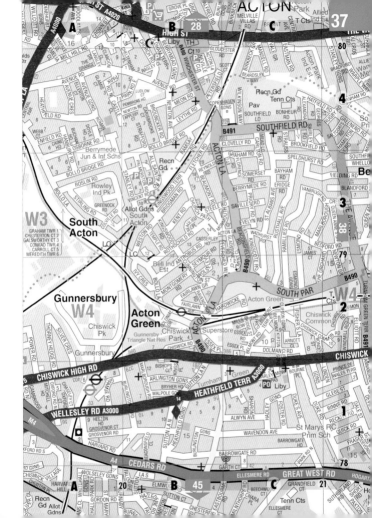

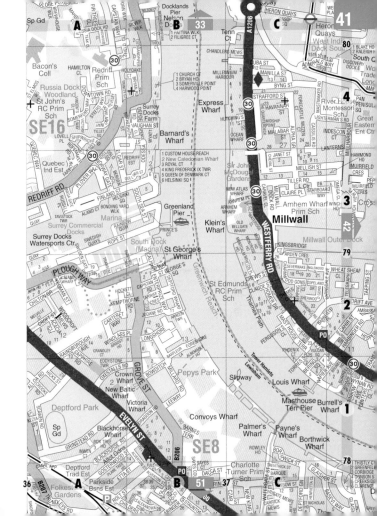

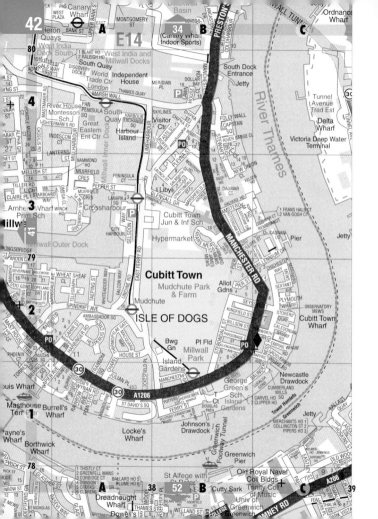

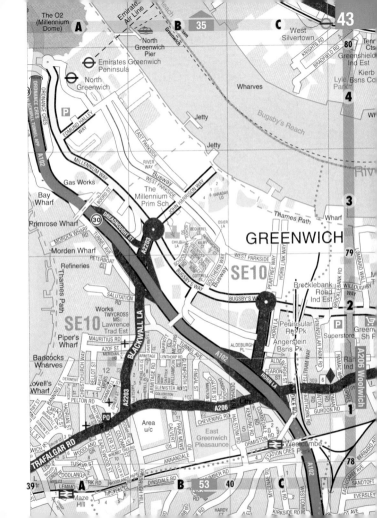

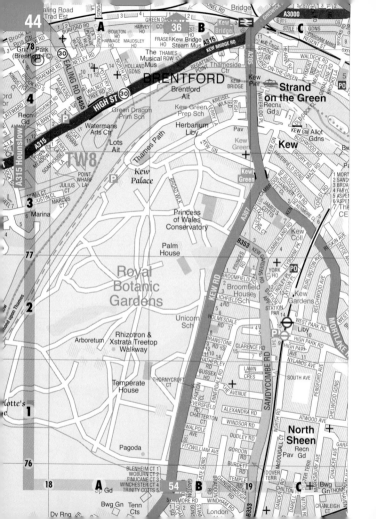

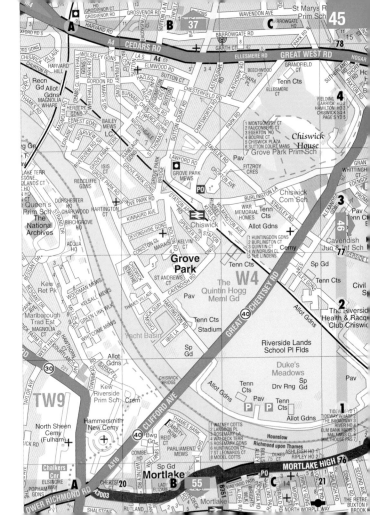

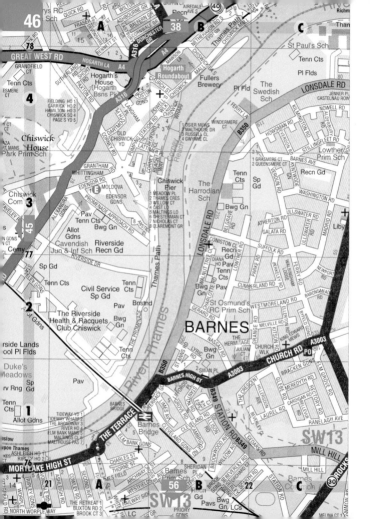

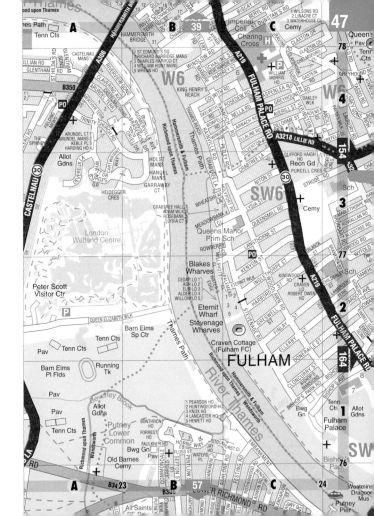

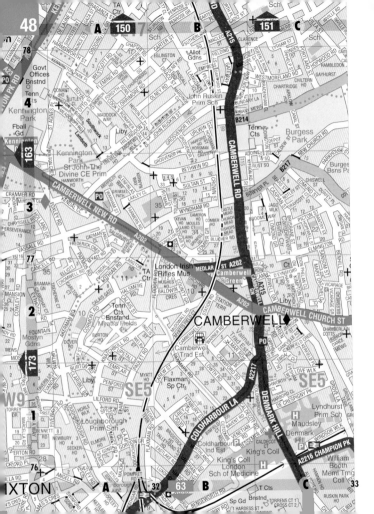

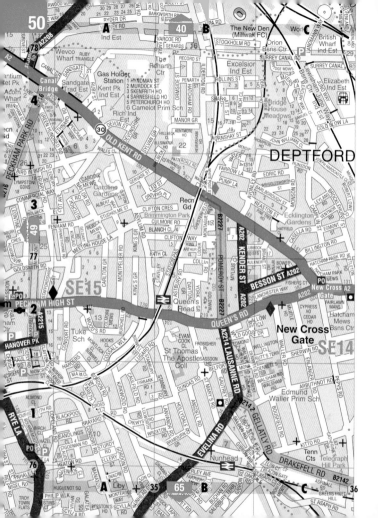

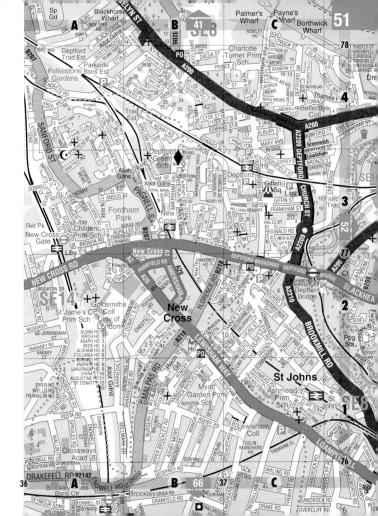

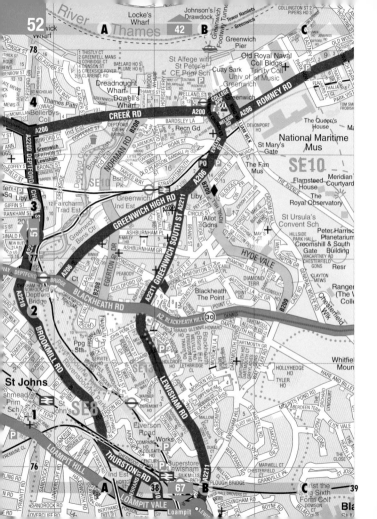

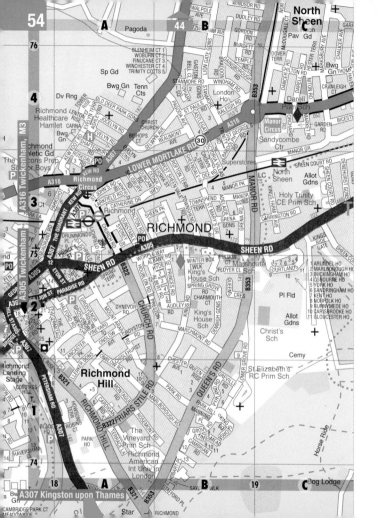

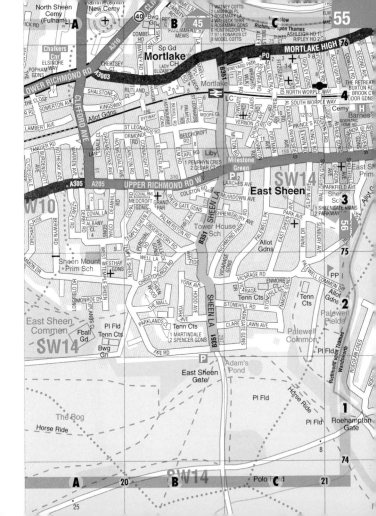

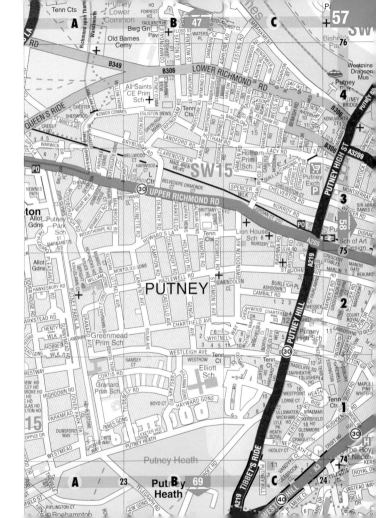

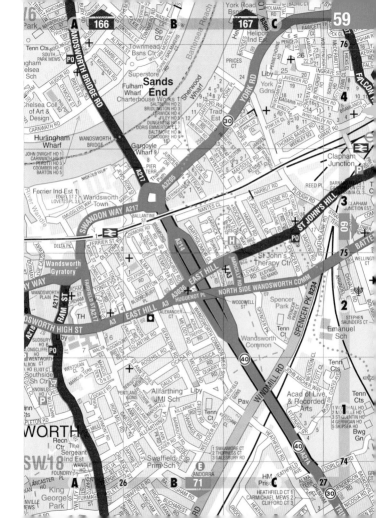

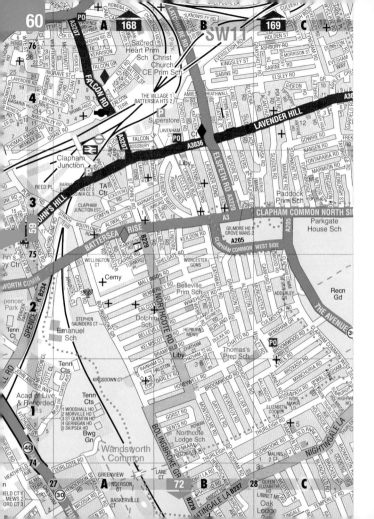

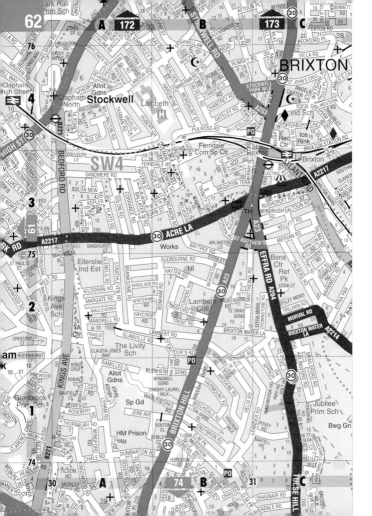

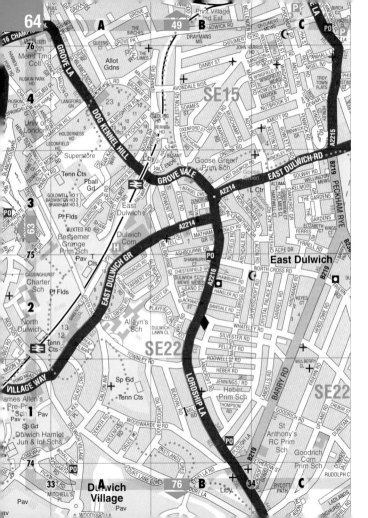

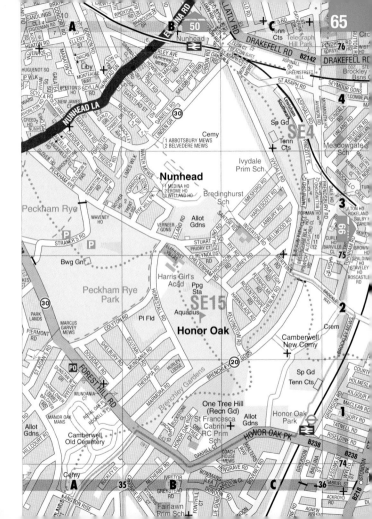

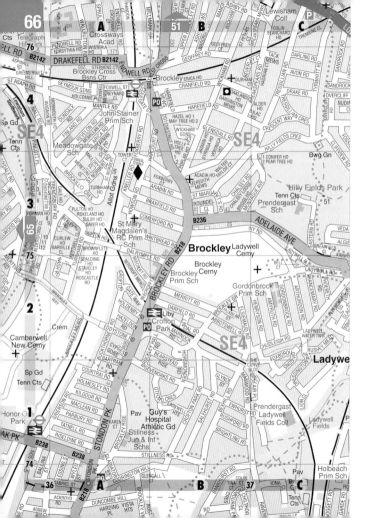

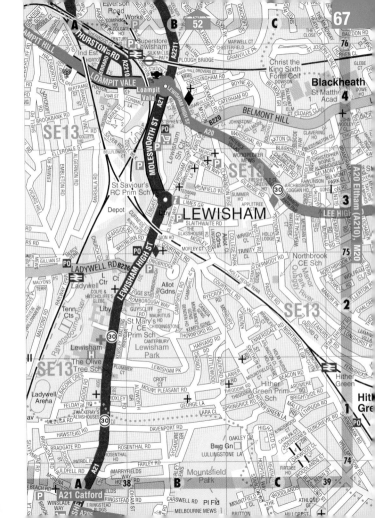

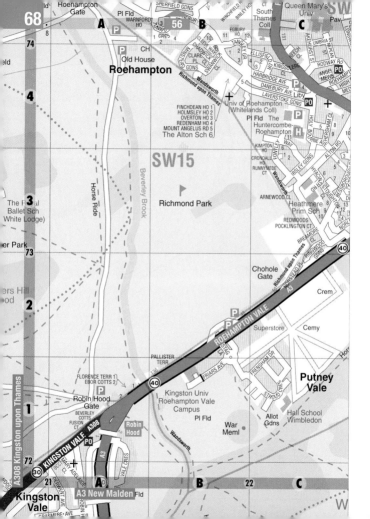

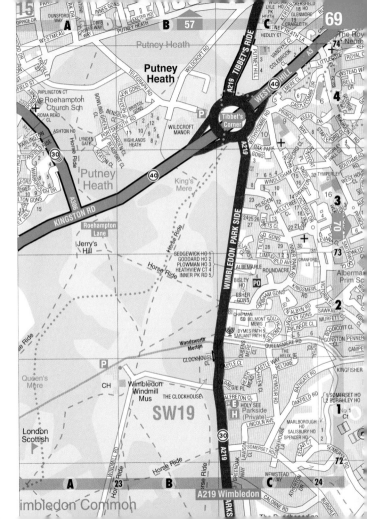

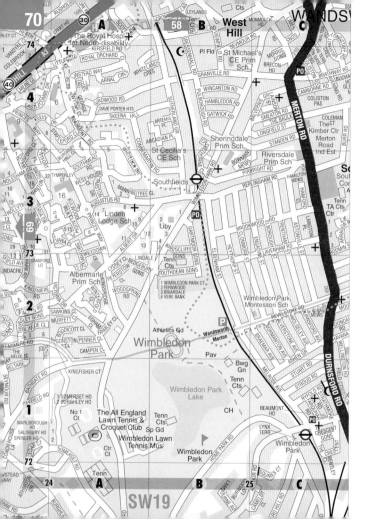

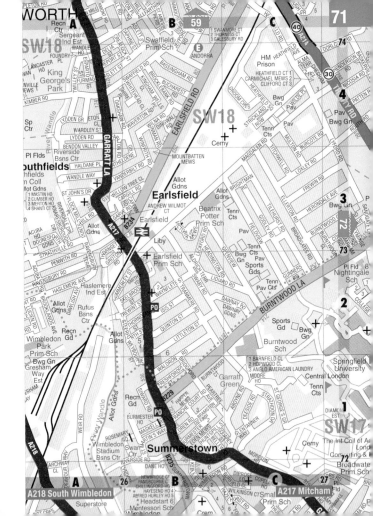

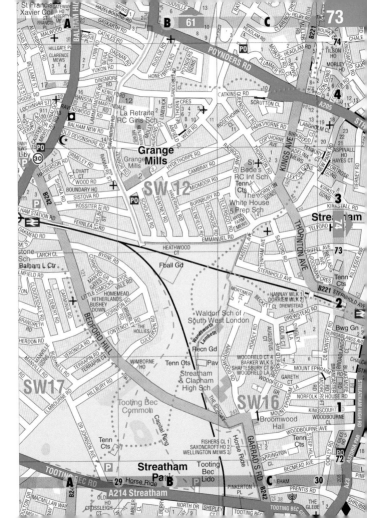

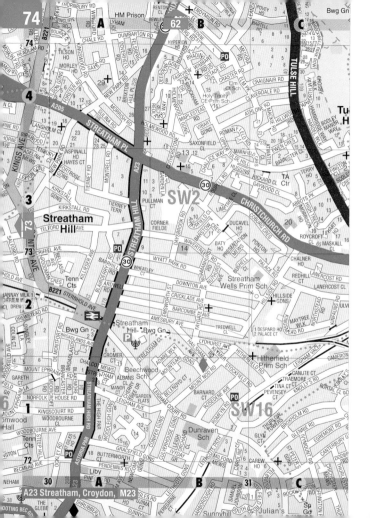

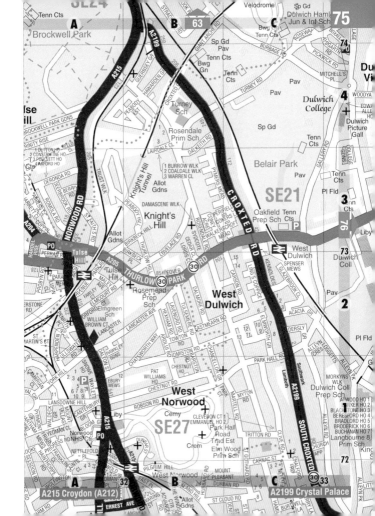

Key to central London map pages

78 79 St John's Wood	Primrose Hill 80 81 Regent's Park	82 83 Somers Town	Islington 84 85 King's Cross	86 87	
Maida Vale 88 89 Westbourne Green	Lisson 90 91 Grove	St Pancras 92 93 Bloomsbury	Finsbury 94 95	Shoreditch 96 97	Bethnal Green 98 99 Spitalfields
Paddington 100 101	Marylebone 102 103	Fitzrovia 104 105	Holborn 106 107 St Giles	City 108 109	110 111 Whitechapel
Notting Hill 112 113	Bayswater 114 115 Kensington Gardens	Mayfair 116 117 Hyde Park	118 119 St James	120 121 South Bank	Southwark 122 123	124 125 St George in the East
Kensington 126 127 Holland Pk West Kensington	Knightsbridge 128 129 Brompton	Green Park 130 131	Westminster 132 133	Waterloo 134 135	The Borough 136 137	Bermondsey 138 139
140 141 Earl's Ct	South Kensington 142 143	144 145 Belgravia	Victoria 146 147 Pimlico	Lambeth 148 149 Vauxhall Kennington	Newington 150 151 Walworth	152 153
West Brompton 154 155 Parsons Green	Chelsea 156 157 Walham Green	158 159 Battersea Park	160 161 Nine Elms	162 163		
Fulham 164 165	Battersea 166 167	168 169	170 171	South Lambeth 172 173 Stockwell		

Congestion Charge Zone

Additional symbols on enlarged maps

All other symbols may be found on page VI

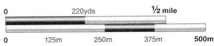

Primary route
– single, dual carriageway

A road
– single, dual carriageway

B road

Through route

Minor road

One way street

No access in direction shown

Congestion Charge Zone
boundary Streets within the zone are outlined in green – for further information call 0845 900 1234

Public building

Railway or bus station building

Place of interest

Embassy, museum, theatre

The map scale on the pages numbered in red is 7 inches to 1 mile
11.04 cm to 1 km • 1 : 9051

0	220yds	½ mile

| 0 | 125m | 250m | 375m | 500m |

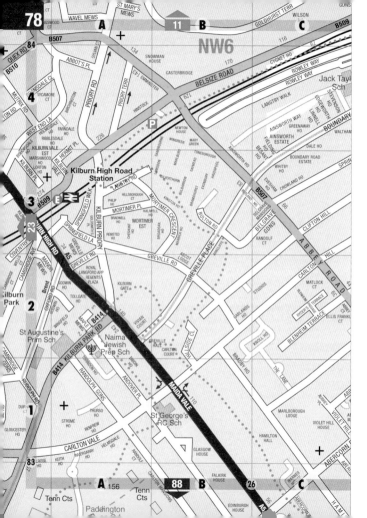

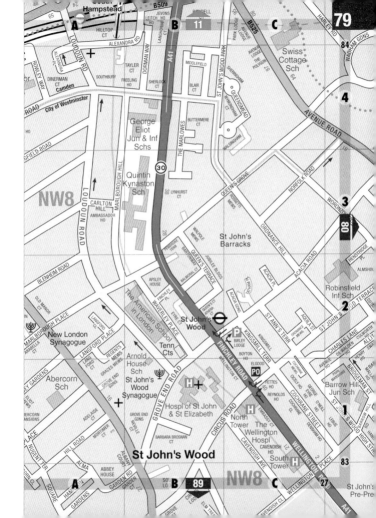

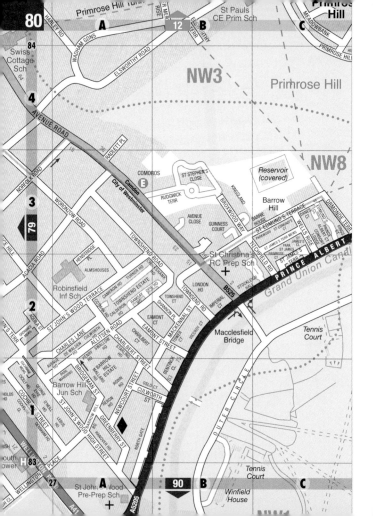

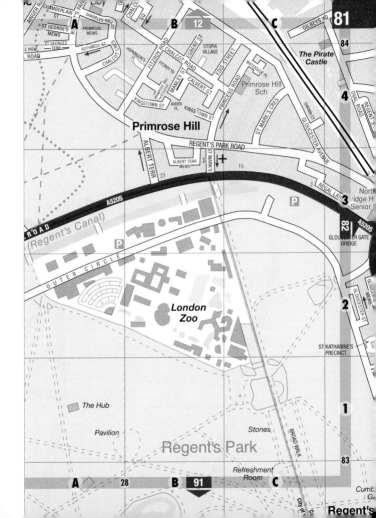

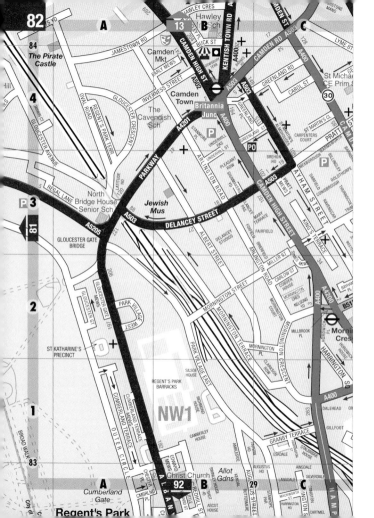

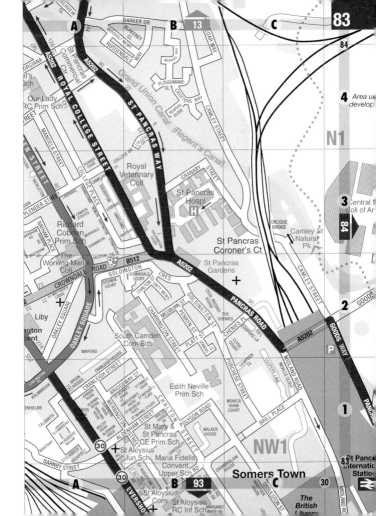

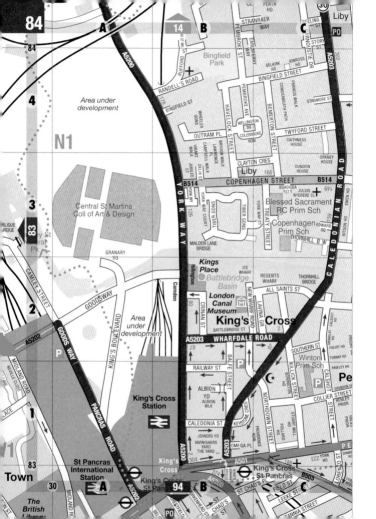

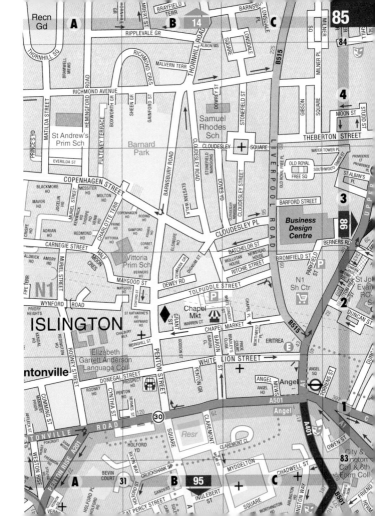

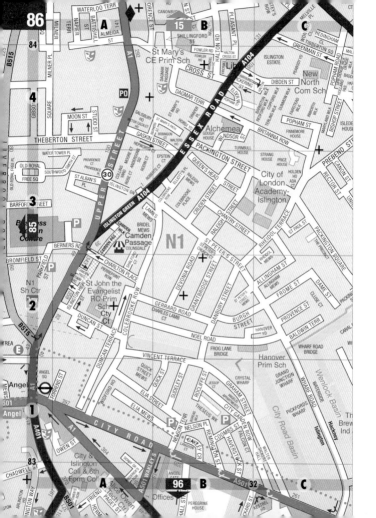

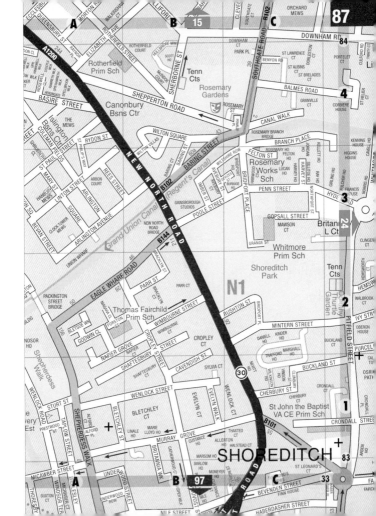

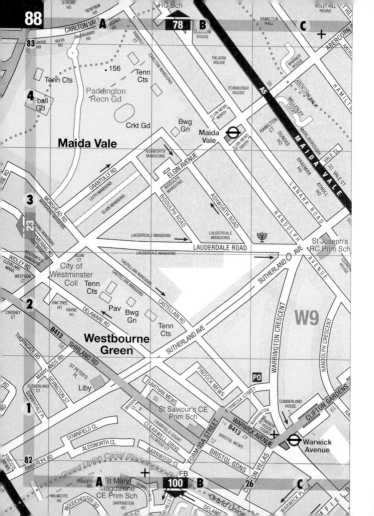

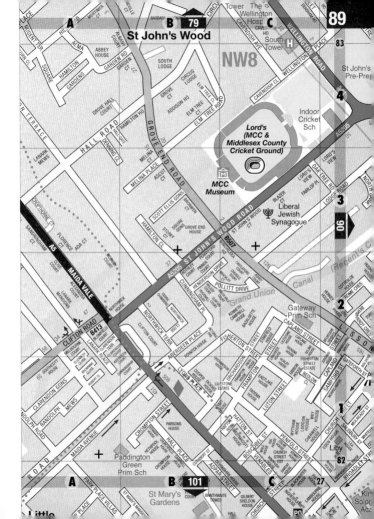

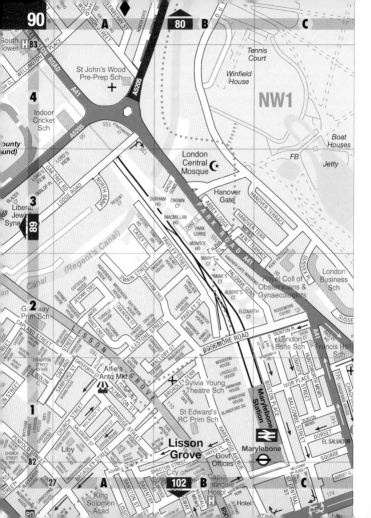

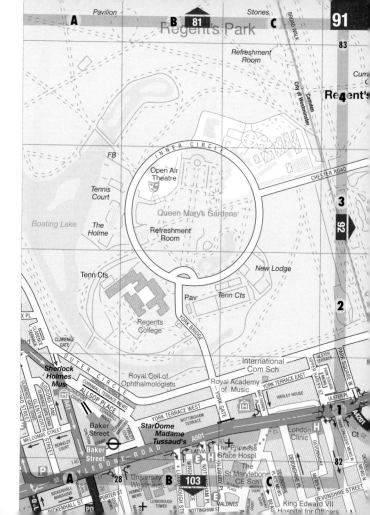

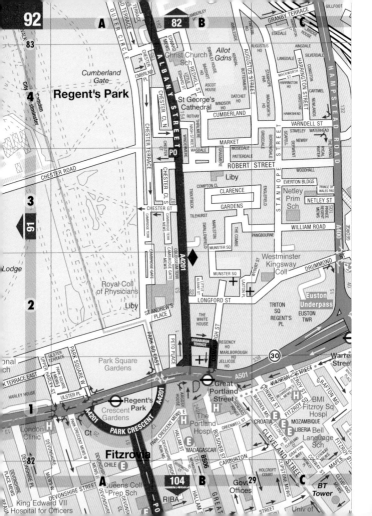

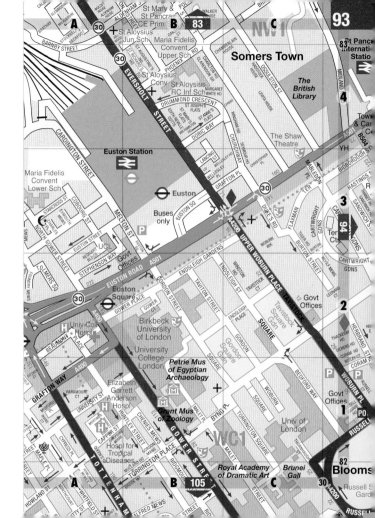

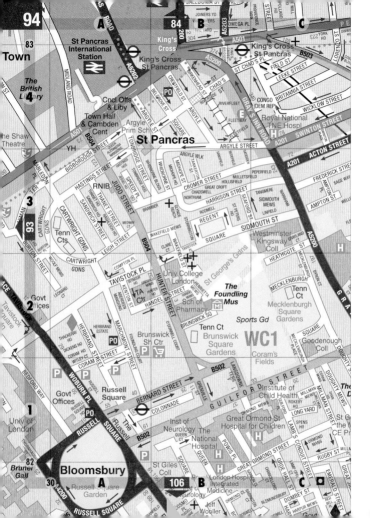

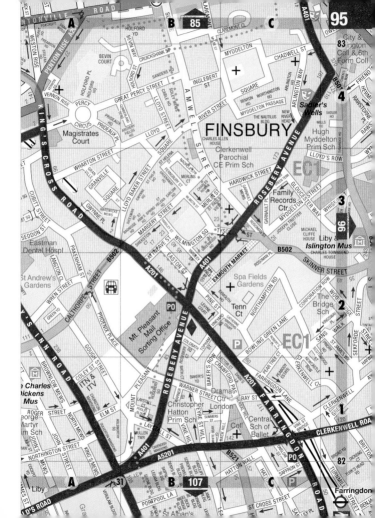

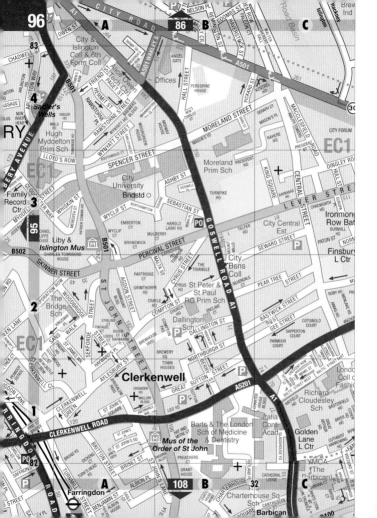

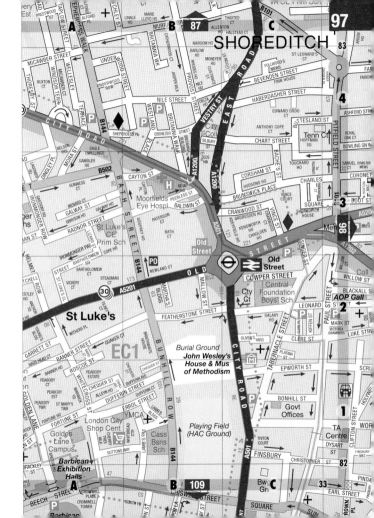

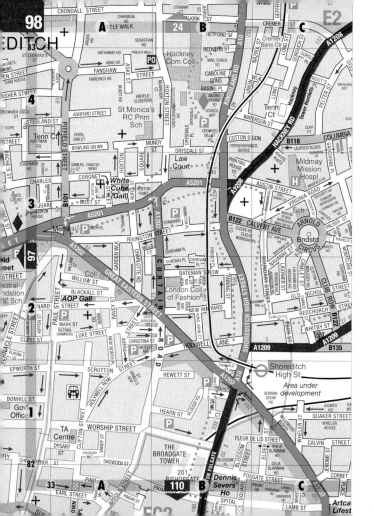

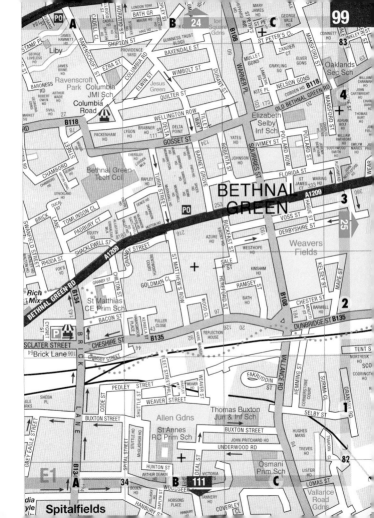

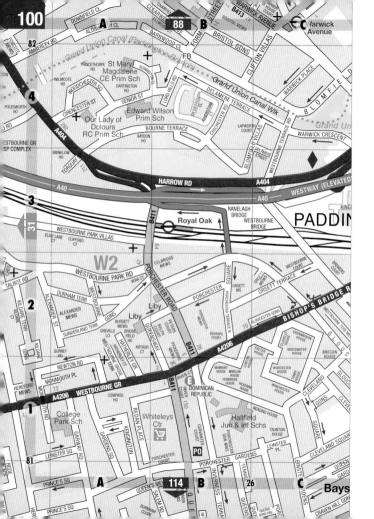

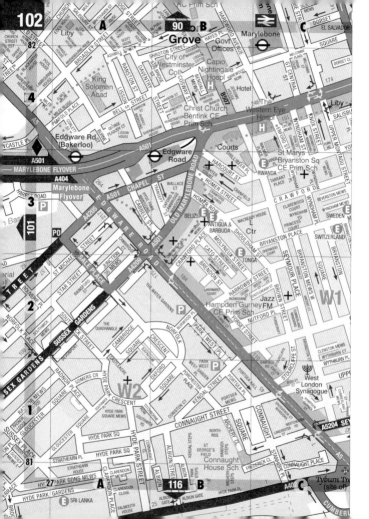

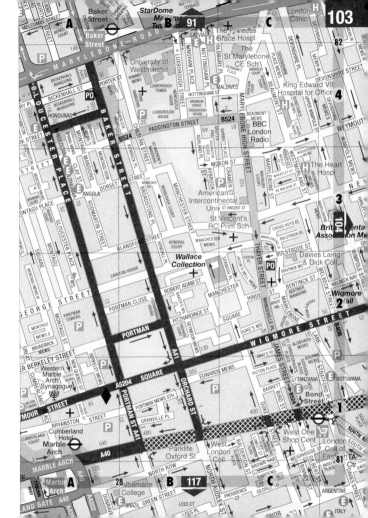

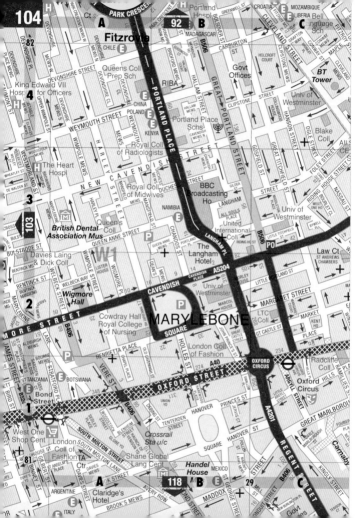

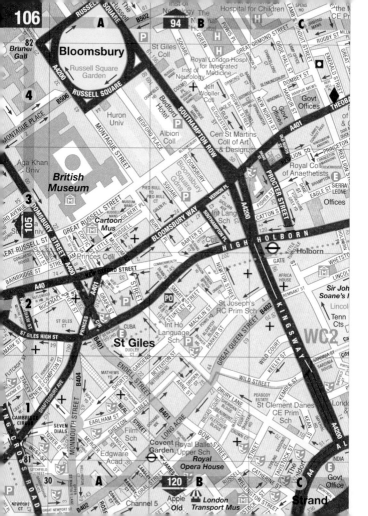

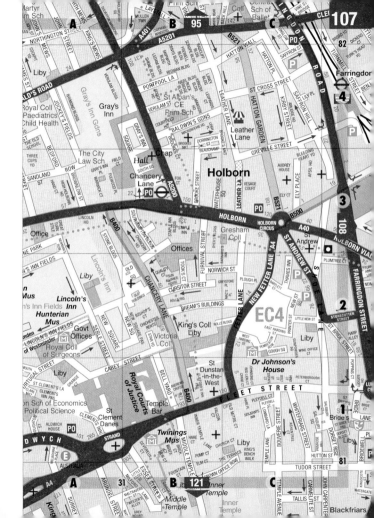

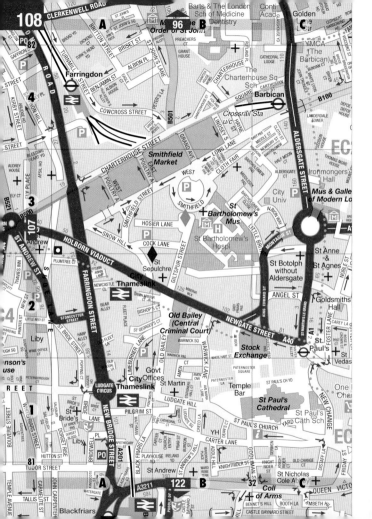

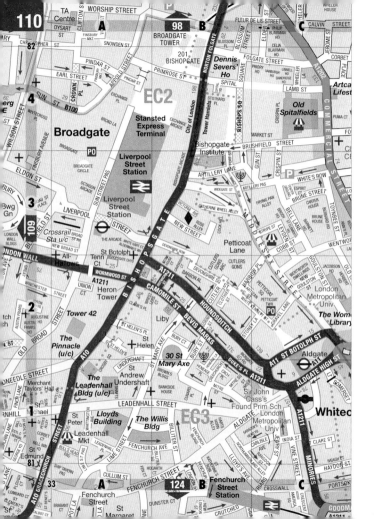

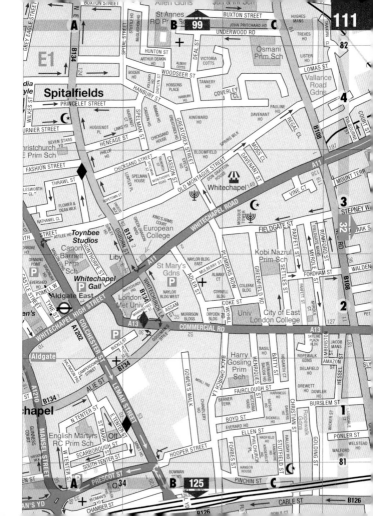

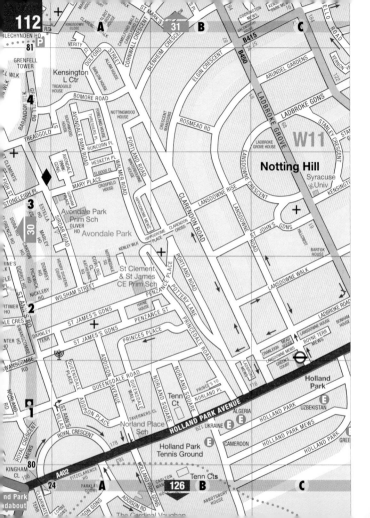

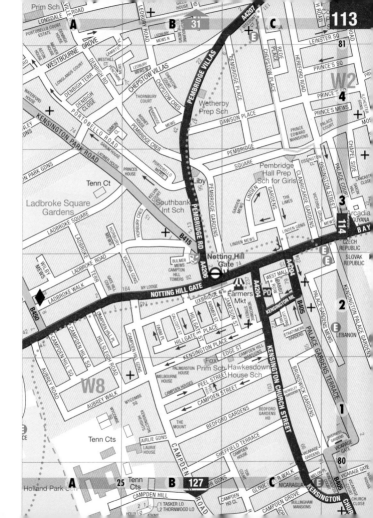

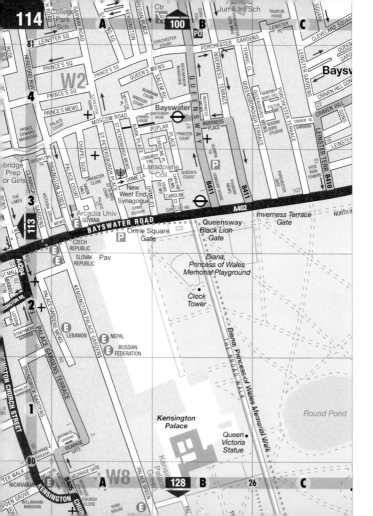

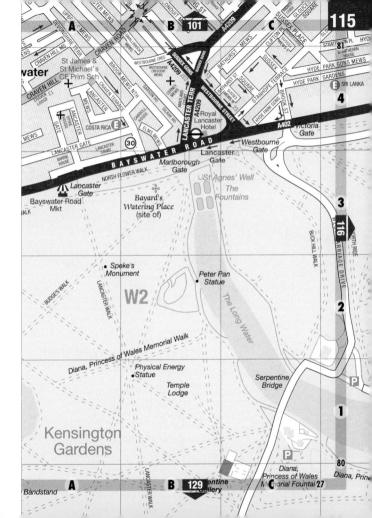

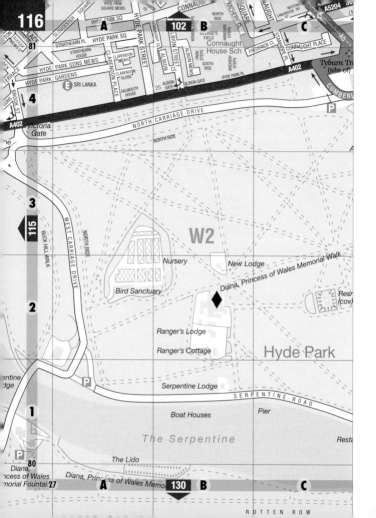

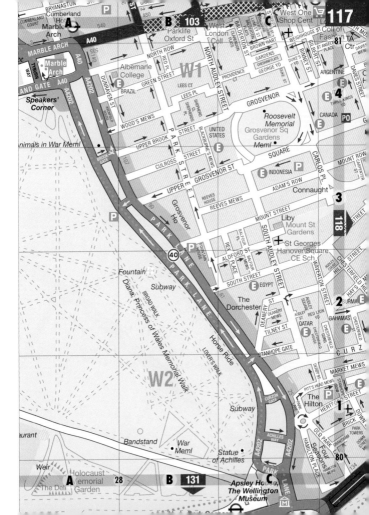

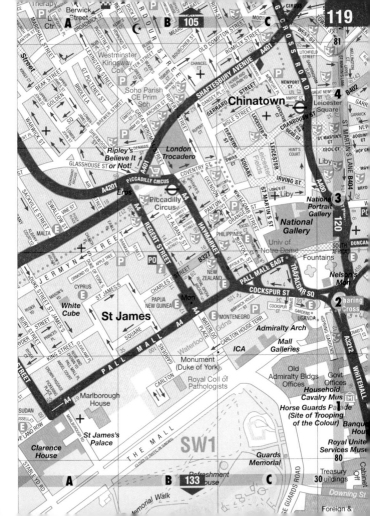

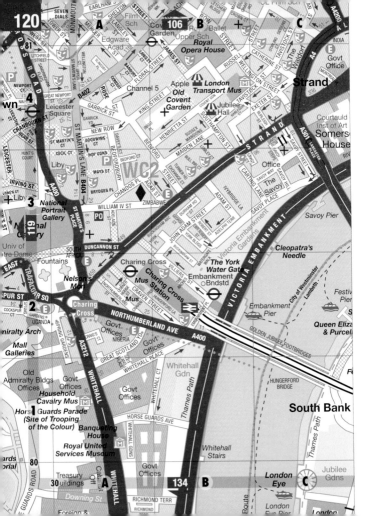

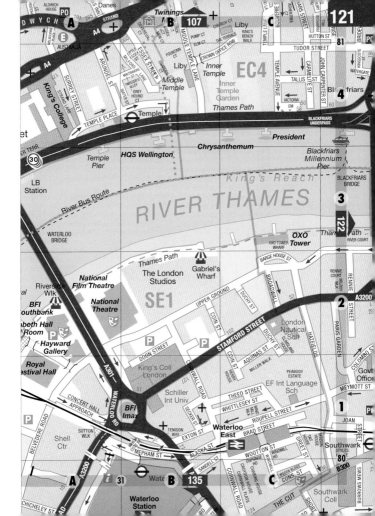

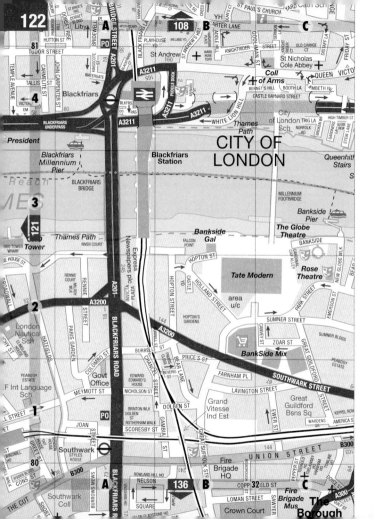

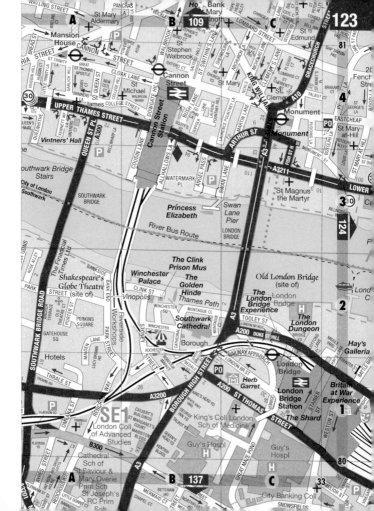

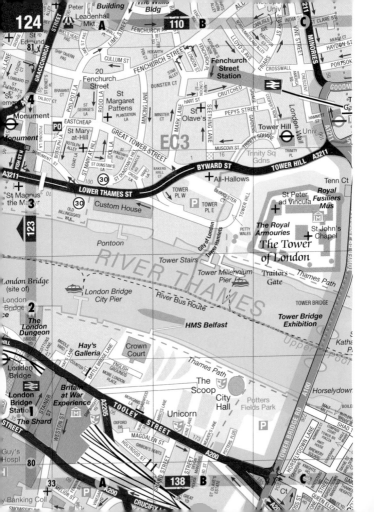

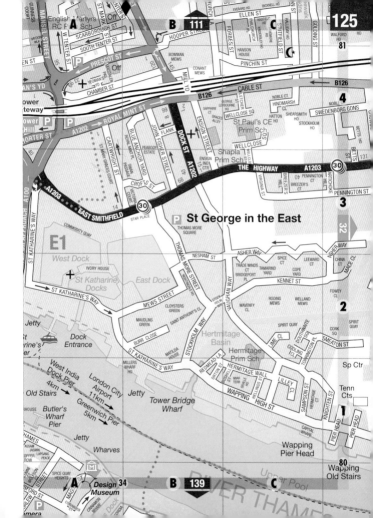

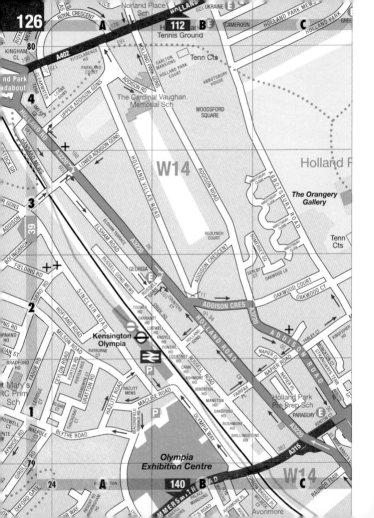

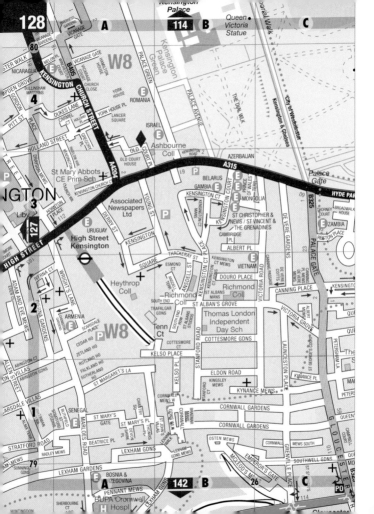

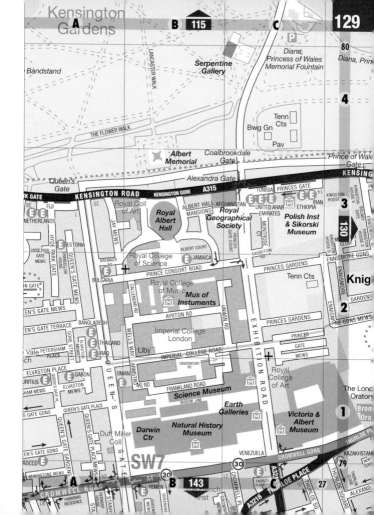

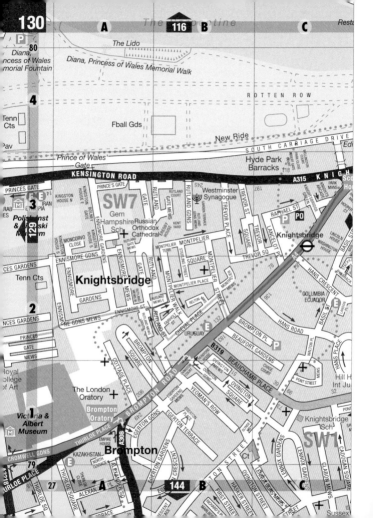

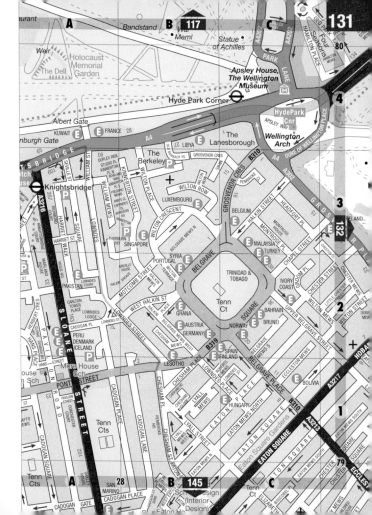

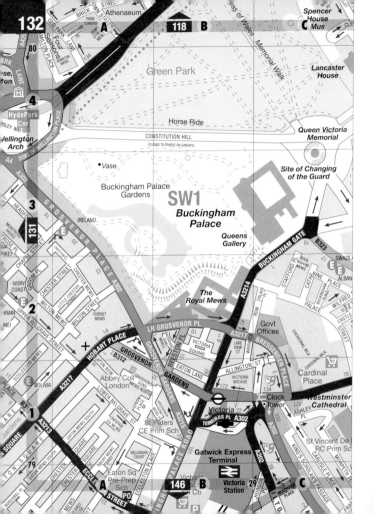

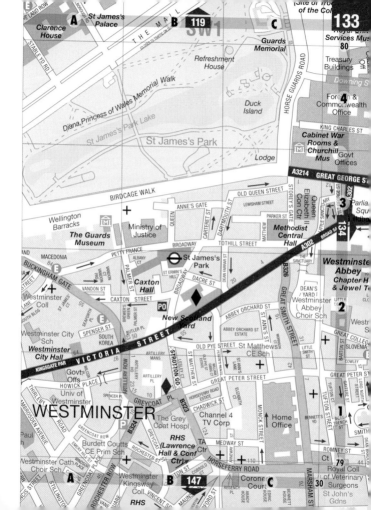

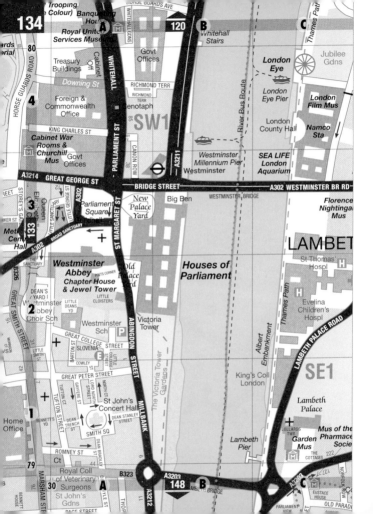

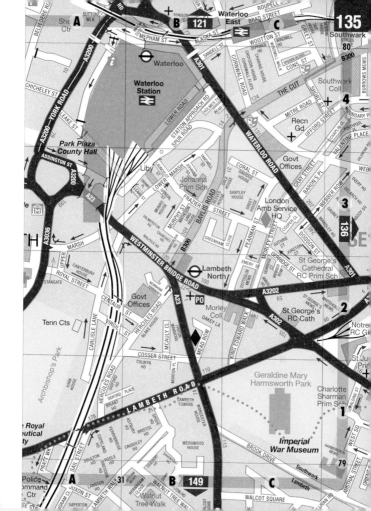

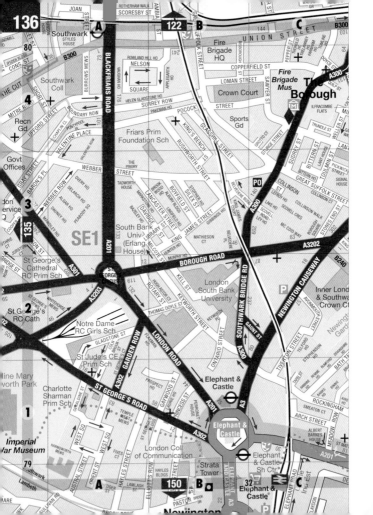

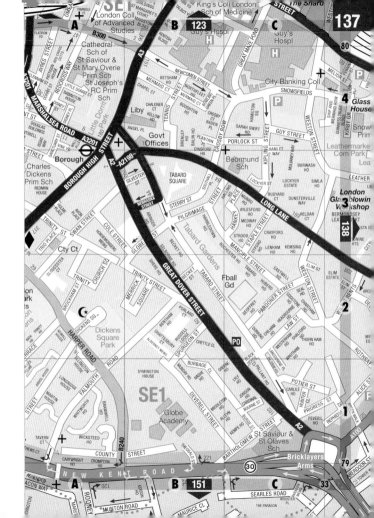

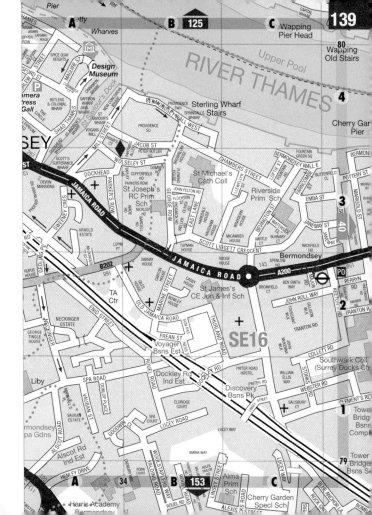

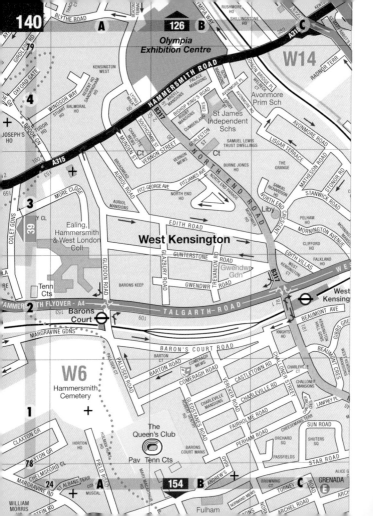

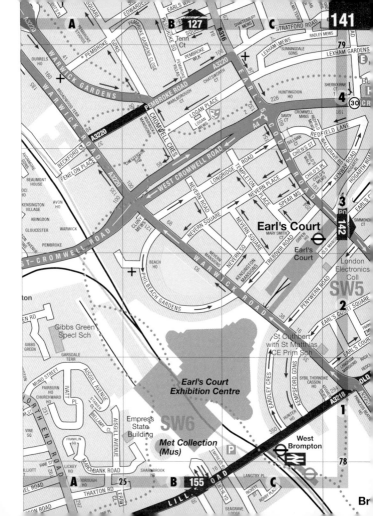

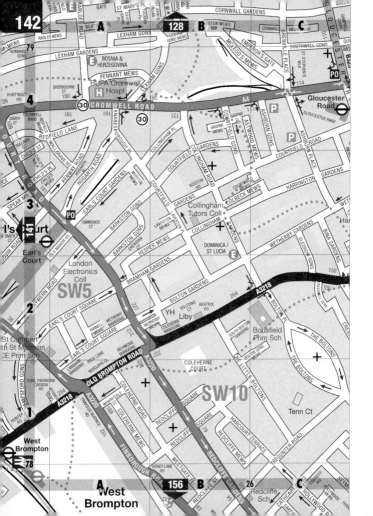

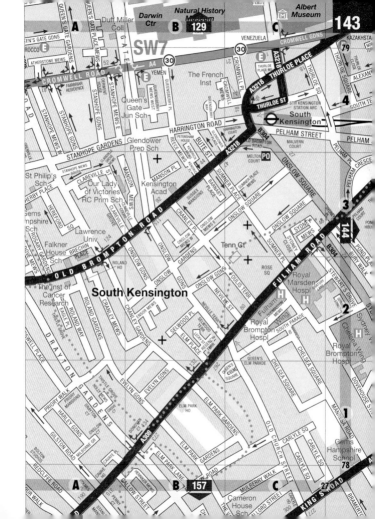

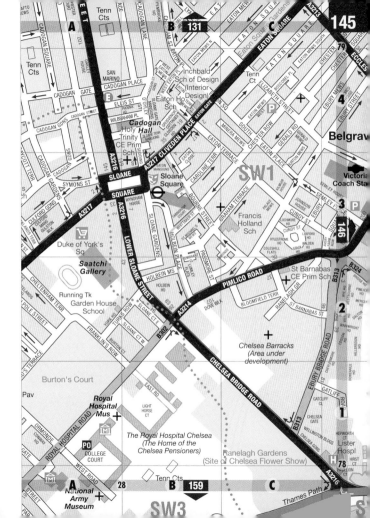

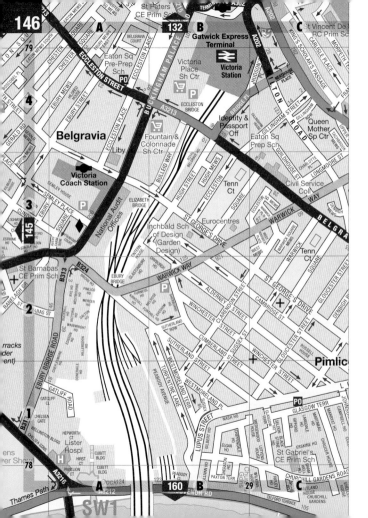

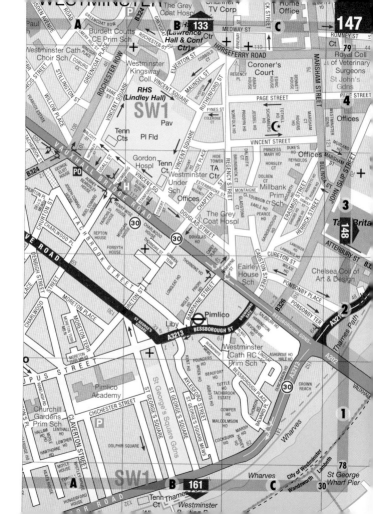

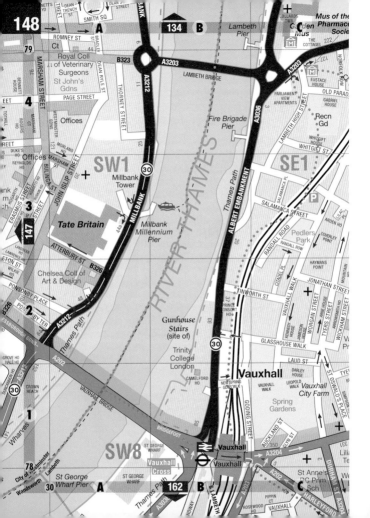

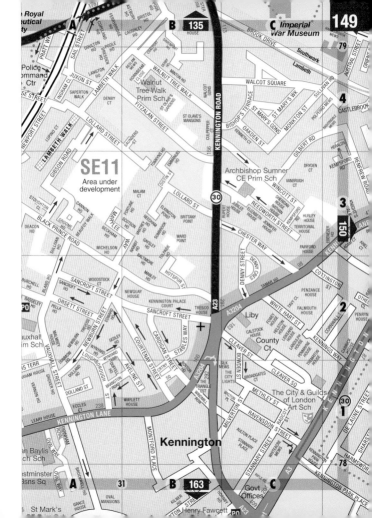

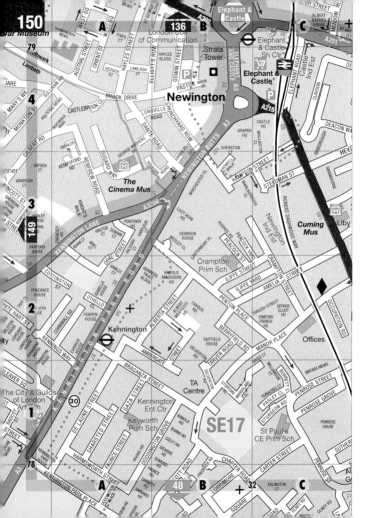

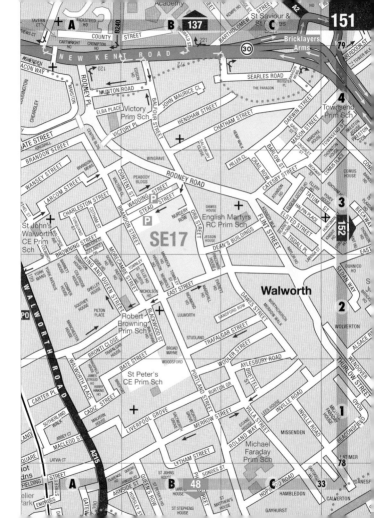

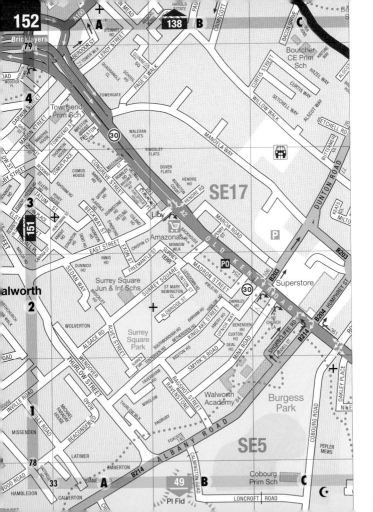

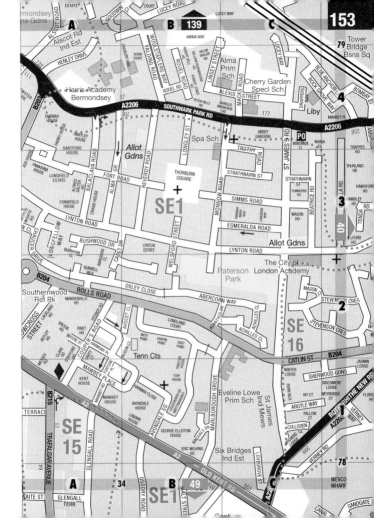

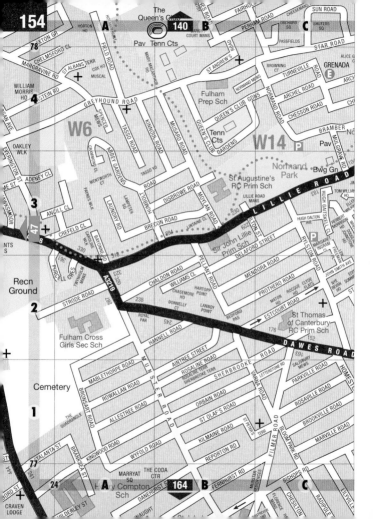

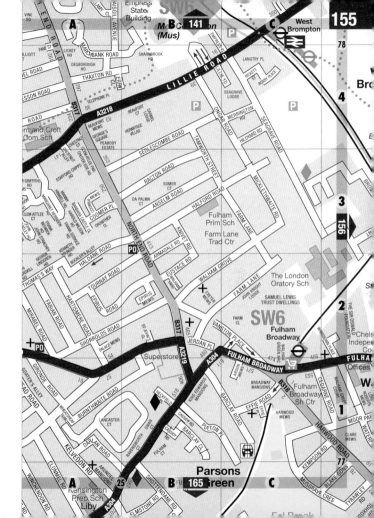

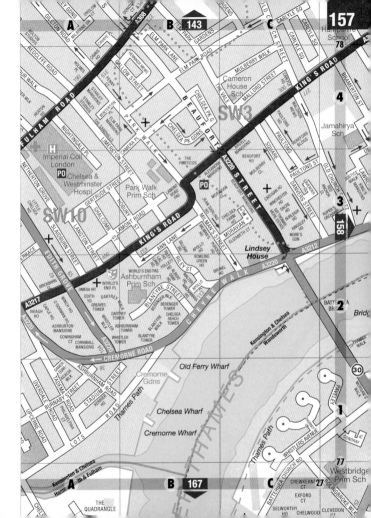

158

Gems
Hampshire
School

A

Offices

144

B

C

KING'S ROAD

A3217

B3004

King's Court N
King's Court E

CHELSEA MANOR

FLOOD WALK

CHELSEA MANOR ST

REDESDALE ST

CHRISTCHURCH STREET

CAVERSHAM ST

HAYDEN PIPER HO

CHELSEA TOWERS

MANOR STREET ESTATE

ALPHA PL

FLOOD STREET

GROVE HO

OAKLEY

ROSSETTI STUDIOS

ST LOO AVE

ROSSETTI GDNS MANSIONS

CHEYNE CT

Christchurch
CE Prim Sch

The
English
Gardening Sch

Chelsea
Physic Garden

Jamahiriya
Sch

BRAMERTON ST

GLEBE PLACE

OAKLEY STREET

MARGARETTA TERR

PHENE ST

GARDENS

SW3

CHEYNE GDNS

PAULTONS

HEREFORD BLDGS

PAULTONS ST

OLD CHURCH STREET

DANVEL STREET

UPPER CHEYNE ROW

JUSTICE WALK

LAWRENCE ST

CHELSEA EMBANKMENT

18 Thames Path

+Carlyle's
House

ADAIR HO

PIER HO

B3004

CHEYNE MEWS

CHEYNE WALK

Cadogan Pier

157

A3212

A2031

ALBERT BRIDGE
(SUSPENSION)

RIVER TH

Chel

30

BATTERSEA
BRIDGE

Bridge Wharf

THAMES WALK

ALBION RIVERSIDE

RIVERSIDE

WATERSIDE POINT

RANSOMES MEWS

GREAT EASTERN WHARF

ANHALT ROAD

CADOGAN CT

Terrace Wa

Thames Path

Old English
Garden

CARRIAGE DRIVE NORTH

Pav

& Chelsea
dsworth

2

30

HESTER ROAD

ELCHO STREET

PARKGATE ROAD

Ransome's
Dock

Bsns
Ctr

Govt
Offices

ALBANY MANSIONS

ST MARY'S

P

P

1

PAVELEY RD

BRIDGE WALK

HOWIE ST

Royal Coll of Art
Sculpture Sch

SEARLES CL

JUER STREET

WORFIELD ST

ALBERT BRIDGE ROAD

BEDFORD MANSIONS

CARRIAGE DRIVE WEST

77

WHISTLERS AVENUE

PAVELEY RD

CONDRAY

CREWKERNE CT

EXFORD CT

SELWORTHY HO

CHELWOOD

CLEVEDON CT

B3305

BATTERSEA BRIDGE ROAD

PO

30

Westbridge
Prim Sch

MUSGRAVE CT

A

HYDE LA

RANDALL CL

WILL

168

B

HERON HO

MASKELYNE

WELBURGA

ETHELBURGA

HENTY CL

JAGGER HO

ALBERT

C

BA

27

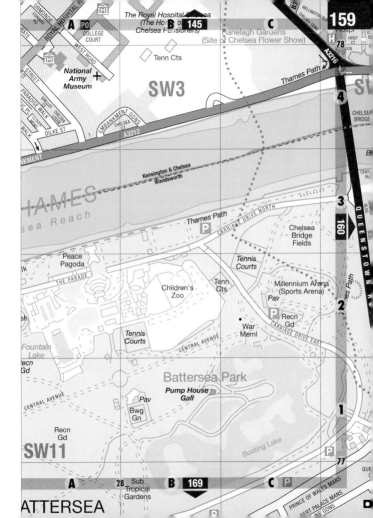

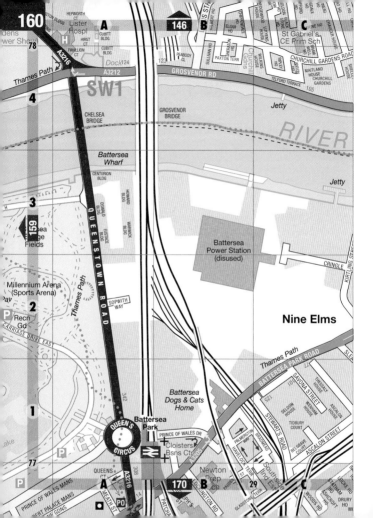

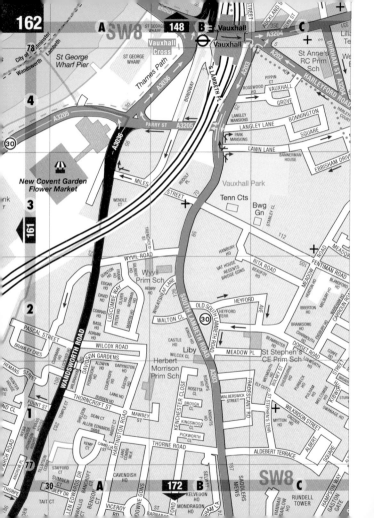

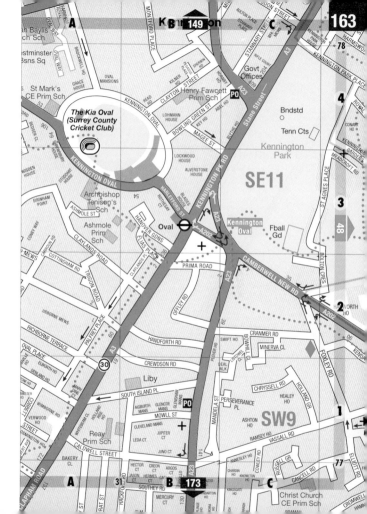

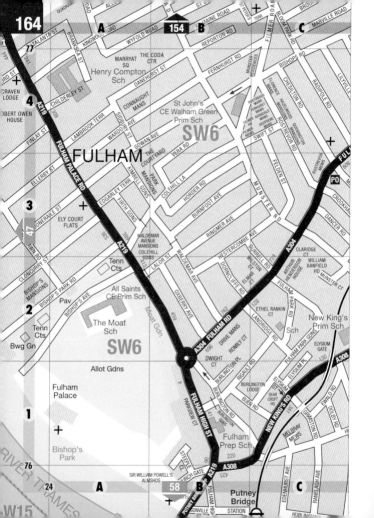

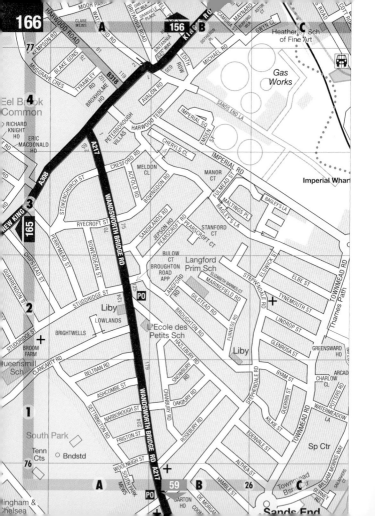

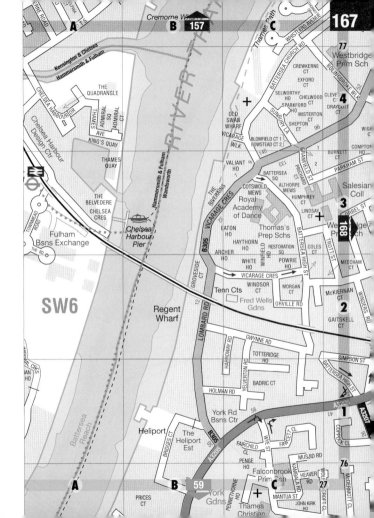

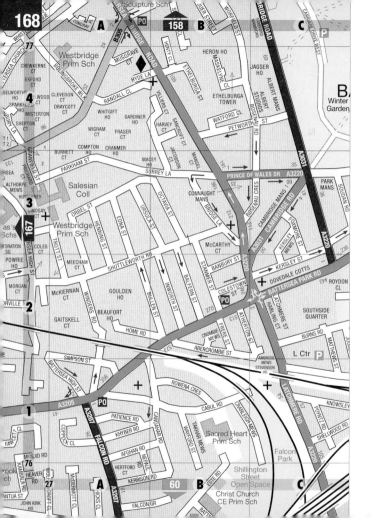

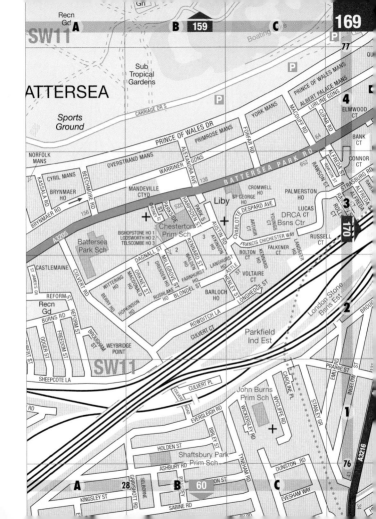

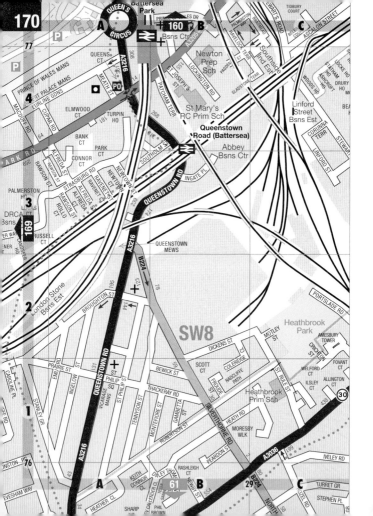

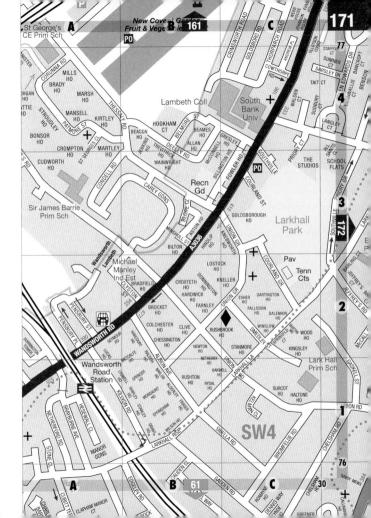

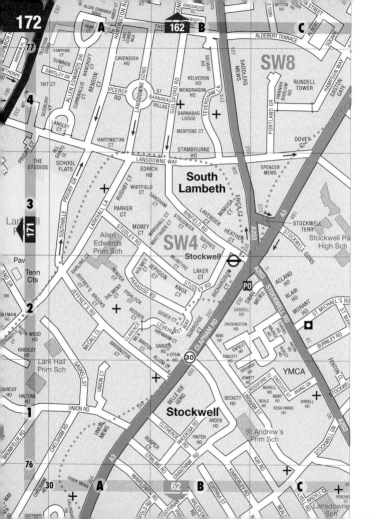

Index

Church Rd **6** Beckenham BR2..........**53** C6 **228** C6

Place name	**Location number**	**Locality, town or village**	**Postcode district**	**Standard scale reference**	**Enlarged scale reference**
May be abbreviated on the map	Present when a number indicates the place's position in a crowded area of mapping	Shown when more than one place (outside London postal districts) has the same name	District for the indexed place	Page number and grid reference for the standard mapping	Page number and grid reference for the central London enlarged mapping, underlined in red

Public and commercial buildings are highlighted in magenta.
Places of interest are highlighted in blue
Cities, towns and villages are listed in CAPITAL LETTERS

Abbreviations used in the index

Acad	Academy	Ct	Court	Int	International	Prom	Promenade
App	Approach	Ctr	Centre	Intc	Interchange	RC	Roman Catholic
Arc	Arcade	Crkt	Cricket	Jun	Junior	Rd	Road
Art Gall	Art Gallery	Ctry Pk	Country Park	Junc	Junction	Rdbt	Roundabout
Ave	Avenue	Cty	County	La	Lane	Ret Pk	Retail Park
Bglws	Bungalows	Ctyd	Courtyard	L Ctr	Leisure Centre	Sch	School
Bldgs	Buildings	Dr	Drive	Liby	Library	Sec	Secondary
Bsns Ctr	Business Centre	Ent Ctr	Enterprise Centre	Mans	Mansions	Sh Ctr	Shopping Centre
Bsns Pk	Business Park	Ent Pk	Enterprise Park	Mdw/s	Meadow/s	Sp	Sports
Bvd	Boulevard	Est	Estate	Meml	Memorial	Specl	Special
Cath	Cathedral, Catholic	Ex Ctr	Exhibition Centre	Mid	Middle	Sports Ctr	Sports Centre
CE	Church of England	Ex Hall	Exhibition Hall	Mix	Mixed	Sq	Square
Cemy	Cemetery	Fst	First	Mkt	Market	St	Street, Saint
Cir	Circus	Gdn	Garden	Mon	Monument	Sta	Station
Circ	Circle	Gdns	Gardens	Mus	Museum	Stad	Stadium
Cl	Close	Gn	Green	Obsy	Observatory	Tech	Technical
Cnr	Corner	Gr	Grove	Orch	Orchard		Technology
Coll	College	Gram	Grammar	Par	Parade	Terr	Terrace
Com	Community	Her Ctr	Heritage Centre	Pas	Passage	Trad Est	Trading Estate
Comm	Common	Ho	House	Pav	Pavilion	Twr/s	Tower/s
Comp	Comprehensive	Hospl	Hospital	Pk	Park	Univ	University
Con Ctr	Conference Centre	Hts	Heights	Pl	Place	Wlk	Walk
Cotts	Cottages	Ind Est	Industrial Estate	Prec	Precinct	Yd	Yard
Cres	Crescent	Inf	Infant	Prep	Preparatory		
Cswy	Causeway	Inst	Institute	Prim	Primary		

2 Willow Rd NW3....**12** A4
3 Mills Studios
E14..................**27** B2
30 St Mary Axe (The
Gherkin) EC2.... **110** B2
176 Gall NW5......**12** C2
201 Bishopsgate
EC2.............. **110** B4

A

Abady Ho SW1 ....**147** C4
Abberley Mews **9**
SW8..................**61** A4
Abbess Cl SW2 ....**75** A3
Abbeville Mews **3**
SW4..................**61** C3
Abbeville Rd SW4 ....**61** C3
Abbey Bsns Ctr
SW8................**170** B4
Abbey Coll London
SW1................**132** A1
Abbey Ct
6 Bedford Pk
W12..................**38** A3
Camberwell SE17...**151** A1
St John's Wood
NW8..................**78** C2
Abbeyfield Rd
SE16................**40** B2
Abbey Gdns
10 Bermondsey
SE16................**153** C4
St John's Wood
NW8..................**79** A1
West Kensington
W6..................**154** A3
Abbey Ho NW8 .....**89** A4
Abbey La E15........**27** C3
Abbey Lo NW8 ......**90** B3
Abbey Orchard St
SW1................**133** C2
Abbey Orchard Street
Est SW1............**133** C2
Abbey Rd
St John's Wood
NW8..................**78** C2
Wembley NW10 .....**20** A3
Abbey St SE1......**138** C2
Abbot Ct SW8 .....**162** A1
Abbot Ho **14** E14 ...**34** A2
Abbotsbury Cl
Kensington W14....**126** C3
Mill Meads E15......**27** B3
Abbotsbury Ho
W14................**126** B4
Abbotsbury Mews
SE15..................**65** B4
Abbotsbury Rd
W14................**126** C3
Abbotshade Rd **15**
SE16..................**32** C1
Abbots Ho
Kensington W14....**126** C1
Pimlico SW1......**147** B1
Abbots La SE1....**124** B1
Abbots Pk SW2....**74** C3
Abbot's PI NW6 ....**78** A4
Abbot St E8 ....**16** B2
Abbotstone Ho **4**
E5....................**7** C2
Abbotstone Rd
SW15..................**57** B4
Abbotswell Rd SE4 ..**66** B2

Abbotswood Rd
London SE22........**64** A3
Streatham SW16....**73** C1
Abbott Ho SW12....**72** B4
Abbott Rd E14.....**34** C3
Abbotts Cl N1......**15** B2
Abbotts Wharf **4**
E14..................**33** C3
Abchurch La EC2,
EC4................**123** C4
Abchurch Yd EC4...**123** B4
Abdale Rd W12......**30** A1
Abel Ho **7** SE11....**163** B4
Aberavon Rd E3....**26** B2
Abercorn Cl NW8....**88** C4
Abercorn Mans
NW8..................**79** A1
Abercorn Mews **16**
TW10..................**54** B3
Abercorn Pl NW8....**78** C1
Abercorn Sch NW8...**79** A1
Abercorn Way
SE1................**153** B2
Abercorn Wlk
NW8..................**88** C4
Abercrombie Ho **1**
W12..................**30** A2
Abercrombie St
SW11................**168** B2
Aberdale Ct **22**
SE16..................**40** C4
Aberdare Gdns
NW6..................**11** A1
Aberdeen Ct
Canonbury N5.......**15** B3
Paddington W9 .....**89** B1
Aberdeen Ctr N5 ...**15** B3
Aberdeen La N5.....**15** B3
Aberdeen Mans
WC1..................**94** A2
Aberdeen Pk N5....**15** B3
Aberdeen Pl NW8 ...**89** B2
Aberdeen Rd
Canonbury N5.......**15** B4
Dudden Hill NW10 ...**8** B3
Aberdeen Terr
SE3..................**52** C1
Aberdour St SE1...**152** A4
Aberfeldy Ho SE5...**48** A3
Aberfeldy St E14 ...**34** B3
Abersham Rd E8 ...**16** B3
Ability Plaza **8** E8 ...**16** B1
Ability Twrs EC1 ...**96** C4
Abingdon W14 .....**141** A3
Abingdon Cl
Fulham SE1........**153** A2
Kentish Town NW1...**13** C2
Abingdon Ct SW8 .**127** C1
Abingdon Gdns
W8..................**127** C1
Abingdon Ho
E2........**24** B1 **98** C2
Abingdon Mans
W8..................**127** B2
Abingdon Rd W8 ..**127** C1
Abingdon St SW1 .**134** A2
Abingdon Villas
W8..................**127** C1
Abinger Gr SE8......**51** B4
Abinger Ho SE1 ...**137** B3
Abinger Mews W9...**23** C1
Abinger Rd W4......**38** A3
Ablett St SE16......**40** B1
Abney Gdns **15**
N16....................**7** B2
Abney Park Cemetery
N16....................**7** A2

Abney Park Ct N16 ...**7** B2
Aborfield **6** NW5 ...**13** B3
Aboyne Rd SW17 ...**71** C1
Abyssinia Cl SW11...**60** A3
Abyssinia Rd
SW11................**60** A3
Acacia Cl SE8......**41** A2
Acacia Gdns NW8 ...**79** C2
Acacia Gr SE21 ....**75** C2
Acacia Ho
Brockley SE4.......**66** B3
Stoke Newington
N16....................**6** C2
Acacia Pl NW8 .....**79** C2
Acacia Rd
Acton W3............**28** B2
St John's Wood
NW8..................**79** C2
Acacia Wlk SW10 .**157** A1
Academy Ct **2** E2 ...**25** B2
Academy Gdns
W8..................**127** B4
Academy Sch The **9**
NW3..................**11** C4
Academy The **2**
N19....................**4** B3
Acad of Live &
Recorded Arts
SW18..................**59** C1
Acanthus Dr SE1 .**153** B2
Acanthus Rd
SW11................**60** C4
Accommodation Rd
London NW11........**1** B3
Acer Ct **2** NW2 .....**9** C4
Acer Rd E8 ....**16** B1
Acfold Rd SW6 ....**166** A3
Achilles Cl SE1 ...**153** C2
Achilles Ho **6** E2 ...**25** A3
Achilles St SE14 ...**51** A3
Achilles Way W1 ..**117** C1
Acklam Rd W10 ....**31** B4
Ackmar Rd SW6 ..**165** B3
Ackroyd Dr E3......**33** C4
Acland Burghley Sch
N19..................**13** A4
Acland Cres SE5 ...**63** C4
Acland Ho SW9 ...**172** C2
Acland Rd NW2......**9** A2
Acol Ct **3** NW6....**10** C1
Acol Rd NW6 ....**11** A1
Acorn Ct **5** E3.....**26** C3
Acorn Gdns W3....**28** C4
Acorn Par **7** SE15...**50** A3
Acorn Production Ctr
N7....................**14** A1
Acorns The **21**
SW19..................**69** C3
Acorn Wharf SE15...**49** C4
Acorn Wlk SE16 ....**33** A1
Acqua Ho TW9 .....**45** A3
Acre Ct SW2........**64** C3
Acre La SW2........**62** B3
Acris St SW18......**59** B2
ACTON................**28** C1
Acton Bsns Ctr
NW10..................**20** C1
Acton Central Ind Est
4 W3................**28** A1
Acton Central Sta
W3..................**28** C1
ACTON GREEN......**37** B2
Acton High Sch
W3..................**36** C4

Acton Hill Mews
W3..................**28** A1
W3..................**28** A1
Acton Ho
16 Acton W3........**28** B3
Acton La
Acton Green W4....**37** B2
Acton W3............**37** B3
Harlesden NW10....**20** C3
Acton Main Line Sta
W3..................**28** B3
Acton Park Ind Est
W3..................**37** C4
Acton St WC1......**94** C3
Acton Town Sta
W3..................**36** C4
Acton Vale Ind Pk
W3..................**29** B2
Acton & West London
Coll **12** W3.......**28** A1
Acuba Ho SW18 ...**71** A3
Acuba Rd SW18 ...**71** A2
Ada Ct
Islington N1........**86** C3
St John's Wood W9 ..**89** A3
Ada Gdns E14......**34** C3
Ada Gdns E15......**27** C4
Adair Ho SW3 ....**158** B4
Adair Rd W10 ......**23** A1
Adair Twr **7** W10...**23** A1
Ada Kennedy Ct **6**
SE10..................**52** B3
Adam Ct SE11 ....**150** A3
Adam & Eve Ct
W1..................**105** A2
Adam & Eve Mews
W8..................**127** C2
Adamfields W13 ...**54** C1
Adams Gardens Est **5**
SE16..................**40** B4
Adams Ho **3** E14...**34** C3
Adams Mews
SW17..................**72** B2
Adamson Rd
Hampstead NW3 ...**11** C1
Newham E16........**35** C3
Adams Pl N7 ......**14** B3
Adam's Row W1 ..**117** C3
Adam St WC2......**120** B3
Adam Wlk SW6......**47** B3
Ada Pl E2 ....**24** C4
Ada Rd SE5 ....**49** A3
Adare Wlk SW16,
SW2..................**74** B2
Ada St E8 ....**25** A4
Adderley Gr SW11...**60** C2
Adderley St E14 ...**34** B3
Addey Ho SE8 ......**51** B3
Addey & Stanhope
Sch **13** SE14 .....**51** C2
Addington Ct **7**
SW14..................**55** C4
Addington Ho **13**
SW9..................**173** A1
Addington Rd E3 ...**26** C2
Addington Sq SE5 ...**48** C3
Addington St SE1 .**135** A3
Addis Ho **13** E11...**32** B4
Addison Ave
W11......**31** A1 **112** A1
Addison Bridge Pl
W14................**140** C4
Addison Cres
W14................**126** B2

Addison Gdns
W14..................**39** C3
Addison Gr W4.....**38** A3
Addison Ho NW8 ...**89** B4
Addison Park Mans **12**
W14..................**39** C4
Addison Pl
W11......**31** A1 **112** A1
Addison Prim Sch
W14..................**39** C3
Addison Rd W14..**126** C2
Addle Hill EC4.....**108** B1
Addlestone Ho **4**
W10..................**30** B4
Addy Ho SE16......**40** B2
Adelaide Ave SE4 ...**66** C3
Adelaide Cl SW9 ...**62** C3
Adelaide Ct
Hackney E5.........**18** A3
St John's Wood
NW8..................**79** A1
Adelaide Gr W12 ...**29** C1
Adelaide Rd
Primrose Hill
NW3..................**12** A1
Richmond TW9 .....**54** B3
2 Wandsworth
SW18..................**58** C2
Adela St W10......**23** A1
Adelina Gr E1......**32** B4
Adelina Mews
SW12..................**73** C3
Adelphi Cl SW12 ..**105** C3
Adelphi Ct **20**
SE16..................**40** C4
Adelphi Terr WC2 .**120** B3
Aden Gr N16.......**15** C4
Aden Ho **16** E1 ....**32** C4
Aden Lo N16 ....**15** C4
Adeyfield Ho EC1 ...**97** C3
Adie Rd W6 ....**39** B3
Adisham Ho **4** E5 ...**17** A3
Adler St E1 ....**111** B2
Adley St E5 ....**18** A3
Admiral Ct
Chelsea SW10 ....**167** A4
Marylebone W1 ...**103** B3
Admiral Hyson Ind Est
SE16..................**40** A1
Admiral Mews
W10..................**22** C1
Admiral Pl SE16 ...**33** A1
Admirals Ct
Bermondsey SE1 .**124** C1
32 Putney SW19 ....**69** C3
Admirals Gate
SE10..................**52** A2
Admiral Sq SW10 .**167** A4
Admiral St SE8 ....**51** C2
Admiral Wlk W9 ...**23** C1
Admiral's Way E14 ...**41** C4
Admiral's Wlk NW3 ..**2** B1
Admiralty Arch
SW1................**119** C2
Admiralty Cl **1**
SW8..................**51** C4
Admiral Wlk W9 ...**23** C1
Adolphus Rd N4....**6** A3
Adolphus St SE8 ...**51** B3
Adpar St W2 ......**101** B4
Adrian Bolt Ho **2**
E2....................**25** A2

Adrian Ho
Islington N1 .... **85** A3
South Lambeth
SW8 .... **162** A2
Stratford E15 .... **19** C1

Adrian Mews
SW10 .... **156** B4

Adriatic Bldg 18
E14 .... **33** A2
Adriatic Ho 15 E16 .. **40** B2
Adron Ho 15 SE16 .. **40** B2
Adstock Ho 5 N1 .. **15** A1
Adventurers Ct 17
E14 .... **34** C2
Adys Lawn NW2 .... **9** A2
Adys Rd SE15 ...... **64** B4
Aegean Apts 7
E16 .... **35** C2
Aegon Ho 8 E14 .. **42** A3
Affleck St N1 ...... **85** A1
Afghan Rd SW11 .. **168** A1
Africa Ho WC2 ..... **106** C2
Afsil Ho EC1 .... **107** C3
Aga Khan Univ
WC1 .... **105** C3
Agamemnon Rd
NW6 .... **10** B3
Agar Gr NW1 .... **13** C1
Agar Pl NW1 .... **13** B1
Agar St WC2 ...... **120** B3
Agate Rd W6 ...... **39** B3
Agatha Cl E1 ...... **32** B1
Agave Rd NW2 ..... **9** B4
Agdon St EC1 ..... **96** A2
Agincourt Rd NW3 .. **12** B4
Agnes Ct 11 SW11 .. **59** C3
Agnes Ho 13 W11 .. **30** C2
Agnes Rd W3 ...... **38** B4
Agnes St E14 ..... **33** B3
Aicon Gall SW1 .... **118** C4
Aigburth Mans 1
SW9 .... **163** B1
Ailsa St E14 ...... **34** B4
Ainger Rd NW3 .... **12** B1
Ainsdale NW1 ..... **92** C4
Ainsdale Dr SE1 .. **153** B1
Ainsley St E2 ..... **25** A2
Ainslie Wlk 8
SW12 .... **73** A4
Ainsty St 16 SE16 .. **40** B4
Ainsworth Cl SE5 .. **49** A1
Ainsworth Est
NW8 .... **78** C4
Ainsworth Ho NW8 **78** B3
Ainsworth Rd E9 .. **17** B1
Ainsworth Way
NW8 .... **78** C4
Aintree St SW6 ... **154** B2
Aird Ho SE1 ...... **136** C1
Airdrie Cl N1 ..... **14** B1
Airedale Ave W4 .. **38** B1
Airedale Ave S W4 **38** B1
Airedale Rd SW12 .. **72** B4
Airlie Gdns
W8 .... **31** C1 **113** B1
Air St W1 .... **119** A3
Aisgill Ave SW5 ... **141** A1
Aiten Pl W6 ...... **38** C2
Aithan Ho 15 E14 .. **33** B3
Aitken Cl E8 ...... **24** C4
Ajax Ho 12 E2 .... **25** A3
Ajax Rd NW6 ..... **10** C3
Akbar Ho 7 E14 .. **42** A2
Akehurst St SW15 .. **68** C4

Akenside Ct 3
NW3 .... **11** C3
Akenside Rd NW3 .. **11** C3
Akerman Rd SW9 .. **48** A2
Akintaro Ho 7
SE8 .... **51** B4
Alamaro Lo 5
SE10 .... **43** B3
Aland Ct SE16 .... **41** A3
Alan Preece Ct
NW6 .... **9** C1
Alaska Bldg 12
SE13 .... **52** A2
Alaska St SE1 ..... **135** A4
Alastor Ho 10 E14 .. **42** B3
Albacore Cres
SE13 .... **67** A1
Alba Mews SW18 .. **70** C2
Albany Ct
College Pk NW10 .. **22** A2
NW8 .... **79** B1
Westminster SW1 .. **133** B2
6 Whitechapel E1 .. **111** B2
Albany Ctyd W1 .. **119** A3
Albany Ho 18 TW8 .. **44** A4
Albany Mans
SW11 .... **158** B1
Albany Mews
Camberwell SE5 .... **48** B4
Islington N1 ...... **14** C1
Albany Par 4
TW8 .... **44** A4
Albany Pas 12
TW10 .... **54** A2
Albany Rd
Camberwell SE5 .... **49** A4
Richmond TW10 .. **54** A2
Albany Terr 6
TW10 .... **54** B2
Alba Pl W11 ...... **31** B3
Albemarle SW19 .. **69** C2
Albemarle Coll
W1 .... **117** A4
Albemarle Ho
2 Brixton SW9 .... **62** C4
Rotherhithe SE8 .. **41** B2
Albemarle Mans
NW3 .... **11** A3
Albemarle Prim Sch
SW19 .... **69** C3
Albemarle St W1 .. **118** C3
Albemarle Way
EC1 .... **96** A1
Alberta Ct 1
TW10 .... **54** B2
Alberta Ho E14 ... **34** B1
Alberta St SE17 .. **150** B2
Albert Ave SW8 .. **162** C1
Albert Barnes Ho
SE1 .... **136** C1
Albert Bigg Point
E15 .... **27** B4
Albert Bridge Rd
SW11 .... **158** C1
Albert Cl 11 E9 ... **25** A4
Albert Cotts 2
E1 .... **111** B4

Albert Ct
Knightsbridge
SW7 .... **129** B3
12 Putney SW19 .. **70** A3
Albert Gate Ct
SW1 .... **130** C3
Albert Gray Ho
SW10 .... **157** B2
Albert Hall Mans
SW7 .... **129** B3
Albert Mans
Battersea SW11 .. **168** C4
Hornsey N8 ...... **5** A4
Albert Meml SW7 .. **129** B3
Albert Mews W8 .. **128** C2
Albert Palace Mans
SW11 .... **169** C4
Albert Rd
Finsbury Pk N4 .... **5** B4
Kilburn NW6 ..... **23** C3
Richmond TW10 .. **54** B2
Albert's Ct NW1 .. **90** B2
Albert Sq SW8 ... **162** C1
Albert St NW1 .... **82** B3
Albert Starr Ho 7
SE8 .... **40** C2
Albert Studios
SW11 .... **168** C4
Albert Terr
Camden Town
NW1 .... **81** B3
Stonebridge NW10 **20** B4
Albert Terr Mews
NW1 .... **81** B3
Albert Way SE15 .. **50** A3
Albert Westcott Ho
SE17 .... **150** B2
Albion Ave SW8 .. **171** B1
Albion Cl W2 ..... **116** B4
Albion Coll WC1 .. **106** B3
Albion Ct 7 W6 .. **39** A1
Albion Dr E8 ..... **16** C1
Albion Est SE16 .. **40** B4
Albion Gdns 1
W6 .... **39** A2
Albion Gr N16 ... **16** A4
Albion Ho
17 Deptford SE8 .. **51** C3
EC1 .... **108** A4
Alberney Ho 20
N1 .... **15** B2
Albion Mews
Bayswater W2 .... **116** A4
6 Hammersmith
W6 .... **39** A2
Islington N1 ..... **85** B4
Albion Pl
Broadgate EC2 ... **109** C3
Clerkenwell EC1 .. **108** A4
Hammersmith W6 .. **39** A2
Albion Prim Sch 34
SE16 .... **40** B4
Albion Rd N16 ... **15** C4
Albion Riverside
SW11 .... **158** A2
Albion Sq E8 ..... **16** B1
Albion St
Bayswater W2 .... **116** B4
Rotherhithe SE16 .. **40** B4
Albion Terr E8 .... **16** B1
Albion Way
Barbican EC1 .... **108** C3
Lewisham SE13 .. **67** B3

Albion Wlk N1 ... **84** B1
Albion Works Studios
14 E8 .... **16** C3
Albion Yd N1 .... **84** B1
Albon Ho SW18 ... **59** A1
Albrighton Rd SE5,
SE22 .... **64** A4
Albury Bldgs SE1 .. **136** B3
Albury Ct SE8 .... **51** C4
Albury Lo 5 SW2 .. **74** B4
Albury St SE8 .... **51** C4
Alchemea Coll of
Audio Engineering
N1 .... **86** B4
Alconbury Rd E5 .. **7** C2
Aldbourne Rd
W12 .... **29** C1
Aldbridge St SE17 .. **152** B2
Aldburgh Mews
W1 .... **103** C2
Aldbury Ho SW3 .. **144** A3
Aldebert Terr
SW8 .... **162** C1
Aldeburgh Pl SE10 .. **43** C2
Aldeburgh St SE10 .. **43** C1
Aldenham Ho NW1 **83** A1
Aldenham St NW1 .. **83** B1
Alden Ho E8 ..... **25** A4
Aldensley Rd W6 .. **39** A3
Alderbrook Prim Sch
12 SW12 .... **73** A4
Alderbrook Rd
SW12 .... **61** A1
Alderbury Rd
SW13 .... **46** C4
Aldergrove Ho 3
E5 .... **7** C2
Alder Ho
Camberwell SE15 .. **49** B4
1 Maitland Pk
NW3 .... **12** B2
St Johns SE4 .... **66** C4
Alderley Ho 30
SW8 .... **171** B1
Alder Lo SW6 .... **47** C2
Aldermanbury
EC2 .... **109** A2
Aldermanbury Sq
EC2 .... **109** A3
Alderman's Wlk
EC2 .... **110** A3
Alderney Ho 20
N1 .... **15** B2
Alderney Mews
SE1 .... **137** B2
Alderney Rd E1 ... **25** C1
Alderney St SW1 .. **146** B2
Alder Rd SW14 ... **55** C4
Aldersford Cl SE4 .. **65** C3
Aldersgate St EC1 .. **108** C3
Aldersgate St EC1 .. **108** C2
Aldershot Rd NW6 .. **23** B4
Alderson St W10 .. **23** A1
Alderton Rd SE24 .. **63** B4
Alderville Rd SW6 .. **165** A2
Alderwick Ct N7 .. **14** B2
Aldford St W1 ... **117** C2
Aldgate EC3 ...... **110** B1
Aldgate East Sta
E1 .... **111** A2
Aldgate High St
EC3 .... **110** B1
Aldgate Sta EC3 .. **110** C1
Aldham Ho SE4 .. **51** B4

Aldine Ct W12 ... **30** B1
Aldine St W12 .... **39** B4
Aldington Ct 1
E8 .... **16** C1
Aldred Rd NW6 .. **10** C3
Aldren Rd SW17 .. **71** B1
Aldrich Terr SW18 .. **71** B2
Aldrick Ho N1 .... **85** A2
Aldridge Ct W11 .. **31** B4
Aldridge Rd Villas
W11 .... **31** B4
Aldsworth Cl W9 .. **88** A1
Aldwich Ho WC2 .. **107** A1
Aldworth Gr SE13 .. **67** B1
Aldwych WC2 .... **107** A1
Aldwych Bldgs
WC2 .... **106** B2
Aldwyn Ho SW8 .. **162** A1
Alexander Ave
NW10 .... **9** A1
Alexander Ct
SW18 .... **59** B2
Alexander Fleming
Laboratory Mus
W2 .... **101** C2
Alexander Ho 15
E14 .... **41** C3
Alexander Mews 2
W2 .... **100** A2
Alexander Pl SW7 .. **144** A4
Alexander Rd N19 .. **5** A2
Alexander Sq
SW3 .... **144** A4
Alexander St W2 .. **31** C3
Alexandra Ave
SW11 .... **169** B3
Alexandra Cl SE8 .. **51** B4
Alexandra Cotts
SE14 .... **51** B2
Alexandra Ct
Paddington W9 ... **89** A2
9 Shacklewell N16 .. **16** B4
5 Shepherd's Bush
W12 .... **38** C3
Alexandra Gdns
W4 .... **46** A3
Alexandra Gr N4 .. **6** A3
Alexandra Ho 13
W6 .... **39** B1
Alexandra Mans
Chelsea SW3 ... **157** B3
Cricklewood NW2 .. **9** C3
6 Hampstead
NW6 .... **10** C3
5 Shepherd's Bush
W12 .... **38** C3
Alexandra National Ho
N4 .... **6** B2
Alexandra PI NW8 .. **79** A4
Alexandra Rd
Acton W4 ...... **37** C3
Hampstead NW8 .. **11** C1
Mortlake SW14 .. **55** C4
Richmond TW9 .. **44** B1
Alexandra St
5 Deptford SE14 .. **51** A3
Newham E16 .... **35** C4
Alex Gossip Ho
SW6 .... **165** B3
Alexis St SE16 ... **153** C4
Alfearn Rd E5 .... **17** B4
Alfie's Antique Mkt
NW8 .... **90** A1
Alford Ct N1 ..... **87** A1
Alford Pl N1 ..... **87** A1
Alfreda Ct SW11 .. **170** A3

Alfreda St SW11 . . . . **170** A3

Alfred Butt Ho
SW17 . . . . **72** B1
Alfred Cl W4 . . . . . . **37** C2
Alfred Ho E9 . . . . . . **18** A3
Alfred Mews W1,
WC1 . . . . **105** B4
Alfred Nunn Ho
NW10 . . . . **21** B4
Alfred Pl WC1 . . . . **105** B4
Alfred Rd
Acton W3 . . . . **28** B1
Paddington W2 . . . . **31** C4
Alfred Salter Ho
SE1 . . . . **153** A3
Alfred Salter Prim Sch
SE16 . . . . **40** C4
Alfred St E3 . . . . . . **26** B2
Alfredon Cl SW9 . . . **69** C1
Alfriston Rd SW11 . **60** B2
Algar Ho SE1 . . . . . **136** A3
Algarve Rd SW18 . . **71** A3
Algernon Rd
Kilburn NW6 . . . . . . **23** C4
Lewisham SE13 . . . . **67** A2
Algiers Rd SE13 . . . **66** C3
Alice Gilliott Ct
W14 . . . . **155** A4
Alice La E3 . . . . **26** B4
Alice Owen Tech Ctr
EC1 . . . . **96** A4
Alice Shepherd Ho **12**
E14 . . . . **42** B4
Alice St SE1 . . . . . **138** A1
Alice Walker Cl **3**
SE24 . . . . **63** A3
Alie St E1 . . . . **111** A1
Aliwal Rd SW11 . . . . **60** A3
Alkerden Rd W4 . . . . **38** A1
Alkham Rd N16 . . . . **7** B2
Allam Ho
W11 . . . . . **31** A2 **112** A4
Allanbridge N16 . . . . **7** A4
Allan Ho SW8 . . . . **171** B4
Allan Way W3 . . . . . **28** B4
Allard Gdns SW4 . . **61** C2
Allardyce St SW4,
SW9 . . . . **62** B3
Allbrook Ho **4**
SW15 . . . . **68** C4
Allcroft Rd NW5 . . . . **12** C3
Allendale Cl SE5 . . . **48** C2
Allen Edwards Dr
SW8 . . . . **172** A4
Allen Edwards Prim
Sch SW4 . . . . . . **172** A3
Allenford Ho
SW15 . . . . **56** B1
All England Lawn
Tennis & Croquet
Club The SW19 . . . **70** A1
Allen Ho W8 . . . . . **127** C2
Allen Mans W8 . . . **127** C2
Allen Rd
Old Ford E3 . . . . . . **26** B3
Stoke Newington
N16 . . . . **16** A4
Allensbury Pl
7 Camden Town
NW1 . . . . **13** C1
Camden Town NW1 . **14** A1
Allen St W8 . . . . . **127** C2
Allenswood **12**
SW19 . . . . **70** A3
Allerdale Ho **7** N4 . . **6** C4
Allerton Ho N1 . . . . **87** C1

Allerton Rd N16 . . . . . **6** B2
Allerton St N1 . . . . . **97** C4
Allerton Wlk **11** N7 . . **5** B2
Allestree Rd SW6 . . **154** A1
Alleyn Cres SE21 . . . **75** C2
Alleyn Ho
Bermondsey SE1 . . . **137** B1
St Luke's EC1 . . . . . . **97** A1
Alleyn Pk SE21 . . . . **76** A1
Alleyn Rd SE21 . . . . **76** A1
Alleyn's Sch SE22 . . **64** A2
Allfarthing JMI Sch
SW18 . . . . **59** B1
Allfarthing La
SW18 . . . . **59** B1
Allgood St E2 . . . . . **24** B3
Allhallows La EC4 . . **123** B3
Alliance Ct W3 . . . . . **28** A4
Allianced Rd W3 . . . . **28** A1
Allied Ind Est W3 . . . **29** A1
Allied Way W3 . . . . . **38** A4
Allingham Ct NW3 . . **12** A3
Allingham Mews
N1 . . . . **86** C2
Allingham St N1 . . . . **86** C2
Allington Ct **8**
SW8 . . . . **170** C1
Allington Rd W10 . . . **23** A3
Allington St SW1 . . **132** B1
Allison Cl SE10 . . . . . **52** B2
Allison Gr SE21 . . . . **76** A3
Allison Rd W3 . . . . . **28** B2
Alliston Ho **27**
E2 . . . . **24** B2 **99** A3
Allitsen Rd NW8 . . . . **80** A2
All Nations Ho **10**
E8 . . . . **25** A4
Allnutt Way SW4 . . . **61** C2
Allom Ct **1** SW4 . . **172** B1
Allonby Ho E14 . . . . . **33** A4
Alloway Rd E3 . . . . . **26** A2
Allport Ho SE5 . . . . . **63** C4
Allport Mews **44**
E1 . . . . **25** B1
All Saints CE Prim Sch
6 Fulham SW6 . . . **164** A2
Putney SW15 . . . . . . **57** B4
All Saints' CE Prim
Sch
Blackheath Vale
SE3 . . . . **53** A1
Child's Hill NW2 . . . . **1** B2
All Saints Church **9**
N19 . . . . **4** C1
All Saints Ct
Lower Clapton E5 . . . **17** B4
10 Shadwell E1 . . . . **32** B2
All Saints Dr SE3 . . . **53** B1
All Saints Ho **2**
W11 . . . . **31** B4
All Saints Pas
SW18 . . . . **58** C2
All Saints Rd W11 . . **31** B3
All Saints Rd W3 . . . **37** B3
All Saints St N1 . . . . **84** C2
All Saints Sta E14 . . **34** A2
Allsop Pl NW1 . . . . . **91** A1
All Souls Ave
NW10 . . . . **22** A4
All Souls CE Prim Sch
W1 . . . . **104** C4
All Souls Pl W1 . . . **104** B3
Alma Birk Ho **1**
NW6 . . . . **10** B1
Almack Rd E5 . . . . . . **17** B4
Alma Gr SE1 . . . . . **153** A3

Alma Ho **7** TW8 . . . . . **44** A4
Alma Pl NW10 . . . . . **22** A2
Alma Prim Sch **3**
SE16 . . . . **153** C4
Alma Rd SW18 . . . . . **59** B2
Alma Sq NW8 . . . . . **89** A4
Alma St
Camden Town
NW5 . . . . **13** A2
Stratford New Town
E15 . . . . **19** C2
Alma Terr
Earl's Ct W8 . . . . . . **127** C1
Wandsworth SW18 . . **71** C4
Almeida St **10** N1 . . . **15** A1
Almeric Rd SW11 . . . **60** B3
Almington St N4 . . . . **5** B3
Almond Ave W5 . . . . **36** A3
Almond Cl SE15 . . . . **49** C1
Almond Ho SE4 . . . . **51** B1
Almond Rd SE16 . . . . **40** A2
Almorah Rd N1 . . . . . **15** C1
Al-Muntada Islamic
Sch SW6 . . . . **165** A4
Alperton St W10 . . . . **23** B1
Alphabet Sq E3 . . . . **33** C4
Alpha Cl NW8 . . . . . . **90** B3
Alpha Ct **7** NW5 . . . **13** A2
Alpha Gr E14 . . . . . . **41** C4
Alpha Ho
9 Brixton SW4 . . . **62** B3
Kilburn NW6 . . . . . . **23** C3
Lisson Gr NW8 . . . . . **90** B1
Alpha Pl
Chelsea SW3 . . . . . **158** B4
Kilburn NW6 . . . . . . **23** C3
Alpha Rd SE14 . . . . . **51** B2
Alpha St SE15 . . . . . **49** C1
Alpine Gr **9** E9 . . . . **17** B1
Alpine Rd SE16 . . . . . **40** C1
Alroy Rd N4 . . . . **5** C4
Alsace Rd SE17 . . . **152** A2
Al Sadiq High Sch for
Boys & Al Zahra
Girls Sch NW6 . . . . **23** A4
Alscot Rd SE1 . . . . **139** A1
Alscot Rd Ind Est
SE1 . . . . **139** A1
Alscot Way SE1 . . . **152** C4
Altair Ct N1 . . . . **15** C2
Altenburg Gdns
SW11 . . . . **60** B3
Althea St SW6 . . . . . **59** A4
Althorpe Mews
SW11 . . . . **167** C3
Althorp Rd SW17 . . . **72** B3
Altima Ct SE22 . . . . **64** C3
Alton Ho **3** E3 . . . . . **27** A2
Alton Rd
Richmond TW10,
TW9 . . . . **54** A3
Roehampton SW15 . . **68** C3
Alton St E14 . . . . **34** A4
Alumni Ct SE1 . . . . **139** A4
Alvanley Ct NW3 . . . . **11** A3
Alvanley Gdns
NW6 . . . . **11** A3
Alvaney Rd NW1 . . . . . (blank)
Alverstone Ave SW18,
SW19 . . . . **70** C2
Alverstone Ho **3**
SE11 . . . . **163** B3
Alverstone Rd NW2 . . **9** B1
Alverton St SE8 . . . . **51** B4
Alvey St SE17 . . . . . **152** A2

Alvington Cres E8 . . . **16** B3
Alwyn Ave W4 . . . . . **37** C1
Alwyne La N1 . . . . . . **15** A1
Alwyne Pl N1 . . . . . . **15** B2
Alwyne Rd N1 . . . . . . **15** B1
Alwyne Sq N1 . . . . . . **15** B2
Alwyne Villas N1 . . . **15** A1
Alwyn Gdns W3 . . . . **28** A3
Alzette Ho **11** E2 . . . **25** B3
Aman Dalvi Ho **2**
SE18 . . . . **70** A4
Amazonas SE1 . . . . **152** B3
Amazon St E1 . . . . . **32** A3
Ambassador Ct **3**
NW6 . . . . **10** C3
Ambassador Ho
NW8 . . . . **79** A3
Ambassador Sq
E14 . . . . **42** A2
Amber Ct N7 . . . . . . **14** C2
Ambergate St
SE17 . . . . **150** B2
Amberley Ct **2**
SW9 . . . . **63** A4
Amberley Rd W9 . . . . **31** C4
Amber Wharf **2**
E2 . . . . **24** B4
Ambler Prim Sch
N4 . . . . **6** A2
Ambler Rd N4 . . . . **6** A1
Ambleside
13 Putney SW19 . . . **70** A3
Regent's Pk NW1 . . . **82** B1
Ambleside Cl E9 . . . . **17** B3
Ambleside Point **1**
SE15 . . . . **50** B3
Ambleside Rd
NW10 . . . . **8** B1
Ambrosden Ave
SW1 . . . . **133** A1
Ambrose Ho **5**
E14 . . . . **33** C4
Ambrose Mews **2**
SW11 . . . . **168** C2
Ambrose St SE16 . . . **40** A2
Ambrose Wlk E3 . . . . **26** C3
AMC Bsns Ctr
NW10 . . . . **20** A2
Amelia Cl W3 . . . . . . **37** A4
Amelia Ho **5** W6 . . . **39** B1
Amelia St SE17 . . . . **150** C2
Amen Cnr EC4 . . . . **108** B1
Amen Ct EC4 . . . . . **108** B1
American
Intercontinental
Univ W1 . . . . **103** C3
American Sch in
London The NW8 . . **79** B2
American Univ in
London The **3** N7 . . **5** B1
America Sq EC3 . . . **124** C4
America St SE1 . . . . **122** C1
Amerland Rd
SW18 . . . . **58** B1
Amersham Gr SE14 . **51** B3
Amersham Rd
SE14 . . . . **51** B3
Amersham Vale SE14,
SE8 . . . . **51** B4
Amery Gdns NW10 . . **22** A4
Amery Ho SE17 . . . . **152** B2
Amesbury Ave
SW2 . . . . **74** B2
Amesbury Twr **4**
SW8 . . . . **170** C2

Ames Cotts **13** E3 . . . **33** A4
Ames Ho E2 . . . . **25** C3
Amethyst Rd E15 . . . **19** C4
Amhurst Ct N4 . . . . . . **6** C4
Amhurst Par N16 . . . . **7** B4
Amhurst Pk N4, N16 . **7** A4
Amhurst Rd E8,
N16 . . . . **16** C4
Amhurst Terr E8 . . . . **16** C4
Amias Ho EC1 . . . . . . **96** C2
Amiel St **13** E1 . . . . . **25** B1
Amies St SW11 . . . . **60** B4
Amigo Ho SE1 . . . . **135** C2
Amina Way SE16 . . . **139** B1
Amner Rd SW11 . . . . **60** C1
Amor Rd W6 . . . . **39** B3
Amory Ho N1 . . . . . . **85** A2
Amott Rd SE15 . . . . . **64** C4
Amoy Pl E14 . . . . **33** C2
Ampton Pl WC1 . . . . **94** C3
Ampton St WC1 . . . . **94** C3
Amstel Ct **12** SE15 . . **49** B3
Amsterdam Rd
E14 . . . . **42** B3
Amundsen Ct **7**
E14 . . . . **41** C1
Amwell St EC1 . . . . . **95** B4
Amyruth Rd SE4 . . . . **66** C2
Anatola Rd N19 . . . . . **4** B2
Anchorage Point **1**
E14 . . . . **41** C4
Anchor Mews
SW12 . . . . **61** A1
Anchor Ret Pk E1 . . . **25** B1
Anchor St SE16 . . . . **40** A2
Anchor Terr SE1 . . . **123** A2
Anchor Yd EC1 . . . . . **97** A2
Ancill Cl W6 . . . . . . **154** A3
Ancona Rd NW10 . . . **21** C3
Andalus Rd SW9 . . . **62** A4
Andaman Ho **3**
E1 . . . . **33** A4
Andersens Wharf **9**
E14 . . . . **33** B3
Anderson Cl W3 . . . . **28** C3
Anderson Ho
11 E14 . . . . **34** B2
5 Tufnell Pk N7 . . . **14** C4
Andersons Sq N1 . . . **86** A3
Anderson St SW3 . . **144** C2
Anderson Way
SE5 . . . . **63** C4
Andover Ho **3** N7 . . . . **5** B2
Andover Pl NW6 . . . . **78** A1
Andover Rd N7 . . . . . . **5** B2
Andoversford Ct **2**
SE15 . . . . **49** A4
Andre St E8 . . . . **16** C3
Andrew Borde St
WC2 . . . . **105** C2
Andrew Ct SE22 . . . **109** A3
Andrewes Ho EC2 . . **109** A3
Andrew Logan's
Glasshouse SE1 . . **138** A4
Andrew Marvell Ho **12**
N16 . . . . **16** A4
Andrew Pl SW8 . . . . **171** C4
Andrew Reed Ho **3**
SW18 . . . . **70** A4
Andrews Crosse
WC2 . . . . **107** B1
Andrew's Ho SE8 . . . **25** A4

Andrew St E14 . . . . 34 B3
Andrews Wharf 14
E8 . . . . 25 A4
Andrews Wlk SE17 . . 48 A4
Andrew Wilmot Ct
SW18 . . . . 71 B3
Anfield Cl SW12 . . . . 73 B4
Angel EC1 . . . . 86 B1
Angela Carter Cl
SW9 . . . . 62 C4
Angela Davis Ind Est
20 SW9 . . . . 63 A3
Angel Ct
Broadgate EC2 . . . 109 C2
St James SW1 . . . . 119 A1
5 Willesden NW2 . . . 8 C3
Angel Gate EC1 . . . . 96 B4
Angel Ho N1 . . . . 85 C1
Angelina Ho 3
SE15 . . . . 49 C2
Angelis Appartments
N1 . . . . 86 B1
Angel La E15 . . . . 19 C2
Angell Park Gdns 3
SW9 . . . . 62 C4
Angell Rd SW9 . . . . . 63 A4
Angel Mews
Finsbury N1 . . . . . . 85 C1
Putney SW15 . . . . . . 68 C4
Stepney E1 . . . . 32 A2
Angel Pas EC4 . . . . . 123 B3
Angel Pl SE1 . . . . . . 137 B4
Angel Sq N1 . . . . 85 C1
Angel St EC1 . . . . . . 108 C2
Angel Wlk W6 . . . . . . 39 B2
Angerstein Bsns Pk
SE10 . . . . 43 C2
Angerstein La SE3 . . 53 B2
Anglebury 5
W2 . . . . 31 C3
Anglers La NW5 . . . . 13 A2
Anglesey Ho 11
E14 . . . . 33 C3
Anglia Ho 8 E14 . . . . 33 A3
Anglo American
Laundry SW17 . . . . . 71 B1
Anglo Rd 18 E3 . . . . . 26 B3
Angrave Ct 3 E8 . . . . 24 B4
Angrave Pas 5 E8 . . . 24 B4
Angus Ho 12
SW12 . . . . 73 C4
Angus St SE14 . . . . . 51 A3
Anhalt Rd SW11 . . . 158 B2
Animals in War Meml
W1 . . . . 117 A4
Anley Rd W14 . . . . . . 39 C4
Annabel Cl E14 . . . . . 34 A3
Anna Cl E8 . . . . 24 B4
Annandale Rd
Chiswick W4 . . . . . . 38 A1
Greenwich SE10 . . . 43 B1
Anne Goodman Ho 3
E1 . . . . 32 B3
Anne Kerr Ct 12
SW15 . . . . 57 C1
Anne's Ct NW8 . . . . . 90 B2
Annesley Ho 5
SW9 . . . . 173 B4
Annesley Wlk N19 . . . 4 B2
Annette Cres 2
N1 . . . . 15 B1
Annette Ct N7 . . . . 5 B1
Annette Rd N7 . . . . . 14 B4

Annie Besant Cl
E3 . . . . 26 B4
Anning St
EC2 . . . . 24 A1 98 B2
Annis Rd E9 . . . . 18 A2
Ann La SW10 . . . . . . 157 B3
Ann Moss Way
SE16 . . . . 40 B3
Ann's Cl SW1 . . . . . . 131 B3
Ann's Pl E1 . . . . 110 C3
Ansdell Rd SE15 . . . . 50 B1
Ansdell St W8 . . . . . 128 B2
Ansdell Terr W8 . . . . 128 B2
Ansell Ho E1 . . . . 32 B4
Ansell Rd SW17 . . . . 72 B1
Anselm Rd SW6 . . . . 155 B3
Ansleigh Pl W11 . . . . 30 C2
Anson Ho
Pimlico SW1 . . . . . . 160 C4
3 Tower Hamlets
E1 . . . . 26 A1
Anson Prim Sch
NW2 . . . . 9 C3
Anson Rd
Cricklewood NW2 . . . . 9 B3
Tufnell Pk N7 . . . . . . 13 C4
Anstey Gn 5 W3 . . . . 37 A4
Anstey Ho 7 E9 . . . . . 25 B4
Anstey Rd SE15 . . . . 64 C4
Anstice Cl W4 . . . . . . 46 A3
Antenor Ho 11 E2 . . . 25 A3
Anthony Cope Ct
N1 . . . . 97 C4
Anthony Ho NW8 . . . 90 A1
Anthony St E1 . . . . . . 32 A3
Antill Rd
E3 . . . . 26 A2
Tottenham N15 . . . . . . 7 C3
Antill Terr 5 E1 . . . . . 32 C3
Antonine Hts SE1 . . . 138 A3
Anton St E8 . . . . 16 C3
Antony Ho
2 Deptford SE14 . . . 50 C3
5 Rotherhithe
SE16 . . . . 40 B2
Antrim Gr NW3 . . . . . 12 B2
Antrim Ho SW11 . . . . 60 C4
Antrim Mans NW3 . . 12 B2
Antrim Rd NW3 . . . . . 12 B2
Antrobus Rd W4 . . . . 37 B3
AOP Gall EC2 . . . . . . 98 A2
Apex Ind Est NW10 . . 21 B1
Aphrodite Ct 11
E14 . . . . 41 C2
Apollo Bldg 2
E14 . . . . 41 C2
Apollo Ho
Chelsea SW10 . . . . 157 B3
32 Hackney E2 . . . . . 25 A3
Highgate N6 . . . . 3 B4
Apollo Ind Bsns Ctr 20
SE8 . . . . 50 C4
Apollo Pl SW10 . . . . 157 B2
Apollo Studios 13
NW5 . . . . 13 C3
Apothecary St
EC4 . . . . 108 A1
Appach Rd SW2 . . . . 62 C1
Appleby Ct W3 . . . . . 37 B4
Appleby Rd
Hackney E8 . . . . 16 C1
Newham E16 . . . . . . 35 C3
Appleby St E2 . . . . . . 24 B3
Appledore Cl SW12,
SW17 . . . . 72 B2

Appleford 8 NW5 . . . 13 B3
Appleford Ho 6
W10 . . . . 23 A1
Appleford Rd W10 . . 23 A1
Applegarth Ho
Borough The SE1 . . 136 B4
6 Camberwell
SE15 . . . . 49 C3
Applegarth Rd
W14 . . . . 39 C3
Appleshaw Ho 3
SE5 . . . . 64 A4
Appleton Ct 30 E8 . . 17 A3
Appletree Ct SE13 . . 67 C3
Apple Tree Yd
SW1 . . . . 119 A2
Appold St EC2 . . . . . 110 A4
Appollo Ct 7
SE1 . . . . 173 B4
Apprentice Way 5
E5 . . . . 17 A4
Approach Cl N16 . . . 16 A4
Approach Rd E2 . . . . 25 B3
Approach The W3 . . . 28 C3
April Ct 21 E2 . . . . . . 24 C3
April St E8 . . . . 16 B4
Apsley Ho
Stepney E1 . . . . 32 B4
St John's Wood
NW8 . . . . 79 B2
Apsley Ho, The
Wellington Mus
SW1 . . . . 131 C4
Apsley Way W1 . . . . 131 C4
Aquila St NW8 . . . . . 79 C2
Aquinas St SE1 . . . . 121 C1
Arabella Dr SW6 . . . 47 B3
Arabella St E14 . . . . 56 A3
Arabian Ho 8 E1 . . . . 26 A1
Aragon Twr SE8 . . . . 41 B2
Arakan Ho 6 N16 . . . 15 C4
Aral Ho 4 E1 . . . . 25 C1
Arapiles Ho 6
E14 . . . . 34 C3
Arbery Rd E3 . . . . . . 26 A3
Arbon Ct N1 . . . . 87 A3
Arbor Ct N16 . . . . 6 C2
Arborfield Cl SW2 . . 74 B3
Arborfield Ho 7
E14 . . . . 33 C2
Arbour Ho 8 E1 . . . . . 32 C3
Arbour Sq E1 . . . . . . 32 C3
Arbuthnot Rd
SE14 . . . . 50 C1
Arbutus St E8 . . . . . . 24 B4
Arcade The
Broadgate EC2 . . . . 110 A3
1 Tufnell Pk N7 . . . . 14 A4
Arcadian Ho W6 . . . 167 A1
Arcadian Pl SW18 . . 70 B4
Arcadia St E14 . . . . . 33 C3
Arcadia Univ W1 . . . 114 A3
Archangel St SE16 . . 40 C4
Archbishop Coggan
Ho SE13 . . . . 67 C3
Archbishop's Pl 1
SW2 . . . . 74 B4
Archbishop Sumner
CE Prim Sch
SE11 . . . . 149 C3
Archbishop Tenison's
Sch SE11 . . . . 163 A3
Archdale Ct W12 . . . 30 A1
Archdale Ho SE1 . . . 138 A2

Archdale Rd SE22 . . . 64 B3
Archel Rd W14 . . . . . 154 C4
Archer Ho
1 Battersea
SW11 . . . . 167 C2
5 Hoxton N1 . . . . . . 24 A4
1 New Cross SE14 . . 51 A2
Notting Hill
W11 . . . . 31 B2 113 A4
Archers Lo 2
SE1 . . . . 153 C1
Archer Sq SE14 . . . . 51 A3
Archer St W1 . . . . . . 119 B4
Archer Way 1 E1 . . . . 32 C2
Archery Cl W2 . . . . . 102 B1
Archery Fields Ho
WC1 . . . . 95 B4
Archery Stps 7 W2 . . 116 B4
Arches The W2 . . . . . 120 B2
Archibald Mews
W1 . . . . 118 A3
Archibald Rd N7 . . . . 13 C4
Archibald St E3 . . . . . 26 C2
Archie St SE1 . . . . . . 138 B3
Arch St SE1 . . . . 136 C1
Archway N19 . . . . 4 B2
Archway Bsns Ctr 5
N19 . . . . 4 C1
Archway Cl
North Kensington
W10 . . . . 30 C4
2 Upper Holloway
N19 . . . . 4 B2
Archway Hts 5 N19 . . 4 B3
Archway L Ctr N19 . . 4 B2
Archway Mews
SW15 . . . . 58 A3
Archway Rd N6 . . . . . . 4 A4
Archway St SW13,
SW14 . . . . 56 A4
Archway Sta N19 . . . . 4 B2
Arcola St E8 . . . . 16 B3
Arctic St NW5 . . . . . . 13 A3
Ardbeg Rd SE24 . . . . 63 C2
Arden 17 SW19 . . . . . 69 C3
Arden Cres E14 . . . . . 41 C2
Arden Ho
13 Hoxton N1 . . . . . . 24 A3
22 Stockwell SW9 . . 172 B1
Vauxhall SE11 . . . . . 148 C3
Ardent Ho 33 E3 . . . . 26 A3
Ardilaun Rd N5 . . . . . 15 B4
Ardleigh Rd N1 . . . . . 16 A2
Ardlui Rd SE27 . . . . . 75 B2
Ardmere Rd SE13 . . . 67 C1
Ardoch Rd SE6 . . . . . 67 C4
Ardshiel Cl
SW15 . . . . 57 C4
Ardwell Rd SW2 . . . . 74 A2
Ardwick Rd NW2 . . . 10 C4
Ares Ct 16 E14 . . . . . . 41 C2
Arethusa Ho 8
E14 . . . . 42 A2
Argo Bsns Ctr 7
NW6 . . . . 23 C2
Argon Mews SW6 . . 155 C1
Argos Ct 5 SW9 . . . . 173 B4
Argos Ho 8 E2 . . . . . 25 A3
Argosy Ho
Fitzrovia W1 . . . . . . 92 B1
Rotherhithe SE8 . . . 41 A2
Argyle Ho E14 . . . . . . 42 B3
Argyle Mans 4
NW2 . . . . 9 C2
Argyle Pl W6 . . . . 39 A2
Argyle Prim Sch
WC1 . . . . 94 A4
Argyle Rd E1 . . . . 25 C1

Argyle Sq WC1 . . . . . 94 B4
Argyle St WC1 . . . . . . 94 B4
Argyle Way SE16 . . . 153 C1
Argyle Wlk WC1 . . . . 94 B3
Argyll Cl SW9 . . . . . . 62 B4
Argyll Ct 15 SW2 . . . 74 A4
Argyll Mans
Chelsea SW3 . . . . . 157 C4
West Kensington
W14 . . . . 140 B4
Argyll Rd W8 . . . . . . 127 C3
Argyll St W1 . . . . . . 104 C1
Arica Ho SE16 . . . . . . 40 A3
Arica Rd SE4 . . . . 66 A4
Ariel Ct
5 Hammersmith
W12 . . . . 38 C3
Newington SE11 . . . 150 A3
Ariel Rd NW6 . . . . . . 10 C2
Ariel Way W1 . . . . . . 30 B1
Aristotle Rd SW4 . . . 61 C4
Arizona Bldg 10
SE13 . . . . 52 A2
Arkansas Ho 21
N19 . . . . 4 C4
Ark Ct N16 . . . . 7 B2
Arklow Ho SE17 . . . . 48 C4
Arklow Rd SE14 . . . . 51 B4
Arklow Road Trad Est
SE14 . . . . 51 B4
Arkwright Ho 23
SW2 . . . . 74 A4
Arkwright Mans 1
NW3 . . . . 11 B3
Arkwright Rd NW3 . . 11 B3
Arlesey Cl SW15 . . . . 58 A2
Arlesford Rd SW9 . . . 62 A4
Arlidge Ho EC1 . . . . 107 C4
Arlingford Rd
SW2 . . . . 62 C1
Arlington Ave N1 . . . 87 A3
Arlington Cl SE13 . . . 67 C2
Arlington Ct 13
W3 . . . . 28 A1
Arlington Gdns
Chiswick W4 . . . . . . 37 B1
Ilford IG1 . . . .
Arlington Ho
2 Deptford SE8 . . . . 51 B4
Finsbury EC1 . . . . . . 95 C4
1 Shepherd's Bush
W12 . . . . 30 A1
Arlington Lo SW2 . . . 62 B3
Arlington Park Mans
4 W4 . . . . 37 B1
Arlington Pl 7
SE10 . . . . 52 B3
Arlington Rd NW1 . . . 82 B3
Arlington Sq N1 . . . . 87 A3
Arlington St SW1 . . . 118 C2
Arlington Way EC1 . . 95 C4
Armada Ct 11 SE8 . . . 51 C4
Armadale Rd
SW6 . . . . 155 B3
Armada St 10 SE8 . . . 51 C4
Armagh Rd E3 . . . . . . 26 B4
Arminger Rd W12 . . . 30 A1
Armitage Ho NW1 . . 102 B4
Armitage Rd
Golders Green
NW11 . . . . 1 B3
Greenwich SE10 . . . 43 B1
Armour Cl N7 . . . . . . 14 B2
Armoury Ho E3 . . . . . 26 A4
Armoury Rd SE8 . . . . 52 A1

Armoury Way
SW18 . . . . 58 C2

Armsby Ho **17** E1 . . . . . . 32 B4

Armstrong Ho **8**
SW15 . . . . 57 C1

Armstrong Rd
East Acton W3 . . . . 29 A1
Knightsbridge
SW7 . . . . 129 B1
11 Willesden NW10 . . . . 8 A1

Arnal Cres SW18 . . . . . . 70 A4

Arncliffe Ho **6** 78 B3

Arndale Wlk **6**
SW18 . . . . 59 A2

Arne Ho SE11 . . . . 148 C2

Arne St WC2 . . . . 106 B1

Arneway St SW1 . . . . . . 133 C1

Arnewood Cl
SW15 . . . . 68 C3

Arnhem Pl E14 . . . . 41 C3

Arnhem Way **3**
SE22 . . . . 64 A2

Arnhem Wharf
E14 . . . . 41 C3

Arnhem Wharf Prim
Sch E14 . . . . 41 C3

Arnold Cir
E2 . . . . 24 B2 98 C3

Arnold Est SE1 . . . . 139 A3

Arnold Ho
Newington SE17 . . . . . . 150 B1
9 Stoke Newington
N16 . . . . 7 A1

Arnold House Sch
NW8 . . . . 79 B1

Arnold Rd E3 . . . . 26 C2

Arnot Ho **27** SE5 . . . . . . 48 B3

Arnott Cl W4 . . . . 37 C2

Arnould Ave SE5 . . . . . . 63 C3

Arnside Ho **2**
SE17 . . . . 48 B4

Arnside St SE17 . . . . 48 B4

Arodene Rd SW2 . . . . . . 62 B1

Arragon Rd SW18 . . . . . . 70 C3

Arran Ho
5 Canary Wharf
E14 . . . . 34 B1
Stoke Newington N16 . . . 7 B3

Arran Wlk N1 . . . . 15 B1

Arrol Ho SE1 . . . . 137 A1

Arrowe Ct **6** E5 . . . . 17 A4

Arrow Ho **28** N1 . . . . 24 A4

Arrow Rd E3 . . . . 27 A2

Arrowsmith Ho
SE11 . . . . 148 C2

Arsenal Sta N5 . . . . 5 C1

Arta Ho **8** E1 . . . . 32 B3

Artcadia Lifestyle
EC2 . . . . 110 C4

Artemis Ct **4** E14 . . . . . 41 C2

Artemis PI SW18 . . . . . . 70 B4

Artesian Rd W2 . . . . 31 C3

Arthur Ct
Battersea SW11 . . . . . . 169 C3
North Kensington
W10 . . . . 30 C3
Paddington W2 . . . . 100 A2

Arthur Deakin Ho **1**
E1 . . . . 111 B4

Arthurdon Rd SE4 . . . . . . 66 C2

Arthur Henderson Ho
9 Crouch End N19 . . . . . 4 C4
2 Fulham SW6 . . . . . . 164 C2

Arthur Newton Ho **11**
SW11 . . . . 59 C4

Arthur Rd N7 . . . . 14 B4

Arthur St EC4 . . . . 123 C4

Arthur Wade Ho **7**
E2 . . . . 24 B2 99 A4

Artichoke Hill **8**
E1 . . . . 32 A2

Artichoke Mews **5**
SE5 . . . . 48 C2

Artichoke PI SE5 . . . . . . 48 C2

Artillery Ho
Bow E3 . . . . 26 A4
Westminster SW1 . . . . . 133 B1

Artillery La
Broadgate E1 . . . . 110 B3
North Kensington
W12 . . . . 29 C3

Artillery Pas E1 . . . . . . 110 B3

Artillery PI SW1 . . . . . . 133 B1

Artillery Row
SW1 . . . . 133 B1

Artisan Ct **8** E8 . . . . 16 C2

Artisan Mews **9**
NW10 . . . . 22 C2

Artisan Quarter **10**
NW10 . . . . 22 C2

Artizan St E1 . . . . 110 B2

Arton Wilson Ho **6**
SW15 . . . . 56 C2

Arts Educational Sch
The **14** W4 . . . . 38 A2

Arundel Bldgs
SE1 . . . . 138 B1

Arundel Cl SW11 . . . . . . 60 A2

Arundel Ct
Barnes SW13 . . . . 47 A4
Chelsea SW3 . . . . 144 B2
Putney SW15 . . . . 57 C2

Arundel Gdns
W11 . . . . 31 B2 112 C4

Arundel Ho
Islington N1 . . . . 86 B4
Richmond TW10 . . . . . . 54 C2
3 South Acton W3 . . . . 37 A4

Arundel Lo **9** N19 . . . . . . 5 A2

Arundel Mans
Barnes SW13 . . . . 47 A4
Fulham SW6 . . . . 165 A4

Arundel PI N1, N7 . . . . . . 14 C2

Arundel Sq N7 . . . . 14 C2

Arundel St WC2 . . . . . . 121 A4

Arundel Terr
SW13 . . . . 47 A4

Arungford Mews **12**
SW2 . . . . 62 C2

Arvon Rd N5 . . . . 14 C3

Asaph Ho SE14 . . . . 51 B2

Ascalon Ct **18** SW2 . . . . 74 B4

Ascalon Ho SW8 . . . . . 160 C1

Ascalon St SW8 . . . . . . 160 C1

Ascham St NW5 . . . . 13 B3

Ascot Ct
8 Brixton SW4 . . . . . . 62 A3
St John's Wood
NW8 . . . . 89 B3

Ascot Ho
6 Acton Green
W4 . . . . 37 B1
Regent's Pk NW1 . . . . . . 92 B4

Ascot Lo NW6 . . . . 78 B2

Ascot Par **2** SW4 . . . . . 62 A3

Ascott Ave W5 . . . . 36 A4

Ashbourne Coll
W8 . . . . 128 A3

Ashbourne Ct E5 . . . . . . 18 A4

Ashbourne Gr
Chiswick W4 . . . . 38 A1
East Dulwich SE22 . . . . . 64 B3

Ashbridge Ct **1**
W6 . . . . 39 A3

Ashbridge St NW8 . . . . . 90 A1

Ashbrook Rd N19 . . . . . . 4 C2

Ashburn Gdns
SW5 . . . . 142 C4

Ashburnham Gr
SE10 . . . . 52 A3

Ashburnham PI
SE10 . . . . 52 A3

Ashburnham Prim Sch
SW10 . . . . 157 B2

Ashburnham Rd
Chelsea SW10 . . . . 157 A1
Kensal Rise NW10 . . . . . 22 B2

Ashburnham Retreat **4**
SE10 . . . . 52 A3

Ashburnham Twr
SW10 . . . . 157 B2

Ashburn PI SW7 . . . . . . 142 C3

Ashburton Mans
SW10 . . . . 157 A2

Ashburton Rd E16 . . . . . . 35 C3

Ashbury Rd SW11 . . . . . 60 C4

Ashby Ct NW8 . . . . 89 C2

Ashby Gr N1 . . . . 15 B1

Ashby Ho
5 Brixton SW9 . . . . . . 48 A1
17 Islington N1 . . . . . . 15 B1

Ashby Mews
4 Clapham Pk
SW2 . . . . 62 A2
New Cross SE4 . . . . 51 B1

Ashby Rd SE4 . . . . 51 B1

Ashby St EC1 . . . . 96 B3

Ashchurch Ct **2**
W12 . . . . 38 C3

Ashchurch Gr
W12 . . . . 38 C3

Ashchurch Park Villas
W12 . . . . 38 C3

Ashchurch Terr
W12 . . . . 38 C3

Ashcombe Ct **4**
SW15 . . . . 58 B2

Ashcombe Ho **39**
E3 . . . . 27 A2

Ashcombe St
SW6 . . . . 166 A1

Ashcroft Ho **8** SW8 . . . 170 C4

Ashcroft Sq **5** W6 . . . . . 39 B2

Ashcroft Tech Acad
SW15 . . . . 58 B2

Ash Ct
Clapham SW11 . . . . 60 A4
Marylebone W1 . . . . 102 C2
6 Rotherhithe
SE16 . . . . 33 A1
10 Upper Holloway N19 . . 4 B2

Ashdale Ho N4 . . . . 6 C4

Ashdene **5** SE15 . . . . . . 50 A3

Ashdon Rd NW10 . . . . . . 21 B4

Ashdown SW15 . . . . 57 C2

Ashdown Cres
NW5 . . . . 12 C3

Ashdown Ct SE22 . . . . . . 76 C3

Ashdown Ho **7** E5 . . . . . . 7 C2

Ashdown Way
SW17 . . . . 72 C2

Ashdown Wlk **29**
E14 . . . . 41 C2

Ashenden SE17 . . . . . . 151 A4

Ashenden Rd E5 . . . . 18 A3

Ashen Gr SW19 . . . . 70 C2

Ashentree Ct EC4 . . . . . 107 C1

Asher Way E1 . . . . 125 C3

Ashfield Ho **5** N5 . . . . . . 15 B3

Ashfield Rd W3 . . . . 29 B1

Ashfield St
E1 . . . . 32 B4

Ashfield Yd **28** E1 . . . . . 32 B4

Ashford Ct NW2 . . . . 9 C4

Ashford Ho
5 Brixton SW9 . . . . . . 63 A3
3 Deptford SE8 . . . . . . 51 B4

Ashford Rd NW2 . . . . 9 C4

Ashford St
N1 . . . . 24 A2 98 A4

Ash Gr
Cricklewood NW2 . . . . . . 10 A4
Ealing W5 . . . . 36 A3
Hackney E8 . . . . 25 A4

Ashgrove Ct **2**
W9 . . . . 31 C4

Ashgrove Ho SW1 . . . . . 147 C2

Ash Ho
1 Canary Wharf
E14 . . . . 42 B4
Fulham SE1 . . . . 153 A3

Ashington **1** NW5 . . . . . 13 A2

Ashington Ho **13**
E1 . . . . 25 A1

Ashington Rd
SW6 . . . . 165 A1

Ashland PI W1 . . . . 103 B4

Ashleigh Ho SW14 . . . . . 56 A4

Ashleigh Rd SW14 . . . . . 56 A4

Ashley Cres
Hampstead NW3 . . . . . . 11 A3
10 Kingsland N16 . . . . . 16 A3

Ashley PI SW1 . . . . 132 C1

Ashley Rd
Hornsey N19 . . . . 5 A4
Richmond TW9 . . . . 54 A4

Ashlar Ct
8 Lo SW6 . . . . 47 C2
Ashlone Rd SW15 . . . . . . 57 C4

Ashmead Bsns Ctr **2**
E16 . . . . 27 C1

Ashmead Ho **9**
E9 . . . . 18 A3

Ashmead Mews **1**
SE8 . . . . 51 C1

Ashmead Prim Sch
SE8 . . . . 51 C1

Ashmead Rd SE8 . . . . . . 51 C1

Ashmere Gr **11** SW2,
SW4 . . . . 62 A3

Ashmere Ho **10**
SW2 . . . . 62 A3

Ashmill St NW8 . . . . 102 A4

Ashmole Prim Sch
SW8 . . . . 163 A3

Ashmole St SW8 . . . . . . 163 A3

Ashmore NW1 . . . . 13 C1

Ashmore Cl SE15 . . . . . . 49 B3

Ashmore Ho W14 . . . . . 126 B1

Ashmore Rd W9 . . . . 23 B2

Ashmount Prim Sch
N19 . . . . 4 B4

Ashmount Rd N19 . . . . . . 4 C4

Ashness Rd SW11 . . . . . 60 B2

Ashpark Ho **4**
E14 . . . . 33 A3

Ashstead Ct **13**
SW19 . . . . 69 C3

Ashtead Rd E5 . . . . 7 C4

Ashton Ho
13 Kennington
SW9 . . . . 163 C1
Roehampton SW15 . . . . 69 A4

Ashton Rd E15 . . . . 19 C3

Ashton St E14 . . . . 34 B2

Ashurst Lo **4** N5 . . . . . . 15 A3

Ashwin St E8 . . . . 16 B2

Ashworth Cl SE5 . . . . . . 48 C1

Ashworth Mans
W9 . . . . 88 B3

Ashworth Rd W9 . . . . 88 B3

Aske Ho
N1 . . . . 24 A2 98 A4

Asker Ho N7 . . . . 14 A4

Aske St N1 . . . . . . 24 A2 98 C4

Askew Cres W12 . . . . 38 C4

Askew Mans **14**
W12 . . . . 38 C4

Askew Rd W12 . . . . 38 C4

Askham Ct W12 . . . . 29 C1

Askham Rd W12 . . . . 29 C1

Askill Dr SW15 . . . . 58 A2

Asland Rd E15 . . . . 27 C4

Aslett St SW18 . . . . 71 B4

Asmara Rd NW2 . . . . 10 A3

Asolando Dr SE17 . . . . . 151 A3

Aspect Ho **2** E14 . . . . . . 42 B4

Aspen Cl
Ealing W5 . . . . 36 B4
1 Upper Holloway
N19 . . . . 4 B2

Aspen Ct
18 Acton W3 . . . . 28 B3
32 Hackney E8 . . . . . . 16 C3
Richmond TW9 . . . . 44 C3

Aspen Gdns **2**
W6 . . . . 39 A1

Aspen Ho
6 Deptford SE15 . . . . . 50 B4
Maitland Pk
NW3 . . . . 12 B2
Richmond TW9 . . . . 44 C3

Aspenlea Rd W6 . . . . 47 C4

Aspen Way E14 . . . . 34 B2

Aspern Gr NW3 . . . . 12 A3

Aspinall Ho SW12 . . . . . . 74 A3

Aspinall Rd SE4 . . . . 65 C4

Aspinden Rd SE16 . . . . . 40 A2

Aspire Bld **10**
SW15 . . . . 58 B2

Aspley Rd SW18 . . . . 59 A2

Assam St E1 . . . . 125 A1

Assam St E1 . . . . 111 B2

Assembly Pas E1 . . . . . . 32 B4

Assisi Ct SW12 . . . . 72 B3

Astbury Bsns Pk **5**
SE15 . . . . 50 B2

Astbury Ho SE11 . . . . . . 135 B1

Astbury Rd SE15 . . . . . . 50 B2

Astell St SW3 . . . . 144 B2

Aster Ho **3** SE13 . . . . . . 52 B1

Aste St E14 . . . . 42 B4

Astey's Row **1** N1 . . . . . 15 B1

Astle St SW11 . . . . 169 C2

Astley Ave NW2 . . . . 9 B3

Astley Ho
Fulham SE1 . . . . 153 A2
Paddington W2 . . . . 31 C4

Aston Ho N4 . . . . 6 B2

Aston Ho
Notting Hill
W11 . . . . 31 B2 113 A4

Aston Ho *continued*
South Lambeth
SW8 . . . . **171** B3
Astonville St
SW18 . . . . .70 C3
Aston St E14 . . . . . . .33 A4
Astor Ct SW6 . . . . . **156** C1
Astoria Mans 10
SW16 . . . . .74 A1
Astoria Par SW16 . . .74 A1
Astoria Wlk SW9 . . . .62 C4
Astra Ho
4 Bow E3 . . . . .26 B2
Hornsey N4 . . . . .5 B4
Astrop Mews W6 . . . .39 B3
Astrop Terr W6 . . . . .39 B4
Astwood Mews
SW7 . . . . **142** C4
Asylum Rd SE15 . . . .50 A3
Atalanta St
SW6 . . . . . .47 C3 **154** A1
Atheldene Rd
SW18 . . . . .71 B3
Athelstan Gr E3 . . . . .26 B3
Athelstane Mews
N4 . . . . .5 C3
Athelstan Gdns 8
NW6 . . . . .10 A1
Athelstan Ho
Hackney Wick E9 . . . .18 B3
Stoke Newington
N16 . . . . .16 A4
Athena Ct
Bermondsey SE1 . . . **138** A3
St John's Wood
NW8 . . . . .79 B2
Athenia Ho 7 E14 . . .34 C3
Athenlay Rd SE15 . . .65 C2
Athenoeum Ct N5 . . . .15 B4
Athens Gdns W9 . . . .23 C1
Atherden Rd E5 . . . . .17 B4
Atherfield Ct
SW18 . . . . .59 A1
Atherfold Rd SW9 . . .62 A4
Atherstone Ct W2 . . **100** B4
Atherstone Mews
SW7 . . . . **143** A4
Atherton Rd SW13 . . .46 C3
Atherton St SW11 . . **168** B2
Athlone Cl 24 E5 . . . .17 A3
Athlone Ho
16 Camden Town
NW5 . . . . .12 C2
1 Stepney E1 . . . . . . .32 B3
Athlone Rd SW2 . . . . .74 C4
Athlone St NW5 . . . . .12 C2
Athol Ct 19 N4 . . . . . .5 B2
Atholl Ho W9 . . . . . . .88 C3
Athol Sq E14 . . . . . . .34 B3
Atkins Ct 13 E3 . . . . .26 B4
Atkins La W8 . . . . . **127** B4
Atkinson Ho
Battersea SW11 . . . **169** B3
15 Hackney E2 . . . . .24 C3
Walworth SE17 . . . . **151** C3
Atlanta Bldg 4
SE13 . . . . .52 A2
Atlantic Ct 11 E14 . .34 C2
Atlantic Ho
1 Putney SW15 . . . . .58 B2
4 Tower Hamlets
E1 . . . . .33 A4

Atlantic Rd SW2, SW9,
SE24 . . . . .62 C3
Atlas Mews
Dalston E8 . . . . .16 B2
Islington N7 . . . . .14 B2
Atlas Rd NW10 . . . . . .21 A2
Atney Rd SW15 . . . . .58 A3
Atterbury St SW1 . . **147** C3
Attilburgh Ho SE1 . . **138** C2
Attlee Ho 1 . . . . . . **111** A3
Attneave St WC1 . . . .95 B3
Atwater Cl SW2 . . . . .74 C3
Atwell Rd 6 SE15 . . .49 C1
Atwood Ave TW9 . . . .44 C1
Atwood Ho SE21 . . . .76 A1
Atwood Rd W6 . . . . . .39 A2
Aubert Ct N5 . . . . . . .15 A4
Aubert Pk N5 . . . . . . .15 A4
Aubert Rd N5 . . . . . . .15 A4
Aubrey Beardsley Ho
SW1 . . . . **147** A3
Aubrey Mans
NW1 . . . . **102** A4
Aubrey Moore Point 5
E15 . . . . .27 B3
Aubrey Pl NW8 . . . . .78 C1
Aubrey Rd
W14 . . . . . .31 B1 **113** A1
Aubrey Wlk
W14 . . . . . .31 B1 **113** A1
Auburn Cl SE14 . . . . .51 A3
Aubyn Sq SW15 . . . . .56 C2
Auckland Ho 11
W12 . . . . .30 A2
Auckland Rd
SW11 . . . . .60 A3
Auckland St SE11 . . **148** C1
Auden Pl NW1 . . . . . .81 B4
Audley Cl 5 SW11 . . .60 C4
Audley Ct W1 . . . . . **118** A2
Audley Rd TW10 . . . .54 B2
Audley Sq W1 . . . . . **117** C2
Audley St W1 . . . . . **117** C2
Audrey Ho EC1 . . . . **107** C3
Audrey St E2 . . . . . . .24 C3
Augusta St E14 . . . . .34 A3
Augustine Ho
Broadgate EC2 . . . . **109** C2
New Cross SE4 . . . . . .51 B2
Augustine Rd W14 . . .39 C3
Augustines Ct E9 . . . .17 B3
Augustus Cl 2
W12 . . . . .39 A3
Augustus Ct
8 Putney SW19 . . . . .70 A3
Streatham SW16 . . . .73 C2
Augustus Ho NW1 . . .92 C4
Augustus Rd
Putney SW19 . . . . . . .69 C3
Putney SW19 . . . . . . .70 A3
Augustus St NW1 . . . .92 B4
Aulton Pl SE11 . . . . **149** C1
Aura Ho 3 TW9 . . . . .45 A2
Auriga Mews N1 . . . .15 C3
Auriol Mans W14 . . **140** A3
Auriol Rd W14 . . . . **140** A3
Aurora Bldg 4
E14 . . . . .34 B1
Aurora Ho E14 . . . . . .34 A3
Austen Ho 3 NW6 . . .23 C2
Austin Friars EC2 . . **109** C2
Austin Friars Ho
EC2 . . . . **109** C2
Austin Friars Sq
EC2 . . . . **109** C2
Austin Ho
6 Brixton SW2 . . . . . .62 B2

Austin Rd *continued*
1 New Cross SE14 . . .51 B3
Austin St E2 . . . . . . **24** B2
Austins Ct SE15 . . . . .64 C4
Austral Ct 22 E2 . . . **98** C3
Australia Rd W12 . . . .30 A2
Austral St SE11 . . . . **150** A4
Autumn Rise 2
W4 . . . . .37 C1
Autumn St E3 . . . . . . .26 C4
Avalon Rd SW6 . . . . **166** A4
Avebury Ct N1 . . . . . .87 B3
Avebury St N1 . . . . . .87 B3
Aveline St SE11 . . . . **149** B1
Aveling Ho 15 N19 . . .4 B1
Ave Maria La EC4 . . **108** B1
Avenell Mans N5 . . . .15 A4
Avenell Rd N5 . . . . . .6 A1
Avenfield Ho W1 . . . **117** A4
Avening Rd SW18 . . . .70 C4
Avening Terr
SW18 . . . . .70 C4
Avenue Cl NW8 . . . . .80 B3
Avenue Cres W3 . . . .37 A4
Avenue Ct
Chelsea SW3 . . . . . **144** C3
Cricklewood NW2 . . . .1 A1
Avenue Gdns
Mortlake SW14 . . . . . .56 A4
South Acton W3 . . . . .37 A4
Avenue Ho
St John's Wood
NW8 . . . . .80 A1
Upper Clapton N16. . . .7 C2
Willesden Green
NW10 . . . . .22 A3
Avenue Lo 12
NW8 . . . . .11 C1
Avenue Mans
Clapham SW11 . . . . . .60 C3
Hampstead NW3 . . . . .11 A3
Willesden NW2 . . . . . .9 A2
Avenue Park Rd SE21,
SE27 . . . . .75 A2
Avenue Rd
Crouch End N6 . . . . . .4 C4
Harlesden NW10 . . . . .21 B3
Primrose Hill NW8 . . . .80 A4
South Acton W3 . . . . .37 A4
Avenue The
Bedford Pk W4 . . . . . .38 A3
Brondesbury Pk
NW6 . . . . .23 A4
Clapham SW4 . . . . . . .60 C2
Greenwich SE10 . . . . .52 C3
Richmond TW9 . . . . . .44 C2
Wandsworth SW18,
SW12 . . . . .72 A4
Averill St W6 . . . . . **47** C4
Avery Farm Row
SW1 . . . . **146** A3
Avery Hill Coll (Mile
End Annexe) E3 . . . . .26 B3
Avery Row W1 . . . . **118** B4
Aviary Cl E16 . . . . . . .35 B4
Avignon Rd SE4 . . . . .65 C4
Avingdon Ct 10
SW8 . . . . .34 B1
Avington Ct SE1 . . . **152** B3
Avis Sq E1 . . . . .32 C3
Avocet Cl SE1 . . . . . **153** B2
Avon Ct
1 Acton W3 . . . . .28 B3
11 Putney SW15 . . . .58 A2
Avondale Ho SE14 . .62 B2

Avondale Ho
11 Bermondsey
SE1 . . . . **153** B1
6 Mortlake SW14 . . . .55 C4
Avondale Mans
SW6 . . . . **164** C4
Avondale Park Gdns
W11 . . . . . .31 A2 **112** A3
Avondale Park Rd
W11 . . . . . .31 A2 **112** A4
Avondale Rd
Mortlake SW14 . . . . . .55 C4
Newham E16 . . . . . . .35 A4
Avondale Rise
SE15 . . . . .64 B4
Avondale Sq SE1 . . **153** B1
Avon Ho
2 Islington N1 . . . . . .14 C1
13 Stoke Newington
N16 . . . . .15 C4
West Kensington
W14 . . . . **141** A3
Avonhurst Ho
NW6 . . . . .10 A1
Avonley Rd SE14 . . . .50 B3
Avonmore Gdns
W14 . . . . **141** A3
Avonmore Pl W14 . . **140** B4
Avonmore Prim Sch
W14 . . . . **140** B4
Avonmore Rd
W14 . . . . **140** C4
Avonmouth St
SE1 . . . . **136** C2
Avon Pl SE1 . . . . . . **137** A3
Avon Rd SE4 . . . . . . .66 C4
Avriol Ho W12 . . . . . .30 A1
Avro Ct E9 . . . . .18 A3
Axford Ho SW2 . . . . .75 A3
Axis Ct SE10 . . . . . . .53 A4
Axminster Rd N7 . . . . .5 B1
Aybrook St W1 . . . . **103** B3
Aycliffe Rd W12 . . . . .29 C1
Aylesbury Ho 15
SE15 . . . . .49 C4
Aylesbury Rd
SE17 . . . . **151** C1
Aylesbury St EC1 . . . .96 A1
Aylesford Ho SE1 . . **137** C3
Aylesford St SW1 . . **147** B1
Aylesham Sh Ctr
SE15 . . . . .49 C2
Aylestone Ave
NW6 . . . . .22 C4
Aylmer Ho SE10 . . . .42 C1
Aylmer Rd W12 . . . . .38 B4
Aylton Est 23 SE16 . .40 B4
Aylward St E1 . . . . . .32 C3
Aylwin Est SE1 . . . . **138** B2
Aynhoe Mans W14 . . **39** C3
Aynhoe Rd W14 . . . . .39 C3
Ayres St SE1 . . . . . **137** A4
Ayrsome Rd N16 . . . . .7 A1
Ayrton Gould Ho 6
E2 . . . . .25 C2
Ayrton Rd SW7 . . . . **129** B2
Aysgarth Rd SE21 . . .76 A4
Ayshford Ho E2 . . . . .25 A2
Ayston Ho 10 SE8 . . .40 C2
Aytoun Ct 3 SW9 . . **173** A1
Aytoun Pl SW9 . . . . **173** A1
Aytoun Rd SW9 . . . **173** A1
Azalea Ho SE14 . . . . .51 B3
Azania Mews NW5 . . .13 A2

Azenby Rd SE15 . . . .49 B1
Azof St SE10 . . . . . . .43 A2
Azov Ho 10 E1 . . . . . .26 A1
Aztec Ct 3 N16 . . . . .16 A2
Azure Ho 28
E2 . . . . .24 C2 **99** B3

B

Baalbek Rd N5 . . . . . .15 A3
Babington Ct
WC1 . . . . **106** B4
Babington Ho
SE1 . . . . **137** A4
Babmaes St SW1 . . **119** B3
Bacchus Wlk 12
N1 . . . . .24 A3
Bache's St N1 . . . . . .97 C4
Back Church La
E1 . . . . **111** B1
Back Hill EC1 . . . . . . .95 C1
Backhouse Pl SE1 . . **152** B3
Back La N4 . . . . .5 C3
Bacon Gr SE1 . . . . . **138** C1
Bacon's Coll SE16 . . .41 A4
Bacon's La N6 . . . . . . .3 C3
Bacon St E2 . . . .24 B1 **99** A2
Bacton NW5 . . . . .12 C3
Bacton St E2 . . . . . . .25 B2
Baddeley Ho SE11 . **149** A2
Baddow Wlk N1 . . . . .86 C4
Baden Pl SE1 . . . . . **137** B4
Badminton Ct
N4 . . . . .6 B4
Badminton Ho
SE22 . . . . .64 A3
Badminton Mews
E16 . . . . .35 C1
Badminton Rd
SW12 . . . . .60 C1
Badric Ct SW11 . . . **167** C1
Badsworth Rd 3
SE5 . . . . .48 B2
Bagley's La SW6 . . **166** B3
Bagnigge Ho WC1 . . .95 B3
Bagshot Ho NW1 . . . .92 B4
Bagshot St SE17 . . . **152** B1
Baildon 8 E2 . . . . . . .25 B3
Baildon St SE8 . . . . . .51 B3
Bailey Ct 9 W12 . . . . .38 C4
Bailey Ho SW10 . . . **156** B2
Bailey Mews
Brixton SW2 . . . . .62 C2
Chiswick W4 . . . . .45 A3
Bainbridge St
WC1 . . . . **105** C2
Bain Ho 8 SW9 . . . . **172** B2
Baird Ho 22 W12 . . . .30 A2
Baird St EC1 . . . . .97 A2
Baizdon Rd SE3 . . . . .53 A1
Baker Ho 12 E3 . . . . .27 A2
Baker Rd NW10 . . . . .21 A4
Bakers Field N7 . . . . .14 A4
Bakers Hall Ct
EC3 . . . . **124** B3
Baker's Mews W1 . . **103** B2
Bakers Pas 22
NW3 . . . . .11 B4
Bakers Rents 13
E2 . . . . .24 B2 **98** C3
Baker's Row E1 . . . . .95 B1
Baker St W1 . . . . . . **103** A4
Baker Street W1. . . **103** A4
Baker Street Sta
NW1 . . . . .91 A1

Baker's Yd EC1 . . . . . . **95** B1
Bakery Cl SW9 . . . . . . **163** A1
Balaclava Rd SE22 . . . . 65 A1
Balchier Rd SE22 . . . . . 65 A1
Balcombe Ho
  Lisson Gr NW1 . . . . . . **90** C2
  Streatham SW2 . . . . . 74 B3
Balcombe St NW1 . . . . **90** C1
Balcorne St E9 . . . . 17 B1
Balderton Flats
  W1 . . . . **103** C1
Balderton St W1 . . . . **103** C1
Baldock Ho **51** SE5 . . . 48 B1
Baldock St E3 . . . . 27 A3
Baldrey Ho
  SE10 . . . . 43 B1
Baldwin Cres SE5 . . . . . 48 B2
Baldwin Ho **18**
  SW2 . . . . 74 C3
Baldwin Rd SW12 . . . . . 60 C1
Baldwin's Gdns
  EC1 . . . . **107** B4
Baldwin St EC1 . . . . . **97** B3
Baldwin Terr N1 . . . . . **86** C2
Baldwyn Gdns W3 . . . . 28 C2
Balearic Apts **3**
  E16 . . . . 35 C2
Bale Rd E1 . . . . 33 A4
Bales Coll W10 . . . . . . 22 C2
Balfern Gr W4 . . . . 38 A1
Balfern St SW11 . . . . **168** B2
Balfe St N1 . . . . **84** B1
Balfour Ho
  W10 . . . . 30 C4
Balfour Mews W1 . . . **117** C2
Balfour Pl
  Mayfair W1 . . . . . . **117** C3
  Putney SW15 . . . . . . 57 A3
Balfour Rd
  Highbury N5 . . . . 15 B4
  North Acton W3 . . . . . 28 C3
Balfour St SE17 . . . . **151** B4
Balfron Twr
  E14 . . . . 34 B3
BALHAM 72 C3
Balham Gr SW12 . . . . . 72 C4
Balham High Rd SW12,
  SW17 . . . . 72 C3
Balham Hill SW12 . . . . . 61 A1
Balham L Ctr
  SW12 . . . . 73 A2
Balham New Rd
  SW12 . . . . 73 A4
Balham Park Mans
  SW12 . . . . 72 C3
Balham Park Rd SW12,
  SW17 . . . . 72 C3
Balham Sta SW12 . . . . 73 A3
Balham Station Rd
  SW12 . . . . 73 A3
Balin Ho SE1 . . . . . . **137** B4
Balkan Wlk E1 . . . . 32 A2
Balladier Wlk E14 . . . . . 34 A4
Ballance Rd E9 . . . . . . 18 A2
Ballantine St
  SW18 . . . . 59 B3
Ballantrae Ho
  NW2 . . . . 10 B1
Ballard Ho SE10 . . . . . 52 A4
Ballast Quay SE10 . . . . 42 C1
Ballater Rd SW2,
  SW4 . . . . 62 A3
Ball Ct EC3 . . . . **109** C1
Ballin Ct E14 . . . . 42 B4
Ballingdon Rd
  SW11 . . . . 60 C1

Ballinger Point **18**
  E3 . . . . 27 A2
Balliol Ho **11**
  SW15 . . . . 57 C1
Balliol Rd W10 . . . . . . 30 C3
Ballogie Ave NW10 . . . . 8 A4
Ballow Cl SE5 . . . . 49 A3
Ball's Pond Pl **3**
  N1 . . . . 15 C2
Ball's Pond Rd N1 . . . . 16 A2
Balman Ho
  SE16 . . . . 40 C2
Balmer Rd E3 . . . . 26 B3
Balmes Rd N1 . . . . . . **87** C4
Balmoral Cl
  SW15 . . . . 57 C1
Balmoral Ct
  21 Rotherhithe
  SE16 . . . . 32 C1
  St John's Wood
  NW8 . . . . **79** B2
Balmoral Gr N7 . . . . . . 14 B2
Balmoral Ho
  1 Isle Of Dogs
  E14 . . . . 42 A3
  West Kensington
  W14 . . . . **140** A4
Balmoral Mews
  W12 . . . . 38 B3
Balmoral Rd NW2 . . . . . 9 A2
Balmore Cl E14 . . . . . . 34 B3
Balmore St N19 . . . . . . 4 A2
Balmuir Gdns
  SW15 . . . . 57 B3
Balnacraig Ave
  NW10 . . . . 8 A4
Balniel Gate SW1 . . . **147** C2
Balsam Ho **9** E14 . . . . 34 A2
Baltic Apts E16 . . . . . . 35 C2
Baltic Ho **7** SE5 . . . . . 48 B1
Baltic St E EC1 . . . . . **96** C1
Baltic St W EC1 . . . . . **96** C1
Baltimore Ho
  Clapham SW18 . . . . . 59 B3
  Kennington SE11 . . . **149** B2
Balvaird Pl SW1 . . . . **147** C1
Balvernie Gr SW18 . . . . 70 C4
Bamber Rd **8**
  SE15 . . . . 49 B2
Bamborough Gdns **12**
  W12 . . . . 39 B4
Banbury Ct WC2 . . . . **120** A4
Banbury Ho **5** E9 . . . . 17 C1
Banbury Rd E9 . . . . . . 17 C1
Banbury St **3**
  SW11 . . . . **168** B2
Bancroft Ho E1 . . . . . . 25 B1
Bancroft Rd **11** E1 . . . . 25 C1
Bancroft Rd E1 . . . . . . 25 C1
Banfield Rd SE15 . . . . . 65 A4
Banff Ho NW3 . . . . 12 A2
Bangabandhu Prim
  Sch **32** E2 . . . . 25 B2
Bangalore St
  SW15 . . . . 57 B4
Banim St W6 . . . . 39 A2
Banister Ho
  Hackney E9 . . . . 17 C3
  Nine Elms SW8 . . . . **172** A4
  9 West Kilburn
  W9 . . . . 23 A2
Banister Rd W10 . . . . . 22 C2
Bank Ct SW11 . . . . . **170** A4
Bank End SE1 . . . . . **123** A2
Bank La SW15 . . . . . . 56 A2

Bank of England
  EC2 . . . . **109** B1
Bank of England Mus
  EC2 . . . . **109** B1
Banks Ho SE1 . . . . . **136** C1
Bankside
  Borough The SE1 . . **122** C3
  Borough The SE1 . . **123** A2
Bankside Ave **1**
  SE13 . . . . 67 B4
Bankside Gall
  SE1 . . . . **122** B3
Bankside Ho EC3 . . . **110** B1
Bankside Mix SE1 . . . **122** B2
Bankside Pier
  SE1 . . . . **121** C2
Bank St E14 . . . . 34 A1
Bank Sta EC3 . . . . . **109** C1
Bank The N6 . . . . 4 A3
Bankton Rd SW2 . . . . . 62 C3
Banner Ho **12**
  SW8 . . . . **162** C3
Banner St EC1 . . . . . **97** A2
Bannerman Ho
  SW8 . . . . **162** C3
Banner St EC1 . . . . . **97** A2
Banning Ho
  SW19 . . . . 69 C3
Banning St SE10 . . . . . 43 A1
Bannister Cl SW2 . . . . . 74 C3
Bannister Ho **28**
  SE14 . . . . 50 C4
Banyan Ho
  NW3 . . . . 11 A2
Banyard Rd SE16 . . . . . 40 A3
Baptist Gdns NW5 . . . . 12 C2
Barandon Wlk
  W11 . . . . 30 C2
Barbanel Ho **28** E1 . . . 25 B1
Barbara Brosnan Ct
  NW8 . . . . **79** B1
Barbara Castle Cl
  SW6 . . . . **155** A3
Barbara Rudolph Ct
  5 N5 . . . . 15 B4
Barbauld Rd N16 . . . . . 7 A1
Barber Beaumont Ho
  1 E1 . . . . 25 C2
Barbers Rd E15 . . . . . . 27 A3
BARBICAN **109** A4
Barbican Ctr EC2 . . . **109** A4
Barb Mews W6 . . . . . . 39 B3
Barbon Alley EC3 . . . **110** B2
Barbon Cl WC1 . . . . **106** C4
Barbrook Ho E9 . . . . . . 17 B2
Barchard St SW18 . . . . 59 A2
Barchester St E14 . . . . 34 A4
Barclay Cl SW6 . . . . **155** B1
Barclay Ho **9** E9 . . . . . 17 B1
Barclay Rd SW6 . . . . **155** C1
Barcombe Ave
  SW2 . . . . 74 B2
Bardell Ho **17** SE1 . . . **139** B3
Bardolph Rd
  Richmond TW9 . . . . . 54 B4
  Tufnell Pk N7 . . . . . . 14 A4

Bard Rd W10 . . . . 30 C2
Bardsey Pl **41** E1 . . . . 25 B1
Bardsey Wlk **5**
  N1 . . . . 15 B2
Bardsley Ho **6**
  SE10 . . . . 52 B4
Bardsley La SE10 . . . . . 52 B4
Barents Ho **1** E1 . . . . 25 C1
Barfett St W10 . . . . . . 23 B1
Barfleur La SE8 . . . . . . 41 B2
Barford Ho **3** E3 . . . . 26 B3
Barford St N1 . . . . . . **85** C3
Barforth Rd SE15 . . . . . 65 A4
Barge House St
  SE1 . . . . **121** C2
Barge La **10** E3 . . . . . 26 B4
Barham Ho SE17 . . . . **152** B2
Baring Ct N1 . . . . . . **87** B3
Baring Ho **14** E14 . . . . 33 C3
Baring St N1 . . . . . . **87** B3
Barker Cl TW9 . . . . . . 45 A1
Barker Ho
  Dulwich SE21 . . . . . . 76 A1
  Walworth SE17 . . . . **152** A3
Barker Mews SW4 . . . . 61 A3
Barker St SW10 . . . . **156** C4
Barker Wlk SW16 . . . . . 73 C1
Bark Pl W2 . . . . **114** A4
Barkston Gdns
  SW5 . . . . **142** A3
Barkway Ct N4 . . . . 6 B2
Barkwith Ho **24** SE14 . . 50 C4
Barkworth Rd
  SE16 . . . . 40 B1
Barlborough St
  SE14 . . . . 50 C3
Barlby Gdns W10 . . . . . 22 C1
Barlby Prim Sch
  W10 . . . . 22 C1
Barlby Rd W10 . . . . . . 30 C4
Barleycorn Way
  E14 . . . . 33 B2
Barley Mow Pas
  Chiswick W4 . . . . 37 C1
  Clerkenwell EC1 . . . **108** B3
Barley Shotts Bsns Pk
  W10 . . . . 23 A1
Barling **6** NW1 . . . . . 13 A1
Barling Cl **11**
  SW4 . . . . **172** A2
Barlings Ho **2**
  SE4 . . . . 65 C3
Barloch Ho
  SW11 . . . . **169** B2
Barlow Ho
  Bermondsey SE16 . . . 40 A2
  16 Notting Hill
  W11 . . . . . . **31** A2 **112** A4
  Shoreditch N1 . . . . . **97** B4
Barlow Pl W1 . . . . . . **118** B3
Barlow Rd
  Acton W3 . . . . 28 A1
  Brondesbury NW6 . . . 10 B2
Barlow St SE17 . . . . **151** C3
Barmouth Ho **7** N7 . . . 5 B2
Barmouth Rd
  SW18 . . . . 59 B1
Barnabas Ho EC1 . . . . **96** C3
Barnabas Lo SW8 . . . **172** B4
Barnabas Rd E9 . . . . . 18 A3
Barnaby Pl SW7 . . . . **143** B3
Barnard Ct SW16 . . . . . 74 B1
Barnard Ho **17** E2 . . . . 25 A2

Barnard Lo **10** W9 . . . 31 C4
Barnard Mews
  SW11 . . . . 60 A3
Barnardo Gdns **1**
  E1 . . . . 32 C2
Barnardo St E1 . . . . . . 32 C3
Barnard Rd SW11 . . . . 60 A3
Barnard's Inn EC4 . . . **107** C2
Barnbrough NW1 . . . . **82** C3
Barnby St NW1 . . . . . **93** A4
Barnersbury Ho
  N7 . . . . 14 A4
Barn Elms Sp Ctr
  SW13 . . . . 47 B2
BARNES 46 A4
Barnes Ave SW13 . . . . 46 C3
Barnes Bridge Sta
  SW13 . . . . 46 A1
Barnes Common
  SW13 . . . . 56 C4
Barnes Ct N1 . . . . 14 C1
Barnes High St
  SW13 . . . . 46 B1
Barnes Ho
  14 Bethnal Green
  E2 . . . . 25 B3
  Camden Town NW1 . . **82** B4
  22 Deptford SE14 . . . 50 C4
  Hornsey N19 . . . . 5 A4
Barnes Hospl
  SW14 . . . . 56 A4
Barnes Prim Sch
  SW13 . . . . 56 B4
Barnes St E14 . . . . . . 33 A3
Barnes Terr SE8 . . . . . 41 B1
Barnet Gr
  E2 . . . . **24** C2 **99** B3
Barnet Ho **36** SE5 . . . 48 B1
Barnett Ho E1 . . . . . **110** C3
Barnett St **32** E1 . . . . 32 A3
Barn Field NW3 . . . . . . 12 B3
Barnfield
  London N4 . . . . 5 A4
  Wandsworth SW17 . . . 71 B1
Barnfield Cl
  SW17 . . . . 71 B1
Barnfield Pl E14 . . . . . 41 C2
Barnham St SE1 . . . . **138** B4
BARNSBURY 14 A1
Barnsbury Gr N7 . . . . . 14 B1
Barnsbury Ho **12**
  SW4 . . . . 61 C1
Barnsbury Pk N1 . . . . . 14 C1
Barnsbury Rd N1 . . . . **85** B3
Barnsbury Sq N1 . . . . . 14 C1
Barnsbury St N1 . . . . . 14 C1
Barnsbury Terr N1 . . . . 14 B1
Barnsdale Ave E14 . . . . 41 C2
Barnsdale Rd W9 . . . . . 23 B1
Barnsley St E1 . . . . . . 25 A1
Barn St N16 . . . . 7 A2
Barnstaple La
  SE13 . . . . 67 B3
Barnston Wlk N1 . . . . **86** C4
Barnwell Ho **1**
  SE5 . . . . 49 A2
Barnwell Rd SW2 . . . . . 62 C2
Barnwood Cl W9 . . . . **88** B1
Baron Cl N1 . . . . **85** B2
Baroness Rd **5**
  E2 . . . . **24** B2 **99** A4
Barons Court Mans
  W14 . . . . **140** B1

Baron's Court Rd
W14 .... **140** B2
Barons Court Sta
W14 .... **140** A2
Barons Gate B
W4 .... **37** A3
Barons Keep W14 ... **140** A2
Barons Lo E1 .... **42** B2
Baronsmead Rd
SW13 .... **46** C2
Baronsmede W5 .... **36** B4
Baron's Pl SE1 .... **135** C3
Baron St N1 ...... **85** B2
Baron Wlk E16 .... **35** B4
Barque Mews SE8 .... **51** C4
Barradell Ho B
W14 .... **39** C3
Barrat Ho E N1 .... **15** A1
Barratt Ind Pk E3 .... **27** A1
Barret Ho NW6 .... **23** C4
Barrett Ct B
NW10 .... **21** A3
Barrett's Gr N16 .... **16** A3
Barretts Green Rd
NW10 .... **20** C3
Barrett St W1 .... **103** C1
Barrhill Rd SW2 .... **74** A2
Barriedale SE14 .... **51** A1
Barrie Ho
Acton W3 .... **37** B4
Bayswater W2 .... **115** A3
Primrose Hill NW8 ... **80** B3
B Stoke Newington
N16 .... **7** A1
Barrington Cl
NW5 .... **12** C3
Barrington Cl
B Acton W3 .... **37** A4
Kentish Town NW5 .... **12** C3
B South Lambeth
SW9 .... **172** B1
Barrington Rd
SW9 .... **63** A4
Barrowgate Ho B
W4 .... **37** C1
Barrowgate Rd
W4 .... **37** C1
Barrow Hill Est
NW8 .... **80** A1
Barrow Hill Jun Sch
NW8 .... **80** A1
Barrow Hill Rd
NW8 .... **80** A1
Barry Ct SW4 .... **61** B1
Barry Ho E16 .... **40** A1
Barry Lo N4 ...... **5** B4
Barry Rd SE22 .... **64** C2
Barset Rd SE15 .... **65** B4
Barston Rd SE27 .... **75** B1
Barston Cres SW2 .. **74** B3
Bartell Ho SW2 .... **62** C1
Barter St WC1 .... **106** B3
Bartholomew Cl
Barbican EC1 .... **108** C3
Wandsworth SW18 .... **59** B3
Bartholomew Ct B
E14 Blackwall E14 .... **34** C2
St Luke's EC1 .... **97** A2
Bartholomew Ho B
SE5 .... **48** B1
Bartholomew La
EC2 .... **109** C1

Bartholomew Pas
EC1 .... **108** B3
Bartholomew Pl B
EC1 .... **108** C3
Bartholomew Rd
NW5 .... **13** B2
Bartholomew Sq
B Bethnal Green
E1 .... **25** A1
St Luke's EC1 .... **97** A2
Bartholomew St
SE1 .... **137** C1
Bartholomew Villas
NW5 .... **13** B2
Bartle Rd W11 .... **31** A3
Bartlett Ct E14 .... **33** C3
Bartlett Ct EC4 .... **107** C2
Bartok Ho
W11 .... **31** B2 **112** C3
Barton Cl
Hackney E9 .... **17** B3
Peckham SE15 .... **65** A4
Barton Ct
B South Lambeth
SW4 .... **172** A1
West Kensington
W14 .... **140** B2
Barton Ho
B Bromley E3 .... **27** A2
Islington N1 .... **15** A1
Sands End SW6 ...... **59** A4
Barton Rd W14 .... **140** B1
Barton St SW1 .... **134** A2
Bartonway NW8 .... **79** B2
Bartram Rd SE4 .... **66** A1
Bartrip St E9 .... **18** B2
Barville Cl SE4 .... **66** A3
Barwell Ho B E2 .. **24** C1 **99** C2
Barwick Ho B W3 .. **37** B4
Bascome St B
SW2 .... **62** C1
Base Apartments B
N1 .... **15** B1
**Baseline Business
Studios** B W11 .... **30** C2
Basevi Way SE8 .... **52** A4
Bashley Rd NW10 .. **20** C1
Basildon Ct W1 .. **103** C4
Basil Ho
South Lambeth
SW8 .... **162** A2
B Whitechapel E1 .. **111** C2
Basil Mans SW1 .. **130** C3
Basil St
Knightsbridge
SW1 .... **130** C3
Basin App E E14 .. **33** A3
Basing Ct E SE15 .. **49** B2
Basingdon Way
SE5 .... **63** C3
Basinghall Ave
EC2 .... **109** B2
Basinghall St EC2 .. **109** B2
Basing Hill NW11 .. **1** B3
Basing House Yd B
E2 .... **24** A2 **98** B4
Basing Pl E2 .. **24** A2 **98** B4
Basing St W11 .... **31** B3
Basire St N1 ...... **87** A4

Baskerville Ct
SW18 .... **72** A4
Baskerville Gdns
NW10 .... **8** A4
Baskerville Rd
SW18 .... **72** A4
Baslow Wlk E5 .... **17** C4
Basnett Rd B
SW11 .... **60** C4
Basque Ct B SE16 .. **40** C4
Bassano St SE22 .. **64** B2
Bassein Park Rd
W12 .... **38** B4
Bassett Ho
SW19 .... **30** C3
Bassett Rd W10 .... **30** C3
Bassett St NW5 .... **12** C2
Bassingbourn Ho B
N1 .... **15** A1
Bassingham Rd
SW18 .... **71** B4
Bassishaw Highwalk
EC2 .... **109** B3
Basswood Cl B
SE15 .... **65** A4
Basterfield Ho B
EC1 .... **96** C1
Bastion Highwalk
EC2 .... **108** C3
Bastwick St EC1 .... **96** C2
Basuto Rd SW6 .. **165** C3
Batavia Ho B
SE14 .... **51** A3
Batavia Mews B
SE14 .... **51** A3
Batavia Rd
SE14 .... **51** A3
Batchelor St N1 .... **85** C3
Bateman Ho B
SE17 .... **48** A4
Bateman's Bldgs
W1 .... **105** B1
Bateman's Row
EC2 .... **24** A1 **98** B2
Bateman St W1 .. **105** B1
Bate St B E14 .... **33** B2
Bath Cl SE15 ...... **50** A3
Bath Ct
Finsbury EC1 .... **97** B3
B Forest Hill SE26 .. **76** C1
Holborn EC1 .... **95** B1
Bathgate Ho B
SW9 .... **48** A2
Bathgate Rd SW19 . **69** C1
Bath Gr B E2 .... **24** C3
Bath Ho
Bethnal Green
E2 .... **24** C1 **99** C2
B Borough The SE1 . **137** A2
Bath Pl
B Hammersmith
W6 .... **39** B1
B Shoreditch
EC2 .... **24** A2 **98** B3
Bath Rd W4 ...... **38** A2
Bath St EC1 ...... **97** B3
Bath Terr SE1 .... **136** C2
Bathurst Gdns
NW10 .... **22** A3
Bathurst Ho B
W12 .... **30** A2
Bathurst Mews
W2 .... **115** C4
Bathurst St W2 .. **115** C4
Batley Pl B N16 .. **7** B1
Batley Rd N16 .... **7** B1
Batman Cl W12 .... **30** A1
Batoum Gdns W6 .. **39** B3

Batson Ho B E1 .. **111** C1
Batson St W12 .... **38** C4
Batten Ho
B London SW4 ...... **61** B2
B West Kilburn
W10 .... **23** A2
Batten St SW11 .... **60** A4
BATTERSEA **169** A4
Battersea Bridge Rd
SW11 .... **158** A1
Battersea Bsns Ctr B
SW11 .... **60** C4
Battersea Church Rd
SW11 .... **167** B1
**Battersea Dogs & Cats
Home** SW8 .... **160** B1
Battersea High St
SW11 .... **167** B1
Battersea Hts B
SW11 .... **60** B4
Battersea Park **159** B1
Battersea Park Rd
SW11, SW8 .... **169** A3
Battersea Park Sch
SW8 .... **160** A1
**Battersea Power
Station(dis)**
SW8 .... **160** B4
Battersea Rise
SW11 .... **60** A3
Battersea Sq B
SW11 .... **167** B3
Battishill St N1 .... **15** A1
Battlebridge Ct
N1 .... **84** B2
Battle Bridge La
SE1 .... **124** A1
Battledean Rd N5 .. **15** A3
Battle Ho B SE15 .. **49** C4
Batty St E1 ...... **111** C2
Baty Ho SW2 ...... **74** B3
Baulk The SW18 .. **70** C4
Bavaria Rd N19 .... **5** A2
Bavent Rd SE5 .... **48** B1
Bawdale Rd SE22 .. **64** B2
Bawtree Rd SE14 .. **51** A3
Baxendale St
E2 .... **24** C2 **99** B4
Baxter Ho B E3 .. **27** A2
Baxter Rd N1 ...... **15** C2
Baycliffe Ho B E9 . **17** C2
Bay Ct
Ealing W5 .... **36** A3
B Stepney E1 .... **25** C1
Bayer Ho EC1 .... **96** C1
Bayes Ct NW3 .... **12** B1
Bayfield Ho B
SE4 .... **65** C3
Bayford Rd NW10 .. **22** C2
Bayford St E8 .... **17** A1
Bayham Pl NW1 .. **83** A3
Bayham Rd W4 .... **37** C3
Bayham St NW1 .. **82** C3
Bayhurst Ho N4 .. **6** B4
Bayley St WC1 .. **105** B3
Baylis Rd SE1 .... **135** B3
Baynes Mews B
NW3 .... **11** C2
Baynes St NW1 .... **13** B1
Bayon Ho N19 .... **4** C4
Bayonne Rd W6 .. **154** A3

Bayston Rd N16 .... **7** B1
BAYSWATER **114** C4
Bayswater Rd W2 . **115** B3
Bayswater Mkt
W2 .... **115** A3
Bayswater Sta
W2 .... **114** B4
Bayton Ct B E2 .. **16** C2
Baytree Rd SW2 .. **62** B3
Bazalgette Ho
NW8 .... **89** C2
Bazeley Ho SE1 .. **136** A3
Bazely St E14 .... **34** B2
BBC Television Ctr
W12 .... **30** B1
Beach Ho SW5 .. **141** B2
Beachy Rd E3 .... **18** C1
**Beaconfield Terrace
Rd** W14 .... **126** A1
Beacon Gate SE14 . **65** C4
Beacon Hill N7 .... **14** A3
Beacon Ho
B Camberwell
SE5 .... **49** A3
B Isle Of Dogs
E14 .... **42** A1
South Lambeth
SW8 .... **171** B4
Beacon Rd SE13 .. **67** C1
Beaconsfield Cl
Acton Green W4 .... **37** B1
Greenwich SE3 .... **53** C4
Beaconsfield Rd
Acton W4 .... **37** C3
Greenwich SE3 .... **53** C4
Walworth SE17 .... **152** A1
Willesden NW10 .... **8** B2
Beaconsfield Wlk
SW6 .... **165** A3
Beadon Rd W6 .... **39** B2
Beak St W1 ...... **119** A4
Beale Ho B SW9 . **172** C1
Beale Pl E3 ...... **26** B3
Beale Rd E3 ...... **26** B4
Beames Ho SW8 . **171** B4
Beames Rd NW10 . **20** C4
Beaminster Ho B
SW8 .... **162** C2
Beamish Ho B
SE16 .... **40** B2
Beanacre Cl E9 ... **18** B2
Bear Alley EC4 .. **108** A2
Bear Croft Ho B
SW6 .... **164** C1
Beardsley Way
W3 .... **37** C4
Bear Gdns SE1 .. **122** C2
Bear La SE1 ...... **122** B1
Bear St WC2 .... **119** C4
Bearstead Rise
SE4 .... **66** B2
Beaton Cl SE15 .. **49** B2
Beatrice Ho
B Brixton SW2 .... **62** B2
B Hammersmith
W6 .... **39** B1
B Stepney E1 .... **32** C4
Beatrice Pl W8 .. **128** A1
Beatrice Rd
Bermondsey SE1 .. **153** C3
Finsbury Pk N4 .... **5** C4
B Richmond TW10 . **54** B2
Beatrice Tate Sch B
E2 .... **25** A2
Beatrice Webb Ho B
E3 .... **26** A3

Beatrix Ho SW5 .... **142** B2
Beatrix Potter Prim Sch SW18 .... 71 B3
Beatson Wlk 28 SE16 .... 32 C1
Beattie Ho SE1 .... **171** A4
Beatty Ho E14 .... 41 C4
Beatty Rd N16 .... 16 A4
Beauchamp Cl 17 W4 .... 37 B3
Beauchamp Pl SW3 .... **130** B1
Beauchamp Rd SW11 .... 60 B3
Beauchamp St EC1 .... **107** B3
Beauchamp Terr SW15 .... 57 A4
Beauclerc Rd W6 .... 39 A3
Beauclerk Ho 10 SW16 .... 74 A1
Beaufort Cl SW19 .... 69 A4
Beaufort Ct SW6 .... **155** B4
Beaufort Gdns SW3 .... **130** B2
Beaufort Ho
  Battersea SW11 .... **168** A2
  Chelsea SW3 .... **157** C3
  28 Millwall E14 .... 41 C4
  Pimlico SW1 .... **147** B1
Beaufort Mans SW3 .... **157** C3
Beaufort Mews SW6 .... **155** A4
Beaufort St SW3 .... **157** B4
Beaufoy Ho
  South Lambeth SW8 .... **162** C2
  5 West Norwood SE27 .... 75 A1
Beaufoy Rd 11 SW8 ....
Beaufoy Wlk SE11 149 A3
Beaulieu Cl SE5 .... 63 C4
Beaulieu Pl W4 .... 37 B3
Beaumanor Mans W2 .... **114** B4
Beaumaris Twr 2 W3 .... 37 A4
Beaumont Ave
  Richmond TW9 .... 54 B4
  West Kensington W14 .... **140** C2
Beaumont Bldgs WC2 .... **106** B1
Beaumont Cres W14 .... **140** C1
Beaumont Ct
  10 Acton Green W4 .... 37 B1
  Marylebone W1 .... **103** C4
  2 Mile End E1 .... 26 C2
Beaumont Gdns NW3 .... 1 C1
Beaumont Gr E1 .... 25 C1
Beaumont Ho
  1 Streatham SW2 .... 74 A3
  West Kensington W14 .... **141** A3
  Wimbledon SW19 .... 70 C1
Beaumont Lo E8 .... 16 C2
Beaumont Pl NW1, WC1, ... **93** A2

Beaumont Rd
  Putney SW15, SW19 .... 70 A4
  South Acton W4 .... 37 B3
Beaumont Rise N19 .... 4 C3
Beaumont Sq E1 .... 32 C4
Beaumont St W1 .... **103** C4
Beaumont Wlk NW3 .... 12 B1
Beauvale 6 NW1 .... 12 C1
Beavis Ho N16 .... 7 A1
Beavor La W6 .... 38 C1
Beccles St E14 .... 33 B2
Beck Cl SE13 .... 52 A2
Beckers The N16 .... 16 C4
Becket Ho SE1 .... **137** B3
Becket St SE1 .... **137** B2
Beckett Cl
  Streatham SW16 .... 73 C2
  Willesden NW10 .... 8 A2
Beckett Ho
  22 London SW9 .... **172** B1
  1 Stepney E1 .... 32 B4
Beckfoot NW1 .... **83** A1
Beckford Cl W14 .... **141** A3
Beckford Ho 18 N16 .... 16 A3
Beckford Prim Sch NW6 .... 10 B3
Beckham Ho SE11 .... **149** A3
Beck Ho N16 .... 7 A1
Beckington 15 NW5 .... 12 C2
Beckley Ho E3 .... 26 B1
Becklow Gdns
  Chiswick W12 .... 38 B4
  1 Shepherd's Bush W12 .... 38 C4
Becklow Mews 7 W12 .... 38 C4
Becklow Rd W12 .... 38 C4
Beck Rd E8 .... 25 A4
Beckton Rd E16 .... 35 B4
Beckway St SE17 .... **152** A3
Beckwith Ho 22 E2 .... 25 A3
Beckwith Rd SE24 .... 63 C2
Bective Pl SW15 .... 58 B3
Bective Rd SW15 .... 58 B3
Bedale St SE1 .... **123** B1
Bedefield WC1 .... **94** B3
Bede Ho
  London SE14 .... 51 B2
  5 Putney SW15 .... 57 C1
Bedford Ave WC1 .... **105** C3
Bedfordbury WC2 .... **120** A3
Bedford Cl W4 .... 46 B4
Bedford Cnr 3 W4 .... 38 A2
Bedford Court Mans WC1 .... **105** C3
Bedford Ct
  6 Richmond TW9 .... 54 B3
  St James WC2 .... **120** A3
Bedford Gardens Ho W8 .... **31** C1 **113** C1
Bedford Hill SW12 .... 73 A2
Bedford Ho
  2 Acton W4 .... 38 A2
  7 Stockwell SW4 .... 62 A3
BEDFORD PARK 38 A3

Bedford Park Cnr 5 W4 .... 38 A2
Bedford Park Mans W4 .... 37 C2
Bedford Pas SW6 .... **154** B2
Bedford Pl WC1 .... **106** A4
Bedford Rd
  Acton W4 .... 38 A3
  Stockwell SW2, SW4 .... 62 A3
Bedford Row WC1 .... **107** A3
Bedford Sq WC1 .... **105** C3
Bedford St WC2 .... **120** B3
Bedford Way WC1 .... **93** C1
Bedgebury Gdns SW19 .... 70 A2
Bedlam Mews SE11 .... **149** B4
Bedlow Cl NW8 .... **89** C1
Bedser Cl SE11 .... **163** A4
Bedser Ct 7 SW4 .... **172** A2
Bedwell Ho 18 SW9 .... **173** B1
Beech Ave W3 .... 29 A1
Beech Cl
  Deptford SE8 .... 51 B4
  Putney SW15 .... 68 C4
Beechcroft Ave NW11 .... 1 B4
Beechcroft Ct
  3 Golders Green NW11 .... 1 B4
  4 Greenwich SE3 .... 53 C2
Beech Croft Ct N5 .... 15 A4
Beechcroft Rd
  Mortlake SW14 .... 55 B4
  Upper Tooting SW17 .... 72 A2
Beechcroft Way N19 .... 4 C3
Beech Ct
  Child's Hill NW2 .... 1 B2
  Marylebone W1 .... **102** C2
  18 Notting Hill W2 .... 31 C4
  7 Rotherhithe SE16 .... 33 A1
Beechdale Rd SW2 .... 62 B1
Beechdene 4 SE15 .... 50 A2
Beeches The 1 N19 .... 5 A3
Beechey Ho 20 E1 .... 32 A1
Beech Gdns W5 .... 36 A3
Beech Ho
  6 Maitland Pk NW3 .... 12 B2
  2 Rotherhithe SE16 .... 40 B4
  3 Stoke Newington N16 .... 6 C2
Beechmore Rd SW11 .... **169** A3
Beech St EC2 .... **109** A4
Beech Tree Cl N1 .... 14 C1
Beechwood Ave TW9 .... 44 C2
Beechwood Ct
  Chiswick W4 .... 45 C4
  Stamford Hill N16 .... 7 A4
Beechwood Gr W3 .... 29 A2
Beechwood Ho 28 E2 .... 24 C3

Beechwood Rd E8 .... 16 B2
Beechworth Cl NW3 .... 1 C1
Beecroft La SE4 .... 66 A2
Beecroft Mews SE4 .... 66 A2
Beecroft Rd SE4 .... 66 A2
Beehive Cl E8 .... 16 B1
Beehive Pl SW9 .... 62 C4
Beeston Cl 5 E8 .... 16 C3
Beeston Pl SW1 .... **132** B2
Beeston's Ho SE15 .... 65 A4
Beethoven St W10 .... 23 A2
Begbie Ho SW9 .... **173** A2
Begonia Wlk W12 .... 29 B3
Beira St SW12 .... 73 A4
Beis Chinuch Lebonos Girls Sch N4 .... 6 B4
Beis Malka Girls Sch N16 .... 7 B3
Beis Hamedrash Elyon NW11 .... 1 A4
Beis Rochel d'Satmar Girls Sch 11 N16 .... 7 A4
Bekesbourne St 17 E14 .... 33 A3
Beldanes Lo NW10 .... 8 C1
Belenoyd Ct SW16 .... 74 B1
Belfast Rd N16 .... 7 B2
Belfont Wlk N7 .... 14 A4
Belford Ho 7 E8 .... 24 B4
Belfort Rd SE15 .... 50 B1
Belfry Cl 22 SE16 .... 40 A1
Belgrade Ho N16 .... 16 A4
Belgrade Rd N16 .... 16 A4
Belgrave Cl 1 W3 .... 37 B4
Belgrave Ct
  4 Acton Green W4 .... 37 B1
  22 Limehouse E14 .... 33 B2
  Nine Elms SW8 .... **160** C1
Belgrave Gdns
  Kilburn NW8 .... **78** C3
  St John's Wood NW8 .... **78** C3
Belgrave Mans NW8 .... **78** C3
Belgrave Mews N SW1 .... **131** B3
Belgrave Mews S SW1 .... **131** C2
Belgrave Mews W SW1 .... **131** B2
Belgrave Pl SW1 .... **131** C1
Belgrave Rd
  Barnes SW13 .... 46 B3
  Westminster SW1 .... **146** C3
Belgrave Sq SW1 .... **131** B2
Belgrave St E1 .... 32 C3
Belgrave Yd SW1 .... **132** A1
Belgravia Ct SW1 .... **132** A1
BELGRAVIA **146** A4
Belgravia Ho 11 SW4 .... 61 C1
Belham Wlk 6 SE5 .... 48 C2
Belinda Rd 5 SW9 .... 63 A4
Belitha Villas N1 .... 14 C1
Bellamy Cl
  18 Millwall E14 .... 41 C4
  West Kensington SW5 .... **141** A1
Bellamy's Ct 15 SE16 .... 32 C1

Bellamy St SW12 .... 73 A4
Bellasis Ave SW2 .... 74 A2
Bell Ct SE13 .... 66 C2
Bell Dr SW18 .... 70 A4
Bellefields Rd SW9 .... 62 B4
Bellenden Prim Sch 5 SE15 .... 65 A4
Bellenden Rd SE15 .... 49 B1
Bellenden Rd Rtl Pk SE15 .... 49 C2
Bellenden Road Bsns Ctr SE15 .... 49 B1
Bellerbys Coll SE8 .... 51 C4
Belleville Prim Sch SW11 .... 60 B2
Belleville Rd SW11 .... 60 B2
Belle Vue Gdns SW9 .... **172** B1
Bellevue Pl E1 .... 25 B1
Bellevue Rd
  Barnes SW13 .... 46 C1
  Upper Tooting SW17 .... 72 B3
Bellew St SW17 .... 71 B1
Bell Flats 4 NW2 .... 8 C2
Bellflower Ct SE13 .... 67 A3
Bellgate Mews NW5 .... 4 A1
Belgrave Lo 9 W4 .... 37 A1
Bell Ho
  Greenwich SE10 .... 52 B4
  1 Streatham SW2 .... 74 B4
Bellina Mews NW5 .... 13 B4
Bell Ind Est 2 W4 .... 37 B2
Bell Inn Yd EC3 .... **109** C1
Bell La
  Newham E16 .... 35 C1
  Spitalfields E1 .... **110** C3
Bell Language Sch W1 .... **92** C1
Bellmaker Ct 8 E3 .... 33 C4
Bell Moor NW3 .... 2 B1
Bello Cl SE24, SW2 .... 75 A3
Bellot Gdns 1 SE10 .... 43 A1
Bellot St SE10 .... 43 A1
Bell St NW1 .... **102** A4
Bell Wharf La EC4 .... **123** A4
Bellwood Rd SE15 .... 65 C3
Bell Yard Mews SE1 .... **138** B3
Bell Yd WC2 .... **107** B2
Belmont Cl SW4 .... 61 B4
Belmont Ct
  Highbury N5 .... 15 B4
  6 Stamford Hill N16 .... 7 A3
Belmont Gr
  Chiswick W4 .... 37 C2
  Lewisham SE13 .... 67 C4
Belmont Hall Ct SE13 .... 67 C4
Belmont Mews SW19 .... 69 C2
Belmont Prim Sch 10 W4 .... 37 C2
Belmont Rd
  Clapham SW4 .... 61 B4
  London W4 .... 37 C2
Belmont St NW1 .... 12 C1

Belmont Terr W4 ....37 C2
Belmore Ho N7....13 C3
Belmore La N7.....13 C3
Belmore St SW8 . **171** B4
Beloe Cl SW15.....56 C3
Belper Ct **11** E5 ....17 A4
Belsham St E9 ......17 B2
Belsize Ave NW3 ..12 A3
Belsize Court Garages
 1 NW3 ....11 C2
Belsize Cres NW3 ..11 C2
Belsize Ct NW3 ....11 C3
Belsize Gr NW3.....12 A2
Belsize La NW3 ....11 C3
Belsize Mews
 NW3 ....11 C2
Belsize Park Gdns
 NW3 ....12 A2
Belsize Park Mews **1**
 NW3 ....11 C2
Belsize Park Sta
 NW3 ....12 A3
Belsize Pk NW3 ....11 C2
Belsize Pl NW3 ....11 C2
Belsize Rd NW6 . **78** B4
Belsize Sq NW3 ....11 C2
Belsize Terr NW3 ..11 C2
Beltane Dr SW19 ..69 C1
Belthorn Cres
 SW12 ....73 B4
Belton Rd NW2 .....8 C2
Belton Way E3 ....33 C4
Beltran Rd SW6 . **166** A1
Belvedere Bldgs
 SE1 ....**136** B3
Belvedere Ct
 Brondesbury NW2 . . .9 C2
 7 Clapham Pk
 SW4 ....61 C1
 Putney SW15 ......57 B3
 13 Shoreditch N1 .24 A4
Belvedere Htss
 NW8 ....**90** A2
Belvedere Mews
 SE15 ....65 B4
Belvedere Pl
 Brixton SW2 ......62 B3
 Lambeth SE1 ...**136** B3
Belvedere Rd SE1 **121** A1
Belvedere The
 SW10 ....**167** A3
Belvoir Lo SE22 . **76** C4
Belvoir Rd SE22 ...76 C4
Bembridge Cl
 NW6 ....10 A1
Bembridge Ho
 8 Deptford SE8 .41 B2
 Wandsworth SW18 . .59 A1
Bemerton St N1 . **84** C4
Bemish Rd SW15 ...57 C4
Benabo Ct **6** E8 ..16 C3
Benbow Ho **12**
 SE8 ....51 C4
Benbow Rd W6 .....39 A3
Benbow St SE8 ....51 C4
Bence Ho **15** SE8 . . .41 A2
Bendall Mews
 NW1 ....**102** B4
Bendemeer Rd
 SW15 ....57 C4
Benden Ho SE13 . . .67 B2
Bendon Valley
 SW18 ....71 A4

Benedict Rd SW9 . **62** B4
Benenden Ho
 SE17 ....**152** B2
Ben Ezra Ct SE17 **151** A3
Benfleet Ct **6** E8 . .24 B4
Bengal Ct EC3.....**109** C1
Bengal Ho E1 .....32 C4
Bengeworth Rd
 SE5 ....63 B4
Benham Ho SW10 **156** B2
Benham's Pl **11**
 NW3 ....11 B4
Benhill Rd SE5 ...48 C2
Benington Ct E5 ..17 C4
Benjamin Cl E8 ....24 C4
Benjamin Franklin
 House SW1 .....**120** A2
Benjamin Ho **1**
 W3 ....28 A1
Benjamin Mews
 SW12 ....73 B4
Benjamin St EC1 . **108** A4
Ben Jonson Ct **1**
 N1 ....24 A3
Ben Jonson Prim Sch
 E1 ....26 A1
Ben Jonson Rd E1 .33 A4
Benledi St E14....34 C3
Bennelong Cl W12 .30 A3
Bennerley Rd
 SW11 ....60 B2
Bennet's Hill EC4 **122** B4
Bennett Ct
 Hampstead NW6 . . .11 A2
 Lower Holloway N7 . .5 B1
 7 South Acton W3 . .37 A4
Bennett Gr SE13 . .52 A2
Bennett Ho
 2 Streatham
 SW4 ....73 C4
 Westminster SW1 . **147** C4
Bennett St
 Chiswick W4 ......38 A1
 St James SW1 ....**118** C2
Bennett's Yd SW1 **133** C1
Benn Ho E2 ..24 C2 **99** B3
Benn St E9 ....18 A2
Benns Wlk **6** TW9 . .54 A3
Bensbury Cl SW15 .69 B4
Ben Smith Way **21**
 SE16 ....**139** C2
Benson Ct
 South Lambeth
 SW8 ....**172** A4
 2 Tufnell Pk N19 . .13 B4
Benson Ho
 Lambeth SE1 .....**121** C1
 Shoreditch
 E2 ....24 B1 **98** C2
Benson Quay E1... **32** B2
Benthal Ct N16....17 C1
Benthal Prim Sch
 N16...............7 C1
Benthal Rd N16....7 C1
Bentham Ct **11** N1 . .15 B1
Bentham Ho SE1 . **137** B2
Bentham Rd E9 ...17 C2
Bentinck Cl NW8 . **80** B1
Bentinck Ho **6**
 W12 ....30 A2
Bentinck Mans
 W1 ....**103** C2
Bentinck Mews
 W1 ....**103** C2
Bentinck St W1 . **103** C2
Bentley Cl SW19 ..70 C1

Bentley Ct SE13 ...67 B3
Bentley Dr NW2 ..10 B1
Bentley Ho
 5 Bow E3 ....26 C1
 6 Camberwell SE5 . .49 A2
Bentley Rd N1 .....16 A2
Bentworth Ct **1**
 E2 ....24 C1 **99** B2
Bentworth Prim Sch
 W12 ....30 A3
Bentworth Rd
 W12 ....30 A3
Benwell Rd N7 ....14 C3
Benwick Cl SE16 . .40 A2
Benworth St E3 ...26 B2
Benyon Ho **1** ...**95** C4
Benyon Rd N1 . **87** C4
Benyon Wharf **51**
 E8 ....24 A4
Beormund Sch
 SE1 ....**137** C3
Bequerel Ct SE10 .43 B3
Berberis Ho **17** E3 . .33 C4
Berber Pl E14 ....33 C2
Beresford Ho
 Dulwich SE21 ....76 A1
 15 Stockwell SW4 . .62 A3
Beresford Rd N5 ..15 C3
Beresford Terr **3**
 N5................15 C3
Bere St E1 ....32 C2
Berestede Rd **4**
 W6................38 B1
Bergen Ho SE5 ....48 B1
Bergen Sq SE16 ....41 A3
Berger Prim Sch **38**
 E9 ....17 C2
Berger Rd E9 ......17 C2
Berghem Mews
 W14 ....39 C3
Berglen Cres N16... **7** A4
Bergholt Cres N16... **7** A4
Bergholt Mews **4**
 NW1 ....13 C1
Bering Sq E14 ....41 C1
Berisford Mews
 SW18 ....59 B1

Berkshire Ho
 WC2 ....**106** A2
Berkshire Rd E9 ..18 B2
Bermans Way NW10 . .8 A4
BERMONDSEY 40 A3
Bermondsey Leather
 Mkt SE1 ....**138** A2
Bermondsey Sq
 SE1 ....**138** A2
Bermondsey St
 SE1 ....**138** A3
Bermondsey Sta
 SE16 ....40 A3
Bermondsey Trad Est
 SE16 ....40 B1
Bermondsey Wall E
 SE16 ....40 A4
Bermondsey Wall W
 SE1, SE16 ......**139** B4
Bernard Angell Ho **3**
 SE10 ....52 C4
Bernard Cassidy St **2**
 E16 ....35 B4
Bernard Ho E1 . **110** C3
Bernard Shaw Ct **5**
 NW1 ....13 B1
Bernard Shaw Ho **9**
 NW10 ....20 C4
Bernard St WC1 . **94** B1
Berners Ho N1 . **85** B2
Berners Mews
 W1 ....**105** A3
Berners Pl W1 ...**105** A2
Berners Rd N1 ....86 A3
Berners St W1 . **105** A2
Bernay's Gr SW9 .. **62** B3
Berner Terr **2** E1 **111** C1
Bernhard Baron Ho **3**
 E1 ....**111** C1
Bernhardt Cres
 NW8 ....**90** A2
Bernie Grant Ho **6**
 E9 ....17 B1
Bernwood Ho **6**
 N4 ....6 C4
Berridge Mews
 NW6 ....10 C3
Berriman Rd N7.....5 B1
Berry Cotts **2** E14 . .33 A3
Berryfield Rd
 SE17 ....**150** B2
Berry Ho
 16 Battersea
 SW11 ....**169** A2
 2 Bethnal Green
 E1................25 A1
Berrymead Gdns
 W3................37 A4
Berrymede Inf Sch
 W4................37 B4
Berrymede Jun Sch
 W4................37 A4
Bermede Rd W4. **37** C3
Berry Pl EC1 .....**96** B3
Berry St EC1 ......**96** B1
Berry Way W3.....37 A3
Bertha Neubergh Ho **4**
 SE5 ....**48** B2
Berthon St SE8 ...51 C4
Bertie Rd NW10 ....8 C2
Bertram St N19 ....4 A2
Bertrand Ho **11**
 SW16 ....74 A1
Bertrand St SE13 . .67 A4
Bertrum House Sch
 SW17 ....72 C2

Berwick St W1....**105** A1
Berwick Street Mkt
 W1 ....**105** A1
Berwyn Ho **3** N16... **7** B3
Berwyn Rd
 Mortlake SW14,
 TW10 ....55 A3
 Streatham SE24 ...75 A3
Beryl Rd W6.......39 C1
Besant Ct N1......15 C3
Besant Ho NW8 . **78** C3
Besant Pl SE22 . **64** B3
Besant Rd NW2 ...10 A4
Besant Wlk N7 .....5 B2
Besford Ho **2** E2 . .24 C3
Bessant Dr TW9 . **45** A2
Bessborough Gdns
 SW1 ....**147** C2
Bessborough Pl
 SW1 ....**147** C2
Bessborough Rd
 SW15 ....68 C3
Bessborough St
 SW1 ....**147** B2
Bessemer Ct **7**
 NW1 ....13 B1
Bessemer Grange
 Prim Sch SE5 ....64 A3
Bessemer Park Ind
 Est **3** SE24.......75 A3
Bessemer Rd SE5... **48** B1
Bessingham Wlk
 SE4 ....65 C2
Besson St SE14....50 C2
Bessy St E2 ....25 B2
Bestwood St SE8 . .40 C2
Beswick Mews **1**
 NW6 ....11 A2
Beta Pl **23** SW4....62 A3
Betchworth Ho **8**
 N7................13 C3
Bethersden Ho
 SE17 ....**152** B2
Bethlehem Ho **13**
 E14 ....33 B2
BETHNAL GREEN ..25 A2
Bethnal Green Rd
 Bethnal Green
 E2 ....24 C2 **99** B3
 Shoreditch E1,
 E2 ....24 B2 **99** A2
Bethnal Green Sta
 Bethnal Green E1 . .25 A1
 Globe Town E2 . **25** B2
Bethnal Green Tech
 Coll **15** E2 ..24 B2 **99** A3
Bethune Rd
 North Acton
 NW10 ....20 C1
 Stamford Hill N16... **7** A4
Bethwin Rd SE5 . **48** B3
Betsham Ho SE1... **137** B4
Betterton Ho
 WC2 ....**106** A1
Betterton St WC2 **106** A1
Bettridge Rd SW6 **165** A1
Betts Ho E1 ....32 A2
Betts St E1 ....32 A2
Betty Layward Prim
 Sch **1** N16........ **7** A1
Betty May Gray Ho **2**
 E14 ....42 B2
Bevan St N1 ...**87** A3
Bev Callender Cl **1**
 SW8 ....61 A4

Bevenden St N1 . . . . . **97** C4
Beveridge Rd **1**
NW10 . . . . 8 A1
Beverley Cl
Barnes SW13 . . . . . . 46 C1
6 Wandsworth
SW11 . . . . 59 C3
Beverley Cotts
SW15 . . . . 68 A1
Beverley Ct **1**
1 Acton Green
W4 . . . . 37 B1
4 Acton W12 . . . . . 38 A4
Brockley SE4 . . . . . . 66 B4
Islington N5 . . . . . . 15 A2
Beverley Gdns
Barnes SW13 . . . . . . 56 B4
Hendon NW11 . . . . . 1 A4
Beverley Lo **6**
TW10 . . . . 54 A2
SW13 . . . . 46 B1
Beverley Path **9**
SW13 . . . . 46 B1
Beverley Rd
Barnes SW13 . . . . . . 56 B4
Chiswick W4 . . . . . . 38 B1
Beversbrook Rd
N19 . . . . 4 C1
Beverston Rd
SW2 . . . . 62 B2
Beverston Mews
NW1 . . . . **102** C3
Bevin Ct SE16 . . . . . 33 A1
Bevin Ct W1 . . . . 95 A4
Bevington Prim Sch
18 W10 . . . . 31 A4
Bevington Rd W10 . . 31 A4
Bevington St
SE16 . . . . **139** C3
Bevin Ho
5 Bethnal Green
E2 . . . . 25 B2
8 Bow E3 . . . . 26 C2
Bevin Sq SW17 . . . . . 72 B1
Bevin Way N1 . . . . . . **95** B4
Bevis Marks EC3 . . . **110** B2
Bew Ct SE21 . . . . . . 76 C4
Bewdley Ho N4 . . . . . . 6 B4
Bewdley St N1 . . . . . 14 C1
Bewick Mews
SE15 . . . . 50 A3
Bewick St SW8 . . . . **170** B1
Bewley Ho **7** E1 . . . 32 A2
Bewley St E1 . . . . . . 32 A2
Bexhill Rd
Catford SE4 . . . . . . 66 B1
Mortlake SW14 . . . . 55 B4
Bexley Ho SE4 . . . . . 66 A3
BFI Imax (Cinema)
SE1 . . . . **121** B1
BFI Southbank
SE1 . . . . **121** A2
Bianca Rd SE1
SE15 . . . . 49 C4
Bicester Rd TW9 . . . . 55 A4
Bickenhall Mans
W1 . . . . **103** A4
Bickenhall St W1 . . . **103** A4
Bickerton Rd N19 . . . . 4 B2
Bickley Ho **11** E1 . . . **111** C3
Bicknell Rd SE5 . . . . 63 B4
Bicknor Ho **2** E5 . . . 17 A3
Bidborough St N1,
WC1 . . . . **94** A3
Biddenham Ho **18**
SE16 . . . . 40 C2

Bidder St E16 . . . . . . 35 A4
Biddesden Ho
SW3 . . . . **144** C3
Biddestone Rd N7 . . 14 B4
Biddulph Mans
W9 . . . . 88 B3
Biddulph Rd W9 . . . . 88 B3
Bidwell St SE15 . . . . 50 A2
Big Ben SW1 . . . . . . **134** B3
Biggerstaff Rd E15 . . 27 B4
Biggerstaff St N4 . . . 5 C2
Bigg's Row SW15 . . . 57 C4
Biggs Sq E9 . . . . 18 B2
Bigland Green Prim
Sch **12** E1 . . . . . . 32 A3
Bigland St E1 . . . . . . 32 A3
Bilberry Ho **13** E3 . . 33 C4
Billie Holiday Ct
NW10 . . . . 20 C3
Billing Ho **7** E1 . . . 32 C3
Billing Pl SW10 . . . **156** B2
Billing Rd SW10 . . . **156** B2
Billing St SW10 . . . **156** B2
Billingsgate Mkt
E14 . . . . 34 A1
Billing St SW10 . . . **156** B2
Billington Ho
SW8 . . . . **171** C3
Billington Rd SE14 . 50 C3
Billiter Sq EC3 . . . . **110** B1
Billiter St EC3 . . . . **110** B1
Billson St E14 . . . . . 42 B2
Bilton Ho SW8 . . . . **171** B3
Bilton Twrs W1 . . . . **103** A1
Bina Gdns SW5 . . . **142** C3
Binbrook Ho **13**
W10 . . . . 30 B4
Binden Rd W12 . . . . 38 B3
Binfield Ct SE5 . . . . 48 B1
Binfield Rd SW4 . . . **172** B3
Bingfield St N1 . . . . 84 C4
Bingham Pl W1 . . . . **103** B4
Bingham St N1 . . . . 15 C2
Binley Ho SW15 . . . 56 B1
Binney St W1 . . . . . **103** C1
Binnie Ct SE10 . . . . 52 A3
Binnie Ho SE1 . . . . **136** C1
Binns Rd W4 . . . . . . 38 A1
Binns Terr **3** W4 . . 38 A1
Binstead Ho SW18 . 59 A1
Binyon Ho **3** N16 . . 16 A4
Birbeck Ho **4** N19 . 4 C3
Bircham Path SE4 . . 65 C3
Birch Cl
Newham E16 . . . . . 35 A4
Peckham SE15 . . . . 49 C1
Upper Holloway N19 . 4 B2
Birchdown Ho **2**
E3 . . . . 27 A2
Birches The SE5 . . . 49 A1
Birchfield Ho **3**
E14 . . . . 33 C2
Birchfield St E14 . . . 33 C2
Birchgrove Ho
TW9 . . . . 45 A3
Birch Ho
New Cross Gate
SE14 . . . . 51 B2
3 Tulse Hill SW2 . 62 C1
Birchington Ct **2**
NW6 . . . . 78 A4
Birchington Ho **1**
E5 . . . . 17 A3
Birchington Rd
NW6 . . . . 23 C4

Birchin La EC3 . . . . **109** C1
Birchlands Ave
SW12 . . . . 72 B4
Birchmere Ct **18**
SE21 . . . . 40 A1
Birchmere Row
SE3 . . . . 53 B1
Birchmore Wlk N5 . . 6 B1
Birch Vale Ct NW8 . 89 C2
Birchwood Dr NW3 . 2 A4
Birdcage Wlk
SW1 . . . . **133** B3
Birdhurst Rd
SW18 . . . . 59 B2
Bird In Bush Rd
SE15 . . . . 49 C3
Bird In Hand Yd **3**
NW3 . . . . 11 B4
Birdsall Ho **5** SE5 . 64 A4
Birdsfield La **12**
E3 . . . . 26 B4
Bird St W1 . . . . **103** C1
Birdwood Ave **4**
SE13 . . . . 67 C1
Birkbeck Ave W3 . . . 28 B2
Birkbeck Coll W1 . **105** B2
Birkbeck Gr W3 . . . . 37 C4
Birkbeck Hill SE21 . . 75 A3
Birkbeck Mews **15**
E8 . . . . 16 B3
Birkbeck Pl SE21 . . . 75 B2
Birkbeck Rd
Acton W3 . . . . 28 C1
Dalston E8 . . . . 16 B3
Birkbeck St E2 . . . . 25 A2
Birkbeck Univ of
London W1 . . . . . . 93 B2
Birkdale Cl **30**
SE16 . . . . 40 A1
Birkenhead Ho **11**
N7 . . . . 14 C3
Birkenhead St
WC1 . . . . 94 B4
Birkwood Cl SW12 . . 73 C4
Birley Lo NW8 . . . . . 79 C2
Birley St SW11 . . . . **169** B1
Birnam Rd N4 . . . . . . 5 B2
Birrell Ho **3** SW9 . **172** C1
Birse Cres NW10 . . . 8 A4
Birtwhistle Ho **3**
E3 . . . . 26 B4
Biscay Ho **11** E1 . . 25 C1
Biscoe Way SE13 . . . 67 C4
Biscott Ho **3** E3 . . 27 A1
Bisham Gdns N6 . . . . 3 C3
Bishop Challoner
Collegiate Sch **28**
E1 . . . . 32 B3
Bishop Ct **20** SW2 . 62 C1
Bishop Duppa's
Almshouses **7**
TW10 . . . . 54 A2
Bishop King's Rd
W14 . . . . **140** B4
Bishop's Ave SE16 . **164** A3
Bishop's Bridge Rd
W2 . . . . **100** C2
Bishops Cl SW4 . . . . 37 B1
Bishop's Cl N19 . . . . 4 B1
Bishops Ct
13 Bayswater
W2 . . . . **100** B2
Richmond TW9 . . . . 54 A4

Bishop's Ct
Holborn EC4 . . . . . **108** A2
Holborn WC2 . . . . . **107** B2
Bishopsdale Ho **5**
NW6 . . . . 23 C4
Bishopsgate EC2 . . **110** A2
Bishopsgate Arc
E1 . . . . **110** B3
Bishopsgate
Churchyard EC2 . **110** A3
Bishopsgate Inst
EC2 . . . . **110** B3
Bishops Ho SW8 . . **162** B1
Bishop's Mans
SW6 . . . . 47 C1
Bishops Mead SE5 . 48 B3
Bishop's Park Rd
SW6 . . . . 47 C1
Bishops Rd SW6 . . **164** C1
Bishops Sq E1 . . . . **110** B4
Bishop St N1 . . . . . . 86 C4
Bishop's Terr
SE11 . . . . **149** C4
Bishopstone Ho **1**
SW11 . . . . **169** B2
Bishop's Way E2 . . . 25 B3
Bishopswood Rd
N6 . . . . 3 A4
Bishop Wilfred Wood
Cl SE15 . . . . 49 C1
Bisley Ho SW19 . . . . 69 C2
Bissextile Ho SE13 . 52 A1
Bisson Rd E15 . . . . . 27 B3
Bittern Ct **7** SE8 . . 51 C4
Bittern Ho SE1 . . . . **136** C3
Bittern St SE1 . . . . **136** C3
Blackall St
EC2 . . . . 24 A1 98 A2
Blackburn Ct **8**
SW2 . . . . 62 C1
Blackburne's Mews
W1 . . . . **117** B3
Blackburn Rd
NW6 . . . . 11 A2
Blackdown Ho E8 . . 16 C4
Blackett St SW15 . . 57 C4
Blackfriars Bridge
EC4 . . . . **122** A3
Blackfriars Ct
EC4 . . . . **122** A4
Black Friars La
EC4 . . . . **108** A1
Blackfriars Pas
EC4 . . . . **122** A4
Blackfriars Pier
EC4 . . . . **122** A4
Blackfriars Underpass
EC4 . . . . **121** C4
Blackheath SE3 . . . . 53 A3
Blackheath Ave
SE3 . . . . 53 A3
Blackheath Bsns Est
SE10 . . . . 52 B2
Blackheath High Jun
Sch SE3 . . . . 53 A1
Blackheath High Sch
SE3 . . . . 53 A1
Blackheath Hill
SE10 . . . . 52 B2
Blackheath Prep Sch
SE3 . . . . 53 C3
Blackheath Rd
SE10 . . . . 52 A2

Blackheath Rise
SE13 . . . . 52 B1
BLACKHEATH
VALE 53 B1
Blackheath Vale
SE3 . . . . 53 B1
Blackheath Village
SE3 . . . . 53 B1
Black Horse Ct
SE1 . . . . **137** C2
Blackhorse Rd
SE8 . . . . 51 A4
Blacklands Terr
SW3 . . . . **145** A3
Black Lion La W6 . . . 38 C2
Black Lion Mews **4**
W6 . . . . 38 C2
Blackmore Ho
Islington N1 . . . . . . 85 A3
2 Wandsworth
SW18 . . . . 59 A2
Blackmore Twr **1**
W3 . . . . 37 A3
Blackpool Rd SE15 . 50 A1
Black Prince Rd
SE1, SE11 . . . . **149** A3
Black Roof Ho **5**
SE5 . . . . 48 A2
Black's Rd W6 . . . . . 39 B2
Blackstock Ho **2**
N5 . . . . 6 A1
Blackstock Mews
N4 . . . . 6 A1
Blackstone Ho
Dulwich SE21 . . . . 76 A1
Pimlico SW1 . . . . . **146** C1
Blackstone Rd NW2 . 9 B4
Black Swan Yd
SE1 . . . . **138** A4
Blackthorn Ct
20 Camberwell
SE15 . . . . 49 B3
4 Leyton E15 . . . . 19 C4
Blackthorne Ct SE3 . 26 C1
Blacktree Mews **11**
SW9 . . . . 62 C4
BLACKWALL 34 B2
Blackwall Sta E14 . . 34 B2
Blackwall Trad Est
E14 . . . . 34 C2
Blackwall Tunnel E14,
SE10 . . . . 34 C4
Blackwall Tunnel App
SE10 . . . . 43 A4
Blackwall Tunnel
Northern Approach
E14, E3 . . . . 27 B1
Blackwall Way 34 B2
Blackwater Ho
NW8 . . . . **101** C4
Blackwater St
SE22 . . . . 64 B2
Blackwell Cl **10** E5 . 17 C4
Blackwell Ho **3**
SW4 . . . . 61 C1
Blackwood Ho **11**
E1 . . . . 25 A1
Blackwood St
SE17 . . . . **151** B2
Blade Mews SW15 . 58 B3
Bladen Ho **4** E1 . . 32 C3

Blades Ct
4 Hammersmith
W6 .... 39 A1
Putney SW15 .... 58 B3

Blades Ho 4
SE11 .... 163 B3
Blades Lo 15 SW2 .. 62 C1
Blagdon Rd SE13 ..... 67 A1
Blagrove Rd 1
W10 .... 31 B4
Blair Cl N1 .... 15 B2
Blair Ct NW8 .... 79 B4
Blairderry Rd SW2 ... 74 A2
Blairgowrie Ct 13
E14 .... 34 C3
Blair Ho SW9 .... 172 C2
Blair St E14 .... 34 C3
Blake Coll W1 .... 104 C4
Blake Ct
8 Bermondsey
SE16 .... 40 A1
Kilburn NW6 .... 23 C2
Blake Gdns SW6 .... 166 A4
Blake Ho
2 Deptford SE8 ...... 51 C4
Isle Of Dogs E14 ..... 42 A4
1 Kentish Town
N19 .... 13 C3
Lambeth SE1 .... 135 B2
14 Stoke Newington
N16 .... 16 A4
Blake Mews 15
TW9 .... 44 C2
Blakemore Rd
SW16 .... 74 A1
Blakeney Cl
5 Camden Town
NW1 .... 13 C1
4 Dalston E8 .... 16 C3
Blakenham Ct
W12 .... 29 C1
Blaker Rd E15 .... 27 B4
Blakes Cl W10 .... 30 B4
Blake's Rd SE15 ..... 49 A3
Blanchard Way E8 .. 16 C2
Blanch Cl SE15 .... 50 B3
Blanchedowne
SE5 .... 63 C3
Blandfield Rd
SW12 .... 72 C4
Blandford Ct
Brondesbury Pk
NW6 .... 10 A1
6 De Beauvoir Town
N1 .... 16 A1
Blandford Ho
SW8 .... 162 C2
Blandford Rd W4 ..... 38 A3
Blandford Sq NW1 .. 90 B1
Blandford St W1 .... 103 B3
Bland Ho SE11 .... 149 A2
Blantyre St SW10 .. 157 B2
Blantyre Twr
SW10 .... 157 B2
Blantyre Wlk
SW10 .... 157 B2
Blashford NW3 ...... 12 B1
Blasker Wlk 8
E14 .... 42 A1
Blaxland Ho 12
W12 .... 30 A2
Blazer Ct NW8 .... 89 C3

Blechynden Ho 17
W10 .... 30 C3
Blechynden St 8
W10 .... 30 C3
Bleeding Heart Yd
EC1 .... 107 C3
Blemundsbury
WC1 .... 106 B4
Blendworth Point 4
SW15 .... 69 A3
Blenheim 28 SW19 .. 69 C3
Blenheim Cres
Notting Hill W11 .... 31 A3
Notting Hill
W11 .... 112 A4
Blenheim Ct
Barnsbury N7 .... 14 A2
Richmond TW9 .... 54 B4
17 Rotherhithe
SE16 .... 32 C1
Blenheim Gdns
Clapham Pk SW2 ..... 62 B1
Dollis Hill NW2 .... 9 B3
Blenheim Gr SE15 .. 49 C1
Blenheim Pas NW8 . 78 C2
Blenheim Rd
Acton W4 .... 38 A3
St John's Wood
NW8 .... 79 A2
Blenheim St W1 .... 104 A1
Blenheim Terr
NW8 .... 78 C2
Blenkarne Rd
SW11 .... 60 C1
Blessed Sacrament
RC Prim Sch N1 ...... 84 C3
Blessington Cl
SE13 .... 67 C4
Blessington Rd
SE13 .... 67 C3
Bletchley Ct N1 ...... 87 B1
Bletchley St N1 ...... 87 A1
Bletsoe Wlk N1 ...... 87 A2
Blick Ho 5 SE16 ..... 40 B3
Blincoe Cl SW19 ... 69 C2
Blissett St SE10 .... 52 B2
Bliss Mews 14
W10 .... 23 A2
Blisworth Ho 2
E2 .... 24 C4
Blithfield St W8 .... 128 A1
Bloemfontein Ave
W12 .... 30 A1
Bloemfontein Rd
W12 .... 30 A2
Blomfield Ct
Battersea SW11 .... 167 C4
Paddington W9 .... 89 A2
Blomfield Ho 4
E14 .... 34 A2
Blomfield Mans 3
W12 .... 30 B1
Blomfield Rd W9 ... 100 C4
Blomfield St EC2 .. 109 C3
Blomfield Villas
W9 .... 100 C4
Blondel St SW11 .. 169 B2
Blondin St E3 .... 26 C3
Bloomburg St
SW1 .... 147 A3
Bloomfield Ho 19
E1 .... 111 B3
Bloomfield Pl W1 .. 118 B4

Bloomfield Terr
SW1 .... 145 C2
Bloom Gr SE27 ...... 75 A1
Bloom Park Rd
SW6 .... 154 C1
BLOOMSBURY 106 A4
Bloomsbury Ct
WC1 .... 106 B3
Bloomsbury Ho 10
SW4 .... 61 C1
Bloomsbury
International
Language Sch
WC1 .... 106 B3
Bloomsbury Pl
London SW18 .... 59 B2
St Giles WC1 .... 106 B3
Bloomsbury Sq
WC1 .... 106 B3
Bloomsbury St
WC1 .... 105 C3
Bloomsbury Way
WC1 .... 106 B3
Blore Cl SW8 .... 171 B3
Blore Ct W1 .... 119 B4
Blore Ho SW10 ..... 156 B2
Blossom Cl W5 ...... 36 A4
Blossom Pl
E1 .... 24 A1 98 B1
Blossom St
E1 .... 24 A1 98 B1
Blount St E14 .... 33 A3
Blucher Rd SE5 ...... 48 B3
Blue Anchor Alley 4
TW9 .... 54 A3
Blue Anchor La
SE16 .... 40 A2
Blue Anchor Yd
E1 .... 125 B4
Bluebell Cl 10 E9 ... 25 B4
Blue Gate Fields Jun
& Inf Schs E1 ...... 32 B2
Bluegate Mews E1 . 32 A2
Blue Lion Pl SE1 ... 138 A2
Blueprint Apartments
5 SW12 .... 73 B4
Blundell Cl E8 .... 16 C4
Blundell St N7 .... 14 A2
Blurton Rd E5 .... 17 C4
Blyth Cl 2 E14 .... 42 C2
Blythe Ho 8 SE11 . 163 C4
Blythe Mews 2
W14 .... 39 C3
Blythendale Ho 8
E2 .... 24 C3
Blythe Rd W14 ...... 126 A1
Blyth's Wharf E14 .. 33 A2
Blythwood Rd N4 ... 5 B4
BMI Fitzroy Square
Hospl W1 .... 92 C1
Bnois Jerusalem Girls
Sch N16 .... 6 C4
Boades Mews 3
NW3 .... 11 C4
Boadicea St N1 ...... 84 C4
Boardwalk Pl E14 .. 34 B1
Boarley Ho SE17 ... 152 A3
Boathouse Ctr The
W10 .... 22 B1
Boathouse Wlk 24
SE15 .... 49 B3
Boat Lifter Way 16
SE16 .... 41 A2
Bobbin Cl SW4 .... 61 B3

Bob Marley Way 10
SE24 .... 62 C3
Bobov Foundation
Sch 4 N16 .... 7 B4
Bocking St E8 .... 25 A4
Boddicott Cl SW19 . 70 A2
Boddington Gdns
W3 .... 36 C4
Boddington Ho 2
SE14 .... 50 B2
Boden Ho 4 E1 ...... 111 B4
Bodington Ct 2
W12 .... 39 B4
Bodley Manor Way
SE24 .... 63 C2
Bodmin St SW18 ... 70 C3
Bodney Rd E5, E8 .. 17 A3
Bogart Ct 15 E14 ... 33 C2
Bohemia Pl 1 E8 ... 17 A2
Bohn Rd E1 .... 33 A4
Boileau Rd SW13 .. 47 A3
Boilerhouse SE1 ... 124 C1
Boisseau Ho 5 E1 .. 32 B4
Boldero Pl NW8 ..... 90 A1
Boldero Pl NW8 ..... 90 A1
Boleyn Rd N16 .... 16 A3
Bolina Rd SE16 ...... 40 B1
Bolingbroke Gr
SW11 .... 60 B1
Bolingbroke Ho 4
W14 .... 39 C3
Bolingbroke Rd
W14 .... 39 C3
Bolingbroke Wlk
SW11 .... 168 A4
Bollo Bridge Rd
W3 .... 37 B4
Bollo Ct 2 W3 .... 37 B3
Bollo La W3 .... 37 A4
Bolney Gate SW7 .. 130 A3
Bolney St SW8 ..... 162 C1
Bolsover St W1 ...... 92 B1
Bolt Ct EC4 .... 107 C1
Bolton Cres SE5 .... 48 A3
Bolton Ct SW11 ..... 169 C3
Bolton Gdns
Kensal Rise
NW10 .... 22 C3
South Kensington
SW5 .... 142 B2
Bolton Gdns Mews
SW5 .... 142 C2
Bolton Ho 4 SE10 .. 43 A1
Bolton Pl SW5 ...... 142 C2
Bolton Rd
Chiswick W4 .... 45 B3
Harlesden NW10 ..... 21 A4
Kilburn NW8 .... 78 B3
Boltons Ct SW5 .... 142 B2
Bolton St W1 .... 118 B2
Boltons The
SW10 .... 142 C2
Bolton Studios
SW10 .... 143 A1
Bolton Wlk N7 .... 5 B2
Bombay Ct 8
SE16 .... 40 B4
Bombay St SE16 .... 40 A2
Bomore Rd
W11 .... 31 A2 112 A4
Bonar Rd SE15 .... 49 C3
Bonchurch Rd
W10 .... 31 A4
Bond Ho 4 NW6 .... 23 B3

Bonding Yard Wlk
SE16 .... 41 A3
Bond St W4 .... 37 C2
Bond Street Sta
W1 .... 103 C1
Bondway SW8 ...... 162 B4
Bonfield Rd SE13 ... 67 B3
Bonham Ho
W11 .... 31 B1 112 C2
Bonham Rd SW2 ... 62 B2
Bonheur Rd W4 ..... 37 C4
Bonhill St EC2 ...... 97 C1
Bonington Ho N1 ... 84 C1
Bonita Mews SE15 . 65 C4
Bonner Ho 3
SW15 .... 56 C2
Bonner Prim Sch 30
E2 .... 25 B2
Bonner Rd E2 .... 25 B3
Bonner St E2 .... 25 B3
Bonneville Gdns
SW4 .... 61 B1
Bonneville Prim Sch
SW4 .... 61 B1
Bonnington Sq
SW8 .... 162 C4
Bonny St NW1 .... 13 B1
Bonsor Ho SW8 .... 171 A4
Bonsor St SE5 .... 49 A3
Bonthron Ho
SW15 .... 47 B1
Booker Cl 11 E3 .... 33 B4
Boord St SE10 .... 43 A3
Boothby Rd N19 .... 4 C2
Booth Cl 10 E9 ...... 25 A4
Booth Ho 2 SW2 .. 74 C4
Booth La EC4 .... 122 C4
Booth's Pl W1 .... 105 A3
Boot St N1 .... 24 A2 98 A4
Bordon Wlk 5
SW15 .... 68 C4
Boreas Wlk N1 ...... 86 B1
Boreham Ave E16 .. 35 C3
Boreman Ho 11
SE10 .... 52 B4
Borland Rd SE15 .... 65 B3
Borneo St SW15 .... 57 B4
Borough High St
SE1 .... 123 B2
Borough Mkt SE1 .. 123 B1
Borough Rd SE1 ... 136 B2
Borough Sq SE1 ... 136 C3
Borough Sta SE1 .. 136 C4
BOROUGH THE 136 C4
Borrett Cl SE17 ..... 150 C1
Borrodaile Rd
SW18 .... 59 A1
Borrowdale NW1 ... 92 C3
Borthwick St SE8 .. 41 C1
Boscastle Rd NW5 . 4 A1
Boscobel Ho 4
E8 .... 17 A2
Boscobel Pl SW1 .. 145 C4
Boscobel St NW8 .. 89 C1
Boscombe Cl E5 .... 18 A3
Boscombe Rd
W12 .... 38 C4
Boss Ho SE1 .... 138 C4
Boss St SE1 .... 138 C4
Boston Gdns W4 ... 46 A4
Boston Ho
3 Camberwell
SE5 .... 48 B1
Earl's Ct SW5 .... 142 B3
Lisson Gr NW1 .... 90 C2
Boston Pl NW1 ..... 90 C1

Bosun Cl **22** E14.....41 C4
Boswell Ct
Bloomsbury WC1 ... **106** B4
9 Hammersmith
W6 .... **39** C3
Boswell Ho W10 ......**23** A1
Boswell St WC1 ... **106** B4
Bosworth Ho **4**
W10 ....**23** A1
Bosworth Rd W10 ...**23** A1
Bothwell Cl E16 ...... **35** B4
Bothwell St W6 ...**47** C4
Botolph Alley EC3 **124** A4
Botolph La EC3 ... **124** A4
Bott's Mews W2 ....**31** C3
Boughton Ho E1 **137** B4
Bouicott St E1 ......**32** C3
Boulevard The
Chelsea SW6 ... **167** A3
4 Upper Tooting
SW17 ....**72** C2
Boulogne Ho SE1 **138** C2
Boulter Ho **4**
SE14 ....**50** B2
Boulton Ho W3 .....**36** A1
Boundaries Mans **3**
SW12 ....**72** C3
Boundaries Rd
SW12 ....**72** C3
Boundary Ho
Balham SW12.....**73** A3
1 Camberwell SE5 ..**48** C3
15 Notting Hill W11 ..**30** C1
Boundary La SE17 ..**48** C4
Boundary Pas
E2 ....**24** B1 **98** C2
Boundary Rd NW8. **79** A4
Boundary Road Est
NW8 ....**78** C3
Boundary Row
SE1 ....**136** A4
Boundary St
E2 ....**24** B1 **98** C2
Bourchier St W1 .. **119** B4
Bourdon Pl W1 ... **118** B4
Bourdon St W1 ... **118** B3
Bourke Cl
London SW4 ....**62** A1
Willesden NW10.....**8** A2
Bourlet Cl W1 .... **104** C3
Bourne Cl W4 ....**45** B3
Bourne Ho **6** SW4 ..**61** B3
Bourne Mews W1 **103** C1
Bournemouth Cl
SE15 ....**49** C1
Bournemouth Rd
SE15 ....**49** C1
Bourne St SW1 ... **145** C3
Bourne Terr W2 ... **100** B4
Bousfield Prim Sch
SW10 .... **142** C2
Bousfield Rd SE14 ..**50** C1
Boutcher CE Prim Sch
SE1 .... **152** C4
Boutflower Rd
SW11 ....**60** A3
Bouverie Mews N16 ..**7** A2
Bouverie Pl W2 ... **101** C2
Bouverie Rd N16 .....**7** A2
Bouverie St EC4 .. **107** C1
Bovingdon Cl **4**
N19 ....**4** B2
Bovingdon Rd
SW6 .... **166** B3
BOW **26** B3

Bowater Cl SW2 ....**62** A1
Bowater Ho EC1 ....**97** A1
Bow Brook The **20**
E2 ....**25** C3
Bow Church Sta
E3 ....**26** C2
Bow Common La
E3 ....**26** B1
Bowden Ho **25** E3 ..**27** A2
Bowden St SE11 .. **149** C1
Bowditch SE8 ....**41** B1
Bowen Ct **2** N5 .....**15** A4
Bowen Dr SE21 .....**76** A1
Bowen St E14 ....**34** A3
Bower Ave SE3 .....**53** A3
Bowerdean St
SW6 .... **166** A2
Bower Ho SE14 ....**50** C2
Bowerman Ave
SE14 ....**51** A4
Bowerman Ct **1**
N19.................**4** C2
Bower St E1 ....**32** C3
Bowes-Lyon Hall **8**
E16 ....**35** C1
Bowes Rd W3 ......**29** A2
Bowfell Rd W6 .....**47** B4
Bowhill Cl SW9 .. **163** C2
Bow Ho **1** E3 ......**26** C2
Bowie Cl SW4 ......**73** C4
Bow La EC2, EC4 . **109** A1
Bowland Ho N4 ......**6** B4
Bowland Rd SW4 ..**61** C3
Bowland Yd SW1 . **131** A3
Bowl Ct EC2...**24** A1 **98** B1
Bowles Rd **1** SE1 ..**49** C4
Bowley Ho **6**
SE16 .... **139** B2
Bowling Green Cl
SW19 ....**69** A4
Bowling Green Ho
SW10 .... **157** B2
Bowling Green La
EC1 ....**95** C2
Bowling Green Pl
SE1 .... **137** B4
Bowling Green St
SE11 .... **163** B4
Bowling Green Wlk
N1 ....**24** A2 **98** A4
Bowman Ave E16...**35** B2
Bowman Mews
St George in East
E1 ....**125** C4
Wandsworth SW18 ..**70** B3
Bowman's Mews
N7 ....**5** A1
Bowman's Pl N7 .....**5** A1
Bowmore Wlk
NW1 ....**13** C1
Bowness Cl **5** E8 ..**16** B2
Bowness Ho SE15 ..**50** B3
Bowood Rd SW11 ..**60** C2
Bow Rd E3 ....**26** C2
Bow Road Sta E3 ..**26** C2
Bowry Ho **4** E14 ..**33** B4
Bow Sec Sch **18**
E3 ....**26** C2
Bowsprit Point **1**
E14 ....**41** C3
Bow St WC2 ...... **106** B1
Bowstead Ct
SW11 .... **167** C3
Bow Triangle Bsns Ctr
17 E3 ....**26** C1

Bowyer Ho
27 Shoreditch N1.....**24** A4
Wandsworth SW18 ..**59** A1
Bowyer Pl SE5......**48** B3
Bowyer St **10** SE5 ..**48** B3
Boxall Rd SE21 .....**64** A1
Boxley Ho **8** E5 ...**17** A3
Boxmoor Ho
16 Hackney E2 ......**24** C4
9 Shepherd's Bush
W11 ....**30** C1
Box Tree Ho SE8 ..**41** A1
Boxworth Gr N1 .....**85** A4
Boyce Ho **9** W10 ..**23** B2
Boyd Ct SW15 ......**57** B1
Boydell Ct NW8 ....**11** C1
Boyd St E1 .... **111** C1
Boyfield St SE1 .. **136** B3
Boyle St W1 ..... **118** C4
Boyne Ct NW10 .....**8** C1
Boyne Rd SE13 .....**67** C4
Boyne Terr Mews
W11 ....**31** B1 **112** C2
Boyson Rd **10**
SE17 ....**48** C4
Boyton Cl E1 ....**25** C1
Boyton Ho
Kennington SE11 .. **149** B1
St John's Wood
NW8 ....**79** C2
Brabant Ct EC3 ... **124** A4
Brabazon St E14 ...**34** A4
Brabner Ho **9**
E2 ....**24** C2 **99** B4
Brabourn Gr SE15 ..**50** B1
Bracer Ho **1** N1 ...**24** A3
Bracewell Rd W10 ..**30** B4
Bracey Mews **1** N4 ..**5** A2
Bracey St N4 ....**5** A2
Bracken Ave SW12 ..**72** C4
Brackenbury N4 .....**5** B3
Brackenbury Gdns
W6 ....**39** A3
Brackenbury Prim Sch
4 W6 ....**39** B3
Brackenbury Rd
W6 ....**39** A3
Bracken Gdns
SW13 ....**46** C1
Bracken Ho **15** E3 ..**33** C4
Brackley Ave SE15 ..**65** B4
Brackley Ct NW8 ....**89** C2
Brackley Rd W4 ....**38** A1
Brackley St EC1 ... **109** A4
Brackley Terr **5**
W4 ....**38** A1
Bracklyn Ct N1 .....**87** B2
Bracklyn St N1 .....**87** B2
Bracknell Gate
NW3 ....**11** A3
Bracknell Gdns
NW3 ....**11** A4
Bracknell Way
NW3 ....**11** A4
Bradbeer Ho **24**
E2 ....**25** B2
Bradbourne St
SW6 .... **165** C2
Bradbury Ct **2**
SE3 ....**53** C3
Bradbury Ho E1 .. **111** A2
Bradbury St **28**
N16 ....**16** A3
Bradby Ho NW8 ....**78** B1
Braddon Rd TW9 ...**54** B4
Braddyll St SE10 ...**43** A1

Bradenham **11**
SE17 ....**48** C4
Bradenham Cl
SE17 ....**48** C4
Braden St W9 ..... **88** A1
Bradfield Ct **14**
NW1 ....**13** A1
Bradford Ho **15**
SW8 .... **171** B2
Bradford Ho **4**
W14 ....**39** C3
Bradford Rd W3 ....**38** A4
Bradgate Rd SE6 ..**67** A1
Brading Rd SW2 ...**74** B4
Brading Terr W12 ..**38** C3
Bradiston Rd W9 ...**23** B2
Bradley Cl N7 ....**14** B2
Bradley Ho
Bermondsey SE16 ...**40** A2
1 Bromley E3 ......**27** A2
Bradley Mews
SW12 ....**72** B3
Bradley's Cl N1 .....**85** C2
Bradford Ho SE21...**76** A1
Bradmead SW8.... **160** C1
Bradmore Park Rd
W6 ....**39** A2
Brad St SE1 ...... **121** C1
Bradstock Ho E9 ...**18** A1
Bradstock Rd E9 ...**17** C2
Bradwell Ho **8**
NW6 .... **78** A3
Bradwell St **24** E1 ..**25** C2
Brady Ho
London SW4 ....**61** C2
South Lambeth
SW8 .... **171** A4
Brady St E1 ....**25** A1
Braefoot Ct SW15 ..**57** C2
Braemar SW15 .....**57** C1
Braemar Ave SW18,
SW19 ....**70** C2
Braemar Ho W9 ... **88** C3
Braemar Mans
W8 .... **128** B1
Braes St N1 ....**15** A1
Braganza St SE17 **150** A1
Braham Ho SE11 . **149** A1
Brahma Kumaris
World Spiritual Univ
NW10 ....**9** A3
Braid Ave W3 ......**29** A3
Braid Ho SE10......**52** B2
Braidwood St SE1 **124** A1
Brailsford Rd SW2 ..**62** C1
Braintree Ho **6**
E1 ....**25** B1
Braintree St E2.....**25** B2
Braithwaite
EC1 ....**97** B2
Braithwaite Twr
W2 .... **101** B4
Bramah Gn SW9 .. **173** C4
Bramall Cl E15 .....**14** B2
Bramber WC1 ......**94** A3
Bramber Ct TW8....**36** A2
Bramber Rd W14 . **154** C4
Brambledown **8**
N4 ....**5** A4
Bramble Gdns
W12 ....**29** B2
Bramble Ho **15** E3 ..**33** C4
Brambling Ct **25**
SE8 ....**51** B4
Bramcote Gr SE16 ..**40** B1

Bramcote Rd
SW15 ....**57** A3
Bramerton NW6 .....**9** C1
Bramerton St
SW3 .... **158** A4
Bramfield Ct N4 .....**6** B2
Bramfield Rd
SW11 ....**60** B2
Bramford Rd
SW18 ....**59** B3
Bramham Gdns
SW5 .... **142** B2
Bramham Ho SE22..**64** A3
Bramlands Cl
SW11 ....**60** A4
Bramley Cres
SW8 .... **161** C2
Bramley Ct SE13...**67** C2
Bramley Ho
10 North Kensington
W10 ....**30** C3
Roehampton SW15 ..**56** B1
Bramley Rd W10 ...**30** C3
Brampton WC1 ... **106** C3
Bramshaw Rd E9 ..**17** C2
Bramshill Gdns
NW5 ....**4** A1
Bramshill Rd
NW10 ....**21** B3
Bramshurst NW8 .. **78** B3
Bramston Rd
Harlesden NW10 ...**21** C3
Wandsworth SW17 ..**71** B1
Bramwell Ho
Borough The SE1 . **137** A1
Chelsea SW1 .... **160** C4
Bramwell Mews
N1 ....**85** A4
Brancaster Ho
22 Globe Town
E1 ....**25** C2
Islington N5 ....**15** A3
Brancaster Rd
SW16 ....**74** A1
Branch Hill NW3 .....**2** B1
Branch Pl N1 ......**87** C4
Branch Rd E14 .....**33** A2
Branch St SE15 ....**49** A3
Brand Cl N4 ....**6** A3
Branden Lo **3** W4 ..**37** B1
Brandlehow Prim Sch
SW15 ....**58** B3
Brandlehow Rd
SW15 ....**58** B3
Brandon Mews
Barbican EC2 .... **109** B4
Walworth SE17 ... **151** A3
Brandon Rd N7.....**14** A1
Brandon St SE17 . **151** A3
Brandrett Wharf
SE16 ....**40** B4
Brandreth Rd
SW17 ....**73** A2
Brand St SE10 .....**52** B3
Brangton Rd SE11 **149** A1
Brangwyn Ct W14 **126** A1
Branksea St SW6 **154** A1
Branksome Ho
SW8 .... **162** C2
Branksome Rd
SW2 ....**62** A2
Bransby Ct **4** N16..**16** A4
Branscombe NW1 ..**83** A3

Branscombe St
SE13 . . . . .67 A4
Bransdale Cl NW6 . .23 C4
Branstone Ct **9**
TW9 . . . . .44 B2
Branstone Rd TW9 . .44 B2
Branston Ho N7 . . . . .14 C3
Brantwood Ho **9**
SE5 . . . . .48 B3
Brantwood Rd
SE24 . . . . .63 B2
Brasenose Dr
SW13 . . . . .47 B4
Brashley Road Cvn
Site NW10 . . . . .21 A2
Brassey Ho **1** E14 . .42 A2
Brassey Rd NW6 . . . .10 B2
Brassey Sq SW11 . . .60 C4
Brassie Ave W3 . . . . .29 A3
Brass Talley Alley **31**
SE16 . . . . .40 C4
Brathay NW1 . . . . . . .83 A1
Brathway Rd
SW18 . . . . .70 C4
Bratley St **11**
E1 . . . . .24 C1 99 B1
Bravington Pl W9 . . .23 B1
Bravington Rd W9 . .23 B2
Brawne Ho **12**
SE17 . . . . .48 A4
Braxfield Rd SE4 . . . .66 B3
Bray NW3 . . . . .12 A1
Brayard's Rd SE15 . .50 A1
Braybrook St W12 . .29 B3
Brayburne Ave
SW4 . . . . .171 A1
Bray Cres SE16 . . . . .40 C4
Braydon Rd N16 . . . . .7 C3
Bray Dr E16 . . . . .35 B2
Brayfield Terr N1 . . .14 C1
Brayford Sq **12** E1 . .32 B3
Bray Pl SW3 . . . . . .144 C3
Bread St EC2, EC4 . .109 A1
Breakspeare SE21 . . .76 B1
Breakspears Mews
SE4 . . . . .51 C1
Breakspears Rd
SE4 . . . . .66 C4
Breakwell Ct **16**
W10 . . . . .23 A1
Breamore Cl
SW15 . . . . .68 C3
Breamore Ho **4**
SE15 . . . . .49 C3
Bream's Bldgs
EC4 . . . . .107 B2
Bream St E3 . . . . .18 C1
Breasley Cl SW15 . . .57 A3
Brechin Pl SW7 . . . .143 A3
Brecknock Prim Sch
10 N7 . . . . .13 C2
Brecknock Rd N19 . .13 C3
Brecon Ho
Stamford Hill N16 . . . . .7 B3
Wandsworth SW18 . . .70 C4
Brecon Rd W6 . . . . .154 B3
Bredel Ho **1** E14 . . .33 C4
Bredgar SE13 . . . . . .67 A2
Bredgar Rd N19 . . . . .4 B2
Bredinghurst SE22 . .76 C4
Bredinghurst Sch
SE15 . . . . .65 C3
Bredin Ho SW10 . . .156 B2
Breer St SW6 . . . . . .59 A4

Breezer's Ct **22**
E1 . . . . .125 C3
Breezer's Hill E1 . . .125 C3
Brehon Ho N1 . . . . . .82 C3
Bremans Row **1**
SW18 . . . . .71 B2
Bremner Rd SW7 . .129 A2
Brenchley Gdns SE15,
SE22, SE23 . . . . .65 C1
Brenda Rd SW17 . . . .72 B2
Brendon Ave NW10 . .8 A4
Brendon Ho W1 . . . .103 B4
Brendon St W1 . . . .102 B2
Brenley Ho SE1 . . . .137 B4
Brennands Ct **14**
N19 . . . . .4 B1
Brent Adult Comm
Education Service
Coll **8** NW10 . . . .20 C4
Brent Ct **5** W12 . . .38 A3
Brentfield Fountain L
Ctr W4 . . . . .36 C1
Brent Ho **18** E9 . . . .17 B2
Brenthouse Rd E9 . .17 B2
Brenthurst Rd
NW10 . . . . .8 B2
Brent Mus NW10 . . . .9 A2
Brent New Ent Ctr
NW10 . . . . .8 B2
Brenton Ct E9 . . . . . .18 A3
Brenton St E14 . . . . .33 A3
Brent Rd E16 . . . . . . .35 C4
Brent Trad Est
NW10 . . . . .8 A3
Brentwick Gdns
TW8 . . . . .36 A2
Brereton Ho **4**
SW2 . . . . .74 C4
Bressenden Pl
SW1 . . . . .132 C2
Breton Ho
Bermondsey SE1 . . . .138 C2
St Luke's EC2 . . . . . . .97 A1
Brett Cl N16 . . . . .7 A2
Brett Cres NW10 . . . .20 C4
Brett Ho **1** SW15 . .69 C4
Brett Ho Cl **2**
SW15 . . . . .69 C4
Brettinghurst **8**
SE1 . . . . .153 B1
Bretton Ho N19 . . . . .5 A3
Brett Pas **28** E8 . . . . .17 A3
Brett Rd E8 . . . . .17 A3
Brewers Bldgs EC1 . .96 A4
Brewers Ct W2 . . . .100 C2
Brewer's Gn SW1 . .133 B2
Brewer's Hall Gdns
EC2 . . . . .109 A3
Brewer St W1 . . . . .119 A4
Brewery Ind Est The
N1 . . . . .87 A1
Brewery Rd N7 . . . . .14 A2
Brewery Sq
Bermondsey SE1 . . . .124 C1
Clerkenwell EC1 . . . . .96 B2
Brewhouse La
Putney SW15 . . . . . . .58 A4
Wapping E1 . . . . .32 A1
Brewhouse Wlk
SE16 . . . . .33 A1
Brewhouse Yd EC1 . .96 A2
Brewster Gdns
W10 . . . . .30 B4
Brewster Ho
Bermondsey SE1 . . . .153 A4

Brewster Ho continued
Poplar E14 . . . . .33 B2
Briant Ho SE1 . . . . .135 A1
Briant St SE14 . . . . . .50 C3
Briar Ct
7 Bow E3 . . . . . . .26 C3
3 Dalston E8 . . . . . .16 B1
Briardale SW19 . . . . .70 B3
Briardale Gdns
NW3 . . . . .1 C1
Briardale Ho **12**
N16 . . . . .7 A3
Briar Rd NW2 . . . . . . .9 B4
Briar Wlk
Putney SW15 . . . . . . .57 A3
West Kilburn W10 . . . .23 A1
Briarwood Rd
SW4 . . . . .61 C2
Briary Cl NW3 . . . . . .12 A1
Briary Ct **16** E16 . . .35 B3
Brickbarn Cl
SW10 . . . . .157 A2
Brick Ct EC4 . . . . . .107 B1
Brick Farm Cl
TW9 . . . . .45 A2
Brick La
Shoreditch
E2 . . . . .24 B2 99 A3
Spitalfields
E1 . . . . .24 B1 99 A1
Brick Lane Mkt E2. .99 A2
Bricklayers Arms
SE1 . . . . .137 C1
Brickwood Ho **28**
SW9 . . . . .173 C4
Brideale Cl SE15 . . . .49 B4
Bride Ct EC4 . . . . . .108 A1
Bride La EC4 . . . . . .108 A1
Bridel Mews N1 . . . .86 A3
Bride St N7 . . . . .14 B2
Bridewain St SE1 . .138 C2
Bridewell Pl
Holborn EC4 . . . . . . .108 A1
22 Wapping E1 . . . .32 A1
Bridford Mews
W1 . . . . .104 B4
Bridge Acad The
E2 . . . . .24 B4
Bridge App NW3 . . . .11 B3
Bridge Ave W6 . . . . .39 B1
Bridge Avenue Mans
1 W6 . . . . .39 B1
Bridge Ct **13** W10 . .30 C3
Bridge Ct
8 Blackwall E14 . . . .34 C2
22 Wapping E1 . . . . .32 A1
Bridge Field Ho **7**
W2 . . . . .100 A2
Bridgefoot SE1 . . . .148 B1
Bridge Gdns N16 . . .15 C4
Bridge Ho
Brockley SE4 . . . . . . .66 B3
1 Camden Town
NW1 . . . . .12 C1
Homerton E9 . . . . . . .17 C3
Bridge House Quay
E14 . . . . .34 B1
Bridge La SW11 . . . .168 B3
Bridgeland Rd E16 . .35 C2
Bridgeman Ho **19**
E9 . . . . .17 B1
Bridgeman Rd N1 . .14 B1
Bridgeman St NW8 . .80 A1
Bridge Meadows
SE14 . . . . .50 C4

Bridgen Rd SW18 . .59 B3
Bridgen Ho **9** E1 . . .32 A3
Bridge Pk **7**
SW18 . . . . .58 C2
Bridge Pl SW1 . . . .146 B4
Bridgeport Pl **4**
E1 . . . . .125 C2
Bridge Rd
Stratford Marsh
E15 . . . . .27 C4
Willesden NW10 . . . . .8 A2
Bridge Sch The
Clerkenwell EC1 . . . . .96 A2
Lower Holloway N7 . . .14 A3
Bridges Ct SW11 . . .167 B1
Bridges Ho **15** SE5 . .48 C3
Bridge St
Chiswick W4 . . . . . . .37 C2
Westminster SW1 . . .134 B3
Bridge Terr **1** E15 . .19 C1
Bridgeview **2** W6 . .39 B1
Bridgewater Rd
E15 . . . . .27 B4
Bridgewater Sq
EC2 . . . . .108 C4
Bridgewater St
EC2 . . . . .108 C4
Bridgeway St NW1 . .83 A1
Bridge Wharf **18**
E2 . . . . .25 C3
Bridge Yd SE1 . . . . .123 C2
Bridgford St SW17,
SW18 . . . . .71 B1
Bridgman Rd W4 . . .37 B3
Bridgnorth Ho **10**
SE15 . . . . .49 C4
Bridgwater Ho
W2 . . . . .100 C2
Bridle La W1 . . . . . .119 A4
Bridlington Ho
SW18 . . . . .59 B3
Bridport SE17 . . . . .151 A1
Bridport Ho N1 . . . . .87 C3
Bridport Pl N1 . . . . . .87 C3
Bridstow Pl W2 . . . . .31 C3
Brief St SE5 . . . . .48 A2
Brierfield NW1 . . . . .82 C3
Brierley Rd
Leyton E11 . . . . .19 C4
Upper Tooting
SW12 . . . . .73 B2
Brierly Gdns E2 . . . . .25 B3
Brigade St SE3 . . . . .53 B1
Briggeford Cl **5** E5 . .7 C2
Briggs Ho **22**
E2 . . . . .24 B2 99 A3
Brightling Rd SE4 . . .66 B1
Brightlingsea Pl **5**
E14 . . . . .33 B2
Brightman Rd
SW18 . . . . .71 C3
Brighton Bldgs
SE1 . . . . .138 A1
Brighton Gr SW15 . .58 B1
Brighton Gr SE14 . . .51 A2
Brighton Ho **7**
SE5 . . . . .48 C2
Brighton Rd N16 . . . .16 A4
Brighton Terr SW9 . .62 B3
Brightside Rd
SE13 . . . . .67 C1
Bright St E14 . . . . . . .34 A4
Brightwell Ct N7 . . .14 B3
Brightwells **1**
SW6 . . . . .166 A2
Brig Mews SE8 . . . . .51 C4

Brigstock Ho SE5 . . .48 B1
Brill Pl NW1 . . . . .83 C1
Brimsdown Ho E3 . . .27 B1
Brindley Ho
37 Notting Hill
W2 . . . . .31 C4
22 Streatham
SW2 . . . . .74 A4
Brindley St SE14 . . . .51 B2
Brine Ho **11** E3 . . . .26 A3
Brinklow Ho W2 . . .100 A3
Brinkworth Way
E9 . . . . .18 B2
Brinsley Ho **17** E1 . . .32 B3
Brinsley St **21** E1 . . .32 A3
Brinton Wlk SE1 . . .122 A1
Brion Pl E14 . . . . . . .34 B4
Brisbane Ho **3**
W12 . . . . .30 A2
Brisbane St SE5 . . . .48 C3
Briset St EC1 . . . . . .96 A1
Briset Way N7 . . . . . . .5 B2
Bristol Gdns
Putney SW15 . . . . . . .69 B4
Westbourne Green
W9 . . . . .88 B1
Bristol Ho SE11 . . . .135 B1
Bristol Mews W9 . . . .88 B1
Bristowe Ct **24**
SW2 . . . . .62 C1
Britannia Building
N1 . . . . .97 B4
Britannia Cl SW4 . . .61 C3
Britannia Gate **11**
E16 . . . . .35 C1
Britannia Junc
NW1 . . . . .82 B4
Britannia L Ctr N1. .24 A4
Britannia Rd
23 Millwall E14 . . . . .41 C2
Walham Green
SW6 . . . . .156 A1
Britannia Row **1** N1 . .86 C4
Britannia St WC1 . . .94 C4
Britannia Way
NW10 . . . . .20 A1
Britannia Wlk N1 . . .97 B4
British Coll of
Osteopathic
Medicine NW3 . . . .11 B2
British Dental
Association Mus
N1 . . . . .104 A3
British Gr W4 . . . . . .38 B1
British Grove Pas **2**
W4 . . . . .38 B1
British Grove S **3**
W4 . . . . .38 B1
British Library The
WC1 . . . . .93 C4
British Mus WC1. .106 A3
British Optical
Association Mus
SW1 . . . . .120 A2
British St E3 . . . . .26 B2
British Wharf Ind Est
SE14 . . . . .50 C4
Britley Ho **18** E14 . .33 B3
Brittage Rd **11**
NW10 . . . . .8 A1
Brittany Ho SW15 . .57 B3
Brittany Point
SE11 . . . . .149 B3
Britten Cl NW11 . . . . .2 A3
Britten Ho SW3 . . . .144 B2
Britten St SW3 . . . .144 B2

Britton St EC1 . . . . **96 A1**
BRIXTON **62 C4**
Brixton Day Coll 🄶
SW2 . . . . .62 A4
Brixton Hill SW2 . . . .62 B2
Brixton Hill Ct 🄱 62 B2
SW2 . . . . .62 B2
Brixton Hill Pl
SW2 . . . . .74 A4
Brixton Mkt SW9 . . . **173 B2**
Brixton Rd SW9 . . . . **173 B2**
Brixton Rec Ctr
SW9 . . . . .62 C4
Brixton Sta SW9 . . . .62 C3
Brixton Station Rd
SW9 . . . . .62 C4
Brixton Water La
SW2 . . . . .62 B2
Broadbent Cl N16 . . . 6 A3
Broadbent St W1 . . . **118 A4**
Broadbridge Cl
SE3 . . . . .53 C3
Broad Common Est
N16 . . . . 7 C3
Broad Ct WC2 . . . . . **106 B1**
Broadfield NW6 . . . . .11 A2
Broadfield La
NW1 . . . . .14 A1
Broadfields Way
NW10 . . . . 8 B3
Bradford Ho 🄵🄶
E1 . . . . 26 A1
BROADGATE **110 A4**
Broadgate EC2 . . . . . **110 A4**
Broadgate Circ
EC2 . . . . **110 A3**
Broadgates Ct
SE11 . . . . **149 C1**
Broadgates Rd
SW18 . . . . .71 C3
Broadgate Twr The
EC2 . . . . .98 B1
Broadhinton Rd
SW4 . . . . .61 B4
Broadhurst Cl
Hampstead NW6 . . . .11 B2
◨ Richmond TW10 . .54 B2
Broadhurst Gdns
NW6 . . . . .11 A2
Broadhurst Mans
NW6 . . . . .11 A2
Broad La EC2 . . . . . . **110 A4**
Broadlands N6 . . . . . .3 C4
Broadlands Ave
SW16 . . . . .74 A2
Broadlands Cl
Highgate N6 . . . . .3 C4
Streatham SW16 . . . .74 A2
Broadlands Ct
TW9 . . . . .44 C3
Broadlands Lo N6 . . . .3 B4
Broadlands Mans 🄻
SW16 . . . . .74 A2
Broadlands Rd N6 . . . 3 B4
Broadley St NW8 . . . **102 A4**
Broadley Terr
NW1 . . . . .90 B1
Broadmayne SE17 **151 B2**
Broadmead W14 . . . **140 A3**
Broadoak Ct 🄱
SW9 . . . . .62 C4
Broadoak Ho 🄻🄻
NW6 . . . . .78 B3
Broad St Ave EC2 . . . **110 A3**
Broad Sanctuary
SW1 . . . . **134 A3**

Broadstone Ho
SW8 . . . . **162 C1**
Broadstone Pl
W1 . . . . **103 B3**
Broad Street Pl
EC2 . . . . **109 C3**
Broadwalk Ho
SW7 . . . . **128 C3**
Broadwalk La NW11 . 1 B4
Broadwall SE1 . . . . . **121 C2**
Broadway
Stratford E15 . . . . . . 19 C1
Westminster SW1 . . **133 B2**
Broadway Arc 🄱
W6 . . . . 39 B2
Broadway Ho 🄶
E8 . . . . 25 A4
Broadway Mans
SW6 . . . . **155 C1**
Broadway Market
E8 . . . . 25 A4
Broadway Market
Mews 🄵 E8 . . . . . . 25 C4
Broadway Mews E5 . 7 B4
Broadway Mkt E8 . . . 25 A4
Broadway Ret Pk
NW2 . . . . .9 C4
Broadway Sh Ctr 🄶
W6 . . . . 39 B2
Broadway The
Barnes SW13 . . . . . . 46 A1
South Acton W3 . . . . 36 C4
Broadway Wlk 🄵
E14 . . . . 41 C3
Broadwick St W1 . . . **105 A1**
Broad Wlk
Mayfair W1 . . . . **117 B2**
Regent's Pk NW1 . . . **81 C1**
Richmond TW9 . . . . . 44 A3
Broad Wlk The
W8 . . . . **114 B1**
Broadwood Terr
W14 . . . . **141 A4**
Broad Yd EC1 . . . . . . **96 A1**
Brocas Cl NW3 . . . . . 12 A1
Brockbridge Ho
SW15 . . . . .56 B1
Brocket Ho 🄻🄾
SW8 . . . . **171 B2**
Brockham Dr SW2 . .74 B4
Brockham Ho
Camden Town
NW1 . . . . .83 A3
◨ Streatham SW2 . .74 B4
Brockham St SE1 . . . **137 B2**
Brockhurst Ho N4 . . . 6 C4
Brockill Cres SE4 . . . 66 A3
Brocklebank Rd
SW18 . . . . .71 B4
Brocklebank Road Ind
Est SE7 . . . . 43 C2
Brocklehurst St
SE14 . . . . 50 C3
BROCKLEY 66 B3
Brockley Cross
SE4 . . . . 66 A4
Brockley Cross Bsns
Ctr SE4 . . . . 66 A4
Brockley Gdns SE4 . 51 B1
Brockley Gr SE4 . . . . 66 B2
Brockley Hall Rd
SE4 . . . . 66 A2
Brockley Mews
SE4 . . . . 66 A2

Brockley Prim Sch
SE4 . . . . 66 B2
Brockley Rd SE4 . . . . 66 B2
Brockley Sta SE4 . . . 66 A4
Brockley Way SE4 . . 66 A3
Brockmer Ho 🄵
E1 . . . . 32 A2
Brock Pl E3 . . . . 27 A1
Brock St SE15 . . . . . . 65 B4
Brockweir 🄶🄶 E2 . . . 25 B3
Brockwell Ct 🄶
SW2 . . . . .62 C2
Brockwell Ho
SE11 . . . . **163 A4**
Brockwell Lido 63 A1
Brockwell Park 63 A1
SE24 . . . . 63 A1
Brockwell Park Gdns
SE24 . . . . 75 A4
Brockwell Park Row
SE24 . . . . 62 C1
Broderick Ho
SE21 . . . . 76 A1
Brodia Rd N16 . . . . . 7 A1
Brodick Ho 🄶 E3 . . . 26 B3
Brodie Ho SE1 . . . . . **153 A2**
Brodie St SE1 . . . . . . **153 A2**
Brodlove La E1 . . . . . 32 C2
Brodrick Rd SW17 . . 72 A2
Brody Ho 🄻 E1 . . . . **110 C3**
Broken Wharf
EC4 . . . . **122 C4**
Brokesley St E3 . . . . 26 B2
Broke Wlk
Hackney E8 . . . . 24 B4
🄻 Hackney E8 . . . . . 24 C4
Bromar Rd SE5 . . . . . 64 A4
Bromehead St 🄻
E1 . . . . 32 B3
Bromell's Rd SW4 . . 61 B3
Bromfelde Rd
SW4 . . . . **171 C1**
Bromfield Ct 🄶🄾
SE16 . . . . **139 C2**
Bromfield St N1 . . . . 85 C2
Bromleigh Ho
SE1 . . . . **138 C2**
BROMLEY E3 . . . . . . 27 A2
Bromley-by-Bow Sta
E3 . . . . 98 A4
Bromley Hall Rd
E14 . . . . 34 B4
Bromley High St
E3 . . . . 27 A2
Bromley Lo 🄶 W3 . . 28 B3
Bromley Pl W1 . . . . . **104 C4**
Bromley St E1 . . . . . . 32 C3
BROMPTON **130 A1**
Brompton Arc
SW1 . . . . **131 A3**
Brompton Oratory
SW3 . . . . **130 A1**
Brompton Park Cres
SW6 . . . . **156 A3**
Brompton Pl SW3 **130 B2**
Brompton Rd
SW3 . . . . **130 A1**
Brompton Sq
SW3 . . . . **130 A2**
Bromstone Ho 🄻🄾
SW9 . . . . **173 B3**
Bromwich Av N6 . . . 3 C2
Bromwich Ho 🄱
TW10 . . . . 54 A1
Bromyard Ave W3 . . 29 A2

Bromyard Ho
Acton W3 . . . . 29 A1
🄱 Peckham SE15 . . . 50 A3
Bron Ct NW6 . . . . . . 23 C4
BRONDESBURY 10 A2
Brondesbury Coll for
Boys 🄵🄶 NW6 . . . . 10 A1
Brondesbury Ct
NW2 . . . . .9 C2
Brondesbury Mews 🄻🄻
NW6 . . . . .10 C1
BRONDESBURY
PARK 22 C4
Brondesbury Park
NW6 . . . . .23 A4
Brondesbury Pk
NW6 . . . . .9 C1
Brondesbury Rd
NW6 . . . . .23 C3
Brondesbury Sta
NW6 . . . . .10 B1
Brondesbury Villas
NW6 . . . . .23 C3
Bronsart Rd SW6 . . . **154 A1**
Bronte Ct 🄱 W14 . . 39 C3
Bronte Ho
Kilburn NW6 . . . . . . 23 C2
🄢 Stoke Newington
N16 . . . . 16 A3
Bronti Cl SE17 . . . . . **151 A2**
Bronwen Ct NW8 . . . **89 B3**
Bronze St SE8 . . . . . . 51 C3
Brookbank Rd
SE13 . . . . 67 A4
Brook Cl SW17 . . . . . 72 C2
Brook Com Prim Sch
E8 . . . . 16 C3
Brook Ct SW14 . . . . . 56 A3
Brookdale Rd SE6 . . 67 A1
Brook Dr SE11 . . . . . **150 A4**
Brook Ct W10 . . . . . . 23 A3
Brooke Ho 🄶
SE14 . . . . 51 A2
Brooke Rd E5, N16 . . 7 C1
Brookes Ct EC1 . . . . . **107 B4**
Brooke's Mkt EC1 . . . **107 C4**
Brooke St EC1 . . . . . . **107 B3**
Brookfield
Dartmouth Pk N6 . . . 3 C1
◨ Finsbury Pk N4 . . 5 B2
Brookfield Ho 🄶🄶
E2 . . . . 25 A3
Brookfield Pk NW5 . . 4 A1
Brookfield Prim Sch
N19 . . . . 4 A2
Brookfield Rd
Acton W4 . . . . 37 C4
Homerton E9 . . . . . . 18 A2
Brookgate N16 . . . . . 6 C2
Brook Gate W1 . . . . . **117 A3**
Brook Gdns SW13 . . 56 B4
Brook Ho W6 . . . . . . 39 C2
BROOK GREEN 39 C2
Brook Green Flats 🄻
W14 . . . . 39 C3
Brook Ho
🄢 Clapham Pk
SW4 . . . . .61 B2
Ealing W3 . . . . 36 C4
🄸 Hammersmith
W6 . . . . 39 B2
Maidenhead WC1 . . **105 B4**
Brook Hos NW1 . . . . 83 A1
Brooklands Ave
SW18 . . . . .71 A4

Brooklands Court
Apartments 🄱
NW6 . . . . .10 B1
Brooklands Ct 🄶
NW6 . . . . .10 B1
Brooklyn Ct W12 . . . 30 B1
Brookmarsh Ind Est
SE10 . . . . .52 A3
Brook Mews N
W2 . . . . **115 A4**
Brookmill Rd SE8 . . . 51 C2
Brooksbank Ho 🄷
E9 . . . . 17 B2
Brooksbank St 🄶
E9 . . . . 17 B2
Brooksby Ho 🄶
N1 . . . . 14 C1
Brooksby Mews
N1 . . . . 14 C1
Brooksby St N1 . . . . 14 C1
Brooksby's Wlk E9 . . 17 C3
Brooks Ct
🄢 London SW4 . . . . **172 A2**
Nine Elms SW8 . . . . **161 A2**
Brooks Ho 🄶 SW2 . 74 C3
Brookside Rd N19 . . 4 B2
Brooks La W4 . . . . . . 44 C4
Brook's Mews W1 . . **118 A4**
Brooks Rd W4 . . . . . 36 C1
Brook St
Bayswater W2 . . . . . **115 C4**
Mayfair W1 . . . . **118 A4**
Brookstone Ct
SE15 . . . . 65 A3
Brooksville Ave
NW6 . . . . .23 A4
Brookville Rd
SW6 . . . . **154 C1**
Brookwood Ave
SW13 . . . . .46 B1
Brookwood Ho
SE1 . . . . **136 B3**
Brook Ct 🄱 70 C2
Broome Ct 🄱
TW9 . . . . .44 C2
Broome Ho 🄷 E5 . . 17 A3
Broome Way SE5 . . . 48 C3
Broom Farm SW6 **165 C2**
Bromfield 🄷
NW1 . . . . .12 C1
Bromfield Ho
SE17 . . . .**152 A3**
Broomfield House Sch
TW9 . . . . .44 B2
Broomfield Rd
TW9 . . . . .44 B2
Broomfield St E14 . . 34 A4
Broomgrove Rd
SW9 . . . . **173 A1**
Broomhill Rd
SW18 . . . . .58 C2
Broomhouse La
SW6 . . . . .58 C1
Broomhouse Rd
SW6 . . . . **165 B2**
Broomsleigh St
NW6 . . . . .10 B3
Broomwood Hall
(Lower Sch) 🄵
SW12 . . . . .60 C1
Broomwood Hall
(Lower Sch)
SW16 . . . . .73 C1

Broomwood Hall Sch
(Upper Sch) **2**
SW12 . . . . .72 C4

Broomwood Rd
SW11 . . . . .60 C2

Brougham Rd
Acton W3 . . . . .28 B4
Hackney E8 . . . . .24 C4

Brougham St
SW11 . . . . .169 A2

Brough Cl SW8 . . . . . .162 B1

Broughton Dr **10**
SW9 . . . . .63 A3

Broughton Rd
SW6 . . . . .166 B2

Broughton Road App
SW6 . . . . .166 A2

Broughton St
SW8 . . . . .170 A2

Brouncker Rd W3 . . . . .37 B4
Browne Ho **13** SE8 . . . .51 C3
Brownfield St E14 . . . .34 B3
Brownflete Ho
SE4 . . . . .66 A3

Brown Hart Gdns
W1 . . . . .117 C4
Browning Cl W9 . . . . . .89 A1
Browning Ct W14 . . . .154 C4
Browning Ho
1 London SE14 . . . . . .51 A2
7 Shepherd's Bush
W12 . . . . .30 B3
10 Stoke Newington
N16 . . . . .16 A4

Browning Mews
W1 . . . . .103 C3
Browning St SE17 . . . .151 A3
Brownlow Ho **10**
SE16 . . . . .139 B3

Brownlow Mews
WC1 . . . . .95 A1

Brownlow Rd
Hackney E8 . . . . .24 C4
Willesden NW10 . . . . . . .8 A1
Brownlow St WC1 . . . .107 A3
Brown's Bldgs
EC3 . . . . .110 B1
Brown St W1 . . . . .102 C2
Brownswood Rd N4 . . .6 B2
Broxash Rd SW11 . . . . .60 C1
Broxbourne Ho **1**
E3 . . . . .27 A1
Broxholme Ho
SW6 . . . . .166 A4
Broxholm Rd SE27,
SW16 . . . . .74 C1
Broxwood Way
NW8 . . . . .80 B3
Bruce Cl W10 . . . . .30 C4
Bruce Glasier Ho **13**
N19 . . . . .5 A3
Bruce Ho
4 Clapham Pk
SW4 . . . . .61 C1
3 North Kensington
W10 . . . . .30 C4
Putney SW15 . . . . .57 A2
Bruce Rd E3 . . . . .27 A2
Bruckner St W10 . . . . .23 B2
Bruges PI **18** NW1 . .13 B1
Brune Ho E1 . . . . .110 C3
Brunei Gall WC1 . . . . .105 C4
Brunel Cl **5** SW13. . . .46 B3
Brunel Est W2 . . . . . . .31 C4

Brunel Ho
Chelsea SW10 . . . . .157 C2
4 Gospel Oak
NW5 . . . . .13 A4
Millwall E14 . . . . .42 A1
New Cross SE8. . . . . .51 B3
2 Streatham SW2 . . .74 A4
Brunel Mews
NW10 . . . . .22 C2
Brunel Mus SE16 . . . . .40 B4
Brunel Rd
Acton W3 . . . . .29 A4
Wapping SE16 . . . . . . .32 B1
Brunel St E16 . . . . .35 B3
Brune St E1 . . . . .110 C3
Brunlees Ho SE1 . . . . .137 A1
Bruno Ct **14** E8 . . . . .16 C2
Brunswick Cl
Bermondsey SE1 . . .138 B4
Finsbury EC1 . . . . .96 A3
Westminster SW1 . . .147 C3
Brunswick Gdns
W8 . . . . .31 C1 113 C4
Brunswick Ho
4 Haggerston E2 . . .24 B3
Lisson Gr NW1 . . . . . . .90 C2
Brunswick Mews
W1 . . . . .103 A2
Brunswick Park Prim
Sch **22** SE5 . . . . .48 C3
Brunswick Pk SE5 . . . .49 A2
Brunswick PI N1 . . . . . .97 C3
Brunswick Quay
SE16 . . . . .40 C3
Brunswick Rd E14 . . . .34 B3
Brunswick Sh Ctr
WC1 . . . . .94 B2
Brunswick Sq WC1 . . . .94 B2
Brunswick Villas **3**
SE5 . . . . .49 A2
Brunton PI E14 . . . . . . .33 A3
Brushfield St E1 . . . . .110 C4
Brussels Rd SW11 . . . .59 C3
Bruton La W1 . . . . . . .118 B3
Bruton PI W1 . . . . .118 B3
Bruton St W1 . . . . .118 B3
Brutus Ct SE11 . . . . . .150 A3
Bryan Ave NW10 . . . . . .9 A1
Bryan Ct W1 . . . . .102 C2
Bryan Ho SE16 . . . . . . .41 B4
Bryan Rd SE16 . . . . . . .41 B4
Bryanston Ho **12**
SE15 . . . . .49 B2
Bryanston Mans
W1 . . . . .102 C4
Bryanston Mews E
W1 . . . . .102 E
Bryanston Mews W
W1 . . . . .102 C2
Bryanston PI W1 . . . . .102 C3
Bryanston Sq W1 . . . .102 C2
Bryanston St W1 . . . . .103 A1
Bryant Ct
Acton W3 . . . . .28 C1
Haggerston E2 . . . . . . .24 B3
Bryantwood Rd N5,
N7 . . . . .14 C3
Bryce Ho **23** SE14. . . .50 C4
Brydale Ho **2**
SE16 . . . . .40 C2
Brydges PI WC2 . . . . .120 A3
Brydges Rd E15 . . . . . .19 C3
Brydon Wlk N1 . . . . . . .84 B4
Bryer Ct EC2 . . . . .108 C4
Bryett Rd N7 . . . . .5 A1

Bryher Ho W4 . . . . .37 B1
Brymay Cl E3 . . . . .26 C3
Brymon Ct W1 . . . . . . .103 A3
Brynmaer Ho
SW11 . . . . .169 A3
Brynmaer Rd
SW11 . . . . .169 A3
Bryony Rd W12 . . . . . . .29 C2
BT Twr W1 . . . . .104 C4
Buccleuch Ho E5 . . . . . .7 C4
Buchanan Ct **18**
SE16 . . . . .40 C2
Buchanan Gdns
NW10 . . . . .22 B3
Buchan Ho
Dulwich SE21 . . . . . . .76 A1
Wandsworth SW18 . .70 C4
Buchan Rd SE15 . . . . . .65 B4
Bucharest Rd
SW18 . . . . .71 B4
Buckfast St
E2 . . . . .24 C2 99 C3
Buck Hill Wlk W2 . . . .115 C3
Buckhold Rd
SW18 . . . . .58 C1
Buckhurst Ho **16**
N7 . . . . .13 C3
Buckhurst St E1 . . . . . .25 A1
Buckingham Ave
SW1 . . . . .120 B3
Buckingham Gate
SW1 . . . . .133 A2
Buckingham Ho
Finsbury Pk N4 . . . . . . .6 B3
Richmond TW10 . . . . .54 C2
Buckingham Mans
NW6 . . . . .11 A3
Buckingham Mews
Harlesden NW10 . . . . .21 B3
7 Kingsland N1 . . . . .16 A2
Westminster SW1 . . .132 C2
Buckingham Pal
SW1 . . . . .132 C3
Buckingham Palace
Rd SW1 . . . . .146 B4
Buckingham Rd
Harlesden NW10 . . . . .21 B3
Kingsland N1 . . . . .16 A2
Buckingham St
WC2 . . . . .120 B3
Buckland Cres
NW3 . . . . .11 C2
Buckland Ct **6** N1 . . .24 A3
Buckland Ho **3**
N1 . . . . .14 C1
Buckland St N1 . . . . . . .87 C1
Buckland Wlk **2**
W3 . . . . .37 B4
Buckler's Alley
SW6 . . . . .155 A2
Bucklersbury EC2,
EC4 . . . . .109 B1
Buckle St
15 Whitechapel
E1 . . . . .111 B2
Whitechapel E1 . . . . .111 A2
Buckley Ct **5**
NW6 . . . . .10 B1
Buckley Rd NW6 . . . . . .10 B1
Buckmaster Cl **1**
SW9 . . . . .62 C4

Buckmaster Ho **1**
N7 . . . . .14 B4
Buckmaster Rd
SW11 . . . . .60 A3
Bucknall Sch WC1 . . . .106 B3
Bucknall St WC2 . . . . .106 A2
Buckner Rd SW2 . . . . . .62 B3
Buckridge Bldg
EC1 . . . . .107 B4
Buckshead Ho **19**
W2 . . . . .31 C4
Buck St NW1 . . . . .13 A1
Buckstone Cl SE23. . . .65 B1
Buckters Rents
SE16 . . . . .33 A1
Buckthorne Rd
SE4 . . . . .66 A1
Budge Row EC4 . . . . . .109 B1
Budge's Wlk W2 . . . . .115 A2
Budleigh Ho **15**
SE15 . . . . .49 C3
Buer Rd SW6 . . . . .164 B1
Bugsby's Way
SE10 . . . . .43 B2
Buick Ho **4** E3 . . . . . . .26 C1
Building Crafts Coll
The E15 . . . . .19 C1
Bulbarrow NW8 . . . . . . .78 B3
Bulinga St SW1 . . . . . .147 C3
Bullace Row SE5 . . . . . .48 C2
Bullards PI **13** E2 . . . .25 C2
Bulleid Way SW1 . . . .146 B3
Bullen Ho **13** E1 . . . . .25 A1
Bullen St SW11 . . . . . .168 B2
Buller Cl SE15 . . . . .49 C3
Buller Rd NW10 . . . . . .22 C2
Bullfinch Ct **4**
SE21 . . . . .75 C2
Bullingham Mans
W8 . . . . .127 C4
Bull Inn Ct WC2 . . . . . .120 B3
Bullivant St **4** E14 . . .34 B2
Bulls Alley SW14 . . . . .45 C1
Bull's Gdns SW3 . . . . .144 B4
Bulls Head Pas
EC3 . . . . .110 A1
Bull Yd SE15 . . . . .49 C2
Bulmer Mews
W11 . . . . .31 C1 113 B2
Bulow Ct **3** SW6 . . . .166 B2
Bulstrode PI W1 . . . . .103 C3
Bulstrode St W1 . . . . .103 C2
Bulwer St W12 . . . . . . .30 B1
Bunbury Ho SE15 . . . . .49 C3
Bunhill Row EC1 . . . . . .97 B1
Bunhouse PI SW1 . . . .145 C2
Bunkers Hill NW11 . . . . .2 B4
Bunning Ho N7 . . . . . . .14 A4
Bunning Way N7 . . . . . .14 B1
Bunsen Ho **2** E3 . . . . .26 A3
Bunsen St **3** E3 . . . . .26 A3
Bunyan Ct EC2 . . . . . .108 C4
Buonaparte Mews
SW1 . . . . .147 B2
Burbage Cl SE1 . . . . . .137 B1
Burbage Ho
16 Deptford SE14 . .50 C4
Shoreditch N1 . . . . . . .87 C3
Burbage Rd SE21,
SE24 . . . . .75 C2
Burbage Sch **54**
N1 . . . . .24 A3
Burcham St E14 . . . . . .34 B3
Burchell Ho SE11 . . . .149 A2
Burchell Rd SE15 . . . . .50 A2

Burcher Gale Gr **5**
SE15 . . . . .49 B3
Burcote Rd SW18. . . . .71 C4
Burden Ho SW8 . . . . . .162 A1
Burdenshott Ave
TW10 . . . . .55 A3
Burder Cl N1 . . . . .16 A2
Burder Rd N1 . . . . .16 A2
Burdett Coutts &
Townshend CE Prim
Sch SW1 . . . . .147 C3
Burdett Mews **4**
W2 . . . . .100 A2
Burdett Rd
Richmond TW9 . . . . . .54 B4
Tower Hamlets E3 . . . .33 B4
Burdon Ct **3** E8 . . . . . .16 C2
Burford Ct SE8 . . . . . . .51 C4
Burford Ho
1 Brentford
TW8 . . . . .36 A1
5 South Lambeth
SW9 . . . . .173 A1
Burford Rd
Brentford TW8 . . . . . .36 A1
6 Stratford Marsh
E15 . . . . .27 C4
Burford Wlk SW6 . . . .156 B1
Burgate Ct **9**
SW9 . . . . .62 C4
Burges Gr SW13. . . . . .47 A3
Burgess Bsns Pk
SE5 . . . . .48 C3
Burgess Hill NW2 . . . . .10 C4
Burgess Ho **3** SE5 . . .48 B3
Burgess Park Mans
NW6 . . . . .10 C4
Burgess St E14 . . . . . . .33 C4
Burge St SE1 . . . . .137 C1
Burgh House &
Hampstead Mus
NW3 . . . . .11 C4
Burghley Hall Cl
SW19 . . . . .70 A3
Burghley Ho SW19. . . .70 A1
Burghley Rd NW5 . . . . .13 A4
Burghley Twr W3 . . . . .29 B2
Burgh St N1 . . . . .86 B2
Burgon St EC4 . . . . . . .108 B1
Burgos Gr SE10 . . . . . .52 A2
Burgoyne Rd SW9 . . . .62 B4
Burhan Uddin Ho
E1 . . . . .24 B1 98 C1
Buriton Ho **9**
SW15 . . . . .69 A3
Burke Cl SW15 . . . . . . .56 A3
Burke Ho **1** SW11 . . .59 C3
Burke St E16 . . . . .35 C4
Burland Rd SW11 . . . . .60 B2
Burleigh Coll W6 . . . . .39 B2
Burleigh Ho
Chelsea SW3 . . . . . .157 C3
3 North Kensington
W10 . . . . .30 C4
Burleigh PI SW15. . . . .57 C2
Burleigh St WC2 . . . . .120 C4
Burley Ho E1 . . . . .32 C3
Burlington Arc
W1 . . . . .118 C3
Burlington Ave
TW9 . . . . .44 C2
Burlington Cl
Brondesbury NW9 . . . .23 C3
Burlington Ct
Chiswick W4 . . . . .45 B3
Highgate N6 . . . . .3 C3

Burlington Danes
Acad W12 . . . . 30 A3
Burlington Gdns
Acton Green W4 . . . . 37 B1
Acton W3 . . . . 28 B1
4 Fulham SW6 . . . . . . 164 B1
Marylebone W1 . . . . 118 C3
Burlington Ho
NW3 . . . . 11 C3
Burlington La W4 . . 45 C3
Burlington Lodge
SW6 . . . . 164 B1
Burlington Mews
Acton W3 . . . . 28 B1
2 Putney SW15 . . . . 58 B2
Burlington Pl
SW6 . . . . 164 B1
Burlington Rd
Acton Green W4 . . . . 37 B1
Fulham SW6 . . . . 164 B1
Burma Rd N16 . . . . . 15 C4
Burmarsh 8 NW5 . . 12 C2
Burmester Ho
SW17 . . . . 71 B1
Burmester Rd
SW17 . . . . 71 B1
Burnaby Cres W4 . . 45 B4
Burnaby St 8
SE16 . . . . 139 C3
Burnaby Gdns W4 . . 45 A4
Burnaby St SW10 . . 157 A1
Burnand Ho 8
W14 . . . . 39 C3
Burnbury Rd SW12 . . 73 B3
Burne Jones Ho
W14 . . . . 140 B3
Burnell Ho 18
SW2 . . . . 74 C3
Burnell Wlk SE1 . . 153 A2
Burness Cl 8 N7 . . . 14 B2
Burne St NW1 . . . . 102 A4
Burnett Cl E9 . . . . 17 B3
Burnett St SW11 . . 168 A3
Burnett Ho 6
SE13 . . . . 52 B1
Burney St SE10 . . . . 52 B3
Burnfoot Ave
SW6 . . . . 164 B3
Burnham NW3 . . . . . 12 A1
Burnham Cl SE1 . . . 153 A3
Burnham Ct W2 . . 114 B4
Burnham Est 8
E2 . . . . 25 B2
Burnham St E2 . . . . . 25 B2
Burnhill Ho EC1 . . . . 96 C3
Burnley Rd
London SW9 . . . . . . 172 C2
Willesden NW10 . . . . 8 C3
Burnsall St SW3 . . 144 B2
Burns Ho
8 Bethnal Green
E2 . . . . 25 B2
1 Islington N7 . . . . . 14 B2
Kennington SE17 . . 150 B1
3 Stoke Newington
N16 . . . . 16 A4
Burn's Ho NW10 . . . 21 A4
Burnside Cl SE16 . . . 32 C1
Burns Rd SW11 . . . 168 C2
Burn's Rd NW10 . . . 21 B4
Burnthwaite Rd
SW6 . . . . 155 A1
Burntwood Cl
SW18 . . . . 72 A3
Burntwood Ct
SW17 . . . . 71 B1

Burntwood Grange Rd
SW18 . . . . 72 A3
Burntwood La
SW17 . . . . 71 C2
Burntwood Sch
SW17 . . . . 71 C2
Buross St E1 . . . . . . 32 A3
Burrage Ct 17
SE16 . . . . 40 C2
Burrard Ho 11 E2 . . 25 B3
Burrard Rd NW6 . . . 10 C4
Burr Cl E1 . . . . 125 B2
Burrell St SE1 . . . . 122 A2
Burrell's Wharf Sq
E14 . . . . 42 A1
Burrhill Ct SE16 . . . 40 C3
Burrow Ho 19
SW9 . . . . 173 A1
Burrow Rd SE22 . . . 64 A3
Burrows Mews
SE1 . . . . 136 A4
Burrows Rd NW10 . . 22 B2
Burrow Wlk SE21 . . 75 B4
Burr Rd SW18 . . . . . 70 C4
Bursar St SE1 . . . . 124 A1
Burslem St 8 E1 . . 111 C1
Burstock Rd SW15 . . 58 A3
Burston Rd SW15 . . 57 C2
Burtley Cl N4 . . . . 6 B3
Burton Bank N1 . . . . 15 C1
Burton Ct SW3 . . . . 145 A2
Burton Gr SE17 . . . 151 B1
Burton Ho
8 Bermondsey
SE16 . . . . 40 A4
8 Brixton SE5 . . . . . 48 A2
Burton Lo 6
SW15 . . . . 58 B2
Burton Mews
SW1 . . . . 145 C3
Burton Pl WC1 . . . . . 93 C3
Burton Rd
8 Brixton SW9 . . . 173 B2
Brixton SW9 . . . . 48 A1
Brondesbury NW6 . . 10 B1
Burtons Ct E15 . . . . 19 C1
Burton St WC1 . . . . . 93 C2
Burtonwood Ho N4 . . 6 C4
Burtt Ho 8
N1 . . . . 24 A2 98 A4
Burwash Ho SE1 . . 137 C3
Burwell Cl 27 E1 . . . . 32 A3
Burwell Wlk 8 E3 . . 26 C1
Burwood Ho 11
SW9 . . . . 63 A3
Burwood Pl W2 . . . 102 B2
Bury Cl SE16 . . . . 32 C1
Bury Ct EC3 . . . . 110 B2
Buryfield Ct 28
SE8 . . . . 40 C2
Bury Pl WC1 . . . . . . 106 B3
Bury St
St James SW1 . . . . 119 A2
Whitechapel EC3 . . 110 B2
Bury Wlk SW3 . . . . 144 A2
Busbridge Ho 24
E14 . . . . 33 C4
Busby Mews 8
NW1 . . . . 13 C2
Busby Pl NW5 . . . . . 13 C2
Bushbaby Cl SE1 . . 138 A1
Bushberry Rd E9 . . . 18 A2
Bush Cotts 12
SW18 . . . . 58 C2
Bush Ct **7** W12 . . . . 39 C4
Bushell Cl SW2 . . . . 74 B2

Bushell St 18 E1 . . . 125 C2
Bushey Down
SW12 . . . . 73 A2
Bushey Hall SE5 . . . 48 B2
Bushey Hill Rd
SE5 . . . . 49 B2
Bushfield Ho N5 . . . 15 B3
Bush Ind Est
NW10 . . . . 20 C1
Bush La EC4 . . . . . . 123 B4
Bushnell Rd SW17 . . 73 A1
Bush Rd
Bermondsey SE8 . . . 40 C2
Hackney E8 . . . . 25 A4
Richmond TW9 . . . . . 44 B4
Bushwood Dr SE1 . 153 A3
Bushwood Rd
TW9 . . . . 44 C4
Business Design Ctr
N1 . . . . 85 C3
Buspace Studios 8
W10 . . . . 23 A1
Butcher Row E1 . . . . 32 C3
Butchers Rd E16 . . . 35 C3
Bute Gdns W6 . . . . . 39 C2
Bute House Prep Sch
2 W6 . . . . 39 C2
Bute St SW7 . . . . . . 143 B4
Bute Wlk **18** N1 . . . . 15 C2
Butfield Ho 6 E9 . . . 17 B2
Butler Ho
8 Bethnal Green
E2 . . . . 25 B2
8 Brixton SW9 . . . . 48 A2
8 Poplar E14 . . . . . 33 B3
Butler Pl SW1 . . . . . 133 B2
Butler Rd NW10 . . . . 8 B1
Butlers & Colonial
Wharf SE1 . . . . . . 139 A4
Butler St **8** E2 . . . . . 25 B2
Butler's Wharf W
SE1 . . . . 124 C1
Butley Ct 8 E3 . . . . . 26 A3
Butterfield Cl 8
SE16 . . . . 40 A4
Butterfly Wlk 2
SE5 . . . . 48 C2
Buttermere Cl
Bermondsey SE1 . . 152 C3
Leyton E11 . . . . 19 C4
Buttermere Ct
NW8 . . . . 79 B4
Buttermere Dr
SW15 . . . . 58 A2
Buttermere Wlk 8
E8 . . . . 16 B2
Butterwick W6 . . . . . 39 B2
Buttesworth Ct
SE16 . . . . 54 A1
Buttesland St N1 . . . 97 C4
Buxhall Cres E9 . . . . 18 B2
Buxted Rd
Camberwell SE22 . . 64 A3
Dalston E8 . . . . 16 B1
Buxton Ct N1 . . . . 97 A4
Buxton Gdns W3 . . 28 A2
Buxton Ho **3**
SW11 . . . . 59 C3
Buxton Mews
SW4 . . . . 171 C2
Buxton Rd
Mortlake SW14 . . . . 56 A4
Upper Holloway N19 . 4 C3

Buxton Rd continued
Willesden NW2 . . . . . . 9 A2
Buxton St
E1 . . . . 24 B1 99 A1
Byam Shaw Sch of Art
8 N19 . . . . 4 C2
Byam St SW6 . . . . . 166 C1
Byards Ct SE16 . . . . 40 C3
Byas Ho **3** E3 . . . . . 26 B2
Byefield Cl SE16 . . . . 41 A4
Byelands Cl 17
SE16 . . . . 32 C1
Bye The W3 . . . . 29 A3
Byeway The SW14 . . 55 B4
Byfeld Gdns SW13 . . 46 C2
Bygrove Prim Sch 21
E14 . . . . 34 A3
Bygrove St E14 . . . . . 34 A3
Byng Pl WC1 . . . . . . 93 B1
Byng St E14 . . . . 41 C4
Byrne Ho 11 SW2 . . 62 B2
Byrne Rd SW12 . . . . 73 A2
Byron Cl E8 . . . . 24 C4
Byron Ct
Chelsea SW3 . . . . . . 144 B3
Dulwich SE21 . . . . . . 76 C3
1 Hampstead
NW6 . . . . 11 B1
Paddington W9 . . . . 23 C1
St Pancras WC1 . . . . 94 C2
Byron Mews
Hampstead NW3 . . . 12 A4
2 Maida Vale W9 . . 23 C1
Byron St E14 . . . . 34 B3
Bythorn St SW9 . . . . 62 B3
Byward St EC3 . . . . 124 B3
Bywater Pl SE16 . . . . 33 A1
Bywater St SW3 . . . 144 C2
Bywell Pl W1 . . . . . 104 C3
Bywrth Wlk N1 . . . . . 15 A2

C

Cabbell St NW1 . . . 102 A3
Cabinet Off SW1 . . 134 A4
Cabinet War Rooms &
Churchill Mus
SW1 . . . . 133 C4
Cable Ho WC1 . . . . . 95 B4
Cable Pl SE10 . . . . . 52 B2
Cable St E1 . . . . 32 A2
Cabot Ct SE16 . . . . . 40 C3
Cabot Sq E14 . . . . . . 33 C1
Cabul Rd SW11 . . . 168 B1
Cactus Cl SE5 . . . . . 49 A1
Cactus Wlk W12 . . . 29 B3
Cadbury Way 1
SE1 . . . . 153 B4
Caddington Rd
NW2 . . . . 1 A1
Cadell Cl E2 . . . . 24 B3
Cadell Ho 2 E2 . . . . 24 B3
Cade Rd SE10 . . . . . 52 C2
Cader Rd SW18 . . . . 59 B1
Cadet Dr SE1 . . . . . 153 A2
Cade Tyler Ho 10
SE10 . . . . 52 B2
Cadiz St SE17 . . . . . 151 A1
Cadman Cl SW9 . . . 48 A3
Cadmore Ho 8
N1 . . . . 15 A1
Cadmus Cl 6
SW4 . . . . 61 C4
Cadmus Ct 8
SW9 . . . . 173 B4

Bur–Cal 191

Cadnam Lo E14 . . . . 42 C3
Cadnam Point 15
SW15 . . . . 69 A3
Cadogan Cl E9 . . . . . 18 B1
Cadogan Ct SW3 . . 144 C3
Cadogan Ct Gdns
SW1 . . . . 145 B4
Cadogan Gate
SW1 . . . . 145 A4
Cadogan Gdns
SW3 . . . . 145 A3
Cadogan Hall
SW1 . . . . 145 B4
Cadogan Ho SW3 . 157 C3
Cadogan Lane SW1 . 131 B1
Cadogan Pier
SW3 . . . . 158 B3
Cadogan Pl SW1 . . 131 A1
Cadogan Sq SW1 . . 131 A1
Cadogan St SW3 . . 144 C3
Cadogan Terr E9 . . . 18 B1
Caedmon Rd N7 . . . . 14 B4
Caernarvon Ho
W2 . . . . 100 C2
Caesar Ct **2** E2 . . . . 25 C3
Cahill St EC1 . . . . . . 97 A1
Cahir St E14 . . . . 42 A2
Caine Ho W3 . . . . . . 37 A4
Caird St W10 . . . . . . 23 B2
Cairns Ho **3** N7 . . . . 14 B4
Cairns Rd SW11 . . . 60 A2
Caister Ho
Balham SW12 . . . . . . 73 A4
8 Islington N7 . . . . . 14 B2
Caistor Mews
SW12 . . . . 73 A4
Caistor Rd SW12 . . 73 A4
Caithness Ho N1 . . . 84 C4
Caithness Rd W14 . . 39 C3
Calabria Rd N5 . . . . 15 A3
Calais Gate SE5 . . . . 48 A2
Calais St SE5 . . . . . 48 A2
Calbourne Rd
SW12 . . . . 72 C4
Calcraft Ho **10** E2 . . 25 B3
Caldecot Ct SE5 . . . 48 B1
Caldecot Rd SE5 . . . 48 B1
Calder Ct SE16 . . . . 33 B1
Calderon Ho NW8 . . 80 A2
Calderon Pl 20
W10 . . . . 30 B4
Caldervale Rd
SW4 . . . . 61 C2
Caldew St SE5 . . . . . 48 C3
Caldwell St SW9 . . 163 A1
Caldy Wlk **8** N1 . . . . 15 B2
Caleb St SE1 . . . . . . 137 A4
Caledonia Ho 15
E14 . . . . 33 A3
Caledonian Market
SE1 . . . . 138 B2
Caledonian Rd
Islington N1 . . . . 84 C3
Lower Holloway N7 . . 14 B2
Caledonian Road &
Barnsbury Sta
N7 . . . . 14 B1
Caledonian Rd Sta
N7 . . . . 14 B2
Caledonian Sq 6
NW1 . . . . 13 C2
Caledonian Wharf Rd
E14 . . . . 42 C2
Caledonia St N1 . . . . 84 B1

Cale St SW3 . . . . **144** A2
Caletock Way
SE10 . . . . 43 B1
Calgarth NW1 . . . . . **83** A1
Calgary Ct 30 SE16 . . 40 B4
Caliban Twr 9 N1 . . 24 A3
Calico Ho 4 SW11 . . 59 B4
Calico Row 5
SW11 . . . . 59 B4
Calidore Cl SW2 . . . 62 B1
California Bldg 2
SE13 . . . . 52 A2
Callaby Terr 11
N1 . . . . 15 C2
Callahan Cotts 8
E1 . . . . 32 B4
Callan Sch The
W1 . . . . **105** A2
Callcott Ct NW6 . . . . 10 B1
Callcott Rd NW6 . . . 10 B1
Callcott St
W8 . . . . . . .31 C1 **113** B2
Callendar Rd
SW7 . . . . **129** B2
Callingham Ho 3
E14 . . . . 33 B4
Callingham Ho 1
SW4 . . . . 62 A4
Callow St SW3 . . . . **157** B4
Calmington Rd
SE5 . . . . 49 A4
Calshot Ho N1 . . . . **84** C2
Calshot St N1 . . . . . **84** C1
Calstock NW1 . . . . . **83** B3
Calstock Ho SE11 . **149** C2
Calthorpe St WC1 . . **95** A2
Calton Ave SE21 . . . 64 A1
Calver 3 NW5 . . . . . 13 A4
Calverley Gr N19 . . 4 C3
Calvert Ave
E2 . . . . .24 B2 **98** C3
Calvert Ct
1 London N19 . . . . 4 B3
5 Richmond TW9 . . 54 B3
Calvert Ho 9 W12 . . 30 A2
Calverton SE5 . . . . . 49 A4
Calvert Rd SE10 . . . 43 B1
Calvert's Bldgs
SE1 . . . . **123** B1
Calvert St NW1 . . . . **81** B4
Calvin St E1 . .24 B1 **98** C1
Calypso Cres 6
SE15 . . . . 49 B3
Calypso Way SE8,
SE16 . . . . 41 B2
Cambalt Ho 3
SW15 . . . . 57 C2
Cambalt Rd SW15 . . 57 C2
Cambay Ho 7 E1 . . 26 A1
Camber Ho 4
SE15 . . . . 50 B4
Camberley Ho
NW1 . . . . **82** B1
CAMBERWELL 48 C2
Camberwell Bsns Ctr
SE5 . . . . 48 C3
Camberwell Church St
SE5 . . . . 48 C2
Camberwell Coll of
Arts
16 Camberwell
SE5 . . . . 49 A2
22 Camberwell
SE15 . . . . 49 B3

Camberwell Glebe
SE5 . . . . 49 A2
Camberwell Gn
SE5 . . . . 48 C2
Camberwell Gr
SE5 . . . . 49 A1
Camberwell Green
SE5 . . . . 48 B2
Camberwell New Rd
SW9 . . . . 48 A3
Camberwell Rd
SE5 . . . . 48 B3
Camberwell Station
Rd SE5 . . . . 48 B2
Camberwell Trad Est
SE5 . . . . 48 B2
Camborne Rd
SW18 . . . . 70 C4
Cambourne Mews 6
W11 . . . . 31 A3
Cambray Rd SW12 . . 73 B3
Cambria Ho 14
E14 . . . . 33 A3
Cambria Lo 3
SW15 . . . . 58 B2
Cambrian Cl SE27 . . 75 A1
Cambrian Rd
TW10 . . . . 54 B1
Cambria St SW6 . . . 63 B4
Cambria St SW6 . . **156** B1
Cambridge Ave
NW6 . . . . 23 C3
Cambridge Cir
WC2 . . . . **105** C1
Cambridge Cotts
TW9 . . . . 44 C4
Cambridge Cres 26
E2 . . . . 25 A3
Cambridge Ct
28 Bethnal Green
E2 . . . . 25 A3
2 Hammersmith
W6 . . . . 39 B2
6 Kilburn NW6 . . . 23 C3
Marylebone W2 . . **102** A3
Stamford Hill N16 . . 7 A4
Cambridge Gate
NW1 . . . . **92** A2
Cambridge Gate
Mews 2 NW1 . . . **92** B2
Cambridge Gdns
Kilburn NW6 . . . . . . 23 C3
North Kensington
W10 . . . . 31 A3
Cambridge Gr W6 . . 39 A2
Cambridge Heath Rd
E1, E2 . . . . 25 A2
Cambridge Heath Sta
E2 . . . . 25 A3
Cambridge Ho
SW6 . . . . 58 A4
Cambridge Mans
SW11 . . . . **168** C3
Cambridge Pas 9
E9 . . . . 17 B1
Cambridge Pl W8 . **128** B3
Cambridge Rd
Barnes SW13 . . . . . . 46 B1
Battersea SW11 . . **168** C3
Kilburn NW6 . . . . . . 23 C2
Kilburn NW6 . . . . . . 23 C3
Richmond TW9 . . . . 44 C3
Cambridge Rd N
W4 . . . . 37 A1
Cambridge Rd S 3
W4 . . . . 37 A1

Cambridge Sch 15
W6 . . . . 39 A2
Cambridge Sq
W2 . . . . **102** A2
Cambridge Terr
SW1 . . . . **146** C2
Cambridge Terr Mews
NW1 . . . . **92** B3
Cambus Rd E16 . . . 35 C4
Cam Ct 2 SE15 . . . 49 B4
Camden Coll of
English 8 NW1 . . 12 C1
Camden Gdns
NW1 . . . . 13 A1
Camden High St
NW1 . . . . **82** C3
Camden Ho 6
SE8 . . . . 41 B1
Camdenhurst St
E14 . . . . 33 A3
Camden Lock Mkt
NW1 . . . . 13 A1
Camden Lock Pl
NW1 . . . . 13 A1
Camden Mews
NW1 . . . . 13 C2
Camden Mkt NW1 . **82** B4
Camden Park Rd
NW1 . . . . 13 C2
Camden Pas N1 . . **86** A3
Camden Rd NW1 . . **82** B4
Camden Road Sta
NW1 . . . . 13 B1
Camden Row SE3 . . 53 A1
Camden Sch for Girls
The NW5 . . . . 13 B2
Camden Sq NW1 . . 13 C2
Camden St NW1 . . **83** A3
Camden Studios
NW1 . . . . 83 A3
Camden Terr 17
NW1 . . . . 13 C2
CAMDEN TOWN . . 82 B4
Camden Town Sta
NW1 . . . . **82** B4
Camden Wlk N1 . . **86** A3
Cameford Ct 20
SW12 . . . . 74 A4
Camelford NW1 . . . **83** A3
Camelford Ct 13
W11 . . . . 31 A3
Camelford Ho
SE1 . . . . **148** B1
Camelford Wlk 13
W11 . . . . 31 A3
Camellia Ho SE8 . . . 51 B3
Camellia St SW8 . . **162** A1
Camelot Ho 15
NW1 . . . . 13 C2
Camelot Prim Sch
SE15 . . . . 50 A4
Camera Pl SW10 . . **157** B4
Camera Press Gall
SE1 . . . . **138** C4
Cameret Ct 6
W11 . . . . 30 C1
Cameron Ct 3
SW19 . . . . 70 A3
Cameron Ho
Camberwell SE5 . . . 48 B3
St John's Wood
NW8 . . . . **80** A2
Cameron House Sch
SW10 . . . . **157** C4

Cameron Pl SW16 . **74** C2
Camerton Cl 8 E8 . 16 B2
Camilla Rd SE16 . . . 40 A2
Camlet St
E2 . . . . . . .24 B1 **98** C2
Camley St Natural Pk
NW1 . . . . 83 C2
Camley St NW1 . . **83** C2
Camomile St EC3 . **110** B2
Campaign Ct W9 . . . 23 B1
Campana Rd SW6 . **165** C3
Campbell Ct
Dulwich SE21 . . . . . 76 C3
South Kensington
SW7 . . . . **128** C1
Campbell Gordon Way
NW2 . . . . 9 A4
Campbell Ho
Paddington W2 . . . **89** B1
Pimlico SW1 . . . . . **146** C1
30 Shepherd's Bush
W12 . . . . 30 A2
Campbell Rd E3 . . . 26 C2
Campbell Wlk N1 . . **84** B4
Campdale Rd N7 . . . 4 C4
Campden Gr W8 . . **127** C4
Campden Hill W8 . **127** C3
Campden Hill Ct
W8 . . . . **127** C4
Campden Hill Gate
W8 . . . . **127** B4
Campden Hill Gdns
W8 . . . . . . .31 C1 **113** B2
Campden Hill Mans
W8 . . . . **113** B2
Campden Hill Pl
W14 . . . . . . .31 B1 **113** A2
Campden Hill Rd
W8 . . . . **127** B3
Campden Hill Sq
W8 . . . . . . .31 B1 **113** A2
Campden Ho 4
W8 . . . . **127** C4
Campden Hos
NW1 . . . . 16 A3
Campden House Cl
W8 . . . . **127** C4
Campden St
W8 . . . . . . .31 C1 **113** B1
Campen Cl SW19 . . 70 A2
Camperdown St
E1 . . . . **111** A1
Campion Ho 19
N16 . . . . 16 A3
Campion Rd SW15 . 57 B2
Campion St SE14 . . 50 C3
Campshill Pl SE13 . . 67 B2
Campshill Rd SE13 . 67 B2
Campton Hill Twrs
W8 . . . . . . .31 C1 **113** B2
Camsey Ho 3
SW2 . . . . 62 B2
Canada Cres W3 . . . 20 B1
Canada Gdns SE13 . 67 B2
Canada Rd W3 . . . . 28 B4
Canada Sq E14 . . . . 34 A1
Canada Water Sta
SE16 . . . . 40 C3
Canada Way W12 . . 30 A2
Canal App SE8 . . . . 51 A4
Canal Bldg N1 . . . . **86** C2
Canal Bridge SE15 . 49 C4
Canal Bvd 7
NW1 . . . . 13 C2

Canal Cl
Mile End E1 . . . . 26 A1
North Kensington
W10 . . . . 22 C1
Canal Gr SE15 . . . . . 50 A4
Canal Head Public Ho
1 SE15 . . . . 49 C2
Canal Path E2 . . . . . **24** B4
Canalside Studios 28
N1 . . . . 24 A4
Canal St SE5 . . . . . 48 C4
Canal Way W10 . . . . 22 C1
Canal Wlk N1 . . . . **87** C4
CANARY WHARF . . 34 A1
Canary Wharf Pier
E14 . . . . 33 B1
Canary Wharf Sta
E14 . . . . 34 A1
Canary Wharf Sta
(DLR) E14 . . . . 33 C1
Canberra Prim Sch
W12 . . . . 30 A2
Canbury Mews
SE26 . . . . 76 C1
Cancell Rd SW9 . . **173** C4
Candahar Rd
SW11 . . . . **168** B1
Candida Ct 3
NW1 . . . . 13 A1
Candishe Ho SE1 . **138** C4
Candle Gr SE15 . . . 65 A4
Candlemakers 24
SW11 . . . . 59 C4
Candover St W1 . . **104** C3
Candy St E3 . . . . . . 26 B4
Canfield Gdns
NW6 . . . . 11 A1
Canfield Pl NW6 . . . 11 B2
Canford Rd SW11 . . 60 C2
Canham Rd W3 . . . . 38 A4
Cann Ho W14 . . . . **126** B1
Canning Cross
SE5 . . . . 49 A1
Canning Pas W8 . **128** C2
Canning Pl W8 . . . **128** C2
Canning Pl Mews
W8 . . . . **128** C2
Canning Rd N5 . . . . 6 A1
Cannington 14
NW5 . . . . 12 C2
CANNING TOWN . . 35 B3
Canning Town
E16 . . . . 35 A3
Canning Town Sta
E16 . . . . 35 B3
Cannock Ho N4 . . . 6 C4
Cannon Dr 21 E14 . 33 C2
Cannon Hill NW6 . . 10 C3
Cannon Ho SE11 . **149** A3
Cannon La NW3 . . . 2 C1
Cannon Pl NW3 . . . 2 C1
Cannon St EC4 . . . **123** A4
Cannon Street Rd
E1 . . . . 32 A3
Cannon Street Sta
EC4 . . . . **123** B4
Cannon Wharf Bsns
Ctr 17 SE8 . . . . . . 41 A2
Canon Barnett Prim
Sch E1 . . . . **111** A2
Canon Beck Rd
SE16 . . . . 40 B4
CANONBURY 15 B2

Canonbury Bsns Ctr
N1............**87** A4

Canonbury Cres
N1............15 B1

Canonbury Ct **21**
N1............15 A1

Canonbury Gr N1....15 B1

Canonbury Hts **6**
N1............15 C2

Canonbury La N1...15 A1

Canonbury Pk N
N1............15 B2

Canonbury Pk S
N1............15 B2

Canonbury Pl N1...15 A2

Canonbury Prim Sch
N1............15 A2

Canonbury Rd N1..15 A1
Canonbury Sq N1...15 B1
Canonbury St N1...15 B1

Canonbury Sta N1,
N5............15 B3

Canonbury Villas
N1............15 A1

Canonbury Yd E **8**
N1............15 B2

Canon Murnane Rd
SE1............**138** C1
Canon Row SW1..**134** A3
Canons Cl N2.......2 C4
Canon St N1......**86** C3
Canrobert St E2....**25** A2
Cantelowes Rd
NW1............13 C2
Canterbury SE13...67 B2
Canterbury Cl **4**
SE5............48 B1
Canterbury Cres
SW9............62 C4
Canterbury Ct
Acton W3........29 A1
Kilburn NW6.....23 C3
Canterbury Gr SE27,
SW16...........74 C1
Canterbury Ho
6 Bromley E3....**27** A2
Lambeth SE1...**135** A2
Canterbury Ind Pk **15**
SE15...........50 B4
Canterbury Mans
NW6............11 A2
Canterbury Pl
SE17..........**150** B3
Canterbury Rd
NW6............23 C3
Canterbury Terr
NW6............23 C3
Cantium Ret Pk
SE1............49 C4
Canton St E14.....33 C3
Cantrell Rd E3.....26 C1
Canute Ct SW16...74 C1
Canute Gdns SE16..40 C2
Canvey St SE1....**122** C2
Cape Henry Ct **15**
E14............**34** C2
Capel Ho **17** E9....**17** B1
Capel Lo
5 Richmond
TW9............44 B2
12 Streatham SW2..74 B4
Capener's Cl SW1...**131** B3
Capern Rd SW18...71 B3
Capio Nightingale
Hospl NW1.....**102** B4

Capital City Acad
NW10...........22 A4
Capital East Apts **8**
E16............35 C2
Capital Interchange
Way TW8.......36 C1
Capital Sh Ctrs
SW1...........**133** B3
Capital Wharf **14**
E1............**125** C1
Capland Ho NW8...**89** C2
Capland St NW8....**89** C2
Caple Ho SW10...**157** A2
Caple Rd NW10....21 B3
Capper St WC1....**93** A1
Capstan Ho **6** E14..42 B2
Capstan Rd SE8....41 B2
Capstan Sq E14.....42 B4
Capstan Way SE16..33 A1
Capulet Mews **1**
E16............35 C1
Caradoc Cl W2....31 C3
Caradoc St SE10...43 A1
Cara Ho **10** N1....14 C1
Caranday Villas **5**
W11............30 C1
Caravel Cl E14.....41 C3
Caravel Mews **14**
SE8............51 C4
Caraway Hts E14...34 B2
Carbery Ave W3...36 B4
Carbis Rd E14.....33 B3
Carbroke Ho **9**
E9............25 B4
Carburton St W1...92 B1
Cardale St **11** E14..42 B3
Carden Rd SE15...65 A4
Cardiff Ho **9** SE15..49 C4
Cardigan Rd
Barnes SW13.....46 C1
Bow E3..........26 B3
Richmond TW10...54 A1
Cardigan St SE11..**149** B2
Cardigan Wlk **19**
N1............15 B1
Cardinal Bourne St
SE1............**137** C1
Cardinal Cap Alley
SE1............**122** C3
Cardinal Hinsley Cl
NW10...........21 C3
Cardinal Hinsley
Mathematics &
Computing Coll
NW10...........21 C4
Cardinal Pl SW15...57 C3
Cardinal Pl SW1..**132** C2
Cardinal Pole RC Sch
London E9.......17 C1
London E9.......18 A3
Cardinals Way N19...4 C3
Cardinal Vaughan
Meml Sch The
W14...........**126** A4
Cardinal Wlk SW1.**132** C1
Cardine Mews
SE15...........50 A3
Cardington St
NW1............93 A3
Cardozo Rd N7....14 A3
Cardross St W6...39 A3
Cardwell Rd **3** N7..14 A4
Career Ct **3** SE16...40 C4
Carew Cl N7.......5 B2
Carew Ct **14** SE14..50 C4
Carew Ho SW16...74 C1

Carew St SE5......48 B1
Carey Ct **29** SE5...48 B3
Carey Gdns SW8..**171** B3
Carey La EC2.....**108** C2
Carey Pl SW1....**147** B3
Carey St WC2....**107** A1
Carfax Pl SW4.....61 C3
Carfree Cl **3** N1...14 C1
Cargill Rd SW18...71 B3
Carinthia Ct **5**
SE8............41 A2
Carisbrooke Ct
Acton W3........37 B4
1 Streatham
SW16...........74 B1
Carisbrooke Gdns
SE15...........49 B3
Carisbrooke Ho
TW10...........54 C2
Carker's La
Crouch End N19...4 C4
Gospel Oak NW5...13 A3
Carleton Gdns
N19............13 B3
Carleton Rd N7....13 C4
Carlile Cl E3......26 B3
Carlile Ho SE1...**137** C1
Carlingford Rd
NW3............11 C4
Carlisle Ave
Acton W3........29 A3
Whitechapel EC3..**110** C1
Carlisle Ho SE5....4 B1
Carlisle La SE1...**135** A2
Carlisle Pl SW1..**132** C1
Carlisle Rd
Finsbury Pk N4....5 C4
Kilburn NW6.....23 A4
Carlisle St W1....**105** B1
Carlisle Wlk **6** E8..16 B2
Carlos Pl W1.....**118** A3
Carlow St NW1....**82** C2
Carlson Ct SW13...58 B3
Carlton Cl NW3....1 C2
Carlton Ct
Brixton SW9......48 A2
Kilburn NW6......78 B2
8 Willesden NW2....9 B2
Carlton Dr SW15...58 A2
Carlton Gdns
SW1...........**119** B1
Carlton Gr SE15...50 A2
Carlton Hill NW8...**78** C2
Carlton Ho
5 Kilburn NW6...23 B3
Kilburn NW6.....23 C3
Marylebone W1..**103** A2
Carlton House Terr
SW1...........**119** C2
Carlton Lo N4......5 C4
Carlton Mans
Brixton SW9......62 C3
Cricklewood NW2....9 C3
Kensington W14..**126** B4
Maida Vale W9....**88** B4
5 South Hampstead
NW6............10 C1
Stamford Hill N16....7 B3
Carlton Prim Sch
NW5............12 C3
Carlton Rd
Acton W4........37 C4
Finsbury Pk N4....5 C4
Mortlake SW14....55 B3
Carlton Sq **1** E1...25 C1
Carlton St SW1...**119** B3

Carltons The **5**
SW15...........58 B2
Carlton Tower Pl
SW1...........**131** A2
Carlton Vale NW6..23 C3
Carlton Vale Inf Sch
NW6...........23 B2
Carlyle Ho
4 Camberwell
SE5............48 B3
Chelsea SW3....**157** C3
12 Stoke Newington
N16............7 A1
Carlyle Mans
SW3...........**158** A3
Carlyle Mews **2**
E1............25 C1
Carlyle Pl SW15...57 C3
Carlyle Rd **1**
NW10...........20 C4
Carlyle's Ho SW3.**158** A3
Carlyle Sq SW3...**143** C1
Carmalt Gdns
SW15...........57 B3
Carmarthen Ho **6**
SW15...........69 B4
Carmarthen Pl
SE1............**138** A4
Carmel Ct W8...**128** A4
Carmelite St EC4..**121** C4
Carmel Lo SW6...**155** B4
Carmen St E14.....34 A3
Carmichael Cl **8**
SW11...........59 C4
Carmichael Ct **5**
SW13...........46 B1
Carmichael Ho **7**
E14............34 B2
Carmichael Mews
SW18...........71 C4
Carminia Rd SW17..73 A2
Carnaby St W1...**104** C1
Carnac St SE21,
SE27...........75 C1
Carna Ct TW9.....54 A4
Carnegie Ho NW3...2 C1
Carnegie Pl SW19..69 C1
Carnegie St N1....85 A3
Carnicot Ho **9**
SE15...........50 A2
Carnoustie Dr N1..14 B1
Carnwath Ho SW6..59 A4
Carnwath Rd SW6..59 A4
Caroline Cl
Bayswater W2...**114** B3
Streatham SW16...74 B1
Caroline Ho
Bayswater W2...**114** B3
20 Hammersmith
W6............39 B1
Caroline Martyn Ho **8**
N19............4 C4
Caroline Pl
Bayswater W2...**114** B3
Clapham SW11..**169** C1
Caroline Pl Mews
W2............**114** B3
Caroline St E1....32 C3
Caroline Terr
SW1...........**145** B3
Caroline Wlk W6..**154** A3
Carol St NW1.....**82** C4
Caronia Ct **4**
SE16...........41 A2

Carpenter Ho
11 Tower Hamlets
E14............**33** C4
5 Tufnell Pk N19...13 C4
Carpenters Ct
NW1...........**82** C4
Carpenter's Pl
SW4............61 C3
Carpenters Prim Sch
E15...........**27** B4
Carradale Ho **2**
E14............34 B3
Carrara Cl **13** SW9..63 A3
Carrara Wharf
SW6............58 A4
Carriage Dr E
SW11..........**159** C2
Carriage Drive E
SW11..........**159** C2
Carriage Drive N SW11,
SW8...........**159** C3
Carriage Dr N
Battersea SW8,
SW11..........**158** C2
Battersea SW8,
SW11..........**159** C3
Carriage Dr S
SW11..........**169** B4
Carriage Dr W
SW11..........**158** C1
Carrick Ho
Islington N7......14 B2
Kennington SE11..**150** A2
Carrick Mews SE8..51 C4
Carrington Ct
SW11...........60 A3
Carrington Ho
W1...........**118** A1
Carrington Lo **3**
TW10...........54 A2
Carrington Rd
TW10...........54 C3
Carrington St W1.**118** A1
Carroll Cl NW5....13 A4
Carron Cl E14.....34 A3
Carroun Rd SW8..**162** C2
Carr St **11** E14.....33 A3
Carslake Rd SW15...57 B1
Carson Rd
Dulwich SE21.....75 C2
Newham E16.....35 C4
Carter Ct EC4....**108** B1
Carteret Ho **3**
W12............30 A2
Carteret St SW1..**133** B2
Carteret Way SE8..41 A2
Carter Ho
1 London SW2....62 C2
Spitalfields E1...**110** C3
Carter La EC4....**108** B1
Carter Pl SE17...**151** A1
Carter's Cl **1** N12...5 C2
Carters St SE17..**151** C1
Carthew Rd W6...39 A3
Carthew Villas W6..39 A3
Carthusian St EC1.**108** C4
Cartier Circ E14....34 B1
Carting La WC2...**120** B3

Cartmel NW1..... _92_ C4

Carton Ho
4 Bermondsey
SE16........... _139_ B2
3 Shepherd's Bush
W11...........30 C2

Cartoon Mus The
WC1........... _106_ A3

Cartwright Gdns
WC1...........94 A3

Cartwright Ho
SE1........... _137_ A1

Cartwright St E1. _125_ A3

Cartwright Way
SW13...........47 A3

Carvel Ho E14.....42 B1
Carver Cl W4.....37 B3
Carver Rd SE24.....63 B1
Carville Cres TW8..36 A2
Caryl Ho W9.......69 C3
Carysfort Rd N16..15 C4
Casby Ho **7** SE16 _139_ B2
Casella Rd SE14.....50 C3
Casey Cl NW8.....90 B3
Casino Ave SE24.....63 C2
Caspian Ho **11** E1..32 C4
Caspian St SE5.....48 C3
Cassandra Ct **7**
NW2...........9 B2
Cass Bsns Sch EC1 _97_ B1
Cassell Ho **21**
SW9........... _172_ B2
Casserley Ho W4...37 C3
Cass Ho **2** E9.....17 C2
Cassidy Rd SW6.. _155_ B1
Cassilis Rd E14.....41 C4
Cassinghurst SE24..63 C2
Cassland Rd E9.....17 C2
Casson Ho **1** E1.. _111_ B4
Casson St E1..... _111_ B3
Castalia Sq **6** E14..42 B4
Castellain Mans
W9...........88 A2
Castellain Rd W9...88 A2
Castell Ho **11** SE8.. _51_ C3
Castello Ave SW15..57 B2
Castelnau SW13.....47 A3
Castelnau Gdns
SW13...........47 A4
Castelnau Mans
SW13...........47 A4
Castelnau Row
SW13...........47 A4
Casterbridge
Kilburn NW6..... _78_ B4
3 Notting Hill W11.. _31_ C3
Casterton St E3.....27 A2
Castleacre W2.... _102_ A1
Castle Baynard St
EC4........... _122_ C4
Castlebrook Cl **1**
SE11........... _150_ A4
Castle Cl
12 Acton W3.....37 B4
Homerton E9.......18 A3
South Acton W3.....37 A4
Wimbledon SW19...69 C1
Castlecombe Dr
SW19...........69 C4
Castle Ct EC3.... _109_ C1
Castleden Ho
NW6...........11 C1
Castleford Ct NW8. _89_ C2

Castlefrank Ho **20**
N1...........24 A2 _98_ B4
Castlegate TW9.....54 B4
Castlehaven Rd
NW1...........13 A1
Castle Ho
Newington SE1.. _150_ C4
South Lambeth
SW8........... _162_ B2
Castle Ind Est
SE17........... _150_ C4
Castle La SW1.... _132_ C2
Castlemaine
SW11........... _169_ A2
Castlemaine St **2**
E1...........32 A4
Castle Mead SE5... _48_ B3
Castle Mews NW1..13 A2
Castle Pl **4**
8 Acton W4.......38 A2
Camden Town NW1. _13_ A2
Castle Rd NW1.....13 A2
Castlereagh St
W1........... _102_ C2
Castleton Ho **3**
E14...........42 B2
Castleton Rd
SW14........... _140_ B1
Castleview Cl N4...6 B2
Castle Way SW19...69 C1
Castlewood Ho
NW1........... _105_ C2
Castle Yd
Highgate N6.......3 C4
Lambeth SE1.... _122_ B2
Castor La E14.....34 A2
Catalpa Ct SE13.....67 C1
Caterham Rd SE13..67 C4
Catesby Ho **23** E9.. _17_ B1
Catesby St SE17.. _151_ C3
Cathay Ho SE16.....40 A4
Cathay St SE16.....40 A4
Cathcart Hill N19...4 B1
Cathcart Rd SW10 _156_ C4
Cathcart St NW5...13 A2
Cathedral Ct EC4.. _108_ B1
Cathedral Lo EC1.. _108_ C4
Cathedral Sch of St
Saviour & St Mary
Overie Prim Sch
SE1........... _137_ A4
Cathedral St SE1. _123_ B2
Cathedral Wlk
SW1........... _132_ C2
Catherall Rd N5,
N16...........6 B1
Catherine Baird Ct **12**
SW12...........73 A4
Catherine Dr TW9..54 A3
Catherine Gr SE10. _52_ A2
Catherine Griffiths Ct
EC1...........95 C2
Catherine Ho **8**
N1........... _24_ A4
Catherine Pl SW1 _132_ C2
Catherine Wheel Alley
E1........... _110_ B3
Catherine Wheel Yd
SW1........... _118_ C1
Catherwood Ct N1. _87_ B1
Cathles Rd SW12...61 A1
Cathnor Rd W12.....39 A4
Catlin St SE16.....40 A1
Catman Ho N4.....5 B3
Cato St W1.......61 C3

Cator St
Camberwell SE15..... _49_ B3
Camberwell SE15..... _49_ B4
Cato St W1....... _102_ B2
Catton St WC1.... _106_ C3
Caughley Ho
SE11........... _135_ B1
Caulfield Ct **18**
NW1...........13 B1
Caulfield Rd SE15.. _50_ A1
Causeway The
SW18...........59 A2
Causton Cotts **3**
E14...........33 A3
Causton Ho SE5.....48 B3
Causton Rd N6.....4 A4
Causton St SW1.. _147_ C2
Cautley Ave SW4...61 B2
Cavalry Gdns
SW15...........58 B2
Cavaye Ho SW10.. _157_ A4
Cavaye Pl SW10.. _143_ A1
Cavell Ct **3** N19.....4 B2
Cavell Ho **4** N1.....24 A4
Cavell St E1.......32 A4
Cavendish Ave
NW8...........79 C1
Cavendish Cl
Brondesbury NW6.. _10_ B2
3 Putney SW15.....57 C2
St John's Wood
NW8...........89 C4
Cavendish Coll
WC1........... _105_ B4
Cavendish Ct EC2. _110_ B2
Cavendish Gdns
SW4...........61 B1
Cavendish Ho
South Lambeth
SW8........... _172_ A4
St John's Wood
NW8...........79 C1
Cavendish Mans
1 Clapham Pk
SW12...........61 B1
Hackney E5.......17 B3
Holborn EC1..... _95_ B1
1 West Hampstead
NW6...........10 C3
Cavendish Mews N
W1........... _104_ B3
Cavendish Mews S
W1........... _104_ B3
Cavendish Par
SW12...........61 A1
Cavendish Pl
Balham SW4.....61 A1
Brondesbury NW2.. _9_ C2
Marylebone W1.. _104_ B2
Cavendish Rd
Brondesbury NW6.. _10_ B1
Chiswick W4.....45 B2
Clapham Pk SW12.. _61_ A1
Cavendish Sch **14**
NW1...........82 B4
Cavendish Sch The
NW1...........82 B4
Cavendish Sq W1. _104_ B2
Cavendish Terr **3**
E3...........26 B2
Cavendish The
NW11...........2 A4

Caversham Ho **7**
SE15...........49 C4
Caversham Rd
NW5...........13 B2
Caversham St
SW3........... _158_ C4
Caverswall St W12. _30_ B3
Cavour Ho SE17.. _150_ B2
Cawdor Cr E23.....26 C2
Caxton Gr E3.......27 A2
Caxton Hall SW1. _133_ B2
Caxton Rd W12.....39 C4
Caxton St N E16.....35 B3
Caxton St SW1.... _133_ B2
Caxton Wlk WC2.. _105_ C1
Cayford Ho **1**
NW3...........12 B3
Cayley Prim Sch **22**
E14...........33 A3
Cayton Pl EC1.... _97_ B3
Cayton St EC1.... _97_ B3
Cazenove Mans **1**
N16...........7 C2
Cazenove Rd N16...7 C2
Cecil Ct
Chelsea SW10.. _156_ C4
South Hampstead
NW6...........11 A1
St James SE27.. _120_ A3
Cecilia Rd E8.....16 C3
Cecil Mans **2**
SW17...........72 C2
Cecil Rd
Acton W3.......28 B4
Harlesden NW10.. _21_ A4
Cecil Rhodes Ho
NW1...........83 B2
Cedar Cl
Old Ford E3.....26 B4
West Norwood
SE21...........75 B2
Cedar Ct
Islington N1.....15 B1
Marylebone W1.. _102_ B2
Mortlake SW14.....45 B3
Wimbledon SW19...69 C1
Cedar Gr W5.......36 A3
Cedar Ho
5 Cubitt Town
E14...........42 B4
Kensington W8.. _128_ A2
New Cross Gate
SE14...........50 C2
7 Richmond TW9.. _45_ A2
16 Rotherhithe
SE16...........40 C4
Cedar Lo
Brondesbury NW2.. _10_ B2
Fulham SW6..... _47_ C2
Cedarne Rd SW6.. _156_ A1
Cedar Rd NW2.....9 B4
Cedars Cl SW13.....47 A3
Cedars Ct SW15.....57 C4
Cedars Ho **4** SW2. _62_ B3
Cedars Mews SW4..61 A3
Cedars Rd
Barnes SW13.....46 C1
Clapham SW4.....61 A3
Cedars The E9..... _17_ C1
Cedar Terr TW9.....54 A3
Cedar Way NW1.. _83_ B4
Cedric Chambers
NW8...........89 B2
Celandine Cl E3,
E14...........33 C4
Celandine Dr E8.. _16_ B1

Celbridge Mews
W2........... _100_ B2
Celestial Gdns
SE13...........67 C3
Celia Biarmi Ho
E1........... _110_ C4
Celia Ct **7** TW9... _44_ B2
Celia Ho **10** N1.....24 A3
Celia Rd N19.....13 B4
Celtic St E14.....34 A4
Cenacle Cl NW3.....1 C1
Cenotaph SW1.... _134_ A4
Centaur Ct **3**
TW8...........36 A1
Centaur St SE1.. _135_ A2
Central Ave SW11. _159_ A1
Central Bsns Ctr
NW10...........8 A3
Central Foundation
Boys' Sch EC2... _97_ C2
Central Foundation
Lower Girls Sch The
E3...........26 A2
Central Foundation
Upper Girls Sch The
7 E3........... _26_ B3
Central Ho E15... _27_ B3
Central Middlesex
Hospl NW10...... _20_ B2
Central Par W3.....37 A4
Central St Martins
Coll EC1....... _95_ C1
Central St Martins
College of Art &
Design N1..... _84_ A3
Central St Martins
Coll of Art & Design
W1........... _105_ C1
Central St Martins
Coll of Art & Design
(The London Inst)
WC1........... _106_ A3
Central Sch of Ballet
EC1...........95 C1
Central Sch of Speech
& Drama NW3..... _11_ C1
Central St Martins
Coll N1....... _96_ C1
Central Way NW10. _20_ B2
Centre Acad **1**
SW11...........59 C3
Centre Ave W3.....28 C1
Centre Bldg SE17 _151_ A4
Centre Hts **5**
NW3...........11 C1
Centre Point **3**
SE1........... _153_ B2
Centre Point Ho
WC2........... _105_ C2
Centre St E2.....25 A3
Centurion Bldg
SW8........... _160_ A3
Centurion Cl N7.. _14_ B1
Centurion La E3... _26_ B3
Century Ho SE13.. _52_ A1
Cephas Ave E1.....25 B1
Cephas Ho **5** E1.. _25_ B1
Cephas St E1.....25 B1
Cerise Rd SE15.....49 C2
Cerney Mews W2. _115_ B4
Cervantes Ct **12**
W2........... _100_ C1
Cester St E2.....24 C4
Ceylon Rd
6 Hammersmith
W14...........39 C3
Kensington W14.. _126_ A1

Chabot Dr SE15 ....65 A4
Chadacre Ho 10
SW9 ....63 A3
Chadbourn St E14..34 A4
Chadston Ho 11
N1 ....15 A1
Chadswell WC1......94 B3
Chadwell St EC1....95 C4
Chadwick Cl SW15..68 B4
Chadwick Rd
Harlesden NW10 ....21 B4
Peckham SE15 ......49 B1
Chadwick St SW1. 133 B1
Chadworth Ho
Finsbury EC1 ....96 C3
Finsbury Pk N4......6 B3
Chagford Ho
40 Bromley E3......27 A2
Marylebone NW1....90 C1
Chagford St NW1...91 A1
Chalbury Ho 8
SW9 ....62 B3
Chalbury Wlk N1...85 B2
Chalcot Cres NW1..81 A4
Chalcot Gdns NW3 .12 B2
Chalcot Mews
SW16 ....74 A1
Chalcot Rd NW1....81 B4
Chalcot Sch 21
NW1...............13 A1
Chalcot Sq NW1....12 C1
Chaldon Rd SW6 .156 B2
Chale Rd SW2 .....62 A1
Chalfont Ct NW1...91 A1
Chalfont Ho 2
SE16 ....40 A3
Chalford 7 NW3 ..11 B2
Chalford Ct 15
SW15 ....57 C2
Chalkers Cnr TW9 ..55 A4
Chalk Farm Sta
NW3 ....12 C1
Chalk Hill Rd W6 ..39 C2
Chalkwell Ho 10
E1 ....32 C3
Challenge Cl
NW10 ....21 A4
Challenger Ho 7
E14 ....33 A2
Challice Way SW2 ..74 B3
Challoner Cres
W14 ....140 C1
Challoner Mans
W14 ....140 C1
Challoner St W14 .140 C1
Chalmers Ho 13
SW11 ....59 B4
Chalmer's Wlk 24
SE17 ....48 A4
Chalner Ho SW2...74 C3
Chaloner Ct SE1 ..137 B4
Chalsey Lodge
SE4 ....66 B3
Chalsey Rd SE4....66 B3
Chalton St NW1....83 B1
Chamberlain Cotts
SE5 ....48 C2
Chamberlain Ho 1
E1 ....32 B2
Chamberlain St 7
NW1...............12 B1
Chamberlayne Ho
3 NW10 ....22 C2
Chamberlayne Rd
NW10 ....22 B4
Chambers La NW10..9 B1

Chambers Rd N7 ...14 A1
Chambers St
SE16 ....139 C3
Chamber St E1....125 A4
Chambon Pl 7
W6 ....38 C2
Chambord Ho 24
E2 ....24 B2 99 A3
Chambord St
E2 ....24 B2 99 A3
Champion Gr SE5...63 C4
Champion Hill SE5 .49 B1
Champion Pk SE5 ..48 C1
Champlain Ho 28
W12 ....30 A2
Chancel Ct W1 ...119 B4
Chancellor Gr
SE21 ....75 B1
Chancellor Ho
South Kensington
27 Wapping E1....32 A1
Chancellor Pas
E14 ....33 C1
Chancellors' Ct
WC1 ....106 C4
Chancellor's Rd
W6 ....39 B1
Chancellors St W6..39 B1
Chancellors Wharf 21
W6 ....39 B1
Chancel St SE1 ...122 A1
Chancery Bldgs 14
E1 ....32 B2
Chancery Ho WC2 107 B3
Chancery La EC4 ..107 B2
Chancery Lane Sta
WC1 ....107 B3
Chancery Mews
SW17 ....72 A2
Chance St
E2 ....24 B1 98 C2
Chandler Ave E16 ..35 C4
Chandlers Mews
E14 ....41 C4
Chandler St E1.....32 A1
Chandlers Way 11
SE24 ....74 C4
Chandler Way
SE15 ....49 B3
Chandley Ho 28
E1 ....111 B1
Chandos Pl WC2 ..120 A3
Chandos Rd
Cricklewood NW2.....9 B3
Old Oak Comm
NW10 ....21 A1
Stratford New Town
E15 ....19 C3
Chandos St W1....104 B3
Chandos Way NW11 .2 A3
Change Alley EC3 .109 C1
Channel Gate Rd
NW10 ....21 A2
Channel Ho E14 ...33 A4
Channel Sea Bsns Ctr
E15 ....27 C4
Channelsea Rd
E15 ....27 C4
Channing Jun Sch
N6................4 A3
Chantrey Rd SW9 ..62 B4
Chantry Cl W9.....23 B1
Chantry Cres NW10..8 B2
Chantry Ct SW6 ...58 A4

Chantry Sq W8 ...128 A1
Chantry St N1.....86 B3
Chant Sq E15......19 C1
Chant St E15......19 C1
Chapel Cl NW10 ....8 B2
Chapel Ct SE1 ....137 B4
Chapel House St
E14 ....42 A2
Chapel Mkt N1 ....85 B2
Chapel Pl
Islington N1 ....85 C2
Marylebone W1 ...104 A1
20 Shoreditch
EC2..........24 A2 98 A3
Chapel Side W2 ..114 A3
Chapel St
Paddington NW1 ..102 A3
Westminster SW1 .131 C3
Chapleton Ho
SW2 ....62 C2
Chaplin Cl SE1 ...136 A4
Chaplin Ho 6
SW9 ....62 C3
Chaplin Rd NW2 ...8 C2
Chaplow Cl SW6 ..166 C1
Chapman Ho
28 Stepney E1 .....32 A3
2 West Norwood
SE27 ....75 A1
Chapman Rd E9 ...18 B2
Chapmans Park Ind
Est NW10 ....8 B2
Chapman Sq
SW19 ....69 C2
Chapman St E1.....32 A2
Chapone Pl W1 ...105 B1
Chapter Cl 13 W4..37 B3
Chapter House &
Jewel Twr SW1 ...134 A2
Chapter Rd
Kennington SE17 ..150 B1
Willesden NW2 .....8 C3
Chapter St SW1 ..147 B3
Chara Rd 8 W4....45 C4
Charcot Ho SW9...56 B1
Charcroft Ct 11
W14 ....39 C4
Chard Ho 7 N7....5 B2
Chardin Ho 30
SW9 ....173 C4
Chardin Rd 11 W4 .38 A2
Chardmore Rd N16 ..7 C3
Charecroft Way
W12 ....39 C4
Charfield Ct W9 ...88 B1
Charford Rd E16...35 C4
Chargrove Cl 24
SE16 ....40 C4
Charing Cross
SW1 ....120 A2
Charing Cross Hospl
W6 ....39 C1
Charing Cross Sta
WC2 ....120 B2
Chariot Cl 3 E3....26 C4
Charlbert Ct NW8 ..80 A2
Charlbert St NW8 ..80 A2
Charles Allen Ho
EC1 ....95 B4
Charles Auffray Ho 30
E1 ....32 B4
Charles Barry Cl
SW4 ....61 B4

Charles Burton Ct
E5 ....18 A4
Charles Coveney Rd
4 SE15 ....49 B2
Charles Darwin Ho 5
E2 ....25 A2
Charles Dickens Ho 1
E2 ....25 A2
Charles Dickens Mus
The WC1 ....95 A1
Charles Dickens Prim
Sch SE1 ....152 C3
Charles Edward
Brooke Sch 11
SW9 ....48 A2
Charles Edward
Brooke Sch (Dennen
Site) 10 SE5 ......48 B2
Charles Flemwell
Mews 2 E16 ....35 C1
Charles Haller St 25
SW2 ....74 C4
Charles Harrod Ct
SW13 ....47 B4
Charles Hocking Ho
8 W3..............37 B4
Charles II Pl SW3 144 C1
Charles II St SW1 .119 B2
Charles La NW8 ....80 A2
Charles Lamb Ct
N1 ....86 B2
Charles Mackenzie Ho
7 SE16 ....153 C4
Charles Pl NW1 ....93 A3
Charles Rowan Ho
WC1 ....95 B3
Charles Sq N1 .....97 C3
Charles St
Barnes SW13 ....46 A1
Mayfair W1 ....118 A2
Chelsea
SE17 ....151 A3
Charles Townsend Ho
EC1 ....96 A2
Charles Utton Ct
E8 ....16 C4
Charlesworth Ho 6
E14 ....33 C3
Charleville Ct
SW5 ....140 C1
Charleville Mans
W14 ....140 B1
Charleville Rd
W14 ....140 C1
Charlotte Ct 10
W6 ....38 C2
Charlotte Despard
Ave SW11 ....169 C3
Charlotte Ho 9
W6 ....39 B1
Charlotte Mews
Marylebone W1 ...105 A4
North Kensington
W10 ....30 C4
West Kensington
W14 ....140 A4
Charlotte Pl
Marylebone W1 ...105 A3
Westminster SW1 .146 C3
Charlotte Rd
Barnes SW13 ....46 B2
Shoreditch
EC2 ....24 A1 98 A2

Charlotte Row
SW4 ....61 B4
Charlotte Sharman
Prim Sch SE1 ....136 A1
Charlotte Sq 5
TW10 ....54 B1
Charlotte St W1 ..105 A4
Charlotte Terr N1 ..85 A3
Charlotte Turner Prim
Sch SE8 ....51 C4
Charlton Ct
22 Hackney E2....24 B4
17 Kentish Town
N7.................5 B2
Charlton Ho
5 Brentford
TW8 ....44 A4
Somers Town NW1 ..93 B4
Charlton King's Rd
NW5 ....13 C3
Charlton Pl N1 ....86 A2
Charlton Rd NW10 .21 A4
Charlton Way SE10,
SE3 ....53 A2
Charlwood Ho
Richmond TW9 .....45 A3
1 Streatham SW2 .74 B3
Westminster SW1 .147 B3
Charlwood Pl
SW1 ....147 A3
Charlwood Rd
SW15 ....57 C3
Charlwood St
SW1 ....147 A2
Charlwood Terr 6
SW15 ....57 C3
Charman Ho
16 London SW8 ...62 C1
South Lambeth
SW8 ....162 A2
Charmian Ho 18
N1 ....24 A3
Charmouth Ct
TW10 ....54 B2
Charmouth Ho
SW8 ....162 C2
Charnock Ho 22
W12 ....30 A2
Charnwood Gdns
E14 ....41 C2
Charrington Ho 42
E1 ....25 B1
Charrington St
NW1...............83 B2
Charter Bldgs 14
SE10 ....52 A2
Charter Ct
Finsbury Pk N4.....5 C3
Marylebone NW1 ..102 B3
Charter Ho WC2 ..106 B1
Charterhouse Bldgs
EC1 ....96 C1
Charterhouse Mews
EC1 ....108 B4
Charterhouse Rd
E8.................16 C3
Charterhouse Sq
EC1 ....108 B4
Charterhouse Square
Sch The EC1 .....108 B4
Charterhouse St
EC1 ....108 A3
Charterhouse Works
SW18 ....59 B3

Charteris Rd
  Finsbury Pk N4........5 C3
  Kilburn NW6..........23 B4
Charteris Sp Ctr
  NW6..................23 C4
Charter Sch SE24.....63 C2
Chartes Ho SE1.....138 B2
Chartfield Ave
  SW15.................57 B2
Chartfield Sq
  SW15.................57 C2
Chartham Ct 2
  SW9..................62 C4
Chartham Gr SE27...75 A1
Chartham Ho SE1...137 C2
Chart House Ho 5
  E14..................42 A1
Chartridge SE17......48 C4
Chart St N1............97 C4
Chartwell 28
  SW19.................69 C3
Chase Ct SW3........130 C1
Chase Ctr The
  NW10.................20 C2
Chaseley Ct W4........37 A1
Chaseley St E14......33 A3
Chasemore Ho
  SW6.................154 B2
Chase Rd NW10......20 C1
Chase Road Trad Est
  NW10.................20 C2
Chase The SW4.......61 A4
Chater Ho 6 E2.......25 C2
Chatfield Rd SW11...59 B4
Chatham Cl SW1.....60 B2
Chatham Ho 7
  SE5..................49 A1
Chatham Pl E9........17 B2
Chatham Rd SW11...60 B2
Chatham St SE17....151 C4
Chatsworth Ct
  Brondesbury NW2.....9 C2
  Clapton Pk E5........17 C4
  Earl's Ct W8........141 B4
Chatsworth Est E5...17 C4
Chatsworth Gdns
  W3...................28 A1
Chatsworth Lo 1
  W4...................37 C1
Chatsworth Rd
  Brondesbury NW2.....9 C2
  Chiswick W4..........45 B4
  Clapton Pk E5........17 C4
Chatsworth Way
  SE27.................75 B1
Chattenden Ho 8
  N4.....................6 C4
Chatterton Ct TW9...44 B1
Chatterton Rd N4......6 A1
Chatto Rd SW11......60 B2
Chaucer Ave TW9....44 C1
Chaucer Ct 7 N16..16 A4
Chaucer Dr SE1.....153 A3
Chaucer Ho SW1...146 C1
Chaucer Rd
  Acton W3.............28 B1
  Herne Hill SE24.....63 A2
Chauldon Ho EC1....97 C3
Cheadle Ct NW8......89 C2
Cheadle Ho 8
  E14..................33 B3
Cheam St 6 SE15....65 A4
Cheapside EC2.....109 A1
Chearsley SE17.....151 A4

Cheddington Ho 9
  E2...................24 C4
Chedworth Cl E16...35 B3
Chedworth Ho 2
  E5.....................7 C2
Cheesemans Terr
  W14.................140 C1
Chelmer Rd E9........17 C3
Chelmsford Cl W6...47 C4
Chelmsford Ho 5
  N7....................14 B4
Chelmsford Sq
  NW10.................22 B4
CHELSEA.............144 B1
Chelsea Antiques Mkt
  SW3.................144 B1
Chelsea Barracks
  SW1.................145 C2
Chelsea Bridge
  SW1.................160 A4
Chelsea Bridge Rd
  SW1.................145 C1
Chelsea Cl NW10....20 C4
Chelsea Cloisters
  SW3.................144 B3
Chelsea Coll of Art &
  Design SW1.......148 A2
Chelsea Cres
  Brondesbury NW2...10 B2
  Chelsea SW10.......167 A3
Chelsea Ct SW3.....159 B4
Chelsea Emb
  SW3.................158 C3
Chelsea Est SW3....158 C3
Chelsea Farm Ho
  SW10................157 C3
Chelsea Gate
  SW1.................145 C1
Chelsea Gdns
  SW1.................145 C1
Chelsea Harbour
  Design Ctr
  SW10................167 A4
Chelsea Harbour Dr
  SW10................167 A4
Chelsea Harbour Pier
  SW10................167 A4
Chelsea Ind Coll
  SW6.................156 A1
Chelsea Lo SW3.....159 A4
Chelsea Manor Ct
  SW3.................158 B4
Chelsea Manor Gdns
  SW3.................144 B1
Chelsea Manor St
  SW3.................144 B1
Chelsea Manor
  Studios SW3.......144 B1
Chelsea Mus SW6..156 B2
Chelsea Park Gdns
  SW3.................157 B4
Chelsea Physic Gdn
  SW1.................158 C4
Chelsea Reach Twr
  SW10................157 B2
Chelsea Sp Ctr
  SW3.................144 B1
Chelsea Sq SW3....143 C1
Chelsea Twrs
  SW3.................158 B4
Chelsea &
  Westminster Hospl
  SW10................157 A3
Chelsfield Ho
  SE17.................152 A3

Chelsfield Point 3
  E9....................17 C1
Chelsham Ho 1
  SW4..................61 C4
Chelsham Rd SW4..61 C4
Cheltenham Pl
  10 Acton W3.......28 A1
  Acton W3............37 B4
  1 South Acton W3..37 A4
Cheltenham Rd
  SE15.................65 B2
Cheltenham Terr
  SW3.................145 A2
Chelverton Ct
  SW15.................57 C3
Chelverton Rd
  SW15.................57 C3
Chelwood Ho
  W2...................101 C1
Chelwood Nw5.......12 C3
Chelwood Ct
  SW11................167 C4
Chelwood Gdns
  TW9..................44 C1
Chenappa Cl 6
  E13..................68 C3
Cheney Ho W2......114 A4
Cheniston Gdns
  W8..................128 A2
Chepstow Cl SW15..58 A2
Chepstow Cres
  W11.................31 C2 113 B4
Chepstow Pl
  W2.................31 C2 113 C4
Chepstow Rd W2...31 C3
Chepstow Villas
  W11.................31 C2 113 B4
Chequers Ct EC1....97 B1
Chequers Ho NW8...90 A2
Chequer St EC1......97 A1
Cherbury Ct N1......87 C1
Cherbury St N1.......87 C1
Cheriton Ho 2 E5...17 A3
Cheriton Sq SW12..72 C2
Cherry Cl 7 SW2....74 C4
Cherry Ct
  Acton W3............29 A1
  5 Rotherhithe
  SE16..................33 A1
Cherry Garden Ho 7
  SE16..................40 A4
Cherry Garden Sch 1
  SE16.................153 C4
Cherry Garden St
  SE16..................40 A4
Cherry Laurel Wlk
  SW2..................62 B1
Cherry Tree Cl 11
  E9....................25 B4
Cherry Tree Ct
  1 Camden Town
  NW1....................13 B1
  11 Peckham SE15...50 A2
Cherry Tree Dr
  SW16..................74 A1
Cherrytree Ho 8
  W10...................22 C2
Cherry Trees Sch The
  22 E3..................26 C2

Cherry Tree Terr
  SE1.................138 B4
Cherry Tree Wlk
  EC1...................97 A1
Cherrywood Cl E3...26 A2
Cherrywood Dr
  SW15.................57 C2
Chertsey Ct SW14...55 A4
Chertsey Ho 37
  E2................24 B2 98 C3
Cherwell Ho NW8...89 C1
Cheryls Cl SW6......166 B4
Chesham Cl SW1...131 B1
Chesham Ct SW18..71 C4
Chesham Flats
  W1..................117 C4
Chesham Ho SW1..131 B1
Chesham Mews
  SW1.................131 B2
Chesham Pl SW1...131 B1
Chesham St SW1...131 B1
Cheshire St
  E2................24 B1 99 A2
Chesholm Rd N16....7 A1
Cheshunt Ho 9
  NW6..................78 A3
Chesil Ct
  17 Bethnal Green
  E2....................25 B3
  Chelsea SW3.......158 C4
Chesilton Rd SW6..164 C4
Chesney Ct W9......23 C1
Chesney Ho SE13...67 C3
Chesney St SW11...169 B3
Chessington Ho 10
  SW8.................171 B2
Chesson Rd W14...155 A4
Chessum Ho E8.....16 C2
Chester Ave TW10..54 B1
Chester Ct
  Barnes SW13......57 A4
  Knightsbridge
  SW1..................132 A3
  1 Richmond TW10..54 B1
Chester Close S
  NW1...................92 B4
Chester Cres E8......16 B3
Chester Ct
  Bermondsey SE8...40 C1
  4 Camberwell SE5..48 C3
  Gospel Oak NW5...12 C4
  Regent's Pk NW1...92 B3
Chesterfield Ct
  SE13...................67 B4
Chesterfield Gdns
  Greenwich SE10....52 C3
  Mayfair W1..........118 A2
Chesterfield Gr
  SE22...................64 B2
Chesterfield Hill
  W1..................118 A2
Chesterfield Ho
  Highgate N6...........3 C3
  Mayfair W1..........117 C2
Chesterfield Rd
  W4.....................45 B4
Chesterfield St
  W1..................118 A2
Chesterfield Way
  SE15...................50 B3
Chesterford Gdns
  NW3...................11 A4
Chester Gate NW1..92 B3

Chester Ho
  Dartmouth Pk N19....4 A2
  1 Deptford SE8.....51 B4
Chesterman Ct
  W4.....................46 A3
Chester Mews
  SW1..................132 A2
  2 Richmond TW10...92 A4
Chester Rd
  Dartmouth Pk N19....4 A2
  Regent's Pk NW1...92 A4
Chester Row SW1..145 C4
Chester Sq SW1....146 A4
Chester Sq Mews
  SW1.................132 A1
Chester St
  Bethnal Green
  E2................24 C1 99 C2
  Westminster SW1..131 C2
Chester Terr NW1...92 A4
Chesterton Cl
  SW18.................58 C2
Chesterton Ct 3 W3..37 A3
Chesterton Ho
  20 Battersea
  SW11.................59 C4
  8 Kensal Town
  W10...................31 A4
Chesterton Prim Sch
  SW11................169 B3
Chesterton Rd
  W10...................31 A4
Chesterton Sq
  W8...................141 B3
Chester Way SE11.149 C3
Chestnut Alley
  SW6.................155 A3
Chestnut Ave 11
  SW14..................55 C4
Chestnut Cl
  New Cross Gate
  SE14...................51 B2
  1 Stoke Newington
  N16.....................6 C2
Chestnut Ct SW6...155 A4
Chestnut Gr SW12..72 C3
Chestnut Grove Sch
  6 SW12...............72 C3
Chestnut Ho
  1 Acton W4..........38 A2
  Brockley SE4..........66 B4
  7 Maitland Pk
  NW3...................12 B2
  West Norwood
  SE27...................75 B1
Chestnut Rd SE21,..
  SE27...................75 B1
Chestnuts The 1
  N5......................15 A3
Chettle Cl SE1......137 B2
Chetwode Ho NW8..90 A2
Chetwode Rd
  SW17...................72 B1
Chetwynd Rd NW5...4 A1
Cheval Ct SW15......57 A3
Cheval Pl SW7......130 B2
Cheval St E14.........41 C3
Chevening Rd
  Cubitt Town SE10...43 B1
  Kilburn NW6..........23 B4
Cheverell Ho 28
  E2....................24 C3
Cheverton Rd N19...4 C3
Chevet St E9..........18 A3
Chevington NW2......10 B2
Cheviot Ct 18 SE14..50 B3

Cheviot Gate NW2 . . . . 1 A2
Cheviot Gdns NW2 . . . . 1 A2
Cheviot Ho N16 . . . . . . 7 B3
Chevron Cl E16 . . . . . . 35 C3
Cheylesmore Ho
SW1 . . . . 146 A2
Cheyne Ct SW3 . . 158 C4
Cheyne Gdns
SW3 . . . . 158 B3
Cheyne Mews
SW3 . . . . 158 B3
Cheyne Pl SW3 . . 158 C4
Cheyne Row SW3 . . 158 A3
Cheyne Wlk SW10 157 B2
Cheyney Ho **2** E9 . .17 C2
Chichele Mans
NW2 . . . . .9 C3
Chichele Rd NW2 . . . . .9 C3
Chicheley St SE1 . 135 A4
Chichester Ct **2**
NW1 . . . . .13 B1
Chichester Ho
NW6 . . . . .23 C3
Chichester Rd
Bayswater W2 . . . . 100 B4
Kilburn NW6 . . . . . . .23 C3
Chichester Rents
WC2 . . . . 107 B2
Chichester St
SW1 . . . . 147 A1
Chichester Way
E14 . . . . .42 C2
Chicksand Ho **14**
E1 . . . . 111 B4
Chicksand St E1 . . 111 A3
Chicksand Street
E1 . . . . 111 B3
Chiddingstone
SE13 . . . . .67 B2
Chiddingstone St
SW6 . . . . 165 C2
Chigwell Ct **1** E9 . .18 A2
Chigwell Hill E1 . . . .32 A2
Chiham Ho **5**
SE15 . . . . .50 B4
Chilcombe Ho **6**
SW15 . . . . .68 C4
Chilcot Cl **11** E14 . . .34 A3
Childebert Rd
SW17 . . . . .73 A2
Childeric Prim Sch
SE14 . . . . .51 A3
Childeric Rd SE14 . .51 A3
Childerley St
SW6 . . . . 164 B4
Childers St SE8 . . . .51 B4
Child La SE10 . . . . . . .43 B3
Childrens House
Upper Sch **15** N1 . .16 A2
CHILD'S HILL 1 C2
Child's Hill Sch
NW2 . . . . .1 A1
Child's Mews
SW5 . . . . 141 C3
Child's Pl SW5 . . . 141 C3
Child's St SW5 . . . 141 C3
Child's Wlk SW5 . . 141 C3
Chilham Ct **13**
SW9 . . . . .62 C4
Chilham Ho SE1 . . 137 C2
Chillington Dr
SW11 . . . . .59 C3
Chillingworth Rd
N7 . . . . .14 C3
Chiltern Ct
18 Deptford SE14 . .50 B3

Chiltern Ct continued
Marylebone NW1 . . **91 A1**
Chiltern Ho
Camberwell SE17 . . .48 C4
4 Kensal Town
W10 . . . . .31 A4
5 Stamford Hill N16 . .7 B3
Chiltern Rd E3 . . . . .26 C1
Chiltern St W1 . . . 103 B4
Chilton Gr SE8 . . . . .41 A2
Chilton Rd TW9 . . . .54 C4
Chilton St
E2 . . . . .24 B1 **99 A2**
Chilver St SE10 . . . . .43 B1
Chilworth Ct **5**
SW19 . . . . .69 C3
Chilworth Mews
W2 . . . . 101 B1
Chilworth St W2 . . 101 A1
Chimney Ct **22** E1 . .32 A1
China Ct **11** E1 . . . . .32 A1
China Hall Mews **16**
SE16 . . . . .40 B3
China Mews **17**
SW2 . . . . .74 B4
Chindit Ho **9** N16 . .15 C4
Ching Ct WC2 . . . . 106 A1
Chinnocks Wharf
E14 . . . . .33 A2
Chipka St E14 . . . . . .42 B4
Chipley St SE14 . . . .51 A4
Chippendale Ho
SW1 . . . . 146 B1
Chippenham Gdns
NW6 . . . . .23 C2
Chippenham Mews
W9 . . . . .23 C1
Chippenham Rd
W9 . . . . .23 C1
Chip St SW4 . . . . .61 C3
Chipstead Ho **5**
SW2 . . . . .74 A3
Chipstead St SW6 165 C2
Chirk Ct SE4 . . . . .51 B1
Chisenhale Prim Sch
16 E3 . . . . .26 A3
Chisenhale Rd E3 . .26 A3
Chisholm Ct **1**
W6 . . . . .38 C1
Chisholm Rd **13**
TW10 . . . . .54 B1
Chisledon Wlk E9 . .18 B2
Chislehurst Rd
TW10 . . . . .54 A2
Chislet **5** NW5 . . . .12 C2
Chiswell St
Barbican EC1 . . . . . 109 B4
Camberwell SE5 . . . .48 C3
CHISWICK 38 B1
Chiswick & Bedford
Park Prep Sch **5**
W4 . . . . .38 A2
Chiswick Common Rd
W4 . . . . .37 C2
Chiswick Com Sch
W4 . . . . .45 C3
Chiswick Green
Studios **1** W4 . . . .37 B2
Chiswick High Rd
W4 . . . . .36 C1
Chiswick High Road
(North Circular Rd)
W4 . . . . .36 C1
Chiswick Ho W4 . . . .45 C4
Chiswick La W4 . . . .38 A1
Chiswick La S W4 . .46 B4

Chiswick Mall W4 . .38 B1
W4 . . . . .46 B4
Chiswick Park Sta
W4 . . . . .37 A2
Chiswick Pier W4 . .46 B3
Chiswick Plaza
W4 . . . . .45 B4
Chiswick Quay W4 . .45 B2
Chiswick Rd W4 . . . .37 B2
Chiswick Rdbt W4 . .36 C1
Chiswick Sq W4 . . . .46 A4
Chiswick Sta W4 . . .45 B3
Chiswick Staithe
W4 . . . . .45 B2
Chiswick Terr **6**
W4 . . . . .37 B2
Chiswick Village
W4 . . . . .45 A4
Chiswick Wharf
W4 . . . . .46 B4
Chitty St W1 . . . . . . 105 A4
Chivalry Rd SW11 . .60 A2
Chivelston **27**
SW19 . . . . .69 C3
Chobham Gdns
SW19 . . . . .69 C2
Chobham Rd E15 . . .19 C3
Cholmeley Cres N6 . .4 A4
Cholmeley Lo N6 . . . .4 A3
Cholmeley Pk N6 . . . .4 A4
Cholmley Gdns
NW6 . . . . .10 C3
Cholmondeley Ave
NW10 . . . . .21 C3
Chopin's Ct **18** E1 . .32 A1
Chopwell Cl E15 . . . .19 C1
Choumert Gr SE15 . .49 C1
Choumert Mews
SE15 . . . . .49 C1
Choumert Rd SE15 . .49 B1
Choumert Sq **4**
SE15 . . . . .49 C1
Chow Sq **2** E8 . . . .16 B3
Chrisp Ho SE10 . . . . .53 A4
Chrisp St E14 . . . . . . .34 A3
Christ Church
TW9 . . . . .54 B4
Christchurch Ave
NW6 . . . . .10 A1
Christ Church
Bentinck CE Prim
Sch NW1 . . . . 102 B4
Christ Church
Brondesbury CE Jun
& Inf Sch NW6 . . . .10 B1
Christchurch CE Prim
Sch SW3 . . . . 158 C4
Christ Church CE
Prim Sch
Battersea SW11 . . . .60 A4
Cubitt Town SE10 . . .43 B1
Christ Church CE
Prim Sch,
Hampstead NW3 . . . .2 B1
Christchurch CE Sch
E1 . . . . 111 C3
Christ Church Ct
1 Brondesbury Pk
NW6 . . . . .10 A1
Harlesden NW10 . . . .21 B3
Christchurch Hill
NW3 . . . . .2 C1
Christchurch Ho **2**
SW2 . . . . .74 A3
Christchurch Pas
NW3 . . . . .2 B1

Christchurch Rd
Mortlake SW14 . . . . .55 B2
Streatham SW2 . . . . .74 B3
Christ Church
Sch W1 . . . . **92 B1**
Christchurch Sq **2**
E9 . . . . .25 B4
Christchurch St
SW3 . . . . 158 C4
Christ Church
Streatham CE Prim
Sch **18** SW2 . . . . .74 B3
Christchurch Terr
SW3 . . . . 158 C4
Christchurch Way
SE10 . . . . .43 A1
Christian Ct SE16 . . .33 B1
Christian St E1 . . . 111 C1
Christie Ct
Maitland Pk NW3 . . .12 A3
1 Upper Holloway
N19 . . . . .4 C2
Christie Ho **2**
SE10 . . . . .43 B1
Christie Rd E9 . . . . . .18 A2
Christina Sq N4 . . . . .6 A3
Christina St
EC2 . . . . .24 A1 **98 A2**
Christopher Boone's
Almshouses
SE13 . . . . .67 C3
Christopher Cl
SE16 . . . . .40 C4
Christopher France
Ho **6** E1 . . . . .26 A2
Christopher Hatton
Prim Sch EC1 . . . **95 B1**
Christopher Lo **2**
N6 . . . . .4 C4
Christopher Pl
NW1 . . . . **93 C3**
Christopher St EC2 **97 C1**
Christ's Sch TW10 . .54 C2
Christ the King RC
Prim Sch N4 . . . . . . .5 B2
Christ the King Sixth
Form Coll SE13 . . . .67 A2
Chryssell Rd SW9 . 163 C2
Chubworthy St **5**
SE14 . . . . .51 A4
Chudleigh Rd
Hampstead NW6 . . . .9 C1
London SE4 . . . . . . .66 C2
Chudleigh St E1 . . . .32 C3
Chumleigh Gdns
SE5 . . . . .49 A4
Chumleigh St SE5 . .49 A4
Church App SE21 . . .75 C1
Church Ave
Camden Town
NW1 . . . . .13 A2
Mortlake SW14 . . . . .55 C4
Church Cl W8 . . . . 128 A4
Church Cres E9 . . . . .17 C1
Churchcroft Cl
SW12 . . . . .72 C4
Church Ct
Holborn EC4 . . . . . 107 C1
Rotherhithe SE16 . . .41 B4
Churchdale Cl **1**
W12 . . . . .38 C4
CHURCH END NW10 . .8 B3
Church Entry EC4 . 108 B1
Church Estate
Almshouses **3**
TW9 . . . . .54 B3

Churchfield Ho
W2 . . . . **89 B1**
Churchfield Mans
SW6 . . . . 165 A1
Churchfield Rd
W3 . . . . .28 B1
Churchfields SE10 . .52 B4
Church Garth **4**
N19 . . . . .4 C2
Church Gate SW6 . . .58 A4
Church Gr SE13 . . . . .67 A2
Church Ho EC1 . . . . **96 B2**
Church Path
Acton W3 . . . . .28 B1
Barnes SW13 . . . . . . .46 C2
Kilburn NW6 . . . . . . .23 B2
Church Rd
Acton W3 . . . . .37 B4
Barnes SW13 . . . . . . .46 C2
2 Canonbury N1 . . .15 B2
Richmond TW10,
TW9 . . . . .54 A2
Willesden NW10 . . . . .8 A1
Willesden NW3,NW11 .1 B4
Church St
Chiswick W4 . . . . . . .46 B4
Lisson Gr NW8 . . . **90 A1**
Church Street East
NW8 . . . . **89 C1**
Church Studios **10**
NW1 . . . . .13 C2
Churchward Ho
Camberwell SE17 . . .48 A4
West Kensington
SW5 . . . . 141 A1
Churchway NW1 . . **93 C4**
Church Wlk
Barnes SW13 . . . . . . .46 C2
Canonbury N16 . . . . .15 C4
Child's Hill NW2 . . . . .1 B1
Dartmouth Pk N6 . . . .3 C1
Churchyard Row
SE11 . . . . 150 B4
Churnfield **2** N4 . . . .5 C2
Churston Cl **16**
SW2 . . . . .74 C3
Churston Mans
WC1 . . . . **95 A1**
Churton Pl
Brentford W4 . . . . . . .45 A4
Pimlico SW1 . . . . . . 147 A3
Churton St SW1 . . 147 A3
Chute Ho **17** SW9 . 173 B1
Chuter Ede Ho
SW6 . . . . 155 A3
Cicada Rd SW18 . . . .59 B2

Cicely Ho NW8 . . . . . . **79** C1
Cicely Rd SE15 . . . . . **49** C2
Cinema Mus The
  SE11 . . . . **150** A3
Cinnabar Wharf
  Central [B] E1 . . . . **125** C2
Cinnabar Wharf East
  [B] E1 . . . . **125** C2
Cinnabar Wharf West
  [B] E1 . . . . **125** C2
Cinnamon Cl [B]
  SE15 . . . . **49** B3
Cinnamon Row [B]
  SW11 . . . . **59** B4
Cinnamon St E1 . . . . **32** A1
Cinnamon Wharf
  SE1 . . . . **139** A4
Circle Ho [B] E14 . . . . **34** C3
Circle The SE1 . . . . . **139** A4
Circus Ho [B] E14 . . . **89** B4
Circus Mews NW1 . . **102** C4
Circus PI EC2 . . . . . **109** C3
Circus Rd NW8 . . . . . **79** B1
Circus St SE10 . . . . . **52** B3
Cirencester St
  W2 . . . . **100** A4
Cissbury Ho [B]
  SE26 . . . . **76** C1
Citadel PI SE11 . . . . **148** C2
Citizen Ho N7 . . . . . . **14** C4
Citizen Rd N7 . . . . . . **14** C4
Citron Terr [B]
  SE15 . . . . **65** A4
Citrus Ho [B] SE8 . . . **41** B1
City Banking Coll
  SE1 . . . . **137** C4
City Bsns Coll EC1 . . **96** B3
City Bsns Ctr [B]
  SE16 . . . . **40** B4
City Central Est
  EC1 . . . . **96** C3
City Coll N1 . . . . **97** B4
City Coll of London
  The WC1 . . . . **107** A3
City Forum EC1 . . . . **96** C4
City Garden Row
  N1 . . . . **86** B1
City Gate EC1 . . . . . . **25** B1
City & Guilds of
  London Art Sch The
  SE11 . . . . **149** C1
City & Hackney Ctr for
  Mental Health
  (Hospl) E9 . . . . . . **18** A3
City Hall SE1 . . . . . **124** B1
City Harbour E14 . . . **42** A3
City & Islington Sixth
  Form Coll EC1 . . . . **96** A4
City & Islington Coll
  (Ctr for Applied
  Sciences) EC1 . . . . **96** A4
City & Islington Coll
  (Ctr for Bsns, Arts &
  Technology) [B]
  N7 . . . . **14** A4
City & Islington Coll
  (Ctr for Health,
  Social & Child Care)
  [B] N7 . . . . **14** B4
City & Islington Coll
  (Ctr for Lifelong
  Learning) [B] N4 . . . **6** A2
City Law Sch The
  EC1 . . . . **107** A3

City Lights The
  SE11 . . . . **149** C1
CITY OF
  LONDON **122** B4
City of London Acad-
  Islington N1 . . . . . **86** C3
City of London Acad
  The SE1 . . . . **153** C2
City of London
  Information Ctr
  EC4 . . . . **108** B1
City of London Sch
  EC4 . . . . **122** C4
City of London Sch for
  Girls EC2 . . . . **109** A4
City of Westminster
  Coll [B] W2 . . . . . . **101** B4
City of Westminster
  Coll, Cosway Street
  NW1 . . . . **102** B3
City of Westminster
  Coll, Maida Vale Ctr
  [B] W9 . . . . **88** A3
City of Westminster
  Coll, Queens Park
  W9 . . . . **23** C2
City Rd EC1 . . . . **97** A4
City Thameslink Sta
  EC4 . . . . **108** A1
City University EC1 . . **96** A3
City Wlk SE1 . . . . . . **138** A3
Civil Service Coll
  SW1 . . . . **144** C4
Clack St SE16 . . . . . . **40** B4
Claire Ct NW2 . . . . . . **10** A2
Claire PI E14 . . . . **41** C3
Clancarty Rd SW6 . **165** C1
Clandon Cl W3 . . . . . **37** A4
Clandon St SE8 . . . . . **51** C1
Clanfield Ho [B]
  SW15 . . . . **68** C3
Clanricarde Gdns
  W2 . . . . **31** C2 **113** C3
Clapham News
  SW1 . . . . **144** C4
CLAPHAM **61** A4
Clapham Common . . **61** A4
Clapham Common
  North Side SW4 . . . **60** C3
Clapham Common
  South Side SW4 . . . **61** B2
Clapham Common Sta
  SW4 . . . . **61** B3
Clapham Common
  West Side
  Clapham SW4,
  SW11 . . . . **60** B3
  Clapham SW11 . . . . . **60** B3
Clapham Computer &
  Secretarial Coll [B]
  SW11 . . . . **60** B2
Clapham Court Terr
  [B] SW4 . . . . **62** A2
Clapham Cres
  SW4 . . . . **61** C3
Clapham Ct [B]
  SW4 . . . . **62** A3
Clapham High St
  SW4 . . . . **61** C3
Clapham High Street
  Sta SW4 . . . . **61** C3
Clapham Junction Est
  SW11 . . . . **60** A3
Clapham Junction Sta
  SW11 . . . . **60** A3

Clapham L Ctr
  SW4 . . . . **61** C4
Clapham Manor Ct [B]
  SW4 . . . . **61** B4
Clapham Manor Prim
  Sch [B] SW4 . . . . . . **61** B4
Clapham Manor St
  SW4 . . . . **61** C4
Clapham Mans
  SW4 . . . . **61** A1
Clapham North Bsns
  Ctr [B] SW4 . . . . . . **172** A2
Clapham North Sta
  SW4 . . . . **62** A4
CLAPHAM PARK . . . **61** C2
Clapham Park Rd
  SW4 . . . . **61** C3
Clapham Park Terr [B]
  SW2 . . . . **62** A2
Clapham Rd SW9 . . **163** A2
Clapham South Sta
  SW4 . . . . **61** A1
Clapton Comm E5 . . . **7** C4
Clapton Girls Tec Coll
  E5 . . . . **17** B4
Clapton Park **17** C4
Clapton Pas E5 . . . . . **17** B3
Clapton Sq E5 . . . . . **17** B3
Clapton Terr E5 . . . . . **7** C3
Clapton Way E5 . . . . **16** C4
Clara Grant Ho [B]
  E14 . . . . **42** A3
Clara Grant Prim Sch
  The [B] E3 . . . . **26** C1
Clare Ct WC1 . . . . . . **94** B3
Claredale Ho [B]
  E2 . . . . **25** A3
Claredale St E2 . . . . . **24** C3
Clare Ho
  Bermondsey SE1 . . **153** A2
  [B] Old Ford E3 . . . . **26** B4
Clare La N1 . . . . **15** B1
Clare Lawn Ave
  SW14 . . . . **55** C2
Clare Mews SW6 . . . **156** A1
Clare Mkt WC2 . . . . **107** A1
Claremont [B]
  SW15 . . . . **58** A2
Claremont Cl
  Finsbury N1 . . . . **85** C1
  [B] Streatham SW2 **74** B3
Claremont Ct [B]
  W9 . . . . **23** B3
Claremont Gr W4 . . . **46** A3
Claremont Rd
  Highgate N6 . . . . **3** C4
  West Kilburn W9 . . . . **23** B3
Claremont Sq N1 . . . **85** B1
Claremont St SE10 . . **52** A4
Clarence Ave SW4 . . **61** C1
Clarence Ct [B]
  W6 . . . . **39** A2
Clarence Gate
  NW1 . . . . **91** A2
Clarence Gate Gdns
  NW1 . . . . **91** A1
Clarence Gdns
  NW1 . . . . **92** B3
Clarence Ho SE17 . . . **48** B4
Clarence Ho NW1 . . **119** A1
Clarence La SW15 . . . **56** B1
Clarence Mews
  Balham SW12 . . . . . **73** A4

Clarence Mews
  continued
  Hackney E5 . . . . **17** A3
  [B] Rotherhithe
    SE16 . . . . **32** C1
Clarence PI [B] E5 . . **17** A3
Clarence Rd
  Brentford W4 . . . . . . **36** C1
  Brondesbury NW6 . . **10** B1
  Greenwich SE8 . . . . **52** A4
  Lower Clapton E5 . . . **17** A4
  Richmond TW9 . . . . **44** C2
Clarence St [B]
  TW9 . . . . **54** A3
Clarence Terr
  NW1 . . . . **91** A2
Clarence Way
  NW1 . . . . **13** A1
Clarence Wlk [B]
  SW4 . . . . **172** A2
Clarendon Cl
  Bayswater W2 . . . . **116** A4
  [B] Hackney E9 . . . . **17** B1
Clarendon Cross
  W11 . . . . **31** A2 **112** B3
Clarendon Ct
  Paddington W9 . . . . **89** A2
  [B] Richmond TW9 . . **44** C2
  Willesden NW2 . . . . . **9** B1
Clarendon Dr
  SW15 . . . . **57** B3
Clarendon Flats
  W1 . . . . **103** C1
Clarendon Gdns
  W9 . . . . **89** A1
Clarendon Gr NW1 . . **93** B4
Clarendon Ho
  NW1 . . . . **83** A1
Clarendon Mews
  W2 . . . . **116** A4
Clarendon PI W2 . . **116** A4
Clarendon Rd
  W11 . . . . **31** A2 **112** B4
Clarendon Rise
  SE13 . . . . **67** B3
Clarendon St
  SW1 . . . . **146** B2
Clarendon Terr
  W9 . . . . **89** A2
Clarendon Wlk [B]
  W11 . . . . **31** A3
Clare PI SW15 . . . . . . **68** B4
Clare Rd
  New Cross SE14 . . . . **51** B2
  Willesden NW10 . . . . . **8** C1
Clare St E2 . . . . **25** A3
Clareville Ct SW7 . . **143** A3
Clareville Gr SW7 . . **143** A3
Clareville Grove Mews
  SW7 . . . . **143** A3
Clareville St SW7 . . **143** A3
Clarewood Ct W1 . . **102** C3
Clarewood Wlk
  SW9 . . . . **62** C3
Clarges Ho [B] W1 . **118** B2
Clarges Mews
  W1 . . . . **118** A2
Clarges St W1 . . . . **118** B2
Clariat Ct W3 . . . . . . **36** C4
Claribel Rd SW9 . . . . **48** A1
Claridge Ct SW6 . . **164** C3
Clarissa Ho [B] E14 . **34** A3
Clarissa St E8 . . . . . . **24** B4
Clarke Ho [B] SW4 . . **61** B4
Clarke Path N16 . . . . . **7** C3

Clarkes Mews W1 . **103** C4
Clark Ho SW10 . . . **156** C2
Clark Lawrence Ct [B]
  SW11 . . . . **59** C4
Clarkson Rd E16 . . . . **35** B3
Clarkson Row
  NW1 . . . . **82** C1
Clarkson St E2 . . . . . **25** A2
Clark's PI EC2 . . . . . **110** A2
Clark St E1 . . . . **32** B4
Classic Mans [B]
  E9 . . . . **17** B1
Classinghall Ho [B]
  SW15 . . . . **57** C2
Claude Rd SE15 . . . . **50** A1
Claude St E14 . . . . . . **41** C2
Claudia Jones Way
  SW2 . . . . **62** A1
Claudia PI SW19 . . . . **70** A3
Clavell St [B] SE10 . . **52** B4
Claverdale Rd
  SW2 . . . . **74** C4
Clavering Ave
  SW13 . . . . **47** A4
Clavering Ho SE13 . . **67** C3
Claverton St SW1 . . **147** A1
Claxton Gr
  W6 . . . . **39** C1 **140** A1
Claybank Gr SE13 . . . **67** A4
Claybrook Rd W6 . . . **47** C4
Claydon SE17 . . . . . **150** C4
Clayhall Ct [B] E3 . . . **26** B3
Claylands PI SW8 . . **163** B2
Claylands Rd
  SW8 . . . . **163** A3
Claypole Rd E15 . . . . **27** B3
Clayponds Ave
  TW8 . . . . **36** A2
Clayponds Hospl
  W5 . . . . **36** A3
Clayponds La TW8 . . **36** A1
Clays Ct N16 . . . . **7** B3
Clay St W1 . . . . **103** A3
Clayton Cres N1 . . . . **84** C3
Clayton Ho [B] E9 . . . **17** B1
Clayton Mews
  SE10 . . . . **52** C2
Clayton Rd SE15 . . . . **49** C2
Clayton St SE11 . . . **163** B4
Clearbrook Way [B]
  E1 . . . . **32** B3
Clear Water Ho [B]
  TW10 . . . . **54** A2
Clearwater Terr [B]
  W11 . . . . **39** C4
Clearwell Dr W9 . . . . **88** B1
Cleaver Ho [B]
  NW3 . . . . **12** B1
Cleaver Sq SE11 . . . **149** C1
Cleaver St SE11 . . . **149** C2
Cleeve Ho [B]
  E2 . . . . **24** A2 **98** B3
Cleeve Way SW15 . . . **68** B4
Cleeve Workshops [B]
  E2 . . . . **24** A2 **98** B3
Clegg St [B] E1 . . . . . **32** A1
Cleland Ho [B] E2 . . . **25** B3
Clematis St W12 . . . . **29** C2
Clem Atlee Par
  SW6 . . . . **155** A3
Clem Attlee Ct
  SW6 . . . . **155** A3
Clemence St E14 . . . **33** B4

Clement Attlee Ho
NW10 . . . . .8 B1
Clement Ave SW4 . .61 C3
Clement Cl
Acton W4 . . . . .37 C2
Hampstead NW6 . . . . . .69 C1
Clement Danes Ho 2
W12 . . . . .30 B3
Clement Ho
14 Deptford SE8 . . . .41 A2
17 North Kensington
W10 . . . . .30 B4
Clements Ave 1
E16 . . . . .35 C2
Clements Inn
WC2 . . . . .107 A1
Clements Inn Pas
WC2 . . . . .107 A1
Clement's La EC2,
EC4 . . . . .123 C4
Clement's Rd SE16 . .40 A3
Clemson Ho 9 E8 . .24 B4
Clennam St SE1 . .137 A4
Clenston Mews
W1 . . . . .102 C2
Clent Ho 1 N16 . . . . .7 B3
Cleopatra's Needle
WC2 . . . . .120 C3
Clephane Rd 13
N1 . . . . .15 B2
Clephane Rd N N1 . .15 B2
Clephane Rd S N1 . .15 C2
Clere Pl EC2 . . . . .97 C2
Clere St EC2 . . . . . . .97 C2
CLERKENWELL 96 A1
Clerkenwell Cl EC1 .95 C1
Clerkenwell Gn
EC1 . . . . .96 A1
Clerkenwell Parochial
CE Prim Sch EC1 . .95 B3
Clerkenwell Rd
EC1 . . . . .96 A1
Clermont Rd E9 . . . .25 B4
Clevedon Ct
Battersea SW11 . . . .168 A4
Dulwich SE21 . . . . . . .75 C1
Clevedon Mans
NW5 . . . . .12 C4
Cleve Ho NW6 . . . . . .11 A1
Cleveland Ave W4 . .38 B2
Cleveland Ct W1 . . . .93 A1
Cleveland Gdns
Barnes SW13 . . . . . . .46 A1
Paddington W2 . . . . .100 C1
Cleveland Gr 30
E1 . . . . .25 B1
Cleveland Mans
8 Brixton SW9 . . . . .163 B1
4 Brondesbury
NW6 . . . . .10 B1
Paddington W9 . . . . .23 C1
Cleveland Mews
W1 . . . . .104 C4
Cleveland Pl SW1 . .119 A2
Cleveland Rd
Barnes SW13 . . . . . . .46 B1
Islington N1 . . . . .15 C1
14 South Acton W4 . .37 B3
Cleveland Row
SW1 . . . . .119 A1
Cleveland Sq W2 . .100 C1
Cleveland St W1 . . . .92 C1
Cleveland Terr
W2 . . . . .101 A2
Cleveland Way E1 . .25 B1
Clevedon Cl N16 . . . .7 A1

Cleve Rd NW6 . . . . . .11 A1
Cleverly Cotts
W12 . . . . .29 B1
Cleverly Est W12 . . .29 C2
Cley Ho SE4 . . . . .65 C3
Clichy Ho 20 E1 . . . .32 B4
Clifden Mews E5 . . .17 C3
Clifden Rd E5 . . . . . .17 C3
Cliff Ct 14 NW1 . . . .13 C2
Cliffe Ho 5 SE10 . . .43 B1
Clifford Ave
Mortlake SW14 . . . . .45 B1
Mortlake SW14,
TW9 . . . . .55 A4
Clifford Ct
Bayswater W2 . . . . . .100 A3
Wandsworth SW18 . . .71 C4
Willesden NW10 . . . . .8 A4
Clifford Dr SW9 . . . .63 A3
Clifford Gdns
NW10 . . . . .22 B3
Clifford Haigh Ho
SW6 . . . . .47 C3
Clifford Ho 4 W14 . .140 C3
Clifford's Inn Pas
EC4 . . . . .107 B1
Clifford St W1 . . . . .118 C3
Clifford Way NW10 . .8 B4
Cliff Rd NW1 . . . . . . .13 C2
Cliff Road Studios 13
NW1 . . . . .13 C2
Cliffsend Ho 85
SW9 . . . . .173 C3
Cliff Terr SE8 . . . . . . .51 C1
Cliffview Rd SE13 . . .66 C4
Cliff Villas NW1 . . . .13 C2
Cliff Wlk E16 . . . . . . .35 B4
Clifton Ave W12 . . . .29 B1
Clifton Cres SE15 . . .50 A3
Clifton Ct
Finsbury Pk N4 . . . . . .5 C2
Paddington NW8 . . . . .89 B2
Peckham SE15 . . . . . .50 A3
Putney SW15 . . . . .57 C2
Clifton Gate
SW10 . . . . .156 C4
Clifton Gdns
Chiswick W4 . . . . .37 C2
Paddington W9 . . . . . .88 C1
Clifton Gr E8 . . . . . . .16 C2
Clifton Hill NW8 . . . .78 C3
Clifton Ho
E2 . . . . .98 C2
Clifton Mans 4
SW9 . . . . .62 C3
Clifton Pl
Paddington W2 . . . . .101 C1
Rotherhithe SE16 . . . .40 B4
Clifton Rd
Harlesden NW10 . . . . .21 C3
Newham E16 . . . . .35 A4
Paddington W9 . . . . . .89 A2
Clifton Rise SE14 . . .51 A3
Clifton St
EC2 . . . . .24 A1 98 A1
Clifton Terr N4 . . . . . .5 C2
Clifton Villas W9 . . . .88 C1
Clifton Way SE15 . . .50 B3
Climsland Ho SE1 . .121 C2
Clinch Ct 11 E16 . . .35 C4
Cline Ho SW15 . . . . .56 C2
Clinger Ct N1 . . . . . . .24 A4
Clink Prison Mus The
SE1 . . . . .123 B2
Clink St SE1 . . . . . . .123 B2
Clinton Rd E3 . . . . . .26 A2

Clipper Appts 12
SE10 . . . . .52 B4
Clipper Cl 3 SE16 . . .40 C4
Clipper Ho E14 . . . . .42 B1
Clipper Way SE13 . . .67 B3
Clipstone Ho 10
SW15 . . . . .56 C2
Clipstone Mews
W1 . . . . .104 C4
Clipstone St W1 . . . .104 C4
Clissold Cres N16 . . .15 C4
Clissold Ct N4 . . . . . . .6 B2
Clissold Ho 1 N16 . . .6 C3
Clissold Rd N16 . . . . .6 C1
Clitheroe Rd SW9 . .172 B1
Clive Ct W9 . . . . .89 A2
Cliveden Ho SW1 . . .145 B4
Cliveden Pl SW1 . . .145 B4
Clive Ho
13 Clapham SW8 . .171 B2
Greenwich SE10 . . . . .52 B4
Clive Rd SE21 . . . . . . .75 C1
Cloak La EC4 . . . . . .123 B4
Clochar Ct NW10 . . . .21 B4
Clock Ho N16 . . . . . . .7 B4
Clockhouse Cl
SW19 . . . . .69 B2
Clockhouse Pl
SW15 . . . . .58 A1
Clockhouse The
SW19 . . . . .69 B1
Clockmakers' Mus
EC2 . . . . .109 A2
Clock Tower Mews
N1 . . . . .87 A3
Clock Tower Pl 1
N7 . . . . .14 A2
Clock View Cres 2
N7 . . . . .14 A2
Cloister Rd
Acton W3 . . . . .28 B4
Child's Hill NW2 . . . . .1 B2
Cloisters The 7 N1 . .16 A1
Cloisters The 22
SW9 . . . . .173 C3
Clonbrock Rd N16 . . .16 A4
Cloncurry St SW6 . . .47 C1
Clone Cl 4 W12 . . . . .38 A3
Clonmel Rd SW6 . . .165 A4
Clonmore St SW18 . .70 B3
Clorane Gdns NW3 . .1 C1
Close The
Lewisham SE3 . . . . . .52 C1
Mortlake SW14 . . . . .55 A4
Cloth Ct EC1 . . . . . . .108 B3
Cloth Fair EC1 . . . . .108 B3
Clothier St E1 . . . . .110 B2
Cloth St EC1 . . . . . . .108 C4
Cloudesdale Rd
SW17 . . . . .73 A2
Cloudesley Mans
N1 . . . . .85 C3
Cloudesley Pl N1 . . .85 C3
Cloudesley Rd N1 . . .85 B3
Cloudesley Sq N1 . . .85 C3
Cloudesley St N1 . . .85 C3
Clove Cres E14 . . . . .34 C2
Clovelly Ct NW2 . . . . .9 B3
Clovelly Ho 2 W2 . .100 C2
Clovelly Rd W4 . . . . .37 C4
Clovelly Way E1 . . . .32 B3
Clover Mews SW3 . .159 A4
Clowes Ho 8 SW4 . .172 A1
Cloysters Gn E1 . . . .125 B2
Club Row E2 . .24 B1 98 C2

Clunbury St N1 . . . . .87 C1
Clunie Ho SW1 . . . .131 A2
Cluny Mews SW5 . .141 B3
Cluny Pl SE1 . . . . . .138 A2
Cluse Ct N1 . . . . .86 C2
Clutton St E14 . . . . . .34 A4
Clyde Ct NW1 . . . . . .83 C2
Clyde Flats SW6 . . .154 C2
Clydesdale Gdns
TW10 . . . . .55 A3
Clydesdale Ho 4
W11 . . . . .31 B3
Clydesdale Rd
W11 . . . . .31 B3
Clyde St SE8 . . . . . . .51 B4
Clynes Ho 3 E2 . . . .25 C2
Clyro Ct N4 . . . . .5 B3
Clyston St SW8 . . . .171 A2
Coach & Horses Yd
W1 . . . . .118 C4
Coach House La
Highbury N5 . . . . .15 A4
Wimbledon SW19 . . . .69 C1
Coach House Mews
SE23 . . . . .65 C1
Coach House Yd 5
NW3 . . . . .11 C4
Coachmaker Mews 5
SW4 . . . . .172 B2
Coalbrook Mans 8
SW12 . . . . .73 A3
Coaldale Wlk SE21 . .75 B4
Coalecroft Rd
SW15 . . . . .57 B2
Coalport Ho SE11 . .149 B4
Coatbridge Ho 8
N1 . . . . .14 B1
Coates Ave SW18 . . .60 A1
Coates Ct NW3 . . . . .12 A3
Coate St E2 . . . . .24 C3
Coates Wlk TW8 . . . .36 A1
Cobbett St SW8 . . . .163 A1
Cobble La N1 . . . . . . .15 A1
Cobble Mews N4,
N5 . . . . .6 B1
Cobbold Ct SW1 . . .147 B4
Cobbold Ind Est
NW10 . . . . .8 B2
Cobbold Mews
W12 . . . . .38 B4
Cobbold Rd
Bedford Pk W12 . . . . .38 B4
Willesden NW10 . . . . .8 B2
Cobb's Hall 1
SW6 . . . . .47 C4
Cobb St E1 . . . . .110 C3
Cobden Bldgs WC1 . .94 C4
Cobden Ho
5 Bethnal Green
E2 . . . . .24 C2 99 C4
Regent's Pk NW1 . . . .82 C2
Cobham Cl SW11 . . .60 A1
Cobham Mews 3
NW1 . . . . .13 C1
Coborn Mews 9
E3 . . . . .26 B2
Coborn Rd E3 . . . . . .26 B2
Coborn St E3 . . . . . . .26 B2
Cobourg Prim Sch
SE5 . . . . .49 B4
Cobourg Rd SE5 . . . .49 B4
Cobourg St NW1 . . . .93 A3
Coburg Cl SW1 . . . .147 A4
Coburg Cres SW2 . . .74 C3
Coburg Dwellings 11
E1 . . . . .32 B2

Cochrane Cl NW8 . . .79 C1
Cochrane Ho 15
E14 . . . . .41 C4
Cochrane Mews
NW8 . . . . .79 C1
Cochrane St NW8 . . .79 C1
Coci Ho W14 . . . . . .141 A3
Cockburn Ho
SW1 . . . . .147 C1
Cock Hill E1 . . . . . . .110 B3
Cock La EC1 . . . . . . .108 B3
Cockpit Yd WC1 . . . .107 A4
Cockspur St SW1 . . .119 C2
Cockspur St SW1 . . .119 C2
Coda Ctr The
SW6 . . . . .164 B4
Code St E1 . .24 B1 99 A1
Codicote Ho 22
SE8 . . . . .40 C2
Codicote Terr N4 . . . .6 B2
Codling Cl E1 . . . . . .125 C2
Codrington Ct 8
SE16 . . . . .33 A1
Codrington Ho 7
E1 . . . . .25 A1
Codrington Mews
W11 . . . . .31 A3
Cody Rd E16 . . . . . . .27 C1
Coffey St SE8 . . . . . . .51 C3
Cohen Lo E5 . . . . . . .18 A3
Coin St SE1 . . . . . . .121 B2
Coity Rd NW5 . . . . . .12 C2
Cokers La SE21 . . . . .75 C2
Coke St E1 . . . . .111 C2
Colas Mews 7
NW6 . . . . .23 C4
Colbeck Mews
SW5 . . . . .142 B3
Colberg Pl N16 . . . . . .7 B4
Colbert 1 SE5 . . . . . .49 B2
Colborne Ho 9
E14 . . . . .33 C2
Colchester Ho 17
SW8 . . . . .171 B2
Colchester St E1 . . .111 A2
Coldbath Sq EC1 . . . .95 B2
Coldbath St SE13 . . .52 A1
Cold Blow La SE14 . .50 C4
Coldharbour E14 . . . .34 B1
Coldharbour Ind Est
SE5 . . . . .48 B1
Coldharbour La
SW9 . . . . .63 A4
Coldharbour Pl
SE5 . . . . .48 C1
Coldstream Gdns
SW18 . . . . .58 B1
Colebeck Mews
N1 . . . . .15 A2
Colebert Ave E1 . . . .25 B1
Colebert Ho 21 E1 . .25 B1
Colebrook Cl
SW19 . . . . .69 C4
Colebrook Ct
SW3 . . . . .144 B3
Colebrooke Pl N1 . . .86 B3
Colebrooke Row
Islington N1 . . . . .84 B4
Islington N1 . . . . .86 A2
Islington N1 . . . . .86 B3
Colebrook Ho 1
E14 . . . . .34 A3
Coleby Path 9
SE5 . . . . .48 C3

Colechurch Ho **9**
SE1 . . . . **153** B1
Colefax Bldg **11**
E1 . . . . **111** C2
Coleford Rd SW18 . . **59** C2
Colegrave Rd E15 . . **19** C3
Colegrave Sch
E15 . . . . **19** C3
Colegrove Rd
SE15 . . . . **49** B4
Coleherne Ct
SW10 . . . . **142** B1
Coleherne Mans
SW5 . . . . **142** B2
Coleherne Mews
SW10 . . . . **142** A1
Colehill Gdns
SW6 . . . . **164** A3
Colehill La SW6 . . . **164** B3
Cole Ho SE1 . . . . . . **135** C3
Coleman Ct SW18 . . **70** C4
Coleman Fields
N1 . . . . **87** A4
Coleman Mans N19 . . **5** A4
Coleman Rd SE5 . . . **49** A3
Coleman St EC2 . . . **109** B2
Coleman Street Bldgs
EC2 . . . . **109** B2
Colenso Rd E5 . . . . **17** B4
Coleraine Rd SE3 . . **53** B4
Coleridge Cl SW8 . . **170** B1
Coleridge Ct SW14 . . **39** C3
Coleridge Gdns
NW6 . . . . **11** B1
Coleridge Ho
Pimlico SW1 . . . . . **147** A1
Walworth SE17 . . . **151** A2
Coleridge Prim Sch
N8 . . . . **4** C4
Coleridge Rd N4,
N7 . . . . **5** C2
Coleridge Sq
SW10 . . . . **156** C2
Coles Cl SW11 . . . . **167** C3
Coleshill Flats
SW1 . . . . **145** C3
Cole St SE1 . . . . . . **137** A3
Colestown St **4**
SW11 . . . . **168** B2
Colet Gdns W14 . . . **39** C2
Colet Ho SE17 . . . . **150** B1
Colette Ct **6** SE16 . . **40** C4
Coley St WC1 . . . . . . **95** A1
Colfe & Hatchcliffe's
Glebe SE13 . . . . . . **67** A2
Colgate Ho SE13 . . . **52** A1
Colin Blanchard Ho
SE4 . . . . **51** C1
Colin Ct SW16 . . . . . **73** C2
Colinette Rd SW15 . **57** B3
Colin Rd NW10 . . . . . **8** C2
Colinsdale N1 . . . . . **86** A3
Colin Winter Ho **16**
E1 . . . . **25** B1
Coliston Pas SW18 . **70** C4
Coliston Rd SW18 . . **70** C4
Collamore Ave
SW18 . . . . **72** A3
Collard Pl NW1 . . . . **13** A1
Collcutt Lo SW4 . . . **62** A3
College App SE10 . . **52** B4
College Cl E5 . . . . . **17** B3

College Cres NW3 . . **11** C2
College Cross N1 . . . **14** C1
College Ct
Chelsea SW3 . . . . . **145** A1
3 Hammersmith
W6 . . . . **39** B1
Hampstead NW3 . . **11** C2
College Gdns
Dulwich SE21 . . . . . **76** A3
Upper Tooting
SW17 . . . . **72** A2
College Gr NW1 . . . . **83** B4
College Green Ct
SW9 . . . . **63** A4
College Hill EC4 . . . **123** A4
College La NW5 . . . . . **13** A4
College Mews **5**
SW18 . . . . **59** A2
College Park Cl
SE13 . . . . **67** C3
College Park Sch
W2 . . . . **100** A1
College Rd
Dulwich SE19,
SE21 . . . . **76** A2
Kensal Green
NW10 . . . . **22** B3
College St EC4 . . . . **123** A4
College Terr E3 . . . . **26** B2
Collent Ho **8** E9 . . . **17** B2
Collent St E9 . . . . . . **17** B2
Collerston Ho
SE10 . . . . **43** B1
Collette Ho N16 . . . . . **7** B3
Collett Ho SE13 . . . . **67** A4
Collett Rd SE16 . . . **139** C2
Colley Ho **17** N7 . . . . **13** C3
Collier St N1 . . . . . . **84** C1
Collingbourne Rd **2**
W12 . . . . **30** A1
Collingham Gdns
SW5 . . . . **142** B3
Collingham Pl
SW5 . . . . **142** B4
Collingham Rd
SW5 . . . . **142** B4
Collingham Tutors
Coll SW5 . . . . **142** B3
Collington St SE10 . . **42** C1
Collingwood Ho
27 Bethnal Green
E1 . . . . **25** A1
Marylebone W1 . . . **104** C4
Collingwood St E1 . **25** A1
Collins Ct E8 . . . . . . **16** C2
Collins Ho
6 Cubitt Town
SE10 . . . . **43** B1
4 Poplar E14 . . . . . . **34** B2
Collinson Ct SE1 . . . **136** C3
Collinson Ho **14**
SE15 . . . . **49** C3
Collinson St SE1 . . . **136** C3
Collinson Wlk
SE1 . . . . **136** C3
Collins Rd N5, N16 . . **15** B4
Collins Sq SE3 . . . . . **53** B1
Collins Yd N1 . . . . . . **86** A3
Collison Pl N16 . . . . . **7** A3
Coll of Arms EC4 . . **122** C4

Coll of Central
London The
EC2 . . . . **24** A1 **98** A2
Coll of Law The
(Bloomsbury)
EC1 . . . . **105** B4
Coll of Law The
(Moorgate) EC1 . . . **97** B1
Coll of NW London **18**
NW6 . . . . **23** C4
Coll of NW London
(Willesden Centre)
NW10 . . . . **8** B3
Coll of Optometrists
The SW1 . . . . **120** A2
Coll Sharp Ct **2**
E2 . . . . **24** B2 **98** C3
Coll's Rd SE15 . . . . . **50** B2
Collyer Pl SE15 . . . . **49** C2
Colmans Wharf **5**
E14 . . . . **34** A4
Colmar Cl **3** E1 . . . . **25** C1
Colmore Mews
SE15 . . . . **50** A2
Colnbrook St SE1 . . **136** A2
Colne Ho NW8 . . . . . **89** C1
Colne Rd E5 . . . . **18** A4
Cologne Rd SW11 . . **59** C3
Colombo St SE1 . . . **122** A1
Colomb St SE10 . . . **43** A1
Colonades The **4**
SE5 . . . . **48** C2
Colonial Dr W4 . . . . **37** B2
Colonnade **3** WC1 . . **94** B1
Colonnade Ho SE3 . . **53** B1
Colonnades The **6**
SE8 . . . . **41** A2
Colonnade The **12**
SE8 . . . . **51** B4
Colorado Bldg **9**
SE13 . . . . **52** A2
Colosseum Terr
NW1 . . . . **92** B2
Colour Ho **5** **138** B3
Colstead Ho **22** E1 . **32** A3
Colston Rd SW14 . . . **55** B3
Colthurst Cres N4 . . . **6** B2
Coltman Ho SE10 . . . **52** B4
Coltman St E14 . . . . **33** A4
Columba Ho SE14 . . **51** B2
Columbas Dr NW3 . . . **2** C3
Columbia Ho **18**
E3 . . . . **26** C2
Columbia Point **7**
SE16 . . . . **40** B3
Columbia Prim Sch
E2 . . . . **24** B2 **99** A4
Columbia Rd
11 Hackney E2 . . . . **24** C3
Shoreditch
E2 . . . . **24** B2 **98** C4
Columbia Road
Flower Mkt
E2 . . . . **24** B2 **99** A4
Colverson Ho **14**
E1 . . . . **32** B4
Colvestone Cres
E8 . . . . **16** B3
Colvestone Prim Sch
E8 . . . . **16** B3
Colville Gdns W11 . . **31** B3
Colville Ho
32 Bethnal Green
E2 . . . . **25** B3
Notting Hill W11 . . . **31** B3

Colville Mews
W11 . . . . **31** B3
Colville Pl W1 . . . . . **105** A3
Colville Prim Sch
W11 . . . . **31** B3
Colville Rd
Notting Hill W11 . . . **31** B3
South Acton W3 . . . **37** A3
Colville Sq W11 . . . . **31** B3
Colville Terr W11 . . . **31** B3
Colwall Ho **18**
SW9 . . . . **173** A1
Colwell Rd SE22 . . . . **64** B2
Colwick Cl N6 . . . . . . **4** C4
Colwith Rd W6 . . . . . **47** B4
Colworth Gr SE17 . . **151** A3
Colwyn Ho SE1 . . . . **135** B1
Colyton Rd SE22 . . . **65** A2
Combe Ave SE3 . . . . **53** B3
Combedale Rd
SE10 . . . . **43** C1
Combe Ho
Mortlake SW14 . . . . **45** B1
20 Paddington W2 . . **31** C4
Combemartin Rd
SW18 . . . . **70** A3
Combe Mews **4**
SE3 . . . . **53** B3
Comber Gr SE5 . . . . **48** B3
Comber Grove Prim
Sch **34** SE5 . . . . . . **48** B3
Comber Ho SE5 . . . . **48** B3
Combermere Rd
SW9 . . . . **62** B4
Combe The NW1 . . . . **92** B3
Com Coll Hackney
The **17** E8 . . . . **25** A4
Comeragh Mews
W14 . . . . **140** B1
Comeragh Rd
W14 . . . . **140** B1
Comerford Rd SE4 . . **66** B3
Comet Pl SE8 . . . . . . **51** C3
Comet St SE8 . . . . . . **51** C3
Comfort St **6**
SE15 . . . . **49** A4
Comins Ho **3** SW4 . . **61** B2
Commercial Rd
Stepney E1 . . . . **32** B3
Whitechapel E1 . . . **111** C2
Commercial St
E1 . . . . **110** C4
Commercial Way
Peckham SE15 . . . . **49** C3
Wembley NW10 . . . . **20** A3
Commerell Pl
SE10 . . . . **43** B1
Commerell St
SE10 . . . . **43** A1
Commodity Quay
E1 . . . . **125** A3
Commodore Ct
SE8 . . . . **51** C2
Commodore Ho **7**
E14 . . . . **34** B2
Commodore St E1 . . **26** A1
Commondale
SW15 . . . . **57** B4
Common Rd SW13 . . **56** C4
Common View
SW15 . . . . **57** B4
Commonwealth Ave
8 W12 . . . . **30** A2
Commonwealth Ho
WC1 . . . . **106** B2
Community La N7 . . . **13** C3

Community Rd
E15 . . . . **19** C3
Comodore Ho
SW18 . . . . **59** B3
Compania Bldg **12**
E1 . . . . **32** C2
Compass Ct SE1 . . . **124** C1
Compass Ho
Bayswater W2 . . . . **100** A1
London SE8 . . . . **52** A1
Compass Point **10**
E14 . . . . **33** B2
Compayne Gdns
NW6 . . . . **11** A1
Compton Ave
Islington N1 . . . . . . **15** A2
London N6 . . . . **3** A4
Compton Cl
Camberwell SE5 . . . **49** B3
Regent's Pk NW1 . . . **92** B3
Compton Cres W4 . . **45** B4
Compton Ho
SW11 . . . . **168** A4
Compton Pas EC1 . . **96** B2
Compton Pl WC1 . . . **94** A2
Compton Rd
Islington N1 . . . . . . **15** A2
Kensal Green
NW10 . . . . **22** C2
Compton St EC1 . . . . **96** B2
Compton Terr N1 . . . **15** A2
Comus Ho SE17 . . . **152** A3
Comus Pl SE17 . . . . **152** A3
Comyn Rd SW11 . . . **60** A3
Comyns Cl E16 . . . . . **35** B4
Conant Ho SE11 . . . **48** A4
Conant Mews **1**
E1 . . . . **125** B4
Concanon Rd SW2,
SW4 . . . . **62** B3
Conant Hall App
SE1 . . . . **121** A1
Concord Bsns Ctr
W3 . . . . **28** A4
Concorde Way
SE16 . . . . **40** C2
Concordia Wharf **10**
E14 . . . . **34** B1
Concord Rd W3 . . . . **20** A1
Condell Rd SW8 . . . **171** A3
Conder St E14 . . . . . **33** A3
Condray Pl SW11 . . **158** A1
Conduit Ct WC2 . . . **120** A4
Conduit Ho SE10 . . . **52** C2
Conduit Mews
W2 . . . . **101** B1
Conduit Pas W2 . . . **101** B1
Conduit Pl W2 . . . . **101** B1
Conduit St W1 . . . . . **118** C4
Conewood St N5 . . . . **6** A1
Coney Acre SE21 . . . **75** B3
Coney Way SW8 . . . **163** A3
Congers Ho SE8 . . . . **51** C3
Congress Ho WC1 . . **105** C2
Congreve Ho **10**
N16 . . . . **16** A3
Congreve St SE17 . . **152** A3
Conifer Ct **21**
SW19 . . . . **69** C3
Conifer Gdns
SW16 . . . . **74** B1
Conifer Ho SE4 . . . . **66** B3
Coniger Rd SW6 . . . **165** B2
Coningham Ct
SW10 . . . . **157** A2

Coningham Mews
W12 . . . . 29 C1
Coningham Rd
W12 . . . . 39 A4
Coningsby Rd N4 . . . 6 A4
Conington Rd
SE13 . . . . 52 B1
Conisbrough NW1 . . 83 C3
Coniston NW1 . . . . 92 C4
Coniston Cl
Barnes SW13 . . . . . 46 B3
Chiswick W4 . . . . . 45 B3
Coniston Ct
Marylebone W2 . . . 102 B1
6 Rotherhithe
SE16 . . . . 40 C4
Conistone Way N7 . 14 A1
Coniston Ho
14 Bow E3 . . . . 26 B2
6 Camberwell SE5 . 48 B3
Coniston Wlk E9 . . 17 B3
Conlan St W10 . . . . 23 A1
Conley Rd NW10 . . . 8 A2
Conley St SE10 . . . . 43 A1
Connaught Ave
SW14 . . . . 55 B3
Connaught Cl W2 . 102 B1
Connaught Ho
College Pk NW10 . . 22 A2
Mayfair W1 . . . . . . 118 A3
Connaught House Sch
W2 . . . . 102 B1
Connaught Lo N4 . . . 5 C4
Connaught Mans
Battersea SW11 . . . 168 B3
3 Brixton SW9 . . . . 62 C3
15 Canonbury N16 . 15 C4
Fulham SW6 . . . . . . 164 A4
Connaught Pl W2 . 102 C1
Connaught Rd
Finsbury Pk N4 . . . . 5 C4
Harlesden NW10 . . . 21 A3
6 Richmond TW10 . 54 B2
Connaught Sq
W2 . . . . 102 C1
Connaught St W2 . 102 B1
Connaught Works
E3 . . . . 26 A4
Connell Ct 6
SE14 . . . . 50 C4
Connor Ct SW11 . . 170 A3
Connor St E9 . . . . . 25 C4
Conrad Ho
8 Limehouse
SE16 . . . . 33 A2
South Lambeth
SW8 . . . . 162 A2
12 Stoke Newington
N16 . . . . 16 A3
Conrad Twr W3 . . . 37 A3
Consort Ho W2 . . . 114 B3
Consort Lo N1 . . . . 80 C3
Consort Rd SE15 . . 50 A1
Cons St SE1 . . . . . . 135 C4
Constable Ct 11
SE16 . . . . 40 A1
Constable Ho
28 Millwall E14 . . . . 41 C4
Primrose Hill NW3 . 12 B1
Constable Wlk
SE21 . . . . 76 A1
Constant Ho 10
E14 . . . . 34 A2
Constantine Ho
SW2 . . . . 75 A3

Constantine Rd
NW3 . . . . 12 A4
Constitution Hill
W1 . . . . 132 B4
Consul Ho **3** E3 . . . 26 C1
Content St **1** SE17 151 B3
Convent Gdns
W11 . . . . 31 B3
**Convent of Jesus &
Mary Language Coll**
NW10 . . . . 22 A3
**Convent of Jesus &
Mary RC Inf Sch 9**
W6 . . . . 9 B2
Conway Gr W3 . . . . 28 C4
Conway Ho
Chelsea SW3 . . . . . 145 A1
6 Millwall E14 . . . . 42 A2
6 Streatham SW2 . 74 A3
Conway Mews W1 . 92 C1
Conway St W1 . . . . 92 C1
Conybeare NW3 . . . 12 A1
Conyer St **3** E3 . . . 26 A3
Cookham Cres
SE16 . . . . 40 C4
Cookham Ho
E2 . . . . 24 B1 98 C2
Cook's Rd
Camberwell SE17 . . 48 A4
Stratford Marsh
E15 . . . . 27 A3
Coomassie Rd W9 . 23 B1
Coombe Ho **13** N7 . 13 C3
Coombe Rd W4 . . . . 38 A1
Coomber Ho SW6 . 59 A4
Coombs St N1 . . . . 86 B1
Coomer Mews
SW6 . . . . 155 A3
Coomer Pl SW6 . . . 155 A3
Cooperage The
SE1 . . . . 124 C1
Cooper Cl SE1 . . . . 135 C3
Cooper Ho NW8 . . . 89 B1
Cooper Rd NW10 . . . 8 C3
Coopersale Rd E9 . . 17 C3
Coopers Ct 3
3 Acton W3 . . . . . . 28 B1
Tower Hamlets E3 . . 26 C1
Coopers La NW1 . . . 83 C1
Coopers Lo SE1 . . . 138 C4
Cooper's Rd SE1 . . 153 A2
Cooper's Row
EC3 . . . . 124 C4
Cooper St **10** E16 . . 35 B4
Coopers Yd N1 . . . . 15 A1
Cope Ho EC1 . . . . . 97 A3
Copeland Dr E14 . . 41 C2
Copeland Ho
SE11 . . . . 135 A1
Copeland Rd SE15 . 50 A1
Copenhagen Gdns
W4 . . . . 37 C4
Copenhagen Ho
N1 . . . . 85 B3
Copenhagen Pl
E14 . . . . 33 C3
Copenhagen Prim Sch
N1 . . . . 84 C3
Cope Pl W8 . . . . . . 127 B1
Cope St SE16 . . . . . 40 C2
Copford Wlk N1 . . . 86 C4
Copleston Rd SE15 . 64 B4
Copley Cl **15** SE17 . 48 A4
Copley St E1 . . . . . 32 C4

Coppedhall 2
SE21 . . . . 75 C2
Copperas St SE8 . . . 52 A4
Copper Beech N6 . . . 3 C4
Copperbeech Cl
NW3 . . . . 11 C3
Copperfield Ho 12
SE1 . . . . 139 B3
Copperfield Rd E3 . 33 A4
Copperfields Ct
W3 . . . . 36 C4
Copperfield St
SE1 . . . . 136 C4
Copper Mews
W4 . . . . 37 B3
Copper Row SE1 . . 124 C1
Coppice Dr SW15 . . 57 A1
Coppin Ho SW2 . . . 75 A3
Coppock Cl SW11 . 168 A1
Copse Ct SW15 . . . 58 A2
Copthall Ave EC2 . 109 C2
Copthall Bldgs
EC2 . . . . 109 C2
Copthall Cl EC2 . . . 109 B2
Copthorne Ave
SW12 . . . . 73 C4
Coptic St WC1 . . . . 106 A3
Copton Cl E3 . . . . . 33 C4
Coral Apts **6** E16 . . 35 C2
Coral Ho **9** E1 . . . . 26 A1
Coral Row SW11 . . . 59 B4
Coral St SE1 . . . . . 135 C3
Coram Ho
Bloomsbury WC1 . . 94 A2
3 Chiswick W4 . . . . 38 A1
Coram Mans WC1 . . 94 A1
Coram St WC1 . . . . 94 A1
Corbden Ct SE15 . . 49 B2
Corbet Ct EC3 . . . . 109 C1
Corbet Ho N1 . . . . . 85 B3
Corbet Pl E1 . . . . . 110 C4
Corbett Ho SW10 . 156 C4
Corbett's La SE16 . 40 B2
Corbetts Pas 8
SE16 . . . . 40 B2
Corbidge Ct SE8 . . . 52 A4
Corbiere Ho **5** N1 . . 24 A4
Corbin Ho **8** E3 . . . 27 A2
Corbridge Cres E2 . 25 A3
Corbyn St N4, N19 . . 5 A3
Corby Rd NW10 . . . 20 C3
Corby Way E3 . . . . . 26 C1
Cordelia Cl SE24 . . . 63 A3
Cordelia Ho **28** N1 . 24 A3
Cordelia St E14 . . . 34 A3
Cording St E14 . . . . 34 A4
Cordwainers Ct 18
E8 . . . . 17 B1
Corfe Ho SW8 . . . . 162 C2
Corfe Lodge 15
SE21 . . . . 75 C2
Corfe Twr **9** W3 . . . 37 B4
Corfield St E2 . . . . . 25 A2
Coriander Ave E14 . 34 C3
Coriander Ct SE1 . 139 A4
Corinne Rd N19 . . . 13 B4
Cork Sq E1 . . . . 32 A1
Cork St Mews W1 . 118 C3
Cork St W1 . . . . . . 118 C3
Corlett St NW1 . . . 102 A4
Cormont Rd SE5 . . . 48 A2
Cormorant Ct
26 Deptford SE8 . . . 51 B4
21 Dulwich SE21 . . . 75 C2

Cornbury Ho 5
SE8 . . . . 51 B4
Cornelia St N7 . . . . 14 B2
Cornell Bldg 7
E1 . . . . 111 B2
Corner Fielde
SW2 . . . . 74 B3
Corner Gn SE3 . . . . 53 C1
Corner House St
WC2 . . . . 120 A2
Cornerstone Ct 3
E1 . . . . 99 C1
Cornerways SW15 . 56 C3
Corney Rd W4 . . . . . 46 A4
Corney Reach Way
W4 . . . . 46 A3
Cornflower Terr
SE22 . . . . 65 A1
Cornford Gr SW12 . 73 A2
Cornhill EC3 . . . . . 109 C1
Cornick Ho 7
Brentford TW8 . . . . 36 A1
7 Camberwell
SE17 . . . . 48 A4
Cornish Ho
Brentford TW8 . . . . 36 B1
7 Camberwell
SE17 . . . . 48 A4
Cornmill La SE13 . . 67 B4
Cornmow Dr NW10 . 8 C3
Cornwall Ave E2 . . . 25 B2
Cornwall Cres
W11 . . . . 31 A3
Cornwall Flats
SE1 . . . . 135 C4
Cornwall Gdns
Kensington SW7 . . 128 B1
Willesden NW10 . . . 9 A2
Cornwall Gdns Wlk
SW7 . . . . 128 B1
Cornwall Gr W4 . . . 38 A1
Cornwall Ho
Marylebone NW1 . . 91 A1
3 Putney SW15 . . . 69 B4
Cornwallis Ct
SW8 . . . . 172 A4
Cornwallis Ho 24
W12 . . . . 30 A2
Cornwallis Rd N19 . . 5 A2
Cornwallis Sq
Finsbury Park
N4 . . . . 5 C2
London N19 . . . . 5 A2
Cornwall Mans
Chelsea SW10 . . . . 157 A2
Marylebone NW1 . . 91 A1
Cornwall Mews S
SW7 . . . . 128 C1
Cornwall Mews W
SW7 . . . . 128 B1
Cornwall Rd
Finsbury Pk N4 . . . . 5 C4
Lambeth SE1 . . . . . 135 C4
Cornwall Sq SE11 . 150 A2
Cornwall St **4** E1 . . 32 A2
Cornwall Terr
NW1 . . . . 91 A1
**Cornwall Terrace
Mews NW1 . . . . 91 A1
Cornwood Dr E1 . . . 32 B3
Coronation Ave 11
N16 . . . . 16 B4
Coronation Ct 19
W10 . . . . 30 B4
Coronet St
N1 . . . . 24 A2 98 A3
Corporation Row
EC1 . . . . 95 C2

Con-Cot 201

Corporation St N7 . 14 A3
**Corpus Christi RC
Prim Sch SW2 . . . . 62 B2
**Corrance Rd SW2,
SW4 . . . . 62 A3
Corringham Ct
N11 . . . . 1 C4
Corringham Ho 11
E1 . . . . 32 C3
Corringham Rd
NW11 . . . . 1 C4
Corringway NW11 . . 2 A4
Corry Dr SW9 . . . . . 63 A3
Corry Ho **2** E14 . . . 34 A2
Corsham St N1 . . . . 97 C3
Corsica St N5 . . . . . 15 A2
Corsley Way E9 . . . 18 B2
Cortayne Rd SW6 . 165 A2
Cortis Rd SW15 . . . 57 A1
Cortis Terr SW15 . . 57 A1
Corunna Rd SW8 . 171 A4
Corunna Terr
SW8 . . . . 170 C4
Corvette 5
SE10 . . . . 52 C4
Coryton Path W9 . . 23 B1
Cosbycote Ave
SE24 . . . . 63 B2
Cosgrove Ho 11
. . . . 24 C4
Cosmo Pl WC1 . . . 106 B4
Cosmur Cl W12 . . . 38 B3
Cossall Wlk SE15 . . 50 A2
Cossar Mews 11
SW2 . . . . 62 C2
Cosser St SE1 . . . . 135 B2
Costa St SE15 . . . . 49 C1
Coston Wlk 4
SE4 . . . . 65 C3
Cosway Mans
NW1 . . . . 102 B4
Cosway St NW1 . . . 102 B4
Cotall St E14 . . . . . 33 C4
Cotes Ho NW8 . . . . 90 A1
Cotham St SE17 . . . 151 A3
Cotherstone Rd
SW2 . . . . 74 B3
Cotleigh Rd NW6 . . 10 C1
Cotman Cl SW15 . . 57 C2
Cotman Ho NW8 . . 80 A2
Cotrill Gdns E8 . . . 17 A2
Cotswold Ct EC1 . . 96 C2
Cotswold Gate NW2 . 1 A3
Cotswold Ho N16 . . 7 B3
Cotswold Mews
SW11 . . . . 167 C3
Cottage Gn SE5 . . . 48 C3
Cottage Gr SW9 . . . 62 A4
Cottage Pl SW3 . . . 130 A1
Cottage St E14 . . . . 34 A2
Cottages The SE1 . 134 C1
Cottage Wlk **2** N16 . 7 B1
Cottenham Ho 5
N19 . . . . 5 A2
Cottesbrook St 9
SE14 . . . . 51 A3
Cottesloe Ho NW8 . 90 A2
Cottesloe Mews
SE1 . . . . 135 C2
Cottesmore Ct
W8 . . . . 128 B2
Cottesmore Gdns
W8 . . . . 128 B2

Cottingham Rd
SW8 . . . . **163** A2
Cottington St
SE11 . . . . **150** A2
Cotton Ave W3 . . . . **28** C3
Cotton Ho
Bedford Pk W12 . . . . **38** B4
18 Streatham
SW12 . . . . **74** A4
Cotton Row SW11 . . **59** C4
Cotton's Gdns
E2 . . . . **24** A2 **98** B4
Cottons La SE1 . . . **123** C2
Cotton St E14 . . . . . **34** B2
Cottrell Ct SE10 . . . **43** B2
Couchman Ho 3
SW4 . . . . **61** B1
Coulgate St SE4 . . . **66** A4
Coulson Ho 5
SW2 . . . . **74** A4
Coulson St SW3 . . . **144** C2
Coulter Rd W6 . . . . **39** A3
Coults Cres NW5 . . . . **3** C1
Councillor St SE5 . . **48** B3
Counters Ct W14 . . . **126** A2
Counter St SE1 . . . . **124** A1
Countess Rd NW5 . . **13** B3
Countisbury Ho
SE26 . . . . **76** C1
County Gr SE5 . . . . . **48** B2
County Ho
22 Herne Hill
SE24 . . . . **63** A3
9 South Lambeth
SW9 . . . . **173** B4
County St SE1 . . . . . **137** A1
Courier Ho 17
SW2 . . . . **74** C4
Courland Gr SW8 . . **171** C3
Courland St SW8 . . **171** C3
Courtauld Ho 12
E2 . . . . **24** C3
Courtauld Inst of Art
WC2 . . . . **120** C4
Courtenay Ave N6 . . . **3** A4
Courtenay Sq
SE11 . . . . **149** B1
Courtenay St
SE11 . . . . **149** B2
Courtfield Gdns
SW5 . . . . **142** B3
Courtfield Ho EC1 . . **107** B4
Courtfield Mews
SW7 . . . . **142** B3
Courtfield Rd
SW7 . . . . **142** C3
Court Gdns N7 . . . . . **14** C2
Courthill Rd SE13 . . . **67** B3
Courthope Ho
14 Rotherhithe
SE16 . . . . **40** B3
South Lambeth
SW8 . . . . **162** A1
Courthope Rd
NW3 . . . . **12** B4
Court La SE21 . . . . . **76** B4
Courtlands TW10 . . . **54** C2
Courtlands Ave
TW9 . . . . **45** A1
Court Lane Gdns
SE21 . . . . **76** A4
Court Mans 8 W6 . . **38** C2

Courtmead Cl
SE24 . . . . **63** B1
Courtnell St W2 . . . . **31** C3
Courtney Ct N7 . . . . . **14** C3
Courtney Ho W14 . . **126** B2
Courtrai Rd SE23 . . . **66** A1
Court Royal SW15 . . **58** A2
Court St 3 E1 . . . . . **32** A4
Courtville Ho 12
W10 . . . . **23** A2
Court Way W3 . . . . . **28** B4
Courtyard The
Fulham SW6 . . . . . . **164** A3
Islington N1 . . . . **14** C1
13 Wandsworth
SW18 . . . . **59** C3
Cousin La EC4 . . . . . **123** B3
Couzens Ho 3 E3 . . . **33** B4
Coval Gdns SW14 . . **55** A3
Coval La SW14 . . . . . **55** A3
Coval Pas SW14 . . . . **55** B3
Coval Rd SW14 . . . . . **55** B3
Covell Ct 3 SE8 . . . . **51** C3
Covent Garden Sta
WC2 . . . . **106** B1
Coventry Cl NW6 . . . **23** C4
Coventry Rd E1 . . . . **25** A1
Coventry St W1 . . . **119** B3
Coverdale Rd
Brondesbury
NW2 . . . . **10** A2
Hammersmith W12 . . **39** A4
Hampstead NW6 . . . . **10** A1
Coverham Ho 5
SE4 . . . . **65** C3
Coverley Cl E1 . . . . **111** C4
Coverley Point
SE11 . . . . **148** C3
Cowcross St EC1 . . . **108** A4
Cowdenbeath Path
N1 . . . . **84** C4
Cowdray Hall Royal
Coll of Nursing
W1 . . . . **104** A2
Cowdray Ho 22
SE22 . . . . **64** A4
Cowdry Rd E9 . . . . . **18** B2
Cowley Rd
Brixton SW9 . . . . . . **173** C4
East Acton W3 . . . . . **29** B2
Mortlake SW14 . . . . . **56** A4
Cowley St SW1 . . . . **134** A1
Cowling Cl
Pimlico SW11 . . . . . **147** C1
Walworth SE17 . . . . **151** A2
Cowper Ho
Acton W3 . . . . **28** C1
Stoke Newington
N16 . . . . **16** A4
Cowper's Ct EC3 . . . **109** C1
Cowper St EC1,EC2 . . **97** C2
Cowper Terr W10 . . . **30** C4
Cowthorpe Rd
SW8 . . . . **172** A4
Cox Ho W6 . . . . **154** A4
Coxson Way SE1 . . . **138** C3
Coysh Ct 5 SW15 . . **58** A2
Crabtree Ct E2 . . . . . **24** C3
Crabtree Hall SW6 . . **47** B3
Crabtree La SW6 . . . **47** C3
Craddock St NW5 . . . **12** C2
Cragie Ho SE1 . . . . . **153** A3
Craigleith SW15 . . . **57** C1

Craignair Rd SW2 . . **74** C4
Craig's Ct SW1 . . . . **120** A2
Craik Ct NW6 . . . . . **23** B3
Crail Row SE17 . . . . **151** C3
Cramer St W1 . . . . . **103** C3
Crammond Cl W6 . . **154** A3
Crampton Prim Sch
SE17 . . . . **150** B2
Crampton St SE17 . . **150** C2
Cranbourn Alley
WC2 . . . . **119** C4
Cranbourne Ct
SW11 . . . . **158** B2
Cranbourn Ho 6
E15 . . . . **19** B4
Cranbourn Pas 5
SE16 . . . . **40** A4
Cranbourn St
WC2 . . . . **119** C4
Cranbrook NW1 . . . . **83** A3
Cranbrook Ho 5
E5 . . . . **17** A3
Cranbrook Rd
Chiswick W4 . . . . **38** A1
St Johns SE8 . . . . **51** C2
Cranbrook St E2 . . . . **25** C3
Cranbury Rd SW6 . . **166** B1
Crandale Ho 5 E5 . . . **17** A3
Crandley Ct SE8 . . . . **41** A2
Crane Ave W3 . . . . . **28** C2
Crane Ct
7 Acton W12 . . . . . . **38** A4
Holborn EC4 . . . . . . **107** C1
Crane Gr N7 . . . . **14** C2
Crane Ho
4 Bow E3 . . . . **26** A3
20 Peckham SE15 . . **49** B2
Crane Mead SE16 . . . **40** C2
Crane St
Greenwich SE10 . . . . **42** C1
8 Peckham SE15 . . . **49** B2
Cranfield Ct NW1 . . **102** B3
Cranfield Ho WC1 . . **106** B4
Cranfield Rd SE4 . . . **66** B4
Cranford Cotts 8
E1 . . . . **32** C2
Cranford Lo SW19 . . **69** C2
Cranford St E1 . . . . . **32** C2
Cranhurst Rd NW2 . . . **9** B3
Cranleigh
W11 . . . . . . **31** B1 **112** C2
Cranleigh Ct
Richmond TW9 . . . . . **54** C4
4 Stamford Hill N16 . . **7** A3
Cranleigh Hos
NW1 . . . . **83** A1
Cranleigh Mews
SW11 . . . . **168** C1
Cranleigh St NW1 . . . **83** A1
Cranley Gdns
SW7 . . . . **143** B2
Cranley Mews
SW7 . . . . **143** A2
Cranley Pl SW7 . . . . **143** B3
Cranmer Ct SW3 . . . **144** B3
Cranmer Ho
SW11 . . . . **168** A4
Cranmer Rd SW9 . . . **163** C2
Cranswick Rd
SE16 . . . . **40** A1
Cranwell Cl E3 . . . . . **27** A1
Cranwich Rd N16 . . . . **7** A4
Cranwood St EC1 . . . **97** C3
Cranwood St EC1 . . . **97** C3

Cranworth Gdns
SW9 . . . . **173** B4
Cranworth Ho 6
N7 . . . . **14** B4
Craster Rd SW2 . . . . **74** B4
Craston Ho 2 SE5 . . . **49** A1
Craven Cl N16 . . . . . . **7** C4
Craven Cottage
(Fulham FC)
SW6 . . . . **47** C2
Craven Hill W2 . . . . **115** A4
Craven Hill Gdns
W2 . . . . **114** C4
Craven Hill Mews
W2 . . . . **115** A4
Craven Ho 2
SW14 . . . . **55** C4
Craven Lo
Bayswater W2 . . . . . **115** A4
Fulham SW6 . . . . **47** C2
Craven Mews 6
SW11 . . . . **60** C4
Craven Park Mews
NW10 . . . . **21** A4
Craven Park Rd
Harlesden NW10 . . . . **21** B4
25 Stoke Newington
N15 . . . . **7** A4
Craven Pas WC2 . . . **120** A2
Craven Pk NW10 . . . . **21** A4
Craven Rd
Paddington W2 . . . . **101** A1
Stonebridge NW10 . . **20** C4
Craven St W2 . . . . . **120** A2
Craven Terr W2 . . . . **115** A4
Craven Wlk E5,N16 . . . **7** C4
Crawford Bldgs
NW1 . . . . **102** B3
Crawford Mews
W1 . . . . **102** C3
Crawford Pas EC1 . . . **95** C1
Crawford Pl W1 . . . **102** B3
Crawford Place
Dwellings W1 . . . . **102** B3
Crawford Point 4
E16 . . . . **35** B3
Crawford Prim Sch
SE5 . . . . **48** B2
Crawford Rd SE5 . . . **48** B2
Crawford St W1 . . . **103** A3
Crawshay Ct SW9 . . **173** C4
Crawshay Ho 13
N16 . . . . **15** C4
Crawthew Gr SE22 . . **64** B3
Crayford Ho
Bermondsey SE1 . . . **137** C3
5 Lower Holloway
N7 . . . . **14** A4
Crayford Rd N7 . . . . **14** A4
Crayle Ho EC1 . . . . . **96** B2
Creasy Est SE1 . . . . **138** A1
Crebor St SE22 . . . . . **64** C1
Credenhill Ho 2
SE15 . . . . **50** A3
Crediton Hill NW6 . . . **11** A3
Crediton Rd NW10 . . . **22** C4
Credon Rd SE16 . . . . **40** A1
Creechurch La
EC3 . . . . **110** B1
Creechurch Pl
EC3 . . . . **110** B1
Creed Ct 8 EC4 . . . . **26** A2
Creed Ho SE15 . . . . . **65** A4
Creed La EC4 . . . . . **108** B1
Creek Ho W14 . . . . **126** B2
Creek Rd SE10,SE8 . . **52** A4

Creek Road Ind Est
SE8 . . . . **52** A4
Creekside SE8 . . . . . **52** A3
Creekside Foyer
SE8 . . . . **52** A4
Crefeld Cl W6 . . . . . **154** A3
Creighton Cl W12 . . . **30** A2
Creighton Rd NW6 . . **22** C3
Cremer Bsns Ctr 8
E2 . . . . **24** B3
Cremer Ho 9 SE8 . . . **51** C3
Cremer St E2 . . . . . . **24** B3
Cremorne Rd
SW10 . . . . **157** B2
Creon Ct 3 SW9 . . . **173** B4
Crescent EC3 . . . . . . **124** C4
Crescent Arc 1
SE10 . . . . **52** B4
Crescent Court Bsns
Ctr 1 E16 . . . . **27** C1
Crescent Ct SW4 . . . **61** C2
Crescent Gdns
SW19 . . . . **70** C1
Crescent Gr SW4 . . . **61** B3
Crescent Ho SE13 . . . **52** A1
Crescent La SW4 . . . **61** C2
Crescent Mans
Islington N5 . . . . **15** A3
Notting Hill
W11 . . . . . **31** A2 **112** B4
Crescent Pl SW3 . . . **144** B4
Crescent Row EC1 . . **96** C1
Crescent St N1 . . . . . **14** B1
Crescent Stables
SW15 . . . . **58** A2
Crescent The
Acton W3 . . . . **29** A3
Barnes SW13 . . . . . . **46** C1
Wimbledon SW19 . . . **70** C1
Crescent Way SE4 . . **66** C4
Crescent Wood Rd
SE26 . . . . **76** C1
Cresford Rd SW6 . . **166** A3
Cressage Ho 2
TW8 . . . . **44** A4
Cressall Ho E14 . . . . **41** C3
Cresset Ho 8 E9 . . . . **17** B2
Cresset Rd E9 . . . . . . **17** B2
Cresset St SW4 . . . . . **61** C4
Cressfield Cl NW5 . . . **12** C3
Cressida Rd N19 . . . . . **4** C3
Cressingham Rd
SE13 . . . . **67** B4
Cressington Cl 4
N16 . . . . **16** A3
Cresswell Gdns
SW5 . . . . **142** C2
Cresswell Pl
SW10 . . . . **143** A2
Cressy Ct
Hammersmith W6 . . . **39** A3
8 Stepney E1 . . . . . . **32** B4
38 Stepney E1 . . . . . **32** B4
Cressy Ho SW13 . . . . **57** A4
Cressy Hos 2 E1 . . . . **32** B4
Cressy Pl E1 . . . . **32** B4
Cressy Rd NW3 . . . . . **12** B4
Cresta Ho
7 Bow E3 . . . . **26** C1
Hampstead NW6 . . . . **11** C1
Crestfield St N1,
WC1 . . . . **94** B4
Crestview NW5 . . . . . . **4** A1
Crestway SW15 . . . . . **57** A1
Creswick Ct W3 . . . . **28** A2
Creswick Rd W3 . . . . **28** A2

Creswick Wlk [7]
E3 . . . . 26 C2

Crewdson Rd
SW9 . . . . 163 B1

Crewe Pl NW10 . . . . 21 B2

Crewkerne Ct
SW11 . . . . 167 C4

Crews St E14 . . . . . 41 C2

Crewys Rd
Child's Hill NW2 . . . . . 1 A1
London SE15 . . . . . . 50 A1

Crichton St SW8 . . 170 C2

Cricketers Mews [4]
SW18 . . . . 59 A2

Cricketfield Rd E5 . . 17 A4

Cricklade Ave
SW2 . . . . 74 B2

CRICKLEWOOD 9 B4

Cricklewood
Broadway NW2 . . . . . 9 C4

Cricklewood La
NW2 . . . . 1 B1

Cricklewood Sta
NW2 . . . . 9 C4

Crieff Rd SW18 . . . . 59 B1

Criffel Ave SW2 . . . 73 C3

Crimscott St SE1 . . 138 B1

Crimsworth Rd
SW8 . . . . 161 C1

Crinan St N1 . . . . . . 84 B2

Cringle St SW8 . . . 160 C2

Cripplegate St
EC1 . . . . 109 A4

Crispe Ho N1 . . . . . 85 A3

Crispian Cl NW10 . . . 8 A4

Crispin Ct SE17 . . . 152 A3

Crispin Pl E1 . . . . . 110 C4

Crispin St E1 . . . . . 110 C3

Crisp Rd W6 . . . . . . 39 B1

Cristowe Rd SW6 . . 165 A1

Criterion Mews
N19 . . . . 4 C2

Crockerton Rd
SW17 . . . . 72 B2

Croft Ct SE13 . . . . . 67 B1

Croftdown Rd NW5 . . . 4 A1

Crofters Ct [9] SE8 . 41 A2

Crofters Way NW1 . . 83 B4

Croft Ho
Putney SW15 . . . . . . 58 A1
[11] West Kilburn
W10 . . . . 23 A2

Crofton Ave W4 . . . . 45 C3

Crofton Gate Way
SE4 . . . . 66 A2

Crofton Park Rd
SE4 . . . . 66 B1

Crofton Park Sta
SE4 . . . . 66 A2

Crofton Rd SE5 . . . . 49 A1

Crofton Terr
Homerton E5 . . . . . . 18 A3
Richmond TW9 . . . . . 54 B3

Crofts Ho [21] E2 . . . 24 C3

Crofts St E1 . . . . . . 125 B3

Croft St SE8 . . . . . . 41 A2

Croft The NW10 . . . 21 B3

Crogsland Rd
NW1 . . . . 12 C1

Cromartie Rd N19 . . . 4 C4

Cromarty Ho [8]
E1 . . . . 33 A4

Crombie Mews [5]
SW11 . . . . 168 B2

Cromdale Ct N16 . . . . 7 B4

Cromer Ct
Streatham SW16 . . . . 74 A1
Wandsworth SW18 . . . 58 B1

Crome Rd NW10 . . . . . 8 A2

Cromer St WC1 . . . . . 94 B3

Cromer Terr E8 . . . . 16 C3

Cromer Villas Rd
SW18 . . . . 58 B1

Cromford Path [1]
E5 . . . . 17 C4

Cromford Rd
SW18 . . . . 58 C2

Crompton Ct SW3 . . 144 A4

Crompton Ho
Borough The SE1 . . . 137 A1
Paddington W2 . . . . . 89 B1
South Lambeth
SW8 . . . . 171 A3

Crompton St W2 . . . . 89 B1

Cromwell Ave
Hammersmith W6 . . . 39 A2
Highgate N6 . . . . 4 A3

Cromwell Cl
Acton W3 . . . . 28 B1
[2] Gunnersbury
W4 . . . . 37 A1

Cromwell Cres
SW5 . . . . 141 B4

Cromwell Ctr
NW10 . . . . 20 C2

Cromwell Gdns
SW7 . . . . 129 C1

Cromwell Gr W6 . . . . 39 B3

Cromwell Ho
Battersea SW11 . . . . 169 C3
Putney SW15 . . . . . . 56 C3

Cromwell Hospl
(BUPA) SW5 . . . . . . 142 A4

Cromwell Lo [46]
E1 . . . . 25 B1

Cromwell Mans
SW5 . . . . 141 C4

Cromwell Mews
SW7 . . . . 143 C4

Cromwell Pl
[8] Acton W3 . . . . . . 28 B1
Barbican EC1 . . . . . 109 A4
Highgate N6 . . . . 4 A3
Mortlake SW14 . . . . . 55 B4
South Kensington
SW7 . . . . 143 C4

Cromwell Rd
Brixton SW9 . . . . 48 A2
South Kensington
SW7 . . . . 143 A4

Cromwell Twr
EC2 . . . . 109 A4

Crondace Rd SW6 . . 165 C3

Crondall Ct [8] N1 . . 24 A3

Crondall Ho SW15 . . 68 C3

Crondall Pl [15] N1 . . 24 A3

Crondall St N1 . . . . . 24 A3

Crone Ct [5] NW6 . . . 23 B3

Cronin St SE15 . . . . 49 B3

Crooked Billet Yd [18]
E2 . . . . 24 A3

Crooke Rd SE8 . . . . . 41 A1

Crookham Rd
SW6 . . . . 164 C3

Croom's Hill SE10 . . 52 C3

Croom's Hill Gr
SE10 . . . . 52 B3

Cropley Ct N1 . . . . . . 87 B2

Cropley St N1 . . . . . . 87 B2

Cropthorne Ct W9 . . 89 A3

Crosby Ct [18] SE1 . 137 B4

Crosby Ho [18] E14 . . 42 B3

Crosby Row SE1 . . . 137 B4

Crosby Sq EC3 . . . . 110 A2

Crosby Wlk
[3] Dalston E8 . . . . . . 16 B2
Streatham SE24 . . . . 74 C4

Crosfield Ct [3]
W10 . . . . 30 C3

Crosfield Ho
W11 . . . . 31 A2 112 A3

Crosland Pl [5]
SW11 . . . . 60 C4

Crossbow Ho [19]
N1 . . . . 24 A4

Cross Cl SE15 . . . . . 50 A1

Cross Ct SE5 . . . . . . 63 C4

Crossfield Rd
NW3 . . . . 11 C2

Crossfield St SE8 . . . 51 C3

Crossford St SW9 . . 172 C1

Crossharbour Sta
E14 . . . . 42 A3

Cross Keys Cl W1 . . 103 C3

Cross La SE5 . . . . . 122 A4

Crossleigh Ct [3]
SE14 . . . . 51 B3

Crosslet St SE17 . . . 151 C4

Crosslet Vale SE10 . 52 A2

Crossley St N7 . . . . . 14 C2

Crossman Hos [1]
SW12 . . . . 74 A4

Crossmount Ho [3]
SE5 . . . . 48 B3

Cross Rd SE5 . . . . . 49 A1

Cross St
Islington N1 . . . . 86 B4
Mortlake SW13 . . . . . 56 A4

Crossthwaite Ave SE5,
SE24 . . . . 63 C3

Crosstrees Ho [7]
E14 . . . . 41 C3

Crosswall EC3 . . . . . 124 C4

Crossway E8, N16 . . 16 A3

Crossway Ct SE4 . . . 51 A1

Crossways Acad
SE4 . . . . 51 A1

Croston St E8 . . . . . 24 C4

Crouch End Hill N8 . . 4 C4

Crouch Hall Ct N19 . . 5 A3

Crouch Hill N4, N8,
N19 . . . . 5 A4

Crouch Hill Sta N4 . . 5 B4

Crouchmans Cl SE21,
SE26 . . . . 76 C1

Crowder St E1 . . . . . 32 A2

Crowfield Ho N5 . . . . 15 B4

Crowfoot Cl E9 . . . . . 18 B3

Crowhurst Cl
SW9 . . . . 173 C2

Crowhurst Ho [21]
SW9 . . . . 173 A1

Crowland Ho NW8 . . 78 C3

Crowland Terr N1 . . . 15 C1

Crowline Wlk [1]
N1 . . . . 15 B2

Crown Ct continued
St John's Wood
NW8 . . . . 90 B3

Crowndale Ct NW1 . . 83 B2

Crowndale Rd
NW1 . . . . 83 A2

Crowne Ho SE1 . . . 123 A1

Crownfield Rd E15 . . 19 C4

Crowngate Ho [33]
E3 . . . . 26 B3

Crownhill Rd
NW10 . . . . 21 B4

Crownleigh
SW2 . . . . 62 C2

Crown Lo SW3 . . . . 144 B3

Crown Mews [9]
E1 . . . . 32 C4

Crown Office Row
EC4 . . . . 121 B4

Crown Pas SW1 . . . 119 A1

Crown Pl
Broadgate EC2 . . . . 110 A4
Kentish Town NW5 . . . 13 A2

Crown Reach
SW1 . . . . 147 C1

Crown St
Acton W3 . . . . 28 A1
Camberwell SE5 . . . . 48 B3

Crownstone Ct [1]
SW2 . . . . 62 C2

Crownstone Rd
SW2 . . . . 62 C2

Crown Terr TW9 . . . . 54 B3

Crows Rd E3, E15 . . 27 C3

Crowther Ave
TW8 . . . . 36 A2

Crowther Cl SW6 . . 155 A3

Crowthorne Cl
SW18 . . . . 70 B3

Crowthorne Rd
W10 . . . . 30 C3

Croxley Ho W9 . . . . . 23 B2

Croxted Cl SE21 . . . . 75 B4

Croxted Rd SE21,
SE24 . . . . 75 C3

Croxteth Ho [1]
SW8 . . . . 171 B2

Croydon Ho SE1 . . . 135 C4

Crozier Ho SW8 . . . 162 C1

Crozier Terr E9 . . . . 17 C3

Crucifix La SE1 . . . . 138 A4

Cruden Ho
[15] Bow E3 . . . . 26 B3
[1] Camberwell
SE17 . . . . 48 A4

Cruden St N1 . . . . . . 86 B3

Cruickshank St
WC1 . . . . 95 B4

Cruikshank Ho
NW8 . . . . 80 B2

Crusader Ho EC1 . . . 96 A1

Crusoe Mews N16 . . . 6 C2

Crutched Friars
EC3 . . . . 124 B4

Crystal Palace Rd
SE22 . . . . 64 C2

Crystal Wharf N1 . . . 86 B1

Cuba St E14 . . . . . . 41 C4

Cubitt Bldg SW1 . . . 146 A1

Cubitt Ho [4] SW4 . . 61 B1

Cubitt St WC1 . . . . . 95 A3

Cubitt Terr SW4 . . . . 61 B4

CUBITT TOWN 42 C2

Cubitt Town Jun & Inf
Sch E14 . . . . 42 C3

Cuddington SE17 . . 151 A4

Cudworth Ho
SW8 . . . . 171 A3

Cudworth St E1 . . . . 25 A1

Cuffley Ho [3] W10 . 30 B4

Cuff Point [2]
E2 . . . . 24 B2 98 C4

Culand Ho SE17 . . . 152 A3

Culford Gdns
SW3 . . . . 145 A3

Culford Gr N1 . . . . . 16 A2

Culford Mans
SW3 . . . . 145 A3

Culford Mews N1 . . . 16 A2

Culford Rd
Kingsland N1 . . . . . . 16 A2
Shoreditch N1 . . . . . 24 A4

Culham Ho
[21] Paddington
W2 . . . . 31 C4
[33] Shoreditch
E2 . . . . 24 B2 98 C3

Cullen Ho W9 . . . . . 23 B3

Cullen Way NW10 . . 20 B1

Culling Rd SE16 . . . . 40 B3

Cullingworth Rd
NW10 . . . . 9 A3

Culloden Cl [2]
SE16 . . . . 153 C1

Culloden Prim Sch [1]
E14 . . . . 34 B3

Cullum St EC3 . . . . 124 A4

Culmore Rd SE15 . . . 50 B3

Culmstock Rd
SW11 . . . . 60 C2

Culpepper Ct
SE11 . . . . 149 B4

Culross Bldgs
NW1 . . . . 84 A2

Culross St W1 . . . . . 117 B3

Culver Ct SW18 . . . . 59 A1

Culverden Rd
SW12 . . . . 73 B2

Culverhouse WC1 . . 106 C3

Culverhouse Gdns
SW16 . . . . 74 B1

Culverin Ct [1] N7 . . 14 B3

Culvert Ct SW11 . . . 169 B2

Culvert Pl SW11 . . . 169 B1

Culvert Rd SW11 . . . 169 A2

Culworth Ho NW8 . . . 80 A1

Culworth St NW8 . . . 80 A1

Cumber Ho SW18 . . . 70 C3

Cumberland Ave
NW10 . . . . 20 A2

Cumberland Bsns Pk
NW10 . . . . 20 A2

Cumberland Cl E8 . . 16 B2

Cumberland Cres
W14 . . . . 140 B4

Cumberland Ct
W1 . . . . 103 A1

Cumberland Gate
W1 . . . . 117 A4

Cumberland Gdns
WC1 . . . . 95 B4

Cumberland Ho
Paddington W9 . . . . . 88 C1
[1] Putney SW15 . . . . 69 B4

Cumberland Mans
Marylebone W1 . . . . 102 C2
[7] West Hampstead
NW6 . . . . 10 C3

Cumberland Market
NW1 . . . . 92 B4

204 Cum–Dat

Cumberland Mills Sq
E14 .... 41 B3
Cumberland Park Ind
Est NW10 .... 21 C2
Cumberland Pk
W3 .... 28 B2
Cumberland Pl
NW1 .... 92 A4
Cumberland Rd
Acton W3 .... 28 A2
Barnes SW13 .... 46 C2
Richmond TW9 ...... 44 C3
Cumberland St
SW1 .... 146 B2
Cumberland Terr
NW1 .... 82 A1
Cumberland Terrace
Mews NW1 .... 82 A1
Cumberland Villas
W3 .... 28 B2
Cumberland Wharf 12
SE16 .... 40 B4
Cumbrian Gdns
NW2 .... 1 A2
Cuming Mus SE17 130 C3
Cumming St N1 .... 85 A1
Cumnor Cl 23
SW9 .... 173 A2
Cunard Pl EC3 .... 110 B1
Cunard Rd NW10 ... 20 C2
Cunard Wlk 5
SE16 .... 41 A3
Cundy St SW1 .... 145 C3
Cureton St SW1 .. 147 C3
Curlew Ho
Brockley SE4 ...... 66 A3
7 Peckham SE15 ... 49 B2
Curlew St SE1 ... 139 A4
Curness St SE13 .. 67 B3
Curran Ho SW3 ... 144 A3
Curricle St W3 .... 29 A1
Currie Ho 13
SW12 .... 159 C4
Cursitor St EC4 .. 107 B2
Curtain Pl
EC2 .... 24 A1 98 B2
Curtain Rd
EC2 .... 24 A1 98 B2
Curtis Dr W3 ...... 28 C3
Curtis Ho SE17 ... 151 B2
Curtis St SE1 .... 152 C4
Curtis Way SE1 .. 152 C4
Curve Bldg The
SE4 .... 66 B2
Curwen The W12 .. 38 C4
Curwen Gall W1 .. 105 B3
Curwen Rd W12 ... 38 C4
Curzon Cres NW10 .. 8 A1
Curzon Gate W1 .. 117 C1
Curzon Sq W1 .... 117 C1
Curzon St W1 .... 118 A2
Custance Ho N1 ... 87 C1
Custance St N1 ... 97 B4
Custom House

Custom House Reach
SE16 .... 41 B3
Cutbush Ho N7 .... 13 C3
Cutcombe Rd SE5 .. 48 B1
Cuthbert Harrowing
Ho EC1 .... 96 C1
Cuthbert Ho W2 .. 101 B4
Cuthbert St W2 ... 89 B1
Cuthill Wlk 3 SE5 . 48 C2
Cutlers Gdns EC3 . 110 B2
Cutlers Gdns Arc
EC2 .... 110 B2
Cutlers Sq E14 ... 41 C2
Cutler St EC2 .... 110 B2
Cut The SE1 ..... 135 C4
Cutty Sark SE10 .. 52 B4
Cutty Sark Ho 10
E14 .... 42 A2
Cutty Sark Sta
SE10 .... 52 B4
Cuxton Ho SE17 .. 152 B2
Cyclops Mews 12
E14 .... 41 C2
Cygnet House N 8
E14 .... 34 B3
Cygnet House S 6
E14 .... 34 A3
Cygnet St
E1 .... 24 B1 99 A2
Cygnus Bsns Ctr
NW10 .... 8 B2
Cynthia St N1 .... 85 A1
Cyntra Pl 8 E8 .... 17 A1
Cypress Cl 5 E5 ... 7 C2
Cypress Ct 5 E11 . 19 C4
Cypress Gdns SE4 . 66 A2
Cypress Ho SE14 .. 50 C2
Cypress Pl W1 .... 93 A1
Cyprus Pl 2 E2 ... 25 B3
Cyprus St E2 ...... 25 B3
Cyrena Rd SE22 ... 64 B2
Cyril Jackson Prim
Sch (North Bldg) 4
E14 .... 33 B2
Cyril Jackson Prim
Sch (South Bldg) 4
E14 .... 33 B2
Cyril Mans SW11 . 169 A3
Cyril Thatcher Ho
SW6 .... 165 C3
Cyrus Ho EC1 ..... 96 B2
Cyrus St EC1 ..... 96 B2
Czar St SE8 ...... 51 C4

D

Dabb's La EC1 .... 95 C1
Dabin Cres SW10 .. 50 C3
Dacca St SE8 ..... 51 B4
Dace Rd E3 .... 26 C4
Dacre Ho SW3 .... 157 C3
Dacre St SW1 .... 133 B2
Daffodil St W12 ... 29 B2
Dafforne Rd SW17 72 C1
Dagmar Ct E14 ... 42 B3
Dagmar Gdns
NW10 .... 22 C3
Dagmar Pas N1 ... 86 B4
Dagmar Rd
Camberwell SE5 ... 49 A2
Finsbury Pk N4 .... 5 C4
Dagmar Terr N1 .. 86 B4
Dagnall St SW11 . 169 B3
Dagnan Rd SW12 . 73 B4

Dagobert Ho 27
E1 .... 32 B4
Daimler Ho 8 E3 . 26 C1
Dainton Ho 22 W2 31 C4
Daintry Way E9 ... 18 B2
Dairy Cl NW10 ... 21 C4
Dairyman Cl NW2 . 1 A1
Daisy Dormer Ct 11
SW9 .... 62 B3
Daisy La SW6 .... 58 C4
Dakin Pl 1 E1 .... 33 A4
Dakota bldg 6
SE13 .... 52 A2
Dalberg Rd SW2 .. 62 C2
Dalbury Ho 6
SW9 .... 62 B3
Dalby Rd SW18 ... 59 B3
Dalby St NW5 .... 13 A2
Dalebury Rd SW17 72 B2
Dale Croft N4 .... 6 B1
Dalehead NW1 .... 82 C1
Daleham Gdns
NW3 .... 11 C2
Daleham Mews
NW3 .... 11 C2
Dale Ho
London SE4 .... 66 A3
St John's Wood
NW8 .... 78 C4
Dalemain Ho 8
SW8 .... 171 C2
Dalemain Mews 12
E16 .... 35 C1
Dale Rd
Camberwell SE17 .. 48 A4
Gospel Oak NW5 .. 12 C3
Dale Row W11 .... 31 A3
Dale St W4 .... 38 A1
Daley Ho 6 W12 .. 30 A3
Daley St E9 ...... 17 C2
Daley Thompson Way 2
7 SW8 .... 61 A4
Dalgarno Gdns
W10 .... 30 B4
Dalgarno Way
W10 .... 22 B1
Daling Way E3 .... 26 A3
Dalkeith Ho 6
SW9 .... 48 A2
Dalkeith Rd SE21 . 75 B4
Dalling Rd W6 .... 39 A2
Dallington Sch
EC1 .... 96 B2
Dallington St EC1 . 96 B2
Dalmeny Ave N7 .. 13 C3
Dalmeny Avenue Est
3 N7 .... 13 C3
Dalmeny Ct 4
SW4 .... 172 A2
Dalmeny Rd N7 ... 13 C4
Dalmeyer Rd NW10 8 B2
Dalmore Rd SE21 . 75 B2
Dalrymple Rd SE4 . 66 A3
DALSTON 16 C2
Dalston Jct 6 E8 . 16 B1
Dalston Junction Sta
.... 16 A2
Dalston Kingsland Sta
.... 16 A3
Dalston La E8 .... 16 C3
Dalton Ho
8 Balham SW12 ... 73 A4
10 Bow E3 .... 26 A3
8 Deptford SE14 . 50 C4
Dalton St SE27 ... 75 A1

Dalwood St SE5 .. 49 A2
Dalyell Rd SW9 ... 62 B4
Damascene Wlk
SE21 .... 75 B3
Damer Ho 5
TW10 .... 54 B1
Damer Terr SW10 157 A1
Dame St N1 .... 86 C2
Damien Ct 12 E1 . 32 A3
Damien St E1 ..... 32 A3
Damory Ho 1
SE16 .... 40 B2
Dan Bryant Ho 8
SW12 .... 73 B4
Danbury St N1 ... 86 B2
Danby Ho
32 Hackney E9 ... 17 B1
2 West Kilburn
W10 .... 23 A2
Danby St SE15 ... 64 B4
Dancer Rd
Fulham SW6 ..... 164 C3
Richmond TW9 ... 54 C4
Dandridge Cl SE10 43 B1
Dandridge Ho E1 . 110 C4
Danebury 18 W10 . 22 B1
Danebury Ave
SW15 .... 56 B1
Danecroft Rd SE24 63 C2
Dane Ho 16 SE5 .. 48 B1
Danehurst St
SW6 .... 164 A4
Danemere St
SW15 .... 57 B4
Dane Pl 3 E3 ..... 26 B3
Danes Ct 16 NW8 . 80 C3
Danesdale Rd E9 . 18 A2
Danesfield SE5 ... 49 A4
Danes Ho 10 W10 . 30 B4
Daneswood Ave
SE6 .... 67 C1
Daneville Rd SE5 . 48 C2
Daniel Bolt Cl E14 34 A4
Daniel Ct 2 W3 ... 29 A2
Daniel Gdns SE15 . 49 B3
Daniell Ho 11 N1 . 87 C2
Daniel's Rd SE15 . 65 B4
Dan Leno Wlk
SW6 .... 156 A1
Dansey Pl W1 .... 119 B4
Dante Pl SE11 ... 150 A4
Dante Rd SE11 ... 150 A4
Danube Ct 13 SE15 49 B3
Danube St SW3 .. 144 B2
Danvers Ho 14 E1 111 C1
Danvers St SW3 .. 157 C3
Da Palma Ct SW6 155 B3
Daphne St SW18 . 59 B1
Daplyn St 6 E1 .. 111 B4
D'arblay St W1 .. 105 A1
Darcy Ho E8 ...... 25 A4
Darell Prim Sch
TW9 .... 54 C4
Darell Rd TW9 ... 54 C4
Daren Ct N7 ...... 14 A4
Darent Ho NW8 .. 101 C4
Darenth Rd N16 .. 7 B3
Darfield NW1 ..... 82 C3
Darfield Rd SE4 .. 66 B2
Darfield Way W10 . 30 C3
Darfur St 2 SW15 57 C4
Darien Ho
16 London SE4 ... 59 C4
11 Stepney E1 ... 32 C4
Darien Rd SW11 .. 59 C4
Daring Ho 25 E3 . 26 A3
Darlan Rd SW6 .. 155 A1

Darley Ho SE11 .. 148 C1
Darley Ho SW11 .. 60 B1
Darling Rd SE4 ... 66 C4
Darling Row E1 ... 25 A1
Darlington Ho
SW8 .... 161 C1
Darnall Ho 4
SE10 .... 52 B2
Darnay Ho 5
SE16 .... 139 C2
Darnell Ho 9
SE10 .... 52 B3
Darnley Ho 7 E14 33 A3
Darnley Rd E9 ... 17 B2
Darnley Terr 12
W11 .... 30 C1
Darrell Rd SE22 .. 64 C2
Darren Cl N4 ..... 5 B4
Darsley Dr SW8 . 172 A4
Dartford Ho SE1 . 153 A4
Dartford St SE17 . 48 B3
Dartington Ho
Bayswater W2 ... 100 A4
2 London SW8 .. 171 C2
Dartle Ct 23 SE16 139 C3
Dartmoor Wlk 18
E14 .... 41 C2
Dartmouth Cl W11 31 C3
Dartmouth Ct
SE10 .... 52 B2
Dartmouth Gr
SE10 .... 52 B2
Dartmouth Hill
SE10 .... 52 B2
Dartmouth Ho
Dartmouth Pk N19 . 4 A2
Lewisham SE10 ... 52 B1
DARTMOUTH
PARK 4 A1
Dartmouth Park Ave
NW5 .... 4 A1
Dartmouth Park Hill
N19 .... 4 A2
Dartmouth Park Rd
NW5 .... 4 A1
Dartmouth Pl W4 . 46 A4
Dartmouth Rd NW2 9 C2
Dartmouth Row
SE10 .... 52 B2
Dartmouth St
SW1 .... 133 C3
Dartmouth Terr
SE10 .... 52 C2
Darton Ct W3 .... 28 B1
Dartrey Twr
SW10 .... 157 B2
Dartrey Wlk
SW10 .... 157 A2
Dart St W10 ...... 23 B2
Darville Rd N16 .. 7 B1
Darwen Pl E2 .... 25 A4
Darwin Cl N11 ... 81 C4
Darwin Ct NW1 .. 129 B1
Darwin Ho 8
SE13 .... 52 B1
Darwin St SE17 . 151 C4
Daryngton Ho
SW8 .... 162 A1
Dashwood Ho
SE21 .... 76 B1
Data Point Bsns Ctr
E16 .... 27 C1
Datchelor Pl 14
SE5 .... 48 C2
Datchet Ho NW1 . 92 B4

Datchett Ho 49
E2 . . . . .24 B2 98 C3
Datchwood Ct N4 . . . . 6 B1
Datchworth Ho 8
N1 . . . . .15 A1
Date St E17 . . . . . . 151 B1
Daubeney Prim Sch
E5 . . . . .18 A4
Daubeney Rd E5. . . .18 A4
Daubeney Twr 2
SE8 . . . . .51 B4
Dault Rd SW18 . . . . .59 B1
Dauney Ho SE1. . . . 136 A3
Dave Adams Ho 3
E3 . . . . .26 B3
Davenant Ho 20
E1 . . . . 111 C4
Davenant Rd N19. . . . 4 C2
Davenant St E1. . . . 111 C3
Davenport Ho
SE11 . . . . 135 B1
Davenport Mews 2
W12 . . . . .30 A1
Davenport Rd SE6 . . .67 B1
Daventry St NW1 . . 102 A4
Dave Porter Hts
SW19 . . . . .70 A4
Daver Ct SW3 . . . . 144 B1
Davern Cl SE10 . . . . .43 B2
Davey Cl N7 . . . . .14 B2
Davey Rd E9 . . . . . . .18 C1
Davey's Ct WC2. . . . 120 A4
Davey St SE15 . . . . . .49 B4
David Devine Ho 4
E8 . . . . .16 C3
David Game Coll
SW7 . . . . 143 B3
Davidge Ho SE1 . . . 135 C3
Davidge St SE1 . . . . 136 B3
David Hewitt Ho 2
E3 . . . . .34 A4
David Ho
5 Putney SW15 . . . .56 C2
South Lambeth
SW8 . . . . 162 A2
David Mews W1. . . . 103 A4
Davidson Gdns
SW8 . . . . 162 A2
Davidson Ho 7
N19 . . . . .13 B4
David St E15 . . . . . . .19 C3
Davies Laing & Dick
Coll W1 . . . . 103 C2
Davies Mews W1. . . 118 A4
Davies St W1 . . . . . 118 A4
Davina Ho
Brondesbury NW2 . . .10 B2
14 Hackney E5. . . . . .17 A3
Da Vinci Ct 12
SE16 . . . . .40 A1
Davis Ho W12. . . . . .30 A2
Davis Rd W3 . . . . . . .38 B4
Davisville Rd W12 . . .38 C4
Dawes Ho SE17 . . . 151 B3
Dawes St SE17 . . . . 151 C2
Dawlish Ave SW18 . .71 A2
Dawlish Rd NW2 . . . . 9 C2
Dawnay Gdns
SW18 . . . . .71 C2
Dawnay Rd SW17,
SW18 . . . . .71 C2
Dawn Cres E15 . . . . .27 C4
Dawson Ho
28 Bethnal Green
E2 . . . . .25 B2

Dawson Ho continued
5 Camberwell SE5 . . .49 A2
Dawson Pl
W2 . . . . .31 C2 113 C4
Dawson Rd NW2 . . . . 9 B4
Dawson St E2 . . . . . .24 B3
Day Ho 2 SE5. . . . . .48 B3
Daylesford Ave
SW15 . . . . .56 C3
Daynor Ho 4
NW6 . . . . .23 C4
Daysbrook Rd
SW2 . . . . .74 B3
Dayton Gr SE15. . . . .50 B2
Deacon Ho SE11. . . 149 A3
Deacon Mews N1 . . .15 C1
Deacon Rd NW2. . . . . 8 C2
Deacon Way SE17 . . 151 A4
Deal Ho
Deptford SE15 . . . . . .50 C4
Walworth SE17. . . . 152 B2
Deal Porters Way
SE16 . . . . .40 C3
Deal St E1 . . . . 111 B4
Dealtry Rd SW15 . . .57 B3
Deal Wlk 8 SW9 . . . 163 C1
Dean Bradley St
SW1 . . . . 134 A1
Dean Cl
Hackney E9. . . . . . . .17 B3
14 Rotherhithe
SE16 . . . . .32 C1
Dean Coll of London 7
N7 . . . . .14 B2
Deancross St E1. . . . .32 B3
Dean Ct
Acton W3 . . . . .28 C3
South Lambeth
SW8 . . . . 162 A1
Deanery Mews
W1 . . . . 117 C2
Deanery St W1 . . . . 117 C2
Dean Farrar St
SW1 . . . . 133 C2
Deanhill Ct 2
SW14 . . . . .55 A3
Deanhill Rd SW14 . .55 A3
Dean Ho
London N4 . . . . 6 B4
New Cross SE14. . . . .51 B3
Stamford Hill N16. . . 7 B3
8 Stepney E1 . . . . . .32 B3
Dean Rd NW2 . . . . . . 9 B2
Dean Ryle St SW1 . 148 A4
Dean's Bldgs
SE17 . . . . 151 C3
Deans Cl W4 . . . . . . .45 A4
Dean's Ct EC4 . . . . 108 B1
Dean's Gateway 7
SE10 . . . . .52 C2
Deanshanger Ho 21
SE8 . . . . .40 C2
Dean's Mews W1. . . 104 B2
Dean St W1 . . . . . . 105 B1
Dean Stanley St
SW1 . . . . 134 A1
Dean's Yd SW1 . . . . 133 C2
Dean Trench St
SW1 . . . . 134 A1
Dearmer Ho 6
SW2 . . . . .74 C4
Deason St E15 . . . . . .27 B4
Deauville Ct
14 London SW4 . . . .61 B1
7 Rotherhithe
SE16 . . . . .40 C4

Deauville Mans 13
SW4 . . . . .61 B1
De Barowe Mews
4 Highbury N5 . . . . .15 A4
1 London N5. . . . . . .15 A3
Debdale Ho 20 E2 . .24 C4
De Beauvoir Cres
N1 . . . . .24 A4
De Beauvoir Ct N1 . .15 C1
De Beauvoir Pl 5
N1 . . . . .16 A2
De Beauvoir Prim Sch
15 N1 . . . . .16 A2
De Beauvoir Rd
N1 . . . . .16 A1
De Beauvoir Sq
N1 . . . . .16 A1
DE BEAUVOIR
TOWN 16 A1
Debnam Ct SE16 . . .40 B2
Decima St SE1 . . . . 138 A2
Deck Cl SE16 . . . . . .32 C1
De Crespigny Pk
SE5 . . . . .48 C1
Deeley Rd SW8 . . . . 171 B4
Deepdale N4 . . . . 6 A1
Deepdene Gdns
SW2 . . . . .74 B4
Deepdene Ho N16. . . 6 C3
Deepdene Lo 5
SW2 . . . . .74 B4
Deepdene Mans
SW6 . . . . 164 C4
Deepdene Rd SE5,
SE24 . . . . .63 C3
Deerbrook Rd SE24,
SW2 . . . . .75 A3
Deerdale Rd SE24 . .63 B3
Deerhurst Ho 6
SE15 . . . . .49 C4
Deerhurst Rd NW2 . . 9 C2
Deer Lo SW6 . . . . . .58 A4
Deeside Rd SW17 . . .71 C1
Dee St E14 . . . . .34 B3
Defoe Ave TW9 . . . . .44 C3
Defoe Ho
Barbican EC2 . . . . . 108 C4
6 Stoke Newington
N16 . . . . 7 A1
Defoe Pl EC2 . . . . . 108 C4
Defoe Rd
Rotherhithe SE16 . . .41 B4
Stoke Newington
N16 . . . . 7 A1
De Gama Pl 3
E14 . . . . .41 C1
Dekker Ho 19 SE5 . .48 C3
Dekker Rd SE21 . . . .76 A4
Delafield Ho 20
E1 . . . . 111 C1
Delaford Rd SE16 . . .40 A1
Delaford St SW6. . . 154 B3
Delamere Ho 4 N4 . . 6 C4
Delamere Rd W5 . . .36 A4
Delamere St W2 . . . 100 C3
Delamere Terr
W2 . . . . 100 B4
Delancey Pas NW1 . .82 B3
Delancey St NW1 . . .82 B3
Delancey Studios
NW1 . . . . .82 B3
Delany Ho SE10 . . . .52 B4
Delarch Ho SE1 . . . 136 A3
De Laune St SE17 . 150 A1

Delaware Rd W9 . . . 88 A2
Delawyk Cres
SE24 . . . . .63 C1
Delft Way 2 SE22 . .64 A2
Delhi St N1 . . . . 84 B3
Delia St SW18 . . . . . .71 A4
Dellafield N4 . . . . 5 C2
Dell Cl E15 . . . . .27 C4
Dellow Ho 6 E1 . . . 32 A2
Dellow St E1 . . . . . . 32 A2
Dell's Mews SW1 . . 147 A3
Deloraine Ho SE8 . . .51 C2
Deloraine St SE8 . . .51 C2
Delorme St W6 . . . . .47 C4
Delta Bldg 7 E14 . .34 B3
Delta Ho N1 . . . . . . 97 B4
Delta Pk SW18 . . . . .59 A3
Delta Point 5
E2 . . . . .24 C2 99 B4
Delta St 2
E2 . . . . .24 C2 99 B4
Delverton Ho
SE17 . . . . 150 B2
Delverton Rd
SE17 . . . . 150 B1
Delvino Rd SW6 . . . 165 C3
De Montfort Ct 1
SW16 . . . . .74 A1
De Montfort Rd
SW16 . . . . .74 A2
De Morgan Rd
SW6 . . . . .59 A4
Dempster Rd
SW18 . . . . .59 B2
Denbigh Cl
W11 . . . . . . .31 B2 113 A4
Denbigh Gdns
TW10 . . . . .54 B2
Denbigh Ho
Knightsbridge
SW1 . . . . 131 A2
7 Notting Hill W11 . 31 B3
Notting Hill
W11 . . . . . . .31 B2 113 A4
Denbigh Mews
SW1 . . . . 146 C3
Denbigh Pl SW1. . . 146 C2
Denbigh Rd
W11 . . . . . . .31 B2 113 A4
Denbigh St SW1. . . 147 A2
Denbigh Terr
W11 . . . . . . .31 B2 113 A4
Denbury Ho 40 E3 . .27 A2
Denby Ct SE11 . . . . 149 A4
Dence Ho 18
E2 . . . . .24 C2 99 B3
Denchworth Ho 14
SW9 . . . . 173 B1
Dene Cl SE4 . . . . . . .66 A3
Denehurst Gdns
Acton W3 . . . . .28 A1
Richmond TW10. . . . .54 C3
Dene Mans 1
NW6 . . . . .10 C2
Denewood SE24 . . . .63 B2
Denewood Rd N6. . . . 3 B4
Dengie Wlk N1 . . . . .86 C4
Denham Ho 32
W12 . . . . .30 A2
Denham St SE10 . . . .43 C1
Denholme Rd W9 . . .23 B2
Denland Ho SW8 . . 163 A1
Denman Ho N16. . . . 7 A2
Denman Rd SE15 . . .49 B1
Denman St W1 . . . . 119 B3

Denmark Gr N1 . . . . 85 B2
Denmark Hill SE5. . .48 C1
Denmark Hill Sta
SE5 . . . . .48 B1
Denmark Mans 14
SE5 . . . . .48 B1
Denmark Pl
2 Bromley E3 . . . . . .26 C2
Soho WC2 . . . . 105 C2
Denmark Rd
Camberwell SE5 . . . .48 B1
Kilburn NW6. . . . . . .23 B3
Denmark St WC2 . . 105 C2
Denmead Ho
SW15 . . . . .56 B1
Denne Terr 8 . . . . . .24 B4
Dennett's Ct SE14 . .51 A2
Dennett's Rd SE14 . .50 B2
Denning Cl NW8. . . 89 A3
Denning Mews
SW12 . . . . .60 C1
Denning Point 1 E1 112 A2
Denning Rd NW3 . . .11 C4
Dennington Park
Mansions 12
NW6 . . . . .10 C3
Dennington Park Rd
NW6 . . . . .10 C2
Dennis Ct SE10 . . . .52 B2
Dennis Ho 4 E3 . . . .26 B3
Dennison Point
E15 . . . . .19 B1
Dennis Severs' House
E1 . . . . 110 B4
Denny Cres SE11 . . 149 C2
Denny St SE11 . . . . 149 C2
Densham Ho NW8 . . 79 C1
Denstone Ho 5
SE15 . . . . .49 C4
Dent Ho SE17 . . . . 152 A3
Denton NW1 . . . . . . .12 C2
Denton Ho N1 . . . . . .15 A1
Denton St SW18 . . . .59 A1
Dents Rd SW11 . . . .60 B1
Denver Rd N16. . . . . 7 A4
Denyer St
SW3 . . . . 144 B3
Denys Bldg EC1 . . . 107 B4
Denzil Rd NW10 . . . . 8 B3
Deodar Rd SW15 . . .58 A3
Depot App NW2 . . . . 9 C4
Depot Rd W12 . . . . .30 B2
Depot St SE5 . . . . . .48 C4
DEPTFORD 50 C3
Deptford Bridge
SE8 . . . . .51 C2
Deptford Bridge Sta
SE8 . . . . .51 C2
Deptford Broadway
SE8, SE14 . . . . .51 C2
Deptford Church St
SE8 . . . . .51 C3
Deptford Ferry Rd 24
E14 . . . . .41 C2
Deptford Gn SE8 . . .51 C4
Deptford Green Sch
SE14 . . . . .51 B3
Deptford Green Sch
(Annex) 21 SE14 . .51 A3
Deptford High St
SE8 . . . . .51 C3

Deptford Park Prim
Sch **2** SE8........41 A1
Deptford Sta SE8...51 C1
Deptford Trad Est
SE8........................51 A4
Deptford Wharf
SE8........................41 B2
De Quincey Mews **3**
E16........................35 C1
Derby Ct E8 E5......17 C4
Derby Gate NW1..134 A4
Derby Rd SE11....149 B4
Derby Rd
Mortlake SW14.....55 A3
South Hackney E5..17 C4
Derbyshire St
E2.............24 C2 99 C3
Derby St W1......117 C1
Dereham Ho **7**
SE4........................65 A3
Dereham Pl
EC2.............24 A1 98 B2
Derek Walcott Cl
SE24......................63 A2
Dericote St E8......25 A4
Dering St W1.....104 B1
Dermody Gdns
SE13......................67 C2
Dermody Rd SE13..67 C2
Deronda Rd SE24,
SW2........................75 A3
Derrick Ho **13**
SW2........................74 C3
Derrycombe Ho **13**
W2..........................31 C4
Derry St W8......128 A3
Dersingham Rd
NW2.........................1 A1
Derwent NW1....92 C3
Derwent Ct
2 Hammersmith
W6..........................39 B3
6 Rotherhithe
SE16....................40 C4
Derwent Gr SE22..64 B3
Derwent Ho
South Kensington
SW7....................143 A4
Tower Hamlets E3..26 B1
Derwent St SE10..43 A1
Derwentwater Mans
2 W3....................28 B1
Derwentwater Prim
Sch W3...................28 B1
Derwentwater Rd
W3..........................28 B1
Desborough Cl
W2........................100 B4
Desborough Ho
W14......................155 A4
Desenfans Rd
SE21......................64 A1
Design Mus SE1...139 A4
Desmond St SE14..51 A4
Despard Ho SW2...74 C2
Despard Rd N19....4 B3
Desvignes Dr SE13..67 C1
Dethick Ct E3......26 A4
Detling Ho SE17..152 A3
Devas St E3..........27 A1
Dereaux Cres **8**
SE4........................66 A4
De Vere Cotts W8..128 C2
De Vere Gdns W8..128 C3

Deverell St SE1...137 B1
De Vere Mews
W8........................128 C2
Devereux Ct EC4...107 B1
Devereux Ho **7**
SW15......................56 C3
Devereux La SW13..47 A3
Devereux Rd
SW11......................60 B1
Devitt Ho **8** E14..34 A2
Devizes St N1......87 C3
Devonhurst Pl **4**
W4..........................37 C1
Devonia Rd N1......86 B2
Devon Mans SE1..138 A4
Devonport W2....102 A2
Devonport Ho
Greenwich SE10.....52 B4
2 Paddington W2...31 C4
Devonport Rd
W12........................39 A4
Devonport St E1...32 C3
Devonshire Cl
W1........................104 A4
Devonshire Ct
1 Balham SW12...73 A4
6 Richmond TW9...44 C2
Devonshire Dr
SE10......................52 A2
Devonshire Gdns
W4..........................45 B3
Devonshire Gr
SE15......................50 A4
Devonshire Hall **1**
E9..........................17 B2
Devonshire Ho
Brondesbury NW6...10 B2
Newington SE1....136 C2
Paddington W2....101 C4
2 Putney SW15....69 B4
Westminster SW1..147 C2
Devonshire House
Prep Sch NW3......11 B3
Devonshire Mews **2**
W4..........................38 A1
Devonshire Mews N
W1........................104 A4
Devonshire Mews S
W1........................104 A4
Devonshire Mews W
W1........................103 C4
Devonshire Pl
Child's Hill NW2......1 C1
Kensington W8....128 A1
Marylebone W1....103 C4
Devonshire Place
Mews W1..............103 C4
W4..........................38 A1
Devonshire Row
EC2......................110 B3
Devonshire Row
Mews W1................92 B1
Devonshire Sq
EC2......................110 B2
Devonshire St
Chiswick W4............38 A1
Marylebone W1....104 A4
Devonshire Terr
W2........................101 A1
Devons Rd E3........27 A1
Devons Road Sta
E3..........................27 A1
Devon St SE15.....50 A4
De Walden Ho
NW8........................80 A2

De Walden St W1..103 C3
Dewar St SE15....64 C4
Dewberry St E14...34 B4
Dewey Rd N1.......85 B2
Dewhurst Rd W14..39 C3
Dewsbury Ct **5**
W4..........................37 B2
Dewsbury Rd NW10..8 C3
Dewsbury Terr
NW1........................82 B4
D'eynsford Rd SE5..48 C2
Dhonau Ho SE16..153 A4
Diadem Ct W1......105 B2
Dial Wlk The W8..128 B4
Diamond Est
SW17......................72 A1
Diamond Ho **2**
E3..........................26 A3
Diamond St SE15..49 A3
Diamond Terr
SE10......................52 B2
Diana Cl **21** SE8..51 B4
Diana Ho
Barnes SW13.........46 B2
4 Brixton SW2......62 B2
Diana, Princess of
Wales Meml
Fountain W2.......129 C4
Diana, Princess of
Wales Meml Wlk
W2........................114 C1
Dibden Ho **5** SE5..49 A3
Dibden St N1........86 C4
Dibdin Ho W9......78 A1
Dicey Ave NW2......9 B3
Dickens Ct EC1.....96 A1
Dickens Ho
Bloomsbury WC1...94 A2
Kennington SE17..150 B1
Kilburn NW6..........23 C2
Paddington NW8...89 C2
Dickenson Rd N8...5 A4
Dickens Sq SE1...137 A2
Dickens St SW8...170 B2
Dickinson Ho **18**
E2.............24 C2 99 B3
Dicksee Ho NW8...89 B1
Dick Shepherd Ct **7**
SW2........................62 C1
Dickson Ho **4** E1..32 A3
Didbin Ho N7..........5 B2
Digby Bsns Ctr E9..17 C2
Digby Cres N4........6 B2
Digby Mans W6....39 B1
Digby Rd E9..........17 C2
Digby St E2..........25 B2
Dighton Ct SE5....48 B4
Dighton Rd SW18..59 B3
Dignum St N1......85 B2
Digswell St N7......14 C2
Dilke St SW3......159 A4
Dilston Gr SE16....40 B2
Dilton Gdns SW15..69 A3
Dimes Pl **6** W6...39 A2
Dimson Cres E3....26 C2
Dinerman Ho **3**
NW8........................79 A4
Dingle Gdns E14...33 C2
Dingley La SW16...73 C2
Dingley Pl EC1......97 A3
Dingley Rd EC1.....96 C3
Dingwall Rd SW18..71 B4
Dinmont Ho **27** E2..24 C3
Dinmont St **1** E2..25 A3
Dinmore Ho **5** E9..25 B4

Dinnington Ho **17**
E1..........................25 A1
Dinsdale Rd SE3...53 B4
Dinsmore Rd
SW12......................73 A4
Dinton Ho NW8....90 A2
Dinwiddy Ho N1...84 C1
Dionis Ho SW6...165 B2
Disbrowe Rd W6..154 B3
Discovery Bsns Pk **13**
SE16......................139 C1
Discovery Dock E
E14........................42 A4
Discovery Ho **1**
E14........................34 B2
Disney Pl SE1.....137 A4
Disney St SE1.....137 A4
Disraeli Cl **1** W4..37 C2
Disraeli Gdns
SW15......................58 B3
Disraeli Rd
Acton NW10..........20 C3
Putney SW15.........58 A3
Diss St E2...........24 B2 98 C4
Distaff La EC4....122 C4
Distillery La W6...39 B1
Distillery Rd W6...39 B1
Distillery Wlk **14**
TW8........................44 A4
Ditchburn St E14..34 B2
Ditton Ho **10** E5..17 A3
Divis Way SW15...57 A1
Dixon Clark Ct N1..15 A2
Dixon Ho **20** NW10..30 C3
Dixon Rd SE14......51 A2
Dixon's Alley **10**
SE16......................40 A4
Dixon Way **6** NW10..8 A1
Dobree Ave NW10..9 A1
Dobson Cl NW6....11 C1
Dobson Ho **2**
SE14......................50 C4
Doby Ct EC4.......123 A4
Dockers Tanner Rd **26**
E14........................41 C2
Dockhead SE1....139 A3
Dockhead Wharf
SE1........................139 A4
Dock Hill Ave
SE16......................40 C4
Docklands Ct **20**
E14........................33 B3
Docklands Visitor Ctr
E14........................42 B4
Dockley Rd SE16..139 B1
Dockley Road Ind Est
SE16......................139 B1
Dock Offices **12**
SE16......................40 B3
Dock Rd E16........35 B2
Dock St E1..........125 B4
Doctor Spurstowe
Almshouses **9**
E8..........................17 A2
Docura Ho N7........5 B2
Docwras Bldgs N1..16 A2
Dodbrooke Rd
SE27......................75 A1
Dodd Ho **16** SE16..40 A2
Doddington Gr
SE17......................150 B1
Doddington Pl **4**
SE17........................48 A4
Dodson St SE1....135 C3
Dod St E14...........33 C3

Dog & Duck Yd
WC1......................106 A3
Dog Kennel Hill
SE22......................64 A4
Dog Kennel Hill Sch
SE22......................64 A4
Dog La NW10.......8 A4
Dolben Ct SW1...147 C3
Dolben St **1** SE1..122 B1
Dolby Rd SW6....164 C1
Doleman Ho **16**
SE10......................52 A2
Dolland Ho SE11..149 A1
Dolland St SE11..149 A1
Dollar Bay E14....42 B4
DOLLIS HILL...........9 A4
Dollis Hill Sta NW2...8 C3
Dolman Rd W4....37 C2
Dolman St SW4...62 B3
Dolphin Cl **2**
SE16......................40 C4
Dolphin Ct N7......14 A2
Dolphin La E14....34 A2
Dolphin Sch SW11..60 B2
Dolphin Sq SW1..147 L3
Dolphin Twr **21**
SE8........................51 B4
Dombey Ho
16 Bermondsey
SE1........................139 B3
4 Shepherd's Bush
W11......................30 C1
Dombey St WC1..106 C4
Domelton Ho
SW18......................59 A1
Domett Cl SE5.....63 C3
Domfe Pl E5........17 B4
Domingo St EC1..96 C1
Dominion St EC2..109 C4
Donaghue Cotts **11**
E14........................33 A4
Donaldson Rd
NW6........................23 B4
Donegal Ho **2** E1..25 B1
Donegal St N1.....85 A1
Doneraile Ho
SW1......................146 A1
Doneraile St SW6..47 C2
Dongola Rd E1.....33 A4
Don Gratton Ho **2**
E1........................111 B3
Donkey Alley SE22..64 C1
Donkin Ho **15**
SE16......................40 A2
Donne Ct SE24....63 B1
Donne Ho
18 Canonbury
N16........................15 C4
11 Poplar E14.......33 C3
Donnelly Ct SW6..154 B2
Donne Pl SW3....144 B4
Donnington Ct
11 Camden Town
NW1......................13 A1
Willesden NW10....9 A1
Donnington Ho **12**
SW8......................171 B2
Donnington Prim Sch
NW10......................22 A4
Donnington Rd
NW10......................22 A4
Donovan Ct **7**
SW7......................143 B1
Donovan Ho **4** E1..32 B2
Don Phelan Cl
SE5........................48 C2

Doon St SE1 ..... **121** B2
Doradus Ct 20
SW19 ..... 69 C3
Dora Ho
11 Shepherd's Bush
W11 ..... 30 C2
1 Tower Hamlets
E14 ..... 33 B3
Dorando Cl W12 ..... 30 A2
Doran Wlk
Stratford E15 ..... 19 B1
Stratford Marsh
E15 ..... 27 B4
Dora St E14 ..... 33 B3
Dorcas Ct 18
SW18 ..... 59 C3
Dorchester Ct
1 De Beauvoir Town
N1 ..... 16 A2
Herne Hill SE24 ..... 63 B2
Knightsbridge
SW1 ..... **131** A1
5 Streatham
SW16 ..... 74 A2
Dorchester Dr
SE24 ..... 63 B2
Dorchester Gr W4 ..... 38 B1
Dorchester Ho
TW9 ..... 45 A3
Dordrecht Rd W3 ..... 29 A1
Doria Rd SW6 ..... **165** A2
Doric Ho 7 E2 ..... 25 C3
Doric Way NW1 ..... 93 B4
Doris Emmerton Ct
SW18 ..... 59 B3
Dorking Cl SE8 ..... 51 B4
Dorking Ho SE1 ..... **137** C2
Dorland Ct SW15 ..... 58 B1
Dorlcote Rd SW18 ..... 72 A4
Dorleston Ct N1 ..... 87 C4
Dorman Way NW8 ..... 79 A4
Dormay St SW18 ..... 59 A2
Dormstone Ho
SE17 ..... **152** A3
Dornberg Cl SE3 ..... 53 C3
Dorncliffe Rd
SW6 ..... **164** B2
Dorney NW3 ..... 12 A1
Dorney Ct SW6 ..... 58 A4
Dornfell St NW6 ..... 10 C3
Dornoch Ho 28 E3 ..... 26 B3
Dornton Rd SW12,
SW17 ..... 73 B2
Dorothy Charrington
Ho 11 SE22 ..... 64 C2
Dorothy Rd SW11 ..... 60 B4
Dorrell Pl 10 SW9 ..... 62 C4
Dorrien Wlk SW16 ..... 73 C2
Dorrington Point 20
E3 ..... 27 A2
Dorrington St
EC1 ..... **107** B4
Dorrit Ho 20 W11 ..... 30 C1
Dorrit St SE1 ..... **137** A4
Dorset Bldgs EC4 ..... **108** A1
Dorset Cl NW1 ..... **102** C4
Dorset Ct 3 N1 ..... 16 A1
Dorset Mans 2
W6 ..... 47 C4
Dorset Mews
SW1 ..... **132** A2
Dorset Pl E15 ..... 19 C2
Dorset Rd SW8 ..... **162** C2
Dorset Rise EC4 ..... **108** A1
Dorset Sq NW1 ..... 90 C1
Dorset St W1 ..... **103** A3

Dorton Cl 6 SE15 ..... 49 A3
Dorville Cres W6 ..... 39 A3
Doughty Ct 11 E1 ..... 32 A1
Doughty Mews
WC1 ..... 94 C1
Doughty St WC1 ..... 94 C1
Douglas Bldgs
SE1 ..... **137** A4
Douglas Ct 3
NW6 ..... 10 C1
Douglas Gracey Ho 3
SW18 ..... 70 A4
Douglas Ho
Putney SW15 ..... 56 C1
Westminster SW1 ..... **147** B3
Douglas Johnstone
Ho SW6 ..... **154** C3
Douglas Mews NW2 ..... 1 A1
Douglas Path E14 ..... 42 B1
Douglas Rd
Islington N1 ..... 15 B1
Kilburn NW6 ..... 23 B4
Douglas Rd N N1 ..... 15 B2
Douglas Rd S N1 ..... 15 B2
Douglas St SW1 ..... **147** B3
Douglas Waite Ho
NW6 ..... 11 B1
Douglas Way SE8 ..... 51 B3
Doulton Ho SE11 ..... **149** A4
Doulton Mews 4
NW6 ..... 11 A2
Dounesforth Gdns
SW18 ..... 71 A3
Douro Pl W8 ..... **128** B2
Douro St 3 E3 ..... 26 C3
Douthwaite Sq 11
E1 ..... **125** C2
Dovecote Gdns 4
SW14 ..... 55 C4
Dove Ct EC2 ..... **109** B1
Dovedale Cotts 6
SW11 ..... **168** C2
Dovedale Ho N16 ..... 6 C4
Dovedale Rd SE22 ..... 65 A1
Dovehouse St
SW3 ..... **144** A1
Dove Mews SW5 ..... **142** C3
Dovercourt Rd
SE22 ..... 64 B1
Dover Ct
Clerkenwell EC1 ..... 96 A2
17 Greenwich SE10 ..... 52 A2
Dove Rd N1 ..... 15 C2
Doverfield Rd
SW2 ..... 74 A4
Dover Flats SE1 ..... **152** B3
Dover Ho
Brixton SE5 ..... 49 A3
11 Deptford SE15 ..... 50 B4
Dover House Rd
SW15 ..... 57 A2
Dover Mans 18
SW9 ..... 62 C4
Dover Park Dr
SW15 ..... 57 A1
Dover Terr TW9 ..... 44 C1
Dover Yd W1 ..... **118** C2
Doves Yd N1 ..... 85 B3
Doveton Ho 7 E1 ..... 25 B1
Doveton St 5 E1 ..... 25 B1
Dove Wlk SW1 ..... **145** B2
Dovey Lo 4 N1 ..... 14 C1

Dowdeny Cl 11
NW5 ..... 13 B3
Dowdeswell Cl
SW15 ..... 56 A3
Dowding Ho 16 N6 ..... 3 C4
Dowell Ho SE21 ..... 76 B1
Dowes Ho 17
SW16 ..... 74 A1
Dowgate Hill EC4 ..... **123** B4
Dowland St W10 ..... 23 A2
Dowlas St SE5 ..... 49 A3
Dowlen Ct 11 E14 ..... 41 C4
Dowler Ho 62 E1 ..... **111** C1
Downbarton Ho 11
SW9 ..... **173** B4
Downbury Mews 15
SW18 ..... 58 C2
Downend Ct 11
SE15 ..... 49 A4
Downer's Cotts
SW4 ..... 61 B3
Downey Ho 6 E1 ..... 25 C1
Downfield Cl W9 ..... 88 A1
Downham Ct 1
N1 ..... 15 C1
Downham Rd N1 ..... 15 C1
Downing Ho
2 North Kensington
W10 ..... 30 C3
8 Putney SW15 ..... 56 C2
Downing St SW1 ..... **134** A4
Down Pl W6 ..... 39 A1
Down St Mews
W1 ..... **118** A1
Downs Ct 18 E8 ..... 17 A3
Downsell Prim Sch
E15 ..... 19 C4
Downsell Rd E15 ..... 19 C4
Downshire Hill
NW3 ..... 11 C4
Downside 2
SW15 ..... 58 A2
Downside Cres
NW3 ..... 12 A3
Downs La 2 E5 ..... 17 A4
Downs Park Rd E5,
E8 ..... 16 C3
Downs Rd E5, N16 ..... 16 C4
Down St W1 ..... **118** A1
Downsview Sch
E5 ..... 17 A4
Downton Ave SW2 ..... 74 B2
Downtown Rd
SE16 ..... 41 A4
Dowrey St 1 N1 ..... 85 B4
Dowson Cl SE5 ..... 63 C3
Dowson Ct SE13 ..... 67 C4
Dowson Ho 6 E1 ..... 32 C3
Doyce St SE1 ..... **136** C4
Doyle Gdns NW10 ..... 22 A4
Doyle Ho W3 ..... 37 A4
D'Oyley St SW1 ..... **145** B4
Doynton St N19 ..... 4 A2
Draco St SE17 ..... 48 B4
Dragon Ct WC2 ..... **106** B2
Dragon Rd SE15 ..... 49 A4
Dragon Yd WC1 ..... **106** B2
Dragoon Rd SE8 ..... 41 B1
Dragor Rd NW10 ..... 20 B1
Drake Cl 6 SE16 ..... 40 C4
Drake Croft N16 ..... 6 C2
Drakefell Rd SE4,
SE14 ..... 65 C4
Drakefield Rd
SW17 ..... 72 C1

Drake Ho
2 Limehouse
E14 ..... 33 A2
11 Stepney E1 ..... 32 B4
Drakeley Ct N5 ..... 15 A4
Drake Rd SE4 ..... 66 C4
Drakes Ctyd NW6 ..... 10 B1
Drake St WC1 ..... **106** C3
Drama Ctr London
EC1 ..... 95 C1
Draper Ho SE1 ..... **150** B4
Draper Pl N1 ..... 86 B4
Drapers Almshouses 5
E3 ..... 26 C2
Drapers Gdns
EC2 ..... **109** C2
Drapers Rd E15 ..... 19 C4
Drappers Way 8
SE16 ..... **153** C4
Draycott Ave SW3 ..... **144** B3
Draycott Cl SE5 ..... 48 C3
Draycott Ct SW11 ..... **168** A4
Draycott Ho SW3 ..... **144** C3
Draycott Pl SW3 ..... **144** C3
Draycott Terr
SW3 ..... **145** A3
Drayford Cl W9 ..... 23 B1
Dray Gdns SW2 ..... 62 B2
Draymans Ct 4
SW9 ..... 62 B4
Draymans Mews
SE15 ..... 49 B1
Drayson Mews
W8 ..... **127** C3
Drayton Ct SW10 ..... **143** A1
Drayton Gdns
SW10 ..... **143** A1
Drayton Ho 14 SE5 ..... 48 C3
Drayton Park Mews 12
N5 ..... 14 C3
Drayton Park Prim
Sch 13 N5 ..... 14 C3
Drayton Park Sta
N5 ..... 14 C3
Drayton Pk N5, N7 ..... 14 C4
Drayton Rd NW10 ..... 21 B4
DRCA Business Ctr
SW11 ..... **169** C3
Dreadnought St
SE10 ..... 43 A3
Dresden Cl NW6 ..... 11 A2
Dresden Ho
3 Clapham
SW11 ..... **169** B2
Lambeth SE11 ..... **149** A4
Dresden Rd N19 ..... 4 C3
Dressington Ave
SE4 ..... 66 C1
Drewett Ho 31 E1 ..... **111** C1
Drew Ho 12 SW16 ..... 74 A1
Drewstead La
SW16 ..... 73 C2
Drewstead Rd
SW16 ..... 73 C2
Driffield Rd E3 ..... 26 A3
Driftway Ho 11 E3 ..... 26 B3
Drinkwater Ho 11
SE5 ..... 48 C3
Drive Mans 1
SW6 ..... **164** B2
Drive The
Acton W3 ..... 28 B3
Harlesden NW10 ..... 21 B4
Hendon NW11 ..... 1 A4
Islington N7 ..... 14 B2

Dr Johnson Ave
SW17 ..... 73 A1
Dr Johnson's House
EC4 ..... **107** C2
Droitwich Cl SE26 ..... 76 C1
Dromore Rd SW15 ..... 58 A1
Dron Ho E1 ..... 32 B4
Droop St W10 ..... 23 A1
Drovers Ct SE13 ..... 67 B4
Drovers Pl SE15 ..... 50 A3
Drovers Way N7 ..... 12 A4
Druce Rd SE21 ..... 64 A1
Druid St SE1 ..... **138** C2
Drummer Lo N7 ..... 5 B1
Drummond Cres
NW1 ..... 93 B4
Drummond Gate
SW1 ..... **147** C2
Drummond Ho 18
E2 ..... 24 C3
Drummond Rd
SE16 ..... 40 A3
Drummonds Pl
TW9 ..... 54 A3
Drummond St
NW1 ..... 92 C2
Drury Ho SW8 ..... **170** C4
Drury La WC2 ..... **106** B1
Dryad St SW15 ..... 57 C4
Dryborough Ho 3
SW15 ..... 56 C2
Dryburgh Ho SW1 ..... **146** B2
Dryburgh Mans
SW15 ..... 57 B4
Dryburgh Rd
SW15 ..... 57 B4
Dryden Bldg 18
E1 ..... **111** B2
Dryden Cl SW4 ..... 61 C2
Dryden Ct SE11 ..... **149** C3
Dryden Ho
6 Camberwell
SE5 ..... 49 A2
16 Stoke Newington
N16 ..... 7 A1
Dryden St WC2 ..... **106** B1
Dryfield Wlk 8
SE8 ..... 51 C4
Drysdale Flats 3
E8 ..... 16 B3
Drysdale Ho 19
E2 ..... 24 A2 98 B4
Drysdale Pl
N1 ..... 24 A2 98 B4
Drysdale St
N1 ..... 24 A2 98 B4
Dublin Ave E8 ..... 24 C4
Ducal St 25
E2 ..... 24 B2 99 A3
Ducane Cl 6 W12 ..... 30 B3
Du Cane Ct SW12 ..... 72 C3
Du Cane Rd W12 ..... 29 C3
Ducavel Ho SW2 ..... 74 B3
Duchess Mews
W1 ..... **104** B3
Duchess of Bedford
Ho W8 ..... **127** B4
Duchess of Bedford's
Wlk W8 ..... **127** B3
Duchess St W1 ..... **104** B3
Duchy St SE1 ..... **121** C2
Ducie Ho 2 SW15 ..... 57 B2
Ducie St SW4 ..... 62 B3
Duckett St E1 ..... 33 A4
Duck La W1 ..... **105** B1
Du Cros Rd W3 ..... 29 A1

DUDDEN HILL 8 C3
Dudden Hill La
NW10 . . . . 8 B3
Dudley Ct
Marylebone W1 . . **102** C1
St Giles WC2 . . . . . **106** A2
Dudley Ho
13 Brixton SW9 . . . **173** B2
Paddington W2 . . . **101** B3
Dudley Mews 14
SW2 . . . . 62 C1
Dudley Rd
Kilburn NW6 . . . . 23 B3
Richmond TW9 . . . . . 44 B1
Dudley St W2 . . . . . **101** B3
Dudmaston Mews
SW3 . . . . **143** C2
Duffell Ho SE11 . . . **149** A1
Dufferin Ave EC1 . . **97** B1
Dufferin Ct EC1 . . . . **97** B1
Dufferin St EC1 . . . . **97** A1
Duffield Ho N4 . . . . . . 6 B4
Duff Miller Coll
SW7 . . . . **129** A1
Duff St E14 . . . . 34 A3
Dufour's Pl W1 . . . . **105** A1
Dugard Way SE11 **150** A3
Dugdale Ho 10 N7 . . 13 C3
Duke Humphrey Rd
SE3 . . . . 53 A1
Duke of Wellington Pl
SW1, W1 . . . . . . **131** C4
Duke of York's Sq
SW3 . . . . **145** A3
Duke of York St
SW1 . . . . **119** A2
Duke Rd W4 . . . . 37 C1
Duke St Hill SE1 . . **123** C2
Duke St St James's
SW1 . . . . **119** A2
Duke's Ave W4 . . . . . 37 C1
Dukes Ct
Dulwich SE22 . . . . . . 76 C3
East Dulwich SE22 . . 65 A2
Lewisham SE13 . . . . . 52 B1
Mortlake SW14 . . . . . 55 A4
Dukes Gate 4 W4 . . 37 B2
Dukes Head Yd N6 . . . 4 A3
Duke's Ho SW1 . . . **147** C4
Duke Shore Wharf
E14 . . . . 33 B2
Dukes La W8 . . . . . **128** A4
Duke's Mews W1 . . **103** C2
Duke's Pl EC3 . . . . . **110** B1
Dukes Point N6 . . . . . 4 A3
Duke's Rd WC1 . . . . **93** C3
Duke St W1 . . . . . . **103** C1
Duke Street Mans
W1 . . . . **103** C1
Duke's Yd W1 . . . . **117** C4
Dulas St N4 . . . . 5 B3
Dulford St
W11 . . . . . 31 A2 **112** A4
Dulka Rd SW11 . . . . . 60 B2
Dulverton NW1 . . . . **83** A3
Dulverton Mans
WC1 . . . . **95** A1
DULWICH 76 A1
Dulwich Coll SE21 . . 76 A2
Dulwich Coll Prep Sch
SE21 . . . . 76 A1
Dulwich Com Hospl
SE22 . . . . 64 A3

Dulwich Comm
SE21 . . . . 76 A3
Dulwich Hamlet Jun
Sch SE21 . . . . **63** C1
Dulwich Lawn Cl
SE22 . . . . 64 B2
Dulwich L Ctr
SE22 . . . . 64 C3
Dulwich Mead
SE24 . . . . 63 B1
Dulwich Mews
1 East Dulwich
SE22 . . . . 64 B3
East Dulwich SE22 . . 64 B2
Dulwich Oaks The
SE21 . . . . 76 B1
Dulwich Picture Gall
SE21 . . . . 76 A2
Dulwich Rd SE24 . . . 63 A1
DULWICH
VILLAGE 76 A4
Dulwich Village . . . 64 A1
Dulwich Village CE Inf
Sch SE21 . . . . 64 A1
Dumain Ct SE11 . . **150** A3
Du Maurier Ho 2
NW3 . . . . 12 B3
Dumbarton Ct 16
SW2 . . . . 74 A4
Dumbarton Rd
SW2 . . . . 62 A1
Dumont Rd N16 . . . . . 7 A1
Dumphreys Ho 5
SW4 . . . . 73 C4
Dumpton Pl NW1 . . 12 C1
Dunbar St SE27 . . . . 75 B1
Dunbar Wharf 20
E14 . . . . 33 B2
Dunboyne Rd NW3 . 12 B3
Dunbridge Ho
SW15 . . . . 56 B1
Dunbridge St
Bethnal Green
E2 . . . . 24 C1 **99** C2
Bethnal Green E2 . . 25 A1
Duncan Ct 3 E14 . . 34 B4
Duncan Gr W3 . . . . . 29 A3
Duncan Ho 5
NW3 . . . . 12 B3
Duncannon Ho
SW1 . . . . **147** C1
Duncannon St
WC2 . . . . **120** A3
Duncan Rd
Hackney E8 . . . . 25 A4
Richmond TW9 . . . . . 54 A3
Duncan St N1 . . . . . **86** A2
Duncan Terr N1 . . . **86** A2
Dunch St 33 E1 . . . 32 A3
Duncombe Ho 7
SW19 . . . . 69 C3
Duncombe Prim Sch
N19 . . . . 5 A3
Duncombe Rd N19 . . 4 C3
Duncrievie Rd
SE13 . . . . 67 C1
Dundalk Ho 2 E1 . . 32 B3
Dundalk Rd SE4 . . . 66 A4
Dundas Ho 12 E2 . . 25 B3
Dundas Rd SE15 . . . 50 B1
Dundee Ct 8 E1 . . . 32 A1
Dundee Ho W9 . . . . **88** C4
Dundee St E1 . . . . . . 32 A1
Dundee Wharf
E14 . . . . 33 B2

Dundonald Rd
NW10 . . . . 22 C4
Dundry Ho 8
SE26 . . . . 76 C1
Dunelm Gr SE27 . . . 75 B1
Dunelm St E1 . . . . . 32 C3
Dunford Rd N7 . . . . 14 B4
Dungarvan Ave
SW15 . . . . 56 C3
Dungeness Ho
SW18 . . . . 59 B3
Dunhill Point 12
SW15 . . . . 69 A3
Dunkeld Ho 15
E14 . . . . 34 C3
Dunlace Rd E5 . . . . . 17 C4
Dunlin Ct 15 SE21 . 75 C2
Dunlin Ho 16 SE16 . 40 C2
Dunloe Ct 7 E2 . . . 24 B3
Dunloe St E2 . . . . . . 24 B3
Dunlop Pl SE16 . . . **139** A1
Dunmore Point 13
E2 . . . . 24 B2 **98** C3
Dunmore Rd NW6 . . 23 A4
Dunmow Ho SE11 **149** C1
Dunmow Rd E15 . . . 19 C4
Dunmow Wlk N1 . . **86** C4
Dunnage Cres
SE16 . . . . 41 A2
Dunne Mews 11
NW5 . . . . 13 B3
Dunnet Ho 27 E3 . . 26 B3
Dunnico Ho SE17 . **152** A2
Dunn's Ct 11
SW10 . . . . 21 A1
Dunn's Pas WC1 . . **106** B2
Dunn St E8 . . . . 16 B3
Dunollie Pl NW5 . . . 13 B3
Dunollie Rd NW5 . . . 13 B3
Dunoon Ho N1 . . . . **84** C3
Dunraven Ho 12
TW9 . . . . 44 B2
Dunraven Rd W12 . 29 C1
Dunraven Sch
SW16 . . . . 74 B1
Dunraven St W1 . . **117** A4
Dunrobin Ct NW3 . . 11 A3
Dunsany Rd W14 . . . 39 C3
Dunsfold Ho 4
SW2 . . . . 74 B4
Dunsford Way
SW15 . . . . 57 A1
Dunsmure Rd N16 . . 7 A3
Dunstable Ct 3
SE3 . . . . 53 C3
Dunstable Mews
W1 . . . . **103** C4
Dunstable Rd TW10,
TW9 . . . . 54 A3
Dunstall Ho 9
SE15 . . . . 49 C2
Dunstan Ho SE4 . . . 51 B1
Dunstan Hos 5
E1 . . . . 32 B4
Dunstan Rd NW11 . . 1 C3
Dunstan's Gr SE22 . 65 A1
Dunstan's Rd SE22 . 64 C1
Dunster Ct EC3 . . . **124** B4
Dunster Gdns
NW6 . . . . 10 B1
Dunsterville Way
SE1 . . . . **137** C3
Dunston Rd
Clapham SW11 . . . **169** C1
Hackney E8 . . . . 24 B4
Dunston St E8 . . . . . 24 B4

Dunton Ho 14
SW16 . . . . 74 A1
Dunton Rd SE1 . . . **152** C3
Duntshill Rd SW18 . 71 A3
Dunworth Mews
W11 . . . . 31 B3
Duplex Ride SW1 **131** A3
Durand Gdns
SW9 . . . . **173** A4
Durand Prim Sch
SW9 . . . . **173** A4
Durant St E2 . . . 24 C2 **99** B4
Durban Ho 28
W12 . . . . 30 A2
Durdans Ho 3
NW1 . . . . 13 B1
Durfey Pl SE5 . . . . . 48 C3
Durford Cres
SW15 . . . . 69 A3
Durham Ct
Brockley SE4 . . . . . . 66 A3
4 Kilburn NW6 . . . 23 C3
Durham Ho
7 Dartmouth Pk
NW5 . . . . 4 B1
Lisson Gr NW8 . . . . **90** B3
Durham House St
WC2 . . . . **120** B3
Durham PI SW3 . . . **144** C1
Durham Rd N4, N7 . . 5 B2
Durham Row E1 . . . 33 A4
Durham St SE11 . . . **162** C4
Durham Terr W2 . . **100** A2
Durley Rd N16 . . . . . . 7 A4
Durlock Ho 15
SW9 . . . . **173** B4
Durlston Rd E5 . . . . . 7 C2
Durnford St
SE10 . . . . 52 B4
Durnsford Ave SW18,
SW19 . . . . 70 C2
Durnsford Rd SW18,
SW19 . . . . 70 C2
Durrell Rd SW6 . . . **164** C3
Durrels Ho W14 . . . **141** A4
Durrington Rd E5 . . 18 A4
Durrington Terr 2
SW8 . . . . **171** A2
Durrisdeer Ho
NW2 . . . . 10 B4
Durston NW5 . . . . . . 12 C3
Durward St E1 . . . . . 32 A4
Durweston Mews
W1 . . . . **103** A4
Durweston St W1 . **103** A3
Dutch Yd SW18 . . . . 58 C2
Dutton Ho SW2 . . . . 75 A3
Dutton St SE10 . . . . 52 B2
Dwight Ct 3 SW6 **164** B2
Dycer Ho 10 E9 . . . 17 C2
Dye House La E3 . . . 26 C4
Dyer Ho SE4 . . . . 51 A1
Dyer's Bldgs EC1 . **107** B3
Dyer's Hall 11 SW2 . 74 B3
Dylan Rd 2 SE24 . . 63 A3
Dylways SE5 . . . . 63 C3
Dymchurch Ho 12
E5 . . . . 17 A3
Dymes Path SW19 . . 69 C2
Dymock St SW6 . . . 59 A4
Dyne Rd NW6 . . . . . 10 B1
Dynevor Rd
Richmond TW10 . . . . 54 A2
Shacklewell N16 . . . . 7 B1
Dynham Rd NW6 . . . 10 C1

Dyott St
Soho WC1 . . . . **105** C2
St Giles WC1, WC2 **106** A2
Dysart St
EC2 . . . . **24** A1 **98** A1
Dyson Ho 3 SE10 . . 43 B1

E

Eade Rd N4 . . . . 6 B4
Eagle Cl SE16 . . . . . 40 B1
Eagle Ct
10 Dulwich SE21 . . 75 C2
Holborn EC1 . . . . . **108** A4
Eagle Dwellings
EC1 . . . . **97** A4
Eagle Ho
22 Bethnal Green
E1 . . . . 5 B1
Finsbury Pk N7 . . . . . 5 B1
Eagle Hts 10 SW11 . 60 A4
Eagle Lo NW11 . . . . . 1 B4
Eagle Mans N16 . . . 16 B3
Eagle Mews N1 . . . 16 A2
Eagle Pl
South Kensington
SW7 . . . . **143** A2
St James SW1 . . . . **119** A3
Eagle St WC1 . . . . **106** C3
Eagle Wharf SE1 . **124** C1
Eagle Wharf Rd
N1 . . . . **87** A2
Eagle Works
E1 . . . . 24 B1 **99** A1
Eagling Cl E3 . . . . . 26 C2
**Ealing, Hammersmith
& West London Coll**
W14 . . . . **140** A2
Eamann Casey Ho 34
SW9 . . . . **173** C3
Eamont Ct NW8 . . . **80** B2
Eamont St NW8 . . . **80** B2
Eardley Cres SW5 **141** C1
Earldom Rd SW15 . . 57 B3
Earle Ho SW1 . . . . **147** C3
Earlham St WC2 . . **106** A1
Earl Ho NW1 . . . . . . **90** B1
Earlom Ho WC1 . . . **95** B3
Earl Rd SW14 . . . . . . 55 B3
EARL'S COURT . . **141** C3
Earl's Court Ex Ctr
SW5 . . . . **141** B1
Earl's Court Gdns
SW5 . . . . **142** A3
Earl's Court Rd SW5,
W8 . . . . **141** C4
Earl's Court Sq
SW5 . . . . **142** A2
Earl's Court Sta
SW5 . . . . **141** C3
Earlsferry Way N1 . 14 A1
EARLSFIELD 71 B3
Earlsfield Prim Sch
SW18 . . . . 71 B2
Earlsfield Rd
SW18 . . . . 71 B3
Earlsfield Sta
SW18 . . . . 71 B3
Earlsmead Rd
NW10 . . . . 22 B2
Earl St EC2 . . . . . . **110** A4
Earls Terr W8 . . . . . **127** A1
Earlsthorpe Mews 3
SW12 . . . . 60 C1
Earlstoke St EC1 . . **96** A4

Earlston Gr E9 . . . . . .25 A4
Earls Wlk W8 . . . . 127 B1
Earlswood Cl 10
 SE10 . . . . .43 A1
Earlswood Ho 2
 SW2 . . . . .74 B3
Earlswood St SE10 . .43 A1
Early Mews NW1 . . . .82 B4
Earnshaw Ho EC1 . 96 B3
Earnshaw St WC1,
 WC2 . . . . 105 C2
Earsby St W14 . . . . 140 B4
Earth Galleries
 SW7 . . . . 129 C1
Eashing Point 5
 SW15 . . . . .69 A3
Easleys Mews W1 103 C2
EAST ACTON 29 A1
East Acton Arc
 W3 . . . . .29 B3
East Acton La W3 . 29 A2
East Acton Prim Sch
 W3 . . . . .29 B3
East Acton Sta
 W12 . . . . .29 C3
East Arbour St E1 . 32 C3
East Bank N16 . . . . . .7 A4
East Block 6 E1 . 32 C2
Eastbourne Ave
 W3 . . . . .28 C3
Eastbourne Gdns
 SW14 . . . . .55 B4
Eastbourne Mews
 W2 . . . . 101 A2
Eastbourne Rd W4 .45 B4
Eastbourne Terr
 W2 . . . . 101 A2
Eastbury Gr W4 . . 38 A1
Eastbury Terr E1 . . 25 C1
Eastcastle St W1 . 105 A2
Eastcheap EC3 . . 124 A4
East Churchfield Rd
 W3 . . . . .28 C1
Eastcote St SW9 . 172 C1
East Cross Route
 Bow E3 . . . . .26 C4
 Hackney Wick E9 . .18 B3
Eastdown Ho E8 . .16 C4
Eastdown Pk SE13 .67 C3
EAST DULWICH 64 C2
East Dulwich Gr
 SE22 . . . . .64 A2
East Dulwich Rd SE15,
 SE22 . . . . .64 C2
East Dulwich Sta
 SE22 . . . . .64 A3
East End Computing &
 Bsns Coll 8 E1 . . 32 A3
Eastern Rd SE4 . . 66 C3
East Ferry Rd E14 . .42 A2
Eastfields Ave
 SW18 . . . . .58 C3
Eastfields Rd W3 . . 28 B4
Eastfield St E14 . . 33 A4
East Harding St
 EC4 . . . . 107 C2
East Heath Rd NW3 . .2 C1
East Hill SW18. . . . 59 B2
East India Bldgs 9
 E14 . . . . .33 C2
East India Ct 7
 SE16 . . . . .40 B4
East India Dock Basin
 E14 . . . . .35 A2

East India Dock Rd
 E14 . . . . .34 A2
East India Dock Road
 Tunnel 18 E14 . . . .34 C3
East India Sta E14 . 34 C2
East La 5 SE16 . . 139 B3
Eastlake Ho 8
 NW8 . . . . .89 C1
Eastlake Rd SE5 . . 48 B1
Eastlands Cres
 SE21 . . . . .64 B1
Eastleigh Wlk 8
 SW15 . . . . .68 C4
Eastman Dental Hospl
 WC1 . . . . .94 C2
Eastman Ho 8
 SW4 . . . . .61 B1
Eastman Rd W3 . . 37 C4
Eastmearn Rd SE21,
 SE27 . . . . .75 B2
East Mount St E1 . 32 A4
Eastney St SE10 . . 42 C1
Easton Ho 4 SE27. .75 A1
Easton St WC1. . . . 95 B2
East Parkside
 SE10 . . . . .43 B4
East Pas EC1. . . . 108 C4
East Plaza E14 . . 34 A1
East Point 8 SE1 153 B2
East Poultry Ave
 EC1 . . . . 108 A3
East Putney Sta
 SW15 . . . . .58 A2
East Rd
 Chelsea SW1 . . . . 145 B1
 Shoreditch N1 . . . . 97 C4
East Row W10. . . . 23 A1
Eastry Ho SW8 . . 162 A1
EAST SHEEN 55 C3
East Sheen Ave
 SW14 . . . . .55 C3
East Sheen Prim Sch
 SW14 . . . . .56 A3
East Smithfield
 E1 . . . . 125 A3
East Surrey Gr
 SE15 . . . . .49 B3
East Tenter St 1 E1 111 A1
Eastvale W3 . . . . 29 B1
East View NW3 . . . . 2 C2
Eastway E9 . . . . . .26 A4
Eastwell Ho SE1 . 137 C2
Eastwick Ct 2
 SW19 . . . . .69 C3
Eastwood Cl 2
 N7 . . . . .14 C3
Eaton Cl SW1 . . . . 145 B3
Eaton Dr SW9 . . . .63 A3
Eaton Gate SW1 . 145 B4
Eaton Ho
 Battersea SW11 . . 167 C3
 23 Limehouse E14 . 33 B2
Eaton House Sch
 SW1 . . . . 145 B4
Eaton House The
 Manor Sch SW4 . . 61 A3
Eaton La 4 SW1 . 132 B1
Eaton Mans SW1 . 145 B3
Eaton Mews N
 SW1 . . . . 131 C1
Eaton Mews S
 SW1 . . . . 132 A1
Eaton Mews W 7
 SW1 . . . . 145 C4
Eaton Pl SW1 . . . . 131 C1
Eaton Row SW1 . . 132 A1

Eaton Sq SW1 . . . . 131 C1
Eaton Sq Pre-Prep
 Sch SW1 . . . . 146 A4
Eaton Sq Prep Sch
 SW1 . . . . 146 C3
Eaton Terr
 Belgravia SW1 . . . . 145 C4
 Bow E3 . . . . .26 A2
Eaton Terr Mews
 SW1 . . . . 145 B4
Eatonville Rd
 SW17 . . . . .72 B2
Eatonville Villas
 SW17 . . . . .72 B2
Ebbisham Dr SW8 162 C3
Ebbsfleet Rd NW2 .10 A4
Ebenezer Ho
 SE11 . . . . 150 A3
Ebenezer Mussel Ho
 E2 . . . . .25 B3
Ebenezer St N1 . . 97 B4
Ebley Cl SE15. . . . 49 B4
Ebner St SW18 . . 59 A2
Ebony Ho
 7 Bethnal Green
 E2 . . . . 24 C2 99 B3
 10 West Hampstead
 NW3 . . . . .11 A2
Ebor Cotts SW15 . . 68 A1
Ebor St
 E1,E2 . . . . . . 24 B1 98 C2
Eburne Rd N7 . . . . 5 A1
Ebury Bridge Rd
 SW1 . . . . 145 C1
Ebury Mews
 Belgravia SW1 . . . . 146 A4
 West Norwood
 SE27 . . . . .75 A1
Ebury Mews E
 SW1 . . . . 132 A1
Ebury Sq SW1 . . . . 145 C3
Ebury St SW1 . . . . 146 A4
Ecclesbourne Rd
 N1 . . . . .15 B1
Eccles Ct SE11 . . 149 A1
Eccles Rd SW11 . . 60 B3
Eccleston Ho 1
 SW2 . . . . .62 C1
Eccleston Mews
 SW1 . . . . 131 C1
Eccleston Pl SW1 146 A4
Eccleston Sq
 SW1 . . . . 146 B3
Eccleston Sq Mews
 SW1 . . . . 146 C3
Eccleston St SW1 146 A4
Eckford St N1 . . . . 85 B2
Eckstein Rd SW11 .60 A3
Edans Ct W12 . . . . 38 B4
Edbrooke Rd W9 . . 23 C1
Eddisbury Ho 7
 SE26 . . . . .76 C1
Eddiscombe Rd
 SW6 . . . . 165 A2
Eddison Ct N19 . . . .5 A2
Eddystone Rd SE4 .66 A2
Eddystone Twr
 SE8 . . . . .41 A1
Edenbridge Cl 26
 SE16 . . . . .40 A1
Edenbridge Rd E9 .17 C1
Eden Cl
 Child's Hill NW3 . . . . 1 C2
 Kensington W8. . . . 127 C2
Edendale W3. . . . 28 A2

Eden Gr
 Islington N7 . . . . .14 B3
 Willesden NW10 . . . . 9 A2
Edenham Way
 W10 . . . . .31 B4
Eden High Sch 9
 W6 . . . . .38 C1
Eden Ho
 5 Battersea
 6 Battersea
 SW11 . . . . .60 A4
 Lisson Gr NW8 . . . . 90 A1
Edenhurst Ave
 SW6 . . . . .58 B4
Eden Lodge NW6 . . . . 9 C1
Eden Mews SW17 . . 71 B1
Edensmuir Ct SE3 53 C3
Edenvale St SW6 166 C1
Eden Way E3 . . . . 26 B4
Edgar Ho
 Homerton E9 . . . . .18 A3
 South Lambeth
 SW8 . . . . 162 A2
Edgar Kail Way
 SE22 . . . . .64 A3
Edgarley Terr
 SW6 . . . . 164 A3
Edgar Rd E3 . . . . 27 A2
Edgar Wallace Cl 4
 SE15 . . . . .49 A3
Edgcott Ho 2
 W10 . . . . .30 B4
Edgecombe Ho
 4 London SE5 . . . . 49 A1
 Putney SW19 . . . . .70 A4
Edgecote Cl 7
 W3 . . . . .28 B1
Edgehill Ho 9
 SW9 . . . . .48 A1
Edgeley La SW4 . . 61 C4
Edgeley Rd SW4 . . 61 C4
Edge St W8 . . . . 31 C1 113 C2
Edgeworth Ho
 NW8 . . . . .78 C4
Edgson Ho SW1 . 146 A2
Edgware Acad
 WC2 . . . . 106 B1
Edgware Rd W2,
 NW1, NW8 . . . . . . 102 A3
Edgware Road Sta
 (Bakerloo) NW1 102 A3
Edgware Road Sta
 (Met, Distr, Circle)
 NW1 . . . . 102 B3
Edinburgh Cl 7
 E2 . . . . .25 B3
Edinburgh Ct 10
 SE16 . . . . .32 C1
Edinburgh Ho
 3 Acton W3 . . . . 28 C3
 Maida Vale W9 . . . . 88 B4
Edington 20 NW5 . . 12 C2
Edison Bldg 7
 E14 . . . . .41 C4
Edison Ct SE10 . . 43 B3
Edison Ho SE1. . . . 151 B4
Edis St NW1 . . . . 81 C4
Editha Mans
 SW10 . . . . 156 C3
Edith Cavell Cl 2
 N19 . . . . .5 A4
Edith Gr SW10 . . 157 A2
Edith Ho 6 W6 . . 39 B1

Edithna St SW9. . . . 62 A4
Edith Neville Cotts
 NW1 . . . . .93 B4
Edith Neville Prim Sch
 NW1 . . . . .83 B1
Edith Ramsay Ho 7
 E1 . . . . .33 A4
Edith Rd
 Stratford New Town
 E15 . . . . .19 C4
 West Kensington
 W14 . . . . 140 B3
Edith Row SW6. . . . 166 B4
Edith St E2 . . . . 24 C3
Edith Summerskill Ho
 SW6 . . . . 154 C2
Edith Terr SW10 . 156 C2
Edith Villas W14 . 140 C2
Edith Yd SW10 . . . 157 A2
Edmeston Cl E9 . . 18 A2
Edmond Ct SE14 . . 50 B3
Edmonton Ct 5
 SE16 . . . . .40 B3
Edmund Halley Way
 SE10 . . . . .43 A4
Edmund Ho
 Kennington SE17 . 150 B1
 New Cross Gate
 SE14 . . . . .51 B2
Edmundsbury Ct Est
 18 SW9 . . . . .62 B3
Edmund St SE5. . . . 48 C3
Edmund Waller Prim
 Sch SE14 . . . . 50 C1
Ednam Ho SE15 . . 49 C4
Edna St SW11 . . . . 168 A3
Edred Ho E9 . . . . 18 A4
Edrich Ho SW4 . . 172 A3
Edric Ho SW1 . . . . 147 C4
Edric Rd SE14 . . . . 50 C3
Edward St 75 A1
Edward Alleyn Ho
 SE21 . . . . .76 A4
Edward Cl 2 E16. .35 C4
Edward Dodd Ct
 N1 . . . . .97 C4
Edward Edward's Ho
 SE1 . . . . 122 A1
Edwardes Pl W8. . 127 A1
Edwardes Sq W8 . 127 A1
Edward Friend Ho 6
 N16 . . . . .7 A1
Edward Ho
 Paddington W2 . . . . 89 B1
 Vauxhall SE11. . . . 149 A1
Edward Kennedy Ho
 18 W10 . . . . .23 A1
Edward Mann Cl 1
 E1 . . . . .32 C3
Edward Mews
 NW1 . . . . .82 B1
Edward Pl SE8 . . 51 B4
Edward Robinson Ho
 3 SE14 . . . . .50 C3
Edward's Cotts 1
 N1 . . . . .15 A1
Edward's La N16 . .7 A2
Edwards Mews
 Islington N1 . . . . .14 C1
 Marylebone W1 . . 103 B1
Edward Sq
 Islington N1 . . . . .84 C3

Edward Sq continued
1 Rotherhithe
SE16.............33 A1
Edward St SE14......51 B3
Edward VII Mans
NW10...............33 C1
Edward Wilson Prim
Sch 2 W2 ....100 A4
Edwin's Mead E9 ...18 A4
Edwin St
Bethnal Green E1....25 B1
Newham E16.........35 C4
Edwy Ho E9..........18 B4
Edwyn Ho SW18......59 A1
Effie Pl SW6.......155 C1
Effie Rd SW6.......155 C1
Effingham Ho 37
SW8...............171 B1
Effra Ct SW2........62 B2
Effra Par SW2.......62 C2
Effra Pde SW2.......62 C2
Effra Rd SW2........62 C2
Effra Road Ret Pk
SW2...............62 C2
EF International
Language Sch
SE1..............121 C1
Egbert Ho E9........18 A3
Egbert St NW1 ......81 B4
Egbury Ho SW15.....56 B1
Egerton Cres
SW3...............144 B4
Egerton Ct 1
TW10..............54 A2
Egerton Dr SE10....52 A2
Egerton Gdns
Knightsbridge
SW3...............130 A1
Willesden NW10.....22 B4
Egerton Gdns Mews
SW3...............130 B1
Egerton Ho W4......45 B4
Egerton Pl SW3 ....130 B1
Egerton Rd N16 .....7 B4
Egerton Terr SW3 ..130 B1
Egham Cl SW19......70 A2
Eglantine Rd
SW18..............59 B2
Eglington Ct SE17 ..48 B4
Egliston Mews
SW15..............57 B4
Egliston Rd SW15...57 B4
Egmont St SE14.....50 C3
Egremont Ho SE13 ..52 A1
Egremont Rd SE27..74 C1
Egret Ho 11 SE16 ...40 C2
Eider Cl 30 SE8......51 B4
Elaine Ct 5 NW3....12 B2
Elaine Gr NW5 ......12 C3
Elaine Ho N4........5 A3
Elam Cl SE5.........48 A1
Elam St SE5.........48 A1
Elan Ct E1..........32 A4
Eland Rd SW11......60 B4
Elba Pl SE17.......151 A4
Elbe St SW6........166 C2
Elborough St
SW18..............70 C3
Elbury Dr E16.......35 C3
Elcho St SW11.....158 B1
Elcot Ave SE15 .....50 A3
Elderberry Rd W5...36 A4

Elderfield Ho 4
E14...............33 C2
Elderfield Rd E5....17 B4
Elder St E1...24 B1 98 C1
Elder Wlk
Islington N1........86 B4
4 Lewisham SE13...67 B4
Eldon Ct NW6........23 C4
Eldon Gr NW3........11 C3
Eldon Rd W8.......128 B1
Eldon St EC2.......109 C3
Eldon Way NW10....20 A3
Eldridge Ct SE16 ..139 B1
Eleanor Cl 15 SE16 ..40 C4
Eleanor Ct 22 E2....24 C4
Eleanor Gr SW13....56 A4
Eleanor Ho
15 Hammersmith
.................39 B1
4 Kentish Town
NW5...............13 B3
Eleanor Palmer Prim
Sch 12 NW5 ....13 B4
Eleanor Rathbone Ho
6 N6...............4 B4
Eleanor Rd E8.......17 A1
Eleanor St E3........26 C2
Electra Ct 6 NW2....9 B2
Electric Ave SW9....62 C3
Electric Ho 13 E3....26 C2
Electric La 2
.................62 C3
Electric Mans 1
.................62 C3
Elephant & Castle
Newington SE1......136 B1
Newington SE1......150 B4
Elephant & Castle Sh
Ctr SE1...........150 C4
Elephant & Castle
Sta SE1...........150 C4
Elephant La SE16....40 B4
Elephant Rd SE17 ..150 C4
Elfindale Rd SE24....63 B2
Elfort Rd N5........15 A4
Elf Row E1..........32 B2
Elgar Ave W5.......36 A4
Elgar Cl SE8........51 C3
Elgar Ct W14.......126 A1
Elgar Ho
Pimlico SW1.......146 B1
3 South Hampstead
.................11 B1
Elgar St SE16.......41 A3
Elgin Ave
Hammersmith
W12...............38 A3
Westbourne Green
W9................88 A3
Elgin Cres
W11.......31 A2 112 B4
Elgin Ho E14........34 A3
Elgin Mans W9......88 A3
Elgin Mews W11....31 A3
Elgin Mews N 9 W9 .88 B4
Elgin Mews S 11 W9 .88 B4
Elgood Cl
W11...............31 A1 112 A1
Elgood Ho NW8 ....79 C1
Elham Ho 15 E5.....17 A3
Elia Mews N1.......86 A1
Elias Pl SW8.......163 B3

Elia St N1...........86 A1
Elim Est SE1.......138 A2
Elim St SE1........138 A2
Eliot Cotts SE3......53 A1
Eliot Ct SW18.......59 A1
Eliot Gdns SW15....56 C3
Eliot Hill SE13......52 B1
Eliot Ho 10 TW10 ...54 A1
Eliot Mews NW8....78 C1
Eliot Pk SE13........52 B1
Eliot Pl SE3.........53 A1
Eliot Vale SE3.......52 C1
Elizabeth Ave
Islington N1........15 C1
Shoreditch N1.......87 A4
Elizabeth Barnes Ct 1
SW6...............166 B2
Elizabeth Blount Ct 4
E14...............33 A3
Elizabeth Cl
Paddington W9......23 B1
12 Poplar E14......34 A3
Elizabeth Cooper Lo
SW12..............60 C1
Elizabeth Cotts 5
TW9...............44 C2
Elizabeth Ct
Chelsea SW10......157 C3
East Dulwich SE22...64 C3
Marylebone NW8....90 B2
Westminster SW1 ..133 C1
Elizabeth Finn Ho 1
W12...............38 C3
Elizabeth Garrett
Anderson Hospl
NW1...............93 A1
Elizabeth Garrett
Anderson Language
Coll N1............85 A1
Elizabeth Gdns
W3................29 B1
Elizabeth Ho
6 Hammersmith
W6................39 B1
13 Lambeth SE11 ..149 C3
Elizabeth Ind Est
SE14..............50 C4
Elizabeth Kenny Ho
N1................15 B2
Elizabeth Mews
28 Hackney E2......24 C3
Maitland Pk NW3....12 B2
Elizabeth Selby Inf
Sch 19 E2....24 C3 99 C4
Elizabeth Sq 13
SE16..............33 A2
Elizabeth St SW1 ..145 C4
Elkington Point
SE11..............149 B3
Elkstone Rd W10....31 B4
Ellacombe Ho 1
SW2...............74 B4
Ellaline Rd W6......47 C4
Ella Mews NW3.....12 B3
Elland Ho 10 E14....33 B3
Elland Rd SE15......65 B3
Ella Rd N4, N8......5 A4
Ellenborough Ho 5
W12...............30 A2
Ellenborough Pl
SW15..............56 C3
Ellen St E1.........111 C1
Ellen Wilkinson Ho
7 Globe Town
E2................25 C2

Ellen Wilkinson Ho
continued
West Brompton
SW6...............155 A3
Ellerby St SW6......47 C2
Ellerdale Cl 13
NW3...............11 B4
Ellerdale Rd NW3...11 B3
Ellerdale St SE13 ...67 A4
Ellerker Gdns
TW10..............54 A1
Ellerslie Gdns
NW10..............21 C4
Ellerslie Ind Est
SW2...............62 A2
Ellerslie Rd W12.....30 A1
Ellerton St E3........27 A2
Ellerton Rd
Wandsworth SW17,
SW18..............71 C3
Ellery Cl 5 NW10 ...21 A3
Ellery Ho SE17.....151 C3
Ellery St SE15......50 A1
Ellesmere Ct W4....45 B4
Ellesmere Rd
Bow E3.............26 A3
Chiswick W4........45 B4
Willesden NW10.....8 C3
Ellesmere St E14....34 A3
Ellingfort Rd E8.....17 A1
Ellingham Rd
Leyton E15.........19 C4
Shepherd's Bush
W12...............38 C4
Ellington Ho SE1 ..137 A1
Ellington St N7......14 C2
Elliott Rd
Acton W4...........38 A2
Brixton SW9........48 A2
Elliott Sch SW15....57 B1
Elliott's Pl N1......86 B3
Elliott Sq NW3.....12 A1
Elliott's Row SE11 .150 B4
Ellis Cl NW10.......9 B2
Ellisfield Dr SW15 ..68 C4
Ellis Franklin Ct
NW8...............78 C2
Ellis Ho SE17.......151 B2
Ellison Ho 1 SE13 ..52 B1
Ellison Rd SW13....46 B1
Ellis St SW1........145 B4
Ellsworth St E2......25 A2
Ellwood Ct 4 W9....88 B1
Elmar Ct SW6......164 B2
Elm Bank Gdns
SW13..............46 A1
Elm Bank Mans
SW13..............46 A1
Elmbourne Rd
SW17..............73 A1
Elmbridge Wlk E8 ..16 C1
Elm Cl N19..........4 B2
Elmcourt Rd SE21,
SE27..............75 C2
Elm Cres W5........36 A4
Elmcroft N6.........4 B4
Elmcroft Ave NW11..1 B4
Elmcroft Cres
NW11..............1 A4
Elmcroft St E5......17 B4
Elm Ct
Brixton SW9.......173 B4
Lewisham SE13.....67 C4
42 Notting Hill W2 ..31 C4
Strand EC4........121 B4

Elm Ct Sch SE27....74 C1
Elmer Ho NW1 .....102 A3
Elmfield Ho
5 Canonbury N5.....15 B3
Paddington W9......23 C1
Elmfield Mans 7
SW17..............72 C2
Elmfield Rd SW17 ..73 A2
Elmfield Way W9....31 C4
Elm Friars Wlk
NW1...............13 C1
Elm Gn W3..........29 A3
Elm Gr
Cricklewood NW2....9 C4
Peckham SE15......49 C1
Evergreen Sch The
SE27..............75 A2
Elm Grove Rd
Barnes SW13........46 C1
Ealing W5...........36 A4
Elm Ho 4 E14.......42 B4
Elmhurst Mans
SW4...............61 C4
Elmhurst St SW4....61 C4
Elmhurst Villas
SE15..............65 B3
Elmington Rd SE5 ..48 C3
Elmira St SE13......67 A4
Elm Lo SW6.........47 C2
Elmore Ho SW9.....48 A1
Elmore St N1........15 C1
Elm Park Gdns
SW10.............143 B1
Elm Park Ho
SW10.............143 B1
Elm Park La SW3 ..143 B1
Elm Park Mans
SW10.............157 A4
Elm Park Rd SW3 ..157 B4
Elm Pk SW2.........74 B4
Elm Pl SW7........143 B2
Elm Quay Sw8......161 B3
Elm Rd SW14.......55 B3
Elm Row NW3.......2 B1
Elms Cres SW4......61 C1
Elmshaw Rd SW15 ..56 C2
Elmslie Point 2
E3................33 B4
Elms Mews W2.....115 B4
Elms Rd SW4.......61 B2
Elm St WC1.........95 A1
Elms The
Barnes SW13........56 B4
8 Harlesden
NW10..............21 A3
Elmstone Rd SW6 .165 B4
Elm Terr NW2.......1 C1
Elmton Ct NW8.....89 B2
Elm Tree Cl NW8....89 B4
Elm Tree Ct
5 Camberwell
.................48 B2
St John's Wood
NW8...............89 B4
Elm Tree Rd NW8...89 B4
Elm Way NW10......8 A4
Elm Wlk NW3.......1 C2
Elmwood Ct
SW11.............170 A4
Elm Wood Prim Sch
SE27..............75 C1
Elmwood Rd
Chiswick W4........45 B4
Herne Hill SE24.....63 C2
Elmworth Gr SE21..75 C2

Elnathan Mews
W9 .... 88 B1
Elphinstone St N5 ....15 A4
Elrington Rd E8 .....16 C2
Elsa St E1 ....37 A4
Elsdale Ho 9 E9 ....17 B2
Elsdale St E9 ....17 B1
Elsden Mews E2 .....25 B3
Elsenham St
SW19 ....70 B2
Elsfield NW5 ....13 A3
Elsham Rd W14 ....126 A3
Elsham Terr W14 ..126 A3
Elsie Lane Ct W2 ...100 A3
Elsiemaud Rd SE4 ...66 B2
Elsie Rd SE22 ....64 B3
Elsinore Gdns NW2 ...1 A1
Elsinore Ho
12 Camberwell
SE5 ....48 B1
Islington N1 ....85 B3
Elsinore Way TW9 ...55 A4
Elsley Rd SW11 ......60 C4
Elsley Sch 8
SW17 ....72 A2
Elspeth Rd SW11 ....60 B3
Elstead Ho 9 SW2 ..74 B4
Elsted St SE17 ......151 C3
Elstow Grange NW6 ...9 C1
Elswick Rd SE13 .....52 A1
Elswick St SW6 .....166 C2
Elsworthy Rd NW3 ..80 A4
Elsworthy Rise
NW3 ....12 A1
Elsworthy Terr
NW3 ....12 A1
Elsynge Rd SW18 ....59 C1
Elsynge Road Mans
SW18 ....59 B3
Elthiron Rd SW6 ...165 C3
Elthorne Rd N19 ......4 C2
Elthruda Rd SE13 ....67 C1
Elton Ho 3 E3 ....26 B4
Elton Pl N16 ....16 A3
Elton St 11 N16 .....16 A3
Eltringham St
SW18 ....59 B3
Elvaston Mews
SW7 ....129 A2
Elvaston Pl SW7 ...129 A1
Elveden Ho 17
SW9 ....63 A3
Elver Gdns 10
E2 ....24 C2 99 C4
Elverson Rd SE8 .....52 A1
Elverson Rd Sta
SE8 ....52 A1
Elverton St SW1 ...147 B4
Elvin Ho 2 E9 ....17 B2
Elvis Rd NW2 ....9 B2
Elwin St E2 ...24 C2 99 B4
Elwood Ho N5 ....6 A1
Elworth Ho SW8 ....163 A1
Ely Cotts SW8 ......162 C1
Ely Court Flats
SW6 ....164 A3
Ely Ct
Holborn EC1 ......107 C3
3 Maida Vale
NW6 ....23 C3
Ely Ho 22 SE15 ......49 C3
Ely Pl EC1 ....107 C3
Elysium Gate 7
SW6 ....164 C2
Elysium Pl SW6 ....164 C1

Elysium St SW6 ....164 C1
Elystan Ct SW15 .....57 A2
Elystan Pl SW3 .....144 C2
Elystan St SW3 .....144 B3
Elystan Wlk N1 ......85 B3
Emanuel Ave W3 ....28 B3
Emanuel Ct W3 ......28 C3
Emanuel Sch
SW11 ....60 A2
Embankment
SW15 ....47 C1
Embankment Gdns
SW3 ....159 A4
Embankment Pier
WC2 ....120 B2
Embankment Pl
WC2 ....120 B2
Embankment Sta
WC2 ....120 B2
Embassy Ct NW8 ....79 C1
Embassy Ho 2
NW6 ....10 C1
Emba St SE16 ......139 C3
Ember Ct 8 W12 ....38 A3
Emberton SE5 ....49 A4
Emberton Ct 11 .....96 A3
Embleton Rd SE13 ..67 A3
Emden St SW6 .....166 B4
Emerald Rd NW10 ...20 C4
Emerald St WC1 ...106 C4
Emerson Ho N16 .....7 A1
Emerson St SE1 ....122 C2
Emery Hill St
SW1 ....133 A1
Emery St SE1 ....135 C2
Emily St 7 E16 ....35 B3
Emirates Airway
SE10 ....35 B1
Emirates Greenwich
Peninsula SE10 ....43 A4
Emirates Royal Dock
E16 ....35 C2
Emirates Stad
(Arsenal FC) N7 ...14 C4
Emlyn Gdns 3
W12 ....38 A3
Emlyn Rd W12 ....38 A3
Emmanuel CE Prim
Sch NW6 ....11 A2
Emmanuel Ho
Dulwich SE21 ......75 C1
Lambeth SE11 ....149 B3
Emmanuel Rd
SW12 ....73 C3
Emma St E2 ....25 A3
Emminster NW6 .....78 A4
Emmott Cl E1 ....26 A1
Emperor's Gate
SW7 ....142 C4
Empingham 20
SE8 ....40 C2
Empire Ho SW3 ....130 A1
Empire Sq N19 ....5 A1
Empire Wharf E3 ...26 A4
Empire Wharf Rd
E14 ....42 C2
Empress Mews 38
SE5 ....48 B1
Empress Pl SW5 ...141 B1
Empress St SE17 ...48 B4
Empress State
Building SW6 .....141 B1
Empson St E3 ....27 A1
Emsworth St SW2 ...74 B2
Emu Rd SW8 ....170 A1
Enard Ho 28 E3 .....26 B3

Enbrook St W10 .....23 A2
Enclave Ct EC1 ......96 B2
Endell St WC2 .....106 A1
Enderby St SE10 ....43 A1
Endlesham Ct 2
SW12 ....72 C4
Endlesham Rd
SW12 ....72 C4
Endsleigh Gdns
WC1 ....93 B2
Endsleigh Mans 4
SW16 ....74 A1
Endsleigh Pl WC1 ...93 C2
Endsleigh St WC1 ...93 C2
Endwell Rd SE4 .....51 A1
Endymion Rd
Harringay N4 ....6 A4
Tulse Hill SW2 ......62 B1
Energen C1 W13 ....37 A4
Enfield Cloisters 7
N1 ....24 A2 98 A4
Enfield Ho 1
SW9 ....172 B2
Enfield Rd
De Beauvoir Town E8,
N1 ....16 A1
South Acton W3 ....37 A4
Enford St W1 ....102 C4
Engadine St SW18 ..70 C3
Engate St SE13 ......67 B3
England's La NW3 ..12 B2
Englefield NW1 ......92 C3
Englefield Rd N1 ....16 A1
Englewood Rd
SW12 ....61 B1
English Gardening
Sch The SW3 .....158 C4
English Grounds
SE1 ....124 A1
English Martyrs RC
Prim Sch
Walworth SE17 ...151 C3
Whitechapel E1 ...111 A1
English St E3 ....26 B1
Enid St SE16 ....139 A2
Enid Stacy Ho 11
N19 ....5 A4
Enmore Ct SW14 ...55 C2
Enmore Gdns
SW14 ....55 C2
Enmore Rd SW15 ...57 B2
Ennerdale Ho 9
N4 ....5 C2
Ennerdale Rd TW9 .44 B1
Ennersdale Rd
SE13 ....67 C2
Ennis Ho 14 E14 ....34 A3
Ennismore Ave
W4 ....38 B2
Ennismore Gdns
SW7 ....130 A2
Ennismore Gdns
Mews SW7 ....130 A2
Ennismore Mews
SW7 ....130 A2
Ennismore St
SW7 ....130 A2
Ennis Rd N4 ....5 C3
Ensbury Ho SW8 ..162 C2
Ensign Ct 6 E1 ....125 C3
Ensign Ho 10 E14 ...41 C4
Ensign St E1 ....125 B4
Ensor Mews SW7 ..143 B2
Enterprise Ho 38
E9 ....17 B1

Enterprise Way
College Pk NW10 ...21 C2
Wandsworth SW18 ..58 C3
Enterprize Way
SE8 ....41 B2
Epirus Mews SW6 .155 B2
Epirus Rd SW6 ....155 A2
Epping Cl E14 ......41 C2
Epping Ho 5 E5 ......7 C2
Epping Pl N1 ....14 C2
Epple Rd SW6 .....165 A4
Epstein Ct N1 ....86 B3
Epworth St EC2 .....97 C1
Equity Sq 26
E2 ....24 B2 99 A3
Erasmus St SW1 ...147 C3
Erconwald St W12 ..29 B3
Eresby Ho SW7 ....130 B3
Eresby Pl NW6 .....10 C1
Erica Ct SW4 ....172 B3
Erica Ho SE4 ....66 B4
Erica St W12 ....29 C2
Ericcson Cl SW18 ...58 C2
Eric Fletcher Ct 15
N1 ....15 B1
Eric Macdonald Ho
SW6 ....165 C3
Eric Rd NW10 ....8 B2
Ericson Ho
London SE13 ....67 C3
Stamford Hill N16 ...7 B3
Eric St E3 ....26 B1
Eric Wilkins Ho 14
SE1 ....153 B1
Eridge Ho SE22 .....64 B4
Eridge House Sch 13
SW6 ....164 C2
Eridge Rd W4 ....37 C3
Erin Ct NW2 ....9 B2
Erlanger Rd SE14 ...50 C1
Ermine Rd SE13 .....67 A3
Ernest Bevin Coll
SW17 ....72 A2
Ernest Gdns W4 ....45 A4
Ernest Simmonds Ho
SE14 ....50 B1
Ernest St E1 ....25 C1
Ernshaw Pl SW15 ..58 A2
Eros (Shaftesbury
Meml Fountain)
W1 ....119 B3
Erpingham Rd
SW15 ....57 B4
Errington Rd N9 ....23 B1
Errol St EC1 ....97 A1
Erskine Ho SW1 ...146 C1
Erskine Rd NW3 ....12 B1
Escuan Lo N5 ....15 B3
Esher Gdns SW19 ..69 C2
Esher Ho 8 SW8 ..171 C2
Eskdale NW1 ....82 C1
Esk Ho E3 ....26 B1
Esme Ho SW15 ......56 B3
Esmeralda Rd
SE1 ....153 C3
Esmond Ct W8 .....128 B2
Esmond Gdns W4 ..37 C2
Esmond Rd
Acton W4 ....37 C3
Kilburn NW6 ....23 B4
Esmond St SW15 ...58 A3
Esparto St SW18 ...71 A4
Espirit Ct E1 ....110 C3
Espirit Ho 6
SW15 ....58 A2

Essendine Mans
W9 ....23 C2
Essendine Prim Sch
11 W9 ....23 C2
Essendine Rd W9 ...23 C2
Essex Ct
Barnes SW13 ......46 B1
Hammersmith W6 ..39 B3
Holborn EC4 ......107 B1
Essex Ho 2 E14 ....34 A3
Essex Park Mews
W3 ....29 A1
Essex Pl W4 ....37 B2
Essex Place Sq 5
W4 ....37 C2
Essex Rd
Acton W3 ....28 B2
Chiswick W4 ....37 C2
Islington N1 ....86 B4
Willesden NW10 .....8 A1
Essex Road Sta N1 ..15 B1
Essex St WC2 .....121 B4
Essex Villas W8 ...127 B3
Essian St E1 ....33 A4
Essington SW15 ....58 A1
Estcourt Rd SW6 ..154 C2
Estella Ho 18 W11 ..30 C2
Estelle Rd NW3 .....12 B4
Esterbrooke St
SW1 ....147 B3
Este Rd SW11 ....60 A4
Estoria Cl 22 SW2 ..74 C4
Etal Ho N1 ....15 A1
Etchingham Rd
E15 ....19 B4
Eternit Wlk SW6 ....47 C2
Ethelbert Ho E9 ....18 A4
Ethelbert St SW12 ..73 A3
Ethelburga St
SW11 ....168 B3
Ethelburga Twr
SW11 ....168 A3
Ethelden Rd W12 ...30 A1
Ethel Rankin Ct 8
SW6 ....164 C2
Ethel St SE17 ......151 A3
Ethelworth Ct 4
SW2 ....74 C3
Etherow St SE22 ...76 C4
Ethnard Rd SE15 ...50 A4
Eton Ave NW3 ....12 A1
Eton Cl SW18 ....71 A4
Eton College Rd
NW3 ....12 B2
Eton Ct NW3 ....11 C1
Eton Garages 11
NW3 ....12 A2
Eton Hall NW3 ......12 B2
Hackney E9 ....18 B2
Highbury N5 ....15 A4
Eton Pl NW1 ....12 C1
Eton Rd NW3 ....12 B2
Eton Rise NW3 ......12 B2
Eton St TW10 ....54 A2
Eton Villas NW3 ....12 B2
Etta St SE8 ....51 A4
Ettrick St E14 ....34 B3
Eugene Cotter Ho
SE17 ....151 C3
Eugenia Rd SE16 ...40 B2
Eurocentres SW1 .146 B3
Euro Cl NW10 ....8 C2

Eurolink Bsns Ctr
SW2 . . . . .62 C2
Europa Pl EC1 . . . . .96 C3
European Coll ◼
E1 . . . . .111 B2
Eustace Bldg
SW8 . . . . .160 A3
Eustace Ho SE11 . .148 C4
Eustace Rd SW6 . .155 B2
Euston Rd NW1 . . . . .93 A2
Euston Sq NW1 . . . . .93 B3
Euston Square Sta
WC1 . . . . .93 A2
Euston St NW1 . . . . .93 A3
Euston Sta NW1 . . . .93 A3
Euston Underpass
NW1 . . . . .92 C2
Evan Cook Cl SE15 . .50 B2
Evandale Rd SW9 .173 C2
Evangelist Rd
NW5 . . . . .13 A4
Evans Cl E8 . . . . .16 B2
Evans Ho
◼ Shepherd's Bush
W12 . . . . .30 A2
South Lambeth
SW8 . . . . .161 C1
Evelina Children's
Hospl E1 . . . . .134 C2
Evelina Mans ◼
SE5 . . . . .48 C3
Evelina Rd SE15 . . . .50 B1
Eveline Lowe Prim
Sch ◼ SE1 . . . . .153 C1
Evelyn Ct
Marylebone W1 . . . .102 C1
Shacklewell E8 . . . . .16 C4
Shoreditch N1 . . . . . .87 B1
Evelyn Denington Ct
◼ N1 . . . . .15 A1
Evelyn Fox Ct W10 . .30 B4
Evelyn Gdns
Richmond TW9 . . . . .54 A3
South Kensington
SW7 . . . . .143 B2
Evelyn Grace Acad
SE24 . . . . .63 A3
Evelyn Ho
Bedford Pk W12 . . . . .38 B4
◼ Brixton SW2 . . . . .62 B2
◼ Spitalfields E1 . .111 B3
Evelyn Rd
Acton W4 . . . . .37 C3
Richmond TW9 . . . . .54 A3
Evelyn St
Greenwich SE10 . . . .52 B4
SE8 . . . . .41 A1
Evelyn Terr TW9 . . . .54 A4
Evelyn Wlk N1 . . . . .87 B1
Evelyn Yd W1 . . . . . .105 B2
Evenwood Cl
SW15 . . . . .58 A2
Everard Ho ◼ E1 .111 C1
Everatt Cl SW18 . . . .58 B2
Everdon Rd SW13 . . .46 C4
Everest Pl E14 . . . . . .34 B4
Everett Ho
Islington N7 . . . . .14 C4
Walworth SE17 . . . . .151 B2
Evergreen Sq ◼
E8 . . . . .16 B1
Everilda St N1 . . . . . . .85 A3
Evering Rd E5, N16 . .7 C1
Everington St W6 . . . .47 C4

Everitt Rd NW10 . . . .20 C2
Everleigh St N4 . . . . .5 B3
Eversfield Rd TW9 . . .44 B1
Evershed Ho E1 . . . .111 A2
Evershed Wlk W4 . . .37 C2
Eversholt St NW1 . . .93 B4
Evershot Rd N4 . . . . . .5 B3
Eversleigh Rd
SW11 . . . . .169 B1
Eversley Ho ◼
E2 . . . . .24 C2 99 B3
Everthorpe Rd
SE15 . . . . .64 B4
Everton Bldgs
NW1 . . . . .92 C3
Evesham Ct ◼ ◼
TW10 . . . . .54 B1
Evesham Ho
◼ Bethnal Green
E2 . . . . .25 B3
Pimlico SW1 . . . . . . .146 B2
St John's Wood
NW8 . . . . .78 C3
Evesham St W11 . . . .30 C2
Evesham Way
SW11 . . . . .60 C4
Evesham Wlk
Brixton SW9 . . . . . . .173 B2
Camberwell SE5 . . . .48 C1
Ewald Rd SW6 . . . . .164 C1
Ewart Pl ◼ E3 . . . . . .26 B3
Ewe Cl N7 . . . . .14 A2
Ewen Cres SW2 . . . .74 C4
Ewen Henderson Ct
◼ SE14 . . . . .51 A3
Ewer St SE1 . . . . .122 C1
Ewhurst ◼ SW15 . . .57 C1
Ewhurst Cl E1 . . . . . .32 B4
Ewhurst Rd SE4 . . . .66 B1
Exbury Ho
Hackney E9 . . . . .17 B2
◼ London SW9 . . . . .62 B3
Excel Ct WC2 . . . . . .119 C3
Excelsior Gdns
SE13 . . . . .52 B1
Excelsior Ind Est
SE16 . . . . .40 B2
Exchange Arc
EC2 . . . . .110 B4
Exchange Ct WC2 . .120 B3
Exchange Mans ◼
NW11 . . . . .1 B4
Exchange Pl EC2 . . .110 A4
Exeter Ct NW6 . . . . .23 C3
Exeter Ho
Paddington W2 . . . .100 C2
◼ Peckham SE15 . . .49 C4
Putney SW15 . . . . . .57 B1
Exeter Mans NW2 . . .10 A2
Exeter Mews
Fulham SW6 . . . . . . .155 B2
◼ Hampstead
NW6 . . . . .11 A2
Exeter Rd
Brondesbury
NW2 . . . . .10 A2
Newham E16 . . . . . . .35 C4
Exeter St WC2 . . . . .120 C4
Exeter Way ◼
SE14 . . . . .51 B3
Exford Ct SW11 . . . .167 C4
Exhibition Cl W12 . . .30 B2
Exhibition Rd
SW7 . . . . .129 C2
Exmoor Ho ◼ E3 . . .26 A3

Exmoor St W10 . . . . .30 C4
Exmouth Ho
Clerkenwell EC1 . . . .95 C2
◼ Millwall E14 . . . . .42 A2
Exmouth Market
EC1 . . . . .95 C2
Exmouth Mews
NW1 . . . . .93 A3
Exmouth Pl E8 . . . . . .17 A1
Exmouth St E1 . . . . . .32 B3
Exonbury NW8 . . . . .78 B3
Exon St SE17 . . . . . . .152 A3
Explorers Ct ◼
E14 . . . . .34 C2
Express Wharf ◼
E14 . . . . .41 C4
Exton St SE1 . . . . . . .121 B1
Eynella Rd SE21 . . . .76 B4
Eynham Rd W12 . . . .30 B3
Eynsford Coll W1 . . .105 B2
Eynsford Ho
Borough The SE1 . . .137 B4
◼ Deptford SE15 . . .50 B4
Walworth SE17 . . . . .152 A3
Eyot Gdns W6 . . . . . .38 B1
Eyot Gn W4 . . . . .38 B1
Eyre Ct NW8 . . . . . . .79 B2
Eyre St Hill EC1 . . . . .95 B1
Eythorne Rd SW9 . .173 C4
Eza St E2 . . . . . .24 B2 99 A4

F

Fabian Rd SW6 . . . . .155 A2
Fabyc Ho TW9 . . . . . .44 C3
Fairacres SW15 . . . . .56 C3
Fairbairn Gn ◼
SW9 . . . . .48 A2
Fairbriar Residence
SW7 . . . . .143 A4
Fairbridge Rd N19 . . .4 C2
Fairburn Ct SW15 . . .58 A2
Fairburn Ho
◼ Stamford Hill
N16 . . . . .7 A3
West Kensington
SW5 . . . . .141 A1
Fairby Ho SE1 . . . . . .153 A4
Faircharm Trad Est
SE8 . . . . .52 A3
Fairchild ◼
SW11 . . . . .167 C1
Fairchild Ho
◼ Hackney E9 . . . . .17 B1
Pimlico SW1 . . . . . . .147 A3
◼ Shoreditch
N1 . . . . .24 A2 98 A4
Fairchild Pl
EC2 . . . . .110 B4
Fairchild St
EC2 . . . . .24 A1 98 B1
Fairclough St E1 . . . .111 C2
Faircourt ◼ NW3 . . .12 B2
Faircroft N16 . . . . .6 C3
Fairdale Gdns
SW15 . . . . .57 A3
Fairdene Ct N7 . . . . .14 A3
Fairfax Ho
◼ Brixton SW9 . . . .173 C1
Putney SW15 . . . . . . .56 C2
Fairfax Mews
SW15 . . . . .57 A3
Fairfax Pl
Kensington W14 . . . .126 B1

Fairfax Pl continued
South Hampstead
NW6 . . . . .11 B1
Fairfax Rd
Acton W4 . . . . .38 A3
South Hampstead
NW6 . . . . .11 B1
Fairfield
Camden Town
NW1 . . . . .82 C3
◼ Stepney E1 . . . . . .32 B4
Fairfield Ct
Harlesden NW10 . . . .21 C4
◼ London SW18 . . . .59 A2
Fairfield Dr SW18 . . .59 A2
Fairfield Rd E3 . . . . . .26 C3
Fairfield St SW18 . . .59 A2
Fairfoot Rd E3 . . . . . .26 C1
Fairford Ho SE11 . . .149 C3
Fairhazel Gdns
NW6 . . . . .11 B1
Fairheathe SW15 . . .57 C1
Fairholme Rd
W14 . . . . .140 B1
Fairholt Cl N16 . . . . . .7 A3
Fairholt Rd N16 . . . . .6 C3
Fairholt St SW7 . . . .130 B2
Fairhurst ◼ NW6 . . .11 B2
Fairlawn Ave W4 . . . .37 B2
Fairlawn Ct ◼ W4 . . .37 B2
Fairlawn Gr W4 . . . . .37 B2
Fairlawn Mans
SE14 . . . . .50 C2
Fairlead Ho ◼
E14 . . . . .41 C3
Fairley House Sch
SW1 . . . . .147 C2
Fairlie Ct
◼ Bromley E3 . . . . .27 A2
◼ Tufnell Pk N7 . . . .13 C3
Fairlight Ave
NW10 . . . . .21 A3
Fairlight Ct ◼
NW10 . . . . .21 A3
Fairlop Pl NW8 . . . . .89 C3
Fairmead Ho E9 . . . . .18 A4
Fairmead Rd N7,
N19 . . . . .5 A1
Fairmont Ave E14 . . .34 C1
Fairmont Ho ◼
E3 . . . . .26 C1
Fairmount Rd
SW2 . . . . .62 B1
Fair St SE1 . . . .138 C4
Fairstead Wlk N1 . . . .86 C4
Fairthorn Rd SE7,
SE10 . . . . .43 C1
Fairview Ho ◼
SW2 . . . . .74 B4
Fairview Pl SW2 . . . .74 B4
Fairwall Ho ◼
SE5 . . . . .49 A2
Fairway Cl NW11 . . . .2 B4
Fairway Ct ◼
SE16 . . . . .40 C4
Fairway The W3 . . . . .29 A3
Fairweather Ho
N7 . . . . .14 A4
Faith Ct NW2 . . . . .9 A2
Faithfull Ho N5 . . . . .15 B3
Fakruddin St
E1 . . . . .24 C1 99 C1
Falconberg Ct
W1 . . . . .105 C2

Falconberg Mews
W1 . . . . .105 C2
Falconbrook Prim Sch
◼ SW11 . . . . .59 C4
Falcon Cl
Chiswick W4 . . . . . . .45 B4
Lambeth SE1 . . . . . . .122 B2
Falcon Ct
◼ ◼ Dulwich SE21 . .75 C2
Holborn EC4 . . . . . . .107 B1
Islington N1 . . . . .86 B1
Falconer Wlk ◼ N7 . .5 B2
Falcon Ho SE15 . . . . .49 B2
Falcon La SW11 . . . . .60 A4
Falcon Lo
◼ Paddington
W9 . . . . .31 C4
West Hampstead
NW3 . . . . .11 A4
Falcon Pk Ind Est
NW10 . . . . .8 A3
Falcon Point SE1 . . .122 B3
Falcon Rd SW11 . . . .60 A4
Falcons Pre Prep
school The ◼
W4 . . . . .45 A4
Falcons Prep Sch for
Boys The TW9 . . . . . .54 A3
Falcon Terr SW11 . . .60 A4
Falcon Way E14 . . . . .42 A2
Falconwood Ct
SE3 . . . . .53 B1
Falkener Ct SW11 . .169 C3
Falkirk Ct ◼ SE16 . . .32 C1
Falkirk Ho W9 . . . . . .88 B4
Falkirk St N1 . . . . .24 A3
Falkland Ho
Kensington W8 . . . . .128 A1
West Kensington
W14 . . . . .140 C2
Falkland Pl ◼
NW5 . . . . .13 B3
Falkland Rd NW5 . . .13 B3
Falkner House Sch
SW7 . . . . .143 A2
Fallodon Ho
◼ London SW8 . . . .171 C2
Paddington W11 . . . . .31 B4
Fallow Ct ◼ SE16 . .153 C1
Fallowfield N4 . . . . . .5 B2
Falmouth Ho
Bayswater W2 . . . . . .116 A4
Kensington SE11 . . . .149 C2
Falmouth Rd SE1 . . .137 A1
Falstaff Ct SE11 . . . .150 A3
Falstaff Ho ◼ N1 . . . .24 A3
Fane St W14 . . . . .155 A4
Fan Mus The SE10 . .52 B3
Fann St EC1 . . . . .97 A1
Fanshaw St
N1 . . . . .24 A2 98 A4
Fanthorpe St
SW15 . . . . .57 B4
Faraday Cl N7 . . . . . .14 B2
Faraday Ho
◼ Balham SW12 . . .73 A4
◼ Gospel Oak
NW5 . . . . .13 A4
Kensal Town W10 . . .31 A4
◼ Poplar E14 . . . . . .33 B2
Faraday Lo SE10 . . . .43 B3
Faraday Rd
Acton W3 . . . . .28 B2
Kensal Town W10 . . .31 A4

Fareham Ho 13
SW15 . . . . .68 C3

Fareham St W1 . . . . . .105 B2

Farjeon Ho NW6 . . . . .11 C1

Farleigh Pl N16 . . . . . .16 B4

Farleigh Rd N16 . . . . .16 B4

Farley Ct
Kensington W14 . . . . .126 B1
Marylebone NW1 . . . . .91 B1

Farlington Pl
SW15 . . . . .69 A4

Farlow Rd SW15 . . . . .57 C4

Farlton Rd SW18 . . . . .71 A4

Farm Ave NW2 . . . . . . .1 B1

Farm Cl SW6 . . . . . . .155 C2

Farmdale Rd SE10 . . .43 C1

Farmer Ho 4
SE16 . . . . .40 A3

Farmers Mkt W8 . . . .113 C2

Farmers Rd SE5 . . . . .48 A3

Farmer St
W8 . . . . .31 C1 113 B2

Farm La SW6 . . . . . . .155 C2

Farm Lane Trad Ctr
SW6 . . . . .155 C3

Farmleigh Ho
SW9 . . . . .63 A2

Farm Pl
W8 . . . . .31 C1 113 B2

Farm Rd NW10 . . . . . .20 C4

Farm St W1 . . . . .118 A3

Farnaby Ho 2
W10 . . . . .23 B2

Farnborough Ho 7
SW15 . . . . .68 C3

Farncombe St
SE16 . . . . .139 C3

Farndale Ho 3
NW6 . . . . .78 A4

Farnell Mews
SW5 . . . . .142 A2

Farnell Pl W3 . . . . . . .28 A2

Farnfield Ho 3
SW12 . . . . .73 A4

Farnham Ct 2 N16 . . .7 A3

Farnham Ho
Borough The SE1 . . . . .122 C1
Marylebone NW1 . . . . .90 B1

Farnham Pl SE1 . . . . .122 B1

Farnham Royal
SE11 . . . . .149 A1

Farnhurst Ho 7
SW11 . . . . .169 B2

Farningham Ho 4
N4 . . . . .6 C4

Farnley Ho 13
SW8 . . . . .171 B2

Farnsworth Ct
SE10 . . . . .43 B3

Farnworth Ho 5
E14 . . . . .42 C2

Faroe Rd W14 . . . . . . .39 C3

Farquhar Rd SW19 . . .70 C1

Farrance St E14 . . . . .33 C3

Farrant Ho 14
SW11 . . . . .59 C4

Farrell Ho E1 . . . . . . .32 B3

Farrer Ho SE8 . . . . . . .51 C3

Farriers Mews
SE15 . . . . .65 B4

Farrier St NW1 . . . . . .13 B1

Farrier Wlk SW10 . . .156 C4

Farringdon La EC1 . . . .95 C1

Farringdon Rd EC1 . . .95 C1

Farringdon St
EC4 . . . . .108 A2

Farringdon Sta
EC1 . . . . .108 A4

Farrins Rents
SE16 . . . . .33 A1

Farrow La SE14 . . . . . .50 B3

Farrow Pl SE16 . . . . . .41 A3

Farthingale Wlk
E15 . . . . .19 C1

Farthing Alley 8
SE1 . . . . .139 B3

Farthing Fields 8
E1 . . . . .32 A1

Fashion Retail Acad
The W1 . . . . .105 B2

Fashion & Textile Mus
SE1 . . . . .138 A4

Fassett Rd E8 . . . . . . .16 C2

Fassett Sq E8 . . . . . . .16 C2

Fauconberg Ct
W4 . . . . .45 B4

Fauconberg Rd
W4 . . . . .45 B4

Faulkner Ho SW15 . . .47 B1

Faulkner's Alley
EC1 . . . . .108 A4

Faulkner St SE14 . . . .50 B2

Faunce Ho 1
SE17 . . . . .48 A4

Faunce St SE17 . . . . .150 A1

Favart Rd SW6 . . . . . .165 C4

Faversham Ho
Camden Town
NW1 . . . . .83 A3
Walworth SE17 . . . . . .152 A1

Fawcett Cl
SW11 . . . . .167 C1

Fawcett Est E5 . . . . . . .7 C3

Fawcett Ho 23
SW9 . . . . .172 B2

Fawcett Rd NW10 . . . . .8 B1

Fawcett St SW10 . . . .156 C4

Fawe Park Rd
SW15 . . . . .58 B3

Fawe St E14 . . . . .34 A4

Fawkham Ho SE1 . . . .153 A3

Fawley Ct SE27 . . . . . .75 A2

Fawley Lo 2 E14 . . . . .42 C2

Fawley Rd NW6 . . . . . .11 A3

Fawnbrake Ave
SE24 . . . . .63 B2

Fayetville Ho 20
N19 . . . . .4 C4

Faygate Rd SW2 . . . . . .74 B2

Fazerley Ct 10 W2 . . .31 C4

Fearnley Ho SE5 . . . . .49 A1

Fearon St SE10 . . . . . .43 C1

Feathers Pl SE10 . . . . .52 C4

Featherstone St
EC1 . . . . .97 B2

Featley Rd SW9 . . . . . .63 A4

Felbridge Ho 21
SE22 . . . . .64 A4

Felday Rd SE13 . . . . . .67 A1

Felden St SW6 . . . . . .164 C3

Feldman Cl N16 . . . . . .7 C3

Felgate Mews 4
W6 . . . . .39 A2

Felix St 16 E2 . . . . . . .25 A3

Felixstowe Rd
NW10 . . . . .22 A2

Fellbrigg Rd SE22 . . . .64 B2

Fellbrigg St 21 E1 . . . .25 A1

Fell Ho 18 N19 . . . . . . .4 B1

Fellows Ct E2 . . . . . . .24 B3

Fellows Rd NW3 . . . . . .12 A1

Fells Haugh 6
W3 . . . . .28 B3

Felltram Way SE7 . . . .43 C1

Felmersham Cl 2
SW4 . . . . .61 C3

Felsberg Rd SW2 . . . . .74 A4

Felsham Ho 3
SW15 . . . . .57 C4

Felsham Mews 14
SW15 . . . . .57 C4

Felstead St E9 . . . . . . .18 B2

Felstead Wharf
E14 . . . . .42 B1

Felton Ho N1 . . . . . . .87 C3

Felton St N1 . . . . .87 C3

Fenchurch Ave
EC3 . . . . .110 A1

Fenchurch Bldgs
EC3 . . . . .110 B1

Fenchurch Pl EC3 . . .124 B4

Fenchurch St EC3 . . .124 B4

Fenchurch Street Sta
EC3 . . . . .124 B4

Fen Ct EC3 . . . . .124 A4

Fendall St SE1 . . . . . .138 B1

Fender Ct 5 SW4 . . . .172 A2

Fendt Cl 3 E16 . . . . . .35 B3

Fenelon Pl W14 . . . . .141 A3

Fenham Rd SE15 . . . . .50 A3

Fenner Cl SE16 . . . . . .40 A2

Fenner Ho 22 E1 . . . . .32 A1

Fenner Sq 7
SW11 . . . . .59 C4

Fenning St SE1 . . . . .138 A4

Fen St E9 . . . . .17 B3

Fen St E16 . . . . .35 B2

Fenstanton 3 N4 . . . .5 B3

Fenstanton Prim Sch
20 SW2 . . . . .74 C3

Fentiman Rd SW8 . . . .162 C2

Fenton Cl
10 Dalston E8 . . . . . . .16 B2
South Lambeth
SW9 . . . . .172 C1

Fenton Ho SE14 . . . . . .51 A3

Fenton House NW3 . . .2 B1

Fentons SE3 . . . . .53 B3

Fenton St E1 . . . . .32 A3

Fenwick Gr SE15 . . . . .64 C4

Fenwick Pl SW9 . . . . .62 A4

Fenwick Rd SE15 . . . . .64 C4

Ferdinand Ho 1
NW1 . . . . .13 A1

Ferdinand Pl NW1 . . .12 C1

Ferdinand St NW1 . . .12 C1

Ferguson Dr W3 . . . . . .28 C3

Ferguson Ho SE10 . . . .52 B2

Ferguson's Cl E14 . . . .41 C2

Fergus Rd N5 . . . . .15 A3

Fermain Ct E N1 . . . . .24 A4

Fermain Ct N N1 . . . . .24 A4

Fermain Ct W N1 . . . . .24 A4

Fermoy Rd W9 . . . . . . .23 B1

Fernbank Mews
SW12 . . . . .61 B1

Fern Cl 3 N1 . . . . .24 A3

Ferncliff Rd E8 . . . . .16 C3

Ferncroft Ave
NW3 . . . . .10 C4

Fern Ct SE14 . . . . .50 C1

Ferndale Com Sp Ctr
SW9 . . . . .62 B3

Ferndale Ho N16 . . . . . .6 C3

Ferndale Rd SW4,
SW9 . . . . .62 B3

Ferndene Rd SE24 . . . .63 B3

Ferndown Lo 17
E14 . . . . .42 B3

Fernhead Rd W9 . . . . .23 B2

Fernhill Ho E5 . . . . .7 C2

Fernholme Rd
SE15 . . . . .65 C2

Fernhurst Rd
SW6 . . . . .164 B4

Fernie Ho SE22 . . . . . .64 B4

Fernlea Rd SW12 . . . . .73 A3

Fernleigh Cl W9 . . . . . .23 B2

Fernsbury St WC1 . . . .95 B3

Fernshaw Mans
SW10 . . . . .156 C3

Fernshaw Rd
SW10 . . . . .156 C3

Fernside NW11 . . . . . . .1 C3

Fernside Rd SW12 . . . .72 C4

Fern St E3 . . . . .26 C1

Fentower Ho N5 . . . . . . .6 C3

Fern Wlk 18 SE16 . . .153 C1

Fernwood SW19 . . . . . .70 B3

Ferrey Mews 19
SW9 . . . . .173 B1

Ferriby Cl N1 . . . . .14 C1

Ferrier Ind Est
SW18 . . . . .59 A3

Ferrier Point 6
E16 . . . . .35 C4

Ferrier St SW18 . . . . . .59 A3

Ferrings SE21 . . . . . . .76 A1

Ferris Rd SE22 . . . . . . .64 C3

Ferrybridge Ho
SE11 . . . . .135 A1

Ferry La
Barnes SW13 . . . . .46 B4
Brentford TW8 . . . . . . .44 A4
Brentford TW8 . . . . . . .44 B4

Ferry Rd SW13 . . . . . . .46 C2

Ferry Sq 1 TW8 . . . . .44 A4

Ferry St E14 . . . . .42 B1

Festing Rd SW15 . . . . .57 C4

Festival Ct 5 E8 . . . . .16 B1

Festival Pier SE1 . . . .120 C2

Fetter La EC4 . . . . . . .107 C2

Fettes Ho NW8 . . . . . . .79 C1

Ffinch St SE8 . . . . .51 C3

Field Ct
Hampstead NW3 . . . . .11 B3
Holborn WC1 . . . . . . .107 A3
Lower Holloway N7 . . . .14 A3
Wimbledon SW19 . . . . .70 C1

Fieldgate Mans 55
E1 . . . . .111 C3

Fieldgate St E1 . . . . . .111 C3

Fieldhouse Rd
SW12 . . . . .73 B3

Fielding Ho
Chiswick W4 . . . . .46 A4
4 Kilburn NW6 . . . . . .23 C2
St John's Wood
NW8 . . . . .78 C4

Fielding Mews
SW13 . . . . .47 A4

Fielding Rd
Acton W4 . . . . .38 A3
Hammersmith W14 . . . .39 C3

Fielding St SE17 . . . . . .48 B4

Field Lo NW10 . . . . .8 B2

Field Rd W6 . . . . .154 A4

Fields Est E8 . . . . .16 C1

Field St WC1 . . . . .94 C4

Fieldsway Ho N5 . . . . .14 C3

Fieldview SW17,
SW18 . . . . .71 C3

Fieldview Ct 2
N5 . . . . .15 A3

Fieldway Cres N5,
N7 . . . . .14 C3

Fieldwick Ho 11
E9 . . . . .17 C2

Fife Rd
Mortlake SW14 . . . . . .55 B2
Newham E16 . . . . .35 C4

Fife Terr N1 . . . . .85 A2

Fifth Ave W10 . . . . . . .23 A2

Fig Tree Cl NW10 . . . .21 A4

Filey Ave N16 . . . . .7 C3

Filey Ho SW18 . . . . . . .59 B3

Filigree Ct SE16 . . . . .33 B1

Filmer Ho SW6 . . . . . .164 B4

Filmer Mews
SW6 . . . . .164 B4

Filmer Rd SW6 . . . . . .154 C1

Filton Ct 14 SE14 . . . .50 B3

Finborough Rd
SW10 . . . . .156 B4

Finchdean Ho
SW15 . . . . .68 B4

Finch Ho 5 SE8 . . . . . .52 A3

Finch La EC2, EC3 . . .109 C1

Finchley Pl NW8 . . . . . .79 B2

Finchley Rd
Hampstead NW3 . . . . .11 B2
St John's Wood
NW8 . . . . .79 B2

Finchley Road &
Frognal Sta NW3 . . .11 B3

Finchley Road Sta
NW3 . . . . .11 C2

Finch Lo 9 W9 . . . . . .31 C4

Finch Mews 3
SE15 . . . . .49 B2

Finch's Ct 10 E14 . . . .34 A2

Findhorn St 8
E14 . . . . .34 B3

Findon Cl SW18 . . . . . .58 C1

Findon Rd W12 . . . . . . .38 C4

Fineran Ct 8
SW11 . . . . .59 C3

Fingal St SE10 . . . . . . .43 B1

Fingest Ho NW8 . . . . . .90 A2

Finland Rd SE4 . . . . . .66 A4

Finland St SE16 . . . . . .41 A3

Finlay St SW6 . . . . . . .47 C2

Finley Ct 21 SE5 . . . . .48 B3

Finmere Ho 4 N4 . . . . .6 B4

Finnemore Ho N1 . . . .86 C4

Finn Ho N1 . . . . .97 C4

Finnis St E2 . . . . .25 A1

FINSBURY 95 C4

Finsbury Ave EC2 . . .109 C3

Finsbury Cir EC2 . . . .109 C3

Finsbury Ct EC2 . . . .109 B4

Finsbury L Ctr EC1 . . .96 C3

Finsbury Market
EC2 . . . . .110 A4

Finsbury Mkt
EC2 . . . . .24 A1 98 A1

FINSBURY PARK 5 C2

Finsbury Park Rd N4,
N5 . . . . .6 A2

Finsbury Park Sta
N4 . . . . .5 C2

Finsbury Pavement
EC2 . . . . .109 C4

Finsbury Sq EC2 .... **109** C4
Finsbury St EC2 ..... **109** B4
Finsen Rd SE5 .... **63** B4
Finstock Rd W10 .... **30** C3
Finton House Sch
SW17 .... **72** B2
Fincane Ct TW9 ...... **54** B4
Finwhale Ho E14 .... **42** A3
Fiona Ct **8** NW6 .... **23** B3
Firbank Rd SW15 .... **58** A1
Fircroft N1 .... **86** B4
Fircroft Prim Sch
SW17 .... **72** B1
Fircroft Rd SW17 .... **72** B1
Fire Brigade Pier
SE1 .... **148** B4
Firecrest Dr NW3 .... **2** A1
Firle Ho **7** W10 ...... **30** B4
Fir Lo SW15 .... **57** A3
Firmston Ho **8**
SW14 .... **55** C4
Firs Ave SW14 .... **55** B3
Firsby Rd N16 .... **7** C3
First Ave
East Acton W3 ...... **29** B1
Mortlake SW14 ...... **56** A4
West Kilburn W10 ... **23** A2
First St SW3 .... **144** B4
Firth Gdns SW6 ..... **164** A3
Fir Tree Ho **11**
SE14 .... **50** B3
Fir Trees Cl SE16 .... **33** A1
Fisher Ho
Islington N1 .... **85** B3
8 Shadwell E1 ...... **32** B2
2 Tufnell Pk N19 ... **4** B1
Fishermans Dr
SE16 .... **40** C4
Fisherman's Wlk
E14 .... **33** C1
Fishers Cl SW16 ..... **73** C1
Fishers Ct SE14 ...... **50** C2
Fisher's La W4 .... **37** C2
Fisher St
Holborn WC1 .... **106** C3
Newham E16 .... **35** C4
Fisherton St NW8 ... **89** C2
Fisherton Street Est
NW8 .... **89** C1
Fishlock Ct **8**
SW4 .... **172** A2
Fish St Hill EC3 ..... **123** C3
Fitch Ct SW2 .... **62** C1
Fitzalan St SE11 ..... **149** B4
Fitzclarence Ho
W11 .... **126** A4
Fitz-George Ave
W14 .... **140** A3
Fitzgerald Ave
SW14 .... **56** A4
Fitzgerald Ho
15 Brixton SW9 .... **173** B1
4 Poplar E14 ...... **34** A3
Fitzgerald Rd
SW14 .... **55** C4
Fitzhardinge Ho
W1 .... **103** B2
Fitzhardinge St
W1 .... **103** B2
Fitzherbert Ho **11**
TW10 .... **54** B1
Fitzhugh Gr SW18 ... **59** C1
Fitzjames Ave
W14 .... **140** B3

Fitzjohn's Ave
NW3 .... **11** C3
Fitzjohns Mans
NW3 .... **11** B2
Fitzjohns Prim Sch **6**
NW3 .... **11** B2
Fitzmaurice Ho **17**
SE16 .... **40** A2
Fitzmaurice Pl
W1 .... **118** B2
Fitzneal St W12 ...... **29** B3
FITZROVIA **104** A4
Fitzroy Cl N6 .... **3** B3
Fitzroy Cres W4 ..... **45** C3
Fitzroy Ct W1 .... **93** A1
Fitzroy Ho
Bermondsey SE1 ... **153** A2
12 Tower Hamlets
E14 .... **33** B3
Fitzroy Mews W1 .... **92** C1
Fitzroy Pk N6 .... **3** B3
Fitzroy Rd NW1 ...... **81** B4
Fitzroy Sq W1 .... **92** C1
Fitzroy St W1 .... **92** C1
Fitzroy Yd NW1 ...... **81** B4
Fitzwarren Gdns
N19 .... **4** B3
Fitzwilliam Ave
TW9 .... **44** B1
Fitzwilliam Mews
E16 .... **35** C1
Fitzwilliam Rd
SW4 .... **61** B4
Fives Ct SE11 .... **136** A1
Fiveways Rd SW9 ... **173** C1
Flamborough Ho **12**
SE15 .... **49** C2
Flamborough St
E14 .... **33** A3
Flamingo Ct **2**
SE8 .... **51** C3
Flamsteed Ct **18**
SE13 .... **52** A2
Flamsteed Ho **2**
SE10 .... **52** C3
Flanchford Rd
W12 .... **38** B3
Flanders Ho N16 ..... **7** A1
Flanders Mans **4**
W4 .... **38** B2
Flanders Rd W4 ..... **38** A2
Flanders Way E9 .... **17** C2
Flank St **3** E1 ...... **125** B4
Flansham Ho **2**
E14 .... **33** B3
Flask Cotts **4**
NW3 .... **11** C4
Flask Wlk NW3 ...... **11** C4
Flatford Ho **6**
SE6 .... **167** A4
Flatiron Sq SE1 ..... **123** A1
Flatiron Yd SE1 ..... **123** A1
Flavell Mews SE10 .. **43** A1
Flaxman Ct W1 ..... **105** B1
Flaxman Ho
7 Chiswick W4 ..... **38** A1
Newington SE1 ..... **136** B2
Flaxman Rd SE5 .... **48** A1
Flaxman Sp Ctr
SE5 .... **48** B1
Flaxman Terr WC1 .. **93** C3
Flecker Ho **5** SE5 .. **48** C3
Fleece Wlk N7 .... **14** A2
Fleet Ct **1** W12 .... **38** A3
Fleetfield WC1 ...... **94** B4
Fleet Ho
5 Brixton SW2 .... **62** C2
4 Limehouse E14 .. **33** A2

Fleet Pl EC4 .... **108** A2
Fleet Prim Sch **18**
NW3 .... **12** B3
Fleet Rd NW3 .... **12** B3
Fleet Sq WC1 .... **95** A3
Fleet St EC4 .... **107** C1
Fleet Street Hill **6**
E1 .... **24** C1 99 C1
Fleetway WC1 .... **94** B4
Fleet Wood **6** N16 .. **7** B2
Fleetwood Rd
NW10 .... **8** C3
Fleetwood St N16 ... **7** A2
Fleming Cl **4** W9 ... **23** C1
Fleming Ct W2 ..... **101** B4
Fleming Ho
14 Bermondsey
SE16 .... **139** B3
Finsbury Pk N4 ...... **6** B3
Fleming Rd SE17 .... **48** A4
Fletcher Bldgs
WC2 .... **106** B1
Fletcher Ct **5**
NW5 .... **13** A4
Fletcher Ho **10**
N16 .... **16** A4
Fletcher Path **7**
SE8 .... **51** C3
Fletcher Rd W4 ..... **37** B3
Fletcher St **18** E1 . **125** C4
Fleur de Lis St
E1 .... **24** B1 98 C1
Fleur Gates **5**
SW19 .... **69** C4
Flinders Ho **28** E1 .. **32** A1
Flinton St SE17 ..... **152** B2
Flint St SE17 .... **151** C3
Flitcroft St WC2 .... **105** C1
Flitton Ho **7** N1 ..... **15** A1
Flock Mill Pl
SW18 .... **71** A3
Flodden Rd SE5 ..... **48** B2
Flood St SW3 .... **158** B4
Flood Wlk SW3 ..... **158** B4
Flora Cl E14 .... **34** A3
Flora Gardens Prim
Sch **10** W6 .... **39** A2
Flora Gdns **5**
W6 .... **39** A2
Floral St WC2 .... **120** A4
Florence Ct W9 ...... **89** A3
Florence Gdns W4 .. **45** B4
Florence Ho
20 Bermondsey
SE16 .... **40** A1
2 Brixton SW2 .... **62** B2
10 Shepherd's Bush
W11 .... **30** C2
7 Wandsworth
SW18 .... **59** C3
Florence Mans
SW6 .... **164** C4
Florence Nightingale
Ho **4** N1 .... **15** B2
Florence Nightingale
Mus SE1 .... **135** A3
Florence Rd
Acton W4 .... **37** C3
Finsbury Pk N4 ...... **5** C4
New Cross Gate
SE14 .... **51** B2
Florence St N1 ...... **15** A1
Florence Terr
Kingston u T
SW15 .... **68** A1
New Cross Gate
SE14 .... **51** B2

Florence Way
SW12 .... **72** B3
Flores Ho **13** E1 .... **32** C4
Florfield Rd E8 ...... **17** A2
Florian SE5 .... **49** A2
Florian Rd SW15 .... **58** A3
Florida St
E2 .... **24** C2 99 C3
Florida State Univ
WC1 .... **105** C3
Florin Ct **11** SE1 .. **138** C3
Floris Pl **7** SW4 .... **61** B4
Florys Ct **7** SW19 .. **70** A3
Floss St SW15 .... **47** B1
Flower & Dean Wlk
E1 .... **111** A3
Flowersmead
SW17 .... **72** C2
Flowers Mews **1**
N19 .... **4** B2
Flower Wlk The
SW7 .... **129** A4
Floyer Cl TW10 ...... **54** B2
Flynn Ct **14** E14 .... **33** C2
Foley Ho **6** E1 ...... **32** B3
Foley St W1 .... **104** C3
Folgate St E1 .... **110** C4
Foliot Ho N1 .... **84** C2
Foliot St W12 .... **29** B3
Follett Ho SW10 ... **157** B2
Follett St E14 .... **34** B3
Folly Wall E14 .... **42** B4
Fonda Ct **7** E14 .... **33** C2
Fontarabia Rd
SW11 .... **60** C3
Fontenelle SE5 ...... **49** A2
Fontenoy Ho
SE11 .... **150** A3
Fontenoy Rd SW12,
SW17 .... **73** A3
Fonthill Ho
Kensington W14 ... **126** B2
4 Pimlico SW1 ... **146** B2
Fonthill Mews N4 .... **5** B2
Fonthill Rd N4 .... **5** C2
Fontley Way SW15 .. **68** C4
Footpath The
SW15 .... **56** C2
Forber Ho **25** E2 .... **25** B2
Forbes Ho **2** W4 .... **36** C1
Forbes St E1 .... **111** C1
Forburg Rd N16 .... **7** C3
Ford Cl **12** E3 .... **26** A3
Fordcombe **2**
NW5 .... **12** C2
Fordham Ho **11**
SE14 .... **51** A3
Fordham St **18** E1 . **111** C2
Fordingley Rd W9 .. **23** B2
Ford Rd E3 .... **26** B4
Ford Sq E1 .... **32** A4
Ford St
Bow E3 .... **26** A3
Canning Town E16 .. **35** B3
Fordwych Ct NW2 .. **10** A2
Fordwych Rd NW2 .. **10** A3
Fordyce Rd SE13 .... **67** B2
Forecastle Ct E14 .. **41** C4
Foreign &
Commonwealth
Office SW1 .... **134** A4
Foreland Ho
W11 .... **31** A2 112 A4
Foreshore SE8 .... **41** B2
Fore St EC2 .... **109** A3

Forest Cl NW6 .... **10** A1
Forester Rd SE15 ... **65** A4
Forest Gr E8 .... **16** B2
Forest Hill Rd
SE22 .... **65** A1
Forest Rd
Dalston E8 .... **16** B2
Richmond TW9 ...... **44** C3
Fore Street Ave
EC2 .... **109** B3
Forest Way **5** N19 .. **4** B2
Forfar Rd SW11 .... **169** C4
Forge Pl NW1 .... **12** C2
Forman Ho SE4 ..... **14** C3
Formby Ct **9** N7 .... **14** C3
Formosa Ho **1** E1 .. **26** A1
Formosa St W9 ...... **88** B1
Formunt Cl E16 ..... **35** B4
Forrest Ct N7 .... **14** C2
Forrest Ho SW15 ... **47** B1
Forset St W1 .... **102** B2
Forrest St W1 ...... **102** B2
Forster Rd SW2 ..... **74** A4
Forston St N1 .... **87** A2
Forsyth Gdns SE17 . **48** A4
Forsyth Ho
14 Hackney E9 ...... **17** B1
Pimlico SW1 .... **147** A3
Forsythia Ho SE4 ... **66** A4
Fortescue Ave **1**
E8 .... **17** A1
Fortess Gr NW5 .... **13** B3
Fortess Rd NW5 .... **13** B4
Fortess Wlk NW5 ... **13** A3
Forthbridge Rd
SW11 .... **60** C3
Forth Ho **30** E3 .... **26** B3
Forties The **9**
NW5 .... **13** B3
Fortior Ct N6 .... **4** B4
Fortnam Rd N19 ...... **4** C2
Fort Rd SE1 .... **153** A3
Fortrose Cl E14 ..... **34** C3
Fortrose Gdns SW12,
SW2 .... **74** A3
Fort St E1 .... **110** B3
Fortuna Cl N7 .... **14** B2
Fortune Ct **6** E8 .... **16** B1
Fortune Gate Rd
NW10 .... **21** A4
Fortune Green Rd
NW6 .... **10** C4
Fortune Ho
Lambeth SE11 ..... **149** B3
St Luke's EC1 .... **97** A1
Fortune St EC1 ...... **97** A1
Fortune Way
NW10 .... **21** C2
Forty Acre La E16 .. **35** C4
Forum Cl **2** E3 ..... **26** C4
Forward Bsns Ctr The
3 E16 .... **27** C1
Fosbrooke Ho
SW8 .... **162** A1
Fosbury Ho **6**
SW9 .... **62** B3
Fosbury Mews
W2 .... **114** B3
Foscote Mews W9 .. **31** C4
Foskett Rd SW6 ... **165** A1
Fossil Rd SE13 ...... **66** C4
Foster Ct
8 Camden Town
NW1 .... **13** B1
Canning Town E16 .. **35** B2
Foster Ho SE14 ..... **51** B2

Foster La EC2 .... 108 C2
Foster Rd
 Acton W3 .... 29 A2
 Chiswick W4 ...... 37 C1
Foubert's Pl W1 .... 104 C1
Foulden Rd N16 ..... 16 B4
Foulden Terr N16 ... 16 B4
Foulis Terr SW7 ... 143 C2
Foulser Rd SW17 .. 72 C2
Foundary Ho 6
  E14 .... 34 A4
Founders Ct EC2 ... 109 C2
Founders Ho SW1 .. 147 B2
Foundling Ct WC1 .. 94 A2
Foundling Mus The
  WC1 .... 94 B2
Foundry Cl SE16 .... 33 A1
Foundry Mews
  NW1 .... 93 A2
Foundry Pl
  Stepney E1 .... 32 B4
  Wandsworth SW18 .. 71 A4
Fountain & Colonnade
  Sh Ctr SW1 ..... 146 B2
Fountain Ct
  Belgravia SW1 ... 146 A3
  16 Shepherd's Bush
   W11 .... 39 C4
  Strand EC4 ..... 121 B4
  SE16 .... 139 C3
Fountain Ho
  33 Bermondsey
  SE16 .... 139 C3
  18 Brondesbury Pk
   NW6 .... 10 A1
  Mayfair W1 .... 117 B2
Fountain Mews
  1 Highbury N5 ... 15 B4
  Maitland Pk NW3 .. 12 B2
Fountain Pl SW9 .. 173 C3
Fountayne Rd N16 .. 7 C2
Fount St SW8 .... 161 C1
Fournier St E1 ... 111 A4
Fourscore Mans
  E8 .... 16 C1
Four Seasons Cl
  E3 .... 26 C3
Fourth Ave W10 ... 23 A2
Fovant Ct 5 SW8 . 170 C1
Fowey Cl E1 ..... 125 C2
Fowey Ho SE11 ... 149 C2
Fowler Cl SW11 ... 59 C4
Fowler Ho
  5 Camberwell
  SE5 .... 49 A1
  Islington N1 .... 86 B4
  South Lambeth
   SW8 .... 171 C3
Fowler Rd N1 .... 86 B4
Fownes St SW11 ... 60 A4
Fox and Knot St
  EC1 .... 108 B4
Foxberry Ct SE4 ... 66 B3
Foxberry Rd SE4 ... 66 A4
Foxborough Gdns
  SE4 .... 66 C2
Foxbourne Rd
  SW17 .... 72 C2
Fox Cl
  Bethnal Green E1 . 25 B1
  Newham E16 .... 35 C4
Foxcombe Rd 6
  SW15 .... 68 C3
Foxcote SE5 .... 152 B1
Foxcroft WC1 .... 85 A1

Fox Ct EC1 ...... 107 B3
Foxfield NW1 ..... 82 B3
Foxglove St W12 .. 29 B2
Foxham Rd N19 ..... 4 C1
Fox Ho 2 SW11 .... 59 C3
Foxley Cl E8 ..... 16 C3
Foxley Ho 4
  E3 .... 27 A2
Foxley Rd SW9 .... 48 A3
Foxley Sq 3 SW9 .. 48 A2
Foxmore St SW11 . 168 C3
Fox Prim Sch
  W8 .... 31 C1 113 B1
Fox Rd E16 .... 35 B4
Fox's Yd E2 .. 24 B1 99 A2
Foxwell Mews SE4 . 66 A4
Foxwell St SE4 ... 66 A4
Foyle Rd SE3 ..... 53 B4
Fradel Lo N16 ..... 6 C3
Framfield Rd N5 ... 15 A3
Frampton NW1 ..... 13 C1
Frampton Ct 3
  W3 .... 37 B4
Frampton Ho NW8 . 89 C1
Frampton Park Rd
  E9 .... 17 B1
Frampton St NW8 .. 89 C1
Francemary Rd
  SE4 .... 66 C2
Franche Court Rd
  SW17 .... 71 B1
Francis Chichester
  Way SW11 ..... 169 C3
Francis Cl 6 E14 . 42 C2
Francis Ct 12 SE14 . 50 C4
Francis Ho
  Harlesden NW10 .. 21 B4
  16 Shoreditch N1 . 24 A4
  Walham Green
   SW10 .... 156 B2
Francis Holland Sch
  Belgravia SW1 .. 145 C3
  Marylebone NW1 . 90 C2
Francis Snary Lo 11
  SW18 .... 58 C3
Francis St SW1 .. 147 A4
Francis Terr N19 .. 4 B1
Francis Terrace Mews
  10 N19 .... 4 B1
Francis Wlk N1 ... 84 C4
Franconia Rd SW4 . 61 C2
Frank Barnes Sch 13
  NW3 .... 11 C1
Frank Beswick Ho
  SW6 .... 155 A3
Frank Dixon Cl
  SE21 .... 76 A3
Frank Dixon Way
  SE21 .... 76 A3
Frankfurt Rd SE24 . 63 B2
Frankham Ho 8
  SE8 .... 51 C3
Frankham St SE8 .. 51 C3
Frank Ho NW8 ... 162 A2
Frankland Cl SE16 . 40 A2
Frankland Ho 4
  SW12 .... 73 A4
Frankland Rd
  SW7 .... 129 B1
Franklin Bldg 3
  E14 .... 41 C4
Franklin Cl
  Greenwich SE13 .. 52 A2
  West Norwood
   SW27 .... 75 A1
Franklin Ho
  New Cross SE4 ... 51 A1

Franklin Ho continued
  28 Wapping E1 .... 32 A1
Franklin Pl SE13 .. 52 A2
Franklin Sq SW5 . 141 A1
Franklin's Row
  SW3 .... 145 A2
Franklin St 5 E3 . 27 A2
Franklyn Rd NW10 . 8 B2
Frank Soskice Ho 6
  SW6 .... 155 A3
Frank Whymark Ho 4
  SE16 .... 40 B4
Frans Hals Ct E14 . 42 C3
Fraserburgh Ho 20
  E3 .... 26 B3
Fraser Ct SW11 .. 168 A4
Fraser Ho
  Brentford TW8 .... 36 B1
  40 Clapham SW8 . 171 B1
Fraser Regnart Ct 12
  NW5 .... 12 B3
Fraser St W4 ..... 38 A1
Frazier St SE1 ... 135 B3
Frean St SE16 ... 139 B2
Frearson Ho WC1 .. 95 A4
Freda Corbett Cl 18
  SE15 .... 49 C3
Frederica St
  N7 .... 14 B1
Frederick Blg N1 .. 24 A4
Frederick Charrington
  Ho 4 E1 .... 25 B1
Frederick Cl W2 . 116 C4
Frederick Cres
  SW9 .... 48 A3
Frederick Ct SW6 . 58 A4
Frederick's Pl
  EC2 .... 109 B1
Frederick Sq 11
  SE16 .... 33 A2
Frederick's Row
  EC1 .... 96 A4
Frederick St WC1 . 94 C3
Frederick Terr E8 . 24 C4
Frederic Mews
  SW1 .... 131 B3
Freedom St SW11 169 A2
Freegrove Rd N7 . 14 A3
Freeling Ho NW8 . 79 B4
Freeling St 7 N1 . 14 B1
Freeman Ho 13
  SW2 .... 74 A4
Freemantle St
  SE17 .... 152 A2
Freemens Hos 1
  SW9 .... 62 B3
Freke Rd SW11 ... 60 C4
Fremantle Ho 14
  E1 .... 25 A1
Fremont St E9 .... 25 B4
French Inst The
  SW7 .... 143 B4
French Pl
  E1 .... 24 A1 98 B2
Frendsbury Rd
  SE4 .... 66 A3
Frensham Ct N5 ... 15 B3
Frensham Dr
  SW15 .... 68 C2
Frensham St SE15 . 49 C4
Frere St 6 SW11 . 168 B2
Freshfield Ave E8 . 16 B1
Freshfield Cl SE13 . 67 C3
Freshford St SW17,
  SW18 .... 71 B1

Freston Rd W10,
  W11 .... 30 C2
Freswick Ho 6
  SE8 .... 41 A2
Freud Mus The
  NW3 .... 11 B2
Frewell Bldg EC1 . 107 B4
Frewin Rd SW18 .. 71 C3
Friar Mews SE27 . 75 A1
Friars Ave
  Putney SW15 .... 58 A2
  Roehampton SW15 . 68 B1
Friars Cl SE1 .... 122 B1
Friars Gdns W3 .. 28 C3
Friars Mead E14 .. 42 B3
Friars Place La
  W3 .... 28 C2
Friars Prim
  Foundation Sch
  SE1 .... 136 B3
Friars Stile Pl 9
  TW10 .... 54 A1
Friars Stile Rd
  TW10 .... 54 A1
Friar St EC4 .... 108 B1
Friars Way W3 ... 28 C3
Friary Park Ct 12
  W3 .... 28 B3
Friary Rd
  Acton W3 .... 28 C3
  Peckham SE15 .... 49 C3
Friday Grove Mews 11
  SW12 .... 73 B4
Friday St EC4 ... 122 C4
Frideswide Pl
  NW5 .... 13 B3
Friendly Pl 18
  SE13 .... 52 A2
Friendly St SE8 .. 51 C2
Friendly Street Mews
  SE8 .... 51 C1
Friendship Way
  E15 .... 27 B4
Friend St EC1 .... 96 A4
Friern Barnet ....
Frigate Ho 8 E14 . 42 B2
Frigate Mews SE8 . 51 C4
Frimley Cl SW19 .. 70 A2
Frimley Way E1 .. 25 C1
Frinstead Ho 6
  W10 .... 30 C2
Friston St SW6 .. 166 A1
Frith Ho
  Bethnal Green
  E2 .... 24 C2 99 B3
  Paddington NW8 . 89 C1
Frith Rd E11 ..... 19 C4
Frith St W1 ..... 105 B1
Frithville Ct 2
  W12 .... 30 B1
Frithville Gdns
  W12 .... 30 B1
Frobisher Ct
  4 Greenwich
  SE10 .... 52 C4
  3 Shepherd's Bush
  W12 .... 39 B4
Frobisher Ho 31
  E1 .... 32 A1
Frobisher Pas E14 . 33 C1
Frobisher Pl SE14 . 50 B2
Frobisher St SE10 . 53 A4
Frogley Rd SE22 .. 64 B3
Frogmore SW18 .. 58 C2
Frogmore Est
  NW10 .... 20 B2

Frogmore Ind Est
  N5 .... 15 B4
Frognal NW3 ..... 11 B3
Frognal Cl NW3 .. 11 B3
Frognal Ct NW3 .. 11 B2
Frognal Gdns NW3 . 11 B4
Frognal La NW3 .. 11 A3
Frognal Par NW3 .. 11 B2
Frognal Rise NW3 . 11 B4
Frognal Way NW3 . 11 B4
Frome Ho SE15 ... 65 B3
Frome St N1 ..... 86 C2
Fromow's Cnr 16
  W4 .... 37 B1
Frontenac NW10 ... 9 A1
Frostic Wlk E1 .. 111 A3
Froude St SW8 ... 170 B1
Frye Ct 5 E3 ..... 26 B2
Frying Pan Alley
  E1 .... 110 C3
Fry Rd NW10 .... 21 B4
Fulbeck Ho N7 ... 14 B2
Fulbourne St E1 .. 32 A4
Fulbrook Rd N19 .. 13 B4
Fulcher Ct 40 SE8 . 51 B4
Fulcher Ho
  16 Deptford SE8 .. 41 B1
  14 Shoreditch N1 . 24 A4
Fulford Mans 3
  N19 .... 5 A1
Fulford St SE16 ... 40 A4
FULHAM 47 C1
Fulham Broadway
  SW6 .... 155 C1
Fulham Broadway Sh
  Ctr SW6 .... 155 C2
Fulham Broadway Sta
  SW6 .... 155 C2
Fulham Bsns
  Exchange SW6 . 167 A3
Fulham Cross Girls
  Sec Sch SW6 ... 154 A1
Fulham High St
  SW6 .... 164 B1
Fulham Palace Rd SW6,
  W6 .... 47 C4
Fulham Park Gdns
  SW6 .... 164 C2
Fulham Park Rd
  SW6 .... 164 C2
Fulham Prep Sch
  6 Fulham SW6 ... 164 B1
  Fulham W14 .... 154 B4
Fulham Prim Sch
  SW6 .... 155 B3
Fulham Rd
  Chelsea SW10 .. 157 A4
  Fulham SW6 .... 165 A4
Fuller Cl 2
  E2 ..... 24 C1 99 B2
Fullers Ho 6
  SW18 .... 58 C2
Fullerton Rd SW18 . 59 B2
Fullwood's Mews
  N1 .... 97 C4
Fulmar Ct 5 SE21 . 75 C2
Fulmar Ho
  12 Bermondsey
  SE16 .... 40 C2
  Marylebone NW8 . 90 B1
Fulmead St SW6 . 166 B3
Fulneck 1 E1 ..... 32 B4

Fulthorp Rd SE3....53 C1
Fulton Mews W2 ..114 C4
Fulwood Pl WC1...107 A3
Fulwood Wlk
 SW19.............70 A3
Furber St W6.......39 A3
Furley Ho SE15 ...49 C3
Furley Rd SE15 ...49 C3
Furlong Rd N7 ....14 C2
Furmage St SW18 .71 A4
Furness Ho SW1 .146 A2
Furness Lo
 SW14.............55 A3
Furness Prim Sch
 NW10.............21 C3
Furness Rd
 Harlesden NW10 ..21 C3
 Sands End SW6 ..166 B2
Furnival St EC4...107 B2
Furrow La E9......17 B3
Fursecroft W1....102 C2
Furze St E3........33 C4
Fusion Ct SW15 ...68 A1
Futters Ct
 NW10.............21 A3
Fyfield N4..........5 C2
Fyfield Rd SW9 ...62 C4
Fynes St SW1 ....147 B4

G

Gable Ho W4......38 A2
Gables Ct SE5.....49 A2
Gables The
 Clapham SW4 ....61 B4
 Hampstead NW3 ...2 C2
Gabriel Ho SE11 .148 C4
Gabrielle Ct NW3 ..11 C2
Gabriel Mews NW2 .1 B2
Gabriel's Wharf
 SE1.............121 B2
Gaddesden Ho EC1 .97 C3
Gadsden Ho
 Homerton E9.....17 C2
 Kensal Town
 W10.............23 A1
Gagarin Ho SW11 ..59 C4
Gage Rd E16......35 A4
Gage St WC1.....106 B4
Gainford Ho E2...25 A2
Gainford St N1....85 B4
Gainsborough Ct
 Bermondsey
 SE16.............40 A1
 Dulwich SE21 ....76 A2
 Shepherd's Bush
 W12.............39 B4
Gainsborough Gdns
 Golders Green
 NW11..............1 B4
 Hampstead NW3 ...2 C1
Gainsborough Ho
 Finsbury Pk N4 ....5 B3
 Hampstead
 NW3.............11 B4
 Limehouse E14 ..33 A2
 Westminster SW1 .147 C3
Gainsborough Prim
 Sch E9...........18 C2

Gainsborough St
 E9..............18 B2
Gainsborough Studios
 N1..............87 B4
Gainsford St SE1 .139 A4
Gairloch Ho
 NW1.............13 C1
Gairloch Rd SE5 ..49 A1
Gaisford St NW5 ..13 B2
Gaitskell Ho SE17 .168 A2
Gaitskell Way SE1 .136 C4
Galata SW13 .....46 C3
Galatea Sq SE15 ..65 A4
Galaxy Bldg
 E14.............41 C2
Galaxy Ho EC1 ....97 C2
Galbraith St E14...42 B3
Gale Ho SW2 .....62 B2
Galena Ho W6 ....39 A2
Galena Rd W6.....39 A2
Galen Pl WC1 ....106 B3
Galesbury Rd
 SW18.............59 B1
Gales Gdns E2....25 A2
Gale St E3........33 C4
Galgate Cl
 SW19.............70 A3
Galleon Cl SE16 ..40 C4
Galleon Ho E14 ..42 B2
Galleries of Modern
 London EC1 ....108 C3
Gallery Ct SW10 .156 C3
Gallery Rd SE21 ..75 C3
Gallery Wall Rd
 SE16.............40 A2
Galleywall Road Trad
 Est SE16 ....40 A2
Galleywood Ho
 W10.............30 B4
Gallia Rd N5......15 A3
Galloway Rd W12...29 C1
Galsworthy Ave
 E14.............33 A4
Galsworthy Ct W3 ..37 A3
Galsworthy Ho
 W11.............31 A3
Galsworthy Rd
 NW2.............10 A4
Galton St W10 ....23 A2
Galveston Ho
 E1..............26 A1
Galveston Rd
 SW15.............58 B2
Galway Ho
 Finsbury EC1 ....97 A3
 Stepney E1 .....32 C4
Galway St EC1....97 A3
Gambetta St
 SW8............170 B1
Gambia St SE1 ...122 B1
Gambier Ho
 EC1.............97 A3
Gamlen Rd SW15 ..57 C3
Gandolfi St
 SE15.............49 A4
Ganley Ct SW11 ..59 C4
Gannet Ct SE21 ..75 C2
Gannet Ho SE15 ..49 B2
Ganton St W1.....105 A1
Garand Ct N7 ....14 B3
Garbett Ho
 SE17.............48 A4
Garbutt Pl W1 ...103 C3
Garden Cl SW15 ..69 A4

Garden Ct
 Richmond
 TW9.............44 B2
 South Acton W4 ..37 B3
 St John's Wood
 NW8.............89 B4
Garden Flats
 SW16.............74 A1
Garden Ho.......172 B2
Garden House Sch
 SW3.............145 A2
Garden La SW2....74 B3
Garden Mews
 W2 ...31 C2 113 C3
Garden Pl E2.....24 B4
Garden Rd
 Richmond TW9 ...54 C4
 St John's Wood
 NW8.............89 A4
Garden Row
 SE1.............136 A2
Garden Royal
 SW15.............57 C1
Gardens The
 East Dulwich
 SE22.............64 C3
 Stamford Hill N16 ..7 B4
Garden Terr
 Knightsbridge
 SW7.............130 B3
 Pimlico SW1 .....147 B2
Garden Wlk
 EC2 ...24 A2 98 A2
Gardiner Ave NW2 ..9 B3
Gardiner Ct NW10 ..20 C4
Gardiner Ho
 SW11............168 A4
Gardner Ct N5.....15 B4
Gardners La EC4 .122 C4
Gardnor Mans
 NW3.............11 B4
Gardnor Rd NW3 ..11 C4
Gard St EC1.......96 B4
Gareth Ct SW16 ..73 C1
Garfield Ho W2 ...102 C1
Garfield Mews
 SW11.............60 C4
Garford St E14....33 C2
Garland Ct E14 ...33 C2
Garland Ho N16 ...6 C1
Garlands NW8 ....78 B2
Garlinge Ho
 SW9.............173 B4
Garlinge Rd NW2 ..10 B2
Garnault Mews
 EC1.............95 C3
Garnault Pl EC1 ..95 C3
Garner St E2 .....24 C3
Garnet Rd NW10 ...8 A2
Garnet St E1 ......32 B2
Garnett Ho
 NW3.............12 B3
Garnett Rd NW3 ..12 B3
Garnham Cl N16 ...7 B2
Garnham St N16 ...7 B2
Garnies Cl SE15 ..49 B3
Garrad's Rd SW16 .73 C1
Garrard Wlk NW10 ..8 A2
Garratt Ho N16 ...7 A3
Garratt La SW18 ..71 A3

Garratt Park Sec
 Specl Sch
 SW18.............71 A3
Garraway Ct SW13 .47 B3
Garraway Ho SE21 .76 B1
Garrett Cl W3.....28 C4
Garrett St EC1 ...97 A2
Garrick Cl SW18 ..59 B3
Garrick Ho
 Chiswick W4......46 A4
 Mayfair W1.......118 A1
Garrick Rd TW9....44 C1
Garrick St WC2 ..120 A4
Garrick Yd WC2 ..120 A4
Garsdale Terr
 SW5.............141 A3
Garsington Mews
 SE4.............66 B4
Garson Ho W2 ...115 B4
Garston Ho N1 ...15 A1
Garter Way SE16 ..40 C4
Garth Ho NW2 .....1 B2
Garth Rd
 Child's Hill NW2 ...1 B2
 Chiswick W4.....37 C1
Gartmoor Gdns
 SW19.............70 B3
Garton Ho N6 ....4 C4
Garton Pl SW18 ..59 B1
Gartons Way
 SW11.............59 B4
Garway Rd W2 ...100 A1
Gascoigne Pl
 E2 ...24 B2 98 C3
Gascony Ave NW6 .10 C1
Gascoyne Ho
 E9..............17 C1
Gascoyne Rd E9 ..17 C1
Gaselee St E14 ...34 B2
Gasholder Pl
 SE11.............149 A1
Gaskarth Rd SW12 .61 A1
Gaskell St SW4 ..172 A2
Gaskin Ho N16 ....6 C1
Gaskin St N1......86 A4
Gaspar Cl SW7 ..142 B4
Gaspar Mews
 SW5.............142 B4
Gasson Ho
 SE14.............50 C4
Gastein Rd W6 ...47 C4
Gastigny Ho EC1 ..97 A3
Gaston Bell Cl
 TW9.............54 B4
Gaston Gate SW8 .172 C4
Gataker Ho
 SE16.............40 A3
Gataker St
 SE16.............40 A3
Gatcliff Cl SW1 ..145 C1
Gatcombe Ho
 SE22.............64 A4
Gatcombe Rd
 Newham E16 ....35 C1
 Tufnell Pk N19 ....4 C1
Gatefield Ct SE15 .64 C4
Gateforth St NW8 .90 A1
Gate Hill Ct
 W11 ...31 B1 113 A2
Gatehouse Sch
 E2..............25 C3
Gatehouse Sq
 SE1.............123 A2
Gateley Ho SE4 ..65 C3

Gateley Rd SW9....62 B4
Gate Mews SW7...130 B3
Gatesborough St
 EC2 ...24 A1 98 A2
Gates Ct SE17 ...150 C2
Gatesden
 WC1.............94 B3
Gateside Rd SW17 .72 B1
Gate St WC2 .....106 C2
Gateway SE17 ....48 B4
Gateway Arc
 N1..............86 A2
Gateway Ho SW12 .61 A1
Gateway Ind Est
 NW10.............21 C1
Gateway Mews
 E8..............16 B3
Gateway Prim Sch
 NW8.............89 C2
Gateways The
 SW3.............144 B3
Gateway Trad Est
 NW10.............21 B2
Gathorne St E2 ..25 C2
Gatliff Rd SW1 ...146 A1
Gatonby St SE15 ..49 B2
Gatwick Ho E14 ..33 B3
Gatwick Rd SW18 .70 B4
Gauden Cl SW4 ...61 C4
Gauden Rd SW4 ...61 C4
Gaugin Ct SE16 ..40 A1
Gaunt St SE1 ....136 C2
Gautrey Rd SE15 ..50 B1
Gavel St SE17 ...151 C4
Gaverick Mews
 E14.............41 C2
Gaviller Pl E5 ....17 A4
Gawber St E2.....25 B2
Gawthorne Ct E3 ..26 C3
Gay Cl NW2 ....9 A3
Gaydon Ho W2 ...100 A4
Gayfere St SW1 ..134 A1
Gayford Rd W12 ..38 B4
Gay Ho N16 ......16 A3
Gayhurst SE17 ...48 C4
Gayhurst Ho NW8 .90 B2
Gayhurst Prim Sch
 E8..............16 C1
Gayhurst Rd E8 ..16 C1
Gaymead NW8 ....78 B3
Gay Rd E15.......27 C3
Gaysley Ho SE11 .149 B3
Gay St SW15 .....57 C4
Gayton Cres NW3 .11 C4
Gayton Ho E3.....26 C1
Gayton Rd NW3 ..11 C4
Gayville Rd SW11 .60 B1
Gaywood Cl SW2 ..74 C3
Gaywood St SE1 .136 B1
Gaza St SE17 ....150 A1
Gaze Ho E14 .....34 C3
Gean Ct E11 .....19 C4
Geary Ho N7......14 B3
Geary Rd NW10 ...8 C3
Geary St N7......14 B3
Gedling Ho SE22 .64 B4
Gedling Pl SE1 ..139 A2
Gees Ct W1......103 C2
Gee St EC1 ......96 C2
Geffrye Ct N1.....24 A3
Geffrye Mus E2 ...24 B3
Geffrye St E2......24 B3
Geldart Rd SE15 ..50 A3
Geldeston Rd E5 ...7 C2
Gellatly Rd SE14 ..50 C1
Gemini Bsns Ctr
 E16.............27 C1
Gemini Ho E3 ....26 C4

Gems Hampshire Sch (Main Sch) SW7 . . . . **144** A1

Gems Hampshire Sch (The Early Years) SW7 . . . . **143** A3

General Wolfe Rd SE10 . . . . **52** C2

Genesis Bsns Pk NW10 . . . . **20** A3

Geneva Ct
1 Putney SW15 . . . . . **57** C2
Stoke Newington
N16 . . . . **6** C3

Geneva Dr SW9 . . . . . **62** C3
Genoa Ave SW15 . . . . **57** B2
Genoa Ho SE1 . . . . . . **25** C1
Geoffrey Cl SE5 . . . . . **48** B1
Geoffrey Ho SE1 . . . **137** C2
Geoffrey Jones Ct
NW10 . . . . **21** C4
Geoffrey Rd SE4 . . . . **66** B4
George Beard Rd **1**
SE8 . . . . **41** B2
George Beare Lo **3**
SW4 . . . . **61** B2
George Belt Ho **8**
E2 . . . . **25** C2
George Ct WC2 . . . . . **120** B3
George Downing Est
N16 . . . . **7** B2
George Eliot Ho
SW1 . . . . **147** A3
George Eliot Jun & Inf Schs NW8 . . . . **79** B4
George Elliot Ho
SE17 . . . . **150** C2
George Elliston Ho **18**
SE1 . . . . **153** B1
George Eyre Ho
NW8 . . . . **79** C1
George Green's Sch
E14 . . . . **42** B1
George Inn Yd
SE1 . . . . **123** B1
George La SE13 . . . . . **67** B1
George Lansbury Ho
7 Bow E3 . . . . **26** B2
8 Willesden NW10 . . . **8** A4
George Lashwood Ct
12 SW9 . . . . **62** B3
George Leybourne Ho
11 E1 . . . . **125** C4
George Lindgren Ho
SW6 . . . . **155** A2
George Loveless Ho
4 E2 . . . . **24** B2 **99** A4
George Mathers Rd
SE11 . . . . **150** A4
George Mews
27 Brixton SW9 . . . . **173** B1
SW1 . . . . **92** C3
George Peabody Ct
NW1 . . . . **102** A4
George Row SE16 . . . **139** B3
George's Rd N7 . . . . . **14** B3
George's Sq SW6 . . . **155** A4
George St
6 Canning Town
E16 . . . . **35** B3
Marylebone W1 . . . . . **103** A2
George Tingle Ho
SE1 . . . . **139** A2
Georgette Pl SE10 . . . **52** B3
George Vale Ho **58**
E2 . . . . **24** C3

George Walter Ho **11**
SE16 . . . . **40** B2
George Wyver Cl
SW18 . . . . **70** A4
George Yd
City of London
EC3 . . . . **109** C1
Mayfair W1 . . . . **117** C4
Georgiana St NW1 . . . **83** A4
Georgian Ct **12** E9 . . . **25** B4
Georgina Gdns **10**
E2 . . . . **24** B2 **99** A4
Geraldine Rd
Brentford W4 . . . . **44** C4
Wandsworth SW18 . . . **59** B2
Geraldine St SE11 . . . **136** A1
Gerald Mews
SW1 . . . . **145** C4
Gerald Rd SW1 . . . . . **145** C4
Geralds Yd NW1 . . . . . **12** C1
Gerard Ct NW2 . . . . . . **9** C3
Gerard Rd SW13 . . . . . **46** B2
Gerards Cl SE16 . . . . . **40** B1
Gernigan Ho
SW18 . . . . **59** C1
Gernon Rd E3 . . . . **26** A3
Gerrard Ho **5**
SE14 . . . . **50** C3
Gerrard Pl W1 . . . . . . **119** C4
Gerrard Rd N1 . . . . **86** B2
Gerrard St W1 . . . . . . **119** C4
Gerridge Ct SE1 . . . . **135** C2
Gerridge St SE1 . . . . **135** C2
Gerry Raffles Sq
E15 . . . . **19** C2
Gertrude St SW10 . . . **157** A3
Gervase St SE15 . . . . . **50** A3
Getters Talmud Torah
3 N16 . . . . **7** A3
Ghent Way E8 . . . . **16** B2
Gherkin The (30 St Mary Axe) EC2 . . . **110** B2
Giant Arches Rd
SE24 . . . . **63** B1
Gibbings Ho SE1 . . . . **136** B3
Gibbins Rd E15 . . . . . . **19** B1
Gibbon Ho NW8 . . . . . **89** C1
Gibbon Rd
Acton W3 . . . . **29** A2
Nunhead SE15 . . . . . . **50** B1
Gibbons Rd NW10 . . . . **8** A2
Gibbon's Rents
SE1 . . . . **124** A1
Gibbon Wlk SW15 . . . . **56** C3
Gibbs Gn W14 . . . . . . **141** A2
Gibbs Green Rd
W14 . . . . **140** C2
Gibbs Green Specl Sch W14 . . . . **141** A2
Gibbs Ho **5** SW12 . . . **73** A4
Gibraltar Ho
NW10 . . . . **21** A3
Gibraltar Wlk **28**
E2 . . . . **24** B2 **99** A3
Gibson Cl E1 . . . . **25** B1
Gibson Gdns N16 . . . . . **7** B2
Gibson Rd SE11 . . . . . **149** A3
Gibson Sq N1 . . . . **85** C4
Gibson St SE10 . . . . . . **43** A1
Gideon Rd SW11 . . . . . **60** C4
Giesbach Rd N19 . . . . . . **4** C2
Giffen Square Mkt
SE8 . . . . **51** C3
Giffin St SE8 . . . . **51** C3
Gifford Ho
5 Clapham SW4 . . . . . **61** C3
Greenwich SE10 . . . . . **42** C1

Gifford Ho continued
Pimlico SW1 . . . . **146** C1
Gifford Rd NW10 . . . . . **8** A1
Gifford St N1 . . . . **14** A1
Gilbert Ho
Barbican EC2 . . . . . . **109** A3
Deptford SE8 . . . . **51** C4
9 Globe Town E2 . . . . **25** C2
Pimlico SW1 . . . . **146** B1
South Lambeth
SW8 . . . . **162** A2
Gilbert Pl WC1 . . . . . **106** A3
Gilbert Sheldon Ho
W2 . . . . **101** C4
Gilbert St
E14 . . . . **41** C3
W1 . . . . **103** C1
Gilbey's Yd NW1 . . . . . **12** C1
Gilby Ho **5** E9 . . . . . . **17** C2
Gilda Cres N16 . . . . **7** C3
Gildea St W1 . . . . **104** B3
Gilden Cres NW5 . . . . . **12** C3
Giles Ho
8 Bermondsey
SE16 . . . . **139** B2
9 Notting Hill W11 . . . **31** C3
Gilesmead SE5 . . . . . . **48** C2
Gilkes Cres SE21 . . . . . **64** A1
Gilkes Pl SE21 . . . . **64** A1
Gillam Ho **3** SE16 . . . **40** B2
Gill Ave E16 . . . . **35** C3
Gillender St E3 . . . . . . **27** B1
Gillespie Prim Sch
N5 . . . . **6** A1
Gillespie Rd N4, N5 . . . . **6** A1
Gillett Pl **27** E8 . . . . . . **16** A3
Gillett St E8, N16 . . . . . **16** A3
Gillfoot NW1 . . . . **82** C1
Gillian St SE13 . . . . . . **67** A2
Gillies St NW5 . . . . **12** C3
Gilling Ct **5** NW3 . . . . **12** A2
Gillingham Ho
SW1 . . . . **146** C4
Gillingham Mews
SW1 . . . . **146** C4
Gillingham Row
SW1 . . . . **146** C4
Gillingham St
SW1 . . . . **146** C4
Gillison Wlk **11**
SE16 . . . . **139** C2
Gilman Ho **24** E2 . . . . . **24** C3
Gilray Ho SW10 . . . . . **157** B3
Gill St E14 . . . . **33** B2
Gilmore Ho SW4 . . . . . **60** B3
Gilmore Rd SE13 . . . . . **67** C3
Gilpin Ave SW14 . . . . . **55** C3
Gilpin Cl W2 . . . . **101** A4
Gilpin Rd E5 . . . . **18** A4
Gilray Ho W2 . . . . **115** B4
Gilstead Rd SW6 . . . . **166** B2
Gilston Rd SW10 . . . . **143** A1
Gilton Rd SE6 . . . . **68** D4
Giltspur St EC1 . . . . . **108** B2
Gilwell Ct **7** E5 . . . . . . **17** A4
Gipsy Cnr W3 . . . . **28** C4
Gipsy La SW15 . . . . **57** A4
Giraud St E14 . . . . **34** A3
Girdlers Rd W14 . . . . . **39** C2
Girdlestone Wlk
N19 . . . . **4** B2
Girdwood Rd SW18, SW19 . . . . **70** A4
Girling Ho **9** N1 . . . . . **24** A4
Gironde Rd SW6 . . . . . **155** A1

Girton Ho SW15 . . . . . **57** C1
Girton Villas **6**
W10 . . . . **30** C3
Gisburn Ho **23**
SE15 . . . . **49** C3
Gissing Wlk N1 . . . . . . **14** C1
Glade The W12 . . . . . . **39** A4
Glading Terr N16 . . . . . . **7** B1
Gladsmuir Rd N19 . . . . . **4** B3
Gladstone Ct
Westminster
SW1 . . . . **147** C3
Willesden NW2 . . . . **9** A3
Gladstone Park Sch
NW10 . . . . **9** A4
Gladstone Rd W4 . . . . . **37** C3
Gladstone St SE1 . . . . **136** A2
Gladstone Terr
SW8 . . . . **170** B4
Gladwin Ho NW1 . . . . . **83** A1
Gladwyn Rd SW15 . . . . **57** C4
Gladys Rd NW6 . . . . . . **10** C1
Glaisher St SE8 . . . . . . **52** A4
Glamis Ct W3 . . . . **37** A4
Glamis Est **3** E1 . . . . . **32** C2
Glamis Pl E1 . . . . **32** B2
Glamis Rd E1 . . . . **32** B2
Glanville Ho
12 SW12 . . . . **73** B4
Glanville Rd SW2 . . . . . **62** A2
Glasbury Ho **5**
SW9 . . . . **62** B3
Glaserton Rd N16 . . . . . **7** A4
Glasgow Ho W9 . . . . . . **78** B1
Glasgow Terr
SW1 . . . . **146** C1
Glasshill St SE1 . . . . . **136** B4
Glasshouse Fields
E1 . . . . **32** C2
Glasshouse St
W1 . . . . **119** A3
Glasshouse The
SE13 . . . . **67** B3
Glasshouse Wlk
SE11 . . . . **148** C2
Glasshouse Yd EC1 . . . **96** C1
Glass St **4** E2 . . . . **25** A1
Glastonbury Ct **12**
SE14 . . . . **50** B3
Glastonbury Ho
SW1 . . . . **146** A2
Glastonbury Pl **22**
E1 . . . . **32** B3
Glastonbury St
NW6 . . . . **10** B3
Glaucus St E3 . . . . **27** A4
Glazbury Rd W14 . . . . **140** B2
Glazebrook Cl
SE21 . . . . **75** C2
Glebe Cl W4 . . . . **38** A1
Glebe Ho **8** SE16 . . . . . **40** A3
Glebelands Cl SE5 . . . . **64** A4
Glebe Pl SW3 . . . . **158** A4
Glebe Rd
Barnes SW13 . . . . **46** C1
Dalston E8 . . . . **16** B1
Willesden NW10 . . . . . . **8** C2
Gledhow Gdns
SW5 . . . . **142** C3
Gledstanes Rd
W14 . . . . **140** B1
Glegg Pl **3** SW15 . . . . **57** C3
Glenaffric Ave E14 . . . . **42** C2

Glen Albyn Rd
SW19 . . . . **69** C2
Glenalmond Ho **2**
SW15 . . . . **57** C1
Glenarm Rd E5 . . . . . . **17** C4
Glenbrook Prim Sch
SW4 . . . . **61** C1
Glenbrook Rd
NW6 . . . . **10** C3
Glenburnie Rd
SW17 . . . . **72** B1
Glencoe Mans **6**
SW9 . . . . **163** B1
Glendall St SW9 . . . . . . **62** B3
Glendarvon St
SW15 . . . . **57** C4
Glendower Gdns **10**
SW14 . . . . **55** C4
Glendower Pl
SW7 . . . . **143** B4
Glendower Prep Sch
SW7 . . . . **143** B4
Glendower Rd
SW14 . . . . **55** C4
Glendown Ho **2**
E8 . . . . **16** C3
Glendun Ct W3 . . . . **29** A2
Glendun Rd W3 . . . . . . **29** A2
Gleneagles Cl **5**
SE16 . . . . **40** A1
Gleneldon Rd SW16 . . . **74** A1
Glenelg Rd SW2 . . . . . . **62** A2
Glenfield Rd SW12 . . . . **73** B3
Glenfinlas Way
SE5 . . . . **48** A3
Glenforth St SE10 . . . . **43** B1
Glengall Gr E14 . . . . . . **42** B3
Glengall Pass **2**
NW6 . . . . **23** C4
Glengall Rd
Camberwell SE15 . . . . . **49** B4
Kilburn NW6 . . . . **23** B4
Glengall Terr SE15 . . . . **49** B4
Glengarnock Ave
E14 . . . . **42** B2
Glengarry Rd SE22 . . . . **64** B2
Glenhurst Ave
NW5 . . . . **12** C4
Glenilla Rd NW3 . . . . . . **12** A2
Glenister Rd SE10 . . . . **43** B1
Glenkerry Ho **11**
E14 . . . . **34** B3
Glenloch Ct **2**
SW15 . . . . **57** C1
Glenloch Rd NW3 . . . . . **12** A3
Glenluce Rd SE3 . . . . . . **53** C4
Glenmore SW15 . . . . . . **57** C1
Glenmore Ho **6**
TW10 . . . . **54** A1
Glenmore Rd NW3 . . . . **12** A2
Glennie Ct SE21 . . . . . . **76** C3
Glennie Ho SE10 . . . . . **52** B2
Glennie Rd SE27,
SW16 . . . . **74** C1
Glenridding NW1 . . . . . **83** A1
Glenrosa St SW6 . . . . **166** C2
Glenroy St W12 . . . . . . **30** B3
Glensdale Rd SE4 . . . . . **66** B4
Glenshaw Mans **1**
SW9 . . . . **163** B1
Glentanner Way
SW17 . . . . **71** C1
Glentham Gdns
SW13 . . . . **47** A4

Glentham Rd
SW13 . . . . **47** A4
Glenthorne Mews
W6 . . . . **39** A2
Glenthorne Rd W6 . . **39** A2
Glenthorpe SW15 . . **56** C3
Glentworth St
NW1 . . . . **91** A1
Glenville Gr SE8 . . . . **51** B3
Glenville Mews
SW18 . . . . **70** C4
Glenworth Ave
E14 . . . . **42** C2
Gliddon Rd W14 . . **140** A2
Globe Acad SE1 . . **137** C1
Globe Pond Rd
SE16 . . . . **33** A1
Globe Prim Sch **37**
E2 . . . . **25** B2
Globe Rd E1, E2 . . . . **25** B1
Globe St SE1 . . . . . . **137** B3
Globe Terr **5** E2 . . . . **25** B2
Globe Theatre The
SE1 . . . . **122** C3
GLOBE TOWN **25** C2
Globe View EC4 . . **122** C4
Globe Yd W1 . . . . . . **104** A1
Gloucester W14 . . **141** A3
Gloucester Ave
NW1 . . . . **81** C4
Gloucester Cir
SE10 . . . . **52** B3
Gloucester Cres
NW1 . . . . **82** A4
Gloucester Ct
Borough The SE1 . . **137** A2
City of London EC3 . **124** B3
Dulwich SE22 . . . . . . **76** C3
Golders Green NW11 . . **1** B4
Richmond TW9 . . . . . . **44** C3
Gloucester Dr N4 . . . . **6** A2
Gloucester Gate
NW1 . . . . **82** A2
Gloucester Gate Mews
NW1 . . . . **82** A2
Gloucester Gdns
Golders Green
NW11 . . . . **1** B4
Paddington W2 . . . **100** C2
Gloucester Ho
Kilburn NW6 . . . . **23** C3
Richmond TW10 . . . . . **54** C2
Gloucester Mews
W2 . . . . **101** A1
Gloucester Mews W
W2 . . . . **101** A1
Gloucester Pk
SW7 . . . . **142** C4
Gloucester Pl NW1 **103** A4
Gloucester Pl Mews
W1 . . . . **103** A3
Gloucester Prim Sch
SE15 . . . . **49** A3
Gloucester Rd
Acton W3 . . . . **37** B4
Richmond TW9 . . . . . . **44** C3
South Kensington
SW7 . . . . **142** C4
Gloucester Road Sta
SW7 . . . . **142** C4
Gloucester Sq
6 Hackney E2 . . . . . . **24** C4
Paddington W2 . . . **102** A1

Gloucester St
SW1 . . . . **146** C2
Gloucester Terr
W2 . . . . **101** A1
Gloucester Way
EC1 . . . . **95** C3
Glover Ho
London SE15 . . . . **65** A3
2 South Hampstead
NW6 . . . . **11** B1
Glycena Rd SW11 . . . . **60** B4
Glyn Ct SE27 . . . . **74** C1
Glynde Mews
SW3 . . . . **130** B1
Glynde Reach WC1 . **94** B3
Glynde St SE4 . . . . . . **66** B1
Glynfield Rd NW10 . . **8** A1
Glyn Mans W14 . . . **140** B4
Glyn Rd E5 . . . . **17** C4
Glyn St SE11 . . . . . . **148** C1
Goater's Alley
SW6 . . . . **155** A1
Goat Wharf TW8 . . . . **44** A4
Godalming Rd E14 . . **34** A4
Goddard Ho SW19 . . **69** C2
Goddard Pl N19 . . . . . **4** B1
Godfrey Ho EC1 . . . . **97** B3
Godfrey St
Chelsea SW3 . . . . . . **144** B2
Mill Meads E15 . . . . . **27** B3
Goding St SE11 . . . **148** B1
Godley Rd SW18 . . . . **71** C3
Godliman St EC4 . . **122** C4
Godman Rd SE15 . . . . **50** A1
Godolphin Ho
Primrose Hill
NW3 . . . . **12** A1
7 Streatham SW2 . . **74** C3
Godolphin & Latymer
Sch **10** **39** A2
Godolphin Pl W3 . . **28** C2
Godolphin Rd
W12 . . . . **39** A4
Godson St N1 . . . . . . **85** B2
Godstone Ct **11** N16 **7** A3
Godstone Ho SE1 . **137** C2
Godwin Cl N1 . . . . . . **87** A2
Godwin Ct NW1 . . . . **83** A2
Godwin Ho
2 Haggerston E2 . . **24** B3
Kilburn NW6 . . . . **78** A2
Goffers Ho SE3 . . . . . **53** A1
Goffers Rd SE3,
SE13 . . . . **53** A1
Goffton Ho **14**
SW9 . . . . **173** A1
Golborne Gdns
3 Kensal Town
W10 . . . . **23** A1
West Kilburn W10 . . . **23** B1
Golborne Mews **9**
W10 . . . . **31** A4
Golborne Rd W10 . . **31** A4
Golden Cross Mews
2 W11 . . . . **31** B3
Golden Hinde The
SE1 . . . . **123** B2
Golden Hind Pl **5**
SE8 . . . . **41** B2
Golden La EC1 . . . . . . **97** A1
Golden Lane Campus
EC1 . . . . **97** A1
Golden Lane L Ctr
EC1 . . . . **96** C1

Golden Plover Cl
E16 . . . . **35** C3
Golden Sq W1 . . . **119** A4
Golders Ct NW11 . . . . **1** B4
Golders Gdns NW11 . **1** B4
GOLDERS GREEN . . **1** C4
Golders Green Coll
NW11 . . . . **1** C3
Golders Green Cres
NW11 . . . . **1** C4
Golders Green Rd
NW11 . . . . **1** A4
Golders Green Sta
NW11 . . . . **1** C3
Golders Hill Sch
NW11 . . . . **1** C4
Golderslea NW11 . . . . **1** C3
Golders Park Cl
NW11 . . . . **1** C3
Golders Way NW11 . . **1** B4
Goldhawk Ind Est
W6 . . . . **39** A3
Goldhawk Mews **2**
W12 . . . . **39** A4
Goldhawk Rd W12 . . **38** C3
Goldhawk Road Sta
W12 . . . . **39** B4
Goldhurst Terr
NW6 . . . . **11** B1
Goldie Ho N19 . . . . . . **4** C4
Golding St **1** E1 . . **111** C1
Goldington Cres
NW1 . . . . **83** B2
Goldington St
NW1 . . . . **83** B2
Goldman Cl **2**
E2 . . . . **99** B2
Goldney Rd W9 . . . . . **23** C1
Goldsboro Rd
SW8 . . . . **161** C1
Goldsborough Ho
SW8 . . . . **171** C3
Goldsmith Ave **3** W3 **28** C2
Goldsmith Ct
WC1 . . . . **106** B2
Goldsmith Rd
Acton W3 . . . . **28** C1
Peckham SE15 . . . . . . **49** C2
Goldsmiths Bldgs
W3 . . . . **28** C1
Goldsmiths Coll, Univ
of London SE14 . . . . . **51** A3
Goldsmith's Pl **8**
NW6 . . . . **78** A3
Goldsmith's Row
E2 . . . . **24** C3
Goldsmith's Sq **17**
E2 . . . . **24** C3
Goldsmith St EC2 **109** A2
Goldthorpe NW1 . . . **82** C3
Goldwell Ho SE22 . . . **64** A3
Goldwin Cl SE14 . . . . **50** B2
Goldwing Cl E16 . . . . **35** C3
Gomm Rd SE16 . . . . . **40** B3
Gondar Gdns NW6 . . **10** B3
Gondar Mans NW6 . . **10** B3
Gonson St SE8 . . . . . . **52** A4
Gonston Cl SW19 . . . **70** A2
Gonville Ho **6**
SW15 . . . . **57** C1
Gonville St SW6 . . . . **58** A4
Gooch Ho EC1 . . . . **107** B4

Goodall Ho **10** SE4 . . **65** C3
Goodenough Coll
WC1 . . . . **94** C2
Goodfaith Ho **18**
E14 . . . . **34** A2
Goodge Pl W1 . . . . **105** A3
Goodge St W1 . . . . **105** A3
Goodge Street Sta
W1 . . . . **105** B4
Goodhall St NW10 . . **21** B2
Good Hart Pl E14 . . . **33** A2
Goodhope Ho **19**
E14 . . . . **34** A2
Goodinge Cl N7 . . . . . **14** A2
Goodinge Rd N7 . . . . **14** A2
Goodman Cres
SW2 . . . . **73** C2
Goodman's Stile **7**
E1 . . . . **111** B2
Goodman's Yd E1,
EC3 . . . . **124** C4
Goodrich Com Prim
Sch SE22 . . . . **64** C1
Goodrich Ct **9**
W10 . . . . **30** C3
Goodrich Ho
20 Bethnal Green
E2 . . . . **25** B3
Stamford Hill N16 . . . **7** A4
Goodrich Rd SE22 . . . **64** C1
Good Shepherd RC
Prim Sch The
W12 . . . . **38** B4
Goodson Rd NW10 . . **8** A1
Goodspeed Ho **20**
E14 . . . . **34** A2
Goodsway NW1 . . . . **84** A2
Goodway Gdns
E14 . . . . **34** C3
Goodwill Ho **22**
E14 . . . . **34** A2
Goodwin Cl SE16 . . **139** A1
Goodwin Ho **2**
SE15 . . . . **65** A4
Goodwin Rd W12 . . . **38** C4
Goodwin St N4 . . . . . . **5** C2
Goodwood Ct W1 . **104** B4
Goodwood Ho **3**
W4 . . . . **37** B1
Goodwood Mans **3**
SW9 . . . . **62** C4
Goodwood Rd
SE14 . . . . **51** A3
Goose Green Prim
Sch SE22 . . . . **64** B3
Goose Green Trad Est
SE22 . . . . **64** C3
Gophir La EC4 . . . . . **123** B4
Gopsall St N1 . . . . . . **87** C3
Gordon Ave SW14 . . **56** A3
Gordonbrock Prim
Sch SE4 . . . . **66** C2
Gordonbrock Rd
SE4 . . . . **66** C2
Gordon Ct **5** SW12 . . **30** B3
Gordondale Rd SW18,
SW19 . . . . **70** C2
Gordon Gr SE5 . . . . . . **48** A1
Gordon Ho **7** E1 . . . . **32** B2
Gordon Hospl
SW1 . . . . **147** B3
Gordon House Rd
NW5 . . . . **12** C4
Gordon Lo N16 . . . . . . **6** C3
Gordon Mans WC1 . . **93** B1

Gordon Pl W8 . . . . **127** C4
Gordon Rd
Chiswick W4 . . . . **45** A4
Leyton E15 . . . . **19** B4
Peckham SE15 . . . . . . **50** A1
Richmond TW9 . . . . . . **44** B1
Gordon Sq WC1 . . . . . **93** C2
Gordon St WC1 . . . . . **93** B2
Gorefield Ho NW6 . . **23** C3
Gorefield Pl NW6 . . . **23** C3
Gore Rd E9 . . . . **25** B4
Gore St SW7 . . . . . . **129** A2
Gorham Ho **12**
SW4 . . . . **61** B1
Gorham Pl
W11 . . . . **31** A2 **112** A3
Goring St EC3 . . . . . **110** B2
Gorleston St W14 . . **140** B4
Gorse Cl E16 . . . . **35** C3
Gorsefield Ho **6**
E14 . . . . **33** C2
Gorst Rd
London SW11 . . . . **60** B1
North Acton NW10 . . **20** C1
Gorsuch Pl **1**
E2 . . . . **24** B2 **98** C4
Gorsuch St
E2 . . . . **24** B2 **98** C4
Gosberton Rd
SW12 . . . . **72** C3
Gosfield St W1 . . . . **104** C3
Gosford Ho **23** E3 . . . **26** B3
Goslett Yd WC2 . . . **105** C2
Gosling Ho **2** E1 . . . **32** B2
Gosling Way SW9 . **173** B4
Gospatrick Home Ho
SW14 . . . . **56** A4
GOSPEL OAK **12** C4
Gospel Oak Prim Sch
NW5 . . . . **12** C4
Gospel Oak Sta
NW5 . . . . **12** C4
Gosset St E2 . . **24** C2 **99** B4
Gosterwood St
SE8 . . . . **51** A4
Goswell Pl EC1 . . . . . **96** B3
Goswell Rd EC1 . . . . . **96** B4
Gothic Ct **17** SE5 . . . . **48** B3
Gottfried Mews
NW5 . . . . **13** B4
Gough Ho N1 . . . . . . **86** B4
Gough Sq EC4 . . . . **107** C2
Gough St WC1 . . . . . . **95** A1
Gough Wlk **14** E14 . . **33** C3
Goulden Ho SW11 . **168** A2
Gouldman Ho **33**
E1 . . . . **25** B1
Gould Terr **28** E8 . . . . **17** A3
Goulston St E1 . . . . **110** C2
Goulton Rd E5 . . . . . . **17** A4
Govan St **2** E2 . . . . . **24** C4
Gover Ct **3** SW4 . . . **172** B2
Gowan Ave SW6 . . **164** A4
Gowan Ho **2**
E2 . . . . **24** B2 **99** A3
Gowan Rd NW10 . . . . **9** A2
Gower Cl SW4 . . . . . . **61** B1
Gower Ct WC1 . . . . . . **93** B2
Gower Ho SE17 . . . **151** A2
Gower Mews
WC1 . . . . **105** C4
Gower Pl NW1,
WC1 . . . . **93** B2

Gower Sch The **4**
N7 . . . . **14** A2
Gower St WC1 . . . . **93** B1
Gowlett Rd SE15 . . . . **64** C4
Gowrie Rd SW11 . . . . . **60** C4
Gracechurch St EC2,
EC4 . . . . **123** C4
Gracefield Gdns
SW16 . . . . **74** A1
Gracemere **2** E1 . . . . **32** B4
Grace Ho SE11 . . . . **163** A4
Grace PI E3 . . . . **27** A2
Graces Mews SE5 . . . . **49** A1
Grace's Mews SE5 . . . **49** A1
Grace St E3 . . . . **27** A2
Graemesdyke Ave
SW14 . . . . **55** A3
Grafton Cres NW1 . . . **13** A2
Grafton Ct **11** E8 . . . . **16** C3
Grafton Ho
16 Bow E3 . . . . **26** C2
17 Deptford SE8 . . . . **41** B1
Grafton Mans SW4 . . **61** B3
Grafton Mews W1 . . . . **92** C1
Grafton PI NW1 . . . . . **93** C3
Grafton Prim Sch **5**
N7 . . . . **5** A1
Grafton Rd
Acton W3 . . . . **28** B2
Gospel Oak NW5 . . . **12** C3
Grafton Sq SW4 . . . . **61** B3
Grafton St W1 . . . . . **118** B3
Grafton Terr NW5 . . . **12** C3
Grafton Way W1 . . . . **93** A1
Grafton Yd NW5 . . . . **13** A2
Graham Ct **5**
SE14 . . . . **50** C4
Graham Ho
5 Balham SW12 . . . **73** A4
6 Tufnell Pk N19 . . **13** C4
Graham Mans **2**
E8 . . . . **17** A2
Graham Rd
Acton W4 . . . . **37** C3
Dalston E8 . . . . **16** C2
Graham St N1 . . . . . . **86** B1
Graham Terr SW1 . . **145** C3
Graham Twr W3 . . . . **37** A3
Grainger Ct **22**
SE5 . . . . **48** B3
Grampian Gdns
NW2 . . . . **1** A3
Grampians The **10**
W14 . . . . **39** C4
Granard Ave SW15 . . **57** A2
Granard Ho **20** E9 . . **17** C2
Granard Prim Sch
SW15 . . . . **57** A2
Granard Rd SW11,
SW12 . . . . **72** B4
Granary Rd E1 . . . . . **25** A1
Granary Sq
Islington N1 . . . . . **14** C2
N1 . . . . **84** A3
Granary St NW1 . . . . **83** B3
Granary The SE8 . . . . **51** C3
Granby PI SE1 . . . . . **135** B3
Granby St
Bethnal Green
E2 . . . . **24** C1 **99** B2
Shoreditch
E2 . . . . **24** B1 **99** A2
Granby Terr NW1 . . . **82** C1

Grand Ave EC1 . . . . **108** B4
Grandfield Ct W4 . . . . **45** C4
Grandison Rd
SW11 . . . . **60** B2
Grand Junction Wharf
N1 . . . . **86** C1
Grand Par SW14 . . . . **55** B3
Grand Union Cl
W9 . . . . **31** B4
Grand Union Cres
E8 . . . . **24** C4
Grand Union Ind Est
NW10 . . . . **20** A3
Grand Vitesse Ind Est
SE1 . . . . **122** B1
Granfield St
SW11 . . . . **167** C3
Grangecourt Rd
N16 . . . . **7** A3
Grange Ct
Peckham SE15 . . . **49** B1
Strand WC2 . . . . . **107** A1
1 Willesden NW10 . . **8** A4
Grangefield NW1 . . . **14** A1
Grange Gdns NW3 . . . **2** A1
Grange Gr N1 . . . . . . **15** B2
Grange Ho
Bermondsey SE1 . **138** C1
Willesden NW10 . . . **9** A1
Grange La SE21 . . . . **76** B2
Grangemill **11**
NW5 . . . . **13** A4
GRANGE MILLS **73** B3
Grange Mills
SW12 . . . . **73** B3
Grange PI NW6 . . . . . **10** C1
Grange Prim Sch
SE1 . . . . **138** A1
Grange Rd
Barnes SW13 . . . . **46** C2
Bermondsey SE1 . **138** C1
Gunnersbury W4 . . **37** A1
Willesden NW10 . . . **9** A2
Grange St N1 . . . . . . **87** C3
Grange The
Bermondsey SE1 . **138** C1
7 Gunnersbury
W4 . . . . **37** A1
Hammersmith W12 . **39** A3
18 Maitland Pk
NW3 . . . . **12** B2
South Acton W3 . . . **37** A4
West Kensington
W14 . . . . **140** C3
Grangeway NW6 . . . **10** C1
Grange Wlk SE1 . . . **138** C1
Grange Yd SE1 . . . . **138** C1
Granite Apts E15 . . . **19** C2
Grannary The **10**
SE16 . . . . **40** B4
Gransden Ave E8 . . . **17** A1
Gransden Ho **1**
SE8 . . . . **41** B1
Gransden Rd W12 . . . **38** B4
Grantbridge St N1 . . **86** B2
Grantham Ct **9**
SE16 . . . . **40** C4
Grantham Ho **12**
SE15 . . . . **49** C4
Grantham PI W1 . . . **118** A1
Grantham Rd
Chiswick W4 . . . . . **46** A3
South Lambeth
SW9 . . . . **172** B1
Grant Ho
38 Clapham SW8 . . **171** B1

Grant Ho continued
Clerkenwell EC1 . . . **108** B4
Grantley Ho
2 Deptford SE14 . . . **50** C4
5 Putney SW15 . . . . **69** C3
Grantley St E1 . . . . . . **25** C1
Grant Mus of Zoology
WC1 . . . . **93** B1
Grant Rd SW11 . . . . . **60** A4
Grant St N1 . . . . **85** B2
Grantully Rd W9 . . . . **88** A3
Granville Ct
8 Deptford SE14 . . . **51** A3
Shoreditch N1 . . . . **87** C3
Granville Gr SE13 . . . **67** B4
Granville Ho **10**
E14 . . . . **33** C3
Granville Ind Est
NW2 . . . . **1** B2
Granville Mans **8**
W12 . . . . **39** B4
Granville Pk SE13 . . . **67** C4
Granville PI
Marylebone W1 . . . **103** B1
Walham Green
SW6 . . . . **156** A1
Granville Point
NW2 . . . . **1** B2
Granville Rd
Child's Hill NW2 . . . **1** B2
Kilburn NW6 . . . . . **23** C3
Wandsworth SW18 . **70** B4
Granville Sq
1 Camberwell
SE15 . . . . **49** A3
Finsbury WC1 . . . . . **95** A3
Granville St WC1 . . . **95** A3
Grape St WC2 . . . . . **106** A2
Grasgarth Cl W3 . . . . **28** B2
Grasmere NW1 . . . . . **92** B3
Grasmere Ave W3 . . **28** C2
Grasmere Ct
SW13 . . . . **46** C4
Grasmere Ho **20**
N16 . . . . **16** C4
Grasmere Point **2**
SE15 . . . . **50** B3
Grasmere Prim Sch
N16 . . . . **15** C4
Grateley Ho **10**
SW15 . . . . **69** A3
Gratton Rd W14 . . . **126** A1
Graveley Ho **7**
SE8 . . . . **41** A2
Gravel La E1 . . . . . . **110** C2
Gravesend Rd
W12 . . . . **29** C2
Grayfriars Pas
EC1 . . . . **108** B2
Gray Ho SE17 . . . . . **151** A2
Grayland Ct WC1 . . . **94** C3
Grayling Ct W1 . . . . **103** B2
Grayling Sq
E2 . . . . **24** C2 **99** C4
Grayshott Rd
SW11 . . . . **60** C4
Gray's Inn PI WC1 . . **107** A3
Gray's Inn Rd WC1 . . **95** A2
Gray's Inn Sq
WC1 . . . . **107** B4
Grayson Ho EC1 . . . . **97** A3
Gray St SE1 . . . . . . **135** C3
Grayswood Point **14**
SW15 . . . . **68** C3
Gray's Yd W1 . . . . . **103** C2

Grazebrook Rd N16 . . **6** C2
Great Arthur Ho
EC1 . . . . **96** C1
Great Bell Alley
EC2 . . . . **109** B2
Great Castle St
W1 . . . . **104** C2
Great Central St
NW1 . . . . **102** C4
Great Chapel St
W1 . . . . **105** B2
Great Chart St
SW11 . . . . **59** B3
Great Chertsey Rd
SW14, W4 . . . . **45** C2
Great Church La
W6 . . . . **39** C1
Great College St
SW1 . . . . **134** A2
Great Croft WC1 . . . . **94** B3
Great Cross Ave
SE3 . . . . **53** A3
Great Cumberland
Mews W1 . . . . **102** C1
Great Cumberland PI
W1 . . . . **103** A1
Great Dover St
SE1 . . . . **137** B2
Great Eastern Bldgs
10 E8 . . . . **17** A2
Great Eastern Ent Ctr
E14 . . . . **42** A4
Great Eastern Pier
E14 . . . . **41** C1
Great Eastern Rd
E15 . . . . **19** C2
Great Eastern St
EC2 . . . . **24** A1 **98** A2
Great Eastern Wharf
SW11 . . . . **158** B1
Great Field **7**
NW5 . . . . **13** B3
Greatfield Cl
London SE4 . . . . . . **66** C3
4 Tufnell Pk N19 . . **13** B4
Great George St
SW1 . . . . **134** A3
Great Guildford Bsns
Sq SE1 . . . . **122** C1
Great Guildford St
SE1 . . . . **122** C1
Greatham Wlk **8**
SW15 . . . . **68** C3
Great James St
WC1 . . . . **106** C4
Great Marlborough St
W1 . . . . **104** C1
Great Maze Pond
SE1 . . . . **137** C4
Great Newport St
WC2 . . . . **120** A4
Greatorex Ho **18**
E1 . . . . **111** B4
Greatorex St E1 . . . **111** B4
Great Ormond St
Hospl for Children
WC1 . . . . **94** C1
Great Ormond St
WC1 . . . . **94** C1
Great Percy St
WC1 . . . . **95** B4
Great Peter St
SW1 . . . . **133** C1
Great Portland St
W1 . . . . **104** B4

Great Portland Street
Sta W1 . . . . **92** B1
Great Pulteney St
W1 . . . . **119** A4
Great Queen St
WC2 . . . . **106** B2
Great Russell Mans
WC1 . . . . **106** A3
Great Russell St
WC1 . . . . **106** A3
Great St Helen's
EC3 . . . . **110** A2
Great St Thomas
Apostle EC4 . . . . . **123** A4
Great Scotland Yd
SW1, WC2 . . . . **120** A2
Great Smith St
SW1 . . . . **133** C2
Great Spilmans
SE22 . . . . **64** A2
Great Suffolk St
SE1 . . . . **122** B1
Great Sutton St
EC1 . . . . **96** B1
Great Swan Alley
EC2 . . . . **109** B2
Great Titchfield St
W1 . . . . **104** C3
Great Tower St
EC3 . . . . **124** A4
Great Trinity La
EC4 . . . . **123** A4
Great Turnstile
WC2 . . . . **107** A3
Great Western Rd W2,
W9 . . . . **31** B4
Great West Rd W4,
W6 . . . . **45** C4
Great West Road
Cedars Rd W4 . . . . **45** B4
Great West Road
Hogarth La W4 . . . **46** A4
Great Winchester St
EC2 . . . . **109** C2
Great Windmill St
W1 . . . . **119** B4
Great Yd SE1 . . . . . **138** B4
Greaves Cotts **9**
E14 . . . . **33** A4
Greaves Twr
SW10 . . . . **157** A2
Grebe Ct **16** E14 . . . . **42** B4
Greek Ct W1 . . . . . . **105** C1
Greek Sch of London
W3 . . . . **28** A2
Greek St W1 . . . . . . **105** C1
Greenacre Ct E8 . . . . **16** C3
Greenacre Sq **26**
SE16 . . . . **40** C4
Green Arbour Ct
EC1 . . . . **108** A2
Greenaway Gdns
NW3 . . . . **11** A4
Greenaway Ho
Finsbury WC1 . . . . . **95** B3
St John's Wood
NW8 . . . . **78** C4
Green Bank E1 . . . . . **32** A1
Greenberry St
NW8 . . . . **80** A1
Green Cl NW11 . . . . . **2** B4
Greencoat PI
SW1 . . . . **147** A4

Greencoat Row
SW1 . . . . **133** A1
Greencourt Ho 28
E1 . . . . **25** C1
Greencroft Gdns
NW6 . . . . **11** B1
Green Ct 2 NW10 . . . **8** A4
Green Dale SE22 . . . **64** A2
Greendale Cl SE22 . . **64** A2
Green Dragon Ct
SE1 . . . . **123** B1
Green Dragon Ho
WC1 . . . . **106** B2
Green Dragon La
TW8 . . . . **36** B1
Green Dragon Prim
Sch TW8 . . . . **44** A4
Green Dragon Yd 24
E1 . . . . **111** B3
Greene Ct 20 SE14 . . **50** C4
Greene Ho SE1 . . . . **137** B1
Greenend Rd W4 . . . **38** A4
Greener Ho 3
SW4 . . . . **61** C4
Greenfell Mans
SE8 . . . . **52** A4
Greenfield Gdns
NW2 . . . . **1** A1
Greenfield Ho 28
SW19 . . . . **69** C3
Greenfield Rd E1 . . **111** C2
Greenham Cl SE1 . . **135** B3
Greenham Ho 3
E9 . . . . **25** B4
Greenheath Bsns Ctr
3 E2 . . . . **25** A1
Greenhill NW3 . . . . **11** C4
Greenhill Pk
NW10 . . . . **21** A4
Greenhill Rd
NW10 . . . . **21** A4
Greenhill's Rents
EC1 . . . . **108** A4
Greenhills Terr 16
N1 . . . . **15** C2
Green Ho The 5
SW19 . . . . **70** A3
Green Hundred Rd
SE15 . . . . **49** C4
Greening Ho SE13 . . **67** C3
Greenland Ho
Bermondsey SE8 . . . **40** C1
4 Mile End E1 . . . . **26** A1
Greenland Mews
SE8 . . . . **40** C1
Greenland Pier
SE8 . . . . **41** B3
Greenland Pl NW1 . . **82** B4
Greenland Quay
SE16 . . . . **40** C2
Greenland Rd NW1 . . **82** C4
Greenland St NW1 . . **82** B4
Green Lanes N4, N8,
N15 . . . . **6** A4
Greenleaf Cl 8
SW2 . . . . **74** C4
Green Link Wlk
TW9 . . . . **45** A2
Greenman St N1 . . . **86** C4
Greenman Prim Sch
SW15 . . . . **57** A2
Greenock Rd 11
W3 . . . . **37** B3

Green Park SW1,
W1 . . . . **132** B4
Green Park Sta
W1 . . . . **118** C2
Greenroof Way
SE10 . . . . **43** B3
Greens Ct W1 . . . . **119** B4
Green's Ct
W11 . . . . . . **31** B1 **112** C1
Greenside Prim Sch
W12 . . . . **38** C4
Greenside Rd W12 . . **38** C4
Green St W1 . . . . . **117** B4
Greenstead Gdns
SW15 . . . . **57** A2
Greenstreet Hill
SE4 . . . . **65** C4
Greensward Ho
SW6 . . . . **166** C2
Green Terr EC1 . . . . **95** C3
Green The W3 . . . . . **29** A3
Greenview Cl W3 . . . **29** A1
Greenview Ct
East Dulwich
SE22 . . . . **64** C3
Wandsworth SW18 . . **72** A4
Greenway Cl N4 . . . . **6** B2
Greenway W1 . . . . . **92** B1
GREENWICH **43** C3
Greenwich Acad
SE10 . . . . **52** A2
Greenwich Bsns Ctr
SE10 . . . . **52** A3
Greenwich Bsns Pk
SE10 . . . . **52** A3
Greenwich Church St
SE10 . . . . **52** B4
Greenwich Coll 17
SE10 . . . . **52** B3
Greenwich Ct 11
E1 . . . . **32** A3
Greenwich High Rd
SE10 . . . . **52** A3
Greenwich Ho
SE13 . . . . **67** C1
Greenwich Ind Est
SE10 . . . . **52** A3
Greenwich Mkt 2
SE10 . . . . **52** B4
Greenwich Park
Greenwich Park St
SE10 . . . . **53** A3
Greenwich Pier
SE10 . . . . **42** B1
Greenwich Quay
SE8 . . . . **52** A4
Greenwich South St
SE10 . . . . **52** A3
Greenwich Sta
SE10 . . . . **52** B3
Greenwich View Pl
E14 . . . . **42** A3
Green Wlk SE1 . . . **138** A1
Greenwood 8
SW19 . . . . **69** A4
Green Wood NW5 . . **13** B3
Greenwood Ho
Finsbury WC1 . . . . . **95** B3
8 Nunhead SE4 . . . **65** C3
Greenwood Pl
NW5 . . . . **13** A3
Greenwood Rd E8 . . **16** C2
Greenwood Terr
NW10 . . . . **20** C3
Green Yd WC1 . . . . . **95** A2

Greet Ho SE1 . . . . **135** C3
Greet St SE1 . . . . . **121** C1
Gregor Mews SE3 . . **53** C3
Gregory Pl W8 . . . . **128** A4
Grenada Ho 18
E14 . . . . **33** B2
Grenade St E14 . . . . **33** B2
Grena Gdns TW9 . . . **54** B3
Grena Rd TW10,
TW9 . . . . **54** B3
Grendon Ho
22 Hackney E9 . . . . **17** B1
Pentonville N1 . . . . **84** C1
Grendon St NW8 . . . **90** A2
Grenfell Ho SE5 . . . **48** B3
Grenfell Rd W11 . . . **30** C2
Grenfell Twr 5
W11 . . . . **30** C2
Grenfell Wlk 4
W11 . . . . **30** C2
Grenier Apartments
11 SE15 . . . . **50** A3
Grenville Ho
26 Bow E3 . . . . **26** A3
4 Deptford SE8 . . . **51** C4
Grenville Lo N6 . . . . . **4** B4
Grenville Mans
WC1 . . . . **94** A2
Grenville Mews
SW7 . . . . **142** C3
Grenville Pl SW7 . . **142** C4
Grenville Rd N19 . . . . **5** A3
Grenville St WC1 . . . **94** B1
Gresham Almshouses
1 SW9 . . . . **62** C3
Gresham Coll EC1 . **107** C3
Gresham Gdns
NW11 . . . . **1** A3
Gresham Pl 2 N19 . . . **4** C2
Gresham Rd SW9 . . . **62** C4
Gresham St EC2 . . . **109** A2
Gresham Way
SW19 . . . . **70** C1
Gresham Way Est
SW19 . . . . **71** A1
Gresley Ho SW8 . . . **171** C4
Gresley Rd N19 . . . . . **4** B4
Gressenhall Rd
SW18 . . . . **70** B4
Gresse St W1 . . . . . **105** B2
Greswell St SW6 . . . **47** C2
Greta Ho SE3 . . . . . **53** B4
Gretton Ho 2 E2 . . . **25** B2
Greville Hall NW6 . . **78** B2
Greville Ho
Knightsbridge
SW1 . . . . **131** B2
Putney SW15 . . . . . . **57** C4
Greville Lo 8 SW8 . . **78** A3
Greville Mews 5
NW6 . . . . **78** A3
Greville Pl W9 . . . . . **78** B2
Greville Rd
Kilburn NW6 . . . . . . **78** B2
Richmond TW10 . . . . **54** B1
Greville St EC1 . . . **107** C3
Grey Coat Hospital
The (Sch)
SW1 . . . . **147** B3
Greycoat Pl SW1 . . **133** B1
Greycoat St SW1 . . **133** B1
Grey Eagle St
E1 . . . . **24** B1 **99** A1

Greyfriars 16 SE26 . . **76** C1
Greyfriars Ho SE3 . . **53** B4
Grey Ho W12 . . . . . . **30** A2
Greyhound Ct
WC2 . . . . **121** B4
Greyhound Rd
College Pk NW10 . . . **22** A2
Fulham W6 . . . . **154** A4
Greyladies Gdns
SE10 . . . . **52** B1
Greystoke Ho
SE15 . . . . **49** B4
Greystoke Pl EC4 . . **107** C2
Grey Turner Ho
W12 . . . . **29** C3
Grice Ct N1 . . . . . . **15** B2
Grierson Rd SE23 . . **66** A1
Griffin Ct
3 Brentford
TW8 . . . . **44** A4
Chiswick W4 . . . . . . **38** B1
Shepherd's Bush
W12 . . . . **30** A1
Griffin Gate 11
SW15 . . . . **57** C4
Griffon Ho 3
SW11 . . . . **60** A4
Grigg's Pl SE1 . . . . **138** B1
Grimaldi Ho N1 . . . . **84** C2
Grimsby St
8 Bethnal Green
E2 . . . . **24** C1
Shoreditch
E2 . . . . **24** C1 **99** A2
Grimsel Path SE5 . . . **48** A3
Grimshaw Cl N6 . . . . . **3** C4
Grimston Rd SW6 . . **164** C1
Grimthorpe Ho
EC1 . . . . **96** A2
Grimwade Cl SE15 . . **65** B4
Grindall Ho 20 E1 . . . **25** A1
Grindal St SE1 . . . . **135** B3
Grindley Ho 3 E3 . . . **33** B4
Grinling Gibbons Prim
Sch 22 SE8 . . . . . . **51** B4
Grinling Pl SE8 . . . . **51** C4
Grinstead Rd SE8 . . . **41** A1
Grisedale NW1 . . . . **92** C4
Grittleton Rd W9 . . . **23** C1
Groombridge Rd
E9 . . . . **17** C1
Groom Cres SW18 . . **71** C4
Groome Ho SE11 . . . **149** A3
Groom Pl SW1 . . . . **131** C2
Grosse Way SW15 . . **57** A1
Grosvenor Ave
Canonbury N5 . . . . . **15** B3
Mortlake SW14 . . . . . **56** A4
Richmond TW10 . . . . **54** A2
Grosvenor Bridge
SW1 . . . . **160** B4
Grosvenor Cotts
SW1 . . . . **145** B4
Grosvenor Court Mans
W2 . . . . **102** C1
Grosvenor Cres
SW1 . . . . **131** C3
Grosvenor Cres Mews
SW1 . . . . **131** B3
Grosvenor Ct
Brondesbury Pk
NW6 . . . . **22** C4
Gunnersbury W4 . . . **37** A1
21 Poplar E14 . . . . **33** B3
Putney SW15 . . . . . . **58** A2

Grosvenor Gdns
Cricklewood NW2 . . . . **9** B3
Mortlake SW14 . . . . . **56** A4
Westminster SW1 . . **132** B1
Grosvenor Gdns Mews
E SW1 . . . . **132** B2
Grosvenor Gdns Mews
N SW1 . . . . **132** B1
Grosvenor Gdns Mews
S SW1 . . . . **132** C1
Grosvenor Hill
W1 . . . . **118** A4
Grosvenor Hill Ct
W1 . . . . **118** A4
Grosvenor Ho E5 . . . . **7** C3
Grosvenor Park
SE5 . . . . **48** B3
Grosvenor Pier
SW1 . . . . **161** B4
Grosvenor Pk SE5 . . **48** B4
Grosvenor Pl
SW1 . . . . **132** A3
Grosvenor Rd
Acton Green W4 . . . . **37** B1
Pimlico SW1 . . . . . . **161** A4
Richmond TW10 . . . . **54** A2
Grosvenor Residences
2 W14 . . . . **39** C3
Grosvenor Sq W1 . . **117** C4
Grosvenor St W1 . . **118** A4
Grosvenor Terr
SE5 . . . . **48** B4
Grosvenor The
NW11 . . . . **2** A4
Grosvenor Wharf Rd
E14 . . . . **42** C2
Grote's Bldgs SE3 . . **53** A1
Grote's Pl SE3 . . . . . **53** A1
Groton Rd SW18 . . . **71** A2
Grotto Ct SE1 . . . . **136** C4
Grotto Pas W1 . . . . **103** B4
Grove Crescent Rd
E15 . . . . **19** C2
Grove Ct
Camberwell SE5 . . . . **49** A1
Clapham SW4 . . . . . **61** B4
South Kensington
SW10 . . . . **143** A1
St John's Wood
NW8 . . . . **89** B4
Grovedale Rd N19 . . . **4** C2
Grove Dwellings
E1 . . . . **32** B4
Grove End NW5 . . . . **13** A4
Grove End Gdns
NW8 . . . . **79** A1
Grove End Ho
NW8 . . . . **89** B3
Grove End Rd NW8 . . **89** B3
Grove Gdns NW8 . . . **90** B3
Grove Hall Ct
Bow E3 . . . . **26** C3
St John's Wood
NW8 . . . . **89** A4
Grove Hill Rd SE5 . . . **64** A4
Grove Ho
Blackheath SE3 . . . . **53** B1
Chelsea SW3 . . . . . **158** B4
Grove La SE5 . . . . . **64** A4
Groveland Ct EC4 . . **109** A1
Grovelands Cl SE5 . . **49** A1
Grove Lane Terr
SE5 . . . . **48** C1
Groveley Ho 7 N4 . . . **6** B4
Grove Lo SW4 . . . . . **61** B3

Grove Mans
London SW4 . . . . 60 B3
2 Shepherd's Bush
W6 . . . . 39 B4
3 Stamford Hill N16 . . 7 C2
Grove Mews W6 . . . . 39 B3
GROVE PARK W4 . . . . 45 B2
Grove Park Bridge
W4 . . . . 45 B3
Grove Park Gdns
W4 . . . . 45 B3
Grove Park Mews
W4 . . . . 45 B3
Grove Park Prim Sch
W4 . . . . 45 B3
Grove Park Rd W4 . . 45 B3
Grove Park Terr
W4 . . . . 45 A4
Grove Pk SE5 . . . . . . 49 A1
Grove Pl
Acton W3 . . . . 28 B1
Balham SW12 . . . . 61 A1
Hampstead NW3 . . . . 2 C1
Grover Ct SE13 . . . . . 52 A1
Grove Rd
Acton W3 . . . . 28 B1
Barnes SW13 . . . . 46 B1
Bow E3 . . . . 26 A3
Richmond TW10 . . . . 54 B1
Willesden NW2 . . . . . 9 B2
Grover Ho
4 London SW4 . . . . 61 B2
Vauxhall SE11 . . . . . . 149 A1
Groveside
SW11 . . . . 167 B2
Grove St SE8 . . . . . . 41 B1
Grove Terr NW5 . . . . 4 A1
Grove Terrace Mews
NW5 . . . . 4 A1
Grove The
Dulwich SE21 . . . . . . 76 C3
Hendon NW11 . . . . . 1 A4
Highgate N6 . . . . 3 C3
Stroud Green N4 . . . . 5 B4
Grove Vale SE22 . . . . 64 B3
Groveway SW9 . . . . . 173 A3
Grovewood 9
TW9 . . . . 44 C2
Grovewood Ho
NW2 . . . . 1 B2
Grummant Rd
SE15 . . . . 49 B2
Grundy St E14 . . . . . 34 A3
Guardian Angels RC
Prim Sch 3 E3 . . . . 26 A2
Guards Mus The
SW1 . . . . 133 A3
Gubyon Ave SE24 . . . 63 A2
Gudden Dr E5 . . . . . . 17 A4
Guerin Sq E3 . . . . . . 26 B2
Guernsey Gr SE24 . . . 75 B4
Guernsey Ho 10
N1 . . . . 15 B2
Guernsey Rd 11
N1 . . . . 15 B2
Guildford Gr SE10 . . . 52 A2
Guildford Ho 23
SE5 . . . . 48 B1
Guildford Rd SW8 . . 172 B4
Guildhall Art Gall
EC2 . . . . 109 A2
Guildhall Ho EC2 . . 109 C2
Guildhall Sch Music &
Drama EC2 . . . . 109 A3
Guildhall Yd EC2 . . . 109 A2

Guildhouse St
SW1 . . . . 146 C3
Guilford Pl WC1 . . . . 94 C1
Guilford St WC1 . . . . 94 B1
Guillemot Ct 28
SE8 . . . . 51 B4
Guinness Ct
Chelsea SW3 . . . . . . 144 C3
Finsbury EC1 . . . . . . 97 A3
Primrose Hill NW8 . . 80 B3
Whitechapel E1 . . . . 111 A1
Guinness Sq SE1 . . . 152 A4
Guinness Trust Bldgs
Bermondsey SE1 . . . 138 A4
3 Bethnal Green
E2 . . . . 24 C3
Chelsea SW3 . . . . . . 144 C3
Hammersmith W6 . . 39 B1
Kennington SE11 . . . 150 A2
Guion Rd SW6 . . . . . 165 A2
Gujarat Ho 1 N16 . . 7 A1
Gulland Wlk 21 N1 . 15 B2
Gullane Ho 24 E3 . . . 26 B3
Gulliver St SE16 . . . . 41 B3
Gulston Wlk SW3 . . 145 A3
Gunmakers La E3 . . . 26 A4
GUNNERSBURY 37 A2
Gunnersbury Avenue
(North Circular Rd)
W3 . . . . 36 C3
Gunnersbury Cl 3
W4 . . . . 37 A1
Gunnersbury Cres
W3 . . . . 36 C4
Gunnersbury Ct 8
W3 . . . . 37 A4
Gunnersbury Dr
W5 . . . . 36 B4
Gunnersbury Gdns
W3 . . . . 36 C4
Gunnersbury La
W3 . . . . 36 C4
Gunnersbury Mews 6
W4 . . . . 37 A1
Gunnersbury Park
W3 . . . . 36 C3
Gunnersbury Park
Mus W3 . . . . 36 C3
Gunnersbury Sta
W4 . . . . 37 A1
Gunnersbury Triangle
Nat Res W12 . . . . . . 37 B2
Gunners Rd SW18 . . 71 C2
Gunpowder Sq
EC4 . . . . 107 C2
Gun St E1 . . . . 110 C3
Gunstor Rd N16 . . . . 16 A4
Gunter Gr SW6 . . . . 156 C2
Gunterstone Rd
W14 . . . . 140 B2
Gunthorpe St E1 . . . 111 A2
Gunwhale Cl SE16 . . 32 C1
Gun Wharf
Old Ford E3 . . . . 26 A4
Wapping E1 . . . . 32 B1
Gurdon Ho 7 E14 . . 33 C3
Gurdon Rd SE7 . . . . 43 C1
Gurney Ho
3 Bayswater
W2 . . . . 100 A2
14 Bethnal Green
E2 . . . . 24 C3
Gurney Rd SW6 . . . . 59 B4
Guthrie Ct SE1 . . . . 135 C3
Guthrie St SW3 . . . . 144 A2

Gutter La EC2 . . . . . 108 C2
Guyscliff Rd SE13 . . . 67 B2
Guy's Hospl SE1 . . . 137 C4
Guy St SE1 . . . . 137 C4
Gwalior Rd SW15 . . . 57 C4
Gwendolen Ave
SW15 . . . . 57 C2
Gwendolen Cl
SW15 . . . . 57 C2
Gwendwr Rd W14 . . 140 B2
Gwent Ct 13 SE16 . . 32 C1
Gwilym Maries Ho 9
E2 . . . . 25 A2
Gwyn Cl SW6 . . . . . . 156 C1
Gwynne Cl W4 . . . . . 46 B4
Gwynne Ho
Finsbury WC1 . . . . . 95 B3
5 Streatham SW2 . . 74 B3
Whitechapel E1 . . . . 32 A4
Gwynne Pl WC1 . . . . 95 A3
Gwynne Rd SW11 . . 167 C2
Gye Ho 2 SW4 . . . . . 62 A3
Gylcote Cl SE5 . . . . . 63 C3

H

Haarlem Rd 12
W14 . . . . 39 C3
Haberdasher Pl 4
N1 . . . . 24 A2
Haberdashers' Aske's
Hatcham Coll
SE4 . . . . 51 A1
Haberdasher St
N1 . . . . 97 C4
Hackford Rd SW9 . . 173 A4
Hackford Wlk
SW9 . . . . 173 B3
HACKNEY 17 A2
Hackney Central Sta
E8 . . . . 17 A2
Hackney Com Coll 18
N1 . . . . 24 A2 98 A4
Hackney Downs Sta
E8 . . . . 17 A3
Hackney Empire
E8 . . . . 17 A2
Hackney Free &
Parochial CE Sec
Sch 18 E9 . . . . 17 B2
Hackney Gr E8 . . . . . 17 A2
Hackney Rd E2 . . . . . 24 C3
HACKNEY WICK 18 C2
Hackney Wick E9 . . . 18 B2
Hackney Wick Sta
E9 . . . . 18 C2
Hackworth Point 24
E3 . . . . 27 A2
Hacon Sq 11 E8 . . . . 17 A1
Haddo Ho
Gospel Oak NW5 . . . 13 A4
Greenwich SE10 . . . . 52 A4
Haddon Ct W3 . . . . . 29 B2
Haddo St SE10 . . . . . 52 B4
Haden Ct N4 . . . . 5 C2
Hadfield Ho 37
E1 . . . . 111 C1
Hadleigh Cl 17 E1 . . 25 B1
Hadleigh Ho 18 E1 . . 25 B1
Hadleigh St E2 . . . . . 25 B2
Hadley Ct N16 . . . . . 7 C3
Hadley Gdns W4 . . . . 37 C1
Hadley St NW1 . . . . . 13 A2
Hadlow Ho SE17 . . . 152 B2
Hadrian Cl 5 E3 . . . . 26 C4

Hadrian Ct SE4 . . . . . 66 C4
Hadrian Est 33 E2 . . 24 C3
Hadrian St SE10 . . . . 43 A1
Hadstock Ho NW1 . . 93 C4
Hadyn Park Ct 15
W12 . . . . 38 C4
Hadyn Park Rd
W12 . . . . 38 C4
Hafer Rd SW11 . . . . . 60 B3
HAGGERSTON 24 B3
Haggerston Rd E8 . . 24 B4
Haggerston Sch 18
E2 . . . . 24 B3
Haggerston Sta
E2 . . . . 24 B3
Haggerston Studios
30 E8 . . . . 24 B4
Hague Prim Sch 21
E2 . . . . 25 A1
Hague St 30
E2 . . . . 24 C2 99 C3
Haig Ho 4 E2 . . . . . . 24 C3
Hailsham Ave SW2 . . 74 B2
Hainault Ct SE4 . . . . 65 C3
Hainford Cl SE4 . . . . 65 C3
Hainton Cl 8 E1 . . . . 36 C1
Hainton Cl E1 . . . . . . 32 A3
Halcomb St N1 . . . . . 24 A4
Halcrow St E1 . . . . . . 32 A4
Haldane Pl SW18 . . . 71 A3
Haldane Rd SW6 . . . 155 A3
Haldon Rd SW18 . . . 58 B1
Hale Ho SW1 . . . . . . 147 C2
Hales Ho 3 SW12 . . 73 A4
Hales Prior N1 . . . . . 84 C1
Hales St SE8 . . . . 51 C3
Hale St E14 . . . . 34 A2
Halesworth
SE13 . . . . 67 A4
Half Moon Cres
N1 . . . . 85 A2
Half Moon Ct EC1 . . 108 C3
Half Moon La SE24 . . 63 B1
Half Moon Pas E1 . . 111 A1
Half Moon St W1 . . . 118 B1
Halford Ho 9
SW15 . . . . 57 C2
Halford Rd
Richmond TW10 . . . . 54 A2
West Brompton
SW6 . . . . 155 B3
Haliday Ho N1 . . . . . 15 C2
Haliday Wlk 4 N1 . . 15 C2
Halidon Cl E9 . . . . . . 17 B3
Haliwell Ho 10
NW6 . . . . 78 A3
Halkett Ho 1 E2 . . . . 25 B4
Halkin Arc SW1 . . . . 131 A2
Halkin Mews SW1 . . 131 B2
Halkin Pl SW1 . . . . . 131 B2
Halkin St SW1 . . . . . 131 C3
Hallam Ct W1 . . . . . 104 B4
Hallam Ho
17 London SW9 . . . 173 B4
Pimlico SW1 . . . . . . 147 A1
Hallam Mews W1 . . 104 B4
Hallam Rd SW13 . . . 57 A4
Hallam St W1 . . . . . 104 B4
Halley Gdns SE13 . . 67 C3
Halley Ho
16 Bethnal Green
E2 . . . . 24 C3
8 Cubitt Town
SE10 . . . . 43 B1
Halley Prim Sch
E14 . . . . 33 A4
Halley St E14 . . . . . . 33 A4

Hallfield Jun & Inf
Schs 17 W2 . . . . . . 100 B1
Hall Gate NW8 . . . . . 89 A4
Halliday Ho 40 E1 . . 111 C1
Halliday St N1 . . . . . . 15 C1
Halling Ho SE1 . . . . 137 C3
Hall Oak Wlk NW6 . . 10 B2
Hall Pl W2 . . . . 89 B1
Hall Rd
Leyton E15 . . . . 19 C4
St John's Wood
NW8 . . . . 89 A4
Hall Sch The NW3 . . 11 C3
Hall Sch Wimbledon
SW15 . . . . 68 C1
Hall St EC1 . . . . 96 B4
Hallsville Prim Sch
E16 . . . . 35 C3
Hallsville Rd E16 . . . 35 B3
Hall Twr W2 . . . . . . 101 C4
Halpin Pl SE17 . . . . 151 C3
Halsbury Ho 7 N7 . . 14 B4
Halsbury Rd W12 . . . 30 A1
Halsey St SW3 . . . . . 144 C4
Halsmere Rd SE5 . . . 48 A2
Halstead Ct N1 . . . . . 87 C1
Halston Cl SW11 . . . 60 B1
Halstow 12 NW5 . . . 13 C2
Halstow Prim Sch 5
SE10 . . . . 43 C1
Halstow Rd
Greenwich SE3,
SE10 . . . . 43 C1
Kensal Green
NW10 . . . . 22 C2
Halton Cross St
N1 . . . . 86 B4
Haltone Ho 1
SW4 . . . . 171 C1
Halton Ho 22 N1 . . . 15 A1
Halton Mans N1 . . . . 15 A1
Halton Pl N1 . . . . 86 B4
Halton Rd N1 . . . . . . 86 B4
Halyard Ho E14 . . . . 42 B3
Hambalt Rd SW4 . . . 61 B2
Hambledon SE17 . . . 48 C4
Hambledon Chase
N4 . . . . 5 A4
Hambledon Ho E5 . . 17 A4
Hambledon Pl
SE21 . . . . 76 B3
Hambledon Rd
SW18 . . . . 70 B4
Hamble St SW6 . . . . 59 A4
Hambley Ho 5
SE16 . . . . 40 A2
Hamblyn Ct N16 . . . . 7 B4
Hambridge Way
SW2 . . . . 74 C4
Hambrook Ct 12
NW5 . . . . 13 A4
Hamers Ho 10
SW2 . . . . 74 C4
Hamilton Ct
Rotherhithe SE16 . . . 41 A4
St John's Wood
NW8 . . . . 89 B3
Hamilton Gdns NW8 88 C4

Hamilton Gdns
NW8 . . . . **89** A4
Hamilton Hall
NW8 . . . . **78** C1
Hamilton Ho
22 Bow E3 . . . . **26** B2
Chiswick W4 . . . . **46** A4
Kensington W8 . . . . . **128** A4
1 Poplar E14 . . . . **33** B2
Putney SW15 . . . . **56** C2
10 Richmond TW9 . . . **44** C2
St John's Wood
NW8 . . . . **89** A4
Hamilton La N5 . . . . **15** A4
Hamilton Lo 图 E1 . . **25** B1
Hamilton Mews
W1 . . . . **132** A4
Hamilton Pk N5 . . . . **15** A4
Hamilton Pk W N5 . **15** A4
Hamilton Pl W1 . . . **117** C1
Hamilton Rd
Acton W4 . . . . **38** A4
Hendon NW11 . . . . **1** A4
Willesden NW10 . . . . . **8** C3
Hamilton Sq SE1 . . **137** C4
Hamilton St SE8 . . . **51** C4
Hamilton Terr
NW8 . . . . **89** A4
Hamlet Ct
1 Hammersmith
W6 . . . . **38** C2
Kensington SE11 . . . **150** A2
Hamlet Gdns W6 . . **38** C2
Hamlet Ind Ctr E9 . **18** C1
Hamlet Sq NW2 . . . . **1** A1
Hamlets Way E3 . . . **26** B1
Hamlet The SE5 . . . **63** C4
Hamlet Way E14 . **137** C4
Hammelton Gn 图
SW9 . . . . **48** A2
Hammersmith Ho 图
SE14 . . . . **50** B3
HAMMERSMITH . . . **39** B2
**Hammersmith Bridge
Rd** W6, SW13 . . . . . **39** B1
**Hammersmith
Broadway**
Hammersmith W6 . . . **39** B1
1 Hammersmith
W6 . . . . **39** B2
Hammersmith Flyover
W6 . . . . **39** B1
Hammersmith Gr
W6 . . . . **39** B3
Hammersmith Hospl
W12 . . . . **30** A3
Hammersmith Rd
Hammersmith W6 . . . **39** C2
Kensington W14 . . . **140** B4
Hammersmith Sta
W6 . . . . **39** B2
Hammersmith Terr 图
W6 . . . . **38** C1
Hammett St EC3 . . **124** C4
Hammond Ho
10 Deptford SE14 . . . **50** B3
Millwall E14 . . . . **42** A3
Hammond Lo 图
W9 . . . . **31** C4
Hammond St NW5 . **13** B2
Hampden Sq N1 . . . **24** A3
Hampden Cl NW1 . . **83** C2
**Hampden Gurney CE
Prim Sch** W1 . . . . **102** B2

Hampden Gurney St
W1 . . . . **102** C1
Hampden Rd N19 . . . **4** C2
Hampshire Ct 图
SW13 . . . . **46** B1
Hampshire Hog La
3 Hammersmith
W6 . . . . **39** A1
11 Hammersmith
W6 . . . . **39** A2
Hampshire St
NW5 . . . . **13** C2
Hampson Way
SW8 . . . . **172** C4
HAMPSTEAD **11** B2
**Hampstead Coll of
Fine Arts &
Humanities** 图
NW3 . . . . **11** C2
Hampstead Com Mkt
NW3 . . . . **11** C3
Hampstead Gate
NW3 . . . . **11** B3
Hampstead Gn
NW3 . . . . **12** A3
Hampstead Gr NW3 . **2** B1
Hampstead Heath . . **2** C2
**Hampstead Heath Pre
Prep Sch** NW3 . . . **12** B4
Hampstead Heath Sta
NW3 . . . . **12** A4
Hampstead High Sch
图 NW3 . . . . **11** B3
Hampstead High St
NW3 . . . . **11** C4
Hampstead Hill Gdns
图 NW3 . . . . **12** A3
Hampstead Hill Sch
图 NW3 . . . . **12** B3
Hampstead La N6 . . **3** A4
**Hampstead Parochial
CE Prim Sch** 图
NW3 . . . . **11** B4
Hampstead Rd
NW1 . . . . **92** C4
Hampstead Sch
NW3 . . . . **3** B1
Hampstead Sq 图
NW3 . . . . **2** B1
Hampstead Sta
NW3 . . . . **11** B4
Hampstead Theatre
NW3 . . . . **11** C1
Hampstead West 图
NW6 . . . . **10** C2
Hampstead Wlk 图
E3 . . . . **26** B4
Hampton Ct 图
1 Islington N1 . . . . **15** A2
9 Rotherhithe
SE16 . . . . **32** C1
Hampton St SE1 . . **150** B3
Hamstead Gates 图
NW5 . . . . **12** C2
Ham Yd W1 . . . . . . **119** B4
Hana Mews E5 . . . . **17** A4
Hanbury Ho
1 Bethnal Green
E2 . . . . **111** B4
South Lambeth
SW8 . . . . **162** B3
Hanbury Mews N1 . **87** A3
Hanbury Rd W3 . . . **37** A4
Hanbury St E1 . . . **111** A4

Hancock Nunn Ho 图
NW3 . . . . **12** B1
Hancock Rd E3 . . . . **27** B2
Handa Wlk 图 N1 . . . **15** B2
Hand Ct WC1 . . . . **107** A3
**Handel House
Museum** W1 . . . . **118** B4
Handel Mans
Barnes SW13 . . . . . . **47** B3
Bloomsbury WC1 . . . **94** B2
Handel St WC1 . . . . **94** B2
Handforth Rd
SW9 . . . . **163** B2
Handley Rd E9 . . . . **25** B4
Handley Wlk E15 . . . **23** B2
Hanford Cl SW18 . . . **70** C3
Hankey Pl SE1 . . . . **137** C3
Hanley Ct N4 . . . . . . **5** B3
Hanley Gdns N4 . . . **5** B3
Hanley Rd N4, N19 . . **5** A3
Hanmer Wlk N7 . . . . **5** B2
Hannah Mary Way 图
SE1 . . . . **153** C3
Hannay La N8 . . . . . . **4** C4
Hannay Wlk SW16 . **73** C2
Hannell Rd SW6 . . **154** B2
Hannen Ho SE5 . . . . **63** C4
Hannen Rd SE27 . . . **75** A1
Hannibal Rd E1 . . . . **32** B4
Hannington Rd
SW4 . . . . **61** A4
Hanover Ave E16 . . . **35** C1
Hanover Cl TW9 . . . **44** C3
Hanover Ct
Shepherd's Bush
W12 . . . . **29** C1
Stamford Hill N16 . . . **7** B4
Hanover Gate Mans
NW1 . . . . **90** B2
Hanover Gdns
SE11 . . . . **163** B3
Hanover Ho NW8 . . **80** A1
Hanover Mans 图
SW2 . . . . **62** C2
Hanover Pk SE15 . . **49** C2
Hanover Pl
18 Bow E3 . . . . **26** B2
St Giles WC2 . . . . . . **106** B1
Hanover Prim Sch
N1 . . . . **86** C2
Hanover Rd NW10 . . **22** B4
Hanover Sq W1 . . . **104** B1
Hanover St W1 . . . . **104** B1
Hanover Stps W2 . . **102** B1
Hanover Terr NW1 . **90** C3
**Hanover Terrace
Mews** NW1 . . . . . . **90** B3
Hanover West Ind Est
NW10 . . . . **20** C2
Hanover Yd N1 . . . . **86** C2
Hansard Mews
W14 . . . . **39** C4
Hanscomb Mews
SW4 . . . . **61** B3
Hans Cres SW1 . . . **130** C2
Hansler Ct 图
SW19 . . . . **70** A3
Hansler Rd SE22 . . . **64** B2
Hanson Cl
Balham SW12 . . . . . . **73** A4
Mortlake SW14 . . . . . **55** B4
Hanson Ho 图 E1 . . **125** C4
Hanson St W1 . . . . **104** C4
Hans Pl SW1 . . . . . **130** C2
Hans Rd SW3 . . . . . **130** C2
Hans St SW1 . . . . . **131** A1

Hanway Ho 图
SW9 . . . . **173** C4
Hanway Pl W1 . . . . **105** B2
Hanway St W1 . . . . **105** B2
Hanworth Ho SE5 . . **48** A3
Harben Rd NW6 . . . . **11** B1
Harberson Ho
SW12 . . . . **73** A3
Harberton Rd N19 . . **4** B3
Harbet Rd W2 . . . . **101** C3
Harbinger Prim Sch
图 E14 . . . . **42** A2
Harbinger Rd E14 . . **42** A2
Harbin Ho 图 SW2 . . **74** C3
Harbledown Ho
SE1 . . . . **137** B3
Harbledown Rd
SW6 . . . . **165** B4
Harbord Cl
Camberwell SE15 . . . **49** A3
London SE5 . . . . **48** C1
Harbord Ho 图
SE16 . . . . **40** C2
Harbord St SW6 . . . **47** C2
Harbour Ave
SW10 . . . . **167** A3
Harbour Exchange Sq
E14 . . . . **42** B4
Harbour Rd SE5 . . . **63** B4
Harbridge Ave
SW15 . . . . **68** C4
Harbut Rd SW11 . . . **59** C3
Harcombe Rd N16 . . **7** A1
Harcourt Ho
27 Clapham SW8 . . **171** B2
Marylebone W1 . . . **104** A2
4 Willesden NW10 . . **9** A1
Harcourt Rd SE4 . . . **66** B4
Harcourt St W1 . . . **102** B3
Harcourt Terr
SW10 . . . . **142** B1
Hardcastle Ho
3 New Cross Gate
SE14 . . . . **51** A2
5 Peckham SE15 . . **49** C3
Hardel Rise SW2 . . . **75** A3
Hardel Wlk SW2,
SW2 . . . . **74** C3
Harden Ho SE5 . . . . **49** A1
Harders Rd SE15 . . . **50** A1
Hardess St SE24 . . . **63** B4
Hardham Ho 图
SW2 . . . . **62** C1
Harding Cl SE17 . . . **48** B4
Hardinge Rd
NW10 . . . . **22** B4
Harding Ho SW13 . . **47** A4
Hardington 图
NW1 . . . . **12** C1
Hardwick Ho 图
SW8 . . . . **27** A2
Hardwicke Mews
WC1 . . . . **95** A3
Hardwicke Rd W4 . . **37** C2
Hardwick Ho
14 London SW8 . . . **171** B2
Marylebone NW8 . . . . **90** B2
Hardwick St EC1 . . . **95** C3
Hardwick's Way
SW18 . . . . **58** C2
Hardwidge St SE1 . **138** A4
Hardy Ave E16 . . . . **35** C1
Hardy Cl SE16 . . . . . **40** C4
Hardy Cotts 图
SE10 . . . . **52** C4

Hardy Ct SE3 . . . . . **53** B4
Hardy Rd SE3 . . . . . **53** B4
Hare and Billet Rd
SE3 . . . . **52** C1
Harecourt Rd N1 . . . **15** B2
Hare Ct EC4 . . . . . **107** B1
Haredale Ho 图
SE16 . . . . **139** B3
Haredale Rd SE24 . . **63** B3
Harefield Mews
SE4 . . . . **66** B4
Harefield Rd SE4 . . . **66** B4
Hare Marsh
E2 . . . . **24** C1 **99** B2
Hare Pl EC4 . . . . . . **107** C1
Hare Row E2 . . . . . . **25** A3
Hare Wlk N1 . . . . . . **24** A3
Harewood Ave
NW1 . . . . **90** B1
Harewood Pl W1 . . **104** B1
Harewood Row
NW1 . . . . **102** B3
Harfield Gdns 图
SE5 . . . . **64** A4
Harfleur Ct SE11 . . **150** A3
Harford Ho
Camberwell SE5 . . . . **48** B4
Notting Hill W11 . . . . **31** B4
Harford Mews 图
N19 . . . . **4** C1
Harford St E1 . . . . . **26** A1
Hargrave Mans 图
N19 . . . . **4** C2
**Hargrave Park Prim
Sch** 图 N19 . . . . **4** B2
Hargrave Pl N19 . . . . **4** C2
Hargrave Pl N7 . . . . **13** C3
Hargrave Rd N19 . . . **4** B2
Hargraves Ho 图
W12 . . . . **30** A2
Hargwyne St SW9 . . **62** B4
Harkness Ho 图
E1 . . . . **111** C1
Harlech Twr 图
W3 . . . . **37** B4
Harlescott Rd
SE15 . . . . **65** C3
HARLESDEN **21** B4
Harlesden Gdns
NW10 . . . . **21** B4
Harlesden Plaza 图
NW10 . . . . **21** B3
Harlesden Prim Sch
NW10 . . . . **21** A3
Harlesden Rd
NW10 . . . . **22** A4
Harlesden Sta
NW10 . . . . **20** C3
Harleyford Ct
SW8 . . . . **162** C4
Harleyford Manor 图
W3 . . . . **28** B1
Harleyford Rd
SE11 . . . . **162** C4
Harleyford St
SE11 . . . . **163** B3
Harley Gdns
SW10 . . . . **143** A1
Harley Gr E3 . . . . . . **26** B2
Harley Ho NW1 . . . . **91** C1
Harley Pl W1 . . . . . **104** A3
Harley Rd
Hampstead NW3 . . . . **11** C1
Harlesden NW10 . . . . **21** A3
Harley St W1 . . . . . **104** A3

Harley Villas
NW10 . . . . 21 A3
Harling Ct 3
SW11 . . . . 168 C2
Harlowe Ho 18 SE4 . 24 B4
Harlynwood 19
SE5 . . . . 48 B3
Harman Cl
16 Bermondsey
SE1 . . . . 153 B1
Cricklewood NW2 . . . 1 A1
Harman Dr
Cricklewood NW2 . . . 1 A1
Hampstead NW2 . . . . 10 A4
Harman Ho 7 SE8 . 41 B2
Harmood Gr NW1 . . 13 A1
Harmood Ho 2
NW1 . . . . 13 A1
Harmood St NW1 . . 13 A1
Harmsworth St
SE17 . . . . 150 A1
Harnage Ho TW8 . . 36 A1
Harney Ct SE14 . . . 51 A2
Harold Ct SE16 . . . 40 C4
Harold Est SE1 . . . 138 B1
Harold Ho 16 E2 . . . 25 C3
Harold Laski Ho
EC1 . . . . 96 B3
Harold Maddison Ho
SE17 . . . . 150 B2
Harold Rd NW10 . . 20 C2
Harold Wilson Ho
SW6 . . . . 155 A3
Harp Alley EC4 . . . 108 A2
Harpenden Rd SE27,
SW16 . . . . 75 A2
Harpenmead Point
NW2 . . . . 1 B2
Harper Ho 3 SW9 . 63 A4
Harper Mews
SW17 . . . . 71 B1
Harper Rd SE1 . . . 137 A2
Harp La EC3 . . . . . 124 A3
Harpley Sq E1 . . . . 25 C1
Harpsden St
SW11 . . . . 169 B3
Harpur Mews
WC1 . . . . 106 C4
Harpur St WC1 . . . 106 C4
Harrier Ho 9
SW11 . . . . 60 A4
Harriet Cl E8 . . . . . 24 C4
Harriet Ho SW6 . . 156 B1
Harriet St SW1 . . . 131 A3
Harriet Tubman Cl 3
SW2 . . . . 74 C4
Harriet Wlk SW1 . 131 A3
Harrington Ct
South Kensington
SW7 . . . . 143 C4
8 West Kilburn
W9 . . . . 23 B2
Harrington Gdns
SW7 . . . . 142 C3
Harrington Ho
Regent's Pk NW1 . . . 92 C4
Westminster SW1 . . 147 C2
Harrington Rd
SW7 . . . . 143 B4
Harrington Sq
NW1 . . . . 82 C1
Harrington St NW1 92 C3
Harriott Cl SE10 . . 43 B2
Harriott Ho 11
E1 . . . . 32 B3
Harris Acad at
Peckham SE15 . . . . 49 B2

Harris Acad
Bermondsey
SE1 . . . . 153 A4
Harris Girl's Acad
SE15 . . . . 65 B2
Harris Ho
11 Bow E3 . . . . 26 C2
2 Brixton SW9 . . . . 62 C4
Harrison Ho SE17 . 151 B2
Harrison Rd NW10 . 20 C4
Harrisons Ct 1
SE14 . . . . 50 C4
Harrison St WC1 . . 94 B3
Harris St SE5 . . . . 48 C3
Harrodian Sch The
SW13 . . . . 46 B3
Harrogate Ct 2
SE26 . . . . 76 C1
Harrold Ho 1
NW3 . . . . 11 B1
Harroway Rd
SW11 . . . . 167 C2
Harrowby St W1 . . 102 B2
Harrowgate Ho 22
E9 . . . . 17 C2
Harrowgate Rd E9 . 18 A1
Harrow La E14 . . . . 34 B2
Harrow Pl E1 . . . . 110 B2
Harrow Rd
Little Venice W2 . . 101 A3
Westbourne Green W2,
W9 . . . . 23 C1
Harrow St NW1 . . 102 A4
Harry Gosling Prim
Sch LB E1 . . . . . . 111 C1
Harry Hinkins Ho 6
SE17 . . . . 151 A1
Harry Lambourn Ho
15 SE15 . . . . 50 A3
Hartfield Terr E3 . . 26 C3
Hartham Cl N7 . . . . 14 A3
Hartham Rd N7 . . . 14 A3
Hart Ho SW2 . . . . . 74 C3
Hartington Ct
Chiswick W4 . . . . . 45 A3
South Lambeth
SW8 . . . . 172 A4
Hartington Rd
Chiswick W4 . . . . . 45 B2
South Lambeth
SW8 . . . . 162 A1
Hartismere Rd
SW6 . . . . 155 A2
Hartlake Rd E9 . . . 18 A2
Hartland NW1 . . . . 83 A3
Hartland Rd
Camden Town
NW1 . . . . 13 A1
Kilburn NW6 . . . . . 23 B4
Hartley Ho
Bermondsey SE1 . . 153 A4
Putney SW15 . . . . . 56 C2
Hartley St E2 . . . . . 25 B2
Hartnoll Ho 4 N7 . . 14 C3
Hartnoll St N7 . . . . 14 B3
Harton Lodge 2
SE8 . . . . 51 C2
Harton St SE8 . . . . 51 C2
Hartopp Ct 20 N16 . 7 A1
Hartopp Point
SW6 . . . . 154 B2
Hartshorn Alley
EC3 . . . . 110 B1
Hart's La SE14 . . . . 51 A2
Hart St EC3 . . . . . . 124 B4

Hartswood Ho 16
SW2 . . . . 74 A3
Hartswood Rd
W12 . . . . 38 B3
Hartwell Cl 12
SW2 . . . . 74 B3
Hartwell St E8 . . . 16 B2
Harvard Ct NW6 . . 11 A3
Harvard Hill W4 . . 45 A4
Harvard Ho
3 Camberwell
SE17 . . . . 48 A4
Putney SW15 . . . . . 57 C1
Harvard Mans 11
SW11 . . . . 59 C3
Harvard Rd
14 Acton Green
W4 . . . . 37 B1
Gunnersbury W4 . . 37 A1
7 Lewisham SE13 . . 67 B2
Harvey Ct SW11 . . 168 B4
Harvey Ho
1 Bethnal Green
E2 . . . . 25 A3
Brentford TW8 . . . . 36 A1
Pimlico SW1 . . . . . 147 C1
Shoreditch N1 . . . . 87 C3
Harvey Lo 8 W9 . . . 31 C4
Harvey Point 7
E16 . . . . 35 C4
Harvey Rd 5 SE5 . . 48 C2
Harvey St N1 . . . . . 87 C3
Harvington Wlk
E8 . . . . 16 C1
Harvist Rd NW6 . . 23 A3
Harwood Ct
Putney SW15 . . . . . 57 B3
Shoreditch N1 . . . . 87 C3
Harwood Point
SE16 . . . . 41 B4
Harwood Rd SW6 . 156 A1
Harwood Terr
SW6 . . . . 166 A4
Hascombe Ho 11
SW15 . . . . 69 A3
Hascombe Terr 2
SE5 . . . . 48 C1
Haselrigge Rd
SW4 . . . . 61 C3
Hasker St SW3 . . . 144 B4
Haslam Cl N1 . . . . . 14 C1
Haslam Ho 12 N1 . . 15 B1
Haslam St SE15 . . . 49 B2
Haslemere Ave
SW18 . . . . 71 A2
Haslemere Ct 5
N16 . . . . 7 A3
Haslemere Ind Est
SW18 . . . . 71 A2
Haslemere Rd N8 . . 5 A4
Hassard St E2 . . . . 24 B3
Hassett Rd E9 . . . . 18 A2
Hassop Rd NW2 . . . 9 C4
Hastings Cl 17
SE15 . . . . 49 C3
Hastings Ho 18
W12 . . . . 30 A2
Hastings Hos WC1 . 94 A3
Hastings St WC1 . . 94 A3
Hatcham Mews Bsns
Ctr SE14 . . . . 50 C2
Hatcham Park Mews
SE14 . . . . 50 C2
Hatcham Park Rd
SE14 . . . . 50 C2

Hatcham Rd SE15 . . 50 B4
Hatchard Rd N19 . . . 5 A2
Hatchers Mews
SE1 . . . . 138 B3
Hatcliffe Almshouses
SE10 . . . . 43 A1
Hatcliffe St SE10 . . 43 A1
Hatfield Cl SE14 . . . 50 C3
Hatfield Ct SE3 . . . 53 C3
Hatfield Ho EC1 . . . 96 C1
Hatfield Rd W4 . . . . 37 C4
Hatfields SE1 . . . . 121 C2
Hathaway Ho 3
N1 . . . . 24 A3
Hatherley Ct 6
W2 . . . . 100 A2
Hatherley Gr W2 . . 100 A2
Hatherley Rd TW9 . 44 B2
Hatherley St SW1 . 147 A3
Hathersage Ct N1 . . 15 C3
Hathersley Ho 3
SW2 . . . . 74 C4
Hathorne Cl 7
SE15 . . . . 50 A1
Hathway Ho 3
SE15 . . . . 50 B1
Hathway St 4
SE15 . . . . 50 B1
Hatley Rd N4, N7 . . . 5 B2
Hat & Mitre Ct EC1 96 B1
Hatstone Ct 2
NW3 . . . . 11 B2
Hatteraick St 8
SE16 . . . . 40 B4
Hatton Gdn EC1 . . 107 C4
Hatton Ho 17 E1 . . 125 C4
Hatton Pl EC1 . . . . 107 C4
Hatton Row NW8 . . 89 C1
Hatton St NW8 . . . . 89 C1
Hatton Wall EC1 . . 107 C4
Haunch of Venison Yd
W1 . . . . 104 A1
Hauteville Court Gdns
2 W6 . . . . 38 B3
Havana Rd SW18 . . .
SW19 . . . . 70 C2
Havannah St E14 . . 41 C4
Havelock Cl 13
W12 . . . . 30 A2
Havelock Ct 5
SE15 . . . . 50 A3
Havelock St N1 . . . . 84 B4
Havelock Terr
SW8 . . . . 160 B1
Haven Cl SW19 . . . . 69 C1
Havenpool NW8 . . . 78 B3
Haven St 3 NW1 . . 13 A1
Haven The TW9 . . . 54 C4
Havercourt 3
NW3 . . . . 12 A2
Haverfield Gdns
TW9 . . . . 44 C3
Haverfield Rd E3 . . 26 A2
Haverhill Rd SW12 . 73 B3
Havering 8 NW1 . . 13 A1
Havering Ho N4 . . . 6 B4
Havering St E1 . . . . 32 C3
Haversham Lo NW2 . 9 C3
Haversham Pl N6 . . . 3 B2
Haverstock Hill
NW3 . . . . 12 B2
Haverstock Rd
NW5 . . . . 12 C3
Haverstock Sch 22
NW1 . . . . 12 C2
Haverstock St N1 . . 86 B1

Havil St SE5 . . . . . 49 A2
Havisham Ho 25
SE16 . . . . 139 B3
Hawarden Gr SE24 . 75 B4
Hawberry Lo N7 . . 14 A2
Hawes St N1 . . . . . 15 A1
Hawgood St E3 . . . . 33 C4
Hawke Ho 20 E1 . . . 25 C1
Hawke Pl 26 SE16 . . 40 C4
Hawkesbury Rd
SW15 . . . . 57 A2
Hawkesdown House
Sch W2 . . 31 C1 113 C4
Hawkesworth Ho 6
SW4 . . . . 61 B1
Hawke Twr 4
SE14 . . . . 51 A4
Hawk Ho 7 SW11 . . 60 A4
Hawkins Ho 3
SE8 . . . . 51 C4
Hawkins Rd NW10 . 8 A1
Hawksley Gdns
SE27 . . . . 75 A2
Hawkridge 19
NW5 . . . . 12 C2
Hawkshaw Cl 28
SW2 . . . . 74 A4
Hawkshead NW1 . . 92 C4
Hawkshead Rd
Acton W4 . . . . 38 A4
Willesden NW10 . . . 8 B1
Hawkslade Rd
SE15 . . . . 65 C2
Hawksley Rd N16 . . 7 A1
Hawks Mews 10
SE10 . . . . 52 B3
Hawksmoor Mews
E1 . . . . 32 A2
Hawksmoor Pl 3
E2 . . . . 24 C1 99 B2
Hawksmoor St 5
W6 . . . . 47 C4
Hawkstone Rd
SE16 . . . . 40 B2
Hawkwell Wlk N1 . . 87 A4
Hawley Cres NW1 . 13 A1
Hawley Inf Sch 37
NW1 . . . . 13 A1
Hawley Mews 4
NW1 . . . . 13 A1
Hawley Rd 3
NW1 . . . . 13 A1
Hawley St NW1 . . . 13 A1
Haworth Ho 7
SW2 . . . . 62 C1
Hawstead Rd SE6 . . 67 A1
Hawthorn Ct
Putney SW15 . . . . . 57 A4
Richmond TW9 . . . . 45 A2
Hawthorne Ave E3 . 26 B4
Hawthorne Ho
SW1 . . . . 147 A1
Hawthorn Ho SE14 . 51 B2
Hawthorn Rd NW10 . 8 C1
Hawthorn Wlk
W10 . . . . 23 A1
Hawtrey Rd NW3 . . 12 A1
Haycroft Gdns
NW10 . . . . 22 A4
Haycroft Mans
NW10 . . . . 21 C4
Haycroft Rd SW2 . . 62 A2
Hay Currie St E14 . 34 A3

Hayday Rd E16 . . . . . . .35 C4
Hayden Piper Ho
SW3 . . . . .158 C4
Hayden's Pl W11 . . . .31 B3
Haydon St E, EC3 124 C4
Haydon Way SW11 . . .59 C3
Haydon Wlk E1 . . . . .111 A1
Hayes Ct
26 Camberwell
SE5 . . . . .48 B3
Streatham SW12 . . . .74 A3
Hayes Gr SE15,
SE22 . . . . .64 B3
Hayes Pl NW1 . . . . . . .90 B1
Hayfield Pas E1 . . . . .25 B1
Hayfield Yd **43** E1 . .25 B1
Hay Hill W1 . . . . .118 B3
Hayhurst N1 . . . . .86 B4
Hayles Bldgs
SE11 . . . . .150 B4
Hayles St SE11 . . . . .150 A4
Hayling Cl **20** N16 . .16 A3
Haymans Point
SE11 . . . . .148 C2
Haymarket SW1 . . . .119 B3
Haymerle Ho **6**
SE15 . . . . .49 C3
Haymerle Rd SE15 . .49 C4
Haymerle Sch **15**
SE15 . . . . .49 C4
Hayne Ho
W11 . . . . .31 A1 112 A2
Haynes Ho **5** E9 . . . .17 C2
Hayne St EC1 . . . . . .108 B4
Hay's Galleria SW1 124 A2
Hay's La SE1 . . . . . .124 A2
Hay's Mews W1 . . . .118 A2
Hay St E2 . . . . .24 C4
Hayter Ho W12 . . . . .29 C2
Hayter Rd SW2 . . . . .62 B2
Haythorn Ho
SW11 . . . . .167 C3
Hayton Cl **11** E8 . . . .16 B2
Hayward Ct **14**
SW4 . . . . .172 B2
Hayward Gallery
SE1 . . . . .121 A2
Hayward Gdns
SW15 . . . . .57 B1
Hayward Ho N1 . . . . .85 B2
Haywards Pl EC1 . . . .96 A2
Hayward's Pl EC1 . . .96 A2
Haywood Lo **23**
N7 . . . . .13 C3
Hazelbourne Rd
SW12 . . . . .61 A1
Hazel Cl
Peckham SE15 . . . . . .49 C1
Upper Holloway N19 . .4 C2
Hazel Ct **6** SE16 . . .33 A1
Hazeldon Rd SE4 . . . .66 A2
Hazel Ho
London SE4 . . . . .66 B4
12 Maitland Pk
NW3 . . . . .12 B2
Hazellville Rd N19 . . .4 C3
Hazelmere Ct **10**
SW2 . . . . .74 B3
Hazelmere Rd
NW6 . . . . .23 B4
Hazel Rd NW10 . . . . .22 B2
Hazel Way SE1 . . . . .152 C4
Hazelwood Cl W5 . . .36 A4

Hazelwood Ho **11**
SE8 . . . . .41 A2
Hazelwood Mans
SW6 . . . . .164 C4
Hazlebury Rd
SW6 . . . . .166 B2
Hazledene Rd W4 . . .45 B4
Hazlewell Rd
SW15 . . . . .57 B2
Hazlewood Cres
W10 . . . . .23 A1
Hazlewood Twr
W10 . . . . .23 B1
Hazlitt Mews
W14 . . . . .126 A1
Hazlitt Rd W14 . . . . .126 A1
Headbourne Ho
SE1 . . . . .137 C2
Headcorn Ho NW5 . .12 C2
Headfort Pl SW1 . . .131 C3
Headington Rd
SW18 . . . . .71 B2
Headlam Rd SW4 . . .73 C4
Headlam St E1 . . . . . .25 A1
Heads Mews W11 . . .31 C3
Head St E1 . . . . .32 C3
Heald St SE8, SE14 . .51 C2
Healey St NW1 . . . . . .13 A2
Healy Ho **2** E3 . . . . .26 C1
Heanor Ct **5** E5 . . . .17 C4
Hearne Rd W4 . . . . . .44 C4
Hearn's Bldgs
SE17 . . . . .151 C3
Hearnshaw St **1**
E14 . . . . .33 A3
Hearn St
EC2 . . . . . . .24 A1 98 B1
Hearnville Rd
SW12 . . . . .72 C3
Heart Hospl The
N1 . . . . .103 C3
Heart Radio W1 . . . .30 C2
Heathbrook Prim Sch
10 SW4 . . . . .170 C1
Heath Brow NW3 . . . .2 B1
Heath Cl NW11 . . . . . .2 A4
Heathcote Point **25**
E9 . . . . .17 C2
Heathcote St WC1 . . .94 C3
Heathcroft NW11 . . . .2 A4
Heath Ct
8 Hampstead
NW3 . . . . .11 B2
Stoke Newington
N16 . . . . .6 C3
Heath Dr NW3 . . . . . .11 A4
Heather Cl SW8 . . . . .61 A4
Heather Ct SW4 . . . .172 B3
Heather Ho **11** E14 .34 B3
Heatherley Ct N16 . . .7 C1
Heatherley Sch of
Fine Art SW10 . . . .156 C1
Heather Lo N16 . . . . .7 A3
Heather Wlk W10 . . .23 A1
Heathfield Ave
SW18 . . . . .71 C4
Heathfield Ct
1 Bow E3 . . . . .26 C3
5 Chiswick W4 . . . .37 C1
Wandsworth SW18 . . .71 C4
Heathfield Gdns
Acton Green W4 . . . . .37 B1
Blackheath SE3 . . . . .53 A1
Wandsworth SW18 . . .59 C1
Heathfield Ho SE3 . . .53 A1

Heathfield House Sch
15 W4 . . . . .37 B1
Heathfield Pk NW2 . .9 B2
Heathfield Rd
South Acton W3 . . . . .37 A4
Wandsworth SW18 . . .59 C1
Heathfield Sq
SW18 . . . . .71 C4
Heathfield Terr
W4 . . . . .37 C1
Heathgate Pl NW3 . .12 B4
Heath House Prep Sch
1 SE8 . . . . .53 B1
Heath Hurst Rd
NW3 . . . . .12 A4
Heath La SE3 . . . . . . .52 C1
Heathland Rd N16 . . .7 A3
Heath Mans
5 Hampstead
NW3 . . . . .11 B4
Putney SW15 . . . . . . .57 C1
Heathman's Rd
SW6 . . . . .165 A3
Heath Mead SW19 . .69 C1
Heathmere Prim Sch
SW15 . . . . .68 C3
Heath Park Gdns
NW3 . . . . .2 A1
Heathpool Ct **8**
E1 . . . . .25 A1
Heath Rd SW8 . . . . .170 B1
Heath Rise SW15 . . . .57 C1
Heath Royal SW15 . . .57 C1
Heathshott **3**
TW10 . . . . .54 A1
Heathside NW3 . . . . .11 C4
Heathside Prep Sch
SW15 . . . . .57 C3
Heath St NW3 . . . . . .2 B1
Heathstan Rd W12 . .29 C3
Heath View NW5 . . . .12 C4
Heathview Ct
SW19 . . . . .69 C2
Heathview Gdns
SW15 . . . . .69 B4
Heath Villas NW3 . . .2 C1
Heathville Rd N4 . . . . .6 B4
Heathwall St
SW11 . . . . .60 B4
Heathway SE3 . . . . . .53 C3
Heathway Ct
NW3 . . . . .1 C2
Heathwood Ct
SW12 . . . . .73 B3
Heaton Ho
Chelsea SW10 . . . . .157 A4
6 Peckham SE15 . . .50 A1
Heaton Rd SE15 . . . .50 A1
Heaven Tree Cl
N1 . . . . .15 B3
Heaver Rd **25**
SW11 . . . . .59 C4
Hebden Ct **24** E2 . .24 B4
Hebdon Rd SW17 . . .72 A1
Heber Prim Sch
SE22 . . . . .64 B1
Heber Rd
Cricklewood NW2 . . . .9 C4
East Dulwich SE22 . . .64 B1
Hebron Rd W6 . . . . . .39 A3
Heckfield Pl SW6 . . .155 B1
Heckford Ho E14 . . . .34 A3
Heckford St E1 . . . . . .32 C2
Hector Ct
1 London SW9 . . . .173 B4
Putney SW15 . . . . . . .57 C2

Hector Ho **14** E2 . . .25 A3
Heddington Gr N7 . . .14 B3
Heddon St W1 . . . . .118 C4
Hedger's Gr E9 . . . . . .18 A2
Hedger St SE11 . . . .150 A4
Hedingham Cl **6**
N1 . . . . .15 B1
Hedley Ho E14 . . . . . .42 B3
Hedley Row N5 . . . . . .
E2 . . . . .24 B1 98 C2
Heidegger Cres
SW13 . . . . .47 A3
Heights The NW3 . . . .11 B4
Heiron St SE17 . . . . . .48 A4
Helby Rd SW4 . . . . . .61 C1
Heldar Ct SE1 . . . . . .137 C3
Helena Pl **3** E9 . . . . .25 B4
Helena Rd NW10 . . . .9 A3
Helena Sq **12** SE16 . .33 A2
Helen Gladstone Ho
SE1 . . . . .136 A4
Helen Mackay Ho **10**
E14 . . . . .34 C3
Helen Peele Cotts **16**
SE16 . . . . .40 B3
Helenslea Ave
NW11 . . . . .1 C3
Helen Taylor Ho **6**
SE16 . . . . .153 B4
Heliport Ind Est
SW11 . . . . .167 B1
Helix Ct **17** W11 . . .30 C1
Helix Gdns SW2 . . . . .62 B1
Helix Rd SW2 . . . . . . .62 B1
Helix The SW19 . . . . .69 C2
Hellings St E1 . . . . . .125 C2
Helmet Row EC1 . . . .97 A2
Helmsdale Ho
NW6 . . . . .78 A1
Helmsley Pl E8 . . . . . .17 A1
Helmsley St **7** E8 . . .17 A1
Helperby Rd NW10 . . .8 A1
Helsby Ct NW8 . . . . . .89 B2
Helsinki Sq SE16 . . . .41 A3
Helston NW1 . . . . . . .82 C2
Helston Ho SE11 . . . .149 C2
Hemans Est SW8 . . .161 C1
Hemans St SW8 . . . .161 C1
Hemberton Rd
SW9 . . . . .62 A4
Hemingford Rd N1 . .85 A4
Hemlock Rd W12 . . . .29 B2
Hemming St
E1 . . . . .24 C1 99 C1
Hemmingway Cl
NW5 . . . . .12 C4
Hemp Wlk SE17 . . . .151 C4
Hemstal Rd NW6 . . . .10 C1
Hemsworth Ct N1 . . .24 A3
Hemsworth St N1 . . .24 A3
Hemus Pl SW3 . . . . .144 B1
Henchman St W12 . .29 B3
Henderson Ct
8 Deptford SE14 . .50 C4
Hampstead NW3 . . . .11 C3
Wandsworth SW18 . . .72 A4
Henderson Dr
NW8 . . . . .89 B2
Henderson Rd
SW18 . . . . .72 A4

Hendham Rd
SW17 . . . . .72 B2
Hendre Ho SE1 . . . . .152 B3
Hendre Rd SE1 . . . . .152 B3
Hendrick Ave
SW12 . . . . .72 B4
Heneage La EC3 . . . .110 B1
Heneage Pl EC3 . . . .110 B1
Heneage St E1 . . . . . .111 A4
Henfield Cl N19 . . . . . .4 B3
Henley Cl SE16 . . . . . .40 B4
Henley Ct
Brondesbury NW2 . . . .9 C2
Peckham SE15 . . . . . .64 C4
Henley Dr SE1 . . . . . .153 A4
Henley Ho
E2 . . . . .24 B1 99 A3
Henley Prior N1 . . . . .84 C1
Henley Rd NW10 . . . .22 B4
Henley St SW11 . . . .169 C2
Henniker Mews
SW3 . . . . .157 B4
Henniker Rd E15 . . . . .19 C3
Henning St SW11 . . .168 A3
Henrietta Cl SE8 . . . . .51 C4
Henrietta Ho **11**
W6 . . . . .39 B1
Henrietta Mews
WC1 . . . . .94 B3
Henrietta Pl W1 . . . .104 A2
Henrietta St
Strand WC2 . . . . . . .120 B4
Stratford New Town
E15 . . . . .19 B3
Henriques St E1 . . . .111 C1
Henry Cavendish Prim
Sch **18** SW12 . . . .73 B3
Henry Compton Sch
SW6 . . . . .164 A4
Henry Dent Cl SE5 . .63 C4
Henry Dickens Ct
W11 . . . . .31 A1 112 A2
Henry Fawcett Prim
Sch **15** SE11 . . . .163 B4
Henry Ho
Lambeth SE1 . . . . . .121 C1
South Lambeth
SW8 . . . . .162 A2
8 St John's Wood
NW8 . . . . .89 B4
Henry Jackson Ho **4**
SW15 . . . . .57 C4
Henry Jackson Rd
SW15 . . . . .57 C4
Henry Rd N4 . . . . .6 B3
Henryson Rd SE4 . . . .66 C2
Henry Wise Ho
SW1 . . . . .147 A3
Henshall Point **19**
E3 . . . . .27 A2
Henshall St N1 . . . . . .15 C2
Henshaw St SE17 . . .151 B4
Hensley Point **28**
E9 . . . . .17 C2
Henslowe Rd SE22 . .64 C2
Henslow Ho **20**
SE15 . . . . .49 C3
Henson Ave NW2 . . . .9 B3
Henson Ct **3** N5 . . . .15 B4
Henstridge Pl
NW8 . . . . .80 A3
Henty Cl SW11 . . . . .168 B4
Henty Wlk SW15 . . . .57 A2
Hepburn Mews
SW11 . . . . .60 B2
Hepburn Mews
SW11 . . . . .60 B2

Hepplestone Cl
SW15 . . . . 57 A1
Hepscott Rd E9 . . . . 18 C1
Hepworth Ct
Chelsea SW1 . . . . 146 A1
Islington N1 . . . . . 86 A4
Hera Ct E15 . . . . . 41 C2
Heralds Pl E11 . . . 150 A4
Herald St E2 . . . . . 25 A1
Herbal Hill EC1 . . . . 95 C1
Herbert Chapman Ct
N5 . . . . 15 A4
Herbert Cres SW1 . . 131 A2
Herbert Gdns
Chiswick W4 . . . . . 45 A4
Willesden Green
NW10 . . . . 22 A3
Herbert Ho E1 . . . . 110 C2
Herbert Mews
SW2 . . . . 62 C1
Herbert Morrison Ho
SW6 . . . . 154 C3
Herbert Morrison
Prim Sch SW8 . . . 162 A1
Herbert St NW5 . . . . 12 C2
Herbrand Est WC1 . . 94 A2
Herbrand St WC1 . . . 94 A2
Hercules Ct E14 . . . 34 A2
Hercules Pl N7 . . . . 5 A1
Hercules Rd SE1 . . . 135 A1
Hercules St N7 . . . . 5 A1
Hereford Bldgs
SW3 . . . . 157 C4
Hereford Ho
5 Brixton SW2 . . . 62 C3
26 Camberwell SE5 . . 48 B1
Knightsbridge
SW3 . . . . 130 B2
Walham Green
SW10 . . . . 156 B2
Hereford Mans 10
W2 . . . . 31 C3
Hereford Mews 11
W2 . . . . 31 C3
Hereford Pl SE14 . . . 51 B3
Hereford Rd
Acton W3 . . . . 28 B2
Bayswater
W2 . . . . . . 31 C2 113 C4
Hereford Retreat 5
SE15 . . . . 49 C3
Hereford Sq SW7 . . 143 A3
Hereford St
E2 . . . . 24 C1 99 B2
Hereward House Sch
NW3 . . . . 11 C2
Heritage Cl SW9 . . . 63 A4
Heritage Ct SE8 . . . 40 C1
Heritage Ho 22
SW19 . . . . 1 C1
Hermes Cl 5 W9 . . . 23 C1
Hermes Ct 4
SW9 . . . . 173 B4
Hermes St N1 . . . . 85 B1
Hermitage
1 Child's Hill NW2 . . 1 C1
12 Wapping E1 . . . 125 C1
Hermitage Gdns
NW2 . . . . 1 C1
Hermitage La NW2 . . 1 C1
Hermitage Prim Sch
10 E1 . . . . 125 C2
Hermitage Row 6
E8 . . . . 16 C3
Hermitage St W2 . . 101 B3

Hermitage The
Barnes SW13 . . . . . 46 B2
Richmond TW10 . . . . 54 A2
Hermitage Villas
SW6 . . . . 155 B4
Hermitage Wall
E1 . . . . 125 C1
Hermit Ho 2 NW6 . . 78 A3
Hermit St EC1 . . . . 96 A4
Herndon Rd SW18 . . 59 B2
HERNE HILL 63 B2
Herne Hill SE24 . . . . 63 B2
Herne Hill Ho
SE24 . . . . 63 A1
Herne Hill Mans
SE24 . . . . 63 B1
Herne Hill Rd
SE24 . . . . 63 B2
Herne Hill Sch
SE24 . . . . 63 B3
Herne Hill Sta
SE24 . . . . 63 A1
Herne Hill Velodrome
SE24 . . . . 63 C1
Herne Pl SE24 . . . . 63 A2
Heron Cl NW10 . . . . 8 A2
Heron Ct
10 Cubitt Town
E14 . . . . 42 B3
7 Dulwich SE21 . . . 75 C2
Herondale Ave
SW18 . . . . 72 A3
Heron Dr N4 . . . . . 6 B2
Herongate N1 . . . . 87 A4
Heron Ho
Battersea SW11 . . . 168 B4
Peckham SE15 . . . . 49 B2
St John's Wood
NW8 . . . . 80 A1
Heron Pl
Marylebone W1 . . . 103 C2
Rotherhithe SE16 . . . 33 A1
Heron Quays E14 . . . 33 C1
Heron Quays Sta
E14 . . . . 33 C1
Heron Rd SE24 . . . . 63 B3
Heron Trad Est
W3 . . . . 28 A4
Herrick Ho
18 Camberwell
SE5 . . . . 48 C3
17 Canonbury N16 . . 15 C4
Herrick Rd N5 . . . . 6 B1
Herrick St SW1 . . . 147 C3
Herries St W10 . . . 23 A3
Hersant Cl NW10 . . . 21 C4
Herschell's Mews
SE5 . . . . 63 B4
Hersham Cl SW15 . . 68 C4
Hershell Ct 1
SW14 . . . . 56 A3
Hertford Ave
SW14 . . . . 56 A3
Hertford Ct 10
SW11 . . . . 60 A4
Hertford Lo 10
SW19 . . . . 70 A3
Hertford Pl W1 . . . . 93 A1
Hertford Rd N1 . . . . 24 A4
Hertford St W1 . . . 118 A1
Hertmitage The 5
SE13 . . . . 52 B1
Hertslet Rd N7 . . . . 5 B1
Hertsmere Rd E14 . . 33 C2
Heswall Cl SW4 . . . 171 A1

Hesketh Pl
W11 . . . . . 31 A2 112 A3
Heslop Cl 1
SW12 . . . . 72 C3
Heslop Rd SW12 . . . 72 B3
Hesper Mews
SW5 . . . . 142 A3
Hesperus Cres
E14 . . . . 42 A2
Hessel St E1 . . . . . 32 A3
Hestercombe Ave
SW6 . . . . 164 B3
Hester Rd SW11 . . . 158 A1
Hester Terr TW9 . . . 54 C4
Hestia Ho SE1 . . . . 138 A3
Heston St SE14 . . . . 51 C2
Hetherington Rd SW2,
SW4 . . . . 62 A3
Hethpool Ho W2 . . . 89 B1
Hetley Rd W12 . . . . 39 A4
Hetty Rees Ct 8
N5 . . . . 5 A4
Hevelius Cl SE10 . . . 43 B1
Hever Ho SE15 . . . . 50 C4
Heversham Ho
SE15 . . . . 50 B4
Heward Ct SE13 . . . 52 B1
Hewer Ho 6 SW4 . . 61 B2
Hewer St W10 . . . . 30 C4
Hewett Ho SW15 . . . 47 B1
Hewett St
EC2 . . . . . . 24 A1 98 B1
Hewison St E3 . . . . 26 B3
Hewlett Rd E3 . . . . 26 A3
Hewling Ho 1
N16 . . . . 16 A3
Hexagon The N6 . . . . 3 B3
Hexham Rd SE27 . . . 75 B2
Hexton Ct N4 . . . . . 6 B2
Heybridge 3 NW1 . . 13 A2
Heydon Ho 3
SE14 . . . . 50 B2
Heyford Ave SW8 . . 162 B2
Heyford Terr SW8 . . 162 B2
Heygate St SE17 . . . 151 A4
Heylyn Sq E3 . . . . . 26 B2
Heysham La NW3 . . . 2 A1
Heythorp St SW18 . . 70 B2
Heythrop Coll W8 . . 128 A2
Heywood Ho
10 Deptford SE14 . . 50 C4
2 Tulse Hill SW2 . . 62 C1
Heyworth Rd E5 . . . 17 A4
Hibbert Ho 19 E14 . . 41 C3
Hibbert St SW11 . . . 59 C4
Hichisson Rd SE15, . . 65 B2
Hicken Rd SW2 . . . . 62 B2
Hickes Ho 6 NW6 . . 11 C1
Hickey's Almshouses 7
TW9 . . . . 54 B3
Hickin Cl SE7 . . . . . 43 A2
Hickin St 2 E14 . . . 42 B3
Hickleton NW1 . . . . 83 A3
Hickling Ho 8
SE16 . . . . 40 A3
Hickmore Wlk
SW4 . . . . 61 B4
Hicks Cl SW11 . . . . 60 A4
Hicks St SE8 . . . . . 41 A1
Hide Pl SW1 . . . . . 147 B3
Hide Twr SW1 . . . . 147 B3
Hieover SE21 . . . . . 75 B2
Higgins Ho 7 N1 . . . 24 A4

Higginson Ho 2
NW3 . . . . 12 B1
Higgs Ind Est 9
SE24 . . . . 63 A4
Highbridge Ct 13
SE14 . . . . 50 B3
High Bridge Wharf
SE10 . . . . 42 C1
Highbury Mans 33
N1 . . . . 15 A1
HIGHBURY 15 A4
Highbury Cnr N5 . . . 15 A2
Highbury Corner
N5 . . . . 15 A2
Highbury Cres N5 . . . 14 C2
Highbury Fields Sch
4 N5 . . . . 15 A3
Highbury Gr N5 . . . . 15 A3
Highbury Grange
N5 . . . . 15 B4
Highbury Grove Ct
N5 . . . . 15 A2
Highbury Grove Sch
7 N5 . . . . 15 B3
Highbury Hill N5 . . . 15 A4
Highbury & Islington
Sta N1 . . . . 15 A2
Highbury New Pk
N5 . . . . 15 B4
Highbury Pk N5 . . . . 15 A4
Highbury Pl N5 . . . . 15 A3
Highbury Pool N5 . . . 15 A2
Highbury Quadrant
N5 . . . . 6 B1
Highbury Quadrant
Prim Sch N5 . . . . . 15 B4
Highbury Station Rd
N1 . . . . 14 C2
Highbury Terrace
Mews N5 . . . . 15 A3
Highcliffe Dr
SW15 . . . . 56 B1
Highcroft Rd N19 . . . 5 A4
Highcross Way 4
SW15 . . . . 68 C3
Highdown Rd
SW15 . . . . 57 A1
Highfield Ave NW11 . . 1 A4
Highfield Cl SE13 . . . 67 C1
Highfield Mews
NW6 . . . . 11 A1
Highfield Rd W3 . . . 28 B4
Highfields Gr N6 . . . . 3 B3
HIGHGATE 3 C4
Highgate Archway
N6 . . . . 4 A3
Highgate Ave N6 . . . . 4 A4
Highgate Cemetery
N19 . . . . 4 A3
Highgate Cl N6 . . . . 3 C4
Highgate High St
N6 . . . . 3 C4
Highgate Hill N19 . . . 4 B3
Highgate Ho 6
SE26 . . . . 76 C1
Highgate Pre-Prep &
Jun Sch N6 . . . . . 3 A4
Highgate Rd NW5 . . . 13 A4
Highgate Sch N6 . . . . 3 C4
Highgate Sch N6 . . . . 3 C3
Highgate West Hill
Highgate N6 . . . . . 3 C3
London N6 . . . . . . 3 C2
Highgrove Point 2
NW3 . . . . 11 B4

High Holborn
WC1 . . . . 106 C3
High Holborn Ho
WC1 . . . . 107 A3
Highlands Ave W3 . . 28 B2
Highlands Cl N4 . . . . 5 A4
Highlands Heath
SW15 . . . . 69 B4
Highlever Rd W10 . . . 30 B4
High London 8 N6 . . . 4 C4
Highmore Rd SE3 . . . 53 A3
High Mount 11 N4 . . . 5 A4
High Park Ave
TW9 . . . . 44 C2
High Park Rd TW9 . . . 44 C2
High Par The
SW16 . . . . 74 A1
High Point N6 . . . . . 3 C4
High Rd NW10 . . . . . 8 C2
Highshore Rd
SE15 . . . . 49 B1
Highshore Sch 10
SE15 . . . . 49 B2
High St
Acton W3 . . . . 28 A1
Brentford TW8 . . . . 44 A4
Stratford Marsh
E15 . . . . 27 B4
High Street Harlesden
NW10 . . . . 21 B3
High Street
Kensington Sta
W8 . . . . 128 A3
High The SW16 . . . . 74 A1
High Timber St
EC4 . . . . 122 C4
High Trees SW2 . . . . 74 C3
Hightrees Ho
SW12 . . . . 60 C1
Highview N8 . . . . . . 5 A4
Highview Ct 2
SW19 . . . . 70 A3
High View Prim Sch
8 SW11 . . . . 59 C3
Highway Bsns Pk The
E1 . . . . 32 C2
Highway The E1 . . . . 32 B2
Highway Trad Ctr The
E1 . . . . 32 C2
Highwood Rd N19 . . . 5 A1
Highworth St
NW1 . . . . 102 B4
Hilary Cl SW6 . . . . 156 A2
Hilary Rd W12 . . . . 29 B2
Hilborough Ct 1
E8 . . . . 24 B4
Hilborough Rd 1
E8 . . . . 16 B1
Hilda Terr 2
SW9 . . . . 173 C2
Hilditch Ho 7
TW10 . . . . 54 B1
Hildred Ho 1 SW1 . . 146 A4
Hildreth St 8
SW12 . . . . 73 A3
Hildreth Street Mews
2 SW12 . . . . 73 A3
Hildyard Rd SW6 . . 155 C4
Hiley Rd NW10 . . . . 22 B2
Hilgrove Rd NW6 . . . 11 B1
Hillary Ct 13 W12 . . 39 B4
Hillbeck Cl
Deptford SE15 . . . . 50 B3

Hillbeck Cl continued
Deptford SE15 . . . .**50** B4
Hillbrow 7 TW10 . . . .**54** A1
Hillbury Rd SW17 . . .**73** A1
Hillcourt Rd SE22 . . .**65** A1
Hillcrest
Camberwell SE24 . . . .**63** C3
Highgate N6 . . . .**3** C4
Notting Hill
W11 . . .**31** B2 **112** C3
Hillcrest Ct NW2 . . . .**10** A3
Hillcrest Rd W3 . . . .**28** A1
Hill Ct
Hampstead NW3 . . . . .**12** A4
Putney SW15 . . . .**57** C2
Hilldrop Cres N7 . . . .**13** C3
Hilldrop La N7 . . . . . .**13** C3
Hilldrop Rd N7 . . . . .**13** C3
Hillersdon Ave
SW13 . . . .**46** C1
Hillersdon Ho
SW1 . . . .**146** A2
Hillery Cl SE17 . . . . .**151** C3
Hill Farm Rd W10 . . .**30** C4
Hillfield Ho N5 . . . . .**15** B3
Hillfield Mans
NW3 . . . .**12** A3
Hillfield Rd NW6 . . . .**10** C3
Hillgate Pl
Balham SW12 . . . .**73** A4
Kensington
W8 . . . .**31** C1 **113** B2
Hillgate St
W8 . . . .**31** C1 **113** B2
Hill House
International Jun
Sch SW1 . . . .**131** A1
Hilliard Ho 15 E1 . . .**32** A1
Hilliard's Ct E1 . . . . .**32** B1
Hillier Ho 1 NW1 . . .**13** C1
Hillier Rd SW11 . . . .**60** B1
Hillingdon St SE17 . .**48** A4
Hill Lo SW11 . . . .**59** C3
Hillman Dr 12
NW10 . . . .**22** B1
Hillman St E8 . . . . . .**17** A2
Hillmarton Rd N7 . . .**14** A3
Hillmead Dr SW9 . . . .**63** A3
Hill Mead Prim Sch 8
SW9 . . . .**63** A3
Hillmore Ct SE13 . . . .**67** C4
Hill Rd NW8 . . . .**79** A1
Hillrise Mans N19 . . . .**5** A4
Hillrise Rd N19 . . . . . .**5** A4
Hillsboro Rd SE22 . . .**64** A2
Hillsborough Ct 1
NW6 . . . .**78** A3
Hillside
Greenwich SE10 . . . . .**52** C3
Stonebridge NW10 . . .**20** C4
Hillside Cl NW8 . . . . .**78** B2
Hillside Ct NW3 . . . . .**11** A3
Hillside Gdns SW2 . . .**74** C2
Hillside Rd SW2 . . . . .**74** C2
Hillsleigh Rd
W14 . . . .**31** B1 **113** A1
Hills Pl W1 . . . .**104** C1
Hill St W1 . . . .**118** A2
Hillstone Ct 5 E3 . . .**27** A1
Hilltop Ct
12 London SW18 . . . .**59** C3
South Hampstead
NW8 . . . .**11** B1

Hilltop Ho 7 N6 . . . . .**4** C4
Hilltop Rd NW6 . . . . .**10** C1
Hill View NW1 . . . . . .**81** A4
Hillway N6 . . . .**3** C2
Hill Wood Ho NW1 . . .**83** B1
Hillworth Rd SW2 . . .**74** C4
Hillyard St SW9 . . . .**173** B3
Hillyfield Cl E9 . . . . .**18** A3

Hilsea Point 7
SW15 . . . .**69** A3
Hilsea St E5 . . . .**17** B4
Hilton Docklands Pier
SE16 . . . .**33** B1
Hilton Ho
Lower Holloway
N7 . . . .**14** A4
9 **Nunhead SE4** **65** C3
Hilversum Cres 10
SE22 . . . .**64** A2
Hinckley Rd SE15 . . . .**64** C3
Hind Ct EC4 . . . .**107** C1
Hinde Mews W1 . . . .**103** C2
Hinde St W1 . . . .**103** C2
Hind Gr E14 . . . .**33** C3
Hindhead Point 6
SW15 . . . .**69** A3
Hind Ho
13 Deptford SE14 . . .**50** C4
Islington N7 . . . .**14** C4
Hindle Ho E8 . . . .**16** B3
Hindley Ho N7 . . . .**5** B1
Hindlip Ho SW8 . . . .**171** B3
Hindmans Rd
SE22 . . . .**64** C2
Hindmarsh Cl E1 . . .**125** C4
Hindrey Rd E5 . . . . . .**17** A3
Hinstock NW6 . . . . . .**78** A4
Hinton Rd SE24 . . . . .**63** A4
Hippodrome Mews
W11 . . . .**31** A2 **112** A3
Hippodrome Pl
W11 . . . .**31** A2 **112** B3
Hirst Ct SW1 . . . . . .**146** A1
Hitchin Sq E3 . . . . . .**26** A3
Hithe Gr 18 SE16 . . . .**40** B3
Hitherfield Prim Sch
SW16 . . . .**74** C2
Hitherfield Rd SW16,
SW27 . . . .**74** C1
Hither Green La
SE13 . . . .**67** C1
Hither Green Prim
Sch SE13 . . . .**67** C1
Hitherlands SW12 . . .**73** A2
HM Prison
Wormwood Scrubs
W12 . . . .**29** C3
HMS Belfast SE1 . . .**124** B2
Hoadly Rd SW16 . . . .**73** C2
Hobart Pl SW1 . . . . .**132** A2
Hobbes Wlk SW15 . . .**57** A2
Hobbs' Ct SE1 . . . . .**139** A4
Hobbs' Pl N1 . . . .**24** A4
Hobday St E14 . . . . . .**34** A3
Hobhouse Ct SW1 . .**119** C3
Hobsons Pl 7 E1 . . .**111** B4
Hobury St SW10 . . . .**157** B3
Hocker St 18
E2 . . . .**24** B2 **98** C3
Hockett Cl SE8 . . . . . .**41** B2
Hockley Ho 4 E9 . . . .**17** B2
Hockliffe Ho 8
W10 . . . .**30** B4

Hockney Ct 1
SE16 . . . .**40** A1
Hockworth Ho 7
N16 . . . .**7** A3
Hocroft Ave NW2 . . . .**1** B1
Hocroft Ct NW2 . . . . .**1** B1
Hocroft Rd NW2 . . . . .**1** B1
Hocroft Wlk NW2 . . . .**1** B1
Hodford Lo NW11 . . . .**1** C2
Hodford Rd NW11 . . . .**1** C2
Hodister Cl 26 SE5 . .**48** B3
Hodnet Gr SE16 . . . . .**40** B2
Hoffman Sq N1 . . . . .**97** C4
Hofland Rd W14 . . . .**126** A2
Hogan Mews W2 . . .**101** B4
Hogan Way E5 . . . . . .**7** C2
Hogarth Bsns Pk
W4 . . . .**38** A4
Hogarth Ct
6 Camden Town
NW1 . . . .**13** B1
City of London EC3 . .**124** B4
24 **Whitechapel E1** . .**111** C1
Hogarth Ho NW1 . . .**147** C3
Hogarth Ind Est
NW10 . . . .**21** C1
Hogarth La W4 . . . . . .**46** A4
Hogarth Pl SW5 . . . .**142** A3
Hogarth Rd SW5 . . . .**142** A3
Hogarth Roundabout
W4 . . . .**46** A4
Hogarth's House ★
W4 . . . .**46** A4
Holbeach Mews 1
SW12 . . . .**73** A3
Holbeck Row SE15 . . .**49** C3
Holbein Ho SW1 . . . .**145** B2
Holbein Mews
SW1 . . . .**145** B2
Holbein Pl SW1 . . . .**145** B3
Holberton Gdns
NW10 . . . .**22** A2
HOLBORN **107** C3
Holborn EC1 . . . . . .**107** C3
Holborn Cir EC1 . . . .**107** C3
Holborn Ho 1
W12 . . . .**30** A3
Holborn Pl WC1 . . . .**106** C3
Holborn Sta WC1 . . .**106** C3
Holborn Viaduct
EC1 . . . .**108** A3
Holbrook Cl N19 . . . . .**4** A3
Holbrooke Ct N7 . . . .**14** A4
Holbrook Ho
Acton W3 . . . .**28** C4
3 Streatham SW2 . . .**74** B3
Holcombe Ho
SW9 . . . .**62** A4
Holcombe Pl SE4 . . . .**66** A4
Holcombe St W6 . . . .**39** A2
Holcroft Ct W1 . . . . .**92** C1
Holcroft Ho
Battersea SW11 . . . . .**59** C4
Lewisham SE10 . . . . .**52** B2
Holcroft Rd E9 . . . . . .**17** B1
Holdenby Rd SE4 . . . .**66** A2
Holden Ho
2 Deptford SE8 . . . . .**51** C3
Islington N1 . . . .**86** C3
Holden St SW11 . . . .**169** B1
Holderness Ho 8
SE5 . . . .**64** A4

Holdsworth Ho 6
SW2 . . . .**74** C4
Holford Ho
6 Bermondsey
SE16 . . . .**40** A2
Finsbury WC1 . . . .**95** A4
Holford Pl WC1 . . . . .**95** A4
Holford Rd NW3 . . . . .**2** B1
Holford St WC1 . . . . .**95** B4
Holford Yd WC1 . . . . .**85** B1
Holgate Ave SW11 . . .**59** C4
Holland Gdns
Brentford TW8 . . . . . .**44** A4
Kensington W14 . . . .**126** B2
Holland Gr SW9 . . . .**163** C1
Holland Park
W11 . . . .**31** B1 **112** C1
Holland Park Ave
W11 . . . .**31** A1 **112** B1
Holland Park Ct
W14 . . . .**126** B2
Holland Park Gdns
W14 . . . .**126** A4
Holland Park Mews
W11 . . . .**31** B1 **112** C1
Holland Park Pre Prep
Sch W14 . . . .**126** C1
Holland Park Rd
W14 . . . .**127** A1
Holland Park Rdbt
W12 . . . .**39** C4
Holland Park Sch
W8 . . . .**127** A4
Holland Park Sta
W11 . . . .**31** B1 **112** C1
Holland Pas N1 . . . . . .**86** C4
Holland Pl W8 . . . . . .**128** A4
Holland Rd
West Kensington
W14 . . . .**126** B2
Willesden Green
NW10 . . . .**22** A3
Holland Rise Ho
SW9 . . . .**163** A1
Holland St
Kensington W8 . . . . .**127** C4
Lambeth SE1 . . . .**122** B2
Holland Villas Rd
W14 . . . .**126** A3
Holland Wlk
Kensington W14 . . . .**127** A4
Upper Holloway N19 . . .**4** C3
Hollar Rd N16 . . . .**7** B1
Hollen St W1 . . . .**105** B2
Holles Ho 3 SW9 . . . .**173** B2
Holles St W1 . . . .**104** B2
Holley Rd W3 . . . .**38** A4
Holliday Sq 4
SW11 . . . .**59** C4
Hollies The SW12 . . . .**73** B2
Hollies Way 1
SW12 . . . .**72** C4
Hollingbourne Rd
SE24 . . . .**63** B2
Hollins Ho N7 . . . .**14** A4
Hollisfield WC1 . . . . .**94** B3
Holloway Rd
Lower Holloway
N7 . . . .**14** B4
Upper Holloway N19 . . .**4** C2
Holloway Road Sta
N7 . . . .**14** B3
Holloway Sch N7 . . . .**13** C3
Holly Berry La 8
NW3 . . . .**11** B4

Hollybush Gdns
E2 . . . .**25** A2
Holly Bush Hill 4
NW3 . . . .**11** B4
Hollybush Ho 28
E2 . . . .**25** A2
Holly Bush Steps 7
NW3 . . . .**11** B4
Holly Bush Vale 10
NW3 . . . .**8** A1
Holly Cl NW10 . . . .**8** A1
Hollycroft Ave NW3 . . .**1** C1
Hollydale Prim Sch 7
SE15 . . . .**50** B1
Hollydale Rd SE15 . . .**50** B1
Hollydene
Hither Green
SE13 . . . .**67** C1
3 Peckham SE15 . . . .**50** A2
Holly Gr SE15 . . . .**49** C1
Hollyhedge Ho
SE3 . . . .**52** C1
Holly Hedge Terr
SE3 . . . .**53** C1
Holly Hill NW3 . . . . . .**11** B4
Holly Lo W8 . . . .**127** B4
Holly Lodge SE13 . . . .**67** C1
Holly Lodge Gdns
N6 . . . .**3** C3
Holly Lodge Mans
N6 . . . .**3** C2
Holly Mews SW10 . . .**143** A1
Holly Mount NW3 . . . .**11** B4
Hollymount Cl 9
SE10 . . . .**52** B2
Holly Park Est N4 . . . . .**5** B4
Holly Pk N4 . . . .**5** B4
Holly Rd 13 W4 . . . . . .**37** C2
Holly St E8 . . . .**16** B1
Holly Terr N6 . . . .**3** C3
Hollytree Cl SW19 . . . .**69** C3
Holly Tree Ho SE4 . . . .**66** B4
Holly Village N6 . . . . . .**4** A2
Holly Wlk NW3 . . . . . .**11** B4
Hollywood Lofts
E1 . . . . . .**24** B1 **98** C1
Hollywood Mews
SW10 . . . .**156** C4
Hollywood Rd
SW10 . . . .**156** C4
Holman Ho 2 E2 . . . .**25** C2
Holman Hunt Ho
W14 . . . .**140** A1
Holman Rd SW11 . . .**167** B1
Holmbrook NW1 . . . . .**83** A1
Holmbury Ct SW17 . . .**72** B1
Holmbury Ho SW9 . . .**63** A2
Holmbush Rd
SW15 . . . .**58** A1
Holmcote Gdns
N5 . . . .**15** B3
Holmdale Rd NW6 . . .**10** C3
Holmdene Ave
SE24 . . . .**63** B2
Holmead Rd SW6 . . .**156** B1
Holmefield Ct 4
NW3 . . . .**12** A2
Holmefield Ho
W10 . . . .**23** A1
Holmes Cl SE22 . . . . .**64** C3
Holmes Ct
18 South Acton
W4 . . . .**37** B3

Holmes Ct *continued*
18 South Lambeth
SW4 . . . . **172** A2
Holmesdale Ave
SW14 . . . . 55 A3
Holmesdale Ho **12**
NW6 . . . . 23 C4
Holmesdale Rd
Highgate N6 . . . . . . 4 A4
Richmond TW9 . . . . 44 B2
Holmesley Rd
SE23 . . . . 66 A1
Holmes Pl SW10 . . 157 A4
Holmes Rd NW5 . . . 13 A3
Holmes Terr SE1 . . 135 B4
Holmewood Gdns
SW2 . . . . 74 B4
Holmewood Rd
SW2 . . . . 74 B4
Holmhurst SE13 . . . 67 C1
Holmleigh Prim Sch
N16 . . . . 7 A3
Holmleigh Rd N16 . . 7 A3
Holm Oak Cl SW15 . 58 B1
Holmsbury Ho **6**
N7 . . . . 13 C3
Holmside Rd **24**
E14 . . . . 34 A4
Holmside Ct SW12 . 60 C1
Holmside Rd
SW12 . . . . 60 C1
Holmsley Ho SW15 . 68 B4
Holm Wlk SE3 . . . . 53 C1
Holmwood Ct **3**
N16 . . . . 7 C4
Holocaust Meml Gdn
W2 . . . . 131 A4
Holroyd Rd SW15 . . 57 B2
Holsgrove Ct W3 . . 29 A1
Holst Mans W14 . . . 47 B3
Holsworthy Ho **49**
E3 . . . . 27 A2
Holsworthy Sq
WC1 . . . . 95 A1
Holt Ct SE10 . . . . . 52 B4
Holt Ho SW2 . . . . . 62 C1
Holton St E1 . . . . . 25 C1
Holwood Pl **7**
SW4 . . . . 61 C3
Holybourne Ave
SW15 . . . . 68 C4
Holy Cross Prim Sch
SW6 . . . . 165 B4
Holy Family RC Prim
Sch **28** E14 . . . . 33 C2
Holyhead Cl E3 . . . 26 C2
Holyoake Ct SE16 . 41 B4
Holyoak Rd SE11 . 150 B3
Holyport Rd SW6 . . 47 C3
Holyrood Ho N4 . . . . 6 B3
Holyrood Mews
6 Greenwich
SE7 . . . . 43 C1
10 Newham E16 . . 35 C1
Holyrood St SE1 . . 124 A1
Holy Trinity CE Prim
Sch
Belgravia SW1 . . . 145 B4
Dalston E8 . . . . . . 16 B2
16 Hampstead
NW3 . . . . 11 C3
Richmond TW10 . . . 54 C3
Streatham SW2 . . . 74 B4

Holy Trinity & Saint
Silas CE Prim Sch **22**
NW1 . . . . 13 A1
Holywell Cl
56 Bermondsey
SE16 . . . . 40 A1
2 Greenwich SE3 . 53 C4
Holywell La
EC2 . . . . 24 A1 98 B2
Holywell Row
EC2 . . . . 24 A1 98 A1
Homan Ho **6** SW4 . 73 C4
Homecross Ho **7**
W4 . . . . 37 C2
Homefield Rd W4 . . 38 B1
Homefield St **14**
N1 . . . . 24 A3
Homeleigh Ct **8**
SW16 . . . . 74 A1
Homeleigh Rd
SE15 . . . . 65 C2
Homemead SW12 . . 73 A2
Home Office SW1 . 133 C1
Home Park Rd
SW19 . . . . 70 B1
Home Rd SW11 . . 168 A2
Homer Dr E14 . . . . 41 C2
Homer Rd E9 . . . . . 18 A2
Homer Row W1 . . 102 B3
Homer St W1 . . . . 102 B3
HOMERTON 17 C1
Homerton Gr E9 . . . 17 C3
Homerton High St
E9 . . . . 17 C3
Homerton Rd E9 . . 18 B3
Homerton Row E9 . 17 B3
Homerton Terr E9 . 17 B2
Homerton University
Hospl E9 . . . . 17 C3
Homestall Rd SE22 . 65 B2
Homestead Rd
SW6 . . . . 155 A1
Homewoods **2**
SW12 . . . . 73 B4
Homildon Ho **10**
SE26 . . . . 76 C1
Honduras St EC1 . . 96 C2
Honeybourne Rd
NW6 . . . . 11 A3
Honeybrook Rd SW12,
SW4 . . . . 73 B4
Honeyfield N4 . . . . . 5 C2
Honey La EC2 . . . 109 A1
Honey Lane Ho
SW10 . . . . 156 B4
Honeyman Cl NW6 . . 9 C1
Honeywell Jun & Inf
Schs SW11 . . . . . 60 B1
Honeywell Rd
SW11 . . . . 60 B1
Honeywood Ho **5**
SE15 . . . . 49 C2
Honeywood Rd
NW10 . . . . 21 B3
Honiton Gdns **1**
SE15 . . . . 50 B1
Honiton Ho **28** SE5 . 48 B1
Honiton Rd NW6 . . 23 B3
HONOR OAK 65 B2
Honor Oak Park Sta
SE23 . . . . 65 C1
Honor Oak Rise
SE23 . . . . 65 B1

Honwell Ho **24** W2 . 31 C4
Hood Ave SW14 . . . 55 B2
Hood Ct **7** 107 B1
Hood Ho **5** SE5 . . 48 C3
Hook Ho SE10 . . . . 52 B2
Hooke Ho SE12 . . . 26 A1
Hookham Ct SW8 . 171 B4
Hooks Cl SE15 . . . . 50 A2
Hooper Ho **9**
SW18 . . . . 58 B2
Hooper Rd E16 . . . 35 C3
Hooper's Ct SW1 . 130 C3
Hooper's Mews **2**
W3 . . . . 28 B1
Hooper St E1 . . . . 111 B1
Hoop La NW11 . . . . 1 C4
Hope Cl
2 Brentford
TW8 . . . . 36 A1
Canonbury N1 . . . . 15 B2
Hopefield Ave
NW6 . . . . 23 A3
Hope Gdns **4** W3 . 37 A4
Hope St SW11 . . . . 59 C4
Hopetown St E1 . . 111 A3
Hopewell St SE5 . . 48 C3
Hop Gdns WC2 . . . 120 A3
Hopgood St **5**
W12 . . . . 30 B1
Hopkins Ho **7**
E14 . . . . 33 C3
Hopkinson Ho **1**
SW11 . . . . 169 B2
Hopkinson's Pl
NW1 . . . . 81 B4
Hopkins St W1 . . . 105 B1
Hopping La N1 . . . . 15 A2
Hop St SE10 . . . . . 43 B2
Hopton Ho **5**
SW9 . . . . 48 A1
Hopton's Gdns
SE1 . . . . 122 B2
Hopton St SE1 . . . 122 B2
Hopwood Cl SW17 . 71 B1
Hopwood Rd SE17 . 48 C4
Hopwood Wlk E8 . . 16 C1
Horatio Ho **13** E2 . 24 B3
Horatio Pl **1** E14 . 34 B1
Horatio St **1** E2 . . 24 B3
Horbury Cres
W11 . . . . . . 31 C2 113 B3
Horbury Mews
W11 . . . . . . 31 B2 113 A3
Horder Rd SW6 . . 164 B3
Hordle Prom E **1**
SE15 . . . . 49 B3
Hordle Prom N **4**
SE15 . . . . 49 B3
Hordle Prom S **7**
SE15 . . . . 49 B3
Horizon Bldg **22**
E14 . . . . 33 C2
Horizon Ind Est
SE15 . . . . 49 B3
Horizon Sch N16 . . 16 A4
Horle Wlk SE5 . . . . 48 A1
Hormead Rd W9 . . 23 B1
Hornbeam Cl
SE11 . . . . 149 B4
Hornbeam Ho **2**
NW3 . . . . 12 B2
Hornbeam Sq **8**
E3 . . . . 26 B4
Hornblower Cl **2**
SE16 . . . . 40 C2
Hornby Cl NW3 . . . 11 C1

Hornby Ho **6**
SE11 . . . . 163 C4
Horndean Cl **3**
SW15 . . . . 68 C3
Horner Hos **10** N1 . 24 A4
Horner Hos SW15 . 47 B1
Horn La
Acton W3 . . . . 28 B3
Greenwich SE10 . . . 43 C2
Horn Link Way
SE10 . . . . 43 C2
Hornsby Ho SW2 . . 72 C3
Hornsey La N6 . . . . 4 B4
Hornsey Lane Gdns
N6 . . . . 4 B4
Hornsey Rd N7,N19 . 5 B2
Hornsey Rise Gdns
N19 . . . . 5 A4
Hornsey St N7 . . . . 14 B3
Hornshay St SE15 . 50 B4
Hornton Ct W8 . . . 127 C3
Hornton Pl W8 . . . 127 C3
Hornton St W8 . . . 127 C3
Horrocks Ho
SW15 . . . . 68 C4
Horse & Dolphin Yd
W1 . . . . 119 C4
Horseferry Pl SE10 . 52 B4
Horseferry Rd
Limehouse E14 . . . . 33 A2
Westminster SW1 . 147 C4
Horseferry Rd Est
SW1 . . . . 133 B1
Horse Guards Ave
SW1 . . . . 120 A1
Horse Guards Par
SW1 . . . . 119 C1
Horse Guards Rd
SW1 . . . . 133 C4
Horsell Rd N5 . . . . 14 C3
Horselydown La
SE1 . . . . 124 C1
Horselydown Mans
SE1 . . . . 138 C4
Horsemongers Mews
SE1 . . . . 137 A3
Horsendon Ho **3**
N7 . . . . 13 C3
Horseshoe Cl E14 . 42 B1
Horse Yd N1 . . . . . 86 B4
Horsfield Ho **3**
N1 . . . . 15 B1
Horsford Rd SW2 . . 62 B2
Horsley Ct SW1 . . 147 C3
Horsley Ho **11** SE4 . 65 C3
Horsley St **3** SE17 . 48 C4
Horsman St SE5 . . 48 B4
Horsmonden Rd
SE4 . . . . 66 B1
Horston Ho N4 . . . . 6 B4
Hortensia Ho
SW10 . . . . 156 C2
Hortensia Rd
SW10 . . . . 156 C2
Horticultural Pl **6**
W4 . . . . 37 C1
Horton Ave NW2 . . 10 A4
Horton Ho
13 Deptford SE15 . 50 B4
South Lambeth
SW8 . . . . 162 C2
West Kensington
W14 . . . . 140 A1
Horton Rd E8 . . . . 17 A2

Horton St SE13 . . . 67 A4
Horwood Ho
24 Bethnal Green
E2 . . . . 25 A2
Marylebone NW8 . . 90 B2
Hosack Rd SW12,
SW17 . . . . 72 C2
Hosier La EC1 . . . 108 B3
Hoskins St SE10 . . 42 C1
Hospl for Tropical
Diseases NW1 . . . 93 A1
Hospl of St John & St
Elizabeth NW8 . . . 79 B1
Hotham Prim Sch
SW15 . . . . 57 C3
Hotham Rd SW15 . . 57 B4
Hothfield Pl SE16 . 40 B3
Hotspur St SE11 . . 149 B2
Houblon Rd TW10 . 54 A2
Houghton Cl **17**
E8 . . . . 16 B2
Houghton Sq SW9 . 62 A4
Houghton St WC2 . 107 A1
Houndsditch EC3 . 110 B2
Household Cavalry
Mus SW1 . . . . . . 120 A1
Houseman Way **2**
SE5 . . . . 48 C3
House Mill The E3 . 27 B2
Houses of Parliament
SW1 . . . . 134 B2
Hoveden Rd NW2 . . 10 A3
Howard Bldg
SW8 . . . . 160 A3
Howard Cl
Acton W3 . . . . 28 A3
Cricklewood NW2 . . 10 A4
Howard Ct
Lewisham SE10 . . . 52 B2
Peckham SE15 . . . . 64 C4
Howard Ho
6 Brixton SW9 . . 62 C4
14 Deptford SE8 . . 51 B4
Fitzrovia W1 . . . . . 92 B1
Howard Mews N5 . . 15 A4
Howard Rd
Canonbury N1 . . . . 15 C4
Cricklewood NW2 . . . 9 C4
Howard's La SW15 . 57 B3
Howbury Rd SE15 . 65 B4
Howcroft Ho **3**
E3 . . . . 26 B2
Howden St SE15 . . 64 C4
Howell Ho **9** N7 . . 13 C3
Howell Wlk SE1 . . 150 B3
Howgate Rd SW14 . 55 C4
Howick Pl SW1 . . . 133 A1
Howie St SW11 . . . 158 A1
Howitt Cl
6 Maitland Pk
NW3 . . . . 12 A2
Stoke Newington
N16 . . . . 16 A4
Howitt Rd NW3 . . . 12 A2
Howland Ho **6**
SW16 . . . . 74 A1
Howland Mews E
W1 . . . . 105 A4
Howland St W1 . . 105 A4
Howland Way
SE16 . . . . 41 A4
Howletts Rd SE24 . 63 B1
Howley Pl W2 . . . 101 A4

Howsman Rd
SW13 . . . . 46 C4
Howson Rd SE4 . . . . 66 A3
Hoxton Terr
TW10 . . . . 54 A1
How's St E2 . . . . . . 24 B3
HOXTON 24 A3
Hoxton Mkt 10
N1 . . . . 24 A2 **98** A3
Hoxton Point
EC1 . . . . 24 A2 **98** A3
Hoxton Sq
N1 . . . . 24 A2 **98** A3
Hoxton St N1 . . . . . 24 A3
Hoxton Sta E2 . . . . 24 B3
Hoylake Rd W3 . . . 29 A3
Hoyland Cl 4
SE15 . . . . 50 A3
Hoy St E16 . . . . . . 35 B3
Hub Buildings The 4
SW12 . . . . 73 A3
Hub E15 E15 . . . . . 27 A3
Huberd Ho SE1 . . . 137 C2
Hubert Gr SW9 . . . 62 A4
Hubert Ho NW8 . . . 90 A1
Hub The NW1 . . . . 81 A1
Hucknall Ct NW8 . . 89 B2
Huddart St E3 . . . . 33 B4
Huddleston Cl E2 . . 25 B3
Huddlestone Rd
NW2 . . . . 9 A2
Huddleston Rd N7 . . 13 A4
Hudson Cl 15 W12 . . 30 A2
Hudson Ct 1 E14 . . 41 C1
Hudson Ho
Chelsea SW10 . . . 156 C2
5 Notting Hill W11 . . 31 A3
Hudsons Ho N1 . . . 97 C3
Hudson's Pl SW1 . . 146 C4
Huggin Ct EC4 . . . 123 A4
Huggin Hill EC4 . . 123 A4
Huggins Ho 9 E3 . . 26 C2
Huggins Pl SW2 . . 74 B3
Hughan Rd E15 . . . 19 C3
Hugh Astor Ct
SE1 . . . . 136 B2
Hugh Dalton Ave
SW6 . . . . 154 C3
Hughenden Ho
NW8 . . . . 90 A2
Hughenden Terr
E15 . . . . 19 B4
Hughes Ho
20 Bethnal Green
E2 . . . . 25 B2
Camberwell SE5 . . . 48 B2
15 Deptford SE8 . . . 51 C4
Newington SE17 . . . 150 B3
Hughes Mans
E2 . . . . 24 C1 **99** C1
Hughes Terr 6
E16 . . . . 35 B4
Hugh Gaitskell Cl
SW6 . . . . 154 C3
Hugh Gaitskell Ho
Stoke Newington
N16 . . . . 7 B2
Willesden NW10 . . . 8 B1
Hugh Mews SW1 . . 146 B3
Hugh Morgan Ho 6
SW4 . . . . 61 C4
Hugh Myddelton Prim
Sch EC1 . . . . 95 C3

Hugh Platt Ho 20
E2 . . . . 25 A3
Hugh St SW1 . . . . 146 B3
Hugo Ho SW1 . . . 131 A2
Hugon Rd SW6 . . . 59 A4
Hugo Rd N19 . . . . 13 B4
Huguenot Ct 7
E1 . . . . 111 B4
Huguenot Pl
London SW18 . . . . 59 B2
Spitalfields E1 . . . . 111 A4
Huguenot Sq SE15 . . 65 A4
Hullbridge Mews
N1 . . . . 87 B4
Hull Cl SE16 . . . . . 32 C1
Hull Ct SE5 . . . . . . 48 C1
Hull St EC1 . . . . . . 96 C3
Hulme Pl SE1 . . . . 137 A3
Humber Dr W10 . . . 22 C1
Humber Rd SE3 . . . 53 B4
Humberton Cl E9 . . 18 A3
Humbolt Rd W6 . . . 154 A3
Hume Ct N1 . . . . . . 15 A1
Hume Ho 14 W11 . . 30 C1
Humphrey Ct
SW11 . . . . 167 C3
Humphrey St SE1 . . 152 C2
Humphry Ho 10
SW15 . . . . 57 C2
Hungerford Bridge
SW1 . . . . 161 A4
Hungerford Ho
SW1 . . . . 161 A4
Hungerford La
WC2 . . . . 120 B2
Hungerford Prim Sch
N7 . . . . 13 C2
Hungerford Rd
12 Camden Town
N7 . . . . 13 C2
Lower Holloway N7 . . 14 A3
Hungerford St 2
E1 . . . . 32 A3
Hunsdon Rd SE14 . . 50 C3
Hunslett St 12 E2 . . 25 B3
Hunstanton Ho
NW1 . . . . 102 B4
Hunt Cl W11 . . . . . 30 C1
Hunter Cl
Borough The SE1 . . 137 C1
Upper Tooting
SW12 . . . . 72 C3
Huntercombe-
Roehampton Hospl
The SW15 . . . . . . 68 C4
Hunter Ct
8 London SE5 . . . 63 C3
27 Streatham SW2 . . 74 C4
Hunter Ho
Bloomsbury WC1 . . 94 B2
Lambeth SE1 . . . . 136 B3
South Lambeth
SW8 . . . . 161 C1
1 Tufnell Pk N19 . . . 4 B1
West Brompton
SW5 . . . . 141 C1
Hunterian Mus
WC2 . . . . 107 A2
Hunter Lo 9 W9 . . . 31 C4
Hunter St WC1 . . . . 94 B2
Huntingdon Ct
SW14 . . . . 55 B4
Huntingdon Gdns
W4 . . . . 45 B3
Huntingdon Ho
SW5 . . . . 141 C4

Huntingdon St
Canning Town
E16 . . . . 35 B3
Islington N1 . . . . . 14 B1
Huntingfield Rd
SW15 . . . . 56 C2
Huntingford Ho
SW15 . . . . 47 B1
Huntington Ho NW2 . 9 B2
Huntley St WC1 . . . 93 B1
Hunton St E1 . . . . 111 B4
Hunts Cl SE3 . . . . . 53 C1
Hunt's Ct WC2 . . . 119 C3
Huntshaw Ho 37
E3 . . . . 27 A2
Hunt's La E15 . . . . 27 B3
Huntsman St
SE17 . . . . 152 A3
Huntspill St SW17 . . 71 B1
Hunts Slip Rd
SE21 . . . . 76 A2
Huntsworth Mews
NW1 . . . . 90 C1
Hurdwick Ho NW1 . . 82 C2
Hurdwick Pl NW1 . . 82 C2
Hurleston Ho 11
SE8 . . . . 41 B1
Hurley Cres SE16 . . 40 C4
Hurley Ho
Lambeth SE11 . . . 149 C3
34 Shoreditch
E2 . . . . 24 B2 **98** C3
Hurley Lo SE22 . . . 65 B1
Hurlingham Bsns Pk
SW6 . . . . 58 C4
Hurlingham & Chelsea
Sch SW6 . . . . 58 C4
Hurlingham Court
Mans SW6 . . . . . 165 B1
Hurlingham Ct
SW6 . . . . 58 B4
Hurlingham Gdns
SW6 . . . . 58 B4
Hurlingham Rd
SW6 . . . . 165 A1
Hurlingham Sch
SW15 . . . . 58 B3
Hurlingham Sq
SW6 . . . . 59 A4
Hurlock Ho 1 N5 . . . 6 A1
Hurlock St N5 . . . . . 6 A1
Huron Rd SW17 . . . 72 C1
Huron Univ WC1 . . 106 A4
Hurstbourne Ho
SW15 . . . . 56 B1
Hurstdene Gdns
N15 . . . . 7 A4
Hurst Ho N1 . . . . . . 85 A1
Hurst St SE24 . . . . 63 A1
Hurstway Wlk 2
W11 . . . . 30 C2
Husbourne Ho 8
SE8 . . . . 41 A2
Huson Cl NW3 . . . . 12 A1
Hutching's St E14 . . 41 C4
Hutching's Wharf 1
E14 . . . . 41 C4
Hutchins Cl E15 . . . 19 B1
Hutchins Ho 5
SW4 . . . . 73 C4
Hutchinson Ho 9
SE14 . . . . 50 B3
Hutton Ct 4 N4 . . . . 5 B3
Hutton Ho 19
E2 . . . . 24 C2 **99** B3
Hutton St EC4 . . . 107 C1

Huxbear St SE4 . . . 66 B2
Huxley Ho
4 London SW9 . . 172 C2
Paddington NW8 . . . 89 C1
Huxley St W10 . . . . 23 A2
Hyacinth Rd SW15 . . 68 C3
Hyde Farm Mews
SW12 . . . . 73 C3
Hyde La SW11 . . . 168 A4
Hyde Park W2 . . . 116 C1
Hyde Park Cnr
SW1 . . . . 131 C4
Hyde Park Corner Sta
SW1 . . . . 131 C4
Hyde Park Cres
W2 . . . . 102 A1
Hyde Park Gate Mews
SW7 . . . . 129 A3
Hyde Park Gdns
W2 . . . . 115 C4
Hyde Park Gdns Mews
W2 . . . . 116 A4
Hyde Park Mans
NW1 . . . . 102 A3
Hyde Park Pl W2 . . 116 B4
Hyde Park Rd W2 . . 102 A1
Hyde Park Square
Mews W2 . . . . . . 102 A1
Hyde Park St W2 . . 102 A1
Hyde Park Twrs
W2 . . . . 114 C3
Hyde Rd
Richmond TW10 . . . 54 B2
Shoreditch N1 . . . . 24 A4
Hyde's Pl 12 N1 . . . 15 A1
Hyde St SE8 . . . . . 51 C4
Hyde Vale SE10 . . . 52 B3
Hylda Ct NW5 . . . . . 3 C1
Hyndman Ho 4
N19 . . . . 13 C4
Hyndman St SE15 . . 50 A4
Hyperion Ho
28 Bow E3 . . . . . 26 B3
Streatham SW2 . . . 74 B4
Hyson Rd SE16 . . . 40 A1
Hythe Ho 16 SE16 . . 40 B4
Hythe Rd NW10 . . . 21 C1
Hythe Road Ind Est
NW10 . . . . 21 C1

Ice Wharf NW1 . . . . 84 B2
Idaho Bldg 7
SE13 . . . . 52 A2
Ida St E14 . . . . 34 B3
Identity & Passport
Office SW1 . . . . . 146 B4
Idmiston Rd SE21,
SE27 . . . . 75 B2
Idol La EC3 . . . . . . 124 A3
Idonia St SE8 . . . . . 51 C3
Iffley Ho 47
E2 . . . . 24 B2 **98** C3
Iffley Rd W6 . . . . . 39 A3
Ifield Ho SE17 . . . . 152 B2
Ifield Rd SW10 . . . 156 B4
Ifor Evans Pl E1 . . . 25 C1
Ightham Ho SE17 . . 152 A3
Ikon Ho 21 E1 . . . . . 32 B2
Ilbert St W10 . . . . . 23 A2
Ilchester Gdns
W2 . . . . 114 A4
Ilchester Mans
W8 . . . . 127 C2
Ilchester Pl W14 . . 127 A2
Ildersly Ge SE21 . . . 75 C2
Ilderton Prim Sch
SE16 . . . . 40 B1
Ilderton Rd SE15,
SE16 . . . . 50 B4
Ilex Rd NW10 . . . . . 8 B2
Ilford Ho 14 N1 . . . 15 C2
Ilfracombe Flats
SE1 . . . . 137 A4
Iliffe St SE17 . . . . 150 B2
Iliffe Yd SE17 . . . . 150 B2
Ilkeston Ct 7 E5 . . . 17 C4
Ilminster Gdns
SW11 . . . . 60 A3
Ilsley Ct 8 SW8 . . 170 C1
Imber St N1 . . . . . . 87 B3
Imperial Ave 5
N16 . . . . 16 A4
Imperial Cl NW2 . . . 9 A3
Imperial College
London (Charing
Cross) W6 . . . . . . 39 C1
Imperial College
London (Chelsea &
Westminster)
SW10 . . . . 157 A3
Imperial College
London
(Hammersmith)
W12 . . . . 30 A3
Imperial College
London (Royal
Brompton) SW3 . . 144 A2
Imperial College
London (South
Kensington)
SW7 . . . . 129 B2
Imperial College
London (St Mary's)
W2 . . . . 101 C2
Imperial College Rd
SW7 . . . . 129 B2
Imperial Cres
SW6 . . . . 167 A1
Imperial Ct NW8 . . . 80 B2
Imperial Ho
1 Bow E3 . . . . . . 26 A2
2 Poplar E14 . . . . 33 B2
Strand WC2 . . . . . 106 C1
Imperial Rd SW6 . . 166 B4
Imperial Sq SW6 . . 166 B4
Imperial St E3 . . . . 27 B2

Imperial Twrs **3**
NW3 .... 11 B2
Imperial War Mus SE1,
SE11 .... 135 C1
Imperial Wharf Sta
SW10 .... 167 A3
Imre Ct W12 .... 30 A1
Inchbald Sch of
Design (Garden
Design) SW1 ...... 146 B3
Inchbald Sch of
Design (Interior
Design) SW1 ...... 145 B4
Independent PI E8 .16 B3
Indescon Ct E14 .... 42 A4
Indiana Bldg 1
SE8 .... 51 C2
India St E1 .... 110 C1
India Way W12 ...... 30 A2
Indigo Mews N16.....6 C1
Indus Ct 10 SE15...49 B3
Ingate PI SW8 ...... 170 B3
Ingelow Ho W8 ... 128 A4
Ingersoll Rd W12...30 A1
Ingestre PI W1 ... 105 A1
Ingestre Rd NW5 ...13 A4
Ingham Rd NW6 ......10 C4
Inglebert St EC1....95 B4
Ingleborough St
SW9 .... 173 B2
Ingleby Rd N7.........5 A1
Inglefield Sq 12
E1 .... 32 A1
Ingle Ho 5 SW2 ...73 C3
Inglesham Wlk E9 ..18 B2
Ingleside Gr SE3 ...53 B4
Inglethorpe Ho 6
E5 .... 7 C2
Inglethorpe St
SW6 .... 47 C2
Ingleton St SW9 ...173 B2
Inglewood Cl E14 ..41 C2
Inglewood Mans 11
NW6 .... 10 C3
Inglewood Rd
NW6 .... 10 C3
Inglis Ho 1 SW15...57 B2
Inglis St SE5 .... 48 A2
Ingram Ave NW11 ....2 B4
Ingram CI SE11 ... 149 A4
Ingram Ho 2 E3 .....26 A4
Ingram Lo 5 SW4...61 C1
Ingrave St SW11 ...60 A4
Ingrebourne Ho
NW8 .... 101 C4
Ingress 4 SW4 .....38 A1
Inigo PI WC2 ...... 120 A4
Inkerman Rd NW5..13 A2
Inkerman Terr
W8 .... 127 C1
Inkster Ho 8
SW11 .... 60 A4
Inman Rd
Harlesden NW10 ...21 A4
Wandsworth SW18 ..71 B4
Inner Circ NW1 .... 91 B4
Inner Park Rd
SW19 .... 69 C2
Inner Temple EC4 121 B4
Inner Temple La
EC4 .... 107 B1
Innes Gdns SW15 ...57 A2
Innisfree Ho NW2 ....9 C2
Innis Ho SE17 ...... 152 A2
Insley Ho 13 E14 ...27 A2

Institute of Cancer
Research The
SW7 .... 143 A2
Institute PI 11 E8...17 A3
Inst of Child Health
WC1 .... 94 C1
Inst of Neurology
Bloomsbury WC1 ... 106 B4
St Pancras WC1 .... 94 B1
Int Coll of
Accountancy The
SW17 .... 72 B1
Interchange The
NW5 .... 13 A3
International Com Sch
W1 .... 91 C1
International House
Language Sch
WC2 .... 106 B2
International Sch of
London W3 ....36 C2
Inver Ct
11 Bayswater
W2 .... 100 B1
4 Hammersmith
W6 .... 38 C3
Inverforth CI NW3 ...2 B2
Inverforth Ho NW3 ..2 B2
Invergarry Ho
NW6 .... 78 A1
Invermead CI W6 ...38 C2
Inverness Gdns
W8 .... 114 A1
Inverness Mews
W2 .... 114 B4
Inverness PI W2 ... 114 B4
Inverness St NW1 ..82 B4
Inverness Terr
W2 .... 114 B4
Inverton Rd SE15 ..65 C3
Invicta CI 16 E3 ....33 C4
Invicta Plaza SE1 122 A2
Invicta Prim Sch
SE3 .... 53 C3
Invicta Rd SE3, SE7..53 C4
Inville Rd SE17 .... 151 C1
Inwen Ct SE8 .... 41 A1
Inwood Ct 13 NW1...13 B1
Inwood Ho 18
SE22 .... 64 A4
Inworth St SW11 ..168 B2
Inworth Wlk N1 .....86 C4
Ion Ct 3 E2 .... 24 C3
Ionian Bldg 20
E14 .... 33 A2
Ionian Ho 21 E1 ....25 C1
Ipsden Bldgs SE1 ..135 C4
Ipswich Ho SE4.....65 C2
Irby Ho SW2 .... 62 C1
Ireland Yd EC4 .... 108 B1
Irene Rd SW6 ...... 165 C3
Ireton Ho 29 SW9 173 C1
Ireton St 17 E3 .....26 C1
Iris Ct 8 SE15 ...... 50 A1
Iroko Ho 7 NW3 ...11 A2
Iron Bridge CI
NW10 .... 8 A3
Iron Bridge Ho
NW3 .... 12 B1
Irongate Ho EC3 .. 110 A1
Iron Mill PI SW18 ..59 A1
Iron Mill Rd SW18 ..59 A1
Ironmonger La
EC2 .... 109 B1

Ironmonger Pas
EC1 .... 97 A3
Ironmonger Row
EC1 .... 97 A3
Ironmonger Row
Baths EC1 ....97 A3
Ironmongers PI
E14 .... 41 C2
Ironmonger's PI 22
E14 .... 41 C2
Ironside CI SE16....40 C4
Ironside Ho E9 ......18 A4
Ironworks 1 E3 ....26 C4
Irvine Ho N7 .... 14 B2
Irving Gr SW9 ..... 172 C1
Irving Ho SE17 .... 150 A1
Irving Mews N1 ....15 B2
Irving Rd W14 ...... 39 C3
Irving St WC2 ...... 119 C3
Irwell Est 31 SE16 ..40 B4
Irwin Gdns NW10 ..22 A4
Isabella Ho
19 Hammersmith
W6 .... 39 B1
Kennington SE11 .. 150 A2
Isabella Mews 11
N1 .... 16 A2
Isabella Rd E9 ....17 B3
Isabel St SW9 ...... 173 A4
Isambard Mews
E14 .... 42 B3
Isambard PI SE16 ..32 B1
Iseldon Ct N7 .... 14 A4
Isel Way 4 SE22 ...64 A2
Isis CI SW15 .... 57 B3
Isis Ho NW8 .... 89 C1
Isis St SW18 .... 71 B2
Islamia Girls' High Sch
NW6 .... 23 A4
Islamia Prim Sch
NW6 .... 23 A4
Islamic Coll for
Advanced Studies 2
NW10 .... 9 A2
Island Gardens Sta
E14 .... 42 B1
Island Ho E14 .... 27 B2
Island Rd SE16 .....40 C2
Island Row E14 .....33 B3
Islay Wlk 19 N1 .... 15 B2
Isleden Ho N1 ...... 86 C4
Iseldon Rd N4, N5 ...6 C1
Isledon Rd N7 .... 5 C1
ISLE OF DOGS 42 B2
ISLINGTON 14 C2
Islington Arts & Media
Sch 6 N4 .... 5 B3
Islington Est N1 ...86 C4
Islington Gn N1 ....86 A3
Islington High St
N1 .... 86 A2
Islington Mus WC1 96 A3
Islington Park Mews
1 N1 .... 15 A1
Islington Park St
N1 .... 15 A1
Islington Tennis Ctr
N7 .... 14 A2
Islip St NW5 .... 13 B3
Isokon Flats 3
NW3 .... 12 B3

Issac Way SE1 .... 137 A4
Italia Conti Acad of
Theatre Arts EC1 ..96 C1
Ivanhoe Ho
1 Balham SW12.....73 A4
34 Bow E3 .... 26 A3
Ivanhoe Rd SE5.....64 A4
Iveagh CI E9 ....25 C4
Iveagh Ct EC3 ...... 110 C1
Iveagh Ho
2 Brixton SW9 .....48 A1
Chelsea SW10 .... 157 A2
Ivebury Ct 3 W10...30 B3
Iveley Rd SW4 .... 170 C1
Iver Ct N1 .... 15 B2
Iverna Ct W8 ...... 127 C2
Iverna Gdns W8 ..127 C2
Iverson Rd NW6 ...10 C2
Ives Rd E16 .... 35 A4
Ives St SW3 .... 144 B4
Ivimey St E2 .... 24 C2
Ivinghoe Ho N7 .. 13 C3
Ivor Ct NW1 .... 90 C2
Ivories The N1 ......15 B1
Ivor Mayor Lo
SW12 .... 60 C1
Ivor PI NW1 .... 90 C1
Ivor St NW1 .... 13 B1
Ivory Ho
10 London SW11 ...59 B4
St George in East
E1 .... 125 A2
Ivory Sq 10 SW18 ..59 B4
Ivybridge Ho 18
SE22 .... 64 A4
Ivybridge La WC2 ..120 B3
Ivy Church La SE1,
SE17 .... 152 C2
Ivy Cres W4 .... 37 B2
Ivy Ct 15 SE16 ......40 A1
Ivydale Prim Sch
SE15 .... 65 C3
Ivydale Rd SE15 ...65 C3
Ivyday Gr SW16 ...74 B1
Ivy Lo W11 .....31 C1 113 B2
Ivymount Rd SE27 74 C1
Ivy Rd
Brockley SE4 ....66 C3
Cricklewood NW2 ....9 B4
Newham E16 ....35 C3
St Johns SE13 .....67 B2
Ixworth PI SW3 ... 144 A3

J

Jacaranda Gr E8 ...16 B1
Jackman Ho 2 E1 ..32 A1
Jackman St E8 ......25 A4
Jackson Ct N7 .... 14 B3
Jackson Ho 16
SW11 .... 59 C4
Jackson Rd N7 .....14 B4
Jackson's La N16 ....4 A3
Jack Taylor Sch
NW8 .... 78 C4
Jack Tizard Sch
W12 .... 30 A1
Jack Walker Ct
N5 .... 15 A4
Jacobin Lo N7 .... 14 A3
Jacob Mans 15 E1 ..32 A3
Jacobson Ct
SW11 .... 168 B3
Jacobson Ho 11 .. 110 C2

Jacob St SE1 ...... 139 B4
Jacob's Well Mews
W1 .... 103 C2
Jacotts Ho W10 ....22 B1
Jacqueline Ho 8
E1 .... 32 B2
Jacques Prevert Sch
3 W6 .... 39 C2
Jaggard Way
SW12 .... 72 B4
Jagger Ho SW11 ..168 C4
Jago Wlk SE5 ...... 48 C3
Jamahirya Sch
SW3 .... 158 A4
Jamaica Rd
Bermondsey SE1 ..139 A3
Bermondsey SE16 ..40 A3
Bermondsey SE1 ...32 B3
James Allen's Girls'
Sch 9 SE22 ....64 A2
James Allen's Pre-
Prep Sch SE21 .....63 C1
James Allen's Prep
Sch 10 SE22 ....64 A2
James Anderson Ct 2
E2 .... 24 A3
James Ave NW2 .....9 B3
James Brine Ho 1
E2 .... 24 B2
James Campbell Ho
2 E2 .... 25 B3
James Collins Cl
W9 .... 23 B1
James Docherty Ho 4
E2 .... 25 B3
James Hammett Ho
3 E2 .... 24 B3
James Joyce Wlk 7
SE24 .... 63 A3
James Leicester Hall
of Residence N7 ..14 A2
James Lind Ho 6
SE8 .... 41 B2
James Middleton Ho
2 E2 .... 25 A2
James Newman Ct
SE9 .... 77 A4
James Riley Point 4
E15 .... 19 B1
James St
Marylebone W1 ... 103 C1
Strand WC2 .... 120 B4
James Stewart Ho
NW6 .... 10 B1
James Stroud Ho
SE17 .... 151 A1
James Wat
N1 .... 82 A4
Jamestown Rd
NW1 .... 82 A4
Jamestown Way
E14 .... 34 C2
James Voller Way 50
E1 .... 32 B3
James Wolfe Prim
Sch 10 SE10 ....52 B3
Jamiatul Ummah Sch
4 E1 .... 32 B3
Jamuna CI E14 .....33 A4

Jane St E1 ... 32 A3
Janet St E14 ... 41 C3
Janeway Pl **2**
SE16 ... 40 A4
Janeway St SE16 . 139 C3
Jansen Ho **5**
SW15 ... 56 C2
Jansen Wlk SW11 .59 C3
Japan Cres N4 ... 5 B3
Jardine Rd E1 ... 32 C2
Jarman Ho
Bermondsey SE16 .40 C2
18 Stepney E1 ... 32 B4
Jarrett Ct SW2 ... 75 A3
Jarrow Rd SE16 ... 40 A2
Jarrow Way E9 ... 18 A4
Jarvis Ho **3** SE15 .49 C2
Jarvis Rd SE22 ... 64 A3
Jasmin St **1** ... 125 A1
Jasmine Sq **16** E3 . 26 B4
Jasmin Ho SE4 ... 66 B4
Jasmin Lo **17** SE16. .40 A1
Jason Ct
2 London W1 ... 173 B4
Marylebone W1 ... 103 C2
Jasper Wlk N1 ... 97 B4
Java Wharf SE1 ... 139 A4
Jay Ho SW15 ... 47 B1
Jay Mews SW7 ... 129 A3
Jean Darling Ho
SW10 ... 157 B3
Jean Pardies Ho **22**
E1 ... 32 B4
Jebb Ave SW2 ... 62 A1
Jebb St E3 ... 26 C3
Jedburgh St SW11 .60 C3
Jeddo Mews W12 . .38 B4
Jeddo Rd W12 ... 38 B4
Jefferson Bldg **3**
E14 ... 41 C4
Jeffrey's Ct **5**
SW4 ... 172 A2
Jeffrey's Pl NW1 ... 13 B1
Jeffrey's Rd SW4 . 172 A2
Jeffrey's St NW1 . .13 B1
Jeff Wooller Coll
WC1 ... 106 B3
Jeger Ave E2 ... 24 B4
Jelf Rd SW2 ... 62 C2
Jellicoe Ho
5 Bethnal Green
E2 ... 24 C3
Fitzrovia NW1 ... 92 B1
1 Putney SW15 ... 57 C2
Jemotts Ct **9**
SE14 ... 50 C4
Jenkins Ho SW8 . 171 B4
Jenkinson Ho **12**
E2 ... 25 C2
Jenner Ave W3 ... 28 C4
Jenner Ho **3** ... 53 A4
Jenner Rd N16 ... 7 B1
Jennifer Ho SE11 . 149 C3
Jennings Ho SE10 .42 C1
Jennings Rd SE22 .64 B1
Jensen Ho **10** E3 ... 26 C1
Jephson Ct **17**
SW4 ... 172 B1
Jephson Ho **6**
SE17 ... 48 A4
Jephson St SE5 ... 48 C2
Jephtha Rd SW18. .58 C1
Jerdan Pl SW6 ... 155 B2

Jeremiah St **11**
E14 ... 34 A3
Jeremy Bentham Ho
2 E2 ... 24 C2 99 C3
Jermyn St SW1 ... 119 A2
Jerningham
SE14 ... 51 A2
Jerningham Rd
SE14 ... 51 A2
Jerome Cres NW8 .90 A2
Jerome Ho NW1 .. 102 B4
Jerome St
E1 ... 24 B1 98 C1
Jerome Twr **5**
W3 ... 37 A4
Jerrard St SE13 ... 67 A4
Jerrold Lo SW15 ...57 B4
Jerrold St **2** N1 ... 24 A3
Jersey Ho **11** N1 ... 15 B2
Jersey Rd N1 ... 15 B2
Jersey St **2** ... 25 A2
Jerusalem Pas
EC1 ... 96 A1
Jervis Bay Ho **9**
E14 ... 34 C3
Jervis Ct
2 Greenwich
SE10 ... 52 B2
Marylebone W1 ... 104 B1
Jessel Ho
St Pancras WC1 ... 94 A3
Westminster SW1 . 147 C4
Jessica Rd SW18 .59 B2
Jessie Blythe La **4**
N19 ... 5 A4
Jessie Duffett Ho **11**
SE5 ... 48 B3
Jesson Ho SE17 . 151 B3
Jessop Ct N1 ... 86 B1
Jessop Ho **6** W4 . .37 C2
Jessop Sq E14 ... 33 C1
Jeston Ho **10** SE27. .75 A1
Jethou Ho **11** N1 . 15 B2
Jevons Ho **5** NW8 .11 C1
Jewell Ho **5**
SW12 ... 73 B4
Jewish Mus NW1 . .82 B3
Jewry St EC3 ... 110 C1
Jews Row SW18 ... 59 B3
Jeymer Ave NW2 ... 9 B3
Jeypore Rd SW18 . .59 B1
Jim Griffiths Ho
SW6 ... 155 A3
Jim Veal Dr **8**
N17 ... 14 A2
Joanna Ho **4** W6 . .39 B1
Joan St SE1 ... 122 A1
Jocelin Ho N1 ... 85 A3
Jocelyn Rd TW9 ... 54 A4
Jocelyn St SE15 .. .49 C2
Jockey's Fields
WC1 ... 107 A4
Jodane St **8** SE8 .. .41 B2
Jodrell Rd E3 ... 18 B1
Johanna Prim Sch
SE1 ... 135 B3
Johanna St SE1 . 135 B3
John Adam St
WC2 ... 120 B3
John Aird Ct W2 . 101 A4
John Archer Way
SW18 ... 59 C1
John Ashby Cl
SW2 ... 62 A1
John Ball Prim Sch
SE3 ... 53 A1

John Barker Ct
NW6 ... 10 A1
John Betts' Ho
W12 ... 38 C3
John Betts Prim Sch
W6 ... 39 A3
John Bond Ho **2**
E3 ... 26 B3
John Brent Ho **8**
SE8 ... 40 C2
John Buck Ho
NW10 ... 21 B4
John Burns Prim Sch
SW11 ... 169 C1
John Campbell Rd **3**
N16 ... 16 A3
John Carpenter St
EC4 ... 122 A4
John Cartwright Ho
7 E2 ... 25 A2
John Clynes Ct
SW15 ... 57 A3
John Conwey Ho **23**
SW2 ... 62 C1
John Dee Ho **3**
SW14 ... 55 C4
John Donne Prim Sch
15 SE15 ... 50 A2
John Dwight Ho
SW6 ... 59 A4
John Fearon Wlk **5**
W10 ... 23 A2
John Felton Rd **16**
SE16 ... 139 B3
John Fielden Ho **6**
E2 ... 25 A2
John Fisher St E1 . 125 B4
John F Kennedy Specl
Sch **6** E15 ... 27 C4
John Harris Ho
SE15 ... 64 C4
John Harrison Way
SE10 ... 43 B3
John Islip St SW1 . 148 A3
John Keall Ho **5**
SW15 ... 57 C4
John Keble CE Prim
Sch NW10 ... 21 B4
John Kennedy Ct **1**
N1 ... 15 C2
John Kennedy Ho **8**
SE16 ... 40 C2
John Kennedy Lo **2**
N1 ... 15 C2
John King Ct **5**
N19 ... 4 C2
John Kirk Ho **6**
21 Battersea
SW11 ... 59 C4
5 Streatham
SW16 ... 74 A1
John Knight Lo
SW6 ... 155 C2
John McDonald Ho **8**
E14 ... 42 B3
John McKenna Wlk **17**
SE16 ... 139 C2
John Maurice Cl
SE17 ... 151 B4
John Nettleford Ho
2 E2 ... 25 A2
John Orwell Sports
Ctr E1 ... 32 A1
John Parker Sq **7**
SW11 ... 59 C4

John Parry Ct **28**
N1 ... 24 A3
John Paul II Sch **3**
SW19 ... 69 C4
John Penn St
SE13 ... 52 A2
John Perryn Prim Sch
W3 ... 29 A3
John Prince's St
W1 ... 104 B2
John Pritchard Ho **18**
E1 ... 24 C1 99 C1
John Ratcliffe Ho **9**
NW6 ... 23 C2
John Rennie Wlk **1**
E1 ... 32 B1
John Roan Way
SE16 ... 139 C2
John Ruskin Prim Sch
SE5 ... 48 B4
John Ruskin St
SE5 ... 48 B4
John Scurr Ho **7**
E14 ... 33 A3
John Scurr Prim Sch
40 E1 ... 25 B1
John Silkin La **8**
SE8 ... 40 C1
John Smith Ave
SW6 ... 154 C2
John Smith Mews
E14 ... 34 C2
Johnson Ct **8**
E14 ... 33 A3
Johnson Ho
Belgravia SW1 ... 145 C3
28 Bethnal Green
E2 ... 24 C2 99 C3
South Lambeth
SW8 ... 161 C1
Johnson Rd NW10 .20 C4
Johnsons Ct E4 ... 107 C1
Johnson St E1 ... 32 B3
Johnsons Way
NW10 ... 20 A1
John Spencer Sq
N1 ... 15 A2
John's Pl E1 ... 32 A3
John St WC1 ... 95 A1
John Stainer Prim
Sch SE4 ... 66 A4
Johnston Cl SW9 . 173 A3
Johnstone Ho
SE13 ... 67 C4
John Strachey Ho
SW6 ... 155 A3
John Trundle Ct
EC2 ... 108 C4
John Tucker Ho **8**
E14 ... 41 C3
John Wesley's House
& Mus of Methodism
EC1 ... 97 C2
John Wheatley Ho
14 London N19 ... 4 C4
West Brompton
SW6 ... 155 A3
John Williams Cl
SE14 ... 50 C4

Joiners Arms Yd **7**
SE5 ... 48 C2
Joiner St SE1 ... 123 C1
Joiners Yd N1 ... 84 B1
Jolles Ho **9** E3 ... 27 A2
Jonathan Ct **7**
W4 ... 38 A2
Jonathan St SE11 . 148 C2
Jones Ho
4 South Bromley
E14 ... 34 C3
Stamford Hill N16 .... 7 A3
Jones St W1 ... 118 A3
Jones Wlk **6**
TW10 ... 54 B1
Jonson Ho
Borough The SE1 . 137 C1
10 Canonbury N16. .15 C4
11 Dulwich SW1 ... 57 C3
Jordan Ho
12 London SE4 ... 65 C3
Shoreditch N1 ... 87 C3
Jordans Ho NW8 . .90 A1
Joscoyne Ho **5**
E1 ... 32 A3
Joseph Ave W3 ... 28 C3
Joseph Conrad Ho
SW1 ... 147 A3
Joseph Ct N16 ...... 7 A4
Joseph Hardcastle Cl
SE14 ... 50 C3
Josephine Ave
SW2 ... 62 B2
Joseph Irwin Ho **3**
E14 ... 33 B2
Joseph Powell Cl **1**
SW12 ... 73 B4
Joseph Priestley Ho
16 E2 ... 25 A2
Joseph St E3 ... 26 B1
Joseph Trotter Cl
EC1 ... 95 C3
Joshua St E14 ... 34 B3
Joslings Cl W12 ... 29 C2
Josseline Ct **3** E3 . 26 A3
Joubert Mans
SW3 ... 144 B2
Joubert St SW11 . 169 A2
Jowett Ho **7**
SW9 ... 172 B1
Jowett St SE15 ... 49 B3
Jubet Ho **9** N15 ... 15 C4
Jubilee Bldgs NW8 .79 B2
Jubilee Cl
NW10 ... 21 B3
Jubilee Cres E14 .. .42 B3
Jubilee Ho **11**
SE11 ... 84 B4
Jubilee Hall Mkt
WC2 ... 120 B4
Jubilee Ho SE1 ... 149 C3
Jolles Hts NW2 ... 10 B2
Jubilee JMI Sch
N16 ... 7 C2
Jubilee Mans **10**
E1 ... 32 B3
Jubilee Pl SW3 .. 144 B2
Jubilee Prim Sch
SW2 ... 62 C1
Jubilee St E1 ... 32 B3
Jubilee The **2**
SE10 ... 52 A3
Jubilee Yd SE1 ... 138 C4
Judd St WC1 ... 94 A3
Jude St E16 ... 35 B3
Judges' Wlk NW3 ... 2 B1
Juer St SW11 ... 158 B1

Julian Ave W3 . . . . .28 A2
Julian Ct SW13 . . . . . . .46 B2
Julian Pl E14 . . . . .42 A1
Julia St NW5 . . . . .12 C3
Juliet Ho 🔢 N1 . . . . . . .24 A3
Julius Ct E8 . . . . .24 A3
Julius Ho 🔢 E14 . . . . . .34 A3
Julius Nyerere Cl

N1 . . . . .84 C3

Junction App
Battersea SW11 . . . . . .60 A4
Lewisham SE13 . . . . . . .67 B4
Junction Mews
W2 . . . . .102 A2
Junction Pl W2 . . . . . .101 C2
Junction Rd N19 . . . . . . .4 B1
Juniper Cres NW1 . . . .12 C1
Juniper Ct N16 . . . . .6 C2
Juniper Dr SW18 . . . . .59 B3
Juniper Ho
🔢 Peckham SE14,
SE15 . . . . .50 B3
🔢 Richmond TW9 . . . . .45 A2
Juniper St E1 . . . . .32 B2
Juno Ct 🔢 SW9 . . . . .163 B1
Juno Ho 🔢 E3 . . . . . . .26 C3
Juno Way SE14 . . . . . . .50 C4
Juno Way Ind Est

SE14 . . . . .50 C4
Jupiter Ct 🔟

SW9 . . . . .163 B1
Jupiter Way N7 . . . . . . .14 B2
Jupp Rd E15 . . . . .19 C1
Jupp Rd W E15 . . . . . . .27 C4
Jura Ho SE16 . . . . .41 A2
Jurston Ct SE1 . . . . . .135 C3
Justice Wlk SW3 . . . . . .58 A3
Justines Pl E2 . . . . .25 C2
Jutland Cl N19 . . . . .5 A3
Jutland Ho 🔢 SE5 . .48 B1
Juxon St SE11 . . . . . . .149 A4

K

Kambala Rd SW11 . . . .59 C4
Kara Way NW2 . . . . .9 C4
Karen Ct
🔢 Camberwell

SE5 . . . . .64 A4
Forest Hill SE23 . . . . . . .66 A1
Karen Ho 🔢 N16 . . . . .15 C4
Kasmin Ct NW10 . . . . . . .8 A1
Kassala Rd SW11 . . . .169 A3
Katherine Cl 🔢

SE16 . . . . .32 C1
Katherine Ho 🔢

W10 . . . . .23 A1
Katherine Sq

W11 . . . . .31 A1 112 A2
Kathleen Ave W3 . . . . .28 B4
Kathleen Rd SW11 . . . .60 B4
Kay Rd SW9 . . . . .172 C1
Kay St E2 . . . . .24 C3
Kean Ho 🔢 SE17 . . . . .48 A4
Kean St WC2 . . . . .106 C1
Keates Est N16 . . . . .7 B2
Keats Cl
Bermondsey SE1 . . . .152 C3
Hampstead NW3 . . . . . .12 A4
Keats Gr NW3 . . . . .12 A4
Keats Ho
🔢 Bethnal Green

E2 . . . . .25 B2
🔢 Camberwell SE5 . . .48 B3
Chelsea SW1 . . . . .161 A4

Keats House (Mus)

NW3 . . . . .12 A4
Keats Pl EC2 . . . . .109 B3
Keble Ho 🔢 SW15 . . .57 C1
Keble Pl SW13 . . . . . . .47 A4
Kedleston Ct E15 . . . . .48 A4
Kedge Ho 🔢 E14 . . . .41 C3
Kedleston Wlk 🔢

E2 . . . . .25 A2
Keel Cl SE16 . . . . .32 C1
Keel Ct 🔢 E14 . . . . . . .34 C2
Keeley Rd SW4 . . . . . .161 C1
Keeley St WC2 . . . . . . .106 C1
Keeling Ho 🔢 E2 . . . . .25 A3
Keelson Ho 🔢 E14 . . .41 C3
Keen's Yd N1 . . . . .15 A2
Keeper Wharf 🔢 E1 . .32 C2
Keeper Wharf 🔢

E1 . . . . .32 C2
Keep The SE3 . . . . .53 C1
Keeton's Rd SE16 . . . . .40 A3
Keevil Dr SW19 . . . . . . .70 A4
Keighley Cl N7 . . . . .14 A4
Keildon Rd SW11 . . . . .60 B3
Keir Hardie Ho
Fulham W6 . . . . .47 C4
🔢 Upper Holloway

N19 . . . . .4 C4
Willesden NW10 . . . . . . .8 B1
Keir Hardy Prim Sch

E16 . . . . .35 C4
Keith Connor Cl 🔢

SW8 . . . . .61 A4
Keith Gr W12 . . . . .29 C1
Keith Ho NW6 . . . . .78 A1
Kelby Ho N7 . . . . .14 B2
Kelfield Ct 🔟 W10 . . .30 C3
Kelfield Gdns W10 . . . .30 C3
Kelfield Mews

W10 . . . . .30 C3
Kellett Ho N1 . . . . .87 C3
Kellett Rd SW2 . . . . . . .62 C3
Kellow Ho SE1 . . . . . .137 B4
Kell St SE1 . . . . .136 B2
Kelly Ct 🔢 E14 . . . . . . .33 C2
Kelly Mews 🔢 W9 . . . .23 B1
Kelly St NW1 . . . . .13 A2
Kelman Cl SW4 . . . . . .171 C1
Kelmore Gr SE22 . . . . .64 C3
Kelmscott Gdns

W12 . . . . .38 C3
Kelmscott House

W6 . . . . .39 A1
Kelmscott Rd

SW11 . . . . .60 B2
Kelross Rd N5 . . . . .15 B4
Kelsall Mews TW9 . . . .45 A2
Kelsey St E2 . . .24 C1 99 C2
Kelshall Ct N4 . . . . .6 B2
Kelson Ho E14 . . . . . . .42 B3
Kelso Pl W8 . . . . .128 B2
Kelvedon Ho SW8 . . .172 B4
Kelvedon Rd SW6 . . . .155 A1
Kelvin Ct
Chiswick W4 . . . . .45 B3
Notting Hill

W11 . . . . .31 C2 113 B3
Kelvington Rd

SE15 . . . . .65 C2
Kelvin Rd N5 . . . . .15 B4
Kelyway Ho 🔢

SW2 . . . . .74 C4
Kember St N1 . . . . .14 B1
Kemble Ho SW9 . . . . . .63 A4
Kemble St WC2 . . . . . .106 C1
Kemerton Rd SE5 . . . . .63 B4

Kemey's St E9 . . . . .18 A3
Kemp Ct SW8 . . . . . . .162 A1
Kempe Ho SE1 . . . . . .137 C1
Kempe Rd NW6 . . . . . .22 C3
Kemp Ho
Finsbury EC1 . . . . .97 B3
🔢 Globe Town E2 . . . .25 C3
Kempis Way 🔢

SE22 . . . . .64 A2
Kemplay Rd NW3 . . . . .11 C4
Kemp's Ct W1 . . . . .105 B1
Kemps Dr E14 . . . . .33 C2
Kempsford Gdns

SW5 . . . . .141 C1
Kempsford Rd
Lambeth SE11 . . . . . . .149 C3
Newington SE11 . . . . .150 A3
Kemps Gdns SE13 . . . .67 B2
Kempson Rd SW6 . . . .155 C1
Kempthorne Rd

SE8 . . . . .41 B2
Kempton Ct 🔢 E1 . . . .32 A4
Kempton Ho 🔢

N1 . . . . .24 A4
Kemsing Ho SE1 . . . . .137 C3
Kemsing Rd SE10 . . . . .43 C1
Kemsley SE13 . . . . .67 A2
Kenbrook Ho
Kensington W14 . . . . .127 A1
🔢 Kentish Town

NW5 . . . . .13 B3
Kenbury Gdns 🔢

SE5 . . . . .48 B1
Kenbury Mans 🔢

SE5 . . . . .48 B1
Kenbury St SE5 . . . . . .48 B1
Kenchester Cl

SW8 . . . . .162 B1
Kendal Ho N1 . . . . .92 B4
Kendal Ave W3 . . . . . . .28 A4
Kendal Cl SE5 . . . . .48 A3
Kendal Cl NW2 . . . . . . .10 A3
Kendal Ho
🔢 Hackney E9 . . . . . .17 B1
Islington N1 . . . . .85 A2
Kendall Ct 🔢 SE22 . . .64 C2
Kendall Pl W1 . . . . . . .103 B3
Kendal Rd NW10 . . . . . .8 C4
Kendal St W2 . . . . .102 B1
Kendal Steps 🔢

W2 . . . . .102 B1
Kender Prim Sch

SE14 . . . . .50 B2
Kender St SE14 . . . . . . .50 B2
Kendoa Rd 🔢

SW4 . . . . .61 C3
Kendon Ho E15 . . . . . . .19 C1
Kendrick Ct 🔢

SE15 . . . . .50 A2
Kendrick Mews

SW7 . . . . .143 B3
Kendrick Pl SW7 . . . . .143 B3
Keniford Rd

SW12 . . . . .73 A4
Kenilworth Ct

SW6 . . . . .58 A4
Kenilworth Rd
Bow E3 . . . . .26 A3
🔢 Kilburn NW6 . . . . . .23 B4
Kenley Wlk

W11 . . . . .31 A2 112 A3
Kenmont Gdns

NW10 . . . . .22 A2
Kenmont Prim Sch

NW10 . . . . .22 A2
Kenmore Cl TW9 . . . . .44 C3

Kenmore Ct NW6 . . . .10 C1
Kenmure Rd E8 . . . . . .17 A3
Kenmure Yd E8 . . . . . . .17 A3
Kennacraig Cl 🔢

E16 . . . . .35 C1
Kennard Ho 🔢

SW11 . . . . .169 C3
Kennard Rd E15 . . . . . .19 C1
Kennard St 🔢

SW11 . . . . .169 B3
Kennedy Cox Ho 🔢

E16 . . . . .35 B4
Kennedy Ho SE11 . . . .148 C2
Kennedy Wlk

SE17 . . . . .151 C3
Kennet Cl SW11 . . . . . .59 C3
Kennet Ct 🔢 W2 . . . . .31 C4
Kenneth Campbell Ho

NW8 . . . . .89 C2
Kenneth Cres NW2 . . . .9 A3
Kenneth Ct SE11 . . . .149 C4
Kennet Ho NW8 . . . . . .89 C1
Kenneth Younger Ho

SW6 . . . . .155 A3
Kennet Rd W9 . . . . . . .23 B1
Kennet St E1 . . . . .125 C2
Kennett Wharf La

EC4 . . . . .123 A4
Kenning Ho 🔢 N1 . . . .24 A4
Kennings Way

SE11 . . . . .149 C2
KENNINGTON 149 B1
Kennington Ent Ctr

SE17 . . . . .150 A1
Kennington La

SE11 . . . . .149 A1
Kennington Oval

SE11 . . . . .163 A3
Kennington Palace Ct

SE11 . . . . .149 B2
Kennington Park Gdns

SE11 . . . . .150 A2
Kennington Park Ho

SE11 . . . . .149 C1
Kennington Park Pl

SE11 . . . . .150 A2
Kennington Park Rd

SE11 . . . . .150 A2
Kennington Rd

SE11 . . . . .149 B3
Kennington Sta

SE17 . . . . .150 A2
Kennlodes SE21 . . . . . .75 C2
Kenrick Pl W1 . . . . . . .103 B3
KENSAL GREEN . .22 B2
Kensal Green Cemy
(All Souls) NW10 . . . . .22 B2
Kensal Green Sta

NW10 . . . . .22 C3
Kensal Ho W10 . . . . . . .23 A1
KENSAL RISE 22 B3
Kensal Rise Prim Sch

NW6 . . . . .22 C3
Kensal Rise Sta

NW10 . . . . .22 C3
KENSAL TOWN 23 A1
KENSINGTON 127 C3
Kensington Acad

SW6 . . . . .156 A1
**Kensington & Chelsea
Coll**
Chelsea SW10 . . . . . . .156 C2

**Kensington & Chelsea
Coll** *continued*
🔢 Kensal Town

W10 . . . . .31 A4
Kensington Church Ct

W8 . . . . .128 A3
Kensington Church St

W8 . . . . . . .31 C1 113 C1
**Kensington Church
Wlk** W8 . . . . .128 A3
**Kensington Court
Mans** W8 . . . . .128 B3
**Kensington Court
Mews** W8 . . . . .128 B2
Kensington Court Pl

W8 . . . . .128 B2
Kensington Ct

W8 . . . . .128 B3
Kensington Ct Gdns

W8 . . . . .128 B2
Kensington Gardens
W2 . . . . .115 A1
Kensington Gate

W8 . . . . .128 C2
Kensington Gdns Sq

W2 . . . . .100 A1
Kensington Gore

SW7 . . . . .129 B3
Kensington Hall Gdns

W14 . . . . .140 C2
Kensington High St

W8 . . . . .127 C2
Kensington Ho 🔢

NW5 . . . . .13 B3
Kensington Ho

W11 . . . . . . .31 C1 113 B2
Kensington L Ctr

W11 . . . . .31 A2 112 A4
Kensington Mall

W8 . . . . .31 C1 113 C2
Kensington Mans

SW5 . . . . .141 C2
**Kensington Olympia
Sta** W14 . . . . .126 A2
Kensington Pal

W8 . . . . .114 B1
**Kensington Palace
Gdns** W8 . . . . .114 A2
Kensington Park Gdns

W11 . . . . . . .31 B2 113 A3
**Kensington Park
Mews** W11 . . . . .31 B3
Kensington Park Rd

W11 . . . . . . .31 B2 113 A4
Kensington Pl

W8 . . . . .31 C1 113 B2
Kensington Prep Sch

SW6 . . . . .165 A4
Kensington Rd

SW7 . . . . .129 A3
Kensington Sq

W8 . . . . .128 A3
Kensington Village

W14 . . . . .141 A3
Kensington W

W14 . . . . .140 A4
Kenworth Ho EC1 . . . . .97 C3
Kent Ct 🔢 E2 . . . . .24 B3
Kent Ho
Camberwell SE1 . . . . .153 A1
🔢 Chiswick W4 . . . . . .38 A1
Marylebone W1 . . . . . .104 C2
Pimlico SW1 . . . . .147 B1
Richmond TW10 . . . . . .54 C2

Kentish Bldgs
SE1 . . . . **123** B1
KENTISH TOWN **13** B2
Kentish Town CE Prim
Sch **IE** NW5 . . . . . . **13** B3
Kentish Town City
Farm NW5 . . . . **12** C3
Kentish Town Rd
NW1 . . . . **13** A2
Kentish Town Sp Ctr
NW5 . . . . **13** A2
Kentish Town Sta
NW5 . . . . **13** B3
Kentish Town West
Sta NW5 . . . . **13** A2
Kent Lo **9** SW19 . . . **69** C3
Kentmere Ho SE15 . **50** B4
Kenton Ct W14 . . . **126** C1
Kenton Ho
20 Globe Town E1 . . **25** B1
Highbury N5 . . . . **5** C1
Kenton Rd E9 . . . . . **17** C2
Kenton St WC1 . . . . **94** A2
Kent Pas NW1 . . . . . **90** C2
Kent Pk Ind Est
SE15 . . . . **50** A4
Kent Rd
Richmond TW9 . . . . **44** C3
South Acton W4 . . . **37** B3
Kent St E2 . . . . **24** B3
Kent Terr NW1 . . . . . **90** B3
Kentwell Cl SE4 . . . **66** A3
Kentwode Gn
SW13 . . . . **46** C3
Kent Yard SW7 . . . **130** B3
Kenway Rd SW5 . . . **142** A3
Ken Wilson Ho **19**
E2 . . . . **24** C3
Kenwood Cl N6 . . . . . . **4** A1
Kenwood Ct
SW9 . . . . **63** A3
Kenwood Ho NW3 . . . **3** A3
Kenworthy Rd E9 . . . **18** A3
Kenwrick Ho N1 . . . . **85** A3
Kenwyn Rd SW4 . . . . **61** C3
Kenyon Ho SE5 . . . . **48** B3
Kenyon St SW6 . . . . **47** C2
Kepler Ho **5** SE10 . . **43** B1
Kepler Rd SW2,
SW4 . . . . **62** A3
Keppel Ho
Brompton SW3 . . . **144** A3
3 Deptford SE8 . . . **41** B1
Keppel Row SE1 . . . **122** C1
Keppel St WC1 . . . . **105** C4
Kerbela St **3**
E2 . . . . **24** C1 **99** B2
Kerbey St E14 . . . . . **34** A3
Kerfield Cres SE5 . . **48** C2
Kerfield Pl SE5 . . . . **48** C2
Kerridge Ct **10** N1 . . **16** A2
Kerrier Ho SW10 . . . **157** A1
Kerrington Ct **7**
W12 . . . . **39** B4
Kerrison Rd
Battersea SW11 . . . . **60** A4
Mill Meads E15 . . . . **27** C4
Kerry N7 . . . . **14** A2
Kerry Ho **5** E1 . . . . **32** B3
Kerry Path SE8 . . . . **51** B4
Kerry Rd SE8 . . . . . . **51** B4
Kerscott Ho **30** E3 . . **27** A2
Kersfield Ho SW15 . . **57** C1
Kersfield Rd SW15 . . **57** C1

Kershaw Cl SW18 . . **59** C1
Kershaw Ho **7**
SE27 . . . . **75** A1
Kersley Mews
SW11 . . . . **168** C3
Kersley Rd N16 . . . . . **7** A1
Kersley St SW11 . . . **168** C2
Kerwick Cl **1** N7 . . . **14** B1
Keslake Mans
NW10 . . . . **22** C3
Keslake Rd NW6 . . . **22** C3
Keston Ho SE17 . . . **152** B2
Keston Rd SE15 . . . . **64** C4
Kestrel Ave SE24 . . . **63** B2
Kestrel Ho
4 Battersea
SW11 . . . . **60** A4
Finsbury EC1 . . . . . . **96** C4
Kestrel Pl SE14 . . . . **51** A4
Keswick Broadway **1**
SW15 . . . . **58** B2
Keswick Ct **2**
SE22 . . . . **64** C2
Keswick Ho **8**
SE5 . . . . **48** B2
Keswick Hts **9**
SW15 . . . . **58** A1
Keswick Lo SE16 . . . **16** B2
Keswick Rd SW15 . . **58** A2
Kett Gdns SW2 . . . . **62** B2
Kettleby Ho NW9 . . . **63** A4
Ketton Ho **10** W10 . . **22** B1
Kevan Ho SE5 . . . . . **48** B3
KEW **44** C4
Kew Bridge TW8 . . . **36** B1
Kew Bridge Ct **4**
TW8 . . . . **36** B1
Kew Bridge
Distribution Ctr
TW8 . . . . **36** B1
Kew Bridge Rd
TW8 . . . . **36** B1
Kew Bridge Sta
TW8 . . . . **36** B1
Kew Bridge Steam
Mus TW8 . . . . **36** B1
Kew Coll TW9 . . . . . **44** C2
Kew Foot Rd TW9 . . **54** A4
Kew Gardens Rd
TW9 . . . . **44** C2
Kew Gardens (Royal
Botanic) Pm **44** B2
Kew Gardens Sta
TW9 . . . . **44** C2
Kew Gn TW9 . . . . . . **44** C4
Kew Green TW9 . . . . **44** C4
Kew Green Prep Sch
TW9 . . . . **44** B4
Kew Lo TW9 . . . . . . **44** B4
Kew Pal TW9 . . . . . . **44** A3
Kew Pier TW9 . . . . . **44** C4
Kew Rd TW9, W4 . . . **44** C2
Kew Ret Pk TW9 . . . **45** A2
Kew Riverside Prim
Sch TW9 . . . . **45** A1
Key Cl E1 . . . . **25** A1
Keyes Ct SE22 . . . . . **64** C2
Keyes Rd NW2 . . . . . . **9** C3
Keyham Ho **9** W2 . . **31** C4
Key Ho **8** SE11 . . . **163** B4
Keymer Rd SW2 . . . . **74** B2
Keynsham Ho **2**
N4 . . . . **6** B4
Keystone Cres N1 . . **84** B1
Keyworth Cl E5 . . . . **18** A4
Keyworth Pl SE1 . . . **136** B2

Keyworth Prim Sch
SE17 . . . . **150** A2
Keyworth St SE1 . . . **136** B2
Kezia St SE8 . . . . . . **41** A1
Khyber Rd SW11 . . . **168** A1
Kia Oval The (Surrey
Cnty Crkt Club)
SE11 . . . . **163** A4
Kibworth St SW8 . . . **162** C1
Kidbrooke Gdns
SE3 . . . . **53** C2
Kidderpore Ave
NW3 . . . . **10** C4
Kidderpore Gdns
NW3 . . . . **10** C4
Kiffen St EC2 . . . . . . **97** C2
Kilbrennan Ho **9**
E14 . . . . **34** B3
KILBURN **23** C4
Kilburn Bridge **14**
NW6 . . . . **23** C4
Kilburn Gate NW6 . . **78** A2
Kilburn High Rd
NW6 . . . . **78** A3
Kilburn High Road Sta
NW6 . . . . **78** A3
Kilburn Ho **11** W9 . . **23** B2
Kilburn La W10 . . . . **23** A3
Kilburn Park Rd
NW6 . . . . **23** C2
Kilburn Park Sch **10**
NW6 . . . . **23** C3
Kilburn Park Sta
NW6 . . . . **23** C3
Kilburn Pl NW6 . . . . **23** C4
Kilburn Priory
NW6 . . . . **78** A3
Kilburn Sq NW6 . . . . **23** C4
Kilburn Sta NW2 . . . . **10** A2
Kilburn Vale NW6 . . **78** A3
Kilburn Vale Est **33**
NW6 . . . . **23** C4
Kilby Ct SE10 . . . . . **43** B3
Kildare Ct W2 . . . . . **31** C3
Kildare Gdns W2 . . . **31** C3
Kildare Rd E16 . . . . **35** C4
Kildare Terr W2 . . . . **31** C3
Kildare Wlk E14 . . . **33** C3
Kildoran Rd SW2 . . . **62** A2
Kilgour Rd SE23 . . . **66** A1
Kilkie St SW6 . . . . . **166** C1
Killarney Rd SW18 . . **59** B1
Killick St N1 . . . . **84** C1
Killieser Ave SW2 . . **74** A2
Killip Cl E16 . . . . . . **35** B3
Killoran Ho **9** E14 . . **42** B3
Killowen Rd E9 . . . . **17** C2
Killyon Rd SW8 . . . . **171** B1
Kilmaine Rd SW6 . . **154** B1
Kilmarsh Rd W6 . . . **39** B2
Kilmington Rd
SW13 . . . . **46** C4
Kilmore Ho **17** E14 . . **34** A3
Kilmuir Ho SW1 . . . **145** C3
Kiln Ct E14 . . . . **33** B2
Kilner Ho **3** SE11 . . **163** B4
Kilner St E14 . . . . . . **33** C4
Kiln Pl NW5 . . . . **12** C3
Kiloh Ct **1** SW11 . . **60** A4
Kilpatrick Ct N16 . . . . **7** B3
Kilpeck Ho **9** N4 . . . . **6** B4
Kilravock St W10 . . . **23** A2
Kilronan **3** W3 . . . **28** C3
Kimball Gdns
SW6 . . . . **164** A3

Kimber Ctr The
SW18 . . . . **70** C4
Kimberley Ave
SE15 . . . . **65** B4
Kimberley Ct NW6 . . **23** A4
Kimberley Ho **7**
E14 . . . . **42** B3
Kimberley Rd
Kilburn NW6 . . . . . . **23** A4
Stockwell SW9 . . . . **62** A4
Kimber Rd SW18 . . . **71** A4
Kimble Ho
Lisson Gr NW8 . . . . **90** B2
1 Lower Holloway
N7 . . . . **14** A3
Kimpton Ct **5** SE5 . . **48** C2
Kimpton Ho SW15 . . **68** C4
Kimpton Rd SE5 . . . **48** C2
Kinburn St SE16 . . . **40** C4
Kincaid Rd SE15 . . . **50** A3
Kincardine Gdns
W9 . . . . **23** C1
Kindell Ho **4**
SW14 . . . . **55** C4
Kinder Ho N1 . . . . . . **87** C2
Kindersley Ho **38**
E1 . . . . **111** C1
Kinder St **15** E1 . . . **32** A3
Kinefold Ho N7 . . . . **14** A2
Kinfauns Rd SW2 . . . **74** C2
King Alfred Sch
NW11 . . . . **1** C2
King Arthur Cl
SE15 . . . . **50** B3
King Charles Ct **16**
SE17 . . . . **48** A4
King Charles Ho
SW6 . . . . **156** B2
King Charles St
SW1 . . . . **134** A4
King Charles Terr **1**
E1 . . . . **32** A2
King Charles Wlk **6**
SW19 . . . . **70** A3
King David La E1 . . . **32** B2
Kingdom St W2 . . . **100** C3
Kingdon Ho **8**
E14 . . . . **42** B3
Kingdon Rd NW6 . . . **10** C2
Kingdown Cl W10 . . **30** C3
King Edward Mans **17**
E8 . . . . **25** A4
King Edward News
SW13 . . . . **46** C2
King Edwards Mans
SW6 . . . . **155** B1
King Edward's Rd
E9 . . . . **25** B4
King Edward St
EC1 . . . . **108** C2
King Edward The
Third Mews **1**
SE16 . . . . **40** A4
King Edward VII Hospl
for Officers W1 . . . **103** C4
King Edward Wlk
SE1 . . . . **135** C2
King Fahed Acad
The **3** **29** B2
Kingfield St E14 . . . . **42** B2
Kingfisher Ct
11 Battersea
SW11 . . . . **60** A4
17 Cubitt Town E14 . **42** B4

Kingfisher Ct continued
Putney SW19 . . . . . . **70** A2
Kingfisher Ho
16 Battersea
SW18 . . . . **59** B4
Peckham SE15 . . . . . **49** B2
West Kensington
W14 . . . . **126** C2
Kingfisher News
SE13 . . . . **67** A2
Kingfisher Sq **13**
SE8 . . . . **51** B4
King Frederick IX Twr
SE16 . . . . **41** B3
King George Sq
TW10 . . . . **54** B1
King George St
SE10 . . . . **52** B3
Kingham Cl
3 Shepherd's Bush
W11 . . . . **39** C4
Wandsworth SW18 . . **71** B4
Kingham Ind Est
NW10 . . . . **20** C2
King Henry's Rd
NW3 . . . . **12** B1
King Henry's Reach
W6 . . . . **47** B4
King Henry St N16 . . **16** A3
King Henry's Wlk
N1 . . . . **16** A2
King Henry's Yd **5**
N16 . . . . **16** A3
King Henry Terr **10**
E1 . . . . **32** A2
Kinghorn St EC1 . . . **108** C3
King James Ct
SE1 . . . . **136** B3
King James St
SE1 . . . . **136** B3
King John Ct
EC2 . . . . **24** A1 **98** B2
King John St **1** E1 . . **32** C4
Kinglake St SE17 . . . **152** B2
Kingly Ct W1 . . . . . **119** A4
Kingly St W1 . . . . . . **118** C4
King & Queen St
SE1 . . . . **151** A2
King's Arms Ct E1 . . **111** B3
King's Arms Yd
EC2 . . . . **109** B2
Kings Ave SW4 . . . . **62** A1
Kings Avenue Sch
SW4 . . . . **62** A2
King's Bench St
SE1 . . . . **136** B4
King's Bench Wlk
EC4 . . . . **107** C1
King's Boulevard
NW1 . . . . **84** A1
Kingsbridge N16 . . . . **7** C1
Kingsbridge Ave
W3 . . . . **36** B4
Kingsbridge Ct
E14 . . . . **41** C2
Kingsbridge Rd
W10 . . . . **30** B3
Kingsbury Rd N1 . . . **16** A2
Kingsbury Terr N1 . . **16** A2
Kingsclere Cl
SW15 . . . . **68** C4
Kingscliffe Gdns
SW19 . . . . **70** B3
King's Coll SE24 . . . **63** C1

Kings College Ct
NW3 . . . . .12 A1
King's College Hospl
SE5 . . . . .48 C1
Kings College Rd
NW3 . . . . .11 C1
King's Coll London
(Denmark Hill
Campus) SE5 . . . . . .48 B1
King's Coll London
School of Medicine
SE1 . . . . .123 C1
King's Coll London
(Strand Campus)
WC2 . . . . .121 A4
King's Coll London (St
Thomas' Campus)
SE1 . . . . .134 C2
King's Coll London
(Waterloo Campus)
SE1 . . . . .121 B1
Kingscote NW11 . . . .1 B3
Kingscote Rd W4 . . . .37 C3
Kingscote St EC4 . .122 A4
King's Court N
SW3 . . . . .144 A1
Kingscourt Rd
SW16 . . . . .74 A1
King's Court S
SW3 . . . . .144 A1
King's Cres N4, N5 . . .6 B1
Kingscroft SW4 . . . . .62 A2
Kingscroft Rd
NW2 . . . . .10 B2
KING'S CROSS 84 C2
King's Cross WC1 . . .94 B4
King's Cross Bridge
WC1 . . . . .94 B4
King's Cross Rd
WC1 . . . . .95 A3
King's Cross, St
Pancras N1 . . . . . . .94 A4
King's Cross Sta
N1 . . . . .84 B1
Kings Ct
6 Barnsbury N7 . . . .14 B1
Chiswick W6 . . . . . . .38 C2
East Dulwich SE22 . .64 C3
Primrose Hill NW8 . .80 C3
17 Putney SW15 . . . .68 C4
Kingsdale Gdns
W11 . . . . .30 C1
Kingsdale Sch
SE21 . . . . .76 A1
Kingsdown Ave
W3 . . . . .29 A2
Kingsdown Cl
26 Deptford SE16 . . .40 A1
8 Notting Hill W11 . .31 A3
Kingsdown Ct
SW11 . . . . .60 A1
Kingsdown Ho 1
E8 . . . . .16 C3
Kingsdown Rd
N19 . . . . .5 A2
Kings Farm Ave
TW10 . . . . .54 C3
Kingsfield Ho 18
N16 . . . . .7 A1
Kingsford St NW5 . .12 B3
Kingsgate Est N1 . . .16 A2
Kingsgate Ho 2
SW9 . . . . .173 C4
Kingsgate Par
SW1 . . . . .133 A1
Kingsgate Pl NW6 . .10 C1

Kingsgate Prim Sch
NW6 . . . . .10 C1
Kingsgate Rd NW6 . .10 C1
King's Gdns 6
NW6 . . . . .10 C1
King's Gr
Peckham SE15 . . . . .50 A2
Peckham SE15 . . . . .50 A3
Kingshall Mews
SE13 . . . . .67 B4
King's Head Yd
SE1 . . . . .123 B1
Kingshill SE17 . . . . .151 A4
Kings Ho
4 Limehouse
E14 . . . . .33 B2
South Lambeth
SW8 . . . . .162 B2
Kingshold Rd E9 . . . .17 B1
King's House Sch
TW10 . . . . .54 B2
King's House Sch
(Jun) TW10 . . . . .54 B2
King's Keep 6
SW15 . . . . .57 C2
KINGSLAND 16 A2
Kingsland NW8 . . . . .80 B3
Kingsland Gn 1 8,
N1 . . . . .16 A2
Kingsland High St
E8 . . . . .16 B3
Kingsland Pas 2
E8 . . . . .16 A2
Kingsland Rd E2 . . . .24 A3
Kingsland Sh Ctr 2
E8 . . . . .16 B2
Kingslawn Cl
SW15 . . . . .57 A2
Kingsley Cl NW4 . . . . .9 A4
Kingsley Flats
SE1 . . . . .152 B3
Kingsley Ho
Chelsea SW3 . . . . . .157 C3
2 Clapham SW4 . . .171 C2
Kingsley Mews
Kensington W8 . . . .128 B1
18 St George in East
E1 . . . . .32 A2
Kingsley Pl N6 . . . . . . .3 C4
Kingsley Rd NW6 . . .23 B4
Kingsley St SW11 . . .60 B4
Kings Mall Sh Ctr
W6 . . . . .39 B2
King's Mans SW3 . .158 A3
Kingsmead SW15 . . .57 B4
Kingsmead Ct N6 . . . .4 C4
Kingsmead Ho E9 . . .18 A4
Kingsmead Prim Sch
E9 . . . . .18 A4
Kingsmead Rd
SW2 . . . . .74 C2
Kings Mead Way E5, 8
E5 . . . . .18 A4
Kingsmere Cl 18
SW15 . . . . .57 C4
Kingsmere Pl N16 . . . .6 C3
Kingsmere Rd
SW19 . . . . .69 C2
King's Mews
1 Clapham Pk
SW4 . . . . .62 A2
Gray's Inn WC1 . . . . .95 A1
Kingsmill NW8 . . . . . .79 C2
Kingsmill Terr
NW8 . . . . .79 C2

Kingsnorth Ho 12
W10 . . . . .30 C3
King Solomon Acad
NW1 . . . . .102 A4
King's Par
2 Hammersmith
W12 . . . . .38 C3
Willesden NW10 . . . .22 A2
Kings Pl W4 . . . . .37 B2
Kings Pl SE1 . . . . . .124 B2
King's Pl SE1 . . . . . .136 C3
King Sq EC1 . . . . .96 C3
King's Quay SW10 . .167 A4
King's Rd
Richmond TW10,
TW9 . . . . .54 B2
Willesden NW10 . . . . .9 A1
King's Rd
Chelsea SW3 . . . . . .144 B1
Chelsea SW10 . . . . .157 B3
Mortlake SW14 . . . . .55 C4
Kings Ride Gate
TW10 . . . . .54 C3
Kingsridge SW19 . . .70 A2
King's Scholars' Pas
SW1 . . . . .146 C4
King St
Acton W3 . . . . .28 B1
Hammersmith W6 . . .38 C2
St James SW1 . . . . .119 A2
Strand WC2 . . . . . . .120 A4
Whitechapel E2 . . . .24 C4
King Stairs Cl
SE16 . . . . .40 A4
King's Terr NW1 . . . .82 C3
Kingston Ho 4
NW6 . . . . .10 A1
Kingston Ho E
SW7 . . . . .130 A3
Kingston Ho N
SW7 . . . . .130 A3
Kingston Ho S
SW7 . . . . .130 A3
Kingston Rd SW15,
SW19 . . . . .69 A3
Kingston Univ
(Roehampton Vale)
SW15 . . . . .68 A1
Kingston Vale
SW15 . . . . .68 A1
King Street Cloisters
6 W6 . . . . .39 A2
King Street Coll 10
W12 . . . . .39 B2
Kingswater Pl
SW11 . . . . .158 A1
Kingsway
Mortlake SW14,
St Giles WC2 . . . . . .106 C2
Kingsway Coll 12
NW5 . . . . .13 A2
Kingsway Mans
WC1 . . . . .106 C4
Kingsway Pl EC1 . . . .96 A2
Kingswear Rd NW5 . . .4 A1
Kings Well 22
NW3 . . . . .11 B4
Kings Wlk Sh Mall
SW3 . . . . .144 C2
Kingswood 31 E2 . . .25 B3
Kingswood Ave
NW6 . . . . .23 A3
Kingswood Cl
SW8 . . . . .162 B1

Kingswood Ct
Hither Green
SE13 . . . . .67 C1
7 Richmond TW10 . .54 B2
Kings Wood Ct 4
NW6 . . . . .10 C1
Kingswood Rd
South Acton W4 . . . .37 B3
Streatham SW2 . . . . .74 A4
Kingswood Terr
W4 . . . . .37 B3
Kings Yd E15 . . . . . . .18 C2
Kington Ho 18
NW6 . . . . .78 B3
Kingward Ho 1 . . . .111 B4
Kingweston Cl NW2 . .1 A1
King William La 3
SE10 . . . . .43 A1
King William St
EC4 . . . . .123 C4
King William Wlk
SE10 . . . . .52 B4
Kingwood Rd
SW6 . . . . .154 A1
Kinloch St N7 . . . . .5 B1
Kinnaird Ave W4 . . . .45 B3
Kinnear Rd W12 . . . .38 B4
Kinnerton Pl N
SW1 . . . . .131 A3
Kinnerton Pl S
SW1 . . . . .131 A3
Kinnerton St SW1 . .131 B3
Kinnerton Yd
SW1 . . . . .131 B3
Kinnoull Mans 10
E5 . . . . .17 A4
Kinnoul Rd W6 . . . .154 A4
Kinross Ho N1 . . . . . .84 C4
Kinsale Rd SE15 . . . .64 C4
Kinsham Ho 8
E2 . . . . .24 C1 99 C2
Kintore Way SE1 . . .152 C4
Kintyre Ct 17 SW2 . .74 A4
Kintyre Ho 6 E14 . . .34 B1
Kinver Ho 4 N19 . . . .5 A2
Kipling Ho 29 SE5 . . .48 B3
Kipling St SE1 . . . . . .137 C4
Kipling Twr 3 W3 . . .37 B3
Kirby Gr SE1 . . . . . . .138 A4
Kirby St EC1 . . . . . . .107 C4
Kirkeby Bldg EC1 . . .107 B4
Kirkland Wlk 4
E8 . . . . .16 B2
Kirkley Ho N16 . . . . . .7 A3
Kirkman Ho W1 . . . .105 B3
Kirkman Pl W1 . . . . .105 B3
Kirkmichael Rd
E14 . . . . .34 B3
Kirkside Rd SE3 . . . .53 C4
Kirk St WC1 . . . . .94 A1
Kirkstall Gdns
SW2 . . . . .74 A3
Kirkstall Ho SW1 . . .146 A2
Kirkstall Rd SW2 . . .74 A3
Kirkstead Ct E5 . . . . .18 A4
Kirkstone NW1 . . . . .92 C4
Kirkwall Pl E2 . . . . . .25 B2
Kirkwood Rd SE15 . .50 A1
Kirtley Ho SW8 . . . . .171 A4
Kirtling St SW8 . . . . .160 C2
Kirton Cl W4 . . . . . . .37 C2
Kirton Gdns 21 2
E2 . . . . .24 B2 99 A3
Kirwin Way SE5 . . . . .48 A3
Kitcat Terr E3 . . . . . .26 C2

Kite Ho 5 SW11 . . . .60 A4
Kite Pl 9
E2 . . . . .24 C2 99 C4
Kitson Rd
Barnes SW13 . . . . . .46 C2
Camberwell SE5 . . . .48 B3
Kittiwake Ct 28
SE8 . . . . .51 B4
Kitto Rd SE14 . . . . . .50 C1
Kiver Rd N19 . . . . .5 A2
Klea Ave SW4 . . . . . .61 C1
Kleffens Ct 2 SE3 . . .53 B3
Kleine Wharf 30
N1 . . . . .24 A4
Knapp Cl NW10 . . . . . .8 A2
Knapp Rd E3 . . . . . . .26 C1
Knaresborough Dr
SW18 . . . . .71 A3
Knaresborough Ho
N4 . . . . .6 B4
Knaresborough Pl
SW5 . . . . .142 A4
Knatchbull Rd
Brixton SE5 . . . . .48 A2
Stonebridge NW10 . .20 C4
Knebworth Ho
South Lambeth
SW8 . . . . .171 C3
2 Stoke Newington
N16 . . . . .16 A4
Knebworth Rd 3
N16 . . . . .16 A4
Kneller Ho
SW8 . . . . .171 C2
Kneller Rd SE4 . . . . .66 A3
Knighten St E1 . . . . .32 A1
Knighthead Point 2
E14 . . . . .41 C3
Knight Ho SE17 . . . .152 A3
Knightleas Ct NW2 . . .9 B2
Knightrider Ct
EC4 . . . . .122 C4
Knightrider St
EC4 . . . . .122 B4
Knights Arc SW1 . . .130 C3
Knight's Ave W5 . . . .36 A4
KNIGHTSBRIDGE 130 A2
Knightsbridge SW1,
SW7 . . . . .130 C3
Knightsbridge Ct
SW1 . . . . .131 A3
Knightsbridge Gn
SW1 . . . . .130 C3
Knightsbridge Sta
SW1 . . . . .131 A3
Knightsbridge Under
Sch SW7 . . . . .143 A3
Knights Cl 6 . . . . . . .17 B3
Knights Ho
Bermondsey SE1 . . .138 C4
South Lambeth
SW8 . . . . .162 B1
West Kensington
SW5 . . . . .141 C4
Knight's Ho SW10 . .156 C2
Knights Rd E16 . . . . .43 A4
Knight's Wlk SE11 . .150 A3
Knightswood Ct N6 . . .4 C4
Knivet Rd SW6 . . . . .155 B3
Knoll Ho NW8 . . . . . .78 C2
Knoll Rd SW18 . . . . .59 B2

Knolly's Cl SE27,
SW16 . . . . **74** C1
Knolly's Rd SE27,
SW16 . . . . **74** C1
Knot Ho SE1 . . . . . **124** C1
Knottisford St E2 . . **25** B2
Knowlden Ho **5**
E1 . . . . **32** B2
Knowledge Point Sch
6 N7 . . . . **14** B2
Knowles Hill Cres
SE13 . . . . **67** C2
Knowles Ho
Wandsworth
SW18 . . . . **59** A1
Willesden Green
NW10 . . . . **21** C4
Knowles Wlk SW4 . . **61** B4
Knowlton Ho **32**
SW9 . . . . **173** C4
Knowsley Rd
SW11 . . . . **168** C1
Knox Ct **16** SW4 . . **172** B2
Knox Ho SW15 . . . . **47** B1
Knox St W1 . . . . . . **102** C4
Knoyle Ho W14 . . . . **126** B2
Knoyle St SE14 . . . . **51** A4
Kobi Nazrul Prim Sch
41 E1 . . . . **111** C2
Kossuth St SE10 . . . **43** A1
Kotree Way **10**
SE1 . . . . **153** C2
Kramer Mews
SW5 . . . . **142** A1
Kreedman Wlk **7**
E8 . . . . **16** C3
Kreisel Wlk TW9 . . . **44** B4
Kylemore Ct **4**
W12 . . . . **38** A3
Kylemore Rd NW6 . . **10** C1
Kylestrome Ho
SW1 . . . . **145** C3
Kynance Mews
SW7 . . . . **128** B1
Kynance Pl SW7 . . . **128** C1
Kynaston Ho **7**
SW2 . . . . **74** B3
Kynaston Rd N16 . . . . **7** A1
Kyrle Rd SW11 . . . . **60** C1
Kyverdale Rd N16 . . . **7** B3

L

Laburnham Ct NW2 . . **1** A3
Laburnum Ct **5**
SE15 . . . . **50** B3
Laburnum Ct **26**
E2 . . . . **24** B4
Laburnum Ho
New Cross SE4 . . . . **51** B1
6 Stoke Newington
N16 . . . . **6** C2
Laburnum St E2 . . . **24** B4
Lacey Ho **7** SE13 . . **52** B1
Lacey Mews **9** E3 . . **26** C3
Lacine Ct **13** SE16 . . **40** C4
Lackington St
EC2 . . . . **109** C4
Lackland Ho **1** SE1 **153** A2
Lacland Ho SW10 . . **157** B2
Lacon Rd SE22 . . . . **64** C3
Lacy Rd SW15 . . . . . **57** C3

Ladbroke Cres
W11 . . . . **31** A3
Ladbroke Gdns
W11 . . . . . **31** B2 **112** C4
Ladbroke Gr
Kensal Town W10 . . . **31** A4
Notting Hill
W11 . . . . . **31** B2 **112** C4
Ladbroke Grove Ho **1**
W11 . . . . **31** B2
Ladbroke Grove Sta
W10 . . . . **31** A4
Ladbroke Ho E1 . . . **111** A3
Ladbroke Mews
W11 . . . . . **31** A1 **112** B1
Ladbroke Rd
W11 . . . . . **31** B1 **112** C1
Ladbroke Sq
W11 . . . . . **31** B2 **112** C2
Ladbroke Terr
W11 . . . . . **31** B1 **113** A2
Ladbroke Wlk
W11 . . . . . **31** B1 **113** A1
Ladlands SE22 . . . . **76** C4
Ladybower Ct **6**
E5 . . . . **17** C4
Ladycroft Rd SE13 . . **67** A4
Lady Elizabeth Ho
SW4 . . . . **55** B4
Ladyfield Cl SE4 . . . **66** B3
Ladywell Hts SE4 . . . **66** B1
Ladywell Rd SE13 . . **67** A2
Ladywell Sta SE13 . . **67** A2
Ladywell Water Twr
SE4 . . . . **66** C2
Lafitte Ho **32** N19 . . . **4** C4
Lafone Ho **11** SW2 . **74** A4
Lafone St SE1 . . . . **138** C4
Lagado Mews
SE16 . . . . **32** C1
Lagonda Ho **11** E3 . . **26** C1
Lagonier Ho EC1 . . . **97** A3
Laindon Ho **6** N7 . . . . **7** B3
Laing Ho SE5 . . . . . . **48** B3
Lainson St SW18 . . . **70** C4
Lairdale Cl SE21 . . . **75** B4
Laird Ho SE5 . . . . . . **48** B3
Lairs Ct **1** N7 . . . . . **14** A2
Laitwood Rd SW12 . . **73** A3
Lakanal **14** SE5 . . . . **49** A2
Lake Ho SE1 . . . . . **136** C3
Laker Ct SW4 . . . . . **172** B2
Laker Pl SW15 . . . . . **58** A1
Lakeside Ct N4 . . . . . **6** B3
Lakeside Rd W14 . . . **39** C3
Lakeview **25** E3 . . . . **27** A2
Lake View Ct
SW1 . . . . **132** B2
Lakis Ct **3** N19 . . . . . **4** B2
Laleham Ho
E2 . . . . **24** B1 **98** C2
Lalor St SW6 . . . . . **164** B2
Lambard Ho **4**
SE10 . . . . **52** B3

Lamb Ct **16** E14 . . . **33** A2
Lamberhurst Ho **14**
SE15 . . . . **50** B4
Lambert Ave TW9 . . . **55** A4
Lambert Ho
10 Brixton SW9 . . . **173** B1
10 Crouch End N19 . . . **4** C4
Lambert Rd SW2 . . . **62** B2
Lambert St N1 . . . . . **14** C1
LAMBETH **134** C4
Lambeth Acad
SW4 . . . . **61** B2
Lambeth Coll (Brixton
Ctr) SW2 . . . . **62** B2
Lambeth Coll
(Clapham Ctr)
SW4 . . . . **61** B2
Lambeth Coll
(Vauxhall Ctr)
SW8 . . . . **171** B4
Lambeth Ct **8**
SW18 . . . . **58** C2
Lambeth High St
SE1 . . . . **148** B4
Lambeth Hill
EC4 . . . . . . **122** C4
Lambeth Hospl
SW9 . . . . **62** B4
Lambeth North Sta
SE1 . . . . **135** B2
Lambeth Pal Rd SE1 . **134** C1
Lambeth Palace Rd
SE1 . . . . **135** A2
Lambeth Pier SE1 . . **134** B1
Lambeth Rd SE1 . . . **135** B1
Lambeth Twrs
SE11 . . . . **135** B1
Lambeth Wlk
SE11 . . . . **149** A4
Lambfold Ho N7 . . . . **14** A2
Lamb Ho
28 Camberwell
SE5 . . . . **48** B3
11 Camberwell SE5 . . **48** C2
5 Greenwich SE10 . . **52** B4
Lamb La E8 . . . . **17** A1
Lamble St NW5 . . . . **12** C4
Lamb Office St
SE1 . . . . **123** C1
Lambolle Pl NW3 . . . **12** A2
Lambolle Rd NW3 . . **12** A2
Lambourn Cl **9**
NW5 . . . . **13** B4
Lambourne Gr
SE16 . . . . **40** C1
Lambourne Ho
NW8 . . . . **101** C4
Lambourn Rd SW4 . . **61** A4
Lambrook Ho **13**
SE15 . . . . **49** C2
Lambrook Terr
SW6 . . . . **164** A4
Lamb's Bldgs EC1 . . . **97** B1
Lamb's Conduit Pas
WC1 . . . . **106** C4
Lamb's Conduit St
WC1 . . . . **94** C1
Lamb's Mews N1 . . . **86** A3
Lamb's Pass EC1 . . . **97** B1
Lamb St E1 . . . . . . **110** C4
Lambton Ct **2** N19 . . . **5** A3
Lambton Mews **4**
N19 . . . . **5** A3
Lambton Pl
W11 . . . . . **31** B2 **113** A4
Lambton Rd N19 . . . . **5** A3
Lamb Wlk SE1 . . . . **138** A3

Lamerton Lo **10**
TW9 . . . . **44** B2
Lamerton St **8**
SE8 . . . . **51** C4
Lamington St **3**
W6 . . . . **39** A2
Lamlash St SE11 . . . **150** A4
Lamley Ho SE10 . . . . **52** A3
Lammas Rd E9 . . . . . **17** C1
Lammermoor Rd
SW12 . . . . **73** A4
Lamont Rd SW10 . . . **157** B3
Lamont Rd Pas
SW10 . . . . **157** B3
Lampard Gr N16 . . . . . **7** B3
Lampern Sq **11**
E2 . . . . **24** C2 **99** C4
Lampeter Sq W6 . . . **154** A3
Lamplighter Cl **34**
E1 . . . . **25** B1
Lampson Ho **6**
N19 . . . . **13** B4
Lanark Ho **5** SE1 . . . **153** B1
Lanark Mans
Paddington W9 . . . . . **89** A2
16 Shepherd's Bush
W12 . . . . **39** B4
Lanark Mews NW8 . . . **89** A2
Lanark Pl W9 . . . . . . **89** A2
Lanark Rd W9 . . . . . **88** C3
Lanark Sq E14 . . . . . **42** A3
Lanbury Rd SE15 . . . **65** C3
Lancashire Ct W1 . . **118** B4
Lancaster Ave SE21,
SE27 . . . . **75** B2
Lancaster Cl
10 De Beauvoir Town
N1 . . . . **16** A1
Kensington W2 . . . . **114** A3
Lancaster Cotts **1**
TW10 . . . . **54** A1
Lancaster Ct
Bayswater W2 . . . . . **115** A4
Parsons Green
SW6 . . . . **155** A1
West Norwood
SE27 . . . . **75** A2
Lancaster Dr
Canary Wharf E14 . . . **34** B1
Maitland Pk NW3 . . . **12** B2
Lancaster Gate
W2 . . . . **115** A4
Lancaster Gate Sta
W2 . . . . **115** B4
Lancaster Gr NW3 . . **12** A2
Lancaster hall **14**
E16 . . . . **35** C1
Lancaster Ho
SW15 . . . . **57** A4
Lancaster Lo **2**
W11 . . . . **31** A3
Lancaster Mews
Bayswater W2 . . . . . **115** A4
3 Richmond TW10 . . **54** A1
3 Wandsworth
SW18 . . . . **59** A2
Lancaster Pk
TW10 . . . . **54** A2
Lancaster PI WC2 . . **120** C3
Lancaster Rd
Dudden Hill NW10 . . . . **8** C3
Finsbury Pk N4 . . . . . **5** C4

Lancaster Rd continued
Notting Hill W11 . . . . **31** A3
Lancaster St SE1 . . **136** B3
Lancaster Stables **10**
NW3 . . . . **12** A2
Lancaster Terr
W2 . . . . **115** B4
Lancaster Wlk
W2 . . . . **115** A2
Lancefield Ct
SE15 . . . . **65** A3
Lancefield St W10 . . **23** B2
Lancell St N16 . . . . . . **7** A2
Lancelot Pl SW7 . . . **130** C3
Lancer Sq W8 . . . . . **128** A4
Lanchester Way
SE14 . . . . **50** C2
Lancing St NW1 . . . . **93** B3
Lancresse Ct N1 . . . **24** A4
Landale Ct SE10 . . . . **52** B2
Landale Ho **13**
SE16 . . . . **40** B3
Landcroft Rd SE22 . . **64** B1
Landells Rd SE22 . . . **64** C1
Landford Rd SW15 . . **57** B4
Landin Ho **1** E14 . . . **33** C3
Landleys Field **21**
N7 . . . . **13** C3
Landmann Ho **16**
SE16 . . . . **40** A2
Landmann Way
SE14 . . . . **40** C1
Landmark Hts E5 . . . **18** A4
Landon Pl SW1 . . . . **130** C2
Landons Cl E14 . . . . **34** B1
Landor Ho **6** SE5 . . . **48** C3
Landor Rd SW9 . . . . **62** A4
Landor Wlk **11**
W12 . . . . **38** C4
Landrake NW1 . . . . . **83** A3
Landridge Rd
SW6 . . . . **164** C2
Landseer Ct **13** N19 . . **5** A2
Landseer Ho
Battersea SW11 . . . **169** C3
Paddington NW8 . . . . **89** C2
Westminster SW1 . . **147** C3
Landseer Rd N19 . . . . **5** A2
Landulph Ho
SE11 . . . . **149** C2
Landward Ct W1 . . . **102** B2
Lane Cl SW11 . . . . . . **72** B4
Lanercost Cl SW2 . . **74** C2
Lanercost Rd SW2 . . **74** C2
Lane The NW8 . . . . . **78** C1
Laneway SW15 . . . . **57** A2
Laney Bldg EC1 . . . **107** B4
Lanfranc Rd E3 . . . . **26** A3
Lanfrey Pl W14 . . . . **140** C1
Langbourne Ave N6 . . . **3** C2
Langbourne Ho **4**
SW2 . . . . **62** C2
Langbourne Mans
N6 . . . . **3** C2
Langbourne Pl
E14 . . . . **42** A1
Langbourne Prim Sch
SE21 . . . . **76** A1
Langdale NW1 . . . . . **92** C4
Langdale Cl
Camberwell SE17 . . . **48** B4
Mortlake SW14 . . . . **55** A3

Langdale Ho SW1 **146** C1
Langdale Rd SE10 . . **52** B3
Langdale St 2B E1 . . **32** A3
Langdon Ct
 Finsbury EC1 . . . . . **86** B1
 Harlesden NW10 . . . **21** A4
Langdon Ho 3
 E14 . . . . **34** B3
Langdon Park Rd
 N6 . . . . **4** B4
Langdon Park Sch
 E14 . . . . **34** B3
Langdon Park Sta
 E14 . . . . **34** B3
Langdon Pk L Ctr
 E14 . . . . **34** B3
Langdon Pk Sta
 E3 . . . . **34** A4
Langdon Pl SW14 . . **55** B4
Langdon Way 13
 SE1 . . . . **153** C3
Langford Cl
 Shacklewell E8 . . . **16** C3
 St John's Wood
 NW8 . . . . **79** A2
Langford Gdns SE5 . . **64** A4
Langford Ho 5
 SE8 . . . . **51** C4
Langford Pl NW8 . . **79** B2
Langford Prim Sch
 SW6 . . . . **166** B2
Langford Rd 4
 SW6 . . . . **166** B2
Langham Ct 4
 SW15 . . . . **57** C2
Langham Ho SW4 . **61** B2
Langham Mans
 SW5 . . . . **142** A1
Langham Pl
 Chiswick W4 . . . . . **46** A4
 Fitzrovia W1 . . . . **104** B3
Langham St W1 . . . **104** B3
Lang Ho
 South Lambeth
 SW8 . . . . **162** A1
 3 Tufnell Pk N19 . . **4** B1
Langholm Cl
 SW12 . . . . **73** C4
Langhorne Ct 10
 NW8 . . . . **11** C1
Langhurst Ho 10
 SW11 . . . . **169** B2
Langland Gdns
 NW3 . . . . **11** A3
Langland Ho 10
 SE5 . . . . **48** C3
Langland Mans
 NW3 . . . . **11** A3
Langler Rd NW10 . . **22** B3
Langley Ct
 South Lambeth
 SW8 . . . . **172** A4
 Strand WC2 . . . . . **120** A4
Langley Dr W3 . . . **37** A4
Langley Ho
 11 Lower Clapton
 E5 . . . . **17** A3
 30 Paddington W2 . **31** C4
Langley La SW8 . . . **162** B4
Langley Mans
 SW8 . . . . **162** B4
Langley St WC2 . . . **106** A1
Langmead Ho 34
 E3 . . . . **27** A2

Langmore Ho 39
 E1 . . . . **111** C1
Langport Ho 1
 SW9 . . . . **48** A1
Langridge 15 NW5 . . **12** C2
Langroyd Rd SW17 . **72** B2
Langside Ave
 SW15 . . . . **56** C3
Lang St E1 . . . . **25** B1
Langston Hughes Cl
 5 SE24 . . . . **63** A3
Langthorn Ct EC2 . **109** C2
Langthorne Lo 30
 SW2 . . . . **74** C4
Langthorne St
 SW6 . . . . **47** C3
Langton Cl WC1 . . . **95** A2
Langton Ct SW15 . . **58** B1
Langton Ho SE11 . . **149** A3
Langton Pl SW18 . . **70** C3
Langton Rd SW9 . . **48** A3
Langton St SW10 . . **157** A3
Langton Way SE3 . . **53** C3
Langtry Pl SW6 . . . **155** C4
Langtry Rd NW8 . . **78** A3
Langtry Wlk NW8 . . **78** C4
Lanhill Rd W9 . . . . **23** C1
Lanier Rd SE13 . . . **67** C1
Lanner Ho 8
 SW11 . . . . **60** A4
Lannoy Point
 SW6 . . . . **154** B2
Lanrick Rd E14 . . . **35** A3
Lansbury Gdns 1
 E14 . . . . **34** C3
Lansbury Lawrence
 Prim Sch 3 E14 . . **34** A3
Lanscombe Wlk
 SW8 . . . . **162** A1
Lansdell Ho 9
 SW2 . . . . **62** C1
Lansdowne Coll
 W2 . . . . **114** A3
Lansdowne Cres
 W11 . . . . **31** A3 **112** B3
Lansdowne Dr E8 . . **16** C1
Lansdowne Gdns
 SW8 . . . . **172** A4
Lansdowne Gr
 NW10 . . . . **8** A4
Lansdowne Hill
 SE27 . . . . **75** A1
Lansdowne Ho
 W11 . . . . **31** B1 **112** C2
Lansdowne Mews
 W11 . . . . **31** B1 **112** C2
Lansdowne Pl
 SE1 . . . . **137** C2
Lansdowne Rd
 W11 . . . . **31** A2 **112** B3
Lansdowne Rise
 W11 . . . . **31** A2 **112** B3
Lansdowne Row
 W1 . . . . **118** B2
Lansdowne Terr
 WC1 . . . . **94** B1
Lansdowne Way SW4,
 SW8 . . . . **172** B3
Lansdowne Wlk
 W11 . . . . **31** B2 **112** C2
Lansdown Ho 28
 SE5 . . . . **48** B1

Lantern Cl SW15 . . **56** C3
Lantern Ho E14 . . . **41** C4
Lanterns Ct E14 . . **41** C3
Lant Ho SE1 . . . . . **136** C3
Lantry Cl 1 W3 . . . **28** A1
Lant St SE1 . . . . . **137** A3
Lanvanor Rd SE15 . . **50** B1
Lanyard Ho 4 SE8 . **41** B2
Lapford Cl W9 . . . . **23** B1
Lapsing SE1 . . . . . **125** A1
Lapwing Twr 51
 SE8 . . . . **51** B4
Lapworth Ct W2 . . **100** B4
Lara Cl SE13 . . . . . **67** B1
Larch Ave W3 . . . . **29** A1
Larch Cl
 Balham SW12 . . . **73** A2
 1B Deptford SE8 . . **51** B4
 10 Upper Holloway
 N19 . . . . **4** B2
Larch Ct 25 SE16 . . **40** B4
Larchmore Ct N19 . . **5** A2
Larch Rd NW2 . . . . **9** B4
Larcom St SE17 . . . **151** A3
Larden Rd W3 . . . . **38** A4
La Retraite RC Girls
 Sch SW12 . . . . . **73** B4
Larissa St SE17 . . . **151** C3
Larix Ct NW10 . . . . **21** C4
Larkfield Rd 5 TW9 . **54** A3
Larkhall La SW4 . . **172** A3
Larkhall Rise
 SW4 . . . . **171** B1
Lark Row 2 E2 . . . . **25** B4
Larmenier & Sacred
 Heart RC Prim Sch
 41 W6 . . . . **39** C2
Larnaca Ho SE1 . . . **138** C2
Larnach Rd W6 . . . **47** C4
Larpent Ave SW15 . . **57** B2
Lascelles Ho NW1 . . **90** B1
Lascell St SE10 . . . . **43** A1
Lasseter Pl SE3 . . . . **53** B4
Latchmere Rd
 SW11 . . . . **168** C1
Latchmere St 5
 SW11 . . . . **168** C2
Latham Ho 1 E1 . . . **32** C3
Latimer SE17 . . . . . **152** A1
Latimer Ho
 11 Homerton E9 . . **17** C2
 Notting Hill
 W11 . . . . **31** B2 **113** A3
Latimer Ind Est 1
 NW10 . . . . **30** B3
Latimer Pl W10 . . . **30** B3
Latimer Rd W10 . . . **30** B3
Latimer Road Sta
 W10 . . . . **30** B2
Latitude Ho NW1 . . **82** A3
Latona Rd SE15 . . . **49** C4
Lattimer Pl W4 . . . **46** A4
Latvia Ct SE17 . . . **151** A1
Latymer Ct W6 . . . . **39** C2
Latymer Upper Sch 14
 W6 . . . . **38** C2
Lauderdale Mans
 W9 . . . . **88** B3
Lauderdale Rd W9 . . **88** B3

Lauderdale Twr
 EC2 . . . . **108** C4
Laud St SE11 . . . . **148** C2
Laughton Ho 11
 SW2 . . . . **62** C1
Launcelot St SE1 . . **135** B3
Launceston Pl
 W8 . . . . **128** C1
Launch St E14 . . . . **42** B3
Laundress La N16 . . **7** C1
Laundry La 7 N1 . . **15** B1
Laundry Rd W6 . . . **154** A3
Laura Pl E5 . . . . . . **17** B4
Laurel Bank Gdns 3
 SW6 . . . . **165** A2
Laurel Cl 8 N19 . . . **4** B2
Laurel Ct
 Dalston E8 . . . . . **16** B1
 2 Putney SW15 . . . **57** C2
 9 Rotherhithe
 SE16 . . . . **33** A1
Laurel Ho
 8 Deptford SE8 . . **51** B4
 5 Hamstead NW3 . . **11** A2
 4 Richmond TW9 . . **45** A2
Laurel St E8 . . . . . . **16** B2
Laurence Mews 12
 W12 . . . . **38** C4
Laurence Pountney
 Hill EC4 . . . . . . **123** B4
Laurence Pountney La
 EC4 . . . . **123** C4
Laurie Gr SE14 . . . . **51** A2
Laurie Ho
 Newington SE1 . . . **136** B1
 Notting Hill
 W8 . . . . **31** C1 **113** B2
Laurier Rd NW5 . . . **4** A1
Lauriston Ho 6
 E9 . . . . **17** C1
Lauriston Lo NW6 . . **10** B2
Lauriston Prim Sch 5
 E9 . . . . **25** C4
Lauriston Rd E9 . . . **17** C1
Lausanne Rd SE15 . . **50** B2
Lavell St N16 . . . . . **15** C4
Lavender Cl SW3 . . **157** C3
Lavender Ct SW4 . . **172** B3
Lavender Gdns
 SW11 . . . . **60** C3
Lavender Gr E8 . . . . **16** C1
Lavender Hill
 SW11 . . . . **60** C4
Lavender Ho
 8 Richmond
 TW9 . . . . **45** A2
 14 Rotherhithe
 SE16 . . . . **32** C1
Lavender Rd
 Battersea SW11 . . **59** C4
 Rotherhithe SE16 . . **33** A1
Lavender Sweep
 SW11 . . . . **60** B3
Lavender Terr 12
 SW11 . . . . **60** A4
Lavender Wlk
 SW11 . . . . **60** B3
Lavendon Ho NW8 . . **90** B2
Lavengro Rd SE27 . . **75** B2
Lavenham Rd
 SW18 . . . . **70** C3
Laverstoke Gdns
 SW15 . . . . **68** C4
Laverton Mews
 SW5 . . . . **142** B3

Laverton Pl SW5. . **142** B3
Lavina Gr N1 . . . . . **84** C2
Lavington Cl E9 . . . **18** B2
Lavington St SE1 . . **122** B1
Lawdale Jun Sch 27
 E2 . . . . **24** C2 **99** C4
Lawford Rd
 Chiswick W4 . . . . . **45** B3
 De Beauvoir Town
 N1 . . . . **16** A1
 Kentish Town NW5 . **13** B2
Lawfords Wharf 1
 NW1 . . . . **13** B1
Lawless Ho 5 E14 . . **34** B2
Lawless St 2 E14 . . **34** A2
Lawley St E5 . . . . . **17** B4
Lawman Ct 2
 TW9 . . . . **44** B2
Lawn Cres TW9 . . . **44** C1
Lawn Ct SE12 . . . . **97** C1
Lawn House Cl
 E14 . . . . **42** B4
Lawn La SW8 . . . . **162** C4
Lawn Rd NW3 . . . . **12** B3
Lawns The N16 . . . . **16** A3
Lawrence Ave
 NW10 . . . . **20** C4
Lawrence Bldgs 1
 N16 . . . . **7** B1
Lawrence Cl
 Bow E3 . . . . **26** C3
 5 Shepherd's Bush
 W12 . . . . **30** A2
Lawrence Ct
 4 South Acton
 W3 . . . . **37** B3
 Stoke Newington N16 . **7** B1
Lawrence Ho
 20 Camden Town
 NW1 . . . . **13** A1
 Westminster SW1 . **147** C3
Lawrence La EC2 . . **109** A2
Lawrence Mans
 SW3 . . . . **158** A3
Lawrence Pl N1 . . . **84** B3
Lawrence St
 Canning Town
 E16 . . . . **35** B4
 Chelsea SW3 . . . . **158** A3
Lawrence Trad Est
 SE10 . . . . **43** A2
Lawrie Park Gdns
 SW7 . . . . **143** A3
Lawson Cl SW19 . . **69** C1
Lawson Ct 1 N4 . . . **5** B3
Lawson Ho 17
 W12 . . . . **30** A2
Law St SE1 . . . . . . **137** C2
Lawton Rd E3 . . . . . **26** A2
Laxfield Ct E8 . . . . **24** C4
Laxley Cl SE5 . . . . . **48** A3
Laxton Path 1
 SE4 . . . . **65** C3
Laxton Pl NW1 . . . . **92** B2
Layard Rd SE16 . . . **40** A2
Layard Sq SE16 . . . **40** A2
Laybourne Ho 18
 E14 . . . . **41** C4
Laycock Prim Sch 6
 N1 . . . . **15** A2
Laycock St N1 . . . . **14** C2
Layfield Ho 6
 SE10 . . . . **43** C1
Laystall Ct EC1 . . . **95** B1

Laystall St EC1 . . . . . . **95 B1**
Layton Pl TW9 . . . .**44 C2**
Lazar Wlk **2** N7 . . . . . **5 B2**
Leabank Sq E9 . . . .**18 C2**
Leabourne Rd N16 . . . . **7 C4**
Leacroft Ave SW12 .**72 B4**
Lea Ct **3** W12 . . . . . .**38 A4**
Leadenhall Building
   The EC3 . . . .**110 A1**
Leadenhall Mkt
   EC3 . . . .**110 A1**
Leadenhall Pl
   EC3 . . . .**110 A1**
Leadenhall St
   EC3 . . . .**110 A1**
Leadenham Ct **5**
   E3 . . . .**26 C1**
Lea Ho NW8 . . . .**90 A1**
Leahurst Rd SE13 . . .**67 C2**
Lea Int E9 . . . .**18 C3**
Leake St
   Lambeth SE1 . . . . .**135 B3**
   South Bank SE1 . . . **135 A4**
Leamington Ct
   1 Forest Hill
      SE26 . . . .**76 C1**
   North Acton W3 . . . .**28 C4**
Leamington Ho **3**
   W11 . . . .**31 B4**
Leamington Pk
   W3 . . . .**28 C4**
Leamington Rd Villas
   W11 . . . .**31 B4**
Leamore St W6 . . . .**39 B2**
Leamouth Rd E14 . .**34 C3**
Leander Ct
   27 Hackney E9 . . . .**17 B1**
   St Johns SE8 . . . . . .**51 C2**
Leander Rd SW2 . . . .**62 C1**
Leary Ho SE11 . . . . . .**149 A1**
Lea Sq **2** E3 . . . .**26 B4**
Leatherdale St
   37 Bethnal Green
      E1 . . . .**25 B1**
   16 Globe Town E1 .**25 C2**
Leatherhead Cl N16 . .**7 B3**
Leather La EC1 . . . . .**107 C4**
Leather La Mkt
   EC1 . . . .**107 C4**
Leathermarket Ct
   SE1 . . . .**138 A3**
Leathermarket St
   SE1 . . . .**138 A3**
Leathwaite Rd
   SW11 . . . .**60 B2**
Leathwell Rd SE8 . .**52 A1**
Lebanon Gdns
   SW18 . . . .**58 C1**
Lebanon Rd SW18 . .**58 C2**
Lebus Ho NW8 . . . .**80 A1**
Lechmere App **9 A2**
Lechmere Rd NW2 .**9 A2**
Leckford Rd SW18 . .**71 B3**
Leckhampton Pl **7**
   SW2 . . . .**74 C4**
Lecky Ho NW2 . . . .**9 A4**
Lecky St SW7 . . . . . .**143 B2**
L'Ecole des Petits Sch
   SW6 . . . .**166 A2**
Leconfield Ave SW13,
   SW15 . . . .**56 B4**
Leconfield Ho SE5 . .**64 A4**
Leconfield Rd N5 . . .**15 C4**
Lector Ct EC1 . . . .**95 C1**

Leda Ct **3** SW9 . . . .**163 B1**
Ledam Bldg EC1 . . .**107 B4**
Ledbury Ho **12**
   SE22 . . . .**64 A4**
Ledbury Mews N
   W11 . . . .**31 C3**
Ledbury Mews W
   W11 . . . .**31 C2 113 B4**
Ledbury Rd W11 . . . .**31 C3**
Ledbury St SE15 . . . .**49 C3**
Lee Ho **10** N16 . . . . .**15 C4**
Lee Conservancy Rd
   E9 . . . .**18 B3**
Lee Ct SE13 . . . .**67 C3**
Leeds Ct EC1 . . . .**96 A2**
Lee Ho **3** N19 . . . .**13 C3**
Leeke St WC1 . . . .**94 C4**
Leeland Way NW10 . .**8 B4**
Leerdam Dr E14 . . . . .**42 B3**
Lees Ct W1 . . . .**117 B4**
Lees St SE17 . . . .**151 C1**
Leeson Rd **11**
   . . . .**62 C3**
Lees Pl W1 . . . .**117 B4**
Lee St E8 . . . .**24 B4**
Leet Ct N16 . . . .**15 C4**
Leeve Ho **7** W9 . . . .**23 B2**
Leeward Ct **3** E1 .**125 C2**
Leeway SE8 . . . .**41 B1**
Lefevre Wlk E3 . . . . . .**26 C4**
Leffern Rd W12 . . . . .**38 C4**
Leff Ho **9** NW6 . . . . .**10 A1**
Lefroy Ho **8** SW2 . .**74 C4**
Lefroy Rd W12 . . . . . .**38 B4**
Legard Rd N5 . . . .**6 A1**
Leggatt Rd E15 . . . . .**27 B3**
Legge St SE13 . . . .**67 B2**
Leghorn Rd NW10 . . .**21 C3**
Legion Cl N1 . . . .**14 C1**
Legion Terr E3 . . . .**26 C4**
Leicester Ct
   7 Paddington
      W2 . . . .**31 C4**
   St James WC2 . . . .**119 C4**
Leicester Ho
   4 Brixton SW9 . . .**63 A4**
   5 Putney SW15 . . .**69 B4**
Leicester Pl WC2 . .**119 C4**
Leicester Sq WC2 .**119 C3**
Leicester Square Sta
   . . . .**119 C4**
Leicester St WC2 . .**119 C4**
Leigham Ave
   SW16 . . . .**74 A1**
Leigham Cl **5**
   SW16 . . . .**74 A1**
Leigham Court Rd
   SW16 . . . .**74 B1**
Leigham Hall **3**
   SW16 . . . .**74 A1**
Leigham Hall Par **2**
   SW16 . . . .**74 A1**
Leigham Vale SE27,
   SW16,SW2 . . . .**74 C2**
Leigh Ct **2** SW2 . . . .**62 C1**
Leighfield Ho **5** N4 .**6 B4**
Leigh Gdns NW10 . . .**22 B3**
Leigh Ho **5** SW15 . .**56 C2**
Leigh Orchard Cl
   SW16 . . . .**74 B1**
Leigh Pl EC1 . . . .**107 B4**
Leigh Rd N5 . . . .**15 A4**
Leigh St WC1 . . . .**94 A3**
Leighton Cres
   NW5 . . . .**13 B3**

Leighton Gdns
   NW10 . . . .**22 B3**
Leighton Gr NW5 . . . .**13 B3**
Leighton House Mus
   W14 . . . .**127 A2**
Leighton Pl NW5 . . . .**13 B3**
Leighton Rd NW5 . . . .**13 B3**
Leinster Ave SW14 . .**55 B3**
Leinster Gdns
   W2 . . . .**114 C4**
Leinster Mews
   W2 . . . .**114 C4**
Leinster Pl W2 . . . . .**100 A1**
Leinster Sq W2 . . . . .**100 A1**
Leinster Terr W2 . . .**114 C4**
Leitch Ho **8** NW8 . . .**11 C1**
Leithcote Path
   SW16 . . . .**74 B1**
Leithcote Gdns
   SW16 . . . .**74 B1**
Leith Ho
   7 Kentish Town
      N7 . . . .**13 C3**
   18 Streatham SW2 .**74 B4**
Leith Mans W9 . . . . . .**88 A3**
Leith Yd **8** NW6 . . . .**23 C4**
Lelitia Cl E8 . . . .**24 C4**
Leman St E1 . . . .**111 B1**
Le Moal Ho **20** E1 . .**32 B4**
Lemsford Ct N4 . . . . . .**6 B2**
Lena Gardens Prim
   Sch W6 . . . .**39 B3**
Lena Gdns W6 . . . . . .**39 B3**
Lendal Terr **7**
   SW4 . . . .**61 C4**
Len Freeman Pl
   SW6 . . . .**154 C3**
Lenham **11** NW5 . . . .**12 C2**
Lenham Ho SE1 . . . .**137 C3**
Lennon Rd NW2 . . . . . .**9 B2**
Lennox Gdns
   Knightsbridge
      SW1 . . . .**130 C1**
   Willesden NW10 . . . . .**8 B4**
Lennox Gdns Mews
   SW1 . . . .**144 C4**
Lennox Ho **10** E9 . . .**17 B2**
Lennox Rd N4, N7 . . . .**5 C2**
Lenthall Ho SW1 . . .**147 A1**
Lenthall Rd E8 . . . . . .**16 C1**
Lenthorp Rd SE10 . .**43 B2**
Lenton Rise TW9 . . . .**54 A4**
Len Williams Ct
   NW6 . . . .**23 C3**
Leonard Ct
   Bloomsbury WC1 . . . **94 A2**
   Kensington W8 . . . .**127 B2**
Leonard Day Ho **8**
   N7 . . . .**14 B2**
Leonard Pl **6** N16 . .**16 A4**
Leonard St EC2 . . . . . .**97 C2**
Leonora Ho W9 . . . . . .**88 C2**
Leontine Cl SE15 . . . .**49 C3**
Leopards Ct EC1 . . .**107 B4**
Leopold Bldgs **14**
   E2 . . . .**24 B2 98 C4**
Leopold Mews E9 . . . .**25 B4**
Leopold Prim Sch
   NW10 . . . .**8 B1**
Leopold Rd NW10 . . . .**8 A1**
Leopold St E3 . . . .**33 B4**
Leopold Wlk SE11 .**148 C1**
Leo St SE15 . . . .**50 A3**
Leo Yd EC1 . . . .**96 B1**
Leppoc Rd SW4 . . . . . .**61 C2**
Leroy St SE1 . . . .**152 A4**
Lerry Cl W14 . . . .**155 A4**
Lerwick Ho SW18 . . .**59 B3**

Lesley Ct SW1 . . . . .**133 B1**
Leslie Prince Ct **8**
   SE5 . . . .**48 C3**
Leslie Rd E11 . . . .**19 C4**
Lessar Ave SW4 . . . . .**61 B1**
Lessar Ct SW4 . . . .**61 B1**
Lester Ct **42** E3 . . . . .**27 A2**
Leswin Pl N16 . . . .**7 B1**
Leswin Rd N16 . . . .**7 B1**
Letchford Gdns
   NW10 . . . .**21 C2**
Letchford Mews
   NW10 . . . .**21 C2**
Letchmore Ho **7**
   W10 . . . .**22 B1**
Lethaby Ho **15**
   SW4 . . . .**62 B3**
Lethbridge Cl
   SE13 . . . .**52 B1**
Letterstone Rd
   SW6 . . . .**154 C1**
Lettice St SW6 . . . . .**165 A3**
Lett Rd E15 . . . .**19 C1**
Lettsom St SE5 . . . . . .**49 A1**
Levana Cl SW19 . . . .**70 A3**
Levant Ho **11** E1 . . . .**25 C1**
Levehurst Way SW4,
   SW9 . . . .**172 B2**
Leven Rd E14 . . . .**34 C3**
Lever Ct **18** E9 . . . . . .**17 C2**
Leverett St SW3 . . . .**144 B4**
Leverington Pl N1 . . .**97 C3**
Lever St EC1 . . . .**96 C3**
Leverstock Ho
   SW3 . . . .**144 B2**
Leverton Pl NW5 . . . .**13 B3**
Leverton St NW5 . . . .**13 B3**
Levison Way **2**
   N19 . . . .**4 C3**
Levita Ho NW1 . . . . . .**93 C4**
Levyne Ct EC1 . . . .**95 B2**
Lewesdon Cl **13**
   SW19 . . . .**69 C3**
Lewes Ho
   Bermondsey SE1 . . .**138 B4**
   Peckham SE15 . . . . . .**49 C4**
Leweston Pl N16 . . . . .**7 B4**
Lewey Ho E3 . . . .**26 B1**
Lewin Rd SW14 . . . . . .**55 C4**
Lewis Ct **5** SE16 . . . .**40 A1**
Lewis Gr SE13 . . . .**67 B4**
LEWISHAM **67 B3**
Lewisham Bridge
   Prim Sch **3**
      SE13 . . . .**67 A4**
Lewisham Bsns Ctr
   SE14 . . . .**50 C4**
Lewisham Coll
   (Deptford Campus)
      12 SE8 . . . .**51 C2**
Lewisham Coll
   (Lewisham Way
   Campus) SE4 . . . . .**51 C1**
Lewisham High St
   SE13 . . . .**67 A2**
Lewisham Hill
   SE13 . . . .**52 B1**
Lewisham Hospl
   SE13 . . . .**67 A2**
Lewisham Pk SE13 . .**67 B2**
Lewisham Rd SE13 .**52 B1**
Lewisham Sh Ctr
   SE13 . . . .**67 B4**
Lewisham St SW1 .**133 C3**
Lewisham Sta
   SE13 . . . .**67 B4**

Lewisham Way SE4,
   SE14 . . . .**51 B2**
Lewis Pl E8 . . . .**16 C3**
Lewis Silkin Ho **9**
   SE15 . . . .**50 B4**
Lewis St NW1 . . . .**13 A2**
Lexden Rd W3 . . . .**28 A1**
Lexfield Ho N5 . . . .**15 B4**
Lexham Gardens
   Mews W8 . . . .**128 B1**
Lexham Gdns W8 **142 A4**
Lexham Mews
   W8 . . . .**141 C4**
Lexham Wlk W8 . . . .**128 B1**
Lexington St W1 . . . .**119 A4**
Lexton Gdns SW12 .**73 C3**
Leybourne Ho **20**
   SE15 . . . .**50 B4**
Leybourne Rd **7**
   NW1 . . . .**13 A1**
Leybourne St **8**
   NW1 . . . .**13 A1**
Leyden Mans **7**
   N19 . . . .**5 A4**
Leyden St E1 . . . .**110 C3**
Leydon Cl
   Rotherhithe SE16 . . .**32 C1**
   . . . .**32 C1**
Ley Ho SE1 . . . .**136 C3**
Leyland Ho **6** E14 .**34 A2**
Leylands SW18 . . . . . .**58 B1**
Leylang Rd SE14 . . . .**50 C3**
Leys Ct **9** SW9 . . . .**173 B1**
Leysdown **9** NW5 .**12 C2**
Leysdown Ho
   SE17 . . . .**152 B2**
Leysfield Rd W12 . . .**38 C4**
Leythe Rd W3 . . . .**37 B4**
LEYTON **19 C4**
Leyton Mill Ret Pk
   E10 . . . .**19 C4**
Leyton Mills E10 . . . .**19 C4**
Leyton Rd E15 . . . .**19 C2**
Liardet St SE14 . . . . . .**51 A4**
Liberia Rd N5 . . . .**15 A2**
Liberty Mews
   SW12 . . . .**61 A1**
Liberty St SW9 . . . . .**173 A4**
Libra Rd **2** E3 . . . . . .**26 B3**
Library Mans **4**
   W12 . . . .**39 B4**
Library Par NW10 . . .**21 A4**
Library Pl E1 . . . .**32 A2**
Library St SE1 . . . . . .**136 B3**
Lichfield Ct TW9 . . . . .**54 A3**
Lichfield Gdns TW10,
   TW9 . . . .**54 A2**
Lichfield Ho **2**
   SE5 . . . .**48 B1**
Lichfield Rd
   Mile End E3 . . . .**26 A2**
   Richmond TW9 . . . . .**44 C3**
   West Hampstead
      NW2 . . . .**10 A4**
Lichfield Terr **5**
   . . . .**54 A2**
Lickey Ho W14 . . . . .**155 A4**
Lidcote Gdns **22**
   SW9 . . . .**173 A1**
Liddell Gdns
   NW10 . . . .**22 B3**
Liddell Rd NW6 . . . . . .**10 C2**
Lidfield Rd N16 . . . . . .**15 C4**
Lidgate Rd **22**
   SE15 . . . .**49 B3**

Lidiard Rd SW18 . . . . .71 B2
Lidlington Pl NW1 . . .83 A1
Lido The W2 . . . . .116 A1
Lidyard Rd N19 . . . . . .4 B3
Liffey St NW10 . . . . . . .8 C1
Liffords Pl SW13 . . . . .46 B1
Lifford St SW15 . . . . . .57 C3
Lighter Cl E1 SE16 . . . .41 A2
Lighterman Mews 15
E1 . . . . .32 C3
Lighterman's Rd
E14 . . . . .42 A4
Lighterman's Wlk
SW18 . . . . .58 C3
Light Horse Ct
SW1 . . . . .145 B1
Ligonier St
E2 . . . . .24 B1 98 C2
Lilac Ho SE4 . . . . .66 B4
Lilac Pl SE11 . . . . . . .148 C3
Lilac St W12 . . . . .30 A2
Lilestone Est NW8 . . .89 C1
Lilestone Ho NW8 . . .89 C2
Lilestone St NW8 . . . .90 A2
Lilford Ho E5 . . . . . . .48 A1
Lilford Rd SE5 . . . . . . .48 A1
Lilian Baylis Ho
N1 . . . . .15 B2
Lilian Baylis Tech Sch
SE11 . . . . .149 A1
Lilley Cl E1 . . . . .125 C1
Lillian Ave W3 . . . . . .36 C4
Lillian Ho SW15 . . . . .14 A3
Lillie Ho N5 . . . . .14 C3
Lillie Rd SW6 . . . . . . .154 C3
Lillie Road Mans
SW6 . . . . .154 B3
Lillieshall Rd SW4 . . .61 B4
Lillie Yd SW6 . . . . . . .155 B4
Lillingston Ho N7 . . . .14 C4
Lily Cl W14 . . . . .39 C2
Lily Pl EC1 . . . . .107 C4
Lilyville Rd SW6 . . . . .164 C4
Limborough Ho 5
E14 . . . . .33 C4
Limburg Rd SW11 . . . .60 A3
Limeburner La
EC4 . . . . .108 A2
Lime Cl E1 . . . . .125 C2
Lime Gr SW15 . . . . . . .57 A4
Lime Gr W12 . . . . .39 B4
Limeharbour E14 . . . .42 A4
Lime Ho 7 NW5 . . . . . .45 C1
LIMEHOUSE 33 A2
Limehouse Cswy
E14 . . . . .33 B2
Limehouse Ct 5
E14 . . . . .34 A3
Lime House Ct 28
E14 . . . . .33 B3
Limehouse Cut 4
E14 . . . . .34 A4
Limehouse Fields Est
16 E14 . . . . .33 A4
Limehouse Link
(Tunnel) E14 . . . . . .33 B2
Limehouse Sta
E14 . . . . .33 A3
Limekiln Wharf 21
E14 . . . . .33 B2
Limerick Cl SW12 . . . .73 B4
Limerick Ct 1
SW12 . . . . .73 A3
Limerston St
SW10 . . . . .157 A3

Lime St Pas EC3 . . . .124 A4
Limes Ave
Barnes SW13 . . . . . .46 B1
Golders Green NW11 . .1 A4
Limes Ct NW6 . . . . . . .9 C1
Limes Field Rd
SW14 . . . . .56 A4
Limesford Rd
SE15 . . . . .65 C3
Limes Gdns SW18 . . .58 C1
Limes Gr SE13 . . . . . .67 B3
Lime St EC3 . . . . .110 A1
Limes The
Camberwell SE5 . . . .64 A4
Kensington
W2 . . . . . . .31 C2 113 C3
Limes Wlk SE15 . . . . .65 B3
Limetree Cl SW2 . . . .74 B3
Lime Tree Ct 14
E3 . . . . .33 C4
Limpsfield Ave
SW19 . . . . .69 C2
Limscott Ho 13 E3 . . .27 A2
Linacre Cl SE15 . . . . .65 A4
Linacre Ct W6 . . . . . . .39 C1
Linacre Rd NW2 . . . . .9 A2
Linale Ho 1 N1 . . . . . .87 B1
Linberry Wlk 3
SE8 . . . . .41 B2
Lincoln Ave SW19 . . . .69 C1
Lincoln Ct N16 . . . . . . .6 C4
Lincoln Ho
Bloomsbury WC1 . . .107 A3
1 Dartmouth Pk
NW5 . . . . .4 B1
2 Islington N1 . . . . . .15 B1
Knightsbridge
SW1 . . . . .130 C3
Lincoln Mews
NW6 . . . . .23 B4
Lincoln's Inn WC2 . . .107 A2
Lincoln's Inn Fields
WC2 . . . . .107 A2
Lincoln St SW3 . . . . .144 C3
Lindale SW19 . . . . . . .70 A2
Lindal Rd SE4 . . . . . . .66 B1
Linden Ave NW10 . . . .22 C3
Linden Ct
8 Battersea
SW18 . . . . .59 C3
1 Shepherd's Bush
W12 . . . . .30 B1
Linden Gdns
Chiswick W4 . . . . . . .37 C1
Notting Hill
W2 . . . . . . .31 C2 113 C3
Linden Gr SE15 . . . . . .65 B4
Linden Ho 10 SE8 . . .51 B4
Linden Lodge Sch
SW19 . . . . .70 A3
Linden Mans N6 . . . . .4 A3
Linden Mews
Kensington
W2 . . . . . . .31 C2 113 C3
Stoke Newington
N1 . . . . .15 C3
Lindens The W4 . . . . .45 B2
Lindfield Gdns
NW3 . . . . .11 B3
Lindfield Hts NW3 . . .11 B3
Lindfield St E14 . . . . .33 C3
Lindisfarne Way
E9 . . . . .18 A4
Lindley Ho
5 Peckham SE15 . . . .49 C3
1 Stepney E1 . . . . . .32 B4

Lindley Pl TW9 . . . . . .44 C2
Lindley St E1 . . . . .32 B4
Lindop Ho 3 E1 . . . . . .26 A1
Lindore Rd SW11 . . . .60 B3
Lindo St SE15 . . . . . . .50 B1
Lindrop St SW6 . . . . .166 C2
Lindsay Ct SW11 . . . .167 C3
Lindsay Sq SW1 . . . .147 C2
Lindsell St 6
SE10 . . . . .52 B2
Lindsey Ho SW10 . . .157 C2
Lindsey Mews 18
N1 . . . . .15 B1
Lindsey St EC1 . . . . .108 B4
Lind St SE8 . . . . .52 A1
Linfield WC1 . . . . .94 C3
Linford Christie
Stadium The
W12 . . . . .30 A4
Linford Ho 17 E2 . . . .24 C4
Linford St SW8 . . . . .170 C3
Linford Street Bsns
Est SW8 . . . . .170 C4
Lingard Ho 11 E14 . . .42 B3
Lingards Rd SE13 . . . .67 B3
Lingfield Ho
3 Acton Green
W4 . . . . .37 B1
Lambeth SE1 . . . . . .136 B3
Lingham St SW9 . . . .172 C1
Ling Rd E16 . . . . .35 C4
Ling's Coppice
SE21 . . . . .75 C2
Lingwell Rd SW17 . . .72 A1
Lingwood Rd E5 . . . . . .7 C4
Linhope St NW1 . . . . .90 C1
Linkenholt Mans 3
W6 . . . . .38 B2
Link St E9 . . . . .17 B3
Links Yd
10 Spitalfields
E1 . . . . .111 B4
Spitalfields E1 . . . . .111 A4
Link The W3 . . . . .28 A3
Linkway N4 . . . . .6 B4
Linkwood Wlk
NW1 . . . . .13 C1
Linnell Ho
Spitalfields E1 . . . . .110 C4
St John's Wood
NW8 . . . . .78 C4
Linnell Rd SE5 . . . . . .49 A1
Linnet Mews
SW12 . . . . .72 C4
Linom Rd SW4 . . . . . .62 A3
Linscott Rd E5 . . . . . .17 B4
Linsey St
Bermondsey
SE16 . . . . .153 B4
Bermondsey SE16 . .139 C1
Linslade Ho
15 Hackney E2 . . . . .24 C4
Marylebone NW8 . . . .90 B2
Linstead St 8
NW6 . . . . .10 C1
Linstead Way SW18,
SW19 . . . . .70 A4
Lintaine Cl W6 . . . . . .154 B3
Linthorpe Rd N16 . . . . .7 A4
Linton Ho
Lower Holloway
N7 . . . . .14 B4
2 Tower Hamlets
E3 . . . . .33 C4
Linton St N1 . . . . .87 A3
Linver Rd SW6 . . . . . .165 B2

Linwood Cl SE5 . . . . .49 B1
Lion Cl SE4 . . . . .66 C1
Lionel Ho 5 W10 . . . . .31 A4
Lionel Mans 14
W14 . . . . .39 C3
Lionel Mews 15
W10 . . . . .31 A4
Lionel Road N
TW8 . . . . .36 A2
Lionel Road Prim Sch
TW8 . . . . .36 A2
Lionel Road S
TW8 . . . . .36 B1
Lion Gate Gdns
TW9 . . . . .54 B4
Lion Gate Mews
SW18 . . . . .70 C4
Lion House Sch
SW15 . . . . .57 C3
Lion Mills 35 E2 . . . . .24 C3
Lion Yd SW4 . . . . .61 C3
Lipton Rd 1 E1 . . . . . .32 C3
Lisburne Rd NW3 . . . .12 B4
Lisford St SE15 . . . . . .49 B2
Lisgar Terr W14 . . . . .140 C4
Liskeard Gdns SE3 . . .53 C2
Liskeard Ho SE11 . . .149 C2
Lisle Ct NW2 . . . . .1 A1
Lisle St WC2 . . . . . . .119 C4
Lismore Cir NW5 . . . .12 C3
Lismore Wlk 4
N1 . . . . .15 B2
Lissenden Gdns
NW5 . . . . .12 C4
Lissenden Mans
NW5 . . . . .12 C4
Lisson Cotts NW1 . . .102 B4
Lisson Gr NW1,
NW8 . . . . .90 A2
LISSON GROVE 90 B1
Lisson Ho NW1 . . . . .102 A4
Lisson St NW1 . . . . . .102 A4
Lister Ct N16 . . . . .7 A2
Lister Ho
Greenwich SE3 . . . . .53 A4
Marylebone W1 . . . .104 A2
Spitalfields E1 . . . . .111 C4
Lister Hospl SW1 . . . .146 A1
Lister Mews N7 . . . . . .14 B4
Liston Rd SW4 . . . . . .61 B4
Listowel Cl 2
SW9 . . . . .163 C2
Listria Lo N16 . . . . .7 B2
Listria Pk N16 . . . . .7 B2
Litcham Ho 21 E1 . . . .25 C2
Litchfield Gdns
NW10 . . . . .8 C2
Litchfield St WC2 . . .119 C4
Lithos Rd NW3 . . . . . .11 B2
Little Albany St
NW1 . . . . .92 B2
Little Argyll St
W1 . . . . .104 C1
Little Boltons The
SW10 . . . . .142 B1
Little Britain EC1 . . . .108 C3
Littlebury Rd SW4 . . .61 C4
Little Chelsea Ho
SW10 . . . . .157 A3
Little Chester St
SW1 . . . . .132 A2
Little Cloisters
SW1 . . . . .134 A2
Little College St
SW1 . . . . .134 A2

Little Combe Cl 13
SW15 . . . . .57 C1
Littlecote Cl SW19 . . .70 A4
Little Cottage Pl
SE10 . . . . .52 A3
Little Deans Yd
SW1 . . . . .134 A2
Little Dimocks
SW12 . . . . .73 A2
Little Dorrit Ct
SE1 . . . . .137 A4
Little Edward St
NW1 . . . . .92 B4
Little Essex St
WC2 . . . . .121 B4
Littlefield Cl N19 . . . . .13 B4
Little George St
SW1 . . . . .134 A3
Little Green St
NW5 . . . . .13 A4
Little Marlborough St
W1 . . . . .104 C1
Little Newport St
WC2 . . . . .119 C4
Little New St EC4 . . .107 C2
Little Portland St
W1 . . . . .104 C2
Little Russell St
WC1 . . . . .106 A3
Little St James's St
SW1 . . . . .118 C1
Little St Leonards
SW14 . . . . .55 B4
Little Sanctuary
SW1 . . . . .134 A3
Little Smith St
SW1 . . . . .133 C2
Little Somerset St
E1 . . . . .110 C1
Little Titchfield St
W1 . . . . .104 C3
Littleton St SW18 . . . .71 B2
Little Trinity La
EC4 . . . . .123 A4
Little Turnstile
WC1 . . . . .106 C3
LITTLE VENICE 101 A4
Little Venice W9 . . . .100 C4
Littlewood SE13 . . . . .67 B1
Livermere Ct 3
E8 . . . . .24 B4
Livermere Rd E8 . . . . .24 B4
Liverpool Gr SE17 . . .151 B1
Liverpool Ho N7 . . . . .14 C2
Liverpool Rd
Islington N1 . . . . . . .85 C3
Islington N1, N7 . . . .14 C1
Newham E16 . . . . . . .35 A4
Liverpool St EC2 . . . .110 A3
Liverpool Street Sta
EC2 . . . . .110 A3
Livesey Pl SE15 . . . . .49 C4
Livingstone Ho 10
SE5 . . . . .48 B3
Livingstone Lo 13
W9 . . . . .31 C4
Livingstone Pl E14 . .42 B1
Livingstone Rd
6 Battersea
SW11 . . . . .59 C4
Mill Meads E15 . . . . .27 C4
Livity Sch The
SW2 . . . . .62 A2
Livonia St W1 . . . . . .105 A1

Lizard St EC1......97 A3
Llandannor Ho 1
  E14......42 B4
Llanelly Rd NW2...1 B2
Llanvanor Rd NW2...1 B2
Llewellyn Ho 10
  N19......4 B1
Llewellyn St SE16 139 C3
L'Ile aux Enfants
  NW5......12 C3
Lloyd Baker St
  WC1......95 B3
Lloyd Ct
  Ladywell SE13...67 A2
  6 West Norwood
  SE27...75 A1
Lloyd Ho N6......6 C1
Lloyd's Ave EC3 110 B1
Lloyd's Bldg EC3 110 A1
Lloyd's Pl SE3...53 A1
Lloyd Sq WC1...95 B4
Lloyd's Row EC1 96 A3
Lloyd St WC1...95 B4
Lloyd Villas SE4...51 C1
Lloyd Williamson Sch
  17 W10......31 A4
Loampit Hill SE13...52 A1
Loampit Vale SE13 67 B4
Loanda Cl 17 E8...24 B4
Loats Rd SW2......62 A1
Locarno Rd 6 W3...28 B1
Lochaline St W6...47 B4
Lochbie 9 N4......5 A4
Lochinvar St SW12 .73 A4
Lochmore Ho
  SW1......145 C3
Lochnagar St E14 ...34 B4
Lockbridge Ct 8
  W9......31 C4
Locke Ho
  Nine Elms SW8...170 C4
  Stamford Hill N16...7 B3
Lockesfield Pl E14...42 A1
Lockgate Cl E9...18 B3
Lockhart Cl N7...14 B2
Lockhart St E3...26 B1
Lockhurst St E5...17 C4
Lockington Rd
  SW8......170 B4
Lockmead Rd
  SE13......67 B4
Lock Mews 3
  NW1......13 C2
Lockside 17 E14...33 B4
Locksley St E14...33 B4
Lock View Ct 9
  E14......33 C4
Lockwood Ho 10
  SE11......163 B3
Lockwood Sq
  SE16......40 A3
Lockyer Est SE1 137 C3
Lockyer Ho
  7 Greenwich
  SE10......43 B1
  18 Putney SW15 ...57 C4
  South Lambeth
  SW8......162 A2
Lockyer St SE1 137 C3
Locton Gn 4 E3...26 B4
Loddiges Ho 5 E9...17 B1
Loddiges Rd E9...17 B1
Loddon Ho NW8...89 C1
Loder St SE15...50 B3

Lodge Ave SW14...56 A4
Lodge Rd NW8......90 A3
Lodge The 9 W8...38 A3
Lodore St E14......34 B3
Lodsworth Ho
  SW11......169 B3
Loftie St SE16...139 C3
Lofting Ho 8 N1...14 C1
Lofting Rd N1......14 C1
Lofts on the Park 2
  E9......17 C2
Loftus Rd W12...30 A1
Loftus Rd (Queens
  Park Rangers FC)
  W12......30 A1
Logan Mews W8...141 B4
Logan Pl W8......141 B4
Loggetts SE21......76 A2
Lohmann Ho 1
  SE11......163 B4
Lolesworth Cl E1...111 A3
Lollard St SE11...149 B3
Lollards Twr SE1...134 C1
Loman St SE1...136 B4
Lomas Dr 10 E8...16 B1
Lomas St E1......111 C4
Lombard Ct
  13 Acton W3......28 B1
  City of London EC3 123 C4
Lombard La EC4...107 C1
Lombard Rd
  SW11......167 B2
Lombard St EC3 109 C1
Lombardy Pl W2...114 B3
Lomley Ho 10 SW2 .62 C1
Lomond Gn SE5...48 C3
Lomond Ho 10
  SE5......48 C2
Loncroft Rd SE5...49 A4
Londesborough Ho 1
  N16......16 A4
Londesborough Rd
  N16......16 A4
London Acad for
  Higher Education
  The E15......27 C4
London Acad of
  Computing &
  Electronics SW17...72 B1
London Bridge EC4,
  SE1......123 C3
London Bridge City
  Pier
  SE1......124 A2
London Bridge
  Experience The
  SE1......123 C2
London Bridge Hospl
  SE1......123 C2
London Bridge St
  SE1......123 C1
London Bridge Sta
  SE1......123 C1
London Britannia Coll
  N1......87 C1
London Business Sch
  NW1......90 C2
London Canal Mus
  N1......84 B2
London Central
  Mosque NW8...90 B3
London Chest Hospl
  E2......25 B3

London Christian Sch
  SE16......40 C1
London City Sh Ctr
  EC1......97 A1
London Clinic (Hospl)
  NW1......91 C1
London Coll of
  Advanced Studies
  SE1......123 B1
London Coll of Beauty
  Therapy W1...105 A1
London Coll of Bsns &
  Computer Studies 12
  SW4......61 C3
London Coll of
  Communication (Sch
  of Printing &
  Publishing)
  SE11......136 B1
London Coll of
  Economics &
  Science NW10...20 B1
London Coll of
  Fashion (Curtain Rd)
  EC2......24 A1 98 B2
London Coll of
  Fashion (Golden La)
  EC1......96 C1
London Coll of
  Fashion (John
  Prince's St) W1 ...104 A1
London Coll of
  Fashion (Lime
  Grove) W6......39 B4
London Coll of
  Fashion (Mare St)
  E8......17 B1
London Coll of
  International
  Business Studies
  WC1......106 B3
London Ct 8
  SW18......58 C2
London Cty Hall
  SE1......134 C4
London Dungeon The
  SE1......123 C2
London Electronics
  Coll SW5......142 A2
London Eye
  (Millennium Wheel)
  SE1......134 C4
London Fields East
  Side E8......17 A1
London Fields Prim
  Sch E8......25 A4
London Fields Sta
  E8......17 A1
London Fields West
  Side E8......16 C1
London Film Mus
  SE1......134 C4
London Fire Brigade
  SE1......134 C4
London Glassblowing
  Workshop SE1...138 A4
London Ho 19 W6...38 C2
London Ho NW8...80 B2
London Hospital
  Dental Inst E1...32 A4
London Independent
  Hospl The E1...32 C4
London International
  Film Sch WC2...106 A1

London Irish Rifles
  Mus SW9......48 B2
London La E8......17 A1
London Meridian Coll
  2 N7......14 B2
London Metrocity Coll
  21 E3......27 A2
London Metropolitan
  Univ
  Islington N7......14 C4
  Whitechapel E1...110 C1
London Metropolitan
  Univ (Central Ho) 44
  E1......111 A2
London Metropolitan
  Univ (Commercial
  Rd) 57 E1......111 B2
London Metropolitan
  Univ (Ladbrook Ho)
  8 N5......15 A3
London Metropolitan
  Univ (Moorgate)
  EC2......109 C3
London Metropolitan
  Univ (Tower Hill)
  EC3......124 C1
London Metropolitan
  Univ (Spring Ho) 6
  N7......14 C2
London Nautical Sch
  SE1......121 C2
London Oratory Sch
  The SW6......155 C1
London Oratory The
  SW3......130 A1
London Sch of Bsns
  SE1......136 B2
London Sch of
  Economics &
  Political Science
  WC2......107 A1
London South Bank
  Univ SE1......136 B2
London St
  City of London
  EC3......124 B4
  Paddington W2...101 B1
London Stile 5
  W4......36 C1
London Stock
  Exchange EC2...108 C2
London Terr 13 E2...24 C3
London Transport
  Mus WC2......120 B4
London Trocadero
  W1......119 B3
London Wall EC2 109 C3
London Wall Bldgs
  EC2......109 C3
London Wetland Ctr
  SW13......47 A3
London Wharf 4
  E2......25 A3
London Zoo NW1...81 B2
Long Acre WC2...106 B1
Longbeach Rd
  SW11......60 B4
Longberrys NW2...1 B2
Longbridge Way
  SE13......67 B2
Longcliffe Ho
  SW18......59 A2
Long Dr W3......29 A3
Longfellow Way
  SE1......153 A3
Longfield Dr SW14 .55 A2

Longfield Est SE1 153 A3
Longfield St SW18..70 C4
Longford Ct
  1 Bedford Pk
  W12......38 A4
  5 Clapton Pk E5 ...17 C4
Longford Ho 7 E1...32 B3
Longford St NW1...92 B2
Longhope Cl SE15 .49 B4
Longhurst Ho 8
  W9......23 B2
Long La
  Bermondsey SE1 ...137 C3
  Holborn EC1......108 B4
Longland Ct
  Bermondsey SE1 ...153 B2
  Hackney E9......18 A3
Longlands Ct
  W11......31 B2 113 A4
Longleat Ho 5 NW1 147 B2
Longleigh Ho 8
  SE5......49 A2
Longlents Ho 3
  NW10......20 C4
Longley Ho 8 N19...13 C4
Longley St SE1...153 B4
Longman Ho
  2 Globe Town
  ......25 C3
  10 Shoreditch E8...24 B4
Long Meadow 20
  N7......14 C3
Longmoor Point 14
  SW15......69 A3
Longmore St SW1 146 C3
Longnor Rd E1...25 C2
Long Pond Rd SE3 .53 A2
Long Rd SW4......61 B3
Longridge Ho SE1 137 A1
Longridge Rd
  SW5......141 C3
Longs Ct 2 TW9...54 B3
Long's Ct W1...119 C3
Longshore SE8...41 B2
Long St E2......24 B2 98 C4
Longstaff Cres
  SW18......70 C4
Longstaff Rd
  SW18......58 C1
Longstone Ave
  NW10......21 B4
Longthorne Ho 18
  E3......26 B2
Longthorpe Ct 5
  W6......38 B1
Longville Rd SE11 150 B4
Long Wlk SE1......138 B2
Longwood Dr
  SW15......56 C1
Long Yd WC1......94 C1
Lonsdale Ho
  Fulham SW6......58 C4
  8 Stoke Newington
  N4......6 B4
Lonsdale Mews
  Notting Hill W11...31 B3
  4 Richmond TW9...44 C2
Lonsdale Pl N1...14 C1
Lonsdale Rd
  Barnes SW13......46 B3
  Chiswick W4......38 B2
  Kilburn NW6......23 B4
  Notting Hill W11...31 B3

Lonsdale Sq
Islington N1 ....14 C1
Islington N1 ....85 C4
Lopez Ho 4 SW9...62 A4
Loraine Rd
Chiswick W4.....45 A4
Islington N7......14 B4
Lord David Pitt Ho 7
SE24.............62 C3
Lorden Wlk 13
E2..........24 C2 99 B3
Lord Hills Rd W2.100 B4
Lord Holland La 5
SW9.............173 C2
Lord North St
SW1...........134 A1
Lord Roberts Mews
SW6............156 A1
Lord's Cricket Mus
NW8............89 C3
Lordship Gr N16...6 C2
Lordship Ho 3 N16.6 C2
Lordship La SE22..64 B1
Lordship Park Mews
N16.............6 B2
Lordship Pl SW3..158 A3
Lordship Rd N16...6 C2
Lordship Terr N16..6 C2
Lord's Indoor Cricket
Sch NW8.......90 A4
Lord's (MCC &
Middlesex Cty
Cricket Ground)
NW8............89 C3
Lord's View NW8..89 C3
Loreburn Ho 2
N7..............14 B4
Lorenzo St N1,
WC1............94 C4
Loris Ho W6.......39 B1
Lorn Ct SW9......173 B2
Lorne Cl NW8.....90 B3
Lorne Ct SW15....57 C1
Lorne Gdns 5
W11............39 C4
Lorne Ho
Hornsey N4.......5 B4
7 Tower Hamlets
E1..............33 A4
Lorne Rd
Finsbury Pk N4.....5 B3
3 Richmond TW10.54 B2
Lorn Rd SW9.....173 B2
Lorraine Ct 10
NW1............13 A1
Lorrimore Rd
SE17............48 A4
Lorrimore Sq SE17.48 A4
Lorton Ho 9 NW6..23 C4
Lostock Ho 9
SW8............171 B2
Lothair Rd S N4....6 A4
Lothbury EC2.....109 B2
Lothian Rd SW9...48 A2
Lothrop St W10....23 A2
Lots Rd SW10....157 A1
Loudoun Rd NW8..79 A3
Loughborough Ct 7
SW9.............63 A4
Loughborough
Junction Sta
SW9.............63 A4

Loughborough Pk
SW9.............63 A3
Loughborough Prim
Sch SW9........48 A1
Loughborough Rd SE5,
SW9.............48 A1
Loughborough St
SE11...........149 A1
Lough Rd N7......14 B2
Louisa Gdns E1....25 C1
Louisa Ho SW15...56 B3
Louisa St E1......25 C1
Louise Bennett Cl 8
SE24............63 A3
Louise De Marillac Ho
4 E1............32 B4
Louise White Ho 11
N19.............4 C4
Louisville Rd
SW17...........72 C1
Louvaine Rd SW11.59 C3
Lovat La EC3.....124 A3
Lovatt Ct SW12....73 A3
Loveday Ho 2
SW2............74 C3
Lovegrove St SE1..49 C4
Lovegrove Wlk
E14.............34 B1
Love La EC2......109 A2
Lovelace Ho 12 E8..24 B4
Lovelace Rd SE21..75 B3
Lovelinch Cl SE15..50 B4
Lovell Ho E8......24 C4
Lovell Pl SE16.....41 A3
Loveridge Mews
NW6............10 B2
Loveridge Rd NW6.10 B2
Lover's Wlk W1...117 B1
Lovette Ho 4 E3...26 C2
Lovetts Pl SW18...59 A3
Love Wlk SE5.....48 C1
Low Cross Wood La
SE21............76 B1
Lowden Rd SE24...63 B3
Lowder Ho 6 E1...32 A1
Lowe Ave E16.....35 C4
Lowell St E14.....33 A3
Lower Addison Gdns
W14............126 A3
Lower Belgrave St
SW1...........132 A1
LOWER CLAPTON.17 B1
Lower Clapton Rd
E5.............17 B4
Lower Clarendon Wlk
9 W11..........31 A3
Lower Comm S
SW15............57 A4
Lower Grosvenor Pl
SW1...........132 B2
Lower Grove Rd
TW10............54 B2
LOWER
HOLLOWAY.....14 A3
Lower James St
W1...........119 A4
Lower John St
W1...........119 A4
Lower Lea Crossing
E14, E16........35 A2
Lower Marsh SE1.135 B3
Lower Merton Rise
NW3............12 A1

Lower Mortlake Rd
TW9.............54 B4
Lower Pk
Acton W3........20 B1
5 Putney SW15...57 C2
LOWER PLACE...20 B3
Lower Place Bsns Ctr
NW10............20 B3
Lower Rd SE8.....40 B4
Lower Richmond Rd
Mortlake SW14,
TW9.............55 A4
Putney SW15.....57 B4
Lower Robert St
WC2...........120 B3
Lower Sloane St
SW1...........145 B2
Lower Terr NW3...2 B1
Lower Thames St
EC3...........124 A3
Lowerwood Ct
W11.............31 A3
Loweswater Ho E3.26 B1
Lowfield Rd
Dagenham W3....28 B3
Hampstead NW6..10 C1
Lowlands NW3....12 A2
Lowman Rd N7....14 B4
Lowndes Cl SW1.131 C1
Lowndes Ct
Knightsbridge
SW1...........131 A2
Marylebone W1..104 C1
Lowndes Lo SW1..131 A2
Lowndes Pl SW1..131 B1
Lowndes Sq SW1.131 A3
Lowndes St SW1..131 B2
Lowood Ho 12 E1..32 B2
Lowood St E1......32 A2
Lowry Ct 3 SE16...40 A1
Lowther Ho
Pimlico SW1P...147 A1
11 Shoreditch E8..24 B4
Lowther Prim Sch
SW13............46 B2
Lowther Rd
Barnes SW13....46 B2
Islington N7.....14 C3
Lowth Rd SE5......48 B1
Loxford Ho SW1..145 C3
Loxham St WC1....94 B3
Loxley Rd SW18...71 C3
LTC Coll London
W1...........104 C2
Lubavitch Boys Prim
Sch E5...........7 C4
Lubavitch Girls Prim
Sch E5...........7 C3
Lubavitch House Sch
(Jun Boys) E5....7 C4
Lubbock St SE14...50 B3
Lucan Ho N1......87 C3
Lucan Pl SW3....144 B3
Lucas Ct SW11...169 C3
Lucas Ho
2 Clapham SW8..171 B1
Walham Green
SW10...........156 B2
Lucas St SE4, SE8..51 C2
Lucas Vale Prim Sch
SE4.............51 C2
Lucerne Mews
W8.....31 C1 113 C2
Lucerne Rd N5....15 A4

Lucey Rd SE16....139 B1
Lucey Way SE16...153 C4
Lucien Ho SW18...71 A2
Lucraft Ho 12 SW2.74 A4
Lucy Ashe Ho
SE17...........150 B3
Lucy Brown Ho
SE1............123 A1
Lucy Cres W3.....20 B1
Ludgate Broadway
EC4............108 B1
Ludgate Cir EC4..108 A1
Ludgate Hill EC4..108 A1
Ludgate Ho EC4..108 A1
Ludgate Sq EC4...108 A1
Ludham NW5.....12 B3
Ludlow Ct W3.....37 B4
Ludlow St EC1....96 C2
Ludovick Wlk
SW15............56 A3
Ludwell Ho W14..126 B2
Ludwick Mews
SE14............51 A3
Lugard Ho 9 W12.30 A1
Lugard Rd SE15...50 A2
Luke Ho 20 E1.....32 A3
Lukin St E1.......32 B3
Lullingstone Ho 21
SE15............50 B4
Lullingstone La
SE13............67 C1
Lulot Gdns N19....4 A2
Lulworth
Camden Town
NW1.............13 C1
8 Walworth SE17.151 B2
Lulworth Ho SW8.162 C1
Lulworth Rd SE15..50 A1
Lumiere Ct 7
SW17............72 C2
Lumina Bldg 1
E14.............34 B1
Lumley Ct WC2...120 B3
Lumley Flats SW1.145 B2
Lumley St W1.....103 C1
Lumsden Ho
SW15............78 B3
Lunan Ho 16 E3...26 B3
Lund Point E15....27 B4
Luntley Pl E1.....111 B3
Lupin Cl SW2.....75 A2
Lupino Ct SE11...149 A4
Lupin Point SE1..139 A3
Lupton St NW5....13 B4
Lupus St SW1....147 A1
Luralda Gdns E14.42 C1
Lurgan Av W6.....47 C4
Lurline Gdns
SW11...........169 C4
Luscombe Ho
SW18............58 B2
Luscombe Way
SW8............162 A2
Lusher Ho SW15...57 C1
Lushington Rd
NW10............22 A2
Lushington Terr 11
E8..............16 C3
Luton Pl SE10.....52 B3
Luton St NW8.....89 C1
Luttrell Ave SW15..57 A2
Lutyens Ho SW1..146 C1
Luxborough Ho
W1............103 B4
Luxborough St
W1............103 B4

Luxborough Twr
W1............103 B4
Luxemburg Gdns
W6.............39 C2
Luxford St SE16...40 C2
Luxmore St SE4...51 B2
Luxor St SE5......63 B4
Lyall Mews SW1..131 B1
Lyall Mews W
SW1...........131 B1
Lyall St SW1.....131 B1
Lyal Rd E3........26 A3
Lycett Ho 10 SW2..74 A4
Lycett Pl 3 W12...38 C4
Lycott Gr SE22....64 B2
Lydden Gr SW18...71 A4
Lydden Rd SW18..71 A4
Lydford NW1......83 A3
Lydford Cl 22 N16.16 A3
Lydford Rd
Brondesbury NW2..9 C2
Paddington W9....23 B1
Lydgate Ho 8
N16.............16 A3
Lydhurst Ave SW2.74 B2
Lydney Cl
Camberwell SE15..49 A3
Putney SW19.....70 A2
Lydon Rd SW4....61 B4
Lydwell Ho 20
SW8............171 B1
Lyford Rd SW18...72 A3
Lygoe Ho 10 N6....4 C4
Lygon Ho 3
E2.........24 C2 99 B4
Lygon Pl SW1....132 A1
Lyham Cl SW2....62 A1
Lyham Rd SW2....62 A1
Lyle Pk SW15.....57 C1
Lyly Ho SE1......137 C1
Lyme Gr E9.......17 B1
Lyme Grove Ho 8
E9..............17 B1
Lyme St NW1.....82 C4
Lyminge Gdns SW17,
SW18............72 A3
Lymington Mans
NW6............11 A2
Lymington Rd
NW6............11 A2
Lympstone Gdns
SE15............49 C3
Lynbrook Gr SE15.49 B3
Lynch Wlk 2 SE8..51 B4
Lyncott Cres SW4..61 A3
Lyncourt SE3.....52 C1
Lyncroft Gdns
NW6............10 C3
Lyncroft Mans 4
NW6............10 C3
Lyndale NW2.....1 B1
Lyndale Ave NW2..1 B1
Lyndale Cl SE3....53 B4
Lynde Ho 2 SW4..61 C4
Lynden Gate SW15.69 A4
Lyndhurst Gdns
NW3............11 C3
Lyndhurst Gr SE5,
SE15............49 B1
Lyndhurst Ho 2
SW15...........68 C4
Lyndhurst House Prep
Sch NW3.......11 C3

Lyndhurst Lo **3**
E14 . . . . .42 C2
Lyndhurst Rd NW3 . .11 C3
Lyndhurst Sch SE5 . .48 C1
Lyndhurst Sq SE15 . .49 B2
Lyndhurst Terr
NW3 . . . . .11 C3
Lyndhurst Way
SE15 . . . . .49 B1
Lyneham Wlk E5 . . . .18 A3
Lynette Ave SW4 . . . .61 B1
Lynford French Ho
SE17 . . . . .150 C2
Lyngham Ct **11** N4 . . . . .5 C4
Lynhurst Ct NW8 . . . .79 B3
Lyn Mews **2** E3 . . . . .26 B2
Lynmouth Rd N16 . . . .7 B3
Lynne Ct NW6 . . . . . .11 A1
Lynnett Ct E19 . . . . . .4 C3
Lynn Ho SE15 . . . . . .49 C4
Lynn Rd SW12 . . . . . .73 A4
Lynton Cl NW10 . . . . . .8 B3
Lynton Ct **2** W3 . . . .28 B3
Lynton Est **1** SE1 . .153 B3
Lynton Ho **19** W2 . . .100 B1
Lynton Lo N16 . . . . . .15 A3
Lynton Mans SE1 . . .135 B2
Lynton Rd
Acton W3 . . . . .28 A2
Bermondsey SE1 . . . .153 A3
Paddington NW6 . . . .23 B3
Lynton Terr **4** W3 . . .28 B3
Lynx Terr SW19 . . . . .70 C1
Lyon Ho NW8 . . . . . .90 A1
Lyons Pl NW8 . . . . . .89 B1
Lyon St N1 . . . . .14 B1
Lyons Wlk W14 . . . .140 A4
Lyric Rd SW13 . . . . . .46 B2
Lysander Gr N19 . . . . .4 C3
Lysander Ho **10**
E2 . . . . .25 A3
Lysander Mews N19 . .4 B3
Lysia Ct SW6 . . . . . . .47 C3
Lysias Rd SW12 . . . . .61 A1
Lysia St SW6 . . . . . . .47 C3
Lysons Wlk SW15 . . .56 C2
Lytham St SE17. . . . .151 B1
Lyttelton Cl NW3 . . . .12 A1
Lytten Ct **6** W12 . . . .38 C4
Lyttleton Ho **10** N16 .16 A4
Lytton Ct WC1. . . . . .106 B3
Lytton Gr SW15. . . . . .58 A1

M

Mabel Thornton Ho **12**
N16 . . . . .15 C4
Mableton Pl NW1,
WC1 . . . . .93 C3
Mablethorpe Rd
SW6 . . . . .154 A1
Mabley St E9 . . . . . . .18 A3
MacArthur Ho **4**
SW2 . . . . .74 A4
Macartney Ho
SE10 . . . . .52 C3
Macaulay CE Prim
Sch SW4 . . . . .61 A3
Macaulay Ho
2 Kensal Town
W10 . . . . .31 A4

Macaulay Ho continued
10 Stoke Newington
N16 . . . . .7 A1
Macaulay Rd SW4 . . .61 A4
Macaulay Sq SW4 . . .61 A3
McAuley Ct **1** SE1 . .135 B2
Macauley Mews
SE13 . . . . .52 B1
McAusland Ho **5**
E3 . . . . .26 B3
Macbeth Ho **4** N1 . . .24 A3
Macbeth St W6 . . . . .39 A1
McBride Ho **6** E2 . . . .25 A3
McCall Cl SW4 . . . . .172 A2
McCall Ho N7 . . . . . . .14 A4
Mccarthy Ct
SW11 . . . . .168 B3
Macclesfield Rd
EC1 . . . . .96 C4
Macclesfield St
W1 . . . . .119 C4
McCoid Way SE1 . . .136 C3
Mcconnell Ho
SW8 . . . . .171 B3
McCormick Ho **9**
SW2 . . . . .74 C3
McCrone Mews **3**
NW3 . . . . .11 C2
McCullum Rd E3 . . . .26 B4
McDermott Cl
SW11 . . . . .60 A4
McDermott Rd
SE15 . . . . .64 C4
Macdonald Ho **2**
SW11 . . . . .169 B2
Macdonald Rd N19 . . .4 B2
McDougall Ct
TW9 . . . . .44 C1
Mcdougall Ho
E2 . . . . .24 C2
McDowall Cl E16 . . . .35 B4
McDowall Rd SE5 . . .48 B2
Macduff Rd SW11 . .169 C4
Mace Cl E1 . . . . .32 A1
Mace St E2 . . . . .25 C3
McEwan Way E15. . . .27 C4
Macey Ho
Battersea SW11 . . . .168 A3
10 Greenwich SE10 . .52 B4
Macfarlane Rd
W12 . . . . .30 B1
Macfarren Ho **7**
W10 . . . . .23 A2
MacFarren Pl NW1 . . .91 C1
McGlashon Ho **16**
E1 . . . . .24 C1 99 B1
McGregor Ct **3**
N1 . . . . .24 A2 98 B4
McGregor Ho **2**
SW12 . . . . .73 C3
McGregor Rd W11 . . .31 B4
Machell Rd SE15 . . . .65 B4
McIndoe Ct N1 . . . . . .87 B4
McIntosh Ho **14**
SE16 . . . . .40 B2
McIntyre Ct **19**
SW4 . . . . .172 B2
Mackay Ho **33**
W12 . . . . .30 A2
Mackay Rd SW4 . . . .61 A4
McKenna Ho **3**
E3 . . . . .26 B3
Mackennal St NW8 . .80 B2
Mackenzie Cl **7**
W12 . . . . .30 A2
Mackenzie Ho N7. . . .14 B2

Mackenzie Wlk
E14 . . . . .33 C1
McKerrell Rd SE15 . .49 C2
Mackeson Rd NW3 . .12 B4
Mackie Ho **18**
SW2 . . . . .74 C4
Mackie Rd SW4 . . . .74 A4
McKiernan Ct **2**
SW11 . . . . .168 A2
McKinnon Wood Ho
18 E2 . . . . .24 C2 99 B3
Mackintosh La **2** E9 .17 C3
Macklin St WC2 . . . .106 B2
Mackonochie Ho
EC1 . . . . .107 B4
Mackrow Wlk **11**
E14 . . . . .34 B2
Macks Rd SE16 . . . . .153 C4
Mackworth Ho
NW1 . . . . .92 C4
Mackworth St
NW1 . . . . .92 C4
Mac Laren Mews
SW15 . . . . .57 B3
Maclean Rd SE23 . . .66 A1
Macleod Ct SE21 . . . .76 C3
McLeod's Mews
SW7 . . . . .142 B4
Macleod St SE17 . . .151 A1
Maclise Rd W14 . . . .126 A1
McManus Ho **2**
SW11 . . . . .59 C4
Mcmillan Ho SE4 . . . .66 A4
Macmillan Ho
Cricklewood NW4 . . . .9 A4
Lisson Gr NW8 . . . . . .90 B3
McMillan St SE8 . . . .51 C4
Mcmorran Ho **4**
N7 . . . . .14 A4
Macnamara Ho
SW10 . . . . .157 B2
Mcneil Rd SE5 . . . . . .49 A1
McNicol Dr NW10 . . .20 B3
Maconochies Rd **3**
E14 . . . . .42 A1
Macquarie Way
E14 . . . . .42 A2
Macready Ho N1 . . . .102 B3
Macready Pl **2**
N7 . . . . .14 A4
Macroom Ho W9 . . . .23 B2
Macroom Rd W9 . . . .23 B2
Mac's Pl EC4 . . . . . .107 C2
Madame Tussaud's
NW1 . . . . .91 B1
Madani Girls Sch **58**
E1 . . . . .32 A3
Maddams St E3 . . . . .27 A1
Maddocks Ho **3**
E1 . . . . .32 A2
Maddock Way
SE17 . . . . .48 A4
Maddox St W1 . . . . .118 C4
Madinah Rd
7 Dalston E8 . . . . .16 C2
London E8. . . . . .16 C3
Madison Ho E3. . . . . .27 B2
Madras Pl N7 . . . . . . .14 C2
Madrid Rd SW13 . . . .46 C3
Madron St SE17 . . . .152 B2
Mafeking Ave
TW8 . . . . .44 A4
Magdala Ave N19. . . . .5 A2
Magdalene Cl **7**
SE15 . . . . .50 A1

Magdalene Ho **7**
SW15 . . . . .57 C1
Magdalen Pas **6** E1 .125 A4
Magdalen Rd
SW18 . . . . .71 C3
Magdalen St SE1 . . .124 A1
Magee St SE11 . . . . .163 B4
Magellan Ho **8**
SW11 . . . . .168 A2
Magellan Pl **2**
E14 . . . . .41 C2
Magnin Cl **3** E8. . . . .24 C4
Magnolia Ct
Richmond TW9 . . . . . .45 A2
Wandsworth SW11 . . .60 B1
Magnolia Ho **13**
SE8 . . . . .51 B4
Magnolia Pl SW4 . . . .62 A2
Magnolia Rd W4 . . . .45 A4
Magnolia Wharf
W4 . . . . .45 A4
Magpie Ho **7** E3 . . . .26 B4
Magpie Pl SE14 . . . . .51 A4
Magri Wlk **22** E1 . . . .32 B4
Maguire St SE1 . . . .139 A4
Mahatma Gandhi Ind
Est **1** SE24. . . . . . . .63 A3
Mahogany Cl SE16 . .33 A1
Mahoney Ho SE14 . . .51 B2
Maida Ave W2. . . . . . .89 A1
MAIDA VALE 88 A4
Maida Vale W9 . . . . . .88 C3
Maida Vale Sta
W9 . . . . .88 B4
Maiden La
Borough The SE1 . . .123 A2
Camden Town NW1 . .13 C1
Strand WC2 . . . . . . .120 B4
Maidenstone Hill
SE10 . . . . .52 B2
Maidstone Bldgs
SE1 . . . . .123 B1
Maidstone Ho **4**
E14 . . . . .34 A3
Mail Coach Yd **2**
E2 . . . . .24 A2 98 B4
Main Yd **8** E9. . . . . . .18 C2
Maismore St SE15 . . .49 C4
Maitland Cl **3**
SE10 . . . . .52 A3
Maitland Ct **2** 115 B4
Maitland Ho
Chelsea SW1 . . . . . .160 C4
16 South Hackney
E2 . . . . .25 B3
MAITLAND PARK . . .12 B2
Maitland Park Rd
NW3 . . . . .12 B2
Maitland Park Villas
NW3 . . . . .12 B2
Maitland Pl E5 . . . . . .17 B4
Majestic Ct N4 . . . . . . .6 A3
Major Cl SW9 . . . . . .63 A4
Majorie Mews **6**
E1 . . . . .32 C3
Major Rd E15. . . . . . . .19 C3
Makepeace Ave N6. . . .3 C2
Makepeace Mans
N6. . . . . .3 C2
Makins St SW3 . . . . .144 B3
Malabar Ct **20**
W12 . . . . .30 A2
Malabar St E14 . . . . .41 C4
Malam Ct SE11 . . . . .149 B3
Malam Gdns **3**
E14 . . . . .34 A2

Malay Ho **2** E1 . . . . . .32 B1
Malbrook Rd
SW15 . . . . .57 A3
Malcolm Ho **18** N1 . .24 A3
Malcolm Pl E2 . . . . . .25 B1
Malcolm Rd E1 . . . . . .25 B1
Malcolmson Ho
SW1 . . . . .147 C1
Malden Cres NW1 . . .12 C2
Malden Pl NW5. . . . . .12 C3
Malden Rd NW5 . . . . .12 C2
Maldon Cl
Camberwell SE5 . . . .64 A4
Shoreditch N1. . . . . . .87 A4
Stratford New Town
E15. . . . . .19 C3
Maldon Rd W3 . . . . . .28 B2
Malet Pl WC1. . . . . . .93 B1
Malet St WC1 . . . . . .105 C4
Maley Ave SE27. . . . . .75 A2
Malfort Rd SE5 . . . . . .64 A4
Malins Ct SW12 . . . . .60 C1
Mallams Mews **1**
SW9 . . . . .63 A4
Mallard Cl
1 Hackney E9. . . . . .18 B2
2 Kilburn NW6 . . . . .23 C4
Mallard Ho
8 Camberwell
SE5 . . . . .49 B2
St John's Wood
NW8 . . . . .80 A1
Mallard Point **6**
E3 . . . . .26 C2
Mallet Ho **11**
SW15 . . . . .56 C2
Mallet Rd SE13 . . . . .67 C1
Mall Galleries
SW1 . . . . .119 C2
Malling SE13 . . . . . . .67 A2
Mallinson Rd
SW11 . . . . .60 B2
Mallinson Sp Ctr
N6. . . . . .3 B3
Mallon Gdns E1 . . . .111 A3
Mallord St SW3 . . . .157 C4
Mallory Bldgs EC1 . . .96 A1
Mallory Cl SE4 . . . . . .66 A3
Mallory St NW8 . . . . .90 B2
Mallow Ct SE13. . . . . .52 B1
Mallow St EC1. . . . . . .97 B2
Mall Rd W6 . . . . .39 A1
Mall Studios **9**
NW3 . . . . .12 B3
Mall The
Mortlake SW14 . . . . . .55 B2
St James SW1 . . . . .119 B1
Malmesbury **30** E3 . .26 C3
Malmesbury Prim Sch
25 E3 . . . . .26 C3
Malmesbury Rd
Bow E3 . . . . .26 B3
Newham E16 . . . . . . .35 A4
Malmesbury Terr
E16. . . . . .35 B4
Malmsey Ho **31** SE11 149 A2
Malmsead Ho
E9 . . . . .18 A3
Malorees Jun & Inf
Schs NW6 . . . . .9 C1
Malpas Rd
Hackney E8. . . . . .17 A2
New Cross SE4 . . . . . .51 B1
Malta St EC1 . . . . . . .96 B2
Maltby St SE1 . . . . . .138 C2
Malthouse Dr W4. . . . .46 B4

Malthouse Pas
SW13 . . . . .46 A1
Malting Ho E14 . . . . . .33 B2
Maltings W4 . . . . .36 C1
Maltings Cl SW13. . . . .46 A1
Maltings Lo 46 A3
Maltings Pl
Bermondsey SE1 . . **138** B4
Parsons Green
SW6 . . . . .166 B3
Malt Mill **124** C1
Malton Mews **1**
W10 . . . . .31 A3
Malton Rd W10. . . . . .31 A3
Maltravers St
WC2 . . . .**121** B4
Malt St SE1 . . . . .49 C4
Malva Cl SW18 . . . . . .59 A2
Malvern Cl W10 . . . . . .31 A4
Malvern Ct
1B Shepherd's Bush
W12 . . . . .38 C4
South Kensington
SW7 . . . .**143** C4
Malvern Gdns NW2 . . .1 A2
Malvern Ho
London N16 . . . . .7 B3
SE17 . . . .**151** A1
Malvern Mews
NW6 . . . . .23 C2
Malvern Pl NW6 . . . . . .23 B2
Malvern Rd
Dalston E8 . . . . .16 C1
Maida Vale NW6. . . . .23 C2
Upper Holloway N19 . .4 C3
Malvern Terr N1. . . . . .85 B4
Malwood Rd SW12 .61 A1
Malyons Rd SE13 . . . .67 A2
Malyons Terr SE13 . . .67 A2
Managers St **8**
E14 . . . . .34 B1
Manaton Cl SE15 . . . .65 A4
Manbre Rd W6 . . . . . .47 B4
Manchester Dr
W10 . . . . .23 A1
Manchester Gr
E14 . . . . .42 B1
Manchester Ho
SE17 . . . .**151** A2
Manchester Mans
N19 . . . . .4 C4
Manchester Mews
W1 . . . .**103** B3
Manchester Rd
E14 . . . . .42 B3
Manchester Sq
W1 . . . .**103** C2
Manchester St
W1 . . . .**103** B3
Manchuria Rd
SW11 . . . . .60 C1
Manciple St SE1. . . .**137** C2
Mandalay Ho **6**
N16 . . . . .15 C4
Mandalay Rd SW4 . . .61 B2
Mandarin Ct **6**
SE8 . . . . .51 C4
Mandela Cl **3B**
W12 . . . . .30 A2
Mandela Ho **1B**
E2 . . . . .24 B2 98 C4
Mandela Rd E16. . . . .35 C3
Mandela St
Camden Town
NW1 . . . . .83 A4
Kennington SW9 . . .**163** B1

Mandela Way SE1 **152** B4
Manderville Ho
SE1. . . . .**153** A2
Mandeville Cl **5**
SE3 . . . . .53 B3
Mandeville Ct
NW3 . . . . .11 A3
Mandeville Ctyd
SW11 . . . .**169** B3
Mandeville Ho **8**
SW4 . . . . .61 B2
Mandeville Pl W1 **103** C2
Mandrake Rd
Richmond TW10,
TW9 . . . . .54 B3
Mandrake Rd SW17 . .72 B1
Mandrell Rd SW2. . . .62 A2
Manette St W1 . . . . .**105** C1
Manfred Ct **7**
SW15 . . . . .58 B2
Manfred Rd SW15 . . .58 B2
Manger Rd N7 . . . . . .14 A2
Manilla St E14 . . . . . .41 C4
Manitoba Ct **2B**
SE16 . . . . .40 B4
Manley Ct N16 . . . . . .7 C1
Manley Ho SE11 . . .**149** B2
Manley St NW1 . . . . . .81 B4
Mannaby Prior N1. .85 A1
Mannering Ho **6**
SW2 . . . . .62 B2
Manningford Cl
EC1 . . . . .96 A4
Manning Ho **9**
W11 . . . . .31 A3
Manning Pl TW10. .54 B1
Manningtree Cl
SW19 . . . . .70 A3
Manningtree St **2**
E1 . . . .**111** B2
Manny Shinwell Ho
SW6 . . . .**155** A3
Manor Ave SE4 . . . . . .51 B1
Manor Circus TW9 . . .54 C4
Manor Ct
7 Brixton SW2. . . . .62 B2
Camberwell SE15 . . .49 B2
Gunnersbury W3 . . . .36 C2
Parsons Green
SW6 . . . .**166** B3
Streatham SW16 . . . .74 A1
Manorfield Cl **3**
N19 . . . . .13 B4
Manorfield Prim Sch
6 E14 . . . . .34 A4
Manor Gdns
5 Chiswick W4 . . . .38 A1
Clapham Pk
SW4 . . . .**171** A1
Gunnersbury W3 . . . .36 C2
Richmond TW10,
TW9 . . . . .54 B4
Upper Holloway N7 . . .5 A1
Manor Gr
Deptford SE15 . . . . . .50 B4
Richmond TW9 . . . . .54 C4
Manor Gt SW15 . . . . .58 A2
Manor Ho NW1 . . . .**102** B4
Manor House Ct
W9 . . . . .88 C1
Manor House Dr
NW6 . . . . .9 C1
Manor House Sta
N4. . . . . .6 A3
Manor Lo NW2 . . . . . . .9 A2
Manor Mans
7 Hampstead
NW3 . . . . .12 A2
Tufnell Pk N7 . . . . . . .5 A1

Manor Mews
New Cross SE4. . . . . .51 B1
Paddington NW6 . . . .23 C3
Manor Oak Mans
SE22 . . . . .65 A1
Manor Par N16. . . . . . .7 B2
Manor Park Par
SE13 . . . . .67 C3
Manor Park Rd
NW10 . . . . .21 B4
Manor Pk TW9 . . . . . .54 B3
Manor Pl SE17 . . . . .**150** C2
Manor Rd
Richmond TW10,
TW9 . . . . .54 B3
Stamford Hill N16. . . . .7 B4
Manor Specl Sch
NW10 . . . . .22 B4
Manor Street Est
SW3 . . . .**158** B4
Manor The W1 . . . .**118** A3
Manor Way SW3 . . . .36 C2
Manresa Rd SW3 **144** A1
Mansel Ct SW11. . . .**168** B3
Mansell Ho SW8. . .**171** A4
Mansell Rd W3 . . . . . .37 C4
Mansell St E1 . . . . . .**111** A1
Manse Rd N16. . . . . . . .7 B1
Mansfield Ct **27**
E2 . . . . .24 B4
Mansfield Ho
SW15 . . . . .57 C1
Mansfield Mews
W1 . . . .**104** A3
Mansfield Pl **28**
NW3 . . . . .11 B4
Mansfield Rd
Acton W3 . . . . .20 A1
Maitland Pk NW3 . . . .12 B4
Mansfield St W1. . . .**104** A3
Mansford St E2 . . . . .24 C3
Mansion Cl SW9 . .**173** C4
Mansion Gdns NW3. . .2 A1
Mansion Ho EC4. . . .**109** B1
Mansion House Pl EC3,
EC4. . . . .**109** B1
Mansion House St
EC2 . . . .**109** B1
Mansion House Sta
EC4 . . . .**123** A4
Mansions The
NW6 . . . . .10 B3
Manson Mews
SW7 . . . .**143** B3
Manson Pl SW7 . . . .**143** B3
Manston NW1 . . . . . .13 B1
Manstone Rd NW2 . . .10 A3
Manston Ho W14 . .**126** B1
Mantell Ho SW4 . . . . .61 B2
Mantle Rd SE4 . . . . . .66 A4
Manton Ho N16 . . . . . .6 C1
Mantua St **2**
SW11 . . . . .59 C4
Manus Cl **1** SW11 . . . .25 B1
Manus Rd E3 . . . . . . .26 B3
Manville Gdns
SW17 . . . . .73 A1
Manville Rd SW17 . . .73 A2
Manwood Rd SE4 . . . .66 B1
Many Gates SW12 . . .73 A2
Mapesbury Ct
NW2 . . . . .10 A3
Mapesbury Rd
NW2 . . . . .10 A3
Mapeshill Pl NW2 . . . .9 B2
Mapes Ho **7** NW6 . .10 A1

Mape St E2 . . . . .25 A1
Maple Ave W3 . . . . . .29 A1
Maple Cl SW4 . . . . . . .61 C1
Maple Ct **3** NW2 . . . . .9 C4
Mapledene Est E8. . .16 C1
Mapledene Rd E8 . . .16 C1
Maple Ho
4 Maitland Pk
NW3 . . . . .12 B2
5 New Cross SE8 . .51 B3
4 Richmond TW9 . . .45 A2
Maple Leaf Sq **27**
SE16 . . . . .40 C4
Maple Lo SW15. . . . . .58 A1
Maple Mews NW6 . . .78 A2
Maple Pl W1 . . . . . . .93 A1
Maples Pl E1 . . . . . . .32 A4
Maple St
8 Bethnal Green
E2 . . . . .25 A3
Fitzrovia W1 . . . . . . .93 A1
Maplestead Rd
SW2 . . . . .74 B4
Mapleton Cres
SW18 . . . . .59 A1
Mapleton Rd
SW18 . . . . .59 A1
Maple Wlk W10 . . . . .22 C1
Maplin St E3 . . . . . . .26 B2
Marada Ho NW6 . . . . .10 A1
Marais W4 . . . . .45 B3
Marban Rd W9 . . . . . .23 B2
Marble Arch W1 . .**117** A4
Marble Arch Sta
W1 . . . .**103** A1
Marble Cl W3 . . . . . . .28 A1
Marbleford Ct **4**
N6. . . . . .4 C4
Marble Ho W9 . . . . . .23 B1
Marcella Rd SW9 . .**173** B1
Marchant Ho **13**
SW2 . . . . .62 B2
Marchant St SE14 . . .51 A4
Marchbank Rd
W14 . . . .**155** A4
March Ct SW15. . . . . .57 A3
Marchmont Rd
TW10 . . . . .54 B2
Marchmont St
WC1 . . . . .94 A2
Marchwood Cl **9**
SE5 . . . . .49 A3
Marcia Rd SE1 . . . .**152** B3
Marcilly Rd SW18 . . .59 C2
Marcol Ho W1 . . . . .**104** B2
Marcon Ct **8** E8 . . . . .17 A3
Marcon Pl E8 . . . . . . .17 A3
Marco Rd W6 . . . . . . .39 B3
Marcus Ct TW8. . . . . .44 A3
Marcus Garvey Mews
SE22 . . . . .65 A2
Marcus Garvey Way
8 SE24 . . . . .62 C3
Marcus Ho **1**
SE15 . . . . .49 B2
Marcus St SW18 . . . .59 A1
Marcus Terr SW18 . . .59 A1
Marden Ho **6** E8 . . . . .17 A3
Marden Sq SE16. . . . .40 A3
Mardyke Ho SE17 **151** C4
Maresfield Gdns
NW3 . . . . .11 B2
Mare St E8. . . . . .17 A1
Margaret Bondfield
Ho
5 Bow E3 . . . . .26 A3

Margaret Bondfield
Ho continued
2B Kentish Town
N7 . . . . .13 C3
Margaret Ct W1 . . . .**104** C2
Margaret Herbison Ho
SW6 . . . .**155** A3
Margaret Ho **1B**
W6 . . . . .39 B1
Margaret Ingram Cl
SW6 . . . .**154** C3
Margaret Mcmillan
Ho **1B** N19. . . . . .4 C4
Margaret Rd N16 . . . . .7 B3
Margaret Rutherford
Pl **8B** SW12. . . . . . . .73 B3
Margaret St W1 . . . .**104** C2
Margaretta Terr
SW3 . . . .**158** B4
Margaret White Ho
NW1 . . . . .93 B4
Margate Rd SW2 . . . .62 A2
Margery Fry Ct N7 . . . .5 A1
Margery St WC1 . . . . .95 B3
Margravine Gdns
Hammersmith W6 . . .39 C1
West Kensington
W14 . . . .**140** A2
Margravine Rd
W6 . . . .**154** A4
Marham Gdns SW17,
SW18 . . . . .72 A3
Maria Fidelis Convent
Sch (Lower) NW1 **93** A3
Maria Fidelis Convent
Sch (Upper) NW1 **93** A4
Marian Ct E9 . . . . . . .17 B3
Marian Pl E2 . . . . .25 A3
Marian Sq E2 . . . . . . .25 A3
Marian St **2** E2 . . . . . .25 A3
Marian Way NW10. . . .8 B1
Maria Terr E1 . . . . . . .25 C1
Maribor **1B** SE10. . . .52 B3
Marie Curie SE5 . . . . .49 A2
Marie Lloyd Ct **1B**
SW9 . . . . .62 B3
Marie Lloyd Gdns **1**
N19. . . . . .5 A4
Marie Lloyd Ho N1 **87** B1
Marie Stopes Ct **3**
N19 . . . . .5 A4
Marigold St SE16 . . . .40 A4
Marina Ct **12** E3 . . . . .26 C2
Marina Point **4**
E14 . . . . .42 A3
Marinefield Rd
SW6 . . . .**166** B2
Marinel Ho **25** SE5. . . .48 B3
Mariners Mews
E14 . . . . .42 C2
Marine St SE16 . . . .**139** B2
Marine Twr **2B**
SE8 . . . . .51 B4
Marion Richardson
Prim Sch **17** E1. . . . .32 C3
Marischal Rd SE13. . .67 C4
Maritime Greenwich
Coll **1B** SE8. . . . . . .51 C3
Maritime Ho **5**
SW4 . . . . .61 B4
Maritime Quay **5**
E14 . . . . .41 C1
Maritime St E3 . . . . . .26 B1

Marius Mans [3]
  SW17 ... 72 C2
Marius Rd SW17 ... 72 C2
Marjorie Gr SW11 ... 60 B3
Market Ct W1 ... 104 C2
Market La W12 ... 39 B4
Market Mews W1 ... 118 A1
Market Pl
  [3] Acton W3 ... 28 B1
  [1] Bermondsey
  SE16 ... 40 A2
  Marylebone W1 ... 104 C2
Market Rd
  Barnsbury N7 ... 14 A2
  Richmond TW9 ... 54 C4
Market St E1 ... 125 A4
Market St E1 ... 110 C2
Market Studios [14]
  W12 ... 39 B4
Market Way E14 ... 34 A3
Market Yd Mews
  SE1 ... 138 A2
Markham Pl SW3 ... 144 C2
Markham Sq SW3 ... 144 C2
Markham St SW3 ... 144 B2
Mark Ho [3] E2 ... 25 C3
Markland Ho W10 ... 30 C2
Mark Mans W12 ... 38 C3
Marksbury Ave
  TW9 ... 54 C4
Mark Sq EC2 ... 24 A1 98 A2
Mark St EC2 ... 24 A1 98 A2
Markstone Ho
  SE1 ... 136 A3
Markyate Ho [6]
  W10 ... 22 B1
Marland Ho SW1 ... 131 A2
Marlborough
  [11] Putney SW19 ... 69 C3
  St John's Wood W9 ... 88 C4
Marlborough Ave
  E8 ... 24 B4
Marlborough Cl
  SE17 ... 150 B3
Marlborough Cres
  W4 ... 38 A3
Marlborough Ct
  Kensington W8 ... 141 B4
  Marylebone W1 ... 104 C1
Marlborough Flats
  SW3 ... 144 B4
Marlborough Gr
  SE1 ... 153 B1
Marlborough Hill
  NW8 ... 79 A3
Marlborough Ho
  Marylebone NW1 ... 92 B2
  Richmond TW10 ... 54 C2
  Stoke Newington N4 ... 6 B3
Marlborough Ho
  SW19 ... 69 C1
Marlborough Lo
  [3] Hackney E9 ... 25 B1
  St John's Wood
Marlborough Mans [5]
  NW6 ... 10 C3
Marlborough Mews [1]
  SW2 ... 62 B3
Marlborough Pl
  NW8 ... 79 A2

Marlborough Prim
  Sch SW3 ... 144 B3
Marlborough Rd
  Acton Green W4 ... 37 B1
  Richmond TW10 ... 54 B1
  St James SW1 ... 119 A1
  Upper Holloway N19 ... 5 A2
Marlborough St
  SW3 ... 144 B3
Marlborough Trad Est
  TW9 ... 45 A2
Marlborough Yd
  N19 ... 4 C2
Marlbury NW8 ... 78 B3
Marley Ho [14] W11 ... 30 C2
Marley Wlk NW2 ... 9 B3
Marlin Ho SW15 ... 58 A2
Marloes Rd W8 ... 128 A1
Marlow Ct NW6 ... 9 C1
Marlowe Bsns Ctr [2]
  SE14 ... 51 A3
Marlowe Ct SW3 ... 144 B3
Marlowe Ho [15]
  N16 ... 16 A4
Marlowes The
  NW8 ... 79 B4
Marlow Ho
  Bermondsey SE1 ... 138 C2
  [5] Kensington W2 ... 100 C1
  [44] Spitalfields
  E2 ... 24 B2 98 C3
Marlow Studio
  Workshops [43]
  E2 ... 24 B2 98 C3
Marlow Way SE16 ... 40 C4
Marl Rd SW18 ... 59 B3
Marlston Ho [1] ... 92 B3
Marlton St SE10 ... 43 B1
Marmara Apts [4]
  E16 ... 35 C2
Marmion Ho [13]
  SW12 ... 73 A4
Marmion Mews [4]
  SW11 ... 60 C4
Marmion Rd SW11 ... 60 C3
Marmont Rd SE15 ... 49 C3
Marmora Ho E1 ... 33 A4
Marmora Rd SE22 ... 65 B1
Marner Prim Sch [8]
  E3 ... 27 A1
Marne St W10 ... 23 A2
Marney Rd SW11 ... 60 C3
Marnfield Cres
  SW2 ... 74 B3
Marnham Ave
  NW2 ... 10 A4
Marnock Ho SE17 ... 151 B2
Marnock Rd SE4 ... 66 B2
Maroon St E14 ... 33 A4
Marquess Rd N1 ... 15 C2
Marquis Ct N4 ... 5 B3
Marquis Rd
  Finsbury Pk N4 ... 5 C4
  Kentish Town NW1 ... 13 C2
Marrick Cl SW15 ... 56 C3
Marrick Ho [6]
  NW6 ... 78 B3
Marriott Rd N4 ... 5 B3
Marryat Ct [12] W6 ... 39 A2
Marryat Ho SW1 ... 146 C1
Marryat Sq SW6 ... 164 A4
Marsala Rd SE13 ... 67 A3
Marsalis Ho [3] E3 ... 26 C2
Marsden Rd SE15 ... 64 B4
Marsden St NW5 ... 12 C2
Marshall Cl SW18 ... 59 B1

Marshall Ct SW4 ... 172 B3
Marshall Ho
  Paddington NW6 ... 23 B3
  Shoreditch N1 ... 87 C2
  Walworth SE17 ... 151 B2
Marshall Rd E10 ... 19 A4
Marshall St L Ctr
  W1 ... 105 A1
Marshall's Pl
  SE16 ... 139 A1
Marshall St W1 ... 105 A1
Marshalsea Rd
  SE1 ... 137 A4
Marsham Ct
  [19] Putney SW19 ... 69 C3
  Westminster SW1 ... 147 C4
Marsham St SW1 ... 147 C4
Marsh Ct E8 ... 16 C2
Marshfield St E14 ... 42 B3
Marsh Gate Bsns Ctr
  E15 ... 27 B3
Marshgate Sch
  TW10 ... 54 B2
Marsh Hill E9 ... 18 A3
Marsh Ho
  Nine Elms SW8 ... 171 A4
  Pimlico SW1 ... 147 C1
Marsh St E14 ... 42 A2
Marsh Wall E14 ... 42 A4
Marshwood Ho [10]
  NW6 ... 23 C4
Marsland Cl SE17 ... 150 B1
Marsom Ho N1 ... 87 B1
Marston SE17 ... 151 A4
Marston Cl NW6 ... 11 B1
Marston Ho [8]
  SW9 ... 173 C1
Martaban Rd N16 ... 7 B2
Martello St E8 ... 17 A1
Martello Terr E8 ... 17 A1
Martell Rd SE21 ... 75 C1
Martel Pl E8 ... 16 B2
Martha's Bldgs
  EC1 ... 97 B2
Martha St E1 ... 32 B3
Martin Ct [12] E14 ... 42 B4
Martindale SW14 ... 55 B2
Martindale Ave [2]
  E16 ... 35 C2
Martindale Ho [23]
  E14 ... 34 A2
Martindale Rd
  SW12 ... 73 A4
Martineau Ho
  SW1 ... 146 C1
Martineau Mews
  N5 ... 15 A4
Martineau Rd N5 ... 15 A4
Martin Ho
  Newington SE1 ... 137 A1
  South Lambeth
  SW8 ... 162 A2
Martin La EC4 ... 123 C4
Martlett Ct WC2 ... 106 B1
Martlett Lo SW3 ... 11 A4
Martley Ho SW8 ... 171 A4
Martock Ct [10]
  SE15 ... 50 A2
Marton Rd [2] N16 ... 7 A1
Marvel Ho [5] SE5 ... 48 C3
Marville Rd SW6 ... 154 C1
Marvin St [3] E8 ... 17 A2
Marwell Ct SE3 ... 52 C1

Mary Adelaide Cl
  SW15 ... 68 A1
Mary Adelaide Ho
  W2 ... 101 C4
Mary Ann Bldgs
  SE8 ... 51 C4
Mary Datchelor Cl
  SE5 ... 48 C2
Mary Dine Ct
  SW8 ... 163 A1
Mary Gn [3] NW8 ... 78 B4
Mary Ho
  [3] Hammersmith
  W6 ... 39 B1
  [6] Stockwell SW9 ... 172 C1
Mary James Ho [32]
  E2 ... 24 C3
Mary Jones Ho [20]
  E14 ... 33 C2
Maryland Rd
  Paddington W9 ... 23 C1
  Stratford New Town
  E15 ... 19 C3
Maryland Wlk N1 ... 86 C4
MARYLEBONE ... 104 B2
Marylebone Flyover
  NW1 ... 102 A3
Marylebone High St
  W1 ... 103 C4
Marylebone La
  W1 ... 103 C2
Marylebone Mews
  W1 ... 104 A3
Marylebone Pas
  W1 ... 105 A2
Marylebone Rd
  W1 ... 103 A3
Marylebone St
  W1 ... 103 C3
Marylebone Sta
  NW1 ... 90 C1
Marylee Way
  SW11 ... 149 A3
Mary McArthur Ho [7]
  N19 ... 4 C4
Mary Macarthur Ho
  [16] Globe Town
  E2 ... 25 C2
  W14 ... 154 A4
Maryon Mews
  NW3 ... 12 A4
Mary Pl
  W11 ... 31 A2 112 A3
Mary's Ct [2] NW8 ... 90 B2
Mary Secole Cl [21]
  E8 ... 24 B4
Mary Smith Ct
  SW5 ... 141 C3
Mary St
  [5] Canning Town
  E16 ... 35 B4
  Shoreditch N1 ... 87 A3
Mary Terr NW1 ... 82 C3
Mary Wharrie Ho [4]
  NW3 ... 12 B1
Masbro' Rd W14 ... 39 C3
Mascotte Rd [2]
  SW15 ... 57 C3
Masefield Ct N5 ... 15 C3
Masefield Ho [4]
  NW6 ... 23 C2
Mashie Rd W3 ... 29 A3
Maskall Cl SW2 ... 74 C3

Maskell Rd SW17 ... 71 B1
Maskelyne Cl
  SW11 ... 168 B4
Mason Cl
  Bermondsey
  SE16 ... 153 C2
  Newham E16 ... 35 C2
Mason Ho
  [18] Bermondsey
  SE16 ... 153 C2
  [1] Hackney E9 ... 17 B1
Mason's Arms Mews
  W1 ... 118 A3
Mason's Ave EC2 ... 109 B2
Mason's Pl EC1 ... 96 C4
Mason St SE17 ... 151 C4
Mason's Yd
  Finsbury EC1 ... 96 B4
  St James SW1 ... 119 A2
Massie Rd E8 ... 16 C2
Massinger St SE17 ... 152 A3
Massingham St E1 ... 25 C1
Mast Ct [17] SE16 ... 41 A2
Masterman Ho [5]
  SE5 ... 48 C3
Masters Dr SE16 ... 40 A1
Masters Lo [24] E1 ... 32 B3
Masters St [5] E1 ... 32 C4
Mast House Terr
  E14 ... 41 C2
Masthouse Terrace
  Pier SE8 ... 41 C1
Mastin Ho SW18 ... 70 C3
Mast L Ctr The
  SE16 ... 41 A2
Mastmaker Rd
  E14 ... 41 C4
Matara Mews
  SE17 ... 150 C1
Matching Ct [14] E3 ... 26 C2
Matham Gr SE22 ... 64 B3
Matheson Lang Ho
  SE1 ... 135 B3
Matheson Rd
  W14 ... 140 C3
Mathews Yd WC2 ... 106 A1
Mathieson Ct SE1 ... 136 B3
Mathison Ho
  SW10 ... 156 C2
Matilda Gdns [10]
  E3 ... 26 C3
Matilda Ho E1 ... 125 B2
Matilda St N1 ... 85 A4
Matlock Cl
  Camberwell SE24 ... 63 B3
Matlock Ct
  [1] Herne Hill SE5 ... 63 C3
  St John's Wood
  NW8 ... 78 C2
Matlock St E14 ... 33 A3
Maton Ho SW6 ... 154 C2
Matson Ho
  [9] Bermondsey
  SE16 ... 40 A3
  [16] Homerton E9 ... 17 C2
Matthew Cl W10 ... 22 C1
Matthew Parker St
  SW1 ... 133 C3
Matthews Ct N5 ... 15 B4
Matthews Ho [6]
  E14 ... 33 C3
Matthews St
  SW11 ... 168 C2
Matthias Ct [12]
  TW10 ... 54 A1

Matthias Ho **2**
N16 . . . . .16 A3
Matthias Rd N16 . . . . .16 A3
Mattingly Way **3**
SE15 . . . . .49 B3
Maude Ho **3** E2 . . . . . .24 C3
Maude Rd SE5 . . . . . . .49 A2
Maudlins Gn E1 . . . . .125 B2
Maudsley Ho Tw4 . . .36 A1
Maudsley Hospl
SE5 . . . . .48 C1
Maud St E16 . . . . .35 B4
Maud Wilkes Cl **10**
NW5 . . . . .13 B3
Maugham Ct **5**
W3 . . . . .37 B3
Mauleverer Rd
SW2 . . . . .62 A2
Maundeby Wlk
NW10 . . . . .8 A2
Maunsel St SW1 . . . .147 B4
Maurer Ct **2** SE10 . .43 B3
Mauretania Bldg **11**
E1 . . . . .32 C2
Maurice Ct **4** E1 . . . .26 A2
Maurice Ho **1**
SW9 . . . . .172 C2
Maurice St W12 . . . . .30 A3
Mauritius Rd SE10 . . .43 A2
Maury Rd N16 . . . . .7 C1
Maverton Rd E3 . . . . .26 C4
Mavor Ho N1 . . . . .85 A3
Mawbey Ho E1 . . . . . .153 A1
Mawbey Pl SE1 . . . . .153 A1
Mawbey Rd SE1 . . . . .153 A1
Mawbey St SW8 . . . .162 A1
Mawdley Ho SE1 . . . .135 C3
Mawson Ct N1 . . . . . .87 C3
Mawson Ho EC1 . . . .107 B4
Mawson La W4 . . . . . .46 B4
Maxden Ct SE15 . . . . .64 C4
Maxted Rd SE15 . . . . .64 B4
Maxwell Ct SE21 . . . . .76 C3
Maxwell Rd SW6 . . . .156 B1
Maya Cl SE15 . . . . .50 A1
Mayall Rd SE24 . . . . . .63 A2
Maybury Ct W1 . . . . . .103 C3
Maybury Gdns
NW10 . . . . .9 A2
Maybury Mews N6 . . . .4 B4
Maydew Ho SE16 . . . .40 B2
Maydwell Ho **6**
E14 . . . . .33 C4
MAYFAIR 118 B3
Mayfair Pl W1 . . . . . .118 B2
Mayfield Ave W4 . . . . .38 A2
Mayfield Cl
Clapham Pk SW4 . . .61 C2
Dalston E8 . . . . .16 B2
Mayfield Ho
51 Bethnal Green
E2 . . . . .25 A3
Stamford Hill N16 . . . .7 A4
Mayfield Mans
SW15 . . . . .58 C2
Mayfield Rd
Acton W3 . . . . .28 A2
Bedford Pk W12 . . . . .38 A4
Dalston E8 . . . . .16 B1
Mayflower Cl SE16 . . .40 C2
Mayflower Prim Sch
22 E14 . . . . .34 A3
Mayflower Rd
SW9 . . . . .62 A4
Mayflower St **1**
SE16 . . . . .40 B4

Mayford NW1 . . . . . .83 A2
Mayford Cl SW12 . . . .72 B4
Mayford Rd SW12 . . . .72 C4
Maygood Ho N1 . . . . .85 B2
Maygood St N1 . . . . . .85 B2
Maygrove Rd NW6 . . .10 B2
Maylands Ho SW3 . . .144 B3
Maylie Ho **4** SE16 . . .40 A4
Maynard Cl SW6 . . . .156 B1
Maynard Ho E1 . . . . . .26 A2
Maynards Quay E1 . . .32 B2
Mayne Ct E8 . . . . .16 C3
Mayo Ho **10** E1 . . . . . .32 B4
Mayola Rd E5 . . . . . . .17 B4
May's Buildings Mews
SE10 . . . . .52 C3
Mays Ct WC2 . . . . . . .120 A3
Maysoule Rd
SW11 . . . . .59 C3
May St W14 . . . . .141 A1
Mayston Mews **3**
SE10 . . . . .43 C1
Maythorne Cotts
SE13 . . . . .67 C1
Mayton St N7 . . . . .5 B1
May Tree Ho SE4 . . . . .66 B4
Maytree Wlk SW2 . . . .74 C2
Mayward Ho **7**
SE5 . . . . .49 A2
Maze Hill SE10 . . . . . . .53 A4
Maze Hill Lodge **7**
SE10 . . . . .52 C4
Maze Hill Sta SE10 . . .53 A4
Mazenod Ave
NW6 . . . . .10 C1
Mace Rd TW9 . . . . . . .44 C2
Mead Ct **3** NW1 . . . .12 C1
Meadcroft Rd
SE17 . . . . .48 A4
Meade Cl W4 . . . . .44 C4
Meader Ct SE14 . . . . . .50 C3
Mead Ho
W11 . . . . . .31 B1 112 C2
Mead Lo W4 . . . . .37 C4
Meadowbank NW3 . . .12 B1
Meadow Bank **8**
SW15 . . . . .58 B2
Meadowbank Cl
SW6 . . . . .47 B3
Meadow Cl E9 . . . . . . .18 B3
Meadowcroft **1**
W4 . . . . .36 C1
Meadowgate Sch
SE4 . . . . .66 A4
Meadow Mews
SW8 . . . . .162 C3
Meadow Pl
Chiswick W4 . . . . . . .46 A3
South Lambeth
SW8 . . . . .162 B2
Meadow Rd SW8 . . . .162 C2
Meadow Row SE1 . . .136 C1
Mead Row SE1 . . . . . .135 B2
Meadway The SE2 . . . .52 C1
Meakin Est SE1 . . . . . .138 A2
Meakin Ho N7 . . . . . . .14 B3
Meard St W1 . . . . .105 B1
Meath Cres E1, E2 . . . .25 C2
Meath Ho SE24 . . . . . .63 A1
Meath St SW11 . . . . . .170 A4

Mecklenburgh Pl
WC1 . . . . .94 C2
Meldon Cl SW6 . . . . . .166 B4
Mecklenburgh Sq
WC1 . . . . .94 C2
Mecklenburgh St
WC1 . . . . .94 C2
Medburn St NW1 . . . . .83 A2
Medcroft Gdns
SW14 . . . . .55 B3
Medfield St SW15 . . . .69 A4
Medhurst Cl **10** E3 . . .26 A3
Median Rd E5 . . . . .17 B3
Medina Gr N7 . . . . .5 C1
Medina Ho SE15 . . . . .65 B3
Medina Rd N7 . . . . .5 C1
Medlar St SE5 . . . . . . .48 B2
Medley Rd NW6 . . . . . .10 C2
Medora Rd SW2 . . . . . .74 B4
Medresco Ho W14 . . . .11 C3
Medusa Rd SE6,
SE13 . . . . .67 A1
Medway Bldgs E3 . . . .26 A3
Medway Ct WC1 . . . . .94 A3
Medway Ho
Bermondsey SE1 . . .137 C3
Paddington NW8 . . . .102 A4
Stoke Newington
N16 . . . . .7 A1
Medway Mews **38**
E3 . . . . .26 A3
Medway Rd E3 . . . . . . .26 A3
Medway St SW1 . . . . .133 C1
Medwin St SW4 . . . . . .62 B3
Meecham Ct **1**
SW11 . . . . .168 A2
Meeson St E5 . . . . .18 A4
Meeting House Alley
7 E1 . . . . .32 A1
Meeting House La
SE15 . . . . .50 A3
Mehetabel Rd E9 . . . . .17 B3
Melba Way SE13 . . . . .52 A2
Melbourne Ct
Hackney E5 . . . . .18 A4
Paddington W9 . . . . . .89 A2
Melbourne Gr
SE22 . . . . .64 B3
Melbourne Ho
W8 . . . . . .31 C1 113 B1
Melbourne Mews
SW9 . . . . .173 B3
Melbourne Pl
WC2 . . . . .107 A1
Melbourne Sq **21**
SW9 . . . . .173 B3
Melbray Mews **1**
SW6 . . . . .164 C1
Melbreak Ho **11**
SE22 . . . . .64 A4
Melbury Ct W8 . . . . . .127 A2
Melbury Dr SE5 . . . . . .49 A3
Melbury Ho SW8 . . . .162 C2
Melbury Rd W14 . . . . .127 A2
Melchester **5**
W11 . . . . .31 B3
Melchester Ho **1**
N19 . . . . .4 C1
Melcombe Ct
NW1 . . . . .102 C4
Melcombe Ho
SW8 . . . . .162 C1
Melcombe Pl
NW1 . . . . .102 C4
Melcombe Prim Sch
6 W6 . . . . .47 C4

Melcombe St NW1 . . . .91 A1
Meldon Cl SW6 . . . . . .166 B4
Melford Ct
Bermondsey SE1 . . .138 B2
Dulwich SE22 . . . . . .76 C4
Melford Rd SE21,
SE22 . . . . .76 C4
Melgund Rd N5 . . . . . .14 C3
Melina Ct
Putney SW15 . . . . . . .56 C4
St John's Wood
NW8 . . . . .89 B3
Melina Pl NW8 . . . . . . .89 B3
Melina Rd W12 . . . . . .39 A4
Melior Pl SE1 . . . . .138 A4
Melior St SE1 . . . . .138 A4
Melisa Ct N6 . . . . .4 C4
Mellington Ct **2**
N16 . . . . .7 C1
Mellis Ave TW9 . . . . . .45 A2
Mellish Ho **4** E1 . . . . .32 A3
Mellish St E14 . . . . . . .41 C3
Mellitus St W12 . . . . . .29 B3
Mell St **6** SE10 . . . . . .43 A1
Melody La N5 . . . . .15 B3
Melody Rd SW18 . . . . .59 B2
Melon Pl W8 . . . . .127 C4
Melon Rd SE15 . . . . . . .49 C2
Melrose Ave
Cricklewood NW2 . . . .9 B3
Wimbledon SW19 . . . .70 C1
Melrose Cl SE12 . . . . . .97 B4
Melrose Gdns W6 . . . .39 B3
Melrose Ho
Maida Vale NW6 . . . .23 C2
Pimlico SW1 . . . . . . .146 B2
Melrose Rd
1 Barnes SW13 . . . . .46 B1
Wandsworth SW18 . . .58 B1
Melrose Terr W6 . . . . . .39 B3
Melton Ct SW7 . . . . . .143 C3
Melton Ho E5 . . . . .7 C2
Melton St NW1 . . . . . . .93 B3
Melville Court Flats
W12 . . . . .39 A4
Melville Ct
4 Brentford W4 . . . .36 C1
Rotherhithe SE8 . . . . .41 A2
Melville Ho SE10 . . . . .52 B2
Melville Pl **4** N1 . . . . .15 B1
Melville Rd SW13 . . . .46 C2
Melville Villas Rd
W3 . . . . .28 C1
Melvin Ct **11** TW9 . . .44 C2
Melwood Ho **22**
E1 . . . . .32 A3
Melyn Cl N7 . . . . .13 B4
Memel Ct EC1 . . . . . . .96 C1
Memel St EC1 . . . . .96 C1
Menai Pl **2** E3 . . . . . . .26 C3
Menard Ct EC1 . . . . . . .97 A3
Mendham Ho SE1 . . . .138 A2
Mendip Ct
8 Battersea
SW11 . . . . .59 B4
Deptford SE14 . . . . . .50 B4
Mendip Ho **2** N4 . . . . .6 C4
Mendip Ho **15** E2 . . . .25 B2
Mendip Rd SW11 . . . . .59 B4
Mendora Rd SW6 . . . .154 C2
Menelik Rd NW2 . . . . .10 B4
Menorah Prim Sch
NW11 . . . . .1 A4

Mat – Mer 243

Menotti St **6**
E2 . . . . .24 C1 99 C2
Menteath Ho **9**
E14 . . . . .33 C3
Mentmore Terr E8 . . . .17 A1
Mentone Ct SW8 . . . .172 B4
Meon Rd W3 . . . . .37 B4
Mepham St SE1 . . . . . .121 B1
Mepham St SE1 . . . . . .121 B1
Mercator Pl
E14 . . . . .41 C1
Mercator Rd SE13 . . . .67 C3
Merceron Ho **3**
E2 . . . . .25 B2
Merceron St E1 . . . . . .25 A1
Mercers Cl SE10 . . . . . .43 B2
Mercer's Cotts **8**
E3 . . . . .33 A3
Mercers Mews N7 . . . . .13 C4
Mercers Pl W6 . . . . . . .39 C2
Mercers Rd N19 . . . . . .4 C1
Mercer St WC2 . . . . . .106 A1
Merchant Ct E1 . . . . . . .32 B1
Merchants Ho
SE10 . . . . .42 C1
Merchant Sq W2 . . . .101 B3
Merchant St E3 . . . . . . .26 B2
Merchant Taylors' Hall
EC3 . . . . .109 C1
Merchon Ho N7 . . . . . .13 B4
Mercia Gr SE13 . . . . . .67 B3
Mercia Ho **9** SE5 . . . . .48 B1
Mercie Ct SE22 . . . . . . .76 C3
Mercier Rd SW15 . . . . .58 A2
Mercury Ct
8 Brixton SW9 . . . .173 B4
10 Millwall E14 . . . .41 C2
Mercury Ho **3** E3 . . . .26 C4
Mercury Way SE14 . . .50 C4
Mercy Terr SE13 . . . . . .67 A2
Mere Cl SW15,
SW19 . . . . .69 C4
Meredith Ave NW2 . . . .9 B3
Meredith Ho **17**
N16 . . . . .16 A3
Meredith Mews
SE4 . . . . .66 B3
Meredith St EC1 . . . . . .96 A3
Meredith Twr W3 . . . . .37 A3
Meredyth Rd
SW13 . . . . .46 C1
Meretone Cl SE4 . . . . . .66 A3
Mereton Mans **8**
SE8 . . . . .51 C2
Mereworth Ho **3**
SE15 . . . . .50 B4
Merganser Ct **17**
SE8 . . . . .51 B4
Meridan Ct SE13 . . . . .67 C3
Meriden Ct SW3 . . . . .144 A1
Meriden Ho **1** N1 . . . . .24 A4
Meridian Courtyard
SE10 . . . . .52 C4
Meridian Ho SE10 . . . .43 A2
Meridian Pl E14 . . . . . .42 B4
Meridian Prim Sch **3**
SE10 . . . . .52 C4
Meridian Sq E15 . . . . .19 C1
Merivale Rd SW15 . . . .58 A3
Merlin Ho
2 Chiswick W4 . . . .37 C1
West Hampstead
NW3 . . . . .11 A4

Merlin Sch The 1
SW15 ....**58** A2
Merlin Ct WC1 .... **95** B3
Merlin St EC1 ...... **95** B3
Mermaid Ct
Bermondsey SE1 ... **137** B4
Rotherhithe SE16 .... **33** B1
Mermaid Ho 8
E14 ....**34** B2
Mermaid Twr 2
SE8 ....**51** B4
Meroe Ct N16 .... **7** A2
Merredene St
SW2 ....**62** B1
Merriam Ave 6
E9 ....**18** B2
Merricks Ct 5
SW14 ....**55** A3
Merrick Sq SE1 ... **137** B2
Merrington Rd
SW6 ....**155** C4
Merritt Rd SE4 .....**66** B2
Merrivale NW1 .....**83** A3
Merrow St SE17 ...**151** B1
Merrow Wlk SE17 **151** C2
Merryfield SE3 .....**53** B1
Merryweather Ct 13
N19 ....**4** B1
Mersey Ho N7 .....**14** C3
Merstone Ho
SW18 ....**59** A1
Merthyr Terr
SW13 ....**47** A4
Merton Ave W4 .....**38** B2
Merton Ho SW18 ...**70** C3
Merton La N6 ....**3** B2
Merton Rd SW18 ...**70** C4
Merton Rise NW3 ..**12** A1
Merton Road Ind Est
SW18 ....**70** C4
Merttins Rd SE15 ..**65** C2
Meru Cl NW5 ....**12** C3
Mervan Rd SW2 .....**62** C3
Messaline Ave W3 .**28** B3
Messina Ave NW6 ..**10** C1
Messiter Ho N1 .....**85** A3
Metcalfe Ho 28
SW8 ....**171** B2
Met Collection (Mus)
SW6 ....**141** B1
Meteor St SW11 ...**60** C3
Methley Ho 2 N7 ...**5** B2
Methley St SE11 ..**149** C1
Methodist Central
Hall SW1 ....**133** C3
Methwold Rd W10 ..**30** C4
Metropolis
Apartments 5
SW12 ....**73** A3
Metropolitan Benefit
Societies
Almshouses 3
N1 ....**16** A2
Metropolitan Bsns Ctr
N1 ....**16** A1
Metropolitan Cl 22
E14 ....**33** C4
Mews St E1 ....**125** B2
Mews The
Shoreditch N1 ....**87** A4
5 Upper Holloway
N19 ....**4** B2
Mexborough NW1 ..**82** C3
Mexfield Rd SW15 ..**58** B3

Meyer Ho 1
SW12 ....**73** A4
Meymott St SE1 ...**122** A1
Meynell Cres E9 ...**17** C1
Meynell Gdns E9 ..**17** C1
Meynell Rd E9 .....**17** C1
Meyrick Ho 8 E14 .**33** C4
Meyrick Rd
Battersea SW11 ......**60** A4
Willesden NW10 ......**8** C2
Miah Terr 9 E1 ....**125** C1
Micawber Ct N1 .....**97** A4
Micawber Ho 27
SE16 ....**139** C3
Micawber St N1 .....**97** A4
Michael Cliffe Ho
EC1 ....**95** C3
Michael Faraday Ho
SE17 ....**151** C1
Michael Faraday Prim
Sch SE17 ....**151** C1
Michael Manley Ind
Est 23 SW8 ....**171** A2
Michael Rd
SW6 ....**166** B4
Michael Tippett Sch
The SE24 ....**63** B3
Michelangelo Ct 14
SE16 ....**40** A1
Michelle Ct 3 W3 .**28** C2
Michels Almshouses
N1 ....**15** A2
Michelsdale Dr 8
TW9 ....**54** A3
Michelson Ho
SE11 ....**149** A3
Michel's Row 2
TW9 ....**54** A3
Michigan Ho E14 ...**41** C3
Mickledore NW1 ....**83** A1
Micklethwaite Rd
SW6 ....**155** C3
Mickleton Ho 30
W2 ....**31** C4
Middlefield NW8 ....**79** B4
Middle Row W10 ....**23** A1
Middle Row Prim Sch
W10 ....**23** A1
Middlesex Ct 5
W4 ....**38** B2
Middlesex Ho W1 .**105** A4
Middlesex Pas
EC1 ....**108** B3
Middlesex Pl 8
E9 ....**17** B2
Middlesex St E1 ..**110** C2
Middlesex Univ
(Archway Campus)
19 N19 ....**4** B2
Middle St EC1 .....**108** C4
Middle Temple
EC4 ....**121** B4
Middle Temple La
EC4 ....**121** B4
Middleton Dr SE16 .**40** C4
Middleton Gr N7 ...**14** A3
Middleton Ho
Dalston E8 ....**16** B1
Newington SE1 ......**137** B1
Middleton Mews
N7 ....**14** A3
Middleton Pl W1 ..**104** C3
Middleton Rd
Dalston E8 ....**16** B1
Golders Green NW11 .**1** C4
Middleton St E2 .....**25** A2

Middleton Way
SE13 ....**67** C3
Middle Yd SE1 .....**124** A2
Midford Pl W1 ....**93** A1
Midhope Ho WC1 ...**94** B3
Midhope St WC1 ....**94** B3
Midhurst Ct N8 ......**5** A4
Midhurst Ho 7
E14 ....**33** A3
Midhurst Way E5 ..**16** C4
Midland Pl E14 ......**42** B1
Midland Rd NW1 ...**94** A4
Midland Terr
NW10 ....**21** A1
Midlothian Ho NW2 .**9** A2
Midlothian Rd E3 ...**26** B1
Midmoor Rd SW12 .**73** B3
Midship Cl SE16 ....**32** C1
Midship Point E14 .**41** C4
Midstrath Rd NW10 ..**8** A4
Midway Ho EC1 .....**96** B4
Milborne Gr
SW10 ....**143** A1
Milborne Ho 19 E9 .**17** B2
Milborne St E9 ......**17** B2
Milbrook Ct NW3 ....**2** B3
Milcote St SE1 .....**136** B3
Mildmay Ave N1 ....**15** C2
Mildmay Ct N1 ......**15** C3
Mildmay Gr N N1 ..**15** C3
Mildmay Gr S N1 ..**15** C3
Mildmay Ho 6
SW15 ....**57** B2
Mildmay Mission
Hospl 4 E2 ....**98** C3
Mildmay Pk N1 ......**15** C3
Mildmay Rd N1 ......**16** A3
Mildmay St N1 ......**15** C3
Mildmay Way E5 ....**17** A4
MILE END **26** A1
Mile End Hospl E2 .**25** C2
Mile End Park L Ctr 8
E3 ....**33** B4
Mile End Pl E1 ......**25** C1
Mile End Rd E1, E3 .**25** C1
Mile End Sta E3 ....**26** B2
Miles Bldgs NW1 ..**102** A4
Miles Coverdale Prim
Sch W12 ....**39** B4
Miles Ct E1 ....**32** A3
Miles Ho 5 SE10 ...**43** A1
Miles Lo E15 ....**19** C3
Miles Pl NW8 ....**101** C4
Miles St SW8 ......**162** B3
Milestone Green
SW14 ....**55** C3
Milfoil St W12 ......**29** C2
Milford Ct 3 N16 ....**7** A3
Milford La WC2 ....**121** B4
Milford Mews
SW16 ....**74** B1
Milford St EC2 ....**109** A2
Milk St 7
E16 ....**55** B2
Milkwell Yd 7
SE5 ....**48** B2
Milkwood Rd SE24 .**63** A3
Milk Yd E1 ....**32** B2
Millais Rd E11 ....**19** C4
Milland Ho 11
SW15 ....**68** C3
Millard Cl N16 ....**16** A3
Millard Rd SE8 ......**41** B1
Millbank SW1 ....**148** A3
Millbank Millennium
Pier SW1 ....**148** B3
Millbank Prim Sch
SW1 ....**147** C3

Millbrooke Ct 7
SW15 ....**58** A2
Millbrook Ho 4
SE15 ....**49** C4
Millbrook Pl NW1 ...**82** C2
Millbrook Rd SW9 ..**63** A4
Millender Wlk
SE16 ....**40** B2
Millennium Bridge N1
EC4 ....**122** C3
Millennium City Acad
W1 ....**104** B3
Millennium Dr
E14 ....**42** C2
Millennium Harbour
E14 ....**41** C4
Millennium Pl 27
E2 ....**25** A3
Millennium Prim Sch
The SE10 ....**43** B3
Millennium Sq
SE1 ....**139** A4
Millennium Way
SE10 ....**43** A3
Miller Ho 9 SW2 ...**74** A4
Miller's Ave E8,
N16 ....**16** B3
Miller's Ct 1 W4 ...**38** B1
Miller St NW1 ....**82** C2
Miller's Terr 1 E8 ..**16** B3
Miller's Way W6 ....**39** B4
Millers Wharf Ho
E1 ....**125** B1
Miller Wlk SE1 .....**121** C1
Millfield N4 ....**5** C2
Millfield La N6 ....**3** B2
Millfield Pl N6 ....**3** C2
Millfields Com Sch
E5 ....**17** B4
Millgrove St 8
SW11 ....**169** B2
Millharbour E14 ....**42** A4
Mill Hill SW13 ....**56** C4
Mill Hill Gr 11 W3 .**28** A1
Mill Hill Rd
Barnes SW13 ....**46** C1
South Acton W3 ......**37** A4
Mill Hill Terr 9
W3 ....**28** A1
Mill Ho 4 SE13 .....**67** B4
Milligan St E14 ......**33** B2
Millners Ct E14 .....**34** B3
Millington Ho N16 ..**6** C1
Millington Ho N16 ..**6** C1
Mill La NW6 ....**10** B3
Millman Ct WC1 ....**94** C1
Millman Mews
WC1 ....**94** C1
Millman Pl WC1 ....**95** A1
Millman St WC1 .....**94** C1
Millmark Gr SE14 ..**51** A1
MILL MEADS **27** C3
Millner Ct SE4 ......**51** B1
Mill Pl E14 ....**33** A3
Mill Pond Cl SW8 .**161** C1
Millpond Est SE16 ..**40** A4
Mill Row N1 ....**24** A4
Mills Ct EC2 .**24** A2 **98** A3
Mills Gr 1 E14 ......**34** B4
Millshott Cl SW6 ...**47** B2
Mills Row W4 ....**37** C2
Mill St
Bermondsey SE1 ...**139** A4
Mayfair W1 ....**118** C4
Millstone Cl E15 ....**19** C2

Millstream Ho 14
SE16 ....**40** A3
Millstream Rd
SE1 ....**138** C3
Mill Trad Est The
NW10 ....**20** B2
MILLWALL **41** C3
Millwall Dock Rd
E14 ....**41** C3
Millwood St 10
W10 ....**31** A4
Mill Yd E1 ....**125** B4
Mill Rd NW6 ....**23** A3
Milman's Ho
SW10 ....**157** A3
Milman's St SW10 .**157** B3
Milner Bldg N16 .....**6** C1
Milner Ho 1
SW11 ....**59** C4
Milner Pl N1 ....**85** C4
Milner Sq N1 ....**15** A1
Milner St SW3 ......**144** C4
Milnthorpe Rd W4 ..**45** C4
Milo Rd SE22 ....**64** B1
Milrood Ho 5 E1 ...**32** C4
Milroy Wlk SE1 ....**122** A2
Milson Rd W14 ......**39** C3
Milsted Ho 22 E5 ...**17** A3
Milton Ave
Becontree NW10 .....**20** C4
Crouch End N6 ....**4** B4
Stonebridge NW10 ...**20** B4
Milton Cl SE1 ......**152** C3
Milton Court Rd
SE14 ....**51** A4
Milton Ct
Fulham SW6 ....**58** A4
St Luke's EC2 ....**109** B4
9 Wandsworth
SW18 ....**58** C2
Milton Gr N16 ....**16** A4
Milton Ho
16 Bethnal Green
E2 ....**25** B2
2 Camberwell SE5 ..**48** C3
Milton House Mans
E8 ....**16** B4
Milton Pk N6 ....**4** B4
Milton Pl 3 N7 .....**14** C3
Milton Rd
Acton W3 ....**28** C1
Crouch End N6 ....**4** B4
Mortlake SW14 ....**55** C4
Tulse Hill SE24 ....**63** A2
Milton St EC1, EC2 **109** B4
Milverton NW5 ......**12** C3
Milverton Rd NW6 ..**9** C1
Milverton St SE11 .**149** C1
Milward St E1 ....**32** A4
Mimosa SW9 ....**172** B3
Mimosa St SW6 ...**165** A3
Mina Rd SE17 ......**152** B2
Minchin Ho 10
E14 ....**33** C3
Mincing La EC3 ...**124** A4
Minera Mews
SW1 ....**145** C4
Minerva Cl SW9 ...**163** C2
Minerva Rd NW10 ..**20** C1
Minerva St E2 ......**25** A3
Minerva Wlk EC1 ..**108** B2
Minet Ave NW10 ....**21** A3
Minet Gdns NW10 ..**21** A3
Minet Ho 20 E1 ....**111** B1
Minet Rd SE5, SW9 ..**48** A1

Minford Gdns
W14 . . . . 39 C4
Mingard Wlk N7. . . . . 5 B1
Ming St E14. . . . . . . 33 C2
Minnow Wlk SE17 152 B3
Minories EC3. . . . . 124 C4
Minshull St SW8. . . 171 B3
Minson Rd E9 . . . . . 25 C4
Minstead Gdns
SW15. . . . . 68 B4
Minster Ct EC3 . . . 124 B4
Minster Rd NW2. . . . 10 A3
Mint Bsns Pk 12
E16. . . . . 35 C4
Mintern St N1. . . . . 87 C2
Minton Ho SE11 . . . 149 B4
Minton Mews 3
NW6. . . . . 11 A2
Mint St SE1 . . . . . 137 A4
Mirabel Rd SW6. . . 155 A2
Miranda Cl 1 E1. . . 32 B4
Miranda Ho 17 N1. . 24 A3
Miranda Rd N19. . . . 4 B3
Missenden SE17. . 151 C1
Missenden Ho
NW8. . . . . 90 A2
Mission Pl SE15 . . . 49 C2
Mission Sq 13
TW8. . . . . 44 A4
Mission The
13 Bermondsey
SE16. . . . . 40 A4
14 Poplar E14. . . . 33 B3
Misterton Ct
SW11. . . . . 167 C4
Mistral SE5. . . . . . . 49 A2
Mitali Pas 21 E1. . . 111 B1
Mitcham Ho 8
SE5 . . . . 48 B2
Mitchell Brook Prim
Sch NW10. . . . . . . 8 A2
Mitchell Ct SW14. . 56 A3
Mitchell Ho
Gunnersbury W4 . . 37 A1
8 Islington N1. . . . 14 C1
31 Shepherd's Bush
W12. . . . . 30 A2
Mitchell's Pl SE21. . 76 A4
Mitchell St EC1. . . . 97 A2
Mitchison Rd N1. . . 15 C2
Mitford Rd N19. . . . . 5 A2
Mitre Bridge Ind Pk
W10. . . . . 22 A1
Mitre Rd SE1 . . . . 135 C4
Mitre Sq EC3 . . . . 110 B1
Mitre St EC3 . . . . 110 B1
Mitre The 9 E14. . 33 B2
Mitre Way W10. . . . 30 A4
Mizzen Ct E14. . . . . 41 C4
Moatfield NW6. . . . . 10 A1
Moat Pl
Acton W3 . . . . 28 A3
Stockwell SW9 . . . . 62 B4
Moat Sch The 7
SW6 . . . . 164 A2
Moberly Rd SW4. . . 73 C4
Mobey Ct SW4. . . . 172 A3
Mocatta Ho 9 E1. . 25 A1
Modbury Gdns
NW5 . . . . 12 C2
Modder Pl SW15. . . 57 C3
Model Cotts SW14. . 55 B3
Modling Ho 8 E2. . 25 C3
Moelwyn Hughes Ct
N7. . . . . 13 C3
Moffat Ho 24 SE5. . 48 B3

Mohawk Ho 8 E3. . 26 A3
Moira Ct SW17. . . . 72 C2
Moira Ho 18 SW9. . 173 B4
Molasses Ho 1
SW11. . . . . 59 B4
Molasses Row 2
SW11. . . . . 59 B4
Mole Ct 2 W12. . . . 38 A4
Mole Ho NW8 . . . . 89 C1
Molesey Ho
E2. . . . . . . 24 B1 98 C2
Molesford Rd
SW6. . . . . 165 B3
Molesworth Ho 9
SE17. . . . . 48 A4
Molesworth St
SE13. . . . . 67 B4
Molly Huggins Cl
SW12. . . . . 73 B4
Molton Ho N1. . . . . 85 A3
Molyneux Ho W1. . 102 B2
Molyneux St W1. . . 102 B3
Mona Rd SE15. . . . . 50 B1
Mona St E16. . . . . . 35 B4
Monck's Row
SW18. . . . . 58 B1
Monck St SW1 . . . 133 C1
Monckton St SW14 126 C2
Moncorvo Cl SW7. 130 A3
Moncrieff St SE15 . . 49 C1
Mondragon Ho
SW8. . . . . 172 B4
Monet Ct 15 SE16. . 40 A1
Moneyer Ho N1. . . . 97 B4
Monier Rd E3. . . . . 18 C1
Monkbretton Ho
E2. . . . . . . 24 C2 99 B3
Monk Ct 2 W12. . . 29 C2
Monk Dr E16. . . . . 35 C2
Monkridge 3 N8. . . . 4 C4
Monksfield N4. . . . . 5 C2
Monkswell Ho
E2. . . . . . . 24 C2 99 B3
Monkton Ho
3 Bermondsey
SE16. . . . . 40 C4
22 Hackney E5. . . . 17 A3
Monkton St SE11. . 149 C4
Monkwell Sq EC2 . 109 A3
Monmouth Cl W4. . 37 C3
Monmouth Gr
TW8. . . . . 36 A2
Monmouth Ho
4 Camden Town
NW5. . . . . 13 A2
Wandsworth SW18 . 58 C1
Monmouth Pl W2 . 100 A1
Monmouth Rd W2 . 31 C3
Monmouth St
WC2 . . . . 106 A1
Monnery Rd N19 . . . 4 B1
Monnow Rd SE1 . . 153 B3
Monroe Dr SW14. . 55 A2
Monroe Ho
10 Crouch End N19 . 4 C4
Lisson Gr NW8. . . . 90 B3
Monro Ho
16 Hampstead
NW3. . . . . 11 B4
Putney SW15 . . . . 57 A2
Monro Way E5. . . . 16 C4
Monsal Ct E5. . . . . 18 A4
Monsell Ct 4 N4. . . . 6 A1

Monsell Rd N4, N5. . 6 A1
Monson Rd
Deptford SE14. . . . 50 C3
Willesden Green
NW10. . . . . 22 A3
Montagu Ct W1 . . 103 A3
Montague Ave
SE4. . . . . 66 C3
Montague Cl SE1. . 123 B2
Montague Pl WC1 105 C4
Montague Rd
Richmond TW10. . . 54 A1
Shacklewell E8. . . . 16 C3
Montague St
Bloomsbury WC1. . 106 A4
City of London EC1 108 C3
Montagu Mans
W1. . . . . 103 A3
Montagu Mews N
W1. . . . . 103 A3
Montagu Mews S
W1. . . . . 103 A3
Montagu Mews W
W1. . . . . 103 A3
Montagu Pl W1 . . 103 A3
Montagu Row W1 103 A3
Montagu Sq W1 . . 103 A3
Montagu St W1 . . 103 A3
Montaigne Cl
SW1 . . . . 147 C3
Montana Bldg 4
SE13. . . . . 52 A2
Montana Rd SW17 72 C1
Montcalm Ho E14 . . 41 C2
Montclare St
E2. . . . . . . 24 B1 98 C2
Monteagle Ct 2
N1. . . . . 24 A3
Monteagle Way
Nunhead SE15. . . . 65 A4
Shacklewell E5. . . . . 7 C1
Montefiore Ct 2
N16. . . . . 7 B3
Montefiore St 2
SW8. . . . . 170 B1
Montego Cl 8
SW2 . . . . 62 A2
Montem Prim Sch 5
N7. . . . . 14 B4
Montem St N4 . . . . 5 B3
Monteray Studios
W10. . . . . 23 A3
Montesquieu Terr 3
E16. . . . . 35 B3
Montford Pl SE11 . 149 B1
Montfort Ho
4 Bethnal Green
E2. . . . . 25 B2
Cubitt Town E14. . . 42 B3
Montfort Pl SW19 . 69 C3
Montgomery Ct
W4 . . . . 45 B4
Montgomery Ho 5
SW14. . . . . 55 C4
Montgomery Lo 8
E1. . . . . 25 B1
Montgomery Rd
W4 . . . . 37 B2
Montholme Rd
SW11. . . . . 60 B1
Monthope Rd 17
E1. . . . . 111 B3

Montolieu Gdns
SW15. . . . . 57 A2
Montpelier Gr
NW5 . . . . 13 B3
Montpelier Mews
SW7 . . . . 130 B2
Montpelier Pl
Knightsbridge
SW7 . . . . 130 B2
2 Stepney E1. . . . 32 B3
Montpelier Rd
SE15. . . . . 50 A2
Montpelier Rise
NW11. . . . . 1 A4
Montpelier Row
SE3 . . . . 53 B1
Montpelier Sq
SW7 . . . . 130 B3
Montpelier St
SW7 . . . . 130 B2
Montpelier Terr
SW7 . . . . 130 B3
Montpelier Vale
SE3 . . . . 53 B1
Montpelier Way
NW11. . . . . 1 A4
Montpelier Wlk
SW7 . . . . 130 B2
Montreal Pl WC2 . 120 C4
Montrell Rd SW2. . 74 A3
Montrose Ave
NW6 . . . . 23 A3
Montrose Ct SW7 129 C3
Montrose Ho
Belgravia SW1. . . 131 C3
Millwall E14 . . . . . 41 C3
Montrose Pl SW1. 131 C3
Montrose Villas 6
W6 . . . . 38 C1
Montserrat Rd
SW15. . . . . 58 A3
Monument EC3. . 123 C4
Monument Gdns
SE13. . . . . 67 B2
Monument St EC3. 123 C4
Monument Sta
EC3. . . . . 123 C4
Monza Bldg The
E1. . . . . 32 B2
Monza St E1. . . . . 32 B2
Moodkee St SE16. . 40 B3
Moody Rd SE15. . . 49 B2
Moody St E1. . . . . 25 C2
Moon St N1. . . . . . 86 A4
Moorcroft St
W6. . . . . 74 A1
Moore Cl SW14. . . 55 B4
Moore Ct N1. . . . . 86 A3
Moore Ho
6 Bethnal Green
E2. . . . . 25 B2
5 Greenwich SE10. 43 B1
7 Shadwell E1. . . 32 B2
Wandsworth SW17 . 71 C1
Moore Park Ct
SW6 . . . . 156 B2
Moore Park Rd
SW6 . . . . 156 A1
Moore St SW3. . . 144 C4
Moorfields EC2. . 109 B3
Moorfields Eye Hospl
EC1. . . . . 97 B3
Moorfields Highwalk
EC2. . . . . 109 B3
Moorgate EC2. . . 109 B3
Moorgate Pl EC2 . 109 B2

Moorgate Sta
EC2. . . . . 109 B3
Moorgreen Ho EC1 96 B4
Moorhouse Ct . . . 109 B3
Moorhouse Rd
W2. . . . . 31 C3
Moor La EC2. . . . 109 B3
Moorland Rd SW9. 63 A3
Moor Pl EC2. . . . 109 B3
Moor St W1. . . . . 105 C1
Morant St E14. . . . 33 C2
Mora Prim Sch
NW2. . . . . 9 B4
Mora Rd NW2 . . . . 9 B4
Mora St EC1. . . . . 97 A3
Morat St SW9 . . . 173 A4
Moravian Cl SW3 157 C3
Moravian Pl
SW10. . . . . 157 C3
Moravian St 10 E2. 25 B2
Moray Ho 8 E1. . . 26 A1
Moray Mews N4, N7.. 5 B2
Moray Rd N4, N7.. . 5 B2
Mordaunt Ho
4 Becontree 20 C4
24 Clapham SW8. 171 B1
Mordaunt Rd
NW10. . . . . 20 C4
Mordaunt St SW9. 62 B4
Morden Hill SE13. . 52 B1
Morden Ho 10
SW2. . . . . 62 C1
Morden La SE13. . 52 B2
Morden Mount Prim
Sch 1 SE13. . . . . 52 A1
Morden Rd SE3. . . 53 C1
Morden Road Mews
SE3. . . . . 53 C1
Morden St SE13. . 52 A2
Morden Wharf Rd
SE10. . . . . 43 A3
Mordern Ho NW1. . 90 B1
Morecambe Cl 3
E1. . . . . 32 C4
Morecambe St
SE17 . . . . 151 A2
More Cl
Canning Town
E16. . . . . 35 B3
West Kensington
W14 . . . . 140 A3
Moredown Ho 3
E8. . . . . 16 C3
More House Sch
SW1 . . . . 131 A1
Moreland Ct 3
NW2. . . . . 1 C1
Moreland Prim Sch
EC1. . . . . 96 B3
Moreland St EC1. . 96 B4
Morella Rd SW11,
SW12. . . . . 72 B4
Morel Ho 9 SW9 172 C1
More London Pl
SE1. . . . . 124 A1
Moresby Wlk 6
SW8. . . . . 170 B1
More's Gdn SW3 . 157 C3
Moreton Ho SE16. . 40 A3
Moreton Pl SW1. . 147 A2
Moreton St SW1. . 147 B2

Moreton Terr
SW1 .... **147** A2
Moreton Terr Mews N
SW1 .... **147** A2
Moreton Terr Mews S
SW1 .... **147** A2
Moreton Twr **3**
W3 .... 28 A1
Morgan Ct **5**
SW11 .... **167** C2
Morgan Ho
Nine Elms SW8 .... **171** A4
Pimlico SW1 ...... **147** A3
Morgan Rd
Islington N7 ...... 14 C3
Notting Hill W10 ... 31 B4
Morgans La SE1 .. **124** A1
Morgan St
Canning Town
E16 .... 35 B4
Globe Town E3 .... 25 C2
Morgan's Wlk
SW11 .... **158** A1
Moriatry Cl N7 .... 14 A4
Morie St SW18 .... 59 A2
Morkyns Wlk SE21.76 A1
Morland Cl NW11....2 A3
Morland Ct W12....39 A4
Morland Est E8 .... 16 C1
Morland Ho
Kilburn NW6 ...... 23 C4
Notting Hill W11 .... 31 A3
Somers Town NW1 .. **83** A1
Westminster SW1 .. **148** A4
Morland Mews N1 .. 14 C1
Morley Coll SE1 .. **135** C2
Morley Ct SE13 .... 67 B3
Morley Ho
Stoke Newington
N16 .... 7 C2
Streatham SW2 .... 74 A4
W1 .... **104** B2
Morley Rd SE13 .... 67 B3
Morley St SE1 .. **135** C3
Morna Rd SE5 .... 48 B1
Morning La E9 .... 17 B2
Morningside Prim Sch
17 E9 .... **17** C2
Mornington Ave
W14 .... **140** C3
Mornington Avenue
Mans W14...... **140** C3
Mornington Cres
Camden Town
NW1 .... **82** C2
NW1 .... **82** C2
Mornington Crescent
Sta NW1 ...... **82** C2
Mornington Ct
NW1 .... **82** C2
Mornington Gr E3 .. 26 C2
Mornington Mews **2**
SE5 .... 48 B2
Mornington Pl
4 New Cross
SE8 .... 51 B3
Regent's Pk NW1 .. **82** C2
Mornington St SE14.
SE8 .... 51 B3
Mornington St
NW1 .... **82** B2
Mornington Terr
NW1 .... **82** B2
Morocco St SE1 .. **138** A3

Morpeth Gr E9 ....25 C4
Morpeth Rd E9 ....25 C4
Morpeth Sch E2 ......25 B2
Morpeth St E2 ....25 B2
Morpeth Terr
SW1 .... **146** C4
Morrel Ct **11** E2 ....24 C3
Morris Blitz Ct **2**
N16 .... 16 B4
Morris Ct **3** SE5 ...63 C3
Morris Gdns SW18.70 C4
Morris Ho
17 Bethnal Green
E2 .... 25 B2
Lisson Gr NW8 ...... **90** A1
1 Stockwell SW4 ..62 A3
10 Tufnell Pk N19 ..13 B4
Morrish Rd SW2 ....74 A4
Morrison Bldgs **5**
E1 .... **111** B2
Morrison Ho SW2 ..74 C3
Morrison St SW11 ..60 C4
Morris Pl N4 ...... 5 C2
Morris Rd E14......34 A4
Morris St E1 ...... 32 A3
Morriss Ho **9**
SE16 .... 40 A4
Morris St E1 ...... 32 A3
Morshead Mans
W9 .... 23 C2
Morshead Rd W9 ...23 C2
Mortain Ho **9**
SE16 .... 40 A2
Morten Cl SW4 ....61 C1
Mortimer Cl
1 Child's Hill NW2 ..1 B1
Streatham SW16 ....73 C2
Mortimer Cres
NW6 .... 78 A3
Mortimer Ct NW8 .. 79 A1
Mortimer Est NW6. 78 A3
Mortimer Ho
3 Shepherd's Bush
W11 .... 30 C1
West Kensington
W14 .... **140** B3
Mortimer Lo **11**
SW19 .... 70 A3
Mortimer Market
WC1 .... **93** A1
Mortimer Pl NW6.. 78 A3
Mortimer Rd
De Beauvoir Town
N1 .... 16 A1
Kensal Green
NW10 .... 22 B2
Mortimer Sq W11 ..30 C2
Mortimer St W1 .. **105** A3
Mortimer Terr
NW5 .... 13 A4
MORTLAKE 55 B4
Mortlake High St
SW14 .... 55 C4
Mortlake Ho **7**
W4 .... 37 B2
Mortlake Rd SW14,
TW9 .... 44 C2
Mortlake Sta
SW14 .... 55 B4
Mortlock Cl SE15 ..50 A2
Morton Cl **2** E1 ....32 B3
Morton Ho SE17....48 A4
Morton Mews
SW5 .... **142** A3
Morton Pl SE1 .. **135** B1

Morton Rd N1.......15 B1
Morval Rd SW2.......62 C2
Morven Rd SW17 ..72 B1
Morville Ho SW18 ..59 C1
Morville St E3 ......26 C3
Morwell St WC1 .. **105** C3
Moscow Pl W2 .. **114** A4
Moscow Rd W2 .. **114** A4
Mosedale NW1..... **92** B3
Moseley Row SE10..**43** B3
Mosque Tower **26**
E1 .... **111** C3
Mossbourne Com
Acad E8 ....16 C3
Mossbury Rd
SW11 .... 60 A4
Moss Cl E1 ...... **111** C4
Mossford St E3 ....26 B1
Mossington Gdns
SE16 .... 40 B2
Mossop St SW3 .. **144** B4
Mostyn Gdns
NW10 .... 22 C3
Mostyn Gr E3 ......26 C3
Mostyn Lo N5 ...... 15 B4
Mostyn Rd SW9 .. **173** C3
Motcomb St SW1 . **131** B2
Mothers Sq The **13**
E5 .... 17 A4
Motley Ave
EC2 .... 24 A1 98 A2
Motley St SW8 .. **170** C2
Moules Ct SE5 ....48 B3
Moulins Rd E9 ......17 B1
Moulsford Ho
5 Lower Holloway
N7 .... 14 A3
23 Paddington W2 ..31 C4
Mounsey Ho **13**
W10 .... 23 A2
Mount Adon Pk SE21,
SE22 .... 76 C4
Montague Pl **2**
E14 .... 34 A2
Mountain Ho
SE11 .... **148** C2
Mount Angelus Rd
SW15 .... 68 B4
Mount Ararat Rd
TW10 .... 54 A2
Mount Carmel **3**
N7 .... 14 B3
Mount Carmel RC
Tech Coll for Girls
5 N19 .... 4 C3
Mountearl Gdns SW16,
SW2 .... 74 B1
Mount Ephraim La
SW16 .... 73 C1
Mount Ephraim Rd
SW16 .... 73 C1
Mountfield NW2....1 B2
Mountfield Ct
SE13 .... 67 C1
Mount Ford St E1 **111** B2
Mountfort Cres
N1 .... 14 C1
Mountfort Terr **1**
N1 .... 14 C1
Mountgrove Rd N5 ..6 B1
Mountjoy Ho EC2 **108** C3
Mount Lodge SW4..61 C3
Mount Mills EC1... **96** B3

Mount Nod Rd SW16,
SW2 .... 74 B1
Mount Pl **7** W3 ...28 A1
Mount Pleasant
WC1 .... **95** B1
Mount Pleasant Cres
N4 .... 5 B4
Mount Pleasant Rd
Lewisham SE13 ......67 B1
Willesden NW10 ....22 B4
Mount Pleasant Villas
N4 .... 5 B4
Mount Rd SW18,
SW19 .... 70 C3
Mount Row W1 .. **118** A3
Mounts Pond Rd SE3,
SE13 .... 52 C1
Mount Sq The **3**
NW3 .... 2 B1
Mount St W1 .. **117** C3
Mount Terr E1......32 A4
Mount The
Hampstead NW3 ......2 B1
Kensington
W8 .... 31 C1 **113** B1
Mount Tyndal NW3 ..2 C3
Mount Vernon
NW3 .... 11 B4
Mountview **5**
SW16 .... 74 B1
Mountview Cl NW11 ..2 B3
Mount Villas SE27 ..75 A1
Mourne Ho NW3 ....11 B2
Mowatt Cl N19 .... 4 C3
Mowbray Rd NW6 ..10 A1
Mowlem Prim Sch
E2 .... 25 B3
Mowlem St E2 ......25 A3
Mowll St SW9 .. **163** B1
Moxon St W1 .. **103** B3
Moye Cl **10** E2......24 C3
Moylan Rd W6 .. **154** B3
Moyle Ho SW1 .. **161** A4
Moyne Ho **11** SW9 ..63 A3
Mozart St W10 ...... 23 B2
Mudchute Pk & Farm
E14 .... 42 B2
Mudchute Sta E14..42 A2
Mudie Ho **5** SW2 ..74 A4
Mudlarks Blvd **3**
SE10 .... 43 B3
Muirdown Ave
SW14 .... 55 C3
Muir Dr SW18 ......60 A1
Muirfield W3 ......29 A3
Muirfield Cl **22**
SE16 .... 40 A1
Muirfield Cres
E14 .... 42 A3
Mulberry Cl
Chelsea SW3 ...... **157** C3
East Dulwich SE22 ..64 C1
Hampstead NW3 ....11 C4
Mulberry Ct
Finsbury EC1 ...... **96** B3
Islington N5 .... 15 A3
11 Leyton E11 ......19 C4
10 Paddington W9 ..23 B2
Mulberry Ho
5 Bethnal Green
E2 .... 25 B2
6 Deptford SE8......51 B4

Mulberry House Sch
NW2 .... 10 A3
Mulberry Mews
SW6 .... 51 B2
Mulberry Pl W6 ....38 C1
Mulberry Rd E8 ....16 B1
Mulberry Sch for Girls
17 Stepney E1 ......32 A3
10 St George in t East
E1 .... 32 A2
Mulberry St **7**
E1 .... **111** B2
Mulberry Wlk
SW3 .... **157** C4
Mulgrave Rd
West Kensington
W14 .... **154** C4
Willesden NW10 ....8 B4
Mulkern Rd N19.....4 C3
Mullard Ho WC1... **105** B4
Mullens Ho **7**
SW15 .... 57 B2
Mullen Twr EC1 .. **95** B1
Muller Rd SW4......61 C1
Mullet Gdns **7**
E2 .... 24 C2 **99** C4
Mulletsfield WC1 ..**94** B3
Mull Ho **8** E3......26 B3
Mullins Path
SW14 .... 55 C4
Mulready St NW8 ..**90** A1
Multi Way W3......38 A4
Multon Ho E9 ......17 B1
Multon Rd SW18 ..71 C4
Mulvaney Way
SE1 .... **137** C3
Mumford Rd SE24 ..63 A2
Muncaster Rd
SW11 .... 60 C2
Mundania Cl SE22 ..65 A1
Mundania Rd SE22 ..65 B1
Munday Ho SE1 .. **137** B3
Munday Rd E16 ....35 C2
Munden Ho **5** E3 ..27 A2
Munden St W14 .. **140** A4
Mund St W14 .. **141** A1
Mundy Ho **6** W10 ..23 A2
Mundy St
N1 .... 24 A2 **98** B4
Munro Ho
Bermondsey SE1 .. **137** C3
Lambeth SE1 ...... **135** B3
Munro Mews W10 ..31 A4
Munster Ct SW6 .. **164** C2
Munster Rd SW6 .. **154** B2
Munster Residences
SW6 .... **164** B4
Munster Sq NW1 .. **92** B2
Munster Rd SE1,
SE17 .... **151** A4
Murchison Ho **1**
W10 .... 31 A4
Murdoch Ho **4**
SE16 .... 40 B3
Murdock Cl E16 ....35 B3
Murdock St SE15 ..50 A4
Murfett Cl SW19....70 A2
Muriel St N1 ...... 85 A4
Murphy Ho SE1 .. **136** B2
Murphy St SE1 .. **135** B3
Murray Gr N1 ...... 87 C1
Murray Mews
NW1 .... 13 C1
Murray St NW1 ....13 C1
Murray Terr NW3 ..11 C4
Musard Rd W6 .. **154** B4

Musbury St E1 . . . . 32 B3
Muscal W6 . . . . 154 A4
Muscatel Pl SE5 . . . . . 49 A2
Muschamp Rd
SE15 . . . . 64 B4
Muscott Ho 12 E2 . . . 24 C4
Muscovy St EC3 . . . . 124 B4
Museum & Galleries
of Modern London
EC2 . . . . 108 C3
Museum Ho 7 E2 . . . 25 B2
Museum La SW7 . . . 129 B1
Museum Mans
WC1 . . . . 106 A3
Museum of Brands,
Packaging &
Advertising W11 . . 31 B3
Museum of Childhood
(V&A) E2 . . . . 25 B2
Museum of
Instruments
SW7 . . . . 129 B2
Museum of London
EC2 . . . . 108 C3
Museum of London
Docklands E14 . . . 33 C2
Museum of the Order
of St John EC1 . . . 96 A1
Museum of the Royal
Pharmaceutical
Society SE1 . . . . . 148 C4
Museum St WC1 . . . 106 A2
Museum Way W3 . . . 36 C4
Musgrave Cres
SW6 . . . . 165 C4
Musgrave Ct
SW11 . . . . 168 A4
Musgrave Ho 1
E9 . . . . 17 C2
Musgrove Rd SE14 . . 51 A2
Musical Mus The
TW8 . . . . 44 B4
Musjid Rd 7
SW11 . . . . 167 C1
Mustow Pl 2
SW6 . . . . 165 A2
Mutrix Rd NW6 . . . . . 23 C4
Mutton Pl NW1 . . . . . 12 C2
Myatt Garden Prim
Sch SE4 . . . . 51 B1
Myatt Ho SE5 . . . . . . 48 A1
Myatt Rd SW9 . . . . . . 48 A1
Myatts Field Ct
SE5 . . . . 48 B2
Mycenae Rd SE3 . . . 53 C4
Myddelton Pas
EC1 . . . . 95 C4
Myddelton Sq EC1 . . 95 C4
Myddelton St EC1 . . 95 C3
Myddleton Ave N4 . . 6 B2
Myers Ho 5 SE5 . . . . 48 B3
Mylius Cl SE14 . . . . . 50 B2
Mylne Cl W6 . . . . 38 C1
Mylne St EC1 . . . . 85 B1
Mynterne Ct 18
SW19 . . . . 69 C3
Myrdle Ct 14 E1 . . . 111 C2
Myrdle St E1 . . . . 111 C2
Myron Pl SE13 . . . . . . 67 B4
Myrtle Ho SE14 . . . . . 50 C2
Myrtle Rd W3 . . . . . . 28 B1
Myrtle Wlk 82 N1 . . . 24 A3
Mysore Rd SW11 . . . 60 B3
Myton Rd SE21 . . . . . 75 C1
Mytton Ho SW8 . . . 162 C1

N

N1 Sh Ctr N1 . . . . 85 C2
Nags Head N7 . . . . . . 14 B4
Nags Head Ct EC1 . . 97 A1
Nags Head Sh Ctr The
N7 . . . . 14 B4
Naima Jewish Prep
Sch 4 NW6 . . . . 78 A2
Nainby Ho SE11 . . . 149 B3
Nairne Gr SE5,
SE24 . . . . 63 C3
Nairn St E14 . . . . 34 B4
Naldera Gdns SE3 . . 53 C4
Nalton Ho 4 NW6 . . 11 B1
Namco Sta SE1 . . . . 134 C4
Nankin St E14 . . . . . . 33 C3
Nansen Rd SW11 . . . 60 C4
Nant Ct NW2 . . . . 1 B2
Nantes Cl SW18 . . . . 59 B3
Nant Rd NW2 . . . . 1 B2
Nant St E2 . . . . 25 A2
Naoroji St WC1 . . . . . 95 B3
Napier Ave
Deptford E14 . . . . . . 41 C1
Fulham SW6 . . . . 58 B4
Napier Ct
New Cross SE14,
SE8 . . . . 51 B3
West Kensington
W14 . . . . 126 C2
Napier Gr N1 . . . . 87 A2
Napier Ho SE17 . . . . 48 A4
Napier PI W14 . . . . . 126 C1
Napier Rd
College Pk NW10 . . . 22 A2
Kensington W14 . . . 126 C1
Napier Terr N1 . . . . . 15 A1
Narborough St
SW6 . . . . 166 A1
Narcissus Rd NW6 . . 10 C3
Narford Rd E5 . . . . 7 C2
Narrow St
2 Acton W3 . . . . 28 A1
Limehouse E14 . . . . . 33 A2
Nascot St W12 . . . . . 30 B3
Naseby Cl NW6 . . . . . 11 B1
Nashe Ho SE1 . . . . . 137 B1
Nash Ho
1 Millwall E14 . . . 41 C3
Pimlico SW1 . . . . . . 146 B1
Nash Rd SE4 . . . . 66 A2
Nasmyth St W6 . . . . . 39 A3
Nassau Rd SW13 . . . 46 B2
Nassau St W1 . . . . . 104 C3
Nassington Rd
NW3 . . . . 12 B4
Nathan Ho 16 SE11 . 149 C3
Nathaniel Cl E1 . . . 111 A3
National Archives The
TW9 . . . . 45 A3
National Army Mus
SW3 . . . . 159 A4
National Gallery
W1 . . . . 119 C3
National Hospl for
Neurology &
Neurosurgery
WC1 . . . . 94 B1

National Maritime
Mus SE10 . . . . 52 C4
National Portrait
Gallery W1 . . . . 119 C3
National Tennis Ctr
SW15 . . . . 56 A2
National Theatre
SE1 . . . . 121 A2
Natural History Mus
SW7 . . . . 129 B1
Nautilus Bldg The
EC1 . . . . 96 B4
Naval Row E14 . . . . . 34 B2
Navarino Gr E8 . . . . . 16 C2
Navarino Mans 16 C2
Navarino Rd E8 . . . . . 16 C2
Navarre St
E2 . . . . 24 B1 98 C2
Navenby Wlk 13
E3 . . . . 26 C1
Navy St SW4 . . . . 61 C4
Naxos Bldg 3 E14 . 41 C4
Naylor Bldg W 4
E1 . . . . 111 B2
Naylor Ho
11 Clapham SW8 . 171 B1
14 Walsworth SE17 . 151 C2
W10 . . . . 23 B2
Naylor Rd SE15 . . . . 50 A3
Nayor Bldg E 8
E1 . . . . 111 B2
Nazareth Cl SE15 . . 50 A1
Nazrul St E2 . . 24 B2 98 C4
Nealden St SW9 . . . . 62 B4
Neal St WC2 . . . . 106 A1
Neal's Yd WC2 . . . . . 106 A1
Neasden Cl NW10 . . 8 A3
Neasden Junc
NW10 . . . . 8 A4
Neasden La NW10 . . 8 A3
Neasden La N NW10 . 8 A3
Neathouse Pl
SW1 . . . . 146 C4
Nebraska Bldg 11
SE13 . . . . 52 A2
Nebraska St SE1 . . . 137 B3
Neckinger SE16 . . . 139 A2
Neckinger Est
SE16 . . . . 139 A2
Neckinger St SE1 . . 139 A2
Nectarine Way
SE13 . . . . 52 A1
Needham Ho
SE11 . . . . 149 B3
Needham Rd W11 . . 31 C3
Needleman St
SE16 . . . . 40 C4
Needwood Ho N4 . . 6 B3
Neilson-Terry Ct 9
SW9 . . . . 62 B3
Neil Wates Cres 17
SW2 . . . . 74 C3
Nella Rd W6 . . . . 47 C4
Nelldale Rd SE16 . . . 40 B2
Nell Gwynn Ho
SW3 . . . . 144 B3
Nelson Cl 2 NW6 . . 23 C2
Nelson Ct SE16 . . . . 33 B1
Nelson Docks
SE16 . . . . 33 B1
Nelson Gdns
E2 . . . . 24 C2 99 C4
Nelson Pas EC1 . . . . 97 A4

Nelson Pl N1 . . . . 86 B1
Nelson Rd SE10 . . . . 52 B4
Nelson's Monument
WC2 . . . . 120 A2
Nelson Sq SE1 . . . . 136 A4
Nelsons Row SW4 . . 61 C3
Nelson St
Canning Town
E16 . . . . 35 B2
Stepney E1 . . . . 32 A3
Nelsons Yd NW1 . . . 82 C2
Nelson Terr N1 . . . . . 86 B1
Nemoure Rd W3 . . . 28 B2
Nepaul Rd 17
SW11 . . . . 60 A4
Nepean St SW15 . . . 68 C4
Neptune Ct 13 E14 . 41 C2
Neptune Ho
2 Rotherhithe
SE16 . . . . 40 B3
14 Stoke Newington
N16 . . . . 16 A3
Neptune St SE16 . . . 40 B3
Nesham Ho 14 N1 . . 24 A4
Nesham St E1 . . . . . 125 B2
Ness St 2 SE16 . . . 139 B2
Nestor Ho 9 E2 . . . 25 A3
Netheravon Rd
W4 . . . . 38 B1
Netheravon Rd S
W4 . . . . 38 B1
Netherby Ho 3
SW8 . . . . 171 B1
Nethercombe Ho 1
SE3 . . . . 53 C4
Nethercott Ho 22
E3 . . . . 27 A2
Netherfield Rd
SW17 . . . . 72 C1
Netherford Rd
SW4 . . . . 171 B1
Netherhall Gdns
NW3 . . . . 11 B3
Netherhall Int Coll
NW3 . . . . 11 B3
Netherhall Way
NW3 . . . . 11 B3
Netherleigh Cl N6 . . 4 A3
Netherton Gr
SW10 . . . . 157 A3
Netherwood Rd
W14 . . . . 39 C4
Netherwood St
NW6 . . . . 10 C2
Netley SE5 . . . . 49 A2
Netley Prim Sch
NW1 . . . . 92 C3
Netley Rd TW8 . . . . . 44 A4
Netley St NW1 . . . . . 92 C3
Nettlecombe 11
SW11 . . . . 13 C1
Nettleden Ho
SW3 . . . . 144 B3
Nettlefold Pl SE27 . . 75 A1
Nettlefold Ho SE14 . 50 C2
Nettleton Rd SE14 . . 50 C2
Nevada St SE10 . . . . 52 B4
Nevena Ct 3 SW2 . . 62 C2
Nevern Mans
SW5 . . . . 141 B2
Nevern Pl SW5 . . . . 141 C3
Nevern Rd SW5 . . . 141 B3
Nevern Sq SW5 . . . 141 C3
Nevil Ho 3 SW9 . . . . 48 A1
Nevill Ct SW10 . . . . 156 C2

Neville Cl continued
Peckham SE15 . . . . . 49 C2
Somers Town NW1 . . 83 C1
Neville Ct 10 SW12 . 73 B4
Neville Gill Cl
SW18 . . . . 59 A1
Neville Ho N6 . . . . 23 B3
Neville Rd NW6 . . . . . 23 B3
Neville St SW7 . . . . 143 B2
Neville Terr SW7 . . . 143 B2
Nevill Rd N16 . . . . 7 A1
Nevinson Cl SW18 . . 59 C1
Nevis Rd SW17 . . . . . 72 C2
Nevitt Ho N1 . . . . 87 C1
Newall Ho SE1 . . . . 137 A2
Newark Cres
NW10 . . . . 20 C2
Newark Ho 3
SW9 . . . . 48 A1
Newark St E1 . . . . 32 A4
New Atlas Wharf
E14 . . . . 41 C3
New Bentham Ct 10
N1 . . . . 15 B1
Newbery Ho N1 . . . . 15 B1
Newbold Cotts 4
E1 . . . . 32 B3
Newbolt Ho SE17 . . 151 B2
New Bond St W1 . . . 118 B4
New Bridge St
EC4 . . . . 108 A1
New Broad St
EC2 . . . . 110 A3
Newburgh Rd W3 . . 28 B1
Newburgh St W1 . . . 105 A1
New Burlington Mews
W1 . . . . 118 C4
New Burlington Pl
W1 . . . . 118 C4
New Burlington St
W1 . . . . 118 C4
Newburn Ho SE11 . 149 A2
Newburn St SE11 . . 149 A2
Newbury Ct E5 . . . . . 18 A3
Newbury Ho
Brixton SW9 . . . . 48 A1
14 Kensington W2 . 100 B1
Newbury Mews
NW5 . . . . 12 C2
Newbury St EC1 . . . 108 C4
New Butt La SE8 . . . 51 C3
Newby Pl E14 . . . . . . 34 B2
Newby St SW8 . . . . . 61 A4
New Caledonian Mkt
SE1 . . . . 138 B2
New Caledonian
Wharf SE16 . . . . 41 B3
New Campden Ct 9
NW3 . . . . 11 B4
Newcastle Cl EC4 . . 108 A2
Newcastle Ct EC4 . . 123 A4
Newcastle Ho W1 . . 103 B4
Newcastle Pl W2 . . 101 C4
Newcastle Row
EC1 . . . . 95 C1
New Cavendish St
W1 . . . . 104 A3
New Change EC4 . . 108 C1
New Charles St
EC1 . . . . 96 B4

New Church Rd
☒ Camberwell
SE5..................48 B3
Camberwell SE5.....48 C4
New College Ct ☐
NW3..................11 B2
New College Mews
N7..................14 C1
New College Par ☐
NW3..................11 C1
Newcombe Ho N5...15 B3
Newcome St
W8....31 C1 113 C2
Newcomen Ho ☐
N5..................13 A4
Newcomen Rd
SW11..................59 C4
Newcomen St
SE1..................137 B4
New Compton St
WC2..................106 A1
New Concordia Wharf
SE1..................139 A4
Newcourt Ho ☒
E2..................25 A2
Newcourt St NW8..80 A1
New Covent Garden
Flower Market
SW8..................162 A3
New Covent Garden
Fruit & Vegetable
Mkt SW8..............161 B1
New Crane Pl E1...32 B1
New Crescent Yd ☐
NW10..................21 B3
NEW CROSS........51 B3
New Cross SE14...51 B3
**NEW CROSS
GATE**................50 C2
New Cross Gate
SE14..................50 C2
New Cross Gate Sta
SE14..................50 C2
New Cross Rd
SE14..................51 A4
New Cross Sta
SE14..................51 B3
New Ct
City of London
EC4..................107 B1
☒ Hampstead
NW3..................11 B4
Stoke Newington
N16....................6 C3
New Den (Millwall
FC) The SE16......40 B1
Newgate Ho ☐
E14..................33 B3
Newell St E14.....33 B3
New End NW3......2 B1
New End Prim Sch ☐
NW3..................11 B4
New End Sq NW3..11 C4
Newent Cl SE15...49 A3
New Fetter La
EC4..................107 C2
Newfield Prim Sch
NW10....................8 B1
Newgate St EC1..108 B2
New Globe Wlk
SE1..................122 C2
New Goulston St
E1..................110 C2

Newham Sixth Form
Coll (Stratford Ctr)
☐ E15..................19 C1
Newham's Row
SE1..................138 B3
Newhaven La ☐
E16..................35 C4
New Hope Christian
Sch ☒ SE22......64 B3
NEWINGTON.......150 B4
**Newington Barrow
Way** N7...............5 B1
Newington Butts
SE1..................150 B3
Newington Cswy
SE1..................136 C2
Newington Gn
N16..................15 C3
**Newington Green
Mans** N16..........15 C3
**Newington Green
Prim Sch** N16....15 C3
Newington Green Rd
N1..................15 C3
Newington Ind Est
SE17..................150 B3
New Inn Broadway
EC2..................24 A1 98 B2
New Inn Sq
EC2..................24 A1 98 B2
New Inn St
EC2..................24 A1 98 B2
New Inn Yd
EC2..................24 A1 98 B2
New James Ct
SE15..................65 A4
New Kent Rd SE1..151 A4
New King's Prim Sch ☐
SW6..................165 A2
New King's Rd
SW6..................165 C3
New King St SE8..51 C4
Newland Ct EC1...97 B2
Newland Ho ☐
SE14..................50 C4
Newlands NW1......92 C4
Newlands Quay E1..32 B2
New London St
EC3..................124 B4
Newlyn NW1.......83 A3
Newman Pas W1..105 A3
Newman's Ct EC3..109 C1
Newman's Row
WC2..................107 A3
Newman St W1.....105 A3
Newmill Ho E3.......27 B1
Newmount NW3....11 C3
New Mount St E15..19 C1
Newnes Path
SW15..................57 A3
Newnham Ho ☐
SW15..................57 C1
Newnham Terr
SE1..................135 B2
New North Com Sch ☐
N1..................86 C4
New North Pl
EC2..................24 A1 98 A2
New North Rd N1..87 B3
**New North Road
Bridge** N1..........87 B3
New North St
WC1..................106 C4
Newnton Cl N4....6 C4
New Oxford St
WC1..................106 A2

New Palace Yd
SW1..................134 A3
New Park Ct ☒
SW2..................74 A4
New Park Par ☐
SW2..................74 A4
New Park Rd SW2..74 A4
New Place Sq
SE16..................40 A3
Newport Ave E14..34 C2
Newport Ct WC2..119 C4
Newport Ho ☐ E3..26 A2
Newport Pl WC2..119 C4
Newport Rd SW13..46 C2
Newport St SE11..149 B2
New Priory Ct ☐
NW6..................10 C1
New Providence
Wharf E14..........34 C1
Newquay Ho SE11 149 B2
New Quebec St
W1..................103 A1
New Rd E1..........32 A4
New River Ct N5..15 C4
New River Way N4..6 C4
New Row WC2......120 A4
New Sq EC2........107 C2
New St EC2.........110 B3
Newstead Ho N1....85 C2
Newton Ave W3..37 B4
Newton Gr W4......38 A2
Newton Ho
☒ Clapham SW8..171 B2
Paddington NW8...78 B4
☐ Stepney E1.......32 A2
Newton Point ☐
E16..................35 B3
Newton Prep Sch
SW8..................170 B4
Newton Rd
Acton W3...........37 B4
Kensington W2....100 A1
Stratford New Town
E15..................19 C3
Newton St WC2...106 B2
Newton's Yd ☐
SW18..................58 C2
New Tower Bldgs ☒
E1..................32 A1
Newtown St
Battersea SW11...170 A3
Clapham SW4......61 A2
New Union Cl E14..42 B3
New Union St
EC2..................109 B3
New Wharf Rd N1..84 B2
Niagara Cl N1......87 A2
Niagara Ct ☒
SE16..................40 B3
Nicholas Ct
Chiswick W4........46 A3
Golders Green NW11..1 C4
Nicholas Ho ☒
SW15..................56 C2
Nicholas La EC2,
EC4..................123 C4

Nicholas Pas EC3..123 C4
Nicholas Rd
Bethnal Green E1....25 B1
☒ Shepherd's Bush
W11..................30 C2
Nicholay Rd N19....4 C3
Nicholl Ho N4......6 B3
Nicholl St E2.......24 C4
Nichols Cl N4.......5 C3
Nicholson Ho
SE17..................151 B2
Nicholson St SE1..122 A1
Nickleby Ho
☒ Bermondsey
SE1..................139 B3
☐ Shepherd's Bush
W11..................30 C1
Nickols Wlk SW18..59 A3
Nicoll Ct NW10......21 A4
Nicoll Rd NW10....21 A4
Nicosia Rd SW18..72 A4
Nigel Bldg EC1...107 B4
Nigel Playfair Ave
W4..................37 B1
Nigel Rd
SE15..................64 C4
Nightingale W4..45 B4
Nightingale Ct
☐ Cubitt Town
E14..................42 B3
☒ Finsbury Pk N4..5 B3
Nightingale Gr
SE13..................67 C2
Nightingale Ho
☒ Hoxton E1.......24 A4
☒ North Kensington
W12..................30 B3
☐ St George in t East
E1..................125 B2
Nightingale La SW11,
SW12..................60 C1
Nightingale Lo ☐
W9..................31 C4
Nightingale Mans ☐
SW12..................60 C1
Nightingale Mews
☐ Bow E3...........26 A3
Newington SE11...150 A4
Nightingale Pl
SW10..................157 A4
Nightingale Prim Sch ☐
E5..................16 C4
Nightingale Rd
☒ Canonbury N1...15 B2
Dagenham NW10...21 A4
Nightingale Sch
SW17..................72 A2
Nightingale Sq
SW12..................72 C4
Nightingale Wlk SW18,
SW4..................61 A1
Nile Cl N16..........7 B2
Nile Ho N1..........97 B4
Nile St N1...........97 B4
Nile Terr SE1,
SE15..................153 A1
Nimegen Way ☒
SE22..................64 A2
Nimrod Pas ☐ N1..16 A2
NINE ELMS........160 C2
Nine Elms La
SW8..................161 B3
Nisbet Ho E9.......17 C3
Niton Rd TW9......54 C4
Niton St SW6......47 C2
Nobel Ho ☒ SE5..48 B1

Noble Ct E1..........32 A2
Noble St EC2......108 C2
Noel Coward Ho
SW1..................147 A3
Noel Ho ☒ NW3....11 C1
Noel Rd
Acton W3...........28 A3
Islington N1........86 B2
Noel St W1.........105 A1
Noko NW10..........20 B3
Nolan Way E5......16 C4
Noll Ho N7...........5 B2
Norbiton Rd E14..33 B3
Norbroke St W12..29 B2
Norburn St W10....31 A4
Norcombe Ho ☒
N19....................4 C1
Norcott Rd N16.....7 C1
Norcroft Gdns
SE22..................76 C4
Norden Ho ☒ E2..25 A2
Nore Ct NW10......8 C1
Norfolk Cres W2..102 B2
Norfolk Ho
City of London
EC4..................122 C4
Greenwich SE3.....53 A4
☒ Putney SW15....69 B4
Richmond TW9......54 C2
Shacklewell E8.....16 B4
☐ St Johns SE8.....51 C2
Westminster SW1..147 C4
Norfolk House Rd
SW16..................74 A1
Norfolk Mans
Battersea SW11....169 A3
☒ Wandsworth
SW18..................58 C2
Norfolk Mews ☒
W10..................31 A4
Norfolk Pl W2......101 C2
Norfolk Rd
St John's Wood
NW8..................79 C3
Willesden NW10.....8 A1
Norfolk Row SE1,
SE11..................148 C4
Norfolk Sq W2....101 C2
Norfolk Sq Mews
W2..................101 C2
Norgrove St SW12..72 C4
Norland Ho ☒
W11..................30 C1
Norland Pl
W11........31 A1 112 B1
Norland Place Sch
W11........31 A1 112 A1
Norland Rd ☒
W11........31 A1 112 A1
Norland Sq
W11........31 A1 112 B1
Norley Vale SW15..68 C3
Norman Butler Ho ☒
W10..................23 A1
Normanby Cl
SW15..................58 B2
Normanby Rd NW10..8 B4
Norman Ct
Dulwich SE22......76 C4
☒ Finsbury Pk N4....5 C4
Willesden NW10.....8 C1
Normand Croft Com
Sch W14.............155 A4
Normand Mews
W14..................154 B4
Normand Rd W14 154 C4

Normandy Ho **8**
E14 . . . . 42 B4
Normandy Rd
SW9 . . . . **173** B3
Norman Gr E3 . . . . . . 26 A3
Norman Ho SW8 . . **162** A2
Barnsburry N7
SW2 . . . . 74 C2
Norman Rd SE10 . . . . 52 A3
Norman St EC1 . . . . . 97 A3
Normanton Ave SW18,
SW19 . . . . 71 A2
Normanton Ho **6**
SW4 . . . . 61 B1
Norman Way W3 . . . . 28 A3
Norris Ho **7**
10 Hoxton N1 . . . . . . 24 A4
15 South Hackney
E9 . . . . 25 B4
Norris St SW1 . . . . **119** B3
Norroy Rd SW15 . . . . 57 C3
Norse Ho **13** SE5 . . . . 48 B1
Norstead Pl SW15 . . **68** C2
NORTH ACTON 20 C2
North Acton Rd
NW10 . . . . 20 C2
North Acton Sta
W3 . . . . 28 C4
Northampton Gr
N1 . . . . 15 C3
Northampton Pk
N1 . . . . 15 C2
Northampton Rd
EC1 . . . . **95** C2
Northampton Sq
EC1 . . . . **96** A3
Northampton St
N1 . . . . 15 B1
North Audley St
W1 . . . . **117** B4
North Ave **8** TW9 . . 44 C2
Northaw Ho **6**
W10 . . . . 22 B1
North Bank NW8 . . . . 90 A3
North Block **13** E1 . . 32 B2
Northbourne Ho **21**
E5 . . . . 17 A3
Northbourne Rd
SW4 . . . . 61 C2
North Bridge House
Sch **13** NW3 . . . . . . 11 B2
North Bridge House
Senior Sch NW1 . . **82** A3
Northbrook CE Sch
SE12 . . . . 67 C2
Northburgh St EC1 **96** B2
North Carriage Dr
W2 . . . . **116** B4
Northchurch
SE17 . . . . **151** C2
Northchurch Ho **19**
E2 . . . . 24 C4
Northchurch Rd
N1 . . . . 15 C1
Northchurch Terr
N1 . . . . 16 A1
North Circular Rd NW2,
NW10 . . . . 8 A3
North Colonnade The
E14 . . . . 34 A1
Northcote Lodge Sch
SW11 . . . . 60 B1
Northcote Rd
Wandsworth
SW11 . . . . 60 B2
Willesden NW10 . . . . . 8 A1

Northcourt W1 . . . . **105** A4
North Cres
Marylebone WC1 . . **105** A4
Newham E16 . . . . . . 27 C1
Northcroft Ct **8**
W12 . . . . 38 C4
North Cross Rd
SE22 . . . . 64 C2
North Ct SW1 . . . . . **134** A1
Northdown St N1 . . **84** C1
North Dulwich Sta
SE21 . . . . 63 C2
North End NW3 . . . . . 2 B2
North End Ave NW3 . 2 B2
North End Cres
W14 . . . . **140** C3
North End Ho
W14 . . . . **140** B3
North End Par
W14 . . . . **140** B3
North End Rd
Golders Green
NW11 . . . . 2 A3
West Kensington
W14 . . . . **141** A1
North End Way
NW3 . . . . 2 B2
Northern Hts N8 . . . . 4 C4
Northesk Ho **6**
E1 . . . . 25 A1
North Eyot Gdns **5**
W6 . . . . 38 B1
Northey St E14 . . . . 33 A2
Northfield Hall N6 . . 3 C4
Northfield Ho **3**
SE15 . . . . 49 C4
Northfield Rd N16 . . 7 A4
Northfields SW18 . . **58** C3
Northfields Prospect
SW18 . . . . **58** C3
Northfields Rd W3 . . 28 B4
Northfleet Ho
SE1 . . . . **137** B4
North Flower Wlk
W2 . . . . **115** B3
North Gate NW8 . . . **80** A1
Northgate Ct **14**
SW9 . . . . 62 C4
North Gower St
NW1 . . . . **93** A3
North Gr N6 . . . . 3 C4
North Greenwich Pier
SE10 . . . . 35 B1
North Greenwich Sta
SE10 . . . . 43 A4
North Hill N6 . . . . 3 C4
North Ho **3** SE8 . . . 41 B1
Northiam WC1 . . . . **94** B3
Northiam St E9 . . . . 25 A4
Northington St
WC1 . . . . **95** A1
**NORTH
KENSINGTON** 30 C4
Northlands St SE5 . . 48 B1
Northleigh Ho **30**
E3 . . . . 27 A2
North Lo SW4 . . . . . 61 A4
North Lodge Cl
SW15 . . . . 57 C2
North London Science
Ctr **2** N1 . . . . **84** C2
North Mews WC1 . . **95** A1
Northolme Rd N5 . . **15** B4
North Pas SW18 . . **58** C2

Northpoint Sq **1**
NW1 . . . . 13 C2
North Pole Rd
W10 . . . . 30 B4
Northport St N1 . . . **87** C3
North Rd
Barnsbury N7 . . . . . . 14 A2
Brentford TW8 . . . . . 44 A4
Highgate N6 . . . . 3 C4
Richmond TW9 . . . . 44 C1
North Ride W2 . . . **116** A3
North Rise w2 . . . **102** B1
North Row W1 . . . **117** B4
NORTH SHEEN . . . 44 C1
North Sheen Sta
TW10 . . . . 54 C3
**North Side
Wandsworth Comm**
SW18 . . . . 59 C2
North St SW4 . . . . . 61 B4
Northstead Rd
SW2 . . . . 74 C2
North Tenter St
E1 . . . . **111** A1
North Terr SW3 . . **130** A1
Northumberland Alley
EC3 . . . . **110** B1
Northumberland Ave
WC2 . . . . **120** A2
Northumberland Ho
NW5 . . . . 13 B2
Northumberland Mans
E5 . . . . 17 B4
Northumberland Pl
W2 . . . . 31 C3
Northumberland St
WC2 . . . . **120** A2
Northumbria Ct **10**
TW9 . . . . 54 A3
Northumbria St
E14 . . . . 33 C3
North Verbena Gdns
2 W6 . . . . 38 C1
Northview **7** N7 . . . 5 A1
Northview Cres
NW10 . . . . 8 B4
Northview Prim Sch
NW10 . . . . 8 B4
North Villas NW1 . . 13 C2
Northway Rd SE5 . . 63 B4
Northways Par **2**
NW3 . . . . 11 C1
North West London
Jewish Day Sch
NW6 . . . . 10 A1
Northwest Ho **1**
SE1 . . . . 85 C2
North Wharf Rd
W2 . . . . **101** B3
Northwick Cl NW8 . **89** B2
Northwick Ho
NW8 . . . . **89** A2
North Wlk W2 . . . **114** C3
Northwold Prim Sch
E5 . . . . 7 C2
Northwold Rd E5,
N16 . . . . 7 C2
North Wood Lo
NW3 . . . . 11 A4
Northwood Ho N6 . . 4 A4
North Worple Way
SW14 . . . . 55 C4
Norton Folgate
E1 . . . . **110** B4

Norton Ho
14 Globe Town
E2 . . . . 25 C2
30 Stepney E1 . . . . 32 A3
16 Stockwell SW9 . **173** A1
Norval Rd **1** SW9 **173** C2
Norvic Ho **5** SE5 . . 48 B1
Norway Gate SE16 . 41 A3
Norway Pl E14 . . . . 33 B3
Norway St SE10 . . . 52 A4
Norwich Ho **6**
E14 . . . . 34 A3
Norwich St EC4 . . **107** B2
Norwood Cl NW2 . . 1 A1
Norwood Ho **25**
E14 . . . . 34 A2
Norwood NHS Ctr
SE27 . . . . 75 A1
Norwood Rd SE24,
SE27 . . . . 75 A3
Notley St SE5 . . . . 48 C3
Notre Dame RC Girls
Sch SE1 . . . . **136** B1
Notting Barn Rd
W10 . . . . 22 C1
Nottingdale Sq
W11 . . . . . . 31 A1 **112** A2
Nottingham Ct
WC2 . . . . **106** A1
Nottingham Pl
W1 . . . . **103** B4
Nottingham Rd
SW17 . . . . 72 B3
Nottingham St
W1 . . . . **103** B4
Nottingham Terr
NW1 . . . . **91** B1
NOTTING HILL . . . **31** B3
Notting Hill Gate
W11 . . . . 31 C1 **113** B2
Notting Hill Gate Sta
W11 . . . . 31 C1 **113** B2
Notting Hill Prep Sch
W11 . . . . 31 A3
Nottingwood Ho
W11 . . . . . . 31 A2 **112** A4
Nova Bldg **1** E14 . . 41 C2
Nova Ct E **3** E14 . . 34 B1
Nova Ct W **2** E14 . . 34 B1
Novello St SW6 . . **165** B4
Nowell Rd SW13 . . 46 C4
Noyna Rd SW17 . . . 72 B1
Nucleus NW10 . . . . 20 B2
Nuding Cl SE13 . . . 66 C4
Nuffield Lo **10** W9 . 31 C4
Nugent Ct **3** N19 . . 5 A3
Nugent Rd N19 . . . . 5 A3
Nugent Terr NW8 . . 79 A1
Nun Ct EC2 . . . . . **109** B2
NUNHEAD **65** B3
Nunhead Cres
SE15 . . . . 65 A4
Nunhead Gn SE15 . 65 A4
Nunhead Gr SE15 . 65 B4
Nunhead La SE15 . 65 A4
Nunhead La SE15 . 65 A4
Nunhead Sta SE15 . 50 B1
Nursery Cl
New Cross SE4 . . . . 51 B1
Putney SW15 . . . . . 57 C3
Nursery La
North Kensington
W10 . . . . 30 B4

Nursery La continued
Shoreditch E2 . . . . . 24 B4
Nursery Rd
Hackney E9 . . . . 17 B2
Stockwell SW9 . . . . 62 B3
Nursery Row
SE17 . . . . **151** B3
Nursery Wlk NW4 . 10 .23 A2
Nutbourne St W10 . 23 A2
Nutbrook St SE15 . 64 C4
Nutcroft Rd SE15 . 50 A3
Nutfield Rd
East Dulwich
SE22 . . . . 64 B3
Leyton E15 . . . . 19 B4
Nutford Pl W1 . . . **102** C2
Nuthurst Ave SW2 . 74 B2
Nutley Terr NW3 . . 11 C2
Nutmeg La E14 . . . 34 C3
Nuttall St N1 . . . . . 24 A3
Nutt St SE15 . . . . . 49 B3
Nye Bevan Ho
SW6 . . . . **154** C2
Nye's Wharf SE1,
SE15 . . . . 49 C4
Nylands Ave TW9 . 44 C1
Nynehead St SE14 . 51 A3
Nyton Cl N19 . . . . . 5 A3

O

O2 Ctr NW6 . . . . . . 11 B2
O2 Millennium Dome
The SE10 . . . . 35 A1
Oakbank Gr SE24 . 63 B3
Oakbury Rd SW6 . 166 B1
Oakcourt **17** SE15 . 49 B3
Oak Cres E16 . . . . . 35 A4
Oakcroft Ct SE3 . . 53 C2
Oakcroft Rd SE13 . 52 C1
Oakdale Ct N19 . . . 5 A2
Oakdale Rd SE15 . 65 B4
Oakdene **8** SE15 . 50 A2
Oakdene Ho **11** N16 . 7 A3
Oakden St SE11 . **149** C4
Oakeford Ho W14 . 126 B1
Oakend Ho **4** N4 . . 6 C4
Oakeshott Ave N6 . 3 C2
Oakey La SE1 . . . . **135** B2
Oakfield Ct
Clapham Pk SW4 . . 62 A1
Finsbury Pk N8 . . . . 5 A4
Oakfield Prep Sch
SE21 . . . . 75 C3
Oakfield Rd
Finsbury Pk N4 . . . . 5 C4
Wimbledon SW19 . . 69 C1
Oakfield St SW10 **156** C4
Oakford Rd NW5 . . 13 B4
Oakham Ho **5**
W10 . . . . 22 B1
Oakhill Ave NW3 . . 11 A4
Oakhill Ct
Honor Oak SE23 . . 65 B1
Putney SW15 . . . . . 58 B2
Oak Hill Lo NW3 . . 11 A4
Oak Hill Park Mews
NW3 . . . . 11 A4
Oak Hill Pk NW3 . . 11 A4
Oakhill Pl SW15 . . 58 C2
Oakhill Rd SW15 . . 58 C2
Oak Hill Way NW3 . 11 A4

Oak Ho
13 Cubitt Town
E14 . . . . 42 B4
2 Maitland Pk
NW3 . . . . 12 B2
2 Richmond TW9 . . .45 A2
3 Stoke Newington
N16 . . . .
Oakhurst Gr SE22 . . 64 C3
Oakington Rd W9 . . 23 C1
Oakington Way N8 . . 5 A4
Oak La E14 . . . . . 33 B2
Oaklands Ct
Dagenham NW10 . . .21 A4
5 Shepherd's Bush
W12 . . . . .30 A1
Oaklands Gr W12 . . .29 C1
Oaklands Ho SE4 . . .66 B4
Oaklands Mews **1**
NW2 . . . . 9 C4
Oaklands Pas NW2 . . 9 C4
Oaklands Pl **1**
SW4 . . . . 61 C3
Oaklands Rd
Cricklewood NW2 . . . .9 C4
Mortlake SW14 . . . 55 C4
Oaklands Sec Sch **1**
E2 . . . . 25 C2
Oakley Cres EC1 . . . 86 B1
Oakley Dr SE13 . . . .67 C1
Oakley Gdns SW3 . . 158 B4
Oakley Ho SW1 . . . 145 A4
Oakley Pl SE1 . . . . 152 C1
Oakley Rd N1 . . . . .15 C1
Oakley Sq NW1 . . . .83 A2
Oakley St SW3 . . . .158 A4
Oakley Wlk W6 . . . .47 C4
Oak Lodge **14**
SE21 . . . . .75 C2
Oak Lodge Sch
SW12 . . . . 72 C4
Oakman Ho **29**
SW19 . . . . 69 C3
Oakmead Rd
SW12 . . . . 73 A3
Oak Park Gdns
SW19 . . . . 69 C3
Oak Park Mews
N16 . . . . 7 B1
Oakshaw Rd SW18 . .71 A4
Oakshott Ct **1** . . . 83 B1
Oaks Sh Ctr The
W3 . . . . .28 B1
Oaks The
Brondesbury Pk
NW6 . . . .
Willesden NW10 . . . .9 A1
Oak Tree Ct
Acton W3 3
8 Clapham Pk
SW4 . . . . 62 A2
Oak Tree Ho W9 . . . 88 A2
Oak Tree Rd NW8 . . 90 A3
Oakview Lo NW11 . . .1 B4
Oak Village NW5 . . .12 C4
Oak Way W3 . . . . . 29 A1
Oakwell Ho **24**
SW8 . . . . 171 B1
Oakwood Cl SE13 . . .67 C1
Oakwood Ct W14 . . 126 C2
Oakwood La W14 . . 126 C2
Oakworth Rd W10 . .30 C4
Oast Ct **6** E14 . . . .33 B2
Oast Lo W4 . . . . . .46 A3

Oat La EC2 . . . . . 109 A2
Oatlands Ct **3**
SW19 . . . . 69 C3
Oatwell Ho SW3 . . 144 B3
Oban Ho E14 . . . . .34 C3
Oban St E14 . . . . . 34 C3
Oberon Ho **1** N1 . .24 A3
Oberstein Rd **13**
SW11 . . . . 59 C3
Oborne Cl SE24 . . . .63 A2
O'Brian Ho E1 . . . . 25 C2
Observatory Gdns
W8 . . . . 127 C4
Observatory Mews
E14 . . . . .42 C2
Observatory Rd
Kensington SW7 . . . 129 B1
Mortlake SW14 . . . .55 B3
Occupation Rd
SE17 . . . . 150 C2
Ocean St E1 . . . . . .32 C4
Ocean Wharf E14 . . .41 C4
Ockbrook **3** E1 . . .32 B4
Ockendon Rd N1 . . .15 C2
Ockley Rd SW16 . . . 74 A1
Octagon Arc EC2 . . 110 A3
Octagon The W10 . . .3 C4
Octavia Ho W10 . . . 23 A1
Octavia Mews **1**
W9 . . . . .23 B1
Octavia St SW11 . . 168 B3
Octavius St SE8 . . . 51 C3
Odell Wlk SE13 . . . .67 B4
Odeon Ct
Dagenham NW10 . . .21 A4
1 Newham E16 . . .35 C4
Odessa Rd NW10 . . .21 C3
Odessa St SE16 . . . .41 B3
Odette Duval Ho **22**
E1 . . . . .32 B4
Odger St SW11 . . . 169 A2
Odhams Wlk WC2 . . 106 B1
Odin Ho **6** SE5 . . .48 B1
O'Donnell Ct WC1 . . 94 B2
O'Driscoll Ho **4**
W12 . . . . 30 A3
Offa's Mead E9 . . . .18 A4
Offenbach Ho **12**
E2 . . . . .25 C3
Offerton Rd SW4 . . .61 B4
Offley Ho **6** E9 . . .17 C2
Offley Rd SW9 . . . 163 B2
Offord Rd N1 . . . . .14 B1
Offord St N1 . . . . .14 B1
Ogilvie Ho **3** E1 . . .32 C3
Oglander Rd SE15 . . 64 B4
Ogle St W1 . . . . . 104 C4
O'Gorman Ho
SW10 . . . . 157 A2
Ohio Bldg **13** SE13 . .52 A2
Oil Mill La W6 . . . .38 C1
Okehampton Rd
NW10 . . . . 22 C4
Okeover Manor
SW4 . . . . 1 A1
Olaf St W11 . . . . . .30 C2
Old Bailey EC4 . . . 108 B1
Old Bailey (Central
Criminal Court)
EC4 . . . . 108 B2
Old Barrack Yd
SW1 . . . . 131 B3
Old Bellgate Wharf
E14 . . . . 41 C3

Old Bethnal Green Rd
E2 . . . . .25 A2
Old Billingsgate Wlk
EC3 . . . . 124 A3
Old Bldgs WC2 . . . 107 B2
Old Bond St W1 . . 118 C3
Old Brewery Mews
NW3 . . . . .11 C4
Old Broad St EC2 . . 109 C2
Old Brompton Rd SW5,
SW7 . . . . 143 A3
Old Burlington St
W1 . . . . 118 C3
Oldbury Ct E9 . . . . .18 A3
Oldbury Pl W1 . . . 103 C4
Old Castle St E1 . . 111 A2
Old Cavendish St
W1 . . . . 104 A1
Old Change Ct
EC4 . . . . 108 C1
Old Chiswick Yd
W4 . . . . .46 A4
Old Church Rd E1 . . .32 C3
Old Church St
SW3 . . . . 143 C1
Old Compton St
W1 . . . . 105 B1
Old Court Ho W8 . . 128 A3
Old Court Pl W8 . . 128 A3
Old Covent Gdn
WC2 . . . . 120 B4
Old Dairy Mews
1 Balham SW12 . . 72 C3
4 Camden Town
NW5 . . . . .13 A2
Old Deer Park Gdns
TW9 . . . . .54 A4
Old Devonshire Rd
SW12 . . . . 73 A4
Old Dock Cl TW9 . . .44 C4
Oldfield Gr SE16 . . . 40 C2
Oldfield Mews N6 . . .4 B4
Oldfield Rd
Bedford Pk W3,
W12 . . . . 38 B4
Stoke Newington
N16 . . . . 7 A1
Willesden NW10 . . . .8 B1
Old Fish St Hill
EC4 . . . . 122 C4
Old Fleet La EC4 . . 108 A2
OLD FORD 26 B4
Old Ford Prim Sch **53**
E3 . . . . .26 B3
Old Ford Rd E2, E3 . .25 C3
Old Ford Trad Est
E3 . . . . .26 C4
Old Forge Mews
W12 . . . . 39 A4
Old Forge Rd N19 . . .4 C2
Old Gloucester St
WC1 . . . . 106 B4
Oldham Terr W3 . . . 28 B1
Oldhill St N16 . . . . .7 C3
Old Hospital Cl SW12,
SW17 . . . . 72 B3
Olding Ho **5**
SW12 . . . . 73 B4
Old Jamaica Bsns Est
23 SE16 . . . . . 139 B1
Old Jamaica Rd
SE16 . . . . 139 B2
Old James St SE15 . .65 A4
Old Jewry EC2 . . . 109 B1

Old Kent Rd
Deptford SE1,
SE15 . . . . .50 A4
Walworth SE1 . . . . 152 B2
Old Laundry The **14**
SW18 . . . . 59 C3
Old Manor Ct NW8 . 79 A2
Old Manor Yd
SW5 . . . . 142 A3
Old Market Sq **11**
E2 . . . . . 24 B2 99 A4
Old Marylebone Rd
NW1 . . . . 102 B3
Old Mitre Ct EC4 . . 107 C1
Old Montague St
E1 . . . . 111 B3
Old Nichol St
E2 . . . . . 24 B1 98 C2
Old North St WC1 . . 106 C4
OLD OAK
COMMON 21 A3
Old Oak Common La
NW10 . . . . 21 A1
Old Oak La NW10 . . 21 A3
Old Oak Prim Sch
W3 . . . . .29 B3
Old Oak Rd W3 . . . .29 B2
Old Orch The NW3 . . 12 B3
Old Palace Prim Sch
51 E3 . . . . . . 27 A2
Old Paradise St
SE11 . . . . 148 C4
Old Park Ave
SW12 . . . . 60 C1
Old Park La W1 . . . 118 A1
Old Pearson St
SE10 . . . . .52 A3
Old Pye St SW1 . . . 133 B2
Old Pye Street Est
SW1 . . . . 133 B1
Old Quebec St
W1 . . . . 103 A1
Old Queen St
SW1 . . . . 133 C3
Old Royal Free Pl
N1 . . . . .85 C3
Old Royal Free Sq
N1 . . . . .85 C3
Old School Sq **12**
E14 . . . . .33 C3
Old School The
WC1 . . . . 107 A4
Old Seacoal La
EC4 . . . . 108 A1
Old South Lambeth Rd
SW8 . . . . 162 B2
Old Spitalfields Mkt
E1 . . . . 110 C4
Old Sq WC2 . . . . . 107 B2
Old St EC1 . . . . . . 97 C2
Old Stable Mews
N5 . . . . 6 B1
Old Street EC1 . . . .97 C2
Old Swan Wharf
SW11 . . . . 167 C4
Old Theatre Ct
SE1 . . . . 123 A2
Old Town SW4 . . . .61 B4
Old Vicarage Sch
TW10 . . . . 54 A1
Old Woolwich Rd
SE10 . . . . .42 C1
Old York Rd SW18 . .59 A2

O'Leary Sq E1 . . . . .32 B4
Olga Prim Sch **27**
E3 . . . . .26 A3
Olga St **20** E3 . . . .26 A3
Oliphant St W10 . . . 23 A2
Olive Blythe Ho **14**
W10 . . . . 23 A1
Oliver Bsns Pk
NW10 . . . . 20 A3
Oliver Cl W4 . . . . . .45 A4
Olive Rd NW2 . . . . .9 B4
Oliver Goldsmith Prim
Sch **18** SE5 . . . . .49 B2
Oliver Ho
22 Bermondsey
SE16 . . . . 139 B3
Notting Hill
W11 . . . . 31 A2 112 A3
South Lambeth
SW8 . . . . 162 A2
Oliver House Prep
Sch 61 A1
Oliver Mews SE15 . . 49 C1
Oliver's Yd EC1 . . . .97 C2
Olive Tree Ho **7**
SE13 . . . .
Olive Tree Sch The
SE13 . . . . .67 A1
Olivette St **1**
SW15 . . . . 57 C3
Olive Waite Ho
NW6 . . . . .11 A1
Ollerton Gn E3 . . . .26 B4
Ollgar Cl W12 . . . . .29 B1
Olliffe St E14 . . . . .42 B3
Olmar St SE1 . . . . .49 C4
Olney Ho NW8 . . . . 90 B2
Olney Rd SE17 . . . .48 B4
Olympia Ex Ctr
W14 . . . . 126 B1
Olympian Ct **8**
E14 . . . . .41 C2
Olympia Way
W14 . . . . 126 B1
Olympia Yd W2 . . . 114 B3
Olympic Ho **10**
W10 . . . . 30 B3
Olympic Park E15 . . 19 A2
Olympic Stadium
E15 . . . . .19 A1
Olympus Sq E5 . . . . 7 C1
Oman Ave NW2 . . . .9 B4
Oman St NW4 . . . . .9 B4
Ombersley Ho N4 . . .6 B4
Omeara St SE1 . . . 123 A1
Omega Cl E14 . . . . 42 A3
Omega Ho SW10 . . 157 A2
Omega Pl N1 . . . . . 84 B1
Omega St SE14 . . . .51 C2
Omega Works E3 . . .18 C1
Ommaney Rd SE14 . .51 A2
Omnibus Bsns Ctr
N7 . . . . .14 A3
Ondine Rd SE15 . . . 64 B3
Onedin Point **10**
E1 . . . . 125 C3
Onega Gate SE16 . . 41 A3
O'Neill Ho NW8 . . . .79 C1
One New Change Sh
Ctr EC4 . . . . . . 108 C1
One Tree Cl SE23 . . 65 B1
Ongar Ho **3** N1 . . .15 C2
Ongar Rd SW6 . . . 155 C4
Onslow Ave TW10 . . 54 A2
Onslow Avenue Mans
10 TW10 . . . . . .54 A2

Onslow Cl W9 . . . . 23 B2
Onslow Ct SW10 . . . 143 A1
Onslow Gdns
　SW7 . . . . 143 B2
Onslow Lo 20 SW7 . .74 C4
Onslow Mews E
　SW7 . . . . 143 B3
Onslow Mews W
　SW7 . . . . 143 B3
Onslow Rd TW10 . . .54 A2
Onslow Sq SW7 . . . 143 C3
Onslow St EC1 . . . . . .95 C1
Ontario St SE1 . . . . 136 B2
Ontario Way E14 . . .33 C2
Opal St SE11 . . . . . . 150 A2
Open Air Theatre,
　Regent's Pk NW1 91 B3
Openview SW17 . . . .
　SW18 . . . . .71 C2
Opera Ct 7 N19 . . . . .4 C1
Operating Theatre
　Mus & Herb Garret
　The SE1 . . . . 123 C1
Ophelia Gdns NW2 . . .1 A1
Ophir Terr SE15 . . . .49 C2
Opie Ho NW8 . . . . . . .80 B2
Oppenheim Rd
　SE13 . . . . .52 B1
Oppidan Apartments
　NW6 . . . . .10 C2
Oppidans Rd NW3 . .12 B1
Orange Pl SE16 . . . .40 B3
Orangery Gallery The
　W8 . . . . 114 A3
Orange St WC2 . . . 119 C3
Orange Yd WC2 . . . 105 C1
Oransay Rd 21 N1 . .15 B2
Oratory La SW3 . . . 143 C2
Oratory RC Prim Sch
　SW3 . . . . 144 A2
Orbain Rd SW6 . . . 154 B1
Orbel St SW11 . . . . 168 A3
Orb St SE17 . . . . . . 151 B3
Orchard Cl
　Honor Oak SE23 . . . .65 B1
　21 Islington N1 . . . .15 B1
　Kensal Town W10 . .31 A4
Orchard Ct
　Barnes SW13 . . . . . .56 B4
　Marylebone W1 . . . 103 B2
Orchard Dr SE3 . . . .53 A1
Orchard Hill SE13 . .52 A2
Orchard Ho
　Camberwell SE5 . . . .48 B2
　11 Rotherhithe
　SE16 . . . . .40 B3
　Shepherd's Bush
　W12 . . . . .29 C1
Orchard House Sch 15
　W4 . . . . .37 A2
Orchard Mead Ho
　NW11 . . . . .2 A3
Orchard Mews N1 . .15 C1
Orchard Pl E14 . . . . .35 A2
Orchard Prim Sch 17
　E9 . . . . .17 B1
Orchard Rd
　Highgate N6 . . . . .4 A4
　Richmond TW9 . . . .54 C4
Orchard Rise
　TW10 . . . . .55 A3
Orchardson Ho
　NW8 . . . . .89 C1
Orchardson St
　NW8 . . . . .89 C1
Orchard Sq SE17 . . 140 C1

Orchard St W1 . . . . 103 C2
Orchard The
　Acton Green W4 . . . .37 C2
　Lewisham SE13 . . . . .52 C1
Orchid Cl SE13 . . . . .67 C2
Orchid St W12 . . . . .29 C2
Orde Hall St WC1 . . 106 C4
Orde Ho 10 N16 . . . .15 C4
Ordell Ct 6 E3 . . . . .26 B3
Ordell Rd E3 . . . . . . .26 B3
Ordnance Cres
　SE10 . . . . .43 A4
Ordnance Hill
　NW8 . . . . .79 C3
Ordnance Mews
　NW8 . . . . .79 C2
Ordnance Rd E16 . . .35 B4
Oregano Dr E14 . . . .34 C3
Oregon Bldg 5
　SE13 . . . . .52 A2
Orestes Mews 1
　NW6 . . . . .10 C3
Orford Ct SE27 . . . . .75 A2
Oriana Ho 3 E14 . . .33 B2
Oriel Ct NW3 . . . . . .11 B4
Oriel Dr SW13 . . . . .47 B4
Oriel Rd
　Hackney E9 . . . . .18 A2
　Homerton E9 . . . . . .17 C2
Orient St SE11 . . . . 150 A4
Orion Bsns Ctr
　SE14 . . . . .40 C1
Orion Ho 21 E1 . . . .25 A1
Orion Point 5
　E14 . . . . .41 C2
Orkney Ho N1 . . . . . .84 C4
Orkney St SW11 . . . 169 B2
Orlando Rd SW4 . . . .61 C4
Orleston Mews N7 . .14 C2
Orleston Rd N7 . . . .14 C2
Orlop St SE10 . . . . . .43 A1
Orme Ct W2 . . . . . . 114 A3
Orme Ct Mews
　W2 . . . . 114 B3
Orme Ho 8 E8 . . . . .24 B4
Orme La W2 . . . . . . 114 A3
Ormeley Rd SW12 . .73 A3
Ormerod Ho 3
　SW9 . . . . .62 A4
Orme Sq W2 . . . . . . 114 A3
Ormiston Gr W12 . . .30 A1
Ormiston Rd SE10 . .43 C1
Ormond Cl WC1 . . . 106 B4
Ormonde Ct SW15 . .57 B3
Ormonde Gate
　SW3 . . . . 145 A1
Ormonde Mans
　WC1 . . . . 106 B4
Ormonde Pl SW1 . . 145 C3
Ormonde Rd SW14 . .55 B4
Ormonde Terr
　NW8 . . . . .80 C3
Ormond Ho 2 N16 . . .6 C2
Ormond Mans
　WC1 . . . . .94 C1
Ormond Mews
　WC1 . . . . .94 B1
Ormond Rd N4, N19 .5 A3
Ormond Yd SW1 . . . 119 A2
Ormrod Ct W11 . . . .31 B3
Ormsby 7 W4 . . . . . .38 A3
Ormsby Pl N16 . . . . . .7 B1
Ormsby St E2 . . . . . .24 B3
Ornside Ho SE15 . . .50 B4
Oronsay 3 N1 . . . . .15 B2
Orpen Ho SW5 . . . . 141 C3

Orpen Wlk N16 . . . . . .7 A1
Orpheus Ho 25 N19 . .4 C4
Orpheus St SE5 . . . .48 C2
Orsett Mews W2 . . . 100 C2
Orsett St SE11 . . . . 149 A2
Orsett Terr W2 . . . . 100 C2
Orsman Rd N1 . . . . . .24 A4
Orton St E1 . . . . . . 125 B1
Orville Rd SW11 . . . 167 C2
Orwell Ct
　Hackney E8 . . . . .24 C4
　Highbury N5 . . . . . . .15 B4
Orwell Ho W12 . . . . .29 C2
Osbaldeston Rd
　N16 . . . . .7 C2
Osbert St SW1 . . . . 147 B3
Osborn Cl E8 . . . . . .24 C4
Osborne Rd
　Finsbury Pk N4 . . . . . .5 C3
　Hackney E9 . . . . .18 B2
　South Acton W3 . . . .37 A4
　Willesden NW2 . . . . . .9 A2
Osborn St E1 . . . . . 111 A4
Osbourne Ho
　TW10 . . . . .54 C2
Oscar Faber Pl 8
　N1 . . . . .16 A1
Oscar St SE8 . . . . . .51 C1
Oseney Cres NW5 . .13 C2
Osier Ct E1 . . . . .25 C1
Osier La SE10 . . . . . .43 B3
Osier Mews W4 . . . .46 B4
Osiers Rd SW18 . . . .58 C3
Osier St E1 . . . . .25 B1
Oslo Ct NW8 . . . . . . .80 A1
Oslo Ho 50 SE5 . . . .48 B1
Oslo Sq SE16 . . . . . .41 A3
Oslow Cl W10 . . . . . .23 B2
Osmani Prim Sch
　E1 . . . . 111 C4
Osman Rd E6 . . . . . .39 B3
Osmington Ho
　SW8 . . . . 163 A1
Osmund St W12 . . . .29 B4
Osnaburgh St NW1 . .92 B2
Osnaburgh Terr
　NW1 . . . . .92 B2
Osprey Ct SW3 . . . . 144 A3
Osprey Ho
　Camberwell SE15 . . .49 B2
　6 Limehouse E14 . . .33 A2
Ospringe Ho SE1 . . 121 C1
Ospringe Rd NW5 . .13 B4
Osram Ct W6 . . . . . .39 B3
Osric Path 1 N1 . . . .24 A3
Ossian Mews N4 . . . .5 B4
Ossian Rd N4 . . . . . . .5 B4
Ossington Bldgs
　W1 . . . . 103 B3
Ossington Cl
　W2 . . . . .31 C2 113 C3
Ossington St W2 . . . 114 A3
Ossory Rd SE1 . . . . 153 A1
Ossulston St NW1 . . .83 C2
Ostade Rd SW2 . . . . .74 B4
Osten Mews SW7 . . 128 B1
Osterley Ho 5
　E14 . . . . .34 A3
Osterley Rd N16 . . . .16 A4
Oswald Bldg SW8 . . 160 A3
Oswald's Mead E9 . .18 A4
Osward Rd SW12,
　SW17 . . . . .72 B2
Oswell Ho 11 E1 . . .32 A1
Oswin St SE11 . . . . 150 B4
Oswyth Rd SE5 . . . . .49 A1

Otford Cres SE4 . . . .66 B1
Otford Ho
　Bermondsey SE1 . . 137 C3
　6 Deptford SE15 . . . .50 B4
Otha Ho 25 SW9 . . . 172 B2
Othello Cl SE11 . . . . 150 A2
Otis St E3 . . . . .27 B2
Otley Ho N5 . . . . .6 A1
Ottaway Ct E5 . . . . . .7 C1
Ottaway St E5 . . . . . .7 C1
Otterburn Ho 12
　SE5 . . . . .48 B3
Otter Cl E15 . . . . . . .27 B4
Otto St SE17 . . . . . . .48 A4
Our Lady of Dolours
　RC Prim Sch 1
　W2 . . . . 100 A4
Our Lady of Lourdes
　RC Prim Sch
　1 Lewisham
　SE13 . . . . .67 C4
　London NW10 . . . . . .20 B4
Our Lady of Victories
　RC Prim Sch
　7 Putney SW15 . . . .57 C3
　South Kensington
　SW7 . . . . 143 A3
Our Lady Queen of
　Heaven RC Prim Sch
　10 SW19 . . . . .69 C4
Our Lady RC Prim Sch
　Camden Town
　NW1 . . . . .83 A4
　22 Poplar E14 . . . . .33 B3
Our Lady St Joseph
　RC Prim Sch 8
　N1 . . . . .16 A2
Our Lady's Convent
　RC High Sch 3
　N15 . . . . .7 A4
Ouseley Rd SW12 . . .72 B3
Outer Circ NW8 . . . . .81 A1
Outgate Rd NW10 . . .8 B1
Outram Pl N1 . . . . . .84 B4
Outram St N1 . . . . . .84 C4
Outwich St 3 EC3 . . 110 B2
Outwood Ho 3
　SW2 . . . . .74 B4
Oval Mans SE11 . . . 163 A4
Oval Pl SW8 . . . . . . 163 A2
Oval Rd NW1 . . . . . . .82 A4
Oval Sta SE11 . . . . . 163 B3
Oval The E2 . . . . . . .25 A3
Oval Way SE11 . . . . 149 A1
Overbury Ho 5
　E5 . . . . .17 C4
Overbury St E5 . . . . .17 C4
Overcliff Rd SE13 . . .66 C4
Overhill Rd SE21,
　SE22 . . . . .76 C4
Overlea Rd E5 . . . . . .7 C4
Oversley Ho 17
　W2 . . . . .31 C4
Overstone Ho 10
　E14 . . . . .33 C3
Overstone Rd W6 . . .39 B2
Overstrand Mans
　SW11 . . . . 169 B3
Overton Ho SW15 . . .68 A4
Overton Rd SW9 . . . 173 C1
Overy Ho SE1 . . . . . 136 A3
Ovex Cl E14 . . . . . . .42 B4
Ovington Ct SW3 . . 130 B1
Ovington Gdns
　SW3 . . . . 130 B1
Ovington Mews
　SW3 . . . . 130 B1

Ovington Sq SW3 . . 130 B1
Ovington St SW3 . . 144 B4
Owen Ho 11 N19 . . .13 B4
Owen's Ct EC1 . . . . .96 A4
Owen's Row EC1 . . . .96 A4
Owen St EC1 . . . . . .86 A1
Owgan Cl SE5 . . . . . .48 C3
Oxberry Ave SW6 . . 164 B2
Oxbridge Ct 4
　W4 . . . . .37 A1
Oxendon St SW1,
　W1 . . . . 119 B3
Oxenford St SE15 . . .64 B4
Oxenham Ho 13
　SE8 . . . . .51 C4
Oxenholme 11 NW1 .83 A1
Oxestalls Rd SE8 . . .41 A1
Oxford & Cambridge
　Mans NW1 . . . . . . 102 B3
Oxford Cir W1 . . . . 104 C1
Oxford Circus Ave
　W1 . . . . 104 C1
Oxford Circus Sta
　W1 . . . . 104 C1
Oxford Ct
　City of London
　EC4 . . . . 123 B4
　Gunnersbury W4 . . .37 A1
　48 Paddington W2 . .31 C4
Oxford Dr SE1 . . . . 124 A1
Oxford Gardens Prim
　Sch 80 W10 . . . . . .30 C3
Oxford Gate W6 . . . .39 C2
Oxford Gdns
　Brentford W4 . . . . . .44 C4
　North Kensington
　W10 . . . . .30 C3
Oxford Ho N4 . . . . . . .5 C3
Oxford Rd
　Finsbury Pk N4 . . . . . .5 C3
　Paddington NW6 . . .23 C3
　Putney SW15 . . . . . .58 A3
　Stratford E15 . . . . . .19 C2
Oxford Rd N W4 . . . .37 A1
Oxford Rd S W4 . . . .37 A1
Oxford Sq W2 . . . . 102 B1
Oxford St W1 . . . . . 104 B1
Oxley Cl SE1 . . . . . . 153 A2
Oxonian St SE22 . . .64 B3
OXO Tower Wharf
　SE1 . . . . 121 C3
Oxo Tower Wharf
　SE1 . . . . 121 C3
Oxted Ct N16 . . . . . . .7 A3
Oyster Row E1 . . . . .32 B3
Ozolins Way E16 . . . .35 C3

P

Pablo Neruda Cl 4
　SE24 . . . . .63 A3
Pace Pl E1 . . . . .32 A3
Pacific Ho 15 E1 . . . .25 C1
Pacific Rd E16 . . . . .35 C3
Pacific Wharf
　SE16 . . . . .32 C1
Packenham Ho
　24 Crouch End N19 . .4 C4
　21 Spitalfields
　E2 . . . . 24 B2 99 A4
Packington Sq N1 . .86 C4
Packington St N1 . . .86 B3
Padbury SE17 . . . . . 152 B1

Padbury Ct
E2 . . . . 24 B2 **99** A3
Padbury Ho NW8 . . . **90** B2
Paddenswick Ct 2
W6 . . . . .39 A3
Paddenswick Rd
W6 . . . . .38 C3
PADDINGTON . . . 100 C3
Paddington Acad 7
W9 . . . . .23 C1
Paddington Gn
W2 . . . . **101** B4
Paddington Green
Prim Sch NW8 . . . **89** B1
Paddington St
W1 . . . . **103** B4
Paddington Sta
W2 . . . . **101** B2
Paddock Ct 3 SE3 . .53 C1
Paddock Prim Sch
SW11 . . . . .60 C3
Paddock Sch
SW15 . . . . .56 B3
Paddock Way 11
SW15 . . . . .69 B4
Padfield Rd SE5 . . .63 B4
Padstone Ho 20
E3 . . . . .27 A2
Padstow Ho 12
E14 . . . . .33 B2
Pagden St SW8 . . **170** B4
Pageant Cres SE16 .33 B1
Pageantmaster Ct
EC4 . . . . **108** A1
Page Ho SE10 . . . . .52 B4
Page St SW1 . . . **147** C4
Page's Wlk SE1 . . **138** B1
Page's Yd W4 . . . . .46 A4
Paget Ho 18 E2 . . .25 B3
Paget Rd N16 . . . . . .6 C3
Paget St EC1 . . . . .96 A4
Pagham Ho 6
W10 . . . . .22 B1
Pagnell St SE14 . . .51 B3
Pagoda Ave TW9 . . .54 B4
Pagoda Gdns SE3 . .52 C1
Pagoda Gr SE27 . . .75 B2
Paine Ct 1 SE3 . . .53 B4
Painsthorpe Rd 3
N16 . . . . .7 A1
Painswick Ct 1
SE15 . . . . .49 B3
Painters Mews
SE16 . . . . **153** C4
Pakeman Ho SE1 . **136** B4
Pakeman Prim Sch
N7 . . . . .5 B1
Pakeman St N7 . . . . .5 B1
Pakenham Cl
SW12 . . . . .72 C3
Pakenham St WC1 . .95 A2
Palace Ave W8 . . **128** B4
Palace Cl 4 E9 . . .18 B2
Palace Ct
Hampstead NW3 . . .11 A3
Kensington W2 . . . **114** A3
Streatham SW2 . . . .74 C2
Palace Garden Mews
W8 . . . . . .31 C1 **113** C2
Palace Gate W8 . . **128** C3
Palace Gdns Mews
W8 . . . . **114** B1
Palace Gn W8 . . . **114** A1
Palace Mans W14 . **140** B4

Palace Mews
Belgravia SW1 . . . **145** C3
Fulham SW6 . . . . **155** A2
Palace Pl SW1 . . **132** C2
Palace Rd SE27, SW16,
SW2 . . . . .74 C2
Palace St SW1 . . **132** C2
Palatine Ave N16 . . .16 A4
Palatine Rd N16 . . .16 A4
Palazzo Apartments
E1 . . . . .16 A1
SE14 . . . . .50 C2
Palemead Cl SW6 . .47 C2
Palermo Rd NW10 . .21 C3
Palewell Common Dr
SW14 . . . . .55 C2
Palewell Pk SW14 . .55 C3
Palfrey Pl SW8 . . **163** A2
Palgrave Gdns
NW1 . . . . .90 B2
Palgrave Ho
7 Camberwell
SE5 . . . . .48 B3
4 Maitland Pk
NW3 . . . . .12 B3
Palissy St 33
E2 . . . . .24 B2 **98** C3
Pallant Ho SE1 . . **137** C1
Pallester Ct SW11 . .1 A3
Palliser Ct W14 . . **140** A1
Palliser Ho
3 Greenwich
SE10 . . . . .52 C4
6 Mile End
E1 . . . . .25 C1
Palliser Rd W14 . . **140** A1
Pallister Terr
SW15 . . . . .68 B2
Pall Mall SW1 . . **119** B1
Pall Mall E SW1 . **119** C2
Pall Mall Pl SW1 . **119** A1
Palm Ct
18 Camberwell
SE5 . . . . .49 B3
Stoke Newington
N16 . . . . .6 C2
Palmer Ho
6 Deptford SE14 . .50 C3
6 Kentish Town
NW5 . . . . .13 B4
5 Tufnell Pk N19 . .4 B1
Palmer Pl N7 . . . . .14 C3
Palmers Rd
Globe Town E2 . . . .25 C3
8 Mortlake SW14 .55 B4
Palmer St SW1 . . **133** B2
Palmerston Ct 22
E3 . . . . .25 C3
Palmerston Ho
Battersea SW11 . . **169** C3
Kensington
W8 . . . . .31 C1 **113** B1
Palmerston Rd
Acton Green W3 . . .37 B3
Brondesbury NW6 . .10 B1
Hampstead NW6 . . .10 C1
Mortlake SW14 . . . .55 B3
Palmerston Way
SW8 . . . . **160** B1
Palm Gr W5 . . . . . .36 A3
Palm Tree Ho 2
SE14 . . . . .50 C3
Pamela Ct NW10 . . . .8 C1
Pamela Ho 18 E8 . .24 B4
Pamlion Ct N4 . . . . .5 A4
Panama Ho 6 E1 . .32 C4
Pancras La EC2 . . **109** B1

Pancras Rd NW1 . . .83 C2
Pancras Way E3 . . .26 C3
Pandian Way 4
NW5 . . . . .13 C2
Pandora Rd NW6 . . .10 C2
Pangbourne NW1 . . .92 C3
Pangbourne Ave
W10 . . . . .30 B4
Pangbourne Ho 8
N7 . . . . .14 A3
Pankhurst Cl 7
SE14 . . . . .50 C3
Pankhurst Ho 6
NW10 . . . . .30 B3
Panmure Ct N5 . . . .15 A4
Pan Peninsula Sq
E14 . . . . .42 A4
Pansy Gdns W12 . . .29 C2
Panton St SW1 . . **119** B3
Panyer Alley EC2 . **108** C2
Paper Mill Wharf
E14 . . . . .33 A2
Papworth Gdns
N7 . . . . .14 B3
Papworth Way
SW2 . . . . .74 C4
Parade Mans 11
SE5 . . . . .48 B1
Parade Mews SE27,
SW2 . . . . .75 A2
Parade The SW11 . **159** A2
Paradise Pas N7 . . .14 C3
Paradise Rd
Richmond TW10 . . . .54 A2
South Lambeth
SW4 . . . . **172** A2
Paradise Row 4 E2 . .25 A2
Paradise St SE16 . . .40 A4
Paradise Wlk
SW3 . . . . **159** A4
Paragon Christian
Acad E5 . . . . .17 C4
Paragon Cl E16 . . . .35 C3
Paragon Ho SE3 . . .53 B1
Paragon Mews
SE1 . . . . **151** C4
Paragon Pl SE3 . . . .53 B1
Paragon Rd E9 . . . .17 B2
Paragon The
Kidbrooke SE3 . . . .53 C1
Walworth SE17 . . . **151** C4
Paramount Bldg
EC1 . . . . .96 A2
Paramount Ct
WC1 . . . . .93 A1
Parbury Rd SE23 . . .66 A1
Pardoner St SE1 . . **137** C2
Parfett St E1 . . . . **111** C2
Parfitt Cl NW11 . . . . .2 B3
Parfrey St W6 . . . . .47 B4
Paris Gdn SE1 . . . **122** A2
Paris Ho 12 E2 . . . .25 A3
Park Ave
Golders Green
NW11 . . . . .2 A3
Mortlake SW14 . . . .55 C3
32 Hackney E9 . . .17 B1
Willesden NW10 . . . .9 B2
Park Ave N NW10 . . .9 A3
Park Cl
Kensington W14 . . **127** A2
Knightsbridge
SW1 . . . . **130** C3
19 South Hackney
E9 . . . . .25 B4
Park Cres W1 . . . . .92 A1

Park Crescent Mews E
W1 . . . . .92 B1
Park Crescent Mews
W W1 . . . . .92 A1
Park Ct
Battersea SW11 . . **170** A4
Clapham Pk SW4 . . .61 C2
Dulwich SE21 . . . . .75 C1
3 Hammersmith
W6 . . . . .38 C2
Upper Tooting
SW12 . . . . .72 C3
Park Dr
Acton W3 . . . . .36 C3
Golders Green NW11 . .2 A3
Park Dwellings 7
NW3 . . . . .12 B3
Park End NW3 . . . . .12 A4
Parker Ct
Shoreditch N1 . . . . .87 A4
South Lambeth
SW4 . . . . **172** A3
Parke Rd SW13 . . . .46 C2
Parker Mews
WC2 . . . . **106** B2
Parkers Row 13
SE1 . . . . **139** A3
Parker's Row SE1 . **139** A3
Parker St WC2 . . . **106** B2
Parkfield Ave
SW14 . . . . .56 A3
Parkfield Ct SE14 . . .51 B2
Parkfield Ind Est
SW11 . . . . **169** C2
Parkfield Rd
New Cross SE14 . . . .51 B2
Willesden NW10 . . . .9 A1
Parkfields SW15 . . .57 B3
Parkfield St N1 . . . .85 C2
Park Flats N6 . . . . . .3 A4
Parkgate Gdns
SW14 . . . . .55 C2
Parkgate House Sch
SW11 . . . . .60 C3
Parkgate Mews N6 . .4 B4
Parkgate Rd
SW11 . . . . **158** B1
Parkham St SW11 . **168** A3
Park Heights Ct 21
E14 . . . . .33 B3
Park Hill
Clapham Pk SW4 . . .61 C2
Richmond TW10 . . . .54 B1
Park Hill Ct SW17 . .72 B1
Parkhill Rd NW3 . . .12 B3
Park Hill Wlk 18
NW3 . . . . .12 B3
Park Ho
6 Camberwell
SE5 . . . . .48 C2
Finsbury Pk N4 . . . . .6 A2
32 Hackney E9 . . .17 B1
Richmond TW10 . . . .54 A1
Parkholme Rd E8 . . .16 C2
Parkhouse St SE5 . .48 C3
Parkhurst Ct N7 . . . .14 A4
Parkhurst Rd N7 . . .14 A4
Parkinson Ct
Finsbury N1 . . . . . . .97 B3
Shoreditch EC1 . . . .97 C4

Parkinson Ho 8
E9 . . . . .17 B1
Park La
Mayfair W1 . . . . . **117** B3
Mill Meads E15 . . . .27 C3
Parkland Ct W14 . . **126** A4
Parkland Gdns 12
SW19 . . . . .69 C3
Parklands
East Dulwich
SE22 . . . . .65 A2
Highgate N6 . . . . . . .4 A4
Parklands Cl SW14 . .55 B2
Park Lea Ct N16 . . . . .7 A4
Parklife Oxford St
W1 . . . . **103** B1
Park Lo
3 South Hampstead
NW8 . . . . .11 C1
10 Wapping E1 . . .32 A1
Willesden NW2 . . . . .9 B4
Park Lofts 9 SW4 . .62 A2
Park Lorne NW8 . . . .90 B3
Park Mans
Battersea SW11 . . **168** C3
Bedford Pk W6 . . . .38 B3
Fulham SW6 . . . . **164** B3
Knightsbridge
SW1 . . . . **130** C3
St John's Wood
NW8 . . . . .80 A1
Vauxhall SW8 . . . **162** B4
Parkmead SW15 . . .57 A1
Park Mews
Greenwich SE10 . . . .43 B1
Kensal Rise W10 . . .23 A3
Park Par
Acton W3 . . . . .36 C3
Dagenham NW10 . . .21 B3
Park Piazza 3
SE13 . . . . .67 C1
Park Pl
Canary Wharf E14 . .33 C1
Gunnersbury W3 . . .36 C2
Shoreditch N1 . . . . .87 C4
St James SW1 . . . **118** C2
Park Place Dr W3 . . .36 C3
Park Place Ho 8
SE10 . . . . .52 C4
Park Place Villas
W2 . . . . **101** A4
Park Rd
Chiswick W4 . . . . . .45 C4
Dagenham NW10 . . .21 A4
Lisson Gr NW1,
NW8 . . . . .90 B2
Richmond TW10 . . . .54 B1
Park Rd E W3 . . . . .37 B4
Park Rd N
Chiswick W4 . . . . . .37 C1
South Acton W3 . . . .37 A4
Park Road E 11
W3 . . . . .37 A4
Park Row SE10 . . . .52 C4
PARK ROYAL 20 A2
Park Royal Ho NW10 .20 A2
Park Royal Bsns Ctr
NW10 . . . . .20 B1
Park Royal Metro Ctr
NW10 . . . . .20 A1
Park Royal Rd NW10,
W3 . . . . .20 B2
Park S SW11 . . . . **169** B3
Park St James
NW8 . . . . .80 C3

Park Sheen 🔳
SW14 . . . .**55** A3
Parkshot TW9 . . . . .**54** A3
Parkside
East Acton W3 . . . . .**29** A1
Greenwich SE3 . . . . .**53** B3
Park Side NW2 . . . . .**9** A3
Parkside Bsns Est
SE8 . . . .**51** A4
Parkside Cres N7 . . .**5** C1
Parkside Est E9 . . . .**25** C4
Parkside (Private)
Hospl SW19 . . . .**69** C1
Parkside St SW11 **169** B3
Park Sq E NW1 . . . . .**92** B2
Park Square Mews
NW1 . . . .**92** A2
Park Sq NW1 . . . . . .**92** A1
Park St
Borough The SE1. . .**123** A2
Mayfair W1 . . . .**117** B3
Parkstead Rd
SW15 . . . .**57** A2
Parkstone Rd 🔳
SE15 . . . .**49** C1
Park Stps SE1 . .**116** B4
Park The NW11 . . . . .**2** A4
Park Twrs W1 . . . . .**118** A1
Park View
Dagenham W3 . . . . . .**28** B4
Highbury N5 . . . .**15** B4
Willesden NW2 . . . . . .**9** B4
Parkview Ct SW6 . .**164** B1
Park View Ct
SW18 . . . .**58** C1
Park View Ho
SE24 . . . .**63** A1
Park View Mans N4 . .**6** A4
Park View Mews 🔳
SW9 . . . .**172** C2
Park View Rd NW10 . .**8** B4
Park Village E
NW1 . . . .**82** B1
Park Village W
NW1 . . . .**82** A2
Parkville Rd SW6 . .**154** C1
Park Vista SE10. . . .**52** C4
Park Walk Prim Sch
SW10 . . . .**157** B3
Parkwat Cres E15 . .**19** B3
Parkway NW1 . . . . .**82** A3
Park Way W3. . . . . . .**36** C2
Parkway Ho SW14 . .**55** C3
Park West W2 . . . .**102** B1
Park West Pl W1,
W2 . . . .**102** B2
Park Wlk
Chelsea SW10 . . . .**157** B4
Highgate N6 . . . .**3** C4
Parkwood NW8 . .**80** C3
Parkwood Prim Sch
N4 . . . .**6** A2
Parliament Ct
NW3 . . . .**12** A4
Parliament Hill
NW3 . . . .**12** A4
Parliament Hill Mans
NW5 . . . .**12** C4
Parliament Hill Sch
NW5 . . . .**12** C4
Parliament Mews
SW14 . . . .**45** B1
Parliament Sq
SW1 . . . .**134** A3

Parliament St
SW1 . . . .**134** A4
Parliament View
Apartments
SE11 . . . .**148** C3
Parma Cres SW11 . .**60** B3
Parminter Ind Est 🔳
E2 . . . .**25** B3
Parmiter St E2 . . . .**25** A3
Parmoor Ct EC1. . . .**96** C2
Parnell Cl W12 . . . .**39** A3
Parnell Ho WC1 . . .**105** C2
Parnell Rd E3 . . . .**26** B4
Parnham St E14 . . .**33** A3
Parolles Rd N19. . . .**4** B3
Parr Ct N1 . . . .**87** B2
Parrington Ho 🔳
SW4 . . . .**61** C1
Parr Ho E14 . . . . . .**42** B2
Parr St N1 . . . .**87** B2
Parry Ho 🔳 E1 . . . .**32** A1
Parry Rd W10 . . . . .**23** A2
Parry St SW8 . . . .**162** B4
Parsifal Coll 🔳
NW3 . . . .**10** C4
Parsifal Ho NW3. . . .**10** C4
Parsifal Rd NW6. . . .**10** C3
Parsonage St E14 . .**42** B2
Parsons Gn SW6 . .**165** B3
PARSONS
GREEN **165** B4
Parsons Green La
SW6 . . . .**165** B4
Parsons Green Sta
SW6 . . . .**165** B3
Parsons Ho
Paddington W2 . . . . .**89** B1
🔳 Streatham
SW12 . . . .**74** A4
Parsons Lo NW6. . .**11** A1
Parthenia Rd
SW6 . . . .**165** C3
Partington Cl N19 . . .**4** C3
Parton Lo 🔳 E8 . . . .**16** B2
Partridge Ct EC1 . . .**96** A2
Partridge Ho 🔳
E3 . . . .**26** B3
Pascall Ho SE17 . . .**48** B4
Pascal St SW8 . . .**161** C2
Pascoe Rd SE13 . . .**67** C2
Pasley Cl SE17 . . .**150** C1
Passfield Dr E14. . .**34** A4
Passfields W14 . . .**140** C1
Passing Alley EC1 . .**96** B1
Passmore St SW1 .**145** B2
Pastor St SE1,
SE11 . . . .**150** B4
Patcham Terr
SW8 . . . .**170** B4
Patent Ho E14 . . . .**34** A4
Paternoster La
EC4 . . . .**108** B2
Paternoster Sq
EC4 . . . .**108** B2
Pater St W8 . . . . .**127** B1
Patience Rd
SW11 . . . .**168** A1
Patience Villas
SE13 . . . .**67** C4
Patio Cl SW4 . . . . .**61** C1
Patmore Ho 🔳
N16 . . . .**16** A3
Patmore St SW8 . . .**171** A4
Patmos Rd SW9 . . .**48** A2
Paton Cl E3 . . . . . .**26** C2
Paton Ho 🔳 SW9 .**172** C2

Paton St EC1 . . . . .**96** C3
Patrick Coman Ho
EC1 . . . .**96** A3
Patrick Connolly Gdns
🔳 E3 . . . .**27** A2
Patriot Sq E2 . . . . .**25** A3
Patrol Pl SE6 . . . . .**67** A1
Pat Shaw Ho 🔳
E1 . . . .**25** C1
Patshull Pl NW5. . . .**13** B2
Patshull Rd NW5 . . .**13** B2
Patten Ho N4 . . . . . .**6** B3
Patten Rd SW18 . . .**72** A4
Patterdale 🔳
NW1 . . . .**92** B3
Patterdale Rd
SE15 . . . .**50** B3
Pattina Wlk SE16 . .**33** A1
Pattison Point 🔳
E16 . . . .**35** C4
Pattison Ho
Borough The SE1 . .**137** A4
🔳 Stepney E1 . . . .**32** C3
Pattison Rd NW2 . . . .**1** C1
Pat Williams Ho
SE27 . . . .**75** B1
Paul Daisley Ct 🔳
NW6 . . . .**10** A1
Paulet Rd SE5 . . . .**48** A2
Paul Ho 🔳 W10 . . . .**23** A1
Pauline Ho 🔳 E1 . .**111** C4
Paul Julius Cl E14. .**34** C2
Paul St EC2 . . . . .**24** A1 **98** A2
Paultons Ho SW3 . .**157** C4
Paultons Sq SW3 . .**157** C4
Paultons St SW3 . .**157** C3
Pauntley Ho 🔳 N19 . .**4** B3
Pauntley St 🔳 N19 . .**4** B3
Pavan Ct 🔳 E2 . . . .**25** B2
Paveley Dr SW11 . .**158** A1
Paveley Ho N1 . . . .**84** C1
Paveley St NW8 . . .**90** B2
Pavement The
Brentford W5 . . . .**36** A3
🔳 Clapham SW4 . . .**61** B3
Pavilion Ct
🔳 Hampstead
NW3 . . . .**11** B4
🔳 Hampstead NW3 . .**11** C3
🔳 Paddington
NW6 . . . .**23** C2
Pavilion Mans 🔳
SW9 . . . .**62** B3
Pavilion Rd SW1 . .**131** A1
Pavilion Sq SW17 . .**72** B1
Pavilion St SW1 . . .**131** A1
Pavilion Terr 🔳
W12 . . . .**30** B3
Pavillion Ct SW1 . .**160** A4
Pavitt Ct NW10 . . . . .**8** C1
Paxton Cl TW9 . . . .**44** B1
Paxton Ho SE17 . . .**151** A2
Paxton Rd W4 . . . . .**46** A4
Paxton Terr SW1 . .**160** B4
Paymal Ho 🔳 E1 . . .**32** B4
Payne Ho N1 . . . . .**85** A3
Payne Rd E3 . . . . . .**27** A3
Paynesfield Ave
SW14 . . . .**55** C4
Payne St SE8 . . . . .**51** B4
Paynes Wlk W6 . . .**154** A3
Peabody Ave SW1 .**146** B1
Peabody Bldgs
🔳 Camberwell
SE5 . . . .**48** C2
Walworth SE17 . . . .**151** B3
Peabody Cl SW1 . .**160** B4

Peabody Ct
🔳 Camberwell
SE5 . . . .**48** C2
St Luke's EC1 . . . . .**97** A1
Peabody Est
🔳 Bethnal Green
E2 . . . .**25** A3
Borough The SE1 . .**122** C1
Fulham SW6 . . . . . .**155** A4
🔳 Hammersmith
W6 . . . .**39** B1
Holborn EC1 . . . . . .**95** C1
Lambeth SE1 . . . . .**121** C1
North Kensington
W10 . . . .**30** B4
🖪 Ratcliff E1 . . . . . .**32** C2
🖪 St George in East
E1 . . . .**125** B4
St Luke's EC1 . . . . .**97** A1
Strand WC2 . . . . . .**106** C1
Streatham SW1 . . . .**147** A4
Westminster SW1 . .**147** A4
Peabody Hill SE21 . .**75** B2
Peabody Sq SE1. . .**136** A3
Peabody Twr EC1 . .**97** A1
Peabody Yd N1 . . . .**86** C4
Peace Pagoda
SW3 . . . .**159** A2
Peach Rd W10 . . . .**23** A2
Peachum Rd SE3 . .**53** B4
Peach Walk Mews 🔳
E3 . . . .**25** C3
Peacock St SE17 . .**150** B3
Peacock Yd SE17 . .**150** B3
Peak Ho N4 . . . .**6** B3
Pearce Ho
Camden Town N19 . . . .**4** B1
🔳 Streatham SW2 . .**74** A4
Westminster SW1 . .**147** C3
Pear Cl SE14 . . . . .**51** A3
Pear Ct 🔳 SE15. . . .**49** B3
Peardon St SW8 . .**170** B1
Pearfield Ho 🔳
N5 . . . .**15** B3
Pearl St E1 . . . . . .**32** A1
Pearman Ho 🔳
SE13 . . . .**52** B1
Pearman St SE1 . .**135** C3
Pear Pl SE1 . . . . .**135** B4
Pearscroft Ct
SW6 . . . .**166** B3
Pearscroft Rd
SW6 . . . .**166** B3
Pearse St 🔳 SE15 .**49** A4
Pearson Cl 🔳 SE5 . .**48** C2
Pearson Ho SW15 . .**47** B1
Pearson's Ave SE8,
SE14 . . . .**51** C2
Pearson St E2 . . . .**24** B3
Peartree Ave
SW17 . . . .**71** B1
Pear Tree Ct 🔳 E2 . .**24** B4
Pear Tree Ct
Holborn EC1 . . . . . .**95** C1
Putney SW15 . . . . . .**57** A3
Pear Tree Ho SE4 . .**66** B3
Peartree La E1 . . . .**32** B2
Peartree St EC1 . . .**96** C2
Peartree Way
SE10 . . . .**43** C2
Peary Pl E2 . . . . . .**25** B2
Peckarmans Wood
SE21, SE26 . . . . . .**76** C1
Peckett Sq 🔳 N5 . .**15** B4
Peckford Pl SW9 . .**173** C1
PECKHAM **49** C2

Peckham Gr SE15 . .**49** A3
Peckham High St
SE15 . . . .**49** C2
Peckham Hill St
SE15 . . . .**49** C3
Peckham Park Prim
Sch 🔳 SE15 . . . . .**49** C3
Peckham Park Rd
SE15 . . . .**49** C3
Peckham Rd SE5 . .**49** A2
Peckham Rye
East Dulwich
SE22 . . . .**64** C3
Peckham SE15,
SE22 . . . .**64** C3
Peckham Rye Sta
SE15 . . . .**49** C1
Peckwater Ho 🔳
NW5 . . . .**13** C2
Peckwater St NW5 .**13** B3
Pedlars Wlk N7 . . .**14** A3
Pedley St E1 . .**24** B1 **99** A1
Pedro St E5 . . . . . .**17** C4
Pedworth Gdns 🔳
SE16 . . . .**40** B2
Peel Gr E2 . . . .**25** B3
Peel Pass W8 . . . . .**31** C1 **113** B1
Peel Prec NW6 . . . .**23** C3
Peel St W8 . . .**31** C1 **113** B1
Peerless St EC1 . . .**97** B3
Pegasus Cl N16 . . .**15** C4
Pegasus Ct
🔳 Acton W3 . . . . .**28** B3
Brentford TW8 . . . . . .**36** B1
College Pk NW10 . . .**22** A2
🔳 Paddington
NW6 . . . .**23** C3
Pegasus Ho 🔳 E1 . .**25** C1
Pegasus Pl SE11. . .**163** B4
Pegwell Ho 🔳 E5 . .**17** A3
Pekin St E14 . . . . .**33** C3
Pekoe SE1 . . . . . .**138** C3
Peldon Ct TW10 . . .**54** B2
Pelham Cl SE5 . . . .**64** A4
Pelham Cres SW7 .**144** A3
Pelham Ct SW3 . . .**144** A3
Pelham Ho W14 . . .**140** C3
Pelham Pl SW7 . . .**144** A3
Pelham St SW7 . . .**143** C4
Pelican Ho 🔳 SE8 . .**41** B2
Pelican Pas 🔳 E1 . .**25** B1
Pelier St SE17 . . . .**48** B4
Pella Ho SE11 . . . .**149** A2
Pellant Rd SW6 . . .**154** B2
Pellatt Rd SE22 . . . .**64** B2
Pellerin Rd N16 . . .**16** A3
Pellew Ho 🔳 E1 . . .**25** A1
Pelling St E14 . . . .**33** C3
Pelter St E2 . . . .**24** B2 **98** C4
Pelton Rd SE10 . . . .**43** A1
Pember Rd NW10 . .**22** C2
Pemberton Ct 🔳
E1 . . . .**25** C2
Pemberton Gdns
N19 . . . .**4** B1
Pemberton Pl 🔳
E8 . . . .**17** A1
Pemberton Row
EC4 . . . .**107** C2
Pemberton Terr
N19 . . . .**4** B1
Pembridge Cres
W11 . . . .**31** C2 **113** A4
Pembridge Gdns
W2 . . . .**31** C2 **113** B3

Pembridge Hall Prep
Sch for Girls
 W2 . . . . .31 C2 113 C3
Pembridge Mews
 W11 . . . . .31 C2 113 B4
Pembridge Pl
 Notting Hill
 W2 . . . . .31 C2 113 C4
 1 Wandsworth
 SW15 . . . . .58 C2
Pembridge Rd
 W11 . . . . .31 C2 113 C4
Pembridge Sq
 W2 . . . . .31 C2 113 C3
Pembridge Villas
 W11 . . . . .31 C2 113 B4
Pembroke W14 . . . .141 A3
Pembroke Ave N1 . .84 B4
Pembroke Bldgs
 NW10 . . . . .21 C2
Pembroke Cl
 SW1 . . . . .131 C3
Pembroke Gdns
 W8 . . . . .141 A4
Pembroke Gdns Cl
 W8 . . . . .127 B1
Pembroke Ho
 Acton W3 . . . . .37 B4
 Chelsea SW1 . . . . . .131 B1
 5 Clapham Pk
 SW2 . . . . .62 A2
 17 Kensington W2 .100 B1
 Putney SW15 . . . . . .56 C2
Pembroke Lo **2**
 SW16 . . . . .74 B1
Pembroke Mews
 8 Bow E3 . . . . .26 A2
 Kensington W8 . . . . .127 B1
Pembroke Pl W8 . .127 B1
Pembroke Rd W8 . .141 B4
Pembroke Sq W8 . .127 B1
Pembroke Studios
 W8 . . . . .127 A1
Pembroke Terr
 NW8 . . . . .79 B3
Pembroke Villas
 W8 . . . . .141 B4
Pembroke Wlk
 W8 . . . . .141 B4
Pembury Cl E5 . . . .17 A3
Pembury Ho SE5 . . .49 A1
Pembury Pl **8** E5,
 E8 . . . . .17 A3
Pembury Rd E5 . . . .17 A3
Pemell Cl **30** E1 . . .25 B1
Pemell Ho **31** E1 . . .25 B1
Penally Pl N1 . . . . .87 C4
Penang St E1 . . . . .32 A1
Penarth Ctr The
 SE15 . . . . .50 B4
Penarth St SE15 . . .50 B4
Pencombe Mews
 W11 . . . . .31 B2 113 A4
Pencraig Way
 SE15 . . . . .50 A4
Penda's Mead E9 . .18 A4
Pendennis Ho **19**
 SE8 . . . . .41 A2
Penderyn Way N7 . .13 C4
Pendle Ho **13**
 SE26 . . . . .76 C1
Pendley Ho **18** E2 . .24 C4
Pendrell Ho WC2 . .105 C1

Pendrell Rd SE4 . . .51 A1
Penelope Ho **20**
 SW9 . . . . .173 B3
Penfield Lo **7** W9 . .31 C4
Penfields Ho N7 . . .14 A2
Penfold Pl NW1 . . .102 A4
Penfold St NW8 . . .89 C1
Penford St SE5 . . . .48 A1
Penhurst Mans
 SW6 . . . . .164 C4
Peninsula Ct E14 . . .42 A3
Peninsula Ret Pk
 TW9 . . . . .43 C2
Peninsular Park Rd
 SE7 . . . . .43 C2
Penmayne Ho
 SE11 . . . . .149 C2
Pennack Rd SE15 . .49 B4
Penn Almshouses **1**
 SE10 . . . . .52 B2
Pennant Mews
 W8 . . . . .142 A4
Pennard Mans **5**
 W12 . . . . .39 B4
Pennard Rd W12 . . .39 B4
Pennefather Ho
 N1 . . . . .15 C2
Penner Cl SW19 . . .70 A2
Pennethorne Cl
 E9 . . . . .25 B4
Pennethorne Ho
 SW11 . . . . .59 C4
Pennethorne Rd
 SE15 . . . . .50 A3
Penn Ho NW8 . . . . .90 A1
Pennine La NW2 . . . .1 A2
Pennine Mans NW2 . .1 A2
Pennine Par NW2 . . .1 A2
Pennington Ct
 1 Rotherhithe
 SE16 . . . . .33 A1
 22 St George in t East
 E1 . . . . .125 C3
Pennington St E1 . .32 A2
Penn Rd N7 . . . . . . .14 A4
Penn St N1 . . . . . . .87 C3
Penny Ct SW10 . . . .157 A4
Pennyfields E14 . . . .33 C2
Pennyford Ct NW8 . .89 B2
Penny Mews
 SW12 . . . . .73 A4
Pennymore Wlk
 W9 . . . . .23 B1
Penny Rd NW10 . . . .20 A2
Penpoll Rd E8 . . . . .17 A2
Penrhyn Cres
 SW14 . . . . .55 B3
Penrith Cl SW15 . . .58 A2
Penrith Pl SE27 . . . .75 A2
Penrose Gr SE17 . .150 C1
Penrose Ho SE17 . .150 C1
Penrose St SE17 . .150 C1
Penryn Ho SE11 . . .150 A2
Penryn St NW1 . . . .83 B2
Penry St SE1 . . . . .152 B3
Pensbury Pl SW8 . .171 A2
Pensbury St SW8 . .171 A2
Pensford Ave TW9 . .44 C1
Penshurst **2** NW5 . .12 C2
Penshurst Ho **1**
 SE15 . . . . .50 B4
Penshurst Rd E9 . . .17 C1
Pentland Cl NW11 . . .1 A2
Pentland Gdns
 SW18 . . . . .59 B1

Pentland Ho
 17 Camden Town
 NW5 . . . . .12 C2
 7 Stamford Hill N16 . .7 B3
Pentland Rd **1**
 NW6 . . . . .23 C2
Pentland St SW18 . .59 B1
Pentlow St SW15 . . .57 B4
Pentney Rd SW12 . .73 B3
Penton Gr N1 . . . . .85 B1
Penton Ho N1 . . . . .85 B1
Penton Pl SE17 . . . .150 B2
Penton Rise WC1 . . .95 A4
Penton St N1 . . . . . .85 B1
PENTONVILLE 85 A1
Pentonville Rd
 WC1 . . . . .84 C1
Pentridge St SE15 . .49 B3
Penwith Rd SW18 . .71 A2
Penwood Ho
 SW15 . . . . .56 B1
Penywern Rd
 SW5 . . . . .141 C2
Penzance Ho
 SE11 . . . . .149 C2
Penzance Pl
 W11 . . . . .31 A1 112 B2
Penzance St
 W11 . . . . .31 A1 112 A2
Peony Gdns W12 . . .29 C2
Peperfield WC1 . . . .94 C3
Pepler Ho **17** W10 . .23 A1
Pepler Mews SE1 . .152 C1
Peploe Rd NW6 . . . .22 C3
Pepper Mead Sq
 SE13 . . . . .66 C2
Pepper St
 Borough The SE1 . .136 C4
 Millwall E14 . . . . .42 A3
Peppie Cl N16 . . . . . .7 A2
Pepys Cres **26** E16 .35 C1
Pepys Ent Ctr **13**
 SE8 . . . . .41 B2
Pepys Ho
 6 Bethnal Green
 E2 . . . . .25 B2
 Clapham Pk SW4 . . .61 C2
Pepys Rd SE14 . . . .50 C1
Pepys St EC3 . . . . .124 B4
Perceval Ave NW3 . .12 A3
Percheron Ct **3**
 SW9 . . . . .62 B4
Perch St E8 . . . . . . .16 B4
Percival Rd SW14 . .55 B3
Percival St EC1 . . . .96 B3
Percy Cir WC1 . . . . .95 A4
Percy Laurie Ho **6**
 SW15 . . . . .57 C3
Percy Mews W1 . . .105 B3
Percy Pas W1 . . . . .105 B3
Percy Rd
 Newham E16 . . . . . . .35 A4
 Shepherd's Bush
 W12 . . . . .38 C4
Percy St W1 . . . . . .105 B3
Peregrine Ho
 6 Battersea
 SW11 . . . . .60 A4
 Finsbury EC1 . . . . . . .96 B4
Perham Rd W14 . . .140 B1
Perifield SE21 . . . . . .75 B3
Periton Rd SE9 . . . .66 A4
Perkins Rents
 SW1 . . . . .133 B1
Perkins Sq SE1 . . . .123 A2
Perley Ho **9** E3 . . . .33 B4

Perotti Ho SW6 . . . .59 A4
Perran Rd SE24,
 SW2 . . . . .75 A2
Perren St NW5 . . . .13 A2
Perrers Rd W6 . . . . .39 A2
Perring Est E3 . . . . .33 C4
Perronet Ho SE1 . . .136 C1
Perry Ave W3 . . . . . .28 C3
Perry Ct **5** E14 . . . .41 C1
Perry Ho SW2 . . . . .74 A4
Perrymead St
 SW6 . . . . .166 A3
Perryn Ho W3 . . . . .29 A2
Perryn Rd
 Acton W3 . . . . .28 C2
 1 Bermondsey
 SE16 . . . . .40 A3
Perry's Pl W1 . . . . .105 B2
Perrywood Ho **17**
 E5 . . . . .17 A3
Perseverance Works
 3 E2 . . . . .24 A2 98 B4
Perth Ct **5** SE5 . . . .63 C3
Perth Ho N1 . . . . . . .14 B1
Perth Rd N4 . . . . .5 C3
Petchey Acad The
 E8 . . . . .16 B3
Peter Ave NW10 . . . .9 A1
Peter Best Ho **1**
 E1 . . . . .32 A3
Peterboat Cl SE10 . .43 A2
Peterborough Ct
 EC4 . . . . .107 C1
Peterborough Mews
 SW6 . . . . .165 B3
Peterborough Rd
 SW6 . . . . .58 C4
Peterborough Villas
 SW6 . . . . .166 A3
Peter Butler Ho **10**
 SE1 . . . . .139 B3
Peterchurch Ho
 SE15 . . . . .50 A4
Petergate SW11 . . . .59 B3
Peter Harrison
 Planetarium
Peter Heathfield Ho
 4 E15 . . . . .27 C4
Peter Hills Ho **6**
 SE16 . . . . .153 B4
Peter Hills Sch **20**
 SE16 . . . . .32 C1
Peter Shore Ct **9**
 E1 . . . . .25 C1
Peters Ct W2 . . . . .100 B2
Petersfield Rd W3 . .37 B4
Petersfield Rise
 SW15 . . . . .69 A3
Petersham Ho
 SW7 . . . . .143 B4
Petersham La
 SW7 . . . . .128 C2
Petersham Mews
 SW7 . . . . .129 A1
Petersham Pl
 SW7 . . . . .129 A2

Peter's La EC1 . . . . .108 B4
Peter St W1 . . . . . . .119 B4
Peterstow Cl
 SW19 . . . . .70 A2
Petherton Ct
 NW10 . . . . .22 C4
Petherton Ho N4 . . . .6 B3
Petherton Rd N5 . . .15 B3
Petiver Cl **28** E9 . . .17 B1
Petley Rd W6 . . . . . .47 C3
Peto Pl NW1 . . . . . . .92 B2
Peto St N E16 . . . . .35 B3
Petrel Ct **8** SE21 . . .75 C2
Petre Cl NW2 . . . . . .10 A2
Petrie Mus of
 Egyptian
 Archaeology
 WC1 . . . . .93 B1
Petros Gdns **1**
 NW3 . . . . .11 B2
Petticoat Lane Mkt
 EC2 . . . . .110 C3
Petticoat Sq E1 . . . .110 C2
Petticoat Twr E1 . . .110 C2
Pettiward Cl SW15 . .57 B3
Petty France SW1 . .133 B2
Petty Wales EC3 . . .124 B3
Petworth Ho **16**
 SE22 . . . . .64 A4
Petworth St
 SW11 . . . . .168 B4
Petyt Pl SW3 . . . . . .158 A3
Petyward SW3 . . . . .144 B3
Pevensey Ct
 3 South Acton
 W3 . . . . .37 A4
 West Norwood
 SW16 . . . . .74 C1
Pevensey Ho **5**
 E1 . . . . .33 A4
Peveril Ho SE1 . . . .137 C1
Pewsham Ho N4 . . . .6 B3
Peyton Pl SE10 . . . .52 B3
Pharamond NW2 . . . .9 C2
Phelps Ho **11**
 SW15 . . . . .57 C4
Phelp St SE17 . . . . .48 C4
Phene St SW3 . . . . .158 B4
Philadelphia Ct
 SW10 . . . . .157 A1
Philbeach Gdns
 SW5 . . . . .141 B2
Phil Brown Pl **3**
 SW8 . . . . .61 A4
Philchurch Pl **24**
 E1 . . . . .111 C1
Philia Ho **1** NW1 . . .13 B1
Philip Blairman Ho
 E1 . . . . .24 B1 98 C1
Philip Ct W2 . . . . . .101 B4
Philip Ho **4** NW6 . . .78 A3
Philip Turner Est **28**
 N1 . . . . .17 B1
Philip Wlk SE15 . . . .64 C4
Phillimore Ct W8 . . .127 C3
Phillimore Gardens Cl
 W8 . . . . .127 B2
Phillimore Gdns
 Kensington W8 . . . . .127 B3
 Willesden NW10 . . . . .22 B4
Phillimore Pl W8 . . .127 B3
Phillimore Terr
 W8 . . . . .127 C2
Phillimore Wlk
 W8 . . . . .127 C2
Phillip Ho E1 . . . . . .111 A3

Phillipp St N1 ...24 A4
Philpot La EC3 ...124 A4
Philpot Sq SW6 ...59 A4
Philpot St E1 ...32 A3
Phison Mans 13
E1 ...32 A2
Phipps Ho 18 W12 ...30 A2
Phipp St
EC2 ...24 A1 98 A2
Phoebeth Rd SE4 ...66 C2
Phoenix Cl 18 E8 ...24 B4
Phoenix Ct
4 Brentford
TW8 ...36 A1
2 Deptford SE14 ...51 A4
Millwall E14 ...41 C2
Phoenix High Sch
W12 ...29 C2
Phoenix Ho SW1 ...145 B4
Phoenix Lodge Mans
1 W6 ...39 B2
Phoenix PI WC1 ...95 A3
Phoenix Rd NW1 ...93 B4
Phoenix Sch The 18
NW3 ...11 B2
Phoenix Sec & Prim
Sch 28 E3 ...26 B2
Phoenix St WC2 ...105 C1
Phoenix Wharf Rd
SE1 ...139 A3
Phyllis Hodges Ho
NW1 ...83 B1
Physic PI SW3 ...158 C4
Piccadilly W1 ...118 C2
Piccadilly Arc
SW1 ...118 C2
Piccadilly Cir W1 ...119 B3
Piccadilly Circus Sta
W1 ...119 B3
Piccadilly Ct 3
N7 ...14 B2
Piccadilly PI W1 ...119 A3
Pickard St EC1 ...96 B4
Pickering Cl E9 ...17 C1
Pickering Ho
18 Kensington
W2 ...100 B1
Stoke Newington N4 ...6 C4
Pickering Mews
W2 ...100 B2
Pickering PI SW1 ...119 A2
Pickering St N1 ...86 B4
Pickets St SW17 ...73 A4
Pickfords Wharf
N1 ...86 C1
Pickwick Ho
21 Bermondsey
SE16 ...139 B3
9 Shepherd's Bush
W11 ...30 C1
Pickwick Rd SE21 ...76 A4
Pickwick St SE1 ...136 C3
Pickworth Cl SW8 ...162 B1
Picton Ho 1 SW4 ...74 A4
Picton PI W1 ...103 C1
Picton St SE5 ...48 C3
Picture Ho 8
SW16 ...74 A2
Pied Bull Ct WC1 ...106 B3
Pied Bull Yd WC1 ...106 B3
Pier Head E1 ...32 A1
Pierhead Wharf 7
E1 ...32 A1
Pier Ho SW3 ...158 B3

Piermont Rd SE22 ...65 A2
Pierpoint Bldg 4
E14 ...41 C4
Pierrepoint Rd
W3 ...28 A2
Pierrepoint Row
N1 ...86 A2
Pier St E14 ...42 B2
Pier Terr SW18 ...59 B3
Piggott Ho 2 E2 ...25 C3
Pigott St E14 ...33 C3
Pilgrimage St
SE1 ...137 B3
Pilgrim Ho SE1 ...137 C1
Pilgrims Cloisters 6
SE5 ...49 A3
Pilgrims Ct SE3 ...53 C2
Pilgrim's La NW3 ...11 C4
Pilgrims Mews 12
E14 ...34 C2
Pilgrim's PI 6
NW3 ...11 C4
Pilgrim St EC4 ...108 A1
Pilgrims Way N19 ...4 C3
Pilgrims Way Prim
Sch 22 SE15 ...50 B4
Pilkington Rd 4
SE15 ...50 A1
Pilot Ind Ctr NW10 ...21 A1
Pilsden Cl SW19 ...69 C3
Pilton PI SE17 ...151 A2
Pimlico Sta SW1 ...147 B2
PIMLICO ...146 C1
Pimlico Acad
SW1 ...147 A1
Pimlico Rd SW1 ...145 C2
Pimlico Wlk 1
N1 ...24 A2 98 A4
Pinchin St E1 ...125 C4
Pincombe Ho
SE17 ...151 B2
Pincott PI SE4 ...65 C3
Pindar St EC2 ...110 A4
Pindock Mews W9 ...88 B1
Pine Apple Ct
SW1 ...132 C2
Pine Ave E15 ...19 C3
Pine Cl N19 ...4 B2
Pinedene 2 SE15 ...50 A2
Pinefield Cl E14 ...33 C2
Pine Gr N4, N19 ...5 C2
Pine Ho
Bow E3 ...26 A4
21 Rotherhithe
SE16 ...40 B4
Pinehurst Ct 6
W11 ...31 B3
Pinelands Cl 7
SE3 ...53 B3
Pine Lo SW15 ...58 A1
Pine Rd NW2 ...9 C4
Pines Ct 4 SW19 ...69 C2
Pine St EC1 ...95 B2
Pine Tree Ho SE14 ...50 C3
Pine Tree Way 1
SE13 ...67 A4
Pinewood Ct SW4 ...61 C1
Pinkham Mans
W4 ...36 C1
Pinnace Ho E14 ...42 B3
Pinnacle Ho EC3 ...124 A3
Pinnacle The 7
N1 ...15 C2
Pinner Ct NW8 ...89 B2
Pinner Ho 30 SE5 ...48 B1

Pintail Ct 3 SE8 ...51 B4
Pinter Ho 20 SW9 ...172 B1
Pioneer Cl
18 Bow Comm
E14 ...34 A4
London W12 ...30 A3
Pioneer St SE15 ...49 C2
Pioneer Way W12 ...30 B3
Piper Cl N7 ...14 B3
Pipers Ho SE10 ...42 C1
Pippin Ho 17 W10 ...30 C2
Pirate Castle The
NW1 ...82 A4
Pirbright Rd SW18 ...70 C3
Pitcairn Ho 5 E9 ...17 B1
Pitfield Ho N5 ...15 B3
Pitfield St N1 ...24 A3
Pitman Ho 4 SE8 ...51 C2
Pitman St SE5 ...48 B3
Pitmaston Ho 2
SE13 ...52 B1
Pitsea PI E1 ...32 C3
Pitsea St E1 ...32 C3
Pitt Ho 4 SW11 ...59 C3
Pitt's Head Mews
W1 ...117 C1
Pitt St W8 ...127 C4
Pixley St E14 ...33 B3
Planetree Ct W6 ...39 C2
Plane Tree Ho
SE8 ...51 A4
Plantain PI SE1 ...137 B4
Plantation La EC3 ...124 A4
Plantation The
SE3 ...53 C1
Platehouse The 3
E14 ...42 A1
Platina St EC2 ...97 C2
Plato PI 11 SW6 ...165 A2
Plato Rd SW2 ...62 A3
Platt's La NW3 ...1 C1
Platt St NW1 ...83 B2
Plaxdale Ho SE17 ...152 A3
Playfair St W6 ...39 B1
Playfield Cres
SE22 ...64 B2
Playford Rd
Finsbury Pk N4 ...5 B2
Finsbury Pk N4 ...5 C2
Playhouse Yd EC4 ...108 A1
Playon (Canary Wharf
Indoor Sports)
E14 ...34 A1
Plaza Sh Ctr W1 ...105 A2
Pleasance Rd
SW15 ...57 A2
Pleasance The
SW15 ...57 A3
Pleasant Pl N1 ...15 A1
Pleasant Row NW1 ...82 B3
Plender Ct NW1 ...83 A3
Plender St NW1 ...83 A3
Pleshey Rd N7 ...13 C4
Plevna St E14 ...42 B3
Pleydell Ave W6 ...38 B2
Pleydell Ct EC4 ...107 C1
Pleydell St EC4 ...107 C1
Plimsoll Cl E14 ...34 A3
Plimsoll Rd N4 ...6 A1
Plough Ct EC3 ...123 C4
Plough La SE22 ...64 B1
Ploughmans Cl
NW1 ...83 B4
Plough Mews 19
SW11 ...59 C3

Plough Rd SW11 ...59 C3
Plough St 16 E1 ...111 B2
Plough Terr SW11 ...59 C3
Plough Way SE16 ...41 A2
Plough Yd
EC2 ...24 A1 98 B1
Plover Ho 4 SW9 ...163 B2
Plover Way SE16 ...41 A3
Plowman Ho
SW19 ...69 C2
Plumbers Row E1 ...111 C2
Plumbridge St 7
SE10 ...52 B2
Plume Ho SE10 ...52 A4
Plummer Ct SE13 ...67 A1
Plummer Rd SW4 ...73 C4
Plumtree Ct EC4 ...108 A2
Plymouth Ho 20
SE10 ...52 A2
Plymouth Rd E16 ...35 C4
Plymouth Wharf
E14 ...42 C2
Plympton Ave
NW6 ...10 B1
Plympton PI NW8 ...90 A1
Plympton Rd NW6 ...10 B1
Plympton St NW8 ...90 A1
Pocklington Ct
SW15 ...68 C3
Pocklington Lo 6
W12 ...38 C3
Pocock St SE1 ...136 B4
Podmore Rd SW18 ...59 B3
Poets Corner SW1 ...134 A2
Poets Mews 3
SE24 ...63 A2
Poet's Rd N5 ...15 C3
Point Cl SE10 ...52 B2
Pointer Sch The
SE3 ...53 C3
Pointers Cl E14 ...42 A1
Point Hill SE10 ...52 B2
Point Ho SE10 ...52 B2
Point Pleasant
SW18 ...58 C3
Point Wharf La
TW8 ...44 A3
Poland Ho 3 E15 ...27 C4
Poland St W1 ...105 A1
Polesworth Ho 18
W2 ...31 C4
Polish Inst & Sikorski
Mus SW7 ...129 C3
Polish Univ Abroad 1
W6 ...38 C2
Pollard Cl
Islington N7 ...14 B4
Newham E16 ...35 C2
Pollard Ho N1 ...84 C1
Pollard Row
E2 ...24 C2 99 C4
Pollard St
E2 ...24 C2 99 C4
Pollen St W1 ...104 B1
Pollitt Dr NW8 ...89 C2
Pollock Ho W10 ...23 A1
Pollock's Toy Mus
W1 ...105 A4
Polperro Mans 3
NW6 ...10 C3
Polperro Mews
SE11 ...150 A4
Polygon Ho NW1 ...83 B1
Polygon The
1 Clapham SW4 ...61 B3

Polygon The continued
St John's Wood
NW8 ...79 C4
Pomell Way E1 ...111 A2
Pomeroy Ct W11 ...31 A3
Pomeroy Ho 5 E2 ...25 C3
Pomeroy St SE14 ...50 B2
Pomfret Rd SE5 ...63 A4
Pomoja La N19 ...5 A2
Pomona Ho 10
SE8 ...41 A2
Pond Cl SE3 ...53 C1
Pond Cotts SE21 ...76 A3
Ponder St 5 N7 ...14 B1
Pondfield Ho 4
N5 ...15 B3
Pond Ho SW3 ...144 A3
Pond Mead SE21 ...63 C1
Pond PI SW3 ...144 A3
Pond Rd SE3 ...53 B1
Pond Sq N6 ...3 C3
Pond St NW3 ...12 A3
Ponler St 1 E1 ...32 A3
Ponsard Rd NW10 ...22 A2
Ponsford St E9 ...17 B2
Ponsonby Ho 13
E2 ...25 B3
Ponsonby PI SW1 ...147 C2
Ponsonby Rd
SW15 ...69 A4
Ponsonby Terr
SW1 ...147 C2
Ponton Rd SW8 ...74 C3
Ponton Rd SW8 ...161 C3
Pont St Mews
SW1 ...130 C1
Pont St SW1 ...131 A1
Pontypool PI SE1 ...136 A4
Poole Ct N1 ...16 A1
Poole Ho SE11 ...135 A1
Poole Rd E9 ...17 C2
Pooles Bldgs EC1 ...95 B1
Pooles La SW10 ...156 C1
Pooles Park Prim Sch
N4 ...5 B2
Pooles Pk N4 ...5 B2
Poole St N1 ...87 B3
Pooley Ho E1 ...25 C2
Pool Ho NW8 ...101 C4
Poolmans St SE16 ...40 C4
Poonah St E1 ...32 B3
Pope Ho
7 Bermondsey
SE16 ...40 A2
3 Camberwell SE5 ...48 C3
Pope John Prim Sch
W12 ...30 A2
Pope's Head Alley
EC3 ...109 C1
Pope's La W5 ...36 A1
Pope's Rd SW2 ...62 C4
Pope St SE1 ...138 B3
Popham Ct N16 ...7 A1
Popham Gdns
TW9 ...55 A4
Popham Rd N1 ...86 C4
Popham St
Shoreditch N1 ...86 C4
POPLAR ...33 C3
Poplar Bath St 11
E14 ...34 A2
Poplar Bsns Pk
E14 ...34 B2

Poplar Cl E9 . . . . 18 B3
Poplar Ct 4 SW16 . . 74 B1
Poplar Gr W6 . . . . . . 39 B4
Poplar High St
　E14 . . . . 34 A2
Poplar Ho
　Brockley SE4 . . . . . . 66 B3
　19 Rotherhithe
　SE16 . . . . 40 C4
Poplar Mews 4
　W12 . . . . 30 B1
Poplar Pl W2 . . . . . 114 B4
Poplar Rd SE24 . . . 63 B3
Poplars The W5 . . 73 C3
Poplar Wlk SE24 . . 63 B3
Poppins Ct EC4 . . 108 A1
Porchester Ct W2 100 B1
Porchester Gate
　W2 . . . . 114 C3
Porchester Gdn Mews
　W2 . . . . 100 B1
Porchester Ho 3
　E1 . . . . 32 A3
Porchester Mews
　W2 . . . . 100 B2
Porchester Pl W2 102 B1
Porchester Rd
　W2 . . . . 100 B2
Porchester Sq
　W2 . . . . 100 B2
Porchester Terr
　W2 . . . . 114 C4
Porchester Terr N
　W2 . . . . 100 B2
Porden Rd SW2 . . . 62 B3
Porland Ct SE1 . . . 137 B2
Porlock Ho 5
　SE26 . . . . 76 C1
Porlock St SE1 . . . 137 C4
Porson Ct SE13 . . . 67 A4
Portal Cl SE27 . . . . 74 C1
Portal Way W3 . . . . 28 C4
Portbury Cl 17
　SE15 . . . . 49 C2
Portchester Cl
　SE24 . . . . 63 C3
Portelet Ct 1 N1 . . 24 A4
Portelet Rd E1 . . . . 25 C2
Porten Hos W14 . . 126 A1
Porten Rd W14 . . . 126 A1
Porter Sq 1 N19 . . . 5 A3
Porter St
　Borough The SE1 . . 123 A2
　Marylebone W1 . . . 103 A4
Porteus Rd W2 . . . 101 A4
Portfleet Pl 24 N1 . . 24 A4
Portgate Cl W9 . . . 23 B1
Port Ho 6 SW11 . . 59 B4
Port House The 6
　E14 . . . . 42 A4
Portia Way E3 . . . . 26 B1
Porticos The SW3 157 B3
Portinscale Rd
　SW15 . . . . 58 B2
Portishead Ho 25
　W2 . . . . 31 C4
Portland Ave N16 . . 7 B4
Portland Ct
　7 De Beauvoir Town
　N1 . . . . 16 A1
　1 Deptford SE14 . . . 51 A4

Portland Gr SW8 . 172 C4
Portland Ho 19
　SW2 . . . . 74 C3
Portland Hospl for
　Women & Children
　W1 . . . . 92 B1
Portland Mews
　W1 . . . . 105 A1
Portland Pl W1 . . . 104 B3
Portland Place Sch
　W1 . . . . 104 B4
Portland Rd
　Notting Hill
　W11 . . . . . 31 A1 112 B2
　Notting Hill
　W11 . . . . . 31 A2 112 A3
Portland Rise N4 . . . 6 B3
Portland Sq 4 E1 . . 32 A1
Portland St SE17 . . 151 B1
Portland Village
　W6 . . . . 39 B3
Portman Ave
　SW14 . . . . 55 C4
Portman Cl W1 . . . 103 B2
Portman Gate
　NW1 . . . . 90 B1
Portman Hts 1
　NW3 . . . . 1 C1
Portman Mews S
　W1 . . . . 103 B1
Portman Pl E2 . . . . 25 B2
Portman Sq W1 . . . 103 B2
Portman St W1 . . . 103 B1
Portman The NW11 . . 1 C4
Portman Twrs
　W1 . . . . 103 A2
Portnall Rd W9 . . . . 23 B2
Portobello Ct Est
　W11 . . . . 31 B3
Portobello Mews
　W11 . . . . . 31 B2 113 B3
Portobello Rd
　W11 . . . . . 31 B2 113 A4
Portobello Road Mkt
　W10 . . . . 31 A4
Portpool La EC1 . . . 107 B4
Portree St E14 . . . . 34 C3
Port Royal Pl 3
　N16 . . . . 16 A3
Portsea Hall 4 W2 . . 102 B1
Portsea Ho 4
　SW15 . . . . 69 A3
Portsea Mews
　W2 . . . . 102 B1
Portsea Pl W2 . . . 102 B1
Portslade Rd SW8 170 C2
Portsmouth Rd
　SW15 . . . . 69 B4
Portsmouth St
　WC2 . . . . 107 A1
Portsoken St E1 . . . 125 A4
Portswood Pl
　SW15 . . . . 56 B1
Portugal St WC2 . . 107 A1
Poseidon Ct 9
　E14 . . . . 41 C2
Postern The EC2 . . 109 A3
Post Office Way
　SW8 . . . . 161 B2
Potier St SE1 . . . . 137 C1
Potterne Cl 5
　SW19 . . . . 69 C4
Potters Cl 5 SE15 . . 49 A3
Potters Fields
　SE1 . . . . 124 B1

Potters Lo E14 . . . . 42 B1
Potters Rd SW6 . . 166 C1
Pottery La
　W11 . . . . . 31 A1 112 B2
Pottery Rd TW8 . . . 44 A4
Pottery St SE16 . . . 40 A4
Pott St E2 . . . . 25 A2
Poullett Ho SE5 . . . 50 A3
Poulton Cl E8 . . . . . 17 A2
Poultry EC2 . . . . 109 B1
Pound La NW10 . . . . 8 C2
Pountney Rd
　SW11 . . . . 60 C4
Povey Ho
　Tulse Hill SW2 . . . . 62 C1
　Walworth SE17 . . . 152 A3
Powell's Wlk W4 . . . 46 B4
Powergate Bsns Pk
　NW10 . . . . 20 C2
Power Ho 13 TW9 . . 44 C2
Power Ho The W4 . . 38 B2
Power Rd W4 . . . . . 36 C2
Powerscroft Rd
　E5 . . . . 17 B4
Powis Gdns
　Golders Green
　NW11 . . . . 1 B4
　Notting Hill W11 . . 31 B3
Powis Ho WC2 . . . . 106 B2
Powis Mews W11 . . 31 B3
Powis Pl WC1 . . . . . 94 B1
Powis Rd E3 . . . . 27 A2
Powis Sq W11 . . . . . 31 B3
Powis Terr W11 . . . 31 B3
Powlesland Ct 4
　E14 . . . . 33 A3
Powlett Ho NW1 . . . 13 A2
Powlett Pl NW1 . . . 13 A1
Pownall Rd E8 . . . . 24 C4
Pownall Ho 4
　SW15 . . . . 167 C2
Poynder Ct 3 N7 . . . 14 A3
Poynders Ct 5
　SW4 . . . . 61 B1
Poynders Gdns
　SW12 . . . . 73 B4
Poynders Rd SW12,
　SW4 . . . . 73 C4
Poynings Rd N19 . . . 4 B1
Poynter Ho
　Paddington NW8 . . . 89 B2
　7 Shepherd's Bush
　W11 . . . . 30 C2
Poyntz Rd SW11 . . 168 C1
Poyser St E2 . . . . . . 25 A3
Praed Mews W2 . . 101 C2
Praed St W2 . . . . . 101 C2
Prague Pl SW2 . . . . 62 A2
Prah Rd N4 . . . . 5 C2
Prairie St SW8 . . . 170 A1
Pratt Mews NW1 . . . 82 C3
Pratt St NW1 . . . . . . 82 C4
Pratt Wlk SE1;
　SE11 . . . . 149 A4
Preachers Ct EC1 . . 96 B1
Prebend Gdns W4,
　W6 . . . . 38 B2
Prebend Mans 4
　W4 . . . . 38 B2
Precinct The
　Islington N1 . . . . . . 86 C3
　Islington N5 . . . . . . 15 A2
Premier Corner
　NW6 . . . . 23 B3
Premier Ho 25 N1 . . 15 A1

Premier Park Rd
　NW10 . . . . 20 A3
Premier Pk NW10 . . 20 A3
Premier Pl 17 E14 . . 33 C2
Prendergast Ho 7
　SW4 . . . . 73 C3
Prendergast Ladywell
　Fields Coll SE4 . . . 66 C2
Prendergast Sch
　SE4 . . . . 66 C4
Prescot St E1 . . . . . 125 A4
Prescott Ho 13
　SE17 . . . . 48 A4
Prescott Pl SW4 . . . 61 C3
Presentation Mews
　SW2 . . . . 74 B2
President Dr E1 . . . . 32 A1
President Ho EC1 . . . 96 B3
President St EC1 . . . 96 C4
Prestage Way E3 . . 34 B2
Prested Rd SW11 . . 60 A3
Preston Cl SE1 . . . . 152 A4
Preston Gdns NW10 . . 8 A2
Preston Ho
　Bermondsey SE1 . . 138 C2
　Walworth SE1 . . . . 152 A4
Preston Pl
　Richmond TW10 . . . 54 A2
　Willesden NW2 . . . 8 C2
Preston's Rd E14 . . 34 B1
Prestwich Terr
　SW4 . . . . 61 C2
Prestwood Ho 3
　SE16 . . . . 40 A3
Prestwood St N1 . . . 87 A1
Priam Ho 17 E2 . . . . 25 A3
Price Cl SW17 . . . . . 72 B1
Price Ho N1 . . . . 86 C3
Prices Ct SW11 . . . 59 C4
Price's St SE1 . . . . 122 B2
Price's Yd N1 . . . . . 85 B3
Prichard Ct
　Battersea SW11 . . 167 C3
　Islington N7 . . . . . . 14 B3
Prideaux Ho WC1 . . 95 A4
Prideaux Pl
　Acton W3 . . . . 28 C2
　St Pancras WC1 . . . 95 A4
Prideaux Rd SW9 . . 62 A4
Pridie Ct N1 . . . . 85 C2
Priestley Ho 2
　Camden Town
　NW5 . . . . 13 A2
　St Luke's EC1 . . . . . 97 A2
Priestley Way
　NW2 . . . . 9 A2
Priestman Point 23
　E3 . . . . 27 A2
Priests Bridge
　SW15 . . . . 58 A3
Priests Ct EC2 . . . . 108 C2
Prima Rd SW9 . . . . 163 B2
Primrose Cl 6 E3 . . 26 C3
Primrose Ct
　2 Child's Hill NW2 . . 1 B1
　1 Primrose Hill NW8 . . 80 C3
　11 Streatham
　SW12 . . . . 73 A4
Primrose Gdns
　NW3 . . . . 12 A2
PRIMROSE HILL 12 B1
Primrose Hill EC4 . . 107 C1
Primrose Hill Ct
　NW3 . . . . 12 B1
Primrose Hill Rd NW1,
　NW3 . . . . 12 B1

Primrose Hill Sch
　NW1 . . . . 81 C4
Primrose Hill Studios
　NW1 . . . . 81 B4
Primrose Ho
　7 Peckham SE15 . . 49 C2
　1 Richmond TW9 . . 44 C2
Primrose Mans
　SW11 . . . . 169 B4
Primrose Mews 9
　NW1 . . . . 12 B1
Primrose Sq E9 . . . 25 B4
Primrose St EC2 . . 110 B4
Primrose Wlk 8
　SE14 . . . . 51 A3
Primula St W12 . . . 29 C3
Prince Albert Ct
　NW8 . . . . 80 C3
Prince Albert Rd
　NW8 . . . . 80 C3
Prince Arthur Ct 18
　NW3 . . . . 11 B4
Prince Arthur Mews
　NW3 . . . . 11 B4
Prince Arthur Rd
　NW3 . . . . 11 C3
Prince Charles Rd
　SE3 . . . . 53 B2
Prince Consort Ho
　SE1 . . . . 148 C2
Prince Consort Rd
　SW7 . . . . 129 B2
Princedale Rd
　W11 . . . . . 31 A1 112 B2
Prince Edward Mans
　W2 . . . . . 31 C3 113 C4
Prince Edward Rd
　E9 . . . . 18 B2
Prince George Rd
　N16 . . . . 16 A4
Princelet St E1 . . . 111 A4
Prince of Orange La
　8 SE10 . . . . 52 B3
Prince of Wales Dr
　SW11 . . . . 169 B4
Prince of Wales Mans
　Battersea SW11 . . 169 C4
　Clapham SW4 . . . . . 60 B3
Prince of Wales Pas
　NW1 . . . . 92 C3
Prince of Wales Rd
　Blackheath Vale
　SE3 . . . . 53 B2
　Camden Town NW5 . . 12 C2
Prince of Wales Terr
　Chiswick W4 . . . . . . 38 A1
　Kensington W8 . . . 128 B3
Prince Regent Ct 2
　SE16 . . . . 33 A1
Prince Regent Mews
　NW1 . . . . 92 C3
Princes Arc SW1 . . 119 A2
Princes Ave W3 . . . 36 C3
Princes Cir WC2 . . 106 A2
Princes Cl N4 . . . . . 6 A3
Princes Coll WC1 . . 106 A2
Princes Court Bsns
　Ctr 14 E1 . . . . 32 A3
Princes Ct
　Brondesbury
　NW2 . . . . 10 A3
　Hampstead NW3 . . . 11 C4
　Stepney E1 . . . . 32 A2
Prince's Ct SE16 . . 41 B3
Princes Gate SW7 129 C3

Prince's Gate
SW7 . . . . **130** A3
Princes Gate Ct
SW7 . . . . **129** C3
Princes Gate Mews
SW7 . . . . **129** C2
Princes Gdns
SW7 . . . . **129** C2
Princes Ho
W11 . . . . . **31** C2 **113** B3
Prince's Mews
1 Hammersmith
W6 . . . . **39** A1
Kensington W2 . . . **114** A4
Princes Pl
Notting Hill
W11 . . . . . **31** A1 **112** A2
St James SW1 . . . . **119** A2
Princes Rd
Kew TW9 . . . . **44** B2
Richmond TW10 . . . **54** B2
Prince's Rd SW14 . . **55** C4
Princes Rise SE13 . . **52** B1
Princes Riverside Rd
7 SE16 . . . . **32** C1
**Princess Alexandra
School of Nursing**
8 E1 . . . . **32** A4
Princess Alice Ho 1
W10 . . . . **22** B1
Princess Beatrice Ho
SW10 . . . . **142** A1
Princess Cres N4 . . . . **6** A2
Princess Ct
Hampstead NW6 . . . . **11** A1
Kensington W2 . . . . **114** B4
Marylebone W1 . . . **102** C3
**Princess Frederica CE
Jun & Inf Sch**
NW10 . . . . **22** B3
**Princess Grace Hospl
The** W1 . . . . **91** B1
Princess Louise Cl
W2 . . . . **101** C4
Princess Mary Ho
SW1 . . . . **147** C3
**Princess May Prim
Sch 16** N16 . . . . . **16** B4
Princess May Rd
N16 . . . . **16** A4
Princess Mews
NW3 . . . . **11** C2
Prince's Sq W2 . . . **114** A4
Princess Rd
Camden Town
NW1 . . . . **82** A3
Paddington NW6 . . . **23** C3
Princess St SE1 . . . **136** C1
Princes St W1 . . . . **104** B1
Prince's St
City of London
EC2 . . . . **109** B1
Richmond TW10,
TW9 . . . . **54** A2
Prince St SE8 . . . . **51** B4
Princes Way
Acton W3 . . . . **36** C3
Putney SW15,
SW19 . . . . **70** A3
Princes Yd
W11 . . . . . **31** A1 **112** B1
Princethorpe Ho
W2 . . . . **100** A4
Princeton Ct 12
SW15 . . . . **57** C4

Princeton Mans
WC1 . . . . **106** C3
Princeton St WC1 . . **106** C3
Principal Sq E9 . . . . **17** C3
Printers Mews E3 . . **26** A4
Printer St EC4 . . . . . **107** C2
Printing House Yd 16
E2 . . . . . **24** A2 **98** B3
Printon Ho 18 E3 . . . . **33** B4
Print Village Ind Est
SE15 . . . . **49** B1
Prior Bolton St N1 . . **15** A2
Prioress Ho 2 E3 . . . **27** A2
Prioress Rd SE27 . . . **75** A1
Prioress St SE1 . . . **137** C1
Priors Lo 4 TW10 . . **54** A1
Prior St SE10 . . . . . **52** B3
**Prior Weston Prim
Sch** EC1 . . . . **97** A1
Priory Ave W4 . . . . . **38** A3
Priory Ct
City of London
EC4 . . . . **108** B1
Homerton E9 . . . . . . **17** C3
Nunhead SE15 . . . . **65** B3
Roehampton SW15 . . . **56** B3
South Lambeth
SW8 . . . . **171** C4
Priory Gdns
Barnes SW13 . . . . . . **56** B4
6 Chiswick W4 . . . . **38** A2
Priory Gn N1 . . . . . . **84** C2
Priory Gr SW8 . . . . **172** A3
Priory Ho
Clerkenwell EC1 . . . **96** A2
Pimlico SW1 . . . . . **147** B2
Spitalfields E1 . . . . **110** C4
**Priory Hospl Grange
Roehampton**
SW15 . . . . **56** B3
Priory Hts N1 . . . . . **85** A2
Priory La SW15 . . . . **56** B2
Priory Lo 4 W4 . . . **36** C1
Priory Mans
17 Maitland Pk
NW3 . . . . **12** B2
South Kensington
SW10 . . . . **143** A1
Priory Park Rd
NW6 . . . . **23** B4
Priory Rd
Bedford Pk W4 . . . . **37** C3
Hampstead NW6 . . . **11** A1
Richmond TW9 . . . . **44** C3
Priory St 18 E3 . . . . **27** A2
Priory Terr NW6 . . . **78** A4
Priory The SE1 . . . **136** A3
Priory Wlk SW10 . . **143** A1
Pritchard Ho 8
Pritchard's Rd E2 . . **24** C4
Priter Rd SE16 . . . . **139** C1
Priter Road Hostel 14
SE16 . . . . **139** C1
Probert Rd SW2 . . . **62** C2
Probyn Ho SW1 . . . **147** C4
Probyn Rd SW2 . . . . **75** A2
Procter Ho 19 SE5 . . . **48** C3
Procter St WC1 . . . **106** C3
Proctor Ho 5
SE1 . . . . **153** B1
Prome Ho 3 N16 . . . . **15** C4
**Promenade Approach
Rd** W4 . . . . **46** A3
Promenade The
W4 . . . . **46** A2

Prospect Cotts
SW18 . . . . **58** C3
Prospect Ho
1 Dalston E8 . . . . **16** B2
Islington N1 . . . . . . **85** B1
Newington SE11 . . **136** B1
14 North Kensington
W10 . . . . **30** B3
**Prospect House Sch
11** SW15 . . . . **69** C4
Prospect Pl
2 Child's Hill NW2 . . . **1** B1
3 Chiswick W4 . . . . **37** C1
6 Deptford SE8 . . . . **51** B4
12 Hampstead
NW3 . . . . **11** B4
7 Lower Holloway
N7 . . . . **14** A4
Wapping E1 . . . . . . **32** B1
Prospect Quay
SW18 . . . . **58** C3
Prospect Rd NW2 . . . **1** C1
Prospect St SE16 . . . **40** A4
Prospect Wharf
E1 . . . . **32** B2
Prospero Rd N19 . . . **4** C3
Prothero Rd SW6 . . **154** C2
Proud Ho 10 E1 . . . **32** A3
Prout Gr NW10 . . . . . **8** B4
Provence St N1 . . . . **86** C2
Providence Ct
Islington N1 . . . . . . **86** A3
Mayfair W1 . . . . . **117** C4
Providence Pl N1 . . **86** A3
Providence Row
N1 . . . . **84** C1
Providence Row Cl 30
E2 . . . . **25** A2
Providence Sq 2
SE1 . . . . **139** B4
Providence Yd 1
E2 . . . . . **24** C2 **99** B4
Provost Ct NW3 . . . **12** B1
Provost Rd NW3 . . . **12** B1
Provost St N1 . . . . . **97** B4
Prowse Pl NW1 . . . . **13** B1
Prudent Pas EC2 . . **109** A1
Prusom's Island 8
E1 . . . . **32** B1
Prusom St E1 . . . . . **32** A1
Pryors The NW3 . . . . . **2** C1
Pudding La EC3 . . . **123** C4
Pudding Mill La
E15 . . . . **27** A4
Pudding Mill Lane Sta
E15 . . . . **27** A4
Puddle Dock EC4 . . **122** B4
Pugin Ct N1 . . . . . . **14** C1
Pulborough Rd
SW18 . . . . **70** B4
Pulham Ho SW8 . . . **162** C1
Pullman Ct SW2 . . . **74** B3
Pullman Gdns
SW15 . . . . **57** B1
Pulross Rd SW9 . . . **62** B4
Pulteney Cl 20 E3 . . **26** B4
Pulteney Terr N1 . . . **85** A4
Pulton Ho SE4 . . . . **66** A3
Pulton Pl SW6 . . . . **155** B1
Puma Ct E1 . . . . . . **110** C4
Pump Ct EC4 . . . . . **107** B1
Pump House Cl

**Pumphouse
Educational Mus The**
SE16 . . . . **33** A1
Pump House Gall
SW11 . . . . **159** B1
Pumping Ho 8
E14 . . . . **34** C2
Pumping Station Rd
W4 . . . . **46** A4
Pump La SE14 . . . . **50** B3
Punderson's Gdns
E2 . . . . **25** A2
Purbeck Ho SW8 . . **162** C1
Purbrook Est SE1 . . **138** B3
Purbrook Ho 2
SW15 . . . . **69** A3
Purbrook St SE1 . . . **138** B2
Purcell Cres SW6 . . **154** A2
Purcell Ho SW10 . . **157** B3
Purcell Mews 2
NW10 . . . . **8** A1
Purcell St N1 . . . . . **24** A3
Purchese St NW1 . . **83** C1
Purday Ho 4 W10 . . **23** B2
Purdon Ho 11
SE15 . . . . **49** C2
Purdy St E3 . . . . . . **27** A1
Purley Ave NW2 . . . . **1** A2
Purley Pl N1 . . . . . . **15** A1
Purser Ho 3 SW2 . . **62** C1
Pursers Cross Rd
SW6 . . . . **165** A4
Pusey Ho 20 E14 . . **33** C3
Puteaux Ho 6 E2 . . **25** C3
PUTNEY **57** B2
Putney Bridge App
SW6 . . . . **58** A4
Putney Bridge Rd
SW15 . . . . **58** B3
Putney Bridge Sta
SW6 . . . . **58** B3
Putney Comm
SW15 . . . . **57** B4
**Putney Exchange
Shopping Ctr**
SW15 . . . . **58** B2
PUTNEY HEATH **57** B1
Putney Heath
SW15 . . . . **57** C2
Putney Heath La
SW15 . . . . **57** C1
Putney High Sch
SW15 . . . . **58** A3
Putney High St
SW15 . . . . **58** B2
Putney Hill
7 Putney SW15 . . . . **69** B4
Putney SW15 . . . . . **57** C2
Putney L Ctr SW15 . . **57** C2
Putney Park Ave
SW15 . . . . **56** C2
Putney Park La
SW15 . . . . **57** A3
Putney Park Sch
SW15 . . . . **57** A2
Putney Pier SW15 . . **58** A4
**Putney School of Art
& Design** SW15 . . **58** A3
PUTNEY VALE **68** C1
Putney Wharf Twr
SW15 . . . . **58** B4
Pykewell Lo 13 E8 . . . **16** C3
Pylon Trad Est
E16 . . . . **34** C4

Pymers Mead
SE21 . . . . **75** B3
Pynfolds SE16 . . . . . **40** A4
Pynnersmead
SE24 . . . . **63** B2
Pyrland Ho 1
SW9 . . . . **63** A3
Pyrland Rd
Richmond TW10 . . . **54** B1
Stoke Newington
N5 . . . . **15** C3
Pyrmont Gr SE27 . . . **75** A1
Pyrmont Rd W4 . . . . **44** C4
Pytchley Rd SE22 . . **64** A4

Q

Quadrangle Cl
SE1 . . . . **152** A4
Quadrangle The
Chelsea SW10 . . . . **167** A4
Fulham SW6 . . . . . **164** A1
Herne Hill SE24 . . . **63** B2
3 North Kensington
W12 . . . . **30** B3
Paddington W2 . . . **102** A2
Quadrant Arc W1 . . **119** A3
Quadrant Bsns Ctr
NW6 . . . . **23** A4
Quadrant Gr NW5 . . **12** B3
Quadrant The
4 Kensal Green
W10 . . . . **22** C2
Richmond TW9 . . . . **54** A3
Quaker Ct 1 EC1 . . . **97** A2
Quaker St
E1 . . . . . **24** B1 **98** C1
Quality Ct WC2 . . . **107** B2
Quantock Ho N16 . . . **7** B3
Quantock Mews 3
SE15 . . . . **49** C1
Quarrendon St
SW6 . . . . **165** C2
Quarry Rd SW18 . . **59** B1
Quarterdeck The
E14 . . . . **41** C4
Quayside Ct 6
SE16 . . . . **32** C1
**Quebec & Crown
Wharves** E14 . . . . . **33** B3
Quebec Ind Est
SE16 . . . . **41** A3
Quebec Mews
W1 . . . . **103** A1
Quebec Way SE16 . . **41** A4
Quebec Wharf 12
E8 . . . . **24** A4
Quedgeley Ct 3
SE15 . . . . **49** B4
**Queen Alexandra
Mans** WC1 . . . . **94** A3
Queen Anne Mews
W1 . . . . **104** B3
Queen Anne Rd
E9 . . . . **17** C2
Queen Anne's Gate
SW1 . . . . **133** B3
Queen Anne's Gdns
Bedford Pk W4 . . . . **38** A3
Ealing W5 . . . . **36** A4
Queen Anne's Gr
Bedford Pk W4 . . . . **38** A3
Ealing W5 . . . . **36** A4

Queen Anne St
W1 . . . . **104** A3
Queen Anne Terr 9
E1 . . . . .32 A2
Queen Caroline St
W6 . . . . .39 B1
Queen Charlotte's &
Chelsea Hospl
W12 . . . . .29 C3
Queen Ct WC1 . . . . .94 B1
Queen Elizabeth Ct 5
N1 . . . . .15 C2
Queen Elizabeth Hall
& Purcell Room
SE1 . . . . **121** A2
Queen Elizabeth Ho
SW12 . . . . .72 C4
Queen Elizabeth II
Con Ctr SW1 . . . . **133** C3
Queen Elizabeth II
Jubilee Sch 5
W9 . . . . .23 B1
Queen Elizabeth's Cl
N16 . . . . .6 C2
Queen Elizabeth's Coll
15 SE10 . . . . .52 B3
Queen Elizabeth St
SE1 . . . . **138** C4
Queen Elizabeth's Wlk
N16 . . . . .6 C2
Queen Elizabeth Wlk
SW13 . . . . .47 A2
Queenhithe EC4 . . **123** A4
Queen Margaret Flats
22 E2 . . . . .25 A2
Queen Margarets Ct
N1 . . . . .16 A3
Queen Margaret's Gr
N1 . . . . .16 A3
Queen Mary's Gdns
NW1 . . . . **91** B3
Queen Mary's Univ
Hospl SW15 . . . . . .56 C1
Queen Mary, Univ of
London E1 . . . . .26 A1
Queen Mother Sp Ctr
SW1 . . . . **146** C4
Queen of Denmark Ct
SE16 . . . . .41 B3
Queen St Pl EC4 . . **123** A4
Queensberry Mews W
SW7 . . . . **143** B4
Queensberry Pl
SW7 . . . . **143** B4
Queensberry Way
SW7 . . . . **143** B4
Queensborough Mews
W2 . . . . **114** C4
Queensborough Pas
W2 . . . . **114** C4
Queensborough Terr
W2 . . . . **114** B4
Queensbridge Ct 1
E2 . . . . .24 B3
Queensbridge Inf Sch
15 E8 . . . . .16 B1
Queensbridge Rd
Dalston E8, E2 . . . . .16 B1
Shoreditch E2, E8 . . .24 B4
Queensbury St 22
N1 . . . . .15 B1
Queen's CE Prim Sch
The TW9 . . . . .44 C2
Queen's Cir SW11 **160** A1

Queen's Club Gdns
W14 . . . . **154** B4
Queen's Club The
W14 . . . . **140** B1
Queen's Coll W1 . . **104** A3
Queen's Coll Prep Sch
W1 . . . . **104** A4
Queens Cres TW10 . .54 A2
Queen's Cres NW5 . .12 C2
Queens Ct
Battersea SW11 . . . **170** A4
Camberwell SE5 . . . .49 A1
4 Limehouse E14 . . .33 B2
Queen's Ct
Barnes SW13 . . . . . .56 C4
Kensington W2 . . . . **114** B3
3 Richmond TW10 . .54 B1
St John's Wood
NW8 . . . . .79 B2
Queensdale W11 . . .30 C1
Queensdale Cres
W11 . . . . .30 C1
Queensdale Pl
W11 . . . . . .31 A1 **112** A1
Queensdale Rd
Notting Hill W11 . . . .30 C1
Notting Hill
W11 . . . . . .31 A1 **112** A1
Queensdale Wlk
W11 . . . . . .31 A1 **112** A1
Queensdown Rd
E5 . . . . .17 A4
Queen's Dr N4 . . . . . .6 A2
Queen's Elm Par
SW3 . . . . **143** C2
Queen's Elm Sq
SW3 . . . . **143** C1
Queen's Gallery
SW1 . . . . **132** B3
Queen's Gate
SW7 . . . . **129** A2
Queensgate Gdns
SW15 . . . . .57 A3
Queen's Gate Gdns
SW7 . . . . **129** A1
Queensgate Ho 34
E3 . . . . .26 B3
Queen's Gate Jun Sch
SW7 . . . . **143** B4
Queen's Gate Mews
SW7 . . . . **129** A2
Queensgate Pl 10
NW6 . . . . .10 C1
Queen's Gate Pl
SW7 . . . . **129** A1
Queen's Gate Pl Mews
SW7 . . . . **129** A1
Queen's Gate Terr
SW7 . . . . **129** A2
Queens Gate Villas
E9 . . . . .18 A1
Queen's Gdns W2 **114** C4
Queen's Gr NW8 . . . .79 C3
Queen's Head Pas
EC2 . . . . **108** C2
Queen's Head St
N1 . . . . .86 B3
Queen's Head Yd
SE1 . . . . **123** B1
Queens Ho 1
SE17 . . . . .48 C4
Queen's House The
SE10 . . . . .52 C4
Queensland Rd
N7 . . . . .14 C4

Queens Manor Sch
SW6 . . . . .47 C3
Queens Mans
NW6 . . . . .11 A3
Queen's Mans W6 . . .39 C2
Queensmead NW8 . .79 C4
Queensmere Cl
SW19 . . . . .69 C2
Queensmere Ct
SW13 . . . . .46 C4
Queensmere Rd
SW19 . . . . .69 C2
Queen's Mews
W2 . . . . **114** A4
Queensmill Rd
SW6 . . . . .47 C3
Queensmill Sch
SW6 . . . . **165** C1
Queens Par 3 NW2 . .9 B2
Queens Park Com Sch
NW6 . . . . .22 C4
Queens Park Ct 5
W10 . . . . .22 C2
Queen's Park Prim
Sch 20 W10 . . . . . .23 A1
Queen's Park Sta
NW6 . . . . .23 B3
Queen Sq WC1 . . . **106** B4
Queen's Quay EC4 **123** A4
Queen's Rd
Mortlake SW14 . . . . .55 C4
New Cross Gate SE14,
SE15 . . . . .50 B2
Richmond TW10 . . . .54 B1
Queen's Ride
SW13 . . . . .57 A4
Queen's Rise
TW10 . . . . .54 B1
Queen's Road Sta
SE15 . . . . .50 B2
Queen's Row SE17 . .48 C4
Queen St
City of London
EC4 . . . . **123** A4
Mayfair W1 . . . . . . **118** A2
Queens Terr NW8 . . .79 B2
Queenstown Mews
SW8 . . . . **170** A3
Queenstown Rd
SW8 . . . . **160** A2
Queenstown Road
(Battersea) Sta
SW8 . . . . **170** B4
Queensville Rd SW12,
SW4 . . . . .73 C4
Queensway W2 . . . **114** B4
Queensway Sta
W2 . . . . **114** B3
Queenswood Ct 7
SW4 . . . . .62 A2
Queens Yd E9 . . . . .18 C2
Queen's Yd WC1 . . . .93 A1
Queen Victoria Meml
SW1 . . . . **132** C4
Queen Victoria St
EC4 . . . . **122** C4
Queen Victoria Terr
12 E1 . . . . **125** C2
Quelch Ho 2 N19 . .13 C3
Quemerford Rd
N7 . . . . .14 B3
Quendon Ho 9
W10 . . . . .22 B1
Quenington Ct 5
SE15 . . . . .49 B4

Quenington Mans
SW6 . . . . **164** C4
Quennel Ho 7
SW12 . . . . .73 B4
Querrin St SW6 . . . **166** C1
Quested Ct 27 E8 . .17 A3
Quex Mews NW6 . . .23 C4
Quex Rd NW6 . . . . .23 C4
Quick Rd W4 . . . . . .38 A1
Quick St N1 . . . . . . .86 B1
Quick Street Mews
N1 . . . . .86 A1
Quickswood NW3 . .12 A1
Quill La SW15 . . . . .57 C3
Quill St N4 . . . . .5 C1
Quilp St SE1 . . . . . **136** C4
Quilter St
E2 . . . . .24 C2 **99** B4
Quilting Ct 28
SE16 . . . . .40 C4
Quince Rd SE13 . . . .52 A1
Quintin Ct W4 . . . . .45 B3
Quintin Kynaston Sch
NW8 . . . . .79 B3
Quintock Ho 2
TW9 . . . . .45 A2
Quinton Ho SW8 . . **162** A2
Quinton St SW18 . . .71 B2
Quixley St 1 E14 . . .34 C2
Quorn Rd SE22 . . . .64 A4

R

Rabbit Row
W8 . . . . .31 C1 **113** C2
Raby St E14 . . . . . . .33 A3
Racine 15 SE5 . . . . .49 A2
Racton Rd SW6 . . . **155** B3
Radbourne Ct E5 . . .17 C4
Radbourne Rd
SW12 . . . . .73 C4
Radcliff Bldg EC1 . **107** B4
Radcliffe Ave
NW10 . . . . .21 C3
Radcliffe Coll
Marylebone W1 . . . **104** C1
Soho W1 . . . . **105** B2
Radcliffe Ho 10
SE16 . . . . .40 A2
Radcliffe Path 5
SW8 . . . . **170** B1
Radcliffe Rd SE1 . . **138** B2
Radcliffe Sq SW15 . .57 C1
Radcot St SE11 . . . **149** C1
Raddington Rd
W10 . . . . .31 A4
Radford Ho
7 Bow Comm
E14 . . . . .34 A4
Islington N7 . . . . . . .14 B3
Radford Rd SE13 . . .67 B1
Radipole Rd SW6 . **164** C4
Radland Rd E16 . . . .35 C3
Radlett Pl NW8 . . . .80 A4
Radley Ct 2 SE16 . .40 C4
Radley Ho NW1 . . . .90 C2
Radley Lo 30
SW19 . . . . .69 C3
Radley Mews W8 . . **127** C1
Radley Terr 1
E16 . . . . .35 B4
Radnor Lo W2 . . . . **101** C1
Radnor Mews W2 . **101** C1
Radnor Pl W2 . . . . **102** A1

Radnor Rd
Kensal Rise NW6 . . . .23 A4
Peckham SE15 . . . . .49 B3
Radnor St EC1 . . . . **97** A3
Radnor Terr W14 . . **140** C4
Radnor Wlk W10,20 . .20 A1
Radnor Wlk
Chelsea SW3 . . . . . **144** C1
21 Millwall E14 . . . . .41 C2
Radstock St
SW11 . . . . **158** A1
Radway Ho 38 W2 . .31 C4
Radwell Ho SW2 . . . .62 C2
Raebarn Ct 6
SW16 . . . . .74 A1
Raeburn St SW2 . . . .62 A3
Ragged School Mus
E3 . . . . .33 A4
Raglan Ct SW9 . . . . .62 C4
Raglan St NW5 . . . . .13 A2
Ragley Cl W3 . . . . . .37 B4
Rahere Ho EC1 . . . . **96** C4
Railey Mews NW5 . . .13 B3
Railton Rd SE24 . . . .63 A2
Railway App SE1 . . **123** C2
Railway Ave SE16 . . .40 B4
Railway Cotts W6 . . .39 B4
Railway Gr SE14 . . . .51 B3
Railway Rise SE22 . .64 A3
Railway Side
SW13 . . . . .56 A4
Railway St N1 . . . . . **84** B1
Railway Terr SE13 . .67 A2
Rainbow Ave E14 . . .42 A1
Rainbow Ct 3
SE14 . . . . .51 A4
Rainbow Montessori
Sch NW6 . . . . .11 A1
Rainbow Quay
SE16 . . . . .41 A3
Rainbow Sch 5
SW17 . . . . .71 B2
Rainbow St SE5 . . . .49 A3
Raines Ct N16 . . . . . .7 B2
Raine's Foundation
Lower Sch 32 E2 . . .25 A2
Raine's Foundation
Sch 22 E2 . . . . .25 B3
Raine St E1 . . . . . . .32 A1
Rainford Ho 9 N7 . . .5 B2
Rainham Cl SW11 . . .60 A1
Rainham Ho NW1 . . .83 A3
Rainham Rd NW10 . .22 B2
Rainhill Way E3 . . . .26 C2
Rainsborough Ave
SE8 . . . . .41 A2
Rainsford Ct
NW10 . . . . .20 A3
Rainsford Ho 14
SW2 . . . . .62 B2
Rainsford Rd
NW10 . . . . .20 A3
Rainsford St W2 . . **102** A2
Rainton Rd SE7 . . . .43 C1
Rainville Rd W6 . . . . .47 B4
Raleigh Ct
7 Hammersmith
W12 . . . . .39 A4
2 Rotherhithe
SE16 . . . . .32 C1
Raleigh Gdns SW2 . .62 B1
Raleigh Ho
30 Clapham SW8 . . **171** B2
Isle of Dogs E14 . . . .42 A4
Raleigh Mews N1 . . .86 B3
Raleigh Rd TW9 . . . .54 B4

Raleigh St N1 . . . . 86 B3
Ralph Ct 8 W2 . . . . . 100 B2
Ralston St W3 . . . . . 144 C1
Ramar Ho 1 E1 . . . . 111 B4
Ramillies Cl W4 . . . . . 62 A1
Ramillies Ho W1 . . . . 105 A1
Ramillies Pl W1 . . . . . 104 C1
Ramillies Rd W4 . . . . . 37 C3
Ramillies St W1 . . . . 104 C1
Rampart St E1 . . . . . . 32 A3
Rampayne St
SW1 . . . . 147 B2
Ramsay Ho NW8 . . . . 80 A2
Ramsay Rd W3 . . . . . . 37 B4
Ramsdean Ho 1
 . . . . 69 A3
Ramsden Rd SW12 . 72 C4
Ramsey Ct
 Putney SW15 . . . . . . 57 B1
 6 Upper Holloway
 N19 . . . .
Ramsey Ho
 5 Battersea
 SW11 . . . . 59 C3
 14 Kensington
 SW9 . . . . 163 C1
Ramsey St
 E2 . . . . 24 C1 99 C2
Ramsey Wlk N1 . . . . 15 C2
Ramsfort Ho 4
 . . . . 40 A2
Ramsgate St E8 . . . . 16 B2
Ram St SW18 . . . . . . 59 A2
Randal Cremer JMI
 Sch 12 E2 . . . . 24 B3
Randall Cl SW11 . . 168 A4
Randall Pl SE10 . . . . . 52 B3
Randall Rd SE11 . . 148 C3
Randall Row SE11 148 C3
Randell's Rd N1 . . . . 84 B4
Randolf Ct
 Paddington NW6 . . . 78 A1
 St John's Wood
 NW8 . . . . 78 C2
Randolph Ave W9 . . 88 C3
Randolph Cres W9 . . 88 C2
Randolph Gdns
 NW6 . . . . 78 A1
Randolph Mews
 W9 . . . . 89 A1
Randolph Rd W9 . . . 89 A1
Randolph St NW1 . . 13 B1
Ranelagh Ave
 Barnes SW13 . . . . . 46 C1
 Fulham SW6 . . . . . . 58 B4
Ranelagh Gardens
 Mans SW6 . . . . 58 A4
Ranelagh Gardens
 (site of Chelsea
 Flower Show)
 SW1 . . . . 145 C1
Ranelagh Gdns
 3 Bedford Pk
 W6 . . . . 38 B3
 Chiswick W4 . . . . . . 45 B3
 Fulham SW6 . . . . . . 58 B4
Ranelagh Gr SW1 145 C2
Ranelagh Ho SW3 154 B2
Ranelagh Mans 4
 SW6 . . . . 165 A2
Rangdon St EC3 . . 110 C1

Ranger's House (The
 Wernher Collection)
 . . . . 52 C2
Rangers Sq SE10 . . . 52 C2
Rangoon Ho 5
 N16 . . . . 15 C4
Rankine Ho SE1 . . 136 C1
Ranmere St SW12 . . 73 A3
Rann Ho 1 SW14 . . 55 C4
Rannoch Rd W6 . . . . 47 C4
Ransomes Dock Bsns
 Ctr SW11 . . . . 158 B1
Ransomes Mews
 SW11 . . . . 158 B2
Ranston St NW1 . . 102 A4
Ranulf Rd NW2 . . . . . 10 B4
Ranulf Ct 6 E3 . . 26 B4
Ranwell Ho 17 E3 . 26 B4
Raphael Ct 9
 SE16 . . . . 40 A1
Raphael St SW7 . . 130 C3
Rapley Ho 9
 E2 . . . . 24 C2 99 B3
Rashleigh Ct 5
 . . . . 61 A4
Rashleigh Ho NW1 . 94 A3
Rastell Ave SW2 . . . . 73 C3
RATCLIFF 32 C2
Ratcliffe Cross St
 . . . . 32 C3
Ratcliffe Ho 10
 E14 . . . . 33 A3
Ratcliffe La 10
 E14 . . . . 33 A3
Ratcliffe Orch 9
 . . . . 32 C2
Rathbone Ho
 5 Canning Town
 E16 . . . . 35 B3
 Kilburn NW6 . . . . . . 23 C4
Rathbone Mkt 3
 . . . . 35 B4
Rathbone Pl W1 . . 105 B2
Rathbone St
 Canning Town
 E16 . . . . 35 B3
 Fitzrovia W1 . . . . . 105 A3
Rathgar Rd SW9 . . . 63 A4
Rathmell Dr SW4 . . 61 C1
Rattray Rd SW2 . . . . 62 C2
Raul Rd SE15 . . . . . . 49 C2
Raveley St NW5 . . . . 13 B4
Ravenet Ct
 Battersea SW11 . . 170 A3
 Clapham SW4 . . . . 61 A2
Ravenet St SW11 . . 170 A3
Ravenfield Rd
 SW17 . . . . 72 B1
Raven Ho 10 SE16 . 40 C2
Ravenna Rd SW15 . 57 C2
Raven Row E1 . . . . . 32 A4
Ravensbourne Ho
 NW8 . . . . 102 A4
Ravensbourne Mans
 9 SE8 . . . . 51 C4
Ravensbourne Pl
 SE13 . . . . 52 A1
Ravensbury Rd
 SW18 . . . . 71 A2
Ravensbury Terr
 SW18 . . . . 71 A2
Ravenscar NW1 . . . . 82 C3
Ravenscourt 1 N16 . 7 C1
Ravenscourt Ave
 W6 . . . . 38 C2

Ravenscourt Gdns
 W6 . . . . 38 C2
Ravenscourt Ho 13
 W6 . . . . 39 A2
Ravenscourt Park
 Mans 1 W6 . . . . . . 39 A3
Ravenscourt Park
 Prep Sch W6 . . . . . 38 C2
Ravenscourt Park Sta
 W6 . . . . 39 A2
Ravenscourt Pk
 W6 . . . . 38 C2
Ravenscourt Pl
 W6 . . . . 39 A2
Ravenscourt Rd
 W6 . . . . 39 A2
Ravenscourt Sq
 W6 . . . . 38 C3
Ravenscourt Theatre
 Sch 11 W6 . . . . 39 A2
Ravenscroft Ave
 NW11 . . . . 1 B4
Ravenscroft Cl 4
 E16 . . . . 35 C4
Ravenscroft Ct
 NW11 . . . . 1 B4
Ravenscroft Point 8
 E9 . . . . 17 C2
Ravenscroft Rd
 Acton W4 . . . . 37 B2
 Newham E16 . . . . . . 35 C4
Ravenscroft St
 E2 . . . . 24 B2 99 A4
Ravenshaw St
 NW6 . . . . 10 B3
Ravenslea Rd SW11,
 SW12 . . . . 72 B4
Ravensmede Way
 W4 . . . . 38 B2
Ravenstone SE17 . 152 B1
Ravenstone Prim Sch
 SW12 . . . . 72 C2
Ravenstone St
 SW12 . . . . 72 C3
Ravenswood Rd
 SW12 . . . . 73 A4
Ravensworth Ct
 SW6 . . . . 155 B1
Ravensworth Rd
 NW10 . . . . 22 A2
Raven Wharf SE1 138 C4
Rav Pinter Cl N16 . . 7 A4
Rawlings St SW3 144 C4
Rawlinson Ho
 SE13 . . . . 67 C3
Rawlinson Point 8
 E16 . . . . 35 B4
Rawnsley Ave CR4 . 90 C3
Rawreth Wlk N1 . . . 87 A4
Rawson Ct SW11 . 169 C3
Rawson St SW11 . 170 A3
Rawstone Pl EC1 . . 96 A4
Rawstone St EC1 . . 96 A4
Rayburne Ct W14 . 126 A2
Raydon St N19 . . . . 4 A2
Ray Ho
 7 North Kensington
 W10 . . . . 30 C3
 Shoreditch N1 . . . . 87 C3
Raymede Twr 2
 W10 . . . . 30 C4
Raymond Bldgs
 WC1 . . . . 107 A4

Raymouth Rd
 SE16 . . . . 40 A2
Raynald Ho 15
 SW16 . . . . 74 A1
Rayne Ct SE1 . . . . 138 C4
Rayne Ho
 1 Balham SW12 . . 60 C1
 Paddington W9 . . . 88 A2
Rayner Ct 10 W12 . 39 B4
Rayner's Rd SW15 . 58 A2
Raynes Ct NW2 . . . . 10 A4
Raynham W2 . . . . 102 A2
Raynham Ho 1
 E1 . . . . 25 C1
Raynham Rd W6 . . . 39 A2
Raynor Pl
 2 Canonbury N1 . . 15 B1
 N1 . . . . 87 A4
Ray St EC1 . . . . 95 C1
Ray Wlk N7 . . . . 5 B2
Reachview Cl 17
 NW1 . . . . 13 B1
Reade Ct 9 W3 . . . . 37 B3
Reade Wlk 5
 NW10 . . . . 8 A1
Read Ho 4 SE11 . . 163 B4
Reading Ho
 Paddington W2 . . 100 C1
 Peckham SE15 . . . . 49 C4
Reading La E8 . . . . . 17 A2
Reapers Cl NW1 . . . 83 B4
Reardon Ho 5 E1 . 32 A1
Reardon Path 31
 E1 . . . . 32 A1
Reardon St E1 . . . . . 32 A1
Reaston St SE14 . . . 50 C3
Reay Prim Sch
 SW9 . . . . 163 A1
Reckitt Rd W4 . . . . . 38 A1
Record St SE16 . . . . 50 B4
Rector St N1 . . . . . . 86 C3
Rectory Gdns 4
 SW4 . . . . 61 B4
Rectory Gr SW4 . . . 61 B4
Rectory Rd
 Barnes SW13 . . . . . 46 C1
 1 London SW13 . . 28 B1
 Shacklewell N16 . . . 7 B1
Rectory Road Sta
 N16 . . . . 7 B1
Rectory Sq E1 . . . . . 32 C4
Reculver Ho 2
 SE15 . . . . 50 B4
Reculver Rd SE16 . 40 C1
Red Anchor Cl
 SW3 . . . . 158 A3
Redan Pl W2 . . . . . 100 A1
Redan St W14 . . . . . 39 C3
Redan Terr SE5 . . . . 48 A1
Redbourne Ho 7
 E14 . . . . 33 B3
Redbourn Ho 10
 W10 . . . . 22 B1
Redbridge Gdns
 SE5 . . . . 49 A3
Redburn St SW3 . . 158 C4
Redcar St SE5 . . . . . 48 B3
Redcastle Cl 11 E1 . 32 B2
Redchurch St
 E2 . . . . 24 B1 98 C2
Redcliffe Cl SW5 . 142 A1
Redcliffe Gdns
 Chiswick W4 . . . . . . 45 A3
 Fulham SW10 . . . . 156 B4
Redcliffe Mews
 SW10 . . . . 142 B1

Ral-Red 259

Redcliffe Pl SW10 156 C3
Redcliffe Rd
 SW10 . . . . 157 A4
Redcliffe Sch
 SW10 . . . . 156 C4
Redcliffe Sq
 SW10 . . . . 142 B1
Redcliffe St SW10 156 B4
Redclyf Ho 13 E1 . . 25 B1
Redcroft 5 NW6 . . . 10 C2
Red Cross Cotts
 SE1 . . . . 137 A4
Redcross Way
 SE1 . . . . 123 A1
Reddins Rd SE15 . . 49 C4
Rede Pl
 W2 . . . . 31 C2 113 C4
Redesdale St
 SW3 . . . . 158 C4
Redfern Rd NW10 . . 8 A1
Redfield La SW5 . . 142 A4
Redfield Mews
 SW5 . . . . 141 C4
Rediff Est SE1 . . . . . 41 B3
Redford Wlk N1 . . . 86 C4
Redgate Terr
 SW15 . . . . 57 C1
Redgrave Rd
 SW15 . . . . 57 C4
Redhill Ct SW2 . . . . 74 C2
Redhill St NW1 . . . . 92 B4
Red House Sq 20
 . . . . 15 B1
Redington Gdns
 NW3 . . . . 11 A4
Redington Ho N1 . . 85 A2
Redington Rd
 NW3 . . . . 11 A4
Redlands Prim Sch 1
 E1 . . . . 32 B4
Redlands Way
 SW2 . . . . 74 B4
Red Lion Cl 4
 SE17 . . . . 48 C4
Red Lion Ct EC4 . 107 C1
Red Lion Row
 SE17 . . . . 48 B4
Red Lion Sq WC1 106 C3
Red Lion St WC1 . 106 C3
Red Lion Yd W1 . . 117 C2
Redlynch Ct W14 . 126 B3
Redlynch Ho 20
 SW9 . . . . 173 C4
Redman Bldg 2 EC1 107 B4
Redman Ho SE1 . . 137 A3
Redman's Rd E1 . . . 32 B4
Redmayne Ho 18
 SW9 . . . . 173 A2
Redmead La E1 . . 125 B1
Redmill Ho 24 E1 . . 25 A1
Redmond Ho N1 . . 85 A3
Redmore Rd W6 . . . 39 A2
Red Pl W1 . . . . 117 B4
Red Post Hill SE21,
 SE24 . . . . 63 C2
Redriff Prim Sch
 SE16 . . . . 41 A4
Redriff Rd SE16 . . . 41 A3
Red Rover SW13 . . 56 C4
Redrup Ho 7
 SE14 . . . . 50 C4
Redruth Rd E9 . . . . . 25 B4
Red Sq The N16 . . . 6 C1
Redstart Cl SE14 . . 51 A3

Redvers Ho
E2 . . . . 24 A2 98 B4
Redwald Ho E5 . . . . . . 17 C4
Redwood Cl
4 Bow E3 . . . . 26 C3
Rotherhithe SE16 . . . . 33 A1
Redwood Ct
Brondesbury
NW6 . . . . 10 A1
Crouch End N19 . . . . 4 C4
Redwood Mews
SW4 . . . . 61 A4
Redwoods SW15 . . . . 68 C3
Reece Mews SW7 143 B4
Reed Cl E16 . . . . 35 C4
Reedham St SE15 . . 64 C4
Reed Ho SW15 . . . . 56 C1
Reedholm Villas
N16 . . . . 15 C4
Reed Pl
Battersea SW11 . . . . 60 A3
Clapham SW4 . . . . . 61 C3
Reed's Pl NW1 . . . . 13 B1
Reedworth St
SE11 . . . . 149 C3
Reef Ho E14 . . . . . . 42 B3
Rees St N1 . . . . 87 A3
Reeves Ho
Lambeth SE1 . . . . . 135 B3
Mayfair W1 . . . . . . 117 B3
Reeves Mews W1 117 C3
Reeves Rd E3 . . . . . 27 A1
Reflection Ho 4
E2 . . . . 24 C1 99 B2
Reform St SW11 . . 169 A2
Regal Cl E1 . . . . . . 111 C4
Regal La NW1 . . . . . 81 C3
Regal Pl
8 Tower Hamlets
E3 . . . . 26 B2
Walham Green
SW6 . . . . 156 B1
Regan Way N1 . . . . 24 A3
Regatta Point TW8 . 44 B4
Regency Cl
5 Bow E3 . . . . 26 B3
14 South Hackney
E9 . . . . 25 B4
Regency Ho NW1 . . 92 B2
Regency Lo NW3 . . 11 C1
Regency Mews
Camberwell SW9 . . . 48 A3
1 Willesden NW10 . . 8 C2
Regency Pl SW1 . . 147 C4
Regency St SW1 . . 147 C3
Regency Terr
SW7 . . . . 143 B2
Regency Wlk 3
TW10 . . . . 54 A2
Regeneration Rd
SE16 . . . . 40 C1
Regent Cl
Lisson Gr NW8 . . . . 90 A3
1 Stamford Hill N16 . 7 B4
Regent Ho W14 . . . 140 A4
1 Regent Pl W11 . . 119 A4
Regent Rd SE24 . . . 63 A2
Regents Bridge Gdns
SW8 . . . . 162 B2
Regents Canal Ho 10
E14 . . . . 33 A3
Regent's Coll NW1 91 B2
Regents Ct E8 . . . . 24 C4

Regents Gate Ho 20
E14 . . . . 33 A2
Regents Lo 9
SW2 . . . . 74 B3
Regents Mews
NW8 . . . . 79 A2
REGENT'S PARK . . 92 A4
Regent's Park
NW1 . . . . 81 B1
Regent's Park
Barracks NW1 . . . 82 B1
Camden Town
NW1 . . . . 81 B4
Primrose Hill NW3 . . 12 C1
Regent's Park Rd
NW1 . . . . 92 A1
Regent's Park Terr
NW1 . . . . 82 A4
Regent's Pl SE3 . . 53 C1
Regents Plaza 2
NW6 . . . . 78 A2
Regent Sq
23 Bromley E3 . . . . 27 A2
St Pancras WC1 . . . 94 B3
Regent's Row E8 . . 24 C4
Regent St
Brentford W4 . . . . . 36 C1
1 Kensal Green
NW10 . . . . 22 C2
Mayfair W1 . . . . . . 118 C4
Regents Wharf
3 Hackney E2 . . . . 25 A4
Islington N1 . . . . . . 84 C2
Reginald Pl 6
SE8 . . . . 51 C3
Reginald Rd SE8 . . 51 C3
Reginald Sq SE8 . . 51 C3
Regina Point SE16 . 40 B3
Regina Rd N4 . . . . . 5 B3
Regis Ct NW1 . . . . 102 C4
Regis Pl 17 SW2 . . 62 B3
Regis Rd NW5 . . . . 13 A3
Regnart Bldgs
NW1 . . . . 93 A3
Reid Ct SW14 . . . . 45 B1
Reighton Rd E5 . . . 7 C2
Reizel Ct N16 . . . . . 7 B3
Relay Rd W12 . . . . 30 B1
Relf Rd SE15 . . . . . 64 C4
Reliance Sq
E2 . . . . 24 A1 98 B2
Relton Ct W3 . . . . . 36 C4
Relton Mews
SW7 . . . . 130 B2
Rembrandt Cl E14 . . 42 C3
Rembrandt Ct 10
SE16 . . . . 40 A1
Rembrant Cl SW1 145 B3
Remington St N1 . . 86 B1
Remnant St WC2 . 106 C2
Remsted Ho 7
NW6 . . . . 78 A3
Remus Rd E3 . . . . . 18 C1
Renaissance Wlk 4
SE10 . . . . 43 B3
Renbold Ho 5
SE10 . . . . 52 B2
Rendlesham Ho 3 E5,
N16 . . . . 7 C1
Rendlesham Rd E5 . 7 C1
Renforth St SE16 . . 40 B4
Renfrew Ho NW6 . . 78 A1
Renfrew Rd SE11 . 150 A3
Rennell Ho 10 E9 . . 17 C2
Rennell St SE13 . . 67 B4

Rennie Cotts 29
E1 . . . . 25 B1
Rennie Ct SE1 . . . 122 A2
Rennie Ho SE1 . . . 136 C1
Rennie St SE1 . . . 122 A2
Renoir Ct 7 SE16 . . 40 A1
Renoir Ho NW11 . . . 2 A4
Rephidim St SE1 . 138 A1
Replingham Rd
SW18 . . . . 70 C3
Reporton Rd SW6 154 B1
Repton Ho SW1 . . 147 A3
Repton St E14 . . . . 33 A3
Reservoir Rd SE4 . . 51 A1
Reservoir Studios 14
E1 . . . . 32 C3
Resolution Way 4
SE8 . . . . 51 C3
Restell Cl SE3 . . . . 53 A4
Reston Pl SW7 . . . 128 C3
Restoration Sq
SW11 . . . . 167 C3
Retcar Pl N19 . . . . . 4 A2
Retford St E2 . . . . . 24 A3
Retreat Ho 8 E9 . . 17 B2
Retreat Pl E9 . . . . . 17 B2
Retreat The SW14 . 56 A4
Reunion Row E1 . . . 32 A2
Reveley Sq SE16 . . 41 A4
Revelon Rd SE4 . . . 66 A4
Revelstoke Rd SW18,
SW19 . . . . 71 A2
Reverdy Rd SE1 . . 153 B3
Rewell St SW6 . . . 156 C1
Rewley Rd NW1 . . 117 C2
Reynard Cl SE4 . . . 66 A4
Reynard Pl SE14 . . 51 A4
Reynolds Cl NW11 . . 2 A4
Reynolds Ho
Finsbury Pk N4 . . . . 5 A3
1 South Hackney
E2 . . . . 25 B3
St John's Wood
NW8 . . . . 79 C1
Westminster SW1 . . 147 C3
Reynolds Pl 7
TW10 . . . . 54 B1
Reynolds Rd
Acton Green W4 . . . 37 B3
Nunhead SE15 . . . . 65 B3
Rhayades Sp Ctr
W3 . . . . 29 A3
Rheidol Mews N1 . . 86 C2
Rheidol Terr N1 . . . 86 C3
Rhizotron & Xstrata
Treetop Walkway
TW9 . . . . 44 A3
Rhoda St E2 . . 24 B1 99 A2
Rhodes Ho
Shepherd's Bush
W12 . . . . 30 A1
3 Shoreditch N1 . . 97 B4
Rhodesia Rd SW9 172 B1
Rhodeswell Rd
N14 . . . . 33 B3
E14 . . . . 33 B3
Rhondda Gr E3 . . . 26 B2
Rhyl Prim Sch 21
NW5 . . . . 12 C2
Rhyl St NW5 . . . . . 12 C2
Ribblesdale Ho 11
NW6 . . . . 23 C4
Ribbon Dance Mews
SE5 . . . . 48 C2

Ribstone Ho 12 E9, 17 C2
Ricardo St E14 . . . . 34 A3
Riceyman Ho WC1 . 95 B3
Richard Anderson Ct
1 SE14 . . . . 50 C3
Richard Atkins Prim
Sch 22 SW2 . . . . 74 A4
Richard Burbidge
Mans SW13 . . . . 47 B4
Richard Cloudesley
Sch (Prim Dept)
EC1 . . . . 96 C1
Richard Cloudesley
Sch (Secondary
Dept) EC1 . . . . . . 96 C1
Richard Cobden Prim
Sch NW1 . . . . 83 A3
Richard Fox Ho N4 . 6 B1
Richard Ho 10
SE16 . . . . 40 B2
Richard Knight Ho
SW6 . . . . 165 C4
Richard Neale Ho 2
E1 . . . . 32 A2
Richardson Cl 20
E8 . . . . 24 B4
Richardson Ct 22
SW4 . . . . 172 B2
Richardson Ho 10
E14 . . . . 33 C4
Richardson's Mews
W1 . . . . 92 C1
Richard's Pl SW3 . 144 B4
Richbell Cl SW12 . . 73 A4
Richbell Pl WC1 . . 106 B4
Richborne Terr
SW8 . . . . 163 A2
Richborough Ho
10 Deptford SE15 . 50 B4
4 Hackney E5 . . . 17 A4
Richborough Rd
NW2 . . . . 10 A4
Richbourne Ct
W1 . . . . 102 B2
Richford Gate W6 . 39 B3
Richford St W6 . . . 39 B3
Rich Ind Est SE15 . 50 A4
Rich La SW5 . . . . . 142 A2
Richland Ho 4
SE15 . . . . 49 C2
Richman Ho 10
SE8 . . . . 41 B1
Rich Mix E1 . . . . . . 99 A3
RICHMOND 54 B3
Richmond Ave
Islington N1 . . . . . . 85 A4
Willesden NW10 . . . 22 C4
Richmond Bldgs
W1 . . . . 105 B1
Richmond Circus
TW9 . . . . 54 A3
Richmond Coll
W8 . . . . 128 B2
Richmond Cres N1 . 85 B4
Richmond Gn
SW1 . . . . 131 A3
Richmond Gr N1 . . 15 A1
Richmond Healthcare
Hamlet Hospl
TW9 . . . . 54 A4
Richmond Hill
TW10 . . . . 54 A1
Richmond Hill Ct 5
TW10 . . . . 54 A1

Richmond Ho
12 Forest Hill
SE26 . . . . 76 C1
Regent's Pk NW1 . . 82 B1
Walworth SE17 . . . 151 B2
Richmond
International Bsns
Ctr 3 TW9 . . . . . . 54 B3
Richmond Mans
Earl's Ct SW5 . . . . 142 A2
Putney SW15 . . . . . 58 A4
Richmond Mews
W1 . . . . 105 B1
Richmond Park Rd
SW14 . . . . 55 C3
Richmond Rd
Dalston E8 . . . . 16 C1
Ealing W5 . . . . 36 A4
Richmond Sta
TW9 . . . . 54 A3
Richmond Terr
SW1 . . . . 134 A4
Richmond Way W12,
W14 . . . . 39 C4
Rich St E14 . . . . . . 33 B2
Rickard Cl SW2 . . . 74 C3
Rickett St SW6 . . . 155 C4
Rickman Ho 22 E2 . 25 B1
Rickman St 24 E1 . 25 B1
Rick Roberts Way
E15 . . . . 27 C3
Rickthorne Rd 7
N19 . . . . 5 A2
Riddell Ct SE1 . . . 152 C2
Ridgdale St E3 . . . 27 A3
Ridge Hill NW11 . . . 1 A3
Ridge Rd NW2 . . . . 1 B1
Ridgeway 11
TW10 . . . . 54 A1
Ridgeway Dr W3 . . 36 C3
Ridgeway Gdns The
N6 . . . . 4 B4
Ridgeway The
Acton W3 . . . . 36 C3
Golders Green NW11, 1 B4
Ridgewell Cl N1 . . . 87 A4
Ridgmount Gdns
WC1 . . . . 105 B4
Ridgmount Pl
WC1 . . . . 105 B4
Ridgmount Rd
SW18 . . . . 59 A2
Ridgmount St
WC1 . . . . 105 B4
Ridgway Rd SW9 . . 63 A4
Riding House St
W1 . . . . 104 C3
Ridings Cl N6 . . . . . 4 B4
Riding The NW11 . . 1 A4
Ridley Ho 14
SW11 . . . . 60 A4
Ridley Rd
Dalston E8 . . . . 16 B3
Willesden Green
NW10 . . . . 21 C3
Ridley Road Mkt
E8 . . . . 16 B3
Riffel Rd NW2 . . . . 9 B3
Rifle Ct SE11 . . . . 163 C4
Rifle Pl W11 . . . . . 30 C1
Rifle St E14 . . . . . . 34 A4
Riga Ho 10 E1 . . . . 32 C4
Rigault Rd SW6 . . 164 B1
Rigden St E14 . . . . 34 A3
Rigeley Rd NW10 . . 21 C2
Rigge Pl SW4 . . . . 61 C3
Rigg Ho 2 SW4 . . . 74 A4

Rignold Ho **6** SE5..49 A1

Riley Ho
8 Bow E3 .... 26 C1
Chelsea SW10 .. 157 B3
1 Streatham SW4 . 73 C4
Riley Rd SE1 ...... 138 C2
Riley St SW10 ..... 157 B2
Rili Ho **13** SE5 .... 49 A1
Rimini Ct SW12... 72 B3
Rinaldo Rd SW12 . 73 A4
Ringcroft St N7 .... 14 C3
Ringford Ho SW18 . 58 B2
Ringford Rd SW18 . 58 C1
Ring Ho **15** E1 ..... 32 B2
Ringmer Ave SW6 164 B3
Ringmer Gdns **18**
.... 5 A2
Ringmer Ho **13**
SE22 .... 64 A4
Ring Rd W12 ...... 30 B1
Ringsfield Ho
SE17 .... 151 A1
Ringwood Gdns
17 Millwall E14 ... 41 C2
Roehampton SW15 55 C4
Ripley Gdns SW14 . 55 C4
Ripley Ho
Mortlake SW14 .. 56 A4
Nine Elms SW11 . 160 C4
Ripley's Believe It or
Not! SW1........ 119 B3
Riplington Ct
SW15 .... 69 A4
Ripplevale Gr N1 .. 85 B2
Risborough SE17 . 150 C4
Risborough Ho
NW8 .... 90 B2
Risborough St
SE1 .... 136 B4
Risdon Ho **20** SE16 . 40 B4
Risdon St **27** SE16 . 40 B4
Riseholme Ct E9 ... 18 B2
Riseholme Ho **14**
SE22 .... 64 A4
Riseldine Rd SE23 . 66 A1
Risinghill St N1 .... 85 B2
Rising Sun Ct EC1 108 B3
Risley Ho **7** E9 .... 17 C2
Rita Rd SW8 ...... 162 C2
Ritchie Ho
Crouch End N19 ... 4 C4
8 Rotherhithe
SE16 .... 40 B3
South Bromley
E14 .... 34 C3
Ritchie St N1 ...... 85 C2
Ritherdon Rd
SW17 .... 73 A2
Ritson Ho N1 ...... 84 C3
Ritson Rd E8 ...... 16 C2
Rivaz Pl E9........ 17 B2
Riven Ct **10** W2... 100 B1
Riverains The
SW11 .... 167 B3
River Barge Cl E14 42 B4
Rivercourt Rd W6 . 39 A1
River Ct SW1 ..... 122 A3
Riverdale Dr SW18 71 A3
Riverfleet WC1 .... 94 B4
Riverford Ho **28**
W2 .... 31 C4
River Ho SW13 ... 46 A1
River House
Montessori Sch
E14 .... 42 A4
Rivermead Ct SW6 58 B4

Rivermead Ho E9... 18 A3
River Pl N1 .... 15 B1
River Plate Ho
EC2 .... 109 C3
Riversdale Prim Sch
SW18 .... 71 A3
Riversdale Rd N5 ... 6 B1
Riversdene N5 ..... 6 B1
Rivers Ho **10** TW8 .. 36 C1
Riverside
Battersea SW11... 158 B2
11 Rotherhithe
SE16 .... 40 B4
St Pancras WC1 .. 94 B4
Riverside Bsns Ctr
SW18 .... 71 A3
Riverside Ct SW8 161 C4
Riverside Dr W4 .. 46 A2
Riverside Gdns
W6 .... 39 A1
Riverside Health &
Racquets Club
Chiswick The
W4 .... 46 A2
Riverside Ho **14**
N1 .... 15 B1
Riverside Mans **4**
E1 .... 32 B1
Riverside Prim Sch **27**
SE16 .... 139 C3
Riverside Rd
Mill Meads E15.... 27 B3
Wandsworth SW17,
SW19 .... 71 A1
Riverside Wlk Mkt
WC2 .... 121 A2
Riverside Workshops
SE1 .... 123 A2
River St EC1 ...... 95 B4
River Terr
London W6 ...... 39 B1
St James SW1 ... 120 C3
Riverton Cl W9 .... 23 B2
Riverview Gdns
SW13 .... 47 A4
Riverview Gr W4 .. 45 A4
Riverview Rd W4 .. 45 A4
River Way SE10 ... 43 B3
Rivet Ho SE1 ..... 153 A2
Rivington Ct
NW10 .... 21 C4
Rivington Pl
EC2 .... 24 A2 98 B3
Rivington St
EC2 .... 24 A2 98 A3
Rivington Wlk **4**
E8 .... 24 C4
Rixon St N7........ 5 C1
Roach Rd E3 ...... 18 C1
Roads Pl N19 .... 5 A2
Roan St SE10 ..... 52 A4
Robert Adam St
W1 .... 103 B2
Roberta St
E2 .... 24 C2 99 C3
Robert Bell Ho **2**
SE16 .... 153 B4
Robert Blair Prim Sch
N7 .... 14 A2
Robert Browning Prim
Sch SE17 ...... 151 B3
Robert Cl **13** W9 .. 89 A1
Robert Dashwood
Way SE17 ...... 150 C3
Robert Gentry Ho
W14 .... 140 B1

Robert Jones Ho **3**
SE16 .... 153 B4
Robert Keen Cl **18**
SE15 .... 49 C2
Robert Lowe Cl
SE14 .... 50 C3
Robert Owen Ho
Fulham SW6 ..... 47 C2
8 Spitalfields E2 .. 99 A4
Robert Owen Lo **4**
E5 .... 17 A3
Roberts Ct
Islington N1 ..... 86 B3
Willesden NW10 ... 8 A2
Roberts Ho **5**
SE27 .... 75 A1
Roberts Mews
SW1 .... 131 B1
Robertson Ho **11**
SE10 .... 52 A4
Robertson St
SW8 .... 170 B1
Robert's Pl EC1 ... 95 C2
Robert St
Regent's Pk NW1 . 92 B3
Strand WC2 ..... 120 B3
Robert Sutton Ho **20**
E1 .... 32 B3
Robeson St **7** E3 . 33 B4
Robin Ct SE16 .... 42 B3
Robin Gr
Dartmouth Pk N6 .. 3 C2
Highgate N6 ..... 3 C2
Robin Ho NW8 .... 80 A1
Robin Hood Gdns **12**
E14 .... 34 B2
Robin Hood La
E14 .... 34 B2
Robinscroft Mews **4**
SE10 .... 52 A2
Robins Ct TW10 ... 54 A3
Robin's Ct SW4.... 62 A1
Robinsfield Inf Sch
NW8 .... 80 A2
Robinson Ct
Islington N1 ..... 86 B4
4 Richmond TW9 . 54 B3
Robinson Ho
4 North Kensington
W10 .... 30 C3
12 Tower Hamlets
E14 .... 33 C4
Robinson Rd E2 ... 25 B3
Robinson St SW3 . 158 C4
Robinswood Mews **6**
N5 .... 15 A3
Robsart St SW9 .. 173 B2
Robson Ave NW10 . 8 C1
Robson Rd SE21,
SE27 .... 75 B1
Roby Ho EC1 ..... 96 C2
Rochdale Way **4**
SE8 .... 51 C3
Roche Ho **15** E14 . 33 B2
Rochelle Cl SW11 . 59 C3
Rochelle Ct **1** E1 . 32 B3
Rochelle St **31**
E2 .... 24 B2 98 C3
Rochemont Wlk **2**
E8 .... 24 C4
Roche Sch The **18**
SW18 .... 58 C2

Rochester Ct
1 Bethnal Green
E2 .... 25 A1
1 Camden Town
NW1 .... 13 B1
Rochester Ho
Bermondsey SE1 . 137 C3
14 Deptford SE15.. 50 B4
Rochester Mews
NW1 .... 13 B1
Rochester Pl NW1 . 13 B1
Rochester Rd NW1 . 13 B2
Rochester Row
SW1 .... 147 A4
Rochester Sq NW1 . 13 B1
Rochester St SW1 133 B1
Rochester Terr
NW1 .... 13 B2
Rochester Wlk
SE1 .... 123 B2
Rochford Wlk **8**
E8 .... 16 C1
Rochfort Ho **4**
SE8 .... 41 B1
Rock Ave SW14 ... 55 C4
Rockell's Pl SE22 .. 65 A1
Rockfield Ho SE10 . 52 B4
Rock Grove Way
SE16 .... 153 C4
Rockhall Rd NW2 .. 9 C4
Rockingham Cl
SW15 .... 56 B3
Rockingham St
SE1 .... 136 C1
Rockland Rd
SW15 .... 58 A3
Rockley Ct **14** W14. 39 C4
Rockley Rd W14 .. 39 C4
Rocks La SW13.... 56 C4
Rock St N4 .... 5 C2
Rockstraw Ho **5**
NW3 .... 12 B1
Rockwood Ct N16 .. 7 C4
Rocliffe St N1 ..... 86 B1
Rocque Ho SW6 .. 154 C2
Rodborough Rd
NW11 .... 1 C3
Rodenhurst Ct
SW4 .... 61 C2
Rodenhurst Rd
SW4 .... 61 C1
Roden St N7 ...... 5 B1
Roderick Ho **3**
SE16 .... 40 B2
Roderick Rd NW3 . 12 B4
Rodgers Ho **2**
SW4 .... 73 C4
Rodin Ct N1 ...... 86 A3
Roding Ct **6** W12 . 38 A4
Roding Ho N1 .... 85 B3
Roding Mews E1 . 125 C2
Roding Rd E5 .... 18 A3
Rodmarton St W1 103 A3
Rodmell WC1...... 94 B3
Rodmere St SE10 . 43 A1
Rodney Ct NW8 .. 89 A2
Rodney Ho
Cubitt Town
E14 .... 42 A2
Islington N1 ..... 85 A1
Notting Hill
W11 .... 31 C2 113 B4
Rodney Pl SE17 .. 151 A4
Rodney Rd SE17 .. 151 B3
Rodney St N1 .... 85 A1
Rodway Rd SW15.. 68 C4

Rodwell Rd SE22 .. 64 B1
Roedean Cres
SW15 .... 56 A2
ROEHAMPTON ... 68 A4
Roehampton Church
Sch SW15 ...... 68 C3
Roehampton Cl
SW15 .... 56 C3
Roehampton Ct
SW13 .... 56 C4
Roehampton Gate
SW15 .... 56 B1
Roehampton High St
SW15 .... 68 C3
Roehampton La
Putney SW15 .... 56 C1
Roehampton SW15. 69 A3
Roehampton Vale
SW15 .... 68 B1
Roffey St E14..... 42 B4
Rogate Ho E5 ..... 7 C1
Roger Dowley Ct **8**
E2 .... 25 B3
Roger's Almshouses
2 SW9 .... 62 B3
Rogers Ct **10** E14 . 33 C2
Rogers Est **21** E2 . 25 B2
Rogers Ho SW1 .. 147 C4
Rogers Rd E16 ... 35 B3
Roger St WC1 .... 95 A1
Rokeby Ho
8 Balham SW12 .. 73 A4
Bloomsbury WC1 .. 94 C1
Rokeby Rd SE4 ... 51 B1
Rokeby Sch E15 .. 19 C1
Rokeland Ho SE4 . 66 A3
Roland Gdns SW7 143 A2
Roland Ho SW7 .. 143 A2
Roland Mews **1**
E1 .... 32 C4
Roland Way
South Kensington
SW7 .... 143 A2
Walworth SE17... 151 C1
Rollins St SE15 ... 50 B4
Rollit Ho N7 ...... 14 C3
Rollit St N7 ...... 14 C3
Rollo St SW11 .... 170 A3
Rolls Bldgs EC4 .. 107 C2
Rollscourt Ave
SE24 .... 63 B2
Rolls Pas EC4 .... 107 B2
Rolls Rd SE1 ..... 153 A2
Rolt St SE8 .... 51 A4
Roman Cl W3 ..... 37 A4
Roman Ct **1** N7... 14 B2
Romanfield Rd
SW2 .... 74 B4
Roman Rd
Chiswick W4 ..... 38 B2
Globe Town E2, E3 . 25 C3
25 Old Ford E3 ... 26 B4
Roman Road Mkt **1**
E3 .... 26 B3
Roman Way
Barnsbury N7 .... 14 B2
4 Deptford SE15.. 50 B3
Roma Read Cl
SW15 .... 69 A4
Romayne Ho SW4 . 61 C4
Romberg Rd SW17 72 C1
Romborough Gdns
SE13 .... 67 B2

Romborough Way
SE13 . . . . 67 B2
Romer Ho **2** SW2 . . . 62 B2
Romero Cl SW9 . . . . . . 62 B4
Romeyn Rd SW16 . . . . 74 B1
Romford Ho **17** N1 . . 15 C2
Romford St E1 . . . . . . 32 A4
Romilly Rd N4 . . . . 6 A2
Romilly St W1 . . . . . 119 C4
Romilly Ct **2** SW6 162 B2
Romney Cl
7 Deptford SE14 . . 50 B3
North End NW11 . . . . . 2 B3
Romney Ct
9 Hammersmith
W12 . . . . 39 B4
1 Hampstead
NW3 . . . . 12 A2
Romney Ho **2**
E14 . . . . 34 C2
Romney Mews
W1 . . . . 103 B4
Romney Rd SE10 . . . . 52 C4
Romney St SW1 . . . . 134 A1
Romola Rd SE24,
SW2 . . . . 75 A3
Ronald Ross Prim Sch
6 SW19 . . . . 69 C3
Ronaldshay N4 . . . . 5 C3
Ronalds Rd N5 . . . . . . 14 C3
Ronald St E1 . . . . 32 B3
Rona Rd NW3 . . . . 12 C4
Rona Wlk **20** N1 . . . . 15 C2
Rondu Rd NW2 . . . . . . 10 A3
Roo La EC3 . . . . 124 A4
Rookery Rd SW4 . . . . . 61 B3
Rooke Way SE10 . . . . . 43 B1
Rookwood Rd N16 . . . 7 C4
Roosevelt Ct **13**
SW19 . . . . 70 A3
Rootes Dr W10 . . . . . . 30 C4
Ropemaker Rd
SE16 . . . . 41 A3
Ropemaker's Fields **7**
E14 . . . . 33 B2
Ropemaker St
EC2 . . . . 109 B4
Roper La SE1 . . . . . . 138 B3
Roper's Orch SW3 158 A3
Ropers Wlk **13**
SE24 . . . . 74 C4
Ropery St E3 . . . . 26 B1
Rope St SE16 . . . . 41 A3
Ropewalk Gdns **8**
E1 . . . . 111 C2
Ropley St **6** E2 . . . . . 24 C3
Rosa Alba Mews
N5 . . . . 15 B4
Rosalind Ho **25** N1 . . 24 A3
Rosaline Rd SW6 . . . 154 B1
Rosaline Terr
SW6 . . . . 154 B1
Rosa Parks Ho **8**
SW9 . . . . 172 C1
Rosary Ct **13** E1 . . . . . 32 C4
Rosary Gdns SW7 . . 143 A3
Rosary RC Prim Sch
NW3 . . . . 12 B3
Rosaville Rd SW6 . . 154 C1
Rosbury SW15 . . . . . . 58 A1
Roscastle Rd SE4 . . . . 66 A2
Roscoe St EC1 . . . . . . 97 A1
Roscommon Ho **2**
NW3 . . . . 11 C3

Rose Alley
Borough The SE1 . . . 123 A2
Broadgate EC2 . . . . . 110 B3
Rosebank
2 Dagenham W3 . . 28 C3
Fulham SW6 . . . . 47 B3
Rosebank Gdns
Bow E3 . . . . 26 B3
1 Dagenham W3 . . 28 C3
Rosebank Way
W3 . . . . 28 C3
Rosebank Wlk
NW1 . . . . 13 C1
Rosebay Ho **20** E3 . . 33 C4
Roseberry Pl E8 . . . . . 16 B2
Roseberry St SE16 . . . 40 A2
Rosebery Ave EC1 . . . 95 C3
Rosebery Ct
Holborn EC1 . . . . 95 B2
Mayfair W1 . . . . 118 A2
Rosebery Ho **21**
E2 . . . . 25 B3
Rosebery Sq EC1 . . . . 95 B1
Rosebery Sq EC1 . . . . 95 B1
Rosebery Rd SW6 166 B1
Rose Bush Ct NW3 . . 12 B3
Rosecroft Ave NW3 . . 1 C1
Rose & Crown Ct
EC2 . . . . 108 C2
Rose & Crown Yd
SW1 . . . . 119 A1
Rose Ct
Dalston E8 . . . . 16 B1
Islington N1 . . . . 86 A3
Spitalfields E1 . . . . . 111 A3
Rosedale Ct N5 . . . . . . 15 A4
Rosedale Ho N16 . . . . 6 C3
Rosedale Rd SW4 . . . 61 A3
Rosedale Terr W6 . . . . 39 A3
Rosedene NW6 . . . . . . 22 C4
Rosedene Ave
SW16 . . . . 74 B1
Rosedew Rd W6 . . . . . 47 C4
Rosefield Gdns
E14 . . . . 33 C2
Roseford Ct **18**
W12 . . . . 39 C4
Rosegate Ho **22**
E3 . . . . 26 B3
Rosehart Mews **3**
W11 . . . . 31 C3
Rosehill Rd SW18 . . . 59 B2
Rose Joan Mews
NW6 . . . . 10 C4
Roseland Ho SW6 . . . 58 A4
Roseleigh Ave N5 . . . 15 A4
Rosemary Branch
Bridge N1 . . . . 87 C4
Rosemary Ct **38**
SE8 . . . . 51 B4
Rosemary Dr **10**
E14 . . . . 34 C3
Rosemary Gdns
SW14 . . . . 55 B4
Rosemary Ho
Shoreditch N1 . . . . . . 87 C3
Wilesden NW10 . . . . . 22 A4
Rosemary La
SW14 . . . . 55 B4
Rosemary Rd
Camberwell SE15 . . . . 49 B3
Wandsworth SW17 . . 71 B1
Rosemary St N1 . . . . . 87 C4
Rosemary Works Sch
N1 . . . . 87 C3

Rosemead Prep Sch
SE27 . . . . 75 B2
Rosemont Mans **11**
NW3 . . . . 11 A3
Rosemont Rd
Acton W3 . . . . 28 A2
Richmond TW10 . . . . 54 A1
1 South Hampstead
NW3 . . . . 11 B2
Rosemoor St SW3 144 C3
Rosemount Ct **2**
W3 . . . . 28 A1
Rosemount Lo **2** . . 28 A2
Rosenau Cres
SW11 . . . . 168 C3
Rosenau Rd SW11 168 C4
Rosendale Prim Sch
SE21 . . . . 75 C2
Rosendale Rd SE21,
SE24 . . . . 75 C3
Roseneath Rd
SW11 . . . . 60 C1
Rosenthal Ho SE6 . . . 67 A1
Rosenthal Rd SE6 . . . 67 B1
Rosenthorpe Rd
SE15 . . . . 65 C2
Roserton St E14 . . . . . 42 B4
Rose Sq SW7 . . . . . . 143 C2
Rose St
Holborn EC4 . . . . . . 108 B2
Strand WC2 . . . . 120 A4
Rose Theatre SE1 . . 122 C2
Rosethorn Cl
SW12 . . . . 73 C4
Rosetta Cl SW8 . . . . 162 B1
Roseway SE21 . . . . . . 63 C1
Rosewood Ct **2**
E11 . . . . 19 C4
Rosewood Gdns
SE13 . . . . 52 B1
Rosewood Ho **9**
NW3 . . . . 11 A2
Rosewood Sq W12 . . 29 C3
Rosher Cl E15 . . . . 19 C1
Rosina St E9 . . . . 17 C2
Roskell Rd SW15 . . . . 57 C4
Roslin Ho **2** E1 . . . . . 32 C2
Roslin Rd W3 . . . . 37 A3
Rosmead Rd
W11 . . . . 31 A2 112 B4
Rosoman Pl EC1 . . . . . 95 C2
Rosoman St EC1 . . . . . 95 C3
Ross Ct
1 Hackney E5 . . . . . 17 A4
4 Putney SW15 . . . . 57 C1
Rossdale Rd SW15 . . 57 B3
Rosse Gdns SE13 . . . . 67 C1
Rossendale Way
NW1 . . . . 83 A4
Rossetti Ct WC1 . . . . 105 B4
Rossetti Gdns Mans
SW3 . . . . 158 C4
Rossetti Ho SW1 . . . 147 C3
Rossetti Mews
NW8 . . . . 79 C3
Rossetti Rd SE16 . . . . 40 A1
Rossetti Studios
SW3 . . . . 158 A4
Ross Ho **16** E1 . . . . . . 32 A1
Rossington St E5 . . . . . 7 C2
Rossiter Rd SW12 . . . 73 A3
Rosslyn Ave SW13 . . 56 A4
Rosslyn Ct NW3 . . . . . 12 A3
Rosslyn Hill NW3 . . . 11 C3
Rosslyn Ho **8**
TW9 . . . . 44 B2

Rosslyn Mans
8 Hampstead
NW3 . . . . 11 B2
South Hampstead
NW6 . . . . 11 B2
Rosslyn Mews **7**
NW3 . . . . 11 C4
Rosslyn Park Mews
NW3 . . . . 11 C3
Rossmore Ct NW1 . . . 90 C2
Rossmore Rd NW1 . . . 90 B2
Rostrevor Mans
SW6 . . . . 164 C4
Rostrevor Mews
SW6 . . . . 164 C3
Rostrevor Rd
SW6 . . . . 164 C4
Rotary Lo **12** SE27 . . 75 A1
Rotary St SE1 . . . . . . 136 B2
Rothay NW1 . . . . 92 B4
Rothbury Rd E9 . . . . . 18 C1
Rotheley Ho **31** E9 . . 17 B1
Rotherfield Ct
De Beauvoir Town
N1 . . . . 15 C1
Shoreditch N1 . . . . . . 87 B4
Rotherfield Prim Sch
Islington N1 . . . . 15 B1
Shoreditch N1 . . . . . . 87 A4
Rotherfield St
SE1 . . . . 122 A1
ROTHERHITHE 40 C3
Rotherhithe Bsns Est
8 SE16 . . . . 40 B4
Rotherhithe New Rd
SE16 . . . . 40 A1
Rotherhithe Old Rd
SE16 . . . . 40 C2
Rotherhithe Prim Sch
24 SE16 . . . . 40 C3
Rotherhithe St
SE16 . . . . 40 B4
Rotherhithe Sta
SE16 . . . . 40 B4
Rotherhithe Tunnel
E1 . . . . 32 C1
Rother Ho SE15 . . . . . 65 A3
Rotherwick Rd
NW11 . . . . 1 C4
Rotherwood Rd
SW15 . . . . 57 C4
Rothery St N1 . . . . 86 B4
Rothesay Ave SW14,
TW10 . . . . 55 A3
Rothesay Ct **13**
SE11 . . . . 163 B3
Rothley Ct NW8 . . . . . 89 B2
Rothsay St SE1 . . . . . 138 A1
Rothsay Wlk **19**
E14 . . . . 41 C2
Rothschild Rd W4 . . . 37 B3
Rothwell St
16 Hampstead
NW1 . . . . 12 B1
Primrose Hill NW1 . . . 81 A4
Roth Wlk N7 . . . . 5 B2
Rotten Row SW1 130 C4
Rotterdam Dr E14 . . . 42 B3
Rouel Rd
Bermondsey
SE16 . . . . 139 C1
Bermondsey SE16 . . 139 B1
Roundacre SW19 . . . . 69 C2
Roundel Cl SE4 . . . . . 66 B3

Roundhouse Theatre
NW1 . . . . 12 C1
Roundwood Rd
NW10 . . . . 8 B1
Rounton Rd E3 . . . . . . 26 C1
Roupell Rd SW2 . . . . . 74 B3
Roupell St SE1 . . . . . 121 C1
Rousden St NW1 . . . . 13 B1
Routh Rd SW18 . . . . . 72 A4
Rover Ho **26** N1 . . . . 24 A4
Rowallan Rd SW6 154 A1
Rowan Cl W5 . . . . 36 A4
Rowan Ct
10 Camberwell
SE15 . . . . 49 B3
Wandsworth SW11 . . 60 B1
Rowan Ho
Bow E3 . . . . 26 B4
Dagenham NW10 . . . 21 A1
5 Maitland Pk
NW3 . . . . 12 B2
Rowan Rd W6 . . . . 39 C2
Rowan Terr W6 . . . . . . 39 C2
Rowan Wlk
7 Dartmouth Pk
N19 . . . . 4 B2
Kensal Town W10 . . . 23 A1
Rowberry Cl SW6 . . . . 47 B3
Rowcross St SE1 . . . 153 A2
Rowditch La
SW11 . . . . 169 B2
Rowdon Ave NW10 . . 9 A1
Rowe Ho E9 . . . . 17 B2
Rowe La E9 . . . . 17 B3
Rowena Cres
SW11 . . . . 168 B1
Rowfant Rd SW12,
SW17 . . . . 72 C2
Rowhill Mans **11**
E5 . . . . 17 A4
Rowhill Rd E5 . . . . 17 A4
Rowington Cl W2 . . . 100 A4
Rowland Hill Ho
SE1 . . . . 136 A4
Rowland Hill St
NW3 . . . . 12 A3
Rowley Gdns N4 . . . . . 6 B4
Rowley Ho SE8 . . . . . . 51 C4
Rowley Ind Pk W3 . . . 37 A3
Rowley Way NW8 . . . 78 C4
Rowntree Cl NW6 . . . 10 C2
Rowse Cl E15 . . . . 27 B4
Rowstock **1** NW5 . . 13 C2
Rowstock Gdns
N7 . . . . 13 C3
Roxby Pl SW6 . . . . . 155 C4
Roxford Ho **2** E3 . . . 27 A1
Roxley Rd SE13 . . . . . 67 A1
Roxwell **10** NW1 . . . 13 A2
Roxwell Rd W12 . . . . 38 C4
Royal Academy of
Dramatic Art
WC1 . . . . 105 A4
Royal Acad of Arts
W1 . . . . 118 C3
Royal Acad of Dance
SW11 . . . . 167 C3
Royal Acad of Music
NW1 . . . . 91 C1
Royal Albert Hall
SW7 . . . . 129 B3
Royal Arc W1 . . . . . . 118 C3
Royal Armouries The
E1 . . . . 124 C3
Royal Ave SW3 . . . . 144 C2

Royal Avenue Ho
SW3 . . . . **144** C2

Royal Ballet Upper
Sch The WC2 . . . . . **106** B1

Royal Brompton Hospl
Chelsea SW3 . . . . . **143** B2
Chelsea SW3 . . . . . **144** A2

Royal Cir SE27 . . . . . **75** A1

Royal Cl
Deptford SE8 . . . . . . **51** B4
Putney SW19 . . . . . . **69** C2
Stamford Hill N16 . . . . **7** A3

Royal College of
Physicians Liby
NW1 . . . . **92** B2

Royal College St
NW1 . . . . **83** A4

Royal Coll of
Anaesthetists
WC1 . . . . **106** C3

Royal Coll of Art
SW7 . . . . **129** B3

Royal Coll of Art
Sculpture Sch
SW11 . . . . **158** A1

Royal Coll of
Midwives W1 . . . . **104** A3

Royal Coll of Music
SW7 . . . . **129** B2

Royal Coll of
Obstetricians &
Gynaecologists
NW1 . . . . **90** C3

Royal Coll of
Ophthalmologists
NW1 . . . . **91** B1

Royal Coll of
Paediatrics & Child
Health W1 . . . . . . **107** A4

Royal Coll of
Pathologists
SW1 . . . . **119** B1

Royal Coll of
Physicians NW1 . . . **92** B2

Royal Coll of
Radiologists W1 . . **104** B3

Royal Coll of Science
SW7 . . . . **129** B2

Royal Coll of Speech
Language Therapists
SE1 . . . . **123** B1

Royal Coll of
Surgeons WC2 . . . **107** A2

Royal Coll of
Veterinary Surgeons
SW1 . . . . **134** A1

Royal Courts of
Justice WC2 . . . . . **107** B1

Royal Cres
W11 . . . . . . **31** A1 **112** A4

Royal Crescent Mews
W11 . . . . **30** C1

Royal Ct
City of London
EC3 . . . . **109** C1
Rotherhithe SE16 . . . . **41** B3

Royal Duchess Mews
SW12 . . . . **73** A4

Royal Exchange
EC3 . . . . **109** C1

Royal Exchange Bldgs
EC3 . . . . **109** C1

Royal Festival Hall
SE1 . . . . **121** A1

Royal Free Hospl
NW3 . . . . **12** A3

Royal Fusiliers Mus
E1 . . . . **124** C3

Royal Geographical
Society SW7 . . . . . **129** C3

Royal Hill SE10 . . . . . **52** B3

Royal Hill Ct
SE10 . . . . **52** B3

Royal Horticultural
Society (Lawrence
Hall & Conf Ctr)
SW1 . . . . **133** B1

Royal Horticultural
Society (Lindley
Hall) SW1 . . . . . . **147** B4

Royal Hospital
Chelsea The
SW1 . . . . **145** B1

Royal Hospital Rd
SW3 . . . . **145** A1

Royal Hospl for Neuro-
Disability The
SW15 . . . . **58** A1

Royal Hospl Mus
SW3 . . . . **145** A1

Royal Institute of
British Architects
W1 . . . . **104** B4

Royal Institution Mus
The SW1 . . . . **118** C3

Royal Langford
Apartments **3**
NW6 . . . . **78** A2

Royal London Est The
NW10 . . . . **20** C3

Royal London Hospl
for Integrated
Medicine WC1 . . . **106** B4

Royal London Surgical
Mus E1 . . . . **32** A4

Royal London Hospl
(Whitechapel) The
E1 . . . . **32** A4

Royal Marsden Hospl
SW3 . . . . **143** C2

Royal Mews The
SW1 . . . . **132** B2

Royal Mint Pl **8**
E1 . . . . **125** A4

Royal Mint St E1 . . **125** A4

Royal National
Orthopaedic Hospl
W1 . . . . **92** B1

Royal National TNE
Hospl The WC1 . . . **94** C4

Royal Naval Pl
SE14 . . . . **51** B3

Royal Oak Ct **3**
N1 . . . . **24** A2 **98** A4

Royal Oak Pl SE22 . . . **65** A1

Royal Oak Rd **5**
E8 . . . . **17** A2

Royal Oak Sta W2 **100** B3

Royal Oak Yd SE1 . **138** A3

Royal Observatory
The SE10 . . . . **52** C3

Royal Opera Arc
SW1 . . . . **119** B2

Royal Orchard Cl
SW18 . . . . **70** A4

Royal Par
Blackheath Vale
SE3 . . . . **53** B1
Fulham SW6 . . . . . **154** A2
13 Richmond TW9 . . . . **44** C3

Royal Pl **11** SE10 . . . . **52** B3

Royal Rd SE17 . . . . . . **48** A4

Royal Sch Hampstead
The **8** NW3 . . . . . . **11** C4

Royal St SE1 . . . . . **135** A2

Royalty Ho W1 . . . . **105** B1

Royalty Mews W1 . **105** B1

Royalty Studios
W11 . . . . **31** A3

Royal United Services
Mus SW1 . . . . **120** A1

Royal Veterinary Coll
NW1 . . . . **83** B3

Royal Victoria Sta
E16 . . . . **35** C2

Royal Victor Pl E3 . . **25** C3

Roycroft Cl SW2 . . . . **74** C3

Roydon Cl **7**
SW11 . . . . **168** C2

Roy Ridley Ho **6**
SW4 . . . . **61** C4

Roy Sq E14 . . . . **33** A2

Royston Cl
New Cross SE4 . . . . . . **51** B1
3 Richmond TW10 . . **54** A2

Royston Ho **14**
SE15 . . . . **49** C4

Royston Rd TW10 . . . **54** A2

Royston St **2** E2 . . . . **25** B3

Rozel Ct **3** N1 . . . . . . **24** A4

Rozel Rd SW4 . . . . . . **61** B4

Ruby St SE15 . . . . **50** A4

Ruby Triangle
SE15 . . . . **50** A4

Ruckholt Rd E9,
E10 . . . . **18** C4

Rucklidge Ave
NW10 . . . . **21** C3

Rudall Cres NW3 . . . . **11** C4

Rudbeck Ho **11**
SE15 . . . . **49** C3

Ruddington Cl E5 . . . **18** A4

Rudge Ho **1**
SE16 . . . . **139** C2

Rudgwick Terr
NW8 . . . . **80** B3

Rudhall Ho **4**
SW2 . . . . **62** C1

Rudloe Rd SW12 . . . . **73** B4

Rudolf Pl SW8 . . . . . **162** B3

Rudolph Rd NW6 . . . . **23** C3

Rudstone Ho **10**
E3 . . . . **27** A2

Rudyard Ct SE1 . . . **137** C3

Rufford St N1 . . . . . . **84** B4

Rufford Street Mews
N1 . . . . **14** A1

Rufford St N1 . . . . . . **28** A1

Rufus Bsns Ctr
SW18 . . . . **71** A2

Rufus Ho SE1 . . . . . **139** A2

Rufus St N1 . . . . **24** A2 **98** A3

Rugby Mans W14 . . **140** B4

Rugby Rd W4 . . . . **38** A4

Rugby St WC1 . . . . . . **94** C1

Rugg St E14 . . . . **33** C2

Rugless Ho **2** E14 . . . . **42** B4

Rugmere **4** NW1 . . . . **12** C1

Rumball Ho **14**
SE5 . . . . **49** A3

Rumbold Rd SW6 . **156** B1

Rum Cl E1 . . . . **32** B2

Rumford Ho SE1 . . **136** C1

Rumsey Rd SW9 . . . . **62** B4

Runacres Ct SE17 . **150** C1

Runcorn Pl
W11 . . . . . . **31** A2 **112** A4

Rundell Twr SW8 . . **172** C4

Running Horse Yd **12**
TW8 . . . . **44** A4

Runnymede Ct
SW15 . . . . **68** C3

Runnymede Ho
Hackney E9 . . . . **18** A4
Richmond TW10 . . . . . **54** C2

Rupack St **3** SE16 . . **40** B4

Rupert Ct W1 . . . . . **119** B4

Rupert Gdns SW9 . . . **48** A1

Rupert Ho
SE11 . . . . **149** C3
8 Upper Holloway
N19 . . . . **4** C1

Rupert Rd
Bedford Pk W4 . . . . . **38** A3
Paddington NW6 . . . . **23** B3
Upper Holloway N19 . . **4** C2

Rupert St W1 . . . . . **119** B4

Rusbridge Cl E8 . . . . **16** C3

Ruscoe Rd E16 . . . . . **35** B3

Rusham Rd SW12 . . . **72** B4

Rushbrook Ho **20**
SW8 . . . . **171** B2

Rushby Ct SW4 . . . **172** A3

Rush Common Mews
18 SW2 . . . . **74** B4

Rushcroft Rd SW2,
SW9 . . . . **62** C3

Rushcutters Ct **18**
SE16 . . . . **41** A2

Rushey Mead SE4 . . . **66** C2

Rushford Rd SE4 . . . . **66** B1

Rush Hill Mews **3**
SW11 . . . . **60** C4

Rush Hill Rd SW11 . . **60** C4

Rushlake Ho **10**
SW11 . . . . **169** B2

Rushmead **5** E2 . . . . **25** A2

Rushmere Ho **7**
SW15 . . . . **68** C3

Rushmore Cres **9**
E5 . . . . **17** C4

Rushmore Ho
8 Kentish Town
N7 . . . . **13** C3
W14 . . . . **126** B1

Rushmore Prim Sch
12 E5 . . . . **17** C4

Rushmore Rd
Clapton Pk E5 . . . . . . **17** C4
Hackney E5 . . . . **18** A4

Rusholme Rd
SW15 . . . . **58** A1

Rushton Ho **20**
SW8 . . . . **171** B1

Rushton St N1 . . . . . . **87** C2

Rushworth St SE1 **136** B3

Ruskin Ave TW9 . . . . **44** C3

Ruskin Ct SE5 . . . . . . **63** C4

Ruskin Ho SW1 . . . **147** C3

Ruskin Park Ho
SE5 . . . . **63** C4

Ruskin Wlk SE24 . . . . **63** B2

Rusper Ct SW9 . . . . **172** B1

Russell Cl W4 . . . . . . **46** B4

Russell Ct
Battersea SW11 . . . **169** C3
Bloomsbury WC1 . . . . **94** A1
5 Peckham SE15 . . . . **50** A1
St James SW1 . . . . . **119** A1

Russell Gdns W14 . **126** A2

Russell Gdns Mews
W14 . . . . **126** A2

Russell Gr SW9 . . . . . **173** C4

Russell Ho
21 Poplar E14 . . . . . . **33** C3
SW1 . . . . **146** C2

Russell Kerr Cl
W4 . . . . **45** B3

Russell Lo SE1 . . . . **137** B2

Russell Mans
SW6 . . . . **164** A4

Russell Pickering Ho
2 SW4 . . . . **62** A4

Russell Pl
Hampstead NW3 . . . . **12** A3
Rotherhithe SE16 . . . . **41** A3

Russell Rd W14 . . . **126** B1

Russell Sq WC1 . . . . **94** A1

Russell Square Ho
WC1 . . . . **94** A1

Russell Square Mans
WC1 . . . . **94** A1

Russell Square Sta
WC1 . . . . **106** B4

Russell St WC2 . . . **120** B4

Russell's Wharf **2**
W9 . . . . **23** B1

Russell Wlk **4**
TW10 . . . . **54** B1

Russell Yd SW15 . . . . **58** A3

Russet Cres N7 . . . . . **14** B3

Russett Way SE13 . . . **52** A1

Russia Dock Rd
SE16 . . . . **33** A1

Russia La E2 . . . . **25** B3

Russia Row EC2 . . . **109** A1

Rusthall Ave W4 . . . . **37** C3

Rusthall Mans **5**
W4 . . . . **37** C2

Ruston Mews W11 . . . **31** A3

Ruston St E3 . . . . **26** B4

Rust Sq SE5 . . . . **48** C3

Ruth Ct **18** E3 . . . . . . **26** A3

Rutherford Ho **12**
2 . . . . **25** A3

Rutherford St
SW1 . . . . **147** B4

Ruth Ho W10 . . . . . . **23** A1

Ruthin Rd SE3 . . . . . . **53** C4

Ruthven St E9 . . . . . . **25** C4

Rutland Cl SW14 . . . . **55** B4

Rutland Ct
Herne Hill SE5 . . . . . **63** C3
SW7 . . . . **130** B3

Rutland Gate
SW7 . . . . **130** B3

Rutland Gate Mews
SW7 . . . . **130** A3

Rutland Gdns
SW7 . . . . **130** B3

Rutland Gdns Mews
SW7 . . . . **130** B3

Rutland Gr W6 . . . . . . **39** A1

Rutland Ho
10 Putney SW15 . . . . **69** B4
W8 . . . . **128** A1

Rutland Mews **21**
NW8 . . . . **78** B3

Rutland Mews E
SW7 . . . . **130** B2

Rutland Mews S
SW7 . . . . **130** A2

Rutland Mews W
SW7 . . . . **130** A2

Rutland Park Gdns [1]
NW2 . . . . 9 B2
Rutland Park Mans [1]
NW2 . . . . 9 B2
Rutland Pk NW2 . . . . 9 B2
Rutland Pl EC1 . . . . . . 108 B4
Rutland Rd E9 . . . . 25 C4
Rutland St SW7 . . . . . 130 B2
Rutland Studios
NW10 . . . . 21 C2
Rutley Cl SE11 . . . . 48 A4
Rutt's Terr SE14 . . . . . . 50 C2
Ruvigny Gdns
SW15 . . . . 57 C4
Ruvigny Mans [7]
SW15 . . . . 57 C4
Rycott Path SE22 . . . . . 76 C4
Ryculff Sq SE3 . . . . 53 B1
Rydal Ho [25] SW8 . . . 171 B1
Rydal Rd SW16 . . . . . . 73 C1
Rydal Water NW1 . . . . 92 C3
Ryde Ho [1] NW6 . . . . . 23 C4
Ryder Ct SW1 . . . . 119 A2
Ryder Dr SE16 . . . . 40 A1
Ryder Ho [10] E1 . . . . . . 25 B1
Ryder St SW1 . . . . 119 A2
Ryder's Terr NW8 . . . . . 78 C2
Ryder Yd SW1 . . . . . . 119 A2
Ryde Vale Rd
SW12 . . . . 73 B2
Rydon St N1 . . . . 87 A4
Rydston Cl [2] N7 . . . . . 14 B1
Ryecotes Mead
SE21 . . . . 76 A3
Ryecroft Rd SE13 . . . . . 67 B2
Ryecroft St SW6 . . . . . 166 A3
Ryedale SE22 . . . . 65 A1
Ryefield Path [7]
SW15 . . . . 68 C3
Ryegates [2] SE15 . . . . . 50 A1
Rye Hill Pk SE15 . . . . . 65 B3
Rye Ho [9] SE16 . . . . . . 40 B4
Rye La SE15 . . . . 49 C1
Rye Lane Mkt
SE15 . . . . 49 C1
Rye Oak Sch [1]
SE15 . . . . 65 A4
Rye Rd SE15 . . . . 65 C3
Rye Wlk SW15 . . . . 57 C2
Ryfold Rd SW19 . . . . . . 70 C1
Ryland Rd NW5 . . . . . . 13 A2
Rylett Cres W12 . . . . . . 38 B3
Rylett Rd W12 . . . . 38 B3
Rylston Rd SW6 . . . . . 154 C3
Rymer St SE24 . . . . 63 A1
Rysbrack St SW1 . . . . 130 C2

S

Saatchi Gallery
SW3 . . . . 145 A2
Sabbarton St [9]
E16 . . . . 35 B3
Sabella Ct E3 . . . . 26 B3
Sabine Rd SW11 . . . . . 60 C4
Sable St N1 . . . . 15 A1
Sacketts Ho [24]
SW9 . . . . 173 C4
Sackville Ho [18]
SW16 . . . . 74 A1
Sackville St W1 . . . . . 119 A3
Sacred Heart High
Sch [9] W6 . . . . 39 B2

Sacred Heart Prim
Sch, Battersea
SW11 . . . . 168 B1
Sacred Heart RC Prim
Sch SW15 . . . . 56 C2
Sacred Heart RC Sec
Sch [10] SE5 . . . . 48 B2
Sacred Heart Sch
N7 . . . . 14 B3
Saddlers Mews
SW8 . . . . 172 B4
Sadler Ho
[17] Bromley E3 . . . . . 27 A2
EC1 . . . . 96 A4
Saffron Ave E14 . . . . . . 34 C2
Saffron Ct [3] N1 . . . . . 15 C2
Saffron Hill EC1 . . . . . 107 C4
Saffron St EC1 . . . . . . 107 C4
Saffron Wharf
SE1 . . . . 139 A4
Sage Mews SE22 . . . . . 64 B2
Sage St E1 . . . . 32 B2
Sage Way WC1 . . . . . . 94 C3
Sailacre Ho [10]
SE10 . . . . 43 B1
Sail Ct [11] E14 . . . . . . 34 C2
Sailmakers Ct
SW6 . . . . 59 B4
Sail St SE11 . . . . 149 A4
Sainfoin Rd SW17 . . . . 72 C2
St Agnes Cl E9 . . . . 25 B4
St Agnes Pl SE11 . . . . . 48 A4
St Agnes RC Prim Sch
[18] E3 . . . . 27 A2
London NW2 . . . . 1 A1
St Aidan's Prim Sch
N4 . . . . 5 C2
St Aidan's Rd SE22 . . 65 A2
St Albans Ave W4 . . . . 37 C3
St Alban's CE Prim
Sch EC1 . . . . 107 B4
St Alban's Cl NW11 . . 1 C3
St Alban's Gr W8 . . . . 128 B2
St Albans La NW11 . . . 1 C3
St Albans Mans
W8 . . . . 128 B2
St Alban's Pl N1 . . . . . 86 A3
St Alban's Rd
Dagenham NW10 . . . . 21 A4
Dartmouth Pk NW5 . . . 4 A1
St Alban's St SW1 . . . 119 B3
St Albans Studios
W8 . . . . 128 B2
St Albans Terr
W6 . . . . 154 A4
St Alban's Villas
NW5 . . . . 3 C1
St Alfege Pas SE10 . . 52 B4
St Alfege with St
Peter's CE Prim Sch
SE10 . . . . 52 B3
St Aloysius Convent
NW1 . . . . 93 A4
St Aloysius RC Coll [9]
N19 . . . . 4 B3
St Aloysius RC Inf Sch
NW1 . . . . 93 A4
St Aloysius RC Jun
Sch NW1 . . . . 83 B1
St Alphage Gdn
EC2 . . . . 109 A3
St Alphage Highwalk
EC2 . . . . 109 A3

St Alphonsus Rd
SW4 . . . . 61 C3
St Andrew & St
Francis CE Prim Sch
[6] NW2 . . . . 9 B2
St Andrew's
(Barnsbury) Prim
Sch N1 . . . . 85 A4
St Andrews Chambers
W1 . . . . 105 A2
St Andrews Cl [8]
SE16 . . . . 40 A1
St Andrews Ct W4 . . 45 B2
St Andrew's Ct [2]
SW18 . . . . 71 B2
St Andrew's Gr N16 . . 6 C3
St Andrew's Greek
Sch N4 . . . . 13 B2
St Andrew's Hill
EC4 . . . . 108 B1
St Andrews Ho [1]
SE16 . . . . 40 A3
St Andrews Mans [9]
E5 . . . . 17 A4
St Andrew's Mans
W1 . . . . 103 B3
St Andrews Mews
Greenwich SE3 . . . . . 53 C3
[4] Streatham
SW12 . . . . 73 C3
St Andrew's Mews
N16 . . . . 7 A3
St Andrew's Pl
NW1 . . . . 92 B2
St Andrew's Prim Sch
[22] SW9 . . . . 172 B1
St Andrew's Rd
W3 . . . . 29 A3
St Andrew's Rd
W14 . . . . 154 B4
Willesden NW2 . . . . . . 9 A2
St Andrew's Sq
W11 . . . . 31 A3
St Andrew St EC4 . . 107 C3
St Andrews Way
E3 . . . . 27 A1
St Andrew's Wharf
SE1 . . . . 139 A4
St Anne RC Prim Sch
[18] E1 . . . . 24 C1
St Anne's CE Prim Sch
[6] SW18 . . . . 59 A2
St Anne's Cl N6 . . . . . 3 C1
St Anne's Ct NW6 . . . 23 A4
St Annes Ho [11]
E14 . . . . 105 B1
St Anne's Flats
NW1 . . . . 93 B4
St Anne's Pas E14 . . 33 B3
St Anne's RC Prim Sch
SE11 . . . . 162 C4
St Anne's Row E14 . . 33 B3
St Anne's St E14 . . . . 33 B3
St Anne's Trad Est [2]
E14 . . . . 33 B3
St Ann's Cres
SW18 . . . . 59 B1
St Ann's Gdns
NW5 . . . . 12 C2
St Ann's Hill SW18 . . 59 B1
St Ann's Ho WC1 . . . 95 B3
St Ann's La SW1 . . . . 133 C1
St Ann's Park Rd
SW18 . . . . 59 B1
St Anns Rd
Barnes SW13 . . . . 46 B2

St Anns Rd continued
Shepherd's Bush
W11 . . . . 30 C2
St Ann's St SW1 . . . . 133 C2
St Ann's Terr NW8 . . 79 C2
St Ann's Villas
W11 . . . 31 A1 112 A1
St Anselm's Pl
W1 . . . . 118 A4
St Anselm's RC Prim
Sch SW17 . . . . 72 C1
St Anthonys Cl [5]
SW17 . . . . 72 A2
St Anthony's Cl
[8] E1 . . . . 125 B2
[5] Hackney Wick
E9 . . . . 18 B2
St Anthony's Ct
[2] Balham SW12 . . 60 C1
Upper Tooting
SW17 . . . . 72 C2
St Anthony's Flats
NW1 . . . . 83 B1
St Anthony's RC Prim
Sch SE22 . . . . 64 C1
St Asaph Ct SE4 . . . . 65 C4
St Asaph Rd SE4 . . . . 65 C4
St Aubins Ct N1 . . . . . 87 C4
St Augustine's CE
High Sch [5]
NW6 . . . . 23 C3
St Augustine's Ho
NW1 . . . . 93 B4
St Augustine's Prim
Sch [8] NW6 . . . . 78 A2
St Augustine's RC
Prim Sch W6 . . . . . . 154 B3
St Augustine's Rd
NW1 . . . . 13 C1
St Austell Rd SE13 . . 52 C1
St Barnabas CE Prim
Sch SW1 . . . . 145 C2
St Barnabas Cl [1]
SE22 . . . . 64 A2
St Barnabas & St
Philip CE Prim Sch
W8 . . . . 127 B1
St Barnabas St
SW1 . . . . 145 C2
St Barnabas Terr
E9 . . . . 17 C3
St Barnabas Villas
SW8 . . . . 172 B4
St Bartholomew's
Hospl EC1 . . . . 108 B3
St Bartholomew's Mus
EC1 . . . . 108 B3
St Bede's RC Inf Sch
SW12 . . . . 73 C3
St Benets Cl [8]
SW17 . . . . 72 A2
St Benet's Pl EC3 . . 123 C4
St Bernadette RC Jun
Sch [2] SW12 . . . . . . 73 B4
St Bernard Ho [6]
E14 . . . . 42 B3
St Botolph St E1,
EC3 . . . . 110 C2
St Brelades Ct N1 . . . 87 C4
St Bride's Ave
EC4 . . . . 108 A1
St Bride's Pas
EC4 . . . . 108 A1

St Bride St EC4 . . . . . 108 A2
St Catherines Cl [7]
SW17 . . . . 72 A2
St Catherine's Ct [5]
W4 . . . . 38 A3
St Catherine's Dr
SE14 . . . . 50 C1
St Catherines Mews
SW3 . . . . 144 C4
St Cecilia's CE Sch
SW18 . . . . 70 B3
St Chad's Pl WC1 . . . 94 B4
St Chad's St WC1 . . . 94 B4
St Charles' Hospl
W10 . . . . 30 C4
St Charles Pl W10 . . 31 A4
St Charles RC Prim
Sch [7] W10 . . . . 30 C4
St Charles RC Sixth
Form Coll [6]
W10 . . . . 30 C4
St Charles Sq W10 . . 30 C4
St Christina's RC Prep
Sch NW8 . . . . 80 B2
St Christopher's CE
N19 . . . . 4 B1
St Christopher's Ho
NW1 . . . . 83 B1
St Christopher's Pl
W1 . . . . 103 C2
St Christopher's Sch
[4] NW3 . . . . 11 C3
St Clair Ho [17] E3 . . 26 B2
St Clare St EC3 . . . . 110 C1
St Clement Danes CE
Prim Sch W2 . . . . . . 106 C1
St Clement & St
James CE Prim Sch
W11 . . . 31 A1 112 A1
St Clements Ct
Barnsbury N7 . . . . . . 14 B2
[7] SE14 . . . . 50 C4
[6] Shepherd's Bush
W11 . . . . 30 C2
St Clement's Ct
EC3 . . . . 123 C4
St Clements Ho
E1 . . . . 110 C3
St Clement's La
WC2 . . . . 107 A1
St Clements Mans [3]
SW6 . . . . 47 C4
St Clements St N7 . . 14 C1
St Columb's Ho [11]
W10 . . . . 31 A4
St Crispins Cl
NW3 . . . . 12 A4
St Cross St EC1 . . . . 107 C4
St Cuthbert's Rd
NW2 . . . . 10 B2
St Cuthbert with St
Matthias CE Prim
Sch SW5 . . . . 142 A2
St Davids Cl [27]
SE16 . . . . 40 A1
St David's Sq E14 . . . 42 A1
St Dionis Rd SW6 . . 165 A2
St Dominic RC Prim
Sch [14] NW5 . . . . . . 12 B3
St Dominics RC Prim
Sch [8] E9 . . . . 18 A2
St Donatt's Rd
New Cross Gate
SE4 . . . . 51 B2

St Dunstan Ave
W3 . . . . .28 C2
St Dunstan Gdns
W3 . . . . .28 C2
St Dunstan's Alley
EC3 . . . .**124 A3**
St Dunstan's Ct
EC4 . . . .**107** C1
St Dunstan's Hill
EC3 . . . .**124 A3**
St Dunstan's La
EC3 . . . .**124 A3**
St Dunstan's Rd
W6 . . . . .39 C1
St Edmunds Cl 图
SW17 . . . . .72 A2
St Edmund's Cl
NW8 . . . . .80 C3
St Edmund's Ct
NW8 . . . . .80 C3
St Edmunds RC Prim
Sch E14 . . . . .41 C2
St Edmund's Sq
SW13 . . . . .47 B4
St Edmund's Terr
NW8 . . . . .80 C3
St Edward's RC Prim
Sch NW1 . . . . .90 B1
St Elizabeth RC Prim
Sch 图 E2 . . . . .25 B3
St Elizabeth's RC Prim
Sch W10 . . . . .54 B1
St Elmo Rd W12 . . . .38 B4
St Elmos Rd SE16 . . .41 A4
St Ermin's Hill
SW1 . . . .**133** B2
St Ervan's Rd W10 . .31 B4
St Eugene de
Mazenod RC Prim
Sch 图 NW6 . . . . .10 C1
St Faith's CE Prim Sch
图 SW18 . . . . .59 B3
St Faith's Rd SE24 . .75 A3
St Francesca Cabrini
RC Prim Sch
SE23 . . . . .65 B1
St Francis' Ho
NW1 . . . . .83 B1
St Francis of Assisi
Prim Sch 图 W11 . .30 C2
St Francis Pl
SW12 . . . . .61 A1
St Francis RC Prim
Sch 図 SE15 . . . . . . .49 C3
St Francis Rd
SE22 . . . . .64 A3
St Francis Xavier Coll
SW12 . . . . .61 A1
St Frideswides Mews
图 E14 . . . . .34 B3
St Gabriel's CE Prim
Sch SW1 . . . .**146** C1
St Gabriels Cl 图
E14 . . . . .34 A4
St Gabriel's Rd
NW2 . . . . .9 C3
St George Ho
SW11 . . . .**169** C3
**ST GEORGE IN THE
EAST** 32 A2
St George's Ave
N7 . . . . .13 C4
St George's Bldgs
SE11 . . . .**136** B1
St George's Cath
NW1 . . . . .92 B4

**St George's Cath RC
Prim Sch** SE1 . . . . .**136 A2**
**St George's CE Prim
Sch**
图 SE5 . . . . .49 A3
SW8 . . . .**161** A1
St George's Circ
SE1 . . . .**136 A2**
St Georges Cl
SW8 . . . .**171** A4
St Georges Coll N7 . .5 C1
St Georges Ct
SW15 . . . . .58 B3
St Georges Ct
Brompton SW3 . . . . .**144** A4
Kensington SW7 . . . .**128** C1
Newington SE1 . . . . .**136** A1
St George's Dr
SW1 . . . .**146** C2
St George's Field
W2 . . . .**102** B1
St George's Gr
SW17 . . . . .71 C1
**St Georges Hanover
Sq** Sch W1 . . . . . .**117** C3
St George's Ho
NW1 . . . . .83 A1
St George's La
EC3 . . . .**124** A4
St Georges Mews 图
NW1 . . . . .12 B1
St George's Mews
图 Rotherhithe
SE8 . . . . .41 B2
SE1 . . . .**135** C2
St Georges Pl N7 . .13 C4
St George's Pools
E1 . . . . .32 A2
St George's RC Cath
SE1 . . . .**135** C2
**St George's RC Sec
Sch** W9 . . . . .78 B1
St Georges Rd W4 . .37 C4
St George's Rd
Newington SE1 . . . . .**136** A1
Richmond TW9 . . . . . .54 B4
**St George's
Residences 图**
SW2 . . . . .62 C2
St George's Ct
EC4 . . . .**108** A2
St Georges Sq 图
E14 . . . . .33 A2
St George's Sq
Rotherhithe SE8 . . . . .41 A2
SW1 . . . .**147** B1
**St George's Square
Mews** SW1 . . . . . .**147** B1
St George St W1 . . .**118** B4
St Georges Terr
Hampstead NW1 . . . .12 B1
NW1 . . . . .81 A4
St George's Way
SE15 . . . . .49 C4
**St George the Martyr
CE Prim Sch**
WC1 . . . . .95 A1
St George Wharf
SW8 . . . .**162** A4
St George Wharf Pier
SW8 . . . .**162** A4
St Gerards Cl SW4 . .61 B2
St German's Pl
SE3 . . . . .53 C2
St Gildas' RC Jun Sch
图 N8 . . . . .5 A4

ST GILES **106** A2
St Giles Cir WC1 . . .**105** C2
St Giles Coll WC1 . .**106** A2
St Giles Ct WC2 . . . .**106** A2
St Giles High St
WC2 . . . .**105** C2
St Giles Ho SW16 . . .74 A1
St Giles Pas WC2 . . .**105** C1
St Giles Rd SE5 . . . .49 A2
St Giles Terr EC1 . . .**109** A3
St Giles Twr 图
SE5 . . . . .49 A2
St Gilles Ho 图 E2 . . .25 C3
St Helena Ho WC1 . .95 B3
St Helena Rd SE16 . .40 C2
St Helena St WC1 . . .95 B3
St Helens Gdns
W10 . . . . .30 C3
St Helen's Pl EC3 . . .**110** A2
St Helen's RC Sch 图
SW9 . . . . .62 C4
St Helier Ct 图 N1 . . .24 A4
St Hilda's Cl NW6 . . .9 C1
St Hilda's Ct 图
SW17 . . . . .72 A2
St Hilda's Rd
SW13 . . . . .47 A4
St Hildas Wharf
E1 . . . . .32 B1
St Hubert's Ho 图
E14 . . . . .41 C3
St Hughes Cl 图
SW17 . . . . .72 A2
St Ives Ct NW2 . . . . .10 A2
ST JAMES **119** B2
St James Cl
图 Bethnal Green
E2 . . . . .24 C2 **99** C3
图 Brentford W4 . . . .36 C1
St James' Ct
Bedford Pk W4 . . . . .37 C3
SW1 . . . .**133** A2
St James Ho N5 . . . .14 C3
**St James Independent
Schs** W14 . . . .**140** B4
St James Ind Mews 图
SE1 . . . .**153** C1
St James' Mans
NW6 . . . . .10 C1
St James Mews
E14 . . . . .42 B3
St James's Ave E2 . . .25 B3
**St James's CE Prim
Sch** SE14 . . . . .51 A2
St James School Flats
图 N7 . . . . .14 C3
St James's Cl
NW8 . . . . .80 C3
Upper Tooting
SW17 . . . . .72 B2
St James's Cloisters
図 SE22 . . . . .64 B3
St James's Cres
SW9 . . . . .62 C4
St James's Dr
Balham SW12,
SW17 . . . . .72 B4
Upper Tooting
SW17 . . . . .72 B3

St James's Gdns
W11 . . . . .31 A1 **112** A2
St James's Gr
SW11 . . . .**169** A2
St James's Market
SW1 . . . .**119** B3
St James's Pal
SW1 . . . .**119** A1
St James's Park Sta
SW1 . . . .**133** B2
St James's Pas
EC3 . . . .**110** B1
St James's Pk
SW1 . . . .**133** B4
St James's Pl
SW1 . . . .**118** C2
St James's Rd
Bermondsey SE1,
SE16 . . . .**153** C4
Peckham SE1 . . . . . . .49 C4
St James's Sq
SW1 . . . .**119** A2
St James's St
SW1 . . . .**118** C2
St James's Terr
NW8 . . . . .80 C4
图 Upper Tooting
SW12 . . . . .72 C3
**St James's Terrace
Mews** NW8 . . . . . . .80 C3
**St James The Great
RC Prim Sch 图**
SE15 . . . . .49 B2
St James Wlk EC1 . . .96 A2
**St Joan of Arc RC
Prim Sch** N5 . . . . . .15 B4
**St John of Jerusalem
CE Prim Sch 图**
E9 . . . . .17 B1
ST JOHN'S 51 C1
**St John & St James
CE Prim Sch 图**
E9 . . . . .17 B3
**St John's Angell Town
CE Prim Sch 图**
SW9 . . . .**173** B1
St John's Ave
Dagenham NW10 . . . .21 B4
Putney SW15 . . . . . . .57 C2
St John's CE Prim Sch
图 E2 . . . . .25 B3
**St John's CE Walham
Green Prim Sch**
SW6 . . . .**164** B4
St John's Church Rd
图 E9 . . . . .17 B3
St John's Cl SW6 . . .**155** B2
St John's Concert Hall
SW1 . . . .**134** A1
St John's Cres
SW9 . . . . .62 C4
St Johns Ct 图 E1 . . .32 A1
St John's Ct
Finsbury Pk N4 . . . . . .6 A2
Hammersmith W6 . . . .39 A2
Lewisham SE13 . . . . . .52 B1
图 South Hampstead
NW3 . . . . .11 B2
Saint John's Ct N5 . .15 A4
St John's Dr SW18 . .71 A3
St John's Gdns
W11 . . . . . . .31 B2 **112** C3
St John's Gr
图 Barnes SW13 . . . .46 B1

St John's Gr continued
图 Richmond TW9 . . . .54 A3
Upper Holloway N19 . .4 B2
**St John's Highbury
Vale CE Prim Sch**
N5 . . . . .6 A1
St John's Hill
SW11 . . . . .59 C3
St John's Hill Gr
SW11 . . . . .59 C3
St Johns Ho 图
SE17 . . . . .48 C4
St John's Ho 图
E14 . . . . .42 B3
St John's Lodge 图
SE8 . . . . .51 C2
St John's Mans E5 . .17 B3
St John's Park Mans
N19 . . . . .4 B1
St John's Path EC1 . .96 A1
St John's Pk SE3 . . .53 C3
St John's PI EC1 . . . .96 A1
St John's RC Prim Sch
SE16 . . . . .41 A4
St John's Rd
Battersea SW11 . . . . .60 A3
Canning Town E16 . . .35 C3
Richmond TW9 . . . . . .54 A3
**St John's & St
Clements CE Jun &
Inf Sch** 図 SE15 . . . .64 C4
St Johns Sig SE1 . . .96 A1
St Johns Sig SE1 . . .96 A1
St John St EC1 . . . . .96 A1
St John's Terr
W10 . . . . .22 C1
St John's Therapy Ctr
SW11 . . . . .59 C3
**St John's Upper
Holloway CE Prim**
Sch 図 N19 . . . . .4 C2
St John's Vale SE8 . .51 C1
St John's Villas
Upper Holloway
N19 . . . . .4 C2
W8 . . . .**128** B1
**St John's Walworth
CE Prim Sch**
SE17 . . . .**151** A3
St John's Way N19 . .4 C3
ST JOHN'S WOOD . .79 B1
St John's Wood Ct
NW8 . . . . .89 C3
**St John's Wood High
St** NW8 . . . . .80 A1
St John's Wood Park
NW8 . . . . .79 B4
**St John's Wood Pre-
Prep Sch** NW8 . . . .90 A4
St John's Wood Rd
NW8 . . . . .89 C3
St John's Wood Sta
NW8 . . . . .79 B2
St John's Wood Terr
NW8 . . . . .80 A2
**St John the Baptist
VA CE Prim Sch**
N1 . . . . .87 C1
**St John the Divine CE
Jun & Inf Sch**
SE5 . . . . .48 A3
**St John the Evangelist
RC Prim Sch** N1 . . .86 A2

St Joseph's CI
W10 .... **31** A4
St Josephs Ct **3**
NW10 .... **21** B3
St Joseph's Flats
NW1 .... **93** B4
St Joseph's Ho
W6 .... **39** C2
St Joseph's Hospice E9,
E8 .... **25** A4
St Joseph's RC Inf &
Jun Schs **5** SE5...**48** B3
St Josephs RC Prim
Sch
Chelsea SW3 ... **144** C3
10 Deptford SE8....**51** C3
11 Greenwich SE10 .**43** A1
Paddington W9.... **88** C3
Rotherhithe SE16...**40** B3
St Giles WC2... **106** B2
Upper Holloway N19 .. **4** C3
16 Wandsworth
SW18 .... **58** C2
8 Willesden NW10...**8** A1
St Joseph's St
SW8 .... **170** B4
St Joseph's Vale
SE3 .... **67** C4
St Jude & St Paul's CE
Prim Sch **12** N1 ...**16** A2
St Jude's CE Prim Sch
4 London SE24....**63** A2
E1 .... **136** A1
St Judes Ho **6**
W10 .... **23** B2
St Jude's Rd E2....**25** A3
St Jude St N16....**16** A3
St Julian's Rd
NW6 .... **23** C4
St Katharine's Ho
N1 .... **85** B2
St Katharine's Prec
NW1 .... **82** A2
St Katharine's Way
E1 .... **125** A2
St Katherine's Pier
E1 .... **125** A2
St Katherine's Row
EC3 .... **110** B1
9 Katherine's Wlk
W11 .... **30** C1
St Kilda's Rd N16....**7** A3
St Laurence's CI
NW6 .... **22** C4
St Lawrence Ct N1 **97** C4
St Lawrence Ho
SE1 .... **138** B2
St Lawrence St
E14 .... **34** B1
St Lawrence Terr
W10 .... **31** A4
St Lawrence Way
SW9 .... **173** C2
St Leonards Ct
SW14 .... **55** B4
St Leonard's Ct N1 **97** C4
St Leonard's Hospl
N1 .... **24** A3
St Leonards Rd
SW14 .... **55** B4
St Leonard's Rd
Becontree NW10 .**20** C1
South Bromley E14...**34** B4

St Leonard's Sq
NW5 .... **12** C2
St Leonard's St E3..**27** A2
St Leonard's Terr
SW3 .... **145** A1
St Loo Ave SW3 . **158** B4
St Loo Ct SW3 ... **158** C4
St Luke Prim CE Sch
8 E16 .... **35** B3
ST LUKE'S **97** A2
St Luke's Ave SW4..**61** C3
St Luke's CE Prim Sch
7 Cubitt Town
E14 .... **42** C2
Paddington W9......**23** B2
Shoreditch EC1....**97** A3
St Luke's CI EC1..**97** A2
St Luke's CI W11...**31** B3
St Luke's Mews
W11 .... **31** B3
St Luke's Rd W11..**31** B4
St Luke's Sq E16 ..**35** B3
St Luke's St SW3. **144** B2
St Margaret's Cres
SW15 .... **57** A2
St Margaret's Ct
Putney SW15 ......**57** A3
SE1 .... **123** B1
St Margaret's La
W8 .... **128** A1
St Margarets Lo
W3 .... **37** A4
St Margaret's Rd
Brockley SE4.......**66** B3
Kensal Green
NW10 .... **22** B2
St Margaret's Sch
NW3 .... **11** A4
St Margaret St
SW1 .... **134** A3
St Mark's CE Prim Sch
SE11 .... **163** A4
St Marks CI **5**
SE10 .... **52** B3
St Mark's Cres
NW1 .... **81** C4
St Marks Gate E9..**18** B1
St Mark's Gr
SW10 .... **156** B2
St Marks Ho **6**
SE17 .... **48** C4
St Mark's Mans **14**
N4 .... **5** B2
St Mark's PI W11 ..**31** A3
St Mark's Prim Sch **13**
N19 .... **5** A2
St Marks Rd
15 North Kensington
NW10 .... **30** C3
North Kensington
W10 .... **30** C4
St Mark's Rd W11 .**31** A3
St Mark's Rise E8..**16** B3
St Mark's Sq NW1..**81** B3
St Mark St E1 .... **111** A1
St Martin-in-the-
Fields High Sch **11**
SW2 .... **74** C3
St Martin's
Almshouses **7** NW1 **82** C4
St Martin's CI NW1 **82** C4
St Martin's Ct N1 ..**24** A4
St Martin's Ct
WC2 .... **120** A4
West Norwood
SE27 .... **75** A2

St Martin's La
WC2 .... **120** A3
St Martin's Le Grand
EC1 .... **108** C2
St Martin's PI
WC2 .... **120** A3
St Martin's Rd
SW9 .... **172** C2
St Martin's St
WC2 .... **119** C3
St Martin's Way
SW17 .... **71** B1
St Mary Abbots CE
Prim Sch **8** W8 ..**127** B4
St Mary Abbot's Ct
W14 .... **126** C1
St Mary Abbot's PI
W8 .... **127** A1
St Mary Abbots Terr
W14 .... **127** A1
St Mary at Hill
EC3 .... **124** A3
St Mary Axe EC3 . **110** B2
St Marychurch St
SE16 .... **40** B4
St Mary Graces Ct
E1 .... **125** A3
St Marylebone CE Sch
The W1 .... **103** C4
St Mary le Bow
Church EC2 ..... **109** A1
St Mary-le-Park Ct
SW11 .... **158** B1
St Mary Magdalene
Acad N7 .... **14** C2
St Mary Magdalene
CE Prim Sch
9 Paddington
W2 .... **100** A4
10 Peckham SE15 ..**50** A1
St Mary Magdalen's
RC Prim Sch
Brockley SE4.......**66** A3
4 Mortlake SW14 ..**55** C4
St Mary Magdalen's
RC Jun Sch **1**
SE15 .... **9** A2
St Mary Newington CI
SE17 .... **152** B2
St Mary of the Angels
RC Prim Sch **2**
W2 .... **31** C3
St Mary RC Prim Sch
22 W10 .... **23** A1
St Mary & St Michael
Prim Sch **27** E1....**32** B3
St Mary & St Pancras
CE Prim Sch
NW1 .... **83** B1
St Mary's Bryanston
Square CE Sch
W1 .... **102** C4
St Mary's CE Prim Sch
Islington N1 ......**86** B4
London SE13.......**67** A2
15 Putney SW15 ....**57** C4
Willesden NW10....**8** A2
St Mary's CE Sch W6.**38** B3
St Mary's Est **3**
SE16 .... **40** B4
St Mary's Flats
NW1 .... **93** B4
St Mary's Gate
W8 .... **128** A1
St Mary's Gdns
SE11 .... **149** C4

St Mary's Gr
Barnes SW13 ......**57** A4
Chiswick W4........**45** A4
Islington N1 ...... **15** A2
Richmond TW10,
TW9 .... **54** B3
St Mary's Ho N1 ..**86** B4
St Mary's Hospl
W2 .... **101** C2
St Mary's Hospl
Medical Sch W2 **101** C2
St Mary's Kilburn CE
Prim Sch
NW6 .... **23** C4
St Mary's Mans
Dagenham NW10 ..**21** A4
Paddington W2....**101** B4
St Mary's Mews
NW6 .... **11** A1
St Mary's Path N1 .**86** B4
St Mary's PI W8 ...**31** C4
St Mary's RC Prim Sch
Chiswick W4........**45** A4
11 Clapham Pk
SW4 .... **61** B2
Clapham SW8 .... **170** B4
Hammersmith W14 .**39** C3
Paddington NW6 ..**23** C3
St Mary's Rd
Golders Green
NW11 .... **1** A4
Harlesden NW10 ...**21** A4
Nunhead SE15......**50** B1
St Mary's Sch **5**
Hampstead NW3 ..**11** C4
St Mary's Sq W2 .**101** B4
St Mary's Stoke
Newington CE Prim
Sch **2** N16........**7** A2
St Mary's Terr
W2 .... **101** B4
St Mary's Twr EC1 .**97** A1
St Mary's Wlk
SE11 .... **149** C4
St Matthews Ct
SE1 .... **136** C1
St Matthew's Ho **8**
SE17 .... **48** C4
St Matthew's Lo
NW1 .... **83** A2
St Matthew's Rd
SW2 .... **62** B2
St Matthew's Row
E2 .... **99** B2
St Matthew St
SW1 .... **133** B1
St Matthias CE Prim
Sch E2 .... **24** B1 **99** A2
St Matthias Prim Sch
22 N16 .... **16** A4
St Mauritius Ho
SE13 .... **67** B2
St Maur Rd SW6 . **165** A3
St Michael & All
Angels CE Acad **38**
SE5 .... **48** A3
St Michael's Alley
EC3 .... **109** C1
St Michael's Cath Coll
SE1 .... **139** B3
St Michael's CE Prim
Sch
Camden Town
NW1 .... **82** C4

St Michael's CE Prim
Sch continued
Highgate N6......... **3** C4
Wandsworth SW18 .**70** B4
St Michaels Ct **2**
E14 .... **34** B4
St Michael's Ct
NW11 .... **1** C4
St Michael's Flats
NW1 .... **83** B1
St Michael's Gdns
W10 .... **31** A4
St Michael's Rd
Cricklewood NW2....**9** B4
Stockwell SW9 ... **172** C2
St Michael's St
W2 .... **101** C2
St Michael Steiner
Sch The **18** SW18 ..**58** C2
St Mildred's Ct
EC2 .... **109** B1
St Monica's RC Prim
Sch **2** N1 .... **24** A2 **98** A4
St Nicholas' Flats
NW1 .... **83** B1
St Nicholas Ho
SE8 .... **51** C4
St Nicholas Mans
SW17 .... **72** B2
St Nicholas St SE8 .**51** C2
St Norbert Gn SE4 .**66** A3
St Norbert Rd SE4 .**66** A3
St Olaf's Rd SW6 **154** B1
St Olaves Ct EC2 .**109** B1
St Olave's Ct EC2 .**109** B1
St Olave's Est SE1 **138** B4
St Olaves Gdns
SE11 .... **149** B4
St Olave's Mans
SE11 .... **149** B4
St Olav's Sq **92**
SE16 .... **40** B4
St Osmund's RC Prim
Sch SW13 .... **46** B2
St Oswald's PI
SE11 .... **148** C1
St Oswulf St SW1 **147** C3
St Owen Ho SE1 . **138** B2
ST PANCRAS **94** B4
St Pancras
Almshouses **13**
NW5 .... **12** C3
St Pancras
Commercial Ctr
NW1 .... **83** A4
St Pancras Hospl
NW1 .... **83** B3
St Pancras
International Sta
WC1 .... **94** A4
St Pancras Way
NW1 .... **83** B4
St Patrick's Coll
W1 .... **105** A2
St Patrick's RC Prim
Sch NW5 .... **13** A3
St Paul's Ave
Rotherhithe SE16 ..**32** C1
Willesden NW2......**9** B2
St Paul's Cath
EC4 .... **108** C1
St Paul's Cath Sch
EC4 .... **108** C1
St Paul's CE Prim Sch
23 Hammersmith
W6 .... **39** B1

St Paul's CE Prim Sch
continued
Hampstead NW3 . . . . 12 B1
SE17 . . . . **150** C2
St Paul's Church Yd
EC4 . . . . **108** C1
St Pauls Cl W5 . . . . 36 B4
St Pauls Cres NW1 . . 13 C1
St Paul's Ct
Clapham SW4 . . . . 61 C3
6 Upper Holloway
N19 . . . . 5 A2
St Paul's Dr E15 . . . 19 C3
St Paul's Girls' Sch **1**
W6 . . . . 39 C2
St Pauls Mews
NW1 . . . . 13 C1
St Paul's Pl N1 . . . . 15 C2
St Pauls Rd W9 . . . . 54 B4
St Paul's Rd N1 . . . . 15 B2
St Paul's Sch
SW13 . . . . 39 A3
St Paul's Sta EC2 . . **108** C2
St Pauls Steiner Sch
22 N1 . . . . 15 C1
St Paul St N1 . . . . **87** A3
St Paul's Terr
SE17 . . . . 48 A4
St Pauls View WC1 . . **95** B3
St Paul's Way E3 . . . 33 C4
St Paul's Way Com
Sch **22** E3 . . . . . . 33 C4
St Paul's with St
Michael's Prim Sch
24 E8 . . . . 24 C4
St Paul with St Luke
CE Prim Sch **18**
E3 . . . . 33 B4
St Peter & St Paul RC
Prim Sch EC1 . . . . **96** B2
St Peter's Alley
EC3 . . . . **109** C1
St Peter's Ave **37**
E2 . . . . 24 C3
St Petersburgh Mews
W2 . . . . **114** A4
St Petersburgh Pl
W2 . . . . **114** A3
St Peter's CE Prim
Sch
18 Chiswick W6 . . . 38 C1
6 E1 . . . . 32 B1
6 Paddington W9 . . 23 C1
SE17 . . . . **151** B1
SW1 . . . . **132** B1
St Peter's Church Ct
N1 . . . . **86** B3
St Peters Cl **1**
SW17 . . . . 72 A2
St Peter's Cl E12 . . . 24 C3
St Peters Ct
New Cross SE4 . . . . 51 B1
28 Stepney E1 . . . . 25 B1
St Peter's Gdns
SE27 . . . . 74 C1
St Peter's Gr W6 . . 38 C2
St Peters Ho W1 . . . 94 B3
St Peter's Ho
4 SE17 . . . . . . 48 B4
Stamford Hill N16 . . . 7 A4
St Peter's Pl W9 . . 88 A1
St Peter's Rd W6 . . 38 C1
St Peter's Sq
Chiswick W6 . . . . . 38 B1
Hackney E2 . . . . . 24 C3
St Peter's St N1 . . . **86** B3

St Peter's Street
Mews N1 . . . . . . 86 B2
St Peter's Terr
SW6 . . . . **154** B1
St Peter's Villas **5**
W6 . . . . 38 C2
St Peter's Way N1 . . 16 A1
St Peter's Wharf **8**
W6 . . . . 38 C1
St Philip Ho WC1 . . **95** B3
St Philip Sq **1**
SW8 . . . . **170** A1
St Philip's Rd E8 . . 16 C2
St Philip's Sch
SW7 . . . . **143** A3
St Philip St SW8 . . **170** A1
St Philip's Way N1 . . **87** A3
St Quentin Ho
SW18 . . . . 59 C1
St Quintin Ave
W10 . . . . 30 C4
St Quintin Gdns **1**
W10 . . . . 30 B4
St Regis Hts NW3 . . . 2 A1
St Richard's Ho
NW1 . . . . **93** B4
St Rule St SW8 . . . **170** C1
St Saviours Ho
SE16 . . . . **139** B3
St Saviour & St Olaves
CE Sch SE1 . . . . **137** C1
St Saviour's CE Prim
Sch
6 Bow Comm
E14 . . . . 34 A4
Camberwell SE24 . . 63 B4
28 Paddington W9 . . **88** B1
SE1 . . . . **139** B3
St Saviours Ho
SE1 . . . . **139** B3
St Saviour's RC Prim
Sch SE13 . . . . . . 67 B3
St Saviour's Rd
SW2 . . . . 62 B2
St Saviour's Wharf
SE1 . . . . **139** A4
St Scholastica's RC
Prim Sch **6** E5 . . . 7 C1
St Silas Pl NW5 . . . 12 C2
St Simon's Ave
SW15 . . . . 57 B2
St Stephen's Ave
Acton W3 . . . . . . 28 A1
4 Shepherd's Bush
W12 . . . . 39 A4
St Stephen's CE Prim
Sch
Paddington W2 . . . 31 C4
17 Shepherd's Bush
W12 . . . . 39 B4
2 St Johns SE8 . . . 51 C1
SE8 . . . . **162** C2
St Stephen's Cl
Maitland Pk NW5 . . 12 B3
NW8 . . . . **80** B3
St Stephen's Cres
W2 . . . . 31 C3
St Stephen's Gdns
Notting Hill W2 . . 31 C3
1 Putney SW15 . . 58 B2
St Stephen's Gr
SE13 . . . . 67 B4
St Stephens Ho **7**
SE17 . . . . 48 C4
St Stephen's Mews **8**
W2 . . . . 31 C4
St Stephen's Rd
E3 . . . . 26 B3
St Stephen's Row
EC4 . . . . **109** B1

St Stephen's Terr
SW8 . . . . **162** C1
St Stephen's Wlk
SW7 . . . . **142** C4
St Swithin's La
EC4 . . . . **123** B4
St Swithun's Rd
SE13 . . . . 67 C2
St Theresas Cl E9 . . 18 C4
St Thomas' CE Prim
Sch W10 . . . . . . 23 A1
St Thomas Ct **14**
NW1 . . . . 13 B1
St Thomas Ho **2**
E1 . . . . 32 C3
St Thomas More
Language Coll
SW3 . . . . **144** C3
St Thomas of
Canterbury RC Prim
Sch SW6 . . . . . **154** C2
St Thomas Rd E16 . . 35 C3
St Thomas' Rd W4 . . 45 B4
St Thomas's Gdns
NW5 . . . . 12 C2
St Thomas's Hospl
SE1 . . . . **134** C2
St Thomas's Pl **20**
E9 . . . . 17 B1
St Thomas's Rd
Dagenham NW10 . . 21 A4
Highbury N4, N5 . . . 5 C2
St Thomas's Sq **9** . . 17 B1
St Thomas' St SE1 . . **123** C1
St Thomas's Way
SW6 . . . . **155** A2
St Thomas the
Apostle Coll
SE15 . . . . 50 B2
St Ursula's Convent
Sch SE10 . . . . . . 52 C3
St Vincent De Paul Ho
2 E1 . . . . 32 B4
St Vincent De Paul RC
Prim Sch SW1 . . **133** A2
St Vincent Ho
SE1 . . . . **138** C2
St Vincent's RC Prim
Sch
Acton W3 . . . . . . 28 A2
Marylebone W1 . . **103** C3
St Vincent St W1 . . **103** C3
Salamanca Pl SE1 . . **148** C3
Salamanca St SE1,
SE11 . . . . **148** C3
Salcombe Gdns
SW4 . . . . 61 A3
Salcombe Lo NW5 . . 12 C4
Salcombe Villas **13**
NW1 . . . . 13 A1
Salcot N4 . . . . . . 5 B2
Salcott Rd SW11 . . 60 B2
Salehurst Rd SE4 . . 66 B1
Salem Ho **19** E9 . . 17 C2
Salem Rd W2 . . . **114** B4
Salesian Coll
SW11 . . . . **168** A3
Sale St E2 . . . . . 24 C1 **2 3**
Salford Ho **5** E14 . . 42 B2
Salford Rd SW12,

Salisbury Ct
15 Bermondsey
SE16 . . . . **139** C1
Chiswick W4 . . . . 38 A2
EC4 . . . . **108** A1
Hackney E9 . . . . . 18 A2
Salisbury Ho
2 Islington N1 . . . 15 A2
Islington N1 . . . . **86** A4
3 Poplar E14 . . . . 34 A3
6 Westminster SW1 **147** C2
Wimbledon SW19 . . 69 C1
Salisbury Mews
SW6 . . . . **154** C1
Salisbury Pl
Camberwell SW9 . . 48 A3
Marylebone W1 . . **102** C4
Salisbury Rd TW9 . . 44 B2
Salisbury Sq EC4 . . **107** C1
Salisbury St
11 Acton W3 . . . 37 B1
NW8 . . . . **90** A1
Salisbury Terr
SE15 . . . . 65 B4
Salisbury Wlk N19 . . 4 B2
Salmon La E14 . . . 33 A3
Salmon St **11** E14 . . 33 B3
Saltcoats Rd W4 . . 38 A4
Saltdene N4 . . . . . 5 B3
Salter Rd
Rotherhithe SE16 . . 32 C1
SE16 . . . . 33 A1
Salters' Hall Ct
EC4 . . . . **123** B4
Salters Rd W10 . . . 22 C1
Salter St
College Pk NW10 . . 21 C2
11 Poplar E14 . . . 33 C2
Salterton Rd N7 . . . 5 B1
Saltoun Rd SW2,
SW9 . . . . 62 C3
Saltram Cres W9 . . 23 B2
Saltwell St E14 . . . 33 C2
Saltwood Gr SE17 . . **151** B1
Saltwood Ho **10**
SE15 . . . . 50 B4
Salusbury Prim Sch
NW6 . . . . 23 B4
Salusbury Rd NW6 . . 23 A4
Salutation Rd
SE10 . . . . 43 A2
Salvin Rd SW15 . . 57 C4
Salway Rd E15 . . . 19 C2
Salween Ho **2**
N16 . . . . 7 C1
Sambrook Ho
1 E1 . . . . 32 B4
Samels Ct W6 . . . 38 C1
Samford Ho N1 . . . 85 B3
Samford St NW8 . . **90** A1
Sam Manners Ho **7**
SE10 . . . . 43 A1
Sam March Ho **5**
E14 . . . . 34 C3
Sampson St E1 . . **125** C1
Samuel Cl
SE14 . . . . 50 C4
Shoreditch E8 . . . 24 B4
Samuel Ct
N1 . . . . . . 24 A2 **98** A3
Samuel Ho **8** E8 . . 24 B4
Samuel Jones Ind Est
7 SE15 . . . . . . 49 A3
Samuel Lewis Bldgs
N1 . . . . 14 C2

Samuel Lewis Trust
Dwellings
6 Camberwell
SE5 . . . . 48 B2
Chelsea SW3 . . . **144** A3
Walham Green
SW6 . . . . **155** C2
West Kensington
W14 . . . . **140** B4
Samuel Rhodes Sch
N1 . . . . 85 B4
Samuel Richardson
Ho W14 . . . . . . **140** C3
Samuel's Cl **2** W6 . . 39 B2
Samuel St SE15 . . . 49 B3
Sancroft Ct SW11 . . **168** B4
Sancroft Ho SE11 . . **149** A2
Sancroft St SE11 . . **149** A2
Sanctuary Mews **8**
E8 . . . . 16 B2
Sanctuary St SE1 . . **137** A4
Sanctuary The
35 Wapping E1 . . . 32 A1
Westminster SW1 . . **133** C2
Sandale Cl N16 . . . . 6 C1
Sandall Ho **7** E3 . . . 26 A3
Sandall Rd NW5 . . . 13 B2
Sandalwood Cl **1**
E1 . . . . 26 A1
Sandalwood Ho **6**
NW3 . . . . 11 A2
Sandbourne
4 Kensington
W11 . . . . 31 C3
14 Paddington NW8 . **78** B4
Sandbourne Rd
SE4 . . . . 51 A1
Sandbrook Rd N16 . . 7 A1
Sandby Ho
11 Camberwell
SE5 . . . . 49 A2
5 Kilburn NW6 . . . 23 C4
Sandell St SE1 . . . **135** B4
Sanderling Ct **20**
SE8 . . . . 51 B4
Sanders Ho WC1 . . **95** B4
Sanderson Cl NW5 . . 13 A4
Sanderson Ho **7**
SE8 . . . . 41 B1
Sanderstead Ave
NW2 . . . . 1 A2
Sanderstead Cl
SW12 . . . . 73 B4
Sanders Way **3**
N19 . . . . 4 C3
Sandfield WC1 . . . **94** B3
Sandford Ct N16 . . . 7 A3
Sandford Row
SE17 . . . . **151** C2
Sandford St SW6 . . **156** B1
Sandgate Ho **13**
E5 . . . . 17 A4
Sandgate La SW17,
SW18 . . . . 72 A3
Sandgate St SE15 . . 50 A4
Sandgate Trad Est
SE15 . . . . 50 A4
Sandham Ct SW4 . . **172** B3
Sandhills The
SW10 . . . . **157** A4
Sandhurst Ct SW2 . . 62 A3
Sandhurst Ho **12**
E1 . . . . 32 B4

Sandilands Rd
SW6 .... 166 A3
Sandison St SE15 .....64 C4
Sandland St W1 ....107 A3
Sandlings Cl SE15 ...50 A1
Sandmere Rd SW4 ..62 A3
Sandon Ho **5**
SW2 ....74 A4
Sandown Ho **2**
W4 ....37 B1
Sandpiper Cl SE16 ..41 B4
Sandpiper Ct
13 Cubitt Town
E14 ....42 B3
1 SE8 ....51 C3
Sandridge St **3**
N19 ....4 B2
Sandringham Cl **1**
SW19 ....69 C3
Sandringham Ct
Marylebone W1 .....105 A1
Putney SW15 ....57 C1
18 Rotherhithe
SE16 ....32 C1
St John's Wood W9 .89 A3
Sandringham Flats
WC2 ....119 C4
Sandringham Ho
Richmond TW10 ......54 C2
W14 ....140 A4
Sandringham Rd
Dalston E8 ....16 B3
Golders Green NW11 ..1 A4
Willesden NW2 ....9 A2
Sandrock Rd SE13 ..66 C4
SANDS END 59 B4
Sands End La
SW6 ....166 B4
Sandstone TW9 ......44 C3
Sandstone Pl N19 ....4 A2
Sandways **6** 44 C2
Sandwell Cres **2**
NW6 ....10 C2
Sandwell Mans **3**
NW6 ....10 C2
Sandwich Ho
16 Rotherhithe
SE16 ....40 B4
WC1 ....94 A3
Sandwich St WC1 ....94 A3
Sandycombe Ctr
TW9 ....54 C4
Sandycombe Rd
TW9 ....44 C1
Sandy Lo N6 ....4 C4
Sandy Rd NW3 ....2 A2
Sandy's Row E1 ....110 B3
Sanford La **3** N16 ...7 B2
Sanford La SE14,
SE8 ....51 A4
Sanford Terr N16 ....7 B1
Sanford Wlk
SE14 ....51 A4
4 Stoke Newington
N16 ....7 B3
Sangora Rd **10**
SW11 ....59 B3
San Ho **8** E9 ....17 C2
Sankey Ho **22** E2 ..25 B3
Sansom St
Camberwell SE5 .....48 C2
SE5 ....48 C3
Sans Wlk EC1 ....96 A2
Santley Ho SE1 ....135 C3

Santley St SW4 ....62 B3
Santos Rd SW18 ....58 C2
Sapcote Trad Ctr
NW10 ....8 B2
Saperton Wlk
SE11 ....149 A4
Sapperton Ct EC1 ..96 C2
Sapphire Ct **13**
E1 ....125 B4
Sapphire Rd SE8 ....41 A2
Saracen's Head Yd
EC2 ....110 B1
Saracen St E14 ....33 C3
Sarah Ho
Roehampton
SW15 ....56 B3
8 Stepney E1 ....32 A3
Sarah Swift Ho
SE1 ....137 C4
Sara Lane Ct **31**
N1 ....24 A3
Saratoga Rd E5 ....17 B4
Sardinia Ho WC2 ...106 C1
Sardinia St WC2 ....106 C2
Sarjant Path SW19 .69 C2
Sark Ho **6** N1 ....15 B2
Sarnesfield Ho
SE15 ....50 A4
Sarratt Ho **6** W10 ..30 B4
Sarre Rd NW2 ....10 B3
Sarsden Bldgs
W1 ....103 C1
Sarsfeld Rd SW12,
SW17 ....72 B3
Sartor Rd SE15 ....65 C3
Sarum Hall Sch
NW3 ....12 B1
Sarum Ho
W11 ....31 B2 113 A3
Sassoon Ho SE15 ...50 B1
Satchwell Rd **17**
E2 ....24 C2 99 B3
Saturn Ho **4** E3 ...26 C4
Saul Ct **4** SE15 .....49 B4
Saunders Cl **14**
E14 ....33 B2
Saunders Ho **11**
SW2 ....74 C3
Saunders Ness Rd
E14 ....42 C2
Saunders St SE11 .149 B4
Savage Gdns EC3 .124 B4
Savana N16 ....7 A2
Savannah Cl **2**
SE15 ....49 B3
Savernake Ho N4 ....6 C4
Savernake Rd
NW3 ....12 B4
Saville Rd W4 ....37 C3
Saville Row W1 .....118 C4
Savill Ho **2** SW4 ...61 C1
Savona St SW8 .....160 C1
Savoy Circus **3**
W3 ....29 B2
Savoy Ct
Earl's Ct SW5 ....141 C4
Strand WC2 ....120 B3
Savoy Hill WC2 .....120 C3
Savoy Mews SW9 ...62 A4
Savoy Pier WC2 ....120 C3
Savoy Pl WC2 ....120 C3
Savoy Row WC2 ....120 C3
Savoy St WC2 ....120 C3
Savoy Stps WC2 ....120 C3
Savoy Way WC2 ....120 C3
Sawkins Cl SW19 ...70 A2
Sawley Rd W12 ....29 C1

Sawmill Yd E3 ....26 A4
Sawyer St SE1 ....136 C4
Saxby Rd SW2 ....74 A4
Saxonbury Ct
16 Kentish Town
N7 ....13 C3
1 Lower Holloway
N7 ....14 A3
Saxoncroft Ho
SW16 ....73 C1
Saxon Dr W3 ....28 A4
Saxonfield Cl SW2 ..74 B4
Saxon Hall W1 ......114 A3
Saxon Ho **6** SW4 ..62 A3
Saxon Rd E3 ....26 B3
Saxton Cl SE13 ....67 C4
Sayer Ho SE4 ....66 A3
Sayes Court St
SE8 ....51 B4
Sayes Ct SE8 ....51 B4
Scafell NW1 ....92 C4
Scala St W1 ....105 A4
Scampston Mews **5**
W10 ....30 C3
Scandrett St **3**
E1 ....32 A1
Scarba Wlk N1 ....15 C2
Scarborough Rd N4 ..5 C3
Scarborough St
E1 ....111 A1
Scarlette Manor Wlk
16 SE24 ....74 C4
Scarsbrook Ho **2**
SW2 ....62 C1
Scarsdale Pl W8 ...128 A2
Scarsdale Villas
W8 ....127 B1
Scarth Rd SW13 .....56 B4
Scawen Rd SE8 ......41 A1
Scawfell St E2 ....24 B3
Sceptre Ho **6** E1 ...25 B1
Sceptre Rd E2 ....25 B2
Schiller International
Univ SE1 ....121 B1
Schofield Wlk SE3 ..53 C3
Sch of Pharmacy
WC1 ....94 B2
Sch of the Islamic
Republic of Iran The
8 NW6 ....23 C3
Scholars Ct **5** N19 ..4 C3
Scholars Rd SW12 ..73 B3
Scholefield Rd N19 ..4 C2
Scholey Ho SW11 ...60 A4
Schomberg Ho
SW1 ....147 C4
Schonfeld Sq N16 ...6 C3
School App **21**
E2 ....24 A2 98 B4
Schoolbank Rd
SE10 ....43 B2
School Bell Cloisters
17 E3 ....26 A3
School Flats SW8 ..172 A3
School Ho SE1 ....152 A4
Schoolhouse La
E1 ....32 C2
School Rd NW10 .....20 C1
School Sq SE10 ....43 B3
Schooner Cl
Cubitt Town E14 .....42 C4
1 Rotherhithe
SE16 ....40 C4
Schubert Rd SW15 .58 B2

Science Mus SW7 .129 B1
Sclater St
London E1 .....24 B1 99 A2
Scoles Cres SW2 ....74 C3
Scoresby St SE1 ....122 A1
Scorton Ho **3** N1 ..24 A3
Scotch Ho SW1 .....130 C3
Scoter Ct **28** SE8 ..51 B4
Scotia Bldg **10** E1 .32 C2
Scotia Ct **3** SE16 ..40 B3
Scotia Rd **2** SW2 ..74 C4
Scotland Pl SW1 ...120 A1
Scotney Ho E9 ....17 B2
Scotson Ho SE11 ..149 B3
Scotswood St EC1 ..95 C2
Scott Ave SW15,
SW18 ....58 A1
Scott Ct
Acton W4 ....37 C4
4 Clapham SW11 ..170 B1
17 Stoke Newington
N16 ....7 A1
Scott Ellis Gdns
NW8 ....89 B3
Scott Ho
2 Barnsbury N7 ....14 B2
Islington N1 ....87 B4
Lisson Gr NW8 ....90 A1
22 Millwall E14 ....41 C4
Scott Lidgett Cres
SE16 ....139 C3
Scotts Ct **3** W12 ..39 A4
Scott's Rd W12 ....39 A4
Scott's Sufferance
Wharf SE1 ....139 A3
Scott St E1 ....25 A1
Scott's Yd EC4 ......123 B4
Scoulding Ho **12**
E14 ....41 C3
Scoulding Rd E16 ...35 C3
Scouler St E14 ....34 C2
Scout App NW10 .....8 A4
Scout La SW4 ....61 B4
Scovell Cres SE1 ..136 C3
Scovell Rd SE1 .....136 C3
Scriven Ct **2** E8 .....24 B4
Scriven St E8 ....24 B4
Scrooby St SE6 ....67 A1
Scrope Bldg EC1 ...107 B4
Scrubs La NW10, W10,
W12 ....22 A1
Scrutton Cl SW12 ...73 C4
Scrutton St
EC2 ....24 A1 98 A1
Scutari Rd SE22 .....65 B2
Scylla Rd SE15 ....65 A4
Seabright St **22**
E2 ....25 A2
Seacole Cl W3 ....28 C4
Seacon Twr **8**
E14 ....41 C4
Seaford Ho **15**
SE16 ....40 B4
Seaford St WC1 ....94 B3
Seaforth Cres N5 ...15 B3
Seaforth Lo **2**
SW13 ....46 B1
Seaforth Pl SW1 ...133 A2
Seagrave Lo SW6 ..155 C4
Seagrave Rd SW6 ..155 C4
Seagrove Cl E1 ....32 C4
Seagull La E16 ....35 C2
Seal Ho SE1 ....137 C2
Seal St E8 ....16 B4

Searle Pl N4 ....5 B2
Searles Cl SW11 ...158 B1
Searles Rd SE1 .....151 C4
Searson Ho SE17 ..150 B3
Sear St SE5 ....48 B3
Seasalter Ho **10**
SW9 ....173 B4
Seaton Cl SW13 ......56 C4
Seaton Point E5 ......16 C4
Seavington Ho **3**
SE5 ....64 A4
Sebastian Ho **22**
N1 ....24 A3
Sebastian St EC1 ....96 B3
Sebbon St N1 ....15 A1
Sebright Ho **23** E2 ..24 C3
Sebright Pas **29**
E2 ....24 C3
Sebright Sch **38**
E2 ....24 C3
Secker Ho SW9 ......48 A1
Secker St SE1 ....121 B1
Second Ave
East Acton W3 ....29 B1
Kensal Town W10 ...23 A1
Mortlake SW14 ......55 C4
Sedan Way SE17 ...152 A2
Sedding St SW1 ....145 B4
Seddon Ho EC2 .....108 C4
Seddon St WC1 ....95 A3
Sedgeford Rd
W12 ....29 B1
Sedgewick Ho
SW19 ....69 C2
Sedgley Ho N4 ....5 B2
Sedgmoor Pl SE5 ...49 A3
Sedgwick St E9 ....17 C3
Sedleigh Rd SW18 ..58 B1
Sedlescombe Rd
SW6 ....155 B4
Sedley Ho SE11 ....149 A2
Sedley Pl W1 ....104 A1
Seething La EC3 ....124 B4
Sefton St SW15 ......57 B4
Sekforde St EC1 .....96 A2
Selbie Ave NW10 .....8 B3
Selborne **2** SW11 ..60 C4
Selborne Ho SE1 ..137 B3
Selborne Rd **1**
SE5 ....48 C1
Selby Ho **10** SW4 ..61 B1
Selby Sq **1** W10 ...23 A2
Selby St E1 ....24 C1
Selden Ho **2** SE15 ..50 B1
Selden Rd SE15 ......50 B1
Selden Wlk N7 ....5 B2
Seldon Ho
Nine Elms SW8 .....160 C1
Pimlico SW1 ....146 C1
Selhurst Cl SW19 ...69 C3
Selina Ho NW8 ....89 C2
Selkirk Ho
N1 ....84 C4
4 Stoke Newington
N16 ....7 A1
Sellons Ave NW10 ..21 B4
Selma Ho **9** W12 ...30 A3
Selman Ho **9** E9 ...18 A2
Selsdon Way E14 ...42 A3
Selsea Pl N16 ....16 A3
Selsey St E14 ....33 C4
Selway Ho SW8 ....172 B4
Selwood Pl SW7 ...143 B2
Selwood Terr
SW7 ....143 B2

Selworthy Ho
SW11 .... 167 C4
Selwyn Ave TW9 ... 54 B4
Selwyn Ct 5
TW10 .... 54 B2
Selwyn Ho 3
SW15 .... 57 C1
Selwyn Rd
Bow E3 .... 26 B3
Willesden NW10... 8 A1
Semley Gate E9 .. 18 B2
Semley Ho SW1 .. 146 A3
Semley Pl SW1 ... 146 A3
Senate St SE15 .. 50 B1
Senators Lo 8 E1 .. 26 A3
Sendall Ct 1
SW11 .... 59 C4
Senior St W2 .... 100 A4
Senrab St E1 .... 32 C3
Seraph Ct EC1.... 96 C4
Serenaders Rd 20
SW9 .... 173 B1
Sergeant Ind Est The
SW18 .... 59 A1
Serica Ct 10 SE10 .. 52 B3
Serjeants' Inn
EC4 .... 107 C1
Serlby Ct W14 ... 126 C2
Serle St WC2 .... 107 A2
Sermon La EC4 ... 108 C1
Serpentine Ct EC1
SE16 .... 40 C4
Serpentine Gallery
W2 .... 129 C4
Serpentine Rd
W2 .... 116 C1
Serpentine The
W2 .... 116 B1
Service Route No 1
E15 .... 19 C1
Service Route No 2 1
E15 .... 19 C1
Service Route No 3
E15 .... 19 C1
Servite Ho SE13 .. 52 A2
Servite RC Prim Sch
SW10 .... 156 C4
Setchell Rd SE1 .. 152 C4
Setchell Way SE1 .. 152 C4
Seth St 25 SE16 .. 40 B4
Settlers Ct 11 E14 . 34 C2
Settles St E1 .... 111 C2
Settrington Rd
SW6 .... 166 A1
Seven Dials WC2 .. 106 A1
Seven Islands L Ctr
SE16 .... 40 B3
Seven Mills Prim Sch
27 E14 .... 41 C4
Sevenoaks Rd SE4 . 66 B1
Seven Sisters Rd
Finsbury Pk N4 .... 6 B4
Stoke Newington N4, N7,
N15 .... 6 B4
Seven Stars Cnr
W12 .... 38 C3
Seven Stars Yd
E1 .... 111 A4
Severnake Cl E14 . 41 C2
Severn Ave 2
W10 .... 23 A2
Severn Way NW10 .. 8 B3
Severus Rd SW11 .. 60 A3
Seville Ho 16 E1 .. 125 C1
Seville Mews N1 .. 16 A1
Seville St SW1 ... 131 A3

Sevington St W9 .. 88 A1
Seward St EC1 ... 96 C3
Sewardstone Rd
E2 .... 25 B3
Sewell Ho 10 N16 .. 16 A3
Sextant Ave E14 .. 42 C2
Sexton's Ho 5
SE13 .... 52 B4
Seymour Ct
Putney SW15 ... 57 A3
Upper Clapton N16... 7 C3
Seymour Gdns
SE4 .... 66 A4
Seymour Ho
Bloomsbury WC1 .. 94 A2
1 Clapham SW8 ... 171 A2
Somers Town NW1... 93 C3
Seymour Mews
W1 .... 103 B3
Seymour Pl W1 ... 102 C2
Seymour Rd
Acton W4 ...... 37 B2
Wandsworth SW18 .. 58 B1
Wimbledon SW19 .. 69 C1
Seymour St W1 ... 103 A1
Seymour Wlk
SW10 .... 156 C4
Seyssel St E14 ... 42 B2
Shaa Rd W3 .... 28 C2
Shabana Ct 3
W12 .... 30 A1
Shackleton Ct
3 Dulwich SE21... 75 C2
2 Isle of Dogs E14 . 41 C1
4 Shepherd's Bush
W12 .... 39 A4
Shackleton Ho 5
E1 .... 32 B1
SHACKLEWELL .. 16 B4
Shacklewell Ho 3
E8 .... 16 B4
Shacklewell La E8 .. 16 B3
Shacklewell Prim Sch
5 E8 .... 16 B4
Shacklewell Rd
N16 .... 16 B4
Shacklewell Row
E8 .... 16 B4
Shacklewell St 30
E2 .... 24 B2 99 A3
Shad Thames SE1 .. 139 A4
SHADWELL 32 B2
Shadwell Gdns 1 .. 32 B2
Shadwell Pierhead
E1 .... 32 B2
Shadwell Pl 1 E1 .. 32 B2
Shadwell Sta E1 .. 32 A2
Shaftesbury Ave
W1 .... 119 C4
Shaftesbury Ct
Borough SE1 ... 137 B2
1 Herne Hill SE5 .. 63 C3
Shoreditch N1 ... 87 B1
Streatham SW16 .. 73 C1
Shaftesbury Ctr
NW10 .... 22 C1
Shaftesbury Gdns
NW10 .... 21 A1
Shaftesbury Ho
1 Canning Town
E16 .... 35 B3
13 Stoke Newington
N16 .... 7 A1
W2 .... 114 B4

Shaftesbury Lo 9
E14 .... 34 A3
Shaftesbury Mews
2 Clapham Pk
SW4 .... 61 B2
W8 .... 127 C1
Shaftesbury Park
Chambers 1
SW11 .... 60 C4
Shaftesbury Rd
Finsbury Pk N4,
N19........... 5 A3
Richmond TW9 ... 54 A4
Shaftesbury St N1 . 87 B1
Shafteswood Ct
SW17 .... 72 B1
Shafto Mews
SW1 .... 131 A1
Shafton Rd E9.... 25 C4
Shaftsbury Park Prim
Sch 18 SW11 ... 60 C4
Shafts Ct EC3.... 110 A1
Shahjalal Ho 10
E2 .... 24 C3
Shakespeare Ave 7
NW10 .... 20 C4
Shakespeare Ho 9
E9 .... 17 B1
Shakespeare Rd
Acton W3 ...... 28 B1
Brixton SE24.... 63 A3
Stonebridge NW10.. 20 C4
Shakespeare's Globe
Theatre (site of)
SE1 .... 123 A2
Shakespeare Twr
EC2 .... 109 A4
Shakspeare Mews 7
N16 .... 16 A4
Shakspeare Wlk
N16 .... 16 A4
Shalbourne Sq E9 .. 18 B2
Shalden Ho SW15 .. 56 B1
Shalfleet Dr W10 .. 30 C2
Shalford NW10 ... 21 C4
Shalford Ct N1 ... 86 A2
Shalford Ho SE1 .. 137 C2
Shalimar Gdns W3 . 28 B2
Shalimar Lo W3 .. 28 B2
Shalimar Rd W3 .. 28 B2
Shalstone Rd SW14,
TW9 .... 55 A4
Shamrock St SW4 . 61 C4
Shandon Ct SE4 .. 51 A1
Shandon Rd SW4 . 61 B1
Shand St SE1 .... 138 B4
Shandy St E1 .... 25 C1
Shan Ho WC1 .... 94 C1
Shannon Ct
12 Peckham SE15 .. 49 B3
Stoke Newington
N16 .... 7 A1
Willesden NW10 .. 8 A4
Shannon Gr SW9 .. 62 B3
Shannon Pl NW8 . 80 B2
Shanti Ct SW18 .. 70 C3
Shapla Prim Sch 25
E1 .... 125 C3
Shardcroft Ave
SE24 .... 63 A2
Shardeloes Rd
SE14 .... 51 B1
Shard's Sq SE15 .. 49 C4
Shard The SE1... 123 C1

Sharebourne Ho
SW2 .... 62 C2
Sharman Ho 13
E14 .... 34 B3
Sharnbrook Ho
W6 .... 155 B4
Sharon Gdns E9 .. 25 B4
Sharon Rd W4 ... 37 C1
Sharp Ho SW8.... 61 A4
Sharples Hall St 8
NW1 .... 12 B1
Sharpness Ct 2
SE15 .... 49 B3
Sharratt St SE15 .. 50 B4
Sharsted St SE17 .. 150 A1
Sharwood WC1 ... 85 A1
Shaver's Pl SW1 .. 119 B3
Shawbury Ct SE22 . 64 B2
Shawbury Rd SE22 . 64 B2
Shaw Cres 3 E14 .. 33 A3
Shaw Ct
8 Acton Green
W3 .... 37 B3
11 Battersea SW11.. 59 C4
Upper Holloway N19 . 5 A2
Shawfield St SW3 . 144 B1
Shawford Ct 3
SW15 .... 68 C4
Shaw Rd SE22 ... 64 A3
Shearling Way N7 . 14 A2
Shearsmith Ho 17
E1 .... 125 C4
Shearwater Ct 24
SE8 .... 51 B4
Sheba Pl E1 .. 24 B1 99 A1
Sheen Common Dr
SW14, TW10 .... 54 C2
Sheen Court Rd
TW10 .... 54 C3
Sheen Ct TW10 .. 54 C3
Sheendale Rd
TW9 .... 54 B3
Sheen Gate Gdns
SW14 .... 55 B3
Sheengate Mans
SW14 .... 55 B3
Sheen Gr N1 .... 85 B4
Sheen La SW14... 55 B3
Sheen Mount Prim
Sch SW14 ..... 55 A2
Sheen Pk TW10,
TW9 .... 54 B3
Sheen Rd TW10,
TW9 .... 54 B3
Sheen Wood
SW14 .... 55 B2
Sheepcote La
SW11 .... 169 A1
Sheep La E8 .... 25 A4
Sheffield Ho 18
SE15 .... 49 B2
Sheffield Sq 2 E3 . 26 B2
Sheffield St WC2 .. 106 C1
Sheffield Terr
W8 .... 31 C1 113 C1
Shelbourne Ho 20
N19 .... 4 C4
Shelburne Ct
SW15 .... 57 C2
Shelburne Rd N7 .. 14 B4
Shelbury Rd SE22 . 65 A2
Sheldon Ct SW8 .. 162 A1
Sheldon Ho 9 E9 .. 17 C2
Sheldon Pl E2 ... 25 A3
Sheldon Rd NW2 . 9 C4
Sheldon Sq W2 ... 101 A3

Sheldrake Ho 16
SE16 .... 40 C2
Sheldrick Cl SW19 . 44 B4
Shelduck Ct 37
SE8 .... 51 B4
Shelford Pl N16 .. 6 C1
Shelgate Rd SW11 . 60 B2
Shell Ctr SE1 .... 121 A1
Shelley Cl SE15.. 50 A1
Shelley Ct
Finsbury Pk N4 .... 5 B3
SW3 .... 159 A4
Shelley Ho
8 Bethnal Green
E2 .... 25 B2
Chelsea SW1 .... 160 C4
9 Stoke Newington
N16 .... 16 A4
Walworth SE17 ... 151 A2
Shelley Rd NW10 . 20 C4
Shellgrove Rd 31
N16 .... 16 A3
Shellness Rd E5 .. 17 A3
Shell Rd SE13 ... 67 A4
Shellwood Rd
SW11 .... 168 C1
Shelmerdine Cl
E3 .... 33 C4
Shelton St WC2 .. 106 A1
Shene Bldg EC1 .. 107 B4
Shene Sch SW14 .. 56 A3
Shenfield St N1 .. 24 A3
Shenley Rd SE5 .. 49 A2
Shepard Ho 17
SW11 .... 59 C4
Sheperdess Pl N1 . 97 A4
Shepherd Cl W1 .. 117 B4
Shepherdess Wlk
N1 .... 87 A1
Shepherd Ho
Barnsbury N7 ... 14 A2
10 Poplar E14 ... 34 A3
Shepherd Mkt
W1 .... 118 A1
SHEPHERD'S
BUSH 30 A1
Shepherd's Bush Gn
W12 .... 39 B4
Shepherd's Bush
Market W12 .... 39 B4
Shepherd's Bush Mkt
Sta W12 .... 39 B4
Shepherd's Bush
Overground Sta
W12 .... 39 C4
Shepherd's Bush Pl
W12 .... 39 C4
Shepherd's Bush Rd
W6 .... 39 B3
Shepherds Ct 8
W12 .... 39 C4
Shepherd's La E9 .. 17 C2
Shepherds Pl W1 . 117 B4
Shepherd St W1 .. 118 A1
Shepherd's Wlk
NW3 .... 11 C4
Sheppard Dr SE16 . 40 A1
Sheppard Ho
31 Hackney E2 ... 24 C3
6 Streatham SW2 . 74 C3
Shepperton Rd N1 . 87 B4
Sheppey Ho 18 E5 . 17 A4

Shepton Ct SW11 . . . . . 167 C4
Shepton Hos 11
  E2 . . . . 25 B2
Sherard Ct N19 . . . . 5 A1
Sherard Ho 4 E9 . . . . . 17 B1
Sheraton Ho SW1 . . . 160 B4
Sheraton St W1 . . . . . 105 B1
Sherborne Ho
  Pimlico SW1 . . . . 146 B2
  South Lambeth
  SW8 . . . . 162 C1
Sherborne La EC4 . . . 123 C4
Sherborne St N1 . . . . . 87 B4
Sherbourne Ct
  SW5 . . . . 142 A4
Sherbrooke Ho 9
  E2 . . . . 25 B3
Sherbrooke Rd
  SW6 . . . . 154 B1
Sherbrooke Terr
  SW6 . . . . 154 B1
Shere Ho SE1 . . . . 137 B2
Sherfield Gdns
  SW15 . . . . 56 B1
Sheridan Bldgs
  WC2 . . . . 106 B1
Sheridan Ct
  Earl's Ct SW5 . . . . . 142 A3
  South Hampstead
  NW6 . . . . 11 B1
  South Lambeth
  SW9 . . . . 173 A3
Sheridan Ho
  SE11 . . . . 149 C3
  7 Stoke Newington
  N16 . . . . 7 A1
Sheridan Pl SW13 . . . . . 56 B4
Sheridan St 6 E1 . . . . 32 A3
Sheringdale Prim Sch
  SW18 . . . . 70 B3
Sheringham NW8 . . . . . 79 C4
Sheringham Ho
  NW1 . . . . 102 B4
Sheringham Mews 6
  SW18 . . . . 71 B2
Sheringham Rd
  N7 . . . . 14 C2
Sherlock Ct NW8 . . . . . 79 B4
Sherlock Holmes Mus
  NW1 . . . . 91 A1
Sherlock Mews
  W1 . . . . 103 B4
Sherren Ho 1 E1 . . . . . 25 B1
Sherrick Green Rd
  NW10 . . . . 9 A3
Sherriff Ct NW6 . . . . . 10 C2
Sherriff Rd NW6 . . . . . 10 C2
Sherrin Rd E10 . . . . . . 19 A4
Sherston Ct
  Finsbury WC1 . . . . 95 B3
  Newington SE1 . . . . . 150 B4
Sherwin Ho 1
  SE11 . . . . 163 B4
Sherwin Rd SE14 . . . . . 50 C2
Sherwood NW6 . . . . . . 10 A1
Sherwood Cl
  SW13 . . . . 57 A4
Sherwood Ct
  11 Battersea
  SW11 . . . . 59 B4
  St Johns SE13 . . . . . 52 A1
  W1 . . . . 102 C3
Sherwood Gdns
  Bermondsey SE16 . . . . 40 A1

Sherwood Gdns
  continued
  Millwall E14 . . . . 41 C2
Sherwood Ho N4 . . . . . . 6 B4
Sherwood St W1 . . . . . 119 A4
Shetland Rd E3 . . . . . . 26 B3
Shillaker Ct W3 . . . . . . 29 B1
Shillibeer Pl W1 . . . . . 102 B3
Shillingford Ho 40
  E3 . . . . 27 A2
Shillingford St 2
  N1 . . . . 15 A1
Shillingstone Ho
  W14 . . . . 126 B1
Shinfield St W12 . . . . . 30 B3
Shipka Rd SW12 . . . . . . 73 A3
Ship La SW14 . . . . 45 B1
Shiplake Ho 20
  E2 . . . . 24 B2 98 C3
Shipley Ho 47
  SW8 . . . . 171 B1
Ship & Mermaid Row
  SE1 . . . . 138 A4
Ship St SE8 . . . . 51 C2
Ship Tavern Pas
  EC3 . . . . 124 A4
Shipton Ho
  1 Camden Town
  NW5 . . . . 12 C2
  11 Haggerston E2 . . . 24 B3
Shipton St
  E2 . . . . 24 B2 99 A4
Shipwright Rd
  SE16 . . . . 41 A4
Shipwright Yd
  SE1 . . . . 124 A1
Shirbutt St E14 . . . . . . 34 A2
Shire Pl SW18 . . . . 71 B4
Shirland Mews
  W9 . . . . 23 B2
Shirland Rd W9 . . . . . . 23 C1
Shirley Gr SW11 . . . . . 60 C4
Shirley Ho 15 SE5 . . . . 48 C3
Shirley Rd W4 . . . . 37 C4
Shirley St E16 . . . . 35 B3
Shirlock Rd NW3 . . . . . 12 B4
Shoe La EC4 . . . . 107 C2
Shooters Hill Rd SE3 . .
  SE10 . . . . 53 A2
Shoot-Up Hill
  NW2 . . . . 10 A2
Shopstop SW11 . . . . . . 60 A4
Shore Bsns Ctr 31
  E9 . . . . 17 B1
SHOREDITCH 87 C1
Shoreditch Ct 4
  E8 . . . . 16 B1
Shoreditch High St
  Sta E2 . . . . 24 B1
Shoreditch High St
  E2 . . . . 24 A1 98 B2
Shoreditch Ho N1 . . . . 97 C3
Shoreham Cl
  SW18 . . . . 59 A2
Shore Ho SW8 . . . . 61 A4
Shore Mews 29 E9 . . . . 17 B1
Shore Pl E9 . . . . 17 B1
Shore Rd E9 . . . . 17 B1
Shorncliffe Rd
  SE1 . . . . 152 C2
Shorrolds Rd
  SW6 . . . . 155 A2
Shortcroft Mead Ct
  NW10 . . . . 8 C3
Shorter St EC3 . . . . . . 125 A4
Shortlands W6 . . . . 39 C2

Short Rd W4 . . . . 46 A4
Shorts Gdns WC2 . . . . 106 A1
Short St SE1 . . . . 135 C4
Shottendane Rd
  SW6 . . . . 165 B4
Shottfield Ave
  SW14 . . . . 56 A3
Shottsford 1 W11 . . . . 31 C3
Shoulder of Mutton
  Alley 10 E14 . . . . 33 A2
Shouldham St
  W1 . . . . 102 B3
Shreveport Ho 2
  N19 . . . . 4 C4
Shrewsbury Ave
  SW14 . . . . 55 C3
Shrewsbury Cres
  NW10 . . . . 20 C4
Shrewsbury Ho
  Chelsea SW3 . . . . 158 A3
  Kennington SE11 . . . 163 A3
Shrewsbury Mews 33
  W2 . . . . 31 C4
Shrewsbury Rd
  W2 . . . . 31 C3
Shrewsbury St
  W10 . . . . 22 B1
Shropshire Ho
  WC1 . . . . 93 A1
Shroton St NW1 . . . . . 102 B4
Shrubbery Cl N1 . . . . . 87 A3
Shrubland Rd E8 . . . . . 24 C4
Shrubs Ho SW1 . . . . . 147 C3
Shurland Gdns
  SE15 . . . . 49 B3
Shuters Sq W14 . . . . . 140 C1
Shuttle St
  E1 . . . . 24 C1 99 B1
Shuttleworth Rd
  SW11 . . . . 168 A2
Sibella Rd SW4 . . . . . 171 C1
Sicilian Ave WC1 . . . . 106 B3
Sidbury St SW6 . . . . . 164 A4
Siddons Ct WC2 . . . . . 106 C1
Siddons Ho 3
  NW3 . . . . 12 B3
Siddons La NW1 . . . . . 91 A1
Sidford Ho SE1 . . . . . 135 A1
Sidford Pl SE1 . . . . . . 135 A1
Sidgwick Ho 20
  SW9 . . . . 172 B1
Sidings Mews N7 . . . . . 14 C4
Sidlaw Ho N16 . . . . 7 B3
Sidmouth Ho
  8 Camberwell
  SE15 . . . . 49 C3
  Marylebone W1 . . . . 102 B2
  26 Streatham SW2 . . . 74 C4
Sidmouth Mews
  WC1 . . . . 94 C3
Sidmouth Par NW2 . . . . 9 B1
Sidmouth Rd NW2 . . . . 9 B1
Sidmouth St WC1 . . . . 94 C3
Sidney Boyd Ct
  NW6 . . . . 10 C1
Sidney Godley (VC)
  Ho 11 E2 . . . . 25 B2
Sidney Gr EC1 . . . . 86 A1
Sidney Ho 4 E2 . . . . . . 25 C3
Sidney Miller Ct 1
  W3 . . . . 28 A1
Sidney Rd SW9 . . . . . 173 A1
Sidney Sq E1 . . . . 32 B4
Sidney St E1 . . . . 32 B4
Sidworth St 8 E8 . . . . 17 A1
Siebert Rd SE3 . . . . . . 53 C4

Siege Ho 14 E1 . . . . . . 32 A3
Sigdon Rd E8 . . . . 16 C3
Signal Ho
  9 London E8 . . . . 17 A1
  SE1 . . . . 136 C3
Signmakers Yd
  NW1 . . . . 82 C3
Sigrist Ho 9
  SE26 . . . . 76 C1
Silbury Ho 8
  SE26 . . . . 76 C1
Silbury St N1 . . . . 97 B4
Silchester Rd W10 . . . . 30 C3
Silesia Bldgs E8 . . . . . 17 A1
Silex St SE1 . . . . 136 B3
Silk Mews SE11 . . . . . 149 C2
Silken Mews 24
  SE15 . . . . 49 C3
Silk Mills Path
  SE13 . . . . 67 B4
Silk Mills Sq E9 . . . . . . 18 B2
Silk St EC2 . . . . 109 A4
Sillitoe Ho N1 . . . . 87 C3
Silsoe Ho NW1 . . . . . . 82 B1
Silverbirch Wlk 1
  NW3 . . . . 12 C2
Silverburn Ho 8
  SW9 . . . . 48 A2
Silver Cl SE14 . . . . 51 A3
Silver Cres W4 . . . . . . 37 A2
Silver Ct N19 . . . . 4 B1
Silverdale NW1 . . . . . . 92 C4
Silverdale Ct EC1 . . . . 96 B2
Silvermere Rd SE6 . . . 67 A1
Silver Pl W1 . . . . 119 A4
Silver Rd
  Shepherd's Bush
  W12 . . . . 30 C2
  St Johns SE13 . . . . . . 67 A4
Silverthorn 11
  NW6 . . . . 78 B3
Silverthorne Rd
  SW8 . . . . 170 B1
Silverton Rd W6 . . . . . 47 C4
Silvertown Way
  E16 . . . . 35 C1
Silver Wlk SE16 . . . . . . 33 B1
Silver Ho
  2 Bethnal Green
  E2 . . . . 25 B2
  1 Notting Hill W11 . . . 31 B3
  8 Stepney E1 . . . . . . 32 B3
Silvester Rd SE22 . . . . 64 B2
Silvester St SE1 . . . . . 137 B3
Silwex Ho
  E1 . . . . 24 B1 98 C1
Silwood St SE16 . . . . . 40 B1
Simla Ho SE1 . . . . 137 C3
Simmonds Ct
  SW5 . . . . 142 A3
Simmons Ho
  20 Bethnal Green
  E2 . . . . 24 C2 99 B3
  Finsbury Pk N7 . . . . . . 5 B2
Simms Rd SE1 . . . . . . 153 C3
Simms Ct SW6 . . . . . . 58 A4
Simon Cl
  W11 . . . . . . 31 B2 113 A4
Simon Ct W9 . . . . 23 C2
Simon Lo 5 SW19 . . . . 69 C3
Simon Marks Jewish
  Prim Sch 8 N16 . . . . 7 B2
Simons Wlk E15 . . . . . . 19 C3
Simpson Dr W3 . . . . . . 28 C3
Simpson Ho
  Lisson Gr NW8 . . . . . 90 A3
  Vauxhall SE11 . . . . . 148 C1
Simpson's Rd E14 . . . . 34 A2

Simpson St SW11 . . . . 168 A1
Sinclair Ct N5 . . . . 15 B2
Sinclair Gdns W14 . . . . 39 C4
Sinclair Ho 1
  SW12 . . . . 73 A4
Sinclair Pl SE4 . . . . . . 66 C1
Sinclair Rd W14 . . . . . 126 A2
Sinclair's Ho 13 E3 . . . 26 B3
Singer St EC2 . . . . 97 C3
Sion Ho SE13 . . . . 67 B3
Sion-Manning RC Sch
  for Girls
  11 Kensal Town
  W10 . . . . 31 A4
  3 North Kensington
  W10 . . . . 30 C4
Sir Abraham Dawes
  Cotts SW15 . . . . 58 A3
Sir Alexander Cl
  W3 . . . . 29 B1
Sir Alexander Rd
  W3 . . . . 29 B1
Sirdar Rd
  W11 . . . . . 31 A2 112 A3
Sir Francis Drake
  Prim Sch 1 SE8 . . . . 41 A1
Sirinham Point
  SW8 . . . . 163 A3
Sirius Bldg 18 E1 . . . . 32 C2
Sir James Barrie Prim
  Sch SW8 . . . . 171 A3
Sir John Cass
  Foundation &
  Redcoat CE Sec Sch
  E1 . . . . 32 C4
Sir John Cass's
  Foundation Prim
  Sch EC3 . . . . 110 B1
Sir John Kirk Cl 33
  SE5 . . . . 48 B3
Sir John Lillie Prim
  Sch SW6 . . . . 154 B3
Sir John Soane's Mus
  WC2 . . . . 106 C2
Sir Oswald Stoll
  Foundation The
  SW6 . . . . 156 A2
Sir Thomas Abney
  Prim Sch N16 . . . . 6 C3
Sir Thomas More Est
  SW3 . . . . 157 C3
Sir William Burrough
  Prim Sch 2 E14 . . . . 33 B3
Sir William Powell's
  Almshos SW6 . . . . . . 58 A4
Sise La EC4 . . . . 109 B1
Siskin Ho 14 SE16 . . . . 40 C2
Sispara Gdns
  SW18 . . . . 58 B1
Sissinghurst Ho 17
  SE15 . . . . 50 B4
Sister Mabel's Way 15
  SE15 . . . . 49 C3
Sisters Ave SW11 . . . . 60 B3
Sisters of St
  Marcellina Sch 34
  NW3 . . . . 11 B4
Sistova Rd SW12 . . . . . 73 A3
Sisulu Pl SW9 . . . . 62 C4
Sitarey Ct 4 W12 . . . . 30 A1
Site of Changing of
  the Guard SW1 . . . . 132 C3
Sivill Ho 3
  E2 . . . . 24 B2 99 A4

Siward Rd SW17....71 B1
Six Bridges Ind Est 15
  SE1.............153 C1
Sixth Ave W10.....23 A2
Skardu Rd NW2 ....10 A3
Skeena Hill SW18,
  SW19 ....70 A4
Skeggs Ho 5 E14..42 B3
Skegness Ho 7
  N7 ....14 B1
Skelbrook St
  SW18.............71 B2
Skelgill Rd SW15..58 B3
Skelton Cl 8 E8....16 B2
Skelton Ho N16 ....16 A3
Skelwith Rd W6....47 B4
Skenfrith Ho SE15..50 A4
Sketchley Gdns
  SE16.............40 C1
Skiffington Cl
  SW2 ....74 C3
Skinner Pl SW1...145 B3
Skinners Company
  Sch (Upper) 10
  N16................7 B4
Skinners La EC4...123 A4
Skinner St EC1.....95 C2
Skipsea Ho SW18..59 C1
Skipton Ho SE4....66 A3
Skipwith Bldg
  EC1..............107 B4
Skipworth Rd E9...25 B4
Skua Cl 33 SE8.....51 B4
Skyline Ct SE1....138 C1
Skyline Plaza Bldg 10
  E1...............111 C2
Skylines E14.......42 B4
Slade Ct NW2 ......10 A3
Sladen Pl 12 E5....17 A4
Slagrove Pl SE13 ..67 A2
Slaidburn St
  SW10 ....157 A3
Slaithwaite Rd
  SE13.............67 B3
Slaney Ct NW10 ....9 B1
Slaney Pl 1 N7....14 C3
Sleaford Ho 6 E3..26 C1
Sleaford Ind Est
  SW8 ....161 A1
Sleaford St SW8 ..161 A1
Sleat Ho 13 E3.....26 B3
Slievemore Cl 8
  SW4 ....61 C4
Sligo Ho 8 E1 .....25 C1
Slingsby Pl WC2 ..120 A4
Slippers Pl SE16 ..40 A3
Slipway Ho 1 E14..42 A1
Sloane Ave SW3 ..144 B3
Sloane Avenue Mans
  SW3 ....144 C3
Sloane Ct E SW3 .145 B2
Sloane Ct W SW3 .145 B2
Sloane Gate Mans
  SW1 ....145 B4
Sloane Gdns SW1.145 B3
Sloane Ho 7 E9....17 B1
Sloane Sq SW1 ...145 B3
Sloane Square Sta
  SW1 ....145 B3
Sloane St SW1 ....131 A1
Sloane Terr SW1 ..145 B4
Sloane Terr Mans
  SW1 ....145 B4
Sly St 11 E1........32 A3
Smallbrook Mews
  W2 ....101 B1

Smalley Cl N16.....7 B1
Smart's Pl WC1,
  WC2 ....106 B2
Smart St E2 ....25 C2
Smeaton Ct SE1...136 C1
Smeaton Rd SW18..70 C4
Smeaton St 1 .....32 A1
Smedley St SW4..171 C2
Smeed Rd E3.......18 C1
Smiles Pl SE13 ....52 B1
Smith Cl SE16 ....32 C1
Smithfield Mkt

  EC1..............108 B3
Smithfield St EC1.108 A3
Smith's Ct 1 ......119 B4
Smith Sq SW1 ....134 A1
Smith St SW3 .....144 C1
Smith's Yd SW18..71 B2
Smith Terr SW3 ..144 C1
Smithwood Cl
  SW19 ....70 A2
Smithy St E1.......32 B4
Smithy Street Sch 34
  E1................32 B4
Smugglers Way
  SW18.............59 A3
Smyrk's Rd SE17 .152 B1
Smyrna Mans 8
  NW6 ....10 C1
Smyrna Rd NW6 ..10 C1
Smythe St E14.....34 A2
Snarsgate St W10 .30 B4
Sneath Ave NW11 ..1 B4
Sneyd Rd NW2 .....9 B4
Snowberry Cl E11 ..19 C4
Snowbury Rd 6
  SW6 ....166 B1
Snowden St
  EC2..............24 A1 98 A1
Snowe Ho SE27....75 A1
Snow Hill EC1 ....108 A3
Snowman Ho NW6 .78 B4
Snowsfields SE1...137 C4
Snowsfields Prim Sch
  SE1...............138 A4
Soames St SE15 ...64 B4
Soane Ct 13 NW1..13 B1
Soane Ho SE17 ...151 C1
Soaphouse La
  TW8 ....44 A3
Sobell L Ctr N7.....5 B1
Soho 105 B1
Soho W1 ....105 B2
Soho Parish CE Prim
  Sch W1 ....119 B4
Soho Sq W1 ......105 B2
Soho St W1 ....105 B2
Sojourner-Truth Cl 8
  E8................17 A2
Solander Gdns
  13 Shadwell E1 ..32 B2
  Stepney E1.......32 A2
Soldene Ct N7.....14 B2
Solebay St E1......26 A1
Solent Rd 6 NW6..33 A4
Soley Mews WC1 ..95 B4
Solidarity Ho 6
  NW10.............9 B2
Solna Ave SW15...57 B2
Solomon's Pas
  SE15.............65 A3
Solon New Rd
  SW4 ....62 A3
Solon Rd SW2 .....62 A3
Solway Ho 12 E1 ..25 C1

Solway Rd SE22 ...64 C3
Somali Rd NW2 ...10 B3
Somborne Ho 11
  SW15.............68 C4
Sombrook Ho
  SE11.............149 B3
Somer Ct SW6 ....155 B3
Somerfield Rd N4 ..6 A2
Somerfield St
  SE16.............40 C1
Somerford Gr N16..16 B4
Somerford Grove Est
  N16................16 B4
Somerford St E1 ..25 A1
Somerford Way
  SE16.............41 A4
Somerleyton Rd
  SW9 ....62 C3
Somers Cl NW1 ...83 B2
Somers Cres W2 .102 A1
Somerset Gdns
  Highgate N6.......3 C4
  St Johns SE13 ...52 A1
Somerset Ho
  SW19 ....70 A4
Somerset Ho
  WC2..............121 A4
Somerset Lo
  SW15.............57 A3
Somerset Rd
  Bedford Pk W4 ...37 C3
  Wimbledon SW19..70 C1
Somerset Sq W14 126 C3
Somers Pl SW2....74 B4
Somers Rd SW2 ...62 B1
SOMERS TOWN ...93 C4
Somers Town Est
  NW1..............83 A1
Somerton Ave
  TW9 ....55 A4
Somerton Rd
  Cricklewood NW2 ..1 A1
  Nunhead SE15 ...65 A3
Somerville Ave
  SW13 ....47 B4
Somerville Cl
  SW9 ....173 A2
Somerville Ho 10
  SW15.............57 C1
Somerville Point
  SE16.............41 B4
Sonderburg Rd 13
  N7 ....5 B2
Sondes St SE17 ...48 C4
Sonia Gdns NW10 ..8 B4
Sonning Ho 23
  E2........24 B2 98 C3
Sophia Cl N7......14 B2
Sophia Ho W6.....39 B1
Sophia Sq 15 SE16..33 A2
Sopwith Way
  SW8 ....160 A2
Sorrel La 11 E14 ..34 C3
Sorrell Cl
  6 Brixton SW9 ..173 C2
  SE14..............51 A3
Soseki Mus SW4...61 A4
Sotheby Rd N5 ....15 B4
Sotheran Cl E8....24 C4
Sotherton Pl SW6 .165 C3
Soudan Rd SW11 .168 C3
Souldern Rd 10
  W14...............39 C3
SOUTH ACTON 37 A3
South Acton Sta W3,
  W4................37 B3

South Africa Rd
  W12...............30 A2
Southall Pl SE1...137 B3
Southam Ho 9
  W10...............23 A1
Southampton Bldgs
  WC2..............107 B3
Southampton Pl
  WC1..............106 B3
Southampton Rd
  NW5..............12 B3
Southampton Row
  WC1..............106 B4
Southampton St
  WC2..............120 B4
Southampton Way
  SE5...............49 A3
Southam St W10 ..23 A1
South Audley St
  W1...............117 C2
South Ave TW9 ...44 C1
SOUTH BANK 120 C1
South Bank Bsns Ctr
  SW8 ....161 C3
Southbank
  International Sch 14
  NW3..............11 B2
Southbank
  International Sch
  (Westminster
  Campus) W1 ....104 A4
Southbank Int Sch
  W11.......31 C2 113 B3
South Bank Univ
  SW8 ....171 C4
South Bank University
  (Erlang House)
  SE1...............136 A3
South Bermondsey
  Sta SE16 ....40 B1
South Black Lion La
  W6................38 C1
South Bldg SW1 ..133 A2
South Block 20 E1 .32 B2
South Bolton Gdns
  SW10 ....142 B2
Southborough Ho
  SE17.............152 B2
Southborough Rd
  E9................25 C4
SOUTH BROMLEY..34 C4
South Building
  SE10.............52 C3
Southbury NW8 ...79 A4
South Camden Com
  Sch NW1 ....83 B2
South Carriage Dr SW1,
  SW7 ....130 C4
South Chelsea Coll 22
  SW9 ....62 B3
South Colonnade The
  E14................34 A1
Southcombe St
  W14..............140 A4
Southcote Rd N19 ..13 B4
Southcott Ho
  8 Bromley E3 ....27 A2
  W9................89 A1
South Cres
  Newham E16 .....27 C1
  WC1..............105 B3
Southcroft 8
  NW10.............20 C4
South Ct SW15 ....57 C1
Southdean Gdns
  SW19 ....70 B2

Southdown N7 ....14 A2
South Eastern Univ 8
  N7 ....5 B1
South Eaton Pl
  SW1 ....145 C4
South Edwardes Sq
  W8...............127 B1
South End W8 ....128 B2
South End Cl NW3 .12 A4
South End Gn
  NW3..............12 A4
South End Rd
  NW3..............12 A4
South End Row
  W8...............128 B2
Southgate Way
  SE14..............51 A3
Southern Gr E3....26 B1
Southern Row
  W10...............23 A1
Southern St N1....84 C2
Southern Way
  SE10.............43 B1
Southernwood Ret Pk
  SE1...............152 C4
Southerton Rd W6 .39 B2
Southey Ho SE17 .151 A2
Southey Mews
  E16................35 C1
Southey Rd SW9 .173 B4
Southfield Lo W4 .37 C4
Southfield Prim Sch
  W4................38 A3
Southfield Rd W4 .37 C4
SOUTHFIELDS 71 A3
Southfields Com Coll
  SW18.............70 C4
Southfields Rd
  SW18.............58 C1
Southfields Sta
  SW18.............70 C4
Southgate Ct N1 ..15 C1
Southgate Gr N1 ..15 C1
Southgate Rd N1..87 C4
South Gr No N6.....3 C3
South Grove Ho N6 .3 C3
SOUTH HACKNEY..25 B4
SOUTH
  HAMPSTEAD 11 B1
South Hampstead
  High Sch 11
  NW3..............11 C2
South Hampstead Sta
  NW8..............11 B1
South Hill Pk NW3 .12 A4
South Hill Pk Gdns
  NW3..............12 A4
Southill St E14....34 A3
South Island Pl
  SW9 ....163 B1
SOUTH
  KENSINGTON ...143 A4
South Kensington Sta
  SW7 ....143 C4
South Kensington
  Station Arc SW7 143 C4
SOUTH
  LAMBETH 172 B3
South Lambeth Pl
  SW8 ....162 B4
South Lambeth Rd
  SW8 ....162 B2
Southlands Dr
  SW19 ....69 C2

South Lo NW8......**89** B4
South London Gall
SE5......**49** A2
South London
Montessori Sch
SW11......**168** A3
Southmead Prim Sch
IB SW19......**70** A3
Southmead Rd
SW19......**70** A3
South Molton La
W1......**104** A1
South Molton Rd
E16......**35** C3
South Molton St
W1......**104** A1
Southmoor Way
E9......**18** B3
Southolm St
SW11......**170** B3
South Par W4......**37** C2
South Parade
SW3......**143** C2
South Park Mews
SW6......**59** A4
South Pl EC2......**109** C3
South Pl Mews
EC2......**109** C3
South Quay Plaza
E14......**42** A4
South Quay Sta
E14......**42** A4
South Rise W2......**116** B4
South Row SE3......**53** B1
South Sea St SE16..**41** B3
South Side W6......**38** B3
Southside Ind Est
SW8......**170** C4
Southside Quarter ◳
SW11......**168** C2
Southside Sh Ctr
SW18......**59** A1
South Sq WC1......**107** B3
South St W1......**117** C2
South Tenter St
E1......**111** A1
South Terr SW7..**144** A4
South Thames Coll
(Putney Ctr) IB
SW15......**57** C2
South Thames Coll
(Roehampton Ctr)
SW15......**56** C1
South Thames Coll
(Wandsworth Ctr) ☐
SW18......**59** A2
Southvale Rd SE3..**53** A1
Southview Ave
NW10......**8** B3
South Villas NW1...**13** C2
Southville
London SW8.....**171** C3
South Lambeth
SW8......**172** A3
SOUTHWARK.....**40** B2
Southwark Bridge SE1,
EC4......**123** A3
Southwark Bridge Rd
SE1......**123** A1
Southwark Cath
SE1......**123** B2
Southwark Coll
SE1......**136** A4
Southwark Coll
(Blackfriars Ctr)
SE1......**122** A1
Southwark Coll
(Camberwell Ctr) ◳
SE5......**49** A3
Southwark Coll
(Grange Ctr)
SE1......**138** B1
Southwark Coll
(Surrey Docks Ctr)
SE16......**40** A3
Southwark Park Est
IB SE16......**40** A2
Southwark Park Prim
Sch IB SE16....**40** A3
Southwark Park Rd
SE16......**153** B4
Southwark PE Sports
Complex SE16....**49** B2
Southwark St SE1 **122** C1
Southwark Sta
IB SE1......**122** B1
Southwater CI ☐
SE11......**33** B3
Southway CI ☐
W12......**39** A4
Southwell Gdns
SW7......**142** C3
Southwell Ho
IB Bermondsey
SE16......**40** A2
☐ Stoke Newington
N16......**16** A3
Southwell Rd SE5..**63** B4
South Wharf Rd
W2......**101** C2
Southwick Mews
W2......**101** C2
Southwick PI W2..**102** A1
Southwick St W2..**102** A1
Southwick Yd W2..**102** A1
Southwold Mans
W9......**23** C2
Southwood Ave N6..**4** A4
Southwood Ct EC1..**96** A3
Southwood Ho
W11......**31** A2
Southwood La N6...**3** C4
Southwood La
N6......**3** C4
Southwood Lawn Rd
N6......**3** C4
Southwood Park
N6......**3** C4
Southwood Smith Ho
☐ E2......**25** A2
Southwood Smith St
N1......**86** C4
South Worple Ave
SW14......**56** A4
Southwyck Ho
SW9......**62** C3
South Yd EC1......**109** B4
Sovereign CI E1....**32** A2
Sovereign Cres
SE16......**33** A2
Sovereign Ct
IB Richmond
TW9......**54** B3
IB Stepney E1....**32** A2
Sovereign Ho IB
E2......**24** B3
Sovereign Mews ◳
E2......**24** B3
Sovereign Pk
NW10......**20** A1

Space Bsns Pk
NW10......**20** A2
Spa Ct IB SE16....**139** B2
Spafield St EC1.....**95** B2
Spalding Ho SE4....**66** A2
Spanby Rd E3......**26** C1
Spaniards CI NW11..**2** C3
Spaniards End NW3..**2** C2
Spaniards Rd NW3...**2** B2
Spanish Billingual Sch
W10......**31** A4
Spanish PI W1.....**103** C2
Spanish Rd SW18..**59** B2
Spa Rd SE16......**139** A1
Sparke Terr ☐
E16......**35** B3
Sparkford Ho
SW11......**167** C4
Sparks CI W3......**28** C3
Sparsholt Rd N19....**5** A3
Sparta St SE10....**52** B2
Spa Sch SE1......**153** B4
Spa View SW16....**74** B1
Speakers' Corner
W1......**117** A4
Speakman Ho SE4..**66** A4
Spear Mews SW5 **141** C3
Spears Rd N19......**5** A3
Spectrum Ho NW5.**12** C4
Spedan CI NW3......**2** B1
Speechly Mews
E8......**16** B3
Speed Ho EC2.....**109** B4
Speedwell St IB
SE8......**51** C3
Speedy PI WC1.....**94** A3
Speldhurst Rd
Bedford Pk W4....**37** C3
Homerton E9......**17** C1
Spellbrook Wlk N1 **87** A4
Spelman Ho IB
E1......**111** B3
Spelman St E1.....**111** B4
Spence CI SE16....**41** B4
Spencer Gdns
SW14......**55** B2
Spencer Ho
IB Clapham SW8..**171** B1
② Putney SW19....**69** C3
Vale of Health NW3....**2** C1
Wimbledon SW19....**69** C1
Spencer House Mus
SW1......**118** C1
Spencer Mews
Fulham W6......**154** A4
South Lambeth
SW9......**172** C3
Spencer Park Ct
SW18......**59** C2
Spencer PI SW18...**59** C2
Spencer Pl
IB Islington N1....**15** A1
SW1......**133** A1
Spencer Rd
Acton W3......**28** B1
Chiswick W4......**45** B3
Wandsworth SW18..**59** C2
Spencer Rise NW5...**4** A1
Spencer St EC1.....**96** A3
Spencer Way IB
E1......**32** A3
Spencer Wlk
②③ Hampstead
NW3......**11** B4
Putney SW15....**57** C3
Spencer Yd SE3....**53** B1

Spenlow Ho ②
SE16......**139** C2
Spenser Gr N16....**16** A4
Spenser Mews
SE21......**75** C3
Spenser Rd SE24..**63** A2
Spenser St SW1...**133** A2
Spens Ho WC1.....**94** C1
Spensley Wlk N16...**6** C1
Spert St E14......**33** A2
Spey St E14......**34** B3
Spezia Rd NW10...**21** C3
Spice Ct
IB Battersea
SW11......**59** B4
② St George in East
E1......**125** C2
Spice Quay Htss
SE1......**125** A1
Spicer CI SE5,SW9..**48** A1
Spicer Ho
E2......**24** C2 **99** B3
Spindrift Ave E14...**42** A2
Spinnaker Ho ②
E14......**41** C4
Spinney The
Barnes SW13......**47** A4
Streatham SW16...**73** C1
Spire CI IB NW10...**54** A1
Spire Ho W2......**115** A4
Spirit Quay E1......**32** A1
SPITALFIELDS......**17** C2
Spital Sq E1......**110** B4
Spital St E1......**111** B4
Spital Yd E1......**110** B4
Splendour Wlk
SE16......**40** B1
Spode Ho SE11....**135** B3
Spode Wlk NW3...**11** A3
Sporle Ct ② SW11..**59** C4
Sprewell SW15....**58** A1
Spriggs Ho IB N1...**15** A1
Sprimont Pl SW3 **144** C2
Springall St ②
SE15......**50** A3
Springalls Wharf ②
SE16......**139** B4
Springbank Wlk
NW1......**13** C1
Spring Cott IB
W12......**38** C4
Spring Ct NW2......**10** B2
Springdale Rd
N16......**15** C4
Springett Ho IB
SW2......**62** B2
Springfield Ct
IB Dagenham W3..**28** B3
Hampstead NW3...**12** A1
Springfield Ho
Acton W3......**28** B1
IB Camberwell SE5..**49** A1
IB Dalston E8......**16** B2
Springfield La
NW6......**78** A3
Springfield Rd
NW8......**79** A3
Springfield University
Hospl SW17......**72** A2
Springfield Wlk
NW6......**78** A3
Spring Gdns
Islington N5......**15** B3
SW1......**120** A2
Spring Gr W4......**44** C4

Spring Grove Rd
TW10......**54** B2
Spring Hill E5......**7** C4
Springhill CI SE5...**63** C4
Spring Ho WC1.....**95** B3
Spring Mews W1 **103** A4
Springpark Dr N4....**6** B3
Spring PI NW5......**13** A3
Springrice Rd
SE13......**67** C1
Spring St W2......**101** B1
Spring Terr TW10..**54** A2
Springtide CI ⑩
SE15......**49** C2
Springvale Ave
TW8......**36** A1
Springvale Terr ⑤
W14......**39** C3
Springwater WC1 **106** C4
Springwell Ave
NW10......**21** B4
Spring Wlk ① E1.**111** C4
Springwood CI ☐
E3......**26** C3
Spruce Ct W5......**36** A3
Spruce Ho ⑮
SE16......**40** C4
Sprules Rd SE4....**51** A1
Spurgeon St SE1 **137** B2
Spurling Rd SE22...**64** B3
Spur Rd SE1......**135** B4
Spurstowe Rd E8...**17** A2
Spurstowe Terr
E8......**17** A3
Square Rigger Row ②
SW11......**59** B4
Square The
Hammersmith W6 **39** B1
SW6......**165** B3
Squarey St SW17 **71** B1
Squire Gdns NW8..**89** B3
Squires Ct SW4...**172** B3
Squire's Mount
NW3......**2** C1
Squirrels The
SE13......**67** C3
Squirries St
E2......**24** C2 **99** C3
Stable Ho IB SE16..**40** B4
Stables Way SE11..**149** B2
Stable Way W10....**30** B3
Stable Yd Rd
SW1......**133** A4
Stacey St
Highbury N7......**5** C1
Soho WC2......**105** C1
Stack Ho SW1.....**145** C3
Stackhouse St
SW1......**130** C2
Stadium St SW10 **157** A1
Stafford CI NW6...**23** C2
Stafford Cripps Ho
IB Bethnal Green
E2......**25** B2
SW6......**155** A3
Stafford Ct
Kensington W8....**127** C2
South Lambeth
SW8......**172** A3
Stafford Ho SE1...**153** A2
Stafford Mans
IB Hammersmith
W14......**39** C3
IB Stockwell SW4..**62** A3
SW11......**158** C1

Stafford Pl SW1.. **132** C2
Stafford Rd
Bow E3 .... 26 B3
Maida Vale NW6... 23 C2
Staffordshire St
Peckham SE15 ...... 49 C2
Peckham SE15 ...... 50 A2
Stafford St W1 .. **118** C2
Stafford Terr W8. **127** B2
Stag La SW15 ...... 68 B2
Stagshaw Ho 17
SE22 .... 64 A4
Stainer St SE1.. **123** C1
Staining La EC2.. **109** A2
Stainsby St 26
E2 .... 25 B3
Stainsby Rd E14...33 C3
Stalbridge Flats
W1 .... **103** C1
Stalbridge Ho
NW1 .... **82** C1
Stalbridge St
NW1 .... **102** B4
Stalham St SE16...40 A3
Stambourne Ho
SW8 .... **172** B4
Stamford Bridge
Stadium (Chelsea
FC) SW6 ...... 156 A2
Stamford Brook Ave
W6 .... 38 B3
Stamford Brook Gdns
1 W6 .... 38 B3
Stamford Brook Mans
2 W6 .... 38 B2
Stamford Brook Rd
W6 .... 38 B3
Stamford Brook Sta
W6 .... 38 B2
Stamford Cl 2
NW3 .... 2 B1
Stamford Cotts
SW10 .... **156** B2
Stamford Gr W6.. 38 C2
Stamford Gr E 1
N16 .... 7 C3
Stamford Gr W 2
N16 .... 7 C3
STAMFORD HILL .. 7 A3
Stamford Hill N16.. 7 A3
Stamford Hill Mans 1
N16 .... 7 A4
Stamford Hill Sta
N16 .... 7 A4
Stamford Lo 2 N16. 7 B4
Stamford Mans 2
N16 .... 7 A4
Stamford Rd N1.. 16 A2
Stamford St SE1.. **121** C2
Stamp Pl E2..24 B2 **99** A4
Stanard Cl N16 ...... 7 A4
Stanborough Ho 4
E3 .... 27 A1
Stanborough Pas
E8 .... 16 B2
Stanbridge Mans
SW15 .... 57 B4
Stanbridge Rd
SW15 .... 57 B4
Stanbrook Ct W1.. **118** C2
Stanbury Ct 18
NW3 .... 12 B2
Stanbury Rd
Nunhead SE15 ...... 50 B1
Peckham SE15 ...... 50 A1

Standard Pl 13
EC2 .... 24 A2 **98** B3
Standard Rd
NW10 .... 20 C1
Standen Rd SW18..70 C4
Standish Ho 6
W6 .... 38 C2
Standish Rd W6 .. 38 C2
Stanesgate Ho 29
SE15 .... 49 C3
Stanfield Ho NW8.. **89** C2
Stanfield Rd E14.. 26 A3
Stanford Ct
Kensington W8....**128** B1
Walham Green
SW6 .... **156** B3
Stanford Pl SE1.. **152** B3
Stanford Rd W8.. **128** B2
Stanford St SW1.. **147** B3
Stangate SE1...**135** A2
Stanhope Cl 28
SE16 .... 40 C4
Stanhope Gate
W1 .... **117** C2
Stanhope Gdns
SW7 .... **143** A4
Stanhope Ho
4 Putney SW15..57 B2
8 .... 51 B3
Stanhope Mews E
SW7 .... **143** A4
Stanhope Mews S
SW7 .... **143** A3
Stanhope Mews W
SW7 .... **143** A4
Stanhope Par NW1 **92** C4
Stanhope Pl W2.. **102** C1
Stanhope Rd N6.. 4 B4
Stanhope Row
W1 .... **118** A1
Stanhope St NW1.. **92** C3
Stanhope Terr
W2 .... **115** C4
Stanier Cl SW5.. **141** A1
Stanlake Mews 7
W12 .... 30 B1
Stanlake Rd W12.. 30 B1
Stanlake Villas 8
W12 .... 30 B1
Stanley Cl SW8.. **162** C3
Stanley Cohen Ho
EC1 .... **96** C1
Stanley Cres
W11 .... 31 B2 **112** C4
Stanley Gdns
Bedford Pk W3...... 38 A4
Cricklewood NW2..9 B3
W11 .... 31 B2 **112** C4
Stanley Gr SW11.. **169** C1
Stanley Ho
35 Clapham SW8.. **171** B1
22 Poplar E14 ...... 33 C3
Stanley Holloway Ct
E16 .... 35 C3
Stanley Mans
SW10 .... **157** A4
Upper Tooting
SW17 .... 72 B2
Stanley Rd
Acton Green W3...... 37 B3
Mill Meads E15...... 27 C4
Mortlake SW14 ...... 55 A3
Stanley St SE14,
SE8 .... 51 B3
Stanley Studios
SW10 .... **157** A4

Stanley Terr 8 N19.. 5 A2
Stanliff Ho 8 E14.. 41 C3
Stanmer St SW11.. **168** B2
Stanmore Gdns
TW9 .... 54 B4
Stanmore Ho 21
SW8 .... **171** C2
Stanmore Pl NW1.. **82** B4
Stanmore Rd TW9.. 54 B4
Stanmore St N1.. **84** C4
Stannard Cotts 3
E1 .... 25 B1
Stannard Mews
E8 .... 16 C2
Stannard Rd E8 .. 16 C2
Stannary Pl SE11.. **149** C1
Stannary St SE11.. **149** C1
Stansbury Sq 3
N4 .... 5 B4
Stansfield Rd SW9.. 62 B4
Stanstead Ho 8
E3 .... 27 B1
Stansted Express
Terminal EC2.. **110** A4
Stanswood Gdns
SE5 .... 49 A3
Stanton Ct N16...... 6 C4
Stanton Ho
SE10 .... 52 B4
Stanton Rd SW13.. 46 B1
Stanway Ct 22 N1.. 24 A3
Stanway St N1 ...... 24 A3
Stanwick Rd W14.. **140** C3
Stanworth St SE1.. **139** A3
Staplefield Cl 3
SW2 .... 74 A3
Stapleford Cl
SW19 .... 70 A4
Staplehurst Ct 1
N1 .... **60** B1
Staplehurst Ho 18
E5 .... 17 A3
Staple Inn WC2.. **107** B3
Staple Inn Bldgs
WC2 .... **107** B3
Staples Cl SE16 .. 33 A1
Staple St SE1.. **137** C3
Stapleton Hall N4.. 5 B4
Stapleton Hall Rd
N4 .... 5 B4
Stapleton Ho 19
E2 .... 25 A2
Stapleton Rd
SW17 .... 72 C1
Star Alley EC3 .. **124** B4
Starboard Way
E14 .... 41 C3
Starcross St NW1.. **93** A3
StarDome NW1 ...... **91** B1
Starfield Rd W12.. 38 C4
Star & Garter Mans 8
SW15 .... 57 C4
Star Lane Sta E16.. 35 A4
Starliner Ct N7.. 14 C2
Starling Ho NW8.. **80** A2
Star Pl E1 ...... **125** A3
Star Rd W14...... **140** C1
Star St W2 ...... **102** A2
Star Works NW10.. 21 C2
Star Yd WC2.. **107** B2
Statham Ct N7 ...... 5 A1
Statham Gr N16...... 6 C1
Statham Ho SW8.. **170** C4
Station App
Dagenham NW10.. 21 B2
Fulham SW6 ...... 58 A4

Station App *continued*
Richmond TW9 ...... 44 C2
Station Approach Rd
W4 .... 45 B3
Station Approach
Road SE1 ...... 135 B4
Station Ave
5 Brixton SW9 ...... 63 A4
2 .... 52 A2
Station Cres SE3.. 43 C1
Station Ct 8 SE15.. 50 B1
Stationers Hall Ct
EC4 .... **108** B1
Station Gdns W4.. 45 B3
Station Mews Terr 4
SE3 .... 43 C1
Station Par
Cricklewood NW2...... 9 B2
Richmond TW9 ...... 44 C2
4 Upper Tooting
SW12 .... 72 C3
Station Pas SE15.. 50 B2
Station Pl N4...... 5 C2
Station Rd
Barnes SW13 ...... 46 B1
Camden Town N19.. 4 B1
Harlesden NW10.. 21 B3
Lewisham SE13 ...... 67 B4
Station Rise SE27.. 75 A2
Station St E15...... 19 C1
Station Terr
Camberwell SE5 ...... 48 B2
Kensal Rise NW10.. 22 C3
Staunton Ho SE17 **152** A3
Staunton St SE8.. 51 B4
Staveley NW1 ...... **92** C4
Staveley Cl
Hackney E9...... 17 B3
Lower Holloway N7.. 14 A4
New Cross Gate
SE15 .... 50 B2
8 Peckham SE15 .. 50 A2
Staveley Gdns W4.. 45 C2
Staveley Rd W4.. 45 C4
Staverton Rd NW2.. 9 B1
Stave Yard Rd
SE16 .... 33 A1
Stavordale Lo
W14 .... **127** A2
Stavordale Rd N5.. 15 A4
Stayner's Rd E1.. 25 C1
Steadman Ct EC1.. **97** A2
Stead St SE17.. **151** B3
Stean St E8...... 24 B4
Stebbing Ho 8
W11 .... 30 C1
Stebondale St E14.. 42 B2
Stebon Prim Sch 20
E14 .... 33 C4
Stedham Pl WC1.. **106** A2
Steedman St
SE17 .... **150** C3
Steele Rd
Acton Green W4...... 37 B3
Becontree NW10.. 20 B3
Steele's Mews N
NW3 .... 12 B2
Steele's Mews S
NW3 .... 12 B2
Steele's Rd NW3.. 12 B2
Steel's La 22 E1.. 32 B3
Steen Way 7
SE22 .... 64 A2
Steep Hill SW16.. 73 C1

Steeple Cl SW6.. **164** B1
Steeple Ct 11 E1.. 25 A1
Steeple Wlk N1 ...... **87** A4
Steerforth St
SW18 .... 71 B2
Steers Way SE16.. 41 A4
Stelfax Ho WC1...... **95** A4
Stellman Cl E5 ...... 7 C1
Stephan Cl E8...... 24 C4
Stephen Ct 18
SW19 .... 69 C3
Stephendale Rd
SW6 .... **166** C2
Stephen Fox Ho 7
W4 .... 38 A1
Stephen Hawking Sch
E14 .... 33 A3
Stephen Mews
W1 .... **105** B3
Stephen Pl SW4.. 61 B4
Stephen Saunders Ct
SW11 .... 60 A2
Stephens Ct SE4.. 66 A4
Stephenson Ho
2 Gospel Oak
NW5 .... 13 A4
6 Maitland Pk
NW3 .... 12 B3
Newington SE1.. **136** C2
Stephenson St
Dagenham NW10.. 21 B2
Newham E16 ...... 35 A4
Stephenson Way
NW1 .... **93** A2
Stephen St W1 .. **105** B3
STEPNEY 32 C4
Stepney City E1.. 32 B4
Stepney City Farm
E1 .... 32 C4
Stepney E1...... 32 C4
Stepney Cswy E1.. 32 C3
Stepney Gn E1.. 32 C4
Stepney Greencoat CE
Prim Sch The 26
E14 .... 33 B3
Stepney Green Ct 4
E1 .... 32 C4
Stepney Green Maths
& Computing Coll 19
E1 .... 32 C4
Stepney Green Sta
E1 .... 25 C2
Stepney High St
E1 .... 32 C4
Stepney Way E1.. 32 B4
Sterling Cl NW10...... 8 C1
Sterling Gdns
SE14 .... 51 A4
Sterling Pl W5 ...... 36 A2
Sterling St SW7 .. **130** B2
Sterndale Rd W14.. 39 C3
Sterne St W12...... 39 C4
Sternhall La SE15.. 64 C4
Sternhold Ave SW12,
SW2 .... 73 C2
Sterry St SE1.. **137** B3
Steve Biko Ct W10.. 22 C1
Steve Biko Rd N7.. 5 C1
Stevedore St 3
E1 .... 32 A1
Stevenage Rd
SW6 .... 47 C2
Stevens Ave E9...... 17 B2

Stevenson Cres SE16 ....40 A1
Stevenson Ho
  [1] Battersea SW11 ....168 C1
  [6] Clapham Pk SW2 ....62 A2
  NW8 ....89 B2
Stevens St SE1 ....138 B2
Steventon Rd W12 ....29 B2
Stewart Headlam Prim Sch [28] E1 ....25 A1
Stewart Ho SE1 ....138 A1
Stewart Rd E15 ....19 C4
Stewart's Gr SW3 ....144 A2
Stewart's Rd SW8 ....170 C4
Stewart St E14 ....42 B4
Stew La EC4 ....122 C4
Steyne Ho
  [14] Acton W3 ....28 A1
  [17] Acton W3 ....28 A1
Steyne Rd W3 ....28 A1
Stifford Ho E1 ....32 B4
Stile Hall Gdns W4 ....36 C1
Stile Hall Par [6] W4 ....36 C1
Stileman Ho [4] E3 ....33 B4
Stillingfleet Rd SW13 ....46 C4
Stillington St SW1 ....147 A4
Stillness Jun & Inf Schs SE23 ....66 A1
Stillness Rd SE23 ....66 B1
Stirling Ct Clerkenwell EC1 ....96 A2 / Strand WC2 ....106 C1
Stirling Rd South Acton W3 ....37 A3 / Stockwell SW9 ....172 B1
Stoatley Ho [10] SW15 ....68 C3
Stockbeck NW1 ....83 A1
Stockfield Rd SW16 ....74 B1
Stockholm Ho E1 ....125 C4
Stockholm Rd SE16 ....40 B1
Stockholm Way E1 ....125 B2
Stockhurst Cl SW15 ....47 C1
Stockleigh Hall NW8 ....80 B2
Stock Orchard Cres N7 ....14 B3
Stock Orchard St N7 ....14 B3
Stocks Ct [5] E1 ....25 C1
Stocks Pl [16] E14 ....33 B2
Stockton Ho [16] E2 ....25 A2
STOCKWELL 62 A4
Stockwell Ave SW9 ....62 B4
Stockwell Gdns SW9 ....172 C3
Stockwell Gn SW9 ....172 C1
Stockwell La SW9 ....172 C1
Stockwell Park Cres SW9 ....173 A2

Stockwell Park High Sch SW9 ....172 C3
Stockwell Park Rd SW9 ....173 A3
Stockwell Park Wlk SW9 ....62 C4
Stockwell Prim Sch SW9 ....62 B4
Stockwell St SE10 ....52 B4
Stockwell Sta SW4 ....172 B2
Stockwell Terr SW9 ....172 C3
Stoddart Ho SW8 ....163 A3
Stodmarsh Ho [23] SW9 ....173 B4
Stoford Cl [4] SW19 ....70 A4
Stokenchurch St SW6 ....166 A3
STOKE NEWINGTON 7 A2
Stoke Newington Church St N16 ....7 A2
Stoke Newington Comm N16 ....7 A3
Stoke Newington High St N16 ....7 B2
Stoke Newington Rd N16 ....16 B4
Stoke Newington Sch N16 ....7 A2
Stoke Newington Sta N16 ....7 B3
Stoke Pl NW10 ....21 B2
Stokesley St W12 ....29 B3
Stondon Pk SE23 ....66 A1
Stone Bldgs WC2 ....107 A3
STONEBRIDGE 20 B4
Stonebridge Ctr [3] NW10 ....20 C4
Stonebridge Prim Sch NW10 ....20 B4
Stone Cl SW4 ....171 A1
Stonecutter St EC4 ....108 A2
Stonefield N4 ....5 B2
Stonefield Mans N1 ....85 B3
Stonefield St N1 ....85 C4
Stonegate [8] NW5 ....12 C2
Stonehill Rd Brentford W4 ....36 C1 / Mortlake SW14 ....55 C2
Stonehills Ct SE21 ....76 A1
Stonehill's Mans [7] SW16 ....74 A1
Stonehouse NW1 ....83 A3
Stonehouse Ct EC2 ....110 B2
Stonehouse Ho [21] W2 ....31 C4
Stoneleigh Lo [13] TW9 ....44 B2
Stoneleigh Mews [8] E3 ....26 A3
Stoneleigh Pl W11 ....30 C2
Stoneleigh St W11 ....30 C2
Stoneleigh Terr N19 ....4 A2
Stonell's Rd SW11 ....60 B2
Stonenest St N4 ....5 B3
Stones End St SE1 ....136 C3
Stoneyard La E14 ....34 A2

Stoney La EC3 ....110 B2
Stoney St SE1 ....123 B2
Stonhouse St SW4 ....61 C3
Stonor Rd W14 ....140 C3
Stopes St SE15 ....49 B3
Stopford Rd SE17 ....150 B1
Stopher Ho SE1 ....136 B3
Storace Ho [6]
Storers Quay E14 ....42 C2
Store St Bloomsbury WC1 ....105 B4 / Stratford New Town E15 ....19 C3
Storey Ct NW8 ....89 B3
Storey Ho [13] E14 ....34 A2
Storey's Gate SW1 ....133 C3
Stories Rd SE5 ....64 A4
Storks Rd SE16 ....139 C1
Stormont House Sch E5 ....17 A4
Stormont Rd Clapham SW11 ....60 C3 / Highgate N6 ....3 B4
Storrington WC1 ....94 B3
Story St N1 ....14 B1
Stothard Ho E1 ....25 B1
Stothard Pl E1 ....110 B4
Stothard St [12] E1 ....25 B1
Stott Cl SW18 ....59 C1
Stoughton Cl Roehampton SW15 ....68 C3 / SE11 ....149 A3
Stourcliffe Cl W1 ....102 C2
Stourcliffe St W1 ....102 C2
Stourhead Cl [6] SW19 ....69 C4
Stour Rd E3 ....18 C1
Stowage SE8 ....52 A4
Stowe Ho [11] N16 ....7 A1
Stowe Rd W12 ....30 A1
Stracey Rd NW10 ....20 C4
Stradbroke Rd N5 ....15 B4
Stradella Rd SE24 ....63 B1
Straffan Lo [5] NW3 ....12 A2
Strafford Ho [9] SE8 ....41 B1
Strafford Rd W3 ....37 B4
Strafford St E14 ....41 C4
Strahan Rd E3 ....26 A2
Straightsmouth SE10 ....52 B3
Straker's Rd SE15 ....65 A3
Strale Ho [11] N1 ....24 A4
STRAND 120 C4
Strand WC2 ....120 C4
Strand Dr TW9 ....45 A3
Strand La WC2 ....121 A4
STRAND ON THE GREEN 44 C4
Strand-on-the-Green SchS W4 ....44 C4
Strand-on-the-Green Schs W4 ....44 C4
Strang Ho N1 ....86 C3
Strangways Terr W14 ....126 C1
Stranraer Way N1 ....14 A1
Strasburg Rd SW11 ....170 A3
STRATFORD 19 B2

Stratford Bus Sta E15 ....19 C1
Stratford Coll (Newham 6th Form Coll) E15 ....19 C2
Stratford Gr SW15 ....57 C3
Stratford High St Sta E15 ....27 C4
Stratford International Sta E15 ....19 C2
STRATFORD MARSH 27 A4
STRATFORD NEW TOWN 19 B3
Stratford Pl W1 ....104 A1
Stratford Rd W8 ....127 C1
Stratford Sh Ctr E15 ....19 C1
Stratford Sta E15 ....19 C1
Stratford Studios W8 ....128 A1
Stratford Villas NW1 ....13 C1
Stratford Workshops E15 ....19 C1
Strathan Cl SW18 ....58 A1
Strathblaine Rd SW11 ....59 C3
Strathdon Dr SW17 ....71 C1
Stratheden Ho W2 ....116 A4
Stratheden Par W2 ....116 A4
Stratheden Rd SE3 ....53 C3
Strathearn Ho SW2 ....62 A2
Strathearn Pl W2 ....116 A4
Strathleven Rd SW2 ....62 A2
Strathmore Ct NW8 ....90 A4
Strathmore Gdns W8 ....31 C1 113 C2
Strathnairn St SE1 ....153 C3
Strathray Gdns NW3 ....12 A2
Strath Terr SW11 ....60 A3
Strathville Rd SW18 ....71 A2
Stratton Ct [4] N1 ....16 A1
Strattondale St E14 ....42 B3
Stratton St W1 ....118 B2
Strauss Rd W4 ....37 C4
Streamline Mews SE22 ....76 C3
Streatham Cl SW16 ....74 A2
Streatham & Clapham High Sch SW16 ....73 C1
Streatham Ct SW16 ....74 A2
STREATHAM HILL 74 A3
Streatham Hill SW2 ....74 B3
Streatham Hill & Clapham High Sch [14] SW2 ....74 B3
Streatham Hill Sta SW2 ....74 B4
Streatham Pl SW2 ....74 A4

Streatham St WC1 ....106 A2
Streathbourne Rd SW17 ....72 C2
Streatham Wells Prim Sch SW2 ....74 C2
Streatleigh Par [4] SW16 ....74 A2
Streatly Pl [22] Hampstead NW3 ....11 B4 / Hampstead NW3 ....11 C4
Streatley Rd NW6 ....10 B1
Streimer Rd E15 ....27 B3
Strelley Way W3 ....29 A2
Stretton Mans [16] SE8 ....51 C4
Strickland Ho [20] E2 ....24 B2 99 A3
Strickland Row SW18 ....71 C4
Strickland St SE8 ....51 C2
Stringer Hos [19] N1 ....24 A4
Strode Ho [8] SW2 ....74 C3
Strode Rd Fulham SW6 ....154 A2 / Willesden NW10 ....8 C2
Strome Ho NW6 ....78 A1
Stronsa Rd W12 ....38 B4
Strood Ho SE1 ....137 C3
Stroud Cres SW15 ....68 C3
Stroud Green Prim Sch N4 ....5 C3
Stroud Green Rd N4 ....5 C3
Stroudley Ho SW8 ....171 A4
Stroudley Wlk E3 ....27 A2
Stroud Rd SW19 ....70 C1
Strout's Pl [2] E2 ....24 B2 98 C4
Strudwick Ct SW4 ....172 B3
Strutton Ground SW1 ....133 B1
Strype St E1 ....110 C3
Stuart Ave W3 ....36 B4
Stuart Ho Hammersmith W6 ....39 B3 / [5] Homerton E9 ....17 C1 / [6] Stockwell SW4 ....62 A3 / W14 ....140 A4
Stuart Mill Ho N1 ....84 C1
Stuart Rd Acton W3 ....28 B1 / Maida Vale NW6 ....23 C2 / Nunhead SE15 ....65 B3 / Wimbledon SW19 ....70 C1
Stubbs Dr SE16 ....40 A1
Stubbs Ho Finsbury Pk N4 ....5 B3 / [1] Globe Town E2 ....25 C2 / [6] Tufnell Pk NW1 ....13 A1
Studdridge St SW6 ....165 C2
Studd St N1 ....86 A4
Studholme Ct NW3 ....10 C4
Studholme St SE15 ....50 A3
Studio Pl SW1 ....131 A3
Studios NW8 ....78 C2
Studios The [4] Clapham SW4 ....61 B3

Studios The continued
SW8 . . . . **171** C3
Studland E1 . . . . **32** B3
Studland Ho E14 . . . . **33** A3
Studland St W6 . . . . . **39** A2
Studley Cl E5 . . . . **18** A3
Studley Cl E14 . . . . . **33** C3
Studley Ct E14 . . . . . **34** C2
Studley Rd SW4 . . . . **172** B2
Stukeley St WC2 . . . . **106** B2
Stunell Ho 23
SE14 . . . . **50** C4
Sturdee Ho 2 E2 . . . **24** C3
Sturdy Ho 23 E3 . . . **26** A3
Sturdy Rd SE15 . . . . **50** B1
Sturgeon Rd SE17 . **150** C1
Sturge St SE1 . . . . . **136** C4
Sturmer Way N7 . . . **14** B3
Sturminster Ho
SW8 . . . . **163** A1
Sturry St E14 . . . . **34** A3
Sturt St N1 . . . . **87** A1
Stutfield St E1 . . . . . **111** C1
Stuttle Ho 14
E1 . . . . **24** C1 **99** B1
Styles Gdns SW9 . . . **63** A4
Styles Ho SE1 . . . . . **122** A1
Stylus Apartments 7
E1 . . . . **25** B1
Sudbourne Prim Sch
18 SW2 . . . . **62** B2
Sudbourne Rd
SW2 . . . . **62** B2
Sudbrooke Rd
SW12 . . . . **60** C1
Sudbury Ct SW8 . . **171** C4
Sudbury Ho SW18 . . **59** A2
Sudeley St N1 . . . . . . **86** B1
Sudlow Rd SW18 . . . **58** C2
Sudrey St SE1 . . . . . **136** C3
Suffield Ho SE17 . . **150** B2
Suffolk Ho 6 NW5 . . **4** B1
Suffolk La EC4 . . . . **123** B4
Suffolk Pl SW1 . . . . **119** C2
Suffolk Rd
Barnes SW13 . . . . . . **46** C3
Willesden NW10 . . . . **8** A1
Suffolk St SW1 . . . . **119** C2
Sugar House La
E15 . . . . **27** B3
Sugar Loaf Wlk 6
E2 . . . . **25** B2
Sugden Rd SW11 . . . **60** C3
Sulby Ho SE4 . . . . . . **66** A3
Sulgrave Gdns 11
W6 . . . . **39** B4
Sulgrave Rd W6 . . . . **39** B3
Sulina Rd SW2 . . . . . **74** A4
Sulivan Ct SW6 . . . . **165** B1
Sulivan Ent Ctr
SW6 . . . . **58** C4
Sulivan Prim Sch
SW6 . . . . **165** B1
Sulkin Ho 2 E2 . . . . . **25** C2
Sullivan Cl SW11 . . . **60** A4
Sullivan Ct
Stamford Hill N16 . . . **7** B3
SW5 . . . . **141** C4
Sullivan Ho
Chelsea SW1 . . . . . . **160** B4
Vauxhall SE11 . . . . . **149** A3
Sullivan Rd SE11 . . **149** C4
Sultan St SE5 . . . . . . **48** B3
Sumatra Rd NW6 . . . **10** C2
Sumburgh Rd
SW12 . . . . **60** C1

Summercourt Rd
E1 . . . . **32** B3
Summerfield Ave
NW6 . . . . **23** A3
Summer Ho SE13 . . . **67** C3
Summerhouse Rd
N16 . . . . **7** A2
Summerlands Ave 3
W3 . . . . **28** B2
Summerley St
SW18 . . . . **71** A2
Summers St EC1 . . . . **95** B1
SUMMERSTOWN . . **71** B1
Summit Ct NW2 . . . . **10** A3
Summit Est N16 . . . . . **7** C4
Sumner Ave SE15 . . . **49** B2
Sumner Bldgs
SE1 . . . . **122** C2
Sumner Ct SW8 . . . **172** A4
Sumner Ho 1 E3 . . . **34** A4
Sumner Pl SW7 . . . . **143** C3
Sumner Place Mews
SW7 . . . . **143** C3
Sumner Rd SE15 . . . . **49** B3
Sumner St SE1 . . . . **122** C2
Sumpter Cl NW3 . . . . **11** B2
Sun Alley 6 TW9 . . . **54** A3
Sun Alliance Ho
WC2 . . . . **107** B2
Sunbeam Cres
W10 . . . . **22** B1
Sunbeam Rd
NW10 . . . . **20** C1
Sunbury Ave
SW14 . . . . **55** C3
Sunbury Ct
SE14 . . . . **50** C4
Sunbury Ho 33
E2 . . . . **24** B2 **98** C3
Sunbury La SW11 . . **167** C4
Sunbury Workshops
30 E2 . . . . . . **24** B2 **98** C3
Sun Ct EC3 . . . . **109** C1
Sunderland Ct
SE22 . . . . **76** C4
Sunderland Ho 33
W2 . . . . **31** C4
Sunderland Terr
W2 . . . . **100** A2
Sundew Ave W12 . . . **29** C2
Sundra Wlk 28 E1 . . **25** C1
Sundridge Ho 4
E9 . . . . **17** C1
Sunlight Sq 22 E2 . . **25** A2
Sunningdale Ave
W3 . . . . **29** A2
Sunningdale Cl 22
SE16 . . . . **40** A1
Sunningdale Gdns
W8 . . . . **127** C1
Sunninghill Ct 9
W3 . . . . **37** B4
Sunninghill Rd
SE13 . . . . **52** A1
Sunnyhill Cl E5 . . . . . **18** A4
Sunnymead Rd
SW15 . . . . **57** A1
Sunnyside 4 NW2 . . . **1** B1
Sunnyside Ho 3
NW2 . . . . **1** B1
Sunnyside Rd N19 . . . **4** C4
Sun Pas 8 SE16 . . . **139** B2
Sunray Ave SE5,
SE24 . . . . **63** C3
Sun Rd W14 . . . . . . **140** C1

Sun St Pas EC2 . . . **110** A3
Sunset Rd SE5 . . . . . **63** C3
Sun St EC2 . . . . **109** C4
Sunwell Cl SE15 . . . . **50** A2
Surcot Ho 2
SW4 . . . . **171** C1
Surma Cl E1 . . . . **24** C1 **99** C1
Surrendale Pl W9 . . . **23** C1
Surrey Canal Rd SE14,
SE8 . . . . **50** C4
Surrey Cres 1
W4 . . . . **36** C1
Surrey Docks Farm
SE16 . . . . **41** B4
Surrey Docks
Watersports Ctr
SE8 . . . . **41** B2
Surrey Gr SE17 . . . . **152** A1
Surrey Ho 18 SE16 . . **32** C1
Surrey La SW11 . . . **168** B3
Surrey Lane Est
SW11 . . . . **168** B3
Surrey Quays Rd
SE16 . . . . **40** C4
Surrey Quays Sh Ctr
SE16 . . . . **40** C3
Surrey Quays Sta
SE16 . . . . **40** C2
Surrey Rd SE15 . . . . . **65** C2
Surrey Row SE1 . . . **136** B4
Surrey Sq SE17 . . . . **152** B2
Surrey Square Inf Sch
SE17 . . . . **152** A2
Surrey Square Jun
Sch SE17 . . . . **152** A2
Surrey St WC2 . . . . **121** A4
Surrey Terr SE17 . . **152** B2
Surrey Water Rd
SE16 . . . . **32** C1
Surrey Wharf SE1 . . . **49** C4
Surridge Ct 13
SW9 . . . . **172** B2
Surr St N7 . . . . **14** A3
Susan Constant Ct 18
E14 . . . . **34** C2
Susannah St E14 . . . **34** B3
Sussex Cl
4 Barnes SW13 . . **46** B1
Greenwich SE10 . . . **52** B4
Paddington W2 . . . . **101** B1
Sussex Gdns W2 . . . **101** C1
Sussex Ho
Hampstead NW3 . . . **12** A2
Richmond TW9 . . . . **44** B1
Sussex House Sch
SW3 . . . . **144** C4
Sussex Lo W2 . . . . . **101** C1
Sussex Mans
South Kensington
SW7 . . . . **143** B3
WC2 . . . . **120** B4
Sussex Mews E
W2 . . . . **101** C1
Sussex Mews W
W2 . . . . **115** C4
Sussex Pl
22 Hammersmith
W6 . . . . **39** B1
Lisson Gr NW1 . . . . . **90** C2
Paddington W2 . . . . **101** C1
Sussex Sq W2 . . . . . **115** C4
Sussex St SW1 . . . . **146** B2
Sussex Way
Upper Holloway N7 . . **5** B1
Upper Holloway N7,
N19 . . . . **5** A2
Upper Holloway N19 . . **4** C3

Sutherland Ave
W9 . . . . **88** C2
Sutherland Ct
8 Paddington
W9 . . . . **23** C1
Stoke Newington
N16 . . . . **6** C1
Sutherland Gdns
SW14 . . . . **56** A4
Sutherland Gr SW18,
SW19 . . . . **70** B4
Sutherland Ho
Kensington W8 . . . . **128** A1
7 Putney SW15 . . . **69** B4
9 South Hampstead
NW6 . . . . **11** B1
Sutherland Pl W2 . . **31** C3
Sutherland Rd W4 . . **46** A4
Sutherland Row
SW1 . . . . **146** B2
Sutherland Sq
SE17 . . . . **150** C1
Sutherland St
SW1 . . . . **146** B2
Sutherland Wlk
SE17 . . . . **151** A1
Sutton Court Mans
W4 . . . . **45** B4
Sutton Court Rd
W4 . . . . **45** B4
Sutton Ct
Chiswick W4 . . . . **45** B4
8 Hackney E5 . . . . . **17** A4
Sutton Est SW3 . . . **144** B2
Sutton Est The 8
W10 . . . . **30** B4
Sutton House E9 . . . . **17** B3
Sutton La EC1 . . . . . . **96** B1
Sutton La N W4 . . . . . **37** B1
Sutton La S W4 . . . . . **45** B4
Sutton Row W1 . . . . **105** C2
Sutton Sq E9 . . . . **17** B3
Sutton St E1 . . . . **32** B3
Sutton Way W10 . . . . **22** C1
Sutton Wlk SE1 . . . **121** A1
Swaby Rd SW17,
SW18 . . . . **71** B1
Swaffield Prim Sch
SW18 . . . . **71** B4
Swaffield Rd
SW18 . . . . **71** B4
Swain's La N6 . . . . . . **4** A2
Swainson Ho N7 . . . . **14** C4
Swainson Rd W3 . . . . **38** B4
Swain St NW8 . . . . . . **90** A2
Swallow Cl SE14 . . . . **50** C2
Swallow Cl W9 . . . . . **31** C4
Swallowfield NW1 . . . **92** B3
Swallow Ho NW8 . . . . **80** A2
Swallow Pl
24 Poplar E14 . . . **33** B3
W1 . . . . **104** B1
Swallow St W1 . . . . **119** A3
Swanage Ct 5 N1 . . . **16** A1
Swanage Ho SW8 . . **162** C1
Swanage Rd SW18 . . **59** B1
Swanbourne Ho
NW8 . . . . **90** A2
Swan Bsns Ctr 8
W4 . . . . **37** C2
Swan Ct
Chelsea SW3 . . . . . **144** B1

Swan Ct continued
Parsons Green
SW6 . . . . **155** B1
Poplar E14 . . . . **33** B3
Swan Ctr SW17 . . . . . **71** B1
Swandon Way
SW18 . . . . **59** A3
Swanfield St
E2 . . . . **24** B2 **99** A3
Swan Ho N1 . . . . **15** C1
Swan La EC4 . . . . . . **123** C3
Swan Lane Pier
EC4 . . . . **123** B3
Swanlea Sch E1 . . . . **25** A1
Swanley Ho SE17 . . **152** B2
Swan Mead SE1 . . . **138** A1
Swan Mews
Stockwell SW9 . . . . **172** C2
SW6 . . . . **165** B4
Swanmore Ct
SW18 . . . . **59** B1
Swanne Ho 12
SE10 . . . . **52** B3
Swan Pas 5 E1 . . . . **125** B3
Swan Pl SW13 . . . . . **46** B1
Swan Rd SE16 . . . . . . **40** B4
Swanscombe Ho 11
W11 . . . . **30** C1
Swanscombe Point 7
E16 . . . . **35** B4
Swanscombe Rd
5 Chiswick W4 . . . . **38** A1
Shepherd's Bush
W11 . . . . **30** C1
Swan St SE1 . . . . . . **137** A3
Swanton Gdns
SW19 . . . . **69** C3
Swanwick Cl
SW15 . . . . **68** B4
Swan Wlk SW3 . . . . **158** C4
Swan Yd N1 . . . . **15** A2
Swaton Rd E3 . . . . . . **26** C1
Swaythling Ho
SW15 . . . . **56** B1
Swedenborg Gdns
E1 . . . . **32** A2
Sweden Gate SE16 . . **41** A2
Swedish Quays
SE16 . . . . **41** A3
Swedish Sch The
SW13 . . . . **46** C4
Sweeney Cres
SE1 . . . . **139** A3
Sweyn Pl SE3 . . . . . . **53** C1
Swift Ho
18 Stepney E1 . . . . **32** B3
18 Stoke Newington
N16 . . . . **7** A1
1 SW9 . . . . **163** C2
Swift St SW6 . . . . . **164** C4
Swinbrook Rd
W10 . . . . **31** A4
Swinburne Ct
SE5 . . . . **63** C3
Swinburne Ho 13
E2 . . . . **25** B2
Swinburne Rd
SW15 . . . . **56** C3
Swindon St W12 . . . . **30** B1
Swinford Gdns
SW9 . . . . **63** A4
Swingfield Ho 4
E9 . . . . **25** B4
Swinley Ho NW1 . . . . **92** B4

Swinnerton St E9 ....18 A3
Swinton Ho 21
E2 ....24 C2 99 B3
Swinton Pl WC1 .....94 C4
Swinton St WC1 .....94 C4
Swiss Cottage
NW3 ....11 C1
Swiss Cottage L Ctr
NW3 ....11 C1
Swiss Cottage Sch
14 South Hampstead
NW3 ....11 C1
St John's Wood
NW8 ....79 C4
Swiss Cottage Sta
NW3 ....11 C1
Swiss Ct SW1 ......119 C3
Swiss Terr 7
NW3 ....11 C1
Switch Ho E14 .....34 C2
Sybil Phoenix Cl
SE8 ....40 C1
Sybil Thorndike
Casson Ho SW5 ..141 C4
Sybil Thorndike Ho 12
N1 ....15 B2
Sycamore Ave E3 ...26 B4
Sycamore Cl W3 ....29 A1
Sycamore Ct
Kilburn NW6 ......23 C4
Tufnell Pk N19 .....4 C1
Sycamore Gdns W6,
W12 ....39 A3
Sycamore Gr SE6 ...67 B1
Sycamore Ho
16 Maitland Pk
NW3 ....12 B2
17 Rotherhithe
SE16 ....40 C4
3 Shepherd's Bush
W6 ....39 A4
2 Stoke Newington
N16 ....6 C2
Sycamore Lo
SW15 ....57 A4
Sycamore Mews 4
SW4 ....61 B4
Sycamore St EC1 ...96 C1
Sycamore Wlk 1
W10 ....23 A1
Sydcote SE21 ....75 B3
Sydenham Hill SE21,
SE22, SE23, SE26,
SE19 ....76 C1
Sydenham Hill Sta
SE21 ....76 C1
Sydenham Hill Wood
Nature Reserve
SE26 ....76 C1
Sydner Mews N16 ..16 B4
Sydner Rd N16 .....16 B4
Sydney Cl SW3 ....143 C3
Sydney Ho W4 .....38 A2
Sydney Mews
SW3 ....143 C3
Sydney Pl SW7 ....144 A3
Sydney Rd TW10,
TW9 ....54 A3
Sydney St SW3 ....144 A2
Sylva Cotts 3 SE8 ..51 C2
Sylva St 3 SW15 ...69 C4
Sylvan St 1 NW6 ...78 A4
Sylvan Gr
Hampstead NW2 ....9 C4

Sylvan Gr continued
SE15 ....50 A4
Sylvester Ho 7
E8 ....17 A2
Sylvester Path 8
E8 ....17 A2
Sylvester Rd E8 ....17 A2
Sylvia Ct N1 ....87 B1
Sylvia Pankhurst Ho
17 E2 ....25 C2
Sylvia Young Theatre
Sch NW1 ....90 B1
Symes Mews NW1 ..82 C2
Symington Ho
SE1 ....137 B1
Symington Mews
E9 ....18 A3
Symister Mews
N1 ....24 A2 98 A3
22 Shoreditch
N1 ....24 A2 98 A3
Symons Cl 5 SE15 ..50 B1
Symons St SW3 ...145 A3
Symphony Mews 1
W10 ....23 A2
Syracuse Univ
W11 ....31 B2 112 C3
Syringa Ho SE4 ....66 B3

T

Tabard Ct 8 E14 ...34 B3
Tabard Ho 4
SE1 ....137 C2
Tabard Sq SE1 .....137 B3
Tabard St SE1 .....137 B2
Tabernacle St EC2 ..97 C2
Tableer Ave SW4 ...61 C2
Tabley Rd N7 ......14 A4
Tabor Rd W6 ......39 A3
Tachbrook Est
SW1 ....147 C1
Tachbrook Mews
SW1 ....146 C4
Tachbrook St
SW1 ....147 A3
Tack Mews SE4 ....66 C4
Tadema Ho NW8 ...89 C1
Tadema Rd SW10 ..157 A1
Tadmor St W12 ....30 C1
Tadworth Ho SE1 ..136 A3
Taeping St E14 .....42 A2
Taffrail Ho 2 E14 ..42 A2
Taft Way 23 E3 ....27 A2
Tailworth St 18
E1 ....111 B3
Tait Ct
10 Old Ford E3 ....26 B4
SW8 ....171 C4
Tait Ho
SE1 ....121 C1
2 Tufnell Pk N19 ...4 B1
Takhar Mews
SW11 ....168 B1
Talacre Com Sp Ctr
NW5 ....13 A2
Talacre Rd NW5 ...12 C2
Talbot Ct EC3 .....123 C4
Talbot Grove Ho 10
W11 ....31 A3
Talbot Ho
Highbury N7 ....5 C1
Poplar E14 ....34 A3
Talbot Pl SE3 ......53 A1
Talbot Rd
Camberwell SE22 ..64 A3

Talbot Rd continued
Notting Hill W2 .....31 C3
Notting Hill W11 ...31 A3
Talbot Sq W2 .....101 B1
Talbot Wlk
Notting Hill W11 ...31 A3
Willesden NW10 ....8 A2
Talbot Yd SE1 ....123 B1
Talcott Path 12
SW2 ....74 C3
Talfourd Pl SE15 ..49 B2
Talfourd Rd SE15 ..49 B2
Talgarth Rd
Hammersmith W6 ..39 B1
W14 ....140 B2
Talia Ho E14 ....42 B3
Talleyrand Ho SE5 ..48 B1
Tallis St EC4 ......121 C4
Talma Rd SW2 ....62 C3
Talmud Torah
Machzikei Hadass
Sch E5 ....7 C4
Talmud Torah Tiferes
Shlomo 1 NW11 ...1 C3
Talmud-Torah Yetev-
Lev 8 N16 ....7 A4
Talwin St E3 ....27 A2
Tamar Cl E3 ....26 B4
Tamar Ho
26 Cubitt Town
E14 ....42 B4
SE11 ....149 C2
Tamarind Ct 8
W3 ....28 B3
Tamarind Ho 4
SE15 ....49 C3
Tamarind Yd 1
E1 ....125 C2
Tamarisk Sq W12 ..29 B2
Tamworth N7 ......14 A2
Tamworth St SW6 ..155 B3
Tangier Rd TW10 ..55 A4
Tangley Gr SW15 ..68 B4
Tangmere WC1 ....94 C3
Tanhurst Ho 27
SW2 ....74 A4
Tankerton St WC1 ..94 B3
Tanner Ho SE1 ....138 B3
Tanner's Hill SE8 ..51 C2
Tanners Mews
SE8 ....51 B2
Tanner St SE1 ....138 B3
Tanners Yd 8 E2 ...25 A3
Tannery Ho 22 E1 ..111 B4
Tannington Terr N5 ..5 C1
Tansley Cl N7 .....13 C3
Tanswell St SE1 ...135 B3
Tantallon Rd
SW12 ....72 C3
Tant Ave E16 ......35 B3
Tanza Rd NW3 ....12 B4
Tapley Ho 1 SE1 ..139 B3
Taplow NW3 ......11 C1
Taplow Ho 5
E2 ....24 B2 98 C3
Taplow St N1 ......87 A1
Tappesfield Rd
SE15 ....65 B4
Tapp St E1 ....25 A1
Taranto Ho 14 E1 ..32 C4
Tarbert Rd SE22 ...64 A2
Tarbert Wlk E1 ....32 B2
Tarling Rd E16 ....35 B3
Tarling St E1 ......32 B3
Tarnbrook Ct
SW1 ....145 B3

Tarn St SE1 ....136 C1
Tarns The NW1 ....92 C4
Tarplett Ho 22
SE14 ....50 C4
Tarragon Cl SE14 ..51 A3
Tarranbrae NW6 ...10 A1
Tarrant Ho E2 .....25 B2
Tarrant Pl W1 ....102 C3
Tarranton Ho 6 NW14 ..126 A2
Tarriff Cres SE8 ...41 B2
Tarrington
SW16 ....73 C1
Tartan Ho 6 E14 ..34 B3
Tarver Rd SE17 ...150 B2
Tarves Way SE10 ..52 A3
Tasker Ho 5 E14 ...33 B4
Tasker Lo W8 .....127 B4
Tasker Rd NW3 ....12 B3
Tasman Ct 8 E14 ..42 A2
Tasman Ho 1 E1 ...32 A1
Tasman Rd SW9 ...62 A4
Tasso Rd W6 .....154 A4
Tasso Yd W6 .....154 A4
Tatchbury Ho
SW15 ....56 B1
Tate Britain SW1 ..148 A3
Tate Ho 10 E2 .....25 C3
Tate Modern EC4 ..122 B2
Tatham Pl NW8 ....79 C2
Tatnell Rd SE23 ...66 A1
Tatton Cres E5, N16 ..7 B4
Tatum St SE17 ...151 C3
Tauheed Cl N4 ....6 B2
Taunton Ho W2 ...100 C1
Taunton Mews
NW1 ....90 C1
Taunton Pl NW1 ...90 C2
Taverner Sq 4 N5 ..15 B4
Tavern Cl SE9 ....173 C2
Taverner Ho N16 ...6 C1
Taverners Cl
W11 ....31 A1 112 A4
Taverner Sq 4 N5 ..15 B4
Tavern Ct SW9 ....173 C2
Tavistock Cl N16 ..16 A3
Tavistock Cres
W11 ....31 B4
Tavistock Ct WC1 ..93 C2
Tavistock Ho 3
W11 ....31 B4
Tavistock Mews 3
W11 ....31 B4
Tavistock Pl WC1 ..94 A2
Tavistock Rd
Dagenham NW10 ..21 B3
Notting Hill W11 ...31 B4
Tavistock Sq WC1 ..93 C2
Tavistock St WC2 ..120 B4
Tavistock Terr N19 ..4 C1
Tavistock Twr
SE16 ....41 A3
Taviton St WC1 ....93 B2
Tavy Cl SE11 .....149 C2
Tawhid Boys Sch
N16 ....7 B2
Tawny Way SE16 ..40 C2
Taybridge Rd
SW11 ....60 C3
Tayburn Cl E14 ...34 B3
Tay Ho 10 E3 .....26 B3
Tayler Ct NW8 ....79 B4
Taylor Ave TW9 ...45 A1
Taylor Cl SE8 .....51 B4
Taylor Ho 10 SW2 ..74 C3
Taylor's Gn W3 ....29 A3
Taylor's La NW10 ..8 A1
Tayport Cl N1 .....14 A1

Tayside Ct 6 SE5 ...63 C3
Teak Cl SE16 ......33 A1
Tealby Ct N7 ......14 B2
Teal Ct 30 SE8 ....51 B4
Teale St E2 ....24 C3
Teal St 1 SE10 ....43 B3
Teather St 12 SE5 ..49 A3
Tebbs Ho 11 SW2 ..74 C4
Tedman Ct SE13 ...67 B3
Ted Roberts Ho 2
E2 ....25 A3
Tedworth Gdns
SW3 ....144 C1
Tedworth Sq SW3 .144 C1
Teesdale Cl E2 ....25 A3
Teesdale St E2 ....25 A3
Teesdale Yd 24 E2 ..25 A3
Tee The W3 ....29 A3
Teignmouth Cl 6
SW4 ....61 C3
Teignmouth Rd
NW2 ....9 C2
Telegraph Hill NW3 ..2 A1
Telegraph Pl E14 ..42 A2
Telegraph Rd
SW15 ....69 B4
Telegraph St EC2 ..109 B2
Telephone Pl
SW6 ....155 A4
Telfer Cl 4 W3 ....37 B4
Telfer Ho EC1 .....96 B3
Telferscot Prim Sch
5 SW12 ....73 C3
Telferscot Rd
SW12 ....73 C3
Telford Ave SW12,
SW2 ....74 A3
Telford Avenue Mans
7 SW2 ....74 A3
Telford Ho
W10 ....31 A4
SE1 ....136 C2
Telford Parade Mans
8 SW2 ....74 A3
Telford Rd
Kensal Town
W10 ....31 A4
Telford Rd W10 ....31 A4
Telford Terr SW1 ..160 C4
Telford Way W3 ...29 A4
Tell Gr SE22 ......64 B3
Telscombe Ho
SW11 ....169 B3
Temair Ho 6 SE10 ..52 B3
Temeraire Pl TW8 ..36 B1
Temeraire St SE16 ..40 B4
Temperley Rd
SW12 ....72 C4
Templar Ho NW2 ..10 B2
Templar St SE5 ...48 A1
Temple Ave EC4 ..121 C4
Temple Bar EC4 ...108 B1
Temple Bar EC4 ...108 B1
Templecombe Rd
E9 ....25 B4
Temple Ct
Temperley E1 ......32 C4
SW8 ....162 A1
Temple Dwellings 7
E2 ....25 A3
Temple Gr Hatcham
Sch SE14 ......50 C1
Temple Ho
13 Battersea
SW11 ....60 A4
4 Tufnell Pk N7 .....4 B1
Temple La EC4 ....107 C1

Templemead Cl
W3 . . . . 29 A3
Templemead Ho
E9 . . . . 18 A4
Temple Mills La
London E10, E15. . . . . 19 B4
Stratford E15 . . . . 19 A4
Temple Mills Rd
E9 . . . . 18 C4
Temple PI WC2 . . . 121 A4
Temple Rd
Acton Green W4 . . . . 37 B3
Richmond TW9 . . . . . 54 B4
Temple Sheen
SW14 . . . . 55 B2
Temple Sheen Rd
SW14 . . . . 55 B3
Temple St E2 . . . . . . 25 A3
Temple Sta WC2 . . 121 B4
Templeton PI 25
N16. . . . . 16 A3
Templeton PI
SW5 . . . . 141 C3
Temple West Mews
SE11. . . . . 136 A1
Templewood Ave
NW3 . . . . 2 A1
Templewood Gdns
NW3 . . . . 2 A1
Templewood Point
NW2 . . . . 1 B2
Tenbury Ct SW12 . . 73 C3
Tenby Ho
Islington N7 . . . . 14 C4
W2 . . . . 100 C1
Tench St E1 . . . . 32 A1
Tenda Rd SE16 . . . . 40 A2
Tendring Ho SW2 . . 62 C1
Tenham Ave SW2 . . 73 C2
Tenison Ct W1 . . . 118 C4
Tenison Way SE1 . 121 B1
Tenniel Cl W2 . . . . 114 B4
Tennis St SE1 . . . . 137 B4
Tennyson Ho
SE17 . . . . 151 C2
Tennyson Rd NW6 . 23 B4
Tennyson St SW8 . 170 A1
Tensing Ho N1 . . . . 15 A2
Tenterden Ho
SE17 . . . . 152 B2
Tenterden St W1 . 104 B1
Tenter Ground E1 . 110 C3
Tent St E1 . . . . 25 A1
Tequila Wharf E14 . 33 A3
Terborch Way 6
SE22 . . . . 64 A2
Tercelet Terr NW3 . . 11 B4
Teredo St SE16 . . . . 40 C3
Terling Ho 9 W10 . 30 B4
Terling Wlk N1 . . . . 86 C4
Terminus PI SW1 . 132 B1
Tern Ho 8 SE15 . . . . 49 B2
Terrace Gdns
SW13 . . . . 46 B1
Terrace La TW10. . . 54 A1
Terrace Rd E9 . . . . . 17 B1
Terrace The
Barnes SW13,
SW14 . . . . 46 A1
Kilburn NW6. . . . . . . 23 C4
10 Rotherhithe SE8 . 41 B2
Terrano Ho 1
TW9 . . . . 45 A2
Terrapin Ct SW17 . . 73 A1

Terrapin Rd SW17 . . 73 A1
Terrick St W12 . . . . 30 A3
Territorial Ho
SE11. . . . . 149 C3
Terry Ho SW2 . . . . . 74 C3
Tersha St TW9 . . . . 54 B3
Tessa Sanderson PI 8
SW8 . . . . 61 A4
Testerton Wlk 3
W11 . . . . 30 B2
Tetcott Rd SW10 . 156 C1
Teversham La
SW8 . . . . 172 B4
Teviot St E14 . . . . . 34 B4
Teyham Ct 2
SW11. . . . . 60 B1
Thackeray Ct
Chelsea SW3 . . . . . 144 C2
West Kensington
W14 . . . . 126 A1
Thackeray Ho
College Pk NW10 . . . 21 C2
WC1. . . . . 106 B4
Thackeray Mews 4
E8 . . . . 16 C2
Thackeray Rd
SW8 . . . . 170 B1
Thackeray's
Almshouses SE6 . . 67 A1
Thackeray St W8 . 128 B2
Thalia Cl SE10 . . . . 52 C4
Tham Cl 10 SE24 . . . 63 A4
Thame Rd SE16 . . . . 40 C4
Thames Ave
SW10 . . . . 167 A4
Thames Bank
SW14 . . . . 45 B1
Thames Christian Coll
23 SW11 . . . . 59 C4
Thames Circ E14 . . 41 C2
Thames Cres W4 . . 46 A3
Thames Ct 10
SE15 . . . . 49 B3
Thames Hts SE1 . 138 C4
Thameside Ctr
TW9 . . . . 54 A3
Thames Link Ho 7
TW9 . . . . 54 A3
Thames PI SW15 . . 57 C4
Thames Quay
Millwall E14 . . . . 42 A4
SW10 . . . . 167 A3
Thames Rd W4 . . . . 45 A4
Thames Reach W6 . 47 B4
Thames Row TW9 . . 44 C3
Thames St SE10 . . . 52 A4
Thames Village
W4 . . . . 45 B2
Thames Wlk
SW11 . . . . 158 A2
Thane Mans N7 . . . . 5 B1
Thanet Ho
WC1. . . . . 94 A3
1 West Norwood
SE27 . . . . 75 A1
Thanet Lo NW2 . . . 10 A2
Thanet St WC1 . . . . 94 A3
Thane Villas N7 . . . . 5 B1
Thane Works N7 . . . 5 B1
Thavies Inn EC4 . . 107 C2
Thaxted Ct N1 . . . . 87 C1
Thaxted Ho SE16 . . 40 B2
Thaxton Rd W14 . . 155 A4
Thayer St W1 . . . . 103 C2
Theatre Royal E10 . 19 C2
Theatre St SW11 . . 19 C2

Theatre St SW11 . . 60 B4
Theberton St N1 . . . 86 A4
Theed St SE1 . . . . 121 C1
Thelbridge Ho 28
E3 . . . . 27 A2
Theobalds Ct N4 . . . 6 B2
Theobald's Rd
WC1. . . . . 106 C4
Theodore Ct SE13 . . 67 C1
Theodore Ho 7
SW15 . . . . 56 C2
Theodore Rd SE13 . 67 C1
Therapia Rd SE22 . . 65 B1
Theresa Rd W6 . . . . 38 C2
Thermopylae Gate
E14 . . . . 42 A2
Theseus Ho 2
E14 . . . . 34 C3
Theseus Wlk N1 . . 86 B1
Thessaly Ho SW8 . 160 C1
Thessaly Rd SW8 . 171 A4
Thetford Ho SE1 . 138 C2
Thetis Terr TW9 . . . 44 C4
Third Ave
East Acton W3 . . . . . 29 B1
West Kilburn W10 . . . 23 A2
Thirleby Rd SW1 . 133 A1
Thirlmere NW1 . . . . 92 B4
Thirlmere Ho 19
N16. . . . . 16 A3
Thirsk Rd SW11 . . . . 60 C3
Thistle Gr SW7 . . . 143 A1
Thistle Ho 15 E14 . . 34 B3
Thistlewood Cl 3
N7 . . . . 5 B2
Thistly Ct SE8 . . . . 52 A4
Thomas Baines Rd
SW11 . . . . 59 C4
Thomas Burt Ho 9
E2 . . . . 25 A2
Thomas Buxton Jun &
Inf Sch E1 . . . . 99 C1
Thomas Crowell Ct 29
N1. . . . . 16 A3
Thomas Doyle St
SE1 . . . . 136 B2
Thomas Fairchild
Com Sch N1 . . . . 87 A2
Thomas Ho
5 Hackney E9 . . . . . . 17 B2
8 Stockwell SW4 . . . 62 A3
Thomas Hollywood Ho
3 E2 . . . . 25 B3
Thomas Jones Prim
Sch 16 W11 . . . . 31 A3
Thomas London Ind
Day Sch W8 . . . . . . 128 B2
Thomas Milner Ho 6
SE15 . . . . 49 C3
Thomas More Ho
EC2 . . . . 108 C3
Thomas More Sq
E1 . . . . 125 B3
Thomas More St
E1 . . . . 125 B3
Thomas Neal's Ctr
WC1. . . . . 106 A1
Thomas North Terr 4
E16 . . . . 35 B4
Thomas Rd E14 . . . . 33 C4
Thomas Road Ind Est
2 E14 . . . . 33 C3

Thomas's Prep Sch
Clapham SW11 . . . . 60 B2
Thomas's Prep Schs
SW11 . . . . 167 C3
Thompson Ave
Richmond TW9 . . . . . 54 C4
SE5 . . . . 48 B3
Thompson Ho
11 Kensal Town
W10 . . . . 23 A1
SE14 . . . . 50 C4
Thompson Rd
SE22 . . . . 64 B1
Thomson Ct 4 E8 . . 16 C2
Thomson Ho
SW1 . . . . 147 C1
Walworth SE17 . . . . 152 A3
Thorburn Ho SW1 131 B3
Thorburn Sq SE1 . 153 B3
Thoresby Ho N16 . . . 6 C1
Thoresby St N1 . . . 97 A4
Thornaby Ho 15
E2 . . . . 25 A2
Thornbill Ho 1
SE15 . . . . 49 C3
Thornbury Ct SW16 . 16 A3
Thornbury Ct
W11 . . . . 31 C2 113 B4
Thornbury Ho N6 . . . 4 B3
Thornbury Rd
SW2 . . . . 62 A1
Thornbury Sq N6 . . . 4 B3
Thorncliffe Ct
SW2 . . . . 62 A1
Thorncliffe Rd
SW2 . . . . 62 A1
Thorncombe Rd
SE22 . . . . 64 A2
Thorncroft St
SW8 . . . . 162 A1
Thorndale Ho 10
N16. . . . . 7 A3
Thorndean St
SW18 . . . . 71 B2
Thorndike Cl
SW10 . . . . 156 C2
Thorndike Ho
SW1 . . . . 147 B2
Thorndike Rd 21
N1 . . . . 15 C2
Thorndike St
SW1 . . . . 147 B3
Thorne Ho
24 Bethnal Green
E2 . . . . 25 B2
4 Cubitt Town E14 . 42 B3
Thorne Pas 7
SW13 . . . . 46 A1
Thorne Rd SW8 . . 162 B1
Thorness Ct SW18 . 59 B1
Thorne St SW13,
SW14 . . . . 56 A4
Thornewill Ho 8
E1 . . . . 32 B2
Thorney Cres
SW11 . . . . 157 C1
Thorneycroft Ho 11
W4 . . . . 38 A1
Thorney Ct W8 . . . 128 C3
Thorney Hedge Rd
W4 . . . . 37 A2
Thorney St SW1 . . 148 A4
Thornfield Ho 5
E14 . . . . 33 C2

Thornfield Rd
W12 . . . . 39 A4
Thornford Rd
SE13 . . . . 67 B2
Thorngate Rd W9 . 23 C1
Thornham Gr E15 . . 19 C3
Thorn Ham Ho
SE1 . . . . 137 C2
Thornham St SE10 . 52 A4
Thornhaugh St
WC1 . . . . 93 C1
Thornhill Bridge
Wharf N1 . . . . 84 C3
Thornhill Cres N1 . 14 B1
Thornhill Gr N1 . . . 14 C1
Thornhill Ho
12 Chiswick W4 . . . . 38 A1
Islington N1 . . . . 14 C1
Thornhill Mews
SW15 . . . . 58 B3
Thornhill Prim Sch 11
N1. . . . . 14 C1
Thornhill Rd N1 . . . 85 B4
Thornhill Sq N1 . . . 14 B1
Thornicroft Ho 4
SW9 . . . . 173 A1
Thornley Pl 2
SE10 . . . . 43 A1
Thornsett Rd
SW18 . . . . 71 A3
Thornton Ave
Chiswick W4 . . . . 38 A2
Streatham SW2 . . . . 73 C3
Thornton Ct N7 . . . . 14 A3
Thornton Gdns
SW12 . . . . 73 C3
Thornton Ho
SE17 . . . . 152 A3
Thornton PI W1 . . 103 A4
Thornton Rd
Mortlake SW14 . . . . . 55 C4
Streatham SW12,
SW2 . . . . 73 C3
Thornton St SW9 . 173 B2
Thornville St SE8 . . 51 C2
Thornwood Gdns
W8 . . . . 127 B4
Thornwood Lo
W8 . . . . 127 B4
Thornycroft Ct
TW9 . . . . 44 B1
Thorold Ho
SE1 . . . . 136 C4
6 Streatham SW2 . . 74 A4
Thorparch Rd
SW8 . . . . 161 C1
Thorpebank Rd
W12 . . . . 29 C1
Thorpe Cl W10 . . . . 31 A3
Thorpedale Rd N4 . . 5 B3
Thorpe Ho N1 . . . . 85 A3
Thornverton Rd NW2 . 1 A1
Thoydon Rd E3 . . . . 26 A3
Thrale St SE1 . . . . 123 A1
Thrasher Cl 20 E8 . . 24 B4
Thrawl St E1 . . . . . 111 A3
Thrayle Ho 2
SW9 . . . . 62 B4
Threadgold Ho 8
N1. . . . . 15 C2
Threadneedle St EC2,
EC3 . . . . 109 C1
Three Colts La E2 . . 25 A1
Three Colt St E14 . . 33 B2

Three Cups Yd
WC1 . . . . **107** A3
Three Kings Yd
W1 . . . . **118** A4
Three Mill La E3 . . **27** B2
Three Nun Ct EC2 **109** C2
Three Oak La SE1 **138** C4
Threshers Pl
W11 . . . . . 31 A2 **112** A4
Thring Ho 2 SW9 **173** C4
Throgmorton Ave
EC2 . . . . **109** C2
Throgmorton St
EC2 . . . . **109** C2
Thrush St SE17 . . **150** C2
Thurland Ho 8
SE16 . . . . **40** A3
Thurland Rd SE16 **139** B2
Thurleigh Ave
SW12 . . . . **60** C1
Thurleigh Ct SW12 **60** C1
Thurleigh Rd
SW12 . . . . **60** C1
Thurloe Cl 9 SW7 **144** A4
Thurloe Ct SW3 **144** A3
Thurloe Pl SW7 . **143** C4
Thurloe Place Mews
SW7 . . . . **143** C4
Thurloe Sq SW7 . **144** A4
Thurloe St SW7 . **143** C4
Thurlow Hill SE21 **75** B2
Thurlow Ho 17
SW16 . . . . **74** A1
Thurlow Park Rd SE21,
SE24 . . . . **75** B2
Thurlow Rd NW3 . **11** C3
Thurlow St SE17 . **152** A1
Thurlow Terr NW5 . **12** C3
Thurlow Twrs
SE27 . . . . **74** C1
Thurlow Wlk
SE17 . . . . **152** A1
Thurnscoe NW1 . **82** C3
Thursley Gdns
SW19 . . . . **69** C2
Thursley Ho 10
SW2 . . . . **74** B4
Thurso Ho NW6 . **78** A1
Thurston Ind Est
SE13 . . . . **67** A4
Thurston Rd SE8,
SE13 . . . . **52** A1
Thurtle Rd E2 . . . **24** B3
Tibbatts Rd E3 . . **27** A1
Tibberton Sq N1 . **86** C4
Tibbets Cl SW19 . **69** C3
Tibbet's Corner
SW19 . . . . **69** C4
Tibbet's Ride
SW19 . . . . **69** C4
Tiber Cl 10 E3 . . . **26** C4
Tiber Gdns N1 . . . **84** B3
Tickford Ho NW8 . **90** A3
Tidal Basin Rd E16 **35** B2
Tidbury Ct SW8 . **160** C1
Tidemill Prim Sch 18
SE8 . . . . **51** C3
Tideswell 10 NW5 . **13** A4
Tideswell Rd
SW15 . . . . **57** B3
Tideway Ct 9
SE16 . . . . **32** C1
Tideway Ho E14 . **41** C4

Tideway Ind Est
SW8 . . . . **161** A3
Tideway Wharf
SW13 . . . . **46** A1
Tideway Yd SW13 **46** A1
Tidey St E3 . . . . . **33** C4
Tidworth Ho 3
SE22 . . . . **64** A4
Tidworth Rd E3 . . **26** C1
Tierney Rd SW2 . **74** A3
Tierney Terr SW2 **74** A3
Tiger Ho NW1 . . . **93** C3
Tiger Way E5 . . . . **17** A4
Tignel Ct W3 . . . . **36** C4
Tilbury Cl 14 SE15 **49** B3
Tilbury Ho 3
SE14 . . . . **50** C4
Tildesley Rd SW15 **57** B1
Tilehurst NW1 . . . **92** B3
Tilehurst Rd SW17,
SW18 . . . . **71** C3
Tile Kiln La N6 . . . **4** B3
Tileyard Rd N7 . . . **14** A1
Tilford Gdns SW19 **69** C3
Tilford Ho 5 SW2 **74** B4
Tilia Rd E5 . . . . . . **17** A4
Tilia Wlk 21 SW9 . **63** A3
Tiller Ho 28 N1 . . . **24** A4
Tiller L Ctr E14 . . . **41** C3
Tiller Rd E14 . . . . **41** C3
Tillet Sq SE16 . . . **41** A4
Tillet Way 6
E2 . . . . **99** C4
Tilling Ho 8 SE15 **65** A4
Tilman Ho 3
SW2 . . . . **74** B3
Tilloch St 9 N1 . . . **14** B1
Tilloch St 9 N1 . . . **14** B1
Tillotson Ct SW8 **161** C1
Tilney Ct EC1 . . . **97** A2
Tilney Gdns 12 N1 **15** C2
Tilney St W1 . . . **117** C2
Tilson Gdns SW2,
SW4 . . . . **74** A4
Tilson Ho SW2 . . **74** A4
Tilton St SW6 . . **154** B3
Tiltwood The W3 . **28** B2
Timberland Cl 16
SE15 . . . . **49** C3
Timberland Rd E1 . **32** A3
Timber Mill Way
SW4 . . . . **61** C4
Timber Pond Rd
SE16 . . . . **40** C4
Timberwharf Rd
N16 . . . . **7** C4
Time Sq E8 . . . . . **16** B3
Timothy Cl 1
SW4 . . . . **61** B2
Timsbury Wlk 8
SW15 . . . . **68** C3
Tina Ct SW16 . . . **74** C1
Tindal St SW9 . . . **48** A2
Tinniswood Cl N5 . **14** C3
Tinsley Rd E1 . . . **32** B4
Tintagel Cres SE22 **64** B3
Tintagel Ct EC1 . **96** A2
Tintern Cl SW15 . **58** A2
Tintern Ho
Belgravia SW1 . **146** A3
Regent's Pk NW1 . **82** B1
Tintern St SW4 . . **62** A3
Tinworth St SE11 **148** B2
Tipthorpe Rd
SW11 . . . . **60** C4
Tiptree 7 NW1 . . . **13** A1

Tisbury Ct W1 . . . **119** B4
Tisdall Pl SE17 . . **151** C3
Tissington Ct 4
SE16 . . . . **40** C2
Titan Bsns Est 3
SE8 . . . . **51** C3
Titan Ct 11 W8 . . **30** B2
Titchborne Row
W2 . . . . **102** B1
Titchfield Rd NW8 . **80** C4
Titchwell Rd
SW18 . . . . **71** C3
Tite St SW3 . . . . **158** C4
Titmuss St 11 W12 **39** B4
Tiverton Rd NW6, ... NW10 . . . . **22** C4
Tiverton St SE1 . **136** C2
Tivoli Ct SE16 . . . **33** B1
Tobago St 12 E14 . **41** C4
Tobin Cl NW3 . . . **12** A1
Todber Ho W14 . **126** A2
Todds Wlk N7 . . . . **5** B2
Tokenhouse Yd
EC2 . . . . **109** B2
Token Yd SW15 . . **58** A3
Toland Sq SW15 . **56** C2
Tolchurch 2 W11 . **31** C3
Toldos Sch N16 . . . **7** A3
Tolhurst Dr 4
W10 . . . . **23** A2
Tollbridge Cl W10 . **23** A1
Tollet St E1 . . . . . **25** C1
Tollgate Dr SE21 . **76** A2
Tollgate Ho 1
NW6 . . . . **78** A2
Tollhouse Way N19 . **4** B2
Tollington Ct N4 . . . **5** B2
Tollington Pk N4 . . **5** B2
Tollington Pl N4 . . **5** B2
Tollington Rd N7 . . **14** B4
Tollington Way N7 . . **5** A1
Tolmers Sq NW1 . . **93** A2
Tolpaide Ho SE11 **149** B3
Tolpuddle St N1 . . **85** B2
Tolsford Rd E5 . . . **17** A3
Tom Groves Cl
E15 . . . . **19** C3
Tom Hood Cl E15 . **19** C3
Tom Jenkinson Rd 5
E16 . . . . **35** C1
Tomkyns Ho SE11 **149** B3
Tomline Ho SE1 . **122** C1
Tomlin's Gr E3 . . . **26** C2
Tomlinson Cl
2 Gunnersbury
W4 . . . . **37** A1
2 Spitalfields
E2 . . . . 24 B2 **99** A3
Tomlin's Terr E14 . **33** A3
Tomlins Wlk 4 N7 . **5** B2
Tompion Ho EC1 . **96** B2
Tompion St EC1 . . **96** B3
Tom Smith Cl
SE10 . . . . **53** A4
Tomson Ho SE1 . **138** C2
Tom Williams Ho
SW6 . . . . **154** C3
Tonbridge Hos
WC1 . . . . **94** A3
Tonbridge St WC1 **94** A3
Toneborough 16
NW8 . . . . **78** B3
Tonsley Hill SW18 . **59** A2

Tonsley Pl SW18 . . **59** A2
Tonsley Rd SW18 . **59** A2
Tonsley St SW18 . . **59** A2
Took's Ct EC4 . . . **107** B2
Tooley St SE1 . . . **124** A1
Tooting Bec Sta
SW17 . . . . **72** C1
Topham Ho 8
SE10 . . . . **52** B3
Topham St EC1 . . . **95** B2
Topiary Sq TW9 . . **54** B4
Topmast Point 28
E14 . . . . **41** C4
Torah Vodaas
NW11 . . . . **1** A4
Tora Temimah Prim
Sch NW2 . . . . **9** C2
Torbay Ct 13 NW1 . **13** A1
Torbay Mans NW6 . **23** B4
Torbay Rd NW6 . . . **10** B1
Torbay St 15 NW1 . **13** A1
Tor Ct W8 . . . . . **127** C4
Tor Gdns W8 . . . **127** C4
Tornay Ho
Hackney E9 . . . . **17** B1
N1 . . . . **84** C2
Torquay St W2 . . **100** A3
Torrence Ho 6 N19 . **4** B2
Torrens Ct SE5 . . . **63** C4
Torrens Rd SW2 . . **62** B2
Torrens St EC1 . . . **86** A1
Torres Sq E14 . . . **41** C1
Torriano Ave NW5 . **13** C3
Torriano Cotts
NW5 . . . . **13** A3
Torriano Jun & Inf
Schs 24 NW5 . . . **13** C3
Torriano Mews
NW5 . . . . **13** A3
Torridge Gdns
SE15 . . . . **65** B3
Torridon Ho NW6 . **78** A1
Torrington Pl
Bloomsbury WC1 . **105** B4
St George in East
E1 . . . . **125** C2
Torrington Sq
WC1 . . . . **93** C1
Tortington Ho
SE15 . . . . **50** A3
Torwood Rd SW15 . **56** C2
Tothill Ho 6 SW1 . **147** C4
Tothill St SW1 . . . **133** C3
Totland Ho SW18 . **59** A1
Tottan Terr E1 . . . **32** C3
Tottenhall 5 NW1 . **12** C1
Tottenham Court Rd
W1 . . . . **105** A4
Tottenham Court
Road Sta W1 . . **105** C2
Tottenham Mews
W1 . . . . **105** A4
Tottenham Rd N1 . **16** A2
Tottenham St W1 **105** A4
Totteridge Ho
SW11 . . . . **167** C2
Toulmin St SE1 . . **136** C3
Toulon St SE5 . . . **48** B3
Toulouse Ct 2
SE16 . . . . **40** A1
Tournay Rd SW6 . **155** A2
Toussaint Wlk 18
SE16 . . . . **139** C2
Tovy Ho 6 SE1 . . **153** B1

Towcester Rd E3 . . **27** B1
Tower 42 EC2 . . . **110** A2
Tower Bldgs 11
E1 . . . . **32** A1
Tower Br App E1,
EC3, ... E1 . . . . **124** C2
Tower Bridge Bsns
Complex SE16 . . . **40** A2
Tower Bridge Bsns Sq
SE16 . . . . **40** A2
Tower Bridge Ex
E1 . . . . **124** C2
Tower Bridge Piazza
SE1 . . . . **124** C1
Tower Bridge Prim
Sch SE1 . . . . . . **138** C4
Tower Bridge Rd
SE1 . . . . **138** A3
Tower Bridge Sq
SE1 . . . . **138** C4
Tower Cl NW3 . . . **11** C3
Tower Ct
Brockley SE4 . . . . **66** A3
Stamford Hill E5 . . **7** B4
St Giles WC2 . . . **106** A1
St John's Wood
NW8 . . . . **80** B2
Towergate SE1 . . **152** A4
Towergate Ho 33
E3 . . . . **26** B3
Tower Gateway Sta
EC3 . . . . **124** C4
Tower Hamlets Coll
25 Poplar E14 . . . **34** A2
3 Poplar E14 . . . **34** A2
18 Stepney E1 . . . **32** B3
Tower Hill EC3 . . **125** A3
Tower Hill Sta
EC3 . . . . **124** C4
Tower House Sch
SW14 . . . . **55** B3
Tower Mans SE1 . **138** C1
Tower Mews E5 . . . **18** A3
Tower Millennium
Pier EC3 . . . . . . **124** B2
Tower Mill Rd
7 Camberwell
SE15 . . . . **49** A4
SE15 . . . . **49** A3
Tower of London The
EC3 . . . . **124** C3
Tower Pl E EC3 . . **124** B3
Tower Pl W EC3 . **124** B3
Tower Rd NW10 . . **8** C1
Tower Rise TW9 . . **54** A4
Tower Royal EC4 . **123** B4
Towers Pl TW10 . . **54** A2
Tower St WC2 . . . **106** A1
Towers The
Dartmouth Pk NW5 . **4** A1
1 Richmond TW9 . **54** B3
Tower Terr SE4 . . . **66** A3
Towerview SE13 . . **66** C2
Tower Wharf SE1 **138** C4
Tower Wlk SE1 . . **152** A4
Towncourt Path N4 . **6** B3
Townhall Ave 3
W4 . . . . **37** C1
Town Hall Rd
SW11 . . . . **60** B4
Town Hos EC1 . . . **96** B1
Townley Rd SE22 . **64** A2
Townley St SE17 . **151** B2

Townmead Bsns Ctr
SW6 . . . . .59 B4
Townmead Rd
Richmond TW9 . . . . .45 A1
Sands End SW6 . . . . . 166 C1
Townsend Ho N
SE1 . . . . 153 C3
Townsend Ind Est
NW10 . . . . .20 B3
Townsend Mews 3
SW18 . . . . .71 B2
Townsend Prim Sch
SE17 . . . . 152 A4
Townsend Rd NW8 . . . 80 A2
Townsend St SE1,
SE17 . . . . 152 A4
Townsend Yd N6 . . . . 4 A3
Townshend Ct
NW8 . . . . 80 B2
Townshend Est
NW8 . . . . 80 A2
Townshend Rd
Primrose Hill NW8 . . 80 A3
Richmond TW9 . . . . . . 54 B3
Townshend Terr
TW9 . . . . .54 B3
Towns Ho 4 SW4 . . 61 C4
Towpath Wlk E9 . . . 18 B3
Towton Rd SE27 . . . . 75 B2
Toxteth Ho N4 . . . . . 6 B4
Toynbee St E1 . . . . 110 C3
Toynbee Studios
E1 . . . . 111 A3
Tracey Ave NW2 . . . . 9 B3
Tracy Ho 3 E3 . . . . 26 B2
Tradescant Ho 19
E9 . . . . .17 B1
Tradescant Rd
SW8 . . . . 162 B1
Trade Twr 3
SW11 . . . . .59 B4
Trade Winds Ct 1
E1 . . . . 125 C2
Trading Estate Rd
NW10 . . . . .20 B1
Traemore Ct
SW16 . . . . .74 C1
Trafalgar Ave
SE15 . . . . .49 B4
Trafalgar Cl 1
SE16 . . . . .41 A2
Trafalgar Gdns
Stepney E1 . . . . 32 C4
W8 . . . . 128 B2
Trafalgar Gr SE10 . 52 C4
Trafalgar Ho
SE17 . . . . 151 A2
Trafalgar Mews
E9 . . . . .18 B2
Trafalgar Point 2
N1 . . . . .15 C1
Trafalgar Rd SE10 . . 43 A1
Trafalgar Sq SW1 . 119 C2
Trafalgar St SE17 . 151 C2
Trafalgar Way E14 . 34 B1
Trafford Ho N1 . . . . 87 C2
Tragail SW15 . . . . . . 58 A2
Trahorn Cl E1 . . . . . 25 A1
Traitors Gate EC3 . 124 C2
Tralee Ct 5 SE16 . . 40 A1
Tramway Ave E15 . . 19 C1
Trance Way W3 . . . . 36 C3
Tranmere Ho 7
N7 . . . . .14 C3
Tranmere Rd SW17,
SW18 . . . . .71 B2

Tranquil Pas SE3 . . 53 B1
Tranquil Vale SE3 . . 53 A1
Transept St NW1 . 102 B3
Transom Cl SE16 . . . 41 A2
Transom Sq E14 . . . 42 A1
Tranton Rd SE16 . . . 40 A3
Trappes Ho 2
SE16 . . . . .40 A2
Travers Ho 6
SE10 . . . . .52 C4
Travers Rd N7 . . . . . 5 C1
Travis Ho SE10 . . . . 52 B2
Treadgold Ho 7
W11 . . . . .30 C2
Treadgold St W11 . . 30 C2
Treadway St E2 . . . 25 A3
Treasury Bldgs
SW1 . . . . 134 A4
Treaty St N1 . . . . . . 84 C3
Trebeck St W1 . . . 118 A1
Treborough Ho
W1 . . . . 103 B4
Trebovir Rd SW5 . 141 C3
Treby St E3 . . . . . . 26 B1
Trecastle Way 2
N7 . . . . .13 C4
Tredegar Mews 10
E3 . . . . .26 B2
Tredegar Rd E3 . . . 26 B3
Tredegar Sq E3 . . . 26 B2
Tredegar Terr E3 . . 26 B2
Trederwen Rd E8 . . 24 C4
Tree Ave SW13 . . . . 56 B4
Trees The N16 . . . . . 6 C4
Trefil Wlk N7 . . . . . 14 A4
Trefoil Rd SW18 . . . 59 B2
Tregarvon Rd
SW11 . . . . .60 C3
Trego Rd E9 . . . . . . 18 C1
Tregothnan Rd
SW9 . . . . .62 A4
Tregunter Rd
SW10 . . . . 142 C1
Treherne Ct SW9 . . 48 A2
Trehern Rd 12
SW14 . . . . .55 C4
Trehurst St E5 . . . . 18 A3
Trelawney Est E9 . . 17 B2
Trelawney Ho
SE1 . . . . 136 C4
Trelawn Rd SW2 . . 62 C2
Trellis Sq 1 E3 . . . 26 B2
Tremadoc Rd SW4 . 61 C3
Tremaine Cl SE4 . . . 51 C1
Trematon St E14 . . 34 A3
Trematon Ho
SE11 . . . . 149 C2
Tremlett Gr N19 . . . 4 B1
Tremlett Mews 17
N19 . . . . 4 B1
Trenchard St SE10 . 42 C1
Trenchold St
SW8 . . . . 162 A3
Trendell Ho 3
E14 . . . . .33 C3
Trenmar Gdns
NW10 . . . . .22 A2
Trentham St W3 . . . 28 C4
Trent Ho SE15 . . . . . 65 B3
Trent Rd SW2 . . . . . 62 B2
Treport St SW18 . . . 71 A4
Tresco Ho SE11 . . . 149 B2
Tresco Rd SE15 . . . 65 A3
Tresham Cres
NW8 . . . . 90 A2
Tresham Wlk E9 . . . 17 B3

Tresidder Ho 10
SW4 . . . . .73 C4
Tressel Cl 5 N1 . . . 15 A1
Tressillian Cres
SE4 . . . . .66 C4
Tressillian Rd SE4 . 66 C4
Trevanion Rd
W14 . . . . 140 B2
Trevelyan Gdns
NW10 . . . . .22 B4
Trevelyan Ho
18 Globe Town
E2 . . . . .25 C2
SE5 . . . . .48 A3
Treveris St SE1 . . . 122 B1
Treverton St W10 . . 22 C1
Treverton Twr 1
W10 . . . . .30 C4
Treves Ho
E1 . . . . 24 C1 99 C1
Treville St SW15 . . . 69 A4
Trevithick Ho
13 Bermondsey
SE16 . . . . .40 A2
5 Gospel Oak
NW5 . . . . 13 A4
SW8 . . . . 171 B4
Trevithick St SE8 . . 51 C4
Trevor Pl SW7 . . . . 130 B3
Trevor Roberts Sch
NW8 . . . . .11 C1
Trevor Sq SW7 . . . 130 B3
Trevor St SW7 . . . . 130 B3
Trevose Ho SE11 . . 149 A2
Trewint St SW18 . . . 71 B2
Triangle Ct SE1 . . . 123 A1
Triangle Est The
SE11 . . . . 149 B1
Triangle Ho SE1 . . . 138 C4
Triangle Pl SW4 . . . 61 C3
Triangle Rd 2 E8 . . 25 A4
Triangle The
Crouch End N19 . . . . 4 C4
EC1 . . . . 96 B2
18 Hackney E8 . . . . 25 A4
Trident Ho 14 E14 . . 34 B3
Trident St SE16 . . . 40 C2
Trieste Ct SW12 . . . 72 B3
Trig La EC4 . . . . . . 122 C4
Trigon Rd SW8 . . . . 163 A2
Trillington Ho
W12 . . . . .30 C1
Trimdon NW1 . . . . . 83 A3
Trimmer Wlk 11
TW8 . . . . .44 A4
Trim St SE8 . . . . . . 51 B4
Trinder Gdns N19 . . 5 A3
Trinder Rd N4, N19 . 5 A3
Trinidad Ho 17
E14 . . . . .33 B2
Trinidad St E14 . . . 33 B2
Trinity Church Rd
SW13 . . . . .47 A4
Trinity Church Sq
SE1 . . . . 137 A2
Trinity Cl
3 Clapham SW4 . . 61 B3
Lewisham SE13 . . . 67 C3
Trinity Coll London
SE1 . . . . 148 B1
Trinity Coll of Music
SE10 . . . . .52 B4
Trinity Cotts TW9 . . 54 B4
Trinity Cres SW17 . 72 C2
Trinity Ct
Finsbury WC1 . . . . . . 94 C2

Trinity Ct continued
2 Hoxton N1 . . . . . . 24 A4
Rotherhithe SE16 . . . 41 A4
Willesden NW2 . . . . . 9 B3
Trinity Gdns
E16 . . . . .35 B4
Stockwell SW2,
SW9 . . . . .62 B3
Trinity Gn E1 . . . . . 32 B3
Trinity Gr 5 SE10 . . 52 B2
Trinity Ho SE1 . . . . 137 A2
Trinity Homes 14
SW2 . . . . .62 B3
Trinity Mews
SW18 . . . . .71 B3
Trinity Pl EC3 . . . . 124 C3
Trinity Rd
Richmond TW9 . . . . . 54 B4
Wandsworth SW17,
SW18 . . . . .72 A4
Trinity Rise SE24,
SW2 . . . . .75 A4
Trinity Sq EC3 . . . . 124 B4
Trinity St
9 Newham E16 . . . . 35 C4
SE1 . . . . 137 B2
Trinity Way W3 . . . 29 B2
Trio Pl SE1 . . . . . . 137 B2
Tristan Ct 24 SE8 . . 51 B4
Triton Ct EC2 . . . . . 97 C1
Triton Ho 8 E14 . . . 42 A2
Tritton Rd SE21 . . . 75 C1
Trocette Mans
SE1 . . . . 138 B2
Trojan Ct NW6 . . . . 10 A1
Trojan Ind Est
NW10 . . . . 8 B2
Troon Cl 21 SE16 . . 40 A1
Troon Ho 6 E14 . . . 33 A3
Troon St E1 . . . . . . 33 A3
Tropical Ct 2
W10 . . . . .22 C2
Trossachs Rd
SE22 . . . . .64 A2
Trothy Rd SE1 . . . . 153 C3
Trotman Ho 1
SE14 . . . . .50 B2
Trott St SW11 . . . . 168 A3
Trotwood Ho 3
SE16 . . . . .40 A4
Troubridge Ct 13
W4 . . . . .37 A1
Troutbeck NW1 . . . 92 B3
Troutbeck Rd
SE14 . . . . .51 A2
Trouville Rd SW4 . . 61 B1
Trowbridge Est 6
E9 . . . . .18 B2
Trowbridge Rd E9 . 18 B2
Trower Ho 5 E9 . . . 18 A2
Troy Ct W8 . . . . . . 127 B2
Troyes Ho NW3 . . . 12 B3
Troy Town SE15 . . . 64 C4
Troy Town Flats
SE15 . . . . .64 C4
Truman's Rd 24
N16 . . . . .16 A3
Trump St EC2 . . . . 109 A1
Trundle St SE1 . . . 136 C4
Trundleys Rd SE8 . . 40 C1
Trundley's Rd SE8 . 40 C1
Trundley's Terr
SE8 . . . . .40 C2

Truro Ho 23 W2 . . . 31 C4
Truro St NW5 . . . . . 12 C2
Truro Rd E16 . . . . . 39 B3
Trust Wlk SE21 . . . 75 A3
Tryon Cres E9 . . . . 25 B4
Tryon St SW3 . . . . 144 C2
Tubbs Rd NW10 . . . 21 B3
Tudor Cl
Crouch End N6 . . . . . 4 B4
Hampstead NW3 . . 12 A2
Tulse Hill SW2 . . . . 62 B1
Tudor Coll WC1 . . . 94 A3
Tudor Ct
Kingsland N1 . . . . . 16 A2
5 Rotherhithe
SE16 . . . . .32 C1
South Acton W5 . . . 36 A4
Tudor Est NW10 . . . 20 A3
Tudor Gdns SW14 . 56 A4
Tudor Gr E9 . . . . . . 17 B1
Tudor Ho
Brook Green W14 . . 39 C2
5 Hackney E9 . . . . 17 B1
Tudor Mews 2
NW10 . . . . 8 C2
Tudor Rd E9 . . . . . . 25 A4
Tudor St EC4 . . . . . 121 C4
Tudor Way W3 . . . . 36 C4
Tufnell Ct 13 E3 . . . 26 B4
Tufnell Mans 7
N7 . . . . .14 A4
TUFNELL PARK . . . 13 C4
Tufnell Park Mans 2
N7 . . . . 5 A1
Tufnell Park Prim Sch
N7 . . . . .13 C4
Tufnell Park Rd N19,
N7 . . . . .13 C4
Tufnell Park Sta
N19 . . . . .13 C4
Tufton Ct SW1 . . . 134 A1
Tufton St SW1 . . . 134 A1
Tuke Sch SE15 . . . . 50 A2
Tullis Ho 9 E9 . . . . 17 B1
TULSE HILL 75 A4
Tulse Hill
Tulse Hill SW2 . . . . 74 C4
Tulse Hill SW27 . . . 75 A2
Tulse Hill Sta
SE27 . . . . .75 A2
Tulse Ho SW2 . . . . 62 C1
Tulsemere Rd SE21,
SE27 . . . . .75 C1
Tunbridge Ct 1
SE26 . . . . .76 C1
Tunbridge Ho EC1 . 96 A4
Tunis Rd W12 . . . . . 30 A1
Tunley Gn 12 E14 . . 33 B4
Tunley Rd
Dagenham NW10 . . 21 A4
Upper Tooting SW12,
SW17 . . . . .72 C2
Tunnel Avenue Trad
Est SE10 . . . . 42 C4
Tunnel Rd SE16 . . . 40 B4
Tunstall Ct 14
TW9 . . . . .44 B2
Tunstall Rd SW9 . . 62 B3
Tunstall Wlk 10
TW8 . . . . .44 A4
Tunworth Cres
SW15 . . . . .56 B1
Tun Yd SW8 . . . . . . 61 A4

Tupman Ho 26
SE16 .... 139 B3
Turberville Ho 1
SW9 ....62 B4
Turenne Cl SW18 ..59 B3
Turin St E2 ....24 C2 99 B3
Turk's Head Yd
EC1 .... 108 A4
Turks Row SW3 .. 145 A2
Turle Rd N4 ....5 B3
Turlewray Cl N4 ....5 B3
Turnagain La EC4 108 A2
Turnberry Cl 24
SE1 ....40 A1
Turnberry Quay 1
E14 ....52 A2
Turnbull Ho N1 ...86 B4
Turnchapel Mews 1
SW4 ....61 A4
Turner Cl 7 SW9 ..48 A2
Turner Ct
9 Herne Hill SE5 ..63 C3
24 Rotherhithe
SE16 ....40 B4
Turner Ho
Finsbury Pk N4 ....5 B3
24 Millwall E14 ...41 C4
St John's Wood
NW8 ....80 A2
Strand WC2 ..... 120 B3
Westminster SW1 147 C3
Turner Lo
SW19 ....69 C3
Turner Pl SW11 ...60 A2
Turners Ct E15 ...19 B4
Turner's Rd E3 ...33 B4
Turner St
Canning Town
E16 ....35 B3
Stepney E1 ....32 A4
Turneville Rd
W14 .... 154 C4
Turney Rd SE21 ...75 C4
Turney Sch SE21...75 B4
Turnham Green Sta
W4 ....38 A2
Turnham Green Terr
W4 ....38 A2
Turnham Ho SE4 ..66 A3
Turnham Prim Sch 1
SE4 ....66 A3
Turnham Rd SE4 ..66 A3
Turnmill Ho 8
SW2 ....62 C2
Turnmill St EC1 .. 108 A4
Turnour Ho 31 E1 .32 A3
Turnpike Cl SE8 ...51 B3
Turnpike Ho EC1 ..96 B3
Turnpin La 3
SE10 ....52 B4
Turpentine La
SW1 .... 146 B1
Turpin Ho SW11 . 170 A4
Turpin Way N19 ....4 C3
Turquand St SE17 151 A3
Turret Gr SW4 ....61 B4
Turville Ho NW8 ..90 A2
Turville St
E2 ....24 B1 98 C2
Tuscan Ho 22 E2 ..25 B2
Tuskar St SE10 ...43 A1
Tuttle Ho SW1 ... 147 C1
Tweed Ho E14 .....27 B1

Tweezer's Alley
WC2 .... 121 B4
Twelvetrees Bsns Pk
E16 ....27 C1
Twelvetrees Cres
E3 ....27 B1
Twig Folly Cl 21
E2 ....25 C3
Twilley St SW18 ..71 A4
Twine Ct E1 ....32 B2
Twinings Mus
WC2 .... 107 B1
Twisden Rd NW5 ..13 A4
Twycross Mews
SE10 ....43 A2
Twyford CE High Sch
W3 ....28 B1
Twyford Ho N5 .....6 A1
Twyford Sp Ctr
W3 ....28 A1
Twyford St N1 ....84 C4
Twynholm Mans
SW6 .... 154 A2
Tyburn Tree (site of)
W2 .... 116 C3
Tyburn Way W1 .. 117 A4
Tyer's Est SE1 ... 138 A4
Tyers Gate SE1 .. 138 A3
Tyers St SE11 .... 148 C2
Tyers Terr SE11 .. 149 A1
Tyler Cl E2 ....24 B3
Tyler Ho SE3 .....52 C1
Tyler St
Greenwich SE10 ...43 A1
SE10 ....53 A4
Tylney Ho 10 E1 ..32 A3
Tymperley Ct
SW19 ....70 A3
Tyndale La N1 ....15 A1
Tyndale Mans 1 ..15 A1
Tyndale Terr 18 ..15 A1
Tyne St
Dalston E8 ....16 B2
Hoxton N1 ....16 B2
Tysson Ho E9 .....18 A1
Tyrawley Rd SW6 166 A4
Tyrells Ct 5 SE15 .65 A4
Tyrrell Ho SW1 .. 161 A4
Tyrrell Rd SE22 ...64 C3
Tyrwhitt Rd SE4 ..66 C4
Tysoe St EC1 .....95 B3
Tyssen Com Prim Sch
N16 ....7 C3
Tyssen St
Dalston E8 ....16 B2
Hoxton N1 ....16 B2
Tytherton 28 E2 ..25 B3
Tytherton Rd N19 ..4 C1

U

Uamvar St E14 ....34 A4
Udall St SW1 .... 147 A3
Udimore Ho 11
W10 ....30 B4

Uffington Rd
NW10 ....22 A4
Ufford St SE1 ... 135 C4
Ufton Gr N1 ....15 C1
Ufton Rd N1 ......16 A1
Uhura Sq 28 N16 ..7 A1
Ujima Ct N19 ......5 A3
Ullin St E14 ....34 B4
Ullswater SW15 ..57 C1
Ullswater Ho SE15 .50 B4
Ullswater Rd
Barnes SW13 ....46 C3
West Norwood SE27,
SW16 ....75 A2
Ulster Pl NW1 ....92 A1
Ulster Terr NW1 ..92 A2
Ulundi Rd SE3 ....53 A4
Ulva Rd SW15 ....57 C3
Ulverscroft Rd
SE22 ....64 C2
Ulverstone Rd
SE27 ....75 A2
Ulysses Rd NW6 ..10 B3
Umberston St E1 ..32 A3
Umbria St SW15 ..56 C1
Una Ho 7 NW5 ...13 A2
Undercliff SE10 ...52 B2
Undercliff Rd
SE13 ....67 A4
Underhill Ho 7
E14 ....33 C4
Underhill Pas NW1 82 B4
Underhill St NW1 .82 B3
Undershaft EC3 .. 110 A1
Underwood Ho
W6 ....39 A3
Underwood Rd
E1 ....24 C1 99 C1
Underwood Row
N1 ....97 A4
Underwood St N1 .97 A4
Undine Rd E14 ....42 A2
Unicorn Bldg 14
E1 ....32 C2
Unicorn Sch TW9 .44 C3
Union Cl E11 .....19 C4
Union Ct
45 Paddington
W2 ....31 C4
2 Richmond TW10 .54 A2
South Lambeth
SW4 .... 172 A1
Whitechapel EC2 . 110 A2
Union Dr E1 ....26 A1
Union Gr SW8 ... 171 C2
Union Mews 3
SW9 .... 172 A1
Union Pk 11 SE10 .43 B1
Union Rd SW8 ... 171 C1
Union Sq N1 ......87 A3
Union St
Mill Meads E15 ...27 C4
SE1 .... 122 C1
Union Wharf N1 ..87 A2
Union Wlk
E2 ....24 A2 98 B4
Union Yd W1 .... 104 B1
United International
Coll W1 .... 104 B3
Unity Cl NW10 ....9 A2
Unity Mews NW1 ..83 B2
Unity Way SE18 ..34 C4
Univ Coll Jun Sch 7
NW3 ....11 B4
Univ Coll London
Bloomsbury WC1 ..93 B2
Bloomsbury WC1 ..94 B2

Univ Coll London
(Windeyer Inst)
NW1 .... 105 A4
Univ Coll London
(Wolfson H)
NW1 .... 93 A2
University Coll Hospl
WC1 .... 93 A2
University Sch
NW3 ....11 B4
University Mans 9
SW15 ....57 B4
University St WC1 .93 A1
Univ of California
WC1 .... 105 C3
Univ of East London
(Duncan Ho) 7
E15 ....27 C4
Univ of Greenwich
SE10 ....52 C4
Univ of London
WC1 .... 93 C1
Univ of London
(King's Coll Hall)
SE5 ....63 C4
Univ of London
(Queen Mary &
Westfield Coll)
E1 ....26 A1
Univ of Notre Dame
SW1 .... 119 C2
Univ of Notre Dame
SW1 .... 119 C2
Univ of Roehampton
(Digby Stuart Coll)
SW15 ....56 C2
Univ of Roehampton
(Froebel Coll)
SW15 ....56 B1
Univ of Roehampton
(Southlands Coll)
SW15 ....56 C2
Univ of Roehampton
(Whitelands Coll)
SW15 ....68 C3
Univ of Westminster
(Cavendish Campus)
W1 .... 104 C4
Univ of Westminster
(Marylebone
Campus) W1 ... 103 B4
Univ of Westminster
(Regent Campus)
W1 .... 104 B2
Univ of Westminster
(Regent Campus,
Wigram House
Halls of Residence)
SW1 .... 133 A1
Unwin Cl SE15 ....49 C4
Unwin Rd SW7 .. 129 C2
Upbrook Mews
W2 .... 101 A1
Upcerne Rd SW10 157 A1
Upcott Ho
33 Bromley E3 .....27 A2
4 Hackney E9 ....17 B1
Upgrove Manor Way
12 SE24 ....74 C4
Upham Park Rd
W4 ....38 B2
Upland Rd SE22 ..64 C1
Uplands Cl SW14 .55 A2
Upnall Ho 16 SE15 .50 B4

Upnor Way SE17.. 152 B2
Upper Addison Gdns
W14 .... 126 A4
Upper Bank St
E14 ....34 A1
Upper Bardsey Wlk 7
N1 ....15 B2
Upper Belgrave St
SW1 .... 131 C2
Upper Berkeley St
W1 .... 103 A1
Upper Brockley Rd
SE4 ....51 B1
Upper Brook St
W1 .... 117 B4
Upper Caldy Wlk 18
N1 ....15 B2
Upper Camelford Wlk
14 W10 ....31 A3
Upper Cheyne Row
SW3 .... 158 A4
Upper Clarendon Wlk
17 W11 ....31 A3
Upper Dengie Wlk
N1 ....86 C4
Upper Grosvenor St
W1 .... 117 B3
Upper Ground
SE1 .... 121 B2
Upper Gulland Wlk 25
N1 ....15 B2
Upper Hampstead Wlk
24 NW3 ....11 B4
Upper Handa Wlk 2
N1 ....15 B2
Upper Harley St
NW1 ....91 C1
Upper Hawkwell Wlk
N1 ....87 A4
Upper James St
W1 .... 119 A4
Upper John St
W1 .... 119 A4
Upper Lismore Wlk 8
N1 ....15 B2
Upper Mall W6 ...39 A1
Upper Marsh SE1 135 A2
Upper Montague St
W1 .... 102 C3
Upper North St E3,
E14 ....33 C4
Upper Park Rd
NW3 ....12 B3
Upper Phillimore
Gdns W8 ...... 127 B3
Upper Ramsey Wlk 19
N1 ....15 C2
Upper Rawreth Wlk
N1 ....87 A4
Upper Richmond Rd
SW15 ....57 B3
Upper Richmond Rd W
W TW10, SW14,
SW15 ....55 B3
Upper St Martin's La
WC2 .... 120 A4
Upper St N1 ......86 A3
Upper Tachbrook St
SW1 .... 147 A4
Upper Talbot Wlk 7
W10 ....31 A3
Upper Terr NW3 ...2 B1

Upper Thames St
EC4 . . . . **123** A4
Upper Tollington Pk
N4 . . . . **5** C3
UPPER TOOTING **72** C3
Upper Tooting Pk
Mans **1** SW17 . . . . **72** C2
Upper Tooting Pk
SW17 . . . . **72** B2
Upper Tooting Rd
SW17 . . . . **72** B2
Upper Tulse Hill
SW2 . . . . **74** B3
Upper Wimpole St
W1 . . . . **103** C4
Upstall St SE5 . . . . **48** A2
Upton Cl NW2 . . . . **1** A1
Urban Mews N4 . . . . **6** A4
Urlwin St SE5 . . . . **48** A4
Urlwin Wlk SW9 . . . . . . **48** A2
Urmston Dr SW19 . . . . . **70** A3
Urmston Ho **4**
E14 . . . . **42** B2
Ursula Mews N4 . . . . **6** B3
Ursula St SW11 . . . . . . **168** A3
Urswick Rd E5, E9 . . . . **17** A4
Usborne Mews
SW8 . . . . **163** A2
Usher Rd E3 . . . . **26** B3
Usk Rd SW11 . . . . **59** B3
Usk St E2 . . . . **25** C2
Utah Bldg **3** SE13 . . . . **52** A2
Utopia Ho **3** NW2 . . . . . **8** C2
Utopia Village
NW1 . . . . **81** B4
Uverdale Rd
SW10 . . . . **157** A1
Uxbridge Rd W12 . . . . . **30** A1
Uxbridge St
W8 . . . . **31** C1 **113** B2

V

Vadnie Bish Ho
NW5 . . . . **13** B2
Vaine Ho **4** E9 . . . . **18** A2
Vale Cl W9 . . . . **88** C3
Vale Ct
East Acton W3 . . . . **29** B1
St John's Wood W9 . . . . **88** C3
Vale End SE22 . . . . **64** B3
Vale Est The W3 . . . . **29** A1
Vale Gr
Acton W3 . . . . **28** C1
Stoke Newington N4 . . . . **6** B4
Valens Ho **1** SW2 . . . . . **74** C3
Valentia Pl SW9 . . . . . . **62** C3
Valentine Ho
1 Clapham Pk
SW4 . . . . **61** B1
2 Old Ford E3 . . . . . . **26** B4
Valentine Pl SE1 . . . . . **136** A4
Valentine Rd E9 . . . . . . **17** C2
Valentine Row
SE1 . . . . **136** A3
VALE OF HEALTH **2** C1
Vale of Health NW3 . . . . **2** C1
Vale Rise NW11 . . . . **1** B3
Vale Row N5 . . . . **6** A1
Vale Royal N7 . . . . **14** A1
Vale Sch The
SW7 . . . . **128** C1

Vale The
Cricklewood NW11 . . . . **1** A2
East Acton W3 . . . . **29** A1
SW3 . . . . **157** C4
Valetta Rd W3 . . . . **38** B4
Valette Ho E9 . . . . **17** B2
Valette St E8 . . . . **17** A2
Valiant Ho
9 Cubitt Town
E14 . . . . **42** B4
SW11 . . . . **167** C3
Vallance Rd
E1 . . . . **24** C1 **99** C1
Valliere Rd NW10 . . . . . **21** C2
Val McKenzie Ave
N7 . . . . **5** C1
Valmar Rd SE5 . . . . **48** B2
Valmar Trad Est
SE5 . . . . **48** B2
Valois Ho **1** SE1 . . . . . **138** C2
Valonia Gdns
SW18 . . . . **58** B1
Vanbern Ho NW5 . . . . . **12** C2
Vanbrugh Ct SE11 . . . . **149** C3
Vanbrugh Fields
SE3 . . . . **53** B3
Vanbrugh Hill SE10,
SE3 . . . . **53** B4
Vanbrugh Ho **8**
E9 . . . . **17** B1
Vanbrugh Park Rd
SE3 . . . . **53** B3
Vanbrugh Park Rd W
SE3 . . . . **53** B3
Vanbrugh Pk SE3 . . . . . **53** B3
Vanbrugh Rd W4 . . . . . . **37** C3
Vanbrugh Terr
SE3 . . . . **53** B2
Vanbrugh Ho E11 . . . . . **19** C4
Vancover Ho **33**
E1 . . . . **32** A1
Vanderbilt Rd
SW18 . . . . **71** B3
Vanderbilt Villas **1**
W12 . . . . **39** C4
Vandon Ct SW1 . . . . . . **133** A2
Vandon Pas SW1 . . . . . **133** A2
Vandon St SW1 . . . . . . **133** A2
Vandyke Cl SW15 . . . . . **57** C1
Vandy St
EC2 . . . . **24** A1 **98** A1
Vane Cl NW3 . . . . **11** C4
Vane St SW1 . . . . **147** A4
Vange Ho **12** W10 . . . . . **30** B4
Van Gogh Ct E14 . . . . . **42** C3
Vanguard Bldg **6**
E14 . . . . **41** C4
Vanguard Ho **11**
E8 . . . . **17** A1
Vanguard St SE1 . . . . . . **51** C2
Vanneck Sq SW15 . . . . . **56** C2
Vanner Point **27**
E9 . . . . **17** C2
Vansittart St **7**
SE14 . . . . **51** A3
Vanston Pl SW6 . . . . . . **155** C2
Vantage Mews **3**
E14 . . . . **34** B1
Vantage Pl W8 . . . . **127** C1
Vantrey Ho SE11 . . . . . **149** B3
Vardon Rd SE16 . . . . . . **40** B1
Vardens Rd SW11 . . . . . **59** C3
Varden St E1 . . . . **32** A3
Vardon Cl W3 . . . . **28** C3
Vardon Ho SE10 . . . . . . **52** B2
Varey Ho E1 . . . . **26** A2

Varley Ho **5** NW6 . . . **23** C4
Varma Ct SE3 . . . . **53** C2
Varna Rd SW6 . . . . **154** C2
Varndell St NW1 . . . . . . **92** C4
Varnishers Yard
N1 . . . . **84** B1
Varsity How E14 . . . . . . **45** B1
Vascroft Est NW10 . . . . **20** A1
Vassall Ho **3** E3 . . . . . **26** A2
Vassall Rd SW9 . . . . . . **163** C1
Vat Ho SW8 . . . . **162** B2
Vauban Est SE16 . . . . . **139** A1
Vauban St SE16 . . . . . . **139** A1
Vaudeville Ct N4 . . . . **5** C2
Vaughan Ave W6 . . . . . . **38** B2
Vaughan Est **8**
E2 . . . . **24** B2 **98** C4
Vaughan Ho SE1 . . . . . **136** A4
Vaughan Rd SE5 . . . . . . **63** B4
Vaughan St SE16 . . . . . **41** B4
Vaughan Way E1 . . . . . **125** C2
Vaughan Williams Cl
SE8 . . . . **51** C3
VAUXHALL **148** B1
Vauxhall Bridge Rd
SW1 . . . . **147** A3
Vauxhall City Farm
SE1 . . . . **148** C2
Vauxhall Cross SE1,
SW8 . . . . **148** B1
Vauxhall Gr SW8 . . . . . **162** C4
Vauxhall Prim Sch
SE11 . . . . **149** A2
Vauxhall St SE11 . . . . . **149** A2
Vauxhall St SE11 . . . . . **148** B1
Vauxhall Wlk
SE11 . . . . **148** C2
Vawdrey Cl E1 . . . . **25** B1
Vaynor Ho N7 . . . . **14** A4
Vectis Ct SW18 . . . . **59** A1
Veda Rd SE13 . . . . **66** C3
Velde Way **1**
SE22 . . . . **64** A2
Vellacott Ho **3**
W12 . . . . **30** A3
Velletri Ho **17** E2 . . . . . **25** C3
Venables St NW8 . . . . . **101** C4
Vencourt Pl W6 . . . . **38** C2
Venetian Rd SE5 . . . . . . **48** B1
Venice Ct **5** SE5 . . . . . **48** B3
Venn Ho N1 . . . . **85** A3
Venn St SW4 . . . . **61** B3
Ventnor Rd SE14 . . . . . . **50** C3
Ventura Ho **2**
SW2 . . . . **62** A3
Venue St E14 . . . . **34** B4
Venus Ho
1 Millwall E14 . . . . . . **41** C2
3 Old Ford E3 . . . . . . **26** C4
Vera Ct **1** W2 . . . . **100** A2
Vera Rd SW6 . . . . **164** B4
Verbena Gdns
W6 . . . . **38** C1
Verdun Rd SW13 . . . . . . **46** C3
Vere Bank SW19 . . . . . . **70** B3
Vereker Rd W14 . . . . . . **140** B1
Vere St W1 . . . . **104** A1
Verity Cl W11 . . . . **31** A3
Verity Ho **9** E3 . . . . **26** B2
Vermeer Ct E14 . . . . **42** C3
Vermont Rd SW18 . . . . . **59** A1
Verne Ct **3** W3 . . . . **37** B3
Verneer Gdns
SE15 . . . . **65** B3
Verney Ho
Lisson Gr NW8 . . . . **90** A2

Verney Ho continued
South Kensington
SW10 . . . . **156** C4
Verney Rd SE16 . . . . . . **40** A1
Verney Way SE16 . . . . . **40** A1
Vernon Ct NW2 . . . . **1** B1
Vernon Ho SE11 . . . . . . **149** A1
Vernon Mews
W14 . . . . **140** B3
Vernon Pl WC1 . . . . **106** B3
Vernon Rd
Bow E3 . . . . **26** B3
Mortlake SW14 . . . . **55** C4
Vernon Rise WC1 . . . . . **95** A4
Vernon Sq WC1 . . . . **95** A4
Vernon St W14 . . . . **140** B3
Vernon Yd
W11 . . . . . . **31** B2 **112** C4
Verona Ct
Chiswick W4 . . . . **38** A1
10 SE14 . . . . **50** C4
Veronica Ho
Brockley SE4 . . . . **66** B4
46 Bromley E3 . . . . . . **27** A2
Veronica Rd SW17 . . . . . **73** A2
Verran Rd SW12 . . . . . . **73** A4
Verulam Bldgs
WC1 . . . . **107** A4
Verulam Ho **3**
W6 . . . . **39** B4
Verulam St EC1 . . . . **107** B4
Vervain Ho **2**
SE15 . . . . **49** C3
Verwood Ho SW8 . . . . . **163** A1
Verwood Lo **1**
E14 . . . . **42** C2
Vesage Ct EC1 . . . . **107** C3
Vesey Path **1** E14 . . . . **34** A3
Vespan Rd W12 . . . . **38** C4
Vesta Ct SE1 . . . . **138** A3
Vesta Rd SE4, SE14 . . . . **51** A1
Vestry Mews **2**
SE5 . . . . **49** A2
Vestry Rd SE5 . . . . **49** A2
Vestry St N1 . . . . **97** B4
Viaduct Pl **22** E2 . . . . . . **25** A2
Viaduct St E2 . . . . **25** A2
Vian St SE13 . . . . **67** A4
Vibart Gdns SW2 . . . . . . **74** B4
Vibart Wlk N1 . . . . **84** B4
Vicarage Ave SE3 . . . . . **53** C3
Vicarage Cres
SW11 . . . . **167** B3
Vicarage Ct
7 Putney SW15 . . . . . **68** C4
W8 . . . . **128** A4
Vicarage Dr SW14 . . . . . **55** C2
Vicarage Gate
W8 . . . . **114** A1
Vicarage Gdns
Mortlake SW14 . . . . **55** C2
W8 . . . . **31** C1 **113** C2
Vicarage Gr SE5 . . . . . . **48** C2
Vicarage Rd SW14 . . . . . **55** C2
Vicarage Wlk
SW11 . . . . **167** B3
Vicar's Cl E9 . . . . **25** B4
Vicars Hill SE13 . . . . . . **67** A3
Vicar's Rd NW5 . . . . **12** C3
Viceroy Ct NW8 . . . . **80** B2
Viceroy Rd SW8 . . . . . . **172** A4
Vic Johnson Ho **3**
E3 . . . . **26** B4
Vickery Ct EC1 . . . . **97** A2

Vickery Ho **13**
SW4 . . . . **62** A3
Vickery's Wharf **3**
E14 . . . . **33** C3
Victor Cazalet Ho
N1 . . . . **86** A4
Victoria & Albert Mus
SW7 . . . . **129** C1
Victoria Arc SW1 . . . . . **132** B1
Victoria Ave EC2 . . . . . **110** B3
Victoria Bldgs **13**
E8 . . . . **25** A4
Victoria Chambers
EC2 . . . . **24** A1 **98** A2
Victoria Coach Sta
SW1 . . . . **146** A3
Victoria Coll W7 . . . . . . **107** B2
Victoria Cotts
7 Richmond
TW9 . . . . **44** C2
3 Spitalfields E1 . . . . **111** B4
Victoria Ct
5 Clapham Pk
SW4 . . . . **61** C1
South Acton W3 . . . . **37** A4
4 St George in East
E1 . . . . **125** B3
Victoria Dr SW19 . . . . . . **69** C3
Victoria Emb
WC2 . . . . **121** B3
Victoria Gdns
W11 . . . . **31** C1 **113** B2
Victoria Gr W8 . . . . **128** C2
Victoria Gr Mews
W2 . . . . **114** A3
Victoria Hall **18**
E16 . . . . **35** C1
Victoria Ho
6 Clapham Pk
SW4 . . . . **61** C1
2 Shepherd's Bush
W12 . . . . **38** C4
SW1 . . . . **146** A2
Victoria Ind Est
W3 . . . . **29** A4
Victoria Mans
1 Islington N7 . . . . . **14** C3
Willesden NW10 . . . . **9** A1
Victoria Mews
Kilburn NW6 . . . . **23** C4
Wandsworth SW18 . . . . **71** B3
Victoria Mills **1**
E15 . . . . **27** C4
Victoria Gr N16 . . . . **7** A1
Victorian Rd N16 . . . . . . **7** B1
Victoria Park Ct **11**
E9 . . . . **17** B1
Victoria Park Ind Ctr
E9 . . . . **18** B1
Victoria Park Lofts
E9 . . . . **18** B2
Victoria Park Rd
E9 . . . . **17** C1
Victoria Park Sq
E2 . . . . **25** B2
Victoria Pas NW8 . . . . . **89** B2
Victoria Place Sh Ctr
SW1 . . . . **146** B4
Victoria Rd
Finsbury Pk N4 . . . . **5** B3
Kensington W8 . . . . **128** C2
Kilburn NW6 . . . . **23** B4
Mortlake SW14 . . . . **55** C4
North Acton NW10 . . . . . **21** A1

Victoria Rise SW4 . . . . . . **61** A4
Victoria Sq SW1 . . . . . . **132** B2
Victoria St SW1 . . . . . . **133** A1
Victoria Sta SW1 . . . . . . **146** B4
Victoria Terr
  Dagenham NW10 . . . . 21 A4
  Finsbury Pk N4 . . . . 5 C3
Victoria
(Underground)
SW1 . . . . **132** B1
Victoria Villas
TW9 . . . . **54** B3
Victoria Wharf
E14 . . . . 33 A2
Victoria Yd ❶ E1 . . . **111** C1
Victor Rd NW10 . . . . . . 22 A2
Victory Pl
❻ Limehouse
E14 . . . . 33 A2
SE17 . . . . **151** B4
Victory Pl
SE17 . . . . **151** A4
Victory Way SE16 . . . . . 41 A4
Victory Wlk SE8 . . . . . . 51 C2
Victor Ct N4 . . . . 5 B4
View Ct N6 . . . . 3 B4
Viewfield Rd
SW18 . . . . 58 B1
Viewpoint ❸ N5 . . . . 15 A3
Vigo St W1 . . . . **118** C3
Viking Cl ⓴ E3 . . . . 26 A3
Viking Ho ❸ SE5 . . . . . 48 B1
Village Cl NW3 . . . . 11 C3
Village Mount ❻
NW3 . . . . 11 B4
Village Sch The
NW3 . . . . 12 B2
Village The SW11 . . . . . 60 B4
Village Way SE21 . . . . . 63 C1
Villa Rd SW9 . . . . 62 C4
Villas On The Heath
NW3 . . . . 2 B1
Villa St SE17 . . . . **151** C1
Villiers Ct SW11 . . . . . **168** B4
Villiers Rd NW2 . . . . 8 C2
Villiers St WC2 . . . . . . **120** B2
Vince Ct N1 . . . . **97** C3
Vincent Ct
  Finsbury Pk N4 . . . . 5 A3
  Marylebone N1 . . . **102** C2
  South Lambeth
  SW9 . . . . **173** A3
Vincent Mews ❶
E3 . . . . 26 C3
Vincent Rd W3 . . . . 37 B4
Vincents Cl SE16 . . . . . 41 A4
Vincent St
  Canning Town
  E16 . . . . 35 B4
  Westminster SW1 . . **147** C4
Vincent Terr N1 . . . . . **86** B2
Vince St EC1 . . . . **97** C3
Vine Cl E5 . . . . 16 C4
Vine Ct E1 . . . . **111** C3
Vinegar St E1 . . . . **32** A1
Vinegar Yd SE1 . . . . . **138** A4
Vine Hill EC1 . . . . **95** B1
Vine La SE1 . . . . **124** B1
Vine St E3 . . . . 56 B4
Vine St Bridge EC1 **95** C1
Vine Sq W14 . . . . **141** A1
Vine St
W1 . . . . **119** A3

Vine St continued
  Whitechapel St **110** C1
Vineyard Path
SW14 . . . . 55 C4
Vineyard Prim Sch
  The TW10 . . . . 54 A1
Vineyard The
TW10 . . . . 54 A2
Vineyard Wlk EC1 . . . **95** B2
Viney Ct ❾ SW4 . . . . . 61 C1
Vine Yd SE1 . . . . **137** A4
Viney Rd SE13 . . . . 67 A4
Vining St SW2,
SW9 . . . . 62 C3
Vinson Ho N1 . . . . **87** C1
Vintners Ct EC4 . . . . . **123** A4
Viola Sq W12 . . . . 29 B2
Violet Cl ❷ SE8 . . . . . . 51 B4
Violet Hill NW8 . . . . . . **78** C1
Violet Hill Ho NW8 . . **78** C1
Violet Rd E3 . . . . 27 A1
Violet St E2 . . . . 25 A1
Virgil Pl W1 . . . . **102** C3
Virgil St SE1 . . . . **135** A2
Virginia Ct ❼
SE16 . . . . 40 C4
Virginia Ho ❶ E14 . . 34 B2
Virginia Prim Sch ⓸
E2 . . . . 24 B2 **98** C3
Virginia Rd ⓳
E2 . . . . 24 B2 **98** C3
Virginia St E1 . . . . . . **125** C3
Virginia Wlk SW2 . . . 62 B1
Viscount Ct ❽
W11 . . . . 31 C3
Viscount St EC1 . . . . **108** C4
Vision Coll of
  Theology E3 . . . . 18 B2
Vista Bldgs ⓳ E3 . . . 26 B2
Vitae Apartments ❼
W6 . . . . 38 C3
Vittoria Ho N1 . . . . . **85** A3
Vittoria Prim Sch
N1 . . . . **85** B2
Vivian Comma Cl ❸
N4 . . . . 6 A1
Vivian Ct NW6 . . . . . . **78** A2
Vivian Ho N4 . . . . 6 C4
Vivian Rd E3 . . . . 26 A3
Vivian Sq SE15 . . . . 65 A4
Vogans Mill SE1 . . . . **139** A4
Vogler Ho ❾ E1 . . . . . 32 B2
Vollasky Ho ❺ E1 . . **111** B4
Voltaire
  ❷ Camberwell
  SE5 . . . . 49 B2
  ⓯ Richmond TW9 . . . 44 B2
Voltaire ❼
SW11 . . . . **169** C2
Voltaire Rd SW4 . . . . . 61 C4
Volt Ave NW10 . . . . . . 21 A2
Vorley Rd N19 . . . . 4 B2
Voss St E2 . . . . 24 C2 **99** C3
Voyager Bsns Est ⓰
SE16 . . . . **139** B2
Vulcan Rd SE4 . . . . 51 B1
Vulcan Sq E14 . . . . 41 C2
Vulcan Terr SE4 . . . . . . 51 B1
Vulcan Way N7 . . . . . . 14 B2
Vyner Ct E5 . . . . 7 C2
Vyner Rd W3 . . . . 28 C2
Vyner St E2 . . . . 25 A4

W

Wadcroft Ct SE4 . . . . . **66** B4
Wadding St SE17 . . . . **151** B3
Waddington Rd
E15 . . . . 19 C2
Waddington St
E15 . . . . 19 C2
Wade Ho ⓰ SE1 . . . . **139** B3
Wadeson St E2 . . . . 25 A3
Wade's Pl E14 . . . . 34 A2
Wadham Gdns
NW3 . . . . 80 A4
Wadham Rd SW15 . . . 58 A3
Wadhurst Rd W4 . . . . . 37 C3
Wager St E3 . . . . 26 B1
Waghorn St SE15 . . . . . 64 C4
Wagner St SE15 . . . . . . 50 B3
Wainford Cl SW19 . . . 69 C3
Wainwright Ho ❸
E1 . . . . 32 B1
Waite St SE15 . . . . 49 B4
Waithman St EC4 . . . **108** A1
Wakefield Ho ❻
SE15 . . . . 49 C2
Wakefield Mews
WC1 . . . . **94** B3
Wakefield St WC1 . . **94** B3
Wakeford Cl SW4 . . . . 61 B2
Wakeham St ❾
N1 . . . . 15 C2
Wakehurst Rd
SW11 . . . . 60 B2
Wakeling Ho ⓯ SE27 . . 75 A1
Wakeling St ⓳
E14 . . . . 33 A3
Wakelin Ho ⓳ N1 . . . 15 A1
Wakeman Rd
NW10 . . . . 22 C2
Wakley St EC1 . . . . . . **96** A4
Walberswick St
SW8 . . . . **162** B1
Walbrook EC4 . . . . . . **123** B4
Walbrook Ct ⓲
N1 . . . . **24** A3
Walbrook Wharf
EC4 . . . . **123** B4
Walburgh St E1 . . . . . . 32 A3
Walcorde Ave
SE17 . . . . **151** A3
Walcot Gdns
SE11 . . . . **149** B4
Walcot Ho ❾
SE22 . . . . 64 A4
Walcot Sq SE11 . . . . **149** C4
Walcott St ❸ SW1 . . **147** A4
Waldeck Gr SE27 . . . . 75 A1
Waldeck Rd
  Brentford W4 . . . . 44 C4
  Mortlake SW14 . . . . . . 55 B4
Waldeck Terr
SW14 . . . . 55 B4
Waldegrave Ho ❺
SW15 . . . . 57 B2
Waldemar Ave
SW6 . . . . **164** B2
Waldemar Avenue
  Mans SW6 . . . . **164** A3
Walden Cl SW8 . . . . . **171** C4
Walden Ho
  ❼ Clapham
  SW11 . . . . **169** B2
  SW1 . . . . **145** C3
Walden St E1 . . . . 32 A3

Waldo Cl SW4 . . . . 61 B2
Waldo Rd NW10 . . . . . 22 A2
Waldorf Sch of S W
  London SW16 . . . . . . **73** C2
Waldron Ho ❼
SW2 . . . . **62** B2
Waldron Mews
SW3 . . . . **157** C4
Waldron Rd SW18 . . **71** B1
Waldron Rd SE13 . . . **52** B3
Waleran Flats
SE1 . . . . **152** A4
Wales Cl SE15 . . . . 50 A4
Wales Farm Rd
W3 . . . . 28 C4
Waley St ❶ E1 . . . . . . 33 A4
Walford Ho ❾ E1 . . . . 32 A3
Walford Rd N16 . . . . . . 16 A4
Walham Ct ⓳
NW3 . . . . 12 B2
Walham Gr SW6 . . . **155** B2
WALHAM
GREEN **156** A1
Walham Green Arc
SW6 . . . . **155** B2
Walham Yd SW6 . . . **155** B2
Walker Ho NW1 . . . . . **83** B1
Walker Mews ❾
SW2 . . . . **62** C2
Walkerscroft Mead
SE21 . . . . 75 B2
Walker's Ct W1 . . . **119** B4
Walker's Lo ⓫ E14 . . 42 B4
Walker's Pl SW15 . . 58 A3
Walkinshaw Ct ❽
N1 . . . . 15 B1
Walkynscroft
SE15 . . . . 50 A1
Wallace Collection
  . . . . **103** B2
Wallace Ho N7 . . . . . **14** B2
Wallace Ho N7 . . . . . . 14 B2
Wallace Lo N4 . . . . 5 C3
Wallace Rd N1, N5 . . **15** B2
Wallbutton Rd
SE4 . . . . **51** A1
Wall Ct N4 . . . . 5 B3
Waller Rd SE14 . . . . . **50** C1
Wallett Ct ⓫ NW1 . . **13** B1
Wallflower St W12 . . 29 B2
Wallgrave Rd
SW5 . . . . **142** A3
Wallingford Ave
W10 . . . . 30 C3
Wallis Alley SE1 . . . . **137** A4
Wallis Cl SW11 . . . . . **59** C4
Wallis Ho ❾ SE14 . . **51** A2
Wallis Rd E9 . . . . 18 C2
Wallorton Gdns
SW14 . . . . 55 C3
Wallside EC2 . . . . **109** A3
Wall St N1 . . . . **15** C2
Wallwood St E14 . . . . . 33 C4
Walmer Ho ❽
W10 . . . . 30 C3
Walmer Pl W1 . . . . . **102** C4
Walmer Rd
  North Kensington
  W10 . . . . 30 B3
  W11 . . . . 31 A2 **112** A4
Walney Wlk ❽ N1 . . . 15 B2
Walnut Cl SE8 . . . . 51 B4
Walnut Ho ⓫ E3 . . . . . 26 B4
Walnut Tree Cl
SW13 . . . . 46 B2

Walnut Tree Ho
SW10 . . . . **156** B4
Walnut Tree Rd
  Brentford TW8 . . . . 44 A4
  Greenwich SE10 . . . . . . 43 A1
Walnut Tree Walk
  Prim Sch SE11 . . . . . **149** B4
Walnut Tree Wlk
SE11 . . . . **149** B4
Walpole Ave TW9 . . . 44 B1
Walpole Ct
  ❼ Hammersmith
  W14 . . . . 39 C3
  South Hampstead
  NW6 . . . . 11 B1
Walpole Gdns W4 . . 37 B1
Walpole Mews
NW8 . . . . **79** B3
Walpole St SW3 . . . **145** A2
Walsham Cl N16 . . . . **7** C3
Walsham Ho
  New Cross Gate
  SE14 . . . . 50 C1
  SE17 . . . . **151** B2
Walsham Rd SE14 . . 50 C1
Walsingham NW8 . . **79** C4
Walsingham Lo
SW13 . . . . 46 C2
Walsingham Mans
SW6 . . . . **156** B2
Walsingham Pl SW4,
SW11 . . . . 60 C1
Walsingham Rd E5 . . 7 C1
Walter Besant Ho ⓴
E1 . . . . 25 C2
Walter Ct ❸ W3 . . . 28 B3
Walter Green Ho
SE15 . . . . 50 B2
Walter Ho SW10 . . . **157** B2
Walter Northcott Ho
❷ NW6 . . . . 10 C3
Walters Cl SE17 . . . . **151** A3
Walters Ho
  ❸ Camberwell
  SE5 . . . . 49 A1
  Islington N1 . . . . **86** B4
  ⓰ Kennington
  SE17 . . . . 48 A4
Walter Sickert Hall
N1 . . . . **86** C1
Walter St E2 . . . . 25 C2
Walters Way SE23 . . . 65 C1
Walter Taylor Ct
SE4 . . . . 66 B3
Walter Terr E1 . . . . 32 C3
Walterton Rd W9 . . . 23 C1
Waltham Green Ct
SW6 . . . . **156** A1
Waltham Ho
NW8 . . . . **78** C4
❶ Stockwell SW9 . . **173** A1
Walton Cl SW8 . . . . . **162** B2
Walton Gdns W3 . . . . . 28 A4
Walton Ho
E2 . . . . 24 B1 **99** A2
  Upper Holloway N7 . . 5 B1
  Wandsworth SW18 . . 58 C1
Walton St SW3 . . . . . **130** C2
Walton St SW3 . . . . . **130** B1
Walton Way W3 . . . . . . 28 A4
Walt Whitman Cl ❻
SE24 . . . . 63 A3
WALWORTH **151** C2
Walworth Acad
SE17 . . . . **152** B1
Walworth Pl SE17 . . **151** A1

Walworth Rd
SE17 . . . . **151** A2
Wanborough Dr
SW15 . . . . .69 A3
Wandle Ct **4** W12. .38 A4
Wandle Ho
NW8 . . . . **102** A4
Wandsworth SW18 . .71 A4
Wandle Rd SW17 . . .72 A2
Wandle Way SW18. .71 A4
Wandon Rd SW6 . . .**156** B1
WANDSWORTH 58 C1
Wandsworth Bridge
Rd SW6 . . . .**166** A3
Wandsworth Common
Sta SW12. . . . . .72 B4
Wandsworth Common
West Side SW18 . . . .59 A1
Wandsworth Gyratory
SW18 . . . . .59 A2
Wandsworth High St
SW18 . . . . .59 A2
Wandsworth Plain
SW18 . . . . .59 A2
Wandsworth Rd
SW8 . . . .**162** A1
Wandsworth Road Sta
SW4 . . . .**171** A1
Wandsworth Town Sta
SW18 . . . . .59 A2
Wangford Ho **13**
SW9 . . . . .63 A3
Wanless Rd SE24 . . .63 B4
Wanley Rd SE5 . . . . .63 C3
Wansbeck Rd E3,
E9 . . . . .18 B1
Wansdown Pl
SW6 . . . .**156** A2
Wandsworth Riverside
Quarter Pier
SW6 . . . . .58 C4
Wansey St SE17 . . .**151** A3
WAPPING 32 A1
Wapping Dock St **18**
E1 . . . . .32 A1
Wapping High St
E1 . . . . .32 A1
Wapping La E1 . . . . .32 B1
Wapping Sta E1 . . . .32 B1
Wapping Wall E1 . . .32 B1
Warbeck Rd W12 . . .39 A4
Warburg Ho
E2 . . . . .24 C2 **99** B3
Warburton Cl **6**
N1 . . . . .16 A2
Warburton Ct
SE15 . . . . .64 C4
Warburton Ho **5**
E8 . . . . .25 A4
Warburton Rd **8**
E8 . . . . .25 A4
Warburton St **8**
E8 . . . . .25 A4
Wardalls Ho **12**
SE8 . . . . .51 B4
Wardell Ho **7**
SE10 . . . . .52 B4
Warden Rd NW5 . . .12 C2
Wardens Gr SE1 . . .**122** C1
Wardle St E9 . . . . . . .17 C3
Wardley St SW18 . . .71 A4
Wardlow **8** NW5 . . .13 A4
Wardo Ave SW6 . . .**164** A4
Wardour Mews
W1 . . . .**105** A1
Wardour St W1 . . . .**105** B1

Ward Point SE11 . .**149** B3
Ward Rd
Camden Town N19 . . . .4 B1
Mill Meads E15. . . . . .27 C4
Wardrobe PI EC4 . .**108** B1
Wardrobe Terr
EC4 . . . .**122** B4
Wareham Ct **2**
N1 . . . . .16 A1
Wareham Ho
SW8 . . . .**162** C2
Warfield Rd NW10 .22 C2
Warfield Yd **6**
NW10 . . . . .22 C2
Wargrave Ho
E2 . . . . .24 B2 **98** C3
Warham St SE5 . . . .48 A3
Waring Ho **25**
E2 . . . . .24 C2 **99** C3
Warley Ho N1 . . . . . .15 C2
Warley St E2 . . . . . . .25 C2
Warlock Rd W9. . . . .23 C1
Warlters Cl **7** N7 . . .14 A4
Warlters Rd N7 . . . .14 A4
Warltersville Mans
N19 . . . . .5 A4
Warltersville Rd N4, N8,
N19 . . . . .5 A4
War Meml Homes
W4 . . . . .45 C3
Warmington Rd
SE24 . . . . .63 B1
Warmsworth NW1. .82 C4
Warndon St SE16 . .40 B2
Warneford St E9 . . .25 A4
Warner Ho
4 Homerton E9 . . . .17 C2
Lewisham SE13 . . . . .52 A1
NW8 . . . .**78** B4
Warner PI
E2 . . . . .24 C2 **99** C4
Warner Rd SE5 . . . .48 B2
Warner St EC1. . . . . .95 B1
Warner Yd EC1 . . . . .95 B1
Warnford Ho
SW15 . . . . .56 A1
Warnham WC1 . . . . .94 C3
Warnham Ho **6**
SW2 . . . . .74 B4
Warple Mews W3 . .38 A4
Warple Way W3,
W12 . . . . .38 A4
Warren Ave SW14,
TW10 . . . . .55 A3
Warren Cl SE21. . . .75 B4
Warren Ct N1 . . . . . .85 B2
Warrender Rd N19 .13 B4
Warren Gdns E15 . .19 C3
Warren Ho **21** E3 . . .27 A2
Warren Mews W1 . .92 C1
Warren St W1 . . . . . .92 C1
Warren Street Sta
NW1 . . . . .93 A2
Warriner Gdns
SW11 . . . .**169** B3
Warrington Cres
W9 . . . . .88 C2
Warrington Gdns
W9 . . . . .88 C1
Warspite Ho **3**
E14 . . . . .42 A2
Warton Rd E15 . . . . .27 B4
Warwick **3** W14 . .**141** A3
Warwick Ave W9 . . .88 C1
Warwick Avenue Sta
W9 . . . . .88 C1

Warwick Bldg
SW8 . . . .**160** A3
Warwick Chambers
W8 . . . .**127** B1
Warwick Cres W2 . .**100** C4
Warwick Ct SW15. .**107** A3
Warwick Dr SW15 . .57 A4
Warwick Gdns
W14 . . . .**141** A4
Warwick Ho
10 Brixton SW9 . . .**173** B1
5 Putney SW15 . . .69 B4
Stoke Newington N4 .6 B4
Warwick House St
SW1 . . . .**119** C2
Warwick La EC4 . . .**108** B1
Warwick Lo NW2 . . .10 A3
Warwick Mans
SW5 . . . .**141** B4
Warwick Pas EC4 . .**108** B2
Warwick PI W9 . . . .**100** C4
Warwick PI N
SW1 . . . .**146** C3
Warwick Rd W14,
SW5 . . . .**141** A4
Warwick Row
SW1 . . . .**132** B2
Warwickshire Path
SE8 . . . . .51 B3
Warwick Sq
Holborn EC4 . . . . . .**108** B2
Pimlico SW1 . . . . . .**146** C2
Warwick Sq Mews
SW1 . . . .**146** C3
Warwick St W1 . . .**119** A4
Warwick Way
SW1 . . . .**146** B4
Warwick Yd EC1 . . . .97 A1
Wasdale NW1 . . . . . .92 C3
Washbrook Ho
SW2 . . . . .62 C1
Washington Bldg **1**
SE13 . . . . .52 A2
Washington Ho
SW1 . . . .**130** C3
Washington Rd
SW13 . . . . .46 C3
Watchfield Ct **7**
W4 . . . . .37 B1
Watcombe Cotts
TW9 . . . . .44 C4
Watercress PI **12**
N1 . . . . .16 A1
Waterford Rd
SW6 . . . .**156** A1
Waterford Way
NW10 . . . . .8 C3
Water Gardens The
W2 . . . .**102** B2
Watergate EC4 . . . .**122** A4
Watergate St SE8. . .51 C4
Watergate Wlk
WC2 . . . .**120** B2
Waterhead NW1 . . .92 C4
Waterhouse CI
Hammersmith W6 . . .39 C1
Hampstead NW3 . . . .11 C3
Waterloo Sq
SE1 . . . .**107** B3
Wateridge CI E14 . .41 C3
Water La
18 Camden Town
NW1 . . . . .13 A1
SE14 . . . . .50 B3

Waterloo Bridge SE1,
WC2 . . . .**121** A3
Waterloo CI E9 . . . . .17 B3
Waterloo East Sta
SE1 . . . .**121** C1
Waterloo Gdns
21 Islington N1 . . . .15 A1
South Hackney E2 . . .25 B3
Waterloo Millennium
Pier SE1 . . . .**134** C4
Waterloo PI
Kew TW9 . . . . .44 C4
3 Richmond TW9 . .54 A3
SW1 . . . .**119** B2
Waterloo Rd SE1 . .**135** C4
Waterloo Sta SE1 . .**135** B4
Waterloo Terr N1. . .15 A1
Waterlow Ct NW11 . .2 A4
Waterlow Rd N19 . . .4 B3
Waterman Bldg **2**
E14 . . . . .41 C4
Watermans Arts Ctr
TW8 . . . . .44 A4
Watermans Ct **2**
TW8 . . . . .44 A4
Waterman St
SW15 . . . . .57 C4
Waterman Way E1 . .32 A1
Watermark PI
EC4 . . . .**123** B3
Watermead Ho E9 .18 B3
Watermeadow La
SW6 . . . .**166** C1
Water Mews SE15 . .65 B3
Watermill Ct SE13 . .67 A4
Watermint Quay
N16 . . . . .7 C4
Water's Edge SW6 . .47 B2
Waterside N1 . . . . . .86 C1
Waterside CI
30 Bermondsey
SE16 . . . .**139** C3
Old Ford E3 . . . . .26 B4
Waterside Ct SE13 . .67 C3
Waterside PI NW1 . .81 C4
Waterside Point
SW11 . . . .**158** B2
Waterson St
E2 . . . . .24 B2 **98** C4
Waters PI SW15 . . . .47 B1
Water St WC2 . . . . .**121** B4
Water Tower PI
N1 . . . . .86 A3
Waterview Ho **13**
E14 . . . . .33 A4
Waterway Ave **2**
SE13 . . . . .67 A4
Waterworks Rd
SW2 . . . . .62 B1
Watford CI SW11 . .**168** B4
Watford Rd E16 . . . .35 C4
Watkins Ho **8** E14 .42 B4
Watkinson Rd N7 . .14 B2
Watling Ct EC4 . . . .**109** A1
Watling Gdns
NW2 . . . . .10 A2
Watling St
4 Camberwell
SE15 . . . . .49 A4
City of London EC4 .**109** A1
Watney Cotts
SW14 . . . . .55 B4
Watney Mkt E1 . . . .32 A3
Watney Rd SW14 . . .55 B4
Watney St E1 . . . . . .32 A3
Watson CI N16 . . . . .15 C3

Watson Ho **3**
SW2 . . . . .74 A4
Watsons Mews
W1 . . . .**102** B3
Watson's St SE8 . . .51 C3
Watts Gr E3 . . . . .34 A4
Watts Ho **6** W10 . .31 A4
Watts St
SE15 . . . . .49 B2
Wapping E1 . . . . .32 A1
Wat Tyler Rd SE10 . .52 C2
Wavel Ct
7 Streatham
SW16 . . . . .74 A1
7 Wapping E1 . . . .32 B1
Wavel Mews NW6 . .11 A1
Wavendon Ave
W4 . . . . .37 C1
Waveney Ave SE15 . .65 A3
Waveney CI **20** E1 .**125** C2
Waveney Ho SE15 . .65 A3
Waverley Ct
2 Brondesbury
NW6 . . . . .10 A1
W1 . . . .**103** C4
Waverley Ho
Finsbury Pk N4 . . . . . .6 A3
St John's Wood
NW8 . . . .**79** B2
Waverley Rd N8 . . . . .5 A4
Waverley CI NW3 . . .12 B2
Waverton Ho **2**
E3 . . . . .26 B4
Waverton Rd
SW18 . . . . .71 B4
Waverton St W1 . . .**118** A2
Wavertree Ct **9**
SW2 . . . . .74 B3
Wavertree Rd
SW2 . . . . .74 B3
Waxham NW5 . . . . . .12 B3
Waxlow Rd NW10 . .20 C3
Wayford St SW11 . .**168** B1
Wayland Ave E8 . . . . .5 A3
Wayland Ho **12**
SW9 . . . .**173** B2
Waylett Ho SE11 . .**149** B1
Waylett PI SE27 . . . .75 A1
Wayman Ct E8 . . . . .17 A2
Waynflete Sq
11 North Kensington
W10 . . . . .30 C3
18 Shepherd's Bush
W10 . . . . .30 C2
Waynflete St
SW18 . . . . .71 B2
Wayside
Golders Green
NW11 . . . . .1 A3
Mortlake SW14 . . . . .55 B2
Weald CI **16** SE16 . .40 A1
Weardale Ho N1 . . . .15 B2
Weardale Rd SE13 . .67 C3
Wearmouth Ho **1**
E3 . . . . .33 B4
Wear PI **13** E2. . . . .25 A2
Wearside Rd SE13 . .67 A3
Weatherbury **6**
W2 . . . . .31 C3
Weatherbury Ho **9**
N19 . . . . .4 C1
Weatherley CI E3 . . .33 B4
Weaver Ct **2** E2 . . .25 A1

Weaver Ho 12
E1 . . . . 24 C1 99 B1
Weaver's La SE1 . . . . 124 B1
Weaver St
E1 . . . . 24 C1 99 B1
Weavers Way
6 Camden Town
NW1 . . . . 13 C1
NW1 . . . . 83 B4
Webb Cl NW10 . . . . . 22 B1
Webb Ct W3 . . . . 37 A4
Webber Row SE1 136 A3
Webber St SE1 . . . . 136 A3
Webb Est E5 . . . . 7 C2
Webb Ho SW8 . . . . 161 C1
Webb Pl NW10 . . . . . 21 B2
Webb Rd SE3 . . . . 53 B4
Webb's Rd SW11 . . 60 B2
Webheath 8 NW6 . 10 B1
Webster Ho 18
N16 . . . . 16 A3
Webster Rd SE16 . 139 C1
Weddell Ho 2 E1 . . 25 C1
Wedderburn Rd
NW3 . . . . 11 C3
Wedgewood Ho
SW1 . . . . 146 C1
Wedgewood Mews
W1 . . . . 105 C1
Wedgewood Wlk
NW3 . . . . 11 A3
Wedgwood Ho 17 Globe Town
E2 . . . . 25 C2
SE11 . . . . 135 B1
Wedlake St W10 . . 23 A1
Wedmore Gdns
N19 . . . . 4 C2
Wedmore Mews
N19 . . . . 4 C1
Wedmore St N19 . . 4 C1
Weech Rd NW6 . . . . 10 C4
Weedington Rd
NW5 . . . . 12 C3
Weedon Ho W12 . . 29 C3
Weekley Sq SW11 . 59 C4
Weighouse St
W1 . . . . 103 C1
Weimar St SW15 . . 58 A4
Weir Ho 6 SW12 . . 73 B4
Weir Rd
Streatham SW12 . . . . 73 B4
Wimbledon SW18,
SW19 . . . . 71 A1
Weiss Rd SW15 . . . . 57 C4
Welbeck Ct W14 . . 140 C4
Welbeck Mans 10
NW6 . . . . 10 C3
Welbeck St W1 . . . 104 A2
Welbeck Way W1 104 A2
Welbury Ct E8 . . . . . . 16 A1
Welby Ho N19 . . . . . . 4 C4
Welby St SE5 . . . . . . 48 A2
Weldon Ct SE8 . . . . 51 C1
Welford Ct
12 Camden Town
NW1 . . . . 13 A1
7 Clapham SW8 . . 170 C1
Welland Ho SE15 . . 65 B3
Welland Mews 27
E1 . . . . 125 C2
Welland St SE10 . . 52 B4
Wellclose Sq E1 . . 125 C4

Wellclose St 20
E1 . . . . 125 C3
Well Ct EC4 . . . . . . 109 A1
Welland Ho 2 E9 . . 18 A2
Welldon Ct 1
SE21 . . . . 75 C2
Weller Ho 8
SE16 . . . . 139 B3
Weller St SE1 . . . . 136 C4
Welles Ct 15 E14 . . 33 C2
Wellesley Ave W6 . 39 A3
Wellesley Ct W9 . . 88 C4
Wellesley Ho N1 . . 93 B3
Wellesley Pl
Camden Town
NW1 . . . . 93 B3
NW5 . . . . 12 C3
NW1 . . . . 93 B3
Wellesley Rd
Gospel Oak NW5 . . 12 C3
Gunnersbury W4 . . 37 A1
Wellesley St E1 . . . 32 C4
Wellesley Terr N1 . 97 A4
Wellfit St SE24 . . . 63 A4
Wellgarth Rd NW11 2 A3
Wellington Arch
SW1 . . . . 131 C4
Wellington Bldgs
15 Bow E3 . . . . 26 C2
SW1 . . . . 145 C1
Wellington Cl
Kensington W11 . . 31 C3
New Cross Gate
SE14 . . . . 50 C2
Wellington Gr
SE10 . . . . 52 C3
Wellington Ho 18
NW3 . . . . 12 B2
Wellington Hospl The
NW8 . . . . 79 C1
Wellington Mans
N16 . . . . 16 B4
Wellington Mews
East Dulwich
SE22 . . . . 64 C3
3 Islington N7 . . . . 14 B2
Streatham SW16 . . 73 C1
Wellington Prim Sch
20 E3 . . . . 26 C2
Wellington Rd
Kensal Green
NW10 . . . . 22 C2
St John's Wood
NW8 . . . . 79 C1
Wimbledon SW19 . 70 C2
Wellington Row
E2 . . . . 24 C2 99 B4
Wellington Sq
Islington N1 . . . . . . 84 A4
SW3 . . . . 144 C2
Wellington St
WC2 . . . . 120 C4
Wellington Terr 2
E1 . . . . 32 A1
Wellington Way
E3 . . . . 26 C2
Well La SW14 . . . . . 55 B2
Well Rd NW3 . . . . 2 C1

Wells Ct
21 Hampstead
NW3 . . . . 11 B4
1 Paddington
NW6 . . . . 23 C3
Stoke Newington
N1 . . . . 16 A3
Wells Ho
Finsbury EC1 . . . . . 96 A4
12 Kensal Town
W10 . . . . 23 A1
New Cross Gate
SE14 . . . . 51 A1
6 Rotherhithe
SE16 . . . . 40 B3
Wells Ho The 2
N1 . . . . 1 C4
Wells House Rd
NW10 . . . . 29 A4
Wellside Gdns
SW14 . . . . 55 B2
Wells Mews W1 . . 105 A2
Wells Pl SW18 . . . . 71 B4
Wells Rd W12 . . . . . 39 B4
Wells Rise NW8 . . . 80 C3
Wells Sq WC1 . . . . . 95 A3
Wells St W1 . . . . . . 105 A2
Well St E9 . . . . 17 B1
Wells Terr N4 . . . . . . 5 C2
Wells Way
Brompton SW7 . . 129 B2
Camberwell SE5 . . 49 A4
Well Wlk NW3 . . . . . 2 C1
Welmar Works
SW4 . . . . 61 C3
Welsford St SE1 . . 153 B3
Welsh Ho 14 E1 . . . 32 A1
Welshpool Ho 22
E8 . . . . 24 C4
Welshpool St 1
E8 . . . . 25 A4
Welstead Ho 26
E1 . . . . 32 A3
Welstead Way W4 . 38 B2
Weltje Rd W6 . . . . . . 38 C1
Welton Ct SE5 . . . . . 49 A2
Welton Ho E1 . . . . . 32 C4
Welwyn St E2 . . . . . 25 B2
Wembury Mews N6 . 4 B4
Wembury Rd N6 . . . . 4 A4
Wemyss Rd SE3 . . . 53 B1
Wendell Park Prim
Sch W12 . . . . 38 B4
Wendell Rd W12 . . 38 B4
Wendle Ct SW8 . . . 162 A3
Wendling NW5 . . . . 12 B3
Wendon St E3 . . . . . 26 B4
Wendover SE17 . . . 152 A1
Wendover Ct
Acton W3 . . . . 20 A1
4 Becontree W3 . . 20 B1
4 Child's Hill NW2 . 1 C1
W1 . . . . 103 B3
Wendover Ho W1 . 103 B3
Wendover Rd
NW10 . . . . 21 B3
Wengham Ho 29
W12 . . . . 29 C2
Wenham Ho SW8 . 160 C1
Wenlake Ho 20
EC1 . . . . 97 A3
Wenlock Ct N1 . . . . 87 C1
Wenlock Rd N1 . . . . 87 A1
Wenlock St N1 . . . . 87 B1
Wennington Rd
E3 . . . . 25 C3

Wensdale Ho E5 . . . 7 C2
Wensleydale Ho 8
N4 . . . . 6 B4
Wentworth Cres
SE15 . . . . 49 C3
Wentworth Ct
W6 . . . . 154 A3
SW18 . . . . 59 A1
Wentworth Dwellings
E1 . . . . 110 C2
Wentworth Ho 4
SE3 . . . . 53 C3
Wentworth Mews
E3 . . . . 26 B2
Wentworth St E1 . . 111 A3
Werrington St
NW1 . . . . 83 A1
Werter Rd SW15 . . 58 A3
Wesley Ave NW10 . 20 C2
Wesley Cl
Finsbury Pk N7 . . . . 5 B2
SE17 . . . . 150 B3
Wesley Ct W1 . . . . 103 C3
Wesley Ho SE24 . . . 63 C1
Wesley Rd NW10 . . 20 B4
Wesley Sq W11 . . . 31 A3
Wesley St W1 . . . . 103 C3
Wessex Ct SW15 . . 57 C2
Wessex Gardens Prim
Sch NW11 . . . . 1 A3
Wessex Gdns NW11 . 1 A3
Wessex Ho
SE1 . . . . 153 A1
Wessex St E2 . . . . . 25 B2
Wessex Way NW11 . 1 A3
West 12 Sh Ctr
W12 . . . . 39 C4
Westacott Cl N19 . . 4 C3
West Acton Prim Sch
W3 . . . . 28 A3
West Arbour St E1 . 32 C3
West Bank N16 . . . . . 7 A4
Westbere Rd NW2 . 10 A4
West Block E1 . . . . 132 B2
Westbourne Ave
W3 . . . . 28 C3
Westbourne Cres
W2 . . . . 115 B4
Westbourne Ct
W2 . . . . 100 C2
Westbourne Gdns
W2 . . . . 100 A2
Westbourne Gr
Notting Hill W2,
W11 . . . . 31 C3
W11 . . . . 31 B2 113 A4
WESTBOURNE
GREEN 88 C2
Westbourne Gr Mews
7 W11 . . . . 31 C3
Westbourne Gr Terr
W2 . . . . 100 A1
Westbourne Ho
SW1 . . . . 146 A2
Westbourne Park Rd
Notting Hill W2,
W11 . . . . 31 C3
Notting Hill W11 . . 31 B3
Westbourne Park Sta
W11 . . . . 31 B4
Westbourne Park
Villas W2 . . . . 100 A3
Westbourne Rd
N7 . . . . 14 B2

Westbourne St
W2 . . . . 115 B4
Westbourne Terr
W2 . . . . 101 A2
Westbourne Terrace
Mews W2 . . . . 100 C2
Westbourne Terrace
Rd W2 . . . . 100 C2
Westbridge Cl
W12 . . . . 29 C1
Westbridge Prim Sch
SW11 . . . . 168 A4
Westbridge Rd
SW11 . . . . 168 A4
WEST
BROMPTON 156 C4
West Brompton Sta
SW5 . . . . 141 C1
Westbrook Ho
6 Bethnal Green
E2 . . . . 25 B2
5 Clapham Pk
SW4 . . . . 61 B2
Westbury Ct SW4 . . 61 A1
Westbury Ho
NW10 . . . . 8 A1
Westbush Ct 1
W12 . . . . 39 A4
West Carriage Dr
W2 . . . . 116 A2
West Central St
WC1 . . . . 106 A2
Westchester Ho
W2 . . . . 102 C1
Westcliff Ho 13
N1 . . . . 15 C2
Westcombe Ct 1
SE3 . . . . 53 B3
Westcombe Hill SE3,
SE10 . . . . 53 B4
Westcombe Park Rd
SE3 . . . . 53 A3
Westcombe Park Sta
SE3 . . . . 43 C2
Westcott Ho 1
E14 . . . . 34 A2
Westcott Rd SE17 . 48 A4
West Cotts NW6 . . . 10 C3
Westcroft Cl NW2 . 10 A4
Westcroft Ct 3
W6 . . . . 38 C2
Westcroft Sq W6 . . 38 C2
Westcroft Way
NW2 . . . . 10 A4
West Cromwell Rd
W14 . . . . 141 A2
West Cross Route W10,
W11 . . . . 30 C2
Westdean Cl
SW18 . . . . 59 A1
West End Ct NW6 . . 11 A1
WEST DULWICH . 75 B2
West Dulwich Sta
SE21 . . . . 75 C2
West Eaton Pl
SW1 . . . . 145 B4
West Eaton Pl Mews
SW1 . . . . 145 B4
West Ella Rd NW10 . 8 A1
West End Cl NW10 . 10 A1
West End La NW6 . 11 A2
Westerdale Ct N5 . . 15 A4
Westerdale Rd 2
SE10 . . . . 43 C1
Westerham NW1 . . 82 C3

Westerham Ho
SE1 . . . . **137** C2
Western Ave W3 . . . . . . **28** C3
Western Avenue Bsns
Pk W3 . . . . **20** A1
Western Beach Apts
E16 . . . . **35** C1
Western Ct
4 Dagenham W3 . . **28** C3
5 Kilburn NW3 . . . . **23** B3
Western Eye Hospl
The NW1 . . . . **102** C4
Western Gateway
E16 . . . . **35** C2
Western Ho **5** W9 . . **23** B1
Western La SW12 . . . . **72** C4
Western Mews
W9 . . . . **23** B1
Western Pl **19**
SE16 . . . . **40** B4
Western Rd
Becontree NW10 . . . **20** B1
Brixton SW9 . . . . . . **62** C4
Western Terr **3**
W6 . . . . **38** C1
Western Wharf **2**
SE15 . . . . **49** C4
Westferry Cir E14 . . **33** C1
Westferry Rd E14 . . . **41** C3
Westferry Sta E14 . . **33** C2
Westfield NW3 . . . . . . **10** C4
Westfield Cl
SW10 . . . . **156** C1
Westfield Ct **1**
W10 . . . . **22** C2
Westfield Ho **6**
SE16 . . . . **40** C2
Westfield London Sh
Ctr W12 . . . . **30** C1
Westfields SW13 . . . **56** B4
Westfields Ave
SW13 . . . . **56** A4
Westfields Rd W3 . . **28** A4
Westfield Stratford Sh
Ctr EH15 . . . . **19** B2
Westfield Way E1 . . **26** A1
West Garden Pl
W2 . . . . **102** B1
Westgate Bsns Ctr
2 Kensal Town
W10 . . . . **23** A1
North Kensington
W10 . . . . **22** C1
Westgate Ct **13**
SW9 . . . . **62** C4
Westgate St E8 . . . . **25** A4
Westgate Terr
SW10 . . . . **156** B4
West Gdns E1 . . . . . . **32** A2
West Gr SE10 . . . . **52** C2
Westgrove La
SE10 . . . . **52** B2
West Halkin St
SW1 . . . . **131** B2
West Hall Rd TW9 . . **45** A2
WEST
HAMPSTEAD **10** C4
West Hampstead
Mews NW6 . . . . **11** A2
West Hampstead Sta
NW6 . . . . **10** C2
West Hampstead
Thameslink Sta
NW6 . . . . **10** C2
West Harding St
EC4 . . . . **107** C2

Westhay Gdns
SW14 . . . . **55** A2
West Heath Ave
NW11 . . . . **1** C3
West Heath Cl NW3 . . **1** C1
West Heath Ct
NW11 . . . . **1** C3
West Heath Dr
NW11 . . . . **1** C3
West Heath Gdns
NW3 . . . . **1** C1
West Heath Rd
NW3 . . . . **2** A1
WEST HILL **58** B1
West Hill SW15 . . . . **58** A1
Westhill Ct
W11 . . . . . . **31** B2 **113** A4
West Hill Ct N6 . . . . . . **3** C1
Westhill Pk
Dartmouth Pk N6 . . . **3** C2
Highgate N6 . . . . **3** C1
West Hill Prim Sch **17**
SW18 . . . . **58** C1
West Hill Rd SW18 . . **58** A1
West Ho **9** SW12 . . **73** B4
Westhope Ho **20**
E2 . . . . **24** C2 **99** C3
Westhorpe Rd
SW15 . . . . **57** B4
West House Cl
SW19 . . . . **70** A3
West India Ave
E14 . . . . **33** C1
West India Dock Rd
E14 . . . . **33** C2
West India Ho **1**
E14 . . . . **33** C2
West India Quay Sta
E14 . . . . **33** C2
WEST
KENSINGTON . . **140** B3
West Kensington Ct
W14 . . . . **140** C2
West Kensington
Mans W14 . . . . . . **140** C1
West Kensington Sta
W14 . . . . **140** C2
WEST KILBURN . . **23** A2
West La SE16 . . . . . . **40** A4
Westlake **1** SE16 . . **40** B2
Westland Pl N1 . . . . **97** B4
Westlands Terr **3**
SW12 . . . . **61** B1
Westleigh Ave
SW15 . . . . **57** B2
Westly Ct NW2 . . . . . . **9** C2
Westmacott Ho
NW8 . . . . **89** C1
West Mall
W11 . . . . . . **31** C1 **113** C2
Westmark Point **19**
SW15 . . . . **69** A3
Westmead SW15 . . . **57** A1
West Mews SW1 . . . **146** C3
Westmill Ct N4 . . . . . . **6** B2
WESTMINSTER . . **133** A1
Westminster Abbey
SW1 . . . . **134** A2
Westminster Abbey
Choir Sch SW1 . . **133** C2
Westminster Acad
W2 . . . . **31** C4
Westminster Acad
(Sch of English)
W1 . . . . **105** A2

Westminster Boating
Base SW1 . . . . **161** B4
Westminster Bridge
SE1, SW1 . . . . **134** B3
Westminster Bridge
Rd SE1 . . . . **134** C3
Westminster Cath
SW1 . . . . **132** C1
Westminster Cath
Choir Sch SW1 . . **132** C1
Westminster Cath RC
Prim Sch SW1 . . . **133** B1
Westminster City Hall
SW1 . . . . **133** A2
Westminster City Sch
SW1 . . . . **133** A2
Westminster Coll
W1 . . . . **119** B4
Westminster Ct
22 Rotherhithe
SE16 . . . . **32** C1
5 Wandsworth
SW18 . . . . **58** C2
Westminster
Dragoons Mus
SW6 . . . . **58** A4
Westminster Gdns
SW1 . . . . **148** A4
Westminster
Kingsway Coll
(King's Cross
Centre) WC1 . . . . . **94** C3
Westminster
Kingsway Coll
(Regent's Park Ctr)
NW1 . . . . **92** C2
Westminster
Kingsway Coll
(Victoria Centre)
SW1 . . . . **147** B4
Westminster
Millennium Pier
SW1 . . . . **134** B3
Westminster Pier
SW1 . . . . **134** B3
Westminster Sch
SW1 . . . . **134** A2
Westminster Sta
SW1 . . . . **134** B3
Westminster Under
Sch SW1 . . . . **147** B3
Westmore Ct
SW15 . . . . **58** A2
Westmoreland Ho
NW10 . . . . **21** C2
Westmoreland Pl
SW1 . . . . **146** B1
Westmoreland Rd
Barnes SW13 . . . . . . **46** C2
Camberwell SE17 . . **48** C4
SE17 . . . . **48** C4
Westmoreland Terr
SW1 . . . . **146** B1
WEST NORWOOD . . **75** B1
West Norwood Sta
SE27 . . . . **75** A1
Westonbirt Ct **6**
SE15 . . . . **49** B4
Weston Ct N4 . . . . **6** C1
West One Sh Ctr
W1 . . . . **104** A1
Weston Ho
6 Brondesbury
NW6 . . . . **10** A1

Weston Ho continued
8 South Hackney
E9 . . . . **25** B4
Weston Rd W4 . . . . . . **37** B3
Weston Rise N1,
WC1 . . . . **95** A4
Weston St SE1 . . . . **137** C4
SE1 . . . . **17** A1
Weston Wlk **8** E8,
E9 . . . . **17** A1
Westover Hill NW3 . . **1** C1
Westover Rd
SW18 . . . . **59** B1
West Park Ave
TW9 . . . . **45** A2
West Park Rd TW9 . . **44** C2
West Parkside
Greenwich SE10 . . . **43** B3
Greenwich SE10 . . . **43** C2
West Plaza E14 . . . . **34** A1
Westpoint SW15 . . . . **57** C1
West Point **2**
SE1 . . . . **153** B2
Westpoint Trad Est
W3 . . . . **28** A4
West Poultry Ave
EC1 . . . . **108** A3
West Quarters
W12 . . . . **29** C3
West Rd
Chelsea SW3 . . . . . **159** A4
Clapham Pk SW4 . . **61** C2
Westrow SW15 . . . . . . **57** B1
West Row W10 . . . . . **23** A1
West Sheen Vale
TW9 . . . . **54** B3
Westside **11** W6 . . **38** C2
Westside **5** E1 . . . . **24** A3
W9 . . . . **23** C1
West Silvertown Sta
E16 . . . . **35** C1
West Smithfield
EC1 . . . . **108** B3
West Sq SE11 . . . . . **136** A1
West St
30 Bethnal Green
E2 . . . . **25** A3
Soho WC2 . . . . **105** C1
West Temple Sheen
SW14 . . . . **55** A2
West Tenter St
E1 . . . . **111** A1
Westvale Mews
W3 . . . . **38** A4
Westview Cl
North Kensington
W10 . . . . **30** B3
Willesden NW10 . . . . **8** B3
Westville Rd W12 . . **38** C4
West Warwick Pl
SW1 . . . . **146** C3
Westway W10,
W12 . . . . **29** C2
Westway (Elevated
Rd) W10 . . . . **31** B4
W2 . . . . **31** C4
Westwell **4** NW5 . . **12** C2
Westwick Gdns
W14 . . . . **39** C4
Westwood Bsns Ctr
NW10 . . . . **21** A1
Westwood Gdns
SW13 . . . . **56** B4

Westwood Ho
6 Shepherd's Bush
W12 . . . . **30** B1
3 Stoke Newington
N4 . . . . **6** C4
Westwood Park Trad
Est W3 . . . . **20** A1
Westwood Rd
SW13 . . . . **56** B4
Wetherby Gdns
SW5 . . . . **142** C3
Wetherby Mans
SW5 . . . . **142** A2
Wetherby Mews
SW5 . . . . **142** B2
Wetherby Pl SW7 . . **143** A3
Wetherby Prep Sch
W11 . . . . . . **31** C2 **113** A4
Wetherell Rd E9 . . . . **25** C4
Wevco Wharf
SE15 . . . . **50** A4
Wexford Ho **1** E1 . . **32** B4
Wexford Rd SW12 . . **72** B4
Weybourne St
SW18 . . . . **71** B2
Weybridge Ct **19**
SE16 . . . . **40** A1
Weybridge Ho N4 . . . . **6** B4
Weybridge Point **11**
SW11 . . . . **169** A2
Weydown Cl SW19 . . **70** A3
Weyhill Ho **30**
SE5 . . . . **48** B1
Weyhill Rd E1 . . . . . **111** C2
Wey Ho NW8 . . . . **89** C1
Weymouth Ct
5 Haggerston E2 . . **24** B3
18 Streatham SW2 . . **74** B4
Weymouth Ho
Fitzrovia W1 . . . . . **104** B4
South Lambeth
SW8 . . . . **162** C1
Weymouth Mews
W1 . . . . **104** A4
Weymouth St W1 . . **104** A4
Weymouth Terr
E2 . . . . **24** B3
Whadcoat St N4 . . . . . **5** C2
Whaddon Ho
10 Camberwell
SE5 . . . . **64** A4
SW1 . . . . **131** A3
Wharfdale Rd N1 . . **84** B2
Wharfedale Ct **5**
E5 . . . . **17** C4
Wharfedale St
SW10 . . . . **142** A1
Wharf La **10** E14 . . **33** B3
Wharf Pl E2 . . . . **25** A4
Wharf Rd N1 . . . . **86** C1
Wharfside Rd E16 . . **35** A4
Wharf St E16 . . . . . . **35** A4
Wharf View Ct **18**
E14 . . . . **34** B3
Wharncliffe Ho **3**
SW15 . . . . **57** B2
Wharton Cl NW10 . . . . **8** A2
Wharton Ho SE1 . . . **138** C2
Wharton St WC1 . . . . **95** A3
Whateley Rd SE22 . . **64** B2
Whatman Ho **10**
E14 . . . . **33** B3
Wheatland Ho **7**
SE22 . . . . **64** A4

Wheatlands Rd
SW17 .... 72 C1

Wheatley Ho
Gospel Oak NW5 ..... 13 A4
3 Putney SW15 .... 68 C4

Wheatley St W1 .. 103 C3

Wheat Sheaf Cl
E14 .... 42 A2

Wheatsheaf La
Fulham SW6 .... 47 B3
SW8 .... 162 B2

Wheatsheaf Terr
SW6 .... 155 A1

Wheatstone Ho 7
W10 .... 31 A4

Wheatstone Rd
W10 .... 31 A4

Wheeler Ct 4
SW11 .... 59 C4

Wheeler Gdns N1 .. 84 B4

Wheeler La E1 .... 110 C4

Wheelhouse The 4
E14 .... 42 A1

Wheelwright St
N7 .... 14 B1

Wheldon St E1 .. 138 C4

Wheler Ho
E1 .... 24 B1 98 C1

Wheler St
E1 .... 24 B1 98 C1

Whellock Rd W4 .. 38 A3

Whetstone Park
WC2 .... 106 C2

Whewell Rd N19 ... 5 A2

Whichcote St SE1 121 B1

Whidborne Bldgs
WC1 .... 94 A3

Whidborne Cl SE8 . 51 C1

Whidborne St WC1 94 B3

Whippingham Ho 22
E3 .... 26 B2

Whiskin St EC1 ... 96 A3

Whistler Mews 28
SE15 .... 49 B3

Whistlers Ave
SW11 .... 157 C1

Whistler St N5 ... 15 A3

Whistler Twr
SW10 .... 156 C1

Whistler Wlk
SW10 .... 157 A2

Whiston Ho 16 N1 . 15 A1

Whiston Rd E2 .... 24 C4

Whitbread Ctr EC1 . 97 B1

Whitbread Rd SE4 . 66 B3

Whitburn Rd SE13 . 67 B3

Whitby Ave NW10 . 20 A2

Whitby Ct 6 N7 .. 14 A4

Whitby Ho NW8 ... 78 C3

Whitby St
E1 .... 24 B1 98 C2

Whitcher Cl SE14 . 51 A4

Whitcher Pl NW1 .. 13 B2

Whitchurch Ho 16
W10 .... 30 C3

Whitchurch Rd
W11 .... 30 C2

Whitcomb Ct W1 119 C3

Whitcomb St
WC2 .... 119 C3

Whitcome Mews
TW9 .... 45 A2

Whiteacre Mews
SE11 .... 149 C1

Whiteadder Way
E14 .... 42 A2

Whitear Wlk E15 .. 19 C2

Whitebeam Cl
SW9 .... 163 A1

Whitebeam Ho 3
NW3 .... 12 B2

White Bear Pl 1
NW3 .... 11 C4

White Bear Rd EC1 . 95 B1

WHITECHAPEL ... 110 C1

Whitechapel Gall

Whitechapel High St
E1 .... 111 A2

Whitechapel Mkt
E1 .... 111 C2

Whitechapel Sta
E1 .... 32 A4

Whitechapel Sta
E1 .... 110 C2

Whitechurch La 3
E1 .... 111 B2

Whitechurch Pas 1
E1 .... 111 B2

White City W10 .... 30 B3
White City W12 ... 30 B3

White City Est
W12 .... 30 A2

White City Rd W12 30 B2

White City Sta
W12 .... 30 B2

Whitecliff Ho
SW18 .... 59 A1

White Conduit St
N1 .... 85 C2

Whitecross PI
EC2 .... 109 C4

Whitecross St EC1 . 97 A1

White Cube (Gall)
N1 .... 24 A2 98 A4
SW1 .... 138 B2
SW1 .... 111 A2

Whitefield Cl
SW15 .... 58 A1

Whitefriars St
EC4 .... 107 C1

Whitehall SW1 .. 134 A4

Whitehall Ct SW1 120 B1

Whitehall Gdns
Chiswick W4 .... 45 A4
SW1 .... 120 A1

Whitehall Mans 4
N19 .... 4 B3

Whitehall Park Rd
N19 .... 4 B4

Whitehall Pk N19 ... 4 B3

Whitehall Pl WC2,
SW1 .... 120 A1

White Hart Ct
EC2 .... 110 A3

White Hart La
Mortlake SW13 ...... 56 A4
SW13 .... 56 B4

White Hart St
Holborn EC4 .... 108 B2
Kennington SE11 ... 149 C2

White Hart Yd
SE1 .... 123 B1

Whitehaven St
NW8 .... 90 A1

Whitehead Cl
SW18 .... 71 B4

Whitehead Ho 9
SW15 .... 57 C2

Whitehead's Gr
SW3 .... 144 B3

White Ho
1 Battersea
SW11 .... 167 C2
1 Streatham SW4 . 73 C4

Whitehorn Ho 6
E1 .... 32 B1

White Horse La
E1 .... 32 C4

Whitehorse Mews
SE1 .... 136 A2

Whitehorse Rd E1 . 33 A4

White Horse Rd
E1 .... 33 A4

White Horse St
W1 .... 118 B1

White Horse Yd
EC2 .... 109 B2

White Ho The NW1 92 B2

White House Prep Sch
SW12 .... 73 C3

White Kennett St
E1 .... 110 B2

Whitelands Cres
SW18 .... 70 A4

Whitelands Ho
SW3 .... 145 A2

Whiteley Ho 9
SW4 .... 73 C4

Whiteleys Ctr 16
W2 .... 100 B1

White Lion Ct
EC3 .... 110 A1

White Lion Hill
EC4 .... 122 B4

White Lion St N1 . 85 C1

White Lo NW11 .... 1 B3

Whitelock Ho 21
E9 .... 17 C2

White Lyon Ct
EC2 .... 108 C4

Whiteness Ho 11
SW9 .... 173 B4

White Post La E9 . 18 C2

White Post St
SE15 .... 50 B3

White Rd E15 ..... 19 C1

White's Grounds
SE1 .... 138 B4

White's Grounds Est
SE1 .... 138 B4

White's Row E1 .. 110 C3

White's Sq SW4 ... 61 C3

Whitestone La NW3 . 2 B1

Whitestone Wlk
NW3 .... 2 B1

Whitethorn St E3 .. 33 C4

White Twr Way E1 . 33 A4

Whitfield Ct SW4 172 A3

Whitfield Gdns
W1 .... 105 A4

Whitfield Ho NW8 . 90 A1

Whitfield Pl W1 ... 93 A1

Whitfield St W1 .. 105 A4

Whitgift Ho
Battersea SW11 .... 168 A4
Lambeth SE11 ..... 148 C4

Whitgift St SE11 . 148 C4

Whitington Ave
EC3 .... 110 A1

Whitley Ho SW1 . 161 A4

Whitlock Dr SW19 . 70 A3

Whitman Ho 20 E2 25 B2

Whitman Rd E3 .... 26 A1

Whitmore Gdns
NW10 .... 22 B3

Whitmore Ho 20
E1 .... 24 A4

Whitmore Prim Sch
N1 .... 87 C3

Whitmore Rd N1 .. 24 A4

Whitnell Ct 7
SW15 .... 57 C2

Whitnell Way
SW15 .... 57 C2

Whitney Ho 6
SE22 .... 64 A4

Whitstable Ho 10
W10 .... 30 C3

Whitstters Ho SE1 138 C4

Whittaker Ct SW4 172 B3

Whittaker St SW1 145 B3

Whittaker Way 19
SE1 .... 153 C4

Whittingham Ct
W4 .... 46 A3

Whittingstall Mans
SW6 .... 165 A3

Whittingstall Rd
SW6 .... 165 A3

Whittington Hospl
The N19 .... 4 B2

Whittlebury Ho N4 . 6 B4

Whittlesey St SE1 121 C1

Whitton NW3 ..... 12 B1

Whitton Wlk E3 ... 26 C2

Whitworth Ho
SE1 .... 137 A1

Whitworth St SE10 43 A1

Whorlton Rd SE15 . 65 A4

Whytlaw Ho 10 E3 . 33 B4

Wicker St E1 ..... 32 A3

Wickfield Ho 7
SE16 .... 139 C3

Wickford Ho 5
E1 .... 25 B1

Wickford St E1 ... 25 B1

Wickham Cl E1 .... 32 B4

Wickham Gdns
SE4 .... 66 B4

Wickham Ho
SW15 .... 57 C2

Wickham Mews
SE4 .... 51 B1

Wickham Rd SE4 .. 66 B4

Wickham St SE11 148 C2

Wick La
Hackney E9 .... 18 B2
Stratford Marsh E3 . 26 C4

Wicklow Ho N16 .... 7 B3

Wicksteed Ho SW1 . 94 C4

Wick Rd
Hackney E9 .... 17 C2
Hackney E9 .... 18 A2

Wickstead Ho
The N19 .... 36 B1

Wicksteed Ho
SE1 .... 137 A1

Wick Village 7
E15 .... 19 B3

Wickway Ct 7
SE15 .... 49 B4

Wickwood St SE5 .. 48 A1

Widdenham Rd
N7 .... 14 B4

Widecombe Ho 33
SE5 .... 48 B1

Widegate St E1 .. 110 B3

Widford 8 NW1 .... 13 A2

Widford Ho N1 .... 86 A1

Widley Rd W9 ..... 23 C1

Widnes Ho 8 N7 ... 14 C3

Wigmore Hall W1 104 A2

Wigmore Pl W1 .. 104 A2

Wigmore St W1 .. 103 C2

Wigram Ct SW11 . 168 A4

Wigram Ho 8 E14 . 34 A2

Wigton Pl SE11 .. 149 C1

Wilberforce Ho 3
SW11 .... 59 C4

Wilberforce Mews
SW4 .... 61 C3

Wilberforce Prim Sch
W10 .... 23 A2

Wilberforce Rd
Finsbury Pk N4 ...... 6 A2
Highbury N4, N5 ..... 6 B1

Wilbraham Ho
SW8 .... 162 A1

Wilbraham Pl
SW1 .... 145 B4

Wilby Mews
W11 .... 31 B1 113 A2

Wilcox Cl SW8 .. 162 B2

Wilcox Ho 3 E3 ... 33 B4

Wilcox Pl SW1 ... 133 A1

Wilcox Rd SW8 .. 162 A1

Wildcroft Manor
SW15 .... 69 B4

Wildcroft Rd
SW15 .... 69 B4

Wild Ct WC2 .... 106 C2

Wilde Cl E8 ...... 24 C4

Wilde Pl SW18 ... 71 C4

Wilderness Mews
SW4 .... 61 A3

Wilderton Rd N16 .. 7 A4

Wild Goose Dr
SE14 .... 50 B2

Wilding Ho 17 E9 . 17 C2

Wild's Rents SE1 138 A2

Wild St WC2 ..... 106 C1

Wildwood Gr NW3 .. 2 B3

Wildwood Rd NW11 . 2 B4

Wildwood Rise
NW11 .... 2 B3

Wildwood Terr NW3,
NW11 .... 2 B3

Wilfred Fienburgh Ho
N7 .... 13 C4

Wilfred St SW1 .. 132 C2

Wilfrid Gdns W3 .. 28 B4

Wilkes St E1 .... 111 A4

Wilkie Ho SW1 .. 147 C2

Wilkin St Mews
NW1 .... 13 A2

Wilkins Ho SW1 . 160 C4

Wilkinson Ho N1 .. 87 C1

Wilkinson St SW8 162 C1

Wilkinson Way
W4 .... 37 C4

Wilkin St NW5 .... 13 A2

Wilks Pl N1 ...... 24 A3

Willan Wall E16 .. 35 B2

Willard St SW8 ... 61 A4

Willbury Ho 4 N7 . 13 C3

Willcott Rd W3 ... 28 A1

Willenfield Rd
NW10 .... 20 B3

WILLESDEN 8 B1

Willesden Community
Hospl The NW10 ... 8 C1

**WILLESDEN
GREEN** 22 A4

Willesden Green Sta
NW2 . . . . 9 B2
Willesden Junction
Sta NW10 . . . . 21 B2
Willesden La NW2,
NW6 . . . . 9 C2
Willesden Sports Ctr
W10 . . . . 22 A4
Willes Rd NW5 . . . . 13 A2
Willett Ho NW9 . . . . . . 62 A4
William Banfield Ho
10 NW6 . . . . 164 C2
William Blake Ho **2**
SE15 . . . . 49 B2
William Bonney Est **10**
SW4 . . . . 61 D3
William Booth Meml
Training Coll
SE5 . . . . 48 C1
William Brown Ct
SE27 . . . . 75 A2
William Caslon Ho **28**
E2 . . . . 25 A3
William Channing Ho
6 E2 . . . . 25 A2
William Cl SE13 . . . . 24 C1 99 B2
William Davis Prim
Sch **18** E2 . . 24 C1 99 B2
William Dromey Ct
NW6 . . . . 10 B1
William Dunbar Ho
NW6 . . . . 23 B3
William Ellis Sch
NW5 . . . . 3 C1
William Ellis Way **10**
SE16 . . . . 139 C1
William Evans Ho **9**
SE8 . . . . 40 C2
William Gdns
SW15 . . . . 57 A2
William Guy Gdns **47**
E3 . . . . 27 A2
William Harvey Ho **1**
SW19 . . . . 70 A3
William Hogarth Sch
The **18** W4 . . . . 38 A1
William Hunt Mans
SW13 . . . . 47 B4
William IV St
WC2 . . . . 120 A3
William Margrie Cl **1**
SE15 . . . . 49 C1
William Mews
SW1 . . . . 131 A3
William Morris Acad
W6 . . . . 39 C1
William Morris Ho
W6 . . . . 47 C4
William Morris Way
SW6 . . . . 166 C1
William Patten Prim
Sch **9** N16 . . . . 7 B2
William Pl **17** E3 . . . 26 B2
William Rathbone Ho
3 E2 . . . . 25 A2
William Rd NW1 . . . . . 92 C3
William Rushbrooke
Ho **4** SE16 . . . . 153 B4
William Saville Ho **2**
NW6 . . . . 23 B3
William's Bldgs **1**
E2 . . . . 25 B1
Williams Cl SW6 . . 154 B2
Williams Coll CC1 107 C3
Williams Ho
10 Bow E3 . . . . . . 26 C2

Williams Ho continued
9 Hackney E9 . . . . . 25 A4
14 Streatham SW2 . 74 C3
Williams La SW14 . . 45 B1
Williamson Cl
SE10 . . . . 43 B1
Williamson Ct
SE17 . . . . 150 C1
Williamson St N7 . . 14 A4
William Sq **15**
SE16 . . . . 33 A2
William St SW1 . . . 131 A3
William Tyndale Prim
Sch **27** N1 . . . . 15 A1
William Winter Ct **7**
SW2 . . . . 74 C4
Willingham Cl **4**
NW5 . . . . 13 B3
Willingham Terr
NW5 . . . . 13 B3
Willington Rd
SW9 . . . . 62 A4
Willis Ho **8** E14 . . . . 34 A2
Willis St E14 . . . . 34 A3
Willoughby Ho
1 EC2 . . . . 109 B3
2 Wapping E1 . . . 32 A1
Willoughby Rd
NW3 . . . . 11 C4
Willoughby St
WC1 . . . . 106 A3
Willoughbys The
SW14 . . . . 56 A3
Willow Ave SW13 . . 46 B1
Willowbank SW6 . . 58 A4
Willowbank Rd
SE15 . . . . 49 B4
Willow Bridge Rd
N1 . . . . 15 B2
Willow Cotts TW9 . . 44 C4
Willow Ct
Brixton SW9 . . . . . . 173 B3
Chiswick W4 . . . . 46 A3
EC2 . . . . 24 A1 98 A2
Islington N7 . . . . 14 B3
10 Paddington W2 . 31 C4
1 Streatham
SW16 . . . . 74 B1
Willowdene
Highgate N6 . . . . 3 B4
1 Peckham SE15 . . 50 A2
5 SE15 . . . . 50 A3
Willow Farm La
SW15 . . . . 57 A4
Willow Hall NW3 . . 11 C4
Willow Ho
1 Maitland Pk
NW3 . . . . 12 B2
North Kensington
W10 . . . . 22 C1
Willow Lo
Fulham SW6 . . . . . . 47 C2
Putney SW15 . . . . . . 57 A4
Willow Lodge **10**
SW8 . . . . 61 A4
Willowmere SE13 . . 67 A2
Willow Pl SW1 . . . 147 A4
Willow Rd
Ealing W5 . . . . 36 A4
1 Hampstead
NW3 . . . . 12 A4
Willow St
EC2 . . . . 24 A1 98 A2
Willows Terr
NW10 . . . . 21 B3
Willow Tree Cl
14 Old Ford E3 . . 26 B4

Willow Tree Cl
continued
Wandsworth SW18 . 71 A2
Willow Vale W12 . . . 29 C1
Willow Way **9**
W11 . . . . 30 C2
Willow Wlk SE1 . . 152 C4
Willsbridge Ct **1**
SE15 . . . . 49 B4
Wilman Gr E8 . . . . . . 16 C1
Wilmcote Ho W2 . . 100 A4
Wilmer Gdns **22**
N1 . . . . 24 A4
Wilmer Ho **6** E3 . . . 26 A3
Wilmer Lea Cl E15 . 19 C1
Wilmer Pl N16 . . . . . . 7 B2
Wilmers Ct **5**
NW10 . . . . 20 C4
Wilmington Ave
W4 . . . . 45 C3
Wilmington Sq
WC1 . . . . 95 B3
Wilmington St
WC1 . . . . 95 B3
Wilmot Cl SE15 . . . . 49 C3
Wilmot Pl NW1 . . . . 13 B1
Wilmot St E2 . . . . . . 25 A1
Wilna Rd SW18 . . . . 71 B4
Wilsham St
W11 . . . . . . 31 A1 112 A2
Wilshaw Ho **10**
SE8 . . . . 51 C3
Wilshaw St SE14 . . 51 C2
Wilson Gr SE16 . . . . 40 A4
Wilson Ho
3 Clapham SW8 . 171 B1
South Hampstead
NW6 . . . . 11 B1
Wilson Rd SE5 . . . . . 49 A2
Wilson's Pl E14 . . . . 33 B3
Wilson's Rd W6 . . . . 39 C1
Wilson St EC2 . . . 109 C4
Wiltern Ct NW2 . . . . 10 A2
Wilton Ave W4 . . . . . 38 A1
Wilton Cres SW1 . . 131 B3
Wilton Ct
4 Richmond
TW10 . . . . 54 A2
7 Stepney E1 . . . 32 A3
Wilton Est E8 . . . . . . 16 C2
Wilton Ho **8** SE22 . 64 A4
Wilton Mews
SW1 . . . . 131 C2
Wilton Pl SW1 . . . 131 B3
Wilton Rd SW1 . . . 146 C4
Wilton Row SW1 . 131 B3
Wilton Sq N1 . . . . . . 87 B4
Wilton St SW1 . . . . 132 A2
Wilton Terr SW1 . . 131 B3
Wilton Villas N1 . . . 87 B3
Wilton Way E8 . . . . . 16 C2
Wiltshire Cl SW3 . 144 C3
Wiltshire Ct **2** N4 . . . 5 B3
Wiltshire Rd SW9 . . 62 C3
Wiltshire Row N1 . . 87 C3
Wimbart Rd SW2 . . 74 B4
Wimbledon Lawn
Tennis Mus
SW19 . . . . 70 A1
Wimbledon Park Ct
SW19 . . . . 70 B3
Wimbledon Park
Montessori Sch
SW18 . . . . 70 C2
Wimbledon Park Prim
Sch SW19 . . . . 71 A2

Wimbledon Park Rd
SW18, SW19 . . . . . . 70 B3
Wimbledon Park Side
SW19 . . . . 69 C3
Wimbledon Park Sta
SW19 . . . . 70 C1
Wimbledon Stadium
Bsns Ctr SW17 . . . . 71 A1
Wimbledon Windmill
Mus SW19 . . . . 69 B1
Wimbolt St
E2 . . . . 24 C2 99 B4
Wimborne Ho
Canning Town
E16 . . . . 35 B2
Marylebone NW1 . . . 90 B1
South Lambeth
SW8 . . . . 163 A1
Upper Tooting
SW12 . . . . 73 B1
Wimborne Ct N1 . . . 87 B2
Wimborne St N1 . . . 87 B2
Wimpole Mews
W1 . . . . 104 A3
Wimpole St W1 . . 104 A2
Winans Wlk SW9 . 173 B1
Winant Ho **19** E14 . 34 A2
Wincanton Rd
SW18 . . . . 70 B4
Winchelsea Cl
SW15 . . . . 57 C2
Winchelsea Ho **16**
SE16 . . . . 40 B4
Winchelsea Rd
NW10 . . . . 20 C4
Winchendon Rd
SW6 . . . . 165 A4
Winchester Ave
NW6 . . . . 10 A1
Winchester Cl
SE17 . . . . 150 B3
Winchester Ct
Richmond TW9 . . . . 54 B4
W8 . . . . 128 A4
Winchester Ho
Bayswater W2 . . . . 100 C1
Chelsea SW3 . . . . . 157 C3
21 Tower Hamlets
E3 . . . . 26 B2
Winchester Pal
SE1 . . . . 123 B2
Winchester Pl
6 Dalston E8 . . . . 16 B3
Highgate N6 . . . . 4 A3
Winchester Rd
Highgate N6 . . . . 4 A3
South Hampstead
NW3 . . . . 11 C1
Winchester Sq
SE1 . . . . 123 B2
Winchester St
Acton W3 . . . . 37 B4
SW1 . . . . 146 B2
Winchester Wlk
SE1 . . . . 123 B2
Winchfield Ho
SW15 . . . . 56 B1
Winch Ho
Isle of Dogs E14 . . . 42 A3
SW10 . . . . 157 A2
Winchilsea Ho
NW8 . . . . 89 C3
Wincott St SE11 . . 149 C3
Windermere
NW1 . . . . 92 B4
12 Putney SW15 . 57 C1

Windermere Ave
NW6 . . . . 23 A4
Windermere Ct
SW13 . . . . 46 B4
Windermere Ho
E3 . . . . 26 B1
Windermere Point **3**
SE15 . . . . 50 B3
Windermere Rd
N19 . . . . 4 B2
Winders Rd SW11 168 A2
Windham Rd TW9 . . 54 B4
Windlass Pl SE8 . . . 41 A2
Windlesham Gr
SW19 . . . . 69 C3
Windmill WC1 . . . 106 C4
Windmill Alley **7**
W4 . . . . 38 A2
Windmill Cl
12 Bermondsey
SE1 . . . . 153 C4
4 Lewisham SE13 . 52 B1
Windmill Ct NW2 . . 10 A2
Windmill Dr
Clapham SW4 . . . . . 61 A2
Cricklewood NW2 . . . 1 A1
Windmill Gdns
SW2 . . . . 62 B1
Windmill Hill
1 Hampstead
NW3 . . . . 11 B4
Hampstead NW3 . . . 2 B1
Windmill Ho
4 Millwall E14 . . 41 C2
SE1 . . . . 121 C1
Windmill La E15 . . 19 C2
Windmill Pas **10**
W4 . . . . 38 A2
Windmill Rd
Chiswick W4 . . . . . . 38 A2
Roehampton SW19 . 69 A1
Wandsworth SW18 . 59 C1
Windmill Row
SE11 . . . . 149 B1
Windmill St W1 . . 105 B3
Windmill Wlk SE1 135 C4
Windrose Cl SE16 . 40 C4
Windrush Cl
Battersea SW11 . . . 59 C3
Chiswick W4 . . . . . . 45 B3
4 Hackney E8 . . . 16 C1
Windrush Ho
NW8 . . . . 101 C4
Windrush Rd
NW10 . . . . 20 C4
Windrush Sq
Brixton SW9 . . . . . . 62 C3
SW2 . . . . 62 C3
Windsock Cl **1**
SE16 . . . . 41 B2
Windsor Ct
Battersea SW11 . . 167 C2
Bayswater W2 . . . . 114 A4
Chelsea SW3 . . . . . 144 B2
2 Clapham SW4 . 61 B3
Fulham NW6 . . . . . . 58 A4
20 Rotherhithe
SE16 . . . . 32 C1
4 Wandsworth
SW18 . . . . 58 C2
West Hampstead
NW3 . . . . 10 C4
Windsor Gdns W9 . 23 C1

Windsor Ho
4 Acton Green
W4 . . . . 37 B1
Brondesbury NW2 . . . 10 A2
4 Globe Town E2 . . . . 25 C2
Regent's Pk NW1 . . . . **92** B4
Shoreditch N1 . . . . . . **87** A2
Stoke Newington N4 . . 6 B3
Windsor Pl SW1 . . . . 147 A4
Windsor Rd
Richmond TW9 . . . . . . 44 B1
Upper Holloway N7 . . . 5 A1
Willesden NW2 . . . . . . 9 B2
Windsor St N1 . . . . . . 86 B4
Windsor Terr N1 . . . . 97 A4
Windsor Way
W14 . . . . 140 A3
Windsor Wharf E9 . . **18** B3
Windsor Wlk SW5 . . . . 11 B3
Windspoint Dr
SE15 . . . . 50 A4
Windus Rd N16 . . . . . . 7 B3
Windus Wlk N16 . . . . 7 B3
Wine Cl E1 . . . . 32 B2
Wine Office Ct
EC4 . . . . **107** C2
Winfield Ho 3
SW11 . . . . **167** C2
Winford Ct 18
SE15 . . . . 49 C2
Winford Ho E3 . . . . . 18 B1
Winforton St SE10 . . 52 B2
Winfrith Rd SW18 . . 71 B3
Wingate Ho
26 Bromley E3 . . . . . . 27 A2
8 Stoke Newington
N16 . . . . 16 A4
Wingate Rd W6 . . . . . 39 A3
Wingfield Ct 5
E14 . . . . 34 C2
Wingfield Ho
Paddington NW6 . . . . **78** A2
18 Spitalfields
E2 . . . . 24 B2 **98** C3
Wingfield Mews
SE15 . . . . 64 C4
Wingfield St SE15 . . 64 C4
Wingford Rd SW2 . . 62 A1
Wingham 3 NW5 . . 12 C2
Wingmore Rd
SE24 . . . . 63 B4
Wingrad Ho 11 E1 . . 32 B4
Wingrave SE17 . . . . **151** B3
Wingrave Rd W6 . . . . 47 B4
Wingreen 1 NW8 . . . . 78 C4
Winicotte Ho W2 . . . **101** C4
Winifrede Paul Ho 7
NW5 . . . . 13 A4
Winkley St 8 E2 . . . . 25 A3
Winkworth Cotts 14
E1 . . . . 25 B1
Winnett St W1 . . . . . **119** B4
Winnington Ho
19 Kensal Town
W10 . . . . 23 A1
8 SE5 . . . . 48 B3
Winscombe St N19 . . 4 A2
Winsham Gr SW11 . . 60 C2
Winsham Ho NW1 . . **93** C4
Winsland Rd SE2 . . . 62 A2
Winsland Mews
W2 . . . . **101** B2
Winsland St W2 . . . **101** B2
Winsley St W1 . . . . . **105** A2

Winslow SE17 . . . . **152** A1
Winslow Rd W6 . . . . 47 B4
Winstanley Rd
SW11 . . . . 59 C4
Winston Churchill's
Britain at War
Experience SE1 . . **124** A1
Winston Ho WC1 . . . **93** C2
Winston Rd N16 . . . . 15 C4
Winston Wlk 2
W4 . . . . 37 C2
Winterbourne Ho
W11 . . . 31 A2 **112** A3
Winter Box Wlk
TW10 . . . . 54 B2
Winterbrook Rd
SE24 . . . . 63 B1
Winterfold Cl
SW19 . . . . 70 A2
Winterleys 7
NW6 . . . . 23 B3
Winter Lo 17
SE16 . . . . **153** C1
Winterslow Ho 20
SE5 . . . . 48 B1
Winterton Ho 18
E1 . . . . 32 B3
Winterton Pl
SW10 . . . . **157** A4
Winterwell Rd
SW2 . . . . 62 A2
Winthorpe Rd
SW15 . . . . 58 A3
Winthrop Ho 16
W12 . . . . 30 A2
Winthrop St 1 E1 . . . 32 A4
Winton Prim Sch
N1 . . . . **84** C1
Wirrall Ho 15 SE26 . . 76 C1
Wisbech 5 N4 . . . . . 5 B3
Wisden Ho SW8 . . **163** A3
Wiseton Rd E15 . . . . 27 C4
Wisley Ho SW1 . . . **147** B2
Wisley Ho SW11 . . . 60 C2
Wisteria Ho SE4 . . . . 66 A4
Wisteria Rd SE13 . . . 67 C3
Wistow Ho 14 E2 . . . 24 C4
Witanhurst La N6 . . . 3 C3
Witan St E2 . . . . 25 A2
Witchwood Ho 10
SW9 . . . . 62 C4
Witcombe Point 14
SE15 . . . . 49 C2
Witechapel Sch Ctr
E1 . . . . 32 B4
Witham Ct SW17 . . . 72 B1
Witham Ho 34 SE5 . . 48 B1
Witherington Rd
N5 . . . . 14 C3
Withers Pl EC1 . . . . **97** A2
Withycombe Rd
SW19 . . . . 69 C4
Withy Ho 4 E1 . . . . . 25 C1
Witley Ct WC1 . . . . **94** A1
Witley Ho 2 SW2 . . 74 B4
Witley Point 8
SW15 . . . . 69 A3
Witley Rd N19 . . . . . 4 B2
Wittering Ho 9
SW11 . . . . **169** A2
Wivenhoe Cl SE15 . . 65 A4
Wix Prim Sch SW4 . . 61 A3
Wix's La SW4 . . . . . . 61 A3

Woburn Ct
32 Bermondsey
SE16 . . . . 40 A1
Richmond TW9 . . . . . . 54 B4
Woburn Ho WC1 . . . **93** C2
Woburn Pl WC1 . . . **94** A3
Woburn Sq WC1 . . . **93** C1
Woburn Wlk WC1 . . **93** C3
Wodeham Gdns 1
E1 . . . . 32 A4
Wodehouse Ave
SE15 . . . . 49 B2
Wodehouse Ct 10
W3 . . . . 37 B3
Woking Cl SW15 . . . 56 B3
Wolcot Ho NW1 . . . **83** A1
Wolfe Cres 24
SE16 . . . . 40 C4
Wolfe Ho 19 W12 . . . 30 A2
Wolfson Ct
Golders Green
NW11 . . . . 1 A4
SE1 . . . . **139** A4
Wolftencroft Cl
SW11 . . . . 59 C4
Wollaston Cl SE1 . . **150** C4
Wollotan Ho N1 . . . **85** C2
Wolseley Ave SW18,
SW19 . . . . 70 C2
Wolseley Gdns
W4 . . . . 45 A4
Wolseley Rd W4 . . . . 37 B2
Wolseley St SE1 . . **139** A3
Wolsey Ct NW6 . . . . 11 B1
Wolsey Ho 3
NW5 . . . . 13 C2
Wolsey Mews
NW5 . . . . 13 B2
Wolsey Rd N1 . . . . . 15 C3
Wolsey St 1 E1 . . . . 32 B4
Wolverley St E2 . . . . 25 A2
Wolverton SE17 . . . **152** A2
Wolverton Gdns
W6 . . . . 39 C2
Women's Liby The
EC2 . . . . **110** C2
Wontner Cl 5 N1 . . 15 B1
Wontner Rd SW12,
SW17 . . . . 72 B2
Woodall Cl 18 E14 . . 34 A2
Woodberry Down
N4 . . . . 6 B4
Woodberry Down
Com Prim Sch N4 . . 6 B4
Woodberry Gr N4 . . . 6 B4
Woodbine Terr E9 . . 17 B2
Woodborough Rd
SW15 . . . . 57 A3
Woodbourne Ave
SW16 . . . . 73 C1
Woodbourne Cl
SW16 . . . . 74 A1
Woodbridge Ct 10
N7 . . . . 5 B2
Woodbridge Cl N16 . . 6 C1
Woodbridge St
EC1 . . . . **96** A2
Woodchester Sq
W2 . . . . **100** A4
Woodchurch Ho 4
SW9 . . . . **173** B4
Woodchurch Rd
NW6 . . . . 11 A1
Wood Cl E2 . . . . 24 C1
Woodcock Ho 4
E14 . . . . 33 C4

Woodcote Ho 4
SE8 . . . . 51 B4
Woodcott Ho 1
SW15 . . . . 68 C4
Woodcroft Mews
SE8 . . . . 41 A2
Wood Dene 8
SE15 . . . . 50 A2
Woodfall Rd N4 . . . . 5 C2
Woodfall St SW3 . . **144** C1
Woodfarrs SE5 . . . . . 63 C3
Wood Field NW3 . . . 12 B3
Woodfield Ave
SW16 . . . . 73 C1
Woodfield Ct
SW16 . . . . 73 C1
Woodfield Gr
SW16 . . . . 73 C1
Woodfield La
SW16 . . . . 73 C1
Woodfield Pl W9 . . . 23 B1
Woodfield Rd W9 . . 31 B4
Woodger Rd W12 . . . 39 C4
Woodhall NW1 . . . . **92** C3
Woodhall Ave
SE21 . . . . 76 B1
Woodhall Dr SE21 . . 76 B1
Woodhall Ho
SW18 . . . . 59 C1
Woodheyes Rd
NW10 . . . . 8 A3
Wood Ho
4 Clapham SW4 . . . **171** C2
Paddington
NW6 . . . . 23 B3
Woodhurst Rd W3 . . 28 B2
Woodison St E3 . . . . 26 A1
Wood La W12 . . . . . . 30 B2
Woodland Cres
11 Rotherhithe
SE16 . . . . 40 C4
Woodland Gr SE10 . . 43 A1
Woodland Hts SE3 . . 53 A4
Woodland Mews
SW16 . . . . 74 A1
Woodlands SW4 . . . . 61 A3
Woodlands Ave
W3 . . . . 28 A1
Woodlands Ct
NW10 . . . . 22 C4
Woodlands Gt
SW15 . . . . 58 B2
Woodlands Park Rd
SE10 . . . . 53 A4
Woodlands Rd
SW13 . . . . 56 B4
Woodland St 2
E8 . . . . 16 B2
Woodlands The
Highbury N5 . . . . 15 B4
18 Hornsey N8 . . . . . 5 A4
Woodlands Way
SW15 . . . . 58 B2
Woodland Wlk
9 Greenwich
SE10 . . . . 43 A1
Hampstead NW3 . . . 12 A3
Wood Lane High Sch
W12 . . . . 30 A3
Wood Lane Sta
W12 . . . . 30 B3
Woodlawn Cl
SW15 . . . . 58 B2

Woodlawn Rd
SW6 . . . . 47 C2
Woodlea Rd N16 . . . 7 A1
Woodleigh Gdns
SW16 . . . . 74 A1
Woodman Mews
TW9 . . . . 45 A2
Woodmans Gr
NW10 . . . . 8 B3
Woodmans Mews
W12 . . . . 30 A4
Woodmere Cl 11
SW11 . . . . 60 C4
Woodpecker Mews
SE13 . . . . 67 C3
Woodpecker Rd 7
SE14 . . . . 51 A4
Wood Point 8
E16 . . . . 35 C4
Woodquest Ave
SE24 . . . . 63 B2
Woodruff Ho 12
SW2 . . . . 62 C1
Woodrush Cl 4
SE14 . . . . 51 A3
Woodseer St E1 . . . **111** B4
Woodsford SE17 . . **151** B1
Woodsford Sq
W14 . . . . **126** B4
Woods Ho SW8 . . . **170** C4
Wood's Mews W1 . . **117** B4
Woodsome Rd NW5 . . 4 A1
Wood's Pl SE1 . . . . **138** B1
Woodspring Rd
SW19 . . . . 70 A2
Wood's Rd SE15 . . . 50 A2
Wood St
Chiswick W4 . . . . 38 A1
City of London EC2 . **109** A2
Woodstar Ho 3
SE15 . . . . 49 C3
Woodstock Ave
NW11 . . . . 1 A4
Woodstock Ct
SE11 . . . . **149** A2
Woodstock Gr
W12 . . . . 39 C4
Woodstock Ho 2
N5 . . . . 15 B4
Woodstock Mews
W1 . . . . **103** C3
Woodstock Rd
Bedford Pk W4 . . . . . 38 A3
Finsbury Pk N4 . . . . . 5 C3
Golders Green NW11 . 1 B3
Woodstock St W1 . . **104** A1
Woodstock Studios 17
W12 . . . . 39 C4
Woodstock Terr
E14 . . . . 34 A2
Wood Vale
SW15 . . . . 57 A3
Woodview Cl N4 . . . 6 A4
Woodville Ct 3
SE10 . . . . 52 B2
Woodville Rd SE10 . **138** C2
Woodville Rd
Golders Green
NW11 . . . . 1 A4
Paddington NW6 . . . 23 B3
Stoke Newington
N16 . . . . 16 A3
Woodwarde Rd
SE22 . . . . 64 A1
Woodwell St
SW18 . . . . 59 B2

Wood Wharf SE10 . . .52 B4
Woodyard Cl NW5. . .12 C3
Woodyard La SE21. .76 A4
Woolcombes Ct 4
  SE16. . . . . .32 C1
Wooler St SE17. . . .151 C2
Woolf Ct 7 W3. . . . .37 B3
Woolf Mews WC1. . .94 A2
Woolley Ho SW9. . . .63 A4
Woollon Ho 1 E1. . .32 B3
Woolmore Prim Sch
  14 E14. . . . . .34 B2
Woolmore St E14. . .34 B2
Woolneigh St
  SW6 . . . . .166 A1
Woolpack Ho 1
  E9. . . . . .17 B2
Woolridge Way E9. .17 B1
Woolstaplers Way
  SE16. . . . . .153 B4
Woolstone Ho 7
  E2. . . . . .24 C4
Woolven Ho SE1. . . .24 C4
Wooster Gdns E14. .34 C3
Wooster Pl SE1. . . .151 C4
Wootton St SE1 . . .121 C1
Worcester Ct 44
  W2 . . . . .31 C4
Worcester Dr W4. . .38 A4
Worcester Gdns
  SW11 . . . . .60 B2
Worcester Ho
  Bayswater W2 . . .100 C1
  3 Islington N1 . . . .15 B1
  Lambeth SE1 . . . .135 B1
  2 Putney SW15 . . .69 B4
Worcester Mews 23
  NW6 . . . . .11 A2
Wordsworth Ho
  NW6 . . . . .23 C2
Wordsworth Pl 1
  NW5. . . . . .12 B3
Wordsworth Rd
  Bermondsey SE1 . .153 A3
  Stoke Newington
  N16. . . . . .16 A4
Worfield St SW11. .158 B1
Worgan St
  Rotherhithe SE16. . .40 C2
  SE11 . . . . .148 C2
Working Men's Coll
  The NW1. . . . . .83 A2
World's End Pas
  SW10 . . . . .157 B2
World's End Pl
  SW10 . . . . .157 A2
World Trade Ctr
  London E14 . . . . . .42 A4
Worlidge St W6 . . . .39 B1
Worlingham St
  SE22 . . . . .64 B3
Wormholt Park Prim
  Sch W12 . . . . .29 C2
Wormholt Rd W12. .29 C1
Wormwood St
  EC2. . . . . .110 A2
Wornington Rd
  W10 . . . . .31 A4
Woronzow Rd
  NW8 . . . . .80 A4
Worple St SW14. . . .55 C4

Worple Way TW10 . .54 A3
Worship St
  EC2. . . . . . . .24 A1 98 A1
Worsley Gr E5. . . . .16 C4
Worsopp Dr SW4. . .61 B2
Worth Gr SE17. . . .151 B1
Worthington Ho
  EC1. . . . . .95 C4
  16 Streatham SW2 .74 C4
Wotton Ct 14 E14. . .34 C2
Wotton Rd 18 SE8. .51 B4
Wouldham Rd E16. .35 B3
Wrayburn Ho 28
  SE16. . . . . .139 C3
Wray Cres N4 . . . . . .5 B2
Wray Ct N4 . . . . .5 B2
Wray Ho 11 SW2 . . .74 A3
Wren Ave NW2 . . . . .9 B4
Wren Cl E16. . . . . . .35 B3
Wren Ho
  20 Bow E3 . . . . . . .26 A3
  SW1 . . . . .147 B1
Wren Landing E14. .33 C1
Wrenn Ho SW13. . . .47 B4
Wren Rd SE5 . . . . . .48 C2
Wren St WC1. . . . . .95 A2
Wrentham Ave
  NW10 . . . . .22 C3
Wren View Ho. 4 B3
Wrestlers Ct EC3 . .110 A2
Wrexham Rd E3. . . .26 C3
Wrigglesworth St
  SE14. . . . . .50 C3
Wright Cl SE13 . . . .67 C3
Wright Ho SW15. . . .57 A2
Wright's Gn SW4. . .61 C3
Wright's La W8. . . .128 A2
Wright's Rd E3. . . . .26 B3
Wrights Wlk SW14. .55 C4
Wrotham Ho SE1 .137 C2
Wrotham Rd 19
  NW1 . . . . .13 B1
Wrottesley Rd
  NW10 . . . . .21 C3
Wroughton Rd
  SW11 . . . . .60 B1
Wroxton Rd SE15. . .50 B1
Wulfstan St W12. . . .29 B3
Wyatt Cl SE16 . . . . .41 B4
Wyatt Dr SW13 . . . .47 A3
Wyatt Ho
  Blackheath Vale
  SE3. . . . . .53 B1
  NW8. . . . . .89 C1
Wyatt Park Mans 1
  SW2 . . . . .74 B2
Wyatt Park Rd
  SW2 . . . . .74 B2
Wyatt Rd N5 . . . . . . .6 B1
Wybert St NW1. . . . .92 C2
Wycherley Cl SE3. . .53 B3
Wychwood End N6. . .4 B4
Wychwood Ho N4. . . .6 B4
Wyclif Ct EC1. . . . . .96 A3
Wycliffe Ho 9
  N16. . . . . .16 A4
Wyclif St EC1. . . . . .96 A3
Wycombe Ct SE3. . .53 C3
Wycombe Gdns
  NW11 . . . . .1 C2
Wycombe Ho NW8 .90 A2

Wycombe Pl SW18 .59 B1
Wycombe Sq
  W8 . . . . .31 C1 113 B1
Wyersdale Ho N4. . . .6 B4
Wye St SW11. . . . .167 C1
Wyfold Rd SW6. . . .154 A1
Wyke Rd E3. . . . . . .18 C1
Wyldes Cl NW11. . . . .2 B3
Wyllen Cl E1. . . . . . .25 B1
Wymering Mans 9
  W9 . . . . .23 C2
Wymering Rd W9. . .23 C2
Wymondham Ct
  NW8. . . . . .79 C4
Wymond St SW15. . .57 B4
Wynan Rd E14. . . . .42 A1
Wyndham Cres N19 . .4 B1
Wyndham Deedes Ho
  30 E2 . . . . .24 C3
Wyndham Ho
  SW1 . . . . .145 B3
Wyndham Mews
  W1 . . . . .102 C3
Wyndham Pl W1. . .102 C3
Wyndham Rd SE5 . .48 B3
Wyndhams Ct 4
  E8. . . . . .16 B1
Wyndham St W1. . .102 C4
Wyndham Yd W1. . .102 C3
Wyneham Rd SE24. .63 C2
Wynford Rd N1. . . . .85 A2
Wynne Ho SE14. . . .50 C2
Wynne Rd SW9. . . .173 B1
Wynnstay Gdns
  W8 . . . . .127 C2
Wynter Ho 20
  SW9 . . . . .173 A1
Wynter St SW11. . . .59 B3
Wynton Pl W3. . . . . .28 A3
Wynyard Ho SE11 .149 A2
Wynyard Terr
  SE11 . . . . .149 A2
Wynyatt Ho EC1. . . .96 A4
Wynyatt St EC1. . . . .96 A4
Wytham Ho NW8. . .89 C1
Wythburn Ct W1. . .102 C2
Wythburn Pl W1. . .102 C2
Wyvil Prim Sch
  SW8 . . . . .162 B2
Wyvil Rd SW8 . . . .162 A2
Wyvis St E14 . . . . . .34 A4

Y

Yabsley St E14. . . . .34 B1
Yaldam Ho SE1. . . .152 A3
Yalding Ho 25 E5 . . .17 A3
Yalding Rd SE16. . .153 B4
Yale Ct NW6. . . . . . .11 A3
Yardley St WC1. . . . .95 B3
Yard The N1. . . . . . .84 B1
Yarmouth Pl W1. . .118 A1
Yarnfield Sq 12
  SE15. . . . . .49 C2
Yarrow Ho
  12 Cubitt Town
  E14. . . . . .42 B3
  16 North Kensington
  W10 . . . . .30 B4
Yatesbury Ct E5 . . . .18 A3
Yates Ct NW2. . . . . . .9 C2

Yates Ho 22
  E2. . . . . .24 C2 99 C4
Yatton Ho 15 W10 . .30 B4
Yeadon Ho 14
  W10 . . . . .30 B4
Yearby Ho W10. . . .22 B1
Yeate St N1. . . . . . .15 C1
Yeats Cl NW10. . . . . .8 A2
Yeldham Ho W6. . . .39 C1
Yeldham Rd W6. . . .39 C1
Yelverton Rd
  SW11 . . . . .167 C1
Yeoman Cl SE27. . . .75 A1
Yeoman's Row
  SW3 . . . . .130 B1
Yeoman St SE8 . . . .41 A2
Yeoman's Yd E1 . . .125 A4
Yeo St E3 . . . . .34 A4
Yeovil Ho
  Finsbury Pk N7. . . . .5 B2
  North Kensington
  W10 . . . . .22 B1
Yerbury Prim Sch
  N19. . . . . .5 A2
Yerbury Rd N19 . . . .4 C1
Yeshivo Horomo
  Talmudical Coll
  N16. . . . . .7 C3
Yesodey Hatorah Jun
  Sch for Girls 7
  N16. . . . . .7 B4
Yesodey Hatorah Sec
  Sch for Girls 6
  N16. . . . . .7 B4
Ye Lev Ct E5. . . . . . .7 C2
Yewfield Rd NW10. . .8 B2
Yew Gr NW2. . . . . . . .9 C4
Yew Ho SE14. . . . . .51 B1
Yew Tree Cl 3
  SE13 . . . . .67 B4
Yew Tree Ct 8 N16. .6 C2
Yew Tree Rd W12. . .29 B2
Yoakley Rd N16. . . . .7 A2
Yoke Cl N7 . . . . .14 A2
Yonge Pk N4, N7. . . .5 C1
York Ave
  Mortlake SW14 . . . .55 B2
  Walworth SE17 . . .151 A2
York Bldgs WC2 . . .120 B3
York Bridge NW1. . .91 B2
York Cl 17 SE5. . . . .48 B1
York Gate NW1 . . . .91 C1
York Gr SE15. . . . . .50 B2
York Hall L Ctr E2 . .25 B3
York Hill SE27,
  SW16 . . . . .75 A1
York Ho
  Acton W3 . . . . .28 B2
  Chelsea SW3 . . . .145 A2
  Islington N5 . . . . . .14 C3
  Kensington W8 . . .128 A4
  2 Kentish Town
  N7. . . . . .13 C2
  Kew TW9 . . . . .44 C2
  Lambeth SE1 . . . .135 A1
  Marylebone W1 . . .102 C4
  Pentonville N1 . . . .84 C1
  Richmond TW10. . . .54 C2
York House Pl
  W8 . . . . .128 A4

Yorkley Ho 3
  W10 . . . . .22 B1
York Mans
  Battersea SW11. . .169 C4
  2 Marylebone W1 .103 B4
  Walworth SE17. . . .151 A2
York Mews NW5. . . .13 A3
York Pl
  Battersea SW11. . . .59 C4
  WC2 . . . . .120 B3
York Place Mans
  NW1 . . . . .103 A4
York Rd
  Battersea SW11,
  SW18 . . . . .59 C4
  Dagenham W3 . . . .28 C3
  4 Richmond TW10 .54 B2
  SE1. . . . . .135 A3
York Rise NW5 . . . . .4 A1
York Road Bsns Ctr
  SW11 . . . . .167 B2
York St Chambers
  W1 . . . . .102 C4
Yorkshire Grey Pl 13
  NW3 . . . . .11 B4
Yorkshire Grey Yd
  WC1 . . . . .106 C3
Yorkshire Rd E14. . .33 A3
York Sq 12 E14 . . . .33 A3
York St W1 . . . . . . .103 A4
York Terr E NW1 . . .91 C1
York Terr W NW1 . . .91 B1
Yorkton St E2 . . . . . .24 C3
York Water Gate The
  SW1 . . . . .120 B2
York Way
  Barnsbury N1, N7,
  NW1 . . . . .14 A1
  N1 . . . . .84 B3
York Way Ct
  Islington N1 . . . . . .84 C3
  N1 . . . . .84 B3
Young's Bldgs EC1. .97 A2
Youngs Ct SW11. . .169 C3
Young St W8. . . . . .128 A3
Yoxall Ho 2 W10. . .22 B1
Yukon Rd SW12. . . .73 A4

Z

Zabludowicz
  Collection NW5 . . .12 C2
Zampa Rd SE16. . . .40 B1
Zander Ct
  E2. . . . . .24 C2 99 C4
Zangwill Ho NW6. . .23 B3
Zealand Ho 11 SE5 .48 B1
Zealand Rd E3 . . . . .26 A3
Zennor Rd SW12 . . .73 B3
Zenoria St SE22 . . . .64 B3
Zetland Ho W8. . . .128 A2
Zetland St E14 . . . . .34 B4
Zeus Ho N1 . . . . . . .97 B3
Zion Ho 6 E1 . . . . . .32 B3
Zoar St SE1 . . . . . .122 C2
Zodiac Ho 3 E3. . . .26 C1
Zoffany St N19 . . . . .4 C1

List of numbered locations

This atlas shows thousands more place names than any other London street atlas. In some busy areas it is impossible to fit the name of every place.

Where not all names will fit, some smaller places are shown by a number. If you wish to find out the name associated with a number, use this listing.

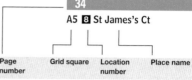

34

A5 8 St James's Ct

Page number | Grid square | Location number | Place name

1

A2 **1** Talmud Torah Tiferes Shlomo
B1 **1** Mortimer Ct
2 Primrose Ct
3 Sunnyside Ho
4 Sunnyside
5 Prospect Pl
B4 **1** Berkeley Ct
2 Exchange Mans
3 Beechcroft Ct
4 Nedahall Ct
C1 **1** Portman Hts
2 Hermitage Ct
3 Moreland Ct
4 Wendover Ct

2

B1 **1** Hampstead Sq
2 Stamford Cl
3 Mount Sq The

4

B1 **1** Hunter Ho
2 Fisher Ho
3 Lang Ho
4 Temple Ho
5 Palmer Ho
6 Durham Ho
7 Suffolk Ho
8 Lincoln Ho
9 Llewellyn Ho
10 Fell Ho
11 Aveling Ho
12 Merryweather Ct
13 Brennands Ct
14 St Christophers Ct
15 Francis Terrace Mews
16 Tremlett Mews
B2 **1** Flowers Mews
2 Archway Cl
3 Sandridge St
4 Bovingdon Cl
5 Cavell Ct
6 Torrence Ho
7 Rowan Wlk
8 Laurel Cl
9 Forest Way
10 Larch Cl
11 Pine Cl
12 Alder Mews

13 Aspen Cl
14 Hargrave Park Prim Sch
15 Middlesex Univ (Archway Campus)
B3 **1** Calvert Ct
2 Academy The
3 Whitehall Mans
4 Pauntley St
5 Archway Hts
6 Pauntley Ho
7 St Aloysius RC Coll
C1 **1** Melchester Ho
2 Norcombe Ho
3 Weatherbury Ho
4 Wessex Ho
5 Archway Bsns Ctr
6 Harford Mews
7 Opera Ct
8 Rupert Ho
9 All Saints Church
C2 **1** Bowerman Ct
2 Gresham Pl
3 Hargrave Mans
4 Church Garth
5 John King Ct
6 Ramsey Ct
7 St John's Upper Holloway CE Prim Sch
8 Byam Shaw Sch of Art
C3 **1** Louise White Ho
2 Levison Way
3 Sanders Way
4 Birbeck Ho
5 Scholars Ct
6 Mount Carmel RC Tech Coll for Girls
C4 **1** Eleanor Rathbone Ho
2 Christopher Lo
3 Monkridge
4 Marbleford Ct
5 High London
6 Garton Ho
7 Hilltop Ho
8 Caroline Martyn Ho
9 Arthur Henderson Ho
10 Margaret Mcmillan Ho
11 Enid Stacy Ho

12 Mary McArthur Ho
13 Bruce Glasier Ho
14 John Wheatley Ho
15 Keir Hardie Ho
16 Monroe Ho
17 Iberia Ho
18 Lygoe Ho
19 Lambert Ho
20 Shelbourne Ho
21 Arkansas Ho
22 Lafitte Ho
23 Shreveport Ho
24 Packenham Ho
25 Orpheus Ho
26 Fayetville Ho
27 Bayon Ho

5

A1 **1** Northview
2 Tufnell Park Mans
3 Fulford Mans
4 Tollington Ho
5 Grafton Prim Sch
A2 **1** Bracey Mews
2 Christie Ct
3 Ringmer Gdns
4 Kingsdown Rd
5 Cottenham Ho
6 St Paul's Ct
7 Rickthorne Rd
8 Stanley Terr
9 Arundel Lo
10 Landseer Ct
11 St Mark's Prim Sch
A3 **1** Beeches The
2 Lambton Ct
3 Nugent Ct
4 Lambton Mews
5 Mews The
A4 **1** Marie Lloyd Gdns
2 Edith Cavell Cl
3 Marie Stopes Ct
4 Jessie Blythe La
5 Barbara Rudolph Ct
6 Hetty Rees Ct
7 Leyden Mans
8 Brambledown
9 Lochbie
10 Lyngham Ct
11 High Mount
12 Woodlands The
13 St Gildas' RC Jun Sch

B1 **1** Pakeman Prim Sch
2 London Meridian Coll
3 American Univ in London The
4 South Eastern Univ
5 Dean Coll of London
6 Montem Prim Sch
B2 **1** Berkeley Wlk
2 Lazar Wlk
3 Thistlewood Cl
4 Tomlins Wlk
5 Andover Ho
6 Barmouth Ho
7 Chard Ho
8 Christ the King RC Prim Sch
9 Methley Ho
10 Rainford Ho
11 Woodbridge Cl
12 Allerton Wlk
13 Falconer Wlk
14 Sonderburg Rd
15 St Mark's Mans
16 Athol Ct
17 Pooles Park Prim Sch
B3 **1** Lawson Ct
2 Wiltshire Ct
3 Fenstanton
4 Hutton Ct
5 Wisbech
6 Islington Arts & Media Sch
C2 **1** Brookfield
2 Churnfield
3 Cornwallis Sq

6

A1 **1** Hurlock Ho
2 Blackstock Ho
3 Vivian Comma Cl
4 Monsell Ct
A2 **1** Parkwood Prim Sch
2 Ambler Prim Sch
3 City & Islington Coll (Ctr for Life-long Learning)
B4 **1** Finmere Ho
2 Keynsham Ho
3 Kilpeck Ho
4 Knaresborough Ho

5 Leighfield Ho
6 Lonsdale Ho
7 Groveley Ho
8 Wensleydale Ho
9 Badminton Ct
C1 **1** Betty Layward Prim Sch
C2 **1** Chestnut Cl
2 Sycamore Ho
3 Lordship Ho
4 Clissold Ho
5 Beech Ho
6 Laburnum Ho
7 Ormond Ho
8 Yew Tree Ct
9 Oak Ho
C4 **1** Selwood Ho
2 Bnois Jerusalem Girls Sch
3 Mendip Ho
4 Ennerdale Ho
5 Getters Talmud Torah
6 Delamere Ho
7 Westwood Ho
8 Bernwood Ho
9 Allerdale Ho
10 Chattenden Ho
11 Farningham Ho
12 Oakend Ho

7

A1 **1** Gujarat Ho
2 Marton Rd
3 Painsthorpe Rd
4 Selkirk Ho
5 Defoe Ho
6 Edward Friend Ho
7 Sheridan Ho
8 Barrie Ho
9 Arnold Ho
10 Macaulay Ho
11 Stowe Ho
12 Carlyle Ho
13 Shaftesbury Ho
14 Lillian Cl
15 Swift Ho
16 Dryden Ho
17 Scott Ct
18 Kingsfield Ho
19 Uhura Sq
20 Hartopp Ct
A2 **1** Denman Ho

2 St Mary's Stoke
Newington CE Prim Sch
A3 1 Godstone Ct
2 Farnham Ct
3 Milford Ct
4 Cranleigh Ct
5 Haslemere Ct
6 Belmont Ct
7 Hockworth Ho
8 Garratt Ho
9 Fairburn Ho
10 Thorndale Ho
11 Oakdene Ho
12 Briardale Ho
A4 1 Beis Rochel
d'Satmar Girls Sch
3 Our Lady's Convent
RC High Sch
B1 1 Lawrence Bldgs
2 Cottage Wlk
3 Batley Pl
B2 1 Garnham St
2 Garnham Cl
3 Sanford La
4 Sanford Wlk
5 Abney Gdns
6 Fleet Wood
8 Simon Marks Jew-
ish Prim Sch
9 William Patten
Prim Sch
B3 1 Stamford Hill Mans
2 Montefiore Ct
3 Berwyn Ho
4 Clent Ho
5 Chiltern Ho
6 Laindon Ho
7 Pentland Ho
B4 1 Regent Ct
2 Stamford Lo
3 Holmwood Ct
4 Bobov Foundation
Sch
5 Yesodey Hatorah
Sec Sch for Girls
6 Lubavitch Boys
Prim Sch
7 Yesodey Hatorah
Jun Sch for Girls
8 Lubavitch Girls
Prim Sch
9 Lubavitch House
Sch (Jun Boys)
10 Skinners Company
Sch (Upper)
C1 1 Ravenscourt
2 Mellington Ct
3 Rendlesham Ho
4 Carroll Ct
5 St Scholastica's RC
Prim Sch
C2 1 Cazenove Mans
2 Chedworth Ho
3 Aldergrove Ho
4 Abbotstone Ho
5 Briggeford Cl
6 Inglethorpe Ho
7 Ashdown Ho
8 Epping Ho
9 Cypress Cl
C3 1 Stamford Gr E
2 Stamford Mans
3 Grove Mans
4 Stamford Gr W
5 Talmud-Torah
Yetev-Lev

8
A1 1 Beveridge Rd
2 Purcell Mews
3 George Lansbury
Ho
4 Charles Hobson Ho
5 Reade Wlk
6 Westbury Ho
7 Bridge Ct
8 St Joseph's RC
Prim Sch
9 Dixon Way
10 Armstrong Rd
11 Brittage Rd
A4 1 Grange Ct
2 Green Cl
C2 1 Regency Mews
2 Tudor Mews
3 Utopia Ho
4 Bell Flats
5 Angel Ct
6 St Andrew & St
Francis CE Prim
Sch

9
A2 1 St Mary Magdelen's
RC Jun Sch
2 Islamic Coll for
Advanced Studies
B2 1 Rutland Park Gdns
2 Rutland Park Mans
3 Queens Par
4 Harcourt Ho
5 Solidarity Ho
6 Electra Ct
7 Cassandra Ct
8 Carlton Ct
9 Convent of Jesus &
Mary RC Inf Sch
C4 1 Oaklands Mews
2 Acer Ct
3 Maple Ct
4 Argyle Mans

10
A1 1 Christ Church Ct
2 Paul Daisley Ct
3 Fountain Ho
4 Kingston Ho
5 Waverley Ct
6 Weston Ho
7 Mapes Ho
8 Athelstan Gdns
9 Leff Ho
10 Brondesbury Coll
for Boys
B1 1 Alma Birk Ho
2 Brooklands St
3 Brooklands Court
Apartments
4 Cleveland Mans
5 Buckley Ct
6 Webheath
C1 1 Linstead St
2 Embassy Ho
3 Acol Ct
4 Kings Wood Ct
5 Douglas Ct
6 King's Gdns
7 Carlton Mans
8 Smyrna Mews
9 New Priory Ct
10 Queensgate Pl
11 Brondesbury Mews
12 St Eugene de Maz-
enod RC Prim Sch

C2 1 Dene Mans
2 Sandwell Cres
3 Sandwell Mans
4 Hampstead West
5 Redcroft
C3 1 Orestes Mews
2 Walter Northcott
Ho
3 Polperro Mans
4 Lyncroft Mans
5 Marlborough Mans
6 Alexandra Mans
7 Cumberland Mans
8 Cavendish Mans
9 Ambassador Ct
10 Welbeck Mans
11 Inglewood Mans
12 Dennington Park
Mansions
C4 1 Parsifal Coll

11
A2 1 Beswick Mews
2 Worcester Mews
3 Minton Mews
4 Doulton Mews
5 Laurel Ho
6 Sandalwood Ho
7 Iroko Ho
8 Banyan Ho
9 Rosewood Ho
10 Ebony Ho
11 Rosemont Mans
12 Exeter Mews
B1 1 Harrold Ho
2 Glover Ho
3 Byron Ct
4 Nalton Ho
B2 1 Petros Gdns
2 Heath Ct
3 Imperial Twrs
4 Fairhurst
5 St John's Ct
6 New College Ct
7 Chalford
8 Rosslyn Mans
9 Sutherland Ho
10 Holy Trinity CE Prim
Sch
11 Phoenix Sch The
12 North Bridge House
Sch
13 Southbank Interna-
tional Sch
B3 1 Arkwright Mans
2 Hatstone Ct
3 Hampstead High
Sch
B4 1 Windmill Mans
2 Highgrove Point
3 Gainsborough Ho
4 Holly Bush Hill
5 Heath Mans
6 Holly Bush Steps
7 Pavilion Ct
8 Holly Berry La
9 New Campden Ct
10 Holly Bush Vale
11 Benham's Pl
12 Prospect Pl
13 Yorkshire Grey Pl
14 Gardnor Mans
15 Ellerdale Cl
16 Monro Ho
17 Prince Arthur
Mews
18 Prince Arthur Ct

19 Village Mount
20 Perrin's Ct
21 Wells Ct
22 Bakers Pas
23 Spencer Wlk
24 Bird In Hand Yd
25 Kings Well
26 New Ct
27 Streatley Pl
28 Mansfield Ct
29 Upper Hampstead
Wlk
30 Hampstead Paro-
chial CE Prim Sch
31 Univ Coll Jun Sch
32 Heathside Prep Sch
33 New End Prim Sch
34 Sisters of St Mar-
cellina Sch
C1 1 New College Par
2 Northways Par
3 Noel Ho
4 Campden Ho
5 Centre Hts
6 Hickes Ho
7 Swiss Terr
8 Leitch Ho
9 Jevons Ho
10 Langhorne Ct
11 Park Lo
12 Avenue Lo
13 Frank Barnes Sch
14 Swiss Cottage Sch
C2 1 Belsize Park Mews
2 Baynes Mews
3 McCrone Mews
4 South Hampstead
High Sch
C3 1 Belsize Court
Garages
2 Roscommon Ho
3 Akenside Ho
4 Fitzjohns Prim Sch
5 St Christopher's
Sch
6 St Anthony's Sch
C4 1 White Bear Pl
2 Wells Ho The
3 Boades Mews
4 Flask Cotts
5 Coach House Yd
6 Pilgrim's Pl
7 Rosslyn Mews
8 Royal Sch Hamp-
stead The
9 Academy Sch The

12
A2 1 Banff Ho
2 Glenloch Ct
3 Havercourt
4 Holmefield Ct
5 Gilling Ct
6 Howitt Cl
7 Manor Mans
8 Straffan Lo
9 Romney Ct
10 Lancaster Stables
11 Eton Garages
12 Hampstead Coll
of Fine Arts &
Humanities
A3 1 Hampstead Hill Sch
B1 1 Hancock Nunn Ho
2 Higginson Ho
3 Duncan Ho
4 Mary Wharrie Ho

12 C2   291

5 Rockstraw Ho
6 Cleaver Ho
7 Chamberlain St
8 Sharples Hall St
9 Primrose Mews
10 Rothwell St
11 St Georges Mews
B2 1 Alder Ho
2 Hornbeam Ho
3 Whitebeam Ho
4 Aspen Ho
5 Rowan Ho
6 Beech Ho
7 Chestnut Ho
8 Oak Ho
9 Willow Ho
10 Sycamore Ho
11 Maple Ho
12 Hazel Ho
13 Elaine Ct
14 Faircourt
15 Walham Ct
16 Stanbury Ct
17 Priory Mans
18 Wellington Ho
19 Grange The
B3 1 Cayford Ho
2 Du Maurier Ho
3 Isokon Flats
4 Palgrave Ho
5 Garnett Ho
6 Stephenson Ho
7 Park Dwellings
8 Siddons Ho
9 Mall Studios
10 Park Hill Wlk
11 Wordsworth Pl
12 Fraser Regnart Ct
13 St Pancras Alm-
shouses
14 St Dominic RC
Prim Sch
15 Fleet Prim Sch
C1 1 Bridge Ho
2 Hardington
3 Mead Cl
4 Rugmere
5 Tottenhall
6 Beauvale
7 Broomfield
8 Camden Coll of
English
C2 1 Silverbirch Wlk
2 Penshurst
3 Wingham
4 Westwell
5 Chislet
6 Burmarsh
7 Shipton Ho
8 Stonegate
9 Leysdown
10 Headcorn
11 Lenham
12 Halstow
13 Fordcombe
14 Cannington
15 Langridge
16 Athlone Ho
17 Pentland Ho
18 Beckington
19 Hawkridge
20 Edington
21 Rhyl Prim Sch
22 Haverstock Sch

13

A1
1 Ferdinand Ho
2 Harwood Ho
3 Hawley Rd
4 Hawley Mews
5 Leybourne St
6 Barling
7 Tiptree
8 Havering
9 Candida Ct
10 Lorraine Ct
11 Donnington Ct
12 Welford Ct
13 Torbay Ct
14 Bradfield Ct
15 Torbay St
16 Water La
17 Leybourne St
18 Haven St
19 Stucley Pl
20 Lawrence Ho
21 Chalcot Sch
22 Holy Trinity & Saint Silas CE Prim Sch
23 Hawley Inf Sch

A2
1 Ashington
2 Priestley Ho
3 Leonard Day Ho
4 Old Dairy Mews
5 Monmouth Ho
6 Alpha Ct
7 Una Ho
8 Widford
9 Heybridge
10 Roxwell
11 Hamstead Gates
12 Kingsway Coll

A4
1 Denyer Ho
2 Stephenson Ho
3 Trevithick Ho
4 Brunel Ho
5 Newcomen Ho
6 Faraday Ho
7 Winifrede Paul Ho
8 Wardlow
9 Fletcher Ct
10 Tideswell
11 Grangemill
12 Hambrook Ct
13 Calver

B1
1 Cherry Tree Ct
2 Chichester Ct
3 Durdans Ho
4 Philia Ho
5 Bernard Shaw Ct
6 Foster Ct
7 Bessemer Ct
8 Hogarth Ct
9 Rochester Ct
10 Soane Ct
11 Wallett Ct
12 Inwood Ct
13 Wrotham Rd
14 St Thomas Ct
15 Caulfield Ct
16 Bruges Pl
17 Reachview Cl
18 Lawfords Wharf

B3
1 Eleanor Ho
2 Falkland Pl
3 Kensington Ho
4 Willingham Cl
5 Kenbrook Ho
6 Aborfield
7 Great Field
8 Appleford
9 Forties The
10 Maud Wilkes Cl
11 Dunne Mews
12 Dowdeny Cl
13 Kentish Town CE Prim Sch

B4
1 Benson Ct
2 Tait Ho
3 Manorfield Cl
4 Greatfield Cl
5 Longley Ho
6 Lampson Ho
7 Davidson Ho
8 Palmer Ho
9 Lambourn Cl
10 Morris Ho
11 Owen Ho
12 Eleanor Palmer Prim Sch

C1
1 Hillier Ho
2 Gairloch Ho
3 Cobham Mews
4 Bergholt Mews
5 Blakeney Cl
6 Weavers Way
7 Allensbury Pl

C2
1 Rawstock
2 Peckwater Ho
3 Wolsey Ho
4 Pandian Way
5 Busby Mews
6 Caledonian Rd
7 Canal Bvd
8 Northpoint Sq
9 Lock Mews
10 Carters Cl
11 York Ho
12 Hungerford Rd
13 Cliff Road Studios
14 Cliff Ct
15 Camelot Ho
16 Church Studios
17 Camden Terr
18 Brecknock Prim Sch
19 Hungerford Prim Sch

C3
1 Blake Ho
2 Quelch Ho
3 Lee Ho
4 Willbury Ho
5 Howell Ho
6 Holmsbury Ho
7 Leith Ho
8 Betchworth Ho
9 Rushmore Ho
10 Dugdale Ho
11 Horsendon Ho
12 Colley Ho
13 Coombe Ho
14 Ivinghoe Ho
15 Buckhurst Ho
16 Saxonbury Ct
17 Charlton Ct
18 Apollo Studios
19 Barn Cl
20 Long Meadow
21 Landleys Field
22 Margaret Bondfield Ho
23 Haywood La
24 Torriano Jun & Inf Schs

C4
1 Fairlie Ct
2 Trecastle Way
3 Dalmeny Avenue Est
4 Hyndman Ho
5 Carpenter Ho
6 Graham Ho
7 Tufnell Mans

14

A2
1 Clock Tower Pl
2 Clock View Cres
3 Jim Veal Dr
4 Gower Sch The

A3
1 Kimble Ho
2 Saxonbury Ct
3 Poynder Ct
4 Moulsford Ho

A4
1 Arcade The
2 Macready Pl
3 Cardwell Rd
4 Mcmorran Ho
5 Crayford Ho
6 Whitby Ct
7 Prospect Pl
8 City & Islington Coll (Ctr for Bsns, Arts & Technology)

B1
1 Kerwick Cl
2 Rydston Cl
3 Skegness Ho
4 Frederica St
5 Ponder St
6 Kings Ct
7 Freeling St
8 Coatbridge Ho
9 Tilloch St

B2
1 Burns Ho
2 Scott Ho
3 Wellington Mews
4 Roman Ct
5 Piccadilly Ct
6 Knowledge Point Sch

B3
1 Culverin Cl
2 Garand Ct
3 Mount Carmel

B4
1 Buckmaster Ho
2 Loreburn Ho
3 Cairns Ho
4 Halsbury Ho
5 Chelmsford Ho
6 Cranworth Ho
7 City & Islington Coll (Ctr for Health, Social & Child Care)

C1
1 Mountfort Terr
2 Avon Ho
3 Buckland Ho
4 Dovey Lo
5 Carfree Cl
6 Mitchell Ho
7 New College Mews
8 Lofting Ho
9 Brooksby Ho
10 Cara Ho
11 Thornhill Prim Sch
12 North London Science Ctr

C2
1 London Metropolitan Univ (Spring Ho)

C3
1 Slaney Pl
2 Eastwood Cl
3 Milton Ho
4 Hartnoll Ho
5 St James School Flats
6 Widnes Ho
7 Tranmere Ho
8 Victoria Mans
9 Formby Ct
10 Mersey Ho
11 Birkenhead Ho
12 Drayton Park Mews
13 Drayton Park Prim Sch

15

A1
1 Islington Park Mews
2 Evelyn Denington Ct
3 Bassingbourn Ho
4 Cadmore Ho
5 Adstock Ho
6 Garston Ho
7 Flitton Ho
8 Datchworth Ho
9 Battishill St
10 Almeida St
11 Edward's Cotts
12 Hyde's Pl
13 Tyndale Terr
14 Spriggs Ho
15 Barratt Ho
16 Spencer Pl
17 Chadston Ho
18 Whiston Ho
19 Wakelin Ho
20 Tressel Cl
21 Canonbury Ct
22 Halton Ho
23 Shillingford St
24 Highbury Mans
25 Premier Ho
26 Waterloo Gdns
27 William Tyndale Prim Sch

A2
1 Hampton Ct
2 Salisbury Ho
3 Canonbury Prim Sch
4 Laycock Prim Sch

A3
1 De Barowe Mews
2 Fieldview Ct
3 Viewpoint
4 Ashurst Lo
5 Highbury Fields
6 London Metropolitan Univ (Ladbroke Ho)
7 Robinswood Mews

A4
1 Chestnuts The
2 Bowen Ct
3 Peckett Sq
4 De Barowe Mews

B1
1 Astey's Row
2 Lincoln Ho
3 Worcester Ho
4 Melville Pl
5 Wontner Cl
6 Hedingham Cl
7 Laundry La
8 Base Apartments
9 Walkinshaw Ct
10 New Bentham Ct
11 Bentham Ct
12 Haslam Ho
13 Horsfield Ho
14 Riverside Ho
15 Eric Fletcher Ct
16 Annette Cres
17 Ashby Ho
18 Lindsey Mews
19 Cardigan Wlk
20 Red House Sq
21 Orchard Cl
22 Queensbury St
23 Raynor Pl

B2
1 Crowline Wlk
2 Upper Handa Wlk
3 Handa Wlk
4 Lismore Wlk
5 Bardsey Wlk
6 Walney Wlk
7 Upper Bardsey Wlk
8 Upper Lismore Wlk
9 Sark Ho
10 Guernsey Ho
11 Guernsey Ho
12 Sybil Thorndike Ho
13 Clephane Rd
14 Florence Nightingale Ho
15 Jersey Ho
16 Jethou Ho
17 Islay Wlk
18 Upper Caldy Wlk
19 Caldy Wlk
20 Alderney Ho
21 Gulland Wlk
22 Nightingale Rd
23 Upper Gulland Wlk
24 Church Rd
25 Oransay Rd
26 Canonbury Yd E

B3
1 Pearfield Ho
2 Larchfield Ho
3 Beresford Terr
4 Pondfield Ho
5 Ashfield Ho
6 Elmfield Ho
7 Highbury Grove Sch

B4
1 Fountain Mews
2 Woodstock Ho
3 Henson Ct
4 Taverner Sq

C1
1 Downham Ct
2 Trafalgar Point

C2
1 John Kennedy Ct
2 John Kennedy Lo
3 Ball's Pond Pl
4 Haliday Wlk
5 Queen Elizabeth Ct
6 Canonbury Hts
7 Pinnacle The
8 Threadgold Ho
9 Wakeham St
10 Saffron Ct
11 Callaby Terr
12 Tilney Gdns
13 Westcliff Ho
14 Ilford Ho
15 Ongar Ho
16 Greenhills Terr
17 Romford Ho
18 Bute Wlk
19 Upper Ramsey Wlk
20 Rona Wlk
21 Thorndike Rd
22 St Pauls Steiner Sch

C3
1 Newington Green Prim Sch

C4
1 Ledo Ho
2 Salween Ho
3 Prome Ho

4 Arakan Ho
5 Rangoon Ho
6 Mandalay Ho
7 Karen Ho
8 Wingate Ho
9 Jubet Ho
10 Orde Ho
11 Chindit Ho
12 Mabel Thornton Ho
13 Crawshay Ho
14 Avon Ho
15 Connaught Mans
16 Jonson Ho
17 Herrick Ho
18 Donne Ho
19 Thirlmere Ho
20 Grasmere Ho

16
A1 1 Dorchester Ct
2 Wareham Ho
3 Dorset Ct
4 Stratton Ct
5 Swanage Ct
6 Blandford Ct
7 Portland Ct
8 Oscar Faber Pl
9 Metropolitan Bsns Ctr
10 Lancaster Ct
11 Palazzo Apartments
12 Watercress Pl
A2 1 Kingsland Gn
2 Kingsland Pas
3 Metropolitan Benefit Societies Almshouses
4 Nimrod Pas
5 De Beauvoir Pl
6 Warburton Ct
7 Buckingham Mews
8 Aztec Ct
10 Kerridge Ct
11 Isabella Mews
12 St Jude & St Paul's CE Prim Sch
13 De Beauvoir Prim Sch
14 Our Lady & St Joseph RC Prim Sch
15 Childrens House Upper Sch
A3 1 Hewling Ho
2 Matthias Ho
3 Port Royal Pl
4 Cressington Cl
5 King Henry's Yd
6 Bronte Ho
7 Sewell Ho
8 Lydgate Ho
9 Patmore Ho
10 Congreve Ho
11 Elton St
12 Conrad Ho
13 Southwell Ho
14 Neptune Ho
15 Campion Ho
16 Webster Ho
17 Meredith Ho
18 Beckford Ho
19 Ashley Ct
20 Hayling Ct
21 Millard Cl
22 Lydford Cl
23 Salcombe Rd

24 Truman's Rd
25 Templeton Cl
26 John Campbell Rd
27 Gillett Pl
28 Bradbury St
29 Thomas Crowell Ct
A4 1 Londesborough Ho
2 Knebworth Ho
3 Knebworth Rd
4 Bransby Ct
5 Imperial Ave
6 Leonard Pl
7 Shakspeare Mews
8 Binyon Ho
9 Shelley Ho
10 Browning Ho
11 Burns Ho
12 Andrew Marvell Ho
13 Wycliffe Ho
14 Blake Ho
15 Marlowe Ho
16 Fletcher Ho
17 Chaucer Ct
18 St Matthias's CE Prim Sch
B1 1 Hilborough Rd
2 Shoreditch Ct
3 Evergreen Sq
4 Wyndhams Ct
5 Festival Ct
6 Fortune Ct
7 Rose Ct
8 Ability Plaza
9 Briar Ct
10 Lomas Dr
11 Queensbridge Jun Sch
B2 1 Prospect Ho
2 Woodland St
3 Crosby Wlk
4 Kirkland Wlk
5 Bowness Cl
6 Carlisle Wlk
7 Skelton Cl
8 Camerton Cl
9 Buttermere Wlk
10 Houghton Cl
11 Hayton Cl
12 Kingsland Sh Ctr
13 Springfield Ho
14 Parton Lo
15 Sanctuary Mews
16 Fenton Cl
B3 1 Miller's Terr
2 Chow Sq
3 Drysdale Flats
4 Gateway Mews
5 Birkbeck Mews
6 Winchester Pl
B4 1 Coronation Ave
2 Morris Blitz Ct
3 Shacklewell Ho
4 Alexandra Ct
5 Shacklewell Prim Sch
6 Princess May Prim Sch
C1 1 Aldington Ct
2 Bayton Ct
3 Rochford Wlk
4 Windrush Ct
5 Gayhurst Prim Sch
C2 3 Burdon Ct
4 Thomson Ct
5 Bruno Ct
6 Thackeray Mews

7 Madinah Rd
C3 1 Kingsdown Ho
2 Glendown Ho
3 Moredown Ho
4 Blakeney Cl
5 Beeston Cl
6 Benabo Ct
7 David Devine Ho
8 Kreedman Wlk
9 Hermitage Row
10 Grafton Ct
11 Lushington Terr
12 Aspen Ct
13 Pykewell Lo
14 Albion Works Studios

17
A1 1 Fortescue Ave
2 Pemberton Pl
3 Weston Wlk
4 Bayford St Ind Ctr
5 Bayford St
6 Sidworth St
7 Helmsley St
8 Cyntra Pl
9 Signal Ho
10 All Nations Ho
11 Vanguard Ho
12 Hacon Sq
A2 1 Bohemia Pl
2 Graham Mans
3 Marvin St
4 Boscobel Ho
5 Royal Oak Rd
6 Colonnades The
7 Sylvester Ho
8 Sylvester Path
9 Doctor Spurstowe Almshouses
10 Great Eastern Bldgs
11 Sojourner-Truth Cl
A3 1 Birchington Ho
2 Bicknor Ho
3 Boxley Ho
4 Adisham Ho
5 Cranbrook Ho
6 Marden Ho
7 Broome Ho
8 Crandale Ho
9 Cheriton Ho
10 Ditton Ho
11 Langley Ho
12 Dymchurch Ho
13 Elham Ho
14 Davina Ho
15 Pembury Ho
16 Downs Ct
17 Perrywood Ho
18 Staplehurst Ho
19 Pegwell Ho
20 Yalding Ho
21 Northbourne Ho
22 Monkton Ho
23 Milsted Ho
24 Athlone Cl
25 Clarence Pl
26 Gould Terr
27 Quested Ct
28 Brett Pas
29 Marcon Ct
30 Appleton Ct
31 Institute Pl
A4 1 Ross Ct
2 Downs La
3 Gaviller Pl
4 Robert Owen Lo

5 Apprentice Way
6 Arrowe Ct
7 Gilwell Ct
8 Sutton Ct
9 St Andrews Mans
10 Kinnoull Mans
11 Rowhill Mans
12 Sladen Pl
13 Mothers Sq The
14 Richborough Ho
15 Sandgate Ho
16 Sheppey Ho
B1 1 Pitcairn Ho
2 Lyme Grove Ho
3 Shakespeare Ho
4 Upcott Ho
5 Loddiges Ho
6 Parkinson Ho
7 Sloane Ho
8 Vanbrugh Ho
9 Cambridge Pas
10 Lyttleton Ho
11 Victoria Park Ct
12 Tullis Ho
13 Fairchild Ho
14 Forsyth Ho
15 Tradescant Ho
16 Mason Ho
17 Capel Ho
18 Cordwainers Ct
19 Bridgeman Ho
20 St Thomas's Pl
21 Barclay Ho
22 Clayton Ho
23 Danby Ho
24 Sherard Ho
25 Catesby Ho
26 Petiver Cl
27 Leander Ct
28 Philip Turner Est
29 Grendon Ho
30 Shore Mews
31 Shore Bsns Ctr
32 Classic Mans
33 Tudor Ho
34 Park Ho
35 Enterprise Ho
36 Alpine Gr
37 Clarendon Cl
38 Rotheley Ho
39 Bernie Grant Ho
40 Orchard Prim Sch
41 St John of Jerusalem CE Prim Sch
B2 1 Woolpack Ho
2 Elvin Ho
3 Thomas Ho
4 Hockley Ho
5 Retreat Ho
6 Butfield Ho
7 Brooksbank Ho
8 Cresset Ho
9 Brooksbank St
10 Lennox Ho
11 Milborne Ho
12 Collent Ho
13 Middlesex Pl
14 Elsdale Ho
15 Devonshire Hall
16 Brent Ho
17 Morningside Prim Sch
18 Hackney Free & Parochial CE Sec Sch

B3 1 St John & St James CE Prim Sch
C1 1 Stuart Ho
2 Gascoyne Ho
3 Chelsfield Point
4 Sundridge Ho
5 Banbury Ho
6 Lauriston Ho
C2 1 Musgrove Ho
2 Cheyney Ho
3 Haynes Ho
4 Warner Ho
5 Gilby Ho
6 Gadsden Ho
7 Risley Ho
8 Baycliffe Ho
9 Sheldon Ho
10 Offley Ho
11 Latimer Ho
12 Ribstone Ho
13 Salem Ho
14 Fieldwick Ho
15 Lever Ct
16 Matson Ho
17 Wilding Ho
18 Rennell Ho
19 Dycer Ho
20 Granard Ho
21 Whitelock Ho
22 Harrowgate Ho
23 Cass Ho
24 Lofts on the Park
25 Heathcote Point
26 Ravenscroft Point
27 Vanner Point
28 Hensley Point
29 San Ho
30 Berger Prim Sch
C4 1 Cromford Path
2 Longford Ct
3 Overbury Ho
4 Heanor Ct
5 Wharfedale Ct
6 Ladybower Ct
7 Ilkeston Ct
8 Derby Ct
9 Rushmore Cres
10 Blackwell Cl
11 Belper Ct
12 Rushmore Prim Sch

18
A2 1 Chigwell Ct
2 Wellday Ho
3 Selman Ho
4 Vaine Ho
5 Trower Ho
6 St Dominics RC Prim Sch
B2 1 Mallard Cl
2 Merriam Ave
3 Gainsborough St
4 Palace Cl
5 St Anthony's Cl
6 Trowbridge Est
B3 1 Wick Village

19
C1 1 Service Route No 2
2 Service Route No 3
3 Newham Sixth Form Coll (Stratford Ctr)

C4 **1** Mulberry Ct
2 Rosewood Ct
3 Gean Ct
4 Blackthorn Ct
5 Cypress Ct

20

C4 **1** Carlyle Rd
2 Bernard Shaw Ho
3 Longlents Ho
4 Mordaunt Ho
5 Wilmers Ct
6 Stonebridge Ctr
7 Shakespeare Ave
8 Southcroft
9 Brent Adult Comm
Education Service
Coll

21

A3 **1** Futters Ct
2 Barrett Ct
3 Elms The
4 Fairlight Ct
B3 **1** New Crescent Yd
2 Harlesden Plaza
3 St Josephs Ct
4 Jubilee Ct
5 Ellery Cl

22

B1 **1** Princess Alice Ho
2 Yoxall Ho
3 Yorkley Ho
4 Northaw Ho
5 Oakham Ho
6 Markyate Ho
7 Letchmore Ho
8 Pagham Ho
9 Quendon Ho
10 Redbourn Ho
11 Ketton Ho
12 Hillman Dr
C2 **1** Westfield Ct
2 Tropical Ct
3 Chamberlayne
Mans
4 Quadrant The
5 Queens Park Ct
6 Warfield Yd
7 Regent St
8 Cherrytree Ho
9 Artisan Mews
10 Artisan Quarter

23

A1 **1** Sycamore Wlk
2 Westgate Bsns Ctr
3 Buspace Studios
4 Bosworth Ho
5 Golborne Gdns
6 Appleford Ho
7 Adair Twr
8 Gadsden Ho
9 Southam Ho
10 Norman Butler Ho
11 Thompson Ho
12 Wells Ho
13 Paul Ho
14 Olive Blythe Ho
15 Katherine Ho
16 Breakwell Ct
17 Pepler Ho

18 Edward Kennedy
Ho
19 Winnington Ho
20 Queen's Park Prim
Sch
21 Middle Row Prim
Sch
22 St Mary RC Prim
Sch
23 St Thomas' CE Prim
Sch
A2 **1** Selby Sq
2 Severn Ave
3 Stansbury Sq
4 Tolhurst Dr
5 John Fearon Wlk
6 Mundy Ho
7 Macfarren Ho
8 Bantock Ho
9 Banister Ho
10 Batten Ho
11 Croft Ho
12 Courtville Ho
13 Mounsey Ho
14 Bliss Mews
15 Symphony Mews
B1 **1** Octavia Mews
2 Russell's Wharf
3 Western Ho
4 Kelly Mews
5 Queen Elizabeth II
Jubilee Sch
B2 **1** Boyce Ho
2 Farnaby Ho
3 Danby Ho
4 Purday Ho
5 Naylor Ho
6 St Judes Ho
7 Leeve Ho
8 Longhurst Ho
9 Harrington Ct
10 Mulberry Ct
11 Kilburn Ho
12 Carlton Vale Inf Sch
B3 **1** Claremont Ct
2 William Saville Ho
3 Western Ct
4 Bond Ho
5 Crone Ct
6 Wood Ho
7 Winterleys
8 Carlton Ho
9 Fiona Ct
C1 **1** Kilburn Park Sch
2 Westside Ct
3 Byron Mews
4 Sutherland Ct
5 Fleming Cl
6 Hermes Ct
7 St Peter's CE Prim
Sch
8 Paddington Acad
C2 **1** Pentland Rd
2 Nelson Cl
3 Pavilion Ct
4 Masefield Ho
5 Austen Ho
6 Fielding Ho
7 Argo Bsns Ctr
8 John Ratcliffe Ho
9 Wymering Mans
10 City of Westminster
Coll, Queens Park
Ctr
11 Essendine Prim
Sch
C3 **1** Wells Ct

2 Cambridge Ct
3 Ely Ct
4 Durham Ct
5 St Augustine's CE
High Sch
6 Sch of the Islamic
Republic of Iran
The
C4 **1** Ryde Ho
2 Glengall Pass
3 Leith Yd
4 Daynor Ho
5 Varley Ho
6 Sandby Ho
7 Colas Mews
8 Bishopsdale Ho
9 Lorton Ho
10 Marshwood Ho
11 Ribblesdale Ho
12 Holmesdale Ho
13 Kilburn Vale Est
14 Kilburn Bridge
15 Coll of NW London
16 St Mary's Kilburn
CE Prim Sch

24

A2 **1** Pimlico Wlk
2 Aske Ho
3 Hathaway Ho
4 Haberdasher Pl
5 Fairchild Ho
6 Burtt Ho
7 Enfield Cloisters
8 McGregor Ct
9 Royal Oak Ct
10 Hoxton Mkt
11 Bath Pl
12 Chapel Pl
13 Standard Pl
14 Cleeve Workshops
15 Cleeve Ho
16 Printing House Yd
17 Perseverance
Works
18 Crooked Billet Yd
19 Drysdale Ho
20 Castlefrank Ho
21 School App
22 Basing House Yd
23 Mail Coach Yd
24 St Monica's RC
Prim Sch
25 Symister Mews
26 Hackney Com Coll
A3 **1** Bracer Ho
2 Scorton Ho
3 Fern Cl
4 Macbeth Ho
5 Oberon Ho
6 Buckland Ct
7 Crondall Ct
8 Osric Path
9 Caliban Twr
10 Celia Ho
11 Juliet Ho
12 Bacchus Wlk
13 Malcolm Ho
14 Homefield St
15 Crondall Ho
16 Blanca Ho
17 Miranda Ho
18 Falstaff Ho
19 Charmian Ho
20 Myrtle Wlk
21 Arden Ho
22 Sebastian Ho

22 Stanway Ct
23 Jerrold St
24 Rosalind Ho
25 Cordelia Ho
26 Monteagle Ct
27 John Parry Ct
28 James Anderson Ct
29 Ben Jonson Ct
30 Sara Lane Ct
31 Walbrook Ct
32 Burbage Sch
A4 **1** Portelet Ct
2 Trinity Ct
3 Rozel Ct
4 St Helier Ct
5 Corbiere Ho
6 Kenning Ho
7 Higgins Ho
8 Cavell Ho
9 Girling Ho
10 Fulcher Ho
11 Francis Ho
12 Norris Ho
13 Kempton Ho
14 Nesham Ho
15 Crossbow Ho
16 Catherine Ho
17 Strale Ho
18 Horner Hos
19 Stringer Hos
20 Whitmore Ho
21 Nightingale Ho
22 Wilmer Gdns
23 Arrow Ho
24 Archer Ho
25 Meriden Ho
26 Rover Ho
27 Bowyer Ho
28 Tiller Ho
29 Canalside Studios
30 Kleine Wharf
31 Benyon Wharf
32 Quebec Wharf
33 Belvedere Ct
34 Portfleet Pl
B2 **1** Gorsuch Pl
2 Strout's Pl
3 Vaughan Est
4 George Loveless Ho
5 Baroness Rd
6 James Brine Ho
7 Arthur Wade Ho
8 Robert Owen Ho
9 Sivill Ho
10 Georgina Gdns
11 Old Market Sq
12 Cuff Point
13 Bakers Rents
14 Leopold Bldgs
15 Dunmore Point
16 Wingfield Ho
17 Gascoigne Pl
18 Mandela Ho
19 Virginia Rd
20 Briggs Ho
21 Packenham Ho
22 Gowan Ho
23 Kirton Gdns
24 Chambord St
25 Ducal St
26 Strickland Ho
27 Alliston Ho
28 Gibraltar Wlk
29 Equity Sq
30 Shacklewell St
31 Rochelle St
32 Sonning Ho

33 Culham Ho
34 Hurley Ho
35 Palissy St
36 Taplow Ho
37 Chertsey Ho
38 Sunbury Ho
39 Sunbury Work-
shops
40 Datchett Ho
41 Hocker St
42 Coll Sharp Ct
43 Marlow Studio
Workshops
44 Marlow Ho
45 Shiplake Ho
46 Wargrave Ho
47 Iffley Ho
48 Virginia Prim Sch
49 Bethnal Green Tech
Coll
B3 **1** Queensbridge Ct
2 Godwin Ho
3 Kent Ct
4 Brunswick Ho
5 Weymouth Ct
6 Sovereign Mews
7 Dunloe Ct
8 Cremer Bsns Ctr
9 James Hammett Ho
10 Allgood St
11 Horatio St
12 Cadell Ho
13 Horatio Ho
14 Shipton Ho
15 Haggerston Sch
16 Randal Cremer JMI
Sch
B4 **1** Hilborough Ct
2 Scriven Ct
3 Livermere Ct
4 Angrave Ct
5 Angrave Pas
6 Benfleet Ct
7 Belford Ho
8 Orme Ho
9 Clemson Ho
10 Longman Ho
11 Lowther Ho
12 Lovelace Ho
13 Harlowe Ho
14 Pamela Ho
15 Samuel Ho
16 Acton Ho
17 Loanda Ct
18 Phoenix Cl
19 Richardson Ct
20 Thrasher Ct
21 Mary Secole Cl
22 Canal Path
23 Pear Tree Ct
24 Hebden Ct
25 Charlton Ct
26 Laburnum Ct
27 Mansfield Ct
28 Garden Pl
29 Amber Wharf
30 Haggerston Studios
C1 **1** Bentworth Ct
2 Hawksmoor Pl
3 Kerbela St
4 Fuller Cl
5 Kinsham Ho
6 Menotti St
7 Barwell Ho
8 Grimsby St
9 Reflection Ho

10 Fleet Street Hill
11 Bratley St
12 Weaver Ho
13 Cornerstone Ct
14 Stuttle Ho
15 McGlashon Ho
16 John Pritchard Ho
17 Thomas Buxton Jun & Inf Sch
18 St Anne RC Prim Sch
19 William Davis Prim Sch
C2 1 Providence Yd
2 Lygon Ho
3 Brabner Ho
4 Delta St
5 Delta Point
6 Tillet Way
7 Mullet Gdns
8 Lampern Sq
9 Kite Pl
10 Elver Gdns
11 Cobden Ho
12 Eversley Ho
13 Lorden Wlk
14 Rapley Ho
15 Dence Ho
16 McKinnon Wood Ho
17 Satchwell Rd
18 Dickinson Ho
19 Hutton Ho
20 Simmons Ho
21 Swinton Ho
22 Yates Ho
23 Johnson Ho
24 Jeremy Bentham Ho
25 Waring Ho
26 St James Ct
27 Ebony Ho
28 Azure Ho
29 Westhope Ho
30 Hague St
31 Elizabeth Selby Inf Sch
32 Lawdale Jun Sch
C3 1 London Terr
2 Sturdee Ho
3 Maude Ho
4 Haig Ho
5 Jellicoe Ho
6 Ropley St
7 Guinness Trust Bldgs
8 Ion Ct
9 Columbia Rd
10 Moye Cl
11 Morrel Ct
12 Courtauld Ho
13 Drummond Ho
14 Gurney Ho
15 Atkinson Ho
16 Halley Ho
17 Goldsmith's Sq
18 Shahjalal Ho
19 Ken Wilson Ho
20 April Ct
21 Crofts Ho
22 Sebright Ho
23 Beechwood Ho
24 Gillman Ho
25 Cheverell Ho
26 Besford Ho
27 Dinmont Ho
28 Elizabeth Mews

29 Sebright Pas
30 Wyndham Deedes Ho
31 Sheppard Ho
32 Mary James Ho
33 Hadrian Est
34 Blythendale Ho
35 George Vale Ho
36 Lion Mills
37 St Peter's Ave
38 Pritchard Ho
39 Sebright Sch
C4 1 Broke Wlk
2 Rochemont Wlk
3 Marlborough Ave
4 Rivington Wlk
5 Magnin Cl
6 Gloucester Sq
7 Woolstone Ho
8 Marsworth Ho
9 Cheddington Ho
10 Linslade Ho
11 Cosgrove Ho
12 Blisworth Ho
13 Eleanor Ct
14 Wistow Ho
15 Muscott Ho
16 Boxmoor Ho
17 Linford Ho
18 Pendley Ho
19 Northchurch Ho
20 Debdale Ho
21 Broadway Market Mews
22 Welshpool Ho
23 Ada Ho
24 St Paul's with St Michael's Prim Sch

25

A1 1 Rochester Ct
2 Weaver Ct
3 Greenheath Bsns Ctr
4 Glass St
5 Herald St
6 Northesk Ho
7 Codrington Ho
8 Heathpool Ct
9 Mocatta Ho
10 Harvey Ho
11 Blackwood Ho
12 Rutherford Ho
13 Bullen Ho
14 Fremantle Ho
15 Pellew Ho
16 Ashington Ho
17 Dinnington Ho
18 Bartholomew Sq
19 Steeple Ct
20 Orion Ho
21 Fellbrigg St
22 Hague Prim Sch
23 Eagle Ho
24 Sovereign Ho
25 Redmill Ho
26 Berry Ho
27 Grindall Ho
28 Collingwood Ho
29 Stewart Headlam Prim Sch
A2 1 Charles Dickens Ho
2 Adrian Bolt Ho
3 William Rathbone Ho
4 Southwood Smith Ho

5 Rushmead
6 William Channing Ho
7 John Cartwright Ho
8 Charles Darwin Ho
9 Thomas Burt Ho
10 John Fielden Ho
11 Gwilym Maries Ho
12 Joseph Priestley Ho
13 Wear Pl
14 John Nettleford Ho
15 Thornaby Ho
16 Stockton Ho
17 Barnard Ho
18 Gainford Ho
19 Stapleton Ho
20 James Middleton Ho
21 Kedleston Wlk
22 Queen Margaret Flats
23 Hollybush Ho
24 Horwood Ho
25 Norden Ho
26 Newcourt Ho
27 Seabright St
28 Viaduct Pl
29 Sunlight Sq
30 Providence Row Cl
31 Oaklands Sec Sch
32 Raine's Foundation Lower Sch
33 Beatrice Tate Sch
A3 1 Dinmont St
2 Marian St
3 Claredale Ho
4 Keeling Ho
5 Maple St
6 Winkley St
7 Temple Dwellings
8 Argos Ho
9 Helen Ho
10 Lysander Ho
11 Antenor Ho
12 Paris Ho
13 Nestor Ho
14 Hector Ho
15 Ajax Ho
16 Achilles Ho
17 Priam Ho
18 Peabody Est
19 Felix St
20 Cambridge Cres
21 Peterley Bsns Ctr
22 Beckwith Ho
23 Brookfield Ho
24 Parminter Ind Est
25 Ted Roberts Ho
26 Cambridge Ct
27 Millennium Pl
28 William Caslon Ho
29 Hugh Platt Ho
30 West St
31 Mayfield Ho
32 Apollo Ho
33 Tanners Yd
34 Teesdale Yd
A4 1 Welshpool St
2 Broadway Ho
3 Regents Wharf
4 Warburton Ho
5 Warburton St
6 Triangle Rd
7 Warburton Rd
8 Williams Ho

10 Booth Cl
11 Albert Cl
12 King Edward Mans
13 Victoria Bldgs
14 Andrews Wharf
15 London Fields Prim Sch
16 Triangle The
17 Com Coll Hackney The
B1 1 William's Bldgs
2 Donegal Ho
3 Pelican Pas
4 Frederick Charrington Ho
5 Wickford Ho
6 Braintree Ho
7 Doveton Ho
8 Doveton St
9 Cephas Ho
10 Sceptre Ho
11 Bancroft Ho
12 Stothard St
13 Redclyf Ho
14 Winkworth Cotts
15 Amiel St
16 Hadleigh Ho
17 Hadleigh Cl
18 Ryder Ho
19 Kenton Ho
20 Colebert Ho
21 Ibbott St
22 Rickman Ho
23 Rickman St
24 Stothard Ho
25 Barbanel Ho
26 Stannard Cotts
27 St Peters Ct
28 Rennie Cotts
29 Pemell Cl
30 Pemell Ho
31 Leatherdale St
32 Gouldman Ho
33 Lamplighter Cl
34 Sherren Ho
35 Marlborough Lo
36 Hamilton Lo
37 Montgomery Lo
38 Cleveland Gr
39 Cromwell Lo
40 Bardsey Pl
41 Charrington Ho
42 Hayfield Yd
43 Allport Mews
44 Colin Winter Ho
45 John Scurr Prim Sch
B2 1 Mulberry Ho
2 Gretton Ho
3 Merceron Ho
4 Montfort Ho
5 Westbrook Ho
6 Sugar Loaf Wlk
7 Museum Ho
8 Burnham Est
9 Globe Terr
10 Moravian St
11 Shepton Hos
12 Mendip Hos
13 Academy Ct
14 Pepys Ho
15 Swinburne Ho
16 Moore Ho
17 Morris Ho
18 Burns Ho
19 Milton Ho
20 Whitman Ho

21 Shelley Ho
22 Keats Ho
23 Dawson Ho
24 Bradbeer Ho
25 Forber Ho
26 Hughes Ho
27 Silvester Ho
28 Rogers Est
29 Pavan Ct
30 Stafford Cripps Ho
31 Sidney Godley (VC) Ho
32 Butler Ho
33 Butler St
34 Thorne Ho
35 Bevin Ho
36 Tuscan Ho
37 Globe Prim Sch
38 Bangabandhu Prim Sch
39 Bonner Prim Sch
B3 1 Evesham Ho
2 James Campbell Ho
3 Thomas Hollywood Ho
4 James Docherty Ho
5 Ebenezer Mussel Ho
6 Jameson Ct
7 Edinburgh Cl
8 Roger Dowley Ct
9 Sherbrooke Ho
10 Calcraft Ho
11 Burrard Ho
12 Dundas Ho
13 Ponsonby Ho
14 Barnes Ho
15 Paget Ho
16 Maitland Ho
17 Chesil Ct
18 Reynolds Ho
19 Cleland Ho
20 Goodrich Ho
21 Rosebery Ho
22 Sankey Ho
23 Cyprus Pl
24 Royston St
25 Stainsbury St
26 Hunslett St
27 Baildon
28 Brockweir
29 Tytherton
30 Malmesbury
31 Kingswood
32 Colville Ho
33 St Elizabeth RC Prim Sch
34 Raine's Foundation Sch
35 St John's CE Prim Sch
36 Mowlem Prim Sch
B4 1 Halkett Ho
2 Christchurch Sq
3 Helena Pl
4 Swingfield Ho
5 Greenham Ho
6 Dinmore Ho
7 Anstey Ho
8 Weston Ho
9 Carbroke Ho
10 Bluebell Cl
11 Cherry Tree Cl

2 Hallings Wharf Studios
3 Poland Ho
4 Peter Heathfield Ho
5 Burford Rd
6 John F Kennedy Spel Sch
7 Univ of East London (Duncan Ho)

28

A1 1 Lantry Ct
2 Rosemount Ct
3 Moreton Twr
4 Acton Central Ind Est
5 Rufford Twr
6 Narrow St
7 Mount Pl
8 Sidney Miller Ct
9 Mill Hill Terr
10 Cheltenham Pl
11 Mill Hill Gr
12 Benjamin Ho
13 Arlington Ct
14 Lombard Ct
15 Steyne Ho
16 Acton & West London Coll
B1 1 Rectory Rd
2 Derwentwater Mans
3 Market Pl
4 Hooper's Mews
5 Cromwell Pl
6 Locarno Rd
7 Edgecote Ct
8 Harleyford Manor
9 Coopers Ct
10 Avingdon Ct
11 Steyne Ho
B3 1 Avon Ct
2 Bromley Lo
3 Walter Ct
4 Lynton Terr
5 Acton Ho
6 Fells Haugh
7 Springfield Ct
8 Tamarind Ct
9 Lynton Ct
10 Aspen Ct
11 Pegasus Ct
12 Friary Park Est
C3 1 Rosebank Gdns
2 Rosebank
3 Edinburgh Ho
4 Western Ct
5 Kilronan

30

A1 1 Arlington Ho
2 Lugard Ho
3 Shabana Ct
4 Sitarey Ct
5 Oaklands Ct
6 Davenport Mews
A2 1 Abercrombie Mews
2 Bathurst Ho
3 Brisbane Ho
4 Bentinck Ho
5 Ellenborough Ho
6 Lawrence Cl
7 Mackenzie Cl
8 Carteret Ho
9 Calvert Ho
10 Winthrop Ho
11 Auckland Ho

12 Blaxland Ho
13 Havelock Cl
14 Hargraves Ho
15 Hudson Cl
16 Phipps Ho
17 Lawson Ho
18 Hastings Ho
19 Wolfe Ho
20 Malabar Ct
21 Charnock Ho
22 Canning Ho
24 Cornwallis Ho
25 Commonwealth Ave
28 Champlain Ho
29 Grey Ho
30 Durban Ho
31 Baird Ho
32 Campbell Ho
33 Mitchell Ho
34 Denham Ho
35 Mackay Ho
36 Evans Ho
37 Davis Ho
38 Mandela Cl
A3 1 Holborn Ho
2 Clement Danes Ho
3 Vellacott Ho
4 O'Driscoll Ho
5 King Ho
6 Daley Ho
7 Selma Ho
8 Garrett Ho
B1 1 Linden Ct
2 Frithville Ct
3 Blomfield Mans
4 Poplar Mews
5 Hopgood St
6 Westwood Ho
7 Stanlake Mews
8 Stanlake Villas
9 Alexandra Mans
B3 1 Latimer Ind Est
2 Pankhurst Ho
3 Quadrangle The
4 Nightingale Ho
5 Gordon Ct
6 Ducane Ct
7 Browning Ho
8 Pavilion Terr
9 Ivebury Ct
10 Olympic Ho
B4 1 Galleywood Ho
2 Edgcott Ho
3 Cuffley Ho
4 Addlestone Ho
5 Hockliffe Ho
6 Sarratt Ho
7 Firle Ho
8 Sutton Est The
9 Terling Ho
10 Danes Ho
11 Udimore Ho
12 Vange Ho
13 Binbrook Ho
14 Yeadon Ho
15 Yatton Ho
16 Yarrow Ho
17 Clement Ho
18 Danebury
19 Coronation Ct
21 St Quintin Gdns
C1 1 St Katherine's Wlk
2 Dorrit Ho
3 Pickwick Ho
4 Dombey Ho

5 Caranday Villas
6 Mortimer Ho
7 Nickleby Ho
8 Stebbing Ho
9 Boxmoor Ho
10 Poynter Ho
11 Swanscombe Ho
12 Darnley Terr
13 Norland Ho
14 Hume Ho
15 Boundary Ho
16 Norland Rd
17 Helix Ct
C2 1 Frinstead Ho
2 Hurstway Wlk
3 Testerton Wlk
4 Grenfell Wlk
5 Grenfell Twr
6 Barandon Wlk
7 Treadgold Ho
8 St Clements Ct
9 Willow Way
10 Dora Ho
11 Carton Ho
12 Agnes Ho
13 Marley Ho
14 Estella Ho
15 Waynflete Sq
16 Pippin Ho
17 Baseline Business Studios
18 St Francis of Assisi Prim Sch
19 Nicholas Rd
C3 1 Kelfield Ct
2 Downing Ho
3 Crosfield Ct
4 Robinson Ho
5 Scampston Mews
6 Girton Villas
7 Ray Ho
8 Walmer Ho
9 Goodrich Ct
10 Arthur Ct
11 Whitstable Ho
12 Kingsnorth Ho
13 Bridge Ct
14 Prospect Ho
15 St Marks Rd
16 Whitchurch Ho
17 Blechynden Ho
18 Waynflete Sq
19 Bramley Ho
20 Dixon Ho
21 Oxford Gardens Prim Sch
22 Bassett House Sch
C4 1 Treverton Twr
2 Raymede Twr
3 Bruce Ho
4 Balfour Ho
5 Burleigh Ho
6 Sion-Manning RC Sch for Girls
7 St Charles RC Prim Sch
8 St Charles RC Sixth Form Coll

31

A3 1 Malton Mews
2 Lancaster Lo
3 Manning Ho
4 Galsworthy Ho
5 Hudson Ho
6 Cambourne Mews

7 Upper Talbot Wlk
8 Kingsdown Cl
9 Lower Clarendon Wlk
10 Talbot Grove Ho
11 Clarendon Wlk
12 Upper Clarendon Wlk
13 Camelford Wlk
14 Upper Camelford Wlk
15 Camelford Ct
16 Thomas Jones Prim Sch
17 Notting Hill Prep Sch
A4 1 Murchison Ho
2 Macaulay Ho
3 Chesterton Ho
4 Chiltern Ho
5 Lionel Ho
6 Watts Ho
7 Wheatstone Ho
8 Telford Ho
9 Golborne Mews
10 Millwood St
11 St Columb's Ho
12 Norfolk Mews
13 Lionel Mews
14 Kensington & Chelsea Coll
15 Bevington Prim Sch
16 Sion-Manning RC Sch for Girls
17 Lloyd Williamson Sch
B3 1 Silvester Ho
2 Golden Cross Mews
3 Tavistock Mews
4 Clydesdale Ho
5 Colville Prim Sch
6 Melchester
7 Pinehurst Ct
8 Denbigh Ho
B4 1 Blagrove Rd
2 All Saints Ho
3 Tavistock Ho
4 Leamington Ho
C3 1 Shottsford
2 Tolchurch
3 Casterbridge
4 Sandbourne
5 Anglebury
6 Weatherbury
7 Westbourne Gr Mews
8 Rosehart Mews
9 Viscount Ct
10 Hereford Mans
11 Hereford Mews
12 St Mary of the Angels RC Prim Sch
C4 1 Ascot Ho
2 Ashgrove Ct
3 Lockbridge Ct
4 Swallow Ct
5 Nightingale Lo
6 Hammond Lo
7 Penfield Lo
8 Harvey Lo
9 Hunter Lo
10 Barnard Lo
11 Falcon Lo
12 Johnson Lo
13 Livingstone Lo
14 Nuffield Lo

15 Finch Lo
16 Polesworth Ho
17 Oversley Ho
18 Derrycombe Ho
19 Buckshead Ho
20 Combe Ho
21 Culham Ho
22 Dainton Ho
23 Devonport Ho
24 Honwell Ho
25 Truro Ho
26 Sunderland Ho
27 Stonehouse Ho
28 Riverford Ho
29 Portishead Ho
30 Mickleton Ho
31 Keyham Ho
32 Moulsford Ho
33 Shrewsbury Mews
34 St Stephen's Mews
35 Westway Lo
36 Langley Ho
37 Brindley Ho
38 Radway Ho
39 Astley Ho
40 Willow Ct
41 Larch Ct
42 Elm Ct
43 Beech Ct
44 Worcester Ct
45 Union Ct
46 Leicester Ct
47 Kennet Ct
48 Oxford Ct
49 Fazerley Ct

32

A1 1 China Ct
2 Wellington Terr
3 Stevedore St
4 Portland Sq
5 Reardon Ho
6 Lowder Ho
7 Meeting House Alley
8 Farthing Fields
9 Oswell Ho
10 Park Lo
11 Doughty Ct
12 Inglefield Sq
13 Chopin's Ct
14 Welsh Ho
15 Hilliard Ho
16 Clegg St
17 Tasman Ho
18 Ross Ho
19 Wapping Dock St
20 Bridewell Pl
21 New Tower Bldgs
22 Tower Bldgs
23 Chimney Ct
24 Jackman Ho
25 Fenner Ho
26 Franklin Ho
27 Frobisher Ho
28 Flinders Ho
29 Chancellor Ho
30 Beechey Ho
31 Reardon Path
32 Parry Ho
33 Vancover Ho
34 Willoughby Ho
35 Sanctuary The
36 Dundee Ct

A1
37 Pierhead Wharf
38 Scandrett St
39 St Johns St

A2 1 Newton Ho
2 Richard Neale Ho
3 Maddocks Ho
4 Cornwall St
5 Brockmer Ho
6 Dellow Ho
7 Bewley Ho
8 Artichoke Hill
9 Queen Anne Terr
10 King Henry Terr
11 King Charles Terr
12 Queen Victoria Terr
13 Sovereign St
14 Princes Court Bsns Ctr
15 Kingsley Mews
16 Mulberry Sch for Girls

A3 1 Peter Best Ho
2 Mellish Ho
3 Porchester Ho
4 Dickson Ho
5 Joscoyne Ho
6 Silvester Ho
7 Wilton Ct
8 Sarah Ho
9 Bridgen Ho
10 Tylney Ho
11 Greenwich Ct
12 Damien Ct
13 Philson Mans
14 Siege Ho
15 Jacob Mans
16 Proud Ho
17 Sly St
18 Barnett St
19 Kinder St
20 Richard St
21 Hungerford St
22 Colstead Ho
23 Melwood Ho
24 Wicker St
25 Langdale St
26 Chapman Ho
27 Burwell Cl
28 Walford Ho
29 Welstead Ho
30 Norton Ho
31 Turnour Ho
32 Luke Ho
33 Dunch St
34 Sheridan St
35 Brinsley St
36 Spencer Way
37 Madani Girls Sch
38 East End Computing & Bsns Coll
39 Mulberry Sch for Girls
40 Jamiatul Ummah Sch
41 Bigland Green Prim Sch

A4 1 Wodeham Gdns
2 Castlemaine St
3 Court St
4 Ashfield St
5 London Hospital Dental Inst

6 Princess Alexandra School of Nursing
B1 1 John Rennie Wlk
2 Malay Ho
3 Wainwright Ho
4 Riverside Mans
5 Shackleton Ho
6 Whitehorn Ho
7 Wavel Ct
8 Prusom's Island
9 St Peter's CE Prim Sch

B2 1 Shadwell Pl
2 Gosling Ho
3 Vogler Ho
4 Donovan Ho
5 Knowlden Ho
6 Chamberlain Ho
7 Moore Ho
8 Thornewill Ho
9 Fisher Ho
10 All Saints Ct
11 Coburg Dwellings
12 Lowood Ho
13 Solander Gdns
14 Chancery Bldgs
15 Ring Ho
16 Juniper St
17 Gordon Ho
18 West Block
19 North Block
20 South Block
21 Ikon Ho
22 Blue Gate Fields Jun & Inf Schs

B3 1 Woollon Ho
2 Dundalk Ho
3 Anne Goodman Ho
4 Newbold Cotts
5 Kerry Ho
6 Zion Ho
7 Longford Ho
8 Bromehead St
9 Athlone Ho
10 Jubilee Mans
11 Harriott Ho
12 Brayford Sq
13 Clearbrook Way
14 Rochelle Ct
15 Winterton Ho
16 Swift Ho
17 Brinsley Ho
18 Dean Ho
19 Foley Ho
20 Robert Sutton Ho
21 Montpelier Pl
22 Glastonbury Pl
23 Steel's La
24 Masters Lo
25 Stylus Apartments
26 Arta Ho
27 St Mary & St Michael Prim Sch
28 Bishop Challoner Collegiate Sch
29 Morton Cl
30 James Voller Way

B4 1 Fulneck
2 Gracehill
3 Ockbrook
4 Fairfield
5 Dunstan Hos
6 Cressy Ct
7 Cressy Hos
8 Callahan Cotts
9 Lindley Ho

10 Mayo Ho
11 Wexford Ho
12 Sandhurst Ho
13 Addis Ho
14 Colverson Ho
15 Beckett Ho
16 Jarman Ho
17 Armsby Ho
18 Wingrad Ho
19 Miranda Cl
20 Drake Ho
21 Ashfield Yd
22 Magri Wlk
23 Jean Pardies Ho
24 St Vincent De Paul Ho
25 Sambrook Ho
26 Louise De Marillac Ho
27 Dagobert Ho
28 Le Moal Ho
29 Odette Duval Ho
30 Charles Auffray Ho
31 Boisseau Ho
32 Clichy Ho
33 Paymal Ho
34 Smithy Street Schs
35 Redlands Prim Sch
36 Cressy Ct

C1 1 Clarence Mews
2 Raleigh Ct
3 Katherine Ct
4 Woolcombes Ct
5 Tudor Ct
6 Quayside Ct
7 Princes Riverside Rd
8 Surrey Ho
9 Tideway Ct
10 Edinburgh Ct
11 Falkirk Ct
12 Byelands Cl
13 Gwent Ct
14 Lavender Ho
15 Abbotsade Rd
16 Bellamy's Ct
17 Blenheim Ct
18 Sandringham Ct
19 Hampton Ct
20 Windsor Ct
21 Balmoral Ct
22 Westminster Ct
23 Beatson Wlk
24 Peter Hills Sch

C2 1 Barnardo Gdns
2 Roslin Ho
3 Glamis Est
4 Peabody Est
5 East Block
6 Highway Trad Ctr The
7 Highway Bsns Pk The
8 Cranford Cotts
9 Ratcliffe Orch
10 Scotia Bldg
11 Mauretania Bldg
12 Compania Bldg
13 Sirius Bldg
14 Unicorn Bldg
15 Keepier Wharf

C3 1 Pattison Ho
2 St Thomas Ho
3 Arbour Ho
4 Bladen Ho
5 Antill Terr
6 Majorie Mews

7 Billing Ho
8 Dowson Ho
9 Lipton Rd
10 Chalkwell Ho
11 Corringham Ho
12 Ogilvie Ho
13 Edward Mann Cl
14 Reservoir Studios
15 Lighterman Mews
16 Tower Hamlets Coll
17 Marion Richardson Prim Sch

C4 1 Roland Mews
2 Beatrice Ho
3 Morecambe Cl
4 Stepney Green Ct
5 Milrood Ho
6 Panama Ho
7 Galway Ho
8 Jacqueline Ho
9 Crown Mews
10 Caspian Ho
11 Darien Ho
12 Riga Ho
13 Flores Ho
14 Taranto Ho
15 Aden Ho
16 Master's St
17 Rosary Ct
18 Stepney Green Maths & Computing Coll
19 Sir John Cass Foundation & Red-coat CE Sec Sch

33

A1 1 Edward Sq
2 Prince Regent Ct
3 Codrington Ct
4 Pennington Ct
5 Cherry Ct
6 Ash Ct
7 Beech Ct
8 Hazel Ct
9 Laurel Ct

A2 1 St Georges Sq
2 Drake Ho
3 Osprey Ho
4 Fleet Ho
5 Gainsborough Ho
6 Victory Pl
7 Challenger Ho
8 Conrad Ho
9 Lock View Ct
10 Shoulder of Mutton Alley
11 Frederick Sq
12 Helena Sq
13 Elizabeth Sq
14 Sophia Sq
15 William Sq
16 Lamb Ct
17 Lockside
18 Adriatic Bldg
19 Ionian Bldg
20 Regents Gate Ho

A3 1 Hearnshaw St
2 Berry Cotts
3 Causton Cotts
4 Elizabeth Blount Ct
5 Carr St
6 Shaw Cres
7 Darnley Ho
8 Mercer's Cotts
9 Troon Ho
10 Ratcliffe Ho

11 Wakeling St
12 York Sq
13 Anglia Ho
14 Cambria Ho
15 Caledonia Ho
16 Ratcliffe La
17 Bekesbourne St
18 John Scurr Ho
19 Regents Canal Ho
20 Basin App
21 Powlesland Ct
22 Cayley Prim Sch
23 Stephen Hawking Sch

A4 1 Waley St
2 Edith Ramsay Ho
3 Andaman Ho
4 Atlantic Ho
5 Pevensey Ho
6 Solent Ho
7 Lorne Ho
8 Cromarty Ho
9 Dakin Pl
10 Greaves Cotts
11 Donaghue Cotts
12 Ames Cotts
13 Waterview Ho
14 Limehouse Fields Est

B2 1 Hamilton Ho
2 Imperial Ho
3 Oriana Ho
4 Queens Ct
5 Brightlingsea Pl
6 Faraday Ho
7 Ropemaker's Fields
8 Oast Ct
9 Mitre The
10 Bate St
11 Joseph Irwin Ho
12 Padstow Ho
13 Bethlehem Ho
14 Saunders Ct
15 Roche Ho
16 Stocks Pl
17 Trinidad Ho
18 Grenada Ho
19 Kings Ho
20 Dunbar Wharf
21 Limekiln Wharf
22 Belgrave Ct
23 Eaton Ho
24 Cyril Jackson Prim Sch (North Bldg)
25 Cyril Jackson Prim Sch (South Bldg)

B3 1 Dora Ho
2 Flansham Ho
3 Gatwick Ho
4 Ashpark Ho
5 Newdigate Ho
6 Midhurst Ho
7 Redbourne Ho
8 Southwater Cl
9 Andersens Wharf
10 Whatman Ho
11 Butler Ho
12 Fitzroy Ho
13 Salmon St
14 Mission The
15 Aithan Ho
16 Britley Ho
17 Cheadle Ho
18 Elland Ho
19 Wharf La
20 Docklands Ct
21 Park Heights Ct

4 Lawrence Ct
5 Maugham Ct
6 Reade Ct
7 Woolf Ct
8 Shaw Ct
9 Verne Ct
10 Wodehouse Ct
11 Greenock Rd
12 Garden Ct
13 Barons Gate
14 Cleveland Rd
15 Carver Cl
16 Chapter Cl
17 Beauchamp Cl
18 Holmes Ct
19 Copper Mews
B4 1 Belgrave Ct
2 Buckland Wlk
3 Frampton Ct
4 Telfer Cl
5 Harlech Twr
6 Corfe Twr
7 Barwick Ho
8 Charles Hocking Ho
9 Sunninghill Ct
10 Salisbury St
11 Jameson Pl
12 Castle Cl
C1 1 Chatsworth Lo
2 Prospect Pl
3 Townhall Ave
4 Devonhurst Pl
5 Heathfield Ct
6 Horticultural Pl
7 Merlin Ho
8 Garth Rd
9 Autumn Rise
C2 1 Disraeli Cl
2 Winston Wlk
3 Rusthall Mans
4 Bedford Park Mans
5 Essex Place Sq
6 Holly Rd
7 Homecross Ho
8 Swan Bsns Ctr
9 Jessop Ho
10 Belmont Prim Sch

38
A1 1 Glebe Cl
2 Devonshire Mews
3 Binns Terr
4 Ingress St
5 Swanscombe Rd
6 Brackley Terr
7 Stephen Fox Ho
8 Manor Gdns
9 Coram Ho
10 Flaxman Ho
11 Thorneycroft Ho
12 Thornhill Ho
13 Kent Ho
14 Oldfield Ho
15 William Hogarth Sch The
A2 1 Chestnut Ho
2 Bedford Ho
3 Bedford Cnr
4 Sydney Ho
5 Bedford Park Cnr
6 Priory Gdns
7 Windmill Alley
8 Castle Pl

9 Jonathan Ct
10 Windmill Pas
11 Chardin Rd
12 Gable Ho
13 Chiswick & Bedford Park Prep Sch
14 Arts Educational Sch The
A3 1 Fleet Ct
2 Ember Ct
3 Emlyn Gdns
4 Clone Ct
5 Brent Ct
6 Abbey Ct
7 Ormsby Lo
8 St Catherine's Ct
9 Lodge The
A4 1 Longford Ct
2 Mole Ct
3 Lea Ct
4 Wandle Ct
5 Beverley Ct
6 Roding Ct
7 Crane Ct
B1 1 Miller's Ct
2 British Grove Pas
3 British Grove S
4 Beresfede Rd
5 North Eyot Gdns
B2 1 Flanders Mans
2 Stamford Brook Mans
3 Linkenholt Mans
4 Prebend Mans
5 Middlesex Ct
B3 1 Stamford Brook Gdns
2 Hauteville Court Gdns
3 Ranelagh Gdns
C1 1 Chisholm Ct
2 North Verbena Gdns
3 Western Terr
4 Verbena Gdns
5 Montrose Villas
6 Hammersmith Terr
7 South Black Lion La
8 St Peter's Wharf
9 Eden High Sch
10 St Peter's CE Prim Sch
C2 1 Hamlet Ct
2 Derwent Ct
3 Westcroft Ct
4 Black Lion Mews
5 St Peter's Villas
6 Standish Ho
7 Chambon Pl
8 Court Mans
9 Longthorpe Ct
10 Charlotte Ct
11 Westside
12 Park Ct
13 London Ho
14 Latymer Upper Sch
15 Polish Univ Abroad
C3 1 Elizabeth Finn Ho
2 Ashchurch Ct
3 King's Par
4 Inver Ct
5 Ariel Ct
6 Popleton Lo
7 Vitae Apartments
C4 1 Becklow Gdns
2 Victoria Ho

3 Lycett Pl
4 Kylemore Ct
5 Alexandra Ct
6 Lytten Ct
7 Becklow Mews
8 Northcroft Ct
9 Bailey Ct
10 Spring Cott
11 Latimer Wlk
12 Laurence Mews
13 Hadyn Park Ct
14 Askew Mans
15 Malvern Ct

39
A1 1 Prince's Mews
2 Aspen Gdns
3 Hampshire Hog La
4 Blades Ct
A2 1 Albion Gdns
2 Flora Gdns
3 Lamington St
4 Felgate Mews
5 Galena Ho
6 Albion Mews
7 Albion Ct
8 King Street Cloisters
9 Dimes Pl
10 Clarence Ct
11 Hampshire Hog La
12 Marryat Ct
13 Ravenscourt Ho
14 Ravenscourt Theatre Sch
15 Cambridge Sch
16 Godolphin & Latymer Sch
17 Flora Gardens Prim Sch
A3 1 Ravenscourt Park Mans
2 Paddenswick Ct
3 Ashbridge Ct
4 Brackenbury Prim Sch
A4 1 Westbush Ct
2 Goldhawk Mews
3 Sycamore Ho
4 Shackleton Ct
5 Drake Ct
6 Scotts Ct
7 Raleigh Ct
8 Melville Court Flats
9 Southway Cl
B1 1 Bridge Avenue Mans
2 Bridgeview
3 College Ct
4 Beatrice Ho
5 Amelia Ho
6 Edith Ho
7 Joanna Ho
8 Mary Ho
9 Adela Ho
10 Sophia Ho
11 Henrietta Ho
12 Charlotte Ho
13 Alexandra Ho
14 Bath Pl
15 Elizabeth Ho
16 Margaret Ho
17 Peabody Est
18 Eleanor Ho
19 Isabella Ho
20 Caroline Ho
21 Chancellors Wharf

22 Sussex Pl
23 St Paul's CE Prim Sch
B2 1 Phoenix Lodge Mans
2 Samuel's Cl
3 Broadway Arc
4 Brook Ho
5 Hammersmith Broadway
6 Broadway Sh Ctr
7 Cambridge Ct
8 Ashcroft Sq
9 Sacred Heart High Sch
10 King Street Coll
B4 1 Verulam Ho
2 Grove Mans
3 Frobisher Ct
4 Library Mans
5 Pennard Mans
6 New Shepherd's Bush Mkt
7 Kerrington Ct
8 Granville Mans
9 Romney Ct
10 Rayner Ct
11 Sulgrave Gdns
12 Bamborough Gdns
13 Hillary Ct
14 Market Studios
15 Lanark Mans
16 Miles Coverdale Prim Sch
17 St Stephen's CE Prim Sch
18 London Coll of Fashion (Lime Grove)
C2 1 St Paul's Girls' Sch
2 Bute House Prep Sch
3 Jacques Prevert Sch
4 Larmenier & Sacred Heart RC Prim Sch
C3 1 Grosvenor Residences
2 Blythe Mews
3 Burnand Ho
4 Bradford Ho
5 Springvale Terr
6 Ceylon Rd
7 Walpole Ct
8 Bronte Ct
9 Boswell Ct
10 Souldern Rd
11 Brook Green Flats
12 Haarlem Rd
13 Stafford Mans
14 Lionel Mans
15 Barradell Ho
C4 1 Vanderbilt Villas
2 Bodington Ct
3 Kingham Cl
4 Clearwater Terr
5 Lorne Gdns
6 Cameret Ct
7 Bush Ct
8 Shepherds Ct
9 Rockley Ct
10 Grampians The
11 Charcroft Ct
12 Addison Park Mans
13 Sinclair Mans
14 Fountain Ct

15 Woodford Ct
16 Roseford Ct
17 Woodstock Studios

40
A1 1 Hockney Ct
2 Toulouse Ct
3 Lowry Ct
4 Barry Ho
5 Lewis Ct
6 Gainsborough Ct
7 Renoir Ct
8 Blake Ct
9 Raphael Ct
10 Rembrandt Ct
11 Constable Ct
12 Da Vinci Ct
13 Gauguin Ct
14 Michelangelo Ct
15 Monet Ct
16 Weald Cl
17 Jasmin Lo
18 Birchmere Ct
19 Weybridge Ct
20 Florence Ho
21 Gleneagles Cl
22 Sunningdale Cl
23 Muirfield Cl
24 Turnberry Cl
25 St Andrews Cl
26 Kingsdown Cl
27 St Davids Cl
28 Galway Cl
29 Edenbridge Cl
30 Birkdale Cl
31 Tralee Ct
32 Woburn Ct
33 Belfry Cl
34 Troon Cl
35 Holywell Cl
A2 1 Market Pl
2 Trappes Ho
3 Thurland Ho
4 Ramsfort Ho
5 Hambley Ho
6 Holford Ho
7 Pope Ho
8 Southwell Ho
9 Mortain Ho
10 Radcliffe Ho
11 Southwark Park Est
12 Galleywall Road Trad Est
13 Trevithick Ho
14 Barlow Ho
15 Donkin Ho
16 Landmann Ho
17 Fitzmaurice Ho
18 Dodd Ho
A3 1 Perryn Rd
2 Chalfont Ho
3 Prestwood Ho
4 Farmer Ho
5 Gataker Ho
6 Gataker St
7 Cornick Ho
8 Glebe Ho
9 Matson Ho
10 Hickling Ho
11 St Andrews Ho
12 Southwark Coll (Surrey Docks Ctr)
13 Southwark Park Prim Sch
A4 1 Butterfield Cl
2 Janeway Pl
3 Trotwood Ho

4 Maylie Ho
5 Cranburn Pas
6 Cranburn Ho
7 Cherry Garden Ho
8 Burton Ho
9 Morriss Ho
10 Dixon's Alley
11 King Edward The Third Mews
12 Cathay St
13 Mission The
14 Millstream Ho
B1 16 Ilderton Prim Sch
B2 1 Damory Ho
2 Antony Ho
3 Roderick Ho
4 Pedworth Gdns
5 Banner Ct
6 Rotherhithe Bsns Est
7 Beamish Ho
8 Corbetts Pas
9 Gillam Ho
10 Richard Ho
11 George Walter Ho
12 Westlake
13 Adron Ho
14 Cavendish Sch
15 McIntosh Ho
B3 1 Blick Ho
2 Neptune Ho
3 Scotia Ct
4 Murdoch Ho
5 Edmonton Ct
6 Niagara Ct
7 Columbia Point
8 Ritchie Ho
9 Wells Ho
10 Helen Peele Cotts
11 Orchard Ho
12 Dock Offices
13 Landale Ho
14 Courthope Ho
15 Hithe Gr
16 China Hall Mews
B4 1 Mayflower St
2 St Mary's Est
3 Rupack St
4 Frank Whymark Ho
5 Adams Gardens Est
6 Hatterack St
7 East India Ct
8 Bombay Ct
9 Stable Ho
10 Grannary The
11 Riverside
12 Cumberland Wharf
13 Seaford Ho
14 Hythe Ho
15 Sandwich Ho
16 Winchelsea Ho
17 Rye Ho
18 Kenning St
19 Western Pl
20 Pine Ho
21 Beech Ho
22 Larch Ho
23 Turner Ct
24 Seth St
25 Risdon Ho
26 Risdon St
27 Aylton Est
28 Manitoba Ct
29 Calgary Ct
30 Irwell Est
31 St Olav's Sq

33 City Bsns Ctr
34 Albion Prim Sch
C2 1 John Kennedy Ho
2 Brydale Ho
3 Balman Ho
4 Tissington Ct
5 Harbord Ho
6 Westfield Ho
7 Albert Starr Ho
8 John Brent Ho
9 William Evans Ho
10 Raven Ho
11 Egret Ho
12 Fulmar Ho
13 Dunlin Ho
14 Siskin Ho
15 Sheldrake Ho
16 Buchanan Ct
17 Burrage Ct
18 Biddenham Ho
19 Ayston Ho
20 Empingham Ho
21 Deanshanger Ho
22 Codicote Ho
23 Buryfield Ct
24 Rotherhithe Prim Sch
C4 1 Schooner Cl
2 Dolphin Cl
3 Clipper Cl
4 Deauville Ct
5 Colette Ct
6 Coniston Ct
7 Virginia Ct
8 Derwent Ct
9 Grantham Ct
10 Serpentine Ct
11 Career Ct
12 Lacine Ct
13 Fairway Ct
14 Harold Ct
15 Spruce Ho
16 Cedar Ho
17 Sycamore Ho
18 Woodland Cres
19 Poplar Ho
20 Adelphi Ct
21 Basque Ct
22 Aberdale Ct
23 Quilting Ct
24 Chargrove Cl
25 Radley Ct
26 Greenacre Sq
27 Maple Leaf Sq
28 Stanhope Cl
29 Hawke Pl
30 Drake Cl
31 Brass Talley Alley
32 Monkton Ho
33 James Ho
34 Wolfe Cres

41
A1 1 Sir Francis Drake Prim Sch
2 Deptford Park Prim Sch
A2 1 Trafalgar Cl
2 Hornblower Cl
3 Cunard Wlk
4 Caronia Ct
5 Carinthia Ct
6 Freswick Ho
7 Graveley Ho
8 Husbourne Ho
9 Crofters Ct
10 Pomona Ho

11 Hazelwood Ho
12 Cannon Wharf Bsns Ctr
13 Bence Ho
14 Clement Ho
15 Pendennis Ho
16 Lighter Cl
17 Mast Ct
18 Rushcutters Ct
19 Boat Lifter Way
B1 1 Gransden Ho
2 Daubeney Twr
3 North Ho
4 Rochfort Ho
5 Keppel Ho
6 Camden Ho
7 Sanderson Ho
8 Berkeley Ho
9 Strafford Ho
10 Richman Ho
11 Hurleston Ho
12 Grafton Ho
13 Fulcher Ho
14 Citrus Ho
B2 1 Windsock Cl
2 St George's Mews
3 Linberry Wlk
4 Lanyard Ho
5 Golden Hind Pl
6 James Lind Ho
7 Harmon Ho
8 Pelican Ho
9 Bembridge Ho
10 Terrace The
11 George Beard Rd
12 Colonnade The
13 Pegys Ent Ctr
14 Hudson Ct
15 Shackleton Ct
16 De Gama Pl
17 Mercator Pl
18 Maritime Quay
19 Perry Ct
20 Amundsen Ct
C2 1 Nova Bldg
2 Apollo Bldg
3 Gaverick Mews
4 Windmill Ho
5 Orion Point
6 Galaxy Bldg
7 Venus Ho
8 Olympian Ct
9 Poseidon Ct
10 Mercury Ct
11 Aphrodite Ct
12 Cyclops Mews
13 Neptune Ct
14 Artemis Ct
15 Hera Ct
16 Ares Ct
17 Ringwood Gdns
18 Dartmoor Wlk
19 Rothsay Wlk
20 Ashdown Wlk
21 Radnor Wlk
22 Ironmonger's Pl
23 Britannia Rd
24 Deptford Ferry Rd
25 Magellan Pl
26 Dockers Tanner Rd
C3 1 Bowsprit Point
2 St Hubert's Ho
3 John Tucker Ho
4 Broadway Wlk
5 Nash Ho
6 Fairlead Ho
7 Crosstrees Ho

8 Stanliff Ho
9 Keelson Ho
10 Clara Grant Ho
11 Gilbertson Ho
12 Scoulding Ho
13 Hibbert Ho
14 Cressall Ho
15 Alexander Ho
16 Kedge Ho
C4 1 Anchorage Point
2 Waterman Bldg
3 Jefferson Bldg
4 Pierpoint Bldg
5 Franklin Bldg
6 Vanguard Bldg
7 Edison Bldg
8 Seacon Twr
9 Naxos Bldg
10 Express Wharf
11 Hutching's Wharf
12 Tobago St
13 Bellamy Cl
14 Dowlen Ct
15 Cochrane Ho
16 Beatty Ho
17 Scott Ho
18 Laybourne Ho
19 Ensign Ho
20 Beaufort Ho
21 Spinnaker Ho
22 Bosun Cl
23 Topmast Point
24 Turner Ho
25 Constable Ho
26 Knighthead Point
27 Seven Mills Prim Sch

42
A1 1 Slipway Ho
2 Taffrail Ho
3 Platehouse The
4 Wheelhouse The
5 Chart House The
6 Port House The
7 Beacon Ho
8 Blasker Wlk
9 Maconochies Rd
A2 1 Brassey Ho
2 Triton Ho
3 Warspite Ho
4 Rodney Ho
5 Conway Ho
6 Exmouth Ho
7 Akbar Ho
8 Arethusa Ho
9 Tasman Ct
10 Cutty Sark Ho
11 Harbinger Prim Sch
A3 1 Turnberry Quay
2 Balmoral Ho
3 Aegon Ho
4 Marina Point
B2 1 St John's Ho
2 Betty May Gray Ho
3 Castleton Ho
4 Urmston Ho
5 Salford Ho
6 Capstan Ho
7 Frigate Ho
8 Galleon Ho
9 Barons Lo
B3 1 Cardale St
2 Hickin St
3 John McDonald Ho
4 Thorne Ho
5 Skeggs Ho

6 St Bernard Ho
7 Kimberley Ho
8 Kingdon Ho
9 Killoran Ho
10 Alastor Ho
11 Lingard Ho
12 Yarrow Ho
13 Sandpiper Ct
14 Nightingale Ct
15 Robin Ct
16 Heron Ct
17 Ferndown Lo
18 Crosby Ho
B4 1 Llandovery Ho
2 Rugless Ho
3 Ash Ho
4 Elm Ho
5 Cedar Ho
6 Castalia Sq
7 Aspect Ho
8 Normandy Ho
9 Valiant Ho
10 Tamar Ho
11 Watkins Ho
12 Alice Shepherd Ho
13 Oak Ho
14 Ballin Ct
15 Martin Ct
16 Grebe Ct
17 Kingfisher Ct
18 Walkers Lo
19 Antilles Bay
C2 1 Verwood Lo
2 Fawley Lo
3 Lyndhurst Lo
4 Blyth Cl
5 Farnworth Ho
6 Francis Cl
7 St Luke's CE Prim Sch

43
A1 1 Bellot Gdns
2 Thornley Pl
3 King William La
4 Bolton Ho
5 Miles Ho
6 Mell St
7 Sam Manners Ho
8 Hatcliffe Alm-shouses
9 Woodland Wlk
10 Earlswood Ct
11 St Joseph's RC Prim Sch
B1 1 Baldrey Ho
2 Christie Ho
3 Dyson Ho
4 Cliffe Ho
5 Moore Ho
6 Collins Ho
7 Halley Ho
8 Kepler Ho
9 Sailacre Ho
10 Union Pk
B3 1 Teal St
2 Maurer Ct
3 Mudlarks Blvd
4 Renaissance Wlk
5 Alamaro Lo
C1 1 Layfield Ho
2 Westerdale Rd
3 Mayston Mews

4 Station Mews Terr
5 Halstow Prim Sch
6 Holyrood Mews

44
A4 1 Ferry Sq
2 Watermans Ct
3 Wilkes Rd
4 Albany Par
5 Charlton Ho
6 Albany Ho
7 Alma Ho
8 Griffin Ct
9 Cressage Ho
10 Tunstall Wlk
11 Trimmer Wlk
12 Running Horse Yd
13 Mission Sq
14 Distillery Wlk
B2 1 Primrose Ho
2 Lawman Ct
3 Royston Ct
4 Garden Ct
5 Capel Lo
6 Devonshire Ct
7 Celia Ct
8 Rosslyn Ho
9 Branstone Ct
10 Lamerton Lo
11 Kew Lo
12 Dunraven Ho
13 Stoneleigh Lo
14 Tunstall Ct
15 Voltaire
C2 1 Clarendon Ct
2 Quintock Ho
3 Broome Ct
4 Lonsdale Mews
5 Elizabeth Cotts
6 Sandways
7 Victoria Cotts
8 North Ave
9 Grovewood
10 Hamilton Ho
11 Melvin Ct
12 Royal Par
13 Power Ho
14 Station Ave
15 Blake Mews
C4 5 Strand-on-the-
Green Schs

45
A2 1 Terrano Ho
2 Oak Ho
3 Aura Ho
4 Maple Ho
5 Cedar Ho
6 Saffron Ho
7 Lime Ho
8 Lavender Ho
9 Juniper Ho
A4 1 Falcons Pre Prep
school The

46
B1 1 Melrose Rd
2 Seaforth Lo
3 St John's Gr
4 Sussex Ct
5 Carmichael Ct
6 Hampshire Ct
7 Thorne Pas
8 Brunel St

9 Beverley Path

47
C4 1 Cobb's Hall
2 Dorset Mans
3 St Clements Mans
4 Bothwell St
5 Hawksmoor St
6 Melcombe Prim
Sch

48
A1 1 Langport Ho
2 Iveagh Ho
3 Newark Ho
4 Edgehill Ho
5 Hopton Ho
6 Ashby Ho
7 Nevil Ho
A2 1 Fairbairn Gn
2 Hammelton Ho
3 Foxley Sq
4 Silverburn Ho
5 Butler Ho
6 Dalkeith Ho
7 Turner Cl
8 Bathgate Ho
9 Black Roof Ho
10 Charles Edward
Brooke Sch (Den-
nen Site)
11 Charles Edward
Brooke Sch
A3 53 St Michael & All
Angels CE Acad
A4 1 Faunce Ho
2 Garbett Ho
3 Harvard Ho
4 Doddington Pl
5 Kean Ho
6 Jephson Ho
7 Cornish Ho
8 Bateman Ho
9 Molesworth Ho
10 Walters Ho
11 Cruden Ho
12 Brawne Ho
13 Prescott Ho
14 Chalmer's Wlk
15 Copley Cl
16 King Charles Ct
B1 1 Bergen Ho
2 Oslo Ho
3 Viking Ho
4 Jutland Ho
5 Norvic Ho
6 Odin Ho
7 Baltic Ho
8 Nobel Ho
9 Mercia Ho
10 Kenbury Gdns
11 Zealand Ho
12 Elsinore Ho
13 Norse Ho
14 Denmark Mans
15 Dane Ho
16 Canterbury Cl
17 York Cl
18 Kenbury Mans
19 Parade Mans
20 Winterslow Ho
21 Lilford Ho
22 Bartholomew Ho
23 Guildford Ho
24 Boston Ho
25 Hereford Ho
26 Weyhill Ho

19 Lichfield Ho
20 Lansdown Ho
21 Honiton Ho
22 Pinner Ho
23 Baldock Ho
24 Widecombe Ho
25 Nottingham Ho
26 Witham Ho
27 Barnet Ho
28 Empress Mews
B2 1 Bertha Neubergh
Ho
2 Mornington Mews
3 Badsworth Ho
4 Pearson Cl
5 Elm Tree Ct
6 Samuel Lewis Trust
Dwellings
7 Milkwell Yd
8 Keswick Ho
9 Mitcham Ho
10 Sacred Heart RC
Sec Sch
B3 1 Boundary Ho
2 Day Ho
3 Burgess Ho
4 Carlyle Ho
5 Myers Ho
6 Thompson Ave
7 Palgrave Ho
8 Winnington Ho
9 Brantwood Ho
10 Lowell Ho
11 Jessie Duffett Ho
12 Otterburn Ho
13 Crossmount Ho
14 Venice Ct
15 Bowyer St
16 Livingstone Ho
17 Gothic Ct
18 Coniston Ho
19 Harlynwood
20 Carey Ct
21 Finley Ct
22 Grainger Ct
23 Hayes Ct
24 Moffat Ho
25 Marinel Ho
26 Hodister Cl
27 Arnot Ho
28 Lamb Ho
29 Kipling Ho
30 Keats Ho
31 Kenyon Ho
32 New Church Rd
33 Sir John Kirk Cl
34 Comber Grove Prim
Sch
35 St Joseph's RC Inf
& Jun Schs
C1 1 Selborne Rd
2 Hascombe Terr
C2 1 Joiners Arms Yd
2 Butterfly Wlk
3 Cuthill Wlk
4 Colonades Ihe
5 Artichoke Mews
6 Peabody Bldgs
7 Brighton Ct
8 Park Ho
9 Peabody Ct
10 Lomond Ho
11 Lamb Ho
12 Kimpton Ct
13 Belham Wlk
14 Datchelor Pl
15 Harvey Rd

C3 1 Masterman Ho
2 Milton Ho
3 Pope Ho
4 Chester Ct
5 Marvel Ho
6 Flecker Ho
7 Landor Ho
8 Leslie Prince Ct
9 Evelina Mans
10 Langland Ho
11 Drinkwater Ho
12 Procter Ho
13 Shirley Ho
14 Drayton Ho
15 Bridges Ho
16 Cunningham Ho
17 Hood Ho
18 Herrick Ho
19 Dekker Ho
20 Houseman Way
21 Coleby Path
22 Brunswick Park
Prim Sch
C4 1 Queens Ho
2 Arnside Ho
3 Horsley St
4 St Peter's Ho
5 St Johns Ho
6 St Marks Ho
7 St Stephens Ho
8 St Matthew's Ho
9 Red Lion Cl
10 Boyson Rd
11 Bradenham

49
A1 1 Springfield Ho
2 Craston Ho
3 Walters Ho
4 Edgecombe Ho
5 Fowler Ho
6 Rignold Ho
7 Chatham Ho
A2 1 Barnwell Ho
2 Brunswick Villas
3 St Giles Twr
4 Bentley Ho
5 Dawson Ho
6 Dryden Ho
7 Mayward Ho
8 Longleigh Ho
9 Fairwall Ho
10 Bodeney Ho
11 Sandby Ho
12 Vestry Mews
13 Netley
14 Lakanal
15 Racine
16 Camberwell Coll of
Arts
A3 1 Tower Mill Rd
2 Tilson Cl
3 Granville Sq
4 Edgar Wallace Cl
5 Potters Cl
6 Dorton Cl
7 Samuel Jones Ind
Est
8 Dibden Ho
9 Marchwood Cl
10 Pilgrims Cloisters
11 Beacon Ho
12 Teather St
13 Stacy Path
14 Rumball Ho
15 Ballow Cl
16 Rill Ho

17 Southwark Coll
(Camberwell Ctr)
18 St George's CE
Prim Sch
A4 1 Downend Ct
2 Andoversford Ct
3 Pearse St
4 Watling St
5 Gandolfi St
6 Comfort St
7 Tower Mill Rd
B2 1 Colbert
2 Voltaire
3 Finch Mews
4 Charles Coveney Rd
5 Bamber Rd
6 Crane St
7 Curlew Ho
8 Mallard Ho
9 Tern Ho
10 Crane Ho
11 Falcon Ho
12 Bryanston Ho
13 Basing Ct
14 Marcus Ho
15 Sheffield Ho
16 Highshore Sch
17 St James The Great
RC Prim Sch
18 Oliver Goldsmith
Prim Sch
B3 1 Painswick Ct
2 Sharpness Ct
3 Mattingly Way
4 Hordle Prom N
5 Burcher Gale Gr
6 Calypso Cres
7 Hordle Prom S
8 Cinnamon Cl
9 Savannah Ct
10 Thames Ct
11 Shannon Ct
12 Amstel Ct
13 Danube Ct
14 Tilbury Cl
15 Hordle Prom E
16 Indus Ct
17 Oakcourt
18 Palm Ct
19 Rowan Ct
20 Blackthorn Ct
21 Pear Ct
22 Lidgate Rd
23 Whistler Mews
24 Boathouse Wlk
25 Camberwell Coll of
Arts
B4 1 Willsbridge Ct
2 Cam Ct
3 Quedgeley Ct
4 Saul Ct
5 Quenington Ct
6 Westonbirt Ct
7 Wickway Ct
C1 1 William Margrie Cl
2 William Blake Ho
3 Quantock Mews
4 Choumert Sq
5 Parkstone Rd
6 Atwell Rd
C2 1 Canal Head Public
Sq
2 Angelina Ho
3 Jarvis Ho
4 Richland Ho
5 Honeywood Ho
6 Wakefield Ho

7 Primrose Ho
8 Hardcastle Ho
9 Dunstall Ho
10 Springtide Cl
11 Purdon Ho
12 Flamborough Ho
13 Lambrook Ho
14 Witcombe Point
15 Yarnfield Sq
16 Winford Ho
17 Portbury Cl
18 Robert Keen Cl
C3 1 Thornhill Ho
2 Vervain Ho
3 Woodstar Ho
4 Tamarind Ho
5 Hereford Retreat
6 Haymerle Ho
7 Furley Ho
8 Thomas Milner Ho
9 Applegarth Ho
10 Freda Corbett Cl
11 Rudbeck Ho
12 Henslow Ho
13 Lindley Ho
14 Collinson Ho
15 Sister Mabel's Way
16 Timberland Cl
17 Hastings Cl
18 Sidmouth Ho
19 Budleigh Ho
20 Stanesgate Ho
21 Breamore Ho
22 Ely Ho
23 Gisburn Ho
24 Silkin Mews
25 Peckham Park Prim Sch
26 St Francis RC Prim Sch
C4 1 Bowles Rd
2 Western Wharf
3 Northfield Ho
4 Millbrook Ho
5 Denstone Ho
6 Deerhurst Ho
7 Caversham Ho
8 Battle Ho
9 Cardiff Ho
10 Bridgnorth Ho
11 Exeter Ho
12 Grantham Ho
13 Aylesbury Ho
14 Royston Ho
15 Haymerle Sch

50
A1 1 Walkynscroft
2 Ryegates
3 Hathorne Cl
4 Pilkington Rd
5 Russell Ct
6 Heaton Ho
7 Magdalene Cl
8 Iris Ct
9 St Mary Magdalene CE Prim Sch
A2 1 Willowdene
2 Pinedene
3 Oakdene
4 Beechdene
5 Hollydene
6 Wood Dene
7 Staveley Cl
8 Carnicot Ho
9 Martock Ct
10 Cherry Tree Ct

12 Kendrick Ct
13 John Donne Prim Sch
A3 1 Tortington Ho
2 Credenhill Ho
3 Bromyard Ho
4 Hoyland Cl
5 Willowdene
6 Ashdene
7 Acorn Par
8 Havelock Ct
9 Springall St
10 Harry Lambourn Ho
11 Grenier Apartments
B1 1 Honiton Gdns
2 Selden Ho
3 Hathway Ho
4 Hathway Ho
5 Station Ct
6 Symons Ct
7 Hollydale Prim Sch
B2 1 Trotman Ho
2 Boddington Ho
3 Heydon Ho
4 Boulter Ho
5 Astbury Bsns Ctr
B3 1 Ambleside Point
2 Grasmere Point
3 Windermere Point
4 Roman Way
5 Laburnum Cl
6 Juniper Ho
7 Romney Cl
8 Hammersley Ho
9 Hutchinson Ho
10 Hammond Ho
11 Fir Tree Ho
12 Glastonbury Ct
13 Highbridge Ct
14 Filton Ct
15 Chiltern Ct
16 Cheviot Ct
B4 1 Penshurst Ho
2 Reculver Ho
3 Mereworth Ho
4 Camber Ho
5 Chiham Ho
6 Otford Ho
7 Olive Tree Ho
8 Aspen Ho
9 Lewis Silkin Ho
10 Richborough Ho
11 Dover Ho
12 Eynsford Ho
13 Horton Ho
14 Lamberhurst Ho
15 Canterbury Ind Pk
16 Upnall Ho
17 Sissinghurst Ho
18 Rochester Ho
19 Saltwood Ho
20 Leybourne Ho
21 Lullingstone Ho
22 Pilgrims Way Prim Sch
C3 1 Richard Anderson Ct
2 Palm Tree Ho
3 Edward Robinson Ho
4 Antony Ho
5 Gerrard Ho
6 Palmer Ho
7 Pankhurst Cl
C4 1 Harrisons Ct
2 Grantley Ho
3 Sunbury Ct

11 Tilbury Ho
2 Graham Ct
3 Connell Ct
4 St Clements Ct
5 Henderson Ct
6 Jemotts Ct
7 Verona Ct
8 Heywood Ho
9 Francis Ct
10 Hind Ho
11 Donne Ho
12 Carew Ct
13 Burbage Ho
14 Newland Ho
15 Dobson Ho
16 Dalton Ho
17 Greene Ct
18 Redrup Ho
19 Tarplett Ho
20 Stunell Ho
21 Gasson Ho
22 Bryce Ho
23 Barnes Ho
24 Barkwith Ho
25 Bannister Ho
26 Apollo Ind Bsns Ctr

51
A2 1 Archer Ho
2 Browning Ho
3 Hardcastle Ho
4 Brooke Ho
5 Wallis Ho
A3 1 Batavia Ho
2 Marlowe Bsns Ctr
3 Batavia Mews
4 Woodrush Cl
5 Alexandra St
6 Primrose Wlk
7 Vansittart St
8 Granville Ct
9 Cottesbrook St
10 Ewen Henderson Ct
11 Fordham Ho
12 Deptford Green Sch (Annex)
A4 1 Portland Ct
2 Phoenix Ct
3 Rainbow Ct
4 Hawke Twr
5 Chubworthy Ct
6 Woodpecker Rd
7 Hercules Ct
B3 1 Austin Ho
2 Exeter Way
3 Crossleigh Ct
4 Mornington Pl
5 Maple Ho
B4 1 Chester Ho
2 Lynch Wlk
3 Arlington Ho
4 Woodcote Ho
5 Cornbury Ho
6 Prospect Pl
7 Akintaro Ho
8 Mulberry Ho
9 Laurel Ho
10 Linden Ho
11 Ashford Ho
12 Wardalls Ho
13 Magnolia Ho
14 Howard Ho
15 Larch Cl
16 Ibis Ct
17 Merganser Ct
18 Wotton Rd
19 Kingfisher Sq

20 Sanderling Ct
21 Dolphin Twr
22 Mermaid Twr
23 Scoter Ct
24 Shearwater Ct
25 Brambling Ct
26 Kittiwake Ct
27 Diana Cl
28 Guillemot Ct
29 Marine Twr
30 Teal Ct
31 Lapwing Twr
32 Violet Cl
33 Skua Ct
34 Tristan Ct
35 Rosemary Ct
36 Cormorant Ct
37 Shelduck Ct
38 Eider Ct
39 Pintail Ct
40 Fulcher Ct
41 Grinling Gibbons Prim Sch
C1 1 Ashmead Mews
2 St Stephen's CE Prim Sch
A2 1 Admiralty Ct
2 Harton Lodge
3 Sylva Cotts
4 Pitman Ho
5 Heston Ho
6 Mereton Mans
7 Indiana Bldg
8 St John's Lodge
9 Dean's Gateway
10 Lucas Vale Prim Sch
11 Addey & Stanhope Sch
12 Lewisham Coll (Deptford Campus)
C3 1 Sandpiper Ct
2 Flamingo Ct
3 Titan Bsns Est
4 Rochdale Way
5 Speedwell St
6 Reginald Pl
7 Fletcher Path
8 Frankham Ho
9 Cremer Ho
10 Wilshaw Ho
11 Castell Ho
12 Holden Ho
13 Browne Ho
14 Resolution Way
15 Lady Florence Ctyd
16 Covell Ct
17 Albion Ho
18 Maritime Greenwich Coll
19 St Joseph's RC Prim Sch
C4 1 Dryfield Wlk
2 Blake Ho
3 Hawkins Ho
4 Grenville Ho
5 Langford Ho
6 Mandarin Ct
7 Bittern Ct
8 Lamerton St
9 Ravensbourne Mans
10 Armada St
11 Armada Ct
12 Benbow Ho
13 Oxenham Ho

14 Caravel Mews
15 Hughes Ho
16 Stretton Mans

52
A1 1 Morden Mount Prim Sch
A2 1 Washington Bldg
2 California Bldg
3 Utah Bldg
4 Montana Bldg
5 Oregon Bldg
6 Dakota bldg
7 Idaho Bldg
8 Atlanta Bldg
9 Colorado Bldg
10 Arizona Bldg
11 Nebraska Bldg
12 Alaska Bldg
13 Ohio Bldg
14 Charter Bldgs
15 Flamsteed Ct
16 Friendly Pl
17 Dover Ct
18 Robinscroft Mews
19 Doleman Ho
20 Plymouth Ho
A3 1 Finch Ho
2 Jubilee The
3 Maitland Cl
4 Ashburnham Retreat
B1 1 Ellison Ho
2 Pitmaston Ho
3 Aster Ho
4 Windmill Cl
5 Hertmitage The
6 Burnett Ho
7 Lacey Ho
8 Darwin Ho
9 Pearmain Ho
B2 1 Penn Almshouses
2 Jervis Ct
3 Woodville Ct
4 Darnall Ho
5 Renbold Ho
6 Lindsell St
7 Plumbridge St
8 Trinity Gr
9 Hollymount Cl
10 Cade Tyler Ho
11 Robertson Ho
B3 1 Temair Ho
2 Royal Hill Ct
3 Prince of Orange La
4 Lambard Ho
5 St Marks Cl
6 Ada Kennedy Ct
7 Arlington Pl
8 Topham Ho
9 Darnell Ho
10 Hawks Mews
11 Royal Pl
12 Swanne Ho
13 Maribor
14 Serica Ct
15 Queen Elizabeth's Coll
16 James Wolfe Prim Sch
B4 1 Greenwich Coll
2 Crescent Arc
3 Greenwich Mkt

304 **52 B4**

3 Turnpin La
4 Durnford St
5 Sexton's Ho
6 Bardsley Ho
7 Wardell Ho
8 Clavell St
9 Stanton Ho
10 Macey Ho
11 Boreman Ho
12 Clipper Appts

C4 1 Frobisher Ct
2 Hardy Cotts
3 Palliser Ho
4 Bernard Angell Ho
5 Corvette Sq
6 Travers Ho
7 Maze Hill Lodge
8 Park Place Ho
9 Meridian Prim Sch

53

B1 1 Heath House Prep
Sch
B3 1 Westcombe Ct
2 Kleffens Ct
3 Ferndale Ct
4 Combe Mews
5 Mandeville Cl
6 Pinelands Cl
C3 1 Mary Lawrenson Pl
2 Bradbury Ct
3 Dunstable Ct
4 Wentworth Ho
C4 1 Nethercombe Ho
2 Holywell Cl

54

A1 1 Lancaster Cotts
2 Lancaster Mews
3 Bromwich Ho
4 Priors Lo
5 Richmond Hill Ct
6 Glenmore Ho
7 Hillbrow
8 Heathshott
9 Friars Stile Pl
10 Spire Ct
11 Ridgeway
12 Matthias Ct
13 Old Vicarage Sch
A2 1 Lichfield Terr
2 Union Ct
3 Carrington Lo
4 Wilton Ct
5 Egerton Ct
6 Beverley Lo
7 Bishop Duppa's
Almshouses
8 Regency Wlk
9 Clear Water Ho
10 Onslow Avenue
Mans
11 Michels Alm-
shouses
12 Albany Pas
13 Salcombe Villas
A3 1 St John's Gr
2 Michel's Row
3 Michelsdale Dr
4 Blue Anchor Alley
5 Clarence St
6 Sun Alley
7 Thames Link Ho
8 Benns Wlk

9 Waterloo Pl
10 Northumbria Ct
B1 1 Chester Cl
2 Evesham Ct
3 Queen's Ct
4 Russell Wlk
5 Charlotte Sq
6 Jones Wlk
7 Hilditch Ho
8 Isabella Ct
9 Damer Ho
10 Eliot Ho
11 Fitzherbert Ho
12 Reynolds Pl
13 Chisholm Rd
B2 1 Alberta Ct
2 Beatrice Rd
3 Lorne Rd
4 York Rd
5 Connaught Rd
6 Albany Terr
7 Kingswood Cl
8 Selwyn Ct
9 Broadhurst Cl
B3 1 Towers The
2 Longs Ct
3 Sovereign Ct
4 Robinson Ct
5 Calvert Ct
6 Bedford Ct
7 Hickey's Alm-
shouses
8 Church Estate
Almshouses
9 Richmond Interna-
tional Bsns Ctr
10 Abercorn Mews

55

A3 1 Hershell Ct
2 Deanhill Ct
3 Park Sheen
4 Furness Lo
5 Merricks Ct
C4 1 Rann Ho
2 Craven Ho
3 John Dee Ho
4 Kindell Ho
5 Montgomery Ho
6 Avondale Ho
7 Addington Ct
8 Dovecote Gdns
9 Firmston Ho
10 Glendower Gdns
11 Chestnut Ave
12 Trehern Rd
13 Rock Ave
14 St Mary Magdalen's
RC Prim Sch

56

C2 1 Theodore Ho
2 Nicholas Ho
3 Bonner Ho
4 Downing Ho
5 Jansen Ho
6 Fairfax Ho
7 Devereux Ho
8 David Ho
9 Leigh Ho
10 Clipstone Ho
11 Mallet Ho
12 Arton Wilson Ho

57

B2 1 Inglis Ho
2 Ducie Ho

3 Wharncliffe Ho
4 Stanhope Ho
5 Waldegrave Ho
6 Mildmay Ho
7 Mullens Ho
C1 1 Balmoral Ho
2 Glenalmond Ho
3 Selwyn Ho
4 Keble Ho
5 Bede Ho
6 Gonville Ho
7 Magdalene Ho
8 Armstrong Ho
9 Newnham Ho
10 Somerville Ho
11 Balliol Ho
12 Windermere
13 Little Combe Cl
14 Classinghall Ho
15 Chalford Ct
16 Garden Royal
17 South Ct
18 Anne Kerr Ct
19 Ewhurst
C2 1 Geneva Ct
2 Laurel Ct
3 Cambalt Ho
4 Langham Ct
5 Lower Pk
6 King's Keep
7 Whitnell Ct
8 Whitehead Ho
9 Halford Ho
10 Humphry Ho
11 Jellicoe Ho
12 South Thames Coll
(Putney Ctr)
C3 1 Olivette St
2 Mascotte Rd
3 Glegg Pl
4 Crown Ct
5 Charlwood Terr
6 Percy Laurie Ho
7 Our Lady of Victo-
ries RC Prim Sch
C4 1 Griffin Gate
2 Darfur St
3 John Keall Ho
4 Henry Jackson Ho
5 Felsham Ho
6 Ardshiel Cl
7 Ruvigny Mans
8 Star & Garter Mans
9 University Mans
10 Lockyer Ho
11 Phelps Ho
12 Princeton Ct
13 Kingsmere Cl
14 Felsham Mews
15 St Mary's CE Prim
Sch

58

A2 1 Claremont
2 Downside
3 Cavendish Cl
4 Ashcombe Ct
5 Carltons The
6 Espirit Ho
7 Millbrooke Ct
8 Coysh Ct
9 Keswick Hts
10 Avon Ct
11 Merlin Sch The
B2 1 Keswick Broadway
2 Burlington Mews
3 Cambria Lo

4 St Stephen's Gdns
5 Atlantic Ho
6 Burton Lo
7 Manfred Ct
8 Meadow Bank
9 Hooper Ho
10 Aspire Bld
C2 1 Pembridge Pl
2 Adelaide Rd
3 London Ct
4 Windsor Ct
5 Westminster Ct
6 Fullers Ho
7 Bridge Pk
8 Lambeth Ct
9 Milton Ct
10 Norfolk Mans
11 Francis Snary Lo
12 Bush Cotts
13 Downbury Mews
14 Newton's Yd
15 Roche Sch The
16 St Joseph's RC
Prim Sch
17 West Hill Prim Sch
18 St Michael Steiner
Sch The

59

A2 1 Fairfield Ct
2 Blackmore Ho
3 Lancaster Mews
4 Cricketers Mews
5 College Mews
6 Arndale Wlk
7 St Anne's CE Prim
Sch
8 South Thames Coll
(Wandsworth Ctr)
B2 1 St Faith's CE Prim
Sch
B4 1 Molasses Ho
2 Molasses Row
3 Cinnamon Row
4 Calico Ho
5 Calico Row
6 Port Ho
7 Square Rigger Row
8 Trade Twr
9 Ivory Ho
10 Spice Ct
11 Sherwood Ct
12 Mendip Ct
13 Chalmers Ho
14 Coral Row
15 Ivory Sq
16 Kingfisher Ho
C3 1 Burke Ho
2 High View Prim Sch
3 Centre Acad
4 Fox Ho
5 Buxton Ho
6 Pitt Ho
7 Ramsey Ho
8 Beverley Cl
9 Florence Ho
10 Linden Ct
11 Dorcas Ct
12 Johnson Ct
13 Agnes Ct
14 Hilltop Ct
15 Courtyard The
16 Old Laundry The
17 Oberstein Rd
18 Fineran Ct
19 Sangora Rd
20 Harvard Mans

10 Plough Mews
C4 2 Milner Ho
3 McManus Ho
4 Wilberforce Ho
5 Wheeler Ct
6 Sporle Ct
7 Holliday Sq
8 John Parker Sq
9 Carmichael Ct
10 Fenner Sq
11 Clark Lawrence Ct
12 Shaw Ct
13 Sendall Ct
14 Livingstone Rd
15 Farrant Ho
16 Jackson Ho
17 Darien Ho
18 Shepard Ho
19 Ganley Ct
20 Arthur Newton Ho
21 Chesterton Ho
22 John Kirk Ho
23 Mantua St
24 Heaver Rd
25 Candlemakers
26 Thames Christian
Coll
27 Falconbrook Prim
Sch

60

A4 1 Kiloh Ct
2 Lanner Ho
3 Griffon Ho
4 Kestrel Ho
5 Kite Ho
6 Peregrine Ho
7 Hawk Ho
8 Inkster Ho
9 Harrier Ho
10 Eagle Hts
11 Kingfisher Ct
12 Lavender Terr
13 Temple Ho
14 Ridley Ho
15 Eden Ho
16 Hertford Ct
17 Nepaul Rd
B1 1 Staplehurst Ct
2 Teyham Ct
3 Honeywell Jun &
Inf Schs
B2 1 Clapham Computer
& Secretarial Coll
C1 1 Rayne Ho
2 St Anthony's Ct
3 Earlsthorpe Mews
4 Nightingale Mans
C4 1 Shaftesbury Park
Chambers
2 Selborne
3 Rush Hill Mews
4 Marmion Mews
5 Crosland Pl
6 Craven Mews
7 Garfield Mews
8 Audley Cl
9 Basnett Rd
10 Tyneham Cl
11 Woodmere Cl
D1 5 Broomwood Hall
(Lower Sch)

61

A1 1 Oliver House Prep
Sch
A4 1 Turnchapel Mews

2 Redwood Mews
3 Phil Brown Pl
4 Bev Callender Cl
5 Keith Connor Cl
6 Tessa Sanderson Pl
7 Daley Thompson Way
8 Rashleigh Ct
9 Abberley Mews
10 Willow Lodge
11 Beaufoy Rd
B1 1 Joseph Powell Cl
2 Cavendish Mans
3 Westlands Terr
4 Cubitt Ho
5 Hawkesworth Ho
6 Normanton Ho
7 Eastman Ho
8 Couchman Ho
9 Poynders Ct
10 Selby Ho
11 Valentine Ho
12 Gorham Ho
13 Deauville Mans
14 Deauville Ct
B2 1 Timothy Cl
2 Shaftesbury Mews
3 Brook Ho
4 Grover Ho
5 Westbrook Ho
6 Hewer Ho
7 Batten Ho
8 Mandeville Ho
9 George Beare Lo
10 St Mary's RC Prim Sch
B3 1 Polygon The
2 Windsor Ct
3 Trinity Cl
4 Studios The
5 Bourne Ho
B4 1 Clapham Manor Ct
2 Clarke Ho
3 Gables The
4 Sycamore Mews
5 Maritime Ho
6 Rectory Gdns
7 Floris Pl
8 Clapham Manor Prim Sch
C1 1 Parrington Ho
2 Savill Ho
3 Blackwell Ho
4 Bruce Ho
5 Victoria Ct
6 Victoria Ho
7 Belvedere Ct
8 Ingram Lo
9 Viney Ct
10 Bloomsbury Ho
11 Belgravia Ho
12 Barnsbury Ho
C3 1 Kendoa Rd
2 Felmersham Cl
3 Abbeville Mews
4 Saxon Ho
5 Gifford Ho
6 Teignmouth Cl
7 Holwood Pl
8 Oaklands Pl
9 Wilberforce Mews
10 William Bonney Est
11 London Coll of Bsns & Computer Studies
C4 1 Chelsham Ho
2 Lynde Ho

3 Greener Ho
4 Towns Ho
5 Hugh Morgan Ho
6 Roy Ridley Ho
7 Lendal Terr
8 Slievemore Cl
9 Cadmus Cl
10 Clapham North Bsns Ctr

62
A2 1 King's Mews
2 Clapham Court Terr
3 Clapham Ct
4 Clapham Park Terr
5 Pembroke Ho
6 Stevenson Ho
7 Queenswood Ct
8 Oak Tree Ct
9 Park Lofts
10 Ashby Mews
A3 1 Morris Ho
2 Gye Ho
3 Clowes Ho
4 Thomas Ho
5 Stuart Ho
6 Storace Ho
7 Bedford Ho
8 Ascot Ct
9 Ascot Par
10 Ashmere Ho
11 Ashmere Gr
12 Ventura Ho
13 Vickery Ho
14 Stafford Mans
15 Beresford Ho
A4 1 Callingham Ho
2 Russell Pickering Ho
3 Ormerod Ho
4 Lopez Ho
5 Coachmaker Mews
6 Brixton Day Coll
B2 1 Beatrice Ho
2 Florence Ho
3 Evelyn Ho
4 Diana Ho
5 Brixton Hill Ct
6 Austin Ho
7 Manor Ct
8 Camsey Ho
9 Romer Ho
10 Gale Ho
11 Byrne Ho
12 Farnfield Ho
13 Marchant Ho
14 Rainsford Ho
15 Springett Ho
16 Mannering Ho
17 Waldron Ho
18 Sudbourne Prim Sch
19 Corpus Christi RC Prim Sch
B3 1 Freemens Hos
2 Roger's Alm-shouses
3 Gresham Alm-shouses
4 Exbury Ho
5 Glasbury Ho
6 Dalbury Ho
7 Fosbury Ho
8 Chalbury Ho
9 Neilson-Terry Ct
10 Pavilion Mans
11 Daisy Dormer Ct

12 George Lashwood Ct
13 Marie Lloyd Ct
14 Trinity Homes
15 Lethaby Ho
16 Edmundsbury Ct Est
17 Regis Pl
18 Marlborough Mews
19 Alpha Ho
20 Beta Pl
21 Cedars Ho
22 South Chelsea Coll
B4 1 Turberville Ho
2 Thrayle Ho
3 Percheron Ct
4 Draymans Ct
5 Lansdowne Sch
C1 1 Eccleston Ho
2 Scarsbrook Ho
3 Purser Ho
4 Rudhall Ho
5 Hardham Ho
6 Heywood Ho
7 Haworth Ho
8 Birch Ho
9 Lansdell Ho
10 Lomley Ho
11 Laughton Ho
12 Woodruff Ho
13 Bascome St
14 Dudley Mews
15 Herbert Mews
16 Blades Lo
17 Dick Shepherd Ct
18 Morden Ho
19 Bishop Ct
20 Blackburn Ct
21 Leigh Ct
22 John Conwey Ho
23 Bristowe Ct
C2 1 Crownstone Ct
2 Brockwell Ct
3 Nevena Ct
4 St George's Residences
5 Hanover Mans
6 Fleet Ho
7 Langbourne Ho
8 Turnmill Ho
9 Walker Mews
10 Cossar Mews
11 Carter Ho
12 Arungford Mews
C3 1 Electric Mans
2 Electric La
3 Connaught Mans
4 Clifton Mans
5 Hereford Ho
6 Chaplin Ho
7 Lord David Pitt Ho
8 Marcus Garvey Way
9 Montego Cl
10 Bob Marley Way
11 Leeson Rd

11 Blacktree Mews
12 Chartham Ct
13 Chilham Ct
14 Northgate Ct
15 Westgate Ct
16 Dover Mans
17 St Helen's RC Sch
18 Dorrell Pl

63
A3 2 Poets Mews
3 St Jude's CE Prim Sch
A3 1 Mahatma Gandhi Ind Est
2 Dylan Rd
3 Bessemer Park Ind Est
4 Pablo Neruda Cl
5 Langston Hughes Cl
6 Walt Whitman Cl
7 James Joyce Wlk
8 Alice Walker Cl
9 Louise Bennett Cl
10 Chadacre Ho
11 Burwood Ho
12 Pyrford Ho
13 Wangford Ho
14 Ashford Ho
15 Kenwood Ho
16 Moyne Ho
17 Elveden Ho
18 Carrara Cl
19 Broughton Dr
20 Angela Davis Ind Est
21 Tilia Wlk
22 County Ho
23 Hill Mead Prim Sch
A4 1 Mallams Mews
2 Amberley Ct
3 Harper Ho
4 Leicester Ho
5 Station Ave
6 Wellfit St
7 Loughborough Ct
8 Belinda Rd
9 Higgs Ind Est
10 Tham Cl
C3 1 Shaftesbury Ct
2 Mayhew Ct
3 Morris Ct
4 Swinburne Ct
5 Perth Ct
6 Tayside Ct
7 Matlock Ct
8 Hunter Ct
9 Turner Ct

64
A2 1 Velde Way
2 Delft Way
3 Arnhem Way
4 Isel Way
5 Kempis Way
6 Terborch Way
7 Steen Way
8 Deventer Cres
9 Nimegen Way
10 Hilversum Cres
11 St Barnabas Cl
12 James Allen's Girls' Sch
13 James Allen's Prep Sch
A4 1 Harfield Gdns

2 Karen Ct
3 Seavington Ho
4 Appleshaw Ho
5 Birdsall Ho
6 Whitney Ho
7 Wheatland Ho
8 Wilton Ho
9 Walcot Ho
10 Whaddon Ho
11 Melbreak Ho
12 Ledbury Ho
13 Tidworth Ho
14 Riseholme Ho
15 Ringmer Ho
16 Petworth Ho
17 Stagshaw Ho
18 Ivybridge Ho
19 Inwood Ho
20 Gatcombe Ho
21 Felbridge Ho
22 Cowdray Ho
23 Dog Kennel Hill Sch
B3 1 Dulwich Mews
2 New Hope Christian Sch
3 St James's Cloisters
C2 1 Dorothy Charrington Ho
2 Keswick Ct
3 Kendall Ct
4 Halliwell Ct
C4 1 St John's & St Clements CE Jun & Inf Sch
2 Bellenden Prim Sch

65
A4 1 Tilling Ho
2 Goodwin Ho
3 Tyrells Ct
4 Citron Terr
5 Basswood Cl
6 Cheam St
7 Rye Oak Sch
C3 1 Laxton Path
2 Barlings Ho
3 Bayfield Ho
4 Coston Wlk
5 Coverham Ho
6 Gateley Ho
7 Dereham Ho
8 Greenwood Ho
9 Hilton Ho
10 Goodall Ho
11 Horsley Ho
12 Jordan Ho

66
A3 1 Turnham Prim Sch

67
A4 1 Pine Tree Way
2 Waterway Ave
3 Lewisham Bridge Prim Sch
B4 1 Bankside Ave
2 Elder Wlk
3 Yew Tree Cl
4 Mill Ho
C1 1 Park Piazza
2 Birdwood Ave

C4 **1** Our Lady of Lourdes RC Prim Sch

68
C3 **1** Farnborough Ho
2 Rushmere Ho
3 Horndean Cl
4 Highcross Way
5 Timsbury Wlk
6 Foxcombe Rd
7 Ryefield Path
8 Greatham Wlk
9 Gosport Ho
10 Stoatley Ho
11 Milland Ho
12 Clanfield Ho
13 Fareham Ho
14 Grayswood Point
C4 **1** Woodcott Ho
2 Lyndhurst Ho
3 Wheatley Ho
4 Allbrook Ho
5 Bordon Wlk
6 Chilcombe Ho
7 Vicarage Ct
8 Shawford Ct
9 Eastleigh Wlk
10 Kings Ct
11 Somborne Ho

69
A3 **1** Ramsdean Ho
2 Purbrook Ho
3 Portsea Ho
4 Blendworth Point
5 Eashing Point
6 Hindhead Point
7 Hilsea Point
8 Witley Point
9 Buriton Ho
10 Grateley Ho
11 Hascombe Ho
12 Dunhill Point
13 Westmark Point
14 Longmoor Point
15 Cadnam Point
B4 **1** Cumberland Ho
2 Devonshire Ho
3 Cornwall Ho
4 Norfolk Ho
5 Leicester Ho
6 Warwick Ho
7 Sutherland Ho
8 Carmarthen Ho
9 Worcester Ho
10 Rutland Ho
11 Paddock Way
12 Putney Hill
C3 **1** Sandringham Ct
2 Eastwick Ct
3 Oatlands Ct
4 Banning Ho
5 Grantley Ho
6 Caryl Ho
7 Duncombe Ho
8 Chilworth Ct
9 Kent Lo
10 Turner Lo
11 Marlborough
12 Parkland Gdns
13 Lewesdon Cl
14 Pines Ct
15 Ashtead Ct
16 Mynterne Ct

70
A3 **1** William Harvey Ho
2 Highview Ct
3 Cameron Ct
4 Galgate Cl
5 Green Ho The
6 King Charles Wlk
7 Florys Ct
8 Augustus Ct
9 Albert Ct
10 Hertford Lo
11 Mortimer Lo
12 Allenswood
13 Ambleside
14 Hansler Ct
15 Roosevelt Ct
16 Southmead Prim
Sch
A4 **1** Douglas Gracey Ho
2 Aman Dalvi Ho
3 Andrew Reed Ho
4 Stoford Cl
5 Ronald Ross Prim
Sch

71
B2 **1** Bremans Row
2 St Andrew's Ct
3 Townsend Mews
4 Sheringham Mews
5 Rainbow Sch
6 Garratt Park Sec
Specl Sch

72
A2 **1** St Peters Cl
2 St Hildas Cl
3 St Edmunds Cl
4 St Hughes Cl
5 St Anthonys Cl
6 St Benets Cl
7 St Catherines Cl
8 Elsley Sch
C2 **1** Upper Tooting Park
Mans

17 Arden
18 Stephen Ct
19 Marsham Ct
20 Doradus Ct
21 Acorns The
22 Heritage Ho
23 Conifer Ct
24 Spencer Ho
25 Chartwell
26 Blenheim
27 Chivelston
28 Greenfield Ho
29 Oakman Ho
30 Radley Lo
31 Simon Lo
32 Admirals Ct
33 Augustus Rd
C4 **1** Brett Ho
2 Brett House Cl
3 Sylva Ct
4 Ross Ct
5 Potterne Cl
6 Stourhead Cl
7 Fleur Gates
8 Greenwood
9 John Paul II Sch
10 Our Lady Queen of
Heaven RC Prim
Sch
11 Prospect House
Sch

73
A3 **1** Holbeach Mews
2 Hildreth Street
Mews
3 Coalbrook Mans
4 Hub Buildings The
5 Metropolis Apart-
ments
6 Hildreth St
A4 **1** Meyer Ho
2 Faraday Ho
3 Hales Ho
4 Frankland Ho
5 Graham Ho
6 Gibbs Ho
7 Dalton Ho
8 Ainslie Wlk
9 Rokeby Ho
10 Caistor Ho
11 Ivanhoe Ho
12 Catherine Baird Ct
13 Marmion Ho
14 Devonshire Ct
15 Blueprint Apart-
ments
16 Royal Duchess
Mews
17 Alderbrook Prim
Sch
B3 **2** Henry Cavendish
Prim Sch
3 Margaret Ruther-
ford Pl
B4 **1** Limerick Ct
2 Homewoods
3 Jewell Ho
4 Glanville Ho
5 Dan Bryant Ho
6 Olding Ho
7 Quennel Ho
8 Weir Ho
9 West Ho
10 Neville Ct
11 Friday Grove Mews
12 St Bernadette RC
Jun Sch
C3 **1** Sinclair Ho
2 MacGregor Ho
3 Ingle Ho
4 St Andrews Mews
5 Telferscot Prim Sch
C4 **1** Riley Ho
2 Bennett Ho
3 White Ho
4 Rodgers Ho

2 Cecil Mans
3 Marius Mans
4 Boulevard The
5 Elmfield Mans
6 Holderness Rd
7 Lumiere Ct
C3 **1** St James's Terr
2 Boundaries Mans
3 Station Par
4 Old Dairy Mews
5 Chestnut Grove Sch
6 Hornsby House Sch
7 Trinity St Mary's
Prim Sch
C4 **1** Hollies Way
2 Endlesham Ct
3 Broomwood Hall
Sch (Upper Sch)
4 Holy Ghost RC Prim
Sch

74
A1 **1** De Montfort Ct
2 Leigham Hall Par
3 Leigham Hall
4 Endsleigh Mans
5 John Kirk Ho
6 Raeburn Ct
7 Wavel Ct
8 Homeleigh Ct
9 Howland Ho
10 Beauclerk Ho
11 Bertrand Ho
12 Drew Ho
13 Dowes Ho
14 Dunton Ho
15 Raynald Ho
16 Sackville Ho
17 Thurlow Ho
18 Astoria Mans
A2 **1** Wyatt Park Mans
2 Broadlands Mans
3 Stonehill's Mans
4 Streatleigh Par
5 Dorchester Ct
6 Picture Ho
A3 **1** Beaumont Ho
2 Christchurch Ho
3 Stapleford Cl
4 Chipstead Ho
5 Coulsdon Ho
6 Conway Ho
7 Telford Avenue
Mans
8 Telford Parade
Mans
9 Wavertree Ct
10 Hartswood Ho
11 Wray Ho
A4 **1** Picton Ho
2 Rigg Ho
3 Watson Ho
4 MacArthur Ho
5 Sandon Ho
6 Thorold Ho
7 Pearce Ho
8 Mudie Ho
9 Miller Ho
10 Lycett Ho
11 Lafone Ho
12 Lucraft Ho
13 New Park Par
14 Freeman Ho
15 Argyll Ct
16 Dumbarton Ct
17 Kintyre Ct
18 Cotton Ho
19 Crossman Hos
20 Camelford Ct
21 Parsons Ho
22 Brindley Ho
23 Arkwright Ho
24 Perry Ho
25 Brunel Ho
26 New Park Ct
27 Tanhurst Ho
28 Hawkshaw Cl

5 Dumphreys Ho
6 Homan Ho
7 Prendergast Ho
8 Hutchins Ho
9 Whiteley Ho
10 Tresidder Ho
11 Primrose Ct
12 Angus Ho
13 Currie Ho

5 Dumphreys Ho
6 Homan Ho
7 Prendergast Ho
8 Hutchins Ho
9 Whiteley Ho
10 Tresidder Ho
11 Primrose Ct
12 Angus Ho
13 Currie Ho

20 Richard Atkins
Prim Sch
B1 **1** Carisbrooke Ct
2 Pembroke Lo
3 Willow Ct
4 Poplar Ct
5 Leigham Ct
6 Mountview
7 Spa View
B3 **1** Charlwood Ho
2 Earlswood Ho
3 Balcombe Ho
4 Claremont Cl
5 Holbrook Ho
6 Gwynne Ho
7 Kynaston Ho
8 Tillman Ho
9 Regents Lo
10 Hazelmere Ct
11 Dykes Ct
12 Hartwell Ct
13 Christ Church
Streatham CE Prim
Sch
14 Streatham Hill &
Clapham High Sch
B4 **1** Archbishop's Pl
2 Witley Ho
3 Outwood Ho
4 Dunsfold Ho
5 Deepdene Lo
6 Warnham Ho
7 Albury Lo
8 Tilford Ho
9 Elstead Ho
10 Thursley Ho
11 Brockham Ho
12 Capel Lo
13 Leith Ho
14 Fairview Ho
15 Weymouth Ho
16 Ascalon Ct
17 China Mews
18 Rush Common
Mews
C3 **1** Valens Ho
2 Loveday Ho
3 Strode Ho
4 Ethelworth Ct
5 Harbin Ho
6 Brooks Ho
7 Godolphin Ho
8 Sheppard Ho
9 McCormick Ho
10 Taylor Ho
11 Saunders Ho
12 Talcott Path
13 Derrick Ho
14 Williams Ho
15 Baldwin Ho
16 Churston Cl
17 Neil Wates Cres
18 Burnell Ho
19 Portland Ho
20 Fenstanton Prim
Sch
21 St Martin-in-the-
Fields High Sch
C4 **1** Ellacombe Ho
2 Booth Ho
3 Hathersley Ho
4 Brereton Ho
5 Holdsworth Ho
6 Dearmer Ho
7 Cherry Cl
8 Greenleaf Cl
9 Longford Wlk

www.philips-maps.co.uk

First published in 2001 by
Philip's, a division of
Octopus Publishing Group Ltd
www.octopusbooks.co.uk
Endeavour House,
189 Shaftesbury Avenue
London WC2H 8JY
An Hachette UK Company
www.hachette.co.uk

Fifth edition 2012
First impression 2012
LONEA

© Philip's 2012

Spiral-bound
ISBN 978-1-84907-208-3

Perfect-bound
ISBN 978-1-84907-209-0

Hardback (red)
ISBN 978-1-84907-210-6

Hardback (navy)
ISBN 978-1-84907-211-3

Hardback (Union Jack)
ISBN 978-1-84907-228-1

This product includes mapping data licensed
from Ordnance Survey® with the permission
of the Controller of Her Majesty's Stationery
Office. © Crown copyright 2012. All rights
reserved. Licence number 100011710.

No part of this publication may be
reproduced, stored in a retrieval system or
transmitted in any form or by any means,
electronic, mechanical, photocopying,
recording or otherwise, without the
permission of the Publishers and the
copyright owner.

While every reasonable effort has been made
to ensure that the information compiled in
this atlas is accurate, complete and up-to-
date at the time of publication, some of this
information is subject to change and the
Publisher cannot guarantee its correctness or
completeness.

The information in this atlas is provided
without any representation or warranty,
express or implied and the Publisher cannot
be held liable for any loss or damage due
to any use or reliance on the information in
this atlas, nor for any errors, omissions or
subsequent changes in such information.

The representation in this atlas of a road,
track or path is no evidence of the existence
of a right of way.

Ordnance Survey and the OS symbol are
registered trademarks of Ordnance Survey,
the national mapping agency of Great Britain

Data for the speed cameras supplied by
PocketGPSWorld.com Ltd

Post Office is a trade mark of Post Office Ltd
in the UK and other countries.

Printed and bound in China

NOTES

NOTES

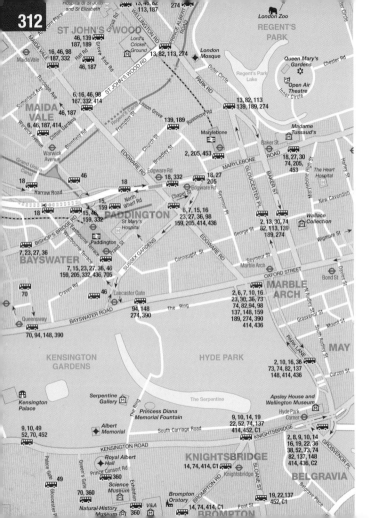

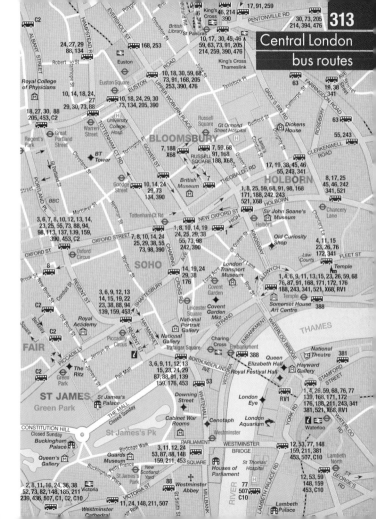

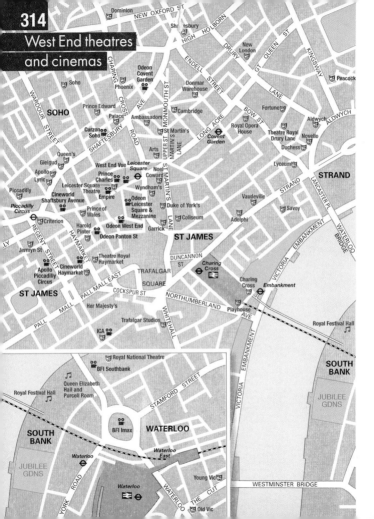